THE INTERNATIONAL TEN
FEDERATION

World of Tennis

1988

The year 1987 saw the dawning of a new era in the women's game. The astonishing West German teenager, Steffi Graf, set new records by reaching the final of all thirteen of the tournaments she entered, and in August deposed Martina Navratilova from the world No. 1 ranking, which she had made her own for so long. Not that the former Czech lost her crown without a fight; she beat Steffi to win both Wimbledon and the US Open singles titles, also achieving the triple at Flushing Meadow. In the men's game Ivan Lendl of Czechoslovakia successfully held off the challenge from the young Swedes, Stefan Edberg and Mats Wilander, to remain undisputed World Champion for the third time and winner of the Masters for a record fifth, while Australia's Pat Cash warmed the hearts of all who watched him win Wimbledon. The extraordinary successes and fascinating struggles are all covered in this twentieth anniversary issue of *World of Tennis*, which provides a comprehensive view of all that is happening in the game. Again published in association with the International Tennis Federation, who celebrate their 75th anniversary in 1988, *World of Tennis* has long been recognised as the sport's foremost reference book. In 1988 it is bigger than ever, with 512 pages packed with photographs, accounts and results of all the world's major tournaments including: the four Grand Slam events; the women's International Series; the men's Grand Prix; international team competitions such as the *Davis Cup*, *Federation Cup* and Wightman Cup; as well as the satellite circuits and Junior and Veteran tennis. The detailed reference section contains biographies of more than 200 top players, with portraits of the all-time greats, plus the Championship Rolls. In special feature articles, Lance Tingay looks back in celebration of 75 years of the International Tennis Federation, and Steve Flink examines what could be the rivalry of the future in the women's game between Steffi Graf and the enchanting Argentinian, Gabriela Sabatini.

THE INTERNATIONAL TENNIS FEDERATION

World of Tennis

1988

Edited by John Barrett
Compiled by Lance Tingay

Willow Books
Collins
8 Grafton Street, London
1988

Editorial and design preparation for Willow Books by Christine Forrest

Abbreviations used in this book

ARG	Argentina	**FIN**	Finland	**MEX**	Mexico
AUS	Australia	**FRA**	France	**NIG**	Nigeria
AUT	Austria	**FRG**	West Germany	**NZL**	New Zealand
BEL	Belgium	**GBR**	Great Britain	**PAK**	Pakistan
BER	Bermuda	**GDR**	East Germany	**PAR**	Paraguay
BOL	Bolivia	**GRE**	Greece	**PER**	Peru
BRA	Brazil	**HKG**	Hong Kong	**POR**	Portugal
BUL	Bulgaria	**HOL**	Netherlands	**RSA**	South Africa
CAN	Canada	**HUN**	Hungary	**SUI**	Switzerland
CHI	Chile	**INA**	Indonesia	**SWE**	Sweden
CHN	People's Republic of China	**IND**	India	**TCH**	Czechoslovakia
COL	Colombia	**IRL**	Ireland	**TUR**	Turkey
DEN	Denmark	**IRN**	Iran	**URS**	USSR
ECU	Ecuador	**ISR**	Israel	**USA**	United States of America
EGY	Arab Republic of Egypt	**ITA**	Italy	**YUG**	Yugoslavia
ESP	Spain	**JPN**	Japan	**ZIM**	Zimbabwe
		LUX	Luxembourg		

Cover photograph: Steffi Graf (Michael Cole Camerawork)

Willow Books, William Collins & Sons Ltd
London · Glasgow · Sydney · Auckland · Toronto · Johannesburg
Published in Great Britain 1988

British Library Cataloguing in Publication Data

World of tennis – 1988
1. Tennis – Periodicals
I. International Tennis Federation
796.342'05 GV991

ISBN: 0 00 218269 6

Typeset, printed and bound in Great Britain by
Hazell Watson & Viney Limited
Member of the BPCC plc
Aylesbury Bucks

CONTENTS

PREFACE

It is 20 years now since Lawn Tennis (as it was known then) went 'Open'. In each of those years this publication has chronicled the game's erratic progress, as it sought to reconcile the conflicting needs and ambitions of the Establishment, the new breed of managerial entrepreneurs and the liberated professional players, men and women. Thanks to the skill and co-operation over that period of so many of the world's leading tennis writers and photographers, these 20 volumes present a consistent historical record of our growing sport.

The growth of the amateur and professional game in those two decades has indeed been impressive. Although we have no precise figures, it is estimated that there are more than twice as many people playing tennis in the world today as there were in 1968. The growth in France and Germany, the pace-setters in Europe, has been phenomenal. There are now 13 times more registered players in France and six times more in Germany than there were 20 years ago. The number of clubs has risen by a factor of seven in each country and the number of courts by about five. When you consider the vast numbers of completely new players who have taken up the sport in the underdeveloped countries in Asia and Africa as a result of the pioneering work undertaken by the ITF over the past seven years, you begin to understand the extent of the revolution that has taken place. In future years we shall know much more accurately what the true figures are, because in 1988 the ITF, to mark its 75th anniversary, is publishing the results of the first survey among its member nations to reveal basic information about the game in each country.

The growth of the professional game, where we do have more accurate figures, is truly astonishing. In the first year of Open tennis (nine months really, because the first Open tournament did not begin until 22 April), the total amount of prize money divided between some 250 men and women professionals at 17 Open tournaments in eight countries was less than $500,000. In 1988, some 450 men and 300 women will divide a total cake of $40 million from official events alone. Add their rewards from special events, and the figure rises by several more million dollars.

Our beginnings as chroniclers of the game resulted from a discussion I had with some fellow journalists over a meal at an indoor tournament in Stalybridge in 1967. Everyone was bemoaning the lack of a tennis reference book since the demise in 1958 of the Dunlop annual, itself the successor to the excellent Ayres Almanacks edited by Wallis Myers for 31 years (1908–1938). We all agreed that it was about time someone produced a new one, and because no-one else seemed too keen to take on the task, I did. My long-suffering wife, Angela, has cursed that day ever since!

The BP Yearbook Of World Tennis, published in 1969 to reflect the happenings of the first year of Open tennis, was one of many contributions to the game undertaken by the BP International Tennis Fellowship, which I had founded with the support of the oil company the previous year. Without the encouragement of Julius Edwardes and John Gearing at BP, the book would never have appeared.

That first issue was a slender volume, a modest affair that looked as if it had been thrown together in rather a hurry, as indeed it had been. It might appear curious that within its 272 pages there is no report of the world's first Open tournament, the Hard Court Championships of Great Britain, played at the West Hants Club, Bournemouth, in April 1968. It happened thus. I had commissioned the Bournemouth story from Bill Edwards, a respected member of the British Tennis Writers Association. The story duly arrived and went, along with everything else, to be set. We had selected as publishers Ward Lock,

In 1969 John Barrett, aware of the need for an authoritative tennis reference book, inspired the first edition of World of Tennis, *which in 1988 celebrates its 20th edition. (M. Cole)*

because an old school friend, Barrie Knight, was the Sales Director there at the time and had offered us good terms.

When, in due course, all the galley proofs had been corrected, it was time to do the paste-up. We had no professional designer, so this tedious job was accomplished on my dining-room table at home, with the help of Peter West, who had compiled the tournament results and the player biographies for that first issue. Peter had also had some experience of this job as editor of the *Playfair Rugby Annual*. Inevitably we were short of time and, having no previous issue to guide us, we simply arranged the material in as logical an order as possible. But when we had finished, despite using up every spare scrap of space, we found to our horror that there was still some material left over – including Bill Edwards' story. Nothing could be done. There was simply insufficient time to do a complete rejig.

There have been other horror stories. In 1969 an indignant Ilie Nastase approached me one day at the French Championships, and said, 'John, why you say I was a shepherd boy? I never been a shepherd boy. I only chase sheep when I want to sleep!' I remembered the reference in Ilie's biography for that first year which had surprised me when I had seen it at the proof stage. I turned it up once more. Sure enough, there were the words 'ex-shepherd boy with a lively temperament'. Investigation revealed that during one of the previous season's tournaments in Europe, a journalist had jokingly thrown this colourful piece of misinformation into a conversation during the busy hour in the press-room when all the scribes were sweating over their stories. A colleague, short of background and on a tight deadline, had overheard the remark and gratefully included it in his story. Peter West, carefully collecting material for the biographies, found this fascinating fact among his press clippings and in it went!

In a publication of this sort, so full of facts and figures, it is virtually impossible to avoid occasional mistakes. However hard you try to check both facts and proofs, errors do slip through – perhaps an incorrect player's initial or nationality, or a score that doesn't make sense, or perhaps a reversed date. Confusion can easily arise in this area when 1/5/87 is translated the American way as 5 January, instead of 1 May, for instance. Even the printer can let you down by reversing photographs at the eleventh hour. When Jimmy Arias pointed out last year that we had printed a picture of him as a left-hander in the 1986 edition, I congratulated him on being in good company. The same thing had happened to Lew Hoad many years earlier!

In those early days we had difficulty in persuading the National Associations to provide their ranking lists in time for publication. The Iron Curtain countries were particularly reticent, and for some years there was a deafening silence from Moscow in response to our repeated requests for the lists. It was as though we were trying to steal state secrets! To the rescue came Geoff Miller of AP, whose team of overseas correspondents knew the trick of prising such information from the grasp of such bureaucrats.

For the second edition in 1970 we changed our publishers. John Gearing had a contact at Clipper Press whose attractive proposal was accepted. Unfortunately the printers were based in Hungary! You can imagine the difficulties we had with communications, especially at the stage of correcting the proofs. It amazed us all that the book came out on time – but it did and was a great improvement on our first effort. This time Lance Tingay provided the bulk of the results, as he has done every year since, aided and abetted by his patient wife, Daphne. The debt we all owe to Lance is enormous.

Peter West continued to supply the biographical material until 1976, when a remarkable young American, Steve Flink, took over. Steve's encyclopaedic memory for results and for the minutiae of a player's career made him the ideal choice for this time-consuming task. It was only his growing responsibilities at *World Tennis* magazine that forced him reluctantly to hand over the baton this year to Christine Forrest. Happily he continues his link with us as the author of a colourful account of the growing rivalry between Steffi Graf and Gabriela Sabatini.

In 1971 we began an association with Alan Smith that still prospers. First with Queen Anne Press (1971–1983), and now with Collins Willow (1984–1988), Alan and his team of house editors and designers helped us to restructure the material so that it was more attractive, both physically and commercially.

It was at Alan's suggestion in 1971 that we published a two-part Ken Rosewall coaching segment, intended for the junior members of the BPITF. Ken and Rod Laver were the two Professional Advisers to the Fellowship at that time. This proved to be surprisingly popular, with general readers as well as with our young members, but the constraints of space and cost precluded a continuance of the coaching feature after 1972. That year, and for the three following years, we published an American edition – in 1972 and 1973 with Simon and Schuster and in 1974 and 1975 with Popular Library. However, the problem of getting copies printed before half the next year had gone inevitably limited our potential sales and made it uneconomic to continue in the United States. Similarly the flirtation with a colour section in 1974 and 1975 proved only that such costly luxuries were not practical in a publication of this nature.

In order to recognise the growing importance of the Grand Prix, we embraced Commercial Union, the sponsors of that competition, as partners in 1973. The link with CU, through

Geoff Mullis and John Beddington, was a happy and successful one that continued until their departure from the tennis scene in 1976. Five years later, in 1981, BP decided to end their association with the publication that they had launched in 1969. It was a happy chance that the world's oldest surviving sports goods company, Slazengers Ltd, were due to celebrate their centenary that same year and, as part of that celebration, asked if they could take on the sponsorship of *World of Tennis*. This was a particularly appropriate link because Slazengers had absorbed the Ayres company soon after the war. In a sense, therefore, we were reviving the work of Wallis Myers.

At the same time the International Tennis Federation expressed an interest in becoming associated with the publication. Thus, in 1981, *World of Tennis* for the first time also became the official yearbook of the ITF. After three years it became apparent that, with all the companies who were members of the ITF's Foundation now having the opportunity each year to advertise in *World of Tennis*, it was no longer appropriate for a single commercial organisation to be directly associated with the governing body's official yearbook. Therefore in 1984 Slazengers Ltd gracefully withdrew.

In 1982 came the transition to computerised production, when the typesetting and printing moved to Hazell Watson and Viney, to whom we are annually indebted for our ability to bring the book out on time. Their good-natured assistance to meet ever tighter deadlines is much appreciated.

Six years on *World of Tennis* has expanded to 512 pages – confirmation, as if any were needed, that the game, fanned by ITF initiatives at junior and veteran level, continues its pattern of growth. This present volume is more than ever the creation of our Production Editor, Christine Forrest, who has been associated with our annual effort since 1980. Because of my own enforced absences she has single-handedly tackled the design, the picture selection and the captions as well as contributing for the first time the all-important player biographies, which have been completely overhauled. It has been a monumental labour, and to Christine I extend my grateful thanks and my congratulations.

I have already recognised the contribution made annually by the indefatigable Lance Tingay whom, it seems, age cannot dim nor effort weary. Long may he retain his enthusiasm as well as his sharp attention to detail! Once again my talented colleagues from the international press corps, both the writers and the photographers, have answered the call to deadline with marvellous dependability. I think they know just how grateful I am. At the ITF Kay Peters has admirably co-ordinated the production of vital information, while Erika Harris, in her first year of involvement with *World of Tennis*, has cheerfully and efficiently produced the mountains of material we require, often at very short notice. My thanks to them both, and also to Ruth Garrett, who helped with some of the proof-reading.

The two players' Associations have once again been of enormous help – Temple Pouncey and Greg Sharko at ATP, Rick Remmert and Maureen Hanlon at WITA. At the MIPTC offices Reg Lansbury and Catalina Cox, plus those delightful ladies on the road, Micky den Tuinder, Lori Stukes and Wendy Miller, have all been unfailingly helpful. So too have those Virginia Slims stalwarts – Ted Tinling, the only man I know who can out-talk a computer, and Annalee Thurston who can actually make a computer talk. To them all our combined thanks. Finally a word of gratitude for the efficient way in which Louise Haines, Commissioning Editor at Collins Willow, accepts the challenge of each new title. Her calming influence is much appreciated.

Looking back over these 20 years the outstanding impression has been the tremendous camaraderie that exists between all members of the tennis fraternity. The hard work entailed in producing this annual reflection on the tennis scene has been made bearable only by the friends around the world who have selflessly given of their time or experience to help us on our way. If it had not been fun, I doubt if I would have continued. To all those unnamed friends and colleagues may I simply say 'Thank You', with the hope that they, along with all our readers, enjoy this latest offering, which celebrates 75 years of the ITF's existence.

JOHN BARRETT
London, March 1988

OBITUARIES 1987

During the course of 1987, tennis lost several distinguished friends, among them the following men, whose contribution to the development of the game, each in his own sphere, was immense.

Henri Cochet, who passed away in April after a long illness, was one of the most gifted players ever to lift a tennis racket. His five French, two Wimbledon and one US Championship titles between 1922 and 1932 bear witness to his stature as one of the game's great champions. However, statistics alone can never reveal the nature of Henri's sleight-of-hand genius which his contemporaries claim has never been equalled. A true patriot, Henri was never happier than when competing for France in the *Davis Cup*. The six Challenge Round triumphs he shared with his fellow 'Musketeers' – Borotra, Lacoste and Brugnon – from 1927–32 were the high-water-mark of French tennis. In 1933 Henri turned professional and played in many tournaments with Bill Tilden and others but he was reinstated as an amateur after the war. He then devoted himself to encouraging young players and took a leading role in the affairs of the French International Club as captain and President.

Derek Hardwick, who died at the end of May after a short illness, was a former British junior doubles champion who was to become the nation's leading international tennis administrator. A Dorset farmer, Derek was always forthright in his opinions and fearless in defence of causes which were closest to his heart. In 1968, as the Chairman of the LTA, he energetically supported the All England Club's decision to hold an Open Wimbledon. For 21 years he served on the joint Championships Committee at Wimbledon and became President of the International Tennis Federation in 1975, a post he held for two years. As a member of the original Men's International Professional Tennis Council until his retirement, Derek continued to exert a powerful influence on affairs. His wise counsel and unrivalled knowledge of the game will be missed.

Basil Reay, who died last autumn, was another leading administrator, intimately involved in the game's evolution. As Secretary of the LTA in Britain and Honorary Secretary of the International Lawn Tennis Federation from 1948–73, and then for three more years the General Secretary of both the ITF (they had dropped 'Lawn' by then) and of the *Davis Cup* nations, Basil Reay had a greater influence upon the development of the world game than any other individual. In recognition of those services, he was made an Honorary Life Councillor of the ITF in 1976, 19 years after being awarded the OBE for services to British tennis.

Don Butler's death at the age of 77 ends another link with players of the pre-war era whose best years were lost to the armed conflict. As a young man in Worcester, Don was the county closed champion for six successive years. He won the Plate event at Wimbledon in 1938, the year he was first selected to the *Davis Cup* team, and he was included again in the 1948 team against Sweden. A small man who kept himself very fit, Don went to live in Seaburn, Co. Durham where he became the area representative for En Tout Cas.

Benjamin Howard-Baker's passing has meant a loss to three major sports, for in his youth this great all-rounder excelled as an athlete, a footballer and a tennis player. Between 1912 and 1920 Benjamin competed in every Olympic Games and for 20 years held the world high jump record. During this same period he earned 15 amateur caps for England on the soccer field. Tennis had always been Benjamin's main summer sport, and although he never aspired to *Davis Cup* honours he served Lancashire nobly as their representative on the LTA in two periods, 1931–36 and 1945–70. In recognition of this service, his county made him an Honorary Life Vice-President in 1978.

Although the Wimbledon title eluded him again, Ivan Lendl won both the French and US titles for the third time, as well as taking a record fifth Masters and five other titles to end the year as he began it – at the top. *(T. Hindley)*

FOREWORD

This 20th edition of *World of Tennis*, coincides with a whole series of anniversaries within the game itself. Most significant, of course, for all of us at the International Tennis Federation, is the fact that we are celebrating our own 75 years in existence.

On a broader scale 1988 also sees the 20th year of Open tennis, the 100th anniversary of the Lawn Tennis Association in Great Britain, the 60th birthday for Roland Garros and, perhaps most exciting of all, the return of tennis as a fully competitive sport to the Olympic Games in Seoul in September. Between these pages you will find all these facets of the tennis world, and many more, accurately reflected and chronicled, especially those which fall under the care and encouragement of the ITF at a time when our work is forever expanding.

Tennis is a sport for everyone, increasingly, it seems, being played from the cradle to the grave. Indeed at times it is difficult to keep pace with the growth not only of big prize-money events which attract most of the publicity from day to day, but also the many international junior and veteran events.

World of Tennis 1988 provides the most comprehensive record of the game's progress on all these fronts, highlighting not only the matches but also the personalities who help to make it so special to us all. I trust that, as in the past, you will find this a publication which is informative, reflective and stimulating.

PHILIPPE CHATRIER
President, International Tennis Federation

THE YEAR IN REVIEW

Ronald Atkin

It was fitting that professional tennis should move into this, the 20th anniversary of the Open game, with an extravagant flourish – the inauguration of the world's most stunning setting for the sport at the 1988 Australian Open in Melbourne. The cost of the new stadium, with its spectacular sliding roof, adds up to just another series of noughts in a sport already laden with such statistics. In 1987 Wimbledon announced a profit in excess of £7 million, an 18-year-old German girl won more than a million dollars in prize money, and everywhere the pickings on offer to the top people continued to soar towards the point where the cracks are beginning to show.

The rehabilitation of the Australian Open will undoubtedly be one of the highlights of 1988. It was not so long ago that the event's future as one of the four Grand Slam tournaments looked to be in doubt, but improved organisation, better prize money – which in turn brought a higher quality of entry – and now the new stadium should have done enough to ensure Australia's lasting place as one of the world's Big Four.

Much hard work was also put in during 1987 to bring to fruition what the International Tennis Federation's president, Philippe Chatrier, referred to as 'a dream come true' – the readmission of tennis to the Olympic Games at Seoul in September 1988. Chatrier described his efforts to achieve that goal as 'a long, exhausting, and at times frustrating, struggle'.

After that struggle was won, many of the players who had earlier been dismissive about tennis at the Olympics adjusted their attitudes, so that by the end of the year there was a strong surge in favour of joining the Olympic parade. There were also, sport being indivisible from politics despite the wishful thinking of many officials, the first rumblings of dissension concerning the names of some who were planning to play in Seoul. Boris Becker, for instance, lost his job as goodwill ambassador to the United Nations Children's Fund (UNICEF), because he refused to sign a statement pledging never again to play in South Africa while that country's apartheid policy remained in effect. Becker, opposed to apartheid, is not planning any future commitment in that country but the young West German viewed signing a UN statement as accepting an ultimatum. Becker had appeared at Sun City in an exhibition event similar to the one which caused Ivan Lendl's final severance of courtesies with the Czech Tennis Federation, and Third World countries were not slow to air their displeasure at the former Wimbledon champion's action.

The subject of South Africa also had a thorough airing at the season's-end debating forum, the Nabisco Masters in New York. The reason was that both Pat Cash, the 1987 Wimbledon champion, and Brad Gilbert had played in the Johannesburg tournament late in the year in search of points to ensure their qualification for the Masters.

Having succeeded in that quest, both players were subjected to a roasting, mainly by the American media, when they reached New York. So persistent was this questioning about the attitudes of individual players that the Men's International Professional Tennis Council chose to issue a statement rather ambiguous in its wording: that the Council reaffirmed its disapproval of apartheid, while claiming that withdrawing approval from the Johannesburg event as a protest against the South African government's policies amounted in itself to discrimination. The further comment that 'the MIPTC is a sport-

Jimmy Connors (right) played the match of the year against Mikael Pernfors in the last 16 at Wimbledon, recovering from 2 sets and 1–4 down to advance to the quarter-finals, where he downed Zivojinovic before bowing to Cash. *(T. Hindley)*

based organisation and is non-political' was clearly well out of court. Unfortunately, in so many fields nowadays, sport *is* politics.

On a happier note, the MIPTC was able to celebrate in August the dismissal of the law suit brought against it by three organisations, the Volvo North American Corporation, the International Management Group and ProServ Inc. These companies had challenged the MIPTC's running of the Nabisco Grand Prix and its use of bonus monies, but the arguments were thrown out by Judge Kevin Thomas Duffy in the US District Court for the Southern District of New York. The litigation is not yet ended, however, for the counter-claims filed by the MIPTC have yet to come to court.

Charges continue to be levelled at the MIPTC by some players and other interested parties, such as agents and managers, about the organisation of the Grand Prix. The most consistent of these accusations is that the year-long grind of tournaments is unwieldy and over demanding. There is a growing concentration of opinion from the opposition that, rather than a calendar containing 80 or so events, the official year should consist of the four Grand Slam Championships, plus either 12 or 16 tournaments comprising the Grand Prix, rather on the lines of motor racing, with all the other competitions attracting the talent as best they can against exhibitions and special events.

The higher up the earning scale, the more vociferous the complaints and the louder the breakaway threats. Such threats seem empty since the Association of Tennis Professionals has allied itself to the MIPTC and the Grand Prix for the next five years as part of a pact which will also see the introduction of a deferred compensation scheme (or pension plan) for players, with an implementation age of 50. Player compensation at Super Series events will also increase in 1988 by 41 per cent. Although the player commitment to Grand Prix competitions remains unchanged at 14 self-designations, the MIPTC agreed to make exceptions in the cases of Lendl and John McEnroe, who were granted a reduction from 14 to 12 because of their long service to the Grand Prix schedule.

Others who find that chasing a tennis ball can be an arduous and damaging business were not so fortunate. Jimmy Arias, limbs cocooned in ice bags, appeared at a Press conference in Monte Carlo, complaining, 'I'm only 22 but my body is about 80', while Stefan Edberg announced at the Masters his intention to abandon most of his doubles commitments because they were affecting his chances in the singles, especially at Grand Slams – something which Bjorn Borg, Jimmy Connors and Lendl acknowledged long ago.

Lendl completed his third year as the official world No. 1 by winning the French and US Opens, five other Grand Prix events and capturing the Masters for a record fifth time. As Philippe Chatrier said, 'Lendl was in a class above everyone else at the Masters' in recording his third successive triumph on the Madison Square Garden carpet.

All Lendl's big wins – at Roland Garros, Flushing Meadow and the Garden – came against the same final opponent, Mats Wilander. The Swede salvaged a set in both the French and US Championships, but at the Masters he was obliterated, claiming only seven games. Lendl hit his stride comparatively late in the year because of a knee operation. He did not win a tournament until the German Open at the beginning of May, but after that he was always the man to beat, and there was an ominous quote for the opposition after that Masters victory: 'There are still a million ways I can improve.'

One who *did* overturn Lendl, and who did it in that most visible of all tennis occasions – the Wimbledon final – was Pat Cash. It was Cash who provided the memorable moment of the year, and probably for many years to come, when he climbed into the Centre Court audience and up to his family, friends and coach, Ian Barclay, in the competitors' box. Asked what Cash had said as he hugged Barclay, the silver-haired coach replied, '"We showed 'em Barkers" . . . that was with the expletives deleted, of course'.

If Cash offered the public the most cherishable moment of 1987, Jimmy Connors, the perennial alley-cat, and Steffi Graf, the new No. 1 of the women's game, were involved in the most memorable matches of the year. It was in the fourth round at Wimbledon that Connors, trailing by two sets and 4–1 to Mikael Pernfors, staged one of the most eye-popping comebacks of even his spectacular career to win in five sets.

Miss Graf prevailed in a marvellous French Open final, after Martina Navratilova had led 5–3 in the third set, and Steffi ended the year with a stupendous record, winning 75 of

In an improved year, Sylvia Hanika of West Germany achieved the upset of the season at the Virginia Slims Championships, when she defeated Chris Evert in the first round before going on to reach the semi-finals. *(Carol L. Newsom/Virginia Slims)*

her 77 matches. Her only defeats came against Miss Navratilova in the Wimbledon and US Open finals, and her position as the new top cat in women's tennis was already assured before she climaxed an unforgettable year by capturing the Virginia Slims Championships crown at Madison Square Garden in November. There she downed her teenage friend, doubles partner and closest young rival, Gabriela Sabatini, in the final.

Steffi matched Martina's earlier achievement by becoming the only other woman to top $1 million in prize money in a year, and she outdid her distinguished senior when she entered the record books as the only player ever to reach the final of every tournament (of which there were 13) that she played in 1987. She also put up another record of sorts by appearing seven times out of 12 on the cover of the monthly newspaper, *Inside Women's Tennis.* As usual, Billie Jean King had the right word for the new phenomenon: 'She has oomph, and you get that feeling only from champions.'

Nobody who lifts both the Wimbledon and US titles can be disappointed about her year, and those victories by Miss Navratilova in the two most important tournaments gave impetus to her contention that the coronation of Queen Steffi may be seriously disputed for a while longer. The Wimbledon success was Martina's first title of the year and the one she wanted more than any other. It was her sixth successive triumph on the Centre Court and equalled Helen Wills Moody's record of eight Wimbledon singles titles. This year the Navratilova sights will be set firmly on a ninth championship at the All England Club. As that three-time Wimbledon winner Maria Bueno said, 'Martina wants to be remembered as the greatest player in history and I don't think she's too far from that'.

Miss Navratilova's win in the US Open was her fourth in the singles there. She also went on to complete the tournament triple crown by winning the women's doubles with Pam Shriver (their 17th Grand Slam title together) and the mixed with Emilio Sanchez. It was the first time anyone had pulled off the triple since Billie Jean King did so at Wimbledon in 1973.

For Chris Evert the year ended disappointingly when she went out in the first round of the Virginia Slims Championships to Sylvia Hanika, but along the way she amassed more statistics for the memory cupboard – her 100th victory at the US Open and the 1,200th match win of her career.

The *Davis Cup* season opened sensationally with defeats for the United States and Czechoslovakia, and closed tamely with Sweden's 5–0 roll over India in the final. The Americans were relegated from the World Group into a regional section, from which they may find it difficult to escape as long as they are condemned to play on clay in Latin America, and until some young successor emerges to follow Connors and McEnroe.

West Germany were the winners of the 25th *Federation Cup*, held in Vancouver, in a tremendous final against the United States, which went to the last set of the deciding rubber. In 1988 the event will be staged in Australia, for the fourth time. On the first occasion, 1963, there were 11 entries. In 1971 that figure had edged up to 14. By 1978 it had mushroomed to 36, and in 1988 it seems certain to exceed the Vancouver total of 42 nations.

There were notable changes in 1987. Hamilton Jordan, a former White House chief of staff in the President Carter regime, became the new executive director of the Association of Tennis Professionals. Jordan replaced Mike Davies, who found a new home as director of marketing for the International Tennis Federation. The MIPTC increased its number of professional chair umpires to five by appointing Rudy Berger of Germany to join Richard Kaufman (US), Richard Ings (Australia), Gerry Armstrong (Britain) and Paulo Pereira (Brazil). The number of full-time MIPTC supervisors was also boosted to five by the selection of Eduardo Menga of Brazil and Dr Edward Hardisty of Britain.

A piece of history was made during the year when the sportswear company Nike reached agreement with officials from the Sports Committee of the Soviet Union to provide shoes and clothing for Russian players on the men's and women's circuits. And there was also a piece of nostalgia: Bjorn Borg, chic and shorn, took himself around the world once more – this time selling his own name brand of men's toiletries, clothes and luggage.

Finally, things seem to be on the move at last in Britain. Bolstered by the injection of another whopping donation from the Wimbledon profits, the Lawn Tennis Association was able to report progress on the mass construction of indoor facilities (with the first one due for completion in spring 1988, the LTA's centenary), an expansion of the Mortgage Corporation Indoor League from 8 to 12 teams, and the appointment of the Australian, Warren Jacques as the new men's international squad director, in charge of guiding the British game out of the backwaters. Jacques is under no illusions about the demands of his five-year assignment: 'It's the toughest tennis job in the world', he said.

PLAYERS OF THE YEAR

Lance Tingay

IVAN LENDL

In a year when he seemed to become more American than Czech, Ivan Lendl, who was 27 in March, 1987, was *the* player. He was not without failure, for in the last instance he again faltered and fell when the still-elusive Wimbledon title was within his grasp, but overall his rugged and ruthless perfectionism, his ability to transpose the ball into a bullet, was awesome. One may suspect that he has sacrificed more than most would like to do in order to hone his skills. Ceaseless training, a diet of values more scientific than palatable, a wholly disciplined life – on such rigours has he grown his success. One may wonder how his fellow-Czech, Kafka, would have written of a man who turned himself, not into the beetle of *Metamorphosis*, but into a machine.

He began the year as a World Champion who might be slipping. Pat Cash ousted him in Australia, and then it was not a fellow-Czech but a Slovak, Miloslav Mecir, who beat him in the Lipton tournament in Florida. He soon avenged himself against Mecir in Paris, where he retained his title for the third time in four years. He hoped to avenge his loss to Cash in the Wimbledon final but the Australian kicked him hard for the second time. Queen Mary, the Tudor monarch, declared that 'Calais' was written on her heart; 'Cash' may be inscribed on the heart of Lendl, for he was the bugbear of his year.

Lendl, for all the world as if he were American, thrived in the strident atmosphere of Flushing Meadow. For him it was a crescendo of form all the way. John McEnroe, in the quarter-final, might have been a child; Jimmy Connors, in the semi-final, could have been an old man. Had he won either of two points for the first set, Lendl would not have been disturbed by Mats Wilander in the final. So in three years he was US Open Champion for the third time. The last man to do that was McEnroe, and Lendl looked good enough to continue his dominance.

PAT CASH

There are some players of consequence who embrace Wimbledon as though it is their natural home. They do so like a monarch coming to his kingdom, the throne belonging to him by inalienable right. Pat Cash was one such in 1987, as Boris Becker had been in 1985 and 1986. He, alas, fell among robbers and did not complete the journey, but then it is the fate of kings to be deposed. Cash is a no-nonsense Australian through and through. You don't play tennis for the sake of having long rallies in the sun in pleasant company. It is more fun to hit the ball hard so that it does not come back, and if in the course of so doing you knock the other chap off the court, too bad! You are not out there to play chess. Cash was made for grass and grass made for Cash, so it was little wonder that he was at home at Wimbledon.

Injury and sickness have plagued him, but when cast down did ever a young man bounce back better? When in the summer of 1987 he hit the winning shot against Ivan Lendl, he did what no other champion has ever done. He turned towards his family and friends in the special stand reserved for such folk and ran towards them across the court. He forced himself through the spectators, appraised the concrete wall before him like a mountaineer, took a handhold, a foothold here and there, and was up embracing them to the astonishment of all. No champion more obviously delighted in his triumph. He had

The men's Grand Slam finals were contested between the four players of the year: Stefan Edberg (above left) triumphed in Australia over Pat Cash (below left) who went on to win Wimbledon. There he overcame Ivan Lendl (above right), the victor over Mats Wilander (below right) in both New York and Paris. *(T. Hindley, Carol L. Newsom)*

conquered Wimbledon and he knew, as we all knew, that no one had a more natural right to do so.

The citadel had not surrendered to him easily. He was first at Wimbledon when he was 16, in 1981. Then he lost the final of the boys' event to Matt Anger, but he was back a year later to win that same event over Henrik Sundstrom. His initial bid in the adult meeting, in 1983, augured well. He penetrated the last 16, yielding to Lendl, and a year later many could see him as a champion. It was John McEnroe who killed him in the semi-final. The low point came in 1985 with the loss to Acuna in the second round, and in 1986 Leconte played brilliantly against him in the quarter-final. But in 1987 Cash was irresistible. Looking back on the year it seemed to matter not that he could fail elsewhere, in the US Open, for example. He was the Wimbledon champion and Australia could look the game in the face again. It was 16 years since brave, brawny and consistent John Newcombe had taken what then seemed an Australian-owned crown for perpetuity. It seems a shame that Australia should give up grass now that they at last have a real grass-court player.

STEFAN EDBERG

Of the plethora of magnificent Swedish players we have seen in recent years I suppose one could name the three most prominent as Bjorn Borg (of course), Mats Wilander and Stefan Edberg. All were precociously skilled, both Borg and Wilander winning Grand Slam titles while still juniors. Edberg has been unique, among that trio, in revealing his talents to the world not so much as a junior among seniors but as a junior among juniors. In 1983 he won all four of the major junior titles, a junior Grand Slam, as it were. As the tardiest among the three to emphasise his mercurial qualities where they matter more, Edberg did not gain his first Grand Slam singles title until the Australian Open in 1985. Now he has done the same for 1987. Oddly he followed Wilander in that, his *Davis Cup* colleague having won in the two preceding years. Edberg was a player who mattered a lot in 1987, and it will be surprising if he does not matter more in 1988.

MATS WILANDER

The last Grand Slam title won by Wilander was his second French Open in 1985, which means that both 1986 and 1987 were blank in that regard. Yet in 1987 Wilander, 23 in August, might have won the French again but for the problem of Lendl in the final, and he might have won the US Open, but for the renewed problem of Lendl in that final also. The third repetition of that tale was at the Masters. He lost earlier at Wimbledon, for grass does not yet seem to be his *forte*. Then he fell in the quarter-finals, and the player who ousted him was the man who took the title, Cash. But you could not move far in the top game of 1987 without bumping into Wilander.

MARTINA NAVRATILOVA

It happened in 1987 that the vagaries of the computer dispossessed this great player from the number one position in the ranking list, overtaken by the younger Steffi Graf. But that she was a player of the year is as certain as anything can be in sport; rather I would say she stands as the player of the decade. In fact, even more, for on the score of her Wimbledon triumph she made herself the player of the half-century. It was in 1938 when Helen Wills Moody acquired her eighth singles title at Wimbledon, a tally which stood on its own until Martina equalled it – and equalled it, moreover, with a unique run of six in a row.

Yet in the first half of the year Steffi seemed not only to have caught up with her senior rival, she seemed to have passed her. There was an unaccustomed trail of defeats for the World Champion, including two, in the French final and the Lipton semi-final, by Graf. It seemed scarcely possible, but by the start of Wimbledon Martina Navratilova had not won a tournament in 1987! Then came her Wimbledon success, which was forthright and sure. The same pattern was repeated at Flushing Meadow. The champion was right back at the top, nearly 31 years old but as good as ever.

The crowning glory in New York was embellished, for she made herself triple champion, a rare feat indeed. It meant, too, that in her career to that date she had won no less than 47 Grand Slam titles, of which singles championships made up 17. She would have taken 61 had she won all her finals, for she was beaten 14 times in the title match – but never, interestingly, in a Wimbledon singles final.

STEFFI GRAF

The Grand Slam citadel was broken at last! Steffi Graf became 18 only in June 1987 but such had been the impact of this hard-hitting and beautiful player that it seemed as if she were fulfilling the promise of many years. The big one was the French Championships and she beat Martina Navratilova in the final to take it. That was the climax of one of the most breathtaking and spectacular sequences of success seen for years. Steffi had by that time shown herself to be invincible. She took apart the best opposition in tournament after tournament. She beat Helena Sukova to win in Boca Raton, Chris Evert to take Key Biscayne, then Manuela Maleeva at Hilton Head, Hana Mandlikova in Amelia Island, Gabriela Sabatini in Rome and Claudia Kohde-Kilsch in Berlin. As for Navratilova, she had been semi-final fodder in Key Biscayne. The crux was the French final. It was touch and go, but Steffi made it – 6–4 4–6 8–6 – a match and a result to remember.

So it was that in the computer rankings Steffi Graf stepped into the top place. She was the world's No. 1. But the old ones don't yield as easily as that! Navratilova was well on top in the Wimbledon final, just as she was when the two great players had their second momentous meeting in the last match of the US Open. On that occasion Steffi clearly had a cold, which was bad luck. But the time when Steffi Graf had to prove herself in 1987 had passed. She was very much one of the players of the year. Maybe, like Navratilova, she is entering into the vistas of immortality, for in 1988 she will be but 19 with the world before her.

GABRIELA SABATINI

The *motif* of the last decade of the women's game was the rivalry between Chris Evert and Martina Navratilova, both Americans (by adoption, anyway). It will be surprising if the *motif* of the decade to come is not Steffi Graf versus Gabriela Sabatini, the former a German, the latter an Argentinian – and both still teenagers.

Sabatini, who became 17 in the course of 1987, did not win a major title, for the two that were missed by Graf were taken by Navratilova. But as Graf achieved the breakthrough to the top, so it seemed as if this entrancing young Latin was also on the verge of doing so. She missed the big ones, but missed only narrowly. She came close in Italy, where she beat Navratilova in the semi-final before losing in three sets to Graf in the final. In the French Open she yielded to Graf again in the semi-final and again in three sets. At Wimbledon it was Graf once more – and in three sets. At Flushing Meadow it was different in that she lost to Navratilova in the quarter-final.

With the Virginia Slims Championships at Madison Square Garden, where the women's rivalries are particularly acute, she dispossessed Navratilova in the quarters and went on to dispute the title with Graf in the final. The score then would have been three sets in the best of three, but as they were playing the best of five it went to four. Amid all the shining gold at the top of the women's game Sabatini, youngest of all, shone like silver. She became one whom all must watch.

The Lipton's trophy was the second of 11 won in 1987 by Steffi Graf (below), who was beaten only by Martina Navratilova (above right) – in the Wimbledon and US Open finals. Although Gabriela Sabatini (above left) has yet to win a match against the new No. 1, she frequently threatened to do so. *(T. Hindley, M. Cole)*

THE ITF YEAR

THE ITF YEAR
DAVIS CUP
FEDERATION CUP

Despite being troubled during the year by a recurring knee injury, Ramesh Krishnan helped India to the final of the Davis Cup *for the first time since 1966 – when his father played.* *(T. Hindley)*

NIKE
NIKE

THE ITF YEAR

John Parsons

Of all the developments, innovations and progress involving the International Tennis Federation during 1987, perhaps the most important was the move into headquarters of their own at last. After 74 years of relying on other people's hospitality, most notably provided by the French Tennis Federation and the Lawn Tennis Association in Britain, and more recently on the forbearance of landlords at the All England Club, the former offices of the LTA in London were purchased. Yet the switch, coming in time for the Federation to celebrate their 75th anniversary this year with a home of their own, was not achieved without mishaps. At the height of the move, for instance, one of the builders accidentally fractured a pipe which left the basement, and much of the equipment which was there at the time, swirling in several inches of water.

Perhaps this excitement was appropriate in a year of considerable activity on and off the courts, when one of the features of the Grand Slam tournaments was the amount of rain from which they all suffered. Australia, saying farewell to Kooyong and grass courts, suffered least of all, but it was a measure of the strength and reputation of the Grand Slam tournaments, which are the pride and joy of the ITF as well as of the Nabisco Grand Prix, that all triumphed handsomely, despite the frustrations enforced by the weather.

In Paris, Ivan Lendl managed to beat Mats Wilander over four long sets in the men's singles final moments before the rain, which had been falling steadily and had twice interrupted play, became a deluge. At Wimbledon, the first week of the Championships was badly hit, with not a single ball struck on the first day. As usual, however, such problems were shrugged aside by Wimbledon, where the organisation, benefiting from more than a century of experience, takes such matters in its stride, and everything was completed on time with panache and its customary style.

The United States Tennis Association were less fortunate, for the foulest of the weather there hit Flushing Meadow on what should have been the last day, offering no scope for catching up. Everyone had to return the following day to see Martina Navratilova become the first to achieve a triple crown at a Grand Slam tournament since Billie Jean King did so at Wimbledon in 1973, and to admire the persistent strength of Lendl's play as he repeated his Roland Garros success over Wilander, virtually assuring himself of retaining the ITF's official world title.

Lendl had added a third successive Masters title and a record fifth in all by the time the ITF panel of great former champions – Fred Perry, Tony Trabert and, by telephone, Frank Sedgman – met to declare the French and US Open winner the World Champion for at least another year, even though he was again unable to master his doubts on grass. In Australia Stefan Edberg retained the title, and at Wimbledon Lendl was beaten in the final for the second successive year, this time by Pat Cash.

For the first time in six years, however, the ITF welcomed a new women's World Champion in Steffi Graf. Although Martina Navratilova gave Miss Graf her only defeats during her brilliantly successful year – in the finals of the world's two most important events, at Wimbledon and the US Open – there was no doubt in the end that Miss Graf, who wound up her programme in fine style by winning the Virginia Slims Championships, was the Player of the Year in women's tennis. She was also the key player as West

Natalia Zvereva of the USSR was the world's top junior in 1987, winning junior Grand Slam titles in Paris, New York and Wimbledon, where she also reached the last 16 of the senior tournament, to end the year ranked 19. (T. Hindley)

Germany won the ITF's major women's team event, the *Federation Cup*, for the first time. It was successfully staged in Vancouver, with a record entry and with added impetus given to the competition because those nations reaching the quarter-finals were automatically guaranteed an extra player in the 1988 Olympic Games.

There was also a record entry for the *Davis Cup* which, for the first time, included a qualifying African Zone to underline the all-round growth of the game. A total of 75 nations, another record, entered the 1988 *Davis Cup*, which is sponsored, like the *Federation Cup*, by NEC. At the annual meeting of the ITF it was agreed to make changes within the Groups, allowing the weaker nations to play off against each other before the reputedly stronger teams, including those relegated from the World Group, join in.

Sweden, playing in their fifth successive final, regained the trophy to become *Davis Cup* champions for the third time in four years. The final, against India, was one-sided, but on the way there had been a series of upsets and momentous events. These included India's astonishing first-round comeback against Argentina and their semi-final triumph in Australia, after the holders lost Pat Cash from the singles through injury. Yet perhaps the most significant event was the relegation, for the first time, of the United States, one of the competition's founder nations. Their home defeat by West Germany in the relegation play-off came after the Americans had lost in Paraguay and West Germany had been defeated in Spain, where Sergio Casal beat Boris Becker.

Administratively 1987 involved many changes for the ITF. In April a new Marketing Division, based in Dallas and under the direction of former ATP Executive Director, Mike Davies, was formed. Later in the year, Shirley Woodhead, the General Secretary and one of the ITF's best-known figures, resigned for personal reasons, and responsibilities within the London headquarters were reorganised. Then Tony Gathercole, an assistant referee for many years at Wimbledon, was appointed to look after the increasingly popular veterans' tennis.

Nowhere is the ITF work more essential, or rewarding, than in the field of development. It is doubtful whether many who live in the fully developed tennis world, or amid the atmosphere of the major professional circuits, realise just what facilities still need to be provided or what potential sources of tennis talent remain untapped. Whether in terms of providing courses for coaches, officials and administrators, or by enabling players to take their first steps on the fiercely competitive international ladder, the ITF, through the initiatives and energy of Director of Development Doug MacCurdy and his staff, carry out a vital role.

All of this naturally requires money, and the ITF are immensely grateful for the continuing help they receive from those commercial organisations who are members of the ITF Foundation and also from the Grand Slam Trust Fund. The latter operates through grants made by the four Grand Slam tournaments at Wimbledon, the US Open, the French Open and the Australian Open. The money is then used to fund schemes, such as satellite events in parts of the world where they would not otherwise be possible, or travel grants to outstanding individuals or teams of players from a part of the world where there are still insufficient domestic opportunities for them to advance.

This provides another excellent example of how money which the game itself has generated is going back into tennis to encourage and inspire the next wave of players coming along. Not everyone, including some of the top players it seems, understands that the prize money received from Grand Slam events, while perhaps a relatively modest proportion of the event's total income, is but a small proportion of the amount that is ploughed straight back into tennis at all levels and for all age groups, to the benefit of their colleagues past, present and future.

The value of the work, in particular, at grass roots level, is certainly being reflected where it counts most at this stage – among the nations represented on the ITF's Junior World Rankings. Among the boys, ten different nations had players ranked among the top 16, four of them countries who will not be in the World Group of the *Davis Cup* in 1988. There is a similarly healthy spread of talent among the leading girls.

Competition to become Junior World Champion, among the boys, was especially keen. No less than 582 boys established singles rankings but it was not until the Orange Bowl

– the very last of a record 106 tournaments in a record 65 countries, compared with 95 events in 62 countries in 1986 – that the winner was declared, Jason Stoltenberg of Australia finally heading both the singles and doubles rankings. A smart piece of observation on the part of John Treleven, the ITF's Junior Administrator, made sure that Natalia Zvereva's dominance, not least in the junior events at Paris, Wimbledon and the US Open, was properly reflected. Without his prompting she may not have played in the Orange Bowl, and would not then have competed in enough circuit events to qualify as Junior World Champion.

There is no doubt that in tennis success breeds success. Bjorn Borg and Sweden set the pattern which is happily being followed by an increasing number of countries, and nowhere is that situation better reflected than in parts of Africa. The number of countries taking part in the 1987 ITF/West African Junior Championships increased by a third, encouraged by the success of neighbouring countries.

Large crowds attended the third staging of the World Youth Cup, the ITF 16 and Under team event. It was held for the first time in Freiburg, West Germany, with Australia winning both the boys' and girls' events, the Australian boys enjoying their third consecutive victory.

Throughout the year the ITF continued to play their full part in the administration of the international game's two governing bodies, the Men's International Professional Tennis Council and the Women's International Professional Tennis Council. For both, the calendar for each succeeding year remains the most enduring problem as they endeavour to find the right formula and mix. On the men's side, the most heartening news was that the United States District Court for the Southern District of New York dismissed the lingering law suit filed by Volvo North America Corporation, the International Management Group and ProServ Inc against the MIPTC, its Administrator, Marshall Happer, and ITF President Philippe Chatrier as former chairman of the MIPTC. The issues remain subject to a countersuit and appeal.

Finally, no review of the ITF year would be complete without reference to the death during the year of Derek Hardwick, a former President, and for almost 40 years a devout campaigner for all that he believed was best for tennis. He was a member of the management committee at Wimbledon for 21 years, the ITF from 1968, a leading advocate in the old days for Open tennis and with a special love always for the *Davis Cup*. His successor as ITF President, Philippe Chatrier, paid him a fitting tribute when he said, 'The game has lost probably its greatest fighter'.

ITF WORLD CHAMPIONS

The ITF Men's World Champion is decided by the ITF's panel of former champions: Fred Perry, Frank Sedgman and Tony Trabert. The ITF Women's World Champion title is awarded to the player who heads the Virginia Slims points table for the year.

	MEN	WOMEN
1978	Bjorn Borg	Chris Evert
1979	Bjorn Borg	Martina Navratilova
1980	Bjorn Borg	Chris Evert Lloyd
1981	John McEnroe	Chris Evert Lloyd
1982	Jimmy Connors	Martina Navratilova
1983	John McEnroe	Martina Navratilova
1984	John McEnroe	Martina Navratilova
1985	Ivan Lendl	Martina Navratilova
1986	Ivan Lendl	Martina Navratilova
1987	Ivan Lendl	Steffi Graf

Note: ITF Junior and Veteran rankings and results can be found on pages 476 and 486 respectively.

Above: The victorious Swedish team who regained the Davis Cup*: (l-r) Stefan Edberg, Anders Jarryd, Hans Olsson (captain), Mats Wilander and Joakim Nystrom. Below: The Indian team, finalists for the first time since 1966: (l-r) Anand Amritraj, Vijay Amritraj, Ramesh Krishnan and Srinivasan Vasudevan.* *(T. Hindley)*

THE *DAVIS CUP* by NEC

Richard Evans

Sweden re-claimed the *Davis Cup*, which they had lost in Australia the previous year, when India were defeated 5–0 in Gothenburg in a final that was not so much a massacre as a celebration. Vijay Amritraj's team, every member of which having been born and bred in Madras, were the least likely finalists since Britain had bucked the odds and made similar progress before falling to the United States in Palm Springs. If anything, India's road to the final had followed an even more improbable path, and when Sweden elected to lay another clay court in the vast Scandinavium Stadium, just as they had for the final against Arthur Ashe's Americans in 1984, Vijay knew that his team's Christmas quest would become just so much tinsel and holly with which to decorate another Swedish triumph.

So although disappointed that they didn't make a better match of it, India were simply happy to be there, and the 12,000 Swedes who packed the stadium for the first two days were equally happy that Santa Claus had no nasty surprises beneath his beard. What the final lacked in competitive edge, it made up for in a spirit of friendship and good sportsmanship that was not only in keeping with the festive season but which went some way to eradicating the unhappy memories of America's boorish behaviour there three years before.

For the record, Mats Wilander defeated Ramesh Krishnan in the opening singles, and then Anders Jarryd continued his career-long domination over India's captain by beating Amritraj, also in straight sets. That was not the draw India had been hoping for, nor was Jarryd's appearance in place of the injured Stefan Edberg a welcome sight for the visitors. 'Frankly we felt Ramesh would have a better chance against Edberg on clay and, at the very least, we were hoping that he would not have to play Wilander first off', admitted Amritraj. 'But I suppose it was too much to hope that our fairy-tale year would have a proper ending.'

The doubles was more competitive with Vijay, joined by his older brother Anand, playing excellently in the first couple of sets and winning the second, before Wilander and his partner Joakim Nystrom improved the power and accuracy of their dipping service returns and completely dominated the remainder of the match. Strangely, the previous time a pair of brothers had appeared in a *Davis Cup* final had been in 1978 when John and David Lloyd had played singles and doubles respectively in the 1–4 loss to the Americans in the California desert. Siblings must improve the odds for rank outsiders.

In winning a set the Indians had at least done as well as that powerful US team in 1984, for Jimmy Connors and John McEnroe also lost their live singles in straight sets and McEnroe and Peter Fleming, suffering their first *Davis Cup* defeat, could manage only one set in the doubles.

The fact that the Americans had fared just as badly in Gothenburg was significant, because it highlighted the fact that Sweden would have crushed all but two or three nations in the world on their own clay court. One would have had to have given Czechoslovakia a chance, and possibly France, but the next country which comes to mind is Spain, and they couldn't even beat the Swedes on a wet clay court in Barcelona in the semi-final. So, after a hiccup in Melbourne, Sweden's dominance of the world's premier team competition was restored. The 1986 final had caught Hans Olsson's team in a rare moment of disarray. Wilander had opted out because of his marriage; Edberg was jaded after a tough year, and most of the team looked as if they would rather have been at home for

Christmas. This time they were and, as if to make up for his earlier absence, it had been Wilander who had done most to ensure that they would be.

Winning every live singles he played, the world No. 3 was the lynch pin of a squad that was represented by a typically wide assortment of players during the year. Mikael Pernfors had the unhappy experience of kicking off the 1987 campaign by losing to Italy's Paolo Cane in the opening rubber in Prato – that turned out to be Sweden's only live singles reverse in the whole competition – and by the time Olsson took the squad to the Roman Arena in Frejus for the quarter-final against France, Kent Carlsson was fit to replace Pernfors and unleash his extraordinary style with devastating effect on both Thierry Tulasne and Henri Leconte. But the demands he put on his body with that excessive top-spin strokeplay takes its toll on Carlsson, and he was injured again when the Swedes went to Barcelona.

No matter. Olsson merely called up the second-ranked player in the world and, ignoring the fact that many experts in Sweden were sceptical of Edberg's solidity as a *Davis Cup* player, especially on clay, asked Stefan to play singles only while giving Jarryd Wilander as a doubles partner. Edberg brushed aside the younger Sanchez brother, Javier, who was making a nervous *Davis Cup* début and then, after Sergio Casal and Emilio Sanchez had kept Spain in the tie by winning the doubles, proved all his critics wrong by serving and volleying his way to a tremendously impressive straight-sets victory over the older Sanchez in the fourth rubber.

All that only proved that the odd injury is of little concern to a team as strong as Sweden have at their disposal now and, indeed, for the foreseeable future. This was their fifth consecutive appearance in the final, their third victory in that period – only at Kooyong, it seems, are they fallible – and their fourth in all; Bjorn Borg having started it all in more ways than one by leading his nation to victory over the Czechs in 1975.

Such are the margins that divide the quick and dead in sport that one backhand volley, made or missed, probably determined whether India would reach the final for the third time in their history, or be relegated. Vijay Amritraj was match-point down to Martin Jaite in the fourth set, with Argentina leading by two rubbers to one in New Delhi in March. Calling on more than fifteen years' experience of top-class match play, the 33-year-old Amritraj charged the net and put away the backhand volley. Having been two sets down, he went on to win 6–2 in the fifth, and Krishnan then wrapped up the tie by beating Horacio de la Pena. Had India lost, they would have had to have played Czechoslovakia.

Grass was obviously India's best friend and Amritraj was so disturbed when Israel caused the biggest shock of the first round by defeating the Czechs at Hradec Kralove – Amos Mansdorf's great wins over Miloslav Mecir and Karel Novacek being the key – that he headed off a looming political problem by going straight to Prime Minister Ghandi. In fact India's captain made two trips to Delhi. On the first he persuaded the Prime Minister to let the match be played somewhere and so avoid a repeat of the terrible disappointment of 1974, when India were forced to default the final to South Africa. Then, although India and Israel do not enjoy diplomatic relations because of the Commonwealth nation's support of the PLO, Amritraj pointed out on his second audience that the only real chance his team had of winning was to bring the Israelis to India as the draw permitted. Mr Ghandi relented and ordered up one of the most comprehensive security blankets ever thrown over a sporting event. Inside the stadium there was one armed soldier for every spectator and both teams were guarded day and night on the corridor of their hotel.

But Vijay's plan worked, primarily because he came through once again with what cricketers would call a real captain's knock by beating the dangerous Mansdorf in straight sets. And when Anand helped him to an equally decisive victory over Shlomo Glickstein and Gilad Bloom in the doubles, it was all over, 3–0.

Australia, of course, presented a wholly different problem. But two factors emerged to suggest that the right karma was guiding Indian tennis in 1987. First the tie was going to be played on grass at Sydney's White City and then, most crucially, Pat Cash, the new Wimbledon champion, announced that a knee injury would prevent him playing singles. Suddenly India were in with a chance, and when Krishnan beat John Fitzgerald, the captain went out and did his stuff once again by recovering from a one-set deficit to beat Wally

Taking no chances, Sweden laid a clay court at the huge Scandinavium Stadium in Gothenburg for the Davis Cup *final against India.* *(T. Hindley)*

Masur. Cash played the doubles which Vijay virtually conceded by opting to rest himself, and even though he could not beat Fitzgerald, Krishnan laid claims to deeds as great as those of his famous father by taking India into the final with a coolly constructed defeat of Masur.

Suddenly Australia had lost the Cup and lost it moreover at home. It was a stunning setback for Neale Fraser but he had none the less maintained his admirable record of having taken Australia at least as far as the semi-final every year but one since assuming the captaincy in 1970, and even Olsson is going to have to work a bit to emulate that kind of record.

So it was an extraordinary *Davis Cup* year, made all the more so by the fact that, while India, with a part-time actor as playing captain and a 35-year-old doubles player whose ranking has disappeared off the bottom of the computer, were reaching the final, the once mighty United States were being relegated as a result of losing their play-off encounter with Boris Becker and West Germany in Hartford, Connecticut. From all accounts that tie was as exciting, emotional and, according to those who thought John McEnroe's flag-waving patriotism over the top, as disgraceful as any played all year – except, surely, for the original American defeat itself which I witnessed in Asuncion.

The Paraguayans won, not because of their cynically biased linesmen, nor because of their wildly partisan spectators, who at least had the good manners to keep quiet during the points, nor even because of the inexcusable attempts by the President of the Tennis Federation to interfere with referee Kurt Nielsen's decision making. Paraguay defeated the United States 3–2 because they had, in Victor Pecci, a player who was a class above anyone else on view at the splendid new Golf & Racket Club Paraguayos and, in the little Argentine-born Hugo Chapacu, a player who performed something of a miracle by recovering from a point of near total collapse – and the more serious position of trailing 1–5 in the fifth set against Jimmy Arias – to win it 9–7. The fourth rubber was completed only after 5 hours 20 minutes of brutally competitive clay-court tennis played amidst the most exciting and, in some ways, intimidating atmosphere I have ever experienced.

Paraguay were subsequently banned from playing any more ties at home in 1987, and although that harsh penalty was reduced to just one match when Pecci and a new force for the better in Paraguayan tennis, Richard Kent, pleaded their case with ITF President Philippe Chatrier in Paris, the reduction became academic because Spain beat them in Caracas.

THE *DAVIS CUP* by NEC, 1987

NON-ZONAL COMPETITION

FIRST ROUND - Sweden d. Italy 3–2, Prato (M. Pernfors lost to P. Cane 6–1 2–6 3–6 4–6; M. Wilander d. S. Colombo 6–2 6–3 6–0; A. Jarryd/Wilander d. Cane/Colombo 6–1 6–2 6–2; Jarryd d. Colombo 6–3 6–4 4–6 7–5; Wilander lost to Cane 3–6 6–2 5–7); ***France d. Republic of Korea 5–0, Marcq-en-Baroeul*** (T. Tulasne d. Bong-Soo Kim 6–4 6–2 6–3; G. Forget d. Jin-Sun Yoo 6–3 5–7 6–3 6–3; T. Benhabiles/Forget d. Yoo Dong-Wook Song 4–6 4–6 6–2 6–3 10–8; Tulasne d. Yoo 6–3 4–6 6–3; Forget d. Kim 6–4 7–5); ***Paraguay d. USA 3–2, Asuncion*** (H. Chapacu lost to A. Krickstein 7–5 3–6 1–6 6–4 4–6; V. Pecci d. J. Arias 6–3 4–6 6–4 7–5; F. Gonzalez/Pecci lost to K. Flach/R. Seguso 7–5 11–9 2–6 5–7 4–6; Chapacu d. Arias 6–4 6–1 5–7 3–6 9–7; Pecci d. Krickstein 6–2 8–6 9–7); ***Spain d. West Germany 3–2, Barcelona*** (E. Sanchez lost to B. Becker 4–6 5–7 7–5 6–3 3–6; S. Casal d. E. Jelen 6–4 6–8 7–9 6–3 6–4; Casal/Sanchez lost to Becker/Jelen 5–7 6–4 4–6 3–6; Sanchez d. Jelen 8–6 6–3 6–2; Casal d. Becker 6–2 0–6 6–2 6–3); ***India d. Argentina 3–2, New Delhi*** (R. Krishnan lost to M. Jaite 6–1 6–3 3–6 2–6 3–6; V. Amritraj d. H. de la Pena 9–7 6–3 6–3; An./V. Amritraj lost to J. Frana/C. Miniussi 3–6 4–6 6–3 6–8; V. Amritraj d. Jaite 3–6 3–6 6–4 8–6 6–2; Krishnan d. de la Pena 6–4 7–5 6–2); ***Israel d. Czechoslovakia 3–2, Hradec Kralove*** (A. Mansdorf d. M. Mecir 6–4 6–2 3–6 6–3; S. Glickstein d. M. Srejber 7–5 4–6 3–6 4–6 3–2 ret'd; Glickstein/Mansdorf lost to Mecir/T. Smid 2–6 6–4 6–8 6–8; Glickstein lost to Mecir 3–6 1–6 2–6; Mansdorf d. K. Novacek 6–3 4–6 6–2 6–0); ***Mexico d. Great Britain 5–0, Mexico City*** (F. Maciel d. M. J. Bates 6–3 6–2 7–5; L. Lavalle d. A. Castle 6–2 3–6 6–2 6–4; Lavalle/J. Lozano d. Bates/Castle 6–3 6–2 6–8 6–2; A. Moreno d. Castle 9–7 6–1; Lozano d. Bates 6–4 6–3); ***Australia d. Yugoslavia 4–1, Adelaide*** (P. Cash d. B. Oresar 9–7 6–4 7–5; W. Masur lost to S. Zivojinovic 8–6 6–8 7–9 10–12; Cash/P. Doohan d. I. Flego/Zivojinovic 9–11 7–5 6–3 6–4; Masur d. Oresar 8–6 6–2 6–1; Cash d. Zivojinovic 6–8 7–5 6–1).

QUARTER-FINALS – Sweden d. France 4–1, Frejus (K. Carlsson d. T. Tulasne 6–1 3–6 6–1 6–2; M. Wilander d. H. Leconte 6–3 6–4 6–2; S. Edberg/A. Jarryd lost to G. Forget/Leconte 4–6 2–6 6–3 13–15; Carlsson d. Leconte 7–5 6–2 9–7; Wilander d. Tulasne 6–4 6–3); ***Spain d. Paraguay 3–2, Caracus (Colombia)*** (E. Sanchez d. V. Pecci 6–1 6–4 11–9; S. Casal lost to H. Chapacu 6–2 5–7 1–6 3–6; Casal/Sanchez d. F. Gonzalez/Pecci 6–2 16–18 6–3 14–12; Casal lost to Pecci 6–2 3–6 2–6 2–6; Sanchez d. Chapacu 6–1 6–3 6–0); ***India d. Israel 4–0, New Delhi*** (R. Krishnan d. S. Glickstein 7–5 6–1 6–1; V. Amritraj d. A. Mansdorf 6–4 6–4 7–5; A./An. Amritraj d. S. Bloom/Glickstein 6–2 6–2 7–5; Krishnan d. Mansdorf 10–8 6–0; S. Vasudevan v. Glickstein 10–8 abandoned); ***Australia d. Mexico 4–1, Brisbane*** (P. Cash d. L. Lavalle 6–2 6–1 6–0; W. Masur d. J. Lozano 6–3 6–4 6–4; P. Doohan/Masur d. Lavalle/Lozano 3–6 6–4 4–6 8–6 13–11; Cash d. Lozano 6–3 6–4; Masur lost to Lavalle 5–7 4–6).

SEMI-FINALS – India d. Australia 3–2, Sydney (R. Krishnan d. J. Fitzgerald 6–1 6–2 3–6 8–6; V. Amritraj d. W. Masur 1–6 6–3 12–10 6–4; A. Amritraj/S. Vasudevan lost to P. Cash/P. Doohan 3–6 4–6 4–6; V. Amritraj lost to Fitzgerald 5–7 3–6 3–6; Krishnan d. Masur 8–6 6–4 6–4; ***Sweden d. Spain 3–2, Barcelona*** (M. Wilander d. E. Sanchez 8–6 3–6 6–0 6–2; S. Edberg d. J. Sanchez 6–4 6–2 6–4; A. Jarryd/M. Wilander lost to S. Casal/E. Sanchez 0–6 3–6 6–2 4–6; Edberg d. E. Sanchez 6–4 8–6 6–4; J. Gunnarsson lost to J. Sanchez 3–6 6–3 3–6).

FINAL – Sweden d. India 5–0, Gothenburg (M. Wilander d. R. Krishnan 6–4 6–1 6–3; A. Jarryd d. V. Amritraj 6–3 6–3 6–1; Wilander/J. Nystrom d. An./V. Amritraj 6–2 3–6 6–1 6–2; Jarryd d. Krishnan 6–4 6–3; Wilander d. V. Amritraj 6–2 6–0).

RELEGATION ROUND – Italy d. Republic of Korea 3–2, Seoul (P. Cane lost to Dong-Wook Song 8–10 6–3 4–6 4–6; C. Panatta d. Jin-Sun Yoo 2–6 6–4 6–4 7–9 12–10; Cane/S. Colombo d. Yoo/Song 6–2 6–4 6–4; Panatta lost to Song 1–6 3–6 6–3 2–6; Cane d. Bong-Soo Kim 6–3 6–1 8–6); ***West Germany d. USA 3–2, Hartford, Conn.*** (E. Jelen d. T. Mayotte 6–8 6–2 1–6 6–3 6–2; B. Becker d. J. P. McEnroe 4–6 15–13 8–10 6–2 6–2; Jelen/R. Osterthun lost to K. Flach/R. Seguso 3–6 6–8 12–14;

DAVIS CUP by NEC 1987

Non-Zonal Competition

FIRST ROUND	QUARTER-FINALS	SEMI-FINALS	FINAL	CHAMPION
SWEDEN Italy	SWEDEN 3–2	SWEDEN 4–1	SWEDEN 3–2	SWEDEN 5–0
FRANCE Republic of Korea	FRANCE 5–0			
USA Paraguay	Paraguay 3–2	Spain 3–2		
WEST GERMANY Spain	Spain 3–2			
India ARGENTINA	India 3–2	India 4–0	India 3–2	
Israel CZECHOSLOVAKIA	Israel 3–2			
Great Britain MEXICO	MEXICO 5–0	AUSTRALIA 4–1		
Yugoslavia AUSTRALIA	AUSTRALIA 4–1			

Capital letters denote seeded nations.

RELEGATION ROUND

Italy Republic of Korea	Italy 3–2
USA West Germany	West Germany 3–2
Argentina Czechoslovakia	Czechoslovakia 5–0
Great Britain Yugoslavia	Yugoslavia 3–0

Zonal Competition

AFRICAN ZONE

FIRST ROUND	QUARTER-FINALS	SEMI-FINALS	PROMOTED
	NIGERIA	NIGERIA 3–2	ZIMBABWE 3–2 (to European Zone B)
Tunisia Ivory Coast	Ivory Coast 5–0		
	ZIMBABWE	ZIMBABWE 5–0	
Kenya Djibouti	Kenya w.o.		
Morocco Senegal	Senegal 3–2	Senegal 4–1	Senegal 3–2 (to European Zone A)
	ALGERIA Libya EGYPT	EGYPT w.o.	

AMERICAN ZONE

FIRST ROUND	QUARTER-FINALS	SEMI-FINALS	FINAL	PROMOTED
	ECUADOR Bolivia	ECUADOR 5–0	ECUADOR 3–2	BRAZIL 4–1
	PERU	Canada 3–2		
Venezuela Canada	Canada 4–1			
Uruguay Colombia	Uruguay 5–0			
	BRAZIL	BRAZIL 3–2	BRAZIL 3–2	
Commonwealth Caribbean Cuba	Commonwealth Caribbean 3–2			
	CHILE	CHILE 3–2		

EASTERN ZONE

FIRST ROUND	QUARTER-FINALS	SEMI-FINALS	FINAL	PROMOTED
	NEW ZEALAND	NEW ZEALAND 5–0	NEW ZEALAND 4–1	NEW ZEALAND 4–1
Chinese Taipei Singapore	Chinese Taipei 5–0			
	THAILAND	THAILAND 3–2		
Bangladesh Pakistan	Pakistan 5–0			
Sri Lanka Philippines	Philippines 5–0	CHINA 4–1	CHINA 3–2	
CHINA Indonesia	CHINA 4–1			
Hong Kong Malaysia	Hong Kong 5–0	JAPAN 4–1		
	JAPAN			

EUROPEAN ZONE A

FIRST ROUND	QUARTER-FINALS	SEMI-FINALS	FINAL	PROMOTED
	USSR	USSR 4–1	USSR 4–1	SWITZERLAND 3–2
Syria Turkey	Turkey 5–0			
	NETHERLANDS	NETHERLANDS 4–1		
Malta Ireland	Ireland 4–1			
Norway Senegal	Senegal 3–2	BULGARIA 5–0	SWITZERLAND 5–0	
	BULGARIA			
	BELGIUM SWITZERLAND	SWITZERLAND 5–0		

EUROPEAN ZONE B

FIRST ROUND	QUARTER-FINALS	SEMI-FINALS	FINAL	PROMOTED
	AUSTRIA	AUSTRIA 4–1	AUSTRIA 4–1	DENMARK 3–2
Greece Luxembourg	Greece 5–0			
	HUNGARY	Portugal 5–0		
Monaco Portugal	Portugal 3–2			
Poland Zimbabwe	Poland 3–2	RUMANIA 4–1	DENMARK 3–2	
	RUMANIA			
Finland Cyprus	Finland 5–0	DENMARK 5–0		
	DENMARK			

Jelen lost to McEnroe 5–7 2–6 1–6; Becker d. Mayotte 6–2 6–3 5–7 4–6 6–2); ***Czechoslovakia d. Argentina 5–0, Prague*** (K. Novacek d. M. Jaite 6–3 2–6 6–3 6–1; M. Mecir d. H. de la Pena 8–6 4–6 6–3 6–4; Mecir/T. Smid d. J. Frana/C. Minicus 6–1 4–6 6–3 6–2; Novacek d. de la Pena 6–4 7–5; Mecir d. Jaite 9–7 6–2); ***Yugoslavia d. Great Britain 3–0, Zagreb*** (B. Oresar d. M. J. Bates 6–1 6–0 1–6 6–3; S. Zivojinovic d. S. Shaw 6–3 6–4 6–4; Oresar/Zivojinovic d. Bates/A. Castle 10–8 11–9 12–10).

AFRICAN ZONE

FIRST ROUND – Ivory Coast d. Tunisia 5–0, Abidjan (C. N'Goran d. M. Soudani 6–2 6–0 7–5; A. Beugretche d. H. Soudani 10–8 6–2 6–1; J. Koffi/N'Goran d. M./H. Soudani 6–2 6–4 7–5; N'Goran d. B. Lyes 6–1 6–3; Beugretche d. G. Adel 6–3 6–2); ***Kenya w.o. Djibouti; Senegal d. Morocco 3–2, Dakar*** (A. Berthe lost to M. Dlimi 3–6 6–4 2–6 4–6; Y. Doumbia d. A. Nadani 7–9 6–8 6–3 6–3 6–3; Doumbia/T. Ly d. A. Chekrouni/Dlimi 6–3 6–4 6–4; Berthe lost to Nadani 2–6 5–7 6–3 6–3 2–6; Doumbia d. Dlimi 3–6 4–6 6–3 8–6 6–4).
SECOND ROUND – Nigeria d. Ivory Coast 3–2, Abidjan (R. Akinloye lost to C. N'Goran 8–6 3–6 4–7 1–6; T. Mmoh d. A. Beugretche 6–1 6–3 6–4; J. Atiomo/Mmoh d. J. Amihiake/N'Goran 7–9 1–6 6–2 9–7 15–13; Mmoh d. N'Goran 6–3 3–6 7–5 6–2; Akinloye lost to Beugretche 2–6 6–4 4–6); ***Zimbabwe d. Kenya 5–0, Nairobi*** (B. Black d. P. Wekessa 6–3 6–4 6–2; G. Roger d. E. Polo 6–2 7–5 5–7 6–4; Black/H. Ismail d. K. Bhardwaj/S. Rana 6–3 6–4 6–3; Black d. Polo 6–3 6–1; Roger d. Bhardwaj 9–7 6–2); ***Senegal d. Algeria 4–1, Dakar*** (T. Ly d. Y. Amier 5–7 6–2 6–3 2–6 6–4; Y. Doumbia d. D. E. Boudjemline 6–4 6–0 6–2; Doumbia/Ly d. Amier/Boudjemline 6–3 6–2 8–6; Ly lost to Boudjemline 3–6 7–9; Doumbia d. Amier 8–6 6–2); ***Egypt w.o. Libya.***
SEMI-FINALS – Zimbabwe d. Nigeria 3–2, Harare (B. Black d. T. Mmoh 4–6 1–6 6–4 6–0 4–2 ret'd; G. Rodger lost to N. Odizor 6–8 6–2 1–6 2–6; Black/Rodger d. A. Abdullah/Odizor 8–6 6–1 3–6 6–3; Rodger lost to Abdullah 3–6 4–6 4–6; Black d. Odizor 5–7 6–4 6–3 6–1). Zimbabwe qualified for European Zone B. ***Senegal d. Egypt 3–2, Dakar*** (M. Doumbia lost to K. Baligh 10–12 9–7 6–4 0–6 6–8; Y. Doumbia d. H. Nasser 6–3 6–0 6–0; A. Berthe/Y. Doumbia d. Baligh/Nasser 6–3 5–7 6–4 6–3; M. Doumbia lost to Nasser 5–7 2–6 2–6; Y. Doumbia d. Baligh 6–3 6–4 6–4). Senegal qualified for European Zone A.

AMERICAN ZONE

FIRST ROUND – Canada d. Venezuela 4–1, Caracas (M. Wostenholme d. C. Claverie 3–6 6–3 6–4 6–4; G. Michibata d. N. Pereira 8–6 6–2 6–4; M. Greenan/Michibata d. V. Boccito/I. Calvo 6–8 6–3 6–2 6–4; Wostenholme d. Pereira 8–6 6–4; Michibata lost to Claverie 3–6 7–5 6–8); ***Uruguay d. Colombia 5–0, Bogota*** (D. Perez d. M. Rincon 6–3 6–3 6–3; M. Filippini d. A. Jordan 3–6 3–6 6–2 6–3 17–15; V. Caldaralli/Perez d. Jordan/M. Tobon 6–4 6–4 6–2; Filippini d. Rincon 3–6 6–4 6–0; Perez d. Jordan 6–3 6–2); ***Commonwealth Caribbean d. Cuba 3–2, Nassau*** (D. Burke d. M. I. T. Perez 6–3 8–6 6–2; R. Smith lost to J. P. Perez 6–1 8–10 6–4 2–6 3–6; Burke/Smith d. M. I. T. Perez/W. N. H. Torriente 6–3 7–6 6–3; Smith d. M. I. T. Perez 6–3 6–0 6–4; Burke lost to J. P. Perez 5–7 0–2 ret'd).
QUARTER-FINALS – Ecuador d. Bolivia 5–0, Guayaquil (A. Gomez d. H. Eterovic 6–2 6–0 6–2; R. Viver d. A. Garron 6–1 6–1 6–0; Gomez/H. Nunez d. Eterovic/H. Villarroel 6–2 6–2 7–5; Viver d. Eterovic 6–0 6–2; Gomez d. Garron 6–0 6–0); ***Canada d. Peru 3–2, Lima*** (A. Sznajder lost to P. Arraya 1–6 3–6 6–8; M. Wostenholme d. J. Yzaga 10–8 2–6 7–5 6–2; G. Michibata/M. Laurendeau lost to C. DiLaura/Yzaga 6–4 5–7 4–6 2–6; Sznajder d. Yzaga 9–7 6–4 6–4; Wostenholme d. Arraya 7–5 2–6 5–7 6–1 7–2); ***Brazil d. Uruguay 3–2, Montevideo*** (L. Mattar d. D. Perez 3–6 6–2 4–6 6–3 7–5; I. Kley lost to V. Caldarelli 6–4 4–6 2–6 6–3 3–6; Mattar/C. Motta d. Caldarelli/Perez 6–3 6–4 4–6 4–6 6–4; Kley lost to Perez 2–6 9–11 2–6; Mattar d. Caldarelli 6–3 6–2 3–6 4–6 7–5); ***Chile d. Commonwealth Caribbean 3–2, Nassau*** (R. Ureta lost to R. Smith 10–12 5–7 6–2 5–7; R. Acuna d. D. Burke 6–3 6–3 9–7; Acuna/H. Gildemeister d. Burke/Smith 6–2 6–4 10–8; Ureta lost to Burke 3–6 4–6 6–3 8–6 4–6; Acuna d. Smith 8–6 8–6 3–6 6–8 6–4).
SEMI-FINALS – Ecuador d. Canada 3–2, Edmonton (H. Nunez lost to A. Sznajder 7–9 4–6 6–8; A. Gomez d. G. Michibata 6–1 6–4 6–2; Gomez/Nunez d. G. Connell/M. Greenan 7–5 7–9 6–4 6–1; Nunez lost to Michibata 8–6 3–6 2–6 2–6; Gomez d. Sznajder 4–6 6–4 6–4 5–7 7–5); ***Brazil d. Chile 3–2, Santiago*** (C. Motta lost to P. Rebolledo 1–6 3–6 6–4 3–6; L. Mattar d. R. Acuna 6–2 6–2 10–8; Mattar/Motta d. Acuna/H. Gildemeister 7–5 6–2 6–1; Motta d. Acuna 1–6 6–2 6–2 6–3; Mattar lost to Rebolledo 6–4 1–6 3–6).
FINAL – Brazil d. Ecuador 4–1, Sao Paulo (C. Motta lost to A. Gomez 8–6 7–5 9–7 3–6; L. Mattar d. H. Nunez 6–1 6–1 6–2; R. Acioly/Mattar d. Gomez/Nunez 7–5 6–3 6–8 6–4; Mattar d. Gomez 6–3 1–6 8–10 6–2 6–1; Motta d. Nunez 6–3 6–1).

EASTERN ZONE

FIRST ROUND – Chinese Taipei d. Singapore 5–0, Taipei (Chung-Hsing Lui d. M. Hassan 6–1 6–2 6–3; Chang-Rung Wu d. T. A. Peng 6–1 6–2 6–2; Huang-Jung Hsu/Wu d. Peng/A. Karim 6–0 6–1 6–0; Wu d. Hassan 6–3 7–5; Liu d. Peng 6–2 6–2); ***Pakistan d. Bangladesh 5–0, Dhaka*** (R. Malik d. S. Iftekhar 6–1 7–5 6–4; H. Aslam d. S. Jamaly 14–12 6–2 11–9; Malik/M. Zia d. Iftekhar/M. Rahman 8–6 6–1 6–2; Aslam d. Iftekhar 6–3 6–4; Zia d. Rahman 4–6 6–2 6–0); ***Philippines d. Sri Lanka 5–0, Colombo*** (R. Rafael d. A. Fernando 3–6 4–6 6–4 6–4 6–2; M. Tolentino d. F. Sebaratnam 6–0 6–0 6–2; A. Battad/R. Suarez d. Fernando/Sebaratnam 6–2 6–0 8–6; Battad d. N. Rajapakse 6–3 6–2; Tolentino d. Fernando 8–6 4–6 6–3); ***People's Republic of China d. Indonesia 4–1, Kunming City*** (Shuhua Liu d. T. Wibowo 6–3 9–7 8–6; Kegin Ma Lost to Y. Tarik 4–6 3–6 2–6; Ma/Liu d. Tarik/Wibowo 6–3 6–2 5–7 6–8 6–1; Ma d. Wibowo 6–4 9–7 5–7 7–5; Liu d. Tarik 6–2 6–1); ***Hong Kong d. Malaysia 5–0, Hong Kong*** (M. Bailey d. Y. Kian Wah 6–3 6–1 6–3; C. Grant d. K. Baharom 6–1 6–2 6–1; Bailey/P. Lui d. C. Chin Chuan/Kian Wah 6–4 6–4 7–5; Bailey d. Baharom 6–1 6–2 6–2; Grant d. Loan Wah 6–2 6–1 6–2).

QUARTER FINALS – New Zealand d. Chinese Taipei 5–0, Taipei (B. Derlin d. Chung-Hsing Liu 6–2 6–1 6–1; K. Evernden d. Chang-Rung Wu 6–4 6–2 6–1; Evernden/S. Guy d. Wu/Huang-Jung Hsu 6–3 6–2 6–4; Derlin d. Wu 6–3 12–10; Evernden d. Liu 6–3 6–2); ***Thailand d. Pakistan 3–2, Bangkok*** (T. Srichaphan d. M. Zia 6–3 6–4 6–4; W. Thongkhamchu lost to H. Aslam 9–11 1–6 2–6; Srichaphan/V. Samrej d. Aslam/H. Haq 6–8 6–3 6–4 7–5; Thongkhamchu d. R. Malik 6–2 6–8 3–6 11–9 6–2; Srichaphan lost to Aslam 5–7 2–6); ***People's Republic of China d. Philippines 4–1, Wuham, China*** (Keqin Ma d. M. Tolentino 7–5 6–3 6–4; Skuhua Liu d. A. Battad 10–8 6–0 6–2; Liu/Ma d. R. Suarez/R. Rafael 7–5 6–2 6–4; Ma d. Battad 6–3 6–3; Wei Yu lost to Tolentino 5–7 6–4 1–6); ***Japan d. Hong Kong 4–1, Toyama*** (S. Shiraishi d. M. Bailey 8–10 6–3 6–1 6–2; T. Fukui d. C. Grant 6–2 6–2 6–3; K. Tachibana/M. Takeyari lost to Bailey/Grant 4–6 4–6 4–6; Fukui d. Bailey 6–2 6–3 6–2; Shiraishi d. Grant 6–4 6–4).

SEMI-FINALS – New Zealand d. Thailand 4–1, Bangkok (K. Evernden d. P. Pladchuanil 6–2 8–6 6–2; B. Derlin d. W. Thongkamchu 2–6 6–2 6–1 6–4; Evernden/S. Guy d. V. Samret/T. Schirchaphan 9–7 6–1 7–5; Derlin d. Pladchuanil 5–7 6–3 6–3; Evernden lost to Thongkamchu 0–6 2–6); ***People's Republic of China d. Japan 3–2, Tianjin*** (Shuhua Liu d. S. Matsuoka 4–6 6–1 4–6 7–5 8–6; Keqin Ma lost to T. Fukui 4–6 4–6 4–6; Ma/Liu d. E. Takeuchi/M. Takeyari 6–4 6–4 6–3; Ma lost to Matsuka 7–9 6–8 2–6; Liu d. Fukui 6–1 6–4 1–6 6–3).

FINAL – New Zealand d. People's Republic of China 4–1, Shanghai (B. Derlin d. Shuhua Liu 6–4 6–4 6–1; K. Evernden d. Wei You 6–2 9–7 6–3; Derlin/Evernden d. Keqin Ma/Liu 5–7 6–4 7–5 8–6; Evernden d. Liu 6–4 6–4; Derlin lost to You 8–10 8–6 4–6).

EUROPEAN ZONE A

FIRST ROUND – Turkey d. Syria 5–0, Damascus (N. Demir d. H. Magarian 6–2 7–5 13–11; Y. Erkangil d. D. Danoudian 6–4 8–6 6–1; Demir/A. Kargoz d. Magarian/M. B. Masoun 6–0 6–4 6–4; Demir d. Danoudian 6–2 6–4; Erkangil d. Magarian 6–3 6–2); ***Ireland d. Malta, Marsa, 4–1*** (M. Doyle d. G. Asciak 6–3 6–1 6–1; S. Sorensen d. D. Delicata 6–2 6–3 6–0; Doyle/Sorensen d. Asciak/S. Schranz 6–0 6–4 6–2; Doyle d. Delicata 6–3 6–0; R. Dolan lost to Asciak 2–6 2–6); ***Senegal d. Norway 3–2, Bergen*** (Y. Doumbia d. J. E. Rustad 5–7 6–2 6–4 2–6 7–5; A. Berthe lost to A. Haaseth 2–6 4–6 1–6; Doumbia/Berthe d. A. Jensen/B. O. Pedersen 7–5 6–3 6–4; Berthe lost to Rustad 1–6 1–6 0–6; Doumbia d. Haaseth 6–4 6–4 6–1).

QUARTER-FINALS – USSR d. Turkey 4–1, Istanbul (A. Dolgopolov lost to N. Demir 1–6 6–4 6–4 4–6 3–6; A. Chesnokov d. K. Saydas 6–1 6–0 6–0; A. Zverev/S. Leoniuk d. Demir/A. Karagoz 6–2 6–2 6–4; Dolgopolov d. Saydas 6–1 6–2 6–1; Chesnokov d. Demir 6–2 6–2); ***Netherlands d. Ireland 4–1, Dublin*** (M. Schapers d. E. Collins 6–2 6–1 6–2; T. Nijssen lost to M. Doyle 6–4 3–6 4–6 1–6; Schapers/H. Van Boeckel d. Doyle/S. Sorensen 6–2 6–4 6–4; Schapers d. M. Nugent 6–0 6–0 6–1; Nijssen d. Collins 6–3 6–2); ***Bulgaria d. Senegal 5–0, Haskova*** (J. Stamatov d. Y. Doumbia 6–3 3–6 16–14 6–4; K. Lazarov d. A. Berthe 6–0 6–1 6–0; Stamatov/Lazarov d. Doumbia/Berthe 6–3 6–2 2–1 ret'd; Stamatov d. Berthe 6–1 6–0; Lazarov d. A. Toure 6–1 6–4); ***Switzerland d. Belgium 5–0, Lugano*** (C. Mezzadri d. K. Demuynck 6–1 6–2 6–2; J. Hlasek d. J. Depreter 6–0 6–3 6–1; Hlasek/Mezzadri d. D. Langaskens/J. Van Langendonck 6–4 7–5 8–6; Hlasek d. Demuynck 9–7 6–4; Mezzadri d. Depreter 6–0 6–2).

SEMI-FINALS – USSR d. Netherlands 4–1, Valkenswaard (A. Chesnokov d. M. Schapers 24–22 1–6 6–2 6–2; A. Volkov d. T. Nijssen 8–6 7–5 6–4; S. Leoniuk/A. Zverev lost to Schapers/H. Van Boeckel 6–3 4–6 4–6 4–6; Volkov d. Schapers 6–2 8–6 6–2; Chesnokov d. Nijssen 6–3 6–3); ***Switzerland d. Bulgaria 5–0, Haskova*** (C. Mezzadri d. K. Lazarov 6–1 6–1 6–1; J. Hlasek d. R. Rainov 7–5 6–2 6–3; Mezzadri/R. Stadler d. T. Batchev/Lazarov 6–4 6–4 6–3; Hlasek d. Lazarov 6–0 6–4; Mezzadri d. Rainov 6–4 6–0).

FINAL – Switzerland d. USSR 3–2, Donetsk (C. Mezzadri d. A. Zverev 7–5 6–2 5–6 0–6 6–2; J. Hlasek lost to A. Chesnokov 7–5 7–9 4–6 4–6; Hlasek/H. Gunthardt d. A. Volkov/Zverev 4–6 6–4 6–3 7–5; Mezzadri lost to Chesnokov 2–6 5–7 5–7; Hlasek d. Zverev 6–4 6–3 6–2).

EUROPEAN ZONE B

FIRST ROUND – Greece d. Luxembourg 5–0, Rhodes (G. Kalovelonis d. S. Bruck 6–4 6–1 6–4; T. Bavelas d. J. Goudenbour 3–6 2–6 8–6 6–1 6–3; J. Rigas/F. Vazeos d. Bruck/J. Radoux 1–6 6–4 14–12 6–4; Kalovelonis d. Radoux 6–4 6–3; Bavelas d. Bruck 6–2 6–1); ***Portugal d. Monaco 3–2, Monaco*** (N. Marques d. B. Balleret 6–3 6–1 6–2; J. C. E. Silva lost to G. Ganancia 6–4 4–6 5–7 4–6; P. Cordeiro/Silva d. Balleret/A. Viviani 6–4 6–2 6–4; Marques lost to Ganancia 5–7 2–6 5–7; Silva d. Balleret 6–3 6–4 0–6 7–5); ***Poland d. Zimbabwe 3–2, Harare*** (L. Bienkowski d. M. Gurr 6–0 6–4 0–6 6–0; W. Kowalski lost to B. Black 6–4 7–5 4–6 2–6 1–6; Bienkowski/Kowalski d. Gurr/Black 8–6 1–6 9–7 8–6; Bienkowski lost to Black 1–6 4–6 2–6; Kowalski d. Gurr 3–6 6–3 6–3 6–3); ***Finland d. Cyprus 5–0, Helsinki*** (V. Paloheimo d. A. Papamichael 6–0 6–1 6–1; O. Rahnasto d. Y. Hadjigeorgiou 8–6 6–2 6–0; Rahnasto/M. Hedman d. Hadjigeorgiou/P. Zachariades 6–1 6–2 6–3; Rahnasto d. Papamichael 6–1 6–3; Paloheimo d. Hadjigiorgiou 6–2 6–1).
QUARTER-FINALS – Austria d. Greece 4–1, Bad Kleinkirchen (H. Skoff d. G. Kalovelonis 6–2 6–4 6–3; T. Muster d. A. Bavelas 7–5 6–0 6–1; A. Antonitsch/Muster d. Kalovelonis/J. Rigas 6–2 6–2 6–2; Muster d. Kalovelonis 6–1 7–5; Skoff lost to Bavelas 6–8 6–3 4–6); ***Portugal d. Hungary 5–0, Lisbon*** (J. Cunha e Silva d. A. Lanyi 6–4 6–4 5–7 8–6; N. Marques d. L. Markovits 6–1 6–3 6–0; Cunha e Silva/P. Cordeiro d. Lanyi/S. Kiss 6–2 5–7 6–4 6–2; Marques d. Lanyi 6–0 4–6 6–2; Cunha e Silva d. Markovitz 4–6 6–2 6–1); ***Rumania d. Poland 4–1, Brasov*** (A. Marcu d. W. Kowalski 6–1 6–2 6–2; F. Segarceanu d. L. Bienkowski 6–3 6–1 6–3; A. Dirzu/Segarceanu d. Kowalski/Bienkowski 6–3 7–5 6–3; Kowalski d. M. Vanta 6–8 6–3 7–5; Marcu d. Bienkowski 6–3 6–2); ***Denmark d. Finland 5–0, Helsinki*** (M. Christensen d. O. Rahnasto 1–6 10–8 6–4 7–5; M. Tauson d. V. Paloheimo 3–6 5–7 6–4 6–2 6–2; Christensen/-Tauson d. Rahnasto/K. Alkio 6–2 6–1 6–2; Christensen d. Paloheimo 6–4 13–11).
SEMI-FINALS – Austria d. Portugal 4–1, Oporto (H. Skoff d. N. Marques 8–6 6–3 6–3; T. Muster d. J. Cunha e Silva 6–1 9–7 6–3; A. Antonitsch/Muster d. P. Cordeiro/Cunha e Silva 6–3 4–6 6–4 6–3; Muster d. Marques 6–3 5–7 7–5; Skoff lost to Cunha e Silva 6–4 1–6 3–6); ***Denmark d. Rumania 3–2, Aarhus*** (P. Bastiansen lost to F. Segarceanu 4–6 3–6 6–3 6–3 5–7; M. Tauson d. A. Marcu 6–2 6–2 1–6 4–6 6–3; Bastiansen/M. Mortensen d. A. Dirzu/Segarceanu 10–8 6–3 3–6 6–2; Bastiansen lost to Marcu 1–6 2–6 3–6; Tauson d. Segarceanu 6–4 5–7 6–4 9–7).
FINAL – Denmark d. Austria 3–2, Copenhagen (M. Christensen d. T. Muster 6–4 6–2 6–2; M. Tauson d. H. Skoff 6–4 4–6 6–3 6–2; Christensen/Mortensen lost to A. Antonitsch/Muster 5–7 6–3 10–12 3–6; Christensen lost to Skoff 8–10 6–4 6–8 1–6; Tauson d. Muster 6–8 12–10 2–6 6–3 6–4).

DAVIS CUP PRIZE MONEY (provided by NEC)

NON-ZONAL COMPETITION: Champion nation: $200,000. Runners-up: $100,000. Semi-finalists $75,000. Quarter-finalists $45,000. Play-off winners: $35,000. Play-off losers: $25,000.
ZONAL COMPETITION: $2,800 per tie. ***Bonuses European, American and Eastern Zones:*** Winners: $3,600. Semi-finalists: $2,000. Quarter-finalists: $1,200. First round winners: $800.
Bonuses African Zone: Semi-finalists: $800. Quarter-finalists: $700. First round winners: $600.
Overall total: $1,229,200.

DAVIS CUP by NEC 1988

Non-Zonal Competition

FIRST ROUND 5–7 February	SECOND ROUND 8–10 April	SEMI-FINALS 22–24 July	FINAL 16–18 December
SWEDEN†			
New Zealand			
CZECHOSLOVAKIA†	*		
Paraguay			
AUSTRALIA			
Mexico†		*	
FRANCE	*		
Switzerland†			
Brazil			
WEST GERMANY†		*	
Denmark†	*		
SPAIN			*
Italy†	*		
ISRAEL			
Yugoslavia			
INDIA†			

† Choice of ground.
** Choice of ground if decided by lot.*

Seeded nations in capital letters.
Play-off ties 8–10 April 1988.

Zonal Competition

EURO/AFRICAN ZONE GROUP I

Zone A

FIRST ROUND 6–8 May	SEMI-FINALS 10–12 June	FINAL 22–24 JULY	
	GREAT BRITAIN†		
Finland			Winner promoted to Non-Zonal Group 1989
Belgium†			
Hungary		*	
Nigeria†	AUSTRIA		

Zone B

FIRST ROUND	SEMI-FINALS	FINAL	
	NETHERLANDS†	*	
Senegal†			Winner promoted to Non-Zonal Group 1989
Bulgaria			
Rumania†	*		
Portugal	USSR		

AMERICAN ZONE GROUP I

FIRST ROUND 5–7 February	SEMI-FINALS 8–10 April	FINAL 22–24 July	
	ARGENTINA		
Ecuador†	†		Winner promoted to Non-Zonal Group 1989
Canada			
Peru	†	*	
Chile†	USA		

ASIA/OCEANIA ZONE GROUP I

FIRST ROUND 5–7 February	SEMI-FINALS 8–10 April	FINAL 22–24 July	
	Republic of Korea†		
Japan			Winner promoted to Non-Zonal Group 1989
Philippines†			
Thailand	*		
Indonesia†	CHINA		

EUROPEAN ZONE GROUP II

FIRST ROUND 8–10 April	SECOND ROUND 6–8 May	SEMI-FINALS 10–12 June	FINAL 22–24 July	
	POLAND†	*		
	Luxembourg			
	GREECE†			Winner promoted to Euro/African Zone Group I 1989
	Turkey			
Malta	†			
Norway†	MONACO		*	
	Cyprus			
	IRELAND†	*		

AFRICAN ZONE GROUP II

FIRST ROUND 5–7 February	SECOND ROUND 8–10 April	SEMI-FINALS 6–8 May	FINAL 22–24 July	
	ZIMBABWE†		*	
	Cameroon			
	ALGERIA	*		Winner promoted to Euro/African Zone Group 1 1989
	Ivory Coast†			
	Tunisia†			
	MOROCCO			
Ghana†				
Kenya	EGYPT	*		

ASIA/OCEANIA ZONE GROUP II

FIRST ROUND 5–7 February	SECOND ROUND 8–10 April	SEMI-FINALS 6–8 May	FINAL 22–24 July	
	HONG KONG		*	
	Iraq†			
	SINGAPORE	*		Winner promoted to Asia/Oceania Zone Group 1 1989
Saudi Arabia	†			
Syria†				
	Bangladesh			
	CHINESE TAIPEI†	*		
Sri Lanka	*			
Malaysia†	PAKISTAN			

AMERICAN ZONE GROUP II

FIRST ROUND 5–7 February	SEMI-FINALS 8–10 April	FINAL 22–24 July	
	URUGUAY		
Cuba†	†		Winner promoted to American Zone Group I 1989
Bolivia			
Venezuela†		*	
Colombia			
Jamaica†	*		
HAITI			

Left: Helen Kelesi of Canada, who had earlier beaten Lindqvist to reach the last 16 of the French Open, proudly took her country to the quarter-finals of the Federation Cup. (T. Hindley) Below: The winning West German team. (M. Phillips)

THE *FEDERATION CUP* by NEC

Henry Wancke

The Federal Republic of Germany pulled off one of the most remarkable victories since the start of the competition in 1963 when they won the *Federation Cup* in West Vancouver on 2 August. It was remarkable in that they faced seemingly inevitable defeat in the deciding doubles, yet emerged champions with a display of tennis which stunned their American adversaries and left the packed stadium gasping for more.

This classic match brought the curtain down on a glorious week of tennis, and must have left the local organisers desperate to try to bring international tennis back to the west coast of Canada. After the resounding success in Prague the previous year, Vancouver pulled out all the stops to ensure that the *Federation Cup* continued to grow in prestige. And they were successful. Their efforts brought a new dimension to the event, which attracted more than 61,000 spectators as the record for the number of competing nations was equalled (42), with the teams including most of the best players in the world.

The United States of America, defending champions and top seeds, declared the same team which had successfully recaptured the *Federation Cup* 12 months earlier from Czechoslovakia – Martina Navratilova, Chris Evert, Pam Shriver and Zina Garrison, captained by Marty Riessen. Regrettably Martina, undoubtedly the main attraction, was forced to withdraw the Friday before the event got under way, owing to a basketball accident a few days earlier when she had twisted her ankle. In her place came Elise Burgin, who arrived on the Sunday just in time for the opening ceremony which was cut short by a deluge! Czechoslovakia, the second seeds, included Hana Mandlikova and Helena Sukova in their strong team, whilst Germany, seeded third and led by Steffi Graf, could also call on either Claudia Kohde-Kilsch or Bettina Bunge to represent them. Whilst other nations had their stars, like Argentina with Gabriela Sabatini, Italy with Sandra Cecchini and Raffaella Reggi, Bulgaria with the Maleeva sisters and their mother, Australia with Wendy Turnbull, and Canada with Carling Bassett, most pundits correctly felt that the title of Champion Nation would go to one of the top three seeds.

The USA had the easiest of draws and cruised through to the final without conceding a rubber. West Germany, however, had a rougher ride, dropping a rubber in both their quarter- and semi-final matches, to Argentina and Czechoslovakia respectively.

Whilst historians and those present will remember the final as the outstanding match, the early part of the week definitely belonged to the host nation, Canada. Unseeded and ably assisted by the partisan crowd, they played above themselves to reach the quarter-finals, defeating the Netherlands and the eighth-seeded USSR on the way. Their star proved to be Helen Kelesi, whose never-say-die spirit, coupled with the pride she displayed at representing her country, proved catching. Playing at No. 2, she emerged from the field of battle with flying colours, undefeated in all her singles matches and having captured the scalps of Marianne Van Der Torre (Netherlands, 6–4 6–2), Natalia Zvereva (USSR, 3–6 6–4 6–3) and Helena Sukova (Czechoslovakia, 4–6 6–1 6–2). She also showed her ability as a doubles player, partnering Jill Hetherington to beat the experienced team of Larisa Savchenko and Svetlana Parkhomenko (USSR, 6–4 6–3). However, the Canadian run was brought to an abrupt halt at the quarter-final stage by the second seeds.

Great Britain also provided an early upset to make up for their disastrous first-round exit in Prague the year before. They reached the quarter-finals with wins over Chile (3–0) and the seventh seeds, Italy (2–1), but couldn't make any impression on the defending champions, going down 0–3. However, their quarter-final placing assured them of direct entries into the Olympics at Seoul in 1988.

The lesser tennis nations, having achieved their more realistic goals and provided the stronger countries with suitable warm-ups, now left the stage for the two strongest nations to contest the title. The dominance of the Americans was being challenged by the fast-maturing West German, Steffi Graf, and as the Americans went for their 13th *Federation Cup* title, Marty Riessen fielded his strongest team. Pam Shriver took on Claudia Kohde-Kilsch in the first singles, and destroyed the obviously nervous West German 6–0 in the first set. Although Claudia managed to raise her game to force a tie-break in the second, she eventually had to concede the first rubber to the Americans 6–0 7–6 (7–5). For Pam, this was the first year she had represented her country at singles in *Federation Cup*, and she gave solid performances throughout the week to emerge, at the end, undefeated.

Chris Evert, with only one loss in singles during her long career of international duty for her country (suffered the previous year in Prague) was completely outplayed by Steffi Graf, winning only three games in a match lasting less than an hour.

Then came the classic doubles. Shriver and Evert, the former on a high in view of her record during the week and the latter stung by unfamiliar emotions, bulldozed their way into a winning position, taking the first set 6–1 and leading 4–0 in the second. Then the Germans relaxed and simply hit out. Surprisingly the experienced Evert appeared to be affected by nerves, for she served two double-faults and the Germans suddenly exploded into action. At first it seemed they would merely delay the inevitable, but as they pulled back to 5-all and then took the second set 7–5, it was obvious that anything could happen. The Europeans were playing brilliant tennis, their opponents had not dropped their standard, and the speed of movement, as both sets of players attacked and defended, forced the spectators on to the edges of their seats. Seeming winners were retrieved and converted into attacking thrusts, and the West Germans snatched victory from the face of defeat 1–6 7–5 6–4.

It was West Germany's fifth appearance in a *Federation Cup* final, and they become only the fifth nation to have won this prestigious title. Yet even in victory Steffi Graf maintained it might have been different had Martina been fit to play. That, of course, is pure conjecture. On the day, the better team won, and no-one who witnessed their excellent performance will ever forget it.

THE *FEDERATION CUP* by NEC

VANCOUVER, 26 JULY–2 AUGUST

QUALIFYING ROUND – Chile d. People's Republic of China 2–1 (C. Espinoza d. Xinji Li 0–6 7–6 6–3; M. Miranda lost to Yan Sun 1–6 6–4 4–6; Espinoza/Miranda d. Ni Zhong/Li Xinji 6–4 7–5); ***Ireland d. Taiwan 3–0*** (S. Nicholson d. Su-Lin Lai 6–3 7–5; J. Thornton d. Shin-Min LIn 6–1 6–1; Nicholson/L. Halleran d. Lin/Dai-Hwa Wang 6–2 6–0); ***Indonesia d. Finland 2–1*** (S. Anggarkusumah d. S. Ansio 4–6 6–4 6–4; N. R. Basuki lost to A. Allonen 4–6 5–7; Anggarkusumah/Basuki d. Allonen/Ansio 6–4 6–2); ***Jamaica w.o. Thailand; Denmark d. Luxembourg 3–0*** (L. Vandborg d. G. Huberty 6–0 6–2; T. Scheuer-Larsen d. K. Kschwendt 6–2 3–6 6–4; Scheuer-Larsen/Vandborg d. Huberty/ Kschwendt 6–3 6–3); ***Switzerland d. Malta 3–0*** (E. Zardo d. H. Asciak 7–5 6–1; E. Krapl d. C. Curmi 6–0 6–2; C. Cohen/Krapl d. Curmi/A. Gera 6–2 6–1); ***Norway d. Peru 3–0*** (M. Wiesse d. K. Heck 6–3 4–6 9–7; A. Joensson d. K. Strohmeier 6–0 6–0; Joensson Wiesse d. Collanges/Strohmeier 6–0 7–5); ***Republic of Korea d. Mexico 2–1*** (Il-Soon Kim d. L. Becerra 6–3 6–7 6–3; Eun-Ok Cho lost to C. Hernandez 4–6 0–6; Jeong-Myung Lee/Kim d. Becerra/Hernandez 6–0 7–5); ***Israel d. Zimbabwe 3–0*** (D. Koriat d. P. Iversen 6–4 6–2; I. Berger d. J. Muir 6–1 6–3; Berger/Koriat d. Iversen/Muir 6–1 6–1); ***Poland d. Philippines 2–1*** (E. Zerdecka d. J. Saberon 7–6 6–4; R. Wojtiewicz lost to D. Castillejo 1–6 7–5 3–6; Wojtiewicz/Zerdecka d. Saberson/S. Rafael 6–3 6–4).

FIRST ROUND – USA d. Japan 3–0 (P. H. Shriver d. A. Kijimuta 7–6 6–1; C. M. Evert d. E. Inoue 6–2 6–4; Evert/Z. Garrison d. Inoue/Kijimuta 6–2 7–5); ***France d. Austria 3–0*** (I. Demongeot d. P. Huber 6–1 6–4; N. Tauziat d. J. Polzl Wiesner 6–3 7–5; Demongeot/C. Suire d. Huber/Polzl Wiesner 1–6 6–3 6–1); ***Great Britain d. Chile 3–0*** (S. Gomer d. C. Espinoza 6–3 6–1; J. M. Durie d. M. Miranda 6–2 6–1; Durie/A. E. Hobbs d. Espinoza/Miranda 6–1 6–0); ***Italy d. Belgium 2–1*** (A. M. Cecchini d. S. Wasserman 6–1 6–0; R. Reggi d. A. Devries 6–2 7–5; L. Garrone/C. Nozzoli lost to Devries/Wasserman

3–6 1–6); ***Bulgaria d. Greece 2–1*** (K. Maleeva d. O. Tsarbopoulou 6–0 6–0; M. Maleeva d. A. Kanellopoulou 6–0 6–0; Y. Berberian/D. Rangelova lost to Kanellopoulou/Tsarbopoulou 2–6 4–6); ***Indonesia d. Ireland 3–0*** (A. Anggarkusuma d. S. Nicholson 7–5 6–4 6–3; Nani Rayhaya Basuki/d. J. Thornton 6–4 6–2; Basuki/Waya Walalangi d. Nicholson/Thornton 7–6 6–3); ***Spain d. Jamaica 3–0*** (M. Llorca d. H. Harris 6–1 6–2; A. Sanchez d. J. van Ryk de Groot 6–3 6–1; Llorca/Sanchez d. Harris/van Ryk de Groot 7–6 6–2); ***Australia d. Denmark 3–0*** (A. Minter d. L. Vanborg 6–2 6–0; E. Smylie d. T. Scheuer-Larsen 5–7 6–4 6–0; J. Byrne/W. M. Turnbull d. Scheuer-Larsen/Vanborg 6–4 2–6 6–2); ***Argentina d. Switzerland 3–0*** (G. Sabatini d. E. Krapl 6–2 6–1; B. Fulco d. E. Zardo 6–4 6–2; M. Paz/Sabatini d. C. Cohen/Krapl 6–2 6–0); ***New Zealand d. Brazil 2–1*** (B. Cordwell d. N. Dias 6–1 6–3; J. Richardson lost to P. Medrado 5–7 2–6; Cordwell/Richardson d. Dias/Medrado 4–6 7–5 6–3); ***Republic of Korea d. Norway 2–1*** (Il-Soon Kim lost to A. Joensson 1–6 7–5 9–11; Jeong-Myung Lee d. M. Wiesse 6–0 6–1; Lee/Kim d. Joensson/S. V. Andersen 6–2 6–0); ***West Germany d. Hong Kong 3–0*** (S. Graf d. P. Hy 6–7 6–2 6–4; C. Kohde-Kilsch d. P. Moreno 6–0 6–2; B. Bunge/S. Meier d. Hy/Moreno 6–1 6–1); ***USSR d. Israel 3–0*** (L. Savchenko d. I. Berger 6–3 6–2; N. Zvereva d. D. Koriat 6–1 6–2; Savchenko/S. Parkhomenko d. Berger/Koriat 6–1 6–1); ***Canada d. Netherlands 3–0*** (C Bassett d. M. Mesker 4–6 7–5 6–2; H. Kelesi d. M. Van Der Torre 6–4 6–2; Bassett/J. Hetherington d. Mesker/Van Der Torre 6–4 6–2); ***Yugoslavia d. Poland 2–1*** (S. Goles d. R. Wojtkiewcz 6–3 6–1; K. Skulje lost to E. Zerdecka 5–7 2–6; Goles/R. Sasak d. Wojtkiewcz/Zerdecka 6–2 6–4); ***Czechoslovakia d. Sweden 3–0*** (H. Mandlikova d. C. Lindqvist 6–3 6–2; H. Sukova d. C. Karlsson 6–4 6–4; Mandlikova/J. Novotna d. Lindqvist/M. Lindstrom 6–3 6–2).

SECOND ROUND – USA d. France 3–0 (P. H. Shriver d. I. Demongeot 6–0 7–6; C. M. Evert d. N. Tauziat 6–1 6–0; Evert/Shriver d. Demongeot/C. Suire 6–1 6–0); ***Great Britain d. Italy 2–1*** (S. Gomer d. A. M. Cecchini 6–7 6–1 6–3; J. M. Durie lost to R. Reggi 5–7 4–6; Durie/A. E. Hobbs d. Cecchini/Reggi 7–5 6–4); ***Bulgaria d. Indonesia 2–1*** (K. Maleeva d. S. Anggarkusuma 6–1 6–1; M. Maleeva d. Nani Rahayu Basuki 6–4 6–0; Y. Berberian/D. Rangelova lost to Anggarkusuma/Basuki 0–6 1–6); ***Australia d. Spain 2–1*** (A. Minter lost to J. Llorca 4–6 4–6; E. Smylie d. A. Sanchez 6–1 4–6 6–1; Smylie/W. M. Turnbull d. Llorca/Sanchez 6–1 6–2); ***Argentina d. New Zealand 3–0*** (B. Fulco d. J. Richardson 6–3 6–4; G. Sabatini d. B. Cordwell 6–3 7–5; M. Paz/Sabatini d. Cordwell/Richardson 4–6 6–3 6–1); ***West Germany d. Republic of Korea 3–0*** (C. Kohde-Kilsch d. Jeong-Myung Lee 6–2 6–1; S. Graf d. Il-Soon Kim 6–1 6–1; Graf/Kohde-Kilsch d. Lee/Kim 6–1 6–0); ***Canada d. USSR 2–1*** (H. Kelesi d. N. Zvereva 3–6 6–4 6–3; C. Bassett lost to L. Savchenko 7–5 4–6 4–6; J. Hetherington/Kelesi d. S. Parkhomenko/Savchenko 6–4 6–3); ***Czechoslovakia d. Yugoslavia 3–0*** (H. Sukova d. K. Skulj 6–2 6–3; H. Mandlikova d. S. Goles 6–4 6–3; J. Novotna/R. Rajchrtova d. Goles/R. Sasak 6–4 5–7 6–4).

QUARTER-FINALS – USA d. Great Britain 3–0 (P. H. Shriver d. S. Gomer 6–1 6–3; C. M. Evert d. J. M. Durie 6–3 6–1; E. Burgin/Z. Garrison d. Durie/Hobbs 7–5 7–5); ***Bulgaria d. Australia 2–0*** (K. Maleeva d. A. Minter 6–2 6–2; M. Maleeva d. E. Smylie 6–4 6–4); ***West Germany d. Argentina 2–1*** (C. Kohde-Kilsch d. B. Fulco 6–2 6–2; S. Graf d. G. Sabatini 6–4 6–4; B. Bunge/S. Meier lost to M. Paz/Sabatini 7–6 1–6 2–6); ***Czechoslovakia d. Canada 2–1*** (H. Sukova lost to H. Kelesi 6–4 1–6 2–6; H. Mandlikova d. C. Bassett 6–4 6–1; Mandlikova/Sukova d. Bassett/Kelesi 6–2 6–2).

SEMI-FINALS – USA d. Bulgaria 2–0 (P. H. Shriver d. K. Maleeva 6–3 7–6; C. M. Evert d. M. Maleeva 6–2 2–6 6–4); ***West Germany d. Czechoslovakia 2–1*** (C. Kohde-Kilsch lost to H. Sukova 6–7 5–7; S. Graf d. H. Mandlikova 6–4 6–1; Graf/Kohde-Kilsch d. Mandlikova/Sukova 7–5 6–2).

FINAL – West Germany d. USA 2–1 (C. Kohde-Kilsch lost to P. H. Shriver 0–6 6–7; S. Graf d. C. M. Evert 6–2 6–1; Graf/Kohde-Kilsch d. Evert/Shriver 1–6 7–5 6–4).

FEDERATION CUP by NEC 1987

PRELIMINARY ROUND

People's Republic of China
Chile

Ireland
Taiwan
Finland
Indonesia
Thailand
Jamaica

Denmark
Luxembourg

Switzerland
Malta

Norway
Peru
Mexico
Republic of Korea

Zimbabwe
Israel

Poland
Philippines

FIRST ROUND

USA (1)
Japan
France
Austria
Great Britain
Chile
2–1
Belgium
ITALY (7)
BULGARIA (4)
Greece
Ireland
3–0
Indonesia
2–1
Jamaica
w.o.
Spain
Denmark
3–0
AUSTRALIA (5)
ARGENTINA (6)
Switzerland
3–0
Brazil
New Zealand
Norway
3–0
Republic of Korea
2–1
Hong Kong
WEST GERMANY (3)
USSR (8)
Israel
3–0
Canada
Netherlands
Poland
2–1
Yugoslavia
Sweden
CZECHOSLOVAKIA (2)

SECOND ROUND

USA (1)
3–0
France
3–0
Great Britain
3–0
ITALY (7)
2–1
BULGARIA (4)
2–1
Indonesia
3–0
Spain
3–0
AUSTRALIA (5)
3–0
ARGENTINA (6)
3–0
New Zealand
2–1
Republic of Korea
2–1
WEST GERMANY (3)
3–0
USSR (8)
3–0
Canada
3–0
Yugoslavia
2–1
CZECHOSLOVAKIA (2)
3–0

QUARTER-FINALS

USA (1)
3–0
Great Britain
2–1
BULGARIA (4)
2–1
AUSTRALIA (5)
2–1
ARGENTINA (6)
3–0
WEST GERMANY (3)
3–0
Canada
2–1
CZECHOSLOVAKIA (2)
3–0

SEMI-FINALS

USA (1)
3–0
BULGARIA (4)
2–0
WEST GERMANY (3)
2–1
CZECHOSLOVAKIA (2)
2–1

FINAL

USA (1)
2–0
WEST GERMANY (3)
2–1

WEST GERMANY (3)
2–1

Capital letters denote seeded countries. Number following country's name denotes seeding order.

GRAND SLAM CHAMPIONSHIPS

AUSTRALIAN OPEN CHAMPIONSHIPS
FRENCH OPEN CHAMPIONSHIPS
WIMBLEDON CHAMPIONSHIPS
US OPEN CHAMPIONSHIPS
(Part of the Nabisco Grand Prix and Virginia Slims Series)

Mats Wilander of Sweden finished 1987 ranked No. 3 for the third consecutive year after reaching the final of the French Open, US Open and Masters, as well as winning his first Italian Open crown and four other singles titles. *(T. Hindley)*

In the last Australian Open to be played on grass at Kooyong, Stefan Edberg confirmed his ability on that surface by retaining his singles title, as well as taking the doubles title with his fellow Swede, Anders Jarryd *(R. Gould)*

AUSTRALIAN OPEN CHAMPIONSHIPS

Alan Trengove

By an ironical twist of fate, the last Australian Open to be held at Kooyong – and presumably the last on grass – turned out to be the best yet. Record crowds poured into the 60-year-old stadium, which was to be superseded in 1988 by a new National Tennis Centre at Flinders Park, on the fringe of Melbourne's central business district.

There were good reasons why the tournament, which has so often been plagued by problems, should have enjoyed such resounding success. A return to the old January dates obviously suited the fans; January is a holiday month for the majority of Australians, and the weather is more settled, if hotter, than in late November and early December, the Open's time-slot in recent years. The fields were strong – though notable absentees included Mats Wilander, John McEnroe, Chris Evert Lloyd and Steffi Graf – and public enthusiasm had been whetted by Australia's *Davis Cup* triumph over Sweden at the same venue only a few weeks earlier. Perhaps, above all, many fans simply didn't want to miss attending, for the last time, the courts which had supplied them with so many vivid memories.

Several fascinating questions awaited resolution in the men's singles. Would Ivan Lendl be rewarded for his most painstaking Australian preparation to date by gaining his first grass-court title? Was Boris Becker going to be affected by any traumatic hangover from his early defeat at Kooyong in 1985 by Michiel Schapers? And could Pat Cash follow up his heroic *Davis Cup* performances by becoming the first Australian since Mark Edmondson in 1976 to win his national crown?

To everyone's surprise, the Championship was dominated by none of these players but by Stefan Edberg, the defending champion, who dropped only one set on his way to the final and then beat Cash in a five-set thriller. For all his undoubted ability, Edberg, the No. 4 seed, was not greatly favoured to win again, because he had appeared to lose confidence in the *Davis Cup* final. Very sensibly, however, Edberg took a Queensland holiday after that disappointment and then rebuilt his form in the low-key Western Australian Open, which he won.

Lendl, the top seed, had come to Australia two weeks before the Open, had played in the doubles event at the South Australian Open, and then had played in exhibitions and practised on grass under the shrewd eye of coach Tony Roche. He was as mentally and physically ready for a grass-court championship as he is ever likely to be. But as Lendl – and several other critics – pointed out the Centre Court arena was so devoid of grass it was more of a hard-court surface. As a result of intensive use during the *Davis Cup* period, the three courts in the stadium looked dry and cracked. Becker said the scene resembled the aftermath of an earthquake, while Wendy Turnbull complained that the hard little globules of soil that broke loose made footing treacherous – 'like treading on ball-bearings'.

Whatever the quality of the courts, they didn't seem to worry Lendl unduly. He dropped one set each to Danny Saltz, Matt Anger and Dan Goldie, and in the quarter-finals hammered Anders Jarryd 7–6 6–1 6–3. Becker, though, ventured much more precariously – principally because of his own imperfections rather than any defects in the courts. In his first match, spread over two days, he was taken to five sets by Brod Dyke, the South Australian left-hander who had beaten him at Brussels early in 1986. The match began at about the same time, and was held on the same court, as Becker's match with Schapers in the 1985 Open. He was very nervous and became increasingly exasperated as the tenacious Dyke served and volleyed excellently, and made the most of his opponent's erratic groundstrokes.

There followed another tough match for Becker as he laboured to beat his friend and doubles partner, Slobodan Zivojinovic, in four sets. Having survived that test, it seemed that Becker was due for some light relief as every other seed in his quarter had been eliminated. It was not to be. He departed rather ingloriously in a quarter-final, beaten 4–6 7–6 6–4 6–7 6–2 by Wally Masur. The most astounding feature of his defeat was his failure on the big points. Four times he double-faulted on break-point. Another flaw was his tactical immaturity in the face of Masur's solid all-round play. Instead of blocking some of Masur's better serves, Becker continued to go for aggressive returns, making so many errors that much of the pressure on the Australian was regularly eased.

Even so, Becker should have won after saving three match-points in the fourth-set tie-break and going to a 2–0 lead in the fifth. Who would have thought that it would be the robust dual Wimbledon champion who would crack first, conceding six games in a row? Becker was fined a total of $2,000 for various acts of misbehaviour during a match in which he totally lost control following an overrule. It was a contest he wanted quickly to forget. His torment was prolonged the next day when his coach, Gunther Bosch, announced his resignation. 'There must be something in the air in Australia', mused a gloomy Boris.

Meanwhile, Edberg and Cash fought their way less emotionally to a second confrontation within a month. The low-key Swede improved with every match, dropping only two games to a partly disabled Robert Seguso, and also dispatching in straight sets an in-form Miloslav Mecir and the gallant Masur. His second serve, which kicked head-high, was almost as deadly as his cannonball. Cash, who was recovering from a *Davis Cup* let-down as well as a virus, also played himself into good form while beating Paul Annacone and Yannick Noah. With his relentless serve-and-volley attack, his lightning court coverage and steely resolve, he conquered Lendl in a semi-final, 7–6 5–7 7–6 6–4. It was a long, dour match between two finely tuned athletes, with Cash's volleying flair finally giving him the edge.

The final provided a fitting climax to Kooyong's Grand Slam history. Edberg was unstoppable for much of the first two sets, but Cash grimly began inching his way into the match late in the second set. When Cash won the third set and led 5–1 in the fourth, the crowd began to think he was going to reproduce the kind of comeback that had frustrated Mikael Pernfors in the *Davis Cup*. But, serving for the fourth set at 5–2, the Australian faltered. Again, at 5–4, he lost concentration, serving three successive double-faults; and though Cash still won the set, Edberg had had time to regroup. In the fifth set, the Swede refound his earlier brilliance and stormed to a well-deserved triumph, 6–3 6–4 3–6 5–7 6–3. He also achieved his first Grand Slam doubles title with Anders Jarryd, beating the Australians, Peter Doohan and Laurie Warder, in the final.

The women's singles was much less dramatic than the men's – up to the final. In contrast to previous years, Martina Navratilova, the defending champion, skipped the two lead-up tournaments in Brisbane and Sydney, preferring to take a skiing holiday in Colorado instead. She arrived in Melbourne with a new coach, Randy Crawford, having recently split with her long-time mentor, Mike Estep. Another addition to 'Team Navratilova' was Virginia Wade.

Hana Mandlikova, on the other hand, flew to Australia more than a month before the Open. She spent Christmas with her husband, Jan Sedlak, in Sydney, announced that she was applying for Australian citizenship, and gained valuable acclimatisation and match practice in the earlier tournaments.

The two different approaches appeared of little consequence in the preliminary rounds. It was Navratilova who, as usual, swept all opposition before her. She allowed Zina Garrison, winner of the NSW Classic, only three games, and conceded only five to Catarina Lindqvist, who, for the second Australian Open in a row, bundled out Pam Shriver.

In the bottom half of the draw Elizabeth Smylie's brave defeat of No. 4 seed Helena Sukova, 7–5 3–6 7–5 after trailing 1–4 in the third, was the outstanding feature. The Australian's aggressive brand of tennis also earned her two set-points in her first set against Claudia Kohde-Kilsch, but she eventually went down in three, 7–6 4–6 6–2. Mandlikova dropped a set apiece to Julie Richardson and Carling Bassett before handing out a

6–0 6–0 drubbing to Lori McNeil in the quarter-finals. Her semi-final with Kohde-Kilsch was a typically fluctuating Mandlikova saga, with the West German nervously losing the first set 6–1, winning the second 6–0, and being marginally outplayed in the third, which went to Hana 6–3.

Navratilova began the final almost as though she had a premonition this would not be her day. The defending champion was on a nine-match winning streak against her Czech rival, her last defeat being at the 1985 US Open. But with Mandlikova, statistics often mean so little.

Navratilova was tentative from the start. She had opportunities to win the first set, in which there were seven breaks of serve, and actually served for the set at 5–4. She lost it 7–5. In the second set, Mandlikova led 5–3 and 30–0, only to lose that ninth game and be taken to a tie-break. This she won by 7 points to 1, beating the world's number one both mentally and physically to capture her second Australian crown. Navratilova and Shriver gained some consolation for their singles defeats when they won their fifth Australian Open doubles title – and their fifteenth Grand Slam championship together – by crushing Garrison and McNeil 6–1 6–0.

The tournament featured the re-introduction of the mixed doubles championship, which had not been a part of the Open since 1969 and had not been played at Kooyong since 1968. Once again Navratilova was frustrated in her ambition to win three titles at the one Grand Slam event. She and Paul Annacone were beaten 3–6 7–5 10–8 in the semi-finals by 40-year-old Sherwood Stewart and his partner, Zina Garrison, who went on to take the title over the unseeded Britons, Anne Hobbs and Andrew Castle.

JUNIOR EVENTS

BOYS' SINGLES – Final: J. Stoltenberg d. T. Woodbridge 6–2 7–6.
GIRLS' SINGLES – Final: M. Jaggard d. N. Provis 6–2 6–4.
BOYS' DOUBLES – Final: Stoltenberg/Woodbridge d. S. Barr/B. Roe 6–2 6–4.
GIRLS' DOUBLES – Final: N. Provis/A. Devries d. D. Jones/G. Dwyer 6–3 6–3.

AUSTRALIAN OPEN CHAMPIONSHIPS PRIZE MONEY – $1,372,375

MEN'S SINGLES – Winner $103,875. Runner-up $51,938. Semi-finalists $25,959. Quarter-finalists $13,336. Fourth round losers $7,171. Third round losers $4,172. Second round losers $2,607. First round losers $1,690.
Total: $522,699.
WOMEN'S SINGLES – Winner $115,000. Runner-up $55,000. Semi-finalists $27,000. Quarter-finalists $13,500. Fourth round losers $6,775. Third round losers $3,700. Second round losers $1,900. First round losers: $950.
Total: $482,600.
MEN'S DOUBLES (per team) – Winners 35,518. Runners-up $17,758. Semi-finalists $8,994. Quarter-finalists $4,688. Third round losers $2,520. Second round losers $1,420. First round losers $1,108.
Total: $168,352.
WOMEN'S DOUBLES (per team) – Winners $40,000. Runners-up $20,000. Semi-finalists $12,450. Quarter-finalists $5,250. Second round losers $2,800. First round losers $1,400.
Total: 150,700.
MIXED DOUBLES (per team) – Winners $13,954. Runners-up $6,658. Semi-finalists $2,942. Quarter-finalists $1,666. Second round losers $1,022. First round losers $418.
Total: $48,024.

MEN'S SINGLES

Holder: S. Edberg (SWE)

FIRST ROUND

Bye
D. Saltz (USA)
P. Kuhnen (FRG)
M. Anger (USA)
M. Freeman (USA)
Bye
D. Goldie (USA)
M. DePalmer (USA)
R. Simpson (NZL)
G. Donnelly (USA)
Bye
Bye
Bye
J. Carlsson (SWE)
C. Saceanu (FRG)
B. Derlin (NZL)
A. Castle (GBR)
Bye
P. Doohan
D. Tyson
W. Scanlon (USA)
A. Lane
Bye
Bye
Bye
Bye
S. Davis (USA)
P. McNamara
B. Schultz (USA)
S. Guy (NZL)
N. Fulwood (GBR)
H. Van Boeckel (HOL)
Bye
D. Cahill (USA)
S. Barr
Bye
Bye
C. Pistolesi (ITA)
M. Robertson (SAF)
M. Schapers (HOL)
J. Levine (USA)
Bye
Bye
P. Annacone (USA)
T. Mmoh (NIG)
T. Nelson (USA)
G. Connell (CAN)
Bye

SECOND ROUND

I. LENDL (TCH) (1)
Saltz 6–4 6–3 6–3
Anger 6–4 1–0 ret'd
A. Mansdorf (ISR)
Goldie 1–6 6–4 6–1 6–2
Simpson 7–6 6–7 6–3 7–6
E. Edwards (RSA)
R. KRISHNAN (IND) (16)
A. JARRYD (SWE) (9)
J. Carlsson 4–6 7–6 6–3 7–6
Derlin 6–7 7–5 3–6 7–5 6–1
T. Champion (FRA)
Doohan 7–6 7–6 6–1
Scanlon 6–7 3–6 6–3 6–2 6–2
J. Fitzgerald
K. CURREN (USA) (8)
Y. NOAH (FRA) (3)
D. McPherson
S. Davis 7–6 6–4 2–6 3–6 6–4
Schultz 7–5 6–2 3–6 7–6
Fulwood 6–3 6–4 7–5
M. R. Edmondson
Barr 6–3 6–4 6–4
T. WILKISON (USA) (14)
P. CASH (11)
Pistolesi 5–7 2–6 6–3 7–6 9–7
Schapers 6–1 6–4 6–4
B. Testerman (USA)
S. Wood
Annacone 7–6 7–6 6–4
Nelson 6–4 6–4 6–4
H. LECONTE (FRA) (5)

THIRD ROUND

LENDL (1) 6–4 3–6 6–1 6–1
Anger 7–6 6–3 3–6 6–3
Goldie 6–3 7–6 7–6
KRISHNAN (16) 4–6 5–7 6–1 6–3 6–3
JARRYD (9) 6–0 7–5 6–0
Champion 6–1 3–0 ret'd
Doohan 6–3 1–6 7–5 7–6
CURREN (8) 7–5 6–2 6–7 4–6 6–3
NOAH (3) 4–6 6–1 6–4 6–3
Schultz 4–6 6–1 6–7 6–2 6–3
Edmondson 6–4 4–6 4–6 7–5 9–7
WILKISON (14) 6–2 6–2 3–6 7–6
CASH (11) 7–6 2–6 7–6 6–2
Testerman 7–6 6–1 6–4
Annacone 6–7 4–6 6–3 6–2 6–4
LECONTE (5) 4–6 7–6 6–2 6–3

FOURTH ROUND

LENDL (1) 6–4 6–2 6–7 6–2
Goldie 3–6 7–5 6–7 6–2 6–2
JARRYD (9) 6–0 7–6 2–6 6–2
Doohan 4–6 6–3 6–4 6–4
NOAH (3) 7–6 4–6 4–6 7–6 6–4
WILKISON (14) 6–2 6–1 7–6
CASH (11) 6–3 6–7 6–1 6–2
Annacone 1–6 4–6 6–3 6–4 10–8

QUARTER-FINALS

LENDL (1) 2–6 6–4 7–6 6–3
JARRYD (9) 6–1 6–7 6–4 7–6
NOAH (3) 4–6 4–6 6–3 6–4 6–2
CASH (11) 6–4 6–1 6–7 6–2

SEMI-FINALS

LENDL (1) 7–6 6–1 6–3
CASH (11) 6–4 6–2 2–6 6–0

FINAL

CASH (11) 7–6 5–7 7–6 6–4

6–3 6–4 3–6 5–7 6–3

Bye
Bye
M. Woodforde
M. Baroch
G. Muller (RSA)
S. Denton (USA)
M. Kratzmann
J. Lapidus (USA)
M. Davis (USA)
C. Eagle
Bye
Bye
Bye
Bye
J. Franz (ARG)
G. Michibata (CAN)
A. Maurer (FRG)
S. Youl
Bye
P. Carlsson (SWE)
J. Stoltenberg
J. Letts (USA)
G. Bloom (ISR)
Bye
Bye
B. Drewett
P. McNamee
D. Rostagno (USA)
N. Odizor (NIG)
Bye
Bye
D. Visser (RSA)
L. Shiras (USA)
K. Evernden (NZL)
J. Canter (USA)
Bye
Bye
C. Van Rensburg (RSA)
L. Lavalle (MEX)
W. Masur
J. Sadri (USA)
Bye
Bye
S. Zivojinovic (YUG)
L. Warder
B. Dyke
C. Miniussi (ARG)
Bye

M. MECIR (TCH) (6)
M. J. Bates (GBR)
Woodforde
6–3 6–4 6–4
Muller
6–7 6–3 6–4 6–4
Kratzmann
7–6 4–6 7–6 6–4
M. Davis
7–6 4–6 7–6
K. Flach (USA)
M. SREJBER (TCH) (12)
R. SEGUSO (USA) (13)
R. Green
Franz
6–3 5–7 6–4 6–4
Maurer
6–3 6–3 7–6
J. Frawley
P. Carlsson
6–3 1–6 6–3 6–2
Letts
4–6 7–5 6–4 6–4
S. EDBERG (SWE) (4)
B. GILBERT (USA) (7)
Drewett
6–4 3–6 6–4 6–2
Rostagno
7–5 6–2 6–3
R. Matuszewski (USA)
B. Pearce (USA)
Visser
4–6 6–2 6–3 7–6
Evernden
7–6 6–3 6–4
J. KRIEK (USA) (10)
J. HLASEK (SUI) (15)
Van Rensburg
6–3 6–4 0–6 6–4
Masur
6–3 6–7 6–4 6–0
K. Jones (USA)
C. Limberger (USA)
Zivojinovic
6–7 3–6 6–3 6–4 6–1
Dyke
6–2 6–1 7–5
B. BECKER (FRG) (2)

MECIR (6)
4–6 6–2 6–1 6–3
Muller
7–5 5–7 4–6 7–6 6–4
Kratzmann
6–4 6–2 6–4
Flach
3–6 2–6 7–5 6–3 6–3
SEGUSO (13)
6–3 3–6 7–6 6–4
Franz
2–6 7–5 6–3 6–4
Frawley
6–2 6–3 3–2 ret'd
EDBERG (4)
3–6 6–1 6–0 6–2
GILBERT (7)
7–5 6–3 6–2
Rostagno
7–5 6–1 6–1
Pearce
3–6 7–6 6–3 4–6 12–10
Evernden
6–2 2–6 6–4 6–4
Van Rensburg
4–6 6–3 6–3 6–7 6–4
Masur
6–7 6–2 6–0 6–4
Zivojinovic
6–1 6–4 6–2
BECKER (2)
6–7 6–1 6–4 6–7 6–2

MECIR (6)
6–4 6–4 6–4
Kratzmann
6–4 6–2 6–4
SEGUSO (13)
6–3 3–6 7–5 6–4
EDBERG (4)
6–4 6–3 6–1
Rostagno
4–6 6–2 6–3 6–1
Evernden
6–2 6–2 6–4
Masur
6–3 2–6 7–5 4–6 6–0
BECKER (2)
6–3 6–3 3–6 6–3

MECIR (6)
6–4 6–2 6–2
EDBERG (4)
6–1 6–0 6–1
Evernden
6–7 6–2 6–4 5–7 7–5
Masur
4–6 7–6 6–4 6–7 6–2

EDBERG (4)
6–1 6–4 6–4
Masur
6–3 7–5 6–4

EDBERG (4)
6–2 6–4 7–6

S. EDBERG (SWE) (4)

Capital letters denote seeded players. Number following player's name gives seeding order.

WOMEN'S SINGLES

Holder: M. Navratilova (USA)

FIRST ROUND

Bye
Bye
C. Benjamin (USA)
E. Minter
H. Kelesi (CAN)
C. Monteiro (BRA)
L. Allen (USA)
R. Bryant
Bye
J. Thompson
J. Dingwall
Bye
Bye
J. Byrne
L. O'Neil
Bye
Cammie MacGregor (USA)
C. Karlsson (SWE)
Bye
C. Copeland (USA)
S. Rimes (USA)
E. Okagawa (JAP)
H. Ludloff (USA)
Bye
Bye
A. Moulton (USA)
C. Porwik (FRG)
Bye
L. Field
B. Gerkin (USA)
J. Polzl (FRG)
S. Walsh Pete (USA)
A. Henricksson (USA)
R. Marsikova (TCH)
Bye
Bye

A. Devries (BLL)
K. Okomoto (JAP)
M. C. Calleja (FRA)
M. Yanagi (JAP)
Bye
C. Bartos Cserepy (SUI)
E. Krapl (SUI)
Bye
Y. Kuzumi (JAP)
M. Schropp (FRG)
Bye

SECOND ROUND

M. NAVRATILOVA (USA) (1)
J. Golder (USA)
Benjamin 0–6 6–4 6–4
Kelesi 6–4 6–4
Bryant 6–1 6–3
B. Bowes (USA)
Thompson 5–7 7–6 6–4
R. FAIRBANK (RSA) (16)
W. M. TURNBULL (11)
Byrne 6–4 2–6 6–2
J. Mundel (RSA)
MacGregor 7–5 3–6 6–2
E. Pfaff (FRG)
Rimes 6–2 6–2
Ludloff 7–5 6–3
Z. GARRISON (USA) (7)
P. H. SHRIVER (USA) (3)
Moulton 4–6 6–4 6–3
E. Reinach (RSA)
Field 7–6 1–6 6–4
Polzl 6–2 6–4
Henricksson 6–4 6–4
V. Nelson Dunbar (USA)
J. M. DURIE (GBR) (14)
C. LINDQVIST (SWE) (10)
Devries 6–2 2–6 6–4
Calleja 3–6 6–2 6–2
M. Bollegraf (HOL)
Bartos Csepery 6–3 6–4
A. Scott
Kuzumi 6–1 2–6 6–3
M. MALEEVA (BUL) (6)

THIRD ROUND

NAVRATILOVA (1) 6–0 6–2
Benjamin 4–6 6–4 6–4
Bowes 6–2 6–7 6–3
Thompson 3–6 6–4 8–6
TURNBULL (11) 2–6 6–4 6–3
Mundel 7–5 4–6 6–0
Pfaff 7–5 6–3
GARRISON (7) 6–1 6–1
SHRIVER (3) 6–2 4–6 11–9
Reinach 6–1 6–2
Polzl 7–6 6–4
DURIE (14) 7–5 6–1
LINDQVIST (10) 6–2 6–3
Calleja 4–6 6–4 6–3
Bartos Cserepy 6–3 6–0
MALEEVA (6) 6–4 6–1

FOURTH ROUND

NAVRATILOVA (1) 6–2 6–1
Thompson 6–3 7–5
TURNBULL (11) 4–6 6–1 6–2
GARRISON (7) 6–2 3–6 7–5
SHRIVER (3) 6–2 6–4
DURIE (14) 6–1 6–4
LINDQVIST (10) 4–6 6–1 6–3
MALEEVA (6) 6–3 6–7 7–5

QUARTER-FINALS

NAVRATILOVA (1) 6–4 6–1
GARRISON (7) 6–1 6–3
SHRIVER (3) 6–1 6–2
LINDQVIST (10) 6–3 6–3

SEMI-FINALS

NAVRATILOVA (1) 6–0 6–3
LINDQVIST (10) 6–3 6–1

FINAL

NAVRATILOVA (1) 6–3 6–2

7–5 7–6

Bye
Bye
T. Mochizuki (USA)
M. Van Nostrand (USA)
C. Singer (FRG)
M. Pazderova (TCH)
S. Hanika (FRG)
M. Van Der Torre (HOL)
E. Inoue (JAP)
D. Van Rensburg (RSA)
Bye
Bye
Bye
B. Cordwell (NZ)
T. Holladay (USA)
P. Hy (HKG)
A. Minter
Bye
Bye
B. Nagelsen (USA)
L. Antonoplis (USA)
Hu Na (USA)
M. Jaggard
Bye
Bye
Bye
M. Werdel (USA)
P. Vasquez (PER)
G. Fernandez (USA)
S. McCann
A. E. Hobbs (GBR)
A. M. Fernandez (USA)
S. Gomer (GBR)
A. Betzner (FRG)
Bye
Bye
Bye
Bye
A. Holikova (TCH)
S. Collins (USA)
W. Probst (FRG)
M. Bowrey
A. E. Smith (USA)
V. Paquet (FRA)
Bye
J. Richardson (NZL)
M. Turk
Bye

C. KOHDE-KILSCH (FRG) (5)
N. Provis
Mochizuki 6–1 6–3
Singer 6–1 6–4
Hanika 7–5 5–7 10–8
Inoue 6–3 7–6
A. Kijimuta (JAP)
T. PHELPS (USA) (13)
R. WHITE (USA) (9)
Cordwell 6–2 7–6
Hy 6–4 6–4
Mrs E. Smylie
C. Jolissaint (SUI)
Nagelsen 6–2 6–7 6–1
Hu Na 7–6 2–6 6–0
H. SUKOVA (TCH) (4)
L. McNEIL (USA) (8)
E. Burgin (USA)
Werdel 6–4 6–2
G. Fernandez 6–4 6–3
Hobbs 3–0 ret'd
Gomer 4–6 6–2 8–6
G. Rush (USA)
Mrs D. BALESTRAT (15)
C. BASSETT (CAN) (12)
J. Salmon (GBR)
Holikova 6–1 4–6 6–4
Probst 6–1 6–4
Smith 7–5 6–3
K. Kiel (USA)
Richardson 6–1 6–3
H. MANDLIKOVA (TCH) (2)

KOHDE-KILSCH (5) 6–2 6–2
Mochizuki 6–3 6–3
Hanika 6–4 6–4
Kijimuta 6–3 4–6 6–0
WHITE (9) 6–1 6–4
Smylie 6–2 6–3
Jolissaint 6–4 1–6 6–3
SUKOVA (4) 6–4 7–6
McNEIL (8) 6–3 6–4
Werdel 6–2 6–3
Hobbs 6–2 6–3
BALESTRAT (15) 6–3 4–6 6–2
BASSETT (12) 6–1 6–1
Holikova 5–7 6–4 8–6
Smith 6–2 6–4
MANDLIKOVA (2) 4–6 6–2 6–2

KOHDE-KILSCH (5) 6–2 6–2
Hanika 6–3 6–3
Smylie 6–1 6–2
SUKOVA (4) 6–1 6–2
McNEIL (8) 6–2 7–5
Hobbs 6–4 6–2
BASSETT (12) 6–1 7–6
MANDLIKOVA (2) 6–3 6–2

KOHDE-KILSCH (5) 6–3 6–1
Smylie 7–5 3–6 7–5
McNEIL (8) 7–6 6–3
MANDLIKOVA (2) 6–2 4–6 6–2

KOHDE-KILSCH (5) 7–6 4–6 6–2
MANDLIKOVA (2) 6–0 6–0

MANDLIKOVA (2) 6–1 0–6 6–3

H. MANDLIKOVA (TCH) (2)

Capital letters denote seeded players. Number following player's name gives seeding order.

MEN'S DOUBLES

Holders: P. Annacone (USA)/C. Van Rensburg (RSA)

FIRST ROUND

Bye
McPherson/Youl
Barlow/Felgate
Saceanu/Utzinger
M. Fancutt/Pfister
Bye
Bye
Bloom/Kuhnen
Evernden/Green
Mansdorf/Van Boeckel
Barr/Stoltenberg
Bye
Bye
Fricker/Pfitzner
Bates/Castle
Denton/Dowlen
Limberger/Woodforde
Bye
Bye
Connell/Kennedy
Derlin/Simpson
Richter/Rudeen
Carter/Lane
Bye
Bye
Mecir/Srejber
M. Smith/Siegel
McNamara/McNamee
DePalmer/Testerman
Bye
Bye
K. Jones/Wilkison
Furlong/Miller
Michibata/Schultz
Frana/Miniussi
Bye
Bye
Graham/Matuszewski
Mmoh/Odizor
Drewett/Schapers
Emerson/Tyson
Bye
Bye
Levine/Shiras
Anger/Pawsat
J./P. Carlsson
Letts/Robertson
Bye

SECOND ROUND

EDBERG/JARRYD (1)
McPherson/Youl 6–3 4–6 14–12
Saceanu/Utzinger 7–6 7–6
LAVALLE/PEARCE (15)
MASUR/DYKE (10)
Evernden/Green 6–3 3–6 6–3
Mansdorf/Van Boeckel 6–4 6–4
HLASEK/STEWART (8)
ANNACONE/VAN RENSBURG (4)
Bates/Castle 5–7 6–4 6–2
Denton/Dowlen 6–3 6–2
CURREN/LECONTE (14)
MULLER/NELSON (12)
Connell/Kennedy 6–4 7–6
Richter/Rudeen 7–6 7–6
CASH/DONNELLY (6)
S. DAVIS/GILBERT (5)
Mecir/Srejber 4–6 7–5 15–13
McNamara/McNamee 7–6 6–4
CAHILL/KRATZMANN (11)
EDWARDS/VISSER (13)
Jones/Wilkison 6–3 6–2
Michibata/Schultz 6–3 6–2
FLACH/SEGUSO (3)
FITZGERALD/KRIEK (7)
Mmoh/Odizor 6–3 6–4
Emerson/Tyson 5–7 6–4 6–4
EDMONDSON/WARWICK (9)
DOOHAN/WARDER (16)
Anger/Pawsat 3–6 6–3 6–4
Letts/Robertson 7–6 6–3
BECKER/ZIVOJINOVIC (2)

THIRD ROUND

EDBERG/JARRYD (1) 7–3 6–3
Saceanu/Utzinger 6–4 6–2
MASUR/DYKE (10) 6–7 7–6 6–4
HLASEK/STEWART (8) 6–7 7–5 6–1
ANNACONE/VAN RENSBURG (4) 4–6 6–4 6–4
CURREN/LECONTE (14) 6–3 6–4
MULLER/NELSON (12) 6–3 7–5
CASH/DONNELLY (6) 6–3 6–3
Mecir/Srejber 4–6 6–3 6–3
CAHILL/KRATZMANN (11) 6–2 7–5
EDWARDS/VISSER (13) 6–3 3–6 10–8
FLACH/SEGUSO (3) 7–6 7–6
Mmoh/Odizor 1–6 7–6 6–3
Emerson/Tyson 6–3 6–7 10–8
DOOHAN/WARDER (16) 7–6 6–3
BECKER/ZIVOJINOVIC (2) 2–6 6–4 6–4

QUARTER-FINALS

EDBERG/JARRYD (1) 6–4 2–6 6–2
MASUR/DYKE (10) 6–7 6–1 6–4
ANNACONE/VAN RENSBURG (4) 2–6 7–6 14–12
MULLER/NELSON (12) 7–6 7–5
CAHILL/KRATZMANN (11) 6–7 6–3 6–4
FLACH/SEGUSO (3) 6–3 6–2
Emerson/Tyson 7–6 6–3
DOOHAN/WARDER (16) 6–3 7–6

SEMI-FINALS

EDBERG/JARRYD (1) 6–3 3–6 6–3 3–6 6–4
ANNACONE/VAN RENSBURG (4) 6–7 6–4 7–6 6–2
FLACH/SEGUSO (3) 6–4 6–4 6–4
DOOHAN/WARDER (16) 6–4 6–3 6–4

FINAL

EDBERG/JARRYD (1) 6–3 7–6 6–3
DOOHAN/WARDER (16) 1–6 6–3 1–6 6–4 10–8

S. EDBERG (SWE)/A. JARRYD (SWE) (1) 6–4 6–4 7–6

Capital letters denote seeded pairings. Number following players' names gives seeding order.

Former Czech Hana Mandlikova, who became a naturalised Australian on the first day of 1988, began 1987 in style by taking her second Australian Open title, although she was later restricted by injury. *(R. Gould)*

WOMEN'S DOUBLES

Holders: M. Navratilova (USA)/P. H. Shriver (USA)

FIRST ROUND	SECOND ROUND	QUARTER-FINALS	SEMI-FINALS	FINAL	
NAVRATILOVA/SHRIVER (1)	NAVRATILOVA/SHRIVER (1) 6–1 6–3	NAVRATILOVA/SHRIVER (1) 6–1 7–5	NAVRATILOVA/SHRIVER (1) 6–4 7–5	NAVRATILOVA/SHRIVER (1) 6–1 6–0	M. NAVRATILOVA (USA)/ P. H. SHRIVER (USA) (1) 6–1 6–0
P. Smith/Holladay					
Mundel/Rush	Mundel/Rush 6–1 7–6				
Kelesi/Bollegraf					
A./E. Minter	Cordwell/Field 6–2 6–1	DURIE/HOBBS (8) 7–6 7–5			
Cordwell/Field					
Cammie/Cynthia MacGregor	DURIE/HOBBS (8) 7–6 6–3				
DURIE/HOBBS (8)					
NAGELSEN/SMYLIE (4)	Schropp/Porwik 6–3 6–2	Lindqvist/Pfaff 6–2 6–2	Hy/Inoue 7–5 6–4		
Schropp/Porwik					
Lindqvist/Pfaff	Lindqvist/Pfaff 6–1 6–2				
Bartos Cserepy/Gomer					
Jolissaint/Ludloff	Jolissaint/Ludloff 3–6 6–3 14–12	Hy/Inoue 7–5 6–3			
Yanagi/Hu Na					
Hy/Inoue	Hy/Inoue 6–3 6–3				
BURGIN/FAIRBANK (5)					
GARRISON/McNEIL (7)	GARRISON/McNEIL (7) 6–2 6–1	GARRISON/McNEIL (7) 6–2 6–1	GARRISON/McNEIL (7) 3–6 6–3 8–6	GARRISON/McNEIL (7) 7–6 7–6	
Van Der Torre/Bakkum					
Byrne/Thompson	Byrne/Thompson 6–4 5–7 6–2				
Dingwall/Bryant					
Gerken/Phelps	Gerken/Phelps 7–5 7–6	MANDLIKOVA/TURNBULL (3) 6–3 6–1			
Antonoplis/Monteiro					
Benjamin/Van Rensburg	MANDLIKOVA/TURNBULL (3) 6–3 6–3				
MANDLIKOVA/TURNBULL (3)					
G. FERNANDEZ/R. WHITE (6)	G. FERNANDEZ/R. WHITE (6) 6–1 6–7 8–6	Collins/Walsh Pete 6–4 2–6 6–2	KOHDE-KILSCH/SUKOVA (2) 7–5 6–0		
Moulton/Van Nostrand					
Balestrat/Marsikova	Collins/Walsh Pete 6–1 6–4				
Collins/Walsh Pete					
Reinach/Allen	Reinach/Allen 6–2 6–3	KOHDE-KILSCH/SUKOVA (2) 6–1 6–2			
Holikova/Probst					
Henricksson/Karlsson	KOHDE-KILSCH/SUKOVA (2) 6–2 6–1				
KOHDE-KILSCH/SUKOVA (2)					

Capital letters denote seeded pairings. Number following players' names gives seeding order.

MIXED DOUBLES

Holders (1969): M. C. Riessen (USA)/Mrs B. M. Court (AUS) shared with F. S. Stolle (AUS)/Mrs P. F. Jones (GBR)

FIRST ROUND	SECOND ROUND	QUARTER-FINALS	SEMI-FINALS	FINAL	
FITZGERALD/SMYLIE (1)	FITZGERALD/SMYLIE (1) 6–4 6–7 6–3	Barr/Jaggard 6–3 7–6	Castle/Hobbs 6–4 6–7 6–3	Castle/Hobbs 6–2 6–3	S. E. STEWART (USA)/ Z. GARRISON (USA) (4) 3–6 7–6 6–3
Schapers/Van Der Torre					
Barr/Jaggard	Barr/Jaggard 6–3 6–4				
Mmoh/Benjamin					
Castle/Hobbs	Castle/Hobbs 6–7 7–6 6–1	Castle/Hobbs 6–1 4–6 6–4			
Barlow/Dingwall					
Graham/Burgin	DONNELLY/BASSETT (8) 7–5 6–2				
DONNELLY/BASSETT (8)					
WARWICK/TURNBULL (3)	WARWICK/TURNBULL (3) 6–2 7–5	Utzinger/Jolissaint 6–4 4–6 6–4	Utzinger/Jolissaint 7–6 7–6		
Drewett/Walsh Pete					
Utzinger/Jolissaint	Utzinger/Jolissaint 6–4 3–6 6–4				
Robertson/Reinach					
Warder/P. Smith	Tyson/Thompson 7–6 6–4	Tyson/Thompson 6–4 4–6 6–4			
Tyson/Thompson					
K. Jones/R. White	KRATZMANN/BYRNE (6) 7–6 6–4				
KRATZMANN/BYRNE (6)					
EDMONDSON/FAIRBANK (5)	EDMONDSON/FAIRBANK (5) 7–6 6–1	Doohan/Balestrat 6–4 7–6	STEWART/GARRISON (4) 3–6 7–5 10–8	STEWART/GARRISON (4) 3–6 7–5 10–8	
Evernden/Collins					
Green/Moulton	Doohan/Balestrat 7–5 6–3				
Doohan/Balestrat					
Rudeen/Bakkum	Rudeen/Bakkum 6–3 3–6 7–5	STEWART/GARRISON (4) 5–7 6–3 6–4			
Derlin/Richardson					
McNamara/Provis	STEWART/GARRISON (4) 7–5 2–6 6–4				
STEWART/GARRISON (4)					
LAVALLE/G. FERNANDEZ (7)	Youl/O'Neil 7–6 6–4	Pawsat/McNeil 6–2 6–2	ANNACONE/NAVRATILOVA (2) 7–6 7–6		
Youl/O'Neil					
Pawsat/McNeil	Pawsat/McNeil 6–3 7–6				
M. Fancutt/Mandlikova					
Simpson/Cordwell	Simpson/Cordwell 7–5 6–7 10–8	ANNACONE/NAVRATILOVA (2) 6–2 3–6 6–2			
Kennedy/Rush					
Letts/MacGregor	ANNACONE/NAVRATILOVA (2) 3–6 6–3 6–4				
ANNACONE/NAVRATILOVA (2)					

Capital letters denote seeded pairings. Number following players' names gives seeding order.

OPEL
RVETEMENTS
S·CHEMISES DE

FRENCH OPEN CHAMPIONSHIPS

David Irvine

Next to the tented village at the Stade Roland Garros in Paris lies a court which is nowadays used exclusively for practice during the French Championships. Until quite recently, before the grounds were extended, it was where less prominent players could expect to be banished during the early rounds of competition, and there in 1983 the 1987 champion made her almost anonymous first appearance at the tournament. It was perhaps not surprising, in the circumstances, that when Steffi Graf arrived for that initial match, someone mistook her for a ball-girl. She was, after all, only 13 at the time. Four years later she was to become the youngest player to win the women's title, beating Martina Navratilova, the World Champion, by 6–4 4–6 8–6 just eight days before her 18th birthday for her first Grand Slam title.

Of such things dreams are made and realised. Yet Graf's success merely demonstrated how easily exceptions become rules and activities which, in theory, require above all the benefits of wisdom and experience can still offer almost instant success, if those with the genius, and ability to apply it, do so. There was a time, of course, when Graf's age would have raised quite a few eyebrows. But not any more. If anything the greater surprise was that it took her four years on the circuit to achieve her first major goal. Mats Wilander and Boris Becker, for instance, were still well short of their 18th birthdays when they first won Paris in 1982 and Wimbledon in 1985 respectively. However, in Graf's case (and only time will determine whether this is so) there was a seeming inevitability to it; a widely held feeling that it represented not so much the arrival of a new star as the dawn of a new era. Wilander and Becker emerged from nowhere with their outstanding talents but have not, as yet, offered undisputed leadership. Graf already has.

As far as the men were concerned, in fact, the French ended with Lendl still their undisputed leader. His successful defence, culminating in his 7–5 6–2 3–6 7–6 victory over the in-form Wilander, gave Europe both major individual prizes for the first time since Bjorn Borg and Hana Mandlikova were crowned six years earlier – and left the Americans empty-handed for only the third time in a decade. The men's final, it must be said, exactly matched the weather – damp, colourless and eminently forgettable. It was entirely appropriate that it should have concluded in a downpour with the crowd already making for the exits, for Wilander, whose dashing approach had so illuminated the quarter- and semi-final rounds, was a bitter let-down.

In the main the men's event had produced tennis of high competitive quality, which is why attendance records were again broken. Indeed, the 330,000 who saw the Championships bore every comparison with the numbers guaranteed at Wimbledon and Flushing Meadow – events with which the French Open can now claim to stand four-square.

With the Australian Open having moved back to its old slot as the first of the year's Grand Slam events, Paris clearly meant rather more to Stefan Edberg and Mandlikova – the Melbourne champions – than anyone else. As it turned out, both fell to French opponents on the third day – officially recognised as Children's Day, though turning out, on this particular occasion, to have more in common with the Bastille festival.

Edberg, whose preparations for Paris were not all they might have been, lost 7–6 7–6 7–5 to the little-known Eric Winogradsky from Agen; a wild-card entrant whose style of play, like the Swede's, was not exactly designed for clay. No matter. His was easily the

In a remarkable year Steffi Graf won her first Grand Slam title in Paris by beating Martina Navratilova, from whom she took over the No. 1 ranking in August. *(M. Cole)*

biggest upset produced by a home-based player since Christophe Roger-Vasselin beat Jimmy Connors in the quarters four years earlier.

Mandlikova, the 1981 champion, had to contend with even greater embarrassment, being beaten 6–4 7–6 by Nathalie Herreman, an inoffensive little player who had pulled a muscle so badly in practice three days earlier that she had been advised to withdraw and played only with the help of a heavy leather brace on her right thigh.

Yet John McEnroe, who had spent an unprecedented three-week period acclimatising to the red clay in an attempt to shape a real challenge, made an even faster departure. He failed to survive his first-round test at the hands of the slim-built Argentine Horacio de la Pena, whom he had beaten in Rome two weeks earlier. In a contest of quite stunning ineptitude, which left many on Centre Court wondering if McEnroe had a future (and others asking why the Press made such a fuss of him), McEnroe was skinned 4–6 6–2 6–4 6–2. 'Physically I wasn't up to it', admitted the American, who had also lost his first match at the US Open nine months earlier. 'You need to feel your best coming into an event like this. I feel I let a lot of people down, especially myself.' Others, who had seen him in Rome and Düsseldorf, were rather less surprised.

At least the one-time No. 1 could console himself with the thought that he was not alone in his misery. Pat Cash, soon to become Wimbledon's new hero, and Henri Leconte went out on the same day while other first-round failures included Mikael Pernfors, the Swede who had reached the final unseeded 12 months earlier, and Johan Kriek.

By the time the men's field had been reduced to 32, a total of seven seeds had been uprooted – including all the 1986 semi-finalists bar Lendl – and there was high promise of further drama to follow as the champion, Lendl, and second seed, Boris Becker, prepared to square up for battles with Joakim Nystrom and Jimmy Arias, opponents who had had the better of them in Rome and Monte Carlo respectively. In the end, however, the Swede and the American were made to pay for their impertinence. Nystrom's hopes of stripping Lendl of both his Italian and French titles crumbled after a remarkable contest had been stopped by bad light with Nystrom, who had saved 11 set-points in the third set, leading the No. 1 seed 6–2 1–6 7–5 0–4. Lendl it was, though, who benefited more from the overnight stoppage. Refreshed and eager, he won eight of the last ten games to win in five sets. Arias similarly could not sustain his bright start against Becker, tried to hit him off the court, and was swamped 5–7 6–3 6–2 6–0.

That left the top half of the draw with a distinctly Czechoslovak flavour, with Lendl, Miloslav Mecir and Karel Novacek in contention alongside Andres Gomez, and the lower half featuring a League of Nations look with Yannick Noah, Becker and the veteran Connors bracketed with the emerging favourite, Wilander.

As is so often the case, the quarter-finals marked the moment when sanity returned. Suddenly a competition of surprise and shock became a contest of total predictability. If either Gomez or Mecir had the game to beat the defending champion, they certainly did not have enough belief, while Wilander, the 1982 and 1985 winner, swept past Noah and Becker with such brilliance and aggression that he was, in effect, a totally 'new' player. Until, that is, the final, the less said of which the better.

Apart from Mandlikova's personal disaster – which was by no means her first – the women's singles did little to suggest that, where potential winners are concerned, the number of genuine candidates can no longer be counted on the fingers of one hand. Undistinguished was the only word for the early rounds, though 15-year-old Arantxa Sanchez, sister of Emilio and Javier, rather deservedly attracted attention by sweeping to the quarters without dropping a set. For the old guard (Navratilova and Chris Evert) and the new (Graf and Gabriela Sabatini), it was very much business as usual, however, and no surprise to anyone when they arrived on cue at the semi-finals. Graf alone by then still had an unblemished record whereas Navratilova, Evert and Sabatini had dropped sets to Adriana Villagran, Raffaella Reggi and Camille Benjamin respectively.

Evert and Navratilova met for the 72nd time since 1973, but despite the fact that the former had beaten the latter in the two preceding French finals, it was Navratilova who decisively won this rather rare semi-final clash by 6–2 6–2 – a tame and disappointing match, as it turned out, and totally overshadowed by that between Graf and Sabatini. Here at last was a women's contest offering not only quality but vibrance, spontaneity and wit. Never before in their short rivalry had the Argentine pushed the West German so hard. But it was symptomatic of Graf's class and confidence that despite being 3–5 down in the third set – twice Sabatini was three points from victory – she should recover to win, and quite brilliantly it must be said, by 6–4 4–6 7–5.

In scoring terms the final was effectively a repeat performance. Again Graf faced 3–5 in the third set; again she pulled out of it for a famous first Grand Slam victory. 'I wish I'd won', said Navratilova later, 'but I'm glad she's out here giving women's tennis a shot in the arm and making me work harder'.

There was at least some consolation for Martina in the doubles, when she and Pam Shriver captured their 16th title – and third modern Grand Slam together – at the expense of the Graf–Sabatini combination, while in the men's it was the previously untried partnership of Anders Jarryd and Robert Seguso who confounded home favourites Guy Forget and Noah by 6–7 6–7 6–3 6–4 6–2 in a long, hard-fought final.

For once Shriver finished with more titles than her celebrated partner. Normally Paris is not one of her ports of call but, to support Navratilova, she had agreed to play the doubles instead of going to Beckenham. Not one to waste time, she also entered the mixed with Emilio Sanchez – and won that too. 'Maybe next year I'd better play the singles as well', she said. 'Who knows what might be possible?'

JUNIOR EVENTS

BOYS' SINGLES – Final: G. Perez Roldan (ARG) d. J. Stoltenberg (AUS) 6–3 3–6 6–1.
BOYS' DOUBLES – Final: J. Courier (USA)/J. Stark (USA) d. F. Davin (ARG)/G. Perez Roldan (ARG) 6–7 6–4 6–3.
GIRLS' SINGLES – Final: N. Zvereva (URS) d. J. Pospisilova (TCH) 6–1 6–0.
GIRLS' DOUBLES – Final: N. Medvedeva (URS)/N. Zvereva (URS) d. M. Jaggard (AUS)/N. Provis (AUS) 6–3 6–3.

35 AND OVER

MEN'S DOUBLES – Final: R. Taylor (GBR)/O. Parun (NZL) d. J. Fillol (CHI)/R. D. Ralston (USA) 5–7 6–3 6–4.

FRENCH OPEN CHAMPIONSHIPS PRIZE MONEY – 19,948,960fr

MEN'S SINGLES – Winner 1,303,800fr. Runner-up 651,900fr. Semi-finalists 325,950fr. Quarter-finalists 165,150fr. Fourth round losers 86,900fr. Third round losers 48,625fr. Second round losers 28,700fr. First round losers 17,500fr.
Total: 6,779,800fr.
WOMEN'S SINGLES – Winner 1,178,840fr. Runner-up 594,220fr. Semi-finalists 289,450fr. Quarter-finalists 147,780fr. Fourth round losers 72,370fr. Third round losers 37,320fr. Second round losers 19,780fr. First round losers 10,270fr.
Total: 5,409,400fr.
MEN'S DOUBLES (per team) – Winners 451,000fr. Runners-up 226,000fr. Semi-finalists 113,000fr. Quarter-finalists 57,300fr. Third round losers 29,500fr. Second round losers 15,640fr. First round losers 9,180fr.
Total: 1,912,200fr.
WOMEN'S DOUBLES (per team) – Winners 365,300fr. Runners-up 189,980fr. Semi-finalists 98,600fr. Quarter-finalists 53,800fr. Third round losers 28,320fr. Second round losers 16,100fr. First round losers 7,980fr.
Total: 1,708,200fr.
MIXED DOUBLES (per team) – Winners 86,000fr. Runners-up 52,280fr. Semi-finalists 31,100fr. Quarter-finalists 18,700fr. Second round losers 10,380fr. First round losers 4,480fr.
Total: 430,000fr.
QUALIFYING COMPETITION: Third round losers 5,000fr. Second round losers: 2,500fr. First round losers 1000fr.

MEN'S SINGLES

Holder: I. Lendl (TCH)

FIRST ROUND

- I. LENDL (TCH) (1)
- R. Agenor (HAI)
- L. Warder (AUS)
- J. Canter (USA)
- T. Tulasne
- D. Rostagno (USA)
- J. Gunnarsson (SWE)
- P. Carlsson (SWE)
- M. Robertson (RSA)
- G. Layendecker (USA)
- M. Kratzmann (AUS)
- D. Cahill (AUS)
- M. Vajda (TCH)
- R. Seguso (USA)
- J. Nystrom (SWE)
- J. KRIEK (USA) (16)
- A. GOMEZ (ECU) (10)
- R. Stadler (SUI)
- C. U. Steeb (FRG)
- T. Champion
- P. Vojtisek (FRG)
- L. Mattar (BRA)
- J. Berger (USA)
- C. Pistolesi (ITA)
- P. McNamee (AUS)
- P. Cane (ITA)
- E. Sanchez (ESP)
- S. Zivojinovic (YUG)
- S. Giammalva (USA)
- M. Purcell (USA)
- H. de la Pena (ARG)
- J. P. McENROE (USA) (7)
- S. EDBERG (SWE) (3)
- M. Leach (USA)
- E. Winogradsky
- M. Freeman (USA)
- J. Hlasek (SUI)
- E. Bengoechea (ARG)
- K. Novacek (TCH)
- T. Nijssen (HOL)
- B. Willenborg (USA)
- U. Stenlund (SWE)
- G. Perez Roldan (ARG)
- T. Muster (AUT)
- T. Pham
- P. Kuhnen (FRG)
- H. Schwaier (FRG)
- M. JAITE (ARG) (14)
- P. CASH (AUS) (12)
- J. Pugh (USA)
- S. Ericksson (SWE)
- C. Limberger (AUS)
- P. Kuchna
- G. Michibata (CAN)
- P. Arraya (PER)
- A. Agassi (USA)
- G. Vilas (ARG)
- J. Potier
- A. Mansdorf (ISR)
- M. Srejber (TCH)
- H. Skoff (AUT)
- O. Delaitre
- T. Witsken (USA)
- M. MECIR (TCH) (5)

SECOND ROUND

- LENDL (1) 7–5 7–6 0–6 6–3
- Canter 6–4 6–1 5–7 6–2
- Tulasne 3–6 6–3 1–6 6–4 6–2
- Gunnarsson 6–1 7–6 6–3
- Robertson 6–2 3–6 6–7 7–6 6–1
- Cahill 6–0 6–3 4–6 6–4
- Vajda 6–4 3–6 6–2 7–6
- Nystrom 6–7 6–2 6–2 6–1
- GOMEZ (10) 6–4 6–2 6–1
- Champion 6–2 6–4 2–6 6–4
- Mattar 3–6 0–6 6–4 7–5 6–4
- Berger 6–1 6–3 6–3
- McNamee 6–0 6–3 6–2
- Sanchez 6–4 6–3 3–6 7–6
- Purcell 4–6 6–0 6–2 6–2
- de la Pena 4–6 6–2 6–4 6–2
- EDBERG (3) 6–2 6–3 6–3
- Winogradsky 7–6 7–5 6–3
- Bengoechea 6–4 6–7 7–5 4–6 6–4
- Novacek 6–2 6–1 6–0
- Stenlund 6–2 6–2 6–2
- Muster 6–1 6–3 6–2
- Pham 7–6 6–3 6–2
- JAITE (14) 6–2 6–3 6–4
- Pugh 3–6 6–3 6–2 7–6
- Limberger 3–6 7–6 6–4 6–3
- Kuchna 6–3 6–2 7–6
- Agassi 6–2 4–6 6–1 7–5
- Vilas 6–3 7–6 6–4
- Srejber 5–7 7–6 7–6 6–3
- Skoff 6–4 7–6 6–1
- MECIR (5) 7–5 3–6 2–6 6–2 9–7

THIRD ROUND

- LENDL (1) 3–6 6–1 6–1 6–2
- Tulasne 6–2 6–3 6–3
- Cahill 6–4 7–6 6–3
- Nystrom 6–3 6–3 6–1
- GOMEZ (10) 7–5 6–2 6–2
- Berger 7–6 6–3 6–3
- E. Sanchez 6–3 6–1 6–1
- de la Pena 6–3 6–4 6–3
- Winogradsky 7–6 7–6 7–5
- Novacek 6–0 6–0 6–0
- Muster 6–2 6–2 6–2
- JAITE (14) 6–4 6–2 6–2
- Pugh 6–1 6–2 6–2
- Kuchna 6–4 6–3 6–3
- Srejber 6–3 6–4 6–2
- MECIR (5) 7–5 6–4 6–1

FOURTH ROUND

- LENDL (1) 7–6 6–2 6–2
- Nystrom 6–4 7–6 6–4
- GOMEZ (10) 5–7 6–1 4–6 6–1 6–4
- E. Sanchez 6–3 6–3 4–6 6–3
- Novacek 6–1 6–0 2–6 6–4
- JAITE (14) 6–2 3–6 7–6 6–0
- Kuchna 6–4 6–2 2–6 6–2
- MECIR (5) 6–1 6–2 6–1

QUARTER-FINALS

- LENDL (1) 2–6 6–1 5–7 6–0 6–2
- GOMEZ (10) 5–7 1–6 7–6 7–5 6–4
- Novacek 7–6 6–4 6–7 6–3
- MECIR (5) 6–0 6–1 6–3

SEMI-FINALS

- LENDL (1) 5–7 6–4 6–1 6–1
- MECIR (5) 7–6 6–1 6–2

FINAL

- LENDL (1) 6–3 6–3 7–6

7–5 6–2 3–6 7–6

Y. NOAH (6)
I. Kley (BRA)
J. Carlsson (SWE)
C. Bergstrom (SWE)
S. Davis (USA)
M. Schapers (HOL)
J. P. Fleurian
J. Sanchez (ESP)
G. Bloom (ISR)
F. Yunis (ARG)
T. Smid (TCH)
L. Couteau
S. Casal (ESP)
M. Tauson (DEN)
A. Boetsch
K. CARLSSON (SWE) (11)
M. PERNFORS (SWE) (13)
T. Benhabiles
M. Fioroni (ITA)
A. Jarryd (SWE)
R. Bathman (SWE)
T. Carbonell (ESP)
G. Donnelly (USA)
A. Chesnokov (URS)
L. Wahlgren (SWE)
G. Forget
A. Krickstein (USA)
W. Masur (AUS)
P. Annacone (USA)
C. Motta (BRA)
S. Colombo (ITA)
M. WILANDER (SWE) (4)
J. S. CONNORS (USA) (8)
T. Nelson (USA)
L. Pimek (TCH)
M. Westphal (FRG)
F. Davin (ARG)
J. Vekemans (HOL)
M. Laurendeau (CAN)
A. Antonitsch (AUT)
A. Maurer (FRG)
D. Keretic (FRG)
P. Lundgren (SWE)
M. DePalmer (USA)
J. Fitzgerald (AUS)
M. Anger (USA)
R. Osterthun (FRG)
H. LECONTE (9)
B. GILBERT (USA) (15)
B. Oresar (YUG)
J. Arrese (ESP)
T. Van Den Daele
W. Scanlon (USA)
J. Arias (USA)
J. Svensson (SWE)
L. Shiras (USA)
G. Holmes (USA)
H. Sundstrom (SWE)
T. Hogstedt (SWE)
E. Jelen (FRG)
M. Buckley (USA)
J. Yzaga (PER)
D. Perez (URU)
B. BECKER (FRG) (2)

NOAH (6) 6–0 6–2 6–2
Bergstrom 6–2 6–1 6–3
Schapers 7–6 5–7 6–4 6–4
J. Sanchez 6–2 6–3 6–4
Yunis 6–1 6–3 6–3
Courteau 7–5 6–2 6–3
Casal 6–4 6–1 6–3
K. CARLSSON (11) 6–1 6–0 6–3
Benhabiles 4–6 6–3 6–4 6–0
Jarryd 6–3 4–6 6–3 6–1
Carbonell 5–7 7–5 7–6 6–3
Chesnokov 6–1 6–3 6–2
Wahlgren 6–3 6–4 6–4
Krickstein 6–3 6–3 6–4
Annacone 6–4 6–1 6–3
WILANDER (4) 3–6 6–2 6–1 5–3 ret'd
CONNORS (8) 7–5 6–2 6–2
Westphal 7–5 5–7 6–2 6–3
Davin 7–5 3–6 2–6 6–2 9–7
Antonitsch 6–2 2–6 6–2 7–6
Keretic 6–4 6–2 7–5
DePalmer 7–5 7–5 6–4
Anger 7–6 7–5 6–3
Osterthun 6–3 6–3 6–7 6–1
GILBERT (15) 1–6 7–5 2–6 6–4 6–4
Arrese 6–3 6–2 7–5
Arias 6–2 7–6 6–2
Svensson 6–4 6–0 6–2
Sundstrom 6–3 6–4 7–5
Jelen 6–4 6–0 3–6 6–1
Buckley 2–6 6–1 6–4 7–6
BECKER (2) 6–1 6–1 7–5

NOAH (6) 7–5 6–7 7–5 6–1
Schapers 6–4 6–2 7–5
Yunis 6–0 7–6 6–1
K. CARLSSON (11) 6–3 6–1 6–3
Benhabiles 7–6 0–6 2–6 6–3 9–7
Chesnokov 6–2 6–2 6–0
Krickstein 6–4 6–1 6–1
WILANDER (4) 6–3 6–4 4–6 6–4
CONNORS (8) 6–4 3–6 7–6 6–2
Davin 5–7 6–3 6–2 6–3
Keretic 3–6 6–2 6–2 6–4
Osterthun 6–2 7–6 6–2
Arrese 7–5 6–2 6–1
Arias 7–5 6–1 2–6 6–4
Sundstrom 2–6 6–3 6–0 5–7 8–6
BECKER (2) 6–1 4–6 6–3 6–2

NOAH (6) 6–3 6–3 6–2
CARLSSON (11) 7–5 6–2 6–1
Benhabiles 5–7 6–4 7–5 6–3
WILANDER (4) 6–1 6–7 6–0 6–2
CONNORS (8) 6–3 6–1 6–2
Osterthun 6–4 5–7 6–2 6–4
Arias 4–6 7–6 6–2 4–6 6–2
BECKER (2) 6–1 3–6 6–3 6–1

NOAH (6) 7–6 6–3 6–7 7–5
WILANDER (4) 5–7 6–1 6–3 6–3
CONNORS (8) 4–6 7–5 6–0 6–3
BECKER (2) 5–7 6–3 6–2 6–0

WILANDER (4) 6–4 6–3 6–2
BECKER (2) 6–3 6–3 7–5

WILANDER (4) 6–4 6–1 6–2

I. LENDL (TCH) (1)

Capital letters denote seeded players. Number following player's name gives seeding order.

WOMEN'S SINGLES

Holder: Mrs C. M. Evert Lloyd (USA)

FIRST ROUND

M. NAVRATILOVA (USA) (1)
C. Tanvier
A. Villagran (ARG)
J. Mundel (RSA)
A. Dechaume
L. Vanhille
P. Huber (AUT)
G. Kim (USA)
M. Bollegraf (HOL)
N. Jagerman (HOL)
L. Garrone (ITA)
A. M. Fernandez (USA)
L. Drescher (SUI)
M. Perez Roldan (ARG)
N. Dias (BRA)
S. HANIKA (FRG) (15)
K. RINALDI (USA) (10)
V. Nelson Dunbar (USA)
J. Halard
H. Fukarkova (TCH)
I. Cueto (FRG)
P. Medrado (BRA)
N. Tauziat
J. Byrne (AUS)
C. Bassett (CAN)
A. Kijumuta (JAP)
R. Marsikova (TCH)
B. Bowes (USA)
I. Kuczynska (POL)
M. Van Nostrand (USA)
P. Hy (HKG)
C. KOHDE-KILSCH (FRG) (8)
C. M. EVERT (USA) (3)
E. Pfaff (FRG)
P. Tarabini (ARG)
I. Demongeot
A. Devries (BEL)
E. Krapl (SUI)
V. Ruzici (RUM)
K. Bohmova (TCH)
S. Niox-Chateau
E. Derly
K. Gompert (USA)
E. Reinach (RSA)
M. Calleja
B. Fulco (ARG)
P. Barg (USA)
K. MALEEVA (BUL) (12)
R. REGGI (ITA) (14)
C. Singer (FRG)
L. Gildemeister (PER)
S. Gomer (GBR)
W. Probst (FRG)
A. Minter (AUS)
E. Okagama (JAP)
S. Sloane (USA)
C. Suire
P. Etchemendy
N. Zvereva (URS)
M. Mesker (HOL)
G. Rush Magers (USA)
D. Spence (USA)
D. Van Rensburg (RSA)
H. SUKOVA (TCH) (5)

SECOND ROUND

NAVRATILOVA (1) 6–3 7–6
Villagran 6–0 6–4
Vanhille 6–3 1–6 6–3
Huber 7–5 7–5
Bollegraf 6–3 6–3
Garrone 6–1 6–2
Perez Roldan 0–6 6–0 6–1
HANIKA (15) 6–2 6–1
RINALDI (10) 6–2 6–0
Halard 5–7 7–6 6–2
Cueto 6–3 6–2
Tauziat 7–5 3–6 6–3
Bassett 6–1 6–3
Marsikova 4–6 6–3 6–2
Kuczynska 6–2 6–3
KOHDE-KILSCH (8) 6–2 6–3
EVERT (3) 6–1 6–3
Demongeot 6–2 7–5
Krapl 6–4 6–4
Ruzici 6–3 6–2
Niox-Chateau 2–6 6–4 6–2
Gompert 6–7 6–3 8–6
Fulco 6–0 6–0
K. MALEEVA (12) 6–2 6–1
REGGI (14) 6–4 6–1
Gomer 6–2 6–4
A. Minter 6–3 6–0
Sloane 3–6 7–5 6–1
Suire 3–6 7–5 6–1
Zvereva 6–3 6–3
Rush Magers 6–2 6–3
SUKOVA (5) 6–1 6–1

THIRD ROUND

NAVRATILOVA (1) 6–0 6–2 6–2
Huber 6–3 6–1
Garrone 6–4 2–6 6–3
HANIKA (15) 6–2 6–4
RINALDI (10) 3–6 6–1 7–5
Tauziat 6–2 0–6 6–3
Bassett 6–2 6–7 6–3
KOHDE-KILSCH (8) 6–2 6–2
EVERT (3) 6–3 7–5
Krapl 7–5 5–7 6–4
Gompert 6–4 6–3
K. MALEEVA (12) 6–3 2–6 6–4
REGGI (14) 6–3 6–3
A. Minter 7–6 6–4
Zvereva 6–7 6–3 6–0
SUKOVA (5) 6–3 6–1

FOURTH ROUND

NAVRATILOVA (1) 6–1 6–1
HANIKA (15) 6–4 6–3
Tauziat 6–1 6–3
KOHDE-KILSCH (8) 7–5 6–3
EVERT (3) 6–2 6–0
K. MALEEVA (12) 7–6 6–1
REGGI (14) 7–5 6–2
SUKOVA (5) 6–1 6–3

QUARTER-FINALS

NAVRATILOVA (1) 6–0 6–2
KOHDE-KILSCH (8) 6–1 3–6 6–0
EVERT (3) 6–4 6–1
REGGI (14) 6–3 4–6 6–2

SEMI-FINALS

NAVRATILOVA (1) 6–1 6–2
EVERT (3) 6–2 6–2

FINAL

NAVRATILOVA (1) 6–2 6–2

6–4 4–6 8–6

First round

G. SABATINI (ARG) (7)
M. Van Der Torre (HOL)
K. Karlsson (SWE)
L. Fernando (ITA)
C. Benjamin (USA)
T. Mochizuki (USA)
M. Werdel (USA)
M. Laval
T. Phelps (USA)
R. Rajchrtova (TCH)
J. Pozl Wiesner (AUT)
Mrs E. Smylie (AUS)
M. Lindstrom (SWE)
K. Schimper (RSA)
L. Bonder (USA)
L. McNEIL (USA) (9)
M. GURNEY (USA) (16)
N. Provis (AUS)
S. Mascarin (USA)
B. Paulus (AUT)
A. Croft (GBR)
G. Dinu (FRG)
E. Burgin (USA)
A. Sanchez (ESP)
E. Minter (AUS)
C. Karlsson (SWE)
C. Porwik (FRG)
F. Bonsignori (ITA)
N. Herreman
L. Field
M. Jausovec (YUG)
H. MANDLIKOVA (TCH) (4)
M. MALEEVA (BUL) (6)
A. M. Cecchini (ITA)
T. Holladay (USA)
D. Balestrat (AUS)
B. Herr (USA)
G. Fernandez (USA)
H. Ter Reit (HOL)
S. Wasserman (BEL)
S. Walsh Pete (USA)
A. Kanellopoulou (GRE)
R. Fairbank (RSA)
H. Cioffi (USA)
S. Rehe (USA)
A. Henricksson (USA)
K. Horvath (USA)
M. J. FERNANDEZ (USA) (13)
C. LINDQVIST (SWE) (11)
M. Paz (ARG)
S. Meier (FRG)
H. Kelesi (CAN)
T. Scheuer-Larsen (DEN)
S. Goles (YUG)
K. Okamoto (JAP)
M. Torres (USA)
C. Mozzoli (ITA)
R. Zrubakova (TCH)
J. Novotna (TCH)
J. M. Durie (GBR)
I. Budarova (TCH)
G. Miro (BRA)
C. Bartos Cserepy (HUN)
S. GRAF (FRG) (2)

Second round

SABATINI (7) 6–0 6–2
Fernando 2–6 7–5 6–0
Benjamin 7–5 6–3
Laval 6–2 6–4
Phelps 6–3 0–6 6–4
Wiesner 6–2 6–2
Schimper 7–6 6–2
Bonder 6–3 6–3
Provis 6–4 6–2
Paulus 6–2 6–4
Dinu 2–6 6–3 6–1
Sanchez 7–5 6–3
C. Karlsson 7–5 6–3
Porwik 7–6 6–4
Herreman 6–4 6–2
MANDLIKOVA (4) 6–0 6–0
M. MALEEVA (6) 3–6 6–3 6–3
Balestrat 6–2 6–3
G. Fernandez 6–2 6–4
Wasserman 6–1 6–1
Kanellopoulou 6–2 6–3
Cioffi 6–2 6–3
Rehe 6–3 6–1
M. J. FERNANDEZ (13) 4–6 6–0 6–2
LINDQVIST (11) 6–0 7–6
Kelesi 2–6 6–0 6–2
Scheuer-Larsen 7–5 6–2
Torres 7–6 6–0
Zrubakova 6–4 6–1
Novotna 6–3 6–1
Budarova 7–6 6–3
GRAF (2) 6–1 6–1

Third round

SABATINI (7) 6–2 6–4
Benjamin 6–0 6–2
Phelps 6–3 6–3
Schimper 4–6 6–3 6–4
Paulus 6–4 6–4
Sanchez 6–0 6–2
C. Karlsson 6–4 3–6 9–7
Herreman 6–4 7–6
M. MALEEVA (6) 6–2 6–0
Wasserman 6–3 6–2
Kanellopoulou 6–1 0–6 6–3
Rehe 7–6 1–6 6–4
Kelesi 7–5 7–5
Torres 4–6 6–4 6–3
Novotna 6–3 4–6 6–4
GRAF (2) 6–1 6–1

Fourth round

SABATINI (7) 6–0 2–6 6–2
Schimper 6–7 6–2 6–2
Sanchez 6–4 6–2
C. Karlsson 6–3 4–6 7–6
M. MALEEVA (6) 5–7 6–3 6–1
Rehe 7–6 6–3
Kelesi 6–1 6–3
GRAF (2) 6–0 6–1

Quarter-finals

SABATINI (7) 6–4 6–1
Sanchez 6–1 6–4
M. MALEEVA (6) 7–6 6–1
GRAF (2) 7–6 6–2

Semi-finals

SABATINI (7) 6–4 6–0
GRAF (2) 6–4 6–1

Final

GRAF (2) 6–4 4–6 7–5

Champion

S. GRAF (FRG) (2)

Capital letters denote seeded players. Number following player's name gives seeding order.

MEN'S DOUBLES

Holders: J. Fitzgerald (AUS)/T. Smid (TCH)

FIRST ROUND

FORGET/NOAH (1)
Tyson/Van Boeckel
Fleurian/Winogradsky
Acuna/Pfister
Arrese/De Miguel
Campos/Colombo
T. Meinecke/Osterthun
CANE/OCLEPPO (16)
STEWART/WARWICK (10)
Benhabiles/DiLaura
Baxter/Chamberlain
Pham/Tulasne
Cahill/Kratzmann
Bauer/Fibak
Nijssen/Vekemans
CASAL/SANCHEZ (7)
GILDEMEISTER/GOMEZ (4)
Maurer/Purcell
Scanlon/Steeb
McNamara/McNamee
Freeman/Witsken
Barlow/Mmoh
Luza/Tiberti
WARDER/WILLENBORG (13)
S. DAVIS/DePALMER (11)
Arias/Korita
Champion/Delaitre
Carbonell/Sanchez
Basham/Buffington
Limberger/Woodforde
Mortensen/Nelson
DONNELLY/FLEMING (5)
NYSTROM/WILANDER (6)
Christensen/Wahlgren
Anger/Holmes
Kley/Soares
Gilbert/Van Patten
Dickson/Scott
Schapers/Srejber
MEZZADRI/PUGH (12)
GUNTHARDT/HLASEK (14)
Bates/Castle
Levine/Gimmalva
Evernden/Masur
Bloom/Suk
Bathman/Lundgren
McPherson/Youl
JARRYD/SEGUSO (3)
FITZGERALD/SMID (8)
Boetsch/Courteau
Layendecker/Michibata
Rive/Tarr
Lopez-Maeso/Tous
Krickstein/Yzaga
Mattar/Motta
HOOPER/LEACH (9)
BAHRAMI/PEREZ (15)
Bastiensen/Tauson
Korda/Slozil
Gunnarsson/Svensson
Birner/Navratil
Robertson/Warnecke
Jelen/Kuhnen
ANNACONE/VAN RENSBURG (2)

SECOND ROUND

FORGET/NOAH (1) 6–4 6–3
Fleurian/Winogradsky 6–4 6–1
Arrese/De Miguel 2–6 6–4 8–6
T. Meinecke/Osterthun 6–3 6–2
STEWART/WARWICK (10) 6–0 6–2
Baxter/Chamberlain 6–1 4–6 6–3
Cahill/Kratzmann 6–4 6–1
CASAL/SANCHEZ (7) 6–3 6–4
GILDEMEISTER/GOMEZ (4) 6–3 6–2
Scanlon/Steeb 6–3 6–4
Freeman/Witsken 4–6 6–0 6–0
WARDER/WILLENBORG (13) 7–5 6–3
Arias/Korita 3–6 6–3 6–2
Carbonell/Sanchez 6–7 6–3 6–1
Limberger/Woodforde 6–7 6–3 6–2
DONNELLY/FLEMING (5) 4–6 6–3 7–5
NYSTROM/WILANDER (6) 6–1 4–6 6–0
Kley/Soares 6–4 6–4
Gilbert/Van Patten 1–6 7–6 6–4
Schapers/Srejber 6–1 6–2
Bates/Castle 6–0 4–6 6–2
Evernden/Masur 6–3 6–2
Bloom/Suk 6–3 6–4
JARRYD/SEGUSO (3) 6–2 6–7 6–0
Boetsch/Courteau 7–6 6–4
Rive/Tarr 7–5 7–5
Lopez-Maeso/Tous 7–6 7–6
HOOPER/LEACH (9) 4–6 6–1 6–4
BAHRAMI/PEREZ (15) 6–4 4–6 6–0
Gunnarsson/Svensson 6–4 6–4
Birner/Navratil 6–1 2–6 6–4
ANNACONE/VAN RENSBURG (2) 6–2 6–3

THIRD ROUND

FORGET/NOAH (1) 7–6 7–6
T. Meinecke/Osterthun 6–1 6–2
STEWART/WARWICK (10) 1–6 6–3 6–4
Cahill/Kratzmann 7–5 4–6 12–10
GILDEMEISTER/GOMEZ (4) 6–4 6–4
WARDER/WILLENBORG (13) 6–0 6–4
Arias/Korita 7–5 6–2
DONNELLY/FLEMING (5) 6–3 6–4
NYSTROM/WILANDER (6) 6–1 6–0
Schapers/Srejber 6–2 5–7 6–3
Bates/Castle 6–7 7–6 6–4
JARRYD/SEGUSO (3) 6–2 6–7 6–2
Rive/Tarr 6–1 7–5
Lopez-Maeso/Tous 6–4 6–4 ret'd
BAHRAMI/PEREZ (15) 2–6 6–3 6–4
Birner/Navratil 6–4 4–3 ret'd

QUARTER-FINALS

FORGET/NOAH (1) 7–5 6–3
STEWART/WARWICK (10) 6–2 6–3
WARDER/WILLENBORG (13) 3–6 6–4 7–5
DONNELLY/FLEMING (5) 4–6 6–2 7–5
NYSTROM/WILANDER (6) 7–6 6–3
JARRYD/SEGUSO (3) 7–6 6–3
Lopez-Maeso/Tous 7–5 6–3
Birner/Navratil 6–1 7–5

SEMI-FINALS

FORGET/NOAH (1) 6–2 6–4
DONNELLY/FLEMING (5) 6–3 7–6
JARRYD/SEGUSO (3) 6–3 6–0
Lopez-Maeso/Tous 6–2 6–4

FINAL

FORGET/NOAH (1) 2–6 6–4 6–1 6–1
JARRYD/SEGUSO (3) 4–6 6–1 5–7 6–2 6–3

A. JARRYD (SWE)/R. SEGUSO (USA) (3) 6–7 6–7 6–3 6–4 6–2

Capital letters denote seeded pairings. Number following players' names gives seeding order.

Ivan Lendl won a third French Open title, after playing a long final against Mats Wilander, the winner in 1982 and 1985. *(Carol L. Newsom)*

WOMEN'S DOUBLES

Holders: M. Navratilova (USA)/A. Temesvari (HUN)

FIRST ROUND

NAVRATILOVA/SHRIVER (1)
Gildemeister/Porwik
Cohen/Gomer
Henricksson/Van Nostrand
E./M. Reinach
Croft/Mascarin
Phelps/Reggi
Horvath/Mesker
Demongeot/Tauziat
M. J. Fernandez/Werdel
Cecchini/Goles
Etchemendy/Paquet
Amiach/Herreman
Field/Minter
Jaggard/Bohmova
Bonder/Gompert
KOHDE-KILSCH/SUKOVA (3)
Fukarkova/Zrubakova
Probst/Tarabini
Garrone/Nozzoli
Holladay/Schutte
Betzner/Singer
Balestrat/Bassett
Rush Magers/Walsh Pete
Hetherington/Russell
Bakkum/Van Der Torre
Mochizuki/Phan Thanh
Minter/Mundel
Kuczynska/Rajchrtova
Bollegraf/Lindstrom
Bonsignori/Ter Riet
G. FERNANDEZ/McNEIL (7)
Nagelsen/Smylie
Martin/Niox Chateau
Hansel/Kaplan
Fulco/Mosca
Drescher/O'Neill
Antonoplis/Monteiro
Derly/Laval
Gerken/Hy
Lindqvist/Scheur-Larsen
C. Karlsson/Provis
Golder/Jausovec
Barg/Herr
Perez Roldan/Tiezzi
Byrne/Rinaldi
Jagerman/Steden
BURGIN/FAIRBANK (4)
PAZ/PFAFF (5)
Bartos Cserepy/Huber
P. Smith/Sodupe
Kelesi/Ruzici
A. M. Fernandez/Richardson
Okamoto/Sato
Budarova/Villagran
Novotna/Suire
K./M. Maleeva
Cueto/Sanchez
Schimper/Yanagi
Dias/Medrado
Marsikova/Meier
Benjamin/Van Rensburg
Gurney/Nelson Dunbar
GRAF/SABATINI (2)

SECOND ROUND

NAVRATILOVA/SHRIVER (1) 6–2 6–2
Henricksson/Van Nostrand 6–4 6–4
E./M. Reinach 6–1 6–4
Phelps/Reggi 6–2 6–2
Demongeot/Tauziat 7–6 2–6 6–4
Cecchini/Goles 6–4 6–7 6–3
Amiach/Herreman 6–2 6–4
Jaggard/Bohmova 5–7 7–6 6–1
KOHDE-KILSCH/SUKOVA (3) 6–2 6–0
Probst/Tarabini 6–0 6–3
Betzner/Singer 7–6 6–3
Balestrat/Bassett 7–6 6–3
Bakkum/Van Der Torre 6–4 5–7 6–1
Minter/Mundel 6–4 7–6
Kuczynska/Rajchrtova 6–1 6–4
G. FERNANDEZ/McNEIL (7) 6–1 6–3
Nagelsen/Smylie 7–5 6–3
Fulco/Mosca 6–1 7–6
Antonoplis/Monteiro 7–5 6–1
Derly/Laval 6–3 6–2
Lindqvist/Scheuer-Larsen 7–6 6–2
Barg/Herr 6–1 4–6 6–2
Byrne/Rinaldi 6–1 6–0
BURGIN/FAIRBANK (4) 6–3 6–2
PAZ/PFAFF (5) 6–2 7–6
P. Smith/Sodupe 7–5 7–6
Okamoto/Sato 4–6 6–3 6–4
Novotna/Suire 7–6 6–3
Cueto/Sanchez 6–1 6–4
Schimper/Yanagi 6–1 3–6 11–9
Marsikova/Meier 6–4 7–5
GRAF/SABATINI (2) 6–2 6–2

THIRD ROUND

NAVRATILOVA/SHRIVER (1) 6–0 6–2
Phelps/Reggi 6–2 6–1
Demongeot/Tauziat 2–6 6–1 6–4
Amiach/Herreman 3–6 6–3 6–3
KOHDE-KILSCH/SUKOVA (3) 6–1 6–4
Balestrat/Bassett 4–6 6–4 6–0
Minter/Mundel 7–6 6–7 6–1
G. FERNANDEZ/McNEIL (7) 6–1 6–2
Nagelsen/Smylie 6–3 6–3
Antonoplis/Monteiro 3–6 7–6 6–0
Barg/Herr 6–3 0–6 6–3
Byrne/Rinaldi 0–6 7–5 6–3
PAZ/PFAFF (5) 7–6 6–3
Novotna/Suire 6–3 6–4
Cueto/Sanchez 6–4 6–2
GRAF/SABATINI (2) 6–1 7–6

QUARTER-FINALS

NAVRATILOVA/SHRIVER (1) 6–4 6–4
Demongeot/Tauziat 7–6 6–1
KOHDE-KILSCH/SUKOVA (3) 7–6 6–2
G. FERNANDEZ/McNEIL (7) 6–4 6–4
Nagelsen/Smylie 6–3 6–2
Byrne/Rinaldi 6–3 7–6
PAZ/PFAFF (5) 2–6 6–4 9–7
GRAF/SABATINI (2) 7–6 6–0

SEMI-FINALS

NAVRATILOVA/SHRIVER (1) 6–3 4–6 6–4
KOHDE-KILSCH/SUKOVA (3) 6–7 6–1 6–2
Byrne/Rinaldi 5–7 6–1 6–3
GRAF/SABATINI (2) 6–2 6–3

FINAL

NAVRATILOVA/SHRIVER (1) 7–6 6–3
GRAF/SABATINI (2) 6–1 6–4

M. NAVRATILOVA (USA)/P. H. SHRIVER (USA) (1) 6–2 6–1

Capital letters denote seeded pairings. Number following players' names gives seeding order.

MIXED DOUBLES

Holders: K. Flach (USA)/Miss K. Jordan (USA)

FIRST ROUND

Bye
Roche/Smylie
Cahill/Provis
Chamberlain/Gerken
Courteau/Paquet
Carbonell/Fernandez
Warder/Meier
Warneke/Rush Magers
Campos/Marsikova
Scanlon/Mascarin
Kurz/Sukova
Lesage/Phan Thanh
Rodriguez/Rodriguez
Bye
Bye
Winogradsky/Herreman
Svensson/Lindqvist
Tiberti/Perez Roldan
Pimek/Kaplan
Skoff/Ruzici
Willenborg/Barg
Baxter/Hetherington
Potier/Calleja
Tyson/Field
Bahrami/Amiach
Kuchna/Vanhille
Gildemeister/Bonder
Bye
Bye
Witsken/Benjamin
Dadillon/Martin
Woodforde/Jaggard
Van Den Daele/Quentrec
Davin/Paz
Robertson/Balestrat
Hooper/Werdel
Kley/Dias
Perez Roldan/Drescher
Soares/Medrado
Purcell/Smith
Mancini/Tiezzi
Bye
Bye
Levine/Reinach
Pham/Suire
Boetsch/Derly
Buffington/Antonoplis
Luza/Tarabini
Casal/Reggi
Schapers/Henricksson
Njissen/Bakkum
Errard/Housset
J./A. Sanchez
Champion/Niox-Chateau
Fleurian/Etchemendy
Bye

SECOND ROUND

E. Sanchez/Shriver
Cahill/Provis 6–1 3–6 6–2
Chamberlain/Gerken 2–6 6–4 6–1
Warder/Meier 6–3 6–4
Warneke/Rush Magers 7–6 2–6 7–5
Scanlon/Mascarin 6–4 4–6 6–4
Lesage/Phan Thanh 6–3 7–6
Slozil/Gildemeister
McNamee/Navratilova
Svensson/Lindqvist 6–2 6–3
Pimek/Kaplan 6–4 6–4
Skoff/Ruzici 6–3 7–5
Baxter/Hetherington 7–6 6–3
Tyson/Field 6–4 6–4
Gildemeister/Bonder 6–1 6–0
Mortensen/Scheuer-Larsen
Warwick/Byrne
Witsken/Benjamin 6–3 6–2
Woodforde/Jaggard 6–1 6–1
Robertson/Balestrat 6–3 6–2
Hooper/Werdel 5–7 6–4 6–4
Soares/Medrado 7–5 6–4
Purcell/Smith 6–4 6–3
Stewart/McNeil
Freyss/Laval
Levine/Reinach 6–7 6–3 6–3
Boetsch/Derly 7–5 6–4
Luza/Tarabini 5–7 6–2 6–3
Schapers/Henricksson 7–5 7–6
J./A. Sanchez 6–1 6–1
Fleurian/Etchemendy 6–3 4–6 6–2
Forget/Nagelsen

THIRD ROUND

Sanchez/Shriver 6–4 6–4
Chamberlain/Gerken 4–6 6–4 6–3
Warneke/Rush Magers 7–6 7–5
Slozil/Gildemeister 6–3 6–1
McNamee/Navratilova 6–2 6–2
Skoff/Ruzici 6–2 6–2
Tyson/Field 6–7 6–3 6–2
Mortensen/Scheuer-Larsen 6–0 6–3
Warwick/Byrne 6–4 7–5
Woodforde/Jaggard 6–3 3–6 6–3
Hooper/Werdel 6–3 6–4
Stewart/McNeil 6–4 7–6
Levine/Reinach 6–0 6–2
Luza/Tarabini w.o.
Schapers/Henricksson 6–2 6–2
Forget/Nagelsen 6–3 3–6 6–4

QUARTER-FINALS

Sanchez/Shriver 6–3 6–3
Slozil/Gildemeister 6–2 6–3
McNamee/Navratilova 2–6 6–2 6–3
Mortensen/Scheuer-Larsen 6–2 6–2
Woodforde/Jaggard 6–4 6–7 8–6
Stewart/McNeil 7–5 6–0
Luza/Tarabini 6–3 5–7 6–4
Schapers/Henricksson 6–2 4–6 7–5

SEMI-FINALS

Sanchez/Shriver 6–4 7–5
Mortensen/Scheuer-Larsen 6–4 1–6 6–4
Stewart/McNeil 7–5 3–6 6–3
Schapers/Henricksson 4–6 6–3 7–5

FINAL

Sanchez/Shriver 3–6 6–1 6–1
Stewart/McNeil 6–4 7–5

E. SANCHEZ (ESP)/P. H. SHRIVER (USA) 6–3 7–6

After beginning the year as runner-up in the Australian Open, the popular Australian, Pat Cash, played inspired grass-court tennis at Wimbledon, where he beat Mats Wilander and Ivan Lendl to take his first Grand Slam title. *(A. Evans)*

WIMBLEDON CHAMPIONSHIPS

Lance Tingay

The Lawn Tennis Championships entered a second century with some foreboding, for the opening days of the 101st meeting were persistently and acutely damp and miserable. With no play at all on the first day, but half a day's play from tea time on the second, and only two matches getting on to court on the Thursday, the pessimists were talking of changing the date, changing the site and, maybe, changing the game. Then, magic! The last few days were the most glorious ever, and the meeting finished on time, the only damage being the reduction of the men's doubles to the best of three sets for the first two rounds.

I will note at the start that John McEnroe did not compete; the women's singles missed Hana Mandlikova, who was injured; and Boris Becker was beaten early – in the second round by the unseeded Australian Peter Doohan. So the young German did not win for the third time in a row. He reacted to his loss manfully: 'I lost a tennis match, not a war.' Ivan Lendl was beaten, although that was not until the final, where for the second year the No. 1 player of the world had the ultimate cup of glory snatched from his lips. Pat Cash, who had virtually won the *Davis Cup* for Australia in 1986, now won the singles crown for himself. Vigorous, inspirational, with grass-court serve-and-volley expertise in every inch of him, he triumphed over Mats Wilander, a revived Jimmy Connors and then Lendl. After beating Lendl, he climbed into the stand and up to the players' guests' box to embrace his relatives and friends. It was a mountaineering feat in itself, though not as skilled as the glorious aggression which had made him the first Australian men's singles champion since John Newcombe in 1971.

Here was a brand new champion who had been seeded only 11th, the same lowly position from which Jaroslav Drobny won in 1954. In the women's singles it was as before. Martina Navratilova set new frontiers by winning for the sixth successive year, equalling the feat of Helen Wills Moody by taking the title for the eighth time. It was her first tournament success for 1987, which had, until then, been a dispiriting year for her. However, she set failure behind her; but for the losing finalist, the 18-year-old genius from Germany, Steffi Graf, it was her first check after a series of victories from the start of the year, during which she won in Boca Raton, Key Biscayne, Hilton Head, Amelia Island, Rome, Berlin and Paris.

Apart from Miss Navratilova's, the honours board took on fresh names. That sterling American pair, Ken Flach and Robert Seguso took the men's doubles. Claudia Kohde-Kilsch and Helena Sukova won the women's doubles, in which their most significant victory was in the semi-final, over the Soviet pair of Svetlana Parkhomenko and Larisa Savchenko, who had beaten Miss Navratilova and Pam Shriver in the round before. The outcome of the mixed doubles could bring only chauvinistic cheers, for 44 Championships had passed since Fred Perry and Dorothy Round had last brought an all-British victory in 1936, the later triumphs of Ann Jones and John Lloyd having been shared with partners from abroad. Jeremy Bates and Jo Durie, unseeded and despite being nearly beaten by Kim Warwick and Jenny Byrne in the second round, triumphed hugely.

It was on the first Friday, when the weather had at last improved, that the heavy, dramatic beat of Wimbledon's weighty upsets was sounded. The two-times champion, 19-year-old Becker, was beaten in four sets by Peter Doohan. The Australian, inspired, took to the inevitably dampish court with the flair of one revelling in such conditions. Most notably, he returned service brilliantly, always well and often with venom, while Becker never brought out his victory battle order. On the same day Lendl was pushed all the way by Paolo Cañe, an Italian who might have been born and bred on turf so well did he serve and volley. Lendl, down 1 set to 2, came perilously close to a 3–5 fourth-set deficit before winning in the fifth.

By the end of the second Monday the meeting had taken shape, though with arrears a-plenty to make up. With the last 16 into line, there were eight unseeded players surviving in the men's singles. One was Anders Jarryd, who brought down the fifth-seeded Miloslav Mecir, not normally a great grass-court man in any case. Tim Mayotte, expected by many to flourish, was eliminated after a splendid match by the 1986 French finalist, Mikael Pernfors of Sweden, who manfully recovered from being two sets down. The Frenchman, Yannick Noah, seeded six, did not survive round two, being dispossessed in a 9–7 fifth set by Guy Forget, his doubles partner. Forget continued to flouish, beating Paul Annacone before yielding to the dashing craft of Cash in the last 16.

It was at that stage that the no-longer-young Jimmy Connors, all 34 years of him, began to fill a hero's role. He had lost – or so it seemed – to Pernfors. His jaded strokes giving more away than they won, he dropped the first two sets, and was 1–4 behind in the third. Having hauled that one back, he was within a point of being 0–4 in the fourth, yet the champion of 1974 and 1982 again found his insistent charging strength to survive. In the same round Henri Leconte had a technical seeding triumph when, at number 9, he beat Andres Gomez at number 8.

That put Leconte into an intriguing quarter-final clash with Lendl, although as it happened the sparks were less bright than expected, and Lendl never appeared seriously threatened. Stefan Edberg came through at the expense of Jarryd to face Lendl. Meanwhile in the other half Cash rattled through against Wilander, while Connors renewed his hero's part by coping with the big-serving Yugoslav, Slobodan Zivojinovic. There were murmers of the possibility of Connors reaching the final. The Grand Old Man had renewed his youth! But not, alas, when he met Cash in the semi-final. He was hardly in the match, while Lendl at the same stage had to struggle far harder to overcome Edberg, though when he found his full service strength, his worries were put behind him.

The Cash-Lendl final was a very good but not great contest. On the very dry court, the rallies were brief and the games long. Long in duration, that is, for Lendl's studied approach, his gathering of concentration, made for long, motionless seconds when he stood still and time ran on. In the end the inspirational efforts of Cash were vastly more effective. It took well over an hour for the first set to finish, with the second game going to seven deuces and the tenth to five. In that last marathon episode Lendl saved a set-point – with an ace.

Lendl began the tie-break badly. Not until Cash was 6–1 was he spurred to perfection, but Cash just managed to win at 7–5, so putting himself in the seat of dominance. Indeed, Lendl was for the next set virtually a despondent, broken player. Then he recovered to move well ahead in the third set, only for Cash, again inspired, to pass him and finally serve himself to the title with a superb love game. Thus the Czech, so great a player, was denied yet again the satisfaction of a big title on grass. It seemed very natural and apt that Cash, whose back injury two years earlier might have put him out of things for good, should add to the stock of Australia's Wimbledon titles.

There were, I suppose, six challengers with a chance of taking the women's singles. Miss Navratilova, of course, Miss Graf, invincible this season to date, the much loved Chris Evert, the young Argentinian, Gabriela Sabatini, Helena Sukova, whose mother was the finalist in 1962 and who had beaten Miss Navratilova at Eastbourne, and Pam Shriver. All survived to the last 16 (by which time six seeds had fallen) without undue problems. As for entry to the last eight, Miss Evert lost the middle set to Ros Fairbank and Miss Sabatini the same to the Soviet junior, Natalia Zvereva. Miss Shriver was match-point down and won only 10–8 in the third set against the rejuvenated German, Sylvia Hanika.

Miss Shriver did the same in the quarter-final against Miss Sukova, although her success served merely to make her sacrificial bait to the all-conquering Miss Graf in the semi-final. Very different was the Navratilova-Evert semi-final. This was their 73rd clash since 1973 and one of the best. Miss Evert, whose net skills reached new heights – albeit lacking the natural talents of her opponent in the same area – hardly contrived to look a winner after

Jeremy Bates and Jo Durie thrilled the home crowds by taking the mixed doubles title at Wimbledon. *(A. Evans)*

losing the first set. She won the second which, as it transpired, was the only set yielded by the perpetual champion. Wimbledon thrilled to the sight of an old battle renewed with sparkle. For the record Miss Navratilova was scoring a 39th victory over her old rival.

The final posed a question put with bated breath. There seemed small doubt but that the mantle of World Champion would ultimately fall on the hard-hitting and brilliant Miss Graf. But would she take the Wimbledon crown in 1987 as she had the French?

Miss Navratilova denied her the achievement manfully and soundly, finding a swinging left-handed serve to the German's backhand. But if Miss Graf's capacity for the sizzling pass rose to great heights, the former Czech still contrived to make her volleying effective. There was a climax when Miss Graf was love-40 and 4–5 in the first set. She recouped with verve, but it merely delayed the end. We witnessed one of the finest of women's finals. It was Miss Navratilova's 41st sequential singles win at Wimbledon, and put her tally of Wimbledon Championships to 16, leaving her five more to go to surpass the 20 won by Billie Jean King.

The men's doubles, diminished a little by the initial reduction to the best of three sets, paid scant regard to the seeding order. Flach and Seguso were the winners against the top seeds, Forget and Noah, in the quarter-final, and beat the third seeds, Gomez and Zivojinovic, in the semi-finals. The previous year's winners, Joakim Nystrom and Wilander, were seeded only five, and lost in the second round to the unseeded Carl Limberger and Mark Woodforde. The Spanish pair, Emilio Sanchez and Sergio Casal, who had already won four titles together in the season, made the final. In the event the seventh seeds beat the eighth, although Flach and Seguso lost the first two sets before coming back to win. Such a feat is rare in the final, the last occasion on which it was done being in 1927 by the Americans Frank Hunter and Bill Tilden.

Claudia Kohde-Kilsch and Miss Sukova lost a set only in the semi-final against the Russians on their way to the women's doubles title, although Betsy Nagelsen and Elizabeth Smylie (who was champion with Kathy Jordan in 1985) resisted them in a close final.

Perhaps the mixed doubles reflected the strains of the early bad weather, but be that as it may, Bates and Miss Durie did nobly for Britain. It should be noted, too, that Sara Gomer of Britain won the Plate; the last home winner was Sue Barker in 1979.

MEN'S SINGLES

Holder: B. Becker (FRG)

FIRST ROUND

B. BECKER (FRG) (1)
K. Novacek (TCH)
A. Antonitsch (AUT)
P. Doohan (AUS)
C. Panatta (ITA)
J. Grabb (USA)
M. Kures (USA)
L. Shiras (USA)
N. Odizor (NIG)
S. Giammalva (USA)
P. Fleming (USA)
M. J. Bates
S. Zivojinovic (YUG)
M. Flur (USA)
S. Casal (ESP)
D. PATE (USA) (15)
T. S. MAYOTTE (USA) (10)
J. P. Fleurian (FRA)
T. Wilkison (USA)
J. Pugh (USA)
M. Pernfors (SWE)
R. Seguso (USA)
C. Steyn (RSA)
C. A. Limberger (AUS)
D. Goldie (USA)
K. Evernden (NZL)
D. T. Visser (RSA)
L. Mattar (BRA)
T. Witsken (USA)
S. M. Shaw
M. Davis (USA)
J. S. CONNORS (USA) (7)
M. WILANDER (SWE) (3)
G. Muller (RSA)
M. Leach (USA)
J. Gunnarsson (SWE)
J. B. Svensson (SWE)
S. Youl (AUS)
I. Kley (BRA)
E. Edwards (RSA)
C. J. Van Rensburg (RSA)
T. Hogstedt (SWE)
C. Bergstrom (SWE)
P. Lundgren (SWE)
J. Yzaga (PER)
E. Jelen (FRG)
M. Bauer (USA)
E. SANCHEZ (ESP) (14)
P. CASH (AUS) (11)
M. Freeman (USA)
T. Nelson (USA)
P. McNamee (AUS)
L. Scott (USA)
G. Holmes (USA)
M. Schapers (HOL)
J. Sanchez (ESP)
P. Annacone (USA)
M. Srejber (TCH)
W. Masur (AUS)
C. Motta (BRA)
G. Forget (FRA)
T. Muster (AUT)
B. D. Drewett (AUS)
Y. NOAH (FRA) (6)

SECOND ROUND

BECKER (1) 6–4 6–2 6–4
Doohan 4–6 7–5 6–2 4–6 9–7
Panatta 6–4 6–7 6–7 6–4 6–3
Shiras 6–3 6–4 6–3
Giammalva 6–3 6–7 6–3 6–3
Bates 7–6 7–6 7–6
Zivojinovic 3–6 6–3 6–4 6–0
PATE (15) 6–4 7–6 7–5
MAYOTTE (10) 6–2 6–3 6–3
Wilkison 7–5 6–7 6–4 6–4
Pernfors 3–6 6–3 6–2 6–7 10–8
Steyn 6–3 6–2 6–4
Evernden 6–3 4–6 6–4 7–5
Visser 3–6 7–6 6–4 6–4
Shaw 6–3 6–4 6–3
CONNORS (7) 6–1 7–6 7–6
WILANDER (3) 6–2 6–1 6–4
Gunnarsson 6–4 6–4 6–4
Svensson 5–7 6–1 6–3 2–6 6–3
Edwards 6–4 3–6 7–6 6–3
Van Rensburg 6–4 6–7 7–6 6–3
C. Bergstrom 6–4 6–2 1–6 3–6 13–11
Jelen 7–6 0–6 6–2 4–6 6–2
SANCHEZ (14) 6–4 3–6 6–2 7–5
CASH (11) 6–0 6–3 6–2
McNamee 6–3 6–4 2–6 1–6 19–17
Scott 6–4 6–2 7–6
Schapers 7–5 6–2 6–2
Annacone 7–6 6–4 6–1
Masur 6–2 6–4 6–4
Forget 6–4 6–4 6–4
NOAH (6) 6–4 6–4 6–4

THIRD ROUND

Doohan 7–6 4–6 6–2 6–4
Shiras 6–3 7–6 3–6 7–6
Bates 6–3 6–3 6–2
Zivojinovic 3–6 7–6 6–4 6–1
MAYOTTE (10) 6–3 4–6 6–7 6–2 6–4
Pernfors 6–3 6–3 6–2
Evernden 6–2 7–6 6–1
CONNORS (7) 6–2 2–6 6–3 6–4
WILANDER (3) 6–2 6–1 6–2
Svensson 4–6 6–3 3–6 6–3 8–6
Van Rensburg 6–3 6–2 6–2
SANCHEZ (14) 5–7 6–1 2–6 7–6 6–2
CASH (11) 7–5 6–4 6–2
Schapers 7–6 6–3 6–2
Annacone 6–7 6–4 7–6 6–7 6–3
Forget 3–6 7–6 4–6 6–4 9–7

FOURTH ROUND

Doohan 6–7 4–6 6–3 6–4 12–10
Zivojinovic 7–6 7–5 7–6
Pernfors 2–6 4–6 6–4 6–3 7–5
CONNORS (7) 6–1 6–2 6–7 6–3
WILANDER (3) 7–6 6–1 6–3
SANCHEZ (14) 7–5 6–4 7–6
CASH (11) 7–6 6–2 2–6 6–4
Forget 4–6 6–4 4–6 6–2 6–4

QUARTER-FINALS

Zivojinovic 6–2 6–4 7–6
CONNORS (7) 1–6 1–6 7–5 6–4 6–2
WILANDER (3) 2–6 7–6 6–3 7–5
CASH (11) 6–2 6–3 6–4

SEMI-FINALS

CONNORS (7) 7–6 7–5 6–3
CASH (11) 6–3 7–5 6–4

FINAL

CASH (11) 6–4 6–4 6–1

7–6 6–2 7–5

M. MECIR (TCH) (5)
M. DePalmer (USA)
M. Woodforde (AUS)
K. Jones (USA)
R. Osterthun (FRG)
A. Jarryd (SWE)
D. Rostagno (USA)
B. Dyke (AUS)
W. Scanlon (USA)
T. Mmoh (NIG)
L. Stefanki (USA)
A. Volkov (URS)
G. Donnelly (USA)
C. A. Bailey
S. M. Bale
B. GILBERT (USA) (12)
J. NYSTROM (SWE) (13)
H. Sundstrom (SWE)
T. Smid (TCH)
D. Tyson (AUS)
A. Maurer (FRG)
C. U. Steeb (FRG)
J. B. Fitzgerald (AUS)
J. Hlasek (SUI)
S. Colombo (ITA)
M. W. Anger (USA)
M. Westphal (FRG)
R. Krishnan (IND)
S. Botfield
M. Purcell (USA)
S. Eriksson (SWE)
S. EDBERG (SWE) (4)
A. GOMEZ (ECU) (8)
H. Skoff (AUT)
J. Canter (USA)
U. Stenlund (SWE)
K. Flach (USA)
R. Saad (ARG)
J. Sadri (USA)
J. Carlsson (SWE)
G. Bloom (ISR)
P. Kuhnen (FRG)
P. Vojtisek (FRG)
M. Laurendeau (CAN)
A. Mansdorf (ISR)
N. A. Fulwood
A. Agassi (USA)
H. LECONTE (FRA) (9)
K. CURREN (USA) (16)
B. Testerman (USA)
J. Avendano (ESP)
J. C. Kriek (USA)
D. de Miguel (ESP)
S. E. Davis (USA)
D. Keretic (FRG)
V. Amritraj (IND)
A. Olkhovsky (URS)
A. N. Castle
R. Stadler (SUI)
R. A. Reneberg (USA)
P. Cane (ITA)
J. Arias (USA)
C. Saceanu (RUM)
I. LENDL (TCH) (2)

MECIR (5) 6–3 6–2 7–5
Woodforde 4–6 3–6 6–3 6–3 6–1
Jarryd 6–3 7–6 6–4
Rostagno 6–2 6–3 6–4
Scanlon 4–6 6–7 6–2 6–4 6–4
Volkov 6–4 4–6 6–3 6–4
Bailey 3–6 7–6 7–5 7–6
GILBERT (12) 7–6 6–4 6–3
NYSTROM (13) 6–2 6–7 6–4 6–3
Smid 6–4 6–4 6–7 6–3
Maurer 6–4 6–7 6–4 5–7 11–9
Hlasek 6–1 6–4 7–6
Anger 6–3 7–5 7–6
Krishnan 6–3 6–1 6–3
Purcell 6–1 6–1 6–2
EDBERG (4) 6–0 6–0 6–0
GOMEZ (8) 6–4 6–4 7–6
Stenlund 6–7 6–3 6–4 6–4
Flach 6–1 6–4 6–4
Sadri 6–1 6–4 6–1
Bloom 6–3 6–3 6–2
Laurendeau 7–5 6–3 6–0
Mansdorf 6–2 7–5 6–1
LECONTE (9) 6–2 6–1 6–2
CURREN (16) 7–6 7–6 6–3
Kriek 6–2 6–1 4–6 6–4
Davis 6–1 6–1 6–3
Amritraj 6–2 6–3 7–5
Castle 7–6 6–2 4–6 7–5
Reneberg 6–7 7–6 6–3 7–6
Cane 6–7 6–2 7–6 6–3
LENDL (2) 6–2 3–6 6–3 7–5

MECIR (5) 6–1 6–3 6–3
Jarryd 6–0 6–3 3–6 6–3
Volkov 7–6 7–6 6–2
GILBERT (12) 6–2 6–2 6–4
NYSTROM (13) 6–3 6–1 6–4
Hlasek 6–3 3–6 6–3 6–3
Anger 6–2 6–4 6–2
EDBERG (4) 6–4 6–3 6–4
GOMEZ (8) 6–3 6–2 7–6
Flach 3–6 6–3 7–6 6–3
Bloom 3–6 2–6 6–1 6–3 6–4
LECONTE (9) 6–2 7–6 2–6 1–6 6–2
Kriek 6–4 3–6 6–3 6–2
Davis 6–3 6–0 6–4
Reneberg 6–4 4–6 6–3 6–4
LENDL (2) 3–6 7–6 6–7 7–5 6–1

Jarryd 6–3 6–3 6–3
Volkov 7–6 0–6 6–3 6–4
Hlasek 5–7 6–3 6–0 7–6
EDBERG (4) 7–6 6–2 6–2
GOMEZ (8) 6–4 6–3 3–6 7–5
LECONTE (9) 6–3 7–6 7–5
Kriek 5–7 6–4 6–7 6–1 8–6
LENDL (2) 6–4 6–7 6–3 7–6

Jarryd 7–6 7–5 6–7 6–4
EDBERG (4) 6–3 6–7 6–1 6–4
LECONTE (9) 7–5 7–5 7–5
LENDL (2) 6–3 7–6 6–2

EDBERG (4) 4–6 6–4 6–1 6–3
LENDL (2) 7–6 6–3 7–6

LENDL (2) 3–6 6–4 7–6 6–4

P. CASH (AUS) (11)

Capital letters denote seeded players. Number following player's name gives seeding order.

WOMEN'S SINGLES

Holder: M. Navratilova (USA)

FIRST ROUND

M. NAVRATILOVA (USA) (1)
C. Porwik (FRG)
K. A. Gompert (USA)
E. Inoue (JAP)
Cammie MacGregor (USA)
L. C. Gould
H. L. Cioffi (USA)
T. A. Harper (USA)
A. Sanchez (ESP)
B. J. Cordwell (NZL)
C. Karlsson (SWE)
J. A. Salmon
J. V. Wood
S. Parkhomenko (URS)
G. Fernandez (USA)
K. MALEEVA (BUL) (14)
B. C. POTTER (USA) (13)
C. Suire (FRA)
M. J. Fernandez (USA)
L. J. Bonder (USA)
B. Nagelsen (USA)
A. A. Moulton (USA)
J. Polzl Wiesner (AUT)
N. Provis (AUS)
I. Budarova (TCH)
B. Fulco (ARG)
W. Probst (FRG)
A. E. Hobbs
Mrs C. M. Balestrat (AUS)
J. M. Byrne (AUS)
H. Kelesi (CAN)
M. MALEEVA (BUL) (7)
C. M. EVERT (USA) (3)
S. L. Gomer
L. Golarsa (ITA)
G. M. Kim (USA)
P. Tarabini (ARG)
K. Okamoto (JAP)
C. K. Bassett (CAN)
S. Goles (YUG)
K. Bohmova (TCH)
P. A. Fendick (USA)
R. D. Fairbank (RSA)
M. Werdel (USA)
W. E. White (USA)
M. Jaggard (AUS)
C. J. Wood
B. BUNGE (FRG) (9)
C. LINDQVIST (SWE) (11)
K. Jordan (USA)
N. Bykova (URS)
C. Benjamin (USA)
K. T. Schimper (RSA)
A. E. Smith (USA)
E. M. Burgin (USA)
E. Reinach (RSA)
A. N. Croft
V. Lake
N. P. Dias (BRA)
Mrs E. Smylie (AUS)
M. Torres (USA)
L. Field (AUS)
A. Devries (BEL)
C. KOHDE-KILSCH (FRG) (8)

SECOND ROUND

NAVRATILOVA (1) 6–1 6–0
Inoue 7–5 6–4
Gould 6–3 6–2
Harper 6–2 6–1
Cordwell 6–1 2–6 6–4
Salmon 6–4 4–6 6–3
Parkhomenko 7–5 6–3
G. Fernandez 7–6 1–6 6–4
POTTER (13) 6–4 4–6 6–1
M. J. Fernandez 6–1 6–2
Moulton 6–2 7–5
Polzl Wiesner 5–7 6–1 6–3
Fulco 6–0 6–3
Hobbs 6–2 4–6 6–0
Balestrat 6–4 6–1
M. MALEEVA (7) 6–3 6–2
EVERT (3) 6–1 6–0
Golarsa 6–4 6–1
Okamoto 6–1 6–4
Goles 6–4 0–6 6–4
Fendick 6–1 6–4
Fairbank 6–2 6–3
W. E. White 6–2 7–6
BUNGE (9) 6–3 6–1
LINDQVIST (11) 6–2 6–2
Benjamin 7–5 6–4
Smith 2–6 6–2 6–1
Burgin 6–4 6–3
Croft 6–3 6–1
Smylie 6–2 6–3
Field 7–6 6–1
KOHDE-KILSCH (8) 6–0 6–1

THIRD ROUND

NAVRATILOVA (1) 6–1 6–2
Harper 7–6 6–2
Cordwell 7–6 6–0
G. Fernandez 6–2 3–6 6–4
M. J. Fernandez 6–0 6–1
Moulton 6–4 6–4
Fulco 6–4 6–3
Balestrat 6–7 6–1 8–6
EVERT (3) 7–5 6–0
Okamoto 4–6 6–3 6–0
Fairbank 6–2 5–7 6–2
BUNGE (9) 6–4 6–4
LINDQVIST (11) 7–5 7–6
Burgin 6–4 7–5
Smylie 6–3 6–1
KOHDE-KILSCH (8) 7–6 6–0

FOURTH ROUND

NAVRATILOVA (1) 6–2 6–2
G. Fernandez 7–6 6–1
M. J. Fernandez 7–6 6–2
Balestrat 7–6 6–0
EVERT (3) 7–5 6–0
Fairbank 7–6 6–4
LINDQVIST (11) 6–4 6–1
KOHDE-KILSCH (8) 6–2 6–1

QUARTER-FINALS

NAVRATILOVA (1) 6–3 6–1
Balestrat 7–5 6–2
EVERT (3) 6–2 2–6 7–5
KOHDE-KILSCH (8) 6–4 6–2

SEMI-FINALS

NAVRATILOVA (1) 6–2 6–1
EVERT (3) 6–1 6–3

FINAL

NAVRATILOVA (1) 6–2 5–7 6–4

7–5 6–3

P. H. SHRIVER (USA) (5)
N. Medvedeva (URS)
A. L. Minter (AUS)
Mrs H. A. Mochizuki (USA)
T. A. Catlin
E. A. Herr (USA)
P. Paradis (FRA)
A. H. White (USA)
A. M. Fernandez (USA)
I. Kuczynska (POL)
S. Meier (FRG)
M. L. Piatek (USA)
G. Rush Magers (USA)
L. Savchenko (URS)
D. S. Van Rensburg (RSA)
S. HANIKA (FRG) (16)
R. REGGI (ITA) (15)
B. A. Bowes (USA)
S. P. Sloane (USA)
P. Casale (USA)
R. Marsikova (TCH)
T. Phelps (USA)
V. Nelson Dunbar (USA)
C. Tanvier (FRA)
E. A. Minter (AUS)
M. A. Mesker (HOL)
M. Van Nostrand (USA)
J. M. Durie
R. M. White (USA)
A. L. Grunfeld
J. Louis
H. SUKOVA (TCH) (4)
G. SABATINI (ARG) (6)
B. S. Gerken (USA)
E. K. Horvath (USA)
C. Bartos Cserepy (SUI)
G. Miro (BRA)
I. Demongeot (FRA)
T. A. Holladay (USA)
L. Garrone (ITA)
K. R. Keil (USA)
A. B. Henricksson (USA)
N. Tauziat (FRA)
B. Paulus (AUT)
N. Zvereva (URS)
H. A. Ludloff (USA)
M. C. Calleja (FRA)
L. M. McNEIL (USA) (10)
W. M. TURNBULL (AUS) (12)
D. Spence (USA)
N. Herreman (FRA)
S. Walsh Pete (USA)
R. Reis (USA)
J. Novotna (TCH)
E. S. Pfaff (FRG)
Hu Na (CHI)
M. Paz (ARG)
L. Gildemeister (PER)
P. Hy (HKG)
A. Kijimuta (JAP)
T. Scheuer-Larsen (DEN)
N. A. M. Jagerman (HOL)
A. C. Villagran (ARG)
S. GRAF (FRG) (2)

SHRIVER (5) 6–2 6–1
A. L. Minter 7–5 6–3
Herr 6–1 5–7 6–3
A. H. White 6–3 7–5
Kuczynska 6–4 7–5
Meier 6–2 6–2
Savchenko 3–6 6–4 6–4
HANIKA (16) 7–5 6–2
REGGI (15) 6–4 6–2
Sloane 6–4 2–6 6–2
Marsikova 6–4 6–3
Tanvier 6–1 7–5
Mesker 6–1 6–1
Durie 6–2 6–0
R. M. White 6–1 6–3
SUKOVA (4) 6–1 6–4
SABATINI (6) 6–3 6–3
Bartos Cserepy 6–4 7–5
Demongeot 6–3 6–1
Garrone 3–6 6–3 6–4
Henricksson 6–2 6–1
Tauziat 2–6 6–1 6–1
Zvereva 6–2 6–4
McNEIL (10) 6–2 6–3
TURNBULL (12) 6–4 6–2
Walsh Pete 6–3 3–6 6–4
Novotna 6–3 3–6 8–6
Hu Na 6–2 6–3
Gildemeister 7–5 4–6 6–3
Kijimuta 6–4 7–5
Scheuer-Larsen 6–2 6–0
GRAF (2) 6–0 6–2

SHRIVER (5) 6–2 6–2
Herr 6–1 6–4
Kuczynska 6–3 6–3
HANIKA (16) 6–3 6–3
REGGI (15) 6–2 6–2
Tanvier 6–0 6–2
Durie 6–3 6–3
SUKOVA (4) 6–2 3–6 6–3
SABATINI (6) 6–1 6–3
Demongeot 3–6 6–2 8–6
Henricksson 6–4 6–4
Zvereva 6–4 6–4
Walsh Pete 6–4 6–4
Novotna 6–2 6–3
Gildemeister 6–2 6–4
GRAF (2) 6–0 6–0

SHRIVER (5) 6–2 6–2
HANIKA (16) 6–3 6–4
REGGI (15) 6–3 6–4
SUKOVA (4) 6–1 6–3
SABATINI (6) 6–3 6–4
Zvereva 6–3 6–3
Novotna 6–2 4–6 6–4
GRAF (2) 6–2 6–1

SHRIVER (5) 6–7 7–5 10–8
SUKOVA (4) 6–0 6–0
SABATINI (6) 6–0 2–6 6–4
GRAF (2) 6–4 6–3

SHRIVER (5) 4–6 7–6 10–8
GRAF (2) 4–6 6–1 6–1

GRAF (2) 6–0 6–2

M. NAVRATILOVA (USA) (1)

Capital letters denote seeded players. Number following player's name gives seeding order

MEN'S DOUBLES

Holders: J. Nystrom (SWE)/M. Wilander (SWE)

FIRST ROUND

G. FORGET/Y. NOAH (1)
R. Barlow/H. Rittersbacher
J. Gunnarsson/M. Mortensen
H. Pfister/J. B. Svensson
R. Leach/T. Pawsat
P. McNamara/P. McNamee
K. Evernden/J. C. Kriek
S. E. DAVIS/D. PATE (15)
C. HOOPER/M. LEACH (9)
P. Cane/G. Ocleppo
M. J. Bates/A. N. Castle
R. Bathman/P. Lundgren
R. Baxter/P. Chamberlin
S. Birner/T. Mmoh
B. Gilbert/E. Korita
K. FLACH/R. SEGUSO (7)
A. GOMEZ/S. ZIVOJINOVIC (3)
A. Amritraj/J. Frana
S. Botfield/M. T. Walker
G. Layendecker/G. Michibata
J. Grabb/B. Pearce
R. J. Simpson/L. Stefanki
E. Edwards/J. Letts
A. KOHLBERG/R. W. VAN'T HOF (14)
C. STEYN/D. T. VISSER (11)
D. Cahill/M. Kratzmann
L. Mattar/C. Motta
G. Muller/T. Nelson
M. Schapers/M. Srejber
L. R. Bourne/J. Klaparda
R. Acioly/D. Campos
G. DONNELLY/P. FLEMING (6)
J. NYSTROM/M. WILANDER (5)
L. Lavalle/C. Saceanu
C. A. Limberger/M. Woodforde
T. E./T. R. Gullikson
B. H. Levine/M. Tideman
H. Leconte/M. Mecir
B. D. Drewett/D. Tyson
P. DOOHAN/L. WARDER (12)
S. E. STEWART/K. WARWICK (13)
R. Acuna/M. Freeman
J. M. Lloyd/S. M. Shaw
P. Aldrich/W. B. Green
H. P. Gunthardt/J. Hlasek
P. Slozil/C. Suk
E. Jelen/W. Scanlon
S. EDBERG/A. JARRYD (4)
S. CASAL/E. SANCHEZ (8)
S. Colombo/D. de Miguel
B. Dyke/W. Masur
B. Testerman/T. Wilkison
M. W. Anger/G. Holmes
G. Connell/L. Scott
D. Cassidy/M. Purcell
K. CURREN/M. DePALMER (10)
J. B. FITZGERALD/T. SMID (16)
D. C. Felgate/J. M. Goodall
W. Popp/U. Riglewski
M. Bauer/W. Fibak
C. H. Cox/M. T. Fancutt
G. Bloom/A. Mansdorf
K. Jones/J. Pugh
P. ANNACONE/C. J. VAN RENSBURG (2)

SECOND ROUND

FORGET/NOAH (1) 6–3 7–6
Gunnarsson/Mortensen 6–3 6–4
Leach/Pawsat 7–6 6–4
DAVIS/PATE (15) 6–3 3–6 6–3
HOOPER/LEACH (9) 6–4 6–2
Bates/Castle 6–4 6–3
Baxter/Chamberlin 7–6 6–4
FLACH/SEGUSO (7) 6–4 6–4
GOMEZ/ZIVOJINOVIC (3) 6–2 6–3
Layendecker/Michibata 6–3 7–6
Simpson/Stefanki 6–3 3–6 13–11
KOHLBERG/VAN'T HOF (14) 6–4 3–6 6–3
Cahill/Kratzmann 6–3 6–4
Muller/Nelson 7–5 6–4
Bourne/Klaparda 6–7 6–3 6–4
DONNELLY/FLEMING (6) 6–3 3–6 6–1
NYSTROM/WILANDER (5) 4–6 6–3 9–7
Limberger/Woodforde 7–5 6–7 6–2
Leconte/Mecir 6–2 6–3
DOOHAN/WARDER (12) 6–4 3–6 6–3
Acuna/Freeman 3–6 7–6 6–4
Aldrich/Green 6–4 7–6
Gunthardt/Hlasek 6–1 7–6
EDBERG/JARRYD (4) 6–2 7–5
CASAL/SANCHEZ (8) 6–4 5–7 6–4
Testerman/Wilkison 6–4 6–7 9–7
Anger/Holmes 6–2 7–6
CURREN/DePALMER (10) 6–4 6–4
FITZGERALD/SMID (16) 7–6 6–3
Bauer/Fibak 6–3 6–4
Bloom/Mansdorf 6–3 7–5
ANNACONE/VAN RENSBURG (2) 6–4 7–6

THIRD ROUND

FORGET/NOAH (1) 7–6 7–6
DAVIS/PATE (15) 6–3 7–6
HOOPER/LEACH (9) 6–4 6–4
FLACH/SEGUSO (7) 6–2 6–4
GOMEZ/ZIVOJINOVIC (3) 7–6 6–4
KOHLBERG/VAN'T HOF (14) 6–4 5–7 6–4
Cahill/Kratzmann 6–3 4–6 6–4
Bourne/Klaparda 7–6 6–4
Limberger/Woodforde 3–6 7–6 8–6
DOOHAN/WARDER (12) 4–6 7–6 6–3
Aldrich/Green 7–6 7–6
EDBERG/JARRYD (4) 3–6 6–3 6–4
CASAL/SANCHEZ (8) 6–1 7–6
CURREN/DePALMER (10) 6–4 7–5
FITZGERALD/SMID (16) 6–2 7–6
ANNACONE/VAN RENSBURG (2) 6–2 3–6 6–3

QUARTER-FINALS

FORGET/NOAH (1) 6–7 7–6 6–3 6–4
FLACH/SEGUSO (7) 7–6 7–6 7–6
GOMEZ/ZIVOJINOVIC (3) 6–3 6–4 7–6
Cahill/Kratzmann 6–2 3–6 6–3 6–4
Limberger/Woodforde 7–5 6–4 3–6 7–6
EDBERG/JARRYD (4) 6–3 6–2 6–4
CASAL/SANCHEZ (8) 6–3 7–6 7–6
ANNACONE/VAN RENSBURG (2) 6–7 7–5 6–3 6–4

SEMI-FINALS

FLACH/SEGUSO (7) 7–6 4–6 4–6 6–3 6–4
GOMEZ/ZIVOJINOVIC (3) 2–6 7–6 6–7 7–6 7–5
EDBERG/JARRYD (4) 6–3 3–6 6–3 6–4
CASAL/SANCHEZ (8) 5–7 6–4 7–5 6–4

FINAL

FLACH/SEGUSO (7) 7–6 2–6 7–6 6–4
CASAL/SANCHEZ (8) 6–3 7–5 6–2

K. FLACH (USA)/R. SEGUSO (USA) (7) 3–6 6–7 7–6 6–1 6–4

Capital letters denote seeded pairings. Number following players' names gives seeding order.

Martina Navratilova's first title of 1987 was the one she wanted most – her eighth Wimbledon singles title, equalling Helen Wills Moody's record, although the Czech-American was the first to win six in a row. *(T. Hindley)*

WOMEN'S DOUBLES

Holders: M. Navratilova (USA)/P. H. Shriver (USA)

FIRST ROUND

M. NAVRATILOVA/P. H. SHRIVER (1)
P. Hy/E. Inoue
L. Antonoplis/C. C. Monteiro
J. Novotna/C. Suire
K. T. Schimper/M. Yanagi
B. J. Cordwell/A. L. Minter
K./M. Maleeva
E. A. HERR/A. A. MOULTON (15)
A. E. HOBBS/C. S. REYNOLDS (11)
P. Casale/L. Drescher
E./M. Reinach
B. Fulco/G. Mosca
Mrs T. A. Harper/H. A. Ludloff
K. Okamoto/N. Sato
V. Lake/C. J. Wood
Mrs S. PARKHOMENKO/L. SAVCHENKO (6)
C. KOHDE-KILSCH/H. SUKOVA (3)
D. A. Hansel/J. C. Kaplan
G. Rush Magers/W. E. White
M. Javer/N. Sodupe
A. B. Henricksson/M. Van Nostrand
C. Karlsson/R. Reggi
S. L. Gomer/M. Jaggard
J. M. BYRNE/P. A. FENDICK (13)
K. JORDAN/A. E. SMITH (9)
Mrs K. Bohmova/I. Kucynska
A. Betzner/C. Singer
P. G. Smith/D. S. Van Rensburg
Cammie/Cynthia MacGregor
B. S. Gerken/S. E. Mascarin
C. L. Billingham/K. F. Hunter
B. BUNGE/G. FERNANDEZ (8)
B. NAGELSEN/E. SMYLIE (5)
M. J. Fernandez/M. Werdel
L. Meskhi/L. Zvereva
M. M. Bollegraf/M. Lindstrom
Hu Na/P. Paradis
J. M. Hetherington/J. C. Russell
I. Budarova/A. C. Villagran
M. L. PIATEK/A. H. WHITE (12)
J. M. DURIE/C. TANVIER (16)
N. P. Dias/P. Tarabini
C. K. Bassett/H. Kelesi
Mrs C. M. Balestrat/T. Phelps
C. Bartos Cserepy/N. Provis
B. A. Borneo/J. A. Salmon
W. Probst/A. Sanchez
E. M. BURGIN/R. D. FAIRBANK (4)
L. M. McNEIL/R. M. WHITE (7)
L. K. Allen/C. Benjamin
P. Barg/L. Gildemeister
S. J. Leo/L. O'Neill
S. Meier/C. Porwik
H. A. Crowe/K. A. Steinmetz
L. Field/E. A. Minter
C. LINDQVIST/T. SCHEUER-LARSEN (14)
M. PAZ/E. S. PFAFF (10)
A. M. Fernandez/J. A. Richardson
I. Demongeot/N. Tauziat
N. A. M. Jagerman/M. Van Der Torre
E. K. Horvath/M. A. Mesker
S. I. Collins/S. Walsh Pete
A. N. Croft/R. Marsikova
S. GRAF/G. SABATINI (2)

SECOND ROUND

NAVRATILOVA/SHRIVER (1) 6–1 6–1
Novotna/Suire 6–1 3–6 6–4
Cordwell/A. L. Minter 6–2 6–3
HERR/MOULTON (15) 6–7 6–3 6–3
HOBBS/REYNOLDS (11) 6–1 6–2
E./M. Reinach 6–0 6–2
Harper/Ludloff 6–4 6–3
PARKHOMENKO/SAVCHENKO (6) 6–2 6–0
KOHDE-KILSCH/SUKOVA (3) 6–3 6–4
Rush Magers/W. E. White 6–1 6–0
Henricksson/Van Nostrand 6–4 6–2
BYRNE/FENDICK (13) 6–2 6–2
JORDAN/A. E. SMITH (9) 7–6 6–4
P. G. Smith/Van Rensburg 7–6 6–7 6–4
Cammie/Cynthia MacGregor 6–4 6–3
BUNGE/G. FERNANDEZ (8) 6–0 6–1
NAGELSEN/SMYLIE (5) 7–5 7–6
Bollegraf/Lindstrom 7–5 6–1
Hetherington/Russell 6–4 6–4
PIATEK/A. H. WHITE (12) 6–1 6–2
Dias/Tarabini 7–5 6–4
Bassett/Kelesi 4–6 7–5 6–4
Bartos,Cserepy/Provis 6–7 7–6 6–4
BURGIN/FAIRBANK (4) 6–2 6–2
McNEIL/R. M. WHITE (7) 6–1 6–3
Barg/Gildemeister 6–3 6–3
Crowe/Steinmetz 4–6 6–4 6–3
Field/E. A. Minter 7–5 3–6 6–2
A. M. Fernandez/Richardson 7–6 4–6 6–3
Demongeot/Tauziat 6–1 6–1
Collins/Walsh Pete 6–4 6–2
GRAF/SABATINI (2) 6–4 6–2

THIRD ROUND

NAVRATILOVA/SHRIVER (1) 5–7 6–4 6–4
Cordwell/A. L. Minter 6–4 6–4
HOBBS/REYNOLDS (11) 5–7 6–4 6–1
PARKHOMENKO/SAVCHENKO (6) 6–0 7–6
KOHDE-KILSCH/SUKOVA (3) 6–3 6–2
Henricksson/Van Nostrand 5–7 6–1 9–7
JORDAN/A. E. SMITH (9) 6–4 6–4
BUNGE/G. FERNANDEZ (8) 6–2 6–7 6–3
NAGELSEN/SMYLIE (5) 4–6 6–3 6–4
Hetherington/Russell 7–5 7–6
Dias/Tarabini 7–6 7–6
BURGIN/FAIRBANK (4) 7–5 6–3
McNEIL/R. M. WHITE (7) 6–2 6–4
Field/E. A. Minter 6–2 6–4
A. M. Fernandez/Richardson 6–4 6–2
GRAF/SABATINI (2) 7–5 6–4

QUARTER-FINALS

NAVRATILOVA/SHRIVER (1) 6–4 6–2
PARKHOMENKO/SAVCHENKO (6) 6–0 6–3
KOHDE-KILSCH/SUKOVA (3) 6–3 6–4
JORDAN/A. E. SMITH (9) 7–5 6–3
NAGELSEN/SMYLIE (5) 4–6 6–4 6–2
BURGIN/FAIRBANK (4) 6–3 6–2
McNEIL/R. M. WHITE (7) 2–6 6–2 6–2
A. M. Fernandez/Richardson 4–6 6–2 6–4

SEMI-FINALS

PARKHOMENKO/SAVCHENKO (6) 6–2 6–4
KOHDE-KILSCH/SUKOVA (3) 7–6 7–5
NAGELSEN/SMYLIE (5) 7–6 6–7 6–3
McNEIL/R. M. WHITE (7) 6–3 6–3

FINAL

KOHDE-KILSCH/SUKOVA (3) 1–6 6–4 7–5
NAGELSEN/SMYLIE (5) 6–4 6–7 6–4

C. KOHDE-KILSCH (FRG)/H. SUKOVA (TCH) (3) 7–5 7–5

Capital letters denote seeded pairings. Number following players' names gives seeding order.

MIXED DOUBLES

Holders: K. Flach (USA)/K. Jordan (USA)

FIRST ROUND

K. FLACH/K. JORDAN (1)
C. Motta/C. C. Monteiro
K. Jones/P. Paradis
M. Bauer/C. Benjamin
J. A. Southcombe/S. L. Gomer
S. Youl/L. O'Neill
R. J. Simpson/B. J. Cordwell
R. SEGUSO/C. K. BASSETT (16)
A. KOHLBERG/P. A. FENDICK (13)
R. Baxter/C. S. Reynolds
J. W. Feaver/S. V. Wade
R. Leach/P. Barg
R. Acuna/J. M. Hetherington
C. H. Cox/W. E. White
T. Pawsat/E. A. Herr
M. KRATZMANN/E. M. BURGIN (8)
C. Fancutt/L. Gracie
B. C. Buffington/N. A. M. Jagerman
M. Schapers/A. B. Henricksson
D. Tyson/L. Field
S. Casal/R. Reggi
J. M. Lloyd/W. M. Turnbull
T. Nelson/L. M. McNeil
G. MULLER/A. H. WHITE (11)
S. E. STEWART/A. E. SMITH (10)
D. Cahill/N. Provis
D. MacPherson/D. S. Van Rensburg
P. Doohan/C. M. Balestrat
W. Scanlon/S. E. Mascarin
L. Scott/H. A. Ludloff
M. T. Fancutt/S. Walsh Pete
H. Shirato/M. Yanagi
A. Olkhovsky/L. Meskhi
M. Woodforde/M. Jaggard
J. Grabb/R. M. White
E. Edwards/E. Reinach
T. Woodbridge/P. Moreno
M. J. Bates/J. M. Durie
J. Pugh/C. Suire
K. WARWICK/J. M. BYRNE (9)
M. MORTENSEN/T. SCHEUER-LARSEN (14)
R. Barlow/J. S. Golder
P. Slozil/L. Gildemeister
A. N. Castle/A. E. Hobbs
O. K. Davidson/A. N. Croft
B. D. Drewett/S. L. Collins
P. Chamberlin/B. S. Gerken
P. FLEMING/B. NAGELSEN (3)
D. T. VISSER/R. D. FAIRBANK (7)
M. Purcell/P. G. Smith
C. J. Van Rensburg/M. Reinach
B. H. Levine/M. Van Nostrand
R. D. Ralston/M. J. Fernandez
J. Letts/L. Antonoplis
L. Warder/C. Porwik
R. W. VAN'T HOF/M. L. PIATEK (12)
J. B. FITZGERALD/E. SMYLIE (15)
A. Maasdorp/H. A. Mochizuki
S. Svensson/C. Lindqvist
G. Michibata/P. Hy
K. Evernden/J. C. Kaplan
K. Hutter/S. Norris
G. Connell/H. Kelesi
D. Roberts/T. A. Catlin

SECOND ROUND

FLACH/JORDAN (1) 6–3 6–0
Bauer/Benjamin 6–4 6–4
Southcombe/Gomer 7–5 7–5
Simpson/Cordwell 6–2 4–6 9–7
KOHLBERG/FENDICK (13) 6–4 4–6 6–4
Leach/Barg 6–7 6–4 6–2
Acuna/Hetherington 4–6 7–6 6–2
Pawsat/Herr 6–3 6–7 6–3
Buffington/Jagerman 6–3 6–2
Tyson/Field 7–6 3–6 9–7
Casal/Reggi 2–6 7–5 7–5
MULLER/A. H. WHITE (11) 6–3 6–4
Cahill/Provis 6–4 6–3
Doohan/Balestrat 7–6 7–6
Scott/Ludloff 6–3 6–2
Fancutt/Walsh Pete w.o.
Olkhovsky/Meskhi 6–4 6–3
Edwards/Reinach 7–6 7–5
Bates/Durie 6–1 6–4
WARWICK/BYRNE (9) 7–6 6–4
MORTENSEN/SCHEUER-LARSEN (14) 6–2 6–2
Slozil/Gildemeister 6–4 6–7 7–5
Davidson/Croft 6–7 6–1 9–7
FLEMING/NAGELSEN (3) 6–3 3–6 9–7
VISSER/FAIRBANK (7) 7–5 5–7 6–3
Van Rensburg/Reinach 6–0 6–7 9–7
Letts/Antonoplis 6–4 6–2
Warder/Porwik 6–4 5–7 6–4
FITZGERALD/SMYLIE (15) 6–1 6–1
Svensson/Lindqvist 6–3 6–4
Evernden/Kaplan 6–1 6–1
Connell/Kelesi 6–3 7–5

THIRD ROUND

FLACH/JORDAN (1) 7–6 7–5
Simpson/Cordwell 6–4 6–2
KOHLBERG/FENDICK (13) 6–4 6–4
Acuna/Hetherington 7–5 6–7 6–2
Buffington/Jagerman 6–7 6–3 6–4
Casal/Reggi w.o.
Cahill/Provis 7–5 6–3
Scott/Ludloff 7–6 6–4
Edwards/Reinach 6–1 6–2
Bates/Durie 3–6 7–6 6–4
MORTENSEN/SCHEUER-LARSEN (14) w.o.
FLEMING/NAGELSEN (3) 6–2 6–7 6–3
VISSER/FAIRBANK (7) 6–3 6–2
Warder/Porwik 6–3 6–3
FITZGERALD/SMYLIE (15) 6–0 6–2
Evernden/Kaplan 7–6 6–4

QUARTER-FINALS

FLACH/JORDAN (1) 6–7 7–6 6–3
KOHLBERG/FENDICK (13) 6–4 6–4
Casal/Reggi 6–1 3–6 6–1
Cahill/Provis 6–3 6–3
Bates/Durie 6–3 6–4
MORTENSEN/SCHEUER-LARSEN (14) 6–4 6–3
VISSER/FAIRBANK (7) 6–3 7–6
FITZGERALD/SMYLIE (15) 6–1 6–3

SEMI-FINALS

KOHLBERG/FENDICK (13) 6–3 3–6 8–6
Cahill/Provis 6–4 6–4
Bates/Durie 6–4 7–6
VISSER/FAIRBANK (7) 6–3 5–7 6–4

FINAL

Cahill/Provis 6–3 7–6
Bates/Durie 7–6 6–3

M. J. BATES (GBR)/J. M. DURIE (GBR) 7–6 6–3

Capital letters denote seeded pairings. Number following players' names gives seeding order.

PRIZE MONEY – £2,470,020

MEN'S SINGLES – Winner £155,000. Runner-up £77,500. Semi-finalists £38,750. Quarter-finalists £19,635. Fourth round losers £10,335. Third round losers £5,785. Second round losers £3,410. First round losers £2,080.
Total: £806,020.
WOMEN'S SINGLES – Winner £139,500. Runner-up £69,750. Semi-finalists £33,900. Quarter-finalists £16,690. Fourth round losers £8,270. Third round losers £4,485. Second round losers £2,645. First round losers £1,610.
Total: £669,410.
MEN'S DOUBLES (per team) – Winners £53,730. Runners-up £26,870. Semi-finalists £13,430. Quarter-finalists £6,820. Third round losers £3,510. Second round losers £1,860. First round losers £1,090.
Total: £227,460.
WOMEN'S DOUBLES (per team) – Winners £46,500. Runners-up £23,250. Semi-finalists £10,740. Quarter-finalists £5,460. Third round losers £2,630. Second round losers £1,400. First round losers: £800.
Total: £182,110.
MIXED DOUBLES (per team) – Winners £27,900. Runners-up £13,950. Semi-finalists £6,980. Quarter-finalists £3,240. Third round losers £1,620. Second round losers £810. First round losers £370.
Total: £106,530.
WOMEN'S PLATE – Winner: £3,950. Finalists: £2,560. Semi-finalists: £1,740. Quarter-finalists: £870. Third round losers: £415. Second round losers: £235. First round losers: £165.
Total: £23,190.
35 AND OVER MEN'S SINGLES – Winner £11,300. Runner-up £9,050. Semi-finalists £5,650. Quarter-finalists £3,400. First round losers £2,250.
Total: £63,250.
35 AND OVER MEN'S DOUBLES (per team) – Winners £9,050. Runners-up £6,780. Semi-finalists £4,520. First round losers £2,260.
Total: £33,910
QUALIFYING COMPETITION – MEN'S SINGLES – Third round losers £1,385. Second round losers £695. First round losers £345.
Total: £66,480.
WOMEN'S SINGLES – Third round losers £1,080. Second round losers £540. First round losers £270.
Total: £92,400.

WIMBLEDON PLATE

WOMEN'S SINGLES – Final: S. L. Gomer d. K. A. Gompert (USA) 6–3 6–4.

JUNIOR EVENTS

BOYS' SINGLES – Final: D. Nargiso (ITA) d. J. Stoltenberg (AUS) 7–6 6–4.
BOYS' DOUBLES – Final: Stoltenberg/T. Woodbridge (AUS) d. Nargiso/E. Rossi (ITA) 6–3 7–6.
GIRLS' SINGLES – Final: N. Zvereva (URS) d. J. Halard (FRA) 6–4 6–4.
GIRLS' DOUBLES – Final: M. Medvedeva (URS)/Zvereva d. I. S. Kim ((KOR)/P. M. Moreno (HKG) 2–6 7–5 6–0.

OVER 35 INVITATION EVENTS

MEN'S SINGLES – Final: T. R. Gullikson (USA) d. R. C. Lutz (USA) 6–3 7–6.
MEN'S DOUBLES – Final: T. E./T. R. Gullikson (USA) d. M. C. Riessen (USA)/S. E. Stewart (USA) 7–6 6–4.

At the US Open Martina Navratilova became the first player since Billie Jean King at Wimbledon in 1973 to achieve a Championship triple, winning the women's doubles with Pam Shriver and the mixed with Emilio Sanchez. *(M. Cole, T. Hindley)*

US OPEN CHAMPIONSHIPS

Bud Collins

Nobody has written a song about Flushing in the New York borough of Queens. For good reasons. But Martina Navratilova and Ivan Lendl ought to try. It would be fitting for yet another hit in the Prague's-to-riches repertory of Navratilova and Lendl that was played out in triple-time at the US Open.

For Martina, the rarely accomplished triple – championships in singles, doubles and mixed – stands as unique in her title-studded career, and the first to be registered in 14 years. Billie Jean King was the last such champion, in 1973, at Wimbledon, and also the most recent US citizen to sweep the US Open in 1967, although Australian Margaret Court did it in 1970. Ivan's triple translates as a third straight US Open singles championship. His long day's journey to the conquest of 3rd-seeded Mats Wilander, 6–7 (7–9) 6–0 7–6 (7–4) 6–4, made him the first alien to win three straight years.

Rarer than a triple is thrice winning the daunting double – Wimbledon and US singles in the same year. Helen Wills Moody had it all to herself (1927–29) until Navratilova came along. With a smashing 7–6 (7–4) 6–1 triumph over No. 1 ranked and seeded Steffi Graf, the sinewy 30-year-old left-hander added 1987 to her 1983, 1984 and 1986 London-New York successes. Perhaps her most incredible act of dominance was extending a streak of Grand Slam final-round appearances to 11 (of which she won six), well beyond the previous best runs of six: Maureen Connolly, 1952–53; Margaret Court, 1969–71; and Martina herself, 1983–84.

No title ribbons but a mantle of excitement was worn by 11th-seeded Lori McNeil, whose placid black face appeared in the semi-finals. Not since Althea Gibson won 29 years earlier had a black woman flown so high. Hers was the most scintillating trip of the tourney, although another surprise semi-finalist, 35-year-old James Scott Connors, seeded sixth gave his innumerable admirers more tingles for their money than most could have imagined. Lori's flight to the last four included ducking two-match-points in a 7–6 (7–0) 3–6 7–6 (8–6) stunning of her pal, seventh-seeded Zina Garrison; jack-hammering a hole in the Chris Evert legend in the quarters, 3–6 6–2 6–4; and coming virtually within one shot of beating Graf in the semis, 4–6 6–2 6–4.

Despite McNeil, seldom since the advent of seeding in 1927 had such a thoroughly formful US Championships occurred. Consider these seeds coming through to the semis: 1, 2, 3 and 6 in the men's singles; 1, 2, 6 and 11 in the women's singles; 1, 2, 3 and 4 in the men's doubles; 1, 3, 5 and 8 in the women's doubles; 1, 2 and 6 in the mixed doubles. You have to retreat 31 years to find anything more predictable. Of the handful of disturbances of law-and-order, the loudest was the crash to McNeil of six-time champion Chris Evert, who thus failed to attain the semis for the only time since her 1971 début as a 16-year-old schoolgirl. In fact it was but the second time in 50 Grand Slam starts that Evert couldn't be found among the final four, and marked the end of a remarkable 13-year endurance record. She had won at least one of the Grand Slam titles every year since 1974.

Gone by the second day to Sweden's Peter Lundgren was the Wimbledon king, seventh-seeded Pat Cash. The seventh day provided appropriate Monday blues for both No. 4 seeds, Hana Mandlikova, the 1985 champ, and Boris Becker, who fell in five sets to the 13th seed, Brad Gilbert. Coming apart temperamentally in the fourth round to be nicked for a warning, penalty point and penalty game (resulting in a $500 fine), Hana was ejected in three sets by ninth-seeded Claudia Kohde-Kilsch. Mandlikova's tawdry language directed at court officials wasn't nearly as explicit or expensive as McEnroe's during his five-set third-round win over Bobo Zivojinovic. McEnroe went the warning, point penalty and game penalty route, too, but in light of previous offences, the upshot was $17,500 in fines and an eventual two-month suspension, eliminating him from the Masters.

Lendl's brilliance in the mistreatment of the last American hopes, McEnroe and Connors, was blinding. He might well have whitewashed his foes altogether to equal a quarter-century-old Frank Sedgman record had he capitalised on a set-point in the opening set tie-break against Wilander. At 6–7 in the tie-break, Wilander smacked a winning forehand to cancel the set-point, and kept going to take the set on two more winners. That stopped Lendl's run of 25 consecutive sets since losing one in the 1986 semis to Henri Leconte. Sedgman, an Australian, closed his 1951–52 reign with a string of 28 sets.

In seizing that beginning set, Wilander gave indications in his first Flushing final that he might prevail where his homeland's icon, Bjorn Borg, had stumbled four times. However, Lendl, the sturdy stoic, was just getting warmed up for their mostly baselining struggle of attrition, which, lasting four hours 47 minutes, was the most elongated of Grand Slam finals, exceeding their French Open snoozer by 17 minutes. It would have gone longer had Lendl not abruptly broken through a three-deuce last game with huge forehand and backhand returns. Or if Wilander had plucked one of the set-points hanging there for him at 4–5, 15–40 in the third.

Nevertheless, Sweden did make an initial entry on US Championships rolls in the forms of Stefan Edberg and Anders Jarryd. They won the doubles 7–6 (7–1) 6–2 4–6 5–7 7–6 (7–2) from 1985 champs, Ken Flach and Robert Seguso, who had deposed 1986 champs Andres Gomez and Bobo Zivojinovic in the semis. It was the first fifth-set tie-break to decide a major championship.

In gracing her third Grand Slam final of the year, 18-year-old Steffi Graf was the youngest to play for so many major titles since 1962 when Margaret Court won the Australian and French at 19 and the US after turning 20. But Steffi hadn't faced such a firing squad before. Three successive serve-and-volleyers aimed at her. The first was Pam Shriver who lost 6–4 6–3 in the quarters, but the second, cool, relentless McNeil, nearly triumphed. A missed point-blank volley cost the constantly charging Lori a break-point to 4–3 in the third set. The third, Navratilova, did win. Despite losing the first two games of her sixth US final, Martina retaliated with a service break in the third game, and remained sharp-edged the rest of the way, pressing and pinching Graf without letting up. From 3–3 Martina won four of the last five points, a walloping forehand return took one of the German's serving points to 3–5, and a rib-tickling serve scored the set-point. A run of two games lengthened to four, to 2–0, and then five as Martina served and swerved through five deuces and two break-points. Graf's resistance was crushed.

Only eighth-seeded Gabriela Sabatini, in the quarters, held a set-point against Navratilova: 5–4, 40–30 on the Argentine's serve. But Martina manoeuvred into position for a close-up smash, and escaped 7–5 6–3. That arranged a re-match of the 1986 final, turning into a 6–2 6–2 win over sixth-seeded Helena Sukova.

If Evert was unable to make a 17th semi-final, Connors arrived in his 13th. Could there yet be a late hurrah – a reprise of those glorious 1982–83 championship victories over Lendl? No. Connors was now too long in the tooth and Lendl, at 27, took his 14th straight win over Jimmy, 6–4 6–2 6–2. Meanwhile, Wilander was having some fun with a couple of tormentors: fifth-seeded Miloslav Mecir and second-seeded countryman Stefan Edberg. Wilander finished strongly against the Slovak in a bageled tie-break, outlasting the 1986 finalist 6–3 6–7 (5–7) 6–4 7–6 (7–0), while Edberg wavered before Mats's unusual aggressiveness, 6–4 3–6 6–3 6–4.

A rain-spattered second weekend combined with the customary thoughtless scheduling made a mess of the concluding stages. Navratilova and Graf had to play second racket to the men's semis, waiting around until after 6.00 p.m. to commence their championship bout in threatening weather.

Rain obliterated the Sunday programme, dictating Monday finals for Lendl and Wilander, and Navratilova. She and Shriver recovered from 1–4 in the second set to bring down Liz Smylie and Kathy Jordan, 5–7 6–4 6–2, for their partnership's 17th major title. Taking 90 minutes off for lunch, Martina returned in the company of Emilio Sanchez for a thrilling

6–4 6–7 (6–8) 7–6 (14–12) victory over Betsy Nagelsen and Paul Annacone. No wilder tie-break has concluded a major championship. Navratilova's swooping volley won it on the seventh match-point after she and the Spaniard had rescued two of the same. The day's labours raised Martina to a grand total of 48 major titles, still 18 short of Margaret Court's record. It had taken Martina only 37 minutes more to win her three finals than Lendl devoted to one, and she earned $306,413.50 – more than anyone else has lifted from one tournament.

JUNIOR EVENTS

BOYS' SINGLES – Final: D. Wheaton d. A. Cherkasov (URS) 7–5 6–0.
BOYS' DOUBLES – Final: G. Ivanisevic (YUG)/D. Nargiso (ITA) d. Z. Ali (IND)/B. Steven (NZL) 3–6 6–4 6–3.
GIRLS' SINGLES – Final: N. Zvereva (URS) d. S. Birch 6–0 6–3.
GIRLS' DOUBLES – Final: M. McGrath/K. Po d. Il-Soon Kim (KOR)/Shi-Ting Wang (TPE) 6–4 7–5.

SENIOR EVENTS

SENIOR MEN'S SINGLES – Final: Tom Gullikson d. S. R. Smith 6–4 6–4.
SENIOR MEN'S DOUBLES – Final: Tom Gullikson/R. Stockton d. R. C. Lutz/S. R. Smith 6–3 6–4 (played later).
SENIOR WOMEN'S DOUBLES – Final: W. M. Turnbull (AUS)/S. Walsh Pete d. V. Ziegenfuss/S. V. Wade (GBR) 6–3 7–6.

US OPEN CHAMPIONSHIPS PRIZE MONEY – $3,979,294

MEN'S AND WOMEN'S SINGLES – Winner $250,000. Runner-up $125,000. Semi-finalists $62,500. Quarter-finalists $31,667. Fourth round losers $16,167. Third round losers $9,333. Second round losers $5,502. First round losers $3,353.
Total for each event $1,300,000.
MEN'S AND WOMEN'S DOUBLES (per team) – Winners $86,667. Runners-up $43,333. Semi-finalists $21,667. Quarter-finalists $11,000. Third round losers $5,667. Second round losers $3,000. First round losers $1,750.
Total for each event $366,667.
MIXED DOUBLES (per team) – Winners $26,160. Runners-up $12,480. Semi-finalists $5,520. Quarter-finalists $3,120. Second round losers $1,920. First round losers $780.
Total $90,000.
MEN'S QUALIFYING SINGLES (128 draw) – Third round losers $1,470. Second round losers $1,020. First round losers $570.
Total $92,640.
WOMEN'S QUALIFYING SINGLES (64 draw) – Third round losers $1,470. Second round losers $1,020. First round losers $570.
Total $46,320.
Total for senior events $162,000.
Bonus pools, players' associations & administrative fees $255,000.

MEN'S SINGLES

Holder: I. Lendl (TCH)

FIRST ROUND

I. LENDL (TCH) (1)
B. Moir (RSA)
J. Fleurian (FRA)
S. Colombo (ITA)
J. Pugh
F. Yunis (ARG)
G. Muller (RSA)
R. Osterthun (FRG)
A. Mansdorf (ISR)
C. Pistolesi (ITA)
M. Freeman
D. Visser (RSA)
P. Fleming
J. Arias
R. Acuna (CHI)
A. JARRYD (SWE) (16)
A. GOMEZ (ECU) (9)
M Schapers (HOL)
R. Agenor (HAI)
A. Burrow (RSA)
T. Muster (AUT)
J. Lozano (MEX)
C. Bengstrom (SWE)
M. Pernfors (SWE)
S. Zivojinovic (YUG)
C. Mezzadri (SUI)
B. Dyke (AUS)
M. Purcell
R. Reneberg
A. Antonitsch (AUT)
M. Anger
J. P. McENROE (8)
B. BECKER (FRG) (4)
T. Wilkison
J. Canter
G. Holmes
A. Castle (GBR)
D. Pate
J. Brown
T. Tulasne (FRA)
G. Forget (FRA)
R. Seguso
T. Benhabiles (FRA)
A. Parker
J. Berger
J. Gurfein
P. Doohan (AUS)
B. GILBERT (13)
H. LECONTE (FRA) (11)
A. Agassi
G. Pozzi (ITA)
A. Sznajder (CAN)
N. Odizor (NIG)
T. Nelson
M. Chang
P. McNamee (AUS)
J. Grabb
S. Cannon
R. Smith (BAH)
M. Vajda (TCH)
W. Hearn
U. Stenlund (SWE)
J. Rive
J. S. CONNORS (6)

SECOND ROUND

LENDL (1) 6–0 6–0 6–0
Fleurian 6–0 7–5 6–1
Pugh 6–3 6–2 6–2
Muller 7–5 6–3 6–2
Mansdorf 6–4 6–2 6–3
Freeman 7–5 4–6 6–2 7–5
Fleming 7–6 6–7 6–2 7–6
JARRYD (16) 6–3 6–4 6–4
GOMEZ (9) 7–6 6–4 7–5
Agenor 6–3 6–7 6–3 6–2
Muster 7–6 6–2 6–4
Bengstrom 6–3 ret'd
Zivojinovic 6–3 6–0 6–4
Dyke 6–4 6–3 4–6 6–2
Reneberg 6–3 6–2 6–2
McENROE (8) 6–3 6–2 6–2
BECKER (4) 4–6 4–6 7–5 6–4 6–2
Canter 7–5 6–4 6–0
Castle 7–5 1–6 2–6 7–6 6–4
Brown 6–2 6–4 6–1
Forget 3–6 7–5 6–3 6–2
Benhabiles 6–3 3–6 6–4 6–4
Berger 4–6 6–4 6–2 6–2
GILBERT (13) 6–1 6–2 6–2
LECONTE (11) 6–4 7–6 4–6 6–3
Pozzi 6–3 6–1 6–2
Odizor 2–6 2–6 7–6 7–5 6–3
Chang 6–3 6–7 6–4 6–4
Grabb 6–3 6–2 6–2
Smith 6–2 6–2 6–4
Hearn 4–6 7–6 6–2 6–4
CONNORS (6) 6–1 6–4 6–4

THIRD ROUND

LENDL (1) 6–4 6–2 6–2
Pugh 7–5 6–3 6–4
Mansdorf 2–6 6–3 6–2
JARRYD (16) 6–3 6–4 6–2
GOMEZ (9) 6–4 6–2 4–6 7–6
Muster 6–7 6–2 6–7 6–3 6–4
Zivojinovic 2–6 4–6 6–1 6–2 6–0
McENROE (8) 7–6 2–6 6–4 6–2
BECKER (4) 6–4 6–2 7–6
Castle 7–6 6–1 6–3
Forget 7–6 4–6 4–6 6–3 6–4
GILBERT (13) 4–6 6–2 6–4 6–3
LECONTE (11) 6–3 6–2 6–3
Odizor 6–1 6–2 6–7 3–6 6–4
Grabb 6–0 6–1 6–3
CONNORS (6) 6–3 6–2 6–1

FOURTH ROUND

LENDL (1) 6–1 6–1 6–2
JARRYD (16) 6–3 6–2 6–2
GOMEZ (9) 1–6 6–7 6–3 6–3 6–3
McENROE (8) 6–4 5–7 7–6 6–4 6–3
BECKER (4) 6–4 5–7 6–2 7–5
GILBERT (13) 6–4 6–7 7–5 6–4
LECONTE (11) 6–7 6–2 6–1 6–2
CONNORS (6) 6–3 6–2 6–4

QUARTER-FINALS

LENDL (1) 6–2 7–6 6–4
McENROE (8) 6–4 7–6 6–3
GILBERT (13) 2–6 6–7 7–6 7–5 6–1
CONNORS (6) 6–7 6–4 6–4 6–3

SEMI-FINALS

LENDL (1) 6–3 6–3 6–4
CONNORS (6) 4–6 6–3 6–4 6–0

FINAL

LENDL (1) 6–4 6–2 6–2

6–7 6–0 7–6 6–4

M. MECIR (TCH) (5)
K. Novacek (TCH)
P. Williamson
J. Fitzgerald (AUS)
J. Hlasek (SUI)
S. Davis
J. Navratil (TCH)
M. DePalmer
M. Srejber (TCH)
R. Matuszewski
L. Bourne
A. Volkov (URS)
M. Woodforde (AUS)
W. Scanlon
S. Giammalva
T. MAYOTTE (12)
E. SANCHEZ (ESP) (14)
W. Masur (AUS)
D. Wheaton
T. Witsken
K. Flach
L. Duncan
D. Cahill (AUS)
M. Kures
L. Pimek (TCH)
E. Teltscher
E. Winogradsky (FRA)
S. Kennedy
J. Carlsson (SWE)
K. Jones
J. Ross
M. WILANDER (SWE) (3)
P. CASH (AUS) (7)
P. Lundgren (SWE)
A. Chesnokov (URS)
C. Hooper
D. Perez (URU)
S. Casal (ESP)
E. Jelen (FRG)
B. Oresar (YUG)
B. Testerman
R. Leach
J. Kriek
B. Drewett (AUS)
R. Krishnan (IND)
P. Annacone
J. Sanchez (ESP)
J. NYSTROM (SWE) (10)
M. JAITE (ARG) (15)
T. Smid (TCH)
J. Yzaga (PER)
T. Hogstedt (SWE)
J. B. Svensson (SWE)
P. Cane (ITA)
G. Donnelly
C. Limberger (AUS)
K. Evernden (NZL)
H. Sundstrom (SWE)
M. Flur
C. Saceanu (FRG)
D. Goldie
C. Steyn (RSA)
D. Rostagno
S. EDBERG (SWE) (2)

MECIR (5) 6–3 6–4 7–6
Fitzgerald 6–3 7–5 6–4
Hlasek 3–6 6–3 2–6 6–4 6–4
Navratil 4–6 6–3 1–6 6–2 7–5
Srejber 6–7 7–6 7–5 7–6
Bourne 7–5 6–2 3–6 2–6 7–5
Woodforde 6–2 6–4 6–2
MAYOTTE (12) 6–1 6–0 6–1
SANCHEZ (14) 1–6 6–4 7–6 6–3
Witsken 7–5 5–7 6–3 6–4
Flach 6–2 7–6 6–0
Cahill 6–2 7–5 6–4
Pimek 7–6 6–3 1–6 7–6
Winogradski 6–4 7–5 2–6 7–6
Carlsson 6–2 6–1 6–3
WILANDER (3) 6–1 6–1 6–1
Lundgren 6–4 4–6 6–4 6–4
Chesnokov 6–4 6–1 6–4
Perez 1–6 6–1 5–7 6–4 6–4
Jelen 6–3 6–2 6–4
Leach 7–6 6–3 6–1
Kriek 6–1 6–2 6–1
Krishnan 6–0 7–5 6–1
NYSTROM (10) 7–6 7–6 3–6 6–2
Smid 7–6 6–4 6–2
Yzaga 6–3 6–2 7–6
Svensson 5–7 6–4 6–2 7–6
Donnelly 4–6 6–7 7–5 6–4 6–4
Evernden 6–2 6–2 7–6
Flur 6–1 7–5 6–7 6–4
Goldie 3–6 6–3 7–5 6–7 6–2
EDBERG (2) 6–3 7–6 6–2

MECIR (5) 6–3 6–1 6–0
Hlasek 7–5 7–5 6–4
Srejber 7–6 3–6 6–7 7–5 6–3
Woodforde 7–6 7–6 3–6 2–6 7–6
SANCHEZ (14) 6–1 6–4 6–3
Flach 1–6 6–4 3–6 6–1 7–6
Pimek 6–4 6–0 6–4
WILANDER (3) 6–2 6–3 6–1
Chesnokov 6–2 7–5 2–6 6–0
Perez 2–6 6–2 6–1 6–3
Kriek 6–3 7–6 3–6 6–3
Krishnan 6–4 7–5 6–2
Yzaga 6–3 6–4 6–1
Svensson 5–7 6–4 6–2
Evernden 4–6 7–6 3–6 6–4 6–3
EDBERG (2) 6–7 6–4 6–2 6–4

MECIR (5) 6–4 6–4 2–6 6–4
Woodforde 6–2 6–1 6–1
Flach 5–7 7–6 7–6 7–5
WILANDER (3) 6–2 6–0 6–1
Chesnokov 6–1 6–2 6–2
Krishnan 6–3 6–4 6–3
Svensson 2–6 6–4 3–6 6–2 6–2
EDBERG (2) 6–2 6–1 6–4

MECIR (5) 6–4 3–6 6–2 6–2
WILANDER (3) 6–3 6–3 7–6
Krishnan 6–4 6–1 6–2
EDBERG (2) 6–2 7–6 6–3

WILANDER (3) 6–3 6–7 6–4 7–6
EDBERG (2) 6–2 6–2 6–2

WILANDER (3) 6–4 3–6 6–3 6–4

I. LENDL (TCH) (1)

Capital letters denote seeded players. Number following player's name gives seeding order.

WOMEN'S SINGLES

Holder: M. Navratilova (USA)

FIRST ROUND

S. GRAF (FRG) (1)
B. Fulco (ARG)
P. Huber (AUT)
Cammie MacGregor
P. Tarabini (ARG)
P. Medrado (BRA)
R. Fairbank (RSA)
B. Gerken
I. Demongeot (FRA)
M. Perez Roldan (ARG)
C. Tanvier (FRA)
B. Nagelsen
S. Walsh Pete
S. Meier (FRG)
K. Okamoto (JAP)
S. HANIKA (FRG) (13)
W. M. TURNBULL (AUS) (16)
B. Gadusek
J. Novotna (TCH)
S. Parkhomenko (URS)
J. Halard (FRA)
E. Inoue (JAP)
F. Bonsignori (ITA)
E. Krapl (SUI)
L. Golarsa (ITA)
M. Werdel
L. Garrone (ITA)
L. Gildemeister (PER)
I. Kuczynska (POL)
G. Kim
W. White
P. H. SHRIVER (5)
C. M. EVERT (3)
S. Sloane
N. Dias (BRA)
A. Sanchez (ESP)
N. Zvereva (URS)
P. Paradis (FRA)
E. Pfaff (FRG)
E. Smylie (AUS)
M. J. Fernandez
R. Marsikova (TCH)
L. Savchenko (URS)
K. Horvath
N. Tauziat (FRA)
H. Ludloff
K. Jordan
M. MALEEVA (BUL) (10)
L. McNEIL (11)
R. Zrubakova (TCH)
C. Benjamin
M. Torres
M. Provis (AUS)
C. Porwik (FRG)
K. Keil
B. Herr
K. Maleeva (BUL)
V. Nelson Dunbar
D. Van Rensburg (RSA)
A. Villagran (ARG)
S. Stafford
T. Phelps
T. Scheuer-Larsen (DEN)
Z. GARRISON (7)

SECOND ROUND

GRAF (1) 6–0 6–3
Huber 6–1 6–4
Tarabini 5–7 6–1 6–3
Fairbank 1–6 6–4 6–2
Demongeot 6–2 6–2
Nagelsen 7–6 6–1
Meier 7–5 6–3
HANIKA (13) 6–0 6–1
TURNBULL (16) 6–2 6–1
Novotna 6–1 7–6
Halard 4–6 6–2 7–5
Bonsignori 6–2 6–4
Golarsa 7–5 0–6 6–2
Gildemeister 6–3 2–6 6–4
Kuczynska 6–4 6–1
SHRIVER (5) 6–3 6–3
EVERT (3) 6–1 6–0
Dias 6–4 6–2
Zvereva 6–3 6–3
Smylie 6–4 7–5
M. J. Fernandez 6–3 6–0
Savchenko 6–3 6–4
Tauziat 6–4 6–2
M. MALEEVA (10) 7–5 6–2
McNEIL (11) 6–3 6–1
Benjamin 6–3 7–5
Provis 4–6 7–5 6–1
Keil 6–3 6–1
K. Maleeva 6–1 6–1
Van Rensburg 6–2 6–0
Phelps 6–2 6–4
GARRISON (7) 6–1 6–3

THIRD ROUND

GRAF (1) 6–2 6–3
Tarabini 6–2 4–6 6–3
Demongeot 6–4 6–1
HANIKA (13) 6–3 6–0
Novotna 6–2 6–4
Halard 6–2 7–6
Golarsa 7–6 6–4
SHRIVER (5) 6–3 6–2
EVERT (3) 6–0 6–1
Zvereva 6–3 6–2
M. J. Fernandez 6–1 6–4
M. MALEEVA (10) 6–1 6–3
McNEIL (11) 6–4 6–2
Provis 6–4 6–2
K. Maleeva 6–2 6–3
GARRISON (7) 7–6 6–1

FOURTH ROUND

GRAF (1) 6–2 6–0
HANIKA (13) 6–4 6–2
Novotna 6–4 6–0
SHRIVER (5) 6–1 6–2
EVERT (3) 6–0 6–2
M. MALEEVA (10) 6–2 0–6 6–3
McNEIL (11) 5–7 6–1 7–6
GARRISON (7) 7–6 7–6

QUARTER-FINALS

GRAF (1) 7–5 6–2
SHRIVER (5) 6–3 7–6
EVERT (3) 7–5 6–4
McNEIL (11) 7–6 3–6 7–6

SEMI-FINALS

GRAF (1) 6–4 6–3
McNEIL (11) 3–6 6–2 6–4

FINAL

GRAF (1) 4–6 6–2 6–4

7–6 6–1

First round

H. SUKOVA (TCH) (6)
M. Gurney
E. Burgin
M. Javer
I. Cueto (FRG)
G. Rush Magers
P. Harper
D. Spence
A. E. Hobbs (GBR)
E. Minter (AUS)
A. Croft (GBR)
A. Kanellopoulu (GRE)
A. Devries (BEL)
M. Van Nostrand
A. Kijimuta (JAP)
B. POTTER (15)
C. KOHDE-KILSCH (FRG) (9)
A. Moulton
C. Bassett (CAN)
D. Balestrat (AUS)
A. M. Cecchini (ITA)
A. White
P. Hy (HKG)
R. Reis
R. Reggi (ITA)
M. Grossman
E. Derly (FRA)
N. Arendt
J. M. Durie (GBR)
A. Minter (AUS)
N. Herreman (FRA)
H. MANDLIKOVA (TCH) (4)
G. SABATINI (ARG) (8)
B. Bowes
S. Gomer (GBR)
W. Probst (FRG)
E. Hakami
H. Cioffi
M. Paz (ARG)
G. Fernandez
A. Henricksson
J. Polzl Wiesner (AUT)
K. Schimper (RSA)
J. Russell
P. Fendick
L. Field (AUS)
M. L. Piatek
B. BUNGE (FRG) (12)
C. LINDQVIST (SWE) (14)
A. Frazier
S. Goles (YUG)
D. Schultz (HOL)
H. Kelesi (CAN)
N. Bykova (URS)
Hu Na
E. Reinach (RSA)
L. Bonder
J. Santrock
P. Casale
I. Budarova (TCH)
R. White
T. Mochizuki
K. Gompert
M. NAVRATILOVA (2)

Second round

SUKOVA (6) 6–7 6–3 6–4
Burgin 7–5 6–4
Cueto 1–6 7–5 7–5
Harper 6–4 6–1
Hobbs 6–4 7–5
Croft 7–5 7–5
Devries 6–3 6–2
Kijimuta 7–6 6–3
KOHDE-KILSCH (9) 6–2 7–5
Bassett 6–4 6–2
Cecchini 6–4 6–2
Hy 4–6 6–4 6–2
Reggi 6–4 6–0
Derly 6–3 2–6 6–2
Durie 6–4 6–2
MANDLIKOVA (4) 6–1 6–3
SABATINI (8) 6–3 6–3
Gomer 6–3 6–0
Hakami 6–1 6–1
Paz 6–4 6–2
Henricksson 7–6 6–2
Schimper 6–2 6–3
Fendick 6–3 2–6 6–0
BUNGE (12) 6–3 7–5
LINDQVIST (14) 6–2 6–2
Goles 7–6 6–3
Kelesi 7–6 7–5
Reinach 6–1 6–0
Bonder 6–4 7–5
Casale 7–5 6–2
R. White 7–5 7–5
NAVRATILOVA (2) 6 1 6 1

Third round

SUKOVA (6) 6–3 6–4
Cueto 6–3 6–2
Hobbs 6–2 7–6
Kijimuta 6–3 1–6 6–2
KOHDE-KILSCH (9) 6–4 6–3
Cecchini 6–4 5–7 7–5
Reggi 6–2 4–6 6–3
MANDLIKOVA (4) 6–3 6–7 6–2
SABATINI (8) 6–3 6–1
Hakami 6–2 6–4
Henricksson 6–4 5–7 6–4
BUNGE (12) 6–2 6–4
LINDQVIST (14) 6–2 6–0
Kelesi 4–6 6–1 6–4
Bonder 6–4 6–1
NAVRATILOVA (2) 6 1 6–3

Fourth round

SUKOVA (6) 7–6 6–1
Hobbs 6–4 2–6 6–4
KOHDE-KILSCH (9) 6–4 6–3
MANDLIKOVA (4) 6–3 6–1
SABATINI (8) 6–1 6–3
BUNGE (12) 6–3 6–4
LINDQVIST (14) 4–6 7–5 6–4
NAVRATILOVA (2) 6–2 6–1

Quarter-finals

SUKOVA (6) 6–4 6–2
KOHDE-KILSCH (9) 6–7 6–4 6–1
SABATINI (8) 1–6 6–1 6–1
NAVRATILOVA (2) 6–0 6–4

Semi-finals

SUKOVA (6) 6–1 6–3
NAVRATILOVA (2) 7–5 6–3

Final

NAVRATILOVA (2) 6–2 6–2

Champion

M. NAVRATILOVA (USA) (2)

Capital letters denote seeded players. Number following player's name gives seeding order.

MEN'S DOUBLES

Holders: A. Gomez (ECU)/S. Zivojinovic (YUG)

FIRST ROUND

EDBERG/JARRYD (1)
Tarango/Wheaton
Cahill/Kratzmann
Krishnan/Schapers
Lloyd/McNamee
Cane/Colombo
Aerts/Siegel
JELEN/NAVRATIL (16)
DOOHAN/WARDER (9)
Steyn/Visser
Lozano/Witsken
Muller/Nelson
Caswell/Jensen
Flur/Tarr
Baxter/Rive
MECIR/SMID (7)
CASAL/SANCHEZ (3)
Bloom/Mansdorf
Layendecker/Michibata
Gilbert/Hlasek
Connell/Livingston
Letts/Lundgren
Korita/Warwick
R. LEACH/PAWSAT (14)
S. DAVIS/PATE (11)
Denton/Giammalva
Dowlen/Freeman
Gonzalez/Warneke
Lavalle/Moreno
Bourne/Klaparda
Cox/Mezzadri
DONNELLY/FLEMING (5)
NYSTROM/WILANDER (6)
Pfister/J. B. Svensson
Agassi/Purcell
Antonitsch/Fibak
Acuna/Robertson
Anger/Holmes
Grabb/Jones
PUGH/WILLENBORG (12)
BAHRAMI/PEREZ (13)
Mortensen/Wilkison
Aldrich/Green
Goldie/P. McEnroe
Slozil/Srejber
Odizor/Testerman
Tim/Tom Gullikson
GOMEZ/ZIVOJINOVIC (4)
ANNACONE/DePALMER (8)
DiLaura/J. Sanchez
Evernden/Kriek
Castle/Chamberlin
Berger/Ross
Levine/MacPherson
Arias/Teltscher
HOOPER/M. LEACH (10)
KOHLBERG/R. VAN'T HOF (15)
Dickson/Rudeen
Limberger/Woodforde
Acioly/L. Scott
Dyke/Fancutt
Fitzgerald/Masur
Forget/Leconte
FLACH/SEGUSO (2)

SECOND ROUND

EDBERG/JARRYD (1) 6–2 6–4
Krishnan/Schapers 6–7 7–6 6–3
Lloyd/McNamee 5–3 ret'd
Aerts/Siegel 6–1 4–6 6–2
DOOHAN/WARDER (9) 6–4 7–6
Lozano/Witsken 6–4 7–5
Flur/Tarr 3–6 6–4 6–4
MECIR/SMID (7) 6–2 6–4
CASAL/SANCHEZ (3) 7–6 7–5
Layendecker/Michibata 6–4 6–4
Letts/Lundgren 7–6 6–3
Korita/Warwick 5–7 7–6 6–4
DAVIS/PATE (11) 7–5 1–6 6–2
Dowlen/Freeman 6–4 6–3
Bourne/Klaparda 2–6 6–1 6–4
Cox/Mezzadri 4–6 6–4 6–4
NYSTROM/WILANDER (6) 6–4 6–4
Antonitsch/Fibak 6–3 3–6 7–5
Acuna/Robertson 6–4 5–7 6–4
PUGH/WILLENBORG (12) 6–3 7–5
BAHRAMI/PEREZ (13) 5–7 7–6 6–3
Goldie/McEnroe 6–1 7–5
Odizor/Testerman 6–4 6–2
GOMEZ/ZIVOJINOVIC (4) 7–6 7–6
ANNACONE/DePALMER (8) 6–2 7–6
Evernden/Kriek 6–3 6–3
Berger/Ross 3–6 6–3 6–0
HOOPER/M. LEACH (10) 7–3 6–2
KOHLBERG/VAN'T HOF (15) 7–6 6–3
Acioly/Scott 6–1 6–4
Fitzgerald/Masur 6–4 6–1
FLACH/SEGUSO (2) 5–7 6–3 6–4

THIRD ROUND

EDBERG/JARRYD (1) 6–3 6–2
Aerts/Siegel 6–3 3–6 6–3
Lozano/Witsken 6–4 7–6
MECIR/SMID (7) 6–1 4–6 7–5
CASAL/SANCHEZ (3) 7–6 6–4
Korita/Warwick 4–6 6–2 7–6
DAVIS/PATE (11) 6–7 7–6 6–4
Cox/Mezzadri 7–5 6–2
NYSTROM/WILANDER (6) 7–6 6–4
PUGH/WILLENBORG (12) 7–5 3–6 7–6
BAHRAMI/PEREZ (13) 7–6 6–3
GOMEZ/ZIVOJINOVIC (4) 6–7 7–6 6–2
ANNACONE/DePALMER (8) 6–2 6–1
HOOPER/M. LEACH (10) 7–6 6–2
KOHLBERG/VAN'T HOF (15) 7–6 6–3
FLACH/SEGUSO (2) 6–4 6–4

QUARTER-FINALS

EDBERG/JARRYD (1) 7–5 4–6 6–1
Lozano/Witsken 6–2 6–4
CASAL/SANCHEZ (3) 6–2 6–2
DAVIS/PATE (11) 6–3 7–6
NYSTROM/WILANDER (6) 6–4 6–4
GOMEZ/ZIVOJINOVIC (4) 6–3 3–6 6–1
ANNACONE/DePALMER (8) 6–4 5–7 7–6
FLACH/SEGUSO (2) 6–2 7–6

SEMI-FINALS

EDBERG/JARRYD (1) 6–3 6–4 3–6 6–4
CASAL/SANCHEZ (3) 6–2 6–2 6–4
GOMEZ/ZIVOJINOVIC (4) 6–3 6–2 7–6
FLACH/SEGUSO (2) 3–6 6–4 7–6 6–7 7–5

FINAL

EDBERG/JARRYD (1) 6–4 6–4 6–0
FLACH/SEGUSO (2) 6–3 7–6 7–5

S. EDBERG (SWE)/A. JARRYD (SWE) (1) 7–6 6–2 4–6 5–7 7–6

Capital letters denote seeded pairings. Number following players' names gives seeding order.

Lori McNeil ended Chris Evert's 13-year record of winning at least one Grand Slam title every year when she beat her in the quarter-finals at Flushing Meadow, going on to extend Steffi Graf to three sets in the semis. She was also a major force in doubles, winning six titles and reaching seven more finals. (M. Cole)

WOMEN'S DOUBLES

Holders: M. Navratilova (USA)/P. H. Shriver (USA)

FIRST ROUND

NAVRATILOVA/SHRIVER (1)
Savchenko/Zvereva
Hetherington/Reynolds
Dias/Villagran
Kaplan/Van Rensburg
Budarova/Porwik
Barg/Russell
EVERT/G. FERNANDEZ (11)
PAZ/PFAFF (9)
Hahn/Reis
Balestrat/Hu Na
Harper/Ludloff
Cueto/A. Sanchez
Demongeot/Tauziat
Kuczynska/Medrado
BURGIN/R. WHITE (7)
GRAF/SABATINI (3)
Field/E. Minter
Hy/Inoue
Henricksson/Van Nostrand
Bowes/Gadusek
Phelps/Reggi
Gerken/Hakami
COLLINS/TANVIER (16)
PIATEK/A. WHITE (14)
A. M. Fernandez/Richardson
M. J. Fernandez/Tarabini
Amiach/Herreman
Foxworth/Sands
Cordwell/A. Minter
Gurney/Kelesi
GARRISON/McNEIL (6)
JORDAN/SMYLIE (5)
Herr/Moulton
E./M. Reinach
Holladay/P. Smith
Horvath/Mesker
Bykova/Parkhomenko
Cecchini/Goles
FAIRBANK/POTTER (13)
LINDQVIST/SCHEUER-LARSEN (12)
Durie/Walsh Pete
Rush Magers/W. White
Allen/Benjamin
Bohmova/Provis
Frazier/McCarthy
K./M. Maleeva
MANDLIKOVA/TURNBULL (4)
HOBBS/NAGELSEN (8)
Casale/Mascarin
Mosca/Rapponi-Longo
Crowe/Steinmetz
Byrne/Fendick
Schimper/Yanagi
Hansel/Leo
BUNGE/GILDEMEISTER (10)
NOVOTNA/SUIRE (15)
Salmon/Van Der Torre
Marsikova/Meier
Cammie/Cynthia MacGregor
Antonoplis/Monteiro
Fulco/Holikova
Adams/Donnelly
KOHDE-KILSCH/SUKOVA (2)

SECOND ROUND

NAVRATILOVA/SHRIVER (1) 6–1 6–3
Dias/Villagran 2–6 2–5 ret'd
Kaplan/Van Rensburg 6–3 6–3
EVERT/G. FERNANDEZ (11) 6–1 6–0
PAZ/PFAFF (9) 6–4 6–3
Balestrat/Hu Na 6–3 5–7 6–3
Cueto/Sanchez 6–4 6–2
BURGIN/R. WHITE (7) 7–5 4–6 7–6
GRAF/SABATINI (3) 6–0 6–3
Henricksson/Van Nostrand 7–6 3–6 6–4
Phelps/Reggi 7–5 6–4
Gerken/Hakami 3–6 6–1 6–2
PIATEK/A. WHITE (14) 3–6 7–6 6–3
M. J. Fernandez/Tarabini 7–5 6–4
Cordwell/A. Minter 6–2 6–4
GARRISON/McNEIL (6) 6–1 6–2
JORDAN/SMYLIE (5) 7–5 6–2
E./M. Reinach 7–6 6–2
Bykova/Parkhomenko 6–2 5–7 6–2
FAIRBANK/POTTER (13) 7–6 6–3
Durie/Walsh Pete 6–2 3–6 7–5
Rush Magers/W. White 6–3 7–6
Bohmova/Provis 4–6 6–1 6–2
MANDLIKOVA/TURNBULL (4) 6–4 6–3
HOBBS/NAGELSEN (8) 1–6 6–3 7–6
Mosca/Rapponi-Longo 6–4 6–7 7–6
Byrne/Fendick 3–6 6–2 6–1
BUNGE/GILDEMEISTER (10) 6–3 6–3
NOVOTNA/SUIRE (15) 6–3 6–3
Cammie/Cynthia MacGregor 3–6 6–1 7–6
Antonoplis/Monteiro 7–6 6–3
KOHDE-KILSCH/SUKOVA (2) 6–1 6–1

THIRD ROUND

NAVRATILOVA/SHRIVER (1) 6–1 6–2
EVERT/G. FERNANDEZ (11) 6–3 6–2
Balestrat/Hu Na 7–5 6–4
BURGIN/R. WHITE (7) 6–1 6–1
GRAF/SABATINI (3) 6–3 6–2
Phelps/Reggi 6–1 6–2
PIATEK/A. WHITE (14) 6–1 6–4
GARRISON/McNEIL (6) 6–2 5–7 6–3
JORDAN/SMYLIE (5) 6–3 2–0 ret'd
Bykova/Parkhomenko 7–6 6–4
Durie/Walsh Pete 7–6 3–6 6–4
MANDLIKOVA/TURNBULL (4) 3–6 7–6 6–2
HOBBS/NAGELSEN (8) 6–2 6–2
BUNGE/GILDEMEISTER (10) 3–6 6–1 6–1
NOVOTNA/SUIRE (15) 6–4 6–0
KOHDE-KILSCH/SUKOVA (2) 6–3 6–0

QUARTER-FINALS

NAVRATILOVA/SHRIVER (1) 6–0 6–1
BURGIN/R. WHITE (7) 6–2 6–2
GRAF/SABATINI (3) 6–0 6–3
GARRISON/McNEIL (6) 6–4 6–4
JORDAN/SMYLIE (5) 3–6 6–3 6–1
Durie/Walsh Pete 6–2 7–5
HOBBS/NAGELSEN (8) 7–5 4–6 6–3
KOHDE-KILSCH/SUKOVA (2) 6–3 6–3

SEMI-FINALS

NAVRATILOVA/SHRIVER (1) 6–1 6–3
GRAF/SABATINI (3) 6–4 5–7 6–4
JORDAN/SMYLIE (5) 6–1 6–4
HOBBS/NAGELSEN (8) 3–6 6–3 6–4

FINAL

NAVRATILOVA/SHRIVER (1)• w.o.
JORDAN/SMYLIE (5) 6–3 6–4

M. NAVRATILOVA (USA)/P. H. SHRIVER (USA) (1) 5–7 6–4 6–2

Capital letters denote seeded pairings. Number following players' names gives seeding order.

MIXED DOUBLES

Holders: S. Casal (ESP)/R. Reggi (ITA)

FIRST ROUND	SECOND ROUND	QUARTER-FINALS	SEMI-FINALS	FINAL	
E. SANCHEZ/NAVRATILOVA (1)	SANCHEZ/NAVRATILOVA (1) 6–2 6–2	SANCHEZ/NAVRATILOVA (1) 6–3 6–2	SANCHEZ/NAVRATILOVA (1) 2–6 6–2 6–2	SANCHEZ/NAVRATILOVA (1) w.o.	E. SANCHEZ (ESP)/ M. NAVRATILOVA (USA) (1) 6–4 6–7 7–6
R. Leach/R. White					
Jones/A. White	Jones/A. White 7–5 6–4				
Steyn/Fairbank					
Schapers/Henricksson	Schapers/Henricksson 6–1 6–3	Schapers/Hetherington 6–3 3–6 6–1			
Dickson/Hobbs					
Bahrami/Suire	Bahrami/Suire 7–5 6–2				
Baxter/Hetherington					
WILLENBORG/BURGIN (4)	WILLENBORG/BURGIN (4) 6–4 6–4	Casal/Reggi w.o.	Casal/Reggi 6–1 6–3		
Lloyd/Turnbull					
Scott/Ludloff	Casal/Reggi 7–6 6–4				
Casal/Reggi					
Warwick/Byrne	Warwick/Byrne 6–4 6–4	Warwick/Byrne 7–6 7–6			
R. Van't Hof/Piatek					
M. Leach/Collins	FITZGERALD/SMYLIE (5) 6–2 6–1				
FITZGERALD/SMYLIE (5)					
STEWART/GARRISON (6)	STEWART/GARRISON (6) 6–4 6–7 6–4	STEWART/GARRISON (6) 7–5 7–6	STEWART/GARRISON (6) 6–4 6–3	ANNACONE/NAGELSEN (2) 6–4 6–4	
Stockton/Bunge					
Ralston/Bowes	Gonzalez/Paz 6–2 6–0				
Gonzalez/Paz					
Purcell/P. Smith	Pugh/Phelps 7–6 6–1	Pugh/Phelps 4–6 6–4 7–5			
Pugh/Phelps					
Pawsat/Herr	FLACH/JORDAN (3) 4–6 7–5 6–1				
FLACH/JORDAN (3)					
MORTENSEN/SCHEUER-LARSEN (8)	Woodforde/Field 7–6 5–7 6–4	Kohlberg/Fendick 3–6 6–4 6–2	ANNACONE/NAGELSEN (2) 7–5 6–4		
Woodforde/Field					
Kohlberg/Fendick	Kohlberg/Fendick 6–0 6–2				
Riessen/Louie					
Goldie/McNeil	Goldie/McNeil 6–4 7–5	ANNACONE/NAGELSEN (2) 6–4 6–4			
Doohan/Balestrat					
Bourne/A. M. Fernandez	ANNACONE/NAGELSEN (2) 6–3 6–7 6–4				
ANNACONE/NAGELSEN (2)					

Capital letters denote seeded pairings. Number following players' names gives seeding order.

75 YEARS OF THE ITF

Lance Tingay

The International Federation of Lawn Tennis Associations, soon to be the International Lawn Tennis Federation and, since 1977, the International Tennis Federation, began life in Paris on 1 March, 1913. It was the outcome of a preliminary meeting in the same city in October of the previous year when representatives of a dozen nations agreed that the world-wide growth of tennis demanded a co-ordinating body. The French had called the meeting after discussions with the British at a *Davis Cup* tie in Folkestone. The meeting was chaired by the British delegate, Mr R. J. McNair, and the ITF launched itself with 13 founder members, consisting of Australasia, Austria, Belgium, Denmark, France, Germany, the British Isles, Netherlands, Russia, South Africa, Spain, Sweden and Switzerland. There were joint secretaries – Anthony Sabelli, who had recently been appointed a paid secretary of the British LTA, and Mr R. Galley, of the French Federation. The official language was French, with English translation, and for many years the ITF was more French than otherwise. From the start there was weighted voting, with one to five votes allotted to nations according to their importance. The British Isles, held to be a special case by virtue of their creation of the sport, were given six votes.

The United States were not among the founding nations. Their absence was the more striking because in 1911 Duane Williams, an American diplomat in Switzerland, had suggested just such an association to Mr Charles Barde, a prominent Swiss official, and to Mr Henri Wallet of France. It happened, with the irony of history, that Mr Williams, the father of R. Norris Williams, the US *Davis Cup* player, was lost in 1912 in the sinking of the *Titanic*, and could not urge the USLTA (the senior of such authorities, having been founded in 1881) to co-operate.

The first important move of the infant ITF was to institute 'World Championships', on grass, hard courts and indoors, with the hard-court title going to Paris. The French had anticipated that, for Mr Wallet had inaugurated such an event in 1912, with a cup donated by the late Duane Williams. The grass title went to Wimbledon, while the indoor event was given to Stockholm and then changed year by year.

What the ITF did *not* do was to take over the rules of tennis. At that time they belonged to the British LTA who had acquired them, soon after their creation in 1888, from the All England Club, creators of the original code in 1877 which had been adopted round the world. The LTA delegates had been specifically instructed not to yield the British authority, and the role of the ITF was held to be little more than that of a liaison committee. Nor was the greatest of international competitions, the *Davis Cup*, in any way made the concern of the new body. The Cup having been donated by an American and the event having been first staged when the British Isles challenged in 1900, it was under rules laid down by the United States as presenters of the trophy. In those days it was the duty of the Champion Nation to arrange the play-off among the challengers, although later control was taken over by a Council of *Davis Cup* nations, which convened annually at a different time and a different place from the ITF.

There was a radical difference between the two, for the *Davis Cup* nations operated on the basis of one nation, one vote. There was increasing co-operation over the years, the same personnel being involved among delegates and the secretariat, although it was not until 1978 that it was incorporated into the ITF. Not all ITF founders had competed in the *Davis Cup* by 1914. Denmark, USSR, Spain, Sweden and Switzerland had not done so, while the United States and Canada, neither members of the ITF, had played. The *Davis*

The following tennis manufacturers
and other groups whose interest
lie in the sport are members of the
ITF FOUNDATION

Any commercial tennis organisation is welcome to
apply for membership – details of the
I.T.F. Foundation and the benefits it brings
to both sport and member can be obtained from:-

The ITF Foundation
International Tennis Federation
Palliser Road
Barons Court
London W14 9EN.

Cup nations were not unmindful of their seniority, and no nation may have a representative on the ITF *Davis Cup* Committee without having played for ten years in the *Davis Cup*.

After 1919 and the dead days of the First World War, a spirit of co-operation became manifest. The catalyst was the decision of the USLTA to join the world governing body, which they did on condition that the grandiose 'World Championship' designation be scrapped. What had irked them was Wimbledon's 'in perpetuity' tenure of the title on grass, for their own championships were also on that surface. Accordingly the USA became one of the senior nations governing the world game. In the weighted voting that still pertains, the four senior nations are Great Britain, France, the USA and Australia, all with 12 votes. In the same year, 1924, the ITF took over the rules of the game from the British.

They have never been hotly controversial: the foot-fault rule was amended in 1959; the tie-break was brought in as a permitted, though not mandatory, scoring system in 1974 after experiment. The definition of the racket came late in the day, and for more than a century it was possible for a player, were he eccentric enough, to use a frying pan. In 1978 a standard was decreed about size and stringing, following the Austrian creation of a racket with knotted stringing that threatened to change the nature of the game.

More controversial was the amendment to Rule 30. Generation after generation in the game was reared on the principle 'Play shall be continuous', even though the manifest impossibility of making it that called for compromise and, with some players, a degree of give and take. The demands of the *Davis Cup*, with non-playing captains on court, brought the first amendment, and in 1965 a limit of one minute was laid down for the change of ends. When the top game became rigorously professional, with American TV making demands, a 30-second limit between points and of 90 seconds at the change-over became the rule, with umpires using a stop watch as a matter of course. This was in 1978.

A constant preoccupation was amateurism. The policy of a strictly defined amateur status was adhered to, despite some obvious breaches as early as the 1920s. The United States' request to stage an Open tournament in 1933 met with short shrift, although subsequently reality demanded liberality. 'Expenses' were allowed for eight weeks annually, a period which later became 210 days, then 240. Committee after committee was set up to solve a problem which had no solution.

The year 1960 was a turning point of sorts, when the leading nations were in agreement that Open tournaments should be permitted and a proposal to this effect was expected to be passed at the annual meeting in Paris. However, it was supported by 134 votes to 75, five short of the necessary two-thirds majority. Subsequent years brought incessant wrangling, though support for a change seemed to diminish to the same degree that players and tournaments widened the breach between fact and theory. An impasse was resolved when Great Britain decreed, in defiance of ITF rules and with a penalty of expulsion, that in their country the amateur-professional distinction would be abolished on 22 April, 1968, the first day of the British Hard Court Championships. A special meeting of the ITF was held in Paris on 30 March, 1968, where 47 nations, without dissent, acquiesced in a *fait accompli* and the face of tennis changed for ever.

With Open tennis new problems arose. The first was to find a way for the ITF to work with World Championship Tennis, the Dallas-based commercial corporation with players under contract. The statesmanship revealed in this matter was not of the highest order, and the outcome was the banning of 'contract' players at Wimbledon in 1972, including John Newcombe of Australia, the title holder with hopes of a fourth victory. Between Wimbledon and the US Open in late August, a solution was found.

The onset of Open tennis, the growth of vast sponsorship, and greatly increased opportunities to earn money put an end to the old officer-private relationship between players and their national associations. The pros naturally wanted a say in their own destiny, and to this end, after one or two failures, an Association of Tennis Professionals took strong root in the autumn of 1972. A traumatic dispute arose a few months later when the Yugoslav, Nikki Pilic, was suspended by his association for failing to play in the *Davis Cup*, a suspension endorsed by the ITF. It meant that his entry at Wimbledon had to be refused. ATP asked the British High Court for an injunction on Pilic's behalf against the ITF and the

Nikki Pilic of Yugoslavia whose suspension following his failure to play in the Davis Cup *in 1972 led to a traumatic dispute.* *(A. Cole)*

Wimbledon committee, but the right of the established authorities to suspend a player was upheld. ATP then asked its members to withdraw their entries, 79 doing so and reducing Wimbledon's men's entry to a poor standard. As it turned out, though, the meeting was a great success, for the play was good and public sympathy was almost entirely with Wimbledon. None the less ATP had made their point. They had to have a voice in the future conduct of the game.

To this end they formed the third leg of the tri-part Men's International Professional Tennis Council along with the ITF and tournament representatives. This body was to administer the Grand Prix, the world-wide, year-long circuit of tournaments initiated, under sponsorship, by the ITF in 1970. To some degree the authority of the ITF was watered down, for prize money and discipline came under the control of the new body, with headquarters in New York and a branch in Paris. A like system was formed in the women's game where the ITF joined with the Women's Tennis Association in the equivalent Women's International Professional Tennis Council. Later the tournament directors joined. The relationship with the women's side of the game was warmed when, in 1963, the ITF marked its 50th year by inaugurating the *Federation Cup*. This was the equivalent of the men's *Davis Cup*, differing in being staged over one week at one venue.

The *Federation Cup* became an outstanding success. The first was staged just before the Wimbledon meeting at Queen's Club, London, side by side with the venerable London Championships. It was a way of reducing the cost to nations but was never repeated, and now the competition is sponsored by NEC of Japan, the supporters of the *Davis Cup*. The standard of women's play, especially among the smaller nations, has risen markedly with the *Federation Cup* over the years. By 1987 no less than 57 nations had taken part.

Years of lobbying were rewarded by the admission of tennis as an Olympic sport for Olympiad XXIV in Seoul in 1988. It was included as a demonstration sport in Los Angeles in 1984 and in Mexico in 1968, but as a full-blown event it was last seen in Paris in 1924.

Like most national associations the ITF has taken on a creative role in the game, no longer merely liaising, scheduling and endorsing but promoting at all levels, not least in the junior and grass roots levels where it all has to begin, and latterly at veteran level where it flourishes.

NABISCO GRAND PRIX

GRAND PRIX REVIEW
POINTS AND PRIZE MONEY
POINTS EXPLANATION
NABISCO GRAND PRIX TOURNAMENTS
NABISCO MASTERS
WCT FINALS

Building on his successes of the previous year, Emilio Sanchez of Spain won four singles titles, took six doubles titles and reached the Wimbledon final with Sergio Casal, as well as winning the mixed doubles in Paris with Pam Shriver and at Flushing Meadow with Martina Navratilova. *(T. Hindley)*

Miloslav Mecir underlined his versatility by winning six Grand Prix titles on four different surfaces, as well as winning the Masters doubles with Tomas Smid and the Lipton's mixed doubles with Novotna. *(Carol L. Newsom)*

GRAND PRIX REVIEW

John Parsons

In a year when Boris Becker discovered the perils as well as the pleasures of being Wimbledon champion, and Stefan Edberg crept closer but not close enough to the very top, the master of almost all he desired on the Nabisco Grand Prix year was once again Ivan Lendl. During the early part of the year he was frustrated by injury, so that May had already started before he won the first of his seven Super Series titles on a damp and generally miserable afternoon in Hamburg. Yet Lendl's record, which included the retention of his French and US Open crowns and a win-loss record of 69–7, was only marginally less impressive than the year before, when he won nine titles with a win-loss record of 75–6.

During 1987 Lendl developed, in many people's eyes, into an even more convincing and commanding champion than before. During the Masters he spoke of the nervousness that still afflicts him at the start of matches, particularly in the early stages of a tournament. But whereas a few years ago such nervousness was a destructive force which too often prevented him from reaching his full potential, it is now more of an exciting appreciation of the occasion, which swiftly inspires the adrenalin and the power-packed winners to flow with awesome profusion.

It was a measure of his consistency that he was beaten by only three players not ranked among the top ten at the time – David Pate in Tokyo during Lendl's first week back after knee surgery, Joakim Nystrom in Rome, and Peter Lundgren in San Francisco. Only Pat Cash beat him twice on the Grand Prix circuit during the year, and these were losses which underlined his one lingering disappointment with himself, for they both came on grass: at the semi-finals of the Australian Open and then in the final at Wimbledon, leaving the World Champion with one surface still to conquer.

Including the Masters, there were 77 Grand Prix tournaments during 1987, offering $26.1 million, an increase of seven events and $3.5 million over the previous year. During 1988, the projection is for 79 tournaments and player compensation, as it is called these days, of $31.4 million. In addition to the main events in 1987, there were almost 200 other tournaments offering computer ranking points, spread among more than another 30 countries. The official circuit thus provided opportunities and employment to 1,159 players.

Yet while there is still a long waiting list of cities and tournaments wishing to attach themselves to the bandwagon, and there is no doubt that the protection of the Grand Prix is imperative for the long-term security of the greatest number of players and events, there are differences of opinion about the present structure. Perhaps worthy of the closest examination is the growing belief that there should be a clearly defined season at the highest level, ending in September or not later than mid-October. This suggestion finds favour in wider circles than simply among players who find themselves most in demand for the big money spectaculars which are undoubtedly a threat to the Grand Prix. The idea of a Super-Super Series, based around the four Grand Slam tournaments and no more than a dozen other events and sensibly spread as widely as possible in various parts of the world, should also be re-examined. It might at least help to overcome the identity crisis the Grand Prix undoubtedly suffers among a public sometimes bewildered by the proliferation of other events, whose results are never officially recorded in tennis history.

Ironically, one strong advocate of an earlier end to the season is Brad Gilbert, the American who benefited most from a hectic final three months of the year as, by criss-crossing the world several times, he lifted himself from 16th place in the Nabisco points table at the end of the US Open, to seize the last of the eight places in the Masters – with the points he gained from the very last tournament on the circuit in Itaparica.

Runner-up in five tournaments, Gilbert gained one title success in Scottsdale, which made him one of 34 tournament winners during 1987, representing 18 countries, two more than in 1986. The continuing potent European influence in men's tennis both persisted and strengthened, with players from Sweden and Czechoslovakia winning no less than 32 of the tournaments between them. If Lendl has his way, however, the contribution he makes to this table will one day have to be listed in the United States' column.

Edberg started the year magnificently, retaining his Australian Open crown and going on to win three more Super Series titles in Memphis, Rotterdam and Tokyo by mid-April. As well as heading the impressive Swedish roll of honour, up from 16 to 18 titles, he also matched Lendl's individual circuit record of seven titles. Behind these two came Miloslav Mecir with six titles, Mats Wilander and Tim Mayotte with five each and Emilio Sanchez, building on his breakthrough in 1986, with four. Whereas all of Wilander's successes came in Super Series events, two of Mayotte's and four of Mecir's were in Regular or Open Week tournaments.

Nevertheless Mecir, whose subtleties of pace and direction can turn his tennis on its best days into a rare art form, not only worked hard for his victories but also showed considerable versatility. He played in 21 tournaments leading into the Masters, and his six titles were achieved on four different surfaces – grass (Adelaide and Sydney), hard courts (Key Biscayne), carpet (WCT Finals) and clay (Stuttgart and Hilversum). His most exciting success, of course, was in the Lipton International at Key Biscayne, where in successive matches the big fisherman landed Edberg, Yannick Noah and Lendl on his craftily cast hook. Then came his four-sets defeat of John McEnroe in Dallas, to make him neck and neck with Edberg for honours as the spotlight switched to Europe and the build-up to Paris.

At the end of 1986, on the strength of his impressive record towards the end of the year until Lendl reminded him who was still champion in the final of the Masters, Becker was so confident about the year ahead of him that he was proclaiming 'the future has already started'. Although he won three titles – Indian Wells, Milan and Queen's Club – things started to go wrong for the West German right at the beginning in Australia, where he not only lost in the fourth round to Wally Masur, but also lost his coach, Gunther Bosch. But it was not until Wimbledon, where his two-year reign as champion met with calamity in the second round against another Australian, Peter Doohan, that the cracks in his game, his concentration and finally his confidence began to assume serious levels. The pressures of trying to maintain equanimity in his tennis and his life in the fishbowl existence which comes from having achieved so much, so soon, were too demanding.

With hindsight Becker, who passed his 20th birthday only in November, admits that for his own peace of mind and progress, he would have preferred delaying his Wimbledon achievements a couple of years, when he would have been better able to cope with them. However, his character is as strong as his personality, prompting the observation: 'I've had two years of cream. Eventually the time comes when you're bound to bite into a sour apple, and that is what happened.' Tendonitis in his left knee was also an inhibiting factor, along with a persistent chest virus in the closing period of the year, when he appointed Bob Brett as his new coach. It will certainly not be through lack of willpower if he does not come booming back in 1988.

Becker was by no means alone in finding that 1987 did not bring all that was hoped for. Yannick Noah's game went into sharp decline, and John McEnroe's comeback never materialised – but Jimmy Connors carried on, as if for ever. His comeback in the last 16 at Wimbledon against Mikael Pernfors, after the Swedish player had established a runaway 6–1 6–1 4–1 lead with the American evoking sentimental sympathy from all quarters, will be remembered not only as one of the tournament's greatest comebacks but probably the 'Match of the Year'. It may also prove to have been Connors's last truly great match among so many in his flamboyant career.

At the end of the year 24 countries could point to one or more players among the world's top 100, with the European advance creeping ever forward and the decline in United

As well as reaching the singles final at Wembley, Anders Jarryd of Sweden won eight doubles titles, including the Australian Open and US Open with Edberg and the French Open with Seguso, to finish the year at the top of the Grand Prix doubles points table.
(M. Cole)

States influence demonstrated most sharply by their relegation from the World Group of the *Davis Cup*. Whereas at the end of 1986 there were 33 American players in the world's top 100, by the end of 1987 the figure had drifted to 25. Sweden, on the other hand, had advanced from 12 to 13, Czechoslovakia (still including Lendl) from seven to ten and West Germany from four to eight. Aleksandr Volkov, a qualifier who had an outstanding Wimbledon, joined Andrei Chesnokov to give the USSR a second player in the top 100, at a time when their junior strength is also becoming pronounced.

Twelve players won Nabisco Grand Prix tournaments for the first time, although not surprisingly these were all Regular or Open Week, rather than Super Series events. The most successful were Argentina's Guillermo Perez Roldan, who won Munich, Athens and Buenos Aires to break into the world's top 20, with New Zealander Kelly Evernden and Jaime Yzaga from Peru each winning two titles.

In the too often neglected world of doubles, Anders Jarryd cast aside all his singles cares, in a year when he was recovering from knee surgery, to pip Robert Seguso at the post as winner of the Nabisco Grand Prix doubles points race. During the year Jarryd underlined not only his enthusiasm but also his flexibility on all surfaces by winning titles with four different players, including the French Open with Seguso and the US Open and Australian Open with his most consistent partner, Stefan Edberg.

When it came to the Masters Doubles in London's Royal Albert Hall, however, the last word came from the old maestro, Tomas Smid, a former winner in London with Pavel Slozil before the merging of the WCT and the Nabisco events. He and the even more deceptively talented Miloslav Mecir beat Edberg and Jarryd twice – in the round-robin and the semi-finals – before taking the title from Wimbledon champions Seguso and Ken Flach in the final. It was their fifth tournament win together in 1987 and Smid's 49th Grand Prix title with 18 different partners in 12 years. That is versatility for you.

NABISCO GRAND PRIX 1987

DATE	VENUE	SINGLES FINAL	DOUBLES WINNERS
29 Dec–4 Jan	Adelaide	W. Masur d. W. Scanlon 6–4 7–6	I. Lendl/W. Scanlon
5–11 Jan	Auckland	M. Mecir d. M. Schapers 6–2 6–3 6–4	K. Jones/B. Pearce
12–25 Jan	Melbourne *(Australian Open)*	S. Edberg d. P. Cash 6–3 6–4 3–6 5–7 6–3	S. Edberg/A. Jarryd
26 Jan–1 Feb	Guaruja	L. Mattar d. C. Motta 6–3 5–7 6–2	L. Mattar/C. Motta
26 Jan–1 Feb	Sydney	M. Mecir d. P. Doohan 6–2 6–4	B. Drewett/M. R. Edmondson
2–8 Feb	Philadelphia	T. Mayotte d. J. P. McEnroe 3–6 6–1 6–3 6–1	S. Casal/E. Sanchez
2–8 Feb	Lyons	Y. Noah d. J. Nystrom 6–4 7–5	G. Forget/Y. Noah
9–15 Feb	Memphis	S. Edberg d. J. S. Connors 6–3 2–1 ret'd	A. Jarryd/J. B. Svensson
16–22 Feb	Indian Wells, Cal	B. Becker d. S. Edberg 6–4 6–4 7–5	G. Forget/Y. Noah
23 Feb–8 March	Key Biscayne	M. Mecir d. I. Lendl 7–5 6–2 7–5	P. Annacone/C. Van Rensburg
16–22 March	Orlando	C. Van Rensburg d. J. S. Connors 6–3 3–6 6–1	S. E. Stewart/K. Warwick
16–22 March	Rotterdam	S. Edberg d. J. P. McEnroe 3–6 6–3 6–1	S. Edberg/A. Jarryd
23–29 March	Brussels	M. Wilander d. J. P. McEnroe 6–3 6–4	B. Becker/S. Zivojinovic
23–29 March	Nancy	P. Cash d. W. Masur 6–2 6–3	R. Krishnan/C. Mezzadri
30 March–5 April	Chicago	T. Mayotte d. D. Pate 6–4 6–2	P. Annacone/C. Van Rensburg
30 March–5 April	Milan	B. Becker d. M. Mecir 6–4 6–3	B. Becker/S. Zivojinovic
6–12 April	Dallas *(WCT Finals)*	M. Mecir d. J. P. McEnroe 6–0 3–6 6–2 6–2	—
6–12 April	Bari	C. Pistolesi d. F. Cancellotti 6–7 7–5 6–3	C. Allgardh/U. Stenlund
13–19 April	Nice	K. Carlsson d. E. Sanchez 7–6 6–3	S. Casal/E. Sanchez
13–19 April	Tokyo	S. Edberg d. D. Pate 7–6 6–4	P. Annacone/K. Curren
20–26 April	Monte Carlo	M. Wilander d. J. Arias 4–6 7–5 6–1 6–3	H. Gildemeister/A. Gomez
20–26 April	Seoul	J. Grabb d. A. Agassi 1–6 6–4 6–2	E. Korita/M. Leach
27 April–3 May	Hamburg *(German Open)*	I. Lendl d. M. Mecir 6–1 6–3 6–3	M. Mecir/T. Smid
4–10 May	Forest Hills, NY	A. Gomez d. Y. Noah 6–4 7–6 7–6	Y. Noah/G. Forget
4–10 May	Munich	G. Perez Roldan d. M. Vajda 6–3 7–6	J. Pugh/B. Willenborg
11–17 May	Rome *(Italian Open)*	M. Wilander d. M. Jaite 6–3 6–4 6–4	Y. Noah/G. Forget
18–24 May	Florence	A. Chesnokov d. A. DeMinicis 6–1 6–3	W. Popp/U. Riglewski
25 May–7 June	Paris *(French Open)*	I. Lendl d. M. Wilander 7–5 6–2 3–6 7–6	A. Jarryd/R. Seguso
8–14 June	Queen's Club	B. Becker d. J. S. Connors 6–7 6–3 6–4	Y. Noah/G. Forget
8–14 June	Bologna	K. Carlsson d. E. Sanchez 6–2 6–1	S. Casal/E. Sanchez
15–21 June	Bristol	K. Evernden d. T. Wilkison 6–4 7–6	—
15–21 June	Athens	G. Perez Roldan d. T. Meinecke 6–2 6–3	T. Meinecke/R. Osterthun
22 June–5 July	*Wimbledon*	P. Cash d. I. Lendl 7–6 6–2 7–5	K. Flach/R. Seguso
6–12 July	Boston	M. Wilander d. K. Carlsson 7–6 6–1	H. Gildemeister/A. Gomez
6–12 July	Newport, RI	D. Goldie d. S. Giammalva 6–7 6–4 6–4	D. Goldie/L. Scott
6–12 July	Gstaad	E. Sanchez d. R. Agenor 6–2 6–3 7–6	J. Gunnarsson/T. Smid
13–19 July	Indianapolis	M. Wilander d. K. Carlsson 7–6 6–3	L. Warder/B. Willenborg
13–19 July	Bordeaux	E. Sanchez d. R. Agenor 5–7 6–4 6–4	S. Casal/E. Sanchez
13–19 July	Stuttgart	M. Mecir d. J. Gunnarsson 6–0 6–2	R. Leach/T. Pawsat

DATE	VENUE	SINGLES FINAL	DOUBLES WINNERS
13–19 July	Livingston, NJ	J. Kriek d. S. Saceanu 7–6 3–6 6–2	G. Donnelly/G. Holmes
20–26 July	Schenectady	J. Yzaga d. J. Pugh 0–6 7–6 6–1	G. Donnelly/P. Fleming
27 July–2 Aug	Washington, DC	I. Lendl d. B. Gilbert 6–1 6–0	G. Donnelly/P. Fleming
27 July–2 Aug	Bastad	J. Nystrom d. S. Edberg 4–6 6–0 6–3	S. Edberg/A. Jarryd
27 July–2 Aug	Hilversum	M. Mecir d. G. Perez Roldan 6–4 1–6 6–3 6–2	M. Mecir/W. Fibak
3–9 Aug	Stratton Mountain	J. P. McEnroe v I. Lendl 7–6 1–4 div'd	P. Annacone/C. Van Rensburg div'd with K. Flach/R. Seguso
3–9 Aug	Kitzbuhel	E. Sanchez d. M. Mecir 6–4 1–6 6–4 4–6 6–1	S. Casal/E. Sanchez
10–16 Aug	Montreal	I. Lendl d. S. Edberg 6–4 7–6	P. Cash/S. Edberg
10–16 Aug	St Vincent	P. Rebolledo d. F. Cancellotti 7–6 4–6 6–3	B. Cox/M. Fancutt
10–16 Aug	Prague	M. Vajda d. T. Smid 6–1 6–3	M. Mecir/T. Smid
17–23 Aug	Cincinnati	S. Edberg d. B. Becker 6–4 6–2	K. Flach/R. Seguso
24–30 Aug	Rye Brook, NY	P. Lundgren d. J. Ross 6–7 7–5 6–3	L. Bourne/J. Klaparda
31 Aug–13 Sept	New York *(US Open)*	I. Lendl d. M. Wilander 6–7 6–0 7–6 6–4	S. Edberg/A. Jarryd
14–20 Sept	Geneva	C. Mezzadri d. T. Smid 6–4 7–5	R. Acioly/L. Mattar
14–20 Sept	Madrid	E. Sanchez d. J. Sanchez 6–3 3–6 6–2	C. DiLaura/J. Sanchez
21–27 Sept	Los Angeles	D. Pate d. S. Edberg 6–4 6–4	K. Curren/D. Pate
21–27 Sept	Barcelona	M. Jaite d. M. Wilander 7–6 6–4 4–6 0–6 6–4	M. Mecir/T. Smid
28 Sept–4 Oct	San Francisco	P. Lundgren d. J. Pugh 6–1 7–5	J. Grabb/P. McEnroe
28 Sept–4 Oct	Palermo	M. Jaite d. K. Novacek 7–6 6–7 6–4	L. Lavalle/C. Panatta
5–11 Oct	Scottsdale	B. Gilbert d. E. Teltscher 6–2 6–2	R. Leach/J. Pugh
5–11 Oct	Brisbane	K. Evernden d. E. Jelen 3–6 6–1 6–1	K. Evernden/M. Anger
5–11 Oct	Basle	Y. Noah d. R. Agenor 7–6 6–4 6–4	A. Jarryd/T. Smid
12–18 Oct	Sydney	I. Lendl d. P. Cash 6–4 6–2 6–4	D. Cahill/M. Kratzmann
12–18 Oct	Toulouse	T. Mayotte d. R. Osterthun 6–2 5–7 6–4	W. Fibak/M. Schapers
12–18 Oct	Tel Aviv	A. Mansdorf d. B. Gilbert 3–6 6–3 6–4	G. Bloom/S. Perkis
19–25 Oct	Tokyo	S. Edberg d. I. Lendl 6–7 6–4 6–4	S. Giammalva/J. Grabb
19–25 Oct	Vienna	J. B. Svensson d. A. Mansdorf 1–6 1–6 6–2 6–3 7–5	M. Purcell/T. Wilkison
26 Oct–1 Nov	Hong Kong	E. Teltscher d. J. Fitzgerald 6–7 3–6 6–1 6–2 7–5	M. Kratzmann/J. Pugh
2–8 Nov	Paris	T. Mayotte d. B. Gilbert 2–6 6–3 7–5 6–7 6–3	P. Annacone/C. Van Rensburg
2–8 Nov	Stockholm	S. Edberg d. J. B. Svensson 7–5 6–2 4–6 6–4	S. Edberg/A. Jarryd
9–15 Nov	Wembley, London	I. Lendl d. A. Jarryd 6–3 6–2 7–5	M. Mecir/T. Smid
9–15 Nov	Frankfurt	T. Mayotte d. A. Gomez 7–6 6–4	B. Becker/P. Kuhnen
9–15 Nov	Sao Paulo	J. Yzaga d. L. Mattar 6–2 4–6 6–2	G. Bloom/J. Sanchez
16–22 Nov	Buenos Aires	G. Perez Roldan d. J. Berger 3–2 ret'd	T. Carbonell/S. Casal
16–22 Nov	Johannesburg	P. Cash d. B. Gilbert 7–6 4–6 2–6 6–0 6–1	K. Curren/D. Pate
23–29 Nov	Itaparica	A. Agassi d. L. Mattar 7–6 6–2	S. Casal/E. Sanchez
2–6 Dec	New York *(Masters)*	I. Lendl d. M. Wilander 6–2 6–2 6–3	—
7–13 Dec	London *(Masters Doubles)*	—	M. Mecir/T. Smid

NABISCO GRAND PRIX 1987 – POINTS EXPLANATION

The Nabisco Grand Prix is a world-wide points-linked circuit of 74 tournaments in 22 countries with $24.5 million prize money under the management of the Men's International Professional Tennis Council. There are 18 separate points categories – from the Grand Slam Championships of Australia, France, Wimbledon and the US Open to the Regular Series tournaments with player compensation of $104,900 – $116,000. There are five categories – Grand Slam; other 2-week tournaments; Super Series, Doubles Series, Tournament of Champions; Open Week Series; Regular Series. In addition there are three season-ending play-offs: Buick WCT Finals, Nabisco Masters Singles and Nabisco Masters Doubles. There is no limit to the number of Grand Prix tournaments in which a player may compete each year.

POINTS TABLE

Player Compensation	**Grand Slam**		**Other Two-Week Events**		**Tournament of Champs.**		**$495,000 and over**		**$465,000 to $494,000**		**$435,000 to $464,000**		**$405,000 to $434,000**		**$375,000 to $404,000**		**$345,000 to $374,000**	
	Sgls	Dbls	Sgls	Dbls	Sgls	Dbls	Sgls	Dbls	Sgls	Dbls	Sgls	Dbls	Sgls	Dbls	Sgls	Dbls	Sgls	Dbls
Winner	700	120	550	110	450	90	400	80	375	75	350	70	325	65	300	60	275	55
Runner-up	500	84	350	70	298	63	280	56	263	52	245	49	227	45	210	42	192	38
Losing semi-finalists	350	48	200	40	180	36	160	32	150	30	140	28	130	26	120	24	110	22
Losing quarter-finalists	200	24	100	20	90	18	80	16	75	15	70	14	65	13	60	12	55	11
Losers in round of 16	100	12	50	10	45	9	40	8	37	8	35	7	32	7	30	6	27	6
Losers in round of 32	50	5	25	5	21	—	19	—	18	—	17	—	16	—	15	—	13	—
Losers in round of 64	25	—	12	—	—	—	—	—	—	—	—	—	—	—	—	—	—	—

Player Compensation	**$315,000 to $344,000**		**$285,000 to $314,000**		**$279,000 to $284,000**		**$231,000 to $278,000**		**$202,000 to $230,000**		**$174,000 to $202,000**		**$145,500 to $173,000**		**$117,000 to $145,000**		**$99,900 to $116,000**	
	Sgls	Dbls	Sgls	Dbls	Sgls	Dbls	Sgls	Dbls	Sgls	Dbls	Sgls	Dbls	Sgls	Dbls	Sgls	Dbls	Sgls	Dbls
Winner	250	50	225	45	220	44	200	40	175	35	150	30	125	25	100	20	89	17
Runner-up	175	35	157	31	151	30	140	28	122	24	104	20	87	17	70	14	62	12
Losing semi-finalists	100	20	90	18	88	17	80	16	70	14	60	12	50	10	40	8	36	7
Losing quarter-finalists	50	10	45	9	44	8	40	8	35	7	30	6	25	5	20	4	18	3
Losers in round of 16	25	5	22	5	21	4	20	4	17	3	14	3	12	2	10	2	9	—
Losers in round of 32	12	—	11	—	10	—	10	—	9	—	7	—	6	—	5	—	4	—
Losers in round of 64	—	—	—	—	—	—	—	—	—	—	—	—	—	—	—	—	—	—

Singles and doubles points are earned separately at each tournament and at the year's end the top 64 men on the singles points list divide the bonus pool of $3.25 million and the top 24 doubles players divide $0.75 million. To qualify for a bonus, a player must compete in at least 14 tournaments and these 'self-designations' may be amended by the MIPTC according to an agreed formula in order to maintain the quality of entry for the entire circuit. The Grand Prix year ends with the Nabisco Masters held in New York during December, which in 1987 was again an 8-player round-robin tournament with knockout semi-finals and final. Prize money was $500,000. The following week in London was held the Nabisco Masters Doubles tournament for the top eight pairs on the points list. Prize money was $255,000. Qualification for both singles and doubles is based on points won at Grand Prix tournaments throughout the year. In addition to the main bonus pools for singles and doubles, players who completed a full commitment to the 1986 Grand Prix and also played at least three additional Regular and/or Open week tournaments (or 5 in all) received bonuses for reaching the semi-finals ($2,000), final ($4,000) or for winning ($8,000).

NABISCO GRAND PRIX 1987 – FINAL STANDINGS

SINGLES

		POINTS	BONUS			POINTS	BONUS
1	I. Lendl (TCH)	4,779	$800,000	33	R. Krishnan (IND)	650	$14,000
2	S. Edberg (SWE)	4,354	550,000	34	C. Van Rensburg (RSA)	627	14,000
3	M. Wilander (SWE)	3,519	400,000	35	E. Bengoechea (ARG)	621	14,000
4	M. Mecir (TCH)	2,852	250,000	36	J. Kriek (USA)	619	14,000
5	B. Becker (FRG)	2,368	150,000	37	M. Pernfors (SWE)	616	14,000
6	J. S. Connors (USA)	2,295	100,000	38	L. Mattar (BRZ)	614	12,000
7	P. Cash (AUS)	2,187	75,000	39	T. Wilkison (USA)	608	12,000
8	B. Gilbert (USA)	1,941	55,000	40	C. Mezzadri (SUI)	580	12,000
9	T. Mayotte (USA)	1,815	45,000	41	M. Schapers (HOL)	565	12,000
10	A. Gomez (ECU)	1,792	40,000	42	R. Agenor (HAI)	561	12,000
11	Y. Noah (FRA)	1,533	35,000	43	K. Curren (USA)	547	10,000
12	E. Sanchez (ESP)	1,482	30,000	44	J. Berger (USA)	538	10,000
13	A. Jarryd (SWE)	1,465	26,000	45	U. Stenlund (SWE)	521	10,000
14	M. Jaite (ARG)	1,446	26,000	46	E. Jelen (FRG)	518	10,000
15	J. P. McEnroe (USA)	1,295	26,000	47	J. Pugh (USA)	516	10,000
16	S. Zivojinovic (YUG)	1,110	26,000	48	J. Gunnarsson (SWE)	511	9,000
17	K. Carlsson (SWE)	1,087	26,000	49	D. Rostagno (USA)	510	9,000
18	J. Nystrom (SWE)	1,032	22,000	50	S. Davis (USA)	503	9,000
19	D. Pate (USA)	993	22,000	51	A. Chesnokov (URS)	498	9,000
20	J. Hlasek (SUI)	924	22,000	52	M. Srejber (TCH)	495	9,000
21	A. Mansdorf (ISR)	890	22,000	53	D. Goldie (USA)	482	8,000
22	A. Agassi (USA)	879	22,000	54	M. Vajda (TCH)	481	8,000
23	G. Perez Roldan (ARG)	877	19,000	55	G. Forget (FRA)	476	8,000
24	H. Leconte (FRA)	859	19,000	56	K. Novacek (TCH)	472	8,000
25	J. B. Svensson (SWE)	808	19,000	57	T. Tulasne (FRA)	448	8,000
26	T. Smid (TCH)	798	19,000	58	J. Grabb (USA)	429	6,000
27	W. Masur (AUS)	761	19,000	59	R. Osterthun (FRG)	409	6,000
28	P. Annacone (USA)	754	16,000	60	J. Yzaga (PER)	405	6,000
29	K. Evernden (NZL)	738	16,000	61	H. Skoff (AUT)	392	6,000
30	P. Lundgren (SWE)	704	16,000	62	S. Casal (ESP)	375	6,000
31	E. Teltscher (USA)	687	16,000	63	M. Anger (USA)	365	5,000
32	J. Arias (USA)	653	16,000	64	T. Muster (AUT)	361	5,000

DOUBLES

		POINTS	BONUS			POINTS	BONUS
1	A. Jarryd (SWE)	799	$165,000	13	M. Mecir (TCH)	476	$13,000
2	R. Seguso (USA)	764	120,000	14	A. Gomez (ECU)	416	12,000
3	E. Sanchez (ESP)	714	90,000	15	G. Donnelly (USA)	358	11,000
4	S. Casal (ESP)	688	70,000	16	S. Zivojinovic (YUG)	356	10,000
5	K. Flach (USA)	659	50,000	17	D. Pate (USA)	344	8,000
6	T. Smid (TCH)	651	40,000	18	K. Curren (USA)	318	8,000
7	P. Annacone (USA)	605	30,000	19	B. Becker (FRG)	286	7,000
8	G. Forget (FRA)	598	25,000	20	J. Pugh (USA)	284	7,000
9	S. Edberg (SWE)	553	20,000	21	J. Nystrom (SWE)	274	5,000
10	Y. Noah (FRA)	509	17,000	22	B. Willenborg (USA)	269	5,000
11	C. Van Rensburg (RSA)	502	15,000	23	S. Davis (USA)	263	4,000
12	L. Warder (AUS)	492	14,000	24	P. Doohan (AUS)	254	4,000

DOUBLES TEAMS

		POINTS			POINTS
1	S. Casal (ESP)/E. Sanchez (ESP)	658	7	P. Doohan (AUS)/L. Warder (AUS)	243
2	K. Flach (USA)/R. Seguso (USA)	538	8	S. Davis (USA)/D. Pate (USA)	211
3	G. Forget (FRA)/Y. Noah (FRA)	509	9	G. Donnelly (USA)P. Fleming (USA)	202
4	S. Edberg (SWE)/A. Jarryd (SWE)	480	10	J. Nystrom (SWE)/M. Wilander (SWE)	201
5	P. Annacone (USA)/C. Van Rensburg (RSA)	467	11	H. Gildemeister (CHI)/A. Gomez (ECU)	195
6	M. Mecir (TCH)/T. Smid (TCH)	426	12	L. Warder (AUS)/B. Willenborg (USA)	185

SEGMENT 1: 2 FEBRUARY–22 MARCH

Richard Finn, Karen Rosen, Richard Evans, Ian Barnes and Edward Johnson

US PROFESSIONAL INDOOR CHAMPIONSHIPS ($375,000)

In 1986 it was a disappointed Tim Mayotte who pulled out of the final at the Spectrum before hitting a ball because of badly pulled stomach muscles. In 1987 it was an obviously delighted Tim Mayotte who held up the winner's cheque of $67,500 and the champion's trophy to show to the large championship-day crowd, who had clearly forgiven him for the disappointment of the previous year. 'I hope what I have done this year has made up a little bit for what I did last year', the American told the crowd of 15,240, after his surprisingly easy 3–6 6–1 6–3 6–1 victory over John McEnroe.

Seeded fifth in the 56-player field, Mayotte dropped just one set the entire week on the Supreme court in defeating Gary Muller, Ben Testerman, Paul Annacone, Milan Srejber and then McEnroe, to win his third career Grand Prix singles title and first since winning at Queen's Club in June, 1986. All week Mayotte had displayed improved quickness on court and a better back-court game, facets of his play that he had worked on during a break of more than two months over the New Year. After failing to capitalise on three break-point opportunities in the opening set, Mayotte took command of the match with two service breaks in each of the last three sets to take his first career victory over McEnroe in six meetings.

Mayotte was not the only one who made a triumphant return to this traditional starting point of the US Nabisco Grand Prix indoor season. McEnroe, the fourth seed, was making his eighth appearance here after missing the 1986 contest as part of his six-and-half-month sabbatical from tournament tennis. He has prospered at this event, joining fellow left-handed greats Rod Laver and Jimmy Connors as the only four-time winners in the 26-year history of the tournament. Furthermore McEnroe played well in reaching his first final of the year, not dropping a set on his way past Mel Purcell, Tomas Smid and Jakob Hlasek to the semi-finals. There, however, he had to battle back to defeat a fast-improving Amos Mansdorf, 5–7 6–2 6–3.

As always at this tournament, there were some early-round upsets. Mats Wilander, the favourite, who in two previous appearances had not advanced beyond the third round, this time went out in the second to his doubles partner and fellow-Swede, Jan Gunnarsson. Second-seeded Connors was knocked out 6–3 7–6 in the quarter-finals by the awesome serving of Srejber, who produced nine aces and countless service winners. Brad Gilbert, seeded three, fell in the second round to the Australian, Broderick Dyke.

Upsets were just as numerous in the doubles competition, won by the fifth-seeded Spanish duo of Sergio Casal and Emilio Sanchez over the sixth-seeded South African team of Christo Steyn and Danie Visser. Casal and Sanchez upset the top seeds, Ken Flach of the US and Smid of Czechoslovakia, in the semi-finals, while the second-seeded team of Annacone and the South African, Christo Van Rensburg, fell in the quarter-finals to the American pairing of Mark Dickson and Robert Van't Hof. – R. F.

Although his joy at Wimbledon did not extend beyond the third round, where he fell in five sets to Mikael Pernfors, America's Tim Mayotte won titles in Philadelphia, Chicago, Toulouse, Paris and Frankfurt to finish the year ranked in the top ten for the first time. *(T. Hindley)*

PHILADELPHIA, 2–8 FEBRUARY
MEN'S SINGLES – Quarter-finals: J. P. McEnroe d. J. Hlasek (SUI) 6–2 6–3; A. Mansdorf (ISR) d. K. Novacek (TCH) 6–7 6–3 6–4; T. Mayotte d. P. Annacone 7–5 6–4; M. Srejber (TCH) d. J. S. Connors 6–3 7–6. ***Semi-finals:*** McEnroe d. Mansdorf 5–7 6–2 6–3; Mayotte d. Srejber 6–2 6–2. ***Final:*** Mayotte d. McEnroe 3–6 6–1 6–3 6–1.
MEN'S DOUBLES – Final: S. Casal (ESP)/E. Sanchez (ESP) d. C. Steyn (RSA)/D. Visser (RSA) 3–6 6–1 7–6.

US INDOOR CHAMPIONSHIPS ($250,000)

Jimmy Connors received a standing ovation as he limped off the court at the Racquet Club of Memphis, an ice-bag around his right knee, but it was top-seeded Stefan Edberg who walked off with the US Indoor Championship, 6–3 2–1 retired. Connors, the 34-year-old second seed, who habitually fights off suggestions of retirement, had sprained the medial collateral ligament in his right knee and could not continue. Thus Edberg, the 1985 Memphis champion, extended his winning streak to thirteen matches, including the Australian Open. In his quiet fashion the Swede was enjoying his rise to No. 2 in the world, having recently slipped past Boris Becker by .13 percentage points on the ATP computer.

Connors, a seven-time winner of the US Indoor Championships, had bounced Andrei Chesnokov of the USSR, 6–1 6–3, veteran American Eliot Teltscher, 6–1 4–6 6–1, and Kevin Curren, 6–4 3–6 6–3 in the quarters, before playing the best match of the 48-man tournament the day before the final. After outlasting the No. 3 seed, Mikael Pernfors, 6–7 (6–8) 7–5 6–3 in two hours and 47 minutes, he commented: 'Long after I'm retired you'll say, "Did you see the match he played against Pernfors?" That's what this game's all about . . . and I like that.' Connors made a dramatic recovery after losing the first-set tie-break (where he had a set-point) and his first two service games of the second set to fall behind 3–1. He later made an even more dramatic recovery against the same player at Wimbledon, winning that encounter after being 1–6 1–6 1–4 down.

Pernfors, the little Swede whose back-court retrieving skills match Connors's, equalled his 1986 Memphis performance, but with fewer matches. Last year's event marked Pernfors's breakthrough on the pro tour as he reached his first semi-final, where he lost to Edberg. This year he didn't have to endure any qualifying matches before defeating qualifier Thomas Hogstedt, Amos Mansdorf of Israel and Greg Holmes of the US.

For the first time since the tournament moved to Memphis in 1977, the top four seeds advanced to the semi-finals. In a re-match of the 1986 final, Edberg avenged his loss then by defeating the defending champion and fourth seed, Brad Gilbert of the US, 6–4 7–6 (8–6). The only set Edberg dropped was the one he conceded to Richey Reneberg in the second round, 7–6 (7–5) 2–6 6–4. The Australian Open champion had little trouble with Ramesh Krishnan's smooth groundstrokes or Tim Mayotte's serves.

McEnroe, seeded fifth, defeated home-state hope Paul Annacone in their first re-match since Annacone bumped him in the first round of the US Open. Johan Kriek, restricted to a modified serve by a frustrating shoulder injury, then played what he termed 'a near perfect match' to upset McEnroe, whose stomach was bothering him. Ahead 40–30 on his serve, McEnroe had a chance to go up 5–2 in the first set, but lost the next three points. Kriek, who broke his favourite racket the following morning, fell to Gilbert 6–2 7–6 (7–5) in the quarters.

Unseeded Anders Jarryd and Jonas Svensson won the doubles title, defeating the sixth-seeded Spanish team of Sergio Casal and Emilio Sanchez of Spain 6–4 6–2. The Swedes had ousted the third seeds, Curren and Gilbert, 6–4 6–7 (5–7) 6–4 in a close quarter-final, before defeating Ben Testerman and Tim Wilkison 4–6 6–2 6–3 in the semis. Testerman and Wilkison had in turn surprised top-seeded Ken Flach and Tomas Smid in the second round, 7–5 5–7 6–4. – K. R.

MEMPHIS, 9–15 FEBRUARY
MEN'S SINGLES – Quarter-finals: S. Edberg (SWE) d. T. Mayotte 6–3 6–4; B. Gilbert d. J. Kriek 6–2 7–6; M. Pernfors (SWE) d. G. Holmes 6–4 3–6 6–3; J. S. Connors d. K. Curren 6–4 3–6 6–3. ***Semi-***

finals: Edberg d. Gilbert 6–4 7–6; Connors d. Pernfors 6–7 7–5 6–3. ***Final:*** Edberg d. Connors 6–3 2–1 ret'd.
MEN'S DOUBLES – Final: A. Jarryd (SWE/J. B. Svensson (SWE) d. S. Casal (ESP)/E. Sanchez (ESP) 6–4 6–2.

PILOT PEN CLASSIC ($350,000)

Boris Becker became a Grand Champion in deed and in name when he defeated his arch-rival Stefan Edberg 6–4 6–4 7–5 to win the Pilot Pen Classic at Indian Wells, California. It was, of course, appropriate that Becker should win the first major tournament ever held in the magnificent 10,500-seat stadium built by Charlie Pasarell, because the 19-year-old West German had signed a five-year contract to act as touring pro for the new Grand Champions resort.

But no matter what took place on court, the event had a significance all of its own. Pasarell's vision had provided a fourth and surely final setting for a tournament that had begun life as the American Airlines Tennis Games in Tucson, Arizona, in the mid-seventies. After a couple of years it had moved to Mission Hills at Rancho Mirage and then, with Pasarell at the helm, had travelled to La Quinta. Congoleum became the title-sponsor before handing over to Pilot Pen in 1986, who in 1988 will reluctantly hand over to *Newsweek*.

For a region that boasts more tennis players per head of the population than any other area in the world, Southern California had always been poorly served for tennis stadia, and Pasarell was determined to put that right when he became President of Grand Champions. Alongside the five-star hotel which sprang up out of the desert scrub, Pasarell planned a stadium, complete with air-conditioned sponsors' boxes, that now ranks with those in Melbourne and Tokyo as the most modern in the world.

The tennis fans of Southern California proved some of the local prophets of doom to be very poor judges of Pasarell's marketing expertise and the seemingly endless attraction of the game itself. It had been said the stadium was too big for a mere tennis tournament but by mid-week the 'House Full' notices had been up for two days and, with a tardy sun at last beginning to shine in the prescribed manner, the new stadium presented a truly splendid sight.

Considering four of the world's top five players reached the semi-finals, it was a pity the matches themselves did not quite live up to the occasion. But Edberg, the top seed, and Becker had built up a head of steam during the week and Edberg, in particular, was bubbling at this stage of the year as his decisive 6–1 7–5 victory over no less a rival than Mats Wilander proved. It was Stefan's 15th consecutive singles victory on the Grand Prix tour – a streak that had started at Kooyong.

But Becker was also in fine form, and although Yannick Noah, a former title-holder of the event in its days under the Congoleum banner, had fought his way through a quarter of the draw dominated by all his fellow-Frenchmen, he was no match for the Wimbledon champion and went down 6–4 6–2. In the final Becker took charge right from the start, just as he had done against Noah, by winning the toss, choosing to receive and breaking serve in the opening game of the match. Edberg almost got back on level terms from a 0–3 deficit in the first set but, in truth, he was always fighting a rearguard action and never looked capable of preventing Becker beating him for the seventh consecutive time.

In partnership with his *Davis Cup* colleague, Eric Jelen, Becker also reached the doubles final but Noah, who enjoys the Californian desert, was waiting for him alongside the elegant Guy Forget and, in a match that offered the large American crowd yet another demonstration of the power and skill of European tennis, it was the Frenchmen who prospered, winning a hard-hitting duel 6–4 7–6. – R. E.

INDIAN WELLS, CALIFORNIA, 16–22 FEBRUARY
MEN'S SINGLES – Quarter-finals: S. Edberg (SWE) d. M. Mecir (TCH) 4–6 6–4 6–2; M. Wllander (SWE) d. J. Hlasek (SUI) 6–3 6–0; Y. Noah (FRA) d. T. Tulasne (FRA) 6–0 3–6 6–4; B. Becker (FRG) d. E. Sanchez (ESP) 6–3 7–5. ***Semi-finals:*** Edberg d. Wilander 6–1 7–5; Becker d. Noah 6–4 6–2. ***Final:*** Becker d. Edberg 6–4 6–4 7–5.

MEN'S DOUBLES – Final: G. Forget (FRA)/Noah d. Becker/E. Jelen (FRG) 6–4 7–6.

LIPTON INTERNATIONAL PLAYERS' CHAMPIONSHIPS ($275,000)

Any man who can view a public rubbish tip, look three months ahead and see the panorama of the fifth-biggest tennis tournament in the world has to be an optimist. He also has to be lucky. Butch Buchholz is a lucky optimist, and now that his Lipton International Players' Championship has established what everyone hopes will be a permanent home, after being played at Delray Beach and Boca Raton, he is entitled to an extremely satisfied smile.

The 1987 Lipton Players' Championships had all the ingredients that make a successful tennis tournament: drama and excitement, a lot of good weather (although there was also plenty of rain and wind) and two unexpected champions. Steffi Graf emphasised her arrival as a women's star by beating both Chris Lloyd and Martina Navratilova on her way to the title. Yet perhaps more surprising was the confirmation of Miloslav Mecir as a genuine contender at the biggest tournaments and a threat, on any surface, to anybody. He had followed his final place at the 1986 US Open by winning two of the first five tournaments of the new year and celebrated by inviting his parents, Ladislav and Blazena, to Key Biscayne. The bonus on their first trip to the United States was to see him not only beat World Champion Ivan Lendl for the men's crown, but also take the mixed doubles title with countrywoman Jana Novotna.

The ninth-seeded Mecir's progress through the 128 draw had been solid rather than spectacular. Casio Motta, Jaime Yzaga and Jimmy Arias had each been mesmerised in progressively more difficult three-set matches and the big-serving Yugoslav, Slobodan Zivojinovic, had been the first to take a set off Mecir in the round of sixteen. But from then on, Mecir was on a magical march. Stefan Edberg was unable to unravel the puzzles he set; Yannick Noah was too full of medication to ease the pain of a strained shoulder to offer much resistance in the semi-final, and Lendl, the sometime 'Iron Man', melted away in the title match. Suffering from a knee injury which subsequently required surgery, he was unable to hit his biggest shots.

If Boris Becker, hot from victory in Indian Wells the week before, had been fit enough to play his opening match against Derrick Rostagno – which he conceded because of suspected food poisoning – things might have been different. Becker was in Lendl's half of the draw and would have been fancied to beat both Jimmy Connors and the below-par Lendl. For tension, temper and drama the semi between Lendl and Connors was the match of the tournament. Stretching over 26 hours because of rain delays, it featured the agony and ecstasy of two superbly competitive tie-breaks, and though the noisy Connors fans were undoubtedly disappointed at the final outcome, the uncommitted loved every moment. Lendl won, eventually, 3–6 7–6 (9–7) 7–6 (11–9) 6–3. But the figures tell only half the story. Lendl needed eight set-points for the second set – including five in the tie-break – and seven more in the third-set tie-break, which restarted the match after an overnight delay, for each time Lendl threatened to take command, Connors mounted the sort of charge on which he has built his reputation. Connors also had his chances for a two-sets-to-one lead. 'I tried to go for too much', he said later. But didn't he always? This is what makes him such a great competitor.

Noah's injury ruined the other semi-final. After three five-set matches, against Emilio Sanchez, Ulf Stenlund and in the quarter-finals against Mats Wilander, the flamboyant Noah had gained the affection of the crowd. Their disappointment was as great as his when he was forced to quit against Mecir at 7–5 5–1 down.

Christo Van Rensburg, who was to go on the following week to record his first Grand Prix singles victory by beating Connors at Orlando, took the doubles title with Paul Annacone. They beat Ken Flach and Robert Seguso in straight sets in the final, after coming through a tough semi-final against Andres Gomez and Zivojinovic. Flach and Seguso reached the final on a walk-over against the injured Noah and his compatriot Guy Forget, but nobody could deny they were worth their place. Their three-sets quarter-final win over

Edberg and Anders Jarryd had been as good a match as you could expect at any stage of any tournament. – I. B.

KEY BISCAYNE, FLORIDA, 23 FEBRUARY–8 MARCH
MEN'S SINGLES – Quarter-finals: I. Lendl (TCH) d. J. Berger 6–3 6–1 6–1; J. S. Connors d. D. Rostagno 6–4 4–6 6–1 6–2; Y. Noah (FRA) d. M. Wilander (SWE) 6–4 6–2 4–6 2–6 7–6; M. Mecir (TCH) d. S. Edberg (SWE) 3–6 6–2 6–2 6–4. ***Semi-finals:*** Lendl d. Connors 3–6 7–6 7–6 6–3; Mecir d. Noah 7–5 5–1 ret'd. ***Final:*** Mecir d. Lendl 7–5 6–2 7–5.
MEN'S DOUBLES – Final: P. Annacone/C. Van Rensburg (RSA) d. K. Flach/R. Seguso 6–2 6–4 6–4.

PAINE WEBBER CLASSIC ($250,000)

It was meant to be a celebration for the Grand Old Man of American tennis, the moment when James Scott Connors cast aside his 34 years to record a 106th tournament victory. All the elements were there at the $250,000 Paine Webber Classic – the same hard-court surface on which he had developed his tennis in California, an enthusiastic crowd at the Grand Cypress Resort in Orlando, the TV cameras at courtside to take the action to a nationwide audience, a field that contained none of the men ranked above him and an opponent he had never met before, whose ranking of 68 suggested that this would be a routine win for the favourite.

But Christo Van Rensburg, a stringy six-footer from Uitenhage, had obviously not read the script. Recovering from an understandably nervous start which produced two double-faults to open the match, the 24-year-old right-hander proceeded to outplay his older opponent and record a well merited 6–3 3–6 6–1 victory in his first Grand Prix singles final. During his four years as a professional, the likeable Christo has built quite a reputation as a doubles player, winning the Australian Open in 1985 with his regular partner, Paul Annacone. In singles Christo's best performances had been to reach the semi-final twice in Regular Series tournaments, although at Wimbledon in 1986 he had reached the last 16, and at the US Open that year he had beaten Mats Wilander.

Van Rensburg took full advantage of the unexpected loss of the No. 2 seed, Andres Gomez, to the hustling Californian Derrick Rostagno in round two. After breezing past Sammy Giammalva and Scott Davis for the loss of only eight games, Christo's confidence was high when he met Rostagno. Holding his nerve in a tense final set, the South African won 2–6 6–1 7–5 to set up a semi-final meeting with the No. 3 seed, Tim Mayotte. This was another close affair, fought out mostly in the forecourt, and Van Rensburg prevailed 2–6 7–6 6–4. Later that evening Christo became embroiled in a hard-hitting doubles semi-final with Annacone against Davis and David Pate, finally winning 6–4 6–2 around midnight.

Connors, meanwhile, had accounted for Kelly Evernden and Greg Holmes in straight sets before facing the No. 8 seed, Tim Wilkison, in the quarter-finals. It was unfortunate that an injury forced the North Carolina native to default with Connors leading 6–2 5–2, but it meant that Jimmy was still fresh when he played fourth-seeded Brad Gilbert in the semi-finals. That was just as well, for Gilbert was rallying superbly and moving the ball about at the start, so that he captured the first set 6–3. The loss of his first set during the week seemed to rouse Connors, who began to hit just a little harder and deeper without making too many errors. With Gilbert looking increasingly despondent, Jimmy accelerated to a 3–6 6–4 6–2 victory.

Once he had begun to relax in the final, Van Rensburg played some magnificent forcing tennis. He was helped by the fact that Connors could not find the rhythm on his serve, so that there were many opportunities to charge the net behind returns of Jimmy's second serve. Throughout the South African volleyed very sharply and with good anticipation. To his credit he refused to be deflected from his attacking game, even when Connors charged from 3–3 in the second set to run off four perfect games that left him 1–0 ahead in the decider. It was Van Rensburg's turn to raise the tempo as Connors's serve still refused to function properly. Facing break-points only twice, he swept through the next six games and served his fourth ace at match-point to record the finest victory of his career that earned him $50,000.

In an unhappy year which brought the loss of his Wimbledon and Young Masters titles, as well as a drop from two to five in the rankings, Boris Becker could find consolation in his three tournament wins in Milan, Indian Wells and Queens, and began 1988 in positive mood under the influence of his new coach, Bob Brett. *(T. Hindley)*

Christo was brought back to earth in the doubles final, when he and Annacone fell to the wiles of the near-veteran pair, Sherwood Stewart of Texas (aged 40) and Australia's Kim Warwick (almost 35), who proved too good as they imposed a 2–6 7–6 6–4 victory to claim the first prize of $7,500. – E. J.

ORLANDO, 16–22 MARCH
MEN'S SINGLES – Quarter finals: J. S. Connors d. T. Wilkison 6–2 5–2 ret'd; B. Gilbert d. M. Freeman 4–6 6–3 6–1; C. Van Rensburg (RSA) d. D. Rostagno 2–6 6–1 7–5; T. Mayotte d. P. Annacone 6–1 7–5. ***Semi-finals:*** Connors d. Gilbert 3–6 6–4 6–2; Van Rensburg d. Mayotte 2–6 7–6 6–4. ***Final:*** Van Rensburg d. Connors 6–3 3–6 6–1.
MEN'S DOUBLES – Final: S. E. Stewart/K. Warwick (AUS) d. P. Annacone/Van Rensburg 2–6 7–6 6–4.

SEGMENT 2: 16 MARCH–5 APRIL

John Parsons, Richard Evans, Edward Johnson and Gianni Clerici

ROTTERDAM ($250,000)

When Stefan Edberg had the opportunity to sit back and analyse how, after five consecutive straight-sets defeats, he had at last discovered a way to beat John McEnroe to win the ABN Wereldtennis Toernooi at the Ahoy Stadium, he may well have wondered why he hadn't managed to do it before. For on reflection it was all quite simple. After a tentative start, which was all too typical of his previous clashes with McEnroe, Edberg eventually resolved to do what he does best and should have done before – namely serve well and come in behind the serve to volley with a steadily increasing venom and authority.

Throughout a week which attracted a record 62,000 spectators, McEnroe was concerned not only about his varying form but also his fitness, with a hip problem the latest to be added to his list of strained and painful muscles. Yet against Mecir, for whom a 6–1 7–5 semi-final loss was only his third defeat in 29 matches during the year, McEnroe played near-faultless tennis. Against Edberg, however, those tell-tale signs of weariness, which crept in towards the end of the match with Mecir, could not be hidden any longer.

McEnroe, who once or twice during the week had walked a mental tightrope as he overcome the Russian No. 1, Andrei Chesnokov, Michiel Schapers of Holland, and then the rapidly improving Israeli, Amos Mansdorf, to reach the last four, won the first set on one break in 45 minutes. Edberg, shutting out those inevitable diversions which the American so frequently created, took 69 minutes over winning the next two, mostly in a relentless, workmanlike fashion. 'I've waited a long time for this', said Edberg, whose earlier victims had been the Czech, Stanislav Birner, Andreas Maurer of Germany, fellow-Swede Anders Jarryd and then the American, Jim Grabb, who, with fellow-countryman Chip Hooper, had proved to be the two main surprises of the event.

For Hooper, a qualifier, it was the first time he had really made an impact since being restricted by injuries at the end of 1986. Among others Hooper beat the ailing Joakim Nystrom (who then went home to consult experts about the state of cartilages in his knee), before losing to the lean and lanky Grabb in the semi-finals. Grabb, who had turned professional after leaving Stanford the previous summer, was clearly helped on his way at Rotterdam by his second-round victory over an injured Libor Pimek, who had already removed Mikael Pernfors, the seed who should have been making progress in that quarter.

Earlier in the week Mansdorf had maintained his steady climb up the world rankings with a 7–5 6–2 defeat of the leading Spaniard, Emilio Sanchez. The Israeli had become a national hero for his crucial defeat of Mecir in the *Davis Cup* in Czechoslovakia and, if anything, there was a touch of over-confidence in the approach to his quarter-final with McEnroe, whom he had tested so comprehensively in Philadelphia. A capacity 8,000 crowd watched as McEnroe, for once serving superbly, won 6–4 7–5.

In the doubles, Edberg took the title with Anders Jarryd, beating the rejuvenated Hooper and fellow-American, Mike Leach, in a lively final. The greatest joy for the American pair had come in the semi-finals when they defeated McEnroe and Peter Fleming 6–4 6–4. – J. P.

16–22 MARCH
MEN'S SINGLES – Quarter-finals: M. Mecir (TCH) d. J. B. Svensson (SWE) 6–2 7–5; J. P. McEnroe (USA) d. A. Mansdorf (ISR) 6–4 7–5; J. Grabb (USA) d. C. Hooper (USA) 6–1 7–5; S. Edberg (SWE) d.

Photos: Russ Adams, Angelo Tonelli   Printed in the U.S.A.

***O**nly 75 tournaments in the world qualify to be a part of the Nabisco Grand Prix, the most prestigious circuit of events in tennis, and they are as diverse as the men who play the game. The Nabisco Grand Prix provides both structure and incentive for the hundreds of players who compete: a fixed bonus points system connecting all of the events and offering over $35 million in cash rewards.*

NABISCO GRAND PRIX

Each week players are awarded bonus points for official matches won. At the conclusion of the year, only the elite will have earned enough points for a share of the $4 million Nabisco Grand Prix Bonus Pool, representing twelve months of pushing themselves to the limit under the toughest of conditions. And, in the season-concluding championships, the Nabisco Masters at Madison Square Garden in New York and Nabisco Masters Doubles at the Royal Albert Hall in London, the top points leaders will face each other in one last definitive battle.

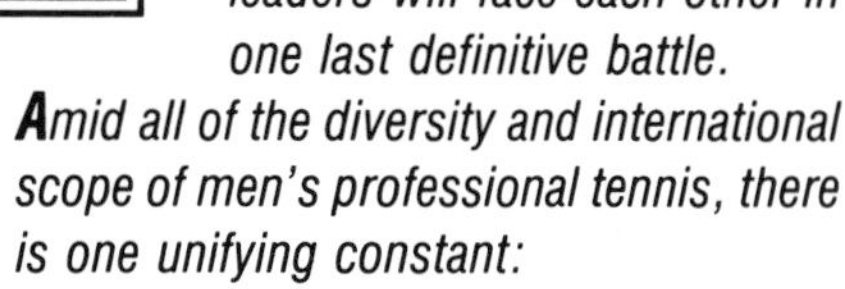

***A**mid all of the diversity and international scope of men's professional tennis, there is one unifying constant:*
***N**abisco...the **N**ame of the **G**ame.*

NABISCO GRAND PRIX
...the name of the game.

A. Jarryd (SWE) 6–4 5–7 6–4. ***Semi-finals:*** McEnroe d. Mecir 6–1 7–5; Edberg d. Grabb 6–3 6–4. ***Final:*** Edberg d. McEnroe 3–6 6–3 6–1.
MEN'S DOUBLES – Final: Edberg/Jarryd d. Hooper/M. Leach (USA) 3–6 6–3 6–4.

BRUSSELS ($250,000)

Mats Wilander, registering his first-ever victory over John McEnroe on an indoor court, retained his Belgian Super Series title at the Brussels Exhibition Centre with a workmanlike victory that suggested tennis was, once again, amongst his list of priorities following a relatively lacklustre year in 1986.

McEnroe, who lost 6–3 6–4 in the final, also had plenty to prove about his commitment to the game, and there was no question about the sincerity of the New Yorker's determination to re-habilitate himself at this stage of the year. He outplayed Miloslav Mecir in the previous week's semi-final in Rotterdam and then, after losing to Stefan Edberg, raced off to London for a brief session with his British physiotherapist, Cynthia Tucker. With continued work from the local doctor and ATP trainer, Todd Snyder, in Brussels, McEnroe managed to keep his back-related hip problems under control throughout a week that saw him produce numerous flashes of the best McEnroe magic.

Having beaten Paolo Cane and Thomas Hogstedt in straight sets, McEnroe was thoroughly tested in the quarters not only by the steadily improving game of Jakob Hlasek but also by his own temperament. Having won the first set 6–3, McEnroe blew up over a bad line call early in the second and was docked a penalty point by MIPTC umpire Richard Ings. Seizing his opportunity with a brilliant backhand return low to the server's feet, Hlasek broke to lead 4–2. McEnroe was still simmering but somehow managed to keep the lid on his emotions. It was interesting to hear just how hard McEnroe was trying to cut out the tantrums and interesting, too, to see how he was able to collect his wits in time to fight back superbly against a worthy opponent. He took Hlasek's serves on the rise with the racket held out in front of the body, and broke through twice to snatch the second set 7–5.

McEnroe's semi-final opponent should have been Boris Becker but it wasn't, for in the quarters Anders Jarryd, who almost always plays well in Brussels, beat Becker who palpably doesn't. Jarryd, who pecks away at his opponents with that darting all-court game that includes some stinging volleys, knew he could beat the big West German because he had done so the year before in the Final of WCT Dallas. So, refusing to be put off by the loss of the first set, he kept on attacking. Jarryd's passing shots were as accurate as Becker's approaches were inconsistent, and once the Swede had secured the vital breakthrough in the ninth game of the third set, he forsook the backcourt completely and served and volleyed his way to an impressive victory. However, he could not reproduce that kind of form the next day, and a very smooth and calm performance from McEnroe took the American through to the final without a tremor, 6–3 6–3.

Of the four Swedes in the quarters, three of them made it to the last four. Jonas Svensson had looked very good in beating Jan Gunnarsson 6–3 6–3 but developed a fever overnight, and went down in straight sets to Wilander after a last-minute decision to play.

The singles final, played before a capacity crowd, was disappointing, for McEnroe never came to terms with the fact that he could not find the timing on his backhand and kept trying to play through the problem. As a result, errors flowed from his racket on the backhand flank and the ever-consistent Wilander feasted off them. The Swede, who had been so distracted by love and marriage, was obviously delighted to have retained his title.

The doubles final was a thriller, with Becker and Slobodan Zivojinovic trading huge serves with the Americans, Chip Hooper and Mike Leach. There are not many bigger servers in the game than this quartet, yet the first-set tie-break saw points going against serve with amazing regularity as everyone went for their returns and stretched it all the way to 15–13. That was in the Yugo-German team's favour as was the next set, which also went to the tie-break, to give Becker and Zivojinovic the title. – R. E.

23–29 MARCH
MEN'S SINGLES – Quarter-finals: A. Jarryd (SWE) d. B. Becker (FRG) 4–6 6–3 6–4; J. P. McEnroe (USA) d. J. Hlasek (SUI) 6–3 7–5; J. B. Svensson (SWE) d. J. Gunnarsson (SWE) 6–3 6–3; M. Wilander (SWE) d. G. Bloom (ISR) 5–7 6–3 6–2. ***Semi-finals:*** McEnroe d. Jarryd 6–3 6–3; Wilander d. Svensson 6–3 6–2. ***Final:*** Wilander d. McEnroe 6–3 6–4.
MEN'S DOUBLES – Final: Becker/S. Zivojinovic (YUG) d. M. Leach (USA)/C. Hooper (USA) 7–6 7–6.

CHICAGO ($300,000)

When Yannick Noah and Jimmy Connors, the top two seeds, fell before the semi-finals, the No. 3 seed, Tim Mayotte, was there to take the major pickings at the $250,000 Volvo Tennis tournament in Chicago. By beating the No. 6 seed, David Pate, 6–4 6–2 in the final, 'Gentleman Tim' not only took home a cheque for $50,000 but also lifted himself back into the top ten on the ATP computer rankings. Not since February 1986 had Tim been among the élite. His dedicated period of fitness training during the winter months had produced a fitter, more confident player.

However, the glory did not belong to Tim alone. Two old-stagers nearly stole the limelight by emerging in the semi-finals, unseeded. When 29-year-old Bill Scanlon beat the No. 4 seed, Brad Gilbert, in straight sets in the second round and, two rounds later, eliminated Scott Davis, seeded 6, also in straight sets, he reminded us what a good player he had been five years earlier when he had won the WCT tournament held in the Windy City.

The achievement of 27-year-old Eliot Teltscher was even more impressive. Having accounted for South Africa's No. 7 seed, Christo Van Rensburg, 6–3 6–2 in the second round, Teltscher proceeded to score a first victory in 16 meetings against the second favourite, Connors. It was an emphatic 6–3 6–1 result, earned on the merits of a fine exhibition of serving and volleying, an art form that the former US *Davis Cup* player had never previously been in danger of mastering. Connors was as surprised as the rest of us. The result left no doubt about the Californian's determination to return from the high 30s to the top 20 after a worrying year following surgery on his right shoulder.

It was Mel Purcell, the likeable lad from Murray, Kentucky, who had caused the tournament's biggest shock when, in the second round, he had defeated the top seed, Noah, 6–4 6–2. The athletic Frenchman had flown to Chicago from Africa at short notice to replace Ivan Lendl and John McEnroe, who had both pulled out of the tournament at a late stage with physical problems. Purcell's unorthodox flair, beautiful to watch but rather lightweight on a Supreme court, was no match for the powerful hitting and sharp volleying of Pate whose 7–5 6–4 win carried him to a meeting with Scanlon in the semi-finals. There he maintained his aggressive form to score a straightforward 6–3 6–2 decision.

The other semi-final proved to be the match of the week. Teltscher built a lead of 5–0, then was 6–3 5–2 with two chances to serve for the match. Mayotte's noted resolve was never more needed, and it did not fail him. Refusing to be put off by some excellent lobs, Tim applied a little extra pressure by thwarting Teltscher's still-effective serve-volley tactics with some beautifully varied returns. Teltscher never did see a match-point as the second set slipped away 7–5, and could offer only token resistance in the decider, after coming from 0–3 to 2–3. Teltscher could only shake his head and murmer, 'I really don't know what happened . . . At 6–3 5–2 I really thought it was mine'.

After preparing properly for his final by warming up for about an hour with brother John, on the advice of his coach Bill Drake, Mayotte served particularly well against a nervous Pate, who was playing in his first Grand Prix final for two years. Pate lost his opening service game of the match and never really recovered. He was not allowed to by a man who feels that his game is now into a new dimension. Pate's five aces took his total for the week to 35 – more than any other player – and so earned him the right to nominate the charity which would receive the $1,000 donated by Faber Castell.

Paul Annacone and Van Rensburg returned to winning doubles form when they took the title and the first prize of $7,500 by beating the Americans, Gary Donnelly and Mike DePalmer, 6–3 7–6. – E. J.

30 MARCH–5 APRIL
MEN'S SINGLES – Quarter-finals: E. Teltscher d. J. S. Connors 6–3 6–1; T. Mayotte d. P. Fleming 6–2 6–3; W. Scanlon d. S. Davis 6–3 6–3; D. Pate d. M. Purcell 7–5 6–4. ***Semi-finals:*** Mayotte d. Teltscher 3–6 7–5 6–2; Pate d. Scanlon 6–3 6–2. ***Final:*** Mayotte d. Pate 6–4 6–2.
MEN'S DOUBLES – Final: P. Annacone/C. Van Rensburg (RSA) d. G. Donnelly/M. DePalmer 6–3 7–6.

Eliot Teltscher enjoyed a successful year in which he beat Connors in Chicago to reach the semi-finals, and in Hong Kong in October his first tournament victory for three years saw him return to the top 20. *(T. Hindley)*

FILA TROPHY ($300,000)

Three features combined to make a success of the International Championships of Italy, played on Supreme Court in Milan. First was the new indoor facility, the Palazzo Trussardi, an enormous futuristic structure, which replaced the Palazzo dello Sport in San Siro that, in 1985, had crashed during a fierce polar storm. The new stadium, home of the Tracer basketball team – the Italian and European champions – can easily accommodate 8,000 spectators, and for the tennis tournament they came in their thousands – Milan's Scala set, singers, actors, fashion designers, beauties of Italy's real capital . . . . This gathering of the cream of Milan society was the second, and excellent, novelty. In these TV-influenced days when people follow their tabloid idols like sheep, hundreds of totally new spectators, as well as the true tennis *afficionados*, followed the fashionable stream, so that by the end of the week almost 48,000 fans had paid to see the tennis.

The third and greatest draw for the tournament was Boris Becker, although at the time few really believed that Boris could win the championship. The media coverage for the top-seeded Wimbledon champion was at least three times as big as that enjoyed by 'Gattone' Mecir, the Big Cat from Czechoslovakia, who had won his Italian nickname – from the ATP road manager, Vittorio Selmi, who is Italian – because he simply belongs there.

Mecir, seeded two, lost only 18 games *en route* to the semi-final where he met Mats Wilander, the third seed, who was well rested after a much needed break from the game. It was a privilege to be in Milan to see the way the creative, amusing game of 'Gattone' was deployed to damage the common-sense game of poor Mats. Slowing down the rallies, then suddenly accelerating, playing first some flat balls, then some that fizzed with side-spin, Mecir mystified the wretched Wilander who lost the first 11 games. It was the same magic that had reduced all the Swedes to impotence against Mecir, whose lifetime record against them in tournaments stood at 27–15. Then, as a desperate Wilander reacted energetically and the Big Cat quietly dozed for a couple of games, the score became less mortifying – 6–0 6–2.

The sharp nails of 'Gattone' did not scratch as effectively in the final against Becker. To perform his conjuring tricks 'Gattone' needed tennis balls, not rockets, but every shot from Boris flew at lightning speed and carried the weight of a meteorite. As long as he was allowed to serve effectively Mecir could stay in the match, so his five double-faults were particularly damaging. When he could get into a rally Mecir could start to work his tricks, often catching the young German unawares with those bemusing, wrong-footing drives that made fun of Becker a couple of times in some deliciously sweet exchanges. But as Becker sprayed his seven aces and 18 other winning shots around the court, poor Gattone was powerless, finishing a 6–4 6–3 victim of German aggression that restricted his income to $27,500, half as much as Becker received. For the winner the result was ample revenge for the humiliation he had suffered at 'Gattone's' hands in the semi-final of the US Open the previous September.

There had been two notable first-round casualties. First the No. 4 seed, Pat Cash, had crashed 6–3 7–6 to the Italian *Davis Cup* man, Paolo Cane, and then Jonas Svensson, the No. 6 seed from Sweden, had been overpowered by the Yugoslav giant, Slobodan Zivojinovic. The two victors met in the quarter-finals with Zivojinovic prevailing 6–1 6–1 to set up a meeting with his doubles partner, Becker. This proved to be another hard-hitting affair with the world's No. 2 beating a man ranked 28 places below him 6–2 3–6 6–2.

Later, as the official favourites, they combined successfully to take the doubles title and the first prize of $8,250 by beating the second-seeded Spaniards, Sergio Casal and Emilio Sanchez, 3–6 6–3 6–4. – G. C.

MILAN 30 MARCH–5 APRIL

MEN'S SINGLES – Quarter-finals: B. Becker (FRG) d. J. Hlasek (SUI) 6–4 6–2; S. Zivojinovic (YUG) d. P. Cane (ITA) 6–1 6–1; M. Mecir (TCH) d. T. Smid (TCH) 6–4 6–4; M. Wilander (SWE) d. E. Sanchez (ESP) 6–3 6–1. ***Semi-finals:*** Becker d. Zivojinovic 6–2 3–6 6–2; Mecir d. Wilander 6–0 6–2. ***Final:*** Becker d. Mecir 6–4 6–3.

MEN'S DOUBLES – Final: Becker/Zivojinovic d. S. Casal (ESP)/Sanchez 3–6 6–3 6–4.

SEGMENT 3: 13 APRIL–17 MAY

Richard Evans, Neil Harman, John Parsons and Peter Alfano

SUNTORY JAPAN OPEN ($400,000)

With an upgrade to Super Series status, a new sponsor in Suntory, and a brand new stadium to house it, the Japan Open was virtually unrecognisable from the autumn event of previous years. Even the date was different and, appropriately, the new-look tournament arrived with the spring – cherry blossom time in the land of the rising sun.

Stefan Edberg saw the sun rise but six times in as swift a round-the-world raid on a Grand Prix event as it would be possible to imagine. Flying in from the WCT finals in Dallas on the Monday and out again to Monte Carlo on the Sunday night, the 21-year-old Swede became the new Japan Open champion with a 7–6 6–4 victory over David Pate in the final. Edberg won just as he had done against the dangerous, free-hitting Andres Gomez in the semi-final; by playing the percentages and heeding the sound advice of the coach, Tony Pickard, to 'Hang in there and concentrate on percentage tennis'.

Harnessing Edberg's stylish serve-and-volley game to the dictates of percentage – and therefore winning – tennis had been Pickard's greatest achievement with his young charge, and it had turned Edberg into the most consistent performer on the tour during the first six months of 1987. The Japan Open was his fourth singles title in seven events.

Edberg might have had a tougher road to the final, because Ivan Lendl, Miloslav Mecir and Jimmy Connors were all in the top half of the draw, but none made it even as far as the semi-finals. It was Lendl's first appearance since his knee operation six weeks before and, as he admitted after Pate had edged him out of the second round in an exciting encounter, 7–6 in the third-set tie-break, he had not expected miracles. Obviously not match tight, the world No. 1 was unable to seize the chances he created for himself, and when he had a clear look at a backhand pass up the line at 3–3 in the deciding tie-break – and missed – it merely emphasised the difficulties facing a top player trying to re-establish himself after injury.

Both Mecir and Connors fell to a man who always seems to do well in the Japanese capital, Scott Davis. In 1983 the tall Californian had reached the final of the Seiko Classic and in 1985 had won the Japan Open when it was still a Regular Series event. Now, once again, the conditions were as favourable for him as they were unfavourable for Mecir, the new WCT Champion, who had managed to beat Tsuyoshi Fukui in the second round but who still looked heavily jet-lagged by the time he met the American. Fast cement courts and rock-hard balls would not be Mecir's idea of heaven in any case and he duly succumbed to Davis's superior fire-power 7–5 6–1.

In the quarters, Davis quickly set about extending his 2–1 career advantage over Connors. Going for his returns and producing a high percentage of first serves, Davis won 6–3 6–4, and was comfortably the better player on the day. Against all the odds, considering the strength of the top half of the draw, Davis then found himself facing his doubles partner in the semi-final. It should have been anybody's match, but Pate dealt with the wind better and served far more consistently to win convincingly, 7–5 6–1.

During this historic week for Japanese tennis Edberg had to share top billing with the new stadium itself, now the centre-piece of the Ariake complex that serves as the headquarters of the game in Japan. Anders Jarryd, who partnered Gomez to the doubles final, where they lost to Kevin Curren and Paul Annacone 6–4 7–6, was just one of many

A springtime winner of the Tournament of Champions in singles, as well as Monte Carlo and Boston in doubles with Gildemeister, the giant Ecuadorian, Andres Gomez, also finished the year on a high note with the birth of his son in December. *(T. Hindley)*

players who enjoyed the atmosphere created inside the 10,000 seat arena. Named the Ariake Coliseum because it has been designed in that circular Roman style, the stadium has benefited considerably from the expert technical advice offered to the architects by the ITF's Asian representative Eiichi Kawatei, who had also been responsible for the development of the future Olympic arena, built along the same lines, in Seoul. – R. E.

TOKYO, 13–19 APRIL
MEN'S SINGLES – Quarter-finals: D. Pate (USA) d. J. Kriek (USA) 7–5 6–2; S. Davis (USA) d. J. S. Connors (USA) 6–3 6–4; A. Gomez (ECU) d. A. Agassi (USA) 6–2 6–0; S. Edberg (SWE) d. A. Jarryd (SWE) 6–3 6–2. ***Semi-finals:*** Pate d. Davis 7–5 6–1; Edberg d. Gomez 4–6 7–6 6–2. ***Final:*** Edberg d. Pate 7–6 6–4.
MEN'S DOUBLES – Final: P. Annacone (USA)/K. Curren (USA) d. Gomez/Jarryd 6–4 7–6.

MONTE CARLO OPEN ($415,000)

When Ion Tiriac chose Wednesday night at the sumptuous Hermitage Hotel to unveil his 'Touch of Class' range of rackets and tennis shoes, he didn't think that Boris Becker, playing in his home tournament, would already be out of the Monte Carlo Open. All the trimmings were there. Caviar flown in fresh from Paris, the best of wines, the most succulent of meats, and Becker, in bow-tie and tails, looking slightly forlorn and out of place. For Boris was the tournament's most surprised and surprising opening-round casualty when Jimmy Arias, whose descent down the rankings had been almost as swift as Becker's progress the other way, stunned the crowd and the West German with a 6–3 6–3 victory.

Arias should not really have been in a fit enough condition to set Becker such a serious test. Having just returned from the United States *Davis Cup* débâcle in Paraguay, he had visited a sports psychologist in an attempt to sort out the mental side of his game. Whatever had been said to him carried Arias all the way to the tournament's final, where he met Sweden's Mats Wilander.

It wasn't always enough to entice the élite of Monaco from their sumptuous lunches, but Wilander's play was impeccable throughout the first real test of the European clay-court season. His methodical, rhythmic march under blessed blue skies and warming sunshine was a foretaste of his summer of plenty. The only set he dropped in the tournament was the first in the final against Arias, the shock of which indiscretion jolted the Swede into a performance of total authority, and a 4–6 7–5 6–1 6–3 victory. 'I feel comfortable here, and this was a very good week for me', said Wilander, who counted Jan Gunnarsson, Thierry Tulasne, and Andrei Chesnokov among his victims on his way to the semi-final, where he met fellow-Swede Ulf Stenlund.

It was Stenlund who had first come to our attention in 1986 when he had beaten Anders Jarryd, among others, to reach the fourth round of the French Open. Earlier in the week, he'd put out Stefan Edberg, the second seed, in three sets, and followed that with a quarter-final success over Martin Jaite of Argentina, 2–6 6–0 7–6 (8–6). So Wilander believed he would be given the toughest test of the week, but instead powered his way to the final 6–2 6–2 against a player who seemed unnerved at the prospect of meeting the world's No. 5.

Arias had steered a safe passage through the other half, with a 7–5 6–1 victory over the 18-year-old Austrian, Horst Skoff, about whom we will undoubtedly hear much in the future. Skoff is a pugnacious, irascible teenager who upset a number of his opponents, notably Andres Gomez, with his constant, irritating querying of line-calls. But there was no doubting his attitude to competition, and clay seems to be the surface on which he will prosper the most.

If Arias, Skoff and even Becker gave us plenty to enjoy from the singles week, then the doubles event was a triumph – or almost – for one of the most spectacular players on the circuit. Mansoor Bahrami is an Iranian now living in France, thick-set, almost portly, sporting a prominent moustache and playing tennis with an indefatigable panache. Everyone wanted him and his Danish partner, Michael Mortensen, to win the doubles final, and they showed in flourishes that they might. But the partnership of Hans Gildemeister and Andres Gomez, among the most formidable in the game, was ultimately too skilful for them and won the final 6–2 6–4. – N. H.

20–26 APRIL
MEN'S SINGLES – Quarter-finals: J. Arias (USA) d. K. Carlsson (SWE) 6–0 2–2 ret'd; H. Skoff (AUT) d. A. Gomez (ECU) 7–5 2–6 6–4; M. Wilander (SWE) d. A. Chesnokov (URS) 6–1 6–3; U. Stenlund (SWE) d. M. Jaite (ARG) 2–6 6–0 7–6. ***Semi-finals:*** Arias d. Skoff 7–5 6–1; Wilander d. Stenlund 6–2 6–2. ***Final:*** Wilander d. Arias 4–6 7–5 6–1 6–3.
MEN'S DOUBLES – Final: H. Gildemeister (CHI)/Gomez d. M. Bahrami (IRN)/M. Mortensen (DEN) 6–2 6–4.

EBEL GERMAN OPEN ($300,000)

The skies were grey and forbidding, the courts often damp and slippery at the Ebel German Open in Hamburg, but there was a record attendance of 89,000, and for Ivan Lendl, striving to prove that his game was starting to flourish again after his arthroscopic knee surgery in March, there was no doubt that spring had arrived.

In his first clay-court tournament since winning the French Open almost a year earlier, Lendl shrugged aside potential disasters in both the quarter- and semi-finals to overwhelm a meagre Miloslav Mecir challenge in the final, 6–1 6–3 6–3. The wonderfully deceptive and exhilarating shots which Mecir had produced to upset his former *Davis Cup* team-mate when they last met in Key Biscayne were a million memories away. As Lendl observed after winning his first Nabisco Grand Prix title of the year: 'Milo played horribly. He didn't do anything right and wasn't able to lift himself out of it.'

Having lost his opening service game in all three sets, Mecir was always under pressure, and at 0–2 in the third set was in such a daze that he went to change ends when it was not time to do so. Yet he had progressed into the final at the expense of Cassio Motta, Milan Srejber, Martin Jaite, and Eduardo Bengoechea without conceding a set.

For Lendl, with Paris 1987 starting to appear in his sights, it was an arduous, sometimes exasperating week, but also a rewarding one. He began with a 6–2 6–1 defeat of Darren Cahill in 56 highly efficient minutes, with six aces. Then Sweden's Jan Gunnarsson was beaten by the same score before Lendl's shortage of match play almost proved his undoing against the Frenchman, Thierry Tulasne. Trailing by a set and 2–4, by which time his forehand had broken down worryingly and his serve was clearly in need of remedial confidence, the top seed was fortunate that Tulasne had neither a sturdy enough game, nor a cool enough temperament to accept the golden opportunity on offer.

The following day Lendl had an even closer call. Sweden's Kent Carlsson, tagged 'the bouncing ball' on the circuit because of the way every shot against him seems to come bouncing back, went within two points of beating the World Champion, but finally lost 3–6 7–5 6–0 in 2 hours 53 minutes. Carlsson, whose punishing style puts as much physical and mental wear on himself as it does on most opponents, took the first set in 52 minutes and then broke for 4–3 in the second. Yet although he reached 30–15 when serving for the match at 5–4, Lendl produced his sternest and most damaging two forehands of the week and the young man's chance was gone.

Lendl was not the only happy man in the rain. The unseeded Eduardo Bengoechea of Argentina, whose drop-shots were a memorable feature of the week, reached his first Super-Series semi-final, beating Swedes Joakim Nystrom and Mikael Pernfors on the way. For the eleven West Germans in the draw, it was a less happy week, only Hans Schwaier and Damir Keretic surviving the first round.

In the doubles, there was a second-round shock for the top seeds, Emilio Sanchez and Sergio Casal of Spain. Their unseeded victors, Claudio Mezzadri and Jim Pugh, went on to reach the final, where, in an an exciting struggle, they went down 4–6 7–6 6–2 to Mecir and Tomas Smid. – J. P.

HAMBURG 27 APRIL–3 MAY
MEN'S SINGLES – Quarter-finals: I. Lendl (TCH) d. T. Tulasne (FRA) 4–6 6–4 6–3; K. Carlsson (SWE)

d. E. Sanchez (ESP) 6–2 6–1; E. Bengoechea (ARG) d. M. Pernfors (SWE) 6–4 6–1; M. Mecir (TCH) d. M. Jaite (ARG) 6–1 6–3. ***Semi-finals:*** Lendl d. Carlsson 3–6 7–5 6–0; Mecir d. Bengoechea 7–6 6–1. ***Final:*** Lendl d. Mecir 6–1 6–3 6–3.
MEN'S DOUBLES – Final: Mecir/T. Smid (TCH) d. C. Mezzadri (ITA)/J. Pugh (USA) 4–6 7–6 6–2.

WCT TOURNAMENT OF CHAMPIONS ($500,000)

The stately Tudor club-house and quaint country-club atmosphere appealed to Andres Gomez. So did the tradition surrounding Forest Hills, once the site of the US Open, where, ten years earlier, Guillermo Vilas of Argentina had won the last Open played at the West Side Tennis Club. Gomez mastered the same Har-Tru clay courts, to defeat defending champion Yannick Noah 6–4 7–6 7–6, and won the Shearson Lehman Brothers Tournament of Champions.

Coming in the middle of the European clay-court season, the tournament is geographically out of place, suffering a depleted field. It is also plagued by the erratic springtime weather in New York, which ranged from rain and a temperature of 38°F on the first day to an unseasonably warm 87°F for Sunday's final. Forest Hills is also one of only three clay-court tournaments remaining in the United States – a number that will decrease to two when Indianapolis switches to hard courts in 1988. 'We do stand out as a sore thumb', said Owen Williams, chief executive officer of WCT. 'But we are committed to the tournament.'

None of this detracted from the way Gomez moved smartly through the field, playing an unspectacular but efficient brand of tennis, built around strong groundstrokes and a better net game than he is generally known for. The 27-year-old fourth seed from Ecuador was quicker than he appeared, moving about like an apparition, materialising in the right place at the right time, as if reading his opponent's mind. Despite having won no tournament since November 1986, he easily advanced to the quarter-finals, before being taken to three sets by Martin Jaite of Argentina. In Saturday's semi-final, he spoiled the prospect of a Yannick Noah-Boris Becker final when he defeated the West German 4–6 6–4 6–3.

Although seeded one in the Tournament of Champions, Becker is not at his best on clay, but he was hoping to show some improvement. He had impressive victories against Horatio de la Pena and Vilas, but lost to Gomez when his serve abandoned him. In the midst of an erratic year, the 19-year-old West German was less than gracious in defeat. 'My serve was terrible', he said. 'I was the better player all the way. I had so many break-points, so many easy shots. And Gomez could have closed his eyes and put the ball in the court.'

Noah had barely perspired as he routed his opponents in the bottom half of the draw, losing his serve only once before the final. An early-season foot injury was no longer troubling him as he showed his customary athletic grace, pausing to exchange pleasantries with the fans and his opponents. 'When I am fit and healthy, I enjoy playing anyone', he said. 'I'm like a racehorse, though. I'm fast, but I break all the time.'

He had defeated Slobodan Zivojinovic in straight sets in the semi-final, although the lumbering serve-and-volleyer from Yugoslavia played surprisingly well on clay. Noah's string of routine victories came to an abrupt halt against Gomez, who won for the fifth time in six matches against the Frenchman. Despite his flamboyant manner, which brought appreciative bursts of applause from the crowd, Noah always found Gomez waiting on the other side of the net, racket poised, ready to hit a winner.

As Gomez signed autographs for fans an hour after his victory, Noah was back on the court, salvaging at least the doubles championship. He and Guy Forget of France defeated Gary Donnelly and Peter Fleming of the US, 4–6 6–4 6–1. – P. A.

FOREST HILLS, NEW YORK, 4–10 MAY
MEN'S SINGLES – Quarter-finals: B. Becker (FRG) d. G. Vilas (ARG) 7–6 6–2; A. Gomez (ECU) d. M. Jaite (ARG) 6–4 3–6 6–4; S. Zivojinovic (YUG) d. P. Annacone 5–7 7–5 6–4; Y. Noah (FRA) d. A. Krickstein 6–2 6–3. ***Semi-finals:*** Gomez d. Becker 4–6 6–4 6–3; Noah d. Zivojinovic 6–3 7–5. ***Final:*** Gomez d. Noah 6–4 7–6 7–6.
MEN'S DOUBLES – Final: Noah/G. Forget (FRA) d. G. Donnelly/P. Fleming 4–6 6–4 6–1.

Clay-court specialist Martin Jaite of Argentina was runner-up in Rome to Wilander, whom he later beat in the final at Barcelona. *(T. Hindley)*

ITALIAN OPEN ($400,000)

Ending a nine-year drought for the Swedes in Rome, Mats Wilander claimed his second clay-court title of Europe's spring season when he defeated the 11th-seeded Argentinian, Martin Jaite, 6–3 6–4 6–4 in a predictably one-sided final. Jaite, small, neat and consistent, had an excellent week and proved he can handle the pressure of an Italian crowd yelling for one of its own when he outfought the talented Paolo Cane over three tough sets in the quarter-finals. Just as impressively Joakim Nystrom was brushed aside 6–3 6–1 in the semis. But Wilander was another story. Although there is much similarity in style between the two men, the Swede is simply one class better than the Argentinian.

Wilander, in fact, was looking a class better than just about everyone for most of the week. The Swede's win in Monte Carlo had fine-tuned his game to what, for his opponents, had become an exasperatingly high level of efficiency. So there was never a great deal of doubt that Wilander would end this strange run of failure for his countrymen at the Foro Italico. Not many Super Series events on the Grand Prix tour have escaped the clutches of this new generation of Swedes, but one had to go back to Bjorn Borg in 1978 to find another Swedish winner in Rome. Nor had Sweden provided a finalist in the intervening years. In fact Wilander was joining a very exclusive club, because prior to Borg Jan-Erik Lundquist in 1964 was the only other Swede to win the Italian title.

Even the United States has produced more champions than that and Americans are not famous for their success on European clay. Like Jimmy Connors, who is still without a singles title on clay in Europe, John McEnroe has always found the surface a hindrance to his ambitions, so it was something of a surprise when the former world No. 1 made a last-minute decision to make his first-ever appearance at the Foro Italico. McEnroe had been warned off Rome numerous times in the past by people who had seen what Italian crowds could do to even the most docile performers. If they had thrown coins at Borg, what would they do with McEnroe?

But those who actually feared for McEnroe's safety were forgetting that he had already pronounced his love for the country after numerous appearances in Milan and, acting on the shrewd advice of his friend, Sergio Palmieri, had accepted Cane as his doubles partner for the week. Sensing that this was something of a special occasion, McEnroe compounded all this good preparation by immediately giving a clenched-fist salute like some Roman Emperor of old when he walked on court for his first-round match against the 17-year-old Franco Davin. Instantly he was annointed by the noisy throng and, to many people's disbelief, there began a love affair between McEnroe and the Roman crowd which lasted throughout the week.

McEnroe's week might have been brief had not some Irish-American gremlin worked its way into the Rome power-plant and switched the lights off. As Davin was leading 6–3 2–0 at the time, McEnroe was more than somewhat relieved. 'That was really nice of them', McEnroe joked afterwards. 'The half-hour break allowed me to get my head together.' A touch of farce invaded the proceedings when the lights went off again four games after the resumption, but McEnroe's humour remained intact and, having finally beaten the promising young Argentinian, he went on to battle his way past three clay-court specialists in Horatio de la Pena, Aaron Krickstein and Claudio Mezzadri.

Although he dropped the first set to Krickstein and the second on the tie-break to Mezzadri, McEnroe survived through a somewhat desperate mixture of dubious defence and hair-raising sorties to the net. There were, however, signs that he was coming to terms with it all, and there was no doubt that he was enjoying it. It was, as he said, a rare experience to have an entire stadium willing him to win, and he responded by behaving in virtually impeccable fashion. The behaviour remained just as good in his semi-final against Wilander but, unfortunately for the crowd, his tennis did not. He served well enough but the volleys which had been giving him so much cause for concern let him down again and Wilander won with embarrassing ease, 6–1 6–3.

The main upset of the week came in the third round when Joakim Nystrom defeated Ivan Lendl, 6–4 2–6 6–3. Tempting fate, Lendl had been saying a couple of days earlier that he was afraid of peaking too soon for the French Open, and perhaps it would not be a bad thing for him to lose a match for a change. He didn't intend to lose to Nystrom, but as soon as the elegant Swede started finding the smooth rhythm on his passing shots, Lendl's aggressive tactics proved pure folly.

The No. 3 seed, Miloslav Mecir, had made an even earlier exit, being beaten 6–1 3–6 6–4 by Anders Jarryd, one of those Swedes he usually beats with ease. But there was an explanation, if not an excuse. Mecir had played an exhibition in Tokyo the week before, giving himself no time to acclimatise.

It was ironic that, during a week that found McEnroe on his best behaviour, his doubles partner, Cane, a volatile character at the best of times, should end up with $4,000-worth of fines for various Code of Conduct infringements. Cane was, however, able to cover some of the cost by reaching the semi-finals of the doubles with McEnroe. They were beaten at that stage by Mecir and Tomas Smid, who eventually lost 6–2 6–7 6–3 in the final to Yannick Noah and Guy Forget, who had also won in New York the week before. – R. E.

ROME, 11–17 MAY
MEN'S SINGLES – Quarter-finals: J. Nystrom (SWE) d. K. Carlsson (SWE) 5–7 7–5 6–1; M. Jaite (ARG) d. P. Cane 3–6 7–6 6–4; J. P. McEnroe (USA) d. C. Mezzadri (SUI) 6–1 6–7 6–3; M. Wilander (SWE) d. A. Gomez (ECU) 6–1 6–2. ***Semi-finals:*** Jaite d. Nystrom 6–3 6–4; Wilander d. McEnroe 6–1 6–3. ***Final:*** Wilander d. Jaite 6–3 6–4 6–4.
MEN'S DOUBLES – Final: G. Forget (FRA)/Y. Noah (FRA) d. M. Mecir (TCH)/T. Smid (TCH) 6–2 6–7 6–3.

SEGMENT 4: 6 JULY–2 AUGUST

Bud Collins, Josh Young and John Feinstein

US PROFESSIONAL CHAMPIONSHIPS ($232,000)

Founded in 1877, the Longwood Club in Boston, which hosted the inaugural *Davis Cup* contest in 1900, supports the longest-running professional tourney, the US Pro. In a foolish time when clay is beginning to seem a species as endangered as grass, Longwood fights almost alone against the insidious and short-sighted rush to pave America and make the game tarmac tennis. Only New York (Forest Hills's Tournament of Champions), Indianapolis (National Clay) and Boston remained as refuges for European, Latin and other determined dirt-kickers. Nobody knew how long the first two would hold their gritty ground, but Longwood members voted down an asphalt proposal, and 65,000 customers for the US Pro seemed to approve.

Celebrating its 60th anniversary, the US Pro has been a haven for Swedes and Spanish-speaking visitors since 1974, when Bjorn Borg began his three-title run, followed by Manolo Orantes, the victor in 1977–78, and José Higueras in 1979. It was '*Heja Sverige*!' (Sweden over all), for sure, this time since the finalists were Mats Wilander from Vaxjo, champion in 1985, and that good-natured son-of-a-twitch, Kent Carlsson from Eskilstuna.

Yet Martin Jaite of Argentina had looked a likely finalist when, in the semis, he was firing at Wilander like Muhammad Ali knocking out Sonny Liston in the first round. Before you could conjugate the Swedish verb *slakt* (to slaughter), Jaite had won the first seven games, and was poised to deliver the *coup de grâce* as he served at 5–3, 30–15 in the second set. Jaite, loser of the two previous Longwood finals (1985 to Wilander, 1986 to Andres Gomez), had turned around a quarter-final to remove the 1984 champ, Aaron Krickstein, 1–6 6–4 6–1. Then it happened to him, two points away from a reversal of the Italian Open final, when he knocked a forehand long to 30-all, and never even got to match-point, as Wilander firmed up suddenly to pull the strange-looking score his way, 0–6 7–5 6–0.

Andres Gomez, who had barely subdued Kent Carlsson in the 1986 semis, couldn't hold off the Swede this time, losing 7–5 4–6 7–5. Even though Gomez broke serve for a 4–3 lead in the third set, and had never before lost to Carlsson, the grunting, quivering Swede finished strongly. Carlsson, who had missed Wimbledon, had arrived in Boston fresh and eager. But he was not ready for Wilander, who prevailed 7–6 (7–5) 6–1 in two topspinning hours, 87 minutes being devoted to the first set, in which Wilander trailed 2–4. But he broke back to win the last two points of a tense tie-break, plus the first eight points of the second set.

Losing only that bageled first set to the Argentinian, Wilander had otherwise breezed to the final. In the quarters he cooled the tourney's unexpected hot-shot, 22-year-old Dutchman Tom Nijssen. Ranked 148th, Nijssen registered his first three Grand Prix singles victories, bumping the eighth and ninth seeds, Tarik Benhabiles and Thierry Tulasne of France, before Wilander got him 6–2 7–5.

Preventing an entirely Swedish gala on finals day, the Chilean-Ecuadorean coalition of Hans Gildemeister and Gomez took their second successive US Pro doubles title, 7–6 (7–3) 3–6 6–1 over Wilander and Joakim Nystrom. – B. C.

BOSTON, 6–12 JULY
MEN'S SINGLES – Quarter-finals: M. Wilander (SWE) d. T. Nijssen (HOL) 6–2 7–5; M. Jaite (ARG) d. A. Krickstein 1–6 6–4 6–1; K. Carlsson (SWE) d. J. Nystrom (SWE) 6–1 7–5; A. Gomez (ECU) d. J.

Kent Carlsson's excessive topspin, while disconcerting his opponents, results in exceptionally long rallies, putting a great strain on his joints. At the age of 19, he underwent arthroscopic knee surgery for the third time in 1987. (Carol L. Newsom)

Arias 2–6 7–5 7–6. ***Semi-finals:*** Wilander d. Jaite 0–6 7–5 6–0; Carlsson d. Gomez 7–5 4–6 7–5. ***Final:*** Wilander d. Carlsson 7–6 6–1.
MEN'S DOUBLES – Final: H. Gildemeister (CHI)/Gomez d. Nystrom/Wilander 7–6 3–6 6–1.

US CLAY COURT CHAMPIONSHIPS ($300,000)

Nothing ever seemed to change in Indianapolis at the US Open Clay Court Championships, until 1987, when the tournament had enough changes to last forever. The draw is virtually the same every year, filled with the world's premier clay-courters but missing the big drawing cards who sell tickets. And Indianapolis has always had both men and women, which is rare for a non-Grand Slam event. This time, though, there was no women's event, mainly because the Pan American Games, which began two weeks after the date when the tournament is traditionally held, forced a change to a time-slot the women's tour couldn't accommodate. But that wasn't the only off-court action going on. The big talk was the possibility of the National Championships dying altogether, as officials announced they were following the trend in the US and paving over the courts for 1988.

On court, the action reached its climax on a traditionally humid Indianapolis afternoon, when Mats Wilander joined the élite list of title holders with a 7–5 6–3 victory over Kent Carlsson in the final. The two Swedes were contesting a final for the second time in as many weeks, with the result the same: Wilander winning a long straight-sets match. Wilander had marched through the tournament without losing a set, and against Carlsson he simply played at a higher level throughout the two hour five minute match. The 22-year-old Wilander attacked behind his ever-improving slice backhand when the opportunity arose, but when Carlsson began hitting those heavy topspin balls, Wilander wore him down at his own game.

The semi-finals were similar to the final, in that it was hot and the rallies were long. Wilander eliminated his friend and doubles partner, Joakim Nystrom, 6–4 7–5, for his eleventh consecutive win in their meetings. Commented Nystrom: 'I know I am going to beat him some day, but it may not be until the over 35s.' In the other semi-final, Carlsson outlasted Guillermo Perez Roldan, whose draw was cleared by South African Gary Muller.

Court One became the burial ground for past champions. First, rookie pro Richey Reneberg, a serve-and-volleyer, upset 1983 champion Jimmy Arias 6–7 (5–7) 6–4 11–9. Reneberg, who had pushed Ivan Lendl to four sets at Wimbledon the month before, fought off seven match-points before coming away with the victory. Like Reneberg, who eventually lost in the quarter-finals to Wilander, Muller served and volleyed his way to a big upset when he eliminated second-seeded Andres Gomez 6–4 4–6 6–4. Gomez, looking for his third Clay Court title in four years, made tired errors the entire match, while Muller played solid tennis for all three sets.

The planned move to hard courts came as no surprise to most people who have watched the US Clay Court attendance figures hit new lows each year. The United States Tennis Association was exploring several new sites, mostly in the southern US, but admitted that it may not be possible to bring the men and women back to the same week. The women's event, planned for Seattle, was not played in 1987, owing to the lack of a sponsor, and nobody will be surprised if the men's event suffers the same fate in 1988. Wilander may prove to have been the last US Clay Court champion.

However, Wilander did not have it all his own way in Indianapolis. In the doubles final he paired with his usual partner, Nystrom, but the Swedes were overwhelmed by the scratch US-Australian pairing of Blaine Willenborg and Laurie Warder whose 6–0 6–3 victory earned them $8,100 each. – J. Y.

INDIANAPOLIS, 13–19 JULY
MEN'S SINGLES – Quarter-finals: M. Wilander (SWE) d. R. Reneberg 6–4 6–4; J. Nystrom (SWE) d. M. Jaite (ARG) 7–6 6–0; K. Carlsson (SWE) d. P. Kuhnen (FRG) 7–6 6–1; G. Perez Roldan (ARG) d. G. Muller (RSA) 1–6 6–3 6–4. ***Semi-finals:*** Wilander d. Nystrom 6–4 7–5; Carlsson d. Perez Roldan 6–2 6–2. ***Final:*** Wilander d. Carlsson 7–5 6–3.
MEN'S DOUBLES – Final: L. Warder (AUS)/B. Willenborg d. Nystrom/Wilander 6–0 6–3.

SOVRAN BANK DC NATIONAL TENNIS CLASSIC ($232,000)

The stars came back to Washington in 1987. For several years the Sovran Bank/DC National Tennis Classic had suffered a definite star-gap, because none of the big names wanted to play a clay-court tournament in sweltering conditions five weeks before the US Open was played on a hard court. So they changed the playing surface, and there were Ivan Lendl, Boris Becker and Jimmy Connors entering the field.

Unfortunately, even with the new DecoTurf II courts in place, few of their high-ranked compatriots accompanied them, most still opting for cooler warm-ups in Vermont or Canada. The top-heavy nature of the field, with three of the world's top six but only four of the top 25, made for a week of less-than-sterling tennis, in which Lendl and Connors produced the best match of the tournament in the semi-finals, Lendl winning 6–4 7–6 (7–3). The final, though, was a cruel joke with Lendl publicly humiliating a nervous Brad Gilbert 6–1 6–0 in 56 minutes.

Gilbert came into the match with an 0–11 career record against Lendl and following a desultory 3–6 6–3 6–0 semi-final win over Becker. It is difficult to play down an upset of Becker, but as Becker himself said, 'It was not me out there all week'. Becker came to Washington the day after West Germany had beaten the United States 3–2 in the *Davis Cup* relegation tie in Hartford. Having played almost seven hours to beat John McEnroe in one singles match, and four hours to beat Tim Mayotte in the deciding match, he was exhausted, drained and nursing an inflamed elbow. He didn't play well to reach the semi-finals and played even worse once there.

Gilbert's week wasn't much better than Becker's, and his first semi-final set was horrendous. 'I was embarrassed to be out there', he said. 'I had no idea what to do. After the first set I realised he wasn't playing much better than I was, and if I could just get into the net a little, I could win. I was surprised though. Boris just played horribly.'

Lendl didn't play much better at the start of the week, losing the first set in his third-round match against 18-year-old American David Wheaton, a wild-card entry. The Czech came back to win 6–7 (7–5) 6–3 6–2, but it wasn't easy in the brutal heat. When the match was over, he had to be treated for heat exhaustion and defaulted his doubles match. The World Champion also needed three sets in the quarter-finals to beat Jimmy Arias, who reached 4-all in the third set, before a couple of crucial errors did him in.

The top four seeds reached the semi-finals for the first time in the 19-year history of the tournament. There Lendl and Connors produced the most entertaining match of the week, in which Connors served for the second set but played, in his words, 'a god-awful game', to let Lendl break back. Lendl then won the tie-break with three extraordinary backhand winners. 'I thought we both played about as well as we can play', Connors said, after losing to Lendl for a 12th straight time. 'That's the best I've seen him serve in a long time. And I still hung right with him.' The next night, Gilbert hung close for two points, reaching 15-all in the opening game, but after that it was all Lendl as he won Washington for the second time.

The doubles was won by Peter Fleming and Gary Donnelly, who took their second title in as many weeks, beating Blaine Willenborg and Laurie Warder 6–2 7–6 (7–2) in the final. Willenborg and Warder had reached the final by saving two match-points on their way past top seeds Paul Annacone and Christo Van Rensburg in the semi-finals. – J. F.

WASHINGTON, DC, 27 JULY–2 AUGUST
MEN'S SINGLES – Quarter-finals: I. Lendl (TCH) d. J. Arias 6–3 4–6 6–4; J. S. Connors d. T. Witsken 6–3 2–6 6–2; B. Gilbert d. M. Davis 6–4 6–4; B. Becker (FRG) d. J. Berger 6–3 6–2. ***Semi-finals:*** Lendl d. Connors 6–4 7–6; Gilbert d. Becker 3–6 6–3 6–0. ***Final:*** Lendl d. Gilbert 6–1 6–0.
MEN'S DOUBLES – Final: G. Donnelly/P. Fleming d. L. Warder (AUS)/B. Willenborg 6–2 7–6.

Still struggling to return to his former fitness and top ranking, John McEnroe reached five finals in 1987 and captivated the crowds at the Italian Open, but could not avoid controversy and finished the year empty-handed and suspended. *(T. Hindley)*

SEGMENT 5: 3–23 AUGUST

Doug Smith and Nora McCabe

VOLVO INTERNATIONAL ($250,000)

Ivan 'Mr Scowl' Lendl and John 'Mr Growl' McEnroe attempted to renew their rivalry in the 1987 final of the $315,000 Volvo International. But the anticipated stormy showdown between two of the game's all-time greats was abandoned – because of stormy weather. McEnroe was leading 7–6 1–4 when a three-hour downpour suspended play and continued the next day. Although tournament director Jim Westhall made several attempts to reschedule the match, no suitable time could be arranged, so both players received runners-up prize money of $20,000 and runners-up Nabisco Grand Prix points of 210 apiece.

McEnroe, seeming ready to make a major step in his comeback bid, won the first set in 58 minutes, but play was halted for the first time in the second set with Lendl ahead 2–1, and umpire Richard Kaufman ordered three other two-minute delays to check the court before suspending play for the day. During the last delay, McEnroe smashed his racket against his equipment bag and complained about the slippery conditions, but while he fumed, Lendl engaged in tomfoolery, joking and chatting with the ESPN courtside cameraman and commentator Cliff Drysdale.

In 1982, when the tournament was held in North Conway, rain forced a 57-day postponement of the final between Lendl and José Higueras, a match which Lendl finally won in seven minutes. A 1984 tournament in Rotterdam between Jimmy Connors and Lendl was stopped because of a bomb scare, with Lendl leading 6–0 1–0, and was never finished. This time the rain wiped out Lendl's chance to score another victory against McEnroe – the player he has learned to hate. But it didn't prevent him from winning a battle of words. At a press conference earlier in the week, McEnroe said that he found the possibility of being Lendl's US *Davis Cup* teammate 'kind of hard to swallow'. (Lendl has applied for US citizenship and wants to play for the US *Davis Cup* team.) He responded: 'It's hard to imagine, with his mouth, he has a hard time to swallow something.'

McEnroe lost only one set in reaching the final, experiencing a mid-match mental lapse against Ben Testerman in the third round, but prevailing 7–6 (7–2) 0–6 6–1. He went on to defeat Brad Gilbert 6–3 6–2 in the quarter-finals and Christo Van Rensburg 6–4 6–2 in the semi-finals. Lendl's route to the final was a bit bumpier. He was pushed to three sets in the third round, defeating Robert Seguso 6–3 6–7 (4–7) 6–2, and also struggled to beat Andre Agassi 6–2 5–7 6–3 in a semi-final match.

Agassi, a 17-year-old from Las Vegas, was ordained the tournament's giant killer after defeating No. 3 seed Pat Cash 7–6 (10–8) 7–6 (8–6) in the second round. Greg Holmes was also impressive, serving 13 aces to upset the second seed, Jimmy Connors, 7–5 7–5 in the first round, and Joey Rive ousted No. 5 Tim Mayotte 7–6 (7–5) 2–6 6–4 in the third round. Holmes went out 6–1 6–4 to Van Rensburg in a third-round match, but Agassi, his two-tone punk hairdo flapping in the wind, stayed tough, eliminating Chip Hooper 6–4 6–7 (5–7) 6–3 in the third round and Rive 6–4 6–2 in the quarter-finals. He played with confidence and a huge forehand that he repeatedly smashed down the line or cross-court for winners.

Tournament officials flew Agassi's parents, Michael and Elizabeth, to Stratton Mountain to see their son test his arsenal against the World No. 1. After the match Agassi, admitting to nerves, said: 'Ivan had too many free points on his serve for me to stay in the match and get him worried. He served pretty big today. I think I have to work on a bigger serve and come in a lot more.'

The doubles final between top seeds Paul Annacone and Van Rensburg and second seeds Ken Flach and Robert Seguso was also cancelled. The week-long tournament had been sold out in advance. Moreover, before the 1987 event had ended, more than 42,000 tickets had been sold for the 1988 event. – D. S.

STRATTON MOUNTAIN, VERMONT, 3–9 AUGUST
MEN'S SINGLES – Quarter-finals: I. Lendl (TCH) d. K. Jones 6–3 6–1; A. Agassi d. J. Rive 6–4 6–2; J. P. McEnroe d. B. Gilbert 6–3 6–2; C. Van Rensburg (RSA) d. D. Visser (RSA) 6–2 6–3. ***Semi-finals:*** Lendl d. Agassi 6–2 5–7 6–3; McEnroe d. Van Rensburg 6–4 6–2. ***Final:*** McEnroe div'd with Lendl 7–6 1–4.
MEN'S DOUBLES – Final: P. Annacone/Van Rensburg div'd with K. Flach/R. Seguso.

PLAYER'S INTERNATIONAL CANADIAN OPEN ($300,000)

Ivan Lendl overcame stomach flu, inclement weather and a strong second-set challenge from the No. 2 seed, Stefan Edberg, to win his fourth Canadian title, 6–4 7–6. The victory was a tribute to the top-ranked Czech's fitness regime, for thanks to the rain that washed out Saturday's semi-finals, Lendl had to battle against a persistent stomach bug, sweltering humidity, and strong, swirling winds as well as Jimmy Connors and Edberg back-to-back on the same day. Only two hours after struggling to find his timing in his 7–5 6–4 win over Connors, Lendl was back on court to play Edberg in a 118-minute final. On this day when the power of his first serve and the accuracy of his passing strokes were also not up to snuff, Lendl took full advantage of the openings offered by the third- and sixth-ranked players.

Against Edberg, who held three break-points in the sixth game of the opening set and a 4–1 second-set lead, Lendl mixed up his deliveries and pressured the Swede's backhand return. This tactic both opened up the court for Lendl's passes and pressed Edberg until his backhand collapsed, producing 14 unforced errors. Not only did the Swede sacrifice some kick on his first and second serves in an unsuccessful attempt to reach the net faster to defend against Lendl's passes, but he also opted to serve primarily to Lendl's backhand, to the point that the Czech was able to anticipate the ball and win two-thirds of the points on his backhand returns. Although Edberg fought off four break-points in the 11th game of the second set to go up 6–5, Lendl held at 15 to force the tie-break which Lendl took 7–2, winning the last four points.

In fairness, Edberg had probably not recovered from the shock of mauling his third-seeded rival, defending champion Boris Becker, 6–2 6–4 in their semi-final. Taking advantage of an out-of-sorts Becker, who had psyched himself into believing he was too tired to play at 10 am after finishing a doubles match at 10 pm on Saturday, Edberg lost only nine points on his own serve and never allowed the West German one break-point during the 71-minute rout.

By contrast, in the other semi, the fourth-seeded Connors was much harder to subdue. Despite squandering three break-points in the fourth game of the match, Connors held serve, dropping only five points until the 11th game when he was double-faulted to be broken at 15. Rebounding, he saved three break-points in the first game of the second set, broke Lendl at deuce and held again for a 3–0 lead before the Czech found his timing, won the next five games and served out the match in the tenth game at 15.

Although both Lendl and Edberg advanced to the final without losing a set, it was the 34-year-old Connors who provided the tournament with its most memorable match: a thrilling three-set quarter-final tussle with sixth-seeded John McEnroe. For drama and sustained quality of all-court shotmaking from both men, Connors's rain-interrupted 6-3 3–6 6–3 victory was as fine a men's match as Canadian fans have witnessed in the past decade.

Connors broke McEnroe twice to take the first set. McEnroe survived two tough service games, then broke Connors in the sixth game to win the second. Undaunted, and aided by a McEnroe double-fault on break-point, Connors took a 2–0 third-set lead when rain forced a 47-minute delay. McEnroe came back recharged, broke Connors and held to even the set at 2–2. Both held for 3–3, then Connors broke again in the eighth game with a forehand service return winner to go up 5–3.

The biggest surprise of the tournament came when the unseeded Peter Lundgren of Sweden first upset fifth-seeded Wimbledon champion Pat Cash, 6–4 7–6, in the third round, then pushed Becker to three sets in the quarters with his steady but powerful backcourt game. Seventh-seeded Tim Mayotte was felled 6–2 5–7 6–3 by New Zealand's Kelly Evernden in his first match in the second round.

Canadian fans were given much to cheer about by two-time national champion Andrew Sznajder. Using his powerful forehand and improved backhand, Sznajder upset first giant-killer Peter Doohan 7–6 2–6 7–6 in the first round, then removed counterpunching American Greg Holmes 7–6 7–6 to reach the third round, where he succumbed 6–1 6–1 to Lendl.

Rain postponed the completion of the doubles final until 31 August at Flushing Meadow, where Cash, playing with Edberg, needed just two minutes to serve out a 6–7 6–4 6–3 win against the young Australians, Peter Doohan and Laurie Warder. – N. M.

MONTREAL, 10–16 AUGUST
MEN'S SINGLES – Quarter-finals: I. Lendl (TCH) d. S. Zivojinovic (YUG) 6–3 7–5; J. S. Connors (USA) d. J. P. McEnroe (USA) 6–3 3–6 6–3; B. Becker (FRG) d. P. Lundgren (SWE) 1–6 6–2 6–1; S. Edberg (SWE) d. K. Curren (USA) 7–6 7–5. ***Semi-finals:*** Lendl d. Connors 7–5 6–4; Edberg d. Becker 6–2 6–4. ***Final:*** Lendl d. Edberg 6–4 7–6.
MEN'S DOUBLES – Final: P. Cash (AUS)/Edberg d. P. Doohan (AUS)/L. Warder (AUS) 6–7 6–3 6–4.

ATP CHAMPIONSHIPS ($300,000)

Sweden's Stefan Edberg breezed through the field at the Thriftway ATP Championships, and defeated his former nemesis, Boris Becker, 6–4 6–1 in the final. His second consecutive victory against the West German, who leads their head-to-head series 7–4, earned him not only $48,000, but also, more importantly, an immeasurable dosage of confidence. Edberg solved the mystery of Becker's powerful serve by standing six feet behind the baseline on the return. He had beaten Becker in Montreal the previous week, but not by returning from that far behind the baseline. 'They used a livelier ball, and it was windy, so he stood back', explained Tony Pickard, Edberg's coach.

Top seed Mats Wilander's early exit gave him a few extra days to prepare for the US Open. He was ousted in the third round by Peter Lundgren, a new Swede on the rise, who beat Wilander 6–1 6–4. Wilander led 4–1 in the second set, but Lundgren then won five consecutive games, ending the match on a volley winner. 'It's the best feeling I've had as a tennis player', said the 22-year-old Lundgren, who used to be Bjorn Borg's opponent in exhibitions. 'Mats is No. 1 in Sweden and No. 2 in the world. That's a very good result.'

Despite Wilander's early demise, four Swedes reached the quarter-finals. Edberg and Lundgren were joined by Anders Jarryd and Mikael Pernfors, while the other quarter-finalists were Jimmy Connors, Nduka Odizor and Brad Gilbert. Jarryd fell 6–3 6–3 to Becker and Edberg stopped Connors 6–2 6–3 in the semis.

Connors, 34, continued his mastery of most of the young pros, eliminating 20-year-old Jay Berger 4–6 6–2 6–1 in the first round. 'He's pretty tough for me to play', said Connors. 'I can't get in against him because he always has that topspin jumping up at me.' Said Berger: 'Even when you're winning, you always have in the back of your mind that this guy is a great player. In my mind he's the greatest. I've never idolised any player, but I really admired and respected him and I admire him a lot more now that I've played him.'

John McEnroe, another American superstar on the decline, continued to suffer injury problems on the comeback trail and fell 7–6 (7–2) 6–4 to Annacone in the first round. The fifth seed, who had missed Wimbledon because of a back problem, experienced back pain while playing Annacone, who went on to defeat John Fitzgerald 6–2 6–1 before losing to Pernfors, 7–6 (7–5) 4–6 6–3, in the third round.

Seventeen-year-old American Andre Agassi upset Pat Cash and took Ivan Lendl to three sets at Stratton Mountain, before finishing the year with his first Grand Prix title at Itaparica. (A. Evans)

The second seeds, Ken Flach and Robert Seguso, won the doubles title, defeating Steve Denton and John Fitzgerald 7–5 6–3 in the final. Denton and Fitzgerald had upset the top-seeded team of Edberg and Jarryd 7–6 (7–4) 4–6 6–3 in the third round. – D. S.

CINCINNATI, 17–23 AUGUST
MEN'S SINGLES – Quarter-finals: A. Jarryd (SWE) d. P. Lundgren (SWE) 6–4 6–4; B. Becker (FRG) w.o. M. Pernfors (SWE); J. S. Connors d. N. Odizor (NIG) 6–1 6–7 6–3; S. Edberg (SWE) d. B. Gilbert 6–1 6–3. ***Semi-finals:*** Becker d. Jarryd 6–3 6–3; Edberg d. Connors 6–2 6–3. ***Final:*** Edberg d. Becker 6–4 6–1.
MEN'S DOUBLES – Final: K. Flach/R. Seguso d. S. Denton/J. Fitzgerald (AUS) 7–5 6–3.

SEGMENT 6: 21 SEPTEMBER–11 OCTOBER

Linda Pentz and Pedro Hernandez

LOS ANGELES ($250,000)

David Pate, seeded third, caused Sweden's Stefan Edberg to score an unwelcome hat-trick of his own at the $250,000 Volvo Tennis/Los Angeles tournament. Edberg was beaten by Pate 6–4 6–4 in the final, marking the third consecutive year in which the Swede has finished as bridesmaid in the Los Angeles event. 'I don't know if I'll ever win here', Edberg said, 'but I'm going to be back.'

Drained after a successful run to the semi-finals of the US Open two weeks earlier, Edberg could muster little inspiration in the final. Pate, on the other hand, enjoyed the support of a vociferous cheering section – many of his family live in LA – and his own explosive serve to keep Edberg at bay. He had struggled past fellow Las Vegan, Andre Agassi, and second-seeded Brad Gilbert in the quarter-finals and semi-finals respectively, both in close three-set matches.

Edberg, on the other hand, had enjoyed a relatively easy time, dismissing an ailing Paul Annacone in the quarter-finals and a tired Tim Wilkison in the semi-finals, both in straight sets. The match with Annacone was extraordinary in that the American began to play better after injuring his back early in the match, while Edberg seemed to fall into a stultified trance, apparently incapable of hitting the ball over the net in the face of his opponent's problems. 'It was the strangest feeling', said Edberg, who recovered consciousness in time to win 6–1 7–5. The match was also a disappointing reversal of their thrilling three-tie-break final of two years earlier, when Annacone had won the LA title.

The tournament's most unusual distinction was the appearance of Edberg's name on the list of code of conduct violations. Although he was not cited during the match, he was subsequently penalised by Grand Prix Supervisor, John Heiss, for unsportsmanlike conduct when he bounced a ball too close to a ballboy. An appeal was still pending at the time of writing.

The Los Angeles event marked the beginning of a renaissance for Eliot Teltscher, 28 and greying, who reached the quarter-finals. He was to repeat the feat a week later in San Francisco, going on to reach the final the following week in Scottsdale, and to take the title in Hong Kong in November. Marty Davis created a record of sorts by playing six consecutive tie-breaks (including one in the qualifying) *en route* to the quarter-finals, where he was beaten by Wilkison in a match that included yet another tie-break.

Pate made it a double payday by winning the doubles title with Kevin Curren, posting a 6–3 6–4 victory over Gilbert and Wilkison. – L. P.

21–27 SEPTEMBER
MEN'S SINGLES – Quarter-finals: S. Edberg (SWE) d. P. Annacone 6–1 7–5; T. Wilkison d. M. Davis 4–6 7–6 6–4; D. Pate d. A. Agassi 5–7 7–6 6–2; B. Gilbert d. E. Teltscher 6–1 6–4. ***Semi-finals:*** Edberg d. Wilkison 6–2 6–3; Pate d. Gilbert 6–3 6–7 6–3. ***Final:*** Pate d. Edberg 6–4 6–4.
MEN'S DOUBLES – Final: K. Curren/D. Pate d. Gilbert/Wilkison 6–3 6–4.

INTERNATIONAL CHAMPIONSHIPS OF SPAIN ($232,000)

By defeating Mats Wilander 7–6 (7–5) 6–4 4–6 0–6 6–4, Martin Jaite was able to overcome his personal psychosis and the hoodoo on Argentinian tennis in Barcelona by winning the Trofeo Conde de Godo. After he had won the first two sets with aggressive tennis, and a fifth set in which his heart carried him through the physical challenge, Jaite ended his

David Pate (left) beat Edberg to win Los Angeles, also taking the doubles title with Curren. In San Francisco the following week Peter Lundgren (below left) beat Jim Pugh (below right) in the final, having beaten Lendl in a sizzling semi.
(A. Evans, M. Cole, T. Hindley)

streak of six losses to Swedish players and became the first Argentinian to succeed in the International Spanish Championship, Guillermo Vilas having lost in the finals from 1980 to 1983. The triumph was significant for Jaite, being his first Super Series win and taking place, as he said, 'in that city where I first dreamed of becoming a professional tennis player'. Born in Buenos Aires, Argentina, but resident in Barcelona until the age of 20, Jaite competed for the Spanish flag in the Galea and Valerio Cups and continues to be a favourite of Barcelona's tennis fans.

Yet Jaite's own success was just a part of the triumphs enjoyed by the rest of the Argentinian contingent in the Real Club de Tenis de Barcelona. For the first time in Argentina's history, three players – Jaite, Eduardo Bengoechea and Guillermo Perez Roldan – reached the semi-finals of a Super Series event. It was also the first time that the Argentine team of Christian Miniussi and Javier Frana had reached the final of a Grand Prix tournament, losing to Miloslav Mecir and Tomas Smid. Two months before the Barcelona success, Jaite, Perez Roldan and Bengoechea had also reached the semi-finals in the Regular Series tournament in Hilversum.

Mats Wilander, whose impressive record in Barcelona showed 23 victories to only one loss before 1987, failed to become the first player to win the Trofeo Conde de Godo for the fourth time. Champion in 1982, 1983 and 1984, Wilander was defeated in 1985 by the Frenchman, Thierry Tulasne, losing the fifth set 0–6.

In 1987 the seeds imposed their authority in the competition, now expanded to 56 players. With the exception of No. 7 Jan Gunnarsson, they all reached the quarter-finals, Gunnarsson's spot being filled by Spain's 19-year-old Tomas Carbonell, a wild-card entry. Playing in his home club, he enjoyed his best career performance in beating Sweden's Bergstrom, Gunnarsson and Claudio Mezzadri of Switzerland. The biggest surprise, though, took place in the quarter-finals with the defeats by the Argentinian heroes of No. 2 Mecir, No. 3 Andres Gomez and fourth-seeded Emilio Sanchez. Bengoechea, seeded eight, defeated Mecir 6–4 6–1, while Perez Roldan continued a successful season, which took him into the top 20, with the help of the shoulder injury that forced Andres Gomez to abandon their match when 3–6 0–1 down.

In their eagerly anticipated quarter-final, Jaite smashed the dreams of local favourite Emilio Sanchez by defeating him 6–3 7–6 (7–0) as the Spanish player suffered from 'the pressure of responsibility of performing well at home'. The only favourite to sail easily into the semi-finals was Mats Wilander, who took 59 minutes to defeat Carbonell 6–0 6–3. Making his task look easy, Wilander then overcame Perez Roldan 6–3 6–0 in the first semi-final, while in the second the Argentine duel brought Jaite a 6–2 6–4 victory over Bengoechea before his final success over Wilander.

Besides pure interest in the sport, two facts positively influenced attendances for the week. The night sessions coincided with the 'fiestas' of the town and encouraged 6,000 spectators to watch Wilander's third-round match against Juan Aguilera. On the other hand, the introduction of IMG to organise and promote the tournament, plus the presence of Winston as the new sponsor, brought significant financial success, along with the creation of a village where the sponsor and VIPs could display their products and hold receptions. – P. H.

BARCELONA, 21–27 SEPTEMBER
MEN'S SINGLES – Quarter-finals: M. Wilander (SWE) d. T. Carbonell 6–0 6–3; G. Perez Roldan (ARG) d. A. Gomez (ECU) 6–3 1–0 ret'd; M. Jaite (ARG) d. E. Sanchez 6–3 7–6; E. Bengoechea (ARG) d. M. Mecir (TCH) 6–4 6–1. ***Semi-finals:*** Wilander d. Perez Roldan 6–3 6–0; Jaite d. Bengoechea 6–2 6–4. ***Final:*** Jaite d. Wilander 7–6 6–4 4–6 0–6 6–4.
MEN'S DOUBLES – Final: Mecir/T. Smid (TCH) d. J. Frana (ARG)/C. Miniussi (ARG) 6–1 6–2.

TRANSAMERICA OPEN ($232,000)

Peter Lundgren of Sweden enjoyed the finest hour of his career in the upset-ridden Transamerica Open at San Francisco's Cow Palace. In a field that was decimated by the pre-tournament withdrawals of John McEnroe and Jimmy Connors and later by a cascade of seeded players, Lundgren emerged as an exciting new star in the men's game. In the semi-finals the Swede faced Ivan Lendl, who had also originally withdrawn, planning to have a cyst removed from his neck that week. But the Czech was talked back into playing and duly reached the semi-finals, where he encountered the brilliance and resilience of the flamboyant Lundgren, whose flowing blond mane and whippy backhand reminded one of Bjorn Borg. Lundgren had not managed to advance beyond the second round of a tournament during the first half of the season, yet now he beat Lendl 6–3 4–6 7–6 in a sizzling match, needing five match-points to do it and fending off two against himself. The match lasted three hours and twelve minutes with scarcely a moment lacking high drama and excitement.

Lundgren, a jitterbug in tennis shoes who rushes from point to point rather like another blonde named Steffi Graf, had already enjoyed a remarkable summer. In the space of four weeks, he had beaten Pat Cash in Montreal, his countryman and hero, Mats Wilander, in Cincinnati, then he had won only the second Grand Prix title of his career in Rye Brook, going on to upset Cash again in the first round of the US Open. At 22, more could be anticipated from Lundgren but no one, least of all Lendl, expected it to come so soon. The Swede sent Lendl hurtling from one corner of the court to another – a penance the World Champion usually likes to inflict on his own victims – but he also proved dramatically incapable of closing out the match when presented with the opportunity.

After saving a match-point against him at 6–5 down in the third set, Lundgren went ahead 6–3 in the tie-breaker, only to deliver a wild forehand that sailed beyond the horizon of the court, followed by two nervous backhand errors to draw the score even. A fourth match-point arrived at 7–6 and Lundgren choked again on another backhand. It seemed inevitable that when the cool and rational Lendl reached match-point again, which he did at 8–7, he would close out the affair with no further ado. Instead, he netted a simple forehand. Lundgren reached match-point for a fifth time at 9–8 and clinched it with a backhand winner down the line, his best shot. The Swede was exultant afterwards. 'It's a dream for a tennis player to beat the number one player in the world', he said. 'To beat Lendl is the best result you can get.'

The next day, Lundgren had to face the rather mundane task of beating Jim Pugh to win the title, which was a more taxing challenge than it appeared, given the cloud on which he was still sailing. But Pugh assisted in the task by playing nervously and serving badly when he held a 3–0 second-set lead, and Lundgren won 6–1 7–5.

Other strange things happened in the Transamerica. When the injured Paul Annacone withdrew, Todd Nelson came in as a lucky loser to enjoy one of the finest weeks of his career, sailing through to the semi-finals before losing a heart-breaker to Pugh, 6–3 6–7 6–4. Eliot Teltscher consolidated his new-found success with his second consecutive quarter-final finish in as many weeks. Four of the eight seeds lost in the first round and these included some highly respectable names such as Tim Mayotte, Henri Leconte and Brad Gilbert. The previous week's champion, David Pate, fell to Lundgren, whom he had beaten easily a few days earlier in Los Angeles.

An amateur – Patrick McEnroe, still at Stanford – won the doubles title in tandem with Jim Grabb by the extraordinary score of 6–2 0–6 6–4 over Glenn Layendecker and Todd Witsken. McEnroe was unable to accept the prize money but Grabb could still pocket only a half share of the loot. – L. P.

SAN FRANCISCO, 28 SEPTEMBER–4 OCTOBER
MEN'S SINGLES – Quarter-finals: I. Lendl (TCH) d. D. Goldie 5–7 6–4 6–3; P. Lundgren (SWE) d. T. Wilkison 6–3 6–4; T. Nelson d. E. Teltscher 6–1 7–6; J. Pugh d. S. Giammalva 6–3 7–5. ***Semi-finals:*** Lundgren d. Lendl 6–3 4–6 7–6; Pugh d. Nelson 6–3 6–7 6–4. ***Final:*** Lundgren d. Pugh 6–1 7–5.
MEN'S DOUBLES – Final: J. Grabb/P. McEnroe d. G. Layendecker/T. Witsken 6–2 0–6 6–4.

Brad Gilbert made a slow start in 1987, doing his best work in the autumn, when he won his first title of the year at Scottsdale. He was a quarter-finalist at the US Open and reached four other finals during the season to qualify for the Masters, where he beat Connors and Becker. *(T. Hindley)*

JOCKEY

SCOTTSDALE OPEN ($232,000)

Brad Gilbert finally consolidated a topsy-turvy year by winning his first title of 1987 at the $232,000 WCT Scottsdale Open. He beat the reburgeoning Eliot Teltscher 6–2 6–2 in a rather flat final that lacked the spark both players had revealed in earlier rounds.

However, Gilbert's success was overshadowed by the exploits of Michael Chang, a 15-year-old wild-card entry. Chang had become the youngest player to win a round at the US Open when he dismissed Paul McNamee on opening day, and although still an amateur at the time, he chose subsequently to play in professional tournaments on wild-cards. The diminutive Chang has solid groundstrokes, and the sheer novelty of his extreme youth seemed to turn his opponents into quivering jellies. He embarrassed Jay Berger, Ben Testerman and Jorge Lozano on his way to the semi-finals, where even the experienced Gilbert became inhibited and pushed the ball around waiting for an error. Chang made a couple of errors himself in convenient places, on which Gilbert capitalised, but the 6–3 6–4 score belied the shaky nature of the match.

Teltscher simply produced that old familiar backhand that was such a weapon in his prime, and stunned opponents with a flowing series of winners as he mowed down Peter Lundgren and David Pate, two players enjoying hot streaks of their own. In the final, Gilbert's game was on and Teltscher's was decidedly off, so that the crowd were thankful for the thrills provided by the subsequent doubles final. Rick Leach and Jim Pugh, both former American collegians, teamed to defeat the 1986 NCCA champion, Dan Goldie, and the ever entertaining Mel Purcell, 6–3 6–2.

The week began with the anxiously awaited arrival of the tournament's top seed, Mats Wilander, who flew in from a rain-delayed *Davis Cup* semi-final in Barcelona. The scheduling was not to the Swede's liking but he nevertheless put up a brave, if lifeless, fight against Goldie in the first round, before losing 7–6 6–3. Goldie had rejoiced on seeing his draw – an unusual reaction when one must face the top seed in the first round – but Dan knew what a gift fate and jet-lag had given him.

Lundgren was thus denied another crack at his countryman in the second round and easily brushed aside Goldie, who was still travelling somewhere in outer space at the time. In the quarter-finals it was Lundgren's turn to waver, losing concentration and a lead of a set and a break as Teltscher stole the match 3–6 6–3 6–4. Pate also let a close one get away from him, losing to Teltscher in the semi-finals 7–6 7–5.

The demise of Tim Mayotte, whose serve took a vacation when perhaps the rest of him should have followed, continued in Scottsdale. Mayotte was a second-round victim of the smooth Mexican, Jorge Lozano, who then became an awkward bag of nerves when faced with Chang, simply losing the quarter-final 6–4 6–1.

Chang was asked throughout the week if he would now turn professional, but insisted the arguments for and against were yet to be weighed, citing the need to be a 'normal 15-year-old', enjoying his friends, and growing up at his own pace as reasons to delay a professional career. They were reasons offered with a mature detachment that belied the young mouth out of which they were uttered. – L. P.

5–11 OCTOBER
MEN'S SINGLES – Quarter-finals: M. Chang d. J. Lozano (MEX) 6–4 6–1; B. Gilbert d. J. Kriek 6–2 6–4; E. Teltscher d. P. Lundgren (SWE) 3–6 6–3 6–4; D. Pate d. K. Curren 6–2 7–6. ***Semi-finals:*** Gilbert d. Chang 6–3 6–4; Teltscher d. Pate 7–6 7–5. ***Final:*** Gilbert d. Teltscher 6–2 6–2.
MEN'S DOUBLES – Final: R. Leach/J. Pugh d. D. Goldie/M. Purcell 6–3 6–2.

SEGMENT 7: 12–25 OCTOBER

John Thirsk and Bryan Cutress

SWAN PREMIUM AUSTRALIAN INDOOR CHAMPIONSHIPS ($275,000)

It was a truly extraordinary week in Sydney. There were things that went bump in the night at the players' hotel and an irresistible force that finally uprooted an immovable object. By the week's end Ivan Lendl had won the $275,000 Swan Premium Open, his second title from four consecutive finals at the Entertainment Centre where record crowds confirmed the popularity of this 15-year-old Australian Indoor Championship.

While Czechoslovakia's World No. 1 gained revenge over the Australian *Davis Cup* idol, Pat Cash, for his straight-sets beating in the Wimbledon final three months earlier, the talk of the tournament was the weird scraping noises and the sounds of ghostly footsteps pacing past the end of Cash's bed. The Aussie strong man had fled to coach Ian Barclay's room to complete a restless night's sleep on a couch. So not surprisingly, when it came to the final, Cash didn't stand the ghost of a chance as Lendl, playing his powerful back-court game with awesome accuracy, demolished the Australian's jaded attacking game 6–4 6–2 6–4.

Lendl had arrived in Sydney after losing to Sweden's Peter Lundgren in the San Francisco semi-final and to Paul Annacone in a special event in Atlanta. In Sydney, though, he easily beat Becker's Wimbledon conqueror, Peter Doohan, in the opening round, and then received a walk-over from the unseeded German, Eric Jelen, who had twisted an ankle in beating the promising Aussie junior, Jason Stoltenberg, 6–4 5–7 6–3 in his first match. Lendl then swept through the delicate defences of the artistic Indian, Ramesh Krishnan, 6–2 6–3 in the quarter-finals and in the semi-finals he reminded Slobodan Zivojinovic of Yugoslavia that power alone is not enough, their thunderous encounter ending in a 6–3 7–5 victory for Lendl.

The immovable object, in the person of defending champion Boris Becker, looked increasingly secure as he swept to the semi-finals past Tim Pawsat, Sammy Giammalva and Paul Annacone for the loss of only 16 games. Not since the early spring had the champion's powerful service looked so well grooved. The irresistible force, in the person of Pat Cash, looked equally determined as he survived two difficult matches. By beating the Brisbane winner, Kelly Evernden, 6–3 7–6, and then revenging himself by the same score against John Frawley, the man who had beaten him in Queensland, Cash revealed a new determination. Looking fitter and faster than at any time since Wimbledon, Cash beat the talented American, Scott Davis, 6–3 7–5 to set up a meeting against Becker.

This semi-final was the match of the tournament. For a set Cash was at his glorious, attacking best as the West German appeared to think he could win from the back of the court. Cash led 6–3 and was volleying superbly, like a cat pouncing on an unfortunate mouse, but Becker, not content to play the mouse, opened his mighty shoulders and for five games became unplayable as he swept from 2–2 to 6–2 and 1–0 in the deciding set with a brand of serve-and-volley tennis that at its best is irresistible. As the games mounted in the final set it was apparent that Cash was equally powerful and adventurous. The tie-break that decided the issue was desperately close and turned on a touch of genius from Cash on the first point when, lunging towards his backhand corner, the Australian flicked up a low, fast lob that evaded Becker's flailing racket and fell, inch-perfect, on the baseline. It was past midnight when Cash delivered a last service winner to claim the tie-break 7–4, having won a personal battle of commitment that was vital for his own peace of mind.

Sadly there was nothing left in the locker when, 13 hours later and with time only for

In the final at Sydney in October, Ivan Lendl gained revenge for his defeat at Wimbledon by Pat Cash (above left), who had beaten Becker in the semis. However, the World Champion was less successful the following week when he lost the Tokyo final to No. 2 Stefan Edberg (above right). *(T. Hindley, Carol L. Newsom)*

six hours' restless sleep, Pat returned to court for the final. Lendl was not about to realise Cash's dream of winning a first major title in Australia following his brave but unavailing loss to Stefan Edberg in the final of the Australian Open in January. Looking every inch the World Champion, Lendl strode majestically to his title against a man who could offer only token resistance.

There was good reason for Australian supporters to celebrate as the final act of the Swan Premium Open was played. The doubles event fell to the educated rackets of Darren Cahill and Mark Kratzmann, two members of the BP Achievers squad and former products of the Australian Institute of Sports in Canberra. In a blistering display of powerful and strategically clever doubles they destroyed the top seeds, Bob Seguso and Boris Becker, 6–3 6–2. It was a triumphant end to a most unusual week. – J. T.

SYDNEY, 12–18 OCTOBER
MEN'S SINGLES – Quarter-finals: I. Lendl (TCH) d. R. Krishnan (IND) 6–2 6–3; S. Zivojinovic (YUG) d. M. Davis (USA) 7–5 6–4; P. Cash d. S. Davis (USA) 6–3 7–5; B. Becker (FRG) d. P. Annacone (USA) 6–3 6–2. ***Semi-finals:*** Lendl d. Zivojinovic 6–3 7–5; Cash d. Becker 6–3 2–6 7–6. ***Final:*** Lendl d. Cash 6–4 6–2 6–4.
MEN'S DOUBLES – Final: D. Cahill/M. Kratzmann d. B. Becker(FRG)/R. Seguso (USA) 6–3 6–2.

SEIKO SUPER TENNIS ($300,000)

Stefan Edberg ended a run of three successive defeats by Ivan Lendl when he took the Seiko Super Tennis title at Yoyogi National Stadium in Tokyo in October. Having waited since the semi-finals of the same event a year earlier to achieve his fourth triumph over the World Champion in ten attempts, he walked off the court with a big smile and a cheque for $60,000. It certainly took him all he had to offer in skill, speed and determination to topple Lendl by 6–7 (4–7) 6–4 6–4. A disputed point in the opening game of the third set, together with Lendl's dislike of the Supreme court, played their part in the result – but not nearly as big a part as Edberg's brilliance. He powered in 65 per cent of his first serves, attacked with confidence at every opportunity, and made few unforced errors. Lendl tried desperately to halt the Swede's rush for revenge but on this day and on this court all he knew was just not good enough.

It was a pity that the dispute rubbed some of the gloss from Edberg's big day. The trouble arose when Lendl, having recovered from 15–40 at the start of the deciding set, faced his third break-point. Lendl was convinced that Edberg's backhand towards the baseline was out, the linesman agreed, but the chair umpire overruled. That cost Lendl his service, and he was never able to make up the leeway on a court which he reckons is such a big handicap to his type of game.

Yet despite the court, Lendl had seemed about to add Edberg to his long list of victims when he took the first-set tie-break. The Swede's problems increased in the second set when he double-faulted twice to move within a point of trailing 2–4, but he survived the crisis, broke Lendl's serve and then took a firm grip on the match. Lendl had one more chance, when he led 30–0 against serve in the eighth game of the final set, but by then Edberg was full of confidence, easily holding off the world No. 1, and moved on to his sixth title of the year.

Edberg had sharpened his game in earlier matches, against Paul Annacone and Slobodan Zivojinovic, both of whom took him the full distance. He lost the opening set to Annacone in the quarter-finals but recovered to win 3–6 6–1 6–2 and then downed the giant Yugoslav 7–6 (7–5) 4–6 6–2. Zivojinovic, accompanied by his wife Zorcia, and small son Filip, who is known on the circuit as Bobolino, had earlier put out defending champion Boris Becker in an acrimonious quarter-final by 6–3 1–6 3–0 retired. Becker was upset because he believed Zivojinovic was stalling and moving around deliberately while he was serving, and the end came when Becker, who had been suffering from a cold and a fever for three weeks, retired because of a painful right thigh muscle.

John Fitzgerald had supplied an early upset with his defeat of Jimmy Connors, seeded fourth, who was lined up for a third-round clash with Mikael Pernfors, the Swede he had teased, tormented and finally beaten at Wimbledon. Fitzgerald, who had qualified, had not beaten Connors in three previous contests and was so sure this match would go the same way as its predecessors that he had packed his bags and left his hotel.

The doubles also produced plenty of suprises before Australian Brod Dyke and Dutchman Tom Nijssen carried off the $18,000 prize with a 6–3 6–2 victory over Americans Sammy Giammalva and Jim Grabb. Dyke and Nijssen had beaten fourth seeds Becker and Eric Jelen in the second round while Giammalva and Grabb had removed the favourites, Robert Seguso and Zivojinovic, 2–6 6–3 6–3 in the semi-finals. – B. C.

TOKYO, 19–25 OCTOBER
MEN'S SINGLES – Quarter-finals: I. Lendl (TCH) d. E. Jelen (FRG) 6–3 6–0; M. Pernfors (SWE) d. J. Fitzgerald (AUS) 6–1 6–2; S. Zivojinovic (YUG) d. B. Becker (FRG) 6–3 1–6 3–0 ret'd; S. Edberg (SWE) d. P. Annacone (USA) 3–6 6–1 6–2. ***Semi-finals:*** Lendl d. Pernfors 6–0 6–2; Edberg d. Zivojinovic 7–6 4–6 6–2. ***Final:*** Edberg d. Lendl 6–7 6–4 6–4.
MEN'S DOUBLES – Final: B. Dyke (AUS)/T. Nijssen (HOL) d. S. Giammalva (USA)/J. Grabb (USA) 6–3 6–2.

SEGMENT 8: 2–22 NOVEMBER

Judith Elian, Bjorn Hellberg, Barry Newcombe and Dena Hardy

PARIS OPEN ($700,000)

Tim Mayotte was understandably elated. 'I'm glad I won and I'm very satisfied with my season. So far I've won four tournaments of which three were Super Series [Philadelphia, Chicago, Paris Open]. This year I've put everything together to overcome the difficulties I had in the past to go all the way in a tournament. It isn't so much the money – although that, of course, is important – but it's the title and the trophy I appreciate. I'll take them home; they belong to me and nobody can take them away.' All the same, the new winner of the $700,000 Paris Indoor Championships did not forget to take home the victor's spoils of $140,000.

In the final Mayotte defeated fellow-countryman Brad Gilbert 2–6 6–3 7–5 6–7 6–3, after a three-and-a-half-hour battle that thrilled the packed stands of the new Bercy stadium. It could have been shorter had Mayotte, leading by two sets to one, taken the point that would have put him ahead 5–3 in the fourth. But Gilbert produced a great service return, Mayotte fluffed two volleys, and dropped his serve. Later, in the tie-break, the tall No. 5 seed was leading 5–4 with two serves to come, but again he couldn't make it. In the fifth set Gilbert, after saving four break-points to reach 3–3, held one himself that would have given him 4–3. He thought Mayotte's forehand volley was out but it was given in, and furious, with his concentration disturbed, Gilbert lost his serve and did not win any more games.

Clashing with the Super Series tournament in Stockholm, the second edition of the Paris Indoor did not enjoy the entry that is expected for such a rich event. None of the world's top four players competed, so that fifth-ranked Miloslav Mecir was the top seed, followed in order by Pat Cash, Yannick Noah, Andres Gomez, Mayotte, Martin Jaite, Gilbert and David Pate.

Mecir disappeared early, beaten in the second round by the former Wimbledon finalist Kevin Curren, whose serve on the fast court was never mastered by the bearded Czech. Gomez, playing his first tournament since injuring his shoulder some weeks earlier, was eliminated in the opening round by Frenchman Thierry Champion. Pate never found his flair at the net against Eduardo Bengoechea, even though the Argentinian hardly ever plays on fast surfaces. Another clay-court specialist, Jaite, was beaten in his opening match by the tall left-handed Russian, Aleksandr Volkov, a qualifier who has improved considerably since he first exploded on the scene at Wimbledon.

The third round produced one exciting match and one disappointment. After Noah's comeback at Basle, everyone was waiting to see how he would do at Bercy, so the public were dismayed when it was announced in the afternoon that he had once again been forced to scratch with an injured stomach muscle. The beneficiary this time was Michiel Schapers of Holland, who had come through tough qualifying rounds before beating Tulasne and Volkov. In the evening session, though, the public were rewarded with a tremendously exciting battle between the other French hero, Henri Leconte, and Australia's Wimbledon champion, Pat Cash. Both players produced some thrilling shots before the home favourite finally prevailed after failing on three match-points in the second set, which he finally lost 9–11 in the tie-break. In the deciding set the left-hander seemed to have a little more stamina than his opponent and he volleyed with rather more efficiency than Cash on the crucial points.

Along with Gilbert, Mayotte and Leconte, the fourth semi-finalist was the unseeded outsider Schapers, then ranked a modest 79 on the ATP computer. The pleasant and modest Dutchman was eventually beaten in three sets by Gilbert but, like Mayotte, he collected his biggest ever pay cheque of $37,000. Leconte, still a little tired from the previous night's matches, was much less sharp against Mayotte than he had been against Cash. His shots lacked their usual sparkle and the American, with his heavy serving and crisp volleying, had little trouble in overpowering a rather flat opponent in the final set.

The doubles event produced some surprises with the title going to the unseeded Swiss pair, Jakob Hlasek and Claudio Mezzadri. They beat Cash and Gomez, second seeds Mecir and Smid, and in the final the unseeded Scott Davis and Pate. Apart from the prize-money of $42,000 which they shared, the Swiss boys each received a magnificent, but unwieldly, large silver plate which they had to carry with them to their next tournaments in London and Johannesburg. – J. E.

2–8 NOVEMBER
MEN'S SINGLES – Final: H. Leconte d. P. Cash (AUS) 6–4 6–7 6–3; T. Mayotte (USA) d. A. Mansdorf (ISR) 6–4 6–2; B. Gilbert (USA) d. K. Curren (USA) 7–5 6–4; M. Schapers (HOL) w.o. Y. Noah. ***Semi-finals:*** Mayotte d. Leconte 6–3 4–6 6–3; Gilbert d. Schapers 7–5 5–7 6–4. ***Final:*** Mayotte d. Gilbert 2–6 6–3 7–5 6–7 6–3.
MEN'S DOUBLES – Final: J. Hlasek (SUI)/C. Mezzadri (SUI) d. S. Davis (USA)/D. Pate (USA) 7–6 6–2.

STOCKHOLM OPEN ($425,000)

It was hardly surprising that Swedish players completely dominated the Stockholm Open, held at the fabulous Royal Club in November. When Boris Becker withdrew shortly before the tournament because of injury, it was an open road for the home players. Swedes occupied seven of the eight seeding positions, with Spanish clay-court specialist Emilio Sanchez at No. 4 being the lone foreigner.

Everything went as planned. For the first time in the 19-year history of the event, Sweden won both the singles and the doubles, title-holder Stefan Edberg becoming the hero of the week, as he captured the singles crown and the doubles together with Anders Jarryd. All the singles semi-finalists were local players – a unique achievement in the Stockholm Open, although in the Swedish Open in Bastad in 1984 Henrik Sundstrom, Anders Jarryd, Joakim Nystrom and Stefan Edberg had taken the first four places. This time, Edberg beat Jonas Svensson 7–5 6–2 4–6 6–4 in a fine final, while Jarryd and the 20-year-old outsider, Magnus Gustafsson of Gothenburg, took care of the remaining spots in the semis.

Edberg had some difficulties in his first three matches: 6–7 6–0 6–2 against Richey Reneberg of the USA, 7–6 6–3 against Ulf Stenlund, and 6–1 7–6 against Peter Lundgren. But he found his magic touch in the semis against Anders Jarryd, destroying his doubles partner 6–4 6–2 after a splendid serve-and-volley performance. In the final, the talented Jonas Svensson fought bravely against Edberg, winning plenty of points with his beautiful lobs and passing shots on the backhand, and he broke his opponent no less than four times. However, in the end Edberg had too many guns for him. Both Stefan and Jonas were born in 1966, and they had played each other often as juniors. At that time, Svensson had a 6–4 edge when he faced his now more famous opponent, but in Grand Prix meetings Edberg leads 2–0, having also beaten his fellow-countryman in straight sets at the US Open two months earlier.

Edberg became the first Swede to win the Stockholm Open twice (Bjorn Borg triumphed in 1980 and Mats Wilander in 1983). In the 1986 final, Edberg had outclassed Wilander 6–2 6–1 6–1 in just 79 minutes. Stefan received his trophy and prize-money from Prince Bertil and Princess Lilian in front of a capacity crowd of almost 4,500 spectators.

Magnus Gustafsson was the talk of the week in Stockholm, leaping up the rankings from 106 to 47 with victories against Francesco Cancellotti of Italy, sixth-seeded Mikael

Pernfors, Eric Jelen of West Germany and American Matt Anger. In the semis, Gustafsson was stopped 6–3 6–4 by Svensson. As proof that it was indeed true, Gustafsson received the honour of being named 'The Surprise of the Year' by Clay & Grass (the Association of Tennis Writers in Sweden).

The shock result of the week was American Jim Grabb's easy 7–5 6–4 victory over Mats Wilander. The Swedish world No. 3 did not even once reach a break-point during the battle! Grabb followed this win with another fine triumph over Sergio Casal of Spain, and then in doubles, Grabb and Jim Pugh reached the final, only to lose 6–3 6–4 against Jarryd and the ruthless Edberg. – B. H.

2–8 NOVEMBER
MEN'S SINGLES – Quarter-finals: S. Edberg d. P. Lundgren 6–1 6–3; A. Jarryd d. M. Laurendeau (CAN) 6–2 6–4; M. Gustafsson d. E. Jelen (FRG) 7–6 6–2; J. Svensson d. J. Grabb (USA) 6–1 6–3. ***Semi-finals:*** Edberg d. Jarryd 6–4 6–2; Svensson d. Gustafsson 6–3 6–4. ***Final:*** Edberg d. Svensson 7–5 6–2 4–6 6–4.
MEN'S DOUBLES – Final: Edberg/Jarryd d. Grabb/J. Pugh (USA) 6–3 6–4.

BENSON AND HEDGES TOURNAMENT ($375,000)

Ivan Lendl's third title in the Benson and Hedges Championships at Wembley, on a court where he has never been beaten in singles, provided a mixed blessing for the sell-out crowd. While enjoying an awesome display by the world No. 1, they knew that Lendl would not be back to defend his title in 1988 because of changes in his tournament schedule. Yet in announcing that he wanted to reduce his match play on Supreme court, the Wembley surface, Lendl acknowledged that one of his best victories outside Grand Slam events was in beating Boris Becker over five sets in the 1985 final. No one looked like properly testing Lendl in the Wembley field as he captured his seventh title of the year. In addition, he took his 1987 prize-money almost to the $1 million mark and clinched top singles place in the Nabisco Grand Prix with its $800,000 reward.

Lendl's task at Wembley was made easier because neither the second seed, Miloslav Mecir, nor the Wimbledon champion, Pat Cash, who were in the opposite half of the draw, took their appointed places in the semi-finals. Mecir fell to Jakob Hlasek 6–3 6–3 in the quarter-finals, and Cash was beaten 3–6 7–6 6–2 at the same stage by Anders Jarryd. Cash had two good reasons for wanting to succeed at Wembley. One was that he simply enjoys playing in London, his adopted home, and the other was that the further he progressed the more he would consolidate his bid to earn a place in the Nabisco Masters. His quarter-final with fifth-seeded Jarryd was tinged with controversy when at 5-all in the second-set tie-break, with Cash just two points from victory, a service return from Jarryd was judged good by the base-line official. Cash, thinking otherwise, believed an overrule would have been the correct decision.

The three British players in the field, Jeremy Bates, Andrew Castle, and Stuart Bale, could not improve on their wild-card status and were beaten in the first round, Bates being particularly disappointed, having led Paul Annacone by a set and 3–0. As Lendl said of that situation: 'Jeremy was probably scared of victory just like I'm scared of defeat. It's a matter of confidence. I can recall so many times where I have won a match only because I have done it before.'

Lendl began the tournament unusually when his first-round match against Ronald Agenor was twice held up because of a leak in the roof. That might have contributed to Lendl's general unease in the early stages, but once he had shaken himself into a more determined mood after losing the first set to Annacone in the quarter-finals, he instantly looked stronger. Strangely Lendl did not play a seed until he met Jarryd in the final. Joakim Nystrom, the fourth seed, was a first-round casualty against Milan Srejber, although it was Henri Leconte who became the front runner in Nystrom's section of the draw, until he found his flamboyance ruined by Lendl's power.

Jarryd's solidity was evident all the way through but he was never in the hunt in the final, which Lendl won 6–3 6–2 7–5. Not once did Jarryd capture Lendl's serve, and though

Jonas Svensson of Sweden ended the year with a flourish, winning his first Grand Prix title in Vienna, and reaching the final at Stockholm, where he extended Stefan Edberg to four sets. *(T. Hindley)*

the Swede employed serve-volley tactics in the third set in a desperate attempt to change the pattern, Lendl's rhythm was not affected for long.

In the doubles final, fourth seeds Mecir and Tomas Smid edged out top-seeded Ken Flach and Robert Seguso 7–5 6–4 to win their fourth title together in 1987. – B. N.

WEMBLEY, LONDON, 10–15 NOVEMBER
MEN'S SINGLES – Quarter-finals: I. Lendl (TCH) d. P. Annacone (USA) 3–6 6–3 6–4; H. Leconte (FRA) d. A. Mansdorf (ISR) 6–7 7–6 6–3; A. Jarryd (SWE) d. P. Cash (AUS) 3–6 7–6 6–2; J. Hlasek (SUI) d. M. Mecir (TCH) 6–3 6–3. ***Semi-finals:*** Lendl d. Leconte 6–4 7–6; Jarryd d. Hlasek 7–6 6–1. ***Final:*** Lendl d. Jarryd 6–3 6–2 7–5.
MEN'S DOUBLES – Final: Mecir/T. Smid (TCH) d. K. Flach (USA)/R. Seguso (USA) 7–5 6–4.

SOUTH AFRICAN CHAMPIONSHIPS ($232,000)

With Zulu ball girls singing *'Thina siyakuthanda u, Pat Cash'* (We love you, Pat Cash), the Altech South African Open reached its high point as the most successful national tournament yet held in Johannesburg. The race for the last two places in the Nabisco Grand Prix Masters resulted in Cash, Gilbert and Gomez joining the safari to the Standard Bank Indoor Arena. As expected, the top seed, Cash, won his first Grand Prix title since Wimbledon; yet it was not easy for the Australian, whose decision to play in South Africa was not popular in certain circles.

The defending champion and fifth seed, Amos Mansdorf, began the defence of his title with his sixth consecutive win over South African Christo Steyn, 7–6 6–2. In the quarter-finals the stocky Israeli nearly came unstuck against Francesco Cancellotti, but after losing the first set to love he got his game together to beat the Italian number two 0–6 6–3 6–3, and earn himself a semi-final appointment with Cash.

The 1986 runner-up and 1985 champion, American Matt Anger, fell in the second round, where Cash, who had handled the high altitude by training at a private court with an oxygen cylinder mask on courtside, now handled Anger's chip-and-charge technique superbly. A thigh injury did not help the American, who lost 6–3 6–2.

The winner in 1983, former South African Johan Kriek, again failed to live up to expectations, being given his marching orders in the third round by Pieter Aldrich, a South African training in the South African Defence Force. Aldrich, a wild-card entry, won 6–3 7–5, but then lost to the third seed, Brad Gilbert. Another former South African, Kevin Curren, fared a little better before coming unstuck against Cash. He started in great style with one of the best sets of his career, but after taking it 6–2 he saw the Wimbledon champion taking command and dictating play from the net to win 2–6 6–3 6–4.

Number six seed, Jakob Hlasek of Switzerland, beat American qualifier, Jim Courier, 6–2 6–2 in the first round, but that was his last match. He received a walkover into the quarter-finals when Simon Youl fell victim to a virus infection, and the same virus then knocked him out, giving Gilbert a walkover into the semi-finals. Frenchman Henri Leconte, the eighth seed, collected a hard-earned 6–4 4–6 6–4 victory in the first round over South African junior Marius Barnard, but then succumbed 6–4 6–4 to the hard-serving local player, Gary Muller. The only seeded South African, No. 7 Christo Van Rensburg, failed even to make it into the main draw, for he withdrew, still suffering from a cold he had caught at the Benson and Hedges tournament in London.

Cash, Mansdorf, Gomez and Gilbert gathered in the semi-finals where Cash beat Mansdorf 6–3 7–6 and Gilbert defeated Gomez 6–4 6–1. In the final, that lasted three hours nine minutes, fortunes fluctuated, with Cash eventually securing his place in the Masters. He took more than an hour to win the first set, on his second set-point in the tie-break – his fourth in the set. But as Gilbert comfortably won the next two sets, Cash looked a beaten man. In the last two sets, however, he showed why he is the Wimbledon champion, allowing Gilbert only eight points in the fourth set which he won 6–0 in 23 minutes. In the final set of 31 minutes Gilbert held serve only in the fifth game, and Cash lost only four points on his own serve.

In the doubles final Curren won his first South African title when, with American David Pate, he beat Eric Korita and Brad Pearce, also of America, 6–4 6–4. – D. H.

JOHANNESBURG, 16–22 NOVEMBER

MEN'S SINGLES – Quarter-finals: P. Cash (AUS) d. K. Curren (USA) 2–6 6–3 6–4; A. Mansdorf (ISR) d. F. Cancellotti (ITA) 0–6 6–3 6–3; B. Gilbert (USA) w.o. J. Hlasek (SUI); A. Gomez (ECU) d. G. Muller 6–1 6–3. ***Semi-finals:*** Cash d. Mansdorf 6–3 7–6; Gilbert d. Gomez 6–4 6–1. ***Final:*** Cash d. Gilbert 7–6 4–6 2–6 6–0 6–1.

MEN'S DOUBLES – Final: Curren/D. Pate (USA) d. E. Korita (USA)/B. Pearce (USA) 6–4 6–4.

OTHER NABISCO GRAND PRIX RESULTS

ADELAIDE ($89,400)

29 DECEMBER–4 JANUARY
MEN'S SINGLES – Quarter-finals: N. Odizor (NIG) d. R. Krishnan (IND) 6–3 6–2; W. Scanlon (USA) d. G. Michibata (CAN) 7–6 7–5; M. Schapers (HOL) d. J. Fitzgerald 7–6 6–4; W. Masur d. A. Mansdorf (ISR) 6–2 6–4. ***Semi-finals:*** Scanlon d. Odizor 6–7 6–4 6–4; Masur d. Schapers 6–4 6–0. ***Final:*** Masur d. Scanlon 6–4 7–6.
MEN'S DOUBLES – Final: I. Lendl (TCH)/Scanlon d. P. Doohan/L. Warder 6–7 6–3 6–4.

AUCKLAND ($89,400)

5–11 JANUARY
MEN'S SINGLES – Quarter-finals: M. Mecir (TCH) d. B. Derlin 6–2 6–2; D. Rostagno (USA) d. R. Krishnan (IND) 6–3 5–7 10–8; C. Limberger (AUS) d. M. Freeman (USA) 6–2 3–6 6–4; M. Schapers (HOL) d. B. Schultz (USA) 3–6 6–2 6–4. ***Semi-finals:*** Mecir d. Rostagno 6–2 6–1; Schapers d. Limberger 2–6 6–3 6–4. ***Final:*** Mecir d. Schapers 6–2 6–3 6–4.
MEN'S DOUBLES – Final: K. Jones (USA)/B. Pearce (USA) d. Limberger/M. Woodforde (AUS) 7–6 7–6.

SYDNEY ($89,400)

26 JANUARY–1 FEBRUARY
MEN'S SINGLES – Quarter-finals: M. Mecir (TCH) d. W. Scanlon (USA) 6–2 6–2; W. Masur d. K. Evernden (NZL) 6–3 6–2; P. Doohan d. N. Odizor (NIG) 6–4 6–3; B. Drewett d. M. Kratzmann 6–2 7–6. ***Semi-finals:*** Mecir d. Masur 6–4 6–2; Doohan d. Drewett 6–7 6–4 6–4. ***Final:*** Mecir d. Doohan 6–2 6–4.
MEN'S DOUBLES – Final: Drewett/M. R. Edmondson d. Doohan/L. Warder 6–4 4–6 6–2.

GUARUJA, BRAZIL ($89,400)

26 JANUARY–1 FEBRUARY
MEN'S SINGLES – Quarter-finals: V. Pecci (PAR) d. J. Lopez-Maeso (ESP) 6–2 4–6 7–5; C. Motta d. R. Acuna (CHI) 7–5 6–2; L. Mattar d. I. Werner 6–3 2–6 7–6; B. Oresar (YUG) d. J. Goes 6–2 6–3. ***Semi-finals:*** Motta d. Pecci 7–5 6–2; Mattar d. Oresar 4–6 7–6 6–4. ***Final:*** Mattar d. Motta 6–3 5–7 6–2.
MEN'S DOUBLES – Final: Mattar/Motta d. T. Meinecke (FRG)/M. Hipp (FRG) 7–6 6–1.

LYON ($150,000)

2–8 FEBRUARY
MEN'S SINGLES – Quarter-finals: J. Nystrom (SWE) d. J. Potier 6–3 6–4; T. Nelson (USA) d. B. Cox (USA) 7–6 6–2; K. Jones (USA) d. G. Forget 5–7 6–1 7–6; Y. Noah d. B. Willenborg (USA) 6–2 6–3. ***Semi-finals:*** Nystrom d. Nelson 7–6 4–6 7–6; Noah d. Jones 1–6 6–1 6–1. ***Final:*** Noah d. Nystrom 6–4 7–5.
MEN'S DOUBLES – Final: Noah/Forget d. Jones/D. Pate (USA) 4–6 6–3 6–4.

NANCY ($89,400)

23–29 MARCH
MEN'S SINGLES – Quarter-finals: P. Cash (AUS) d. J. Grabb (USA) 7–6 6–2; R. Krishnan (IND) d. M.

Claudio Mezzadri, the Swiss No. 2, won his first singles title in Geneva and reached the semi-finals in Gstaad and Vienna, moving more than 100 places up the rankings to finish the year at No. 28. *(T. Hindley)*

Bahrami (IRN) 6–4 4–6 6–4; B. Drewett (AUS) d. C. Bergstrom (SWE) 7–5 0–6 7–6; W. Masur (AUS) d. M. Dickson (USA) 6–4 3–6 6–3. ***Semi-finals:*** Cash d. Krishnan 7–6 6–3; Masur d. Drewett 6–4 7–6. ***Final:*** Cash d. Masur 6–2 6–3.
MEN'S DOUBLES – Final: Krishnan/C. Mezzadri (ITA) d. G. Connell (CAN)/L. Scott (USA) 6–4 6–4.

BARI ($89,400)

6–12 APRIL
MEN'S SINGLES – Quarter-finals: F. Cancellotti d. T. Tulasne (FRA) 6–3 4–6 6–2; H. de la Pena (ARG) d. J. Avendano (ESP) 6–3 1–6 7–6; U. Stenlund (SWE) d. R. Osterthun (FRG) 6–3 1–6 6–1; C. Pistolesi d. F. Davin (ARG) 7–6 6–3. ***Semi-finals:*** Cancellotti d. de la Pena 6–3 6–3; Pistolesi d. Stenlund 6–1 0–6 6–1. ***Final:*** Pistolesi d. Cancellotti 6–7 7–5 6–3.
MEN'S DOUBLES – Final: C. Allgardh (SWE)/Stenlund d. R. Azar/M. Ingaramo 6–3 6–3.

NICE ($89,400)

13–19 APRIL
MEN'S SINGLES – Quarter-finals: K. Carlsson (SWE) d. R. Agenor (HAI) 6–2 6–1; A. Chesnokov (URS) d. M. Jaite (ARG) 7–6 6–2; T. Tulasne d. A. Krickstein (USA) 7–5 7–6; E. Sanchez (ESP) d. M. Vajda (TCH) 6–2 6–2. ***Semi-finals:*** Carlsson d. Chesnokov 6–0 7–6; Sanchez d. Tulasne 7–5 6–2. ***Final:*** Carlsson d. Sanchez 7–6 6–3.
MEN'S DOUBLES – Final: S. Casal (ESP)/Sanchez d. C. Mezzadri (ITA)/G. Ocleppo (ITA) 6–3 6–3.

SEOUL ($89,400)

20–26 APRIL
MEN'S SINGLES – Quarter-finals: J. Grabb (USA) d. M. Schapers (HOL) 6–3 6–3; J. P. Fleurian (FRA) d. J. Sadri (USA) 6–4 1–6 6–3; A. Agassi (USA) d. J. Fitzgerald (AUS) 6–1 6–3; B. Testerman (USA) d. M. Leach (USA) 7–6 6–1. ***Semi-finals:*** Grabb d. Fleurian 6–2 7–6; Agassi d. Testerman 2–6 6–3 6–2. ***Final:*** Grabb d. Agassi 1–6 6–4 6–2.
MEN'S DOUBLES – Final: E. Korita (USA)/M. Leach (USA) d. K. Flach (USA)/Grabb 6–7 6–1 7–5.

MUNICH ($125,000)

4–10 MAY
MEN'S SINGLES – Quarter-finals: M. Purcell (USA) d. C. U. Steeb 6–3 7–6; G. Perez Roldan (ARG) d. S. Casal (ESP) 6–7 7–5 6–1; J. Nystrom (SWE) d. C. Limberger (AUS) 6–3 6–3; M. Vajda (TCH) d. J. Kriek 6–2 7–5. ***Semi-finals:*** Perez Roldan d. Purcell 1–6 7–5 6–1; Vajda d. Nystrom 6–4 6–4. ***Final:*** Perez Roldan d. Vajda 6–3 7–6.
MEN'S DOUBLES – Final: J. Pugh (USA) B. Willenborg (USA) d. Casal/E. Sanchez (ESP) 7–6 4–6 6–4.

FLORENCE ($99,400)

18–24 MAY
MEN'S SINGLES – Quarter-finals: A. Chesnokov (URS) d. J. Yzaga (PER) 7–6 6–1; G. Perez Roldan (ARG) d. C. Panatta 6–3 6–1; A. DeMinicis d. M. Dickson (USA) 6–3 6–1; E. Bengoechea (ARG) d. P. Cane 6–3 6–2. ***Semi-finals:*** Chesnokov d. Perez Roldan 3–6 7–5 7–5; DeMinicis d. Bengoechea 6–4 3–6 6–4. ***Final:*** Chesnokov d. DeMinicis 6–1 6–3.
MEN'S DOUBLES – Final: W. Popp (FRG)/U. Riglewski (FRG) d. P. Cane/G. Ocleppo 6–4 6–4.

STELLA ARTOIS CHAMPIONSHIPS ($250,000)

QUEEN'S CLUB, LONDON, 8–14 JUNE
MEN'S SINGLES – Quarter-finals: B. Becker (FRG) d. D. Pate (USA) 6–4 7–6; T. Mayotte (USA) d. R. Krishnan (IND) 6–2 6–3; J. S. Connors (USA) d. E. Jelen (FRG) 6–4 6–4; P. Cash (AUS) d. S. Edberg (SWE) 7–6 7–6. ***Semi-finals:*** Becker d. Mayotte 4–6 7–6 6–4; Connors d. Cash 7–6 6–4. ***Final:*** Becker d. Connors 6–7 6–3 6–4.
MEN'S DOUBLES – Final: G. Forget (FRA)/Y. Noah (FRA) d. R. Leach (USA)/T. Pawsat (USA) 6–4 6–4.

BOLOGNA ($89,400)

8–14 JUNE
MEN'S SINGLES – Quarter-finals: K. Carlsson (SWE) d. F. Davin (ARG) 6–0 6–0; P. Cane d. T. Tulasne (FRA) 7–5 4–6 6–0; E. Sanchez (ESP) d. B. Willenborg (USA) 6–3 6–3; M. Jaite (ARG) d. J. Brown (USA) 6–1 6–1. ***Semi-finals:*** Carlsson d. Cane 6–1 6–0; Sanchez d. Jaite 6–3 6–0. ***Final:*** Carlsson d. Sanchez 6–2 6–1.
MEN'S DOUBLES – Final: S. Casal (ESP)/E. Sanchez d. C. Panatta (ITA)/Willenborg 6–3 6–2.

BRISTOL ($100,000)

15–21 JUNE
MEN'S SINGLES – Quarter-finals: M. Schapers (HOL) d. H. Leconte (FRA) 7–6 6–7 7–5; T. Wilkison (USA) d. B. Testerman (USA) 6–7 6–2 6–2; K. Evernden (NZL) d. E. Edwards (RSA) 3–6 6–3 6–4; E. Jelen (FRG) d. E. Winogradsky (FRA) 6–4 6–4. ***Semi-finals:*** Wilkison d. Schapers 4–6 6–4 10–8; Evernden d. Jelen 6–7 6–3 6–2. ***Final:*** Evernden d. Wilkison 6–4 7–6.
MEN'S DOUBLES – Abandoned.

ATHENS ($100,000)

15–21 JUNE
MEN'S SINGLES – Quarter-finals: T. Meinecke (FRG) d. P. Rebolledo (CHI) 6–1 6–7 6–3; F. Yunis (ARG) d. J. Navratil (TCH) 6–3 7–5; G. Perez Roldan (ARG) d. M. Vajda (TCH) 6–4 6–4; P. Vojtisek (FRG) d. H. Skoff (AUT) 7–6 6–4. ***Semi-finals:*** Meinecke d. Yunis 6–4 6–4; Perez Roldan d. Vojtisek 6–7 6–4 6–2. ***Final:*** Perez Roldan d. Meinecke 6–2 6–3.
MEN'S DOUBLES – Final: Meinecke/R. Osterthun (FRG) d. Navratil/T. Nijssen (HOL) 6–2 3–6 6–2.

HALL OF FAME CHAMPIONSHIPS ($100,000)

NEWPORT, 6–12 JULY
MEN'S SINGLES – Quarter-finals: W. Masur (AUS) d. J. Fitzgerald (USA) 6–4 6–3; D. Goldie d. M. Flur 6–4 7–5; C. Van Rensburg (RSA) d. J. Rive 2–6 6–3 6–3; S. Giammalva d. B. Drewett (AUS) 7–6 6–1. ***Semi-finals:*** Goldie d. Masur 6–2 4–6 6–2; Giammalva d. Van Rensburg 6–3 6–1. ***Final:*** Goldie d. Giammalva 6–7 6–4 6–4.
MEN'S DOUBLES – Final: Goldie/L. Scott d. C. Hooper/M. Leach 6–3 4–6 6–4.

SWISS CHAMPIONSHIPS ($200,000)

GSTAAD, 6–12 JULY
MEN'S SINGLES – Quarter-finals: E. Sanchez (ESP) d. M. Pernfors (SWE) 5–7 6–4 6–1; E. Bengoechea (ARG) d. A. Tous (ESP) 7–5 3–6 6–4; C. Mezzadri d. G. Forget (FRA) 7–6 6–3; R. Agenor (HAI) d. M. Vajda (TCH) 7–5 6–1. ***Semi-finals:*** Sanchez d. Bengoechea 6–1 7–5; Agenor d. Mezzadri 6–7 6–4 6–3. ***Final:*** Sanchez d. Agenor 6–2 6–3 7–6.
MEN'S DOUBLES – Final: J. Gunnarsson (SWE)/T. Smid (TCH) d. Forget/L. Courteau (FRA) 7–6 6–2.

STUTTGART ($200,000)

13–19 JULY
MEN'S SINGLES – Quarter-finals: M. Mecir (TCH) d. M. Vajda (TCH) 4–6 6–3 6–3; T. Smid (TCH) d. E. Bengoechea (ARG) 6–2 6–2; J. Gunnarsson (SWE) d. J. Hlasek (SUI) 6–4 6–4; C. U. Steeb d. H. Leconte (FRA) 7–5 6–3. ***Semi-finals:*** Mecir d. Smid 6–3 6–3; Gunnarsson d. Steeb 6–4 7–6. ***Final:*** Mecir d. Gunnarsson 6–0 6–2.
MEN'S DOUBLES – Final: R. Leach (USA)/T. Pawsat (USA) d. M. Pernfors (SWE)/M. Tideman (SWE) 6–3 6–4.

BORDEAUX ($125,000)

13–19 JULY
MEN'S SINGLES – Quarter-finals: B. Derlin (NZL) d. D. de Miguel (ESP) 6–3 1–6 6–1; R. Agenor (HAI) d. S. Shaw (GBR) 7–6 6–7 6–4; G. Urpi (ESP) d. M. Cierro (ITA) 6–2 7–6; E. Sanchez (ESP) d. T.

In Adelaide the English-born Australian, Wally Masur, won his first tournament since 1983. He went on to upset Boris Becker at the Australian Open on his way to the semi-finals, and was runner-up to Pat Cash at Nancy. *(A. Evans)*

Champion 6–4 6–2. ***Semi-finals:*** Agenor d. Derlin 6–1 6–3; Sanchez d. Urpi 6–1 6–2. ***Final:*** Sanchez d. Agenor 5–7 6–4 6–4.
MEN'S DOUBLES – Final: S. Casal/Sanchez d. D. Cahill (AUS)/M. Woodforde (AUS) 6–3 6–3.

LIVINGSTON, NEW JERSEY ($89,400)

13–19 JULY
MEN'S SINGLES – Quarter-finals: J. Kriek d. S. Bonneau 6–2 1–6 6–2; A. Antonitsch (AUT) d. M. Freeman 0–6 7–6 6–4; C. Saceanu (FRG) d. K. Flach 6–1 3–6 6–3; M. Flur d. W. Masur (AUS) 6–2 6–3. ***Semi-finals:*** Kriek d. Antonitsch 6–3 2–6 6–4; Saceanu d. Flur 6–3 6–4. ***Final:*** Kriek d. Saceanu 7–6 3–6 6–2.
MEN'S DOUBLES – Final: G. Donnelly/G. Holmes d. Flach/R. Seguso 7–6 6–3.

SCHENECTADY, NEW YORK ($89,400)

20–26 JULY
MEN'S SINGLES – Quarter-finals: J. Yzaga (PER) d. J. Lapidus 6–2 6–0; T. Mmoh (NIG) d. V. Van Patten 6–4 7–5; J. Pugh d. B. Testerman 6–2 6–3; T. Hogstedt (SWE) d. G. Muller (RSA) 7–6 6–3. ***Semi-finals:*** Yzaga d. Mmoh 6–3 6–2; Pugh d. Hogstedt 6–3 6–4. ***Final:*** Yzaga d. Pugh 0–6 7–6 6–1.
MEN'S DOUBLES – Final: G. Donnelly/G. Muller (RSA) d. Pugh/B. Pearce 7–6 6–2.

DUTCH CHAMPIONSHIPS ($150,000)

HILVERSUM, 27 JULY–2 AUGUST
MEN'S SINGLES – Quarter-finals: M. Mecir (TCH) d. H. Skoff (AUT) 7–5 6–2; E. Bengoechea (ARG) d. C. U. Steeb (FRG) 2–6 7–6 6–2; G. Perez Roldan (ARG) d. T. Muster (AUT) 7–6 1–6 6–1; M. Jaite (ARG) d. A. Chesnokov (URS) 6–2 6–4. ***Semi-finals:*** Mecir d. Bengoechea 6–1 7–5; Perez Roldan d. Jaite 3–6 7–5 6–3. ***Final:*** Mecir d. Perez Roldan 6–4 1–6 6–3 6–2.
MEN'S DOUBLES – Final: Mecir/W. Fibak (POL) d. T. Nijssen/J. Vekemans 7–6 6–7 6–2.

SWEDISH CHAMPIONSHIPS ($175,000)

BASTAD, 27 JULY–2 AUGUST
MEN'S SINGLES – Quarter-finals: M. Wilander d. J. Gunnarsson 6–4 7–6; J. Nystrom d. K. Carlsson 6–2 5–7 7–5; E. Sanchez (ESP) d. A. Jarryd 6–3 6–2; S. Edberg d. P. Vojitsek (FRG) 6–3 6–4. ***Semi-finals:*** Nystrom d. Wilander 6–2 6–2; Edberg d. Sanchez 6–4 6–0. ***Final:*** Nystrom d. Edberg 4–6 6–0 6–3.
MEN'S DOUBLES – Final: Edberg/Jarryd d. J./E. Sanchez 7–6 6–3.

KITZBUHEL ($175,000)

3–9 AUGUST
MEN'S SINGLES – Quarter-finals: M. Mecir (TCH) d. R. Agenor (HAI) 6–4 6–4; D. Cahill (AUS) d. R. Osterthun (FRG) 6–3 1–6 7–5; T. Meinecke (FRG) d. G. Perez Roldan (ARG) 6–3 6–3; E. Sanchez (ESP) d. P. Arraya (PER) 6–3 6–2. ***Semi-finals:*** Mecir d. Cahill 6–1 6–2; Sanchez d. Meinecke 6–2 6–2. ***Final:*** Sanchez d. Mecir 6–4 6–1 4–6 6–1.
MEN'S DOUBLES – Final: S. Casal (ESP)/Sanchez d. Mecir/T. Smid (TCH) 7–6 7–6.

PRAGUE ($150,000)

10–16 AUGUST
MEN'S SINGLES – Quarter-finals: J. Navratil d. W. Popp (FRG) 6–4 6–4; T. Smid d. T. Muster (AUT) 7–5 5–7 7–5; M. Vajda d. K. Novacek 6–4 4–6 6–3; G. Vilas (ARG) d. P. Korda 6–3 6–2. ***Semi-finals:*** Smid d. Navratil 6–1 7–5; Vajda d. Vilas 3–6 6–3 6–3. ***Final:*** Vajda d. Smid 6–1 6–3.
MEN'S DOUBLES – Final: M. Mecir/Smid d. S. Birner/Navratil 6–3 6–7 6–3.

ST VINCENT, ITALY ($100,000)

10–16 AUGUST
MEN'S SINGLES – Quarter-finals: F. Cancellotti w.o. K. Carlsson (SWE); P. Cane d. S. Colombo 7–5

6–3; P. Rebolledo (CHI) d. P. McNamee (AUS) 6–2 6–2; C. Pistolesi d. C. Miniussi 6–2 5–7 6–3. ***Semi-finals:*** Cancellotti d. Cane 6–2 6–2; Rebolledo d. Pistolesi 6–1 6–4. ***Final:*** Rebolledo d. Cancellotti 7–6 4–6 6–3.
MEN'S DOUBLES – Final: B. Cox (USA)/M. Fancutt (AUS) d. M. Cierro/A. DeMinicis 6–3 7–4.

RYE BROOK, NEW YORK ($89,400)

24–30 AUGUST
MEN'S SINGLES – Quarter-finals: R. Matuszewski d. M. Flur 7–5 6–1; J. Ross d. T. Muster (AUT) 7–6 6–3; R. Krishnan (IND) d. J. Sanchez (ESP) 6–0 6–1; P. Lundgren (SWE) d. M. Davis 6–2 6–3. ***Semi-finals:*** Ross d. Matuszewski 7–6 4–6 7–5; Lundgren d. Krishnan 6–2 7–5. ***Final:*** Lundgren d. Ross 6–7 7–5 6–3.
MEN'S DOUBLES – Final: L. Bourne/J. Klaparda d. C. Limberger (AUS)/M. Woodforde (AUS) 6–3 6–2.

GENEVA ($200,000)

14–20 SEPTEMBER
MEN'S SINGLES – Quarter-finals: A. Gomez (ECU) d. T. Tulasne (FRA) 7–6 6–4; T. Smid (TCH) d. G. Perez Roldan (ARG) 6–2 7–6; U. Stenlund (SWE) d. H. de le Pena (ARG) 4–6 6–1 7–5; C. Mezzadri d. R. Stadler 6–4 6–1. ***Semi-finals:*** Smid d. Gomez 7–6 4–6 6–0; Mezzadri d. Stenlund 6–2 6–7 7–6. ***Final:*** Mezzadri d. Smid 6–4 7–5.
MEN'S DOUBLES – Final: R. Acioly (BRA)/L. Mattar (BRA) d. M. Bahrami (IRN)/D. Perez (URU) 3–6 6–4 6–2.

MADRID ($89,400)

14–20 SEPTEMBER
MEN'S SINGLES – Quarter-finals: E. Sanchez d. J. Aguilera 6–3 6–0; F. Davin (ARG) d. J. Bardou 3–6 7–5 6–1; J. Sanchez d. P. Rebolledo (CHI) 6–4 6–4; J. Windahl (SWE) d. C. Bergstrom (SWE) 6–2 7–5. ***Semi-finals:*** E. Sanchez d. Davin 7–6 6–1; J. Sanchez d. Windahl 6–3 6–4. ***Final:*** E. Sanchez d. J. Sanchez 6–3 3–6 6–2.
MEN'S DOUBLES – Final: C. DiLaura (ITA)/J. Sanchez d. S. Casal/E. Sanchez 6–3 3–6 7–6.

PALERMO ($100,000)

28 SEPTEMBER–4 OCTOBER
MEN'S SINGLES – Quarter-finals: M. Jaite (ARG) d. L. Duncan (USA) 7–6 6–3; J. Cihak d. C. Miniussi 7–5 7–6; D. Keretic (FRG) d. J. Brown (USA) 6–0 6–3; K. Novacek (TCH) d. J. Arrese (ESP) 6–3 1–6 6–3. ***Semi-finals:*** Jaite d. Cihak 6–2 6–3; Novacek d. Keretic 6–2 6–3. ***Final:*** Jaite d. Novacek 7–6 6–7 6–4.
MEN'S DOUBLES – Final: L. Lavalle (MEX)/C. Panatta d. P. Korda (TCH)/T. Smid (TCH) 3–6 6–4 6–4.

BASLE ($200,000)

5–11 OCTOBER
MEN'S SINGLES – Quarter-finals: Y. Noah (FRA) d. H. Skoff (AUT) 6–2 6–4; G. Forget (FRA) d. S. Zivojinovic (YUG) 5–7 6–4 6–4; A. Agassi (USA) d. J. Navratil (TCH) 6–2 0–6 6–3; R. Agenor (HAI) d. P. Kuhnen (FRG) 7–5 6–7 6–4. ***Semi-finals:*** Noah d. Forget 6–1 6–2; Agenor d. Agassi 6–1 6–4. ***Final:*** Noah d. Agenor 7–6 6–4 6–4.
MEN'S DOUBLES – Final: A. Jarryd (SWE)/T. Smid (TCH) d. S. Birner (TCH)/Navratil 6–4 6–3.

BRISBANE ($150,000)

5–11 OCTOBER
MEN'S SINGLES – Quarter-finals: J. Frawley d. P. Cash 6–4 6–3; K. Evernden (NZL) d. R. Krishnan (IND) 7–6 6–1; M. Freeman (USA) d. B. Dyke 6–3 7–6; E. Jelen (FRG) d. J. Fitzgerald 7–5 6–3. ***Semi-finals:*** Evernden d. Frawley 5–7 6–3 6–4; Jelen d. Freeman 6–2 6–3. ***Final:*** Evernden d. Jelen 3–6 6–1 6–1.
MEN'S DOUBLES – Final: Evernden/M. Anger (USA) d. Dyke/W. Masur 7–6 6–2.

Kelly Evernden of New Zealand, a quarter-finalist at the Australian Open, improved his ranking by more than 250 places in 1987 with a first Grand Prix title at Bristol and singles and doubles titles in Brisbane in October. (P. Shephard-Lewis)

TEL AVIV ($89,400)

12–18 OCTOBER
MEN'S SINGLES – Quarter-finals: J. S. Connors (USA) d. H. Van Boeckel (HOL) 6–1 6–1; A. Mansdorf d. W. Popp (FRG) 6–7 6–4 6–2; P. Lundgren (SWE) d. G. Campbell (RSA) 6–3 3–6 6–2; B. Gilbert (USA) d. G. Bloom 6–3 6–3. ***Semi-finals:*** Mansdorf d. Connors 7–6 6–3; Gilbert d. Lundgren 6–3 6–3. ***Final:*** Mansdorf d. Gilbert 3–6 6–3 6–4.
MEN'S DOUBLES – Final: G. Bloom/S. Perkis d. Popp/Van Boeckel 6–2 6–4.

TOULOUSE ($175,000)

12–18 OCTOBER
MEN'S SINGLES – Quarter-finals: T. Mayotte (USA) d. C. Mezzadri (SUI) 6–2 6–1; J. Hlasek (SUI) d. P. Kuhnen (FRG) 6–4 1–6 6–2; R. Osterthun (FRG) d. L. Mattar (BRA) 3–6 6–4 6–3; T. Wilkison (USA) d. J. Potier (FRA) 6–4 6–7 6–3. ***Semi-finals:*** Mayotte d. Hlasek 6–3 6–1; Osterthun d. Wilkison 5–7 6–4 6–2. ***Final:*** Mayotte d. Osterthun 6–2 5–7 6–4.

MEN'S DOUBLES – Final: W. Fibak (POL)/M. Schapers (HOL) d. K. Jones (USA)/P. Kuhnen (FRG) 6–2 6–4.

VIENNA ($125,000)

19–25 OCTOBER
MEN'S SINGLES – Quarter-finals: T. Muster d. E. Sanchez (ESP) 6–4 6–4; A. Mansdorf (ISR) d. A. Jarryd (SWE) 4–6 7–5 6–2; J. Svensson (SWE) d. M. Srejber (TCH) 6–1 5–7 6–2; C. Mezzadri (SUI) d. T. Mayotte (USA) 7–6 6–7 7–6. ***Semi-finals:*** Mansdorf d. Muster 2–6 6–4 6–2; Svensson d. Mezzadri 6–2 6–3. ***Final:*** Svensson d. Mansdorf 1–6 1–6 6–2 6–3 7–5.
MEN'S DOUBLES – Final: M. Purcell (USA)/T. Wilkison (USA) d. E./J. Sanchez 6–3 7–5.

HONG KONG ($200,000)

26 OCTOBER–1 NOVEMBER
MEN'S SINGLES – Quarter-finals: M. J. Bates (GBR) d. T. Nijssen (HOL) 6–4 6–4; J. Fitzgerald (AUS) d. C. Saceanu (FRG) 6–1 4–6 6–2; E. Teltscher (USA) d. R. Leach (USA) 4–6 6–2 6–3; D. Cahill (AUS) d. J. Ross (USA) 6–4 4–6 6–4. ***Semi-finals:*** Fitzgerald d. Bates 6–3 6–4; Teltscher d. Cahill 7–5 6–0. ***Final:*** Teltscher d. Fitzgerald 6–7 3–6 6–1 6–2 7–5.
MEN'S DOUBLES – Final: M. Kratzmann (AUS)/J. Pugh (USA) d. M. Davis (USA)/B. Drewett (AUS) 6–7 6–4 6–2.

SAO PAULO ($89,400)

9–15 NOVEMBER
MEN'S SINGLES – Quarter-finals: L. Mattar d. M. Filippino (URU) 6–3 6–4; D. Cassidy (USA) d. J. Gurfein (USA) 7–6 2–6 7–6; J. Berger (USA) d. T. Meinecke (FRG) 6–3 6–2; J. Yzaga (PER) d. R. Saad (ARG) 6–4 7–6. ***Semi-finals:*** Mattar d. Cassidy 6–2 6–4; Yzaga d. Berger 6–2 6–1. ***Final:*** Yzaga d. Mattar 6–2 4–6 6–2.
MEN'S DOUBLES – Final: G. Bloom (ISR)/J. Sanchez (ESP) d. T. Carbonell (ESP)/S. Casal (ESP) 6–3 6–7 6–4.

FRANKFURT ($150,000)

9–15 NOVEMBER
MEN'S SINGLES – Quarter-finals: A. Gomez (ECU) d. L. Pimek (TCH) 6–2 6–4; J. Pugh (USA) d. B. Gilbert (USA) 7–5 0–6 6–2; D. Rostagno (USA) d. N. Kroon (SWE) 7–6 4–6 6–1; T. Mayotte (USA) d. D. Goldie (USA) 7–6 6–4. ***Semi-finals:*** Gomez d. Pugh 6–3 6–3; Mayotte d. Rostagno 6–4 6–1. ***Final:*** Mayotte d. Gomez 7–6 6–4.
MEN'S DOUBLES – Final: B. Becker/P. Kuhnen d. S. Davis (USA)/D. Pate (USA) 6–4 6–2.

BUENOS AIRES ($89,400)

16–22 NOVEMBER
MEN'S SINGLES – Quarter-finals: P. Arraya (PER) d. M. Jaite 6–2 1–6 6–4; J. Berger (USA) d. H. de la Pena 6–7 6–3 6–4; G. Perez Roldan d. C. Motta (BRA) 4–6 6–1 6–4; J. Aguilera (ESP) d. G. Garetto 6–2 6–7 6–0. ***Semi-finals:*** Berger d. Arraya 2–6 7–6 6–4; Perez Roldan d. Aguilera 6–3 6–1. ***Final:*** Perez Roldan d. Berger 3–2 ret'd.
MEN'S DOUBLES – Final: T. Carbonell (ESP)/S. Casal (ESP) w.o. Berger/H. de la Pena.

ITAPARICA, BRAZIL ($125,000)

23–29 NOVEMBER
MEN'S SINGLES – Quarter-finals: T. Smid (TCH) d. A. Gomez (ECU) 7–6 7–6; L. Mattar d. S. Casal (ESP) 7–5 5–7 7–6; M. Jaite (ARG) d. T. Meinecke (FRG) 6–2 6–2; A. Agassi (USA) d. B. Gilbert (USA) 6–1 6–3. ***Semi-finals:*** Mattar d. Smid 4–6 7–6 6–4; Agassi d. Jaite 6–2 7–5. ***Final:*** Agassi d. Mattar 7–6 6–2.
MEN'S DOUBLES – Final: Casal/E. Sanchez (ESP) d. J. Lozano (MEX)/D. Perez (URU) 6–2 6–2.

Ivan Lendl was magnificent as he won a record fifth Nabisco Masters, losing only one set along the way – to Boris Becker – and spectacularly overcoming Mats Wilander in the third major final that they contested in 1987. (R. Adams)

THE NABISCO MASTERS

John Barrett

There was good news and bad news at the $500,000 Nabisco Masters in 1987. Let's start with the good things. Ivan Lendl was good, very good. He himself felt it was 'the best match I've played all year . . . possibly the best match I've ever played'. On the receiving end of this explosive expertise was the likeable 22-year-old Swede, Mats Wilander, who was failing against the world's No. 1 for the third time in 1987. Playing in his eighth consecutive final of the climactic event of the Nabisco Grand Prix year, and on the same Supreme court carpet on which he had won the title for the past two years and four times in all, the 27-year-old World Champion was virtually racket-perfect as he swept Wilander from the court 6–2 6–2 6–3 in just 2 hours and 23 minutes. One has to go back to Lendl's own humiliation at the hands of John McEnroe in January 1985 to find a performance to match it.

The organisation was also good. Tournament Director Gene Scott and his Tournament Manager, Sue Rothstein, led an experienced team. Nabisco's hospitality, organised by Ed Redding, was excellent, as were the ladies of the MIPTC's media support group and their master (metaphorically speaking, of course), Reg Lansbury. Full marks also to Bobby Goldwater of MSG, trainer Todd Snyder of ATP, dapper Drysdale, suave Stolle and the supporting cast of ESPN, Referee/Supervisor Ken Farrar of MIPTC, tournament doctors Irving Glick and Charles Goodwin, and the patient ladies at the media coat check-in desk.

The tennis? Oh yes, the tennis. Well, to be quite honest, some of it was not very good. All eight of the points leaders of the Nabisco points table were there, so it should have been good. A cynic might suggest that they all showed up only because unless they did so they could not take their share of the $4 million Nabisco bonus pool, ranging from Lendl's top prize of $800,000 to Brad Gilbert's $55,000. And that is why young Brad earlier went galloping off to Itaparica in Brazil to fight off the challenge of Andres Gomez, who also had his eyes on that little nest egg. The same motive had driven Pat Cash to Johannesburg and persuaded Boris Becker to return to competition despite a knee injury. And for the same reason Jimmy Connors decided to play, despite having announced he would be resting for the remainder of the year after pulling out of the Seiko tournament in Tokyo. Nature took her revenge, though, for Jimmy was forced to retire to Lendl with a respiratory disorder after just seven games of his last group match.

Just for the record, the top-heavy eight split $2,380,000 between them, leaving crumbs of $870,000 for the remaining 56 men on the Nabisco singles table and $750,000 for the top 24 Nabisco doubles players. The two Masters tournaments are the only times the overall sponsor, Nabisco, gets full value for money, although they don't get the profits. Ever since the MIPTC prised control of the event from the grasp of Volvo and ProServ a couple of years ago, they have been able to fund Marshall Happer's growing empire and the cost of all those first-class air fares without threat of insolvency.

Included in the bad-news category is the round-robin system of matches. Commercial it may be, but it is bad for the image of men's tennis. If this purports to be the final showdown of the year between the best eight players of the Grand Prix year, then it must surely reflect the greatest of those championships, the four Grand Slam events, where every match is contested over the full distance. Similarly, to reflect the Grand Prix accurately the Masters must be played on a variety of surfaces and in different continents. In 18 years it has visited only six countries, and has been played continuously at New York's Madison Square Garden since 1978. Tennis is a world sport, not only an American one, and if it is to regain its lost credibility and prestige in the minds of the legions of fans from Tokyo to Timbuctu, then it must be seen to be acting in the best interests of the sport.

And so to the tennis. The players were allocated places in the Rod Laver and Pancho Segura groups according to their ATP rankings. Thus in the first were Lendl (1), Connors (4), Becker (5) and Gilbert (13). In the second were Stefan Edberg (2), Wilander (3), Miloslav Mecir (6) and Cash (7). Each man played every other in his group, three matches being staged on each of the first three evenings beginning at 6.00 pm and three more on the Saturday, starting at noon. Thus every player had one day off. On Sunday the two semi-finals brought together the first and second man in each group, the pairings being decided by lot. The final was played on Monday, 4 December at 8.00 pm, the time being dictated by television. The fact that no national network saw fit to cover the tournament reflects the low standing of tennis compared with American football and basketball, both of which were at the height of their seasons at the time.

Lendl duly headed the Laver group with three wins. He was threatened only briefly on the Saturday, when Becker, by now out of the reckoning unless he could win in straight sets, suddenly caught fire. The 20-year-old West German, after a disappointing season marred by the parting from coach Gunther Bosch in Australia and by some niggling injuries, stormed to success in the second set after a tie-break of glorious free-hitting tennis. This cheered his new coach, Australian Bob Brett, who had taken on the role officially only the previous week at the Waterford Crystal Young Masters. There Becker, returning to competition after an enforced break, had not even reached the semi-finals. Now Lendl raised his game one notch to complete his win 6–4 6–7 6–3. Thus Lendl and Gilbert advanced, Gilbert having beaten both Becker and Connors, whom Becker had also beaten.

Edberg was as devastating in the Segura Group as Lendl was in his. Only one lost set – to Cash on the opening night – spoiled the otherwise perfect record of the 21-year-old former Junior World Champion. On day two he scored a 6–3 6–3 win against a lacklustre Mecir, who looked from the start as if he would much prefer to have been home in Czechoslovakia, fishing. The highlight of Edberg's week was a devastating display against fellow countryman Wilander on the fourth day. His 6–2 7–6 win, gained on the merits of some hard-hit groundstrokes and powerful serves, allied to the usual quota of winning volleys, brought him to 5–7 in matches against Wilander since the older man had won their first meeting as seniors at Bastad in 1983.

By the time he played Edberg, Wilander had also beaten Mecir (6–4 6–1) and Cash (7–6 6–3), so that he, too, was assured of a place in the semi-finals. A spin of the racket decided who would play whom on the Sunday, a method that was supposed to prevent anyone from manipulating the draw in the days when in the semi-finals the winner of each group would always play the second-placed man in the other. As luck would have it, the spin produced a rematch of the two round-robin matches. Predictably enough Lendl inflicted a 14th successive defeat on Gilbert. The score, 6–2 6–4, does not reveal the one-sided nature of the contest. 'I just grew a little bit lazy at the end', confided Lendl afterwards. 'I like to play in New York because I get to stay at home', home being a mansion a short drive away in Greenwich, Connecticut, where he is guarded by the famed German shepherd dogs who, like their master, can be savage when their security is threatened. With Lendl that means his No. 1 world ranking, which he defends with ruthless efficiency.

In the other semi-final Wilander turned the tables on Edberg. He won 6–2 4–6 6–3 against an increasingly despondent opponent, who looked as if he resented having to come out and prove all over again why he was the No. 2 player in the world. 'It feels very strange . . . you play a guy the day before and you really beat him badly . . . the next day you have to come and play him again. They are always going to have that problem with the round-robin', he reflected. Yet one had to admire the skill of Wilander, who was quick, sharp and eager; some of his counter-hitting and retrieving had to be seen to be believed.

Thus we had a final that was a repeat of the deciding matches in two of the major Championships of 1987, in Paris and New York. Lendl had won both to take his life-time tally against the Swede to 12 wins from 18 meetings since 1982. Wilander was 17 years old at the time of that first meeting in Paris during his record-breaking run to a first major title. Lendl was 22, and had yet to win a Grand Slam championship. That improbable fourth-round victory had stamped Wilander as a man of the future, and his two Australian titles in 1983 and 1984, plus another victory over Lendl in the 1985 French Open final, had turned the future into the present. Clearly the young Swede would be a force to be reckoned with for years to come.

Wilander's improvement had indeed been impressive, but Lendl's had been even more spectacular. A strict regime of training and diet, together with shrewd advice from his Australian coach, Tony Roche, had turned the Czech into a veritable iron man – iron in body, iron in will and iron in technique. By the time he had added a third French and a third consecutive US Open title to his tally in 1987, Lendl's powerful game had become irresistible. Only a narrow failure in the semi-finals of the Australian Open and a more decisive beating in the Wimbledon final (both at the hands of Cash) had blemished an otherwise perfect year. As he brushed Wilander aside at the year's end with a blistering display of service and groundstroke strength, Lendl stood unassailable at the head of men's tennis. It was a beautifully symmetrical performance from the World Champion, one that netted him a cool $210,000. The first set occupied 47 minutes, the second 48 and the third 48. While Lendl can produce tennis of this quality to order and as long as the strength of body and mind are maintained, there seems to be no reason why he should not stay there indefinitely.

NABISCO MASTERS ($500,000)

MADISON SQUARE GARDEN, NEW YORK, 2–7 DECEMBER
ROUND ROBIN – ROD LAVER GROUP: 1st I. Lendl (TCH) d. Gilbert 6–2 6–2, d. Connors 4–3 ret'd, d. Becker 6–4 6–7 6–3. ***2nd*** B. Gilbert d. Becker 4–6 6–4 6–4, d. Connors 6–4 7–6. ***3rd*** B. Becker (FRG) d. Connors 7–5 2–6 6–3. ***4th*** J. S. Connors. ***PANCHO SEGURA GROUP: 1st*** S. Edberg (SWE) d. Cash 6–4 4–6 6–1, d. Mecir 6–3 6–3, d. Wilander 6–2 7–6. ***2nd*** M. Wilander (SWE) d. Mecir 6–4 6–1, d. Cash 7–6 6–3. ***3rd*** P. Cash (AUS) d. Mecir 7–5 6–4. ***4th*** M. Mecir (TCH).
PLAY-OFFS – Semi-finals: Lendl d. Gilbert 6–2 6–4; Wilander d. Edberg 6–2 4–6 6–3. ***Final:*** Lendl d. Wilander 6–2 6–2 6–3.

Tomas Smid (above left) and Miloslav Mecir crowned a successful year's partnership by winning the Nabisco Masters doubles at the Royal Albert Hall (below). *(M. Cole)*

NABISCO MASTERS DOUBLES

Modesty Wood

The Nabisco Masters Doubles tournament, held for the second time at the Royal Albert Hall during the week after the singles, was won by Miloslav Mecir, a relative newcomer to the art of doubles, and the 31-year-old Tomas Smid, who was playing with his 18th different partner. Seeded fifth, they beat America's Ken Flach and Robert Seguso in a three-hour final, which could have been settled earlier had the eventual winners capitalised on two break-points in the third set. They earned $72,000, while the losers shared $36,000.

The Czechoslovaks were the only pairing to remain unbeaten in the round-robin stages, although against Stefan Edberg and Anders Jarryd they had to come from behind to win in five sets, as they did again in the semi-final against the same opposition. The Swedish duo, top seeds and defending champions, wasted two match-points in the first of those encounters. They were probably playing their last major doubles tournament together, as Edberg intends to reduce his doubles play to concentrate on singles in 1988. In the same group Paul Annacone and Christo Van Rensburg struggled in five sets to beat Australians Peter Doohan and Laurie Warder 7–6 7–6 2–6 4–6 7–6, finally taking the last tie-break 11–9 after four hours and eleven minutes. Annacone turned an ankle during that tie-break, and they lost the rest of their round-robin matches.

Flach and Seguso secured their place in the semi-final after straight-sets defeats of Americans Scott Davis and David Pate, and the Spanish pairing of Sergio Casal and Emilio Sanchez, the latter a rematch of the Wimbledon final. Perhaps feeling too complacent, they then lost, also in straight sets, to Peter Fleming and Gary Donnelly. The 1986 Wimbledon finalists had squeezed into the tournament when the runners-up of the previous year, Guy Forget and Yannick Noah of France, were prevented from playing by an injury to Noah. In the semi-finals Flach and Seguso again faced Casal and Sanchez, who, after losing the first two sets in 52 minutes, put up a tremendous fight before conceding 6–1 6–2 3–6 5–7 7–5.

The final featured the same contestants with the same outcome as that at Wembley a month earlier. On this occasion, Seguso's serve stuttered, while Flach had trouble returning serves, particularly those to his backhand. The American pair were also confounded by Mecir's subtlety, complemented by Smid's more forthright game, a combination which brought the Czechoslovak *Davis Cup* pairing their sixth title together in 1987.

NABISCO MASTERS DOUBLES ($200,000)

ROYAL ALBERT HALL, LONDON, 9–13 DECEMBER

ROUND ROBIN: GROUP I – 1st: M. Mecir (TCH)/T. Smid (TCH) 3 wins (d. Edberg/Jarryd 2–6 7–6 1–6 7–6 6–3, d. Annacone/Van Rensburg 6–2 6–1 6–4, d. Doohan/Warder 6–4 3–6 6–3 7–5). ***2nd:*** S. Edberg (SWE)/A. Jarryd (SWE) 2 wins (d. Annacone/Van Rensburg 7–6 6–3 6–2, d. Doohan/Warder 4–6 6–3 6–3 7–6). ***3rd:*** P. Annacone (USA)/C. Van Rensburg (RSA) 1 win (d. Doohan/Warder 7–6 7–6 2–6 4–6 7–6). ***4th:*** P. Doohan (AUS)/L. Warder (AUS) No win. ***GROUP II – 1st:*** K. Flach (USA)/R. Seguso (USA) 2 wins, 6–3 sets (d. Casal/Sanchez 6–3 6–3 6–2, d. Davis/Pate 6–2 6–3 6–4). ***2nd:*** S. Casal (ESP)/E. Sanchez (ESP) 2 wins, 6–3 sets (d. Fleming/Donnelly 6–3 6–4 6–4, d. Davis/Pate 7–6 6–4 7–6). ***3rd:*** P. Fleming (USA)/G. Donnelly (USA) 2 wins, 6–4 sets (d. Davis/Pate 6–3 3–6 6–3 6–4, d. Flach/Seguso 6–3 7–6 6–1). ***4th:*** S. Davis (USA)/D. Pate (USA) No win.

PLAY-OFFS – Semi-finals: Mecir/Smid d. Edberg/Jarryd 3–6 6–3 6–3 2–6 6–4; Flach/Seguso d. Casal/Sanchez 6–1 6–2 3–6 5–7 7–5. ***Final:*** Mecir/Smid d. Flach/Seguso 6–4 7–5 6–7 6–3.

5th place play-off: Annacone/Van Rensburg d. Donnelly/Fleming 6–1 3–6 6–1. ***7th place play-off:*** Davis/Pate d. Doohan/Warder 6–4 6–2.

REEBOK

WCT FINALS

Richard Finn

Just as the tournament officials of the Buick WCT Finals in Dallas had their hands full in keeping the prestige of this annual springtime extravaganza up to the high standard set by its predecessors, so the players had their hands full in keeping up with the wizardy of Miloslav Mecir. Even before the action began four top names pulled out of the eight-player field for a variety of reasons. Ivan Lendl was recovering from knee surgery, Henri Leconte was recuperating from back surgery, Nystrom was ailing, and Boris Becker, the previous year's runner-up and already seeded No. 1, withdrew just two days after he had won the Grand Prix title in Milan, and was replaced by Kevin Curren. Becker claimed to be suffering still from the stomach virus that had caused him to withdraw from the Lipton tournament, although tournament staff and media remembered that the previous year he had complained about the scheduling, when he had had to play three best-of-five-sets matches in as many days. Was this his retaliation?

Adding more to the woes of the tournament was the late appearance of Mats Wilander, who skipped Tuesday's mandatory press conference, opting instead to do some furniture shopping in New York with his wife – a spree that would cost him 15 per cent of his Grand Prix bonus cheque at the end of the year. He finally arrived on Thursday afternoon, hours before his opening match against Mecir which, not surprisingly, he lost 6–1 6–1 6–3.

McEnroe, the four-times champion who was making a record seventh appearance, had his opportunity to win a fifth title. He reached the final by virtue of a superb serve-and-volley performance to down Stefan Edberg 7–6 (7–4) 6–7 (5–7) 7–6 (7–3) 6–4 in the semi-finals, but in the Sunday morning final he was thwarted by the quiet, bearded Czech, Mecir, who was fast becoming the most feared player on the tour. Mecir, playing in just his second WCT play-offs, had reached the final with victories over Wilander and Andres Gomez. His career-first victory over McEnroe, 6–0 3–6 6–2 6–2, was worth $200,000, which put Mecir on top of the money-leaders' board. It was Mecir's fourth Grand Prix victory in the young season, and his triumph over McEnroe was his sixth over a top ten player in the year.

McEnroe, who had lost just one point on his serve in the final set against Edberg, did not have such luck against the penetrating and disguised returns of Mecir, who broke serve ten times, three in the first and fourth sets and four times in the third. Said Mecir: 'It showed to me that I can play good and beat some good players.'

WCT FINALS ($500,000)

DALLAS, 7–12 APRIL
MEN'S SINGLES – First round: S. Edberg (SWE) d. T. Mayotte 6–2 5–7 6–7 3–6 6–1; J. P. McEnroe d. Y. Noah (FRA) 7–6 6–2 4–6 6–3; A. Gomez (ECU) d. K. Curren 6–7 7–6 6–7 6–4 6–2; M. Mecir (TCH) d. M. Wilander (SWE) 6–1 6–3 6–3. ***Semi-finals:*** McEnroe d. Edberg 7–6 6–7 7–6 6–4; Mecir d. Gomez 6–7 7–6 6–4 6–2. ***Final:*** Mecir d. McEnroe 6–0 3–6 6–2 6–2.

The wizardry and guile of Miloslav Mecir proved too much of a puzzle for Mats Wilander, Andres Gomez and John McEnroe as the Czech downed them all to win the WCT Finals in Dallas *(T. Hindley)*

HEAD PRO
RACQUETS FOR WINNERS
THE NEW PERFORMANCE PRO
SERIES FOR PLAYERS
WHO WANT TO WIN
To win is the goal of each tennis player. HEAD has an advantage in tennis technology because the computer sophistication of the HEAD CAD-CAM System of racquet engineering with the personal assessment of top ranked professionals the world over. Together, they make it easier to win with HEAD.
The use of space age materials like TWARON® allows for the thinnest racquet profile in the world, and the «spoiler-effect» of the unique C.A.P. System – a protection strip fully integrated into the frame protecting both the racquet and strings – increase aerodynamic efficiency.
Choose the HEAD Pro that fits your game best, and for optimum performance, ask your authorized HEAD dealer for original HEAD strings.
HEAD
HIGH TECHNOLOGY
Henri Leconte

VIRGINIA SLIMS SERIES

VIRGINIA SLIMS SERIES REVIEW
POINTS EXPLANATION
POINTS AND PRIZE MONEY
VIRGINIA SLIMS SERIES TOURNAMENTS
VIRGINIA SLIMS CHAMPIONSHIPS

Although she won five titles, including a record 153rd, Chris Evert Finished 1987 ranked No. 3, her lowest since 1979. For the first time since 1973, she failed to win a Grand Slam title, and after her first-round loss to Sylvia Hanika at the Virginia Slims Championships she was seriously considering her future. *(Carol L. Newsom/Virginia Slims)*

prince

THE VIRGINIA SLIMS YEAR

Barry Wood

Once again the Virginia Slims tour, offering $15 million at 55 tournaments in 18 countries around the world in 1987, provided both a healthy living for some 200 of the world's best women players and also a showcase for their considerable talents. The year without any shadow of a doubt belonged to Steffi Graf, and Sunday, 16 August will live in her memory for ever. It will also go down in tennis history, for it was the day on which Steffi replaced Martina Navratilova as No. 1 in the world. She became the first European and, apart from a brief reign by Tracy Austin, the only player other than Navratilova and Chris Evert to be ranked in that position since computer records began in 1975. The occasion was the final of the Virginia Slims of Los Angeles, a city already close to Graf's heart following her victory in the Olympic Demonstration event there in 1984. She had started the year with a win over Helena Sukova in the final of the Virginia Slims of Florida, she had claimed her first Grand Slam title by defeating Navratilova in Paris, and she finished the year in the way she had begun by beating Gabriela Sabatini in the final of the Virginia Slims Championships. Her record for the year stood at 75–2, the only setbacks being her losses to Navratilova in the Wimbledon and US Open finals. Her last defeat by anyone other than Navratilova was at the hands of Hana Mandlikova in the quarter-finals of the French Open in 1986.

Martina considered that her victories in the two most important tournaments were enough to make her – morally at least – still the real No. 1, especially as her record against Graf stood at 2-all. 'I've played twelve tournaments and won ten of them', Graf responded on the eve of the Championships. 'That's a great thing and very difficult ever to do again, and I would not exchange those ten titles for two Grand Slams. I've had such a consistent year and to me it's fair that I am No. 1'. After the Championships, in which she was beaten by Sabatini in the quarter-finals, Navratilova reluctantly gave up the argument. 'She's No. 1. Which is too bad, because what disappoints me most is that I know I am the better player. I just haven't proved it on the court', she said.

She will find it difficult, if not impossible, to recover the ground she lost in the first half of 1987. While Graf promised after the Championships that even better things may be in store from her in 1988, the dethroned champion is left to contemplate a famine of titles stretching all the way from the 1986 Virginia Slims Championships in November right up to Wimbledon. Graf was No. 1 in most people's minds long before the computer confirmed it on that hot August afternoon. At the season's end the prize money list confirmed it too. For the first time since 1981, when both Evert and Austin were ahead of her, Martina failed to head the earnings table. Miss Graf's $1,063,785 was more than $100,000 ahead of her and meant that the young West German now joined the select band of 22 tennis millionairesses.

However, Martina did carve a place in history for herself during the year. She became the first player since Billie Jean King at Wimbledon in 1973 to win a Grand Slam triple crown. The venue was the US Open, and she added the women's doubles and the mixed doubles to her win over Graf. She was, however, helped along the way by receiving walkovers through the semi-finals of both doubles events. Graf was suffering from the 'flu and so withdrew with Sabatini while defending mixed champions, Sergio Casal and

With four singles titles and a semi-final showing at Wimbledon, Pam Shriver improved her year-end ranking to four, as well as maintaining her excellent record in doubles, in which she completed a third Grand Slam with Martina Navratilova. (T. Hindley)

Raffaella Reggi, had to pull out because rain had caused the event to overrun by a day and Casal had to travel to Europe for another tournament. If there was no challenge in the semis, there certainly was in the finals. In the women's doubles Navratilova and Pam Shriver were down a set and 2–4 to Kathy Jordan and Elizabeth Smylie, and in the mixed, Navratilova and Emilio Sanchez had to save two match-points against Betsy Nagelsen and Paul Annacone before winning 6–4 6–7 (6–8) 7–6 (14–12).

While Graf and Navratilova found triumph in different ways, Evert stood at the cross-roads of her glittering career as the year drew to a close. There were signs, quite understandably after a lifetime in the sport, that the hunger was no longer there. At times she would produce some of the best tennis she has ever played – against Navratilova in Los Angeles and Wimbledon, against Pam Shriver in Dallas for example – but it wasn't there week in, week out as it used to be. She lost to Lori McNeil in the quarter-finals at Flushing Meadow, and she lost twice to Shriver. She had never done that before. Then at the Championships she was outplayed by Sylvia Hanika in the first round – a defeat that saw her returning home to ponder her future after leaving an ominous warning echoing down the corridors. 'I've been on the road since I was 16 and I'm 32 now. I feel like a machine and I just want to be normal and do the things that a normal girl does. I've been a gypsy and I don't want to be a gypsy any more.'

Shriver's victories over Evert helped her reach No. 4 in the world for the first time, a just reward for a year of consistency. Although her game did not perhaps reach the heights demonstrated in the latter part of 1986, she did claim four titles. Sabatini also reached her highest point, ending the year at No. 6. Her game made remarkable progress, largely as a result of her employing Angel Gimenez as her coach in March, immediately following the Lipton tournament. All aspects of her game have improved considerably, especially her serve, which has been converted from a liability into a weapon, as well as her willingness and ability to cover the whole court. As her game matured, so she beat Navratilova for the first time to reach the Italian Open final, and she repeated the f at at Madison Square Garden. Along the way she also won the Pan Pacific Open in Tokyo and the Brighton Classic. Hana Mandlikova, however, suffered a disapppointing year after a bright start in which she won Brisbane, the Australian Open and Washington. Part of her problem was persistent injury, but she didn't suffer as badly as Stephanie Rehe and Kathy Rinaldi, both of whom missed most of the year.

A significant advance was made by the Russians, who ended the year with Larisa Savchenko and Natalia Zvereva in the top 25, with others such as Natalia Bykova and Leila Meskhi also making plenty of ripples. Savchenko, already part of a successful doubles team with Svetlana Parkhomenko, reached the final of the Edgbaston Cup, while Zvereva moved from 92 in the world to 19. The young girl from Minsk, who didn't turn 16 until April, came to world attention when she dismissed McNeil in the second round at Wimbledon and then took a set from Sabatini on Centre Court. She charmed the crowd (and the hardened men of the press) on that occasion, and did so again by reaching the final of the Virginia Slims of Chicago, where she lost to Navratilova. She also reached the final of the Virginia Slims of Arkansas for the second year in a row, and won the French, Wimbledon and US Open junior titles.

Zvereva would be one candidate for the most improved player of the year award, but there are many other contenders. Sylvia Hanika makes a strong bid. She began the year by beating Sabatini and reaching the final in San Francisco, then finished by beating Evert on her way to the semi-finals of the Championships. She rose from 50 – which was already an achievement, as she had slipped below 100 – and finished at No. 14. Barbara Potter too has a strong claim, for overcoming a series of crippling injuries to return to the edge of the top ten. Kathy Jordan, who missed most of 1986, also stormed back again, rising from 100 to 36. Some unexpected names sprang forward during the year too. Elizabeth Smylie, better known as one of the world's top doubles players, reached the quarter-finals of the Australian Open and consolidated that success by beating McNeil in the final of the Virginia Slims of Oklahoma. Those accomplishments pushed her into the top 20 during the year, from a low point of 114.

The award, though, may go to Sandra Cecchini, who has surprised many by reaching

Returning after a series of crippling injuries, Barbara Potter won titles in Kansas and Beckenham, to finish the year ranked just outside the top ten. *(A. Evans)*

the top 20 and strongly challenging Reggi as the Italian No. 1. Her strength of course is clay, and she was successful in reaching the semi-finals of the German Open (where she lost 6–4 in the third set to Graf), as well as the finals of Strasbourg (lost Bassett) and Bastad (beat Lindqvist). She also reached the semi-finals in Hamburg and won Arkansas indoors.

In doubles, Navratilova and Shriver underlined their long-running supremacy by adding seven more titles to their growing list. Their only major disappointment in an otherwise all-conquering year was the loss of their Wimbledon title at the quarter-final stage, where they were beaten by the Russians, Parkhomenko and Savchenko.

VIRGINIA SLIMS WORLD CHAMPIONSHIP SERIES 1987 POINTS EXPLANATION

The Virginia Slims World Championship Series is the equivalent of the men's Grand Prix. The series began on 29 December in Brisbane and ended with the Virginia Slims Championships (prize money $1 million) in November 1987 at Madison Square Garden, New York. There were 55 singles and one doubles tournaments in six points categories scheduled to take place in 18 different countries. The leading 16 singles players and eight doubles pairs on the Virginia Slims points table qualified for the Championships.

Events comprising the 1987 Virginia Slims World Championship Series included:

Grand Slam Championships: Australian Open, French Open, Wimbledon, US Open.

Virginia Slims named events: With prize money of $150,000 or more.

Supported tournaments: Where Virginia Slims is not the named sponsor but contributes to the event, which must have prize money of $150,000 or more.

Named independent series events: Where prize money is $75,000 and Virginia Slims is the named sponsor.

Independent Series events: Where prize money is $50,000 and no contribution is made by Virginia Slims.

All Series tournaments are under the jurisdiction of the Women's International Professional Tennis Council who divide the tournaments into the following points categories. The points given are for singles. Individual players' doubles points are half those awarded for singles.

	Grand Slam and Virginia Slims Championships (singles only)	**Category 4 $200,000+**	**Category 3 $150,000+**	**Category 2 $100,000+**	**Category 1+ $75,000+**	**Category 1 $50,000+**
Winner	700	375	300	200	150	100
Runner-up	490	263	210	140	105	70
Losing semi-finalist	315	169	135	90	68	45
Losing quarter-finalist	161	86	69	46	35	23
Loser – round of 16	84	45	36	24	18	12
Loser – round of 32	42	23	18	12	9	6
Loser – round of 64*	21	11	9	6	4	3
Loser – round of 128*	7	4	3	2	1	1

*Outside Grand Slam events and 64-draw events points to be used for qualifying.

1987 BONUS POOLS ($US) Total $1 million.

SINGLES: **1** 225,000; **2** 170,000; **3** 120,000; **4** 85,000; **5** 45,000; **6** 25,000; **7–8** 15,000; **9–12** 10,000; **13–16** 5,000 (Total $785,000).

DOUBLES: **1** 50,000; **2** 25,000; **3–4** 10,000; **5–8** 5,000 (Total $115,000).

Exempt 'A' player-incentive pool: **1** 30,000; **2** 20,000; **3** 15,000; **4 10,000 (Total $75,000).**

Independent tournament incentive pool (Player ranked 19–40 on 9 August 1986): **1** 10,000; **2** 7,500; **3** 5,000; ***4*** 2,500 (Total $25,000).

Left: *Bettina Bunge, voted WITA Comeback Player of the Year, reached her first final for four years at the Belgian Open.* ***Right:*** *Catarina Lindqvist reached the Australian Open semi-finals and the last 16 of Wimbledon and the US Open. Both qualified for the Virginia Slims Championships.* *(Carol L. Newson/Virginia Slims)*

VIRGINIA SLIMS WORLD CHAMPIONSHIP SERIES 1987 – FINAL STANDINGS AND BONUSES

SINGLES POSITION		SINGLES POINTS	SINGLES BONUS	DOUBLES POSITION	DOUBLES POINTS	DOUBLES BONUS	TOTAL BONUS
1	Steffi Graf (FRG)	5,455	$225,000				$225,000
2	Martina Navratilova (USA)	4,087	170,000	4	3,911	$10,000	180,000
3	Chris Evert (USA)	3,901	120,000				120,000
4	Pam Shriver (USA)	3,426	85,000	3	4,149	10,000	85,000
5	Gabriela Sabatini (ARG)	3,296	45,000				45,000
6	Helena Sukova (TCH)	2,934	25,000	2	4,224	25,000	50,000
7	Hana Mandlikova (TCH)	2,639	15,000				15,000
8	Lori McNeil (USA)	2,331	15,000	1	4,951	50,000	65,000
9	Zina Garrison (USA)	2,274	10,000	6	3,435	5,000	15,000
10	Manuela Maleeva (BUL)	2,182	10,000				10,000
11	Claudia Kohde-Kilsch (FRG)	1,626	10,000	5	3,889	5,000	15,000
12	Sylvia Hanika (FRG)	1,454	10,000				10,000
13	Raffaella Reggi (ITA)	1,332	5,000				5,000
14	Catarina Lindqvist (SWE)	1,260	5,000				5,000
15	Bettina Bunge (FRG)	1,186	5,000				5,000
16	Katerina Maleeva (BUL)	1,174	5,000				5,000
Players with doubles bonuses only							
	Elizabeth Smylie (AUS)			7	2,742	5,000	5,000
	Elise Burgin (USA)			8	2,732	5,000	5,000

VIRGINIA SLIMS 1987

DATE	VENUE	SINGLES FINAL	DOUBLES WINNERS
1–8 Dec	Buenos Aires	G. Sabatini d. A. Sanchez 6–1 6–1	L. McNeil/M. Paz
9–15 Dec	Sao Paulo	V. Nelson Dunbar d. J. Klitch 6–2 7–6	N. Dias/P. Medrado
29 Dec–4 Jan	Brisbane	H. Mandlikova d. P. H. Shriver 6–2 2–6 6–4	H. Mandlikova/W. M. Turnbull
5–11 Jan	Sydney	Z. Garrison d. P. H. Shriver 6–2 6–4	B. Nagelsen/E. Smylie
12–25 Jan	Melbourne (*Australian Open*)	H. Mandlikova d. M. Navratilova 7–5 7–6	M. Navratilova/P. H. Shriver
26 Jan–1 Feb	Tokyo	—	C. Kohde-Kilsch/H. Sukova
26 Jan–1 Feb	Auckland	G. Rush d. T. Phelps 6–2 6–3	J. Richardson/A. M. Fernandez
2–8 Feb	Wichita, Kansas	B. Potter d. L. Savchenko 7–6 7–6	S. Parkhomenko/L. Savchenko
8–15 Feb	San Francisco	Z. Garrison d. S. Hanika 7–5 4–6 6–3	H. Mandlikova/W. M. Turnbull
8–15 Feb	Oklahoma	E. Smylie d. L. McNeil 4–6 6–3 7–5	S. Parkhomenko/L. Savchenko
12–22 Feb	Boca Raton	S. Graf d. H. Sukova 6–2 6–3	S. Parkhomenko/L. Savchenko
23 Feb–8 March	Key Biscayne	S. Graf d. C. M. Evert 6–1 6–2	M. Navratilova/P. H. Shriver
9–15 March	Phoenix	A. White d. D. Balestrat 6–1 6–2	P. Barg/B. Herr
12–14 March	Marco Island	—	C. M. Evert/W. M. Turnbull
16–22 March	Dallas	C. M. Evert d. P. H. Shriver 6–1 6–3	M. L. Piatek/A. White
23–29 March	Washington, DC	H. Mandlikova d. B. Potter 6–4 6–2	E. Burgin/P. H. Shriver
30 March–5 April	Piscataway, NJ	H. Sukova d. L. McNeil 6–0 6–3	G. Fernandez/L. McNeil
30 March–5 April	Charleston	M. Maleeva d. R. Reggi 5–7 6–2 6–3	L. Gildemeister/T. Scheuer-Larsen
6–12 April	Hilton Head	S. Graf d. M. Maleeva 6–2 4–6 6–3	M. Paz/E. Pfaff
13–19 April	Amelia Island	S. Graf d. H. Mandlikova 6–3 6–4	S. Graf/G. Sabatini
13–19 April	Tokyo	K. Maleeva d. B. Gerken 6–2 6–3	K. Jordan/B. Nagelsen
20–27 April	Houston	C. M. Evert d. M. Navratilova 3–6 6–1 7–6	M. Navratilova/K. Jordan
20–27 April	Taipei	A. Minter d. C. Porwik 6–4 6–1	Ca./Cy. MacGregor
27 April–3 May	Tampa	C. M. Evert d. K. Gompert 6–3 6–2	C. M. Evert/W. M. Turnbull
27 April–3 May	Singapore	A. Minter d. B. Gerken 6–4 6–1	A. M. Fernandez/J. Richardson
4–10 May	Rome (*Italian Open*)	S. Graf d. G. Sabatini 7–5 4–6 6–0	M. Navratilova/G. Sabatini
11–17 May	Berlin	S. Graf d. C. Kohde-Kilsch 6–2 6–3	C. Kohde-Kilsch/H. Sukova
18–24 May	Geneva	C. M. Evert d. M. Maleeva 6–3 4–6 6–2	B. Nagelsen/E. Smylie
18–24 May	Strasbourg	C. Bassett d. A. M. Cecchini 6–3 6–4	J. Novotna/C. Suire
25 May–7 June	Paris (*French Open*)	S. Graf d. M. Navratilova 6–4 4–6 8–6	M. Navratilova/P. H. Shriver
8–14 June	Edgbaston	P. H. Shriver d. L. Savchenko 4–6 6–2 6–2	—
15–21 June	Eastbourne	H. Sukova d. M. Navratilova 7–6 6–3	S. Parkhomenko/L. Savchenko
22 June–5 July	Wimbledon	M. Navratilova d. S. Graf 7–5 6–3	C. Kohde-Kilsch/H. Sukova
5–12 July	Bastad	A. M. Cecchini d. C. Lindqvist 6–4 6–4	P. Barg/T. Scheuer-Larsen
5–12 July	Knokke	K. Horvath d. B. Bunge 6–1 7–6	B. Bunge/M. Maleeva
13–19 July	Newport, RI	P. H. Shriver d. W. White 6–2 6–4	G. Fernandez/L. McNeil

DATE	VENUE	SINGLES FINAL	DOUBLES WINNERS
20–26 July	Berkeley, Cal.	E. Hakami d. M. Gurney 6–3 6–2	K. Jordan/R. White
3–9 Aug	San Diego	R. Reggi d. A. Minter 6–0 6–4	J. Novotna/C. Suire
10–16 Aug	Los Angeles	S. Graf d. C. M. Evert 6–3 6–4	M. Navratilova/P. H. Shriver
17–23 Aug	Toronto	P. H. Shriver d. Z. Garrison 6–4 6–1	Z. Garrison/L. McNeil
24–30 Aug	Mahwah, NJ	M. Maleeva d. S. Hanika	G. Fernandez/L. McNeil
31 Aug–13 Sept	New York (*US Open*)	M. Navratilova d. S. Graf 7–6 6–1	M. Navratilova/P. H. Shriver
14–20 Sept	Tokyo	G. Sabatini d. M. Maleeva 6–4 7–6	A. White/R. White
21–27 Sept	Hamburg	S. Graf d. I. Cueto 6–2 6–2	C. Kohde-Kilsch/J. Novotna
21–27 Sept	Athens	K. Maleeva d. J. Halard 6–1 6–0	A. Betzner/J. Wiesner Polzl
28 Sept–4 Oct	New Orleans	C. M. Evert d. L. McNeil 6–3 7–5	Z. Garrison/L. McNeil
12–18 Oct	San Juan	S. Rehe d. C. Benjamin 7–6 7–6	L. Gregory/R. Reis
12–18 Oct	Filderstadt	M. Navratilova d. C. M. Evert 7–5 6–1	M. Navratilova/P. H. Shriver
19–25 Oct	Brighton	G. Sabatini d. P. H. Shriver 7–5 6–4	K. Jordan/H. Sukova
26 Oct–1 Nov	Zurich	S. Graf d. H. Mandlikova 6–2 6–2	N. Herreman/P. Paradis
26 Oct–1 Nov	Indianapolis	H. Cioffi d. A. E. Smith 4–6 6–4 7–6	J. Byrne/M. Jaggard
2–8 Nov	Worcester, Mass.	P. H. Shriver d. C. M. Evert 6–4 4–6 6–0	E. Burgin/R. Fairbank
2–8 Nov	Arkansas	A. M. Cecchini d. N. Zvereva 0–6 6–1 6–3	M. L. Daniels/R. White
9–15 Nov	Chicago	M. Navratilova d. N. Zvereva 6–1 6–2	C. Kohde-Kilsch/H. Sukova
16–22 Nov	New York (*Virginia Slims Champs*)	S. Graf d. G. Sabatini 4–6 6–4 6–0 6–4	M. Navratilova/P. H. Shriver

The remarkable Wendy Turnbull of Australia was still a force to be reckoned with at the age of 35, beating Mandlikova and McNeil in Brisbane and winning four doubles titles in 1987. *(Carol L. Newson)*

SEGMENT 1: 5 JANUARY–8 MARCH

Barry Wood, Jim Sarni, Ronald Atkin

SYDNEY ($150,000)

Hana Mandlikova was the top seed and definitely the player to beat, following her success the week before in Brisbane, where she had won both the singles and doubles titles. The player to do it was veteran Wendy Turnbull, who repeated her 1986 US Open upset with a 6–3 7–5 victory in the third round. The wily Australian is never more dangerous than when she appears to be losing her grip as one of the game's most enduring characters, and in Sydney she was fired by her dismal showing in Brisbane where she had expired with hardly a whimper against Heather Ludloff, although she had won the doubles with Mandlikova. True, it was another of those erratic performances from Hana that we used to witness with depressing regularity but which have now become a rarity, but Hana gave Wendy credit: 'Wendy played very well and didn't miss anything. She mixed up her shots a lot and sometimes served so softly I couldn't do anything with it'.

In fact, she was playing so well, reaching the semi-finals without dropping a set, that there were realistic hopes voiced of her perhaps reaching the final and even winning the event. After wins over Terry Holladay, top Australian junior Nicole Provis and then Mandlikova, Wendy clashed with Lori McNeil. The Texan was an opponent to be wary of, having proved her worth on grass by reaching the quarter-finals at Wimbledon and the final at Newport. Thus, the fact that Turnbull beat her 6–4 7–5 only added to the hopes of the Aussie crowd that their heroine would manage to dismiss Zina Garrison too. But it wasn't to be. Sentiment carried only so far, and Garrison pulled out a 6–3 6–4 victory.

While all the excitement was going on in the top half of the draw, the second seed, Pam Shriver, was making her way confidently through the pack in the bottom half. Sara Gomer fell first, followed by Gretchen Rush, Catarina Lindqvist and then Manuela Maleeva, none winning more than six games. Shriver was out for a title, anxious to make up for her defeat by Hana in Brisbane. The last thing she wanted was to lose two finals in two weeks. But that is what happened, as a quite brilliant Garrison triumphed 6–2 6–4. It was her first grass-court singles success since she claimed the Wimbledon Junior title in 1981.

There were some tremendous performances from lesser players during the week. Anne Minter perhaps worked the hardest, defeating Cammie MacGregor, 7–6 (7–5) 4–6 7–5, and then Anne Hobbs, 2–6 6–3 6–3, before falling 6–4 2–6 6–4 to Etsuko Inoue. Hobbs had had her own tough match in the first round, taking almost three hours to defeat Helen Kelesi 7–6 (7–4) 6–7 (4–7) 6–4. It was all the more unfortunate that the contest ended in such controversial circumstances. Hobbs, leading 5–3 30–30 in the final set, hit what she thought were two aces, but each time they were called out, the call being upheld by umpire Peter Duncan. The tables were then turned dramatically moments later when at 5–4 and match-point to Hobbs, a forehand from Kelesi was called out after landing quite clearly inside the line. The volatile Canadian argued long and hard but to no avail.

The doubles saw a major upset when the unheralded team of Jenny Byrne and Janine Thompson defeated the top seeds, Claudia Kohde-Kilsch and Helena Sukova, 7–5 7–5 in the third round. The Aussies followed that result with a win in three sets over Gigi Fernandez and Robin White to reach the final, where they battled bravely before conceding the match to Betsy Nagelsen and Elizabeth Smylie 6–7 (5–7) 7–5 6–1. – B. W.

5–11 JANUARY
WOMEN'S SINGLES – Quarter-finals: W. M. Turnbull d. L. McNeil (USA) 6–4 7–5; Z. Garrison (USA)

d. H. Sukova (TCH) 6–3 6–1; M. Maleeva (BUL) d. E. Inoue (JAP) 4–6 6–2 6–2; P. H. Shriver (USA) d. C. Lindqvist (SWE) 6–4 6–2. ***Semi-finals:*** Garrison d. Turnbull 6–3 6–4; Shriver d. Maleeva 6–3 6–3. ***Final:*** Garrison d. Shriver 6–2 6–4.
WOMEN'S DOUBLES – Final: B. Nagelsen (USA)/E. Smylie d. J. Byrne/J. Thompson 6–7 7–5 6–1.

VIRGINIA SLIMS OF CALIFORNIA ($150,000)

The Virginia Slims of California, which moved in 1987 from its usual location across the bay in Oakland to downtown San Francisco, was won by Zina Garrison but dominated by a renascent Sylvia Hanika enjoying her tenth year as a professional and determined to regain her place in the top ten. Apparently lacking motivation or interest, she had slipped disastrously from her peak in 1983, when she was ranked five in the world, to a low of 102 in the summer of 1986. In an effort to reverse the trend she competed in a $50,000 event in Greece and, by defeating Angeliki Kanellopoulou in the final, was able to start upon the long road back to respectability, with a rediscovered determination, release from various illnesses, and the loss of 20lb.

In California, fourth-seeded Gabriela Sabatini was the first to suffer from Hanika's revival, losing 4–6 6–1 6–2 in the opening round. Despite a painful ankle injury, Hanika followed that by surrendering just two games to Laura Garrone before defeating sixth-seeded Wendy Turnbull in straight sets to reach the semi-finals. The German left-hander dropped the first set to second seed Kathy Rinaldi, recovered to win, and then fought long and hard before surrendering 7–5 4–6 6–3 to Garrison in the final.

But what of Garrison? She began the year by winning the singles title and reaching the doubles semi-finals in Sydney. That was followed by a quarter-final finish in the Australian Open – where she lost to Martina Navratilova. In doubles, she reached the final with Lori McNeil, where they were overwhelmed by Navratilova and Pam Shriver, and in the mixed doubles she won the title with Sherwood Stewart over Anne Hobbs and Andrew Castle. So, together with Hana Mandlikova – winner in Brisbane and Melbourne – she entered California as the player most in form. When the two met, in the semi-finals, it was Garrison, agile and approaching the net effectively, who kept her momentum going by defeating Mandlikova 7–5 4–6 6–2.

Andrea Temesvari, once ranked in the top ten but now suffering from a seemingly endless round of injuries, made a rare appearance. But after defeating US Open junior champion Elly Hakami in the first round, she offered little resistance to Manuela Maleeva. Meanwhile, Sabatini was not the only seed to fall in the first round, for Robin White, seeded seven, fought out a brave first set against Mary Joe Fernandez, but then collapsed to a 6–7 (7–9) 6–1 6–3 defeat.

The doubles title was won by top seeds Mandlikova and Turnbull for their second success of the year. They followed up their victory in Brisbane with a 6–4 7–6 (7–4) win over second seeds Garrison and Sabatini. The only upset came in the first round, when Alycia Moulton and Molly Van Nostrand, seeded four, fell 6–4 6–7 (5–7) 6–2 to the French girls, Isabelle Demongeot and Nathalie Tauziat, who again caught the eye with matching outfits. – B. W.

SAN FRANCISCO, 9–15 FEBRUARY
WOMEN'S SINGLES – Quarter-finals: H. Mandlikova (TCH) d. M. Maleeva (BUL) 6–3 7–5; Z. Garrison d. W. White 6–1 6–2; S. Hanika (FRG) d. W. M. Turnbull (AUS) 6–4 6–1; K. Rinaldi d. S. Rehe 1–6 6–4 6–4. ***Semi-finals:*** Garrison d. Mandlikova 7–5 4–6 6–2; Hanika d. Rinaldi 1–6 6–3 6–2. ***Final:*** Garrison d. Hanika 7–5 4–6 6–3.
WOMEN'S DOUBLES – Final: Mandlikova/Turnbull d. Garrison/G. Sabatini (ARG) 6–4 7–6.

VIRGINIA SLIMS OF FLORIDA ($250,000)

The Polo Club is Chris Evert's new address in South Florida, but Steffi Graf owns the centre court. Graf won the $250,000 Virginia Slims of Florida there to cap her rise to No. 2 on the WITA computer, while Evert Lloyd, the former No. 2, was forced to watch from the sidelines. Playing her first tournament for five months following a serious knee

Despite being hampered by a stress fracture to her foot, which forced her to withdraw from the French Open and Wimbledon, Zina Garrison won singles titles in Sydney and California, and was runner-up with McNeil in the women's doubles at the Australian Open, where she won the mixed with Stewart. *(T. Hindley)*

injury, Evert Lloyd suffered only her sixth loss in her home state when she fell 4–6 6–4 6–3 in the third round to Kate Gompert, a former All-American at Stanford. 'Kate played a great match', said Evert Lloyd, who had won the tournament the past four years at Key Biscayne and PGA National in Palm Beach Gardens. 'I guess coming into the tournament I didn't expect too much and, as a result, I didn't do too much.'

The local fans who came to see the triumphant return of Evert Lloyd soon found a new heroine in Graf, the West German teenager who had lost in last year's final. Playing her first tournament of the season, she quickly rediscovered the form that won her eight tournaments in 1987, and did not lose a set as she dispatched Angeliki Kanellopoulou, Sara Gomer, Claudia Kohde-Kilsch, Pam Shriver in the semi-finals and Helena Sukova 6–2 6–3 in the final. Graf needed only 59 minutes to beat Sukova, who had rallied to win three-set matches against Patty Fendick, Raffaella Reggi and Gabriela Sabatini on her way to the final. Pavel Slozil, Graf's new coach, watched with wry interest as his pupil dissected Sukova. Before he could start working with Graf, Slozil, a Czech, had to obtain permission from his national tennis federation, whose president is Cyril Suk, the father of Helena Sukova. 'It was a special feeling to watch Steffi play Helena', Slozil said. 'The better player won. I was happy for Steffi, but if Helena had won, I would have been the first to congratulate her.'

There were two surprises in the first round. Sara Gomer upset No. 10 seed Terry Phelps, 7–5 2–6 7–6 (10–8), and Laura Gildemeister defeated the No. 12, Barbara Potter, 6–4 7–5.

Larisa Savchenko and Svetlana Parkhomenko won the doubles, with a 6–0 3–6 6–2 victory in the final over Evert Lloyd and Shriver, who had upset the top-seeded team of Kohde-Kilsch and Sukova 6–7 (8–6) 6–4 7–6 (7–4) in the semi-finals. – J. S.

BOCA RATON, 16–22 FEBRUARY

WOMEN'S SINGLES – Quarter-finals: G. Sabatini (ARG) d. K. Gompert 6–2 6–1; H. Sukova (TCH) d. B. Bunge (FRG) 3–6 6–3 7–5; P. H. Shriver d. G. Fernandez 6–3 6–3; S. Graf (FRG) d. C. Kohde-Kilsch (FRG) 7–6 6–2. ***Semi-finals:*** Sukova d. Sabatini 6–3 6–1; Graf d. Shriver 6–4 6–3. ***Final:*** Graf d. Sukova 6–2 6–3.

WOMEN'S DOUBLES – Final: S. Parkhomenko (URS)/L. Savchenko (URS) d. C. Evert Lloyd/P. H. Shriver 6–0 3–6 6–2.

LIPTON INTERNATIONAL PLAYERS' CHAMPIONSHIPS ($750,000)

The mould of women's tennis was shattered in the sun and gusting wind of Key Biscayne when Steffi Graf beat the Big Two of the women's game to capture the $150,000 first prize at the third Lipton International Players' Championships, played on the site of a former rubbish dump at the tournament's new permanent home, just fifteen minutes' drive from downtown Miami. It wasn't just that Steffi defeated first the number one seed Martina Navratilova and then the second seed, defending champion and the closest thing Florida possesses to royalty – Chris Evert Lloyd – in the final. It was the irresistible fashion in which she overturned Navratilova 6–3 6–2 in the semi-final and then humiliated Evert Lloyd 6–1 6–2 in the title match that suggested the beginning of a new era.

Navratilova survived 56 minutes – the sort of quick-time thrashing she has imposed on others so frequently in the past – and while Evert Lloyd lasted one minute longer she collected two games fewer than Martina. The two women, who between them have dominated the game for 13 years, were generous in their praise of the 17-year-old Graf. After a defeat which reduced her to tears in the privacy of the caravans which served as makeshift locker rooms at the unfinished tournament site, Navratilova said: 'Steffi was the best player in the world today and she will remain so until I beat her.' Evert Lloyd was graphic in her description of what Steffi had done to her: 'She cleaned my clock', said Chris, adding, 'I used to say that Steffi had a bright future. Now I have to say she has a very bright present. Martina is 30 and I'm 32', she continued, 'so neither of us is going to be around much longer. The way Steffi is playing right now she could win everything this year.'

Steffi had, in fact, already won the Virginia Slims of Florida at Boca Raton the previous week, on her return to the circuit following a winter devoted to beefing up her serve, backhand and passing shots under the supervision of newly hired coach Pavel Slozil, the Czech *Davis Cup* player. Improvement was clearly to be seen in all those departments of her game but it was the crunching Graf forehand which inflicted the most telling damage at Key Biscayne. Steffi conceded a mere 20 games in seven matches and, having been blasted off court 6–0 6–1 in the quarter-finals, Lisa Bonder said, 'Nobody hits the ball as hard as Steffi'.

Chris Evert Lloyd, who had practised with men before the final to prepare herself for the barrage, claimed that Graf struck the ball harder than any of those male practice opponents. She walloped three huge forehand winners to break serve in the opening game of the final, and so outplayed was the home crowd's favourite that she held serve only once in eight attempts. For believers in omens there were two buzzards circling high over the court as Evert Lloyd strove desperately to stem the flow of winners from the other side of the net.

Graf's stunning performance tended to overshadow some other notable feats. For instance, Steffi's West German compatriot, Silke Meier, put out the 11th seed, Manuela Maleeva, in her first match and went on to reach the fourth round – surviving three-set battles on each occasion – until she fell to Nathalie Tauziat. Then Mary Joe Fernandez, only 15 years old, rubbed out fifth-seeded Pam Shriver in straight sets in the second round.

There was revenge for Shriver – and for Navratilova, too – when they captured the first prize of $38,000 in the doubles by beating the 'Twin Towers', Claudia Kohde-Kilsch and Helena Sukova, 6–3 7–6 (8–6). Their quarter-final victims were Fernandez and Anne Smith, while in the semi-finals they overwhelmed Graf and Gabriela Sabatini 6–4 6–0. But the player of the tournament was the blonde, smiling German girl who confessed, as she clutched the winner's cheque and the silverware: 'I never thought I would come so far so quickly when I first came into tennis.' As she told the world's press, everything is going her way at the moment. She even has happy dreams, like the one on the night before the final when she dreamed she was riding on the back of a dolphin. With her sort of forehand and those sort of dreams, who knows what successes will remain out of the reach of Steffi Graf? – R. A.

KEY BISCAYNE, FLORIDA, 23 FEBRUARY–8 MARCH
WOMEN'S SINGLES – Quarter-finals: M. Navratilova d. N. Tauziat (FRA) 6–1 6–1; S. Graf (FRG) d. L. Bonder 6–0 6–1; H. Mandlikova (TCH) d. H. Sukova (TCH) 6–4 6–3; C. Evert Lloyd d. C. Kohde-Kilsch (FRG) 6–2 7–5. ***Semi-finals:*** Graf d. Navratilova 6–3 6–2; Evert Lloyd d. Mandlikova 7–5 6–0. ***Final:*** Graf d. Evert Lloyd 6–1 6–2.
WOMEN'S DOUBLES – Final: Navratilova/P. H. Shriver d. Kohde-Kilsch/Sukova 6–3 7–6.
MIXED DOUBLES – Final: M. Mecir (TCH)/J. Novotna (TCH) d. C. Van Rensburg (RSA)/E. Reinach (RSA) 6–3 3–6 6–3.

SEGMENT 2: 16 MARCH–4 APRIL

Jim Sarni, John Feinstein and Barry Wood

VIRGINIA SLIMS OF DALLAS ($250,000)

Chris Evert Lloyd had gone nine months without winning a tournament – failing in five and suffering a five-month lay-off with a knee injury – and 12 years without winning the Virginia Slims of Dallas. Then tennis's all-time tournament champion put an end to both droughts in March, when she defeated second seed Pam Shriver 6–1 6–3 for her 149th title at Moody Coliseum on the campus of SMU. 'I kept hearing that I hadn't won a tournament since the French, and it started to bug me', said Evert Lloyd, who had beaten Virginia Wade to win the 1974 Virginia Slims of Dallas.

Martina Navratilova, a seven-time champion in her hometown, was off skiing, and Steffi Graf was back in West Germany preparing for the clay-court season. That left Shriver and Zina Garrison as the only top ten opposition for Evert Lloyd in Dallas. And except for losing opening sets to Katerina Maleeva in the first round and Garrison in the semi-finals, Evert Lloyd had strolled through the rounds. Carling Bassett managed one game in the second; Stephanie Rehe took one in the quarter-finals; and Garrison lost 12 of her last 13 games after taking the first set 6–3.

'The whole key is that she is very eager', said Shriver, who hadn't lost so badly to Chris since the 1981 Wimbledon semi-finals. 'You can see it. Her shots are very crisp. I felt naked out there. I kept looking down to see if I had my skirt on and my top on. I put a wristband on halfway through to cover my wrists. But I hit one great shot.' It was a Hall of Fame shot. Chasing a lob to the baseline, she whipped a blind crosscourt backhand past Evert Lloyd. Shriver was losing 1–6 1–4 at the time, but the shot inspired her to win the next two games and get back on serve at 3–4. But, as against Garrison in the semi-finals, Evert Lloyd concentrated hard when she needed to.

On her way to the final, Shriver had used her solid serve-and-volley game to achieve a 7–5 6–3 semi-final win over sixth-seeded Lori McNeil, who had pulled off the upset of the tournament in saving three match-points to eliminate fourth-seeded Manuela Maleeva, 5–7 7–6 6–2. The tournament's most exciting match came in the second round, when Bettina Bunge, the fifth seed, outlasted Kate Gompert 6–1 4–6 7–6 (9–7).

The unseeded team of Anne White and Mary Lou Piatek won the doubles, topping Elise Burgin and Wendy White 7–5 6–3 in the finals.

An officiating controversy arose early in the tournament when it was learned that some of the linesmen, pressed into service owing to a boycott caused by a pay dispute between the tournament and the Southwest Tennis Umpires Association, were not certified by the United States Tennis Association. Evert Lloyd, the president of the WITA, complained to tournament director Nancy Jeffett after several bad calls during a doubles match, and certified officials worked all the remaining main matches. – J. S.

16–22 MARCH
WOMEN'S SINGLES – Quarter-finals: C. Evert Lloyd d. S. Rehe 6–1 6–0; Z. Garrison d. B. Bunge (FRG) 6–3 6–4; L. McNeil d. M. Maleeva (BUL) 5–7 7–6 6–2; P. H. Shriver d. W. M. Turnbull (AUS) 6–4 6–4. ***Semi-finals:*** Evert Lloyd d. Garrison 3–6 6–1 6–0; Shriver d. McNeil 7–5 6–3. ***Final:*** Evert Lloyd d. Shriver 6–1 6–3.
WOMEN'S DOUBLES – Final: M. L. Piatek/A. White d. E. Burgin/R. White 7–5 6–3.

Gigi Fernandez of Puerto Rico, an attractive player who likes to laugh with the crowd, enjoyed a successful year, reaching the last 16 at Wimbledon, taking three doubles titles with Lori McNeil and breaking into the top 50. *(Carol L. Newson)*

VIRGINIA SLIMS OF WASHINGTON ($150,000)

It was a week of rest for the Big Three in women's tennis: Martina Navratilova, Steffi Graf and Chris Evert. Which meant that for the next three – Hana Mandlikova, Helena Sukova and Pam Shriver – the $150,000 Virginia Slims of Washington was a wide-open door. When the week was over, Hana Mandlikova had knocked the door down and walked away with her third tournament victory of 1987. Shriver never passed the first round, losing a stunning three-setter 7–6 (7–4) 3–6 7–6 (7–3) to 19-year-old powerhouse Marianne Werdel. Sukova played good tennis all week but had the misfortune to be in Mandlikova's half of the draw, and when the two Czechs met in the semi-finals, the result was an impressive 6–3 6–2 victory for Mandlikova.

Yet the story of the tournament for much of the week was Barbara Potter, ranked 35 in the world. Six years ago, at the age of 19, Potter was a semi-finalist at the US Open, breaking into the top ten that same year; but since then she has been plagued with injuries that seem to come just when she is about to make another big splash. At Washington luck favoured her when Werdel upset Shriver, opening up her quarter of the draw, but her own victories over Catarina Lindqvist in the last 16 and Sylvia Hanika (conqueror of Werdel) in the quarter-finals took some excellent serve-and-volley tennis. She saved three match-points before beating Hanika, but her most impressive victory of the week was in the semi-finals, where she upset Zina Garrison, the No. 7 player in the world and the fourth seed in the tournament.

Potter played the entire match from behind. Garrison won the first set, Potter won the second. Garrison went up a break in the third, led 4–2 and served for the match at 5–3. Potter saved a match-point, broke for 5–4 and held for 5-all. Then, serving at 5–6, Potter saved three more match-points, the last when a Garrison lob landed inches beyond the baseline. They moved to a tie-break, and again Potter was in trouble until Garrison, leading 4–2, suddenly collapsed, making three straight unforced errors. Attacking as always, Potter reached match-point with a forehand volley, and the match ended when Garrison slammed a forehand into the net, with Potter the winner by 3–6 6–3 7–6 (7–4). Potter was ecstatic, to say the least. 'The hustle and competitiveness I showed even surprised me', she said. 'Last August when I was flat on my back I just dreamed of playing again, competing as hard as my heart could possibly allow. Today, I did that for the first time in a complete match in a long time.'

Her giddy run ended the next evening in the final against Mandlikova, who was virtually untouchable all week, never dropping a set. It took Mandlikova just 75 minutes to beat Potter, 6–4 6–2, to earn the $30,500 top prize, while Potter took $13,800. 'I played about as well as I can', Mandlikova said after the match. 'I think any of the top four can win when we are all in a tournament but when the other three aren't playing, I feel as if I should win.' She did just that against both Sukova and Potter, never letting either opponent get into the match as she served superbly and executed near-perfect groundstrokes. Both Sukova and Potter tried to attack and both watched one passing shot after another whistle past them.

The week was not a total loss for Shriver. She rebounded from her singles loss to win the doubles along with childhood pal Elise Burgin, with whom she beat another pair of long-time friends, Garrison and Lori McNeil, 6–1 3–6 6–4 in the final. For Burgin, the victory provided a small measure of revenge since McNeil had come from a set down to beat her in the singles. It was the first professional victory together for Shriver and Burgin who began playing each other at the age of nine in local tournaments in Baltimore. – J. F.

23–29 MARCH

WOMEN'S SINGLES – Quarter-finals: H. Mandlikova (TCH) d. K. Rinaldi 7–5 6–1; H. Sukova (TCH) d. L. McNeil 6–4 2–6 6–1; Z. Garrison d. A. Henricksson 6–2 6–2; B. Potter d. S. Hanika (FRG) 4–6 7–6 7–6. ***Semi-finals:*** Mandlikova d. Sukova 6–3 6–2; Potter d. Garrison 3–6 6–3 7–6. ***Final:*** Mandlikova d. Potter 6–4 6–2.

WOMEN'S DOUBLES – Final: E. Burgin/P. H. Shriver d. Garrison/McNeil 6–1 3–6 6–4.

US INDOOR CHAMPIONSHIPS ($150,000)

Helena Sukova must surely have derived tremendous pleasure from winning the US Indoors after coming so close in 1986, when she lost a dramatic final to Martina Navratilova, on a disputed line-call in a third-set tie-break. In 1987 there were no doubts about her claim to the title as she swept aside Lori McNeil, 6–0 6–3, in a remarkably one-sided match that was all over in 53 minutes. The easy victory could perhaps have been anticipated; the two finalists had met twice before in closely contested three-setters, but somehow one knew that the same would not happen three times in a row. One of them was due an easy victory, and common sense indicated it would be Sukova with her greater experience of the big occasion, her stronger serve and her willingness to come to the net. Sukova, who conceded only eight points in the first set, faced little resistance. 'She was rushing me and kept me from the net', offered the Texan by way of explanation.

The second-seeded Czech progressed to the final without losing a set, defeating Dianne Balestrat, Ann Henricksson, Catarina Lindqvist and surprise semi-finalist Gigi Fernandez along the way. McNeil, seeded four, beat Susan Rimes and Heather Ludloff in straight sets, dropped the first set before ousting Wendy Turnbull, and reached the final with a walkover against top seed Hana Mandlikova, who was suffering from a strained stomach muscle. It was an unhappy week for her, as she came under fierce criticism from several of her colleagues for practising what Fernandez described as 'gamesmanship'. Both Elizabeth Smylie and Hanika refused to walk from the court with her after their defeats, and strongly condemned the Czech's alleged intimidation of the officials. 'If they feel that way that's up to them', she responded. 'I complain if I think the call is wrong.'

One disappointing aspect of the event was the low attendance in the absence of Navratilova, Graf and Evert. Top players were reluctant to play for a number of reasons, which included the fact that the prize money of $150,000 was lower than at most other top-level tournaments, and in 1987 the event was played at the tail-end of the long indoor circuit and immediately before the clay-court season.

One attractive player with flair who found the support of the crowd was Gigi Fernandez, who reached the semi-finals, largely on the strength of her second-round upset of seventh seed Melissa Gurney and a gap left in the draw by the first-round defeat of third-seeded Kathy Rinaldi by Hu Na. She is not afraid to try a spectacular shot and to laugh at herself if it goes wrong, and the crowd likes to laugh with her. She joined with McNeil to win the doubles, beating Smylie and Betsy Nagelsen 6–1 6–4 in the final. In 1986, Smylie had won the title with Kathy Jordan, who tested the waters for a comeback after months of injury by teaming with Sukova. However, they were beaten in their opening match by Balestrat and Terry Phelps. – B. W.

PISCATAWAY, NEW JERSEY, 30 MARCH–4 APRIL
WOMEN'S SINGLES – Quarter-finals: H. Mandlikova (TCH) d. S. Hanika (FRG) 6–4 6–1; L. McNeil d. W. M. Turnbull (AUS) 4–6 6–1 6–2; G. Fernandez d. G. Kim 6–1 7–6; H. Sukova (TCH) d. C. Lindqvist (SWE) 6–4 6–3. ***Semi-finals:*** McNeil w.o. Mandlikova; Sukova d. Fernandez 6–3 7–5. ***Final:*** Sukova d. McNeil 6–0 6–3.
WOMEN'S DOUBLES – Final: Fernandez/McNeil d. B. Nagelsen/E. Smylie (AUS) 6–1 6–4

Manuela Maleeva, the Bulgarian No. 1, won her first title for two years at Wild Dunes, going on to upset Chris Evert at Hilton Head the following week, and winning her second title of the year at Mahwah. She also finished the year on a high note with her marriage to Swiss tennis coach François Fragniere. *(T. Hindley)*

SEGMENT 3: 6 APRIL–3 MAY

Linda Pentz and Josh Young

FAMILY CIRCLE MAGAZINE CUP ($200,000)

Steffi Graf, fresh from her resounding victories at the Lipton International Players' Championships, confirmed that she was the player to beat in 1987 when she won the Family Circle Magazine Cup at Hilton Head, marking her third straight title of the year and extending her tally to 70 matches won and three lost in 15 tournaments, including the *Federation Cup*. The Family Circle victory also marked Graf's first successful defence of a title, for the 17-year-old West German had claimed her first tournament victory just one year earlier at this event. She defeated a resurgent Manuela Maleeva 6–2 4–6 6–3 in the final, after the Bulgarian had scored the biggest victory of her career the previous day in defeating Chris Evert in a thrilling, three-set semi-final, 6–1 2–6 7–6 (7–5).

Indeed, semi-finals day at Hilton Head had proved one of the most dramatic in memory, with the match between Graf and Gabriela Sabatini also going the full distance before Graf won 6–3 2–6 7–6 (7–5). Their dual was one of classic beauty and drama, long rallies being punctuated by low backhand slice winners from Graf and high looping topspin groundstrokes from Sabatini. Having lost control in the second set after Sabatini took a 3–0 lead following a game with seven deuces, Graf missed her first match-point at 5–1 in the third, with Sabatini serving, when she swatted a put-away high forehand deep. Two more came at 5–4 but again Graf failed, watching a Sabatini forehand sail by her for a winner, then missing a backhand.

Sabatini's dramatic fight-back endured for five straight games, giving her a 6–5 lead with Graf's service to come. Two crucial forehand winners gave Graf that game and the match moved into the climactic tie-break. A fourth match-point arrived at 6–4 in the tie-break, but Sabatini scored a forehand winner off a net cord. Graf's forehand, her most lethal weapon, had been temperamental all week, but at 6–5 and the fifth match-point she stood and delivered a stinging forehand return down the line, granting her, at last, the victory.

Maleeva and Evert were hard-pushed to follow the morning's drama. Evert was still recovering from 'flu while Maleeva's confidence was high, following a title victory the week before at Wild Dunes. In the first set she tore Evert's erratic game to shreds with a 6–1 win, which must have stoked Evert's competitive fires, for she broke Maleeva four times in the second set to win it 6–2. Evert's first-set problems with her serve and an errant forehand seemed behind her in the final set as games went with serve, but when Maleeva broke Evert for a 6–5 lead it seemed that the 32-year-old American's comeback was not yet in gear. However, using her superb concentration and overhead skills, Evert broke Maleeva to take the match into the tie-break. Maleeva then led all the way, despite dropping four service points of her own, and won the match 7–5 on her first match-point when Evert knocked a smash wide.

The first set of the final was all Graf as the West German won it 6–2, but a few backhand errors gave her opponent an edge in the second which she won 6–4. Some of the fizz went out of the match in the third set when Graf, leading 4–1, seemed to have it won. Maleeva fought back to 5–3 but didn't have the necessary reserves and Graf broke the Bulgarian for the match 6–3 as Maleeva netted a forehand.

The doubles final featured another player enjoying a comeback as a slimmer Eva Pfaff of West Germany partnered Argentina's Mercedes Paz to defeat Zina Garrison and Lori McNeil, 7–6 7–5. – L. P.

HILTON HEAD, 6–12 APRIL
WOMEN'S SINGLES – Quarter-finals: S. Graf (FRG) d. H. Kelesi (CAN) 6–2 6–2; G. Sabatini (ARG) d. C. Kohde-Kilsch (FRG) 7–6 6–3; M. Maleeva d. Z. Garrison 6–2 7–5; C. M. Evert d. B. Bunge (FRG) 6–3 6–2. ***Semi-finals:*** Graf d. Sabatini 6–3 2–6 7–6; Maleeva d. Evert 6–1 2–6 7–6. ***Final:*** Graf d. Maleeva 6–2 4–6 6–3.
WOMEN'S DOUBLES – Final: M. Paz (ARG)/E. Pfaff (FRG) d. Garrison/L. McNeil 7–6 7–5.

WITA CHAMPIONSHIPS ($275,000)

The Women's International Tennis Association Championships had other claims to fame in 1987, besides being possibly the longest title in the women's circuit. It marked Steffi Graf's 12th tournament title in as many months as she swept through the draw to defeat Hana Mandlikova 6–3 6–4 in the final. Graf collected $40,000, which was $20,000 less than her Hilton Head purse because the Amelia Island tournament donates $100,000 of the prize money to the WITA. Although Graf had been dissatisfied with her play during the Hilton Head week she was in full command at Amelia Island, where she lost only ten games *en route* to the final. She faced Gabriela Sabatini again in the semi-finals, but this time summarily dispatched her rival 6–2 6–2.

Zina Garrison was equally disappointing against Mandlikova in the other semi-final, as the Czech No. 1, who had struggled with her serve in earlier rounds, played confidently to win 6–3 6–3. Graf had beaten Claudia Kohde-Kilsch in the final here a year earlier, but this time the tall West German was upset early on by an exciting new prospect, Canada's Helen Kelesi. Kelesi, whose parents emigrated from Czechoslovakia in 1968, plays a resourceful and athletic groundstroke game and beat Kohde-Kilsch convincingly 6–3 6–4. Kelesi had shed about 15lb in the previous four months and had trained hard for the spring season, running eight miles and working five to six hours a day on court with her coach and father, Milan. Sabatini took care of her in the quarter-finals, but only just, winning 6–4 4–6 6–2.

Manuela Maleeva also got a second crack at Graf at that stage, but the match was a disaster for the Bulgarian, who lost 6–1 6–0. A drained Maleeva had simply played herself to a standstill and was facing a very different Graf from the less-than-confident version she had encountered two weeks earlier in Hilton Head.

Double-faults, of which she served seven in the match, were Mandlikova's downfall in her first set against Graf in the final, for despite breaking her opponent twice in the first set, she double-faulted at break-point down when trailing 3–4, setting up Graf to serve out the set at love. Mandlikova streaked to a 3–0 lead in the second set before Graf edged back to 3–3, broke her in the ninth game for a 5–4 lead, and served out the match at love when Mandlikova missed a backhand return.

Amelia Island introduced fans to yet another exciting Argentinian in the person of Bettina Fulco, another pupil of Sabatini's former coach, Patricio Apey, who also works with the rapidly improving Mercedes Paz. Fulco upset tenth-seeded Stephanie Rehe in the second round before Graf beat her 6–0 6–1.

The doubles title match was a triumph of youth over experience when the flamboyant duo of Graf and Sabatini beat Wendy Turnbull and Mandlikova 3–6 6–3 7–5 in a thrilling final that compensated for the more lacklustre singles that preceded it. – L. P.

AMELIA ISLAND, 13–19 APRIL
WOMEN'S SINGLES – Quarter-finals: S. Graf (FRG) d. M. Maleeva (BUL) 6–1 6–0; G. Sabatini (ARG) d. H. Kelesi (CAN) 6–4 4–6 6–2; Z. Garrison d. K. Rinaldi 6–4 6–4; H. Mandlikova (TCH) d. T. Phelps 7–6 6–2. ***Semi-finals:*** Graf d. Sabatini 6–2 6–2; Mandlikova d. Garrison 6–3 6–3. ***Final:*** Graf d. Mandlikova 6–3 6–4.
WOMEN'S DOUBLES – Final: Graf/Sabatini d. Mandlikova/W. M. Turnbull (AUS) 3–6 6–3 7–5.

Chris Evert (top) enjoyed a purple patch in the late spring, beating Hana Mandlikova and Martina Navratilova to win her 150th title at the Virginia Slims of Dallas, and taking both singles and doubles titles in Tampa the following week. Her victim in the singles final was Kate Gompert (bottom), who had inflicted a rare defeat in her home state on the world No. 3 in February. *(T. Hindley, Carol L. Newsom)*

HEAD

VIRGINIA SLIMS OF HOUSTON

While all eight seeds played through to the quarter-finals and the top four showed up in the semis, few seemed to care about six of those eight, who included Hana Mandlikova (a 6–3 7–5 semi-final loser to Evert) and Gabriela Sabatini, who fell to Mandlikova in the quarter-finals. What did matter was the anticipation among fans, players, and, naturally, tournament organisers of a 71st meeting between Evert and Navratilova. And no one was disappointed after Evert defeated Navratilova 3–6 6–1 7–6 (7–4) in a thrilling final to capture her monumental 150th career title.

Over the past 14 years Evert and Navratilova have created a rivalry for sports fans to cherish long after they both retire. After the two had played a third-set tie-break for only the second time in their 71 meetings, one wondered how much longer they could maintain their high standard of play. 'We're definitely closer to the end than the beginning', said Navratilova, who leads the series 37–34. 'People were complaining beforehand because they wanted some fresh faces, but this week all you heard was how great it would be for Chris and me to play again.' Concurred Evert, 'It's a special feeling every time we play.'

On her way to the final, Navratilova had eliminated the two local girls who were both products of John Wilkerson's public parks programme; Lori McNeil fell 6–1 6–2 in the quarter-finals and Zina Garrison was beaten 6–1 7–6 one round later.

In the final Martina took advantage of two double-faults, one each in the first and seventh games, to break Evert twice in the first set while dropping her own serve only once. Evert, known almost as well for her slow starts as her two-fisted backhand, retaliated by breaking Navratilova all four times she served in the second set.

The third set was a tennis version of a well-played chess match. Navratilova attacked with the caution of a true clay-court player, while Evert added creativity to her backcourt routine with an occasional drop-shot and several lobs that left Navratilova frozen at the net. Neither player reached break-point until Navratilova broke Evert in the eighth game with a brilliant topspin backhand passing shot that prompted a congratulatory nod from Evert. Serving for the match at 5–4, Navratilova belted an ace for 30–15, but Evert sunk two returns at her feet and angled a winning drop volley on break-point for 5–5. Inevitably, each held serve at 15 to force a tie-break.

Deadlocked at three points apiece, Navratilova hit a penetrating backhand approach and crowded the net, only to watch Evert hit a forehand lob out of her reach. Navratilova, worrying about another Evert lob, hit a slice backhand approach long on the next point, and Evert dusted the line with a forehand pass off a nervous approach for 6–3. From there, Evert recounted: 'At 6–3 in the tie-break, I remember thinking, "You have to come in on her backhand." And then she hit the best [backhand] passing shot I've seen from her. Somehow I ended up at the net at 6–4 to win the match.'

Both Navratilova and Evert had cruised through the early rounds of the 32-player draw without dropping a set, as did five of the other six seeds. Only eighth-seeded Raffaella Reggi, a new face amongst seeds at a tournament with a draw this strong, was pushed to three sets. The spunky Italian needed a third-set tie-break to beat Gretchen Rush Magers 6–3 2–6 7–6 (7–5) in a long match that seemed longer. Andrea Jaeger, staging a comeback at 21, could have made things interesting. The one-time finalist at Wimbledon and Paris, playing only her second tournament since February of 1986, resorted to moonballs in her first-round victory over her friend and girlhood rival, Mary Lou Piatek, but then reverted to her chronically injured status of the past four years, withdrawing from her second-round singles and doubles matches with shoulder problems.

The Houston fans were also treated to the doubles final they wanted, featuring their local heroines, Zina Garrison and Lori McNeil. Unfortunately, Martina Navratilova and Kathy Jordan were also there to defeat Garrison and McNeil 6–2 6–4. – J. Y.

20–26 APRIL
WOMEN'S SINGLES – Final: M. Navratilova d. L. McNeil 6–1 6–2; Z. Garrison d. R. Reggi (ITA) 6–1 6–0; C. M. Evert d. K. Gompert 6–3 6–3; H. Mandlikova (TCH) d. G. Sabatini (ARG) 7–5 6–4. ***Semi-finals:*** Navratilova d. Garrison 6–1 7–6; Evert d. Mandlikova 6–3 7–5. ***Final:*** Evert d. Navratilova 3–6 6–1 7–6.
WOMEN'S DOUBLES – Final: Navratilova/K. Jordan d. Garrison/McNeil 6–2 6–4.

ECKERD FLORIDA OPEN ($150,000)

It was the Chris Evert show for the second week in a row when everyone's favourite American tennis player, newly divorced from John Lloyd, took the title at the $150,000 Eckerd Open in Florida. Fresh from her victory at the Virginia Slims of Houston, she enjoyed a confident week, buoyed by the support of her boyfriend, ex-Olympic skier Andy Mill. Evert swept through the week without the loss of a set to defeat fourth-seeded Kate Gompert, 6–3 6–2, in the final, topping off the day by also taking the doubles title, 6–3 6–4, with Wendy Turnbull over Elise Burgin and Ros Fairbank.

Her first opponent was Gabriela Dinu, a little-known Rumanian who was thrashed 6–2 6–1. Then came the wily left-hander, Camille Benjamin, whose forehand gave Evert some trouble in the first set, although she was too nervy in the second to pose a serious threat and lost 6–3 6–1. Another big hitter off the forehand side, Peru's Laura Gildemeister, was Evert's opponent in the quarter-finals, but it proved to be one of the charismatic Peruvian's off days as Evert triumphed 6–2 6–1.

Several amateur players also made their marks at the Eckerd Open. Ronni Reis, finishing her time at the University of Miami, and Gabriela Miro, an exotic Brazilian junior, each reached the quarter-finals, where Gompert dispatched Reis 6–1 3–6 6–1 in a battle of two left-handers, and second-seeded Kathy Rinaldi removed Miro 7–5 6–4. The third amateur was Beverly Bowes, 94 in the world, who toppled seeds Elise Burgin (four) and Terry Phelps (three) before facing Evert in the semis. There here nerves failed her as she was 'double bageled' 6–0 6–0 in under an hour.

If Bowes's undoing was predictable against the world's No. 3, the downfall of Kathy Rinaldi was far more perplexing. She simply lost all control of her serve as she went down 6–0 6–1 to Gompert. She double-faulted three times in a row in the second game of the match, again to go three set-points down before losing the first set at love, and once more in the second game of the second set. In all she projected 12 double-faults in the match, requiring Gompert to do little more than keep her groundstrokes in play.

Gompert battled hard and long against Evert in the final, which lasted an hour and 50 minutes despite its two-set score, and Evert was forced to work for every point. The victory marked her 151st career title, a record for either women's or men's tennis.

Some humour was added to the day's proceedings after Evert and Turnbull won the doubles title. 'It's nice to play with someone near to my own age', said the 34-year-old Turnbull while adding: 'Your cane is waiting by your chair, Chris.' The 32-year-old Evert responded: 'It's really nice to play doubles with Wendy because she's the only player on the tour older than me.' – L. P.

TAMPA, FLORIDA, 27 APRIL–3 MAY
WOMEN'S SINGLES – Quarter-finals: C. M. Evert d. L. Gildemeister (PER) 6–2 6–1; B. Bowes d. T. Phelps 6–3 5–7 6–1; K. Gompert d. R. Reis 6–1 3–6 6–1; K. Rinaldi d. G. Miro (BRA) 7–5 6–4. ***Semi-finals:*** Evert d. Bowes 6–0 6–0; Gompert d. Rinaldi 6–0 6–1. ***Final:*** Evert d. Gompert 6–3 6–2.
WOMEN'S DOUBLES – Final: Evert/W. M. Turnbull (AUS) d. E. Burgin/R. Fairbank (RSA) 6–4 6–3.

SEGMENT 4: 4 MAY–20 JUNE

John Parsons, Chris Martin and Malcolm Folley

ITALIAN CHAMPIONSHIPS ($150,000)

The Italians, so often dismissive of women's tennis in the past, could not have been more hospitable or admiring in welcoming them back to the Foro Italico for the first time since 1979. By the time Steffi Graf took her record for 1987 to 27–0 in terms of matches with a 7–5 4–6 6–0 defeat of Gabriela Sabatini, 61,000 had attended the seven days' play.

Although it was the most recent upstarts on the women's tour, Miss Graf and Miss Sabatini, who produced the most combative and exciting tennis in reaching the final, it was the presence of World Champion Martina Navratilova which proved the greatest fascination for the crowd. Short of match confidence, Martina was stretched in her first match to two tie-breaks, which she won 7–3 and 7–4 to overcome Yugoslavia's Sabrina Goles. Yet there was no doubting her popularity. When, during the second set of Miss Graf's 6–1 7–5 defeat of Sandra Cecchini, Miss Navratilova arrived to take a look at the girl threatening her supremacy, it created the biggest stir of the day.

It was an excellent week for teenagers with four reaching the quarter-finals, three of them at the expense of other teenagers. They include Arantxa Sanchez from Spain – the 15-year-old sister of Emilio and Javier – whose backhand had been such a thorn in Miss Navratilova's side in Key Biscayne a few weeks earlier. Miss Sanchez, who had won a magnificent second-round struggle with the more experienced local favourite, Raffaella Reggi, skilfully used drop-shots, as well as her developing groundstroke command to win 6–3 6–1 against 18-year-old Isabel Cueto from West Germany. And while Miss Sabatini, still only 16, was impressively accounting for Mary Joe Fernandez, aged 15, for the loss of only four games, 18-year-old Bettina Fulco upset the eighth-seeded Katerina Maleeva on her 17th birthday.

By the quarter-finals, however, the top four seeds were still in attendance. Miss Graf (2) steadily wore down Miss Fulco's defences, 6–4 6–4, and went through to face Helena Sukova (3), while Miss Sabatini (4) overwhelmed Miss Sanchez to earn the right to tackle Miss Navratilova (1). The World Champion had won comfortably 6–2 6–3 against Claudia Kohde-Kilsch, who once more failed to match her potential. Miss Sabatini, who did not allow Miss Sanchez even one game, felt bouyant enough later to say that although she had never taken a set from Martina in earlier matches, 'I think I have a chance of beating her this time, because everyone knows she's not playing so well now'.

And so it seemed on the following afternoon when Miss Navratilova, lacking the self-assurance and command she needed on the taunting and teasing red clay, eventually slumped in tears to a 7–6 6–1 defeat. It was another in a lengthy series of punishing blows to her pride, as well as her record, and yet early on there was no hint of the calamity which was to befall her. She led 3–0 and then 5–2 with a set-point in that game and another in the one which followed. Yet it was the way in which she allowed that second opportunity to escape, by becoming not just tentative but apprehensive, which best illustrated the difference between a once wholly assured champion and one who had become so clearly uncertain about her game. Miss Sabatini, who ran down most of Miss Navratilova's drop-shots to turn many of them into spectacular winners of her own, not only broke back, but took firm command in a 7–2 tie-break and then dropped only one more game, as the World Champion wilted visibly.

Miss Graf beat Miss Sukova 6–3 6–3 in the other semi-final, taking frequent and

Fifteen-year-old Arantxa Sanchez, whose backhand had earlier unsettled Martina Navratilova at Key Biscayne, was an unexpected quarter-finalist at the French Open in her first Grand Slam appearance. She had begun the season as runner-up at the Argentine Open to Gabriela Sabatini, who later beat her in both the French and Italian Open quarter-finals. (T. Hindley)

impressive advantage of the Czech's failure to put away enough of her volleys with sufficient accuracy.

The final was the sixth meeting between the confident young lady from West Germany and the attractive teenager from Argentina and, for the fifth time, Miss Sabatini was to take a set, although before an appreciative crowd Miss Graf eventually won 7–5 4–6 6–0. At first Miss Graf's forehand went badly adrift. Miss Sabatini won the first four games and had four points to close out the set at 5–2. Yet Miss Graf suddenly produced a succession of winners which spectacularly and swiftly changed the balance of power. She rattled off the last 15 points of the first set, leaving Miss Sabatini mourning how three times, on her second set-point, she had failed to put the ball away, once on the volley and twice with overheads. Although Miss Graf's concentration wavered briefly again to cost her the second set, she looked irresistible in the third, which she eventually won in a flourish by taking 11 of the last 12 points.

Owing to a misunderstanding, the customary Graf/Sabatini partnership for the doubles was not in action. Instead Miss Sabatini teamed up with Miss Navratilova for one of the World Champion's rare doubles appearances without Pam Shriver alongside her. Needless to say they were the top seeds and they also won the title without dropping a set, beating Miss Sukova and Miss Kohde-Kilsch 6–4 6–1 in a lively but increasingly one-sided final. – J. P.

ROME, 4–10 MAY
WOMEN'S SINGLES – Quarter-finals: M. Navratilova (USA) d. C. Kohde-Kilsch (FRG) 6–2 6–3; G. Sabatini (ARG) d. A. Sanchez (ESP) 6–0 6–0; H. Sukova (TCH) d. J. Polzl (AUT) 6–4 6–2; S. Graf (FRG) d. B. Fulco (ARG) 6–4 6–4. ***Semi-finals:*** Sabatini d. Navratilova 7–6 6–1; Graf d. Sukova 6–3 6–3. ***Final:*** Graf d. Sabatini 7–5 4–6 6–0.
WOMEN'S DOUBLES – Final: Navratilova/Sabatini d. Kohde-Kilsch/Sukova 6–4 6–1.

FILA GERMAN OPEN ($150,000)

Whenever Steffi Graf looks back on 1987, the West German youngster will remember the Fila German Open in West Berlin as perhaps one of her most trying experiences of a hectic year. For Steffi was returning home for the first time since making it quite clear that she was about to emerge as the new world No. 1, and for the first time she was experiencing the sort of pressure Boris Becker had found he could not endure.

To make matters worse, with neither Martina Navratilova nor Chris Evert in the draw, Steffi was the clear favourite, and the large crowds that flocked to the picturesque Rot-Weiss Tennis Club expected her to win. Steffi duly obliged, dropping only one set on her way to her sixth successive title of the year, defeating her *Federation Cup* team-mate, Claudia Kohde-Kilsch, 6–2 6–3 in the final. Despite her obvious delight, Steffi was also somewhat relieved. 'I felt the whole week was very long and very difficult for me', said Steffi. 'It wasn't only the tennis but the surroundings as well. I had to do a lot of interviews and everybody wanted to talk to me.'

On court, only the gritty Italian, Sandra Cecchini, conqueror of Evert Lloyd in the 1986 *Federation Cup*, and ranked 74th in the world, was able to push her to three sets. After Miss Cecchini had dismissed the seventh-seeded Canadian, Helen Kelesi, in the second round, she had predicted: 'I know even if I play well Steffi can beat me love and love because she is such a great player.' As it turned out the Italian was somewhat understating her own ability, for in their semi-final she proceeded to keep Miss Graf occupied for 2 hours and 34 minutes, extending her to the limit before bowing out 6–3 6–7 6–4. Until then Miss Graf had lost just nine games, and in one typically devastating display in the third round, she had conceded only five points in taking the first nine games from compatriot Claudia Porwik before going on to win 6–0 6–1. 'It was so icy cold when we started I thought I had better get it over with quickly', quipped Steffi after the 34-minute massacre.

While Steffi somewhat predictably marched towards the title a number of other seeds fell by the wayside. The biggest surprise was the second-round defeat of the No. 2, Helena Sukova, by West German Silke Meier. Miss Sukova led 4–1 in the final set but collapsed

Sandra Cecchini, with something of a reputation as a giant-killer after her triumph over Evert Lloyd in the 1986 Federation Cup, *was the only player in Berlin able to extend Graf to three sets.* *(T. Hindley)*

to a 6–2 3–6 6–4 defeat after missing an inviting overhead that would have given her a 5–3 lead. Catarina Lindqvist, Jo Durie, Catherine Tanvier, Eva Pfaff, Sabrina Goles and Nathalie Herreman were others who failed to live up to their seedings, while the fourth seed, Bettina Bunge, was forced out before hitting a ball because of a shoulder injury.

Thanks to Bunge's default after play had started, and victories over Isabelle Demongeot and Christina Singer, Australian Lousie Field reached her first quarter-final in a tournament of this size. That feat was also achieved and surpassed by former Junior World Champion Patricia Tarabini, who reached the semis after winning through against Meier, who fell over and had to default with match-point against her. Then the Argentine youngster beat Australia's Nicole Provis, conqueror of Miss Durie in the third round.

Miss Sukova made up for her disappointing singles showing by teaming with the beaten singles finalist, Miss Kohde-Kilsch, to win the doubles title. The aptly nicknamed 'twin towers' defeated Catarina Lindqvist and Tine Scheuer-Larsen, 6–1 6–2. – C. M.

BERLIN, 11–17 MAY
WOMEN'S SINGLES – Quarter-finals: S. Graf d. N. Tauziat (FRA) 6–2 6–1; A. M. Cecchini (ITA) d. L. Field (AUS) 6–2 6–2; P. Tarabini (ARG) d. N. Provis (AUS) 6–2 6–1; C. Kohde-Kilsch d. R. Reggi (ITA) 7–5 6–3. ***Semi-finals:*** Graf d. Cecchini 6–3 6–7 6–4; Kohde-Kilsch d. Tarabini 6–4 7–6. ***Final:*** Graf d. Kohde-Kilsch 6–2 6–3.
WOMEN'S DOUBLES – Final: Kohde-Kilsch/H. Sukova (TCH) d. C. Lindqvist (SWE)/T. Scheuer-Larsen (DEN) 6–1 6–2.

PILKINGTON GLASS CHAMPIONSHIPS ($200,000)

We might expect it to rain at Eastbourne, but we do not expect Martina Navratilova to show up on the South Coast empty-handed, still seeking her first singles title of the season. Martina had taken some time off since losing to Steffi Graf in the final of the French Open on the red clay of Stade Roland Garros, and when she made her entrance at Devonshire Park, she talked enthusiastically about being back on a grass court again. She said she had left Paris with extremely positive vibes, for although she had lost, she felt she had also been on a voyage of discovery in the French capital, not least because she was playing there for the first time with a new racket. Now all she required to propel her towards Wimbledon in a buoyant mood was to win the Pilkington Glass Ladies Championship, and she began in demonstrative fashion, dismissing Californian teenager Marianne Werdel for the loss of a solitary game.

Pam Shriver, enjoying a purple patch, elected to play singles, rather than adopt her usual custom of playing only doubles with Martina. Seeded fourth, she was destined to collide with Martina in the semi-finals. It was an appointment she was able to keep by defeating Jo Louis, Elna Reinach, Liz Smylie and Gabriela Sabatini for the loss of just one set. Pam was bubbly, talkative and keen to meet Martina at a time when the world No. 1 was behaving on the tennis court more like a normal mortal.

Chris Evert, making her first appearance in England since her divorce from John Lloyd, reached the semi-finals in most convincing fashion, dismissing Sharon Walsh Pete, Lisa Bonder, Wendy White and Larisa Savchenko without conceding a set. But if the Eastbourne public were beginning to relish the prospect of a final showdown between Martina and Chris, the script was about to take a dramatic turn, for Helena Sukova from Czechoslovakia was waiting to take centre stage.

Miss Sukova had taken a set from Martina in the Eastbourne final a year earlier and, with her serve and volley game, was ably equipped to pose serious questions again. In the quarter-finals, Helena demonstrated tenacity and an enduring will to win in overcoming Ros Fairbank 6–7 6–3 8–6. Those same qualities would be needed against Miss Evert, and Helena managed to find them. Not even the temporary presence of a brass band, marching in a neighbouring road, could knock the Czech girl out of her stride. Once, Miss Evert would have been too wrapped up in her work to notice such distractions, but on this occasion a television close up showed Miss Evert smiling wryly as the band marched past at the precise moment the match umpire said: 'Quiet please.' Miss Sukova won their semi-final 4–6 6–4 8–6. Later, Miss Evert, now 32, talked about how the grind of playing week in week out, year in year out was beginning take its toll. Her resolve, she said, was no longer what it was.

Miss Shriver, for her part, tested Martina's resolve to the maximum. The world No. 1 survived the examination, but the 6–4 4–6 6–3 scoreline reflects how Miss Navratilova had been made to sweat.

The final, therefore, starred the same two characters as a year earlier. But the plot was decidedly different. The first set was Martina's for the taking, or so she thought as she led 5–2. However, Miss Sukova had other ideas. As Helena's game grew in stature, as she went for bolder winners, as she hugged the net, Martina became riddled with self-doubt once more. Her composure disappeared; her game disintegrated; her will perished. Miss Sukova claimed the first-set tie-break 7–5 and never looked back on her way to a famous triumph, 7–6 6–3. So Miss Navratilova left Eastbourne as professionally destitute as she had arrived, but still clinging to her Wimbledon dream. The rest, as they say, is history.

The Eastern Bloc were to make it a memorable double when Svetlana Parkhomenko, from Moscow, and Miss Savchenko, from the Ukraine, defeated Ros Fairbank and Liz Smylie 7–6 (7–5) 7–5 to win the doubles title. The two Russian girls had earlier beaten Hana Mandlikova and Wendy Turnbull, the No. 2 seeds, 6–3 6–7 (0–7) 6–4 in the semi-finals, at which stage the top seeds, Claudia Kohde-Kilsch and Miss Sukova, had lost to Fairbank and Smylie. – M. F.

EASTBOURNE, 15–20 JUNE

WOMEN'S SINGLES – Quarter-finals: M. Navratilova (USA) d. I. Demongeot (FRA) 7–5 6–3; P. H. Shriver (FRA) d. G. Sabatini (ARG) 6–3 6–3; H. Sukova (TCH) d. R. Fairbank (RSA) 6–7 6–3 8–6; C. M. Evert (USA) d. L. Savchenko (URS) 6–1 6–3. ***Semi-finals:*** Navratilova d. Shriver 6–4 4–6 6–3; Sukova d. Evert 4–6 6–4 8–6. ***Final:*** Sukova d. Navratilova 7–6 6–3.

WOMEN'S DOUBLES – Final: S. Parkhomenko (URS)/L. Savchenko d. R. Fairbank/E. Smylie (AUS) 7–6 7–5.

Helena Sukova of Czechoslovakia beat Chris Evert and Martina Navratilova back-to-back to win Eastbourne, going on to reach the quarter-finals at Wimbledon, where she won the doubles with Claudia Kohde-Kilsch. *(T. Hindley)*

SEGMENT 5: 13 JULY–30 AUGUST

Craig Gabriel, Josh Young, Nora McCabe and Bob Greene

VIRGINIA SLIMS OF NEWPORT ($150,000)

Pam Shriver, fresh from a successful Wimbledon where she had reached the semi-finals only two weeks before, continued her fine run on grass to reach her third straight final at her favourite tournament, the $150,000 Virginia Slims of Newport, before capturing the title for the second consecutive year with a 6–2 6–4 result over eighth-seeded Texan, Wendy White, which earned her $30,000. Shriver, the tournament's top seed, was playing with a renewed enthusiasm for the game. More relaxed and eager, the lanky American served and volleyed her way to victory over White, using all her experience to play the right returns at the right time and rarely making an error.

It was the first time White had reached the final of a big tournament and the lack of experience showed, even though the Texan never gave up trying. She had several chances to score service breaks in the first set, but Shriver usually came up with a big serve, or her longer reach blocked returns as she managed to keep White at arm's length.

White earned $13,800 for the week, winning her first two rounds in straight sets – over Cammie MacGregor and Ann Henricksson – although they both included second-set tie-breaks. In the quarter-finals, against Heather Ludloff, she held three match-points in the second set before winning 6–3 5–7 6–4 and then beat South African Ros Fairbank 6–3 6–4 in the semi-finals.

By contrast Shriver dropped only three games in each of her first two rounds. She opened against former top ten player Kathy Jordan, who had been sidelined with injuries, winning 6–3 6–0, and then equally easily defeated Patty Fendick of Sacramento, who had just won her second NCAA crown.

However, it was the quarter-final match between Shriver and seventh-seeded Gigi Fernandez that produced the week's best tennis. Shriver won the first set 8–6 on a tie-break as both women tried to dominate at the net. Then Fernandez, who has made a jump from 130 to 33 on the computer rankings after a slump, took the second set before the defending champion finally closed out the match, 7–6 4–6 6–2.

Second-seeded Lori McNeil of Texas was upset by fifth-seeded Fairbank 5–7 6–4 6–4 in another tense quarter-final match. McNeil had lost to Shriver in the 1986 final, but was having problems with her serve this time and delivered 48 double-faults in the three singles matches she played. The only two seeds not to make the quarter-finals were No. 3 Wendy Turnbull, dismissed 6–4 6–0 in the second round by Californian Alycia Moulton, who eventually lost in the semi-finals to Shriver, and the No. 4, Melissa Gurney of Palos Verdes, who lost 2–6 6–3 6–1 to qualifier Dee Ann Hansel of Atlanta.

World No. 7 Zina Garrison, recovering from a foot injury that kept her out of the French Open and Wimbledon, played only doubles in Newport, her first tournament after an eight-week gap. She and Ann Henricksson lost in the first round to the eventual finalists, Britain's Anne Hobbs and Jordan, who upset the top seeds Shriver and Turnbull, 6–4 1–6 6–3 in the semi-finals, but lost in the final to the second-seeded pair of Fernandez and McNeil, 7–6 (7–5) 7–5. – C. G.

13–19 JULY
WOMEN'S SINGLES – Quarter-finals: P. H. Shriver d. G. Fernandez 7–6 4–6 6–2; A. Moulton d. T.

Phelps 6–4 6–3; W. White d. H. Ludloff 6–3 5–7 6–4; R. Fairbank (RSA) d. L. McNeil 5–7 6–4 6–4. ***Semi-finals:*** Shriver d. Moulton 6–3 6–2; White d. Fairbank 6–3 6–4. ***Final:*** Shriver d. White 6–2 6–4. ***WOMEN'S DOUBLES – Final:*** G. Fernandez/L. McNeil d. A. E. Hobbs (GBR)/K. Jordan 7–6 7–5.

VIRGINIA SLIMS OF LOS ANGELES ($250,000)

For seven months Steffi Graf had been threatening to take the No. 1 ranking from Martina Navratilova, and coming into the Virginia Slims of Los Angeles, she had lost only one match all year – to Navratilova in the Wimbledon final. Slowly the 18-year-old West German had been closing the gap in the computer rankings, and for many Graf's replacing Navratilova at the top had become a question of when, not if. When the week was over, nobody could say if.

When it was determined at the beginning of the week that Graf could pass Navratilova, the speculation of this actually happening overshadowed the fact that seven of the top ten were in the 56-player singles draw. The tension heightened when the semi-final pairings were decided, for Graf, who had dropped only seven games in her first three matches, would play Gabriela Sabatini, and Navratilova would face third-seeded Chris Evert. And when Evert dispatched Navratilova in a surprisingly easy 6–2 6–1 match, it seemed inevitable.

If Graf, who had beaten Sabatini 7–5 7–5 in the other semi-final, could beat Evert in the final, she would move into the No. 1 spot on the computer by seven-tenths of a point. Everyone knew but Steffi, who was apparently taken by surprise. 'Being number one means the most of anything I've done', she said. Yet ironically, the scenario that enabled Graf to reach that position unfolded in a match in which she was not involved. Had Evert lost to Navratilova in the semi-finals, Graf's elevation would have been delayed.

The 81-minute final, which Graf won 6–3 6–4, offered no surprises, but the mere fact that the number one ranking was on the line ignited the sell-out crowd at the Manhattan Beach Club. Most of the points were played from the baseline. Evert's strategy was simple: keep the ball away from the powerful Graf forehand, but although she was relatively successful, she dropped her serve three times in each set. Navratilova, playing her first tournament since Wimbledon, sat in the stands during the final and watched Graf dethrone her. Navratilova had been No. 1 without interruption since November 1985, and Graf had become only the second player to break the 11-year reign that Navratilova and Evert had enjoyed in the top spot. It was fitting that the only other person to accomplish that feat, Tracy Austin (1980), was also in the stands watching the final.

Yet the biggest upset of the week happened in the quarter-finals when Sabatini surprised fourth-seeded Hana Mandlikova 7–6 (7–3) 2–6 7–5. Still, Sabatini could not get past her doubles partner, Graf, in the next round. In what has been called the rivalry of the future, Graf has beaten Sabatini ten times without loss. While six of the top eight seeds made it to the quarter-finals without losing a set, there were some noteworthy performances in the early rounds. Qualifier Elly Hakami, a 17-year-old Californian who hits with two hands off both wings, won three consecutive three-set matches in the main draw, before falling to Navratilova in the quarter-finals. Another qualifier, Pascale Paradis, showed up in the third round, where she failed to win a game from Graf. A similar fate befell ninth-seeded Bettina Bunge, who upset fifth-seeded Helena Sukova 6–3 2–6 6–3 in the third round but managed to win only two games from Graf the next day.

Navratilova's only consolation was what has become her security blanket – the doubles. She and Pam Shriver, who did not play singles, won yet another doubles title by beating Zina Garrison and Lori McNeil 6–3 6–4 in the final. In contrast, the doubles provided the only disappointment for Graf, she and Sabatini being upset in the second round by Catherine Suire and Jana Novotna. But for Graf, the new No. 1, it was a small price to pay. – J. Y.

10–16 AUGUST
WOMEN'S SINGLES – Quarter-finals: M. Navratilova d. E. Hakami 6–3 6–2; C. M. Evert d. L. McNeil 6–1 6–1; G. Sabatini (ARG) d. H. Mandlikova (TCH) 7–6 2–6 7–5; S. Graf (FRG) d. B. Bunge (FRG) 6–1 6–1. ***Semi-finals:*** Evert d. Navratilova 6–2 6–1; Graf d. Sabatini 7–5 7–5. ***Final:*** Graf d. Evert 6–3 6–4. ***WOMEN'S DOUBLES – Final:*** Navratilova/P. H. Shriver d. Z. Garrison/McNeil 6–3 6–4.

Determined to regain her top ten ranking after slipping to as low as 102, Sylvia Hanika was well on her way at No. 14 by the end of 1987, during which she reached the last 16 in all four Grand Slam Championships. *(T. Hindley)*

PLAYER'S CHALLENGE CANADIAN OPEN ($250,000)

On Saturday, 22 August Pam Shriver wept. She had just beaten Chris Evert 6–4 6–1 for only her second victory since they first met in the final of the 1978 US Open when Shriver was a gangling 16-year-old. This was their 19th meeting and Shriver hadn't won a set from Evert in five years. As the top seed observed wryly: 'This was a match that was long overdue.' The third-seeded Shriver came out swinging and convincingly beat Evert, a four-time Canadian champ, winning 11 of the final 13 games against her increasingly dispirited semi-final opponent.

After trailing 1–3 in the first set, Shriver played virtually immaculate tennis. Ignoring the past, she broke back at love in the sixth game, then sweated out four set-points in the tenth to shatter Evert's defences with a second break. In that first set, Shriver held her own in the back-court, outrallying this most consistent of baseliners when it counted most. In the second, she clobbered Evert from the net. Beaming through her tears, Shriver said: 'To win the match I had to play perfect tennis. I know. I've played 18 imperfect matches against her . . . I thought she'd retire before I won one off her.'

The next day Shriver, the 1986 finalist, came back and, in a near carbon copy victory, whipped fifth-seeded Zina Garrison 6–4 6–1 to win her first Canadian title. In the close first set, Garrison, who missed just four first serves in her five service games, forced Shriver to play very near the top of her serve-and-volley game, particularly in the critical ninth game. Shriver saved three break-points, each time uncorking a whopping big serve down the middle of the deuce court that produced two netted returns and a weak effort that Shriver nailed with a crisp backhand volley winner, then broke Garrison on the fourth break-point to take the set. Whereas Shriver had trouble reading Garrison's backhand passing shots in the first, she surged through the second set, using her immense wing-span at net to crack winning volleys from her shoetops, waist and shoulders or higher as if on a practice court. Breaking Garrison twice, she won the last five games, dropping only four points on her own serve.

In retrospect, the key to Shriver's first hard-court tournament victory in four years may well have been her commanding 6–2 6–1 dismissal of the gifted sixth-seeded Gabriela Sabatini in the quarter-finals. After fighting off a break-point in the second game of the match, Shriver took absolute charge, winning 16 straight points on serve and losing only another six points altogether. Thwarted from executing her new, but still fledgling, serve and volley attack, the by now befuddled Sabatini retreated to the baseline where she went down in a rash of unforced backhand errors. Shriver credited her success to three things: digging her way out of match-point situations two days in a row to reach the Wimbledon semi-finals; her new Yonex racket which increased her confidence in her groundstrokes; and her wide volleys and her new fitness routine.

It was indeed a magnificent run, effectively eclipsing a second-round 6–3 6–1 upset of the defending champion, Helena Sukova, by the unseeded Australian, Anne Minter, as well as some strong performances by Evert, who lost just 11 games on her way to the semis, and by Garrison, who, in struggling to recover form after a two-month injury break, was extended by two tough three-setters before blitzing eighth-seeded Bettina Bunge 6–2 6–3 to reach the final.

There were also noteworthy efforts by ninth-seeded Barbara Potter and the unseeded Canadian national champion, Helen Kelesi. Potter played the match of her career in the third round, using her big southpaw serve to rout second-seeded Hana Mandlikova 6–4 6–4 the day after the erratic Czech had won her 500th career victory. The 17-year-old Kelesi capped a brilliant *Federation Cup* performance, in which she won three singles matches to help Canada qualify for the 1988 Olympics. After upsetting the seventh seed, Claudia Kohde-Kilsch, 6–2 6–3 in the third round, Hurricane Helen ran into Evert who promptly downgraded her to a drizzle. Facing a merciless barrage of accurately placed Evert groundstrokes and passes, Kelesi, who won just 20 points, collapsed 6–2 6–0.

The doubles title fell to the two Houston friends, Garrison and Lori McNeil, who beat the tall Europeans Kohde-Kilsch and Sukova 6–1 6–2. – N. McC.

TORONTO, 17–23 AUGUST
WOMEN'S SINGLES* – *Quarter-finals: C. M. Evert (USA) d. H. Kelesi 6–2 6–0; P. H. Shriver (USA) d. G. Sabatini (ARG) 6–2 6–1; Z. Garrison (USA) d. A. Minter (AUS) 6–1 2–6 6–4; B. Bunge (FRG) d. B. Potter (USA) 6–2 6–0. ***Semi-finals:*** Shriver d. Evert 6–4 6–1; Garrison d. Bunge 6–2 6–3. ***Final:*** Shriver d. Garrison 6–4 6–1.
WOMEN'S DOUBLES* – *Final: Garrison/L. McNeil (USA) d. C. Kohde-Kilsch (FRG)/H. Sukova (TCH) 6–1 6–2.

UNITED JERSEY BANK CLASSIC ($150,000)

Manuela Maleeva of Bulgaria became the 21st millionaire on the women's tennis tour when she swept to the title of the $150,000 United Jersey Bank Classic at Mahwah, New Jersey, the final warm-up stop before the US Open. Seeded third, Manuela had to come from behind to defeat the sixth seed, Sylvia Hanika of West Germany, 1–6 6–4 6–1 in the final. The prize money of $30,000 lifted her career earnings to $1,002,963. Hanika, who had reached the zenith of her career earlier in the decade when she won the Avon Championships in 1982 – surprising Martina Navratilova in the final – and reached the French Open final in 1981, raised her career earnings to $984,147.

Hanika, a strong left-handed serve-and-volley player, completely dominated the first set, losing just eight points, and held serve in the seventh game of the second set for a 4–3 lead. But then her sliced backhand shots began losing depth, and Maleeva used lobs and drop shots, running her opponent all over the court to win nine of the last ten games.

The tournament, played on the hard courts at Ramapo College, began badly when West Germany's Steffi Graf had to withdraw with an infected tooth and Barbara Potter pulled out with a back ailment. Then there was Raffaella Reggi of Italy, who bravely played despite having contracted a bad case of poison ivy. Helena Sukova of Czechoslovakia took over as the top seed, and the field also included Americans Zina Garrison and Lori McNeil, and Sweden's Catarina Lindqvist.

Australian Dianne Balestrat eliminated Garrison, seeded three, 6–4 6–1 in 61 minutes in the second round, before falling to Hanika in the quarter-finals. Maleeva, meanwhile, rolled through the early rounds, breezing past Reggi and France's Nathalie Tauziat and not dropping a set, but playing an emotional semi-final when she faced her younger sister, Katerina. Manuela maintained her record against her sister – in six matches pitting the two Bulgarians, Katerina has yet to win a set, and at Mahwah, Manuela won five of the last six games in their baseline duel. Katerina had earlier beaten the 1983 winner, Jo Durie, and then pulled off the biggest upset of the tournament in the quarter-finals when she eliminated Sukova 6–2 6–3, the Czech double-faulting on match-point.

In the bottom half of the draw, McNeil defeated Sandra Cecchini of Italy and then Lindqvist in a tough three-setter. That set her against Hanika, who had eliminated Isabelle Demongeot of France, veteran American Betsy Nagelsen and Balestrat. Hanika needed two hours and four minutes to advance to her second tournament final of the year. The 27-year-old West German jumped out to a 4–1 lead in the third set before double-faulting away the sixth game to McNeil. But she broke back in the seventh game and fought off four break-points in the eighth to close out the 6–4 2–6 6–2 victory.

McNeil did come out of Mahwah with a title, however, teaming with Gigi Fernandez of Puerto Rico to capture the doubles with a 6–3 6–2 victory over Britain's Anne Hobbs and Australia's Elizabeth Smylie, having eliminated the Maleeva sisters in the second round in straight sets. – B. G.

MAHWAH, NEW JERSEY, 24–30 AUGUST
WOMEN'S SINGLES* – *Quarter-finals: K. Maleeva (BUL) d. H. Sukova (TCH) 6–2 6–3; M. Maleeva (BUL) d. R. Reggi (ITA) 6–4 6–3; S. Hanika (FRG) d. D. Balestrat (AUS) 6–2 7–5; L. McNeil d. C. Lindqvist (SWE) 4–6 6–4 6–3. ***Semi-finals:*** M. Maleeva d. K. Maleeva 6–3 6–4; Hanika d. McNeil 6–2 2–6 6–2. ***Final:*** M. Maleeva d. Hanika 1–6 6–4 6–1.
WOMEN'S DOUBLES* – *Final: G. Fernandez/McNeil d. A. Hobbs (GBR)/E. Smylie (AUS) 6–3 6–2.

At the Canadian Open in August, Pam Shriver was overjoyed to beat Chris Evert for only the second time in 19 meetings since their first encounter in the final of the 1978 US Open. *(Carol L. Newsom)*

SEGMENT 6: 14 SEPTEMBER–4 OCTOBER

Edward Johnson and Herman Fuchs

PAN PACIFIC OPEN ($250,000)

You could say that the talented Argentine beauty, Gabriela Sabatini, finally arrived in Tokyo. By beating the No. 2 seed, Manuela Maleeva of Bulgaria, 6–4 7–6 in the final of the $250,000 Pan Pacific Open, 17-year-old Gabriela was claiming her first major title and her third tournament win on the Virginia Slims tour. Appropriately her first career win had been the 1985 Japan Open, a smaller $50,000 event.

Miss Sabatini justified her top seeding by winning the tournament without losing a set, while Miss Maleeva had dropped sets to American Marianne Werdel (4–6 7–5 6–1) and fifth-seeded Catarina Lindqvist of Sweden (6–3 3–6 6–4) on her way to the final. Miss Werdel had earlier beaten the eighth seed, Gigi Fernandez, in round two, after the No. 7 seed, Helen Kelesi of Canada, had fallen to the local girl, Etsuko Inoue, 6–2 6–2 in the opening round. These were the only upsets as fourth seed Katerina Maleeva and Miss Lindqvist joined Miss Sabatini and Manuela Maleeva in the semi-finals.

When Miss Sabatini led 4–0 in the second set of the final after taking the first 6–4, it seemed she would easily add to her four previous wins in six career meetings with the Bulgarian. But, as so often in the past, Gabriela's concentration wavered, allowing Miss Maleeva to sweep through the next five games to take the lead. 'That made me mad so I worked harder', admitted the winner afterwards. The hard work paid dividends as she steadied herself to capture an exciting tie-break 8–6 and claim the first prize of $50,000. Thus Miss Maleeva was relegated to second place (and $22,500) for the second time in three years, for she had won the tournament in 1985 but lost to Steffi Graf in 1986.

The scratch all-White pairing, Anne and Robin of that ilk, beat the top-seeded Maleeva sisters 6–1 6–2 in a one-sided final to share the winners' prize of $15,000. – E. J.

TOKYO, 14–20 SEPTEMBER
WOMEN'S SINGLES – Quarter-finals: G. Sabatini (ARG) d. E. Inoue 6–2 6–3; K. Maleeva (BUL) d. D. Balestrat (AUS) 6–2 6–0; C. Lindqvist (SWE) d. B. Potter (USA) 7–5 4–6 6–4; M. Maleeva (BUL) d. M. Werdel (USA) 4–6 7–5 6–1. ***Semi-finals:*** Sabatini d. K. Maleeva 7–6 6–4; M. Maleeva d. Lindqvist 6–3 3–6 6–4. ***Final:*** Sabatini d. M. Maleeva 6–4 7–6.
WOMEN'S DOUBLES – Final: A./R. White d. K./M. Maleeva 6–1 6–2.

CITIZEN CUP ($150,000)

The resurrection wasn't under a lucky star exactly. The weather gods went crazy when, after a nine-year break, ladies' tennis returned to Hamburg with the Citizen Cup. Icy cold rain, the like of which not even Wimbledon sees very often, badly disrupted the event. When the quarter-finals were scheduled to have been played, the last 16 players were not yet decided, and the doubles had not even begun.

That the organisers still had a turnout of more than 40,000 fans, that in spite of all adversities there was no deficit, was due only to Steffi Graf. The new No. 1 of women's tennis made the fans forget the rain as well as the cold. Of course, everything was done to present Germany's new tennis darling in a perfect way, and about 7,000 fans turned out for the 'Steffi Day' before the tournament began. Miss Graf played a short set against the German youngster, Carl-Uwe Steeb, and although they played only seven games, Steffi probably stood on the court longer in that encounter than in the following five matches that led to her ninth tournament win of the year. Against Louise Field, Bettina Fulco, Wiltrud Probst, Sandra Cecchini and Isabel Cueto she lost only 17 games.

Claudia Kohde-Kilsch, expected to be Graf's final opponent, was eliminated in round three by Iwona Kuczynska, a Pole who lives in Florida and is ranked some 100 places behind Kohde-Kilsch. Even greater was the difference in ranking between Bettina Bunge, seeded third, and her conqueror; Leila Meskhi of Russia, who started the tournament as the world's No. 171, beat the No. 12 in round two.

It says a lot about the recent German tennis boom that despite the loss of two top players, there was still a second German making it to the final. To get there, though, Isabel Cueto had to work hard. The day before the final she was on court for more than four hours, grinding down first Yugoslavia's Sabrina Goles, then Kathy Horvath, both in three sets. Against Steffi all her strength was gone, but the dark-haired girl with the South American background had already secured the brightest success of her career.

The doubles took one day longer than planned. The top seeds, Graf and Bunge, had lost to Bykova and Meskhi in the quarter-finals, and the young Russians also put up a great fight in the final, at which no admission was charged. Yet they could not keep the winners' prize from Claudia Kohde-Kilsch and Jana Novotna, who were playing together for the first time, two tie-breaks winning the match for the second seeds. – H. F.

HAMBURG, 21–27 SEPTEMBER
WOMEN'S SINGLES – Quarter-finals: S. Graf d. W. Probst 6–2 6–0; A. M. Cecchini (ITA) d. R. Reggi (ITA) 6–3 1–6 6–4; I. Cueto d. S. Goles (YUG) 6–1 3–6 6–1; K. Horvath (USA) d. I. Kuczynska (POL) 6–1 6–7 6–3. ***Semi-finals:*** Graf d. Cecchini 6–0 6–2; Cueto d. Horvath 6–4 1–6 6–2. ***Final:*** Graf d. Cueto 6–2 6–2.
WOMEN'S DOUBLES – Final: C. Kohde-Kilsch/J. Novotna (TCH) d. N. Bykova (URS)/L. Meskhi (URS) 7–6 7–6.

VIRGINIA SLIMS OF NEW ORLEANS ($150,000)

Revenge, they say, is sweet. Chris Evert, the top seed, had a sweet time in October when, in the final of the $150,000 Virginia Slims of New Orleans, she beat third-seeded Lori McNeil 6–3 7–5 to avenge her dramatic loss to the Houston player at the US Open. On a slightly slower indoor Supreme surface, Miss Evert was able to return McNeil's serve better than she had done on the asphalt at Flushing Meadow, timing the ball well and covering the court better than at the US Open where many of her opponent's volleys had left her flat-footed. 'I just played solid tennis', said the winner after receiving a cheque for $30,000. 'You have to concentrate against Lori . . . she's so quick and makes a lot of winners – but she also makes some errors.' This 153rd career title put Miss Evert still further ahead of all players, men or women, in the game's record books. Her former fiancé, Jimmy Connors, heads the men's list with 105 wins.

There had been three seeding upsets in the opening round in New Orleans before sanity prevailed. Left-handed Barbara Potter (4) fell 7–6 6–4 to Robin White; Gigi Fernandez (7) was beaten 6–3 6–1 by Mary Lou Piatek and Wendy White (8) lost 6–3 6–4 to Gretchen Rush Magers. However, the Australian veteran Wendy Turnbull (6) cut down Robin White in the quarter-finals before a foot injury forced her to retire to Miss Evert in the semi-final when trailing 2–4. In the other semi-final Miss McNeil's Houston stablemate Zina Garrison failed once again to turn the tables on her friend. McNeil's 6–2 6–4 win means that she has now won all three of their personal battles – the second being at the US Open.

However, the friends got it all together in the doubles when they beat Peanut Louie Harper and Heather Ludloff 6–3 6–3 for their second title of the year. – E. J.

28 SEPTEMBER–4 OCTOBER
WOMEN'S SINGLES – Quarter-finals: C. M. Evert d. A. E. Smith 6–2 6–0; W. M. Turnbull (AUS) d. R. White 6–2 3–6 6–4; L. McNeil d. K. Gompert 6–4 6–4; Z. Garrison d. M. Werdel 3–6 6–1 6–4. ***Semi-finals:*** Evert d. Turnbull 4–2 ret'd; McNeil d. Garrison 6–2 6–4. ***Final:*** Evert d. McNeil 6–3 7–5.
WOMEN'S DOUBLES – Final: Garrison/McNeil d. H. Ludloff/P. Louie Harper 6–3 6–3.

SEGMENT 7: 12 OCTOBER–1 NOVEMBER

Barry Wood, Hugh Jamieson and Edward Johnson

PORSCHE TENNIS GRAND PRIX ($175,000)

They met for the 75th time, and by resisting Chris Evert's determined first-set challenge Martina Navratilova was able to celebrate her 31st birthday with a 7–5 6–1 victory in the final of the Porsche Tennis Grand Prix. It was her 40th win over her long-time rival, her fourth title at Filderstadt, and her third title of the year following Wimbledon and the US Open. It is unlikely that any of their matches over the last 14 years has changed direction so dramatically. During the first set they conjured up some of the best tennis ever played between them, but a series of exhibitions and a demanding quarter-final against Mary Joe Fernandez had left Evert drained, and she was unable to present any real challenge in the second set, which took only 21 minutes.

Yet the first set was intensely competitive. Evert began well by moving Navratilova all over the court and hitting deep into the corners. They thrilled the crowd with some superb rallies, often using the sharpest of angles as they pulled each other wider and wider. Evert took the first break to lead 4–2, but Navratilova broke straight back and then took the lead for the first time at 6–5. That game contained three deuces and the defending champion needed three break-points to clinch it. She then served out the set and, as she has so often done before – usually against lesser opponents – dominated the remainder of the match. Afterwards Navratilova admitted: 'She was emotionally down and felt it was too far to come back. And of course, by having the first set under my belt I relaxed and played even better.'

Yet some of the blame for Evert's defeat must be laid at the door of Fernandez, who conceded their quarter-final 6–2 5–7 6–4 only after two hours and eight minutes. Victory for the second seed was by no means secure until the final point had been played, and it required a third consecutive break of serve for Evert to win the match. 'I had 6–2 5–3 match point (40–30) and should have clinched it then', said Evert. 'Once it was 5-all Mary Joe started to hit the ball very very hard and started going for all her shots and the end result was that I was lucky to win the match. That's the best she's ever played against me.' The next day she was able to put that struggle behind her and gain revenge against Pam Shriver for the defeat inflicted upon her in Toronto in August. That had been Evert's first loss to Shriver in 19 matches; this time Evert won 7–5 6–3.

Navratilova reached the final with a 6–2 6–2 win over Gabriela Sabatini, who was hampered by a stomach upset. In the quarter-finals the Argentinian justified her advance over Helena Sukova in the computer rankings – they exchanged sixth and seventh positions – by defeating her 6–7 (10–12) 7–6 (7–5) 6–3 in a marathon lasting two hours and 34 minutes. The Czech actually led by a set and 4–1, served for the match at 5–4 and 6–5, and then held a 4–1 lead in the second-set tie-break.

In doubles, top seeds Navratilova and Shriver retained their title with a straightforward 6–1 6–2 win over Zina Garrison and Lori McNeil. The third seeds had reached the final by

A quarter-finalist at the French Open in 1986 when she was still only 14, Mary Joe Fernandez beat Barbara Potter on her way to the last 16 of Wimbledon in 1987, and extended Chris Evert to three tough sets in the quarter-finals at Filderstadt, as well as reaching the same stage in Geneva. *(T. Hindley)*

beating Kathy Jordan and Sukova 6–7 (7–9) 7–6 (7–5) 6–4. Another lengthy encounter took place between the German pair of Andrea Betzner and Christina Singer and one of the most successful new teams on the tour, Jana Novotna and Catherine Suire. The result was a 6–7 (4–7) 6–4 7–6 (7–5) first-round win for the Germans. – B. W.

FILDERSTADT, 12–18 OCTOBER
WOMEN'S SINGLES – Quarter-finals: M. Navratilova (USA) d. L. McNeil (USA) 6–4 6–2; G. Sabatini (ARG) d. H. Sukova (TCH) 6–7 7–6 6–3; P. H. Shriver (USA) d. Z. Garrison (USA) 6–4 6–2; C. M. Evert (USA) d. M. J. Fernandez (USA) 6–2 5–7 6–4. ***Semi-finals:*** Navratilova d. Sabatini 6–2 6–2; Evert d. Shriver 7–5 6–3. ***Final:*** Navratilova d. Evert 7–5 6–1.
WOMEN'S DOUBLES – Final: Navratilova/Shriver d. Garrison/McNeil 6–1 6–2.

VOLVO CLASSIC ($200,000)

The hurricane that had ripped through Brighton only days earlier failed to ruffle the feathers of the elegant Gabriela Sabatini, the 17-year-old Argentinian who was making her début in the Volvo Classic. Miss Sabatini, ranked sixth in the world, celebrated her arrival on the south coast by scooping Europe's richest indoor women's event with a 7–5 6–4 triumph over top-seeded American Pam Shriver. It was Gabby's first-ever win over Miss Shriver, coming just six weeks after she had been allowed a meagre three games by the tall American in Toronto.

When Miss Shriver stormed into a 4–0 lead with some relentless attacking, the Argentinian must have feared the worst, but Miss Sabatini held her nerve and gradually underlined the influence that her coach, Angel Gimenez, the former Spanish *Davis Cup* player, has had on her all-round game since they teamed up nine months earlier. Once she had survived a set-point at 4–5 with a typically glorious backhand, Miss Sabatini increased the doubt in Miss Shriver's mind with the kind of shot-making that had left Helena Sukova wondering what had hit her in the semi-final. Miss Shriver, restricted to just three points after breaking for 4–3 in the second set, had been cut down to size, admitting: 'I was very impressed with Gabriela's performance. I didn't think she could keep up that sort of standard once she had worked her way back into the match. She was prepared to attack me more than she had in Toronto and didn't give me any peace from the back of the court.'

Miss Sabatini's only blemish was a warning for time-wasting from umpire Jeremy Shales as she bounced the ball so many times before serving. Shales' patience finally ran out after Miss Sabatini had bounced the ball 24 times to produce a delay of 42 seconds between points in the third game of the second set. Gabriela's second tournament title of the year and her first in Europe earned her $25,000.

A tournament without Martina Navratilova, Steffi Graf, Chris Evert and Hana Mandlikova needed someone with Miss Sabatini's style and flair – not to mention her beauty – to captivate the crowds, as well as to give hard-working tournament director George Hendon something to smile about. Much to the dismay of LTA supremo, Warren Jacques, British hopes were smashed with almost the same ferocity that the storms had inflicted. Eighteen girls having failed to qualify, home hopes rested on Jo Durie, Sara Gomer, Anne Hobbs and Clare Wood, of whom only Miss Gomer survived into the second round.

Miss Durie was sent packing by the third seed, Miss Sukova, while Miss Hobbs, almost always guaranteed to give anyone a fight, slumped to a 6–2 6–3 defeat against French qualifier Pascale Paradis, who was stopped in the second round by Helena Sukova. At least Miss Wood, the 19-year-old from down the coast at Littlehampton, took French girl Isabelle Demongeot, ranked 118 places above her, to three sets before losing 6–1 3–6 6–4. 'I held back in the final set when I should have gone for my shots. I should be beyond that sort of thing now', she said.

That left 23-year-old Miss Gomer, at 6ft 2in hoping to walk tall after defeating Spanish teenager Arantxa Sanchez. However, Miss Shriver, 6 feet tall and ranked five in the world, had hammered Miss Gomer twice in their previous matches and was in no mood now to look up to the British girl. Putting behind her the worries about her shares on the Stock

Market, she won 6–3 6–3 and then spelled out a timely warning to Miss Gomer, saying: 'If she had a lot more faith in her own physical abilities it could make all the difference. Anyone that size and left-handed has to be taken seriously. If she decided to get herself into tip-top shape then she could do something.'

The doubles title fell to the No. 2 seeds, Kathy Jordan and Sukova, who beat Tine Scheuer-Larsen and Catherine Tanvier 7–5 6–1. – H. J.

BRIGHTON, 19–20 OCTOBER
WOMEN'S SINGLES – Quarter-finals: P. H. Shriver (USA) d. K. Maleeva (BUL) 6–2 6–1; K. Jordan (USA) d. A. M. Cecchini (ITA) 6–1 6–3; G. Sabatini (ARG) d. B. Bunge (FRG) 5–0 ret'd; H. Sukova (TCH) d. S. Hanika (FRG) 6–3 5–7 6–1. ***Semi-finals:*** Shriver d. Jordan 6–1 7–5; Sabatini d. Sukova 6–1 6–3. ***Final:*** Sabatini d. Shriver 7–5 6–4.
WOMEN'S DOUBLES – Final: Jordan/Sukova d. T. Scheuer-Larsen (DEN)/C. Tanvier (FRA) 7–5 6–1.

EUROPEAN INDOOR CHAMPIONSHIPS ($150,000)

Back in Los Angeles it had been the world No. 1 ranking. In Zurich it was the World Champion's crown. These two firsts for the remarkable German teenager, Steffi Graf, were peaks of an incredible year in which she won a first Grand Slam title in Paris and more tournaments than anyone else, man or woman. In the final of the $150,000 European Indoor Championships in Zurich, Steffi beat the erratic Czech, Hana Mandlikova, 6–2 6–2 to claim the $30,000 first prize and the 210 Virginia Slims points that ensured her position as World Champion.

Three of the four top seeds came safely through to the semi-finals in Zurich, the only absentee being fourth-seeded Claudia Kohde-Kilsch, who had to default with a knee injury to Nathalie Tauziat in the second round. Tauziat made the most of her good luck by proceeding to the semi-finals at the expense of qualifier Christina Singer who, herself, had upset her compatriot, the former German No. 1 Sylvia Hanika, 0–6 7–6 7–6 in an exciting second-round match.

This was Miss Graf's tenth singles title of the year and her fourth success against Miss Mandlikova in five career meetings. The customary coolness and punishing power on backhand and forehand demolished her taller opponent in just 66 minutes. 'I had to concentrate hard and stay alert against Hana', said the new European Champion. 'I am very happy with my game.' This was understandable as she had been made to fight in an intriguing semi-final by Manuela Maleeva, who snatched the middle set on an 8–6 tie-break before being overwhelmed in the decider. Miss Mandlikova was allowed no such chances.

The unseeded French pair of Nathalie Herreman and Pascale Paradis won their first tour doubles title together when they beat the fourth seeds, Jana Novotna and Catherine Suire, 6–3 2–6 6–3 in the final to earn the $9,000 first prize which they shared. – E. J.

ZURICH, 26 OCTOBER–1 NOVEMBER
WOMEN'S SINGLES – Quarter-finals: H. Mandlikova (TCH) d. J. Polzl Wiesner (AUT) 6–3 7–5; N. Tauziat (FRA) d. C. Singer (FRG) 7–5 6–4; M. Maleeva (BUL) d. R. Reggi (ITA) 6–2 6–4; S. Graf (FRG) d. K. Maleeva (BUL) 6–2 6–3. ***Semi-finals:*** Mandlikova d. Tauziat 6–1 3–6 6–3; Graf d. M. Maleeva 6–4 6–7 6–1. ***Final:*** Graf d. Mandlikova 6–2 6–2.
WOMEN'S DOUBLES – Final: N. Herreman (FRA)/P. Paradis (FRA) d. J. Novotna (TCH)/C. Suire (FRA) 6–3 2–6 6–3.

Rosalyn Fairbank of South Africa, better known for her doubles play, with titles in Beckenham and New England in 1987, also appeared in the last 16 of the singles at Wimbledon, where she extended Chris Evert to 7–5 in the final set. (T. Hindley)

SEGMENT 8: 2–15 NOVEMBER

Josh Young and Barry Wood

VIRGINIA SLIMS OF NEW ENGLAND ($250,000)

Pam Shriver did not expect much when she arrived in Worcester, Massachusetts in November. A year earlier, she had been humbled when she went to a local book store to peddle her book, *Passing Shots*, and nobody showed up at the book-autographing party. This year, Shriver was peddling her new tennis game, and it turned out to be Chris Evert, her opponent in the final, who was humbled when Shriver authored a best-selling 6–4 4–6 6–0 victory tale in the final. The win came one day after the entire town and a glittering array of tennis personalities had gathered to pay tribute to Evert's 153 career titles. The gala celebration left Evert too tired to clinch number 154.

Shriver called it 'my best final ever', and it certainly was. The six-foot-tall resident of Lutherville, Maryland, became the first woman to win a love set from Evert in a championship final since Evonne Goolagong did so at the 1974 Australian Open. In the past, it would have been Shriver who faded first, but not now. The new edition was fit and confident, and nobody could have agreed more than Evert, who won only seven points in the final set. Shriver's serve clicked like never before, so that Evert broke it only once – in the tenth game to win the second set. Shriver's total confidence in her ability to hold serve allowed her to attack Evert's delivery every time the 32-year-old put the ball in play. When asked why she had suddenly beaten Evert in two of their last three meetings after losing 18 times, Shriver responded: 'My serve. The big difference is that I can rely on it now.'

Evert admitted that the gala had made her tired and also pointed out that third-seeded Gabriela Sabatini had battled her for one hour and 50 minutes before conceding a 6–4 7–6 (7–1) semi-final victory. In the quarter-finals Evert had been scared by another big server, seventh-seeded Barbara Potter, who, behind a barrage of aces and service winners, had taken the first set in 22 minutes, before Evert rallied for a 1–6 6–1 6–3 win. Shriver, however, rolled into the final without the loss of a set, passing fourth-seeded Helena Sukova 7–5 6–3 in the semi-finals after losing a 5–1 lead in each set. Sukova told Shriver afterwards that she wouldn't be able to play that loosely in the final if she wanted to beat Evert. Shriver took Sukova's advice and didn't.

Form held for seven of eight seeds coming into the quarter-finals, the lone exception being the No. 8, Wendy Turnbull, who had fallen 7–5 7–6 (8–6) to Eva Pfaff in the first round. The feeling at the Centrum all week long was that it would be Evert and somebody, probably Shriver or Sukova, in the final. The crowds, as Pam Shriver had learned the year before, weren't interested in casual entertainment. They wanted suspense, drama. The only early-round match that had such potential occurred in the second round between Sabatini and Kathy Jordan. A dangerous serve-and-volleyer and one of the best unseeded players a tournament could hope to have, Jordan is not scared of any player because she has beaten them all. As Sabatini's father paced to and fro, waiting for the match to go on, an extra one thousand people showed up, but all they saw was Jordan take a fall at two-all and leave with an injured knee.

She had to withdraw from the doubles as well, which paved the way for the unseeded team of Elise Burgin of the US and South African Ros Fairbank, whose mission was to win the tournament so that they could qualify for the Virginia Slims Championships. They did it, and thus earned the spot below Shriver's on the Worcester best-seller list for the week. – J. Y.

WORCESTER, MASS., 2–8 NOVEMBER
WOMEN'S SINGLES – Quarter-finals: C. M. Evert d. B. Potter 1–6 6–1 6–3; G. Sabatini (ARG) d. L. McNeil 6–2 6–3; H. Sukova (TCH) d. E. Pfaff (FRG) 6–2 6–1; P. H. Shriver d. B. Bunge (FRG) 6–4 6–4. ***Semi-finals:*** Evert d. Sabatini 6–4 7–6; Shriver d. Sukova 7–5 6–3. ***Final:*** Shriver d. Evert 6–4 4–6 6–0.
WOMEN'S DOUBLES – Final: E. Burgin/R. Fairbank (RSA) d. Bunge/Pfaff 6–4 6–4.

VIRGINIA SLIMS OF CHICAGO ($150,000)

Martina Navratilova may have won the tournament, but 16-year-old Natalia Zvereva won the hearts of the Chicago people as she battled her way to the final. There the defending champion defeated her easily enough, 6–1 6–2, but noted the Russian's potential. 'She'll be around for a while if they keep letting her come out and play', she forecast. 'She doesn't have any real weaknesses. If I were her I'd work on my first serve. Otherwise she's there.'

She certainly is. Natalia came into the tournament fresh from reaching the final of the Virginia Slims of Arkansas, where she lost in three sets to Sandra Cecchini. Coincidentally, her only previous final had also been in Arkansas in 1986, when she lost to Kathy Rinaldi. But it is in the juniors where she had truly excelled, winning the 1987 French, Wimbledon and US Open titles, all without conceding a set. The junior Grand Slam might have been hers had she gone on to compete in the 1988 Australian Open.

'She has the right instincts on the court more than anything', said Barbara Potter, who was beaten 6–4 2–6 6–4 by Zvereva in the semi-finals. The effort she put into beating Potter, playing from the baseline but mixing up her game beautifully with lobs and drop-shots to keep Potter off balance, won her much applause, and in the final, as the underdog facing one of the mightiest players of all time, she could not help but draw the warmth of the crowd to her. Her after-match speech in halting English was merely the icing on the cake. Chicago will keep a welcome for Natalia Zvereva for a long time to come.

If Zvereva took away happy memories, then so too did Kate Gompert who added Hana Mandlikova to her list of surprised victims during the year, Chris Evert at Boca Raton having been the first. This time she inflicted a 6–2 7–6 (7–0) defeat on the Czech No. 1 in the second round. She got no further than the quarter-finals, however, because there she lost 5–7 6–4 6–0 to a certain little Russian girl called Natalia.

Catarina Lindqvist, seeded eight, lost 6–3 6–2 to Potter in the first round, although that was understandable owing to this being her first tournament in two months after recovering from mononucleosis. The second round produced two surprises in addition to Gompert's win over Mandlikova. Russian qualifier Leila Meskhi overcame the seventh seed, Bettina Bunge, 6–4 6–2, while Zvereva brought off another upset by defeating the fifth seed, Claudia Kohde-Kilsch, who was hindered by a knee injury. The quarter-finals found Navratilova easing past Lori McNeil 6–1 6–4, Sukova eventually getting the better of Meskhi by the rather bizarre score of 7–6 (7–4) 0–6 6–0 and Potter upsetting No. 4 Zina Garrison 6–3 6–4. In the semi-finals Navratilova beat Sukova 7–5 7–5, while Zvereva enjoyed that wonderful two-and-a-half-hour win over Potter.

In the doubles final top seeds Kohde-Kilsch and Sukova beat second seeds Garrison and McNeil in straight sets. Mandlikova and Jana Novotna, in the second week of a new partnership, won their first match together against the newly married Mary Lou Piatek Daniels, now a resident of Chicago, and Sharon Walsh Pete. They followed that with a victory over Ros Fairbank and Elise Burgin before losing 6–1 7–6 in the semi-finals to the eventual champions. – B. W.

9–15 NOVEMBER
WOMEN'S SINGLES – Quarter-finals: M. Navratilova d. L. McNeil 6–1 6–4; H. Sukova (TCH) d. L. Meskhi (URS) 7–6 0–6 6–0; N. Zvereva (URS) d. K. Gompert 5–7 6–4 6–0; B. Potter d. Z. Garrison 6–3 6–4. ***Semi-finals:*** Navratilova d. Sukova 7–5 7–5; Zvereva d. Potter 6–4 2–6 6–4. ***Final:*** Navratilova d. Zvereva 6–1 6–2.
WOMEN'S DOUBLES – Final: C. Kohde-Kilsch (FRG)/Sukova d. Z. Garrison/McNeil 6–4 6–3.

As she had at Wimbledon, Natalia Zvereva won the hearts of the Chicago crowds – and compliments from both Martina Navratilova, who beat her, and Barbara Potter, who didn't – when she reached the final there. *(A. Evans)*

OTHER VIRGINIA SLIMS TOURNAMENTS

ARGENTINE OPEN ($50,000)

BUENOS AIRES, 1–8 DECEMBER, 1986
WOMEN'S SINGLES – Quarter-finals: G. Sabatini d. P. Tarabini 6–3 6–0; L. McNeil (USA) d. L. Golarsa 6–2 6–2; A. Sanchez (ESP) d. B. Fulco 6–2 6–4; M. Perez Roldan d. N. Jagerman (HOL) 6–2 6–2. ***Semi-finals:*** Sabatini d. McNeil 6–2 6–3; Sanchez d. Perez Roldan 7–6 7–5. ***Final:*** Sabatini d. Sanchez 6–1 6–1.
WOMEN'S DOUBLES – Final: McNeil/M. Paz d. Jagerman/M. Bollegraf (HOL) 6–1 2–6 6–1.

BRAZILIAN OPEN ($50,000)

SAO PAULO, 8–15 DECEMBER, 1986
WOMEN'S SINGLES – Quarter-finals: K. Keil (USA) d. N. Jagerman (HOL) 6–2 6–0; J. Klitch (USA) d. A. Villagran (ARG) 6–2 6–1; A. Schwartz (USA) d. A. Sanchez (ESP) 6–4 6–1; V. Nelson Dunbar (USA) d. C. Nozzoli (ITA) 7–5 6–2. ***Semi-finals:*** Klitch d. Keil 6–1 4–6 6–3; Nelson Dunbar d. Schwartz 6–4 6–3. ***Final:*** Nelson Dunbar d. Klitch 6–2 7–6.
WOMEN'S DOUBLES – Final: N. Dias/P. Medrado d. L. Gildemeister (PER)/P. Huber (AUT) 4–6 6–4 7–6.

BRISBANE ($100,000)

29 DECEMBER 1986–4 JANUARY
WOMEN'S SINGLES – Quarter-finals: H. Mandlikova (TCH) d. H. Kelesi (CAN) 6–3 6–3; H. Sukova (TCH) d. R. Fairbank (RSA) 7–5 6–3; B. Nagelsen (USA) d. E. Smylie 3–6 6–2 6–3; P. H. Shriver (USA) d. E. Pfaff (FRG) 6–3 6–4. ***Semi-finals:*** Mandlikova d. Sukova 4–6 6–1 6–2; Shriver d. Nagelsen 6–1 6–3. ***Final:*** Mandlikova d. Shriver 6–2 2–6 6–4.
WOMEN'S DOUBLES – Final: Mandlikova/W. M. Turnbull d. Nagelsen/Smylie 6–4 6–3.

AUCKLAND ($50,000)

26 JANUARY–1 FEBRUARY
WOMEN'S SINGLES – Quarter-finals: T. Phelps (USA) d. A. M. Fernandez (USA) 6–4 6–3; E. Minter (AUS) d. M. Jaggard (AUS) 7–5 4–6 7–6; K. Keil (USA) d. A. Devries (BEL) 6–4 2–6 6–1; G. Rush (USA) d. N. Provis (AUS) 6–0 6–1. ***Semi-finals:*** Phelps d. Minter 6–1 7–5; Rush d. Keil 7–6 6–1. ***Final:*** Rush d. Phelps 6–2 6–3.
WOMEN'S DOUBLES – Final: J. Richardson/Fernandez d. Rush/Minter 4–6 6–4 6–2.

BRIDGESTONE DOUBLES ($175,000)

TOKYO, 26 JANUARY–1 FEBRUARY
WOMEN'S DOUBLES – Semi-finals: C. Kohde-Kilsch (FRG)/H. Sukova (TCH) d. G. Fernandez (USA)/R. White (USA) 6–4 1–6 6–2; E. Burgin (USA)/P. H. Shriver (USA) d. S. Collins (USA)/S. Walsh Pete (USA) 6–4 4–6 6–3. ***Final:*** Kohde-Kilsch/Sukova d. Burgin/Shriver 6–1 7–6.

VIRGINIA SLIMS OF OKLAHOMA ($75,000)

OKLAHOMA CITY, 9–15 FEBRUARY
WOMEN'S SINGLES – Quarter-finals: L. McNeil d. Hu Na 6–1 7–6; L. Savchenko (URS) d. N. Bykova (URS) 7–5 7–6; E. Smylie (AUS) d. C. Benjamin 6–2 6–4; C. Lindqvist (SWE) d. E. Minter (AUS) 6–4

Anne Minter of Australia, who raised her ranking to 38, won her first title at Taipei in April, and followed a week later with her second – in Singapore. *(T. Hindley)*

6–2. ***Semi-finals:*** McNeil d. Savchenko 7–6 6–2; Smylie d. Lindqvist 6–4 6–4. ***Final:*** Smylie d. McNeil 4–6 6–3 7–5.
WOMEN'S DOUBLES – Final: S. Parkhomenko (URS)/Savchenko d. McNeil/K. Sands 6–4 6–4.

VIRGINIA SLIMS OF ARIZONA ($75,000)

PHOENIX, 9–15 MARCH
WOMEN'S SINGLES – Quarter-finals: D. Balestrat (AUS) d. C. Suire (FRA) 6–2 6–0; S. Walsh Pete d. A. Henricksson 7–5 6–3; A. White d. C. Jolissaint (SUI) 6–3 6–2; M. Lindstrom (SWE) d. P. Barg 6–7 7–5 6–3. ***Semi-finals:*** Balestrat d. Walsh Pete 7–5 7–5; White d. Lindstrom 6–2 6–4. ***Final:*** White d. Balestrat 6–1 6–2.
WOMEN'S DOUBLES – Final: P. Barg/B. Herr d. M. L. Piatek/A. White 2–6 6–2 7–6.

PLYMOUTH WOMEN'S TEAM CHAMPIONSHIPS ($175,000)

MARCO ISLAND, FLORIDA, 12–14 MARCH
WOMEN'S DOUBLES – Semi-finals: L. McNeil/B. Bunge (FRG) d. E. Smylie (AUS)/C. Tanvier (FRA) 3–6 6–3 6–2; C. M. Evert Lloyd/W. M. Turnbull (AUS) d. B. Nagelsen/R. White 7–6 7–6. ***Final:*** Evert Lloyd/Turnbull d. McNeil/Bunge 6–1 7–5.

WILD DUNES CHARLESTON ($75,000)

30 MARCH–5 APRIL
WOMEN'S SINGLES – Quarter-finals: M. Maleeva (BUL) d. H. Cioffi 6–0 6–4; B. Fulco (ARG) d. S. Cecchini (ITA) 6–0 2–6 6–2; J. Novotna (TCH) d. K. Gompert 6–1 7–6; R. Reggi (ITA) d. W. Probst (FRG) 6–4 7–6. ***Semi-finals:*** Maleeva d. Fulco 6–4 6–1; Reggi d. Novotna 6–3 2–6 7–5. ***Final:*** Maleeva d. Reggi 5–7 6–2 6–3.
WOMEN'S DOUBLES – Final: L. Glldemeister (PER)/T. Scheuer-Larsen (DEN) d. M. Paz (ARG)/C. Reynolds 6–4 6–4.

JAPAN & ASIAN OPEN ($50,000)

TOKYO, 13–19 APRIL
WOMEN'S SINGLES – Quarter-finals: E. Inoue d. M. Gurney (USA) 6–3 6–0; B. Gerken (USA) d. K. Jordan (USA) 6–3 3–6 7–5; B. Nagelsen (USA) d. K. Okamoto 6–3 6–4; K. Maleeva (BUL) d. B. Herr (USA) 6–1 6–1. ***Semi-finals:*** Gerken d. Inoue 6–1 7–6; Maleeva d. Nagelsen 1–6 7–6 6–3. ***Final:*** Maleeva d. Gerken 6–2 6–3.
WOMEN'S DOUBLES – Final: Jordan/Nagelsen d. S. Collins (USA)/S. Walsh Pete (USA) 6–3 7–5.

TAPEI ($50,000)

20–26 APRIL
WOMEN'S SINGLES – Quarter-finals: A. Minter (AUS) d. A. Devries (BEL) 6–2 6–3; A. Villagran (ARG) d. C. Monteiro (BRA) 3–6 6–4 6–1; C. Porwik (FRG) d. L. Golarsa (ITA) 7–6 6–2; H. Ludloff (USA) d. C. Nozzoli (ITA) 6–3 6–4. ***Semi-finals:*** Minter d. Villagran 2–6 6–3 6–1; Porwik d. Ludloff 4–6 6–1 6–1. ***Final:*** Minter d. Porwik 6–4 6–1.
WOMEN'S DOUBLES – Final: Cammie (USA)/Cynthia MacGregor (USA) d. S. Collins (USA)/S. Walsh Pete (USA) 7–6 5–7 6–4.

TAMPA ($150,000)

27 APRIL–3 MAY
WOMEN'S SINGLES – Quarter-finals: C. M. Evert d. L. Gildemeister (PER) 6–2 6–1; B. Bowes d. T. Phelps 6–3 5–7 6–1; K. Gompert d. R. Reis 6–1 3–6 6–1; K. Rinaldi d. G. Miro (BRA) 7–5 6–4. ***Semi-finals:*** Evert d. Bowes 6–0 6–0; Gompert d. Rinaldi 6–0 6–1. ***Final:*** Evert d. Gompert 6–3 6–2.
WOMEN'S DOUBLES – Final: Evert/W. M. Turnbull (AUS) d. E. Burgin/R. Fairbank (RSA) 6–4 6–3.

Elizabeth Smylie of Australia won Oklahoma in singles and took two titles in doubles, as well as being runner-up at Wimbledon with Betsy Nagelsen and at the US Open with Kathy Jordan. (A. Evans)

SINGAPORE OPEN ($50,000)

27 APRIL–3 MAY
WOMEN'S SINGLES – Quarter-finals: E. Okagawa (JAP) d. A. Devries (BEL) 7–6 6–2; B. Gerken (USA) d. Cammie MacGregor (USA) 6–4 6–4; A. Minter (AUS) d. A. Croft (GBR) 6–1 6–0; E. Inoue (JAP) d. C. Porwik (FRG) 6–3 6–2. ***Semi-finals:*** Gerken d. Okagawa 6–4 6–3; Minter d. Inoue 2–6 6–4 6–2. ***Final:*** Minter d. Gerken 6–4 6–1.
WOMEN'S DOUBLES – Final: A. M. Fernandez (USA)/J. Richardson (NZL) d. B. Gerken (USA)/H. Ludloff (USA) 6–1 6–4.

EUROPEAN CHAMPIONS ($100,000)

GENEVA, 18–24 MAY
WOMEN'S SINGLES – Quarter-finals: C. M. Evert (USA) d. M. J. Fernandez (USA) 7–6 6–1; L. McNeil (USA) d. M. Perez Roldan (ARG) 6–1 6–0; R. Reggi (ITA) d. I. Budarova (TCH) 6–4 6–4; M. Maleeva (BUL) d. K. Maleeva (BUL) 6–1 6–2. ***Semi-finals:*** Evert d. McNeil 6–0 6–2; M. Maleeva d. Reggi 6–4 2–6 6–2. ***Final:*** Evert d. M. Maleeva 6–3 4–6 6–2.
WOMEN'S DOUBLES – Final: B. Nagelsen (USA)/E. Smylie (AUS) d. L. Gildemeister (PER)/C. Tanvier (FRA) 4–6 6–4 6–3.

STRASBOURG ($50,000)

18–24 MAY
WOMEN'S SINGLES – Quarter-finals: C. Bassett (CAN) d. V. Ruzici (RUM) 6–4 7–5; N. Tauziat d. T. Phelps (USA) 4–6 6–2 6–4; A. M. Cecchini (ITA) d. I. Cueto (FRG) 6–2 6–3; K. Horvath (USA) d. E. Burgin (USA) 2–6 6–2 6–1. ***Semi-finals:*** Bassett d. Tauziat 6–1 6–1; Cecchini d. Horvath 6–0 7–6. ***Final:*** Bassett d. Cecchini 6–3 6–4.
WOMEN'S DOUBLES – Final: J. Novotna (TCH)/C. Suire (FRA) d. Horvath/M. Mesker (HOL) 6–0 6–2.

DOW CLASSIC ($125,000)

EDGBASTON, BIRMINGHAM, 8–14 JUNE
WOMEN'S SINGLES – Quarter-finals: P. H. Shriver (USA) d. N. Tauziat (FRA) 6–0 6–1; E. Inoue (JAP) d. C. Bassett (CAN) 6–2 6–0; E. Pfaff (FRG) d. E. Smylie (AUS) 6–1 6–3; L. Savchenko (URS) d. R. Fairbank (RSA) 7–5 6–4. ***Semi-finals:*** Shriver d. Inoue 6–2 6–4; Savchenko d. Pfaff 6–3 6–0. ***Final:*** Shriver d. Savchenko 4–6 6–2 6–2.

SWEDISH CHAMPIONSHIPS ($75,000)

BASTAD, 6–12 JULY
WOMEN'S SINGLES – Quarter-finals: C. Lindqvist d. A. Villagran (ARG) 7–6 6–3; J. Polzl Wiesner (AUT) d. K. Karlsson (SWE) 6–4 6–1; A. M. Cecchini (ITA) d. A. Joensson (NOR) 6–4 7–6; K. Maleeva (BUL) d. T. Scheuer-Larsen (DEN) 6–3 6–2. ***Semi-finals:*** Lindqvist d. Polzl Wiesner 6–4 6–3; Cecchini d. Maleeva 4–6 6–3 6–4. ***Final:*** Cecchini d. Lindqvist 6–4 6–4.
WOMEN'S DOUBLES – Final: P. Barg (USA)/T. Scheuer-Larsen (DEN) d. Cecchini/P. Tarabini (ARG) 6–1 6–2.

BELGIUM CHAMPIONSHIPS ($75,000)

KNOKKE-LE-ZOUTE, 6–12 JULY
WOMEN'S SINGLES – Quarter-finals: B. Bunge (FRG) d. I. Cueto (FRG) 6–2 6–1; N. Herreman (FRA) d. M. Paz (ARG) 6–2 3–6 7–6; L. Garrone (ITA) d. F. Bonsignori (ITA) 2–6 7–5 6–3; K. Horvath (USA) d. A. Devries 6–4 6–3. ***Semi-finals:*** Bunge d. Herreman 7–5 6–2; Horvath d. Garrone 6–4 6–2. ***Final:*** Horvath d. Bunge 6–1 7–6.
WOMEN'S DOUBLES – Final: Bunge/M. Maleeva (BUL) d. Horvath/M. Mesker (HOL) 4–6 6–4 6–4.

VIRGINIA SLIMS OF SAN DIEGO ($75,000)

3–9 AUGUST
WOMEN'S SINGLES – Quarter-finals: L. McNeil d. E. Hakami 6–3 7–6; A. Minter (AUS) d. N. Herreman (FRA) 6–2 6–4; R. Reggi (ITA) d. I. Demongeot (FRA) 4–6 6–3 6–4; N. Tauziat (FRA) d. K. Gompert 6–3 2–6 6–4. ***Semi-finals:*** Minter d. McNeil 2–6 6–4 7–5; Reggi d. Tauziat 6–4 6–3. ***Final:*** Reggi d. Minter 6–0 6–4.
WOMEN'S DOUBLES – Final: J. Novotna (TCH)/C. Suire (FRA) d. E. Burgin/S. Walsh Pete 6–3 6–4.

ATHENS ($75,000)

5–11 OCTOBER
WOMEN'S SINGLES – Quarter-finals: I. Cueto (FRG) d. A. Dechaume (FRA) 2–6 7–5 7–5; J. Halard (FRA) d. L. Meskhi (URS) 6–3 1–6 6–3; J. Polzl Wiesner (AUT) d. P. Tarabini (ARG) 7–5 6–0; K. Maleeva (BUL) d. O. Tsarbopoulou 6–1 7–5. ***Semi-finals:*** Halard d. Cueto 7–6 7–6; Maleeva d. Polzl Wiesner 6–3 6–2. ***Final:*** Maleeva d. Halard 6–1 6–0.
WOMEN'S DOUBLES – Final: A. Betzner (FRG)/Polzl Wiesner d. K. Horvath (USA)/D. Van Rensburg (RSA) 6–4 7–6.

VIRGINIA SLIMS OF ARKANSAS ($75,000)

2–8 NOVEMBER
WOMEN'S SINGLES – Quarter-finals: N. Zvereva (URS) d. B. Gerken 6–0 6–3; L. Savchenko (URS) d. M. Bollegraf (HOL) 6–1 6–1; A. E. Smith d. S. Sloane 6–2 6–2; A. M. Cecchini (ITA) d. N. Sodupe 6–4 6–2. ***Semi-finals:*** Zvereva d. Savchenko 6–3 6–1; Cecchini d. Smith 6–4 6–3. ***Final:*** Cecchini d. Zvereva 0–6 6–1 6–3.
WOMEN'S DOUBLES – Final: M. L. Daniels/R. White d. L. Antonoplis/Gerken 6–2 6–4.

VIRGINIA SLIMS CHAMPIONSHIPS

Mark Fogarty

What weighed most heavily on the mind of Steffi Graf on the night of 21 November, 1987, was not the question of how she would beat Gabriela Sabatini the next day in the singles final of the Virginia Slims Championships. Instead, her thoughts were full of the speech she would have to make at the prize-giving dinner hours after the match. Graf, whose nerves of steel on the court in the previous ten months had taken her to No. 1 in the world, lay awake worrying about words.

But the agony over how to describe her ecstacy was worth it, for after defeating Sabatini in an entertaining, if not exciting, four-set match, she charmed the heard-it-all-before tennis Press corps with a refreshingly different summary of her year. 'Last night it took me a long time to fall asleep', she began. 'I was thinking how to describe my year. I decided to describe the year as if I were cooking and making up a menu card. For the appetiser, I took a baked Key Biscayne, with a little bit of Boca Raton, Hilton Head and Amelia Island on the side. Then as a main course I took a huge, tender French Open, topped with Berlin and Rome. On the side was a little bit of Wimbledon and US Open finals. That was the bad thing about my cooking: I didn't take enough salt and pepper on both of them. I like dessert very much, and I started with Hamburg and Zurich, and then the biggest and best thing, New York. That was my description of the year, which was very tasteful.'

Graf had hit a verbal forehand winner down the line – and she knew it. At the Pierre Hotel later that evening, she 'dined out' on the story, delighting guests at the annual Virginia Slims awards dinner. Her speech revealed the human and humorous side of Steffi, who is often accused by fellow players of being aloof. During the night there were further reminders that while she is wise beyond her years on the court, away from tennis she is simply an 18-year-old with the normal interests and anxieties of a teenage girl. Over dinner, Steffi talked of being lonely and having no friends her own age; and later, while the band played, she remained at her table, too shy to suggest a dance and a victim of her own fame in that none of the males was game enough to ask her. When an invitation finally came, just before she was due to leave, she accepted eagerly.

When Graf arrived in the Big Apple for the final stop on the Virginia Slims World Championship Series tour, she was intent on ending the year on the same winning note she had held in ten of her previous twelve tournaments. There was also the question of who would – or, more accurately, should – finish the year as No. 1. There was no dispute as far as the Hewlett-Packard/WITA computer was concerned: Graf was unassailable in the top spot, ahead of Martina Navratilova. But Martina begged to differ, promoting the argument that because she had won two Grand Slam titles (Wimbledon and the US Open) compared with Graf's solo Slam (the French Open), the top ranking was still open to discussion. Navratilova believed that if she won the Championships, then she would have legitimate moral claim to the premier ranking, even though her overall singles record for the year would show only four titles from 12 tournaments.

But she was never able to stake her claim, for Gabriela Sabatini settled the argument with a quarter-final upset win over Navratilova. 'Steffi's No. 1', conceded Martina afterwards. 'Which is too bad because I had such a good year. But she had an unbelievable year. She won so many events, but not so many big ones, besides the French Open. There are a lot of players out there capable of beating her, but she has a lot of confidence right now and they don't think they can beat her. I had a stretch there where I was winning simply because people didn't think they could beat me. To be No. 1 again, I have to beat

With her victory in the Virginia Slims Championships, Steffi Graf (below) dispelled any lingering doubts concerning her position at the top of the women's game, while Martina Navratilova and Pam Shriver (l-r) confirmed their supremacy in doubles by taking their sixth season-end title.

(Carol L. Newsom/Virginia Slims)

her. I know I'm the better player, but I haven't proved it this year. I still believe I have the shots. It's nothing physical, it's mental. I have to believe and go after it.'

The other big upset of the Virginia Slims Championships was Sylvia Hanika's first-night ambush of Chris Evert, who during the year had come to accept her No. 3 world ranking for the achievement it represented rather than regard it as a reminder of her inability to challenge Graf and Navratilova. But to lose so early – and to Hanika who had never previously taken a set from her – was a shock which left Evert pondering her future aloud, something her pride had never before permitted. 'The years are catching up with me. I've been on the road since I was 16 and now I'm 32. I think it's really hitting me more than ever now that I don't want to be a gypsy. I want to do things like a normal girl.'

The fall of the 'Old Guard' contrasted with the rise to their first encounter in a tournament final of Graf and Sabatini, the 'New Guard'. If there were any doubts that the future of women's tennis is in good hands, they were dispelled on the afternoon of Sunday, 22 November, when the 'teen queens' proved there is definitely life after Martina and Chris.

The Virginia Slims Championships were held at New York City's Madison Square Garden with a field consisting of the top 16 Slims series singles points-scorers and the leading eight doubles teams. The format was round-by-round elimination, with play at night for the first five days, switching to afternoon sessions on the weekend. It was the most successful ever, attracting a record total attendance of more than 93,000, and the large crowds got their money's worth from the first session.

Seventh seed Helena Sukova made a faltering start against rising star Lori McNeil in the opening match. The unseeded, but certainly not unheralded, McNeil came out of the blocks like Ben Johnson to grab the first set before the lanky Czech got into her stride in the second and finished strongly to score a 2–6 7–5 6–2 victory. Meanwhile Gabriela Sabatini was wayward in allowing the erratic West German, Bettina Bunge, to take her to a second-set tie-break, whereupon her concentration returned with a vengeance as she blasted Bunge 7–2 for a 6–2 7–6 advance.

There was no such escape for Chris Evert in the other opening-night performance, when, faced with the prospect of extending her unbeaten record against unseeded West German Sylvia Hanika, Evert suffered the fate of many a favourite. Inspired by her newly formed liaison with Team Navratilova reject, Mike Estep, Hanika used her southpaw serve to crash through the Evert brick wall at last, 6–4 6–4. 'I sort of thought I was going to win when I came out tonight', said a drained and disconsolate Evert, 'but when I saw how I was playing, I didn't have a lot of confidence. I felt disappointed that I wasn't playing up to my expectations. I have had four or five matches this year when I played below my standards, and that hasn't happened before. I just have to think nature is taking its course.' It was a discouraging end to a humbling year for Evert, who for the first time in 14 years ended a season without winning a major championship.

Catarina Lindqvist exposed some uncertainty in Martina Navratilova on the second night. Navratilova lacked her usual early-round swagger, and her tentativeness, combined with Lindqvist's doggedness, forced her to resolve the issue in a second-set tie-break. This she did, dispatching the unseeded Swede 7–1 for an untidy 6–4 7–6 progression. Steffi Graf meanwhile dashed Zina Garrison's hopes 6–0 6–3, while Bulgaria's Manuela Maleeva, the No. 8 seed, was tested 4–6 6–3 6–4 by Claudia Kohde-Kilsch. Fourth-seeded Pam Shriver sowed seeds of doubt with a roller-coaster 6–1 3–6 6–3 win over Katerina Maleeva, and the improving Italian, Raffaella Reggi, edged Hana Mandlikova 7–5 in the first set, whereupon the bouncing Czech called it a year. Mandlikova was literally on her last legs, suffering lower back and hamstring injuries.

Also Czech-mated by injury was Sukova. In the second of the Thursday night's two quarter-finals, painful neck muscle spasms prevented her from offering Graf much resistance. After losing the first set 2–6, Sukova delayed the inevitable by calling time out for treatment, and to the surprise of Graf and the gallery, she resumed after a five-minute injury break, only to retire at 0–2 in the second. Earlier, Reggi extended Hanika to three sets in a match which went with serves. In the wake of her 6–2 4–6 6–0 loss, Reggi resolved to work on her weakness. 'If I don't improve my serve, I will not go anywhere in the rankings', said a ruffled Raffaella. 'I must start like a little girl to learn how to serve all over again.'

The following night claimed both Shriver and Navratilova. Neither Shriver nor Manuela Maleeva could serve to save themselves – there were six breaks in the first seven games of their opening set – and were forced to rely on returns, the match being remarkable for the high standard of returning on both sides of the net. But the loss of her serve brought nervous skeletons out of Shriver's closet, while Maleeva's scintillating returns gave her the steadiness and confidence to tip the balance in crucial service games, bringing a 6–2 3–6 7–5 victory, which ended a long losing streak against Shriver. Maleeva felt that her impending marriage brought a lot to her game, while Shriver was of the opinion that 'it was a miracle' the match lasted three sets. 'I served that poorly. I kept thinking that I would hit those big serves. I kept reaching inside, but no one was home.'

Navratilova followed her doubles partner to the singles sidelines, as Sabatini combined her trademark heavy topspin forehand with uncharacteristic aggressiveness at the net and mobility around the court to expose insecurities in virtually every aspect of Navratilova's game. 'Nothing was there', said a bewildered Martina. 'I don't know what to attribute it to except nerves. The whole tournament I felt nervous because it was my chance to prove that I was still No. 1, even though it wouldn't go on the computer. I felt I had a chance to get in there. Normally, when I feel I have a chance, I grab the bull by the horns. She didn't give me a chance, but I didn't create any, either.' In fact, Navratilova squandered two crucial opportunities in the second set, at 2–0 30–0 and at 5–4. Sabatini broke back on both occasions to remove Navratilova 6–4 7–5. She rated disturbing Navratilova's plot at the Garden, where she had reigned on the Supreme since 1984, ahead of her breakthrough win six months earlier in Rome.

The semi-finals were Slims pickings for those who used the rankings as a form guide. Both match-ups were unfamiliar at this stage of a major tournament: Graf v Hanika, followed by Manuela Maleeva v Sabatini. Graf, who had barely worked up a sweat so far, hammered Hanika 6–1 6–4. Sabatini's path to the semi-finals had been more difficult, and her longer matches, later nights and the emotional drain of beating Navratilova showed during her 6–3 4–6 6–3 elimination of Maleeva. The Argentinian suffered an inevitable letdown in the second set, lapsing into defensive backcourt play which allowed Maleeva to control the rallies and force her 17-year-old opponent out of position. Either side of that trough, Sabatini overwhelmed Maleeva with her sheer power off the ground and aggressive all-court play.

So, finally, the future was now. A healthy rivalry already existed between Graf and Sabatini, but none of their previous encounters had been a title match and Graf was a comfortable 10–0 in the series. In the final, though, she would face a more dangerous, stronger, and more confident opponent, for it could be said that Sabatini came of age during the Championships. Her game displayed more authority and variety; she had shown a willingness to go to the net and move her feet. Her main weapons were still those topspin-loaded forehands and backhands, but by adding aggression and mobility to her arsenal, Sabatini had shot closer to the top of the Class of '87. Graf, meanwhile, went into the final without so much as a hint of weakness. Of all her many strengths, though, her stamina as much as her strokes would prove decisive against Sabatini.

The best-of-five-sets final, the only full-length feature in women's tennis, would test the most glaring flaw in Sabatini's game – her staying power. It would be a case of win fast or not at all. In the first set, Graf often over-hit her forehand and struggled to find touch with her backhand slice. Nevertheless, Sabatini had to stave off eight break-points. She scored the early advantage by breaking in the ninth game and then served out the set, finishing with a flourish by sealing it with an ace. But like a Formula One racing driver who had gone too hard, too soon and overheated his tyres, Sabatini began to fall off. Graf lifted her game a vital notch in the second set, hitting harder and better to level the score, and she never looked back. Sabatini, her spirit and stamina broken, faded in the final two terms as tiredness induced tentativeness, particularly on her serve, and allowed Graf to sweep through the third set. Sabatini managed to summon some resistance in the fourth, but by then Graf had created too much momentum, rolling on to a 4–6 6–4 6–0 6–4 victory,

West Germany's Claudia Kohde-Kilsch won the Wimbledon doubles with Sukova, with whom she was a runner-up at the Virginia Slims Championships. *(T. Hindley)*

which took her match record for the year to 75–2. The sparkling Tiffany's crystal Virginia Slims Championship trophy was the 11th she had lifted over her head during the year. 'It feels very good', said Graf of her win. 'I think it's the biggest win I've had. It's the toughest tournament to win. The best players are all here and it's at the end of a long year.' Graf's $125,000 winner's cheque boosted her season's tournament earnings to more than $1.8 million.

In the doubles Navratilova and Shriver won the final after a testing advance. They squeezed past Jana Novotna and Catherine Suire 7–6 (7–1) 5–7 6–4 to meet Graf and Sabatini in the semi-finals. In what was perhaps the best match of the tournament, Navratilova and Shriver survived match-points galore in the second set before asserting their authority in the tie-break. Their dramatic 3–6 7–6 (7–4) 6–1 success earned them a title showdown with Claudia Kohde-Kilsch and Helena Sukova. On their way to the final, Kohde-Kilsch and Sukova struggled to a 6–4 3–6 7–5 triumph over Anne White and Mary-Lou Piatek Daniels, then dispatched Elise Burgin and Ros Fairbank 6–2 6–3 in the semis. Navratilova and Shriver finished yet another dominant year, in which their only failure in a major title was at Wimbledon, with a 6–1 6–1 Championship wipe of Kohde-Kilsch and Sukova.

VIRGINIA SLIMS CHAMPIONSHIPS ($1,000,000)

MADISON SQUARE GARDEN, NEW YORK, 16–22 NOVEMBER
WOMEN'S SINGLES – Quarter-finals: S. Graf (FRG) d. H. Sukova (TCH) 6–2 2–0 ret'd; S. Hanika (FRG) d. R. Reggi (ITA) 6–2 4–6 6–0; M. Maleeva (BUL) d. P. H. Shriver 6–2 3–6 7–5; G. Sabatini (ARG) d. M. Navratilova 6–4 7–5. ***Semi-finals:*** Graf d. Hanika 6–1 6–4; Sabatini d. Maleeva 6–3 4–6 6–3. ***Final:*** Graf d. Sabatini 4–6 6–4 6–0 6–4.
WOMEN'S DOUBLES – Final: Navratilova/Shriver d. C. Kohde-Kilsch (FRG)/Sukova 6–1 6–1.

GRAF AND SABATINI: THE INHERITORS

Steve Flink

Every time you looked up in 1987, in nearly all of the major championships, on almost any conceivable surface, Steffi Graf was confronting Gabriela Sabatini. They clashed at Hilton Head and Amelia Island, the Italian and French Opens, Wimbledon and the *Federation Cup*, Los Angeles, the US Open and the year-end Virginia Slims Championship in New York's incomparable Madison Square Garden. They contested one glorious match after another, unfailingly delighting galleries with their astonishing shotmaking prowess. These confrontations always featured high-quality rallies, uncommon competitive awareness for two teenagers, and unpredictable patterns. But one aspect of the proceedings never altered; Graf always won.

In fact, the disciplined and determined German beat her Argentine rival eight times to extend her career record to 11–0 in their head-to-head series. The fact remains that five of the eight duels did not result in straight-sets verdicts, and Graf emerged with such victories only three times in those eleven career meetings. Furthermore, Sabatini could hardly have come any closer; in the semi-finals of the French Open, she led 5–3 in the final set and served for the match at 5–4. She was three points away from winning that one. It was even closer at Hilton Head Island, where she erased a 1–5 deficit in the final set, led 6–5, and was two points from triumph before surrendering in a tie-break.

That Graf kept winning and Sabatini always fell short was more a tribute to the victor than anything else. After all, Graf won 11 of 13 tournaments across the year, 75 of 77 matches, losing only twice – each time to the same player: Martina Navratilova, in the Wimbledon and US Open finals. You had to cast the mind all the way back to the 1986 French Open quarter-finals against Hana Mandlikova to find Graf's last defeat by anyone other than Navratilova.

Those facts notwithstanding, Sabatini had a superb 1987 season herself. She won the Argentine Open, Tokyo and Brighton, was runner-up to Graf at the Italian Open and the Virginia Slims Championship (defeating Navratilova in straight sets in those two significant events) and lost to only the élite of the sport in practically every case. Competing in 20 tournaments plus the *Federation Cup*, she lost 17 times, but Graf alone accounted for eight of those losses, while Navratilova beat her three times. Pam Shriver defeated her twice, and Chris Evert, Hana Mandlikova and Helena Sukova each stopped her once. The only player outside the world's top ten to beat Sabatini was Sylvia Hanika in her first tournament of the year; her record was that consistent.

How have Graf and Sabatini become so good, so fast? How can two teenagers be playing the game on such a high level, each displaying talent and tenacity of extraordinary promise? To be sure, both are following a trend in the women's professional game which can be traced back to the arrival of Chris Evert in 1972. At 16, she became the youngest semi-finalist ever at the US Open. At 17, the Floridian was one of the three best players in the world; and at 19, Evert was the Wimbledon champion.

Then along came Tracy Austin in 1977 to reach the quarter-finals of the US Open three months before her 15th birthday; at 16, in the summer of 1979, Austin won her first US

The graceful Argentine, Gabriela Sabatini, frequently extended Steffi Graf during 1987, although she never managed to beat her. The meeting of the two teenagers in the final of the Virginia Slims Championships surely confirmed their rivalry as the theme of the future. *(Carol L. Newsom/Virginia Slims)*

Open, to become the youngest winner in the history of the tournament. The swift rise of Andrea Jaeger was similar. An exhuberant baseliner with a first-rate two-handed backhand and a style reminiscent of Evert and Austin, Jaeger burst into the quarter-finals of Wimbledon at 15, becoming the youngest US Open semi-finalist later that summer.

Meanwhile, Martina Navratilova and Evonne Goolagong are two more prime examples of competitors who made their presence known as teenagers, sending ripples of fear throughout the community of women's tennis. Although Martina and Evonne made their marks slightly later in their teens, the fact remains that they arrived in the game's upper levels sooner than expected. Martina upset 1968 champion Nancy Richey on her way to the quarter-finals of the 1973 French Open at the age of 16, and was runner-up to Evert at the Italian Open the following year. At 18, she was among the top four players in the world. Goolagong – carefree, graceful, oblivious to larger names and reputations – won the French Open and Wimbledon at 19, well ahead of schedule.

And so the message seems to be that to make it on a significant scale in women's tennis, to become a player of the highest order, to be a champion, you must make sizeable inroads when you are quite young. Graf and Sabatini have done just that. But why, and how? There is no mistaking the fact that these are two well-schooled individuals, exploiting the privilege of their positions at and near the top of the game.

Peter Graf has fast become one of the tour's most controversial figures, keeping careful track of his daughter at every step of the way on her march to the top of the WITA rankings. But whether you like him or not, there is no question but that he has guided Steffi admirably as a tennis player. By and large, he has been her coach, and he has done an excellent job. But by bringing former Czech *Davis Cup* player Pavel Slozil on as a sparring partner, Peter Graf has made certain that his daughter gets proper workouts and preparation for all her matches.

As for Sabatini, during her first few years on the tour she had as a coach the former Chilean player, Patricio Apey. Apey was probably good for Sabatini during her formative stages, but he seemed to ignore technical flaws in her game and one could question his tactical acuteness. Was it an accident that Sabatini improved to such an extraordinary degree after Apey departed? The evidence strongly suggests that the arrival in March 1987 of Angel Gimenez was fortuitous for Sabatini. The Spanish star seemed better able to bring the best out of his pupil; her topspin forehand became a much more forceful, penetrating stroke, delivered with more consistent depth. Her first serve became a substantial weapon as she altered her toss and got more weight behind the delivery. Her second serve became less vulnerable, and she began at last to grasp the meaning of the volley.

Those improvements were coupled with the continued refinement of her devastatingly effective backhand. She made subtle strides with her underspin backhand, but her topspin backhand flourished. It is already one of the single most potent strokes in the sport, and no male or female can disguise the down-the-line shot as well as Gabriela; not even the deceptive band of two-handers like Evert and Mats Wilander.

If you take those outstanding traits in Sabatini and compare her technically to Graf, you quickly understand why their matches are so marvellous. While Sabatini excels off the backhand, Graf possesses the best female forehand in tennis. In fact, Graf is almost a replica of Ivan Lendl in stylistic terms. She builds her game around her explosive forehand, and is so quick that she can constantly afford to run around her backhand to produce reverse crosscourt forehand winners. Graf's second most formidable weapon is her serve, which features a high toss similar to Lendl's. In time, she will probably lower that toss slightly as Lendl already has, but in any case she has developed a tremendous first serve. If Graf can become more confident about her topspin backhand, and mix it more regularly along with her Ken Rosewall-like underspin shot off that side, then she will step up another level. The reason she lost to Navratilova in the Wimbledon and US finals of 1987 was simple: Martina methodically broke down her backhand with deep first serves, first volleys, and skidding underspin approach shots. Steffi cracked beneath the barrage.

But the precocious German did not fall apart anywhere else. She won seven straight tournaments and 45 consecutive matches until Martina stopped her at Wimbledon. No

Whether they played on the same side of the net or on opposite sides, Gabriela Sabatini and Steffi Graf (right) thrilled spectators throughout the year.
(Carol L. Newsom)

other woman in the Open era had come into the world's premier tournament without a defeat. Furthermore, she reached the final of every tournament she played, which is something else no other woman player had achieved in the past two decades of Open competition. Given those credentials, given the fact that Graf is growing on a number of levels, how can Sabatini expect to deal with her? It is an interesting problem.

However, Gabriela has shown on a consistent basis that she can stay with Steffi. Although Graf is stronger physically and emotionally and can wear her rival down in both departments, the Sabatini of 1987 was also fitter and stronger than ever before. In Paris and Hilton Head, she hung in through three long and hard sets. However, she faded away 0–6 in the final set of the Italian final, and in their last meeting of 1987 at Madison Square Garden, Graf knew before she even walked on court that all she would have to do was split the first two sets in their best-of-five-sets final. Sure enough, the West German did just that, recovering to win 4–6 6–4 6–0 6–4 as Sabatini served 17 double-faults. More importantly, the Argentine discovered that although her strength has improved she needs to build herself into still better condition.

Nevertheless, it is surely only a matter of time before Sabatini will strike the right chord. She is going to beat Graf somehow, somewhere, sometime. Then what? Will the series between them take on a new tone? Yes, and no. When Sabatini finally beats Graf, a burden will be lifted from both players. Sabatini will be delighted to have scored a victory, while Graf will possibly be somewhat relieved to have lost to someone so dangerous after so many close skirmishes.

The view here is that Graf against Sabatini will be along the lines of Evert versus Goolagong, and Court versus Billie Jean King. For a time, Goolagong baffled Evert with her unpredictability. Her streaky, brilliant play gave her a 9–8 lead in her career series with Chris. Then Evert took over and with her superior discipline and more solid groundstrokes, with her more thoughtful approach to match play, she eventually ran away with their career series, finishing with a 25–13 edge. Court and King played 34 officially recorded matches, with Margaret's consistency prevailing nearly twice as often as Billie Jean's inspiration, to give her a winning record of 22–12.

In the end, it is hard to imagine Graf not handling Sabatini in the majority of their contests. Sabatini is a player of dazzling possibilities, and a splendid shotmaker with the instincts of a genius. But Graf is only slightly less naturally talented, and she may tower above Sabatini ultimately as a peerless match player in the way that Helen Wills totally dominated her great rival of the 1930s, Helen Jacobs, to whom she never lost.

In any event, 1988 will surely mark a turning point in the delightful Graf-Sabatini rivalry. I believe that this will be the year when Sabatini will find a way to topple Steffi Graf at least once, and the attractive South American may even end the year as the No. 2 player in the world, overtaking Navratilova, Evert, Shriver and Mandlikova. I can't help thinking, though, that in both the short and the long run Graf will be triumphant against them all.

OTHER OFFICIAL PRO TOURNAMENTS

SATELLITE CIRCUITS
CHALLENGER SERIES
ITF APPROVED WOMEN'S TOURNAMENTS

Radka Zrubakova, a member of the winning Czech team in both the Annie Soisbault Cup and HM Queen Sofia Cup in 1986, won singles titles in Helsinki and Neumunster in 1987, as well as reaching the doubles final in Stavanger. *(T. Hindley)*

MEN'S SATELLITE CIRCUIT 1987

National circuits of four tournaments plus concluding Masters' event. The following were the results of the Masters' singles finals.

VENUE	DATE	SINGLES FINAL
Australia		
Canberra	11–15 March	S. Youl d. J. Frawley w.o.
Milton	21–27 Sept	J. Frawley d. P. Lindgren 6–4 6–2
Melbourne	16–22 Nov	J. Anderson d. J. Frawley w.o.
Belgium		
Brussels	3–9 Aug	W. Kowalski d. J. Bulant 6–3 6–2
Brazil		
Sao Paulo	2–8 March	R. Arguello d. J. Goes 6–1 6–2
Bulgaria		
Varna	28 June–2 July	D. Pollakov d. A. Vysand 6–2 6–2
France		
Pau	10–16 Aug	G. Giussani d. J. Piacentile 2–6 7–6 7–6
Great Britain		
London	23–29 Feb	M. Tauson d. M. Woodforde 6–3 5–7 6–4
Bournemouth	12–16 May	D. Tyson d. T. Theine 6–3 7–6
Hungary		
Budapest	25–31 May	B. Stankovic d. U. Pigato 0–6 6–2 7–5
India		
Bombay	26 Jan–1 Feb	J. P. Fleurian d. A. Olkhovski 6–4 6–4
Indonesia		
Jakarta	24–30 Aug	Suharyadi d. O. Smith 2–6 7–6 6–2
Israel		
Kiryat Shomonah	30 March–5 April	D. Howell d. S. Kennedy w.o.
Jerusalem	30 Nov–6 Dec	C. Falk d. C. Adams 6–3 2–6 7–6
Italy		
Mantova	16–22 March	J. Klaparda d. D. Nargiso 4–6 6–3 7–5
Verona	7–13 Sept	G. Vacarezza d. M. Narducci 6–3 6–3
Cagliari	2–8 Nov	A. Chesnokov d. F. Fioroni 6–4 6–7 7–6
Ivory Coast		
Abidjan	9–14 March	T. Nijssen d. L. Bottazzi 6–3 6–2

Andrei Chesnokov, winner of the Italian Satellite in Cagliari, had earlier reached the last 16 of the US Open, and by winning Florence he became the first Russian to take a Grand Prix title since Metreveli won South Orange in 1974. *(T. Hindley)*

Japan		
Fukuoka	29 June–5 July	F. Barrientos d. B. S. Kim 6–0 6–3
Tachikawa	30 Nov–6 Dec	Man Song Hing d. Tauchihashi 6–1 4–6 7–6
Mexico		
Guadalajara	6–12 April	E. Velez d. S. Bonneau 6–4 7–5
Puerto Vallarta	13–17 May	D. Campos d. D. Montes De Oca 6–2 6–4
North Africa ITF		
Tangier	19–25 Oct	L. Courteau d. M. Zillner 6–4 6–4
Poland		
Warsaw	14–20 Sept	A. Vysand d. J. Krochko w.o.
Portugal		
Lisbon	2–8 Nov	J. Bardou d. L. Jensen 6–4 6–3
Spain		
Barcelona	25–31 May	B. Blair d. F. Roig 6–4 0–6 6–3
Alicante	27 July–2 Aug	J. Clavet d. B. Uribe 6–3 7–5
Ovieda	14–20 Sept	J. A. Fernandez d. M. Filippini 7–5 6–7 6–3
Sweden		
Tumba	1–7 June	M. Gustafsson d. H. Holm 6–1 6–1
Switzerland		
Crans-Montana	10–16 Aug	R. Hertzog d. M. Pacheco 6–0 5–7 6–3
Ecublens	30 Nov–6 Dec	R. Bergh d. H. Nunez 6–4 3–6 7–6
Taiwan		
Taipei	22–28 June	J. S. Yoo d. B. S. Kim 7–6 1–6 7–6
USA		
Mount Pleasant, SC	2–7 June	B. Moir d. J. Ross 6–3 3–6 6–1
Tyler, Texas	7–12 July	M. Keil d. J. Tarango 6–4 6–3
Lake Ozark, Mo.	11–16 Aug	R. Bergh d. R. Smith 7–6 6–2
Honolulu	24–30 Nov	M. Dungo d. G. Michibata 7–6 6–4
West Germany		
Sindelfingen	25 Feb–3 March	J. Goes d. E. Velez 6–1 6–1
Munster	13–19 July	J. Windahl d. A. Lesch 6–4 6–3
Yugoslavia		
Umag	13–19 April	J. Cihak d. N. Devide 6–3 7–5

MEN'S CHALLENGER SERIES

Non Nabisco Grand Prix tournaments carrying ATP points

FINALS

VINA DEL MAR, CHILE 19–25 JANUARY
SINGLES: P. Moraing d. R. Azar 4–6 6–1 6–4.
DOUBLES: F. Gonzalez/V. Pecci d. J. Lopez/A. Tous 3–6 6–3 6–1.

SAO PAULO 2–8 FEBRUARY
SINGLES: P. Vojtischek d. R. Arguello 6–4 2–6 6–3.
DOUBLES: R. Bathman/C. DiLaura d. C. Kist/J. Soares 6–4 6–4.

ENUGU, NIGERIA 2–8 FEBRUARY
SINGLES: B. Dickinson d. S. Birner 2–6 6–2 6–4.
DOUBLES: J. Lozano/Pawsat d. M. J. Bates/Birner 6–1 1–6 6–2.

NAIROBI 2–8 FEBRUARY
SINGLES: L. Bottazzi d. P. Wekesa 6–2 7–6.
DOUBLES: A. Amritraj/S. Vasudevan d. A. Altobelli/G. Lelli Mami 6–3 6–4.

LAGOS 9–15 FEBRUARY
SINGLES:J. Lozano d. N. Odizor 6–4 6–4.
DOUBLES: L. Bourne/J. Klaparda d. L. Courteau/E. Winogradsky 6–7 6–2 7–6.

CHERBOURG 9–15 MARCH
SINGLES: S. Eriksson d. J. Pugh 6–3 6–0.
DOUBLES: P. Chamberlin/L. Shiras d. Pugh/E. Winogradsky 7–5 7–5.

CAIRO 16–22 MARCH
SINGLES: A. Tous d. D. DeMiguel 6–2 6–3.
DOUBLES: L. Courteau/T. Meinecke d. J. Arrese/DeMiguel 2–6 7–6 6–4.

MARRAKECH 23–29 MARCH
SINGLES: T. Benhabiles d. F. Yunis 6–2 7–5.
DOUBLES: Benhabiles/C. DiLaura d. J. Pugh/Tideman 4–6 6–3 6–4.

AGADIR 30 MARCH–5 APRIL
SINGLES: L. Duncan d. J. Pugh 6–4 6–2.
DOUBLES: Pugh/M. Tideman d. T. Meinecke/C. U. Steeb 2–6 7–5 6–2.

VIENNA 30 MARCH–5 APRIL
SINGLES: E. Winogradsky d. M. Woodforde 6–3 6–2.
DOUBLES: J. Navratil/F. Segarceanu d. S. Guy/D. Lewis 6–4 6–4.

GRAZ 6–12 APRIL
SINGLES: C. Saceanu d. M. Woodforde 5–7 6–3 6–4.
DOUBLES: G. Connell/D. Livingston d. C. Limberger/Woodforde 7–5 6–3.

Christian Saceanu of West Germany won Challenger tournaments in Graz and Valkenswaard before reaching his first Grand Prix final at Livingston. (T. Hindley)

MARTINIQUE 6–12 APRIL
SINGLES: P. Doohan d. T. Nelson 6–3 6–2.
DOUBLES: M. Christensen/L. Wahlgren d. M. J. Bates/N. Fulwood 7–6 6–3.

GUADELUPE FWI 13–19 APRIL
SINGLES: J. Canter d. L. Stefanki 6–3 6–4.
DOUBLES: N. Aerts/B. Dickinson d. Canter/D. Langaskens 6–2 6–3.

PARIOLI, ROME 13–19 APRIL
SINGLES: C. DiLaura d. G. Perez Roldan 6–3 6–2.
DOUBLES: M. Basham/B. Buffington d. M. Cierro/A. DeMinicis 4–6 6–2 6–1.

SAN LUIS POTOSI, MEXICO 13–19 APRIL
SINGLES: L. Lavalle d. J. Lozano 6–4 3–6 6–4.
DOUBLES: J. Letts/R. Rudeen d. K. Richter/M. Wooldridge 6–3 6–4.

JERUSALEM 20–26 APRIL
SINGLES: S. Perkis d. C. Saceanu 4–6 7–6 6–2.
DOUBLES: G. Bloom/Perkis d. S. Glickstein/A. Mansdorf 7–5 7–5.

LISBON 20–26 APRIL
SINGLES: C. DiLaura d. J. Coles 6–1 6–3.
DOUBLES: M. Dickson/M. Tideman d. J. Lopez-Maeso/A. Tous 6–2 6–4.

PORTO 27 APRIL–3 MAY
SINGLES: C. Bergstrom d. A. Antonitsch 6–1 6–3.
DOUBLES: S. Svensson/Falk d. R. Bathman/M. Tauson 7–5 5–7 6–3.

NAGOYA 27 APRIL–3 MAY
SINGLES: R. Krishnan d. J. Lapidus 6–3 6–0.
DOUBLES: A. Castle/J. Levine d. S. Guy/D. Mustard 7–6 7–6.

RALEIGH, NC 11–17 MAY
SINGLES: J. Brown d. A. Parker 1–6 6–0 6–1.
DOUBLES: R. Baxter/M. DePalmer d. B. Levine/MacPherson 7–5 2–6 6–4.

WAIBLINGEN, WEST GERMANY 11–17 MAY
SINGLES: A. Tous d. R. Stadler w.o.
DOUBLES: J. Navratil/M. Woodforde d. A. Antonitsch/P. Lundgren 6–3 7–5.

CLERMONT FERRAND 22–28 JUNE
SINGLES: B. Oresar d. L. Pimek 6–2 6–4.
DOUBLES: M. Bahrami/C. Mezzadri d. Lesage/Piacentile 6–3 7–5.

TARBES 29 JUNE–5 JULY
SINGLES: P. Rebolledo d. R. Agenor 6–3 6–4.
DOUBLES: Y. Doumbia/T. Pham d. R. Azar/M. Ingaramo 7–6 6–4.

HANKO, FINLAND 20–26 JULY
SINGLES: P. Henricsson d. M. Gustafsson 6–4 3–6 6–2.
DOUBLES: V. Paloheimi/M. Hedman d. C. Campbell/D. Tyson 5–7 6–3 6–2.

FURTH, WEST GERMANY 20–26 JULY
SINGLES: P. Baur d. E. Mazza 6–3 7–5.
DOUBLES: N. Fulwood/J. Suk d. Hornung/Saniter 4–6 6–3 6–2.

CAMPOS DO JORDAO, BRAZIL 27 JULY–2 AUGUST
SINGLES: L. Mattar d. C. Motta 6–3 6–1.
DOUBLES: I. Kley/J. Soares d. C. Kirmayr/D. Marcellino 6–2 7–6.

NEU ULM, WEST GERMANY 27 JULY–2 AUGUST
SINGLES: T. Smid d. T. Champion 6–3 6–4.
DOUBLES: J. Becka/U. Riglewski div'd with M. Mortensen/M. Bahrami.

SEATTLE 27 JULY–2 AUGUST
SINGLES: A. Sznajder d. L. Bourne 6–4 4–6 6–3.
DOUBLES: R. Leach/P. McEnroe d. B. Levine/D. MacPherson 5–7 6–2 6–3.

SAO PAULO 3–9 AUGUST
SINGLES: M. Filippini d. J. Goes 6–2 7–6.
DOUBLES: J. Daher/Martins d. R. Acioly/D. Campos 6–3 7–6.

NEW HAVEN, CONN. 10–16 AUGUST
SINGLES: D. Cahill d. D. Cassidy 6–0 6–3.
DOUBLES: G. Layendecker/G. Michibata d. G. Bloom/B. Pearce 3–6 6–4 6–2.

KNOKKE, BELGIUM 10–16 AUGUST
SINGLES: E. Mazza d. E. Masso 7–6 6–4.
DOUBLES: Henricsson/Henricksson d. G. Barbosa/N. Devide 6–1 6–3.

WINNETKA, ILL. 17–23 AUGUST
SINGLES: S. Youl d. R. Saad 5–7 7–6 6–3.
DOUBLES: T. Svantesson/Tremi d. Aldrich/Green 6–3 6–4.

ISTANBUL 17–23 AUGUST
SINGLES: B. Stankovic d. F. Segarceanu 6–2 6–1.
DOUBLES: A. Paris/Devide d. G. Marcu/Segarceanu 7–5 6–2.

BUDAPEST 31 AUGUST–6 SEPTEMBER
SINGLES: P. Korda d. A. Zverev 5–7 6–3 6–2.
DOUBLES: J. Cihak/J. Suk d. C. Allgardh/Engel 6–2 7–6.

THESSALONIKI 7–13 SEPTEMBER
SINGLES: M. Laurendeau d. N. Kroon 7–6 6–4.
DOUBLES: P. Henricksson/Holm d. P. Aldrich/M. Christiensen 7–6 3–6 6–3.

BRISBANE 28 SEPTEMBER–4 OCTOBER
SINGLES: J. Frawley d. M. Kratzmann 6–2 6–2.
DOUBLES: J. Stoltenberg/T. Woodbridge d. S. Furlong/P. Wright 6–3 7–5.

ESTORIL 28 SEPTEMBER–4 OCTOBER
SINGLES: G. Bloom d. M. Dickson 7–6 6–3.
DOUBLES: B. Moir/G. Pozzi d. Bloom/N. Kroon 6–4 3–6 7–6.

COQUITLAM, BC, CANADA 28 SEPTEMBER–4 OCTOBER
SINGLES: S. Bonneau d. D. Burke 6–1 0–6 6–4.
DOUBLES: G. Connell/G. Michibata d. J. Rios/R. Smith 7–6 5–7 6–4.

MESSINA 5–11 OCTOBER
SINGLES: H. Schwaier d. M. Racki 6–3 4–6 6–4.
DOUBLES: O. Camporese/D. Nargiso d. D. Campos/B. Dickinson 6–4 6–4.

VANCOUVER 5–11 OCTOBER
SINGLES: G. Connell d. A. Mronz 7–6 6–1.
DOUBLES: Connell/G. Michibata d. Brabanec/Mackin 6–4 6–2.

LAS VEGAS 12–18 OCTOBER
SINGLES: M. Chang d. J. Levine 6–3 4–6 6–2.
DOUBLES: B. Dowlen/G. Layendecker d. Basham/Beckman 6–1 6–2.

Italy's Diego Nargiso, winner of Wimbledon Junior singles and the US Open Junior doubles, was also a finalist in the Munich Challenger tournament, and won the doubles title in Messina with Camporese. *(T. Hindley)*

CASABLANCA 12–18 OCTOBER
SINGLES: L. Duncan d. M. Narducci 7–5 6–1.
DOUBLES: J. Lopez-Maeso/A. Tous d. A. DeMinicis/M. Cierro 7–6 6–2.

BERGEN 26 OCTOBER–1 NOVEMBER
SINGLES: P. Kuhnen d. G. Connell 6–4 3–6 7–6.
DOUBLES: N. Odizor/B. Testerman d. J. Gunnarsson/M. Mortensen 6–3 6–4.

BOSSONNENS, SWITZERLAND 2–8 NOVEMBER
SINGLES: R. Smith d. A. Mronz 7–6 4–6 6–3.
DOUBLES: P. Palanjian/B. Schultz d. H. Moraing/Mronz 6–4 6–3.

JAKARTA 2–8 NOVEMBER
SINGLES: B. Dyke d. P. Chamberlin 6–3 2–0 ret'd.
DOUBLES: S. Guy/J. Levine d. Suharyadi/D. Wallan 6–7 6–4 6–3.

SANTIAGO 2–8 NOVEMBER
SINGLES: J. Frana d. A. Mancini 2–6 6–3 6–4.
DOUBLES: H. Gildemeister/Frana d. A./M. Hocevar 6–4 6–3.

HELSINKI 9–15 NOVEMBER
SINGLES: G. Connell d. A. Zverev 7–6 6–2.
DOUBLES: A. Palandjina/B. Schultz d. N. Utgren/A. Vitarnen 7–6 6–4.

VALKENSWAARD, NETHERLANDS 18–22 NOVEMBER
SINGLES: C. Saceanu d. M. Oosting 2–6 6–4 6–4.
DOUBLES: M. Schapers/H. Van Boeckel d. Carter/L. Shiras 3–6 6–3 6–2.

MUNICH 23–29 NOVEMBER
SINGLES: L. Shiras d. D. Nargiso 7–6 6–4.
DOUBLES: T. Mmoh/R. Smith d. L. Lavalle/Nargiso 7–6 6–4.

BLOEMFONTEIN 23–29 NOVEMBER
SINGLES: P. Johnson d. M. Bauer 6–2 6–4.
DOUBLES: D. Felgate/N. Fulwood d. Bauer/P. Palandjian 6–1 3–6 6–4.

DURBAN 30 NOVEMBER–6 DECEMBER
SINGLES: P. Johnson d. T. Zimmerman 6–2 2–0 ret'd.
DOUBLES: P. Norval/Barnard d. P. Aldrich/W. Green 6–3 6–4.

MUNSTER 30 NOVEMBER–6 DECEMBER
SINGLES: E. Jelen d. J. Gunnarsson 6–4 7–6.
DOUBLES: K. Novaceck/M. Vajda d. A. Antonitsch/T. Mmoh 4–6 7–6 7–6.

SAO PAULO 30 NOVEMBER–6 DECEMBER
SINGLES: I. Kley d. R. Viver 6–4 6–2.
DOUBLES: M. Filippini/Montes de Oca d. J. Frana/Guerrero 7–5 4–6 6–1.

EAST LONDON 7–12 DECEMBER
SINGLES: P. Aldrich d. M. Keil 6–3 6–2.
DOUBLES: L. Jensen/B. Talbot d. S. Medem/G. Roper 6–2 5–7 6–4.

PORT ELIZABETH 14–19 DECEMBER
SINGLES: M. Robertson d. D. Maasdorp 6–4 6–2.
DOUBLES: N. Broad/S. Kruger d. C. Boynton/Mercer 4–6 6–4 6–2.

CAPE TOWN 21–24 DECEMBER
SINGLES: P. Aldrich d. M. Bauer 1–6 6–4 6–2.
DOUBLES: N. Broad/S. Kruger d. Bauter/L. Jensen 6–4 6–2.

1987 ITF APPROVED WOMEN'S EVENTS

The Virginia Slims World Championship Series is the showcase of the women's professional game, consisting of more than 60 tournaments which offer prize money of $50,000 or more, totalling some $14 million, as authorised by the Women's International Professional Tennis Council (WIPTC). In order to be able to compete on this circuit, players must have attained a WITA/Hewlett Packard international computer ranking of about 300 or higher and, with more than 600 players now ranked, it is essential for them to earn their apprenticeship in order to attain an initial ranking and rise up the list.

Low prize money tournaments worldwide have been established to provide this vital apprenticeship and the secondary professional circuit of ITF Approved Events, offering in excess of $1 million in 1987, continues to expand to give young players further opportunity to gain both ranking points and experience of international match play. Tournaments and circuits at this level are approved by the International Tennis Federation and are eligible for WITA/Hewlett Packard computer credit under the ITF regulations governing these events in the following categories:

$20,000 Development Circuits: A circuit of three tournaments, each of $5,000 in prize money, plus a Masters tournament of $5,000 in prize money for the most successful players. Players receive computer points for the Masters event only and therefore these circuits, which are suitable for national unranked players, provide essential match play experience under professional conditions and enable players to start to earn an initial ranking.

$10,000 Satellite Tournaments: Individual tournaments of $10,000 in prize money in which players receive computer points for the main draw only. These events help them to achieve their minimum three tournaments required to appear on the ranking list, and to improve the position of players ranked below 150 on the computer.

Satellite Circuits: A circuit of three or more tournaments, each of $10,000 in prize money, plus a Masters tournament of $10,000 for the most successful players, offering a total of $40,000 in prize money. Players receive computer credit for each tournament played if they reach the main draw, and these circuits provide essential match play experience under more international conditions.

$25,000 Challenger Tournaments: Individual tournaments of $25,000 in prize money, in which players receive computer points for both qualifying and main draw. These events help those ranked higher than 150 on the computer to improve their ranking towards qualification into Virginia Slims Series events of $50,000 or more in prize money.

During 1987 a total of 30 countries organised ITF Approved women's tournaments and circuits, providing players with the opportunity of gaining experience in professional match play, as well as earning both a computer ranking and prize money. Of this total, some six nations, including Argentina, Brazil, Israel, Italy and the Netherlands, staged development circuits, thereby giving many national junior players the chance to play under professional conditions in their own countries for the first time. Grants from the Grand Slam Trust Fund, administered by the ITF on behalf of Wimbledon, the US Open, and the French and Australian Championships, have continued to be a significant catalyst by supporting several of these circuits and other satellite events first established in 1986. Australia, Bulgaria, Colombia, Great Britain, Italy, Japan, Mexico, Peru, Spain, USA, Venezuela, Yugoslavia and the Nordic countries were among those which organised Satellite or Challenger events. In addition to attracting a more international field of entry, these also provided the means for players to achieve their minimum of three events and enabled more players to move up the computer rankings.

Further information on ITF Approved Women's Events eligible for WITA Computer Credit is available upon request from the Director of Women's Tennis at the ITF London office.

RESULTS OF ITF APPROVED WOMEN'S EVENTS 1987

$20,000 DEVELOPMENT CIRCUIT – MASTERS

ARAD, ISRAEL 30 MARCH–5 APRIL
SINGLES: H. Witvoet (HOL) d. I. Berger 6–2 6–1.
DOUBLES: Berger/Y. Shavit d. T. Wilmink (HOL)/Witvoet (HOL) 6–3 6–2.

BAD GASTEIN, AUSTRIA 28–31 MAY
SINGLES: P. Ritter d. H. Witvoet (HOL) 2–6 7–6 6–1.
DOUBLES: Witvoet (HOL)/Y. Der Kinderen (HOL) d. R. Kowaczicz (HUN)/K. Darvas (HUN) 6–2 6–0.

AMERSFOORT, NETHERLANDS 20–26 JULY
SINGLES: Y. Der Kinderen (HOL) d. G. Levers (FRG) 6–2 6–2.
DOUBLES: G. Coorengel/C. Vis d. Der Kinderen/I. Dolman 6–3 3–6 6–1.

SAO PAULO, BRAZIL 28 OCTOBER–1 NOVEMBER
SINGLES: N. Dias d. A. Vieira 2–6 6–3 6–1.
DOUBLES: G. Faria/Dias d. L. Peria/B. Rodrigues (CUB) 6–3 6–2.

BUENOS AIRES, ARGENTINA 24–29 NOVEMBER
SINGLES: C. Tessi d. G. Castro 6–3 6–1.
DOUBLES: F. Labat/F. Haummuller d. S. Correa/M. E. Vago 7–6 6–2.

JERUSALEM, ISRAEL 25–30 NOVEMBER
SINGLES: I. Berger d. D. Coriat 6–3 6–2.
DOUBLES: Berger/R. Benjamini d. S. Rehmke (FRG)/J. Koran (HOL) 6–2 6–1.

PORT ELIZABETH, SOUTH AFRICA 16–20 DECEMBER
SINGLES: L. Barnard d. A. Coetzer 4–6 6–1 6–1.
DOUBLES: Barnard/M. de Swardt d. R. Fourie/B. Haycock 6–4 6–2.

$10,000 SATELLITE TOURNAMENTS

CHICAGO, USA 6–11 JANUARY
SINGLES: B. Schultz (HOL) d. A. Grousbeck 6–4 6–3.
DOUBLES: K. Adams/D. Donnelly d. M. L. Piatek/Y. Vermaak (RSA) 6–4 6–3.

HELSINKI, FINLAND 6–11 JANUARY
SINGLES: R. Zrubakova (TCH) d. P. Thoren 6–2 2–6 6–0.
DOUBLES: N. Dahlman/L. Mannisto d. D. Krajcovicova (TCH)/Zrubakova (TCH) 6–7 7–6 7–6.

KEY BISCAYNE, USA 13–18 JANUARY
SINGLES: S. Stafford d. C. Jones 6–2 7–5.
DOUBLES: Jones/R. Morrison d. R. Baranski (POL)/D. A. Hansel 7–5 7–6.

SAN ANTONIO, USA 20–25 JANUARY
SINGLES: M. Brown d. L. Corsato (BRA) 6–2 6–2.
DOUBLES: J. Goodling/J. Kaplan d. H. Crowe/K. Steinmetz 6–4 6–4.

Nathalie Tauziat of France won singles and doubles titles at the Limoges Challenger tournament, as well as reaching the last 16 of the French Open and the semi-finals in Strasbourg, San Diego and Zurich, to improve her ranking to 25. *(M. Cole)*

FOLKSAM CUP
STOCKHOLM, SWEDEN 19–25 JANUARY

SINGLES: C. Jexell d. J. Pospisilova (TCH) 6–2 2–6 7–5.
DOUBLES: Jexell/E. L. Olsson d. J. Jonerup/M. Strandlund 6–2 6–3.

BAYONNE, FRANCE 19–25 JANUARY

SINGLES: Y. Kuczynska (POL) d. C. Mothes 2–6 6–3 6–4.
DOUBLES: V. Ruzici (ROM)/C. Tanvier d. Kuczynska (POL)/C. Vanier 6–3 6–2.

STAVANGER OPEN, NORWAY 26 JANUARY–1 FEBRUARY

SINGLES: M. Strandlund (SWE) d. P. Thoren (FIN) 7–6 6–2.
DOUBLES: C. Jexell (SWE)/L. Sandin (SWE) d. R. Zrubakova (TCH)/D. Krajcovicova (TCH) 3–6 6–1 6–1.

CODAN CUP
HORSHOLM, DENMARK 3–7 FEBRUARY

SINGLES: L. Sandin (SWE) d. S. Wasserman (BEL) 6–2 6–0.
DOUBLES: M. Strandlund (SWE)/J. Jonerup (SWE) d. M. Ekstrand (SWE)/L. Vandborg 6–1 6–3.

REIMS, FRANCE 10–15 FEBRUARY

SINGLES: M. C. Damas d. R. Rajchrtova (TCH) 6–1 2–6 6–2.
DOUBLES: E. Smith (USA)/R. Szikszay (HUN) d. Rajchrtova (TCH)/A. Vopat (FRG) 6–4 6–3.

MALO, FRANCE 17–22 FEBRUARY

SINGLES: R. Rajchrtova (TCH) d. I. De Ruysscher (BEL) 6–1 6–1.
DOUBLES: E. Smith (USA)/D. Schauerman (GBR) d. V. Paquet/K. Quentrec 6–3 6–2.

CANBERRA, AUSTRALIA 16–22 MARCH

SINGLES: B. Cordwell (NZL) d. A. Jonsson (NOR) 6–3 6–2.
DOUBLES: C. Carney/A. Scott d. K. Deed/B. Potter 7–5 7–6.

TUCSON, USA 17–22 MARCH

SINGLES: S. London d. C. MacGregor 6–2 6–3.
DOUBLES: J. Fuchs/J. Smoller d. L. Bartlett/L. Tanner 6–0 6–4.

MELBOURNE, AUSTRALIA 23–29 MARCH

SINGLES: L. Field d. H. Dahlstrom (SWE) 6–3 6–3.
DOUBLES: Field/B. Cordwell (NZL) d. C. Carney/A. Olsson (SWE) 6–2 3–6 6–3.

FRESNO, USA 24–28 MARCH

SINGLES: C. Jones d. C. Gurney 6–4 6–1.
DOUBLES: L. Seeman/H. Manset d. Gurney/D. Graham 6–3 1–6 7–6.

BARI, ITALY 30 MARCH–5 APRIL

SINGLES: V. Milviskaya (URS) d. A. Halatian (URS) 1–6 6–1 7–5.
DOUBLES: Milviskaya (URS)/Halatian (URS) d. S. Sullivan (GBR)/K. Moos (HOL) 6–2 2–6 7–6.

KAILUA-KONA, USA 31 MARCH—5 APRIL

SINGLES: C. Hernandez (MEX) d. S. Livingston 6–2 6–2.
DOUBLES: C. Jones/R. Morrison d. H. Crowe/K. Steinmetz 7–6 7–5.

HAIFA, ISRAEL 1–4 APRIL

SINGLES: L. Berger d. C. Calmette (FRA) 6–2 6–0.
DOUBLES: T. Wilmink (HOL)/H. Vitvoet (HOL) d. E. Larwig (FRG)/C. Hein (FRG) 6–1 7–6.

CASERTA, ITALY 6–12 APRIL

SINGLES: L. Lapi d. O. Tsarbopoulou (GRE) 6–1 6–3.
DOUBLES: N. Medvedeva (URS)/E. Maniokova (URS) d. H. Thoms (FRG)/Tsarbopoulou 6–3 7–5.

TORINO, ITALY 20–25 APRIL
SINGLES: N. Medvedeva (URS) d. L. Ferrando 6–1 6–3.
DOUBLES: A. Halatian (URS)/V. Milvidskaia (URS) d. H. Fukarkova (TCH)/I. Kuczynska (POL) 7–5 6–3.

LONDON (QUEENS), GREAT BRITAIN 21–25 APRIL
SINGLES: S. Frankl (FRG) d. K. Rickett 6–3 7–5.
DOUBLES: J. Louis/K. Martin (FRA) d. V. Lake/I. De Ruysscher (BEL) 6–1 5–7 6–4.

SUTTON, GREAT BRITAIN 28 APRIL–2 MAY
SINGLES: M. Llorca (ESP) d. S. Niox-Chateau (FRA) 6–4 4–6 7–5.
DOUBLES: L. Barnard (RSA)/B. Borneo d. L. Vandborg (DEN)/T. Wilmink (HOL) 2–6 7–5 7–6.

BOURNEMOUTH, GREAT BRITAIN 5–9 MAY
SINGLES: J. Jonerup (SWE) d. S. Sullivan 2–6 6–3 6–3.
DOUBLES: R. Bielsa (ESP)/A. Segura (ESP) d. L. Vandborg (DEN)/T. Wilmink (HOL) 6–4 7–5.

LEE-ON-SOLENT, GREAT BRITAIN 12–16 MAY
SINGLES: M. Llorca (ESP) d. E. Galphin (USA) 6–1 3–6 6–1.
DOUBLES: V. Lake/A. Tiezzi (ARG) d. I. Berger (ISR)/T. Wilmink (HOL) 6–3 6–2.

ADRIA, ITALY 1–7 JUNE
SINGLES: K. Skulj (YUG) d. O. Tsarbopoulou (GRE) 3–6 6–3 6–3.
DOUBLES: P. Langrova (TCH)/M. Bajchikova (TCH) d. R. Sziksay (HUN)/E. Smith (USA) 6–7 7–5 6–2.

BRANDON, USA 1–7 JUNE
SINGLES: K. Labuschange (RSA) d. L. Gregory (RSA) 4–6 6–3 6–3.
DOUBLES: I. Driehuis (HOL)/Gregory d. K. Foxworth/T. Whittington 7–6 6–7 6–4.

CAPRI, ITALY 8–14 JUNE
SINGLES: K. Caversazio d. L. Lapi 6–1 6–2.
DOUBLES: K. McDonald (AUS)/H. Adamkova (TCH) d. P. Langrova (TCH)/N. Bajchikova (TCH) 6–7 7–5 7–5.

KEY BISCAYNE, USA 9–14 JUNE
SINGLES: S. Stafford d. T. Whittington 7–5 6–3.
DOUBLES: L. Gregory (RSA)/I. Driehuis (HOL) d. K. Foxworth/Whittington 3–6 7–6 6–2.

SALERNO, ITALY 15–21 JUNE
SINGLES: L. Lapi d. A. K. Olsson (SWE) 6–3 6–2.
DOUBLES: D. Moise (ROM)/V. Martinek (FRG) d. K. McDonald (AUS)/H. Adamkova (TCH) 7–6 6–2.

BIRMINGHAM, USA 16–21 JUNE
SINGLES: T. Whittington d. K. Dreyer 2–6 6–1 6–1.
DOUBLES: I. Driehuis (HOL)/L. Gregory (RSA) d. K. Adams/S. Hahn 6–7 6–4 6–2.

FRANCAVILLA, ITALY 22–28 JUNE
SINGLES: F. Bonsignori d. B. Romano 1–6 7–6 6–4.
DOUBLES: M. Pawlik (FRG)/K. McDonald (AUS) d. M. Bowrey (AUS)/C. Radford (AUS) 6–4 6–3.

BRINDISI, ITALY 29 JUNE–5 JULY
SINGLES: I. Varas (ESP) d. S. Sullivan (GBR) 6–2 6–0.
DOUBLES: C. Radford (AUS)/M. Bowery (AUS) d. E. Guerra (ESP)/R. Bielsa (ESP) 6–3 7–6.

MEXICO CITY, MEXICO 29 JUNE–5 JULY
SINGLES: A. Tiezzi (ARG) d. C. Bakkum (HOL) 6–1 7–5.
DOUBLES: Bakkum/T. Zambrzyski (BRA) d. L. Becerra/M. Llamas 6–3 6–4.

LITCHFIELD, USA 30 JUNE–5 JULY
SINGLES: M. Kidowaki (JPN) d. S. Faulkner (AUS) 6–3 6–1.
DOUBLES: I. Driehuis (HOL)/L. Gregory (RSA) d. P. Roux (RSA)/R. Winebarger 7–5 6–2.

PALIANO, ITALY 6–12 JULY
SINGLES: L. Lapi d. S. Kusuma (INA) 4–6 6–1 6–4.
DOUBLES: S. Kusuma (INA)/Y. Basuki (INA) d. B. Romano/Lapi 6–4 2–6 6–0.

SAN LUIS POTOSI, MEXICO 6–12 JULY
SINGLES: C. Hernandez d. M. Yamada (JPN) 6–4 3–6 6–2.
DOUBLES: L. Becerra/M. Llamas d. M. Parun (NZL)/J. Masters (AUS) 6–4 7–6.

JOHNS ISLAND, USA 7–12 JULY
SINGLES: I. Driehuis (HOL) d. E. Galphin 6–2 6–4.
DOUBLES: Driehuis/L. Gregory (RSA) d. K. Foxworth/T. Whittington 6–1 6–2.

SUBIACO, ITALY 13–19 JULY
SINGLES: S. Lucchi d. L. Lapi 1–6 6–1 7–6.
DOUBLES: S. Kasumi (INA)/Y. Basuki (INA) d. I. Leyton (HOL)/B. Pardoel (HOL) 7–5 7–5.

LEON, MEXICO 13–19 JULY
SINGLES: N. Marcucci (ARG) d. J. Masters (AUS) 7–5 6–2.
DOUBLES: M. Parun (NZL)/Masters d. C. Hernandez/L. Herrera 6–4 7–6.

ERLANGEN, WEST GERMANY 13–19 JULY
SINGLES: J. Halard (FRA) d. W. Probst 6–4 4–6 6–2.
DOUBLES: D. Krajcovicova (TCH)/V. Paquet (FRA) d. A. Scott (AUS)/H. Sprung (AUT) 6–1 6–2.

FAYETTEVILLE, USA 14–19 JULY
SINGLES: J. Thomas d. L. Green 6–2 6–0.
DOUBLES: I. Driehuis (HOL)/K. Foxworth d. R. Lamb (AUS)/S. Schenck 6–2 2–6 6–3.

SEZZE, ITALY 20–26 JULY
SINGLES: I. Varas (ESP) d. S. Lucchi 6–2 6–1.
DOUBLES: S. Isidori/C. Casini d. E. Guerre (ESP)/F. Hugonnet 6–2 6–1.

VAIHINGEN, WEST GERMANY 20–26 JULY
SINGLES: D. Krajcovicova (TCH) d. M. Kriebel 6–4 4–6 7–5.
DOUBLES: V. Paquet (FRA)/J. Halard (FRA) d. H. Fukarkova (TCH)/Krajcovicova 6–4 4–6 7–5.

CHATHAM, USA 28 JULY–2 AUGUST
SINGLES: S. Stafford d. A. Leand 7–5 6–2.
DOUBLES: K. Adams/D. Donnelly d. J. Fuchs/R. Lamb (AUS) 7–5 6–3.

RHEDA-WIEDENBRUCK, WEST GERMANY 3–9 AUGUST
SINGLES: T. Weigl d. S. Auer 6–4 6–2.
DOUBLES: H. Fukarkova (TCH)/J. Pospisilova (TCH) d. D. Krajcovicova (TCH)/N. Bajchikova (TCH) 6–2 6–0.

KITZBUHEL, AUSTRIA 3–9 AUGUST
SINGLES: P. Huber d. J. Polzl Wiesner 6–3 3–6 6–1.
DOUBLES: Polzl Wiesner/H. Sprung d. B. Diesner/K. Oberleitner 6–3 6–4.

LEBANON, USA 4–9 AUGUST
SINGLES: S. Stafford d. K. Adams 6–3 6–1.
DOUBLES: J. Fuchs/J. Thomas d. L. Daly (NZL)/J. Kaczmarek 6–1 6–3.

DARMSTADT, WEST GERMANY 10–16 AUGUST
SINGLES: S. Auer d. M. Pawlik 7–5 6–2.
DOUBLES: H. Fukarkova (TCH)/J. Pospisilova (TCH) d. D. Krajcovicova (TCH)/N. Bajchikova (TCH) 6–0 6–3.

KOKSIJDE, BELGIUM 10–16 AUGUST
SINGLES: C. Van Renterghem d. N. Van Dierendonck (HOL) 6–1 6–0 ret'd.
DOUBLES: S. Appelmans/C. Van Renterghem d. K. Schuurmans/J. Tacon (GBR) 6–7 6–2 7–6.

HADDONFIELD, USA 11–16 AUGUST
SINGLES: J. Halard (FRA) d. O. Votavova (TCH) 6–3 6–4.
DOUBLES: L. Eldredge/A. Finerman d. I. Crudo (FRA)/Halard 7–6 6–3.

LISBON, PORTUGAL 17–23 AUGUST
SINGLES: L. Lapi (ITA) d. P. Ritter (AUT) 6–4 4–6 7–5.
DOUBLES: R. Sziskay (HUN)/V. Martinek (FRG) d. S. Dalla Valle (ITA)/B. Diesner (AUT) 7–6 6–7 7–6.

PORTO, PORTUGAL 24–30 AUGUST
SINGLES: L. Lapi (ITA) d. M. Schweda (AUT) 6–4 6–0.
DOUBLES: J./N. Souto (ESP) d. A. Segura (POR)/G. Castro (ARG) 4–6 6–2 6–0.

VILAMOURA, PORTUGAL 31 AUGUST–6 SEPTEMBER
SINGLES: E. Zardo (SUI) d. C. Lechner (FRG) 6–1 6–3.
DOUBLES: A. Segura/G. Castro (ARG) d. S. Jaquet (SUI)/A. Martinelli (SUI) 6–2 6–1.

CARACAS, VENEZUELA 1–6 SEPTEMBER
SINGLES: A. Vieira (BRA) d. G. Faria (BRA) 7–6 6–3.
DOUBLES: A. Schael/H. Gemmer d. R. Cruz-Lima (BRA)/S. Giusto (BRA) 6–4 6–1.

MADEIRA, PORTUGAL 7–13 SEPTEMBER
SINGLES: E. Zardo (SUI) d. C. Bousmans (BEL) 6–3 6–4.
DOUBLES: M. Pawlik (FRG)/V. Martinek (FRG) d. M. Parun (NZL)/J. Masters (AUS) 6–2 6–4.

BOGOTA, COLOMBIA 7–13 SEPTEMBER
SINGLES: L. Tella (BRA) d. M. Strebel (SUI) 3–6 6–4 2–0 ret'd.
DOUBLES: A. Vieira (BRA)/Tella d. M. Miranda (CHI)/C. Espinoza (CHI) 7–5 7–5.

SOFIA, BULGARIA 14–20 SEPTEMBER
SINGLES: E. Maniokova (TCH) d. V. Milvidskaia (URS) 6–1 6–0.
DOUBLES: P. Langrova (TCH)/M. Frimmelova (TCH) d. A. Aallonen (FIN)/E. Larwig (FRG) 6–2 6–2.

LORCA, SPAIN 14–20 SEPTEMBER
SINGLES: J. Suoto d. M. Strandlund (SWE) 1–6 6–4 6–4.
DOUBLES: A. Jonsson (NOR)/P. Moreno (HKG) d. M. Lundquist (SWE)/M. Ekstrand (SWE) 7–6 6–7 7–5.

MEDELLIN, COLOMBIA 15–20 SEPTEMBER
SINGLES: A. Vieira (BRA) d. L. Tella (BRA) 6–1 6–3.
DOUBLES: Vieira/Tella d. A. Tiezzi (ARG)/M. Miranda (CHI) 4–6 7–5 6–3.

SIBENIK, YUGOSLAVIA 21–27 SEPTEMBER
SINGLES: H. Witvoet (HOL) d. J. Jonerup (SWE) 6–3 6–0.
DOUBLES: I. Der Kinderen (HOL)/Witvoet d. M. Strandlund (SWE)/Jonerup 6–3 6–3.

VALENCIA, SPAIN 21–27 SEPTEMBER
SINGLES: M. Llorca d. I. Varas 2–6 6–1 6–2.
DOUBLES: E. Guerra/R. Bielsa d. Varas/Llorca 6–3 3–6 6–3.

LIMA, PERU 21–27 SEPTEMBER

SINGLES: A. Vieira (BRA) d. M. Miranda (CHI) 6–3 7–5.
DOUBLES: Vieira/L. Tella (BRA) d. A. Tiezzi (ARG)/Miranda 7–6 6–3.

BOL NA BRACU, YUGOSLAVIA 28 SEPTEMBER—4 OCTOBER

SINGLES: J. Pospisilova (TCH) d. K. Kschwendt (LUX) 6–3 6–3.
DOUBLES: V. Milvidskaja (URS)/E. Brioukhovets (URS) d. E. Maniukova (URS)/A. Halatian (URS) 6–4 5–7 6–4.

Isabelle Demongeot, France's No. 3, won a doubles title at the Limoges Challenger tournament and was a quarter-finalist in San Diego and San Francisco. *(T. Hindley)*

SANTIAGO, CHILE 28 SEPTEMBER–4 OCTOBER
SINGLES: K. Strohmeier (PER) d. M. Strebel (SUI) 6–4 6–1.
DOUBLES: P. Miller (URU)/Strebel d. A. Tiezzi (ARG)/M. Miranda 6–4 6–1.

RABAC, YUGOSLAVIA 5–11 OCTOBER
SINGLES: H. Witvoet (HOL) d. L. Laskova (TCH) 6–3 6–2.
DOUBLES: K. Kschwendt (LUX)/A. Van Buuren (HOL) d. N./M. Rooimans (HOL) 6–3 6–4.

MALI LOSINJ, YUGOSLAVIA 12–18 OCTOBER
SINGLES: J. Pospisilova (TCH) d. K. Kschwendt (LUX) 6–4 6–4.
DOUBLES: P. Holubova (TCH)/M. Frimelova (TCH) d. Pospisilova/D. Krajcovicova (TCH) 7–5 4–6 7–5.

IBARAKI, JAPAN 12–19 OCTOBER
SINGLES: L. Eldredge (USA) d. J. Fuchs (USA) 7–5 2–6 6–2.
DOUBLES: Eldredge/J. Smoller (USA) d. S. Savides (USA)/A. Scott (AUS) 6–3 7–6.

IBARAKI, JAPAN 19–25 OCTOBER
SINGLES: M. Kidowaki d. M. Mizokuchi 6–4 6–1.
DOUBLES: Y. Basuki (INA)/S. Kusuma (INA) d. S. Savides (USA)/A. Scott (AUS) 6–2 4–6 6–0.

MATSUYAMA, JAPAN 26 OCTOBER–1 NOVEMBER
SINGLES: S. Kusuma (INA) d. M. Kidowaki 6–3 6–3.
DOUBLES: Y. Basuki (INA)/Kusuma d. J. Smoller (USA)/J. Fuchs (USA) 6–4 3–6 6–0.

BRAMHALL, GREAT BRITAIN 26 OCTOBER–1 NOVEMBER
SINGLES: K. Quentrec (FRA) d. M. Pawlick (FRG) 6–2 6–4.
DOUBLES: E. Maniukova (URS)/N. Medvedeva (URS) d. P. Moreno (HKG)/M. Strandlund (SWE) 6–2 7–6.

SYDNEY, AUSTRALIA 26 OCTOBER–1 NOVEMBER
SINGLES: L. Stacey d. J. Morro (RSA) 0–6 7–6 6–2.
DOUBLES: J. A. Faull/R. McQuillan d. C. Thompson/K. Sharpe 4–6 6–3 6–3.

SAGA, JAPAN 2–8 NOVEMBER
SINGLES: S. Savides (USA) d. E. Iida 3–6 7–6 6–1.
DOUBLES: Iida/M. Kidowaki d. N. Sato/K. Okamoto 7–6 3–6 9–7.

TELFORD, GREAT BRITAIN 2–6 NOVEMBER
SINGLES: N. Medvedeva (URS) d. S. Loosemore 6–2 6–2.
DOUBLES: E. Maniukova (URS)/N. Medvedeva (URS) d. S. Hack (FRG)/I. Peltzer (FRG) 6–0 6–2.

KYOTO MASTERS, JAPAN 12–15 NOVEMBER
SINGLES: M. Mizokuchi d. J. Fuchs (USA) 6–0 4–6 6–1.
DOUBLES: M. Kidowaki/E. Iida d. J. Kimura/H. Nakazaka 6–2 6–2.

EASTBOURNE, GREAT BRITAIN 7–13 NOVEMBER
SINGLES: N. Medvedeva (URS) d. E. Maniukova (URS) 6–2 7–5.
DOUBLES: Maniukova/Medvedeva d. P. Etchemendy (FRA)/J. Tacon 6–1 6–1.

CROYDON, GREAT BRITAIN 16–23 NOVEMBER
SINGLES: N. Medvedeva (URS) d. T. Catlin 6–2 6–3.
DOUBLES: V. Milvidskaia (URS)/P. Moreno (HKG) d. E. Maniukova (URS)/Medvedeva 6–4 6–1.

WELS, AUSTRIA 15–22 NOVEMBER
SINGLES: B. Paulus d. D. Krajcovicova (TCH) 6–2 6–2.
DOUBLES: P. Hentschl/E. M. Schurhoff (FRG) d. P. Ritter/Paulus 4–6 6–4 7–6.

BUDAPEST, HUNGARY 30 NOVEMBER–6 DECEMBER
SINGLES: C. Jexell (SWE) d. N. Dahlman (SWE) 6–2 6–2.
DOUBLES: Jexell/M. Lundquist (SWE) d. P. Schmitt/C. Schneider 6–3 6–2.

SYDNEY, AUSTRALIA 30 NOVEMBER—6 DECEMBER
SINGLES: R. McQuillan d. K. Radford 6–4 4–6 6–3.
DOUBLES: McQuillan/J. A. Faull d. S. McCann/Radford 6–3 6–2.

$25,000 CHALLENGER TOURNAMENTS

TARZANA, USA 25 JANUARY–1 FEBRUARY
SINGLES: L. Meskhi (URS) d. C. Wood (GBR) 1–6 6–4 6–2.
DOUBLES: A. Frazier/C. Gurney d. K. Dewis (CAN)/L. Lewis 6–3 6–2.

LIMOGES, FRANCE 27 MARCH–5 APRIL
SINGLES: N. Tauziat d. R. Rajchrtova (TCH) 6–1 2–6 6–1.
DOUBLES: I. Demongeot/Tauziat d. C. Cohen (SUI)/E. Krapl (SUI) 7–5 6–2.

ADELAIDE, AUSTRALIA 30 MARCH–5 APRIL
SINGLES: B. Cordwell (NZL) d. L. Field 6–0 4–6 6–4.
DOUBLES: Field/Cordwell (NZL) d. C. Carney/A. Scott 6–1 1–6 6–4.

KAILUA-KONA, USA 7–12 APRIL
SINGLES: A. Frazier d. H. Crowe 6–2 6–3.
DOUBLES: J. Goodling/W. Wood d. L. Bartlett/L. Tanner 2–6 7–6 6–2.

TARANTO, ITALY 27 APRIL–3 MAY
SINGLES: N. Zvereva (URS) d. R. Rajchrtova (TCH) 7–6 4–6 6–3.
DOUBLES: L. Meskhi (URS)/Zvereva (URS) d. S. Schilder (HOL)/C. Wood (GBR) 6–3 6–2.

AUGUSTA, USA 23–28 JUNE
SINGLES: R. Baranski (POL) d. S. Stafford 7–6 3–6 6–4.
DOUBLES: K. Foxworth/T. Whittington d. J. Fuchs/D. Levy 6–3 7–5.

PHILADELPHIA, USA 21–26 JULY
SINGLES: L. Gregory (RSA) d. J. Santrock 4–6 7–5 7–6.
DOUBLES: I. Driehuis (HOL)/K. Adams d. K. Foxworth/T. Whittington 6–3 6–4.

NEUMUNSTER, WEST GERMANY 27 JULY–2 AUGUST
SINGLES: J. Halard (FRA) d. B. Schultz (HOL) 6–2 6–4.
DOUBLES: D. Krajcovicova (TCH)/R. Zrubakova (TCH) d. I. Budarova (TCH)/N. Bajchikova (URS) 6–2 6–0.

MANHASSET, USA 18–23 AUGUST
SINGLES: G. Dinu (FRG) d. M. Van Der Torre (HOL) 7–6 6–3.
DOUBLES: I. Berger (ISR)/J. Thomas (USA) d. B. Schultz (HOL)/Van Der Torre 6–4 6–1.

BETHESDA, USA 29 SEPTEMBER–4 OCTOBER
SINGLES: J. Hetherington (CAN) d. C. Christian 6–1 6–4.
DOUBLES: Hetherington/I. Driehuis (HOL) d. D. Levy/J. Thomas 6–1 6–3.

CHIBA, JAPAN 5–11 OCTOBER
SINGLES: E. Okagawa d. R. Hiraki 6–2 2–6 6–1.
DOUBLES: E. Iida/A. Nishiya d. N. Sato/K. Okamoto 7–5 6–2.

JOHANNESBURG, SOUTH AFRICA 16–21 NOVEMBER
SINGLES: G. Rush Magers (USA) d. L. Allen (USA) 6–7 7–6 6–4.
DOUBLES: B. Herr (USA)/B. Gerken (USA) d. R. Mentz/M. de Swardt 7–6 6–2.

INTERNATIONAL TEAM COMPETITIONS

WIGHTMAN CUP
WORLD TEAM CUP
BASF EUROPEAN CUP
WOMEN'S EUROPEAN CUP
MAUREEN CONNOLLY BRINKER TROPHY
WHEELCHAIR CHAMPIONSHIPS

Jakob Hlasek of Switzerland helped his country to a second success in the European Cup and beat Joakim Nystrom to reach the last 16 at Wimbledon (T. Hindley)

Above: *Jo Durie (right) prevented a third successive whitewash in the Wightman Cup when she beat Zina Garrison, returning with Anne Hobbs (left) to recover from 0–6 down to beat Garrison and Lori McNeil in the final doubles.* ***Below:*** *The winning US team (l–r) Zina Garrison, Lori McNeil, Gigi Fernandez, Marty Riessen (coach), Robin White and Pam Shriver.* *(R. Adams)*

WIGHTMAN CUP

Barry Wood

Great Britain went into the Wightman Cup with the somewhat dubious cushion of knowing that they could not possibly do worse than people's expectations of them. For they had already been written off before they left for Williamsburg, and a third successive 7–0 whitewash seemed to be a foregone conclusion. Once again calls were being made for a European team to replace the British squad, especially in view of the recent victory of the Ryder Cup team in America. Pam Shriver pondered the idea of a Commonwealth team, while Britain's coach, Warren Jacques, suggested, after the first results had gone against them, that it might be a better idea to play the event every other year, in order to give the British team time to build.

All the negative talk actually served to make the task easier in the minds of the players, because it lifted much of the pressure from them. They were also grateful to be able to play away from home and far from the critical gaze of Fleet Street. While the American team, under the guidance of Shriver, featured four new members – Zina Garrison, Lori McNeil, Robin White and Gigi Fernandez – Britain relied on the experience of Jo Durie and Anne Hobbs, together with Sara Gomer and Clare Wood, who was making her senior international début. Valda Lake also travelled with the team, but did not play.

The only really disappointing British performance came from Gomer, who completely crumbled against McNeil, losing 6–2 6–1. The others performed with credit, their persistence eventually paying off as they won the last two rubbers. It may have been too little too late, but no-one should suggest that with victory assured the Americans were no longer trying. The tears from Garrison, who lost 7–6 6–3 to Durie and then with McNeil lost 0–6 6–4 7–5 against Durie and Hobbs, left no doubt in anyone's mind how important it still was to win. What stung most of all was Britain's comeback in the doubles – from 0–6 in the first set and 1–4 in the third. The American team afterwards seemed surrounded by the aura of a defeated nation.

When the computer rankings of the players currently concerned are examined, Britain should never in theory win a match at all. The fact that occasionally they are able to do so is therefore a bonus. The reasons behind Britain's inability to produce top players is another subject entirely and has, of course, been the centre of much discussion over the years. But Jacques sees hope for the future. 'The material is definitely there to work on', he said. 'I think you have to wait for two or three years, but British tennis is on the upswing. There are a lot of good young girls coming up and I'm quite excited about it.'

WILLIAMSBURG, 29–31 OCTOBER
U.S.A. d. Great Britain 5–2: Z. Garrison d. A. E. Hobbs 7–5 6–2; L. McNeil d. S. Gomer 6–2 6–1; P. H. Shriver d. J. M. Durie 6–1 7–5; G. Fernandez/R. White d. Gomer/C. Wood 6–4 6–1; Shriver d. Hobbs 6–4 6–3; Garrison lost to Durie 6–7 3–6; Garrison/McNeil lost to Durie/Hobbs 6–0 4–6 5–7.

PEUGEOT WORLD TEAM CUP

Chris Martin

Despite being unable to call upon the services of world No. 1 Ivan Lendl, Czechoslovakia, led by the unpredictable Miloslav Mecir, swept to a popular 2–1 victory over the United States to win the World Team Cup for the second time. However, the conclusion of arguably the most smoothly run and best-supported event on the circuit was marred by the sudden walk-out by John McEnroe during the opening rubber of the final.

McEnroe was locked in the third set of a superb struggle with Miloslav Mecir when, without warning, he walked from the court, leaving umpire Richard Kaufman no choice but to default the fiery New Yorker. Mecir, who had just broken serve to lead 2–1, gratefully accepted the victory, although like everyone else he was more than a little puzzled by McEnroe's decision. 'This is not good for tennis', said a somewhat startled Mecir. 'He tried to do the same thing against me in Dallas but after a few minutes they made him play.'

McEnroe's decision to pull out came only moments after he had become embroiled in a heated discussion with Kaufman over a line-call, as a result of which he had received a warning for 'unsportsmanlike conduct'. He marched back on court to face Mecir's serve but at 30–0 refused to ready himself to receive. Kaufman warned him for time delay and issued a penalty point 30 seconds later, whereupon McEnroe walked over to his chair, packed his bags and left, apparently in protest. Some 60 minutes later, after deep consultations with a number of people, McEnroe emerged from the locker room claiming that he had been suffering from a pain in his back and that as far as he was concerned he had simply retired. 'I wasn't aware of the rule which says I need permission to leave the court', he asserted. He was fined a total of $4,500 but subsequently escaped any further punishment. In fact that fine was not the largest to be imposed during the tournament; Pat Cash was fined $5,000 for five separate offences.

While the capacity crowd of 10,000 was still buzzing over McEnroe's decision to quit, Brad Gilbert, who had been promoted to second singles player after Jimmy Connors's withdrawal prior to the start of the event, produced perhaps his best performance of the week to defeat Milan Srejber 6–4 5–7 6–4 and pull the United States level at 1–1. Owing to his earlier transgression, McEnroe, who had played doubles only once in the United States' opening match against Spain, was not now permitted to compete in the decider, so that Gilbert and Robert Seguso were left to face Tomas Smid and Mecir. It turned out to be a somewhat one-sided affair with the Czechs winning 6–3 6–1, much to the delight of the crowd and in particular Mecir, who has never forgotten the previous time he had the chance to win the Cup for his country. On that occasion – in 1985 – Mecir had Jimmy Connors on the ropes but then crumbled to such an extent that he had to serve under-arm.

In fact Mecir almost cost the Czechs the trophy earlier in the week with an alarmingly lacklustre display in a round-robin group match against West Germany who were, as usual, playing without Boris Becker. Then Mecir was crushed 6–1 6–1 by Eric Jelen, who is the first to admit that he is not the strongest player on a clay court.

The Czechs finished their group matches level with Sweden and West Germany, each with two wins and one defeat, but Czechoslovakia qualified by virtue of a better overall win-loss record. The Americans came through their group unscathed, with convincing victories over Spain, Argentina and France, the defending champions. Both France and Australia surprisingly won no match in the tournament, which was sponsored for the first time by Peugeot. Henri Leconte was particularly disappointed, because he had been

John McEnroe was still unable to avoid controversy in 1987. (Carol L. Newsom)

unbeaten in seven singles matches in the competition. This time he lost his very first encounter against Argentina's Martin Jaite, 7–6 7–6.

Sadly, McEnroe's decision to pull out was not the only controversy to plague the tournament. When heavy rain washed out play on the Thursday, the players were told they were required to play at a near-by indoor clay court. The ensuing mini revolt was not settled until Grand Prix supervisor Thomas Karlberg issued an ultimatum, and in the meantime several thousand fans were kept waiting for nearly three hours. Considering the amount of money on offer ($750,000), the tournament, and in particular the mild-mannered but much harrassed tournament director, Horst Klosterkemper, deserved better.

DÜSSELDORF, 18–24 MAY
ROUND ROBIN RED GROUP: Czechoslovakia d. Australia 3–0 (M. Mecir d. P. Cash 6–4 7–6; M. Srejber d. W. Masur 6–3 7–6; Mecir/T. Smid d. Cash/P. McNamee 6–1 6–4); ***Czechoslovakia d. Sweden 3–0*** (Mecir d. A. Jarryd 6–2 6–3; Srejber d. J. Nystrom 6–2 6–2; Mecir/Smid d. Jarryd/Nystrom 6–4 6–2); ***Sweden d. West Germany 2–1*** (S. Edberg d. E. Jelen 6–3 6–7 6–4; Nystrom lost to D. Keretic 6–4 6–2; Edberg/Jarryd d. J./T. Meinecke 6–2 6–3); ***Sweden d. Australia 3–0*** (Nystrom d. McNamee 6–2 6–7 7–6; Jarryd d. Cash 1–6 7–6 7–5; Jarryd/Nystrom d. McNamee/Masur 6–1 3–6 6–2); ***West Germany d. Australia 2–1*** (Jelen lost to Cash 6–7 7–6 3–6; Keretic d. McNamee 6–0 6–0; Jelen/T. Meinecke d. P. McNamara/Masur 6–2 6–2); ***West Germany d. Czechoslovakia 2–1*** (Jelen d. Mecir 6–1 6–1; Keretic lost to Srejber 6–7 4–6; Jelen/T. Meinecke d. Mecir/Smid 6–4 0–6 7–5).
1st: Czechoslovakia 2 wins, 7 rubbers; ***2nd:*** West Germany 2 wins, 5 rubbers, 12 sets; ***3rd:*** Sweden 2 wins, 5 rubbers, 10 sets: ***4th:*** Australia no wins.
ROUND ROBIN BLUE GROUP: USA d. Spain, 2–1 (B. Gilbert d. S. Casal 4–6 6–4 6–3; J. P. McEnroe *d. E. Sanchez 7–5 3–6 7–5; McEnroe/R. Seguso lost to Casal/Sanchez 6–2 4–6 4–6);* ***USA d. Argentina 3–0*** (McEnroe d. M. Jaite 6–4 6–1; Gilbert d. G. Vilas 6–4 6–1; Gilbert/Seguso d. Jaite/Vilas 5–7 6–4 6–2); ***USA d. France 2–1*** (McEnroe d. Leconte 2–6 7–5 6–1; Gilbert lost to Tulasne 1–6 0–6; Gilbert/Seguso d. Forget/Leconte 6–3 2–6 6–4); ***Argentina d. France 2–1*** (Vilas d. Tulasne 7–6 6–2; Jaite d. Leconte 7–6 7–6; Jaite/Vilas lost to Forget/Leconte 4–6 3–6); ***Argentina d. Spain 2–1*** (Vilas d. Casal 7–5 6–4; Jaite d. Sanchez 5–7 6–3 7–5; Vilas/G. Tiberti lost to Casal/Sanchez 5–7 3–6); ***Spain d. France 2–1*** (Casal d. Tulasne 6–4 6–0; Sanchez d. Leconte 6–4 6–3; Casal/Sanchez lost to Forget/Leconte 6–2 5–7 3–6).
1st: USA 3 wins; ***2nd:*** Argentina 2 wins; ***3rd:*** Spain 1 win; ***4th:*** France no wins.
FINAL: Czechoslovakia d. USA 2–1 (Mecir d. McEnroe 7–5 2–6 2–1 disqual.; Srejber lost to Gilbert 4–6 7–5 4–6; Mecir/Smid d. Gilbert/Seguso 6–3 6–1).

OTHER INTERNATIONAL TEAM EVENTS

Peter Blackman and Barry Wood

EUROPEAN CUP

The tiny tennis nation of Switzerland, who until 1985 had not figured prominently in the competition, pulled off their second consecutive European Cup success. The Czechs could argue that they were seriously weakened by the absence of the world No. 1, Ivan Lendl, and Miloslav Mecir, while West Germany could point to the absence of Boris Becker. But that should not minimise Switzerland's achievement in ice-bound Hanover where Britain, most unlikely finalists, gave them a tremendous battle in a final throbbing with excitement and razor-sharp tennis. Britain were trying to win a competition they had dominated in the 1960s but had last won 20 years ago and, as if on cue, Andrew Castle and Jeremy Bates had an inspired week to come within a whisker of landing the main prize.

Switzerland survived a thrilling struggle against Holland, in which Jakob Hlasek beat Michiel Schapers in a crucial singles encounter after Claudio Mezzadri had lost to Menno Oosting. The situation worsened for the relegation-threatened Dutch when they lost to Czechoslovakia, although the clouds cleared for them when they beat Italy, who ended the week beaten also by Britain and West Germany. Throughout the competition bad line-calls first ruffled and then angered the players, but the Italians could not control their tempers sufficiently to keep their games in shape.

The first big surprise was the way in which Switzerland upended the favourites, Czechoslovakia, with Roland Stadler and Hlasek clinching their singles in devastating style. Then the West Germans, having beaten a demoralised Italy, crashed to Britain. The home country badly needed victory, which would have guaranteed live television coverage as well as boosting seat sales dramatically. But Bates was at his competitive best against Patrick Kuhnen, while Castle lost a magnificent battle over three sets to Michael Westphal. That left a nail-biting doubles to settle the issue and the British pair rose superbly to the challenge.

The relegation match involving Italy and Holland caused the final to be delayed two and a half hours – a situation that European Cup officials insist will not be allowed to happen again. So it was nearing midnight before the story finally ended. Bates, determined not to let the delay upset him, gave Britain a brilliant start by beating Stadler, and then Hlasek struggled to beat Castle in three tense sets.

The deciding doubles brought down the curtain on the European Cup with an explosive thump. Some line calls were so bad that they left the players and their captains speechless, creating a tension which in the end seemed to suffocate the proceedings. Britain took the first set and had a match-point at 6–5 in the second set before a backhand volley from Bates flew tantalisingly out by a mere two inches. That shot will surely haunt him for years. Reprieved, the Swiss returned strongly to the battle, making full use of the second chance to run away with the decisive third set. – P. B.

Division 1

HANOVER, 29 JANUARY–1 FEBRUARY

GROUP I: Great Britain d. Italy 2–1 (M. J. Bates lost to S. Colombo 6–3 6–7 6–7; A. Castle d. P. Cane 6–3 6–4; Bates/Castle d. Cane/Colombo 7–6 7–6); ***West Germany d. Italy 2–1; Great Britain d. West Germany 2–1*** (Bates d. P. Kuhnen 6–3 7–6; Castle lost to M. Westphal 7–6 4–6 4–6; Bates/Castle d. Kuhnen/C. U. Steeb 6–3 6–2).

Jeremy Bates (left) and Andrew Castle played Davis Cup *together and were only a match-point away from winning the European Cup over West Germany. (T. Hindley)*

GROUP II: Switzerland d. Netherlands 2–1; Czechoslovakia d. Netherlands 2–1; Switzerland d. Czechoslovakia 3–0.
RELEGATION MATCH: Netherlands d. Italy 2–1.
GROUP FINAL: Switzerland d. Great Britain 2–1 (R. Stadler lost to Bates 6–7 2–6; J. Hlasek d. Castle 6–3 6–7 6–2; Hlasek/Stadler d. Bates/Castle 3–6 7–6 6–0).
Division 2
GROUP FINAL: Sweden d. Finland 2–0.
RELEGATION MATCH: Yugoslavia d. Ireland 2–0.
Division 3
GROUP FINAL: France d. Spain 2–1;
RELEGATION MATCH: Belgium d. Monaco 2–0.
Division 4
GROUP FINAL: Bulgaria d. Norway 3–0.
RELEGATION MATCH: Poland d. Cyprus 3–0.

EUROPEAN CUP – WOMEN

France, perhaps surprisingly, won the 1987 European Women's Team Championship. Represented by Pascale Paradis, Marie-Christine Calleja and Julie Halard, not only were they not seeded to win, West Germany being the official favourites, but they also suffered a set-back when Calleja was injured. Retiring at 1–4 in the final set against Sara Gomer during their semi-final against Britain, she took no further part in the event and France were reduced to just two players. However, they had shown their potential the day before by defeating Czechoslovakia 2–1. Paradis beat Jana Pospisilova in straight sets, and after Jana Novotna had levelled the tie with a win over Halard, Paradis and Calleja narrowly won the doubles over Novotna and Pospisilova. From 4–4 in the final set they claimed the last two games to win 6–2 3–6 6–4. Novotna's expertise in doubles, demonstrated at the Virginia Slims Championships in New York just the week before, counted for nothing on this occasion. The next day France sealed their place in the final with a 2–1 win over Great Britain. Following Calleja's retirement against Gomer, Paradis beat Anne Hobbs and then joined with Halard to win the doubles.

Their opponents in the final were the Netherlands, who inflicted a 3–0 defeat on West Germany before dismissing Sweden 2–1, with Marcella Mesker and Manon Bollegraf winning the doubles over Catarina Lindqvist (at 17, the highest-ranked player in the competition) and Maria Lindstrom. The final day's play produced considerable drama in both the title match and the relegation play-off. France beat the Netherlands 2–0, but only after Mesker had let victory slip from her grasp in the first rubber. She won the first set 6–3 and served for the match at 5–4 in the second, but although she reached 30-all and deuce, that is as close as she came, and Paradis bounced back to claim what had seemed an unlikely win, by 3–6 7–5 6–2. Halard, who at 17 looks no older than 12, then unleashed some astonishing power from her tiny frame to claim the Cup for France with a 6–2 6–4 triumph over Bollegraf.

The relegation tie between the Germans and the Czechs produced a dramatic ending to the tournament as the top-seeded Germans avoided relegation to Division 2 by winning the deciding doubles. First Wiltrud Probst beat Pospisilova 6–3 6–4 for Germany's first win of the event, but Silke Meier was beaten 6–3 3–6 6–1 by Novotna. Probst then teamed with Claudia Porwik to defeat Novotna and Pospisilova 6–0 3–6 7–5, breaking serve in the final game. How cruel it would have been if relegation had been decided on a tie-break.

For Paradis, who won all five of her matches, the success was all part of an ongoing renaissance in her career. Having reached 25 in the world three years ago, she had sunk into the hundreds by the summer of 1987. What turned things around for her was her decision to return to the fold of the French Federation, to ignore the complexities of the game and just to play.

Changes within the Dutch Federation had played a large part in the Netherlands reaching the final, according to the experienced Mesker. 'Until last year the Association would pick a couple of juniors who they would promote at the expense of all the other players. That created a lot of friction because their choices were usually not the best players available and so they were resented', she revealed. 'But last year a couple of new coaches introduced a totally different attitude, and if a player isn't good enough yet then they have to wait. There's a much better atmosphere in the team now and obviously that has helped us to play better and work for each other – B. W.

Division 1

LOMMA-BJARRED, SWEDEN

Netherlands d. West Germany 3–0; Great Britain d. Czechoslovakia 2–1; Sweden d. West Germany 3–0; France d. Czechoslovakia 2–1; Netherlands d. Sweden 2–1; France d. Great Britain 2–1. ***FINAL:*** France d. Netherlands 2–0. ***RELEGATION MATCH:*** West Germany d. Czechoslovakia 2–1.

Division 2

SCHRUNS-TSCHAGGUNS, AUSTRIA

FINAL: USSR d. Belgium 2–1. ***RELEGATION MATCH:*** Italy d. Bulgaria 2–0.

Division 3

MARIBOR, YUGOSLAVIA

FINAL: Yugoslavia d. Hungary 2–1. ***RELEGATION MATCH:*** Spain d. Denmark 2–0.

MAUREEN CONNOLLY BRINKER TROPHY

Women's under 21 team competition between USA and Great Britain

QUEEN'S CLUB, 23–25 SEPTEMBER

Great Britain d. USA 6–5 (L. Gould d. A. Grousbeck 7–6 6–2; T. Catlin d. S. Hahn 4–6 6–1 6–1; C. Wood d. J. Santrock 6–0 6–2; Catlin/Gould lost to Grousbeck/L. Green 6–7 4–6; S. Loosemore lost to Green 6–4 6–7 3–6; V. Lake lost to G. Kim 4–6 5–7; Catlin d. Grousbeck 6–3 6–3; Gould lost to Hahn 4–6 2–6; Lake d. Santrock 7–5 3–6 6–3; Wood d. Kim 6–2 6–4; Lake/Wood lost to Hahn/Santrock 5–7 2–6).

WHEELCHAIR CHAMPIONSHIPS

FRENCH OPEN

PARIS, 21–24 MAY
MEN'S SINGLES – Semi-finals: P. Fusade d. T. Caillier 5–7 6–4 6–3; L. Giammartini d. F. Dessauve 6–1 6–1. ***Final:*** Giammartini d. Fusade 6–2 6–1.
WOMEN'S SINGLES – Semi-finals: M. Vandenbosch d. M. Picard 7–6 6–3; T. Avifhay d. C. Vandierendonck w.o. ***Final:*** Vandenbosch d. Avifhay 6–1 6–2.
MEN'S DOUBLES – Semi-finals: Fusade/Dessauve d. Lechaplain/Estrade 6–2 6–2; Giammartini/Creuzet d. C. Illingsworth/Kleingeld 6–2 6–2. ***Final:*** Giammartini/Creuzet d. Fusade/Dessauve 6–2 6–2.
WOMEN'S DOUBLES – Semi-finals: Picard/Winkelmann d. J. McMorran/Chiari ab; Vandierendonck/Vandenbosch d. Vainstein/Avifhay 6–2 6–0. ***Final:*** Vandierendonck/Vandenbosch d. Picard/Winkelmann 6–1 6–1.

GERMAN OPEN

LOHMAR, 28–30 MAY
MEN'S SINGLES – Semi-finals: Fusade d. Hatt 6–0 6–1; Illingsworth d. Belser 6–0 6–0. ***Final:*** Fusade d. Illingsworth 1–6 6–1 6–2.
WOMEN'S SINGLES – Semi-finals: Vanderbosch d. R. Isecke 6–0 6–1; McMorran d. Scherer 6–0 6–0. ***Final:*** Vanderbosch d. McMorran w.o.
MEN'S DOUBLES – Semi-finals: Fusade/Illingsworth d. Geider/Zielasko 6–1 6–2; Liebl/Kirsch d. T. Holland/Hatt 6–0 6–3. ***Final:*** Fusade/Illingsworth d. Liebl/Kirsch 6–1 6–2.
WOMEN'S DOUBLES – Final: Isecke/Winkelmann d. Scherer/McMorran 6–4 6–0.

ISRAEL OPEN

TEL AVIV, 14–18 JULY
MEN'S SINGLES – Semi-finals: R. Snow d. Paticha 6–4 6–2; Giammartini d. Hagai 6–3 6–1. ***Final:*** Giammartini d. Snow 2–6 6–2 6–3.
WOMEN'S SINGLES – Semi-finals: Vendierendonck d. E. DeLange 6–1 6–4; Vanderbosch d. Avifhay 6–0 6–0. ***Final:*** Vandierendonck d. Vanderbosch 7–6 6–4.
MEN'S DOUBLES – Semi-finals: Giammartini/Fusade d. Sheri/Eval 7–6 6–3; Snow/Itmar d. B. Hagai/Paticha 6–3 5–7 6–3. ***Final:*** Giammartini/Fusade d. Snow/Itmar 6–4 4–6 6–1.
WOMEN'S DOUBLES – Semi-finals: Vandierendonck/Vanderbosch d. DeLange/J. McMorran 6–3 6–1; Avifhay/M. Miller d. N. Yaacov/Avya 7–5 6–2. ***Final:*** Vandierendonck/Vanderbosch d. Avifhay/Miller 6–2 6–1.

DUTCH OPEN

PIJNACKER, 20–25 JULY
MEN'S SINGLES – Semi-finals: Snow d. Fusade 7–6 6–2; Turner d. Giammartini 7–5 6–4. ***Final:*** Snow d. Turner 6–3 6–3.
WOMEN'S SINGLES – Semi-finals: Vandierendonck d. R. Iseche 6–0 6–2; Vanderbosch d. B. White 6–0 6–3. ***Final:*** Vanderbosch d. Vandierendonck 0–6 7–6 6–0.
MEN'S DOUBLES – Semi-finals: Snow/Van de Brock d. Creuzel/Lkeingeid 6–3 6–3; C. Turner/D. Lachman d. Giammartini/Fusade 3–6 7–5 6–3. ***Final:*** Turner/Lachman d. Snow/Van de Brock 6–3 6–4.
WOMEN'S DOUBLES – Final: Vandierendonck/Vanderbosch d. Olsen/White 6–1 6–2.

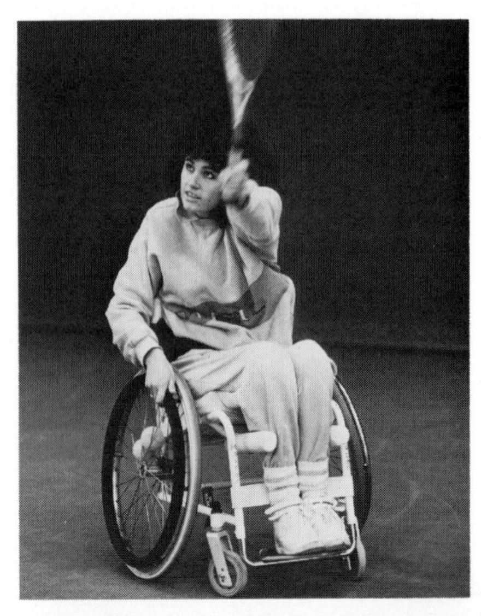

Chantal Vandierendonck (left and below right) was the 1987 Wheelchair Tennis World Champion in singles, doubles – with Monique Vanderbosch (below left) – and mixed doubles. (H. Koster)

US OPEN

RACQUET CLUB OF IRVINE, CALIFORNIA, 9–18 OCTOBER
MEN'S SINGLES – Semi-finals: Giammartini d. Turner; B. Parks d. D. Kiley. ***Final:*** Parks d. Giammartini 6–3 7–5.
WOMEN'S SINGLES – Semi-finals: Vanderbosch d. T. Lewis 6–0 2–6 6–0; Vandierendonck d. DeLange 6–0 6–0. ***Final:*** Vandierendonck d. Vanderbosch 6–4 6–7 6–2.
MEN'S DOUBLES – Final: Kiley/Snow d. Parks/Montgomery 6–7 6–1 6–2.
WOMEN'S DOUBLES – Final: Vandierendonck/Vanderbosch d. White/Olsen 7–5 6–3.
BOYS' SINGLES – Final: Vicaire d. Van Beek 6–2 6–1.
BOYS' DOUBLES – Final: Christensen/Van Beek d. Flores/Le 7–5 6–3.

RANKINGS

WORLD RANKINGS
ATP RANKINGS AND PRIZE MONEY
WITA RANKINGS AND PRIZE MONEY
MISCELLANEOUS EVENTS

Argentina's Guillermo Perez Roldan, ranked 109 at the end of 1986, leapt into the top 20 in 1987 with victories in Munich, Athens and Buenos Aires, as well as taking the French Open Junior singles title. *(T. Hindley)*

Yannick Noah of France did not have so much to smile about in 1987, for although he won Lyon and Basel at either end of the year, and was runner-up in the French Open doubles with Guy Forget, he was discouraged by unexpected losses and during the summer talked of retiring from competitive tennis. *(T. Hindley)*

WORLD RANKINGS

Lance Tingay

WORLD RANKINGS 1987

MEN

1 Ivan Lendl (TCH) (1)
2 Pat Cash (AUS) (—)
3 Stefan Edberg (SWE) (5)
4 Mats Wilander (SWE) (6)
5 Miloslav Mecir (TCH) (4)
6 Boris Becker (FRG) (2)
7 Jimmy Connors (USA) (—)
8 Andres Gomez (ECU) (8)
9 Yannick Noah (FRA) (9)
10 John McEnroe (USA) (—)

1986 ranking in brackets.

WOMEN

1 { Steffi Graf (FRG) (4)
  { Martina Navratilova (USA) (1)
3 Chris Evert (USA) (2)
4 Hana Mandlikova (TCH) (3)
5 Pam Shriver (USA) (6)
6 Gabriela Sabatini (ARG) (9)
7 Helena Sukova (TCH) (5)
8 Lori McNeil (USA) (10)
9 Manuela Maleeva (BUL) (8)
10 Zina Garrison (USA) (—)

Ivan Lendl was the top-ranked man for 1987 without question. He did not win Wimbledon, but with an awe-inspiring record that was topped by the French and US Open Championships, he was outstanding for the third year running. The women, in contrast, raised a burning question. That remarkable teenager Steffi Graf was all but invincible. Statistically she was well in front. But what of Martina Navratilova? Was she deposed at long last? Well, yes and no. The American-Czech was more vulnerable than for many years, suffering defeats from Hana Mandlikova, Chris Evert, Helena Sukova, Gabriela Sabatini – and from Graf. But who ended the season as champion of Wimbledon and the United States? Navratilova. And whom did she beat in both finals? Graf.

I can, then, only fudge the answer and rank Graf and Navratilova jointly in the lead. How can one dethrone the champion of the two master tournaments that mean most to the world and to the players themselves? The wonderful Navratilova, perhaps the most powerful woman player that ever was, must keep her place; but, having to move to make room for another, it looks as though she is unlikely to be there in a year's time. Navratilova will then be 32, Graf a mere 19. There is no need to consult Nostradamus to guess how Graf will stand.

The problem among the men is the position of the Australian, Pat Cash. While Lendl swallowed the two big titles of France and the US (this last for the third year), the biggest of all, the Wimbledon crown, eluded him in the final for the second year. Cash, with injury put behind him at last, took the Wimbledon singles for Australia – and for the personal possession of a vigorous, aggressive grass-court expert who had, half a year earlier, won the *Davis Cup* for his country. Yet elsewhere Cash suffered so many defeats from men below his level that had he been at school his master would have reported, 'Must try harder to do better'. Even so a Wimbledon champion acquires a unique gloss, so although he cannot be number one, nor can he rate less than second best.

There was much in and out form among the top men. Stefan Edberg, more consistent than some, beat Cash to win the Australian Open. The fascinating Miloslav Mecir always made his presence felt and beat Lendl to take what aspires to be next after Grand Slam status, the Lipton event in Florida. He also took Dallas. Mats Wilander, like Mecir and Edberg, won many Grand Prix tournaments, but Boris Becker did not. The two-time Wimbledon champion fell back, but will no doubt find form again, for he will not turn 21 until the end of 1988.

Jimmy Connors came back wonderfully to appear in the semi-finals at both Wimbledon

Hana Mandlikova, as brilliant but erratic as ever, dropped one place down the rankings in 1987. *(T. Hindley)*

and Flushing Meadow, but he was 35 in September 1987, and could not keep his spark glowing to the climax of a tournament. I have him in the top ten for the 14th time, the first having been in 1973. Andres Gomez, the best man in South America, maintained his useful standard on slow courts, while the Frenchman, Yannick Noah, hinted at his high potential, but was bothered with injury and could not achieve his best. The come-back of John McEnroe did not fail altogether, but neither did he rise to anything like his former standard. His old rival, Connors, held his head far higher in the big events, although one must credit McEnroe's best achievement in reaching the Dallas WCT final.

With Navratilova and Graf at the top, who next? There are not, after all, many obviously top-category women. The Australian Championship was the only Grand Slam title not won by them, and there the winner was Mandlikova, as brilliant and as erratic as always. Must it, then, be third place for this Czech, now married to an Australian? I prefer Chris Evert, who beat her twice. One can only extol the continuing virtues of Chris Evert, who was ranked for the first time in 1971 and has been continuously in the list for 17 years, three times at the top. What makes 1987 nostalgic is that it is the first year since 1974 that she has failed to take a Grand Slam title, or play a Grand Slam final. She was 33 at the end of the year. Will one see another of like consistency?

Pam Shriver maintained her standard just below the aristocrats, wth Gabriela Sabatini just behind her, on virtually level terms with Helena Sukova. Lori McNeil did marginally better than a year ago, while Manuela Maleeva more or less maintained herself and Zina Garrison squeezed into the last place.

LANCE TINGAY'S WORLD RANKINGS 1968–1986

MEN

Rank	1968	1969	1970	1971
1	Laver	Laver	Newcombe	Newcombe
2	Ashe	Roche	Rosewall	Smith
3	Rosewall	Newcombe	Laver	Laver
4	Okker	Okker	Roche	Rosewall
5	Roche	Rosewall	Okker	Kodes
6	Newcombe	Ashe	Natase	Ashe
7	Graebner	Drysdale	Richey	Okker
8	Ralston	Gonzales	Ashe	Drysdale
9	Drysdale	Gimeno	Gimeno Pilic	Riessen
10	Gonzales	Stolle	Ralston Taylor	Nastase

Rank	1972	1973	1974	1975
1	Smith	Newcombe	Connors	Ashe
2	Nastase	Smith	Rosewall	Orantes
3	Rosewall	Nastase	Newcombe	Connors
4	Laver	Kodes	Borg	Borg
5	Ashe	Ashe	Nastase	Vilas
6	Newcombe	Rosewall	Smith	Nastase
7	Richey	Laver	Laver	Ramirez
8	Orantes	Gorman	Orantes	Newcombe
9	Gimeno	Connors	Metreveli	Laver
10	Kodes	Okker	Vilas	Tanner

Rank	1976	1977	1978	1979
1	Connors	Borg	Borg	Borg
2	Borg	Vilas	Connors	McEnroe
3	Panatta	Connors	Gerulaitis	Connors
4	Nastase	Gerulaitis	Vilas	Gerulaitis
5	Vilas	Gottfried	Dibbs	Tanner
6	Dibbs	Stockton	Ramirez	Vilas
7	Solomon	Dibbs	Gottfried	Pecci
8	Orantes	Ramirez	Barazzutti	Higueras
9	Ramirez	Solomon	A. Mayer	Dibbs
10	Tanner	Tanner	McEnroe	Solomon

Rank	1980	1981	1982	1983
1	Borg	McEnroe	Connors	McEnroe
2	McEnroe	Borg	Lendl	Connors
3	Connors	Connors	McEnroe	Lendl
4	Vilas	Lendl	Wilander	Wilander
5	Gerulaitis	Clerc	Vilas	Noah
6	Lendl	Pecci	Gerulaitis	Arias
7	Solomon	G. Mayer	Higueras	Higueras
8	G. Mayer	Vilas	Gomez	Vilas
9	Teltscher	Gerulaitis	Noah	Clerc
10	Gottfried	Teacher	Teltscher	Gerulaitis

Rank	1984	1985	1986
1	McEnroe	Lendl	Lendl
2	Lendl	Wilander	Becker
3	Wilander	McEnroe	Leconte
4	Connors	Becker	Mecir
5	Gomez	Edberg	Edberg
6	Cash	Connors	Wilander
7	Sundstrom	Jarryd	Nystrom
8	Curren	Curren	Gomez
9	Aguilera	Noah	Noah
10	Krickstein	Nystrom	Jarryd

WOMEN

	1968	1969	1970	1971
1	King	Court	Court	Goolagong
2	Wade	Jones	King	Court
3	Richey	King	Casals	King
4	Bueno	Richey	Niessen	Casals
5	Court	Heldman	Wade	Melville
6	Jones	Casals	Jones	Dalton
7	Tegart	Melville	Melville	Durr
8	Du Plooy	Bartkowitz	Krantzcke	Wade
9	Bowrey	Wade	Heldman	Masthoff
10	Casals	Bowrey	Durr	Evert

	1972	1973	1974	1975
1	King	Court	Evert	Evert
2	Goolagong	King	King	King
3	Evert	Evert	Goolagong	Cawley
4	Court	Goolagong	Morozova	Navratilova
5	Melville	Melville	Melville	Wade
6	Wade	Wade	Casals	Court
7	Casals	Casals	Wade	Morozova
8	Gunter	Masthoff	Masthoff	Sawamatsu
9	Durr	Morozova	Heldman	Heldman
10	Tuero	Stove	Gunter	Reid

	1976	1977	1978	1979
1	Evert	Evert	Navratilova	Navratilova
2	Cawley	Wade	Evert	Austin
3	Wade	King	Cawley	Evert Lloyd
4	Casals	Navratilova	Wade	King
5	Navratilova	Barker	King	Cawley
6	Fromholtz	Reid	Turnbull	Wade
7	Reid	Turnbull	Ruzici	Fromholtz
8	Barker	Casals	Jausovec	Turnbull
9	Jausovec	Stove	Marsikova	Ruzici
10	Morozova	Jausovec	Shriver	Hanika

	1980	1981	1982	1983
1	Evert Lloyd	Austin	Navratilova	Navratilova
2	Cawley	Evert Lloyd	Evert Lloyd	Evert Lloyd
3	Austin	Mandlikova	Jaeger	Jaeger
4	Navratilova	Navratilova	Mandlikova	Mandlikova
5	Mandlikova	Jaeger	Potter	Hanika
6	King	Ruzici	Austin	Shriver
7	Ruzici	Turnbull	Shriver	Jausovec
8	Jaeger	Shriver	Bunge	Temesvari
9	Turnbull	Hanika	King	King
10	K. Jordan	Jausovec	Hanika	Durie

	1984	1985	1986
1	Navratilova	Navratilova	Navratilova
2	Evert Lloyd	Mandlikova	Evert Lloyd
3	Mandlikova	Evert Lloyd	Mandlikova
4	M. Maleeva	Shriver	Graf
5	K. Jordan	Garrison	Sukova
6	Shriver	Sukova	Shriver
7	Turnbull	Rinaldi	Kohde-Kilsch
8	Kohde-Kilsch	Kohde-Kilsch	M. Maleeva
9	Bassett	M. Maleeva	Sabatini
10	Sukova	Graf	McNeil

HEWLETT-PACKARD ATP RANKINGS AND PRIZE MONEY 1987

The following tables show year-end rankings of the top 200 in singles and top 100 in doubles, and the top 200 prize money winners at all recognised tournaments.

The Hewlett-Packard ATP singles and doubles rankings are based on points awarded for performances at all tournaments with at least $25,000 in prize money, where entry is based upon an approved system of merit, where the conditions laid down for the conduct of tournaments are observed and where there are at least 32 singles players and/or 16 doubles pairs in the draw(s). The level of prize money, the size of the draw and the strength of the field determine the rating a tournament receives. There are also bonus points to be won, on a graded scale, for beating a player ranked in the top 150. A player's ranking, updated weekly, is based on his average number of points (total points divided by the number of tournaments played) over a moving 12-month period. Until he has played 12 tournaments his total is, nevertheless, divided by 12. Since 1984, when a player has completed 14 tournaments in a 52-week period his divisor becomes 13. After 15 tournaments it becomes 14 and so on until, after completing 27 tournaments (by which time the divisor has become 23), it increases by one more point for every tournament played.

SINGLES

		T'MENTS	AVGE POINTS
1	Ivan Lendl (TCH)	15	173.40
2	Stefan Edberg (SWE)	17	142.12
3	Mats Wilander (SWE)	19	118.41
4	Jimmy Connors (USA)	16	88.73
5	Boris Becker (FRG)	15	88.06
6	Miloslav Mecir (TCH)	20	85.55
7	Pat Cash (AUS)	16	82.93
8	Yannick Noah (FRA)	14	65.61
9	Tim Mayotte (USA)	17	62.87
10	John McEnroe (USA)	11	59.33
11	Andres Gomez (ECU)	18	59.11
12	Kent Carlsson (SWE)	11	56.25
13	Brad Gilbert (USA)	22	53.95
14	Martin Jaite (ARG)	19	49.05
15	Anders Jarryd (SWE)	19	48.47
16	Joakim Nystrom (SWE)	17	43.87
17	Emilio Sanchez (ESP)	27	39.37
18	David Pate (USA)	19	33.05
19	Guillermo Perez Roldan (ARG)	19	33.00
20	Eliot Teltscher (USA)	14	31.23
21	Henri Leconte (FRA)	17	31.12
22	Slobodan Zivojinovic (YUG)	22	30.65
23	Jakob Hlasek (SUI)	21	30.63
24	Eduardo Bengoechea (ARG)	17	29.93
25	Andre Agassi (USA)	18	29.76
26	Peter Lundgren (SWE)	21	29.42
27	Amos Mansdorf (ISR)	22	28.75
28	Claudio Mezzadri (SUI)	19	26.58
29	Christo Van Rensburg (RSA)	15	25.71
30	Jonas Svensson (SWE)	19	25.41
31	Tomas Smid (TCH)	27	24.79
32	Paul Annacone (USA)	20	24.77
33	Mikael Pernfors (SWE)	16	24.66
34	Jimmy Arias (USA)	18	23.76
35	Wally Masur (AUS)	20	23.50
36	Kelly Evernden (NZL)	20	22.83
37	Kevin Curren (USA)	16	22.33
38	Luiz Mattar (BRA)	19	22.17
39	Jan Gunnarsson (SWE)	21	21.78
40	Eric Jelen (FRG)	20	21.50
41	Carl-Uwe Steeb (FRG)	14	20.92
42	John Frawley (AUS)	12	20.83
43	Ulf Stenlund (SWE)	20	20.61
44	Ronald Agenor (HAI)	23	20.60
45	Jim Pugh (USA)	25	20.50
46	Marian Vajda (YUG)	20	20.05
47	Jay Berger (USA)	20	19.61
48	Johan Kriek (USA)	21	19.57
49	Michiel Schapers (HOL)	20	19.38
50	Dan Goldie (USA)	20	18.94
51	Paolo Cane (ITA)	16	18.80
52	Andrei Chesnokov (URS)	18	18.76
53	Magnus Gustafsson (SWE)	11	18.58
54	Guy Forget (FRA)	20	18.50
55	Tim Wilkison (USA)	20	18.38
56	Thomas Muster (AUT)	18	18.05
57	Thierry Tulasne (FRA)	20	17.83
58	Ramesh Krishnan (IND)	27	17.62

		T'MENTS	AVGE POINTS			T'MENTS	AVGE POINTS
59	Scott Davis (USA)	21	17.36	117	Greg Holmes (USA)	17	10.25
60	Derrick Rostagno (USA)	23	17.04	118	Marcelo Filippini (URU)	12	10.25
61	Aaron Krickstein (USA)	12	16.66	119	Jerome Potier (FRA)	11	10.25
62	Milan Srejber (TCH)	26	16.60	120	Broderick Dyke (USA)	23	10.15
63	Horst Skoff (FRG)	20	16.55	121	Simon Youl (AUS)	19	10.00
64	Tore Meinecke (FRG)	21	15.84	122	Cassio Motta (BRA)	18	10.00
65	Tarik Benhabiles (FRA)	19	15.70	123	Grant Connell (CAN)	11	10.00
66	Jim Grabb (USA)	20	15.61	124	Marc Flur (USA)	14	9.92
67	Mark Woodforde (AUS)	21	15.42	125	Christian Miniussi (ARG)	14	9.84
68	Gary Muller (RSA)	17	15.25	126	Andreas Maurer (FRG)	18	9.76
69	Christian Bergstrom (SWE)	17	15.12	127	Francisco Yunis (ARG)	18	9.64
70	Jaime Yzaga (PER)	22	15.05	128	Jorge Arrese (ESP)	18	9.64
71	Guillermo Vilas (ARG)	13	14.92	129	Jean-Philippe Fleurian (FRA)	14	9.61
72	Peter Doohan (AUS)	18	14.88	130	Alberto Mancini (ARG)	14	9.53
73	John Fitzgerald (AUS)	18	14.64	131	Eric Winogradsky (FRA)	21	9.47
74	Francesco Cancellotti (ITA)	17	14.43	132	Pablo Arraya (PER)	24	9.38
75	Ricki Osterthun (FRG)	22	14.40	133	Johan Carlsson (SWE)	19	9.35
76	Karel Novacek (TCH)	23	14.30	134	Pieter Aldrich (SWE)	12	9.33
77	Josef Cihak (TCH)	10	13.91	135	Robert Seguso (USA)	16	9.26
78	Jaro Navratil (TCH)	15	13.85	136	Danie Visser (RSA)	18	9.23
79	Richey Reneberg (USA)	13	13.84	137	Javier Frana (ARG)	16	9.13
80	Alberto Tous (ESP)	17	13.81	138	Massimiliano Narducci (ITA)	6	8.91
81	Paul Vojtischek (FRG)	16	13.80	139	Gilad Bloom (ISR)	22	8.90
82	Darren Cahill (USA)	22	13.75	140	Mel Purcell (USA)	23	8.75
83	Patrick Kuhnen (FRG)	17	13.75	141	Juan Aguilera (ESP)	13	8.69
84	Christian Saceanu (FRG)	18	13.70	142	Barry Moir (RSA)	19	8.61
85	Jimmy Brown (USA)	16	12.93	143	Wolfgang Popp (FRG)	19	8.58
86	Branislav Stankovic (TCH)	11	12.83	144	Martin Laurendeau (CAN)	16	8.50
87	Petr Korda (TCH)	12	12.66	145	Blaine Willenborg (USA)	12	8.50
88	Horacio de la Pena (ARG)	19	12.58	146	Roger Smith (USA)	11	8.50
89	Jeremy Bates (GBR)	15	12.57	147	Carl Limberger (AUS)	24	8.42
90	Niclas Kroon (SWE)	13	12.30	148	Rick Leach (USA)	13	8.38
91	Matt Anger (USA)	22	12.30	149	Florin Segarceanu (RUM)	11	8.33
92	Sergio Casal (ESP)	25	12.09	150	Chip Hooper (USA)	11	8.33
93	Lawson Duncan (USA)	16	12.06	151	Stefan Eriksson (SWE)	14	8.30
94	Pedro Rebolledo (CHI)	17	12.00	152	Menno Oosting (HOL)	16	8.26
95	Libor Pimek (TCH)	19	11.94	153	Gianluca Pozzi (ITA)	13	8.07
96	Martin Davis (USA)	18	11.94	154	Brad Drewett (AUS)	19	8.05
97	Claudio Pistolesi (ITA)	17	11.93	155	Mark Dickson (USA)	18	8.05
98	Nduka Odizor (NIG)	21	11.84	156	Kelly Jones (USA)	24	8.00
99	Bill Scanlon (USA)	17	11.81	157	Leif Shiras (USA)	20	8.00
100	Ken Flach (USA)	13	11.53	158	Todd Witsken (USA)	17	7.93
101	John Ross (USA)	10	11.50	159	José Daher (BRA)	10	7.91
102	Joey Rive (USA)	16	11.46	160	Lloyd Bourne (USA)	10	7.91
103	Tom Nijssen (HOL)	16	11.33	161	Marcel Freeman (USA)	20	7.83
104	Aleksandr Volkov (URS)	8	11.33	162	Stephen Shaw (GBR)	13	7.76
105	Thierry Champion (FRA)	16	11.00	163	Michael Chang (USA)	5	7.75
106	Dan Cassidy (USA)	10	11.00	164	Agustin Moreno (MEX)	8	7.75
107	Jorge Lozano (MEX)	15	10.93	165	Julio Goes (BRA)	9	7.75
108	Sammy Giammalva (USA)	21	10.89	166	Franco Davin (ARG)	18	7.58
109	Damir Keretic (YUG)	15	10.78	167	Carlos Dilaura (PER)	13	7.46
110	Javier Sanchez (ESP)	21	10.63	168	Jorgen Windahl (SWE)	15	7.42
111	Bruno Oresar (YUG)	13	10.61	169	Jonathan Canter (USA)	20	7.38
112	Todd Nelson (USA)	19	10.58	170	Hans Schwaier (FRG)	18	7.35
113	Ben Testerman (USA)	21	10.57	171	Stephane Bonneau (CAN)	19	7.33
114	Chris Pridham (CAN)	9	10.50	172	Edoardo Mazza (ITA)	11	7.33
115	Alex Antonitsch (AUT)	19	10.35	173	John Sadri (USA)	13	7.30
116	Diego Perez (URU)	19	10.29	174	Peter Fleming (USA)	15	7.26

		T'MENTS	AVGE POINTS			T'MENTS	AVGE POINTS
175	Marcelo Ingaramo (ARG)	10	7.25	188	David de Miguel (ESP)	13	6.76
176	Andrew Castle (GBR)	22	7.20	189	Loic Courteau (FRA)	10	6.75
177	Roberto Arguello (ARG)	13	7.15	190	Alexander Mronz (FRG)	11	6.75
178	Glenn Michibata (CAN)	15	7.14	191	Diego Nargiso (ITA)	11	6.75
179	Thomas Hogstedt (SWE)	16	7.13	192	Luke Jensen (USA)	8	6.66
180	Markus Rackl (FRG)	10	7.08	193	Patrice Kuchna (FRA)	11	6.58
181	Roland Stadler (FRG)	15	7.07	194	Paul McNamee (AUS)	14	6.46
182	Mark Kratzmann (AUS)	17	7.00	195	Tony Mmoh (NIG)	18	6.41
183	Massimo Cierro (ITA)	17	6.93	196	Mansour Bahrami (IRN)	13	6.30
184	Peter Lindgren (SWE)	16	6.93	197	Richard Matuszewski (USA)	23	6.25
185	Eduardo Masso (ARG)	15	6.92	198	Luca Bottazzi (MEX)	9	6.25
186	Gerald Marzenell (FRG)	10	6.91	199	Ricardo Acuna (CHI)	15	6.21
187	Gustavo Garetto (FRG)	10	6.91	200	Jesus Colas (ESP)	12	6.16

Jay Berger of the US enjoyed a solid year, in which he moved 35 places up the rankings and into the top 50. *(M. Cole)*

DOUBLES

		T'MENTS	AVGE POINTS			T'MENTS	AVGE POINTS
1	Robert Seguso (USA)	17	134.43	51	Wojtek Fibak (POL)	16	27.40
2	Anders Jarryd (SWE)	17	129.12	52	Patrick McEnroe (USA)	8	26.75
3	Stefan Edberg (SWE)	10	113.75	53	Mark Woodforde (AUS)	22	26.20
4	Yannick Noah (FRA)	11	113.00	54	Eddie Edwards (RSA)	14	26.07
5	Ken Flach (USA)	24	88.09	55	Brad Pearce (USA)	24	25.90
6	Guy Forget (FRA)	21	84.78	56	Tim Wilkison (USA)	18	25.76
7	Sergio Casal (ESP)	26	79.39	57	Brad Gilbert (USA)	18	25.52
8	Emilio Sanchez (ESP)	27	79.00	58	Brad Drewett (AUS)	17	25.43
9	Paul Annacone (USA)	21	75.90	59	Tim Pawsat (USA)	26	25.30
10	Christo Van Rensburg (RSA)	18	74.70	60	Darren Cahill (AUS)	24	25.19
11	Andres Gomez (ECU)	17	70.75	61	Mike DePalmer (USA)	18	24.64
12	Miloslav Mecir (TCH)	18	69.47	62	Jonas Svensson (SWE)	15	24.14
13	Tomas Smid (TCH)	27	68.66	63	José Lopez-Maeso (ESP)	16	23.93
14	Slobodan Zivojinovic (YUG)	17	61.81	64	Kelly Jones (USA)	26	23.82
15	David Pate (USA)	17	58.00	65	Jan Gunnarsson (SWE)	20	23.77
16	Boris Becker (FRG)	11	56.75	66	Eric Korita (USA)	10	23.50
17	Blaine Willenborg (USA)	15	54.07	67	Javier Sanchez (ESP)	18	23.23
18	Laurie Warder (AUS)	26	52.60	68	Danie Visser (RSA)	14	23.23
19	Kevin Curren (USA)	15	51.66	69	Ben Testerman (USA)	20	23.11
20	Gary Donnelly (USA)	22	48.80	70	Matt Anger (USA)	21	22.90
21	Peter Fleming (USA)	13	48.15	71	Lloyd Bourne (USA)	18	22.88
22	Hans Gildemeister (CHI)	12	47.66	72	Martin Davis (USA)	13	22.84
23	Scott Davis (USA)	19	46.29	73	Wally Masur (AUS)	17	22.81
24	Joakim Nystrom (SWE)	17	45.31	74	Jeff Klaparda (USA)	18	22.58
25	Mats Wilander (SWE)	15	44.64	75	Tore Meinecke (FRG)	19	22.52
26	Claudio Mezzadri (ITA)	19	44.41	76	Alberto Tous (ESP)	19	22.41
27	Peter Doohan (AUS)	18	43.70	77	Eric Jelen (FRG)	17	22.31
28	Jim Grabb (USA)	14	41.00	78	Michiel Schapers (HOL)	21	22.15
29	Robert Van't Hof (USA)	15	39.71	79	Mark Dickson (USA)	14	21.61
30	Andy Kohlberg (USA)	13	37.38	80	Gary Muller (RSA)	18	21.41
31	Jaro Navratil (TCH)	19	35.82	81	Javier Frana (ARG)	14	21.38
32	Jim Pugh (USA)	26	35.43	82	John McEnroe (USA)	5	21.33
33	Jorge Lozano (MEX)	15	34.64	83	Steve Denton (USA)	18	21.17
34	John Fitzgerald (AUS)	13	33.69	84	Francisco Gonzalez (USA)	15	21.06
35	Jakob Hlasek (SUI)	21	33.00	85	Carl Limberger (AUS)	27	21.04
36	Kim Warwick (AUS)	13	33.00	86	Luiz Mattar (BRA)	16	20.93
37	Sherwood Stewart (USA)	10	32.83	87	Loic Courteau (FRA)	10	20.91
38	Mike Leach (USA)	19	32.29	88	Christian Miniussi (ARG)	13	20.00
39	Pat Cash (AUS)	7	32.25	89	Glenn Layendecker (USA)	20	19.55
40	Chip Hooper (USA)	21	31.68	90	Gilad Bloom (ISR)	22	19.35
41	Diego Perez (URU)	17	31.18	91	Petr Korda (TCH)	15	19.28
42	Todd Witsken (USA)	13	30.92	92	Dan Goldie (USA)	10	19.16
43	Mark Kratzmann (AUS)	22	30.35	93	Broderick Dyke (AUS)	21	19.00
44	Tom Nijssen (HOL)	14	30.00	94	Carlos Dilaura (PER)	17	19.00
45	Rick Leach (USA)	17	29.93	95	Nduka Odizor (NIG)	17	18.62
46	Sammy Giammalva (USA)	14	29.23	96	Grant Connell (CAN)	14	18.53
47	Mansour Bahrami (IRN)	23	29.00	97	Johan Kriek (USA)	14	18.46
48	Kelly Evernden (NZL)	17	28.62	98	Cassio Motta (BRA)	14	18.38
49	Stanislav Birner (TCH)	19	28.05	99	Wolfgang Popp (FRG)	17	18.00
50	Michael Mortensen (SWE)	17	27.50	100	Magnus Tideman (SWE)	9	17.91

PRIZE MONEY

In 1987 four men exceeded $1 million in earnings, and the combined earnings of the top ten were an all-time record at $9,152,179. This upward trend, apparent at all levels, reflects the growing rewards at the top of the game as levels of prize money rise. For six consecutive years now, Ivan Lendl has exceeded $1 million in earnings, and for the first time he exceeded $2 million, becoming the first tennis player to do so. However, although Martina Navratilova failed to reach the $1 million mark in 1987, Lendl still remains behind her in career earnings, with $12,298,031, compared with her $12,724,417. The other men to pass $1 million were Stefan Edberg, Miloslav Mecir and Mats Wilander.

Lower down, all the records of 1985, intact at the end of 1986, were broken in 1987. Sixteen men, compared with 15, passed $300,000; 28, as opposed to 23, passed $200,000; the 67 who passed $100,000 were 14 more than in 1985; and 124 players, 16 more than in 1985, earned $50,000.

Note: The prize money figures include earnings from tournaments, circuit bonuses and play-offs, plus team events, where the entry is based purely on merit. They include WCT earnings but not rewards from *Davis Cup* ties, invitation tournaments, exhibitions and special events; nor do they include income from contracts or endorsements.

The following table shows the top 200 prize money earners in 1987.

		PRIZE MONEY			PRIZE MONEY
1	Ivan Lendl (TCH)	$2,003,656	42	Michiel Schapers (HOL)	148,121
2	Stefan Edberg (SWE)	1,587,467	43	Scott Davis (USA)	145,438
3	Miloslav Mecir (TCH)	1,205,326	44	Ramesh Krishnan (IND)	145,185
4	Mats Wilander (SWE)	1,164,674	45	Eliot Teltscher (USA)	141,888
5	Pat Cash (AUS)	565,934	46	Johan Kriek (USA)	141,398
6	Anders Jarryd (SWE)	561,977	47	Ronald Agenor (HAI)	140,176
7	Boris Becker (FRG)	558,979	48	Jimmy Arias (USA)	129,711
8	Emilio Sanchez (ESP)	538,158	49	Jan Gunnarsson (SWE)	128,239
9	Brad Gilbert (USA)	507,187	50	Tim Wilkison (USA)	127,953
10	Tim Mayotte (USA)	458,821	51	Jim Grabb (USA)	126,208
11	Andres Gomez (ECU)	433,813	52	Marian Vajda (TCH)	119,124
12	Tomas Smid (TCH)	433,783	53	Mikael Pernfors (SWE)	117,133
13	Jimmy Connors (USA)	422,026	54	Karel Novacek (TCH)	115,777
14	Yannick Noah (FRA)	394,503	55	Jaime Yzaga (PER)	114,979
15	John McEnroe (USA)	391,766	56	Andrei Chesnokov (URS)	112,980
16	Robert Seguso (USA)	367,022	57	Eduardo Bengoechea (ARG)	110,748
17	Martin Jaite (ARG)	287,923	58	Ricki Osterthun (FRG)	107,555
18	Sergio Casal (ESP)	269,851	59	Dan Goldie (USA)	107,042
19	Joakim Nystrom (SWE)	268,215	60	Thierry Tulasne (FRA)	105,040
20	Slobodan Zivojinovic (YUG)	256,824	61	Jay Berger (USA)	104,096
21	David Pate (USA)	251,121	62	Ulf Stenlund (SWE)	103,754
22	Paul Annacone (USA)	248,209	63	Derrick Rostagno (USA)	101,908
23	Ken Flach (USA)	226,371	64	Gary Donnelly (USA)	101,647
24	Guy Forget (FRA)	224,273	65	Darren Cahill (AUS)	101,507
25	Milan Srejber (TCH)	214,263	66	Tore Meinecke (FRG)	101,341
26	Christo Van Rensburg (RSA)	210,088	67	Peter Doohan (AUS)	101,020
27	Jakob Hlasek (SUI)	207,416	68	Matt Anger (USA)	97,522
28	Andre Agassi (USA)	205,555	69	Guillermo Vilas (ARG)	92,504
29	Henri Leconte (FRA)	196,190	70	Laurie Warder (AUS)	90,684
30	Amos Mansdorf (ISR)	194,417	71	John Fitzgerald (AUS)	90,384
31	Guillermo Perez Roldan (ARG)	193,226	72	Sammy Giammalva (USA)	86,912
32	Jonas Svensson (SWE)	185,326	73	Carl Limberger (AUS)	86,428
33	Claudio Mezzadri (ITA)	175,282	74	Broderick Dyke (AUS)	84,812
34	Kevin Curren (USA)	171,458	75	Mark Woodforde (AUS)	79,454
35	Peter Lundgren (SWE)	171,038	76	Diego Perez (URU)	79,116
36	Kelly Evernden (NZL)	167,667	77	Javier Sanchez (ESP)	79,084
37	Jim Pugh (USA)	167,568	78	Paolo Cane (ITA)	79,068
38	Kent Carlsson (SWE)	167,541	79	Kelly Jones (USA)	78,929
39	Wally Masur (AUS)	165,259	80	Gilad Bloom (ISR)	78,571
40	Luiz Mattar (BRA)	163,769	81	Mel Purcell (USA)	77,952
41	Eric Jelen (FRG)	162,184	82	Horst Skoff (FRG)	77,508

		PRIZE MONEY
83	Tarik Benhabiles (FRA)	77,350
84	Christian Saceanu (FRG)	77,324
85	Peter Fleming (USA)	75,192
86	Alberto Tous (ESP)	75,065
87	Ben Testerman (USA)	74,303
88	Nduka Odizor (NIG)	73,896
89	Gary Muller (RSA)	73,845
90	Thomas Muster (AUT)	73,325
91	Damir Keretic (FRG)	72,991
92	Bill Scanlon (USA)	71,545
93	Mark Kratzmann (AUS)	69,945
94	Marcel Freeman (USA)	68,284
95	Cassio Motta (BRA)	67,957
96	Brad Drewett (AUS)	67,163
97	Blaine Willenborg (USA)	64,988
98	Martin Davis (USA)	64,976
99	Rick Leach (USA)	64,270
100	Claudio Pistolesi (ITA)	63,384
101	Todd Witsken (USA)	62,787
102	Todd Nelson (USA)	62,657
103	Jaro Navratil (TCH)	61,451
104	Patrick Kuhnen (FRA)	60,912
105	Libor Pimek (TCH)	59,225
106	Jorge Lozano (MEX)	58,705
107	Pedro Rebolledo (CHI)	58,502
108	Danie Visser (RSA)	58,040
109	Francesco Cancellotti (ITA)	57,882
110	Andrew Castle (GBR)	57,296
111	Horacio de la Pena (ARG)	57,177
112	Greg Holmes (USA)	56,447
113	Chip Hooper (USA)	54,311
114	Mansour Bahrami (IRN)	53,570
115	Mike Leach (USA)	53,555
116	Brad Pearce (USA)	53,230
117	Mike DePalmer (USA)	53,204
118	Aaron Krickstein (USA)	53,140
119	Christo Steyn (RSA)	53,093
120	Eddie Edwards (RSA)	52,670
121	Jeremy Bates (GBR)	51,612
122	Pablo Arraya (PER)	50,904
123	Johan Carlsson (SWE)	50,778
124	Christian Bergstrom (SWE)	50,754
125	Richey Reneberg (USA)	49,875
126	Andreas Maurer (FRG)	49,787
127	Leif Shiras (USA)	49,194
128	Alex Antonitsch (AUT)	48,450
129	Tony Mmoh (NIG)	47,904
130	Jonathan Canter (USA)	47,849
131	Stanislav Birner (TCH)	47,511
132	Tom Nijssen (HOL)	46,310
133	Lawson Duncan (USA)	46,293
134	Paul McNamee (AUS)	45,968
135	Simon Youl (AUS)	45,249
136	Claudio Panatta (ITA)	45,051
137	Carl-Uwe Steeb (FRG)	44,880
138	Mark Dickson (USA)	44,245
139	Joey Rive (USA)	43,837
140	Eric Winogradsky (FRA)	43,621
141	Paul Vojtischek (FRG)	43,182

		PRIZE MONEY
142	Simone Colombo (ITA)	42,242
143	Jorge Arrese (ESP)	42,030
144	Thierry Champion (FRA)	41,649
145	Marc Flur (USA)	41,449
146	Richard Matuszewski (USA)	40,871
147	Bruno Oresar (YUG)	40,711
148	Wolfgang Popp (FRG)	39,945
149	Glenn Layendecker (USA)	39,821
150	Franco Davin (ARG)	39,163
151	Aleksandr Volkov (URS)	39,124
152	John Ross (USA)	38,646
153	Barry Moir (RSA)	38,598
154	Jean-Philippe Fleurian (FRA)	37,999
155	Jimmy Brown (USA)	37,586
156	Francisco Yunis (ARG)	37,353
157	Martin Laurendeau (CAN)	37,303
158	Magnus Gustafsson (SWE)	36,960
159	Thomas Hogstedt (SWE)	36,846
160	Ivan Kley (BRA)	36,729
161	Tim Pawsat (USA)	36,490
162	David de Miguel (ESP)	36,276
163	Hans Schwaier (FRG)	34,131
164	Leonardo Lavalle (MEX)	33,778
165	Wojtek Fibak (POL)	33,594
166	Javier Frana (ARG)	33,539
167	Grant Connell (CAN)	33,520
168	Glenn Michibata (CAN)	33,199
169	Christian Miniussi (ARG)	33,122
170	Hans Gildemeister (CHI)	33,063
171	Jon Levine (USA)	32,567
172	Ricardo Acuna (CHI)	32,299
173	Lloyd Bourne (USA)	31,861
174	Roland Stadler (FRG)	31,801
175	Carlos Dilaura (PER)	31,734
176	Michael Westphal (FRG)	30,854
177	Robert Van't Hof (USA)	30,797
178	Charles Bud Cox (USA)	30,751
179	Henrik Sundstrom (SWE)	29,900
180	Michael Robertson (RSA)	28,642
181	Stefan Eriksson (SWE)	28,557
182	Petr Korda (TCH)	28,344
183	Alessandro de Minicis (ITA)	28,342
184	Jose Lopez-Maeso (ESP)	28,330
185	Andy Kohlberg (USA)	27,318
186	Paul Chamberlin (USA)	26,532
187	Juan Aguilera (ESP)	26,389
188	John Sadri (USA)	26,228
189	Larry Scott (USA)	26,137
190	Michael Chang (USA)	25,681
191	Kim Warwick (AUS)	25,678
192	John Frawley (AUS)	25,099
193	Jorgen Windahl (SWE)	24,889
194	Jay Lapidus (USA)	24,845
195	Niclas Kroon (SWE)	24,251
196	Michael Kures (USA)	24,113
197	Roberto Saad (ARG)	23,833
198	Fernando Luna (ESP)	23,546
199	Massimo Cierro (ITA)	22,692
200	Lars Wahlgren (SWE)	22,593

Joakim Nystrom beat Lendl for the first time at the Italian Open, but suffered a mid-year slump which saw his ranking drop as low as 29, before beating Wilander and Edberg to win his first title of the year at Bastad. *(T. Hindley)*

Players who have won more than $1 million in prize money

1	Ivan Lendl	$12,298,031	29	Ken Rosewall	$1,600,300
2	John McEnroe	9,586,625	30	Arthur Ashe	1,584,909
3	Jimmy Connors	7,489,977	31	Sherwood Stewart	1,582.924
4	Mats Wilander	5,101,332	32	Rod Laver	1,564,213
5	Guillermo Vilas	4,838,990	33	Heinz Gunthardt	1,509,335
6	Bjorn Borg	3,607,206	34	Mark Edmondson	1,449,486
7	Stefan Edberg	3,573,502	35	Brad Gilbert	1,430,469
8	Tomas Smid	3,342,005	36	Tim Mayotte	1,427,936
9	Brian Gottfried	2,781,614	37	Brian Teacher	1,426,244
10	Vitas Gerulaitis	2,777,727	38	José Higueras	1,406,355
11	Wojtek Fibak	2,717,213	39	Manuel Orantes	1,398,303
12	Boris Becker	2,658,929	40	Gene Mayer	1,381,562
13	Andres Gomez	2,484,536	41	Bill Scanlon	1,366,150
14	Yannick Noah	2,489,400	42	Balazs Taroczy	1,356,095
15	Anders Jarryd	2,223,259	43	Henri Leconte	1,348,685
16	Paul Ramirez	2,213,581	44	Vijay Amritraj	1,272,077
17	Ilie Nastase	2,070,164	45	Tom Okker	1,257,200
18	Johan Kriek	2,053,250	46	Jimmy Arias	1,256,271
19	Eddie Dibbs	2,016,426	47	Paul McNamee	1,227,459
20	Peter Fleming	1,982,717	48	John Alexander	1,214,079
21	José-Luis Clerc	1,969,334	49	Pat Cash	1,176,962
22	Joakim Nystrom	1,949,162	50	Bob Lutz	1,165,276
23	Miloslav Mecir	1,885,597	51	Tim Gullikson	1,119,910
24	Harold Solomon	1,799,230	52	Steve Denton	1,067,357
25	Kevin Curren	1,785,282	53	Dick Stockton	1,063,385
26	Stan Smith	1,774,811	54	Sandy Mayer	1,057,783
27	Roscoe Tanner	1,696,108	55	Peter McNamara	1,046,145
28	Eliot Teltscher	1,601,173			

ATP 'JAKS' AWARDS 1987

At the 13th annual ATP Tennis Awards Gala, held on 1 December at the New York Hilton Hotel, in aid of the ATP's adopted charity, Cystic Fibrosis, the following awards were made.
Player of the Year – Ivan Lendl.
Doubles Team of the Year – Stefan Edberg and Anders Jarryd.
Newcomer of the Year – Richey Reneberg.
Most Improved Player of the Year – Peter Lundgren.
Sportsmanship Award – Miloslav Mecir.
ATP Super Series Tournament of the Year – Stratton Mountain.
ATP Open and Regular Series Tournament of the Year – Stuttgart.
CF Humanitarian Award – Bob Finkelstein.

HEWLETT-PACKARD WITA RANKINGS AND PRIZE MONEY 1987

RANKINGS

The following tables show the season-end 1987 rankings in singles and doubles. The rankings, compiled for the WITA by Hewlett-Packard and updated every two weeks, form the basis for acceptance at all official tournaments, the criteria for which have been set by the players themselves.

SINGLES

		T'MENTS	AVGE POINTS			T'MENTS	AVGE POINTS
1	Steffi Graf (FRG)	13	280.20	39	Gigi Fernandez (USA)	18	20.02
2	Martina Navratilova (USA)	12	231.21	40	Anne Smith (USA)	10	19.66
3	Chris Evert (USA)	17	165.76	41	Anne Hobbs (GBR)	11	18.87
4	Pam Shriver (USA)	17	137.27	42	Elly Hakami (USA)	17	18.85
5	Hana Mandlikova (TCH)	16	120.96	43	Eva Pfaff (FRG)	20	18.82
6	Gabriela Sabatini (ARG)	19	113.57	44	Bettina Fulco (ARG)	18	18.25
7	Helena Sukova (TCH)	21	92.35	45	Leila Meskhi (URS)	11	17.81
8	Manuela Maleeva (BUL)	17	83.13	46	Laura Gildemeister (PER)	15	17.60
9	Zina Garrison (USA)	19	80.91	47	Jana Novotna (TCH)	20	17.31
10	Claudia Kohde-Kilsch (FRG)	16	65.77	48	Terry Phelps (USA)	22	16.61
11	Lori McNeil (USA)	24	63.68	49	Lisa Bonder (USA)	14	16.03
12	Barbara Potter (USA)	14	47.07	50	Silke Meier (FGR)	13	15.92
13	Katerina Maleeva (BUL)	17	45.97	51	Alycia Moulton (USA)	17	15.76
14	Sylvia Hanika (FRG)	19	44.24	52	Gretchen Rush Magers (USA)	18	15.16
15	Bettina Bunge (FRG)	18	42.23	53	Isabelle Demongeot (FRA)	20	15.07
16	Catarina Lindqvist (SWE)	20	40.36	54	Arantxa Sanchez (ESP)	15	14.93
17	Raffaella Reggi (ITA)	22	37.26	55	Halle Cioffi (USA)	16	14.77
18	Sandra Cecchini (ITA)	19	35.92	56	Robin White (USA)	14	14.75
19	Natalia Zvereva (URS)	13	34.34	57	Anne White (USA)	12	14.71
20	Mary Joe Fernandez (USA)	14	34.10	58	Hu Na (USA)	18	14.61
21	Dianne Balestrat (AUS)	13	33.19	59	Marianne Werdel (USA)	17	14.20
22	Kate Gompert (USA)	18	32.55	60	Ann Henricksson (USA)	23	14.19
23	Wendy Turnbull (AUS)	16	31.37	61	Betsy Nagelsen (USA)	15	14.10
24	Larisa Savchenko (URS)	14	30.60	62	Julie Halard (FRA)	13	13.53
25	Nathalie Tauziat (FRA)	20	29.92	63	Barbara Gerken (USA)	19	13.42
26	Kathy Rinaldi (USA)	8	29.87	64	Sabrina Goles (YUG)	19	13.00
27	Elizabeth Smylie (AUS)	15	28.80	65	Elise Burgin (USA)	21	12.85
28	Stephanie Rehe (USA)	9	27.91	66	Camille Benjamin (USA)	24	12.75
29	Isabel Cueto (FRG)	17	26.41	67	Michelle Torres (USA)	19	12.42
30	Etsuko Inoue (JPN)	16	25.06	68	Kathrin Keil (USA)	17	12.41
31	Kathleen Horvath (USA)	14	23.42	69	Patricia Tarabini (ARG)	18	12.38
32	Carling Bassett Seguso (CAN)	13	23.34	70	Mariana Perez-Roldan (ARG)	19	11.93
33	Helen Kelesi (CAN)	19	22.89	71	Regina Marsikova (TCH)	19	11.92
34	Judith Polzl Wiesner (AUT)	14	22.35	72	Sara Gomer (GBR)	20	11.89
35	Wendy White (USA)	17	22.29	73	Jo Durie (GBR)	17	11.70
36	Kathy Jordan (USA)	10	22.25	74	Heather Ludloff (USA)	18	11.52
37	Rosalyn Fairbank (RSA)	20	22.05	75	Beverly Bowes (USA)	18	11.50
38	Anne Minter (AUS)	23	21.70	76	Elizabeth Minter (AUS)	17	11.38

		T'MENTS	AVGE POINTS
77	Nicole Provis (AUS)	21	11.30
78	Patty Fendick (USA)	9	11.08
79	Akiko Kijimuta (JPN)	14	11.07
80	Barbara Paulus (AUT)	13	10.96
81	Iwona Kuczynska (POL)	15	10.76
82	Christina Singer (FRA)	13	10.68
83	Sharon Walsh Pete (USA)	16	10.60
84	Petra Huber (AUT)	15	10.56
85	Laura Garrone (ITA)	17	10.11
86	Christiane Jolissaint (SUI)	11	9.93
87	Regina Rajchrtova (TCH)	13	9.90
88	Mercedes Paz (ARG)	20	9.89
89	Nathalie Herreman (FRA)	20	9.67
90	Melissa Gurney (USA)	14	9.57
91	Federica Bonsignori (ITA)	16	9.29
92	Mary Lou Piatek Daniels (USA)	12	9.14
93	Natalia Bykova (URS)	16	8.68
94	Elna Reinach (RSA)	21	8.59
95	Catherine Tanvier (FRA)	19	8.57
96	Dinky Van Rensburg (RSA)	21	8.50
97	Peanut Louie Harper (USA)	16	8.37
98	Wiltrud Probst (FRG)	18	8.36
99	Vicki Nelson Dunbar (USA)	21	8.35
100	Ann Devries (BEL)	18	8.15
101	Patricia Hy (HKG)	16	8.12
102	Karen Schimper (RSA)	17	8.08
103	Pascale Paradis (FRA)	18	8.03
104	Claudia Porwik (FRG)	22	7.96
105	Penny Barg (USA)	15	7.93
106	Janine Thompson (AUS)	8	7.89
107	Kumiko Okamoto (JPN)	9	7.79
108	Ronni Reis (USA)	11	7.76
109	Gisele Miro (BRA)	11	7.64
110	Adriana Villagran (ARG)	22	7.59
111	Susan Sloane (USA)	15	7.43
112	Svetlana Parkhomenko (URS)	13	7.42
113	Pam Casale (USA)	11	7.41
114	Louise Field (AUS)	20	7.25
115	Laura Golarsa (ITA)	13	7.21
116	Iva Budarova (TCH)	17	7.03
117	Niege Dias (BRA)	18	7.00
118	Susan Mascarin (USA)	14	6.97
119	Eva Krapl (SUI)	13	6.90
120	Maria Lindstrom (SWE)	19	6.88
121	Manon Bollegraf (HOL)	19	6.74
122	Angeliki Kanellopoulou (GRE)	12	6.66
123	Sandra Wasserman (BEL)	15	6.61
124	Marie Calleja (FRA)	16	6.44
125	Belinda Cordwell (NZL)	16	6.32
126	Beth Herr (USA)	17	6.31
127	Andrea Holikova (TCH)	19	6.22
128	Alexia Dechâume (FRA)	14	6.12
129	Tine Scheuer-Larsen (DEN)	17	6.09
130	Michelle Jaggard (AUS)	14	6.09
131	Grace Kim (USA)	18	6.05
132	Carina Karlsson (SWE)	19	6.04
133	Emanuelle Derly (FRA)	15	6.00
134	Cammie MacGregor (USA)	19	6.00
135	Catherine Suire (FRA)	16	5.92
136	Niurka Sodupe (USA)	11	5.88
137	Anna-Maria Fernandez (USA)	19	5.85
138	Radka Zrubakova (TCH)	14	5.81
139	Tina Mochizuki (USA)	26	5.76
140	Annabel Croft (GBR)	17	5.74
141	Molly Van Nostrand (USA)	15	5.50
142	Virginia Ruzici (RUM)	9	5.48
143	Jenny Byrne (AUS)	20	5.32
144	Hellas Ter Riet (HOL)	22	5.23
145	Marcella Mesker (HOL)	16	5.00
146	Caterina Nozzoli (ITA)	11	4.91
147	Jenny Klitch (USA)	19	4.84
148	Brenda Schultz (HOL)	15	4.78
149	Louise Allen (USA)	16	4.74
150	Pilar Vasquez (PER)	18	4.58
151	Debbie Spence (USA)	11	4.58
152	Csilla Bartos Cserepy (SUI)	10	4.54
153	Linda Ferrando (ITA)	13	4.13
154	Olga Tsarbopoulou (GRE)	10	4.11
155	Julie Richardson (NZL)	15	3.87
156	Dee Ann Hansel (USA)	14	3.85
157	Cecilia Fernandez (USA)	10	3.70
158	Andrea Betzner (FRG)	15	3.57
159	Lea Antonoplis (USA)	17	3.54
160	Amy Schwartz (USA)	18	3.53
161	Emiko Okagawa (JPN)	15	3.50
162	Monique Javer (USA)	14	3.48
163	Katrina Adams (USA)	13	3.47
164	Jennifer Mundel Reinbold (RSA)	15	3.44
165	Jane Forman (USA)	13	3.35
166	Gabriela Dinu (FRG)	15	3.19
167	Lise Gregory (RSA)	12	3.07
168	Pat Medrado (BRA)	15	3.05
169	Clare Wood (GBR)	13	2.94
170	Laura Lapi (ITA)	14	2.88
171	Karolina Karlsson (SWE)	6	2.86
172	Sandy Collins (USA)	12	2.82
173	Nicole Jagerman (HOL)	13	2.82
174	Carol Christian (USA)	14	2.81
175	Claudia Monteiro (BRA)	14	2.68
176	Amy Jonsson (NOR)	21	2.63
177	Hana Fukarkova (TCH)	14	2.61
177	Candy Reynolds (USA)	14	2.61
179	Sybille Niox-Chateau (FRA)	12	2.53
180	Marianne Van Der Torre (HOL)	13	2.51
181	Melissa Brown (USA)	16	2.51
182	Emilse Rapponi Longo (ARG)	12	2.51
183	Rebecca Bryant (AUS)	4	2.50
184	Julie Salmon (GBR)	14	2.46
185	Sylvia La Fratta (ITA)	13	2.45
186	Marie Jose Llorca (ESP)	11	2.43
187	Yukie Koizumi (JPN)	13	2.41
188	Jamie Golder (USA)	16	2.31
189	Valda Lake (GBR)	16	2.27
190	Shaun Stafford (USA)	7	2.27
191	Kim Labuschagne (RSA)	13	2.25
192	Jill Hetherington (CAN)	7	2.23

Left: *Etsuko Inoue, Japan's No. 1, shot 50 places up the rankings in 1987, with semi-final appearances in Tokyo, Singapore and Edgbaston.* ***Below:*** *Raffaella Reggi of Italy moved into the world top 20, winning the Virginia Slims of San Diego and beating Helena Sukova on her way to the French Open quarter-finals. (Carol L. Newson)*

		T'MENTS	AVGE POINTS
193	Cynthia MacGregor (USA)	14	2.20
194	Helena Dahlstrom (SWE)	13	2.19
195	Barbara Romano (ITA)	10	2.09
196	Natalia Medvedeva (URS)	7	2.01
197	Maider Laval (FRA)	7	1.95
198	Paula Smith (USA)	11	1.95
199	Katerina Bohmova (TCH)	6	1.94
200	Amy Frazier (USA)	12	1.93
201	Yvonne Vermaak (RSA)	4	1.93
202	Akemi Nishiya (JPN)	12	1.92
203	Susan Leo (AUS)	10	1.90
204	Jennifer Santrock (USA)	9	1.89
205	Karmen Skulj (YUG)	11	1.77
206	Lisa O'Neill (AUS)	13	1.75
207	Hester Witvoet (HOL)	9	1.72
208	Andrea Vieira (BRA)	8	1.70
209	Maria Strandlund (SWE)	8	1.70
210	Amanda Dingwall (AUS)	9	1.69
211	Susan Rimes (USA)	8	1.68
212	Luciana Corsato (BRA)	17	1.65
213	Heike Thoms (FRG)	8	1.64
214	Yvonne Der Kinderen (HOL)	13	1.61
215	Kim Steinmetz (USA)	15	1.59
216	Elizabeth Galphin (USA)	19	1.57
217	Carin Bakkum (HOL)	18	1.57
218	Donna Faber (USA)	11	1.57
219	Christine Damas (FRA)	14	1.57
220	Noelle Porter (USA)	4	1.54
221	Maya Kidowaki (JPN)	18	1.54
222	Leigh Anne Eldredge (USA)	12	1.54
223	Renata Baranski (POL)	16	1.53
224	Celine Cohen (SUI)	15	1.52
225	Jana Pospisilova (TCH)	11	1.52
226	Tammy Whittington (USA)	10	1.52
227	Andrea Tiezzi (ARG)	18	1.48
228	Claudia Hernandez (MEX)	8	1.47
229	Lisa Pennington (GBR)	15	1.46
230	Luciana Tella (VEN)	8	1.41
231	Sally McCann (AUS)	9	1.40
232	Leslie Allen (USA)	6	1.39
233	Andrea Berger (USA)	4	1.37
234	Mima Jausovec (YUG)	3	1.37
235	Olga Votavova (TCH)	12	1.33
236	Lilian Drescher (SUI)	5	1.33
237	Stephanie Faulkner (AUS)	18	1.32
238	Pascale Etchemendy (FRA)	14	1.31
239	Natasha Marcucci (ARG)	11	1.29
240	Annette Gerber (FRG)	13	1.29
241	Heather Crowe (USA)	10	1.29
242	Katharina Duell (FRG)	7	1.29
243	Lydie Van Hille (FRA)	11	1.28
244	Gabriela Mosca (ARG)	18	1.28
245	Silke Frankl (FRG)	9	1.26
246	Masako Yanagi (JPN)	13	1.26
247	Holly Ann Lloyd (USA)	11	1.26
248	Linda Barnard (RSA)	9	1.26
249	Helena Manset (USA)	8	1.25
250	Lindsay Bartlett (USA)	16	1.21

DOUBLES

1 Martina Navratilova (USA)
2 Pam Shriver (USA)
3 Claudia Kohde-Kilsch (FRG)
4 Lori McNeil (USA)
5 Gabriela Sabatini (ARG)
6 Helena Sukova (TCH)
7 Zina Garrison (USA)
8 Elizabeth Smylie (AUS)
9 Svetlana Parkhomenko (URS)
10 Kathy Jordan (USA)
11 Larisa Savchenko (URS)
12 Hana Mandlikova (TCH)
13 Steffi Graf (FRG)
14 Betsy Nagelsen (USA)
15 Wendy Turnbull (AUS)
16 Elise Burgin (USA)
17 Robin White (USA)
18 Anne Hobbs (GBR)
19 Rosalyn Fairbank (RSA)
20 Gigi Fernandez (USA)
21 Bettina Bunge (FRG)
22 Tine Scheuer-Larsen (DEN)
23 Anne White (USA)
24 Jana Novotna (TCH)
25 Eva Pfaff (FRG)
26 Barbara Potter (USA)
27 Catherine Suire (FRA)
28 Mary Lou Piatek Daniels (USA)
29 Janine Thompson (AUS)
30 Chris Evert (USA)
31 Mercedes Paz (ARG)
32 Jenny Byrne (AUS)
33 Laura Gildemeister (PER)
34 Anne Smith (USA)
35 Catherine Tanvier (FRA)
36 Candy Reynolds (USA)
37 Sharon Walsh Pete (USA)
38 Heather Ludloff (USA)
39 Peanut Louie Harper (USA)
40 Isabelle Demongeot (FRA)
40 Nathalie Tauziat (FRA)
42 Penny Barg (USA)
43 Jo Durie (GBR)
44 Leila Meskhi (URS)
45 Catarina Lindqvist (SWE)
46 Marcella Mesker (HOL)
47 Manuela Maleeva (BUL)
48 Patricia Hy (HKG)
49 Beth Herr (USA)
50 Nathalie Herreman (FRA)

PRIZE MONEY

The following table shows the prize money and bonuses won at all recognised tournaments which adopt the WITA guidelines and where entry is based on merit.

1	Steffi Graf (FRG)	$1,063,785
2	Martina Navratilova (USA)	932,102
3	Chris Evert (USA)	769,943
4	Pam Shriver (USA)	703,030
5	Helena Sukova (TCH)	490,792
6	Gabriela Sabatini (ARG)	465,933
7	Lori McNeil (USA)	401,524
8	Hana Mandlikova (TCH)	340,410
9	Zina Garrison (USA)	328,694
10	Claudia Kohde-Kilsch (FRG)	321,773
11	Manuela Maleeva (BUL)	245,100
12	Wendy Turnbull (AUS)	207,467
13	Bettina Bunge (FRG)	171,855
14	Catarina Lindqvist (SWE)	145,883
15	Elizabeth Smylie (AUS)	145,642
16	Raffaella Reggi (ITA)	138,527
17	Sylvia Hanika (FRG)	135,774
18	Katerina Maleeva (BUL)	135,393
19	Elise Burgin (USA)	130,133
20	Barbara Potter (USA)	114,533
21	Rosalyn Fairbank (RSA)	113,258
22	Gigi Fernandez (USA)	101,841
23	Robin White (USA)	99,752
24	Betsy Nagelsen (USA)	98,786
25	Jana Novotna (TCH)	95,347
26	Nathalie Tauziat (FRA)	92,208
27	Sandra Cecchini (ITA)	88,775
28	Larisa Savchenko (URS)	83,732
29	Jo Durie (GBR)	78,765
30	Kathy Jordan (USA)	78,130
31	Eva Pfaff (FRG)	77,208
32	Anne Hobbs (GBR)	75,733
33	Anne Minter (AUS)	73,972
34	Dianne Balestrat (AUS)	69,245
35	Kathy Rinaldi (USA)	68,479
36	Carling Bassett Seguso (CAN)	67,259
37	Terry Phelps (USA)	67,121
38	Helen Kelesi (CAN)	66,203
39	Camille Benjamin (USA)	65,040
40	Natalia Zvereva (URS)	64,333
41	Ann Henricksson (USA)	61,031
42	Anne White (USA)	60,415
43	Isabelle Demongeot (FRA)	59,810
44	Mary Joe Fernandez (USA)	57,567
45	Svetlana Parkhomenko (URS)	54,642
46	Kate Gompert (USA)	54,603
47	Wendy White (USA)	54,428
48	Gretchen Rush Magers (USA)	54,407
49	Mercedes Paz (ARG)	54,355
50	Tine Scheuer-Larsen (DEN)	52,721
51	Kathleen Horvath (USA)	52,704
52	Sharon Walsh Pete (USA)	52,659
53	Catherine Tanvier (FRA)	52,591
54	Silke Meier (FRG)	52,025
55	Nicole Provis (AUS)	51,695
56	Laura Gildemeister (PER)	50,221
57	Sabrina Goles (YUG)	49,762
58	Barbara Gerken (USA)	49,657
59	Etsuko Inoue (JPN)	49,289
60	Alycia Moulton (USA)	49,224
61	Stephanie Rehe (USA)	49,150
62	Arantxa Sanchez (ESP)	49,125
63	Jenny Byrne (AUS)	48,280
64	Isabel Cueto (FRG)	48,268
65	Catherine Suire (FRA)	46,641
66	Elna Reinach (RSA)	44,788
67	Beth Herr (USA)	44,440
68	Elly Hakami (USA)	43,983
69	Hu Na (USA)	42,547
70	Sara Gomer (GBR)	42,495
71	Lisa Bonder (USA)	42,292
72	Heather Ludloff (USA)	41,548
73	Peanut Louie Harper (USA)	40,929
74	Nathalie Herreman (FRA)	40,561
75	Mary Lou Piatek Daniels (USA)	39,831
76	Bettina Fulco (ARG)	39,620
77	Patricia Tarabini (ARG)	39,560
78	Anne Smith (USA)	38,820
79	Patricia Hy (HKG)	38,403
80	Judith Polzl Wiesner (AUT)	37,569
81	Marianne Werdel (USA)	37,296
82	Louise Field (AUS)	35,688
83	Beverly Bowes (USA)	35,068
84	Halle Cioffi (USA)	34,916
85	Dinky Van Rensburg (RSA)	33,816
86	Regina Marsikova (TCH)	33,382
87	Belinda Cordwell (NZL)	32,629
88	Claudia Porwik (FRG)	31,855
89	Michelle Torres (USA)	31,415
90	Karen Schimper (RSA)	31,328
91	Molly Van Nostrand (USA)	31,135
92	Tina Mochizuki (USA)	30,836
93	Elizabeth Minter (AUS)	30,740
94	Niege Dias (BRA)	30,164
95	Patty Fendick (USA)	30,092
96	Julie Halard (FRA)	29,960
97	Anna Maria Fernandez (USA)	29,644
98	Iwona Kuczynska (POL)	28,656
99	Kathrin Keil (USA)	28,650
100	Carina Karlsson (SWE)	28,626
101	Akiko Kijimuta (JPN)	28,327
102	Laura Garrone (ITA)	28,280
103	Pascale Paradis (FRA)	28,257
104	Melissa Gurney (USA)	28,150
105	Cammie MacGregor (USA)	28,070
106	Vicki Nelson Dunbar (USA)	27,611
107	Sandy Collins (USA)	27,421
108	Petra Huber (AUT)	27,394
109	Adriana Villagran (ARG)	27,217
110	Marcella Mesker (HOL)	26,728
111	Iva Budarova (TCH)	26,505
112	Wiltrud Probst (FRG)	26,411
113	Mariana Perez Roldan (ARG)	26,113
114	Candy Reynolds (USA)	25,854
115	Leila Meskhi (URS)	25,772
116	Penny Barg (USA)	25,532

117	Natalia Bykova (URS)	24,285	159	Brenda Schultz (HOL)	15,315
118	Regina Rajchrtova (TCH)	24,267	160	Gabriella Dinu (RUM)	14,760
119	Annabel Croft (GBR)	24,185	161	JoAnne Russell (USA)	14,753
120	Ann Devries (BEL)	23,910	162	Debbie Spence (USA)	14,653
121	Federica Bonsignori (ITA)	22,661	163	Lise Gregory (RSA)	13,595
122	Janine Thompson (AUS)	22,608	164	Paula Smith (USA)	13,262
123	Andrea Holikova (TCH)	22,007	165	Nicole Jagerman (HOL)	13,226
124	Manon Bollegraf (HOL)	21,788	166	Masako Yanagi (JPN)	13,209
125	Lea Antonoplis (USA)	21,517	167	Shawn Stafford (USA)	13,053
126	Louise Allen (USA)	21,109	168	Monica Reinach (RSA)	12,819
127	Julie Richardson (NZL)	21,084	169	Terry Holladay (USA)	12,720
128	Kumiko Okamoto (JPN)	20,994	170	Amy Frazier (USA)	12,607
129	Maria Lindstrom (SWE)	20,094	171	Julie Salmon (GBR)	12,286
130	Susan Sloane (USA)	19,861	172	Maya Kidowaki (JPN)	11,962
131	Eva Krapl (SUI)	19,812	173	Laura Lapi (ITA)	11,900
132	Pat Medrado (BRA)	19,033	174	Gabriela Mosca (ARG)	11,829
133	Marianne Van Der Torre (HOL)	18,897	175	Carin Bakkum (HOL)	11,636
134	Miki Mizokuchi (JPN)	18,800	176	Alexia Dechaume (FRA)	11,384
135	Michelle Jaggard (AUS)	18,735	177	Gisele Miro (BRA)	11,337
136	Laura Golarsa (ITA)	18,713	178	Kim Steinmetz (USA)	11,310
137	Angeliki Kanellopoulou (GRE)	18,708	179	Dee Ann Hansel (USA)	11,037
138	Christina Singer (FRG)	18,668	180	Niurka Sodupe	11,037
139	Emmanuelle Derly (FRA)	18,597	181	Amy Jonsson (NOR)	10,782
140	Grace Kim (USA)	18,428	182	Monique Javer (USA)	10,779
141	Pam Casale (USA)	18,268	183	Natalia Medvedeva (URS)	10,761
142	Claudia Monteiro (BRA)	18,013	184	Katrina Adams (USA)	10,545
143	Barbara Paulus (FRG)	17,933	185	Katerina Bohmova (TCH)	10,291
144	Clare Wood (GBR)	17,832	186	Pilar Vasquez (PER)	10,270
145	Cynthia MacGregor (USA)	17,478	187	Caterina Nozzoli (ITA)	10,192
146	Radka Zrubakova (TCH)	17,346	188	Linda Ferrando (ITA)	10,022
147	Marie Christine Calleja (FRA)	17,195	189	Hellas Ter Riet (HOL)	9,980
148	Virginia Ruzici (YUG)	16,840	190	Melissa Brown (USA)	9,936
149	Ronni Reis USA)	16,664	191	Heather Crowe (USA)	9,806
150	Valda Lake (GBR)	16,140	192	Jenny Klitch (USA)	9,705
151	Andrea Betzner (FRG)	16,112	193	Ilana Berger (ISR)	9,620
152	Susan Mascarin (USA)	16,101	194	Jennifer Santrock (USA)	9,440
153	Jill Hetherington (CAN)	15,823	195	Jaime Kaplan (USA)	9,071
154	Emiko Okagawa (JPN)	15,792	196	Emilse Rapponi Longo (ARG)	8,907
155	Christiane Jolissaint (SUI)	15,708	197	Denisa Krajcovicova (TCH)	8,862
156	Csilla Bartos Cserepy (SUI)	15,545	198	Marie José Llorca (ESP)	8,770
157	Jennifer Mundel Reinbold (RSA)	15,509	199	Andrea Tiezzi (ARG)	8,708
158	Sandra Wasserman (BEL)	15,430	200	Cecilia Fernandez (USA)	8,582

Players who have won more than $1 million in prize money

1	Martina Navratilova	$12,724,417	12	Evonne Goolagong Cawley	$1,399,431
2	Chris Evert	7,965,861	13	Andrea Jaeger	1,379,066
3	Pam Shriver	3,375,777	14	Kathy Jordan	1,374,114
4	Hana Mandlikova	3,005,091	15	Rosie Casals	1,327,143
5	Wendy Turnbull	2,614,704	16	Zina Garrison	1,198,961
6	Helena Sukova	2,070,485	17	Virginia Ruzici	1,184,478
7	Billie Jean King	1,965,462	18	Barbara Potter	1,169,248
8	Steffi Graf	1,909,312	19	Manuela Maleeva	1,102,030
9	Tracy Austin	1,908,715	20	Bettina Bunge	1,095,881
10	Claudia Kohde-Kilsch	1,617,388	21	Sylvia Hanika	1,049,946
11	Virginia Wade	1,542,276	22	Betty Stove	1,047,356

MISCELLANEOUS TOURNAMENTS AND SPECIAL EVENTS

EEC CHAMPIONSHIPS ($923,000)

ANTWERP, 26 OCTOBER–1 NOVEMBER
MEN'S SINGLES – Quarter-finals: I. Lendl (TCH) d. T. Mayotte (USA) 6–3 6–3; P. Cash (AUS) d. W. Fibak (POL) 4–6 6–3 6–4; M. Mecir (TCH) d. J. P. McEnroe (USA) 6–4 6–4; M. Wilander (SWE) d. B. Gilbert (USA) 6–2 6–4. ***Semi-finals:*** Lendl d. Cash 6–4 7–6; Mecir d. Wilander 6–1 6–3. ***Final:*** Lendl d. Mecir 5–7 6–1 6–4 6–3.

ROYAL BANK OF SCOTLAND SCOTTISH CHAMPIONSHIPS

CRAIGLOCKHART, EDINBURGH, 8–14 JUNE
MEN'S SINGLES – Quarter-finals: I. Lendl (TCH) d. A. D. Roche (AUS) 7–6 7–5; A. Jarryd (SWE) d. D. Tyson (AUS) 6–4 3–6 6–3; J. Kriek (USA) d. J. Canter (USA)7–5 2–6 7–5; A. Gomez (ECU) d. D. Pate 6–2 3–6 6–4. ***Semi-finals:*** Jarryd d. Lendl 2–2 ret'd; Gomez d. Kriek 6–3 6–1. ***Final:*** Jarryd div'd with Gomez.

HAMLET CLASSIC

JERICHO, NY, 24–30 AUGUST
MEN'S SINGLES – Quarter-finals: D. Pate d. I. Lendl (TCH) 6–3 6–7 7–6; P. Annacone d. A. Gomez (ECU) 6–3 6–2; J. B. Svensson (SWE) d. P. Cash (AUS) 6–3 6–2; H. Leconte (FRA) w.o. J. S. Connors. ***Semi-finals:*** Pate d. Annacone 7–6 6–4; Svensson d. Leconte 6–3 6–3. ***Final:*** Pate d. Svensson 7–6 3–6 6–3.

AT & T TOURNAMENT

ATLANTA, 5–11 OCTOBER
MEN'S SINGLES – Semi-finals: P. Annacone d. I. Lendl (TCH) 6–3 6–2; J. P. McEnroe d. J. S. Connors 6–4 6–4. ***Final:*** McEnroe d. Annacone 6–4 7–6.

WATERFORD CRYSTAL YOUNG MASTERS ($150,000)

FRIEDRICHSHAFEN, 17–21 NOVEMBER
21 AND UNDER
Thomas Muster, the 20-year-old Austrian No. 1, became only the second man to win the $150,000 Waterford Crystal Young Masters title when, in Friedrichshafen in November, he outpaced Jonas Svensson of Sweden to win an exciting final 6–4 4–6 7–5 6–2 that earned him $30,000. Boris Becker, the holder for the past three years, returned to competition following an enforced break caused by illness and injury, and was surprisingly beaten in the last of the round-robin matches by Magnus Gustafsson. The improving Swede had lifted his ATP ranking to 51 in the Stockholm tournament three weeks earlier with victories over Mikael Pernfors and Eric Jelen. 'But this was much more satisfying', he said. It was Muster who accounted for Gustafsson 6–2 6–4 in one semi-final while Svensson, playing virtually faultless tennis, had accounted for another Austrian, Alexander Antonitsch, 6–1 6–1 in the other.

RED GROUP: 1st: M. Gustafsson (SWE) d. C. Pistolesi (ITA) 3–6 6–3 6–3; d. N. Kulti (SWE) 6–2 6–1; d. B. Becker 2–6 6–4 6–2. ***2nd:*** Becker d. Kulti 7–5 6–3; d. Pistolesi 6–1 6–2. ***3rd:*** Kulti d. Pistolesi 7–5 3–6 6–2. ***4th:*** Pistolesi.

Tomas Muster won the Austrian National Championships and the Young Masters title, as well as beating Emilio Sanchez to reach the semi-finals in Vienna.
(T. Hindley)

BLUE GROUP: 1st: T. Muster (AUT) d. C. U. Steeb 7–6 6–3; d. F. Schaffner 6–0 6–0; d. E. Winogradsky (FRA) 6–4 3–6 6–3. ***2nd:*** Winogradsky d. Schaffner 6–3 6–3; d. Steeb 7–6 6–2. ***3rd:*** Steeb d. Schaffner 6–4 6–4. ***4th:*** Schaffner.
GREEN GROUP: 1st: A. Antonitsch (AUT) d. U. Stenlund (SWE) 6–2 7–5; d. D. Wheaton (USA) 4–6 7–6 6–0; d. C. Bergstrom (SWE) 3–6 7–6 6–4. ***2nd:*** Wheaton d. Bergstrom 6–4 6–4; d. Stenlund 4–6 6–2 7–5. ***3rd:*** Bergstrom d. Stenlund 3–6 6–1 6–1. ***4th:*** Stenlund.
GOLD GROUP: 1st: J. Svensson (SWE) d. O. Kristiansson (SWE) 6–1 6–2; d. J. Carlsson (SWE) 6–0 6–1; d. P. Kuhnen 6–7 6–3 7–5. ***2nd:*** Kuhnen d. Carlsson 2–6 6–3 7–5; d. Kristiansson 6–1 6–2. ***3rd:*** Carlsson d. Kristiansson 6–3 7–6. ***4th:*** Kristiansson.
Semi-finals: Muster d. Gustafsson 6–2 6–4; Svensson d. Antonitsch 6–1 6–1. ***Final:*** Muster d. Svensson 6–4 4–6 7–5 6–2.

US INTERCOLLEGIATE CHAMPIONSHIPS

MEN'S SINGLES – Quarter-finals: A. Burrow (Miami) d. S. Cannon (Tennessee) 7–6 6–2; M. Kaplan (Cal./Irvine) d. S. Warner (Nevada/Las Vegas) 6–4 2–6 6–4; O. Lorrin (Oklahoma) d. N. Caswell (Furman) 7–6 6–4; D. Goldberg (Michigan) d. G. Van Emburgh (Kentucky) 6–3 6–4. ***Semi-finals:*** Burrow d. Kaplan 7–6 2–6 6–1; Goldberg d. Lorrin 6–4 2–6 6–1. ***Final:*** Burrow d. Goldberg 2–6 6–1 6–4.
MEN'S DOUBLES – Final: R. Leach/S. Melville (S. Cal.) d. J. Barham/D. Yates (Cal./Irvine) 3–6 6–4 7–5.
WOMEN'S SINGLES – Quarter-finals: P. Fendick (Stanford) d. J. Hetherington (Florida) 6–2 6–1; J. Santrock (SMU) d. K. Labuschagne (Texas A & M) 7–5 6–2; L. Green (Stanford) d. T. Whittington (Florida) 6–4 6–3; S. Stafford (Florida) d. B. Bowes (Texas) 6–7 6–3 6–3. ***Semi-finals:*** Fendick d. Santrock 6–1 6–3; Stafford d. Green 6–4 6–0. ***Final:*** Fendick d. Stafford 6–2 5–7 6–2.
WOMEN'S DOUBLES – Final: K. Adams/D. Donnelly (Northwestern) d. Fendick/S. Savides (Stanford) 6–2 6–4.

REFERENCE SECTION

BIOGRAPHIES
ALL-TIME GREATS
CHAMPIONSHIP ROLLS

Illness, injury and the departure of his coach, Gunther Bosch, brought a disappointing year for Boris Becker, who won only three titles and failed in his bid for a third Wimbledon crown when he fell in the second round to Peter Doohan. *(T. Hindley)*

Jana Novotna of Czechoslovakia developed a formidable doubles partnership with Catherine Suire, as well as reaching the last 16 in singles at Wimbledon and the US Open, improving her ranking from 182 to 47. *(A. Evans)*

BIOGRAPHIES

Christine Forrest

Abbreviations used in this section:

f	final	D Cup	Davis Cup
sf	semi-final	Fed Cup	Federation Cup
qf	quarter-final	W Cup	Wightman Cup
r/u	runner-up	FC Cup	Family Circle Cup
def	defaulted	Champ	Championship
retd	retired	Int	International
fs	final set	Inv	Invitation
rr	round-robin	Jun	Junior
b-p	break-point	Nat	National
s-p	set-point	Pro	Professional
m-p	match-point	Tourn	Tournament
t-b	tie-break	CS	Colgate Series
1r	first round	TS	Toyota Series
2s	second set	HC	Hard Court
RH	right-handed	VS	Virginia Slims
LH	left-handed	WCT	World Championship Tennis
2HB	2-handed backhand	WTT	World Team Tennis
2HF	2-handed forehand	GP	Grand Prix
US CC	US Clay Court Championships	LIPC	Lipton International Players Championships

Men and women who appear in the top 100 on the ATP and WITA computer rankings are included below, as well as leading doubles players, a few prominent players who compete less than usual nowadays, plus some newcomers. We gratefully acknowledge the assistance of the Nabisco Grand Prix, ATP, Virginia Slims and WITA in supplying additional biographical information.
The final ranking for each year is shown in brackets following the date.
1986 doubles ranking is shown in brackets after 1987 ranking where applicable.
Note: 1987 rankings for women are season-end rankings, and those for men are year-end rankings.

ANDRE AGASSI (USA)
Born Las Vegas, 29 April, 1970, and lives there; RH; 5ft 10in; 150lb; final 1987 ATP ranking 25; 1987 prize money $205,555.
Suffers from Osgood Schlatter's disease, which causes a bone in the knee to grow improperly. ***1984:*** Ranked 4 in US Boys' 14s and won Nat 14s. ***1985:*** (618) Receiving expert council from Pancho Gonzales, he tested the waters of men's circuit. ***1986:*** (91) Downed Mayotte and S. Davis on way to qf Stratton Mountain. ***1987:*** Reached first GP f at Seoul, won his 1st GP title at Itaparica at end of season and d. Jarryd *en route* to sf Basel. ***1987 HIGHLIGHTS – SINGLES: French Open*** 2r (d. Arraya 6–2 4–6 6–1 7–5, lost Kuchna 6–4 6–3 6–3), ***Wimbledon*** 1r (lost Leconte [seed 9] 6–2 6–1 6–2), ***US OPEN*** 1r (lost Leconte [seed 11] 6–4 7–6 4–6 6–3); ***won*** Itaparica (d. Daher 5–7 6 –0 6–3, Yzaga 6–3 6–4, Gilbert 6–1 6–3, Jaite 6–2 7–5, Mattar 7–6 6–2); ***r/u*** Seoul (d. Cox, Simpson, Fitzgerald 6–1 6–3, Testerman 2–6 6–3 6–2, lost Grabb 1–6 6–4 6–2); ***sf*** Stratton Mountain

(d. Jensen 3–6 6–3 6–3, Cash 7–6 7–6, Hooper 6–4 6–7 6–3, lost Lendl 6–2 5–7 7–3), ***sf*** Basel (d. Jarryd 6–2 6–3, Vajda 6–4 6–3, Navratil 6–2 0–6 6–3, lost Agenor 6–1 6–4).

RONALD AGENOR (Haiti)
Born Rabat, Morocco, 13 November, 1964; lives Bordeaux, France and Port-au-Prince; RH; 5ft 11in; 168lb; final 1987 ATP ranking 44; 1987 prize money $140,176.
Lived some time in Zaire. ***1985:*** (50) With a stream of steady results including six qf showings on GP tour, he moved up 366 places on ATP computer. ***1986:*** (74) Performing solidly on clay again, he beat Pate, Arias, Tulasne and Jaite among others and reached sf Bordeaux. ***1987:*** Took Lendl to 4s French Open before reaching his 1st GP f at Gstaad and being r/u again in Bordeaux and Basel. ***1987 HIGHLIGHTS – SINGLES: French Open*** 1r (lost Lendl 7–5 7–6 0–6 6–3), ***US Open*** 2r (d. Burrow 6–3 6–7 6–3 6–2, lost Gomez [seed 9] 6–4 6–2 4–6 7–6); ***won*** Dortmund Challenger (d. Oresar 4–6 7–5 6–3); ***r/u*** Gstaad (d. Krishnan 6–3 6–3, Smid 6–2 6–3, Vajda 7–5 6–1, Mezzadri 6–7 6–4 6–3, lost E. Sanchez 6–2 6–3 7–6), ***r/u*** Bordeaux (d. Aguilera 4–6 6–3 6–4, Cahill 7–6 4–6 6–3, Shaw 7–6 6–7 6–4, Derlin 6–1 6–3, lost E. Sanchez 5–7 6–4 6–4), ***r/u*** Basel (d. de Miguel 6–1 6–4, Smid 7–5 2–6 6–3, Woodforde 7–5 6–7 6–4, Agassi 6–1 6–4, lost Noah 7–6 6–4 6–4).

MATT ANGER (USA)
Born Walnut Creek, Cal., 20 June, 1963; lives Pleasanton, Cal.; RH; 6ft 2in; 170lb; final 1987 ATP ranking 91; 1987 prize money $97,522.
1981: (361) Coached by Mark Elliott of Pleasanton, he won Wimbledon Jun. ***1984:*** (177) All-American at USC for 3rd straight year. ***1985:*** (31) Began year at 117 but raised level of his game to finish at 31 after winning his first GP title in Johannesburg in autumn. ***1986:*** (59) Last 16 at Wimbledon where he was twice within a point of extending Lendl to 5s; last 16 US Open, r/u Johannesburg. ***1987:*** Sf Beckenham was best showing. Married Kristin Dyan Thomas 28 March. ***1987 HIGHLIGHTS – SINGLES: Australian Open*** 3r (d. Freeman 6–4 1–0 ret'd, Mansdorf 7–6 6–3 3–6 6–3), lost Lendl [seed 1] 6–4 6–2 6–7 6–2), ***French Open*** 2r (d. Fitzgerald 7–6 7–5 6–3, lost Osterthun 6–2 7–6 6–2), ***Wimbledon*** 3r (d. Colombo 6–3 7–5 7–6, Krishnan 6–2 6–4 6–2, lost Edberg [seed 4] 7–6 6–2 6–2), ***US Open*** 1r (lost McEnroe 6–3 6–2 6–2); ***sf*** Beckenham (lost S. Davis 6–1 7–5). ***1987 HIGHLIGHTS – DOUBLES:*** (with Evernden) ***won*** Brisbane (d. Dyke/Masur 7–6 6–2).

PAUL ANNACONE (USA)
Born New York, 20 March, 1963 and lives there; RH; 6ft 1in; 175lb; final 1987 ATP ranking 32 singles, 9 doubles; 1987 prize money $248,209.
Son Nicholas (born June 1987). ***1982:*** (389) All-American at Univ. of Tennessee (and again in 1983). ***1984:*** (94) Surprisingly lost qf NCAA Champ but as qualifier reached qf first Wimbledon. ***1985:*** (13) Surged into top 20 with sizzling autumn including two GP victories in LA and Brisbane, and won Australian Open doubles with Van Rensburg. Married Tracy Kohr Nov. ***1986:*** (43) Joined American D Cup squad and contributed to only victory in 3–1 sf loss to Australia, taking doubles in 5s with Flach over Cash/McNamee. Upset McEnroe 1r US Open. ***1987:*** Last 16 Australian Open; qf Philadelphia and Forest Hills. ***1987 HIGHLIGHTS – SINGLES: Australian Open*** last 16, unseeded (d. Mmoh 7–6 7–6 6–4, Wood 6–7 4–6 6–3 6–2 6–4, Leconte [seed 5] 1–6 4–6 6–3 6–4 10–8, lost Cash [seed 11] 6–4 6–1 6–7 1–6 6–2), ***French Open*** 2r (d. Motta 6–4 6–1 6–3, lost Wilander [seed 4] 6–3 6–4 4–6 6–4), ***Wimbledon*** 3r (d. Srejber 7–6 6–4 6–1, Masur 6–7 6–4 7–6 6–7 6–3, lost Forget 4–6 6–4 4–6 6–2 6–4), ***US Open*** 1r (lost Krishnan 6–0 7–5 6–1). ***1987 HIGHLIGHTS – DOUBLES:*** (with Van Rensburg unless stated) ***won*** LIPC (d. Flach/Seguso 6–2 6–4 6–4), ***won*** Chicago (d. DePalmer/Donnelly 6–3 7–6), [Curren] ***won*** Tokyo (d. Gomez/Jarryd 6–4 7–6), Stratton Mountain divided with Flach/Seguso; ***r/u*** Orlando (lost Stewart/Warwick 2–6 7–6 6–4). ***1987 HIGHLIGHTS – MIXED DOUBLES:*** (with Nagelsen) ***r/u US Open*** (lost Navratilova/E. Sanchez 6–4 6–7 7–6). ***CAREER HIGHLIGHTS – SINGLES: Wimbledon – qf 1984*** (d. Kriek, lost Connors 6–2 6–4 6–2). ***CAREER HIGHLIGHTS – DOUBLES:*** (with Van Rensburg) ***Australian Open – won 1985*** (d. Edmondson/Warwick 3–6 7–6 6–4 6–4); ***LIPC – won 1985*** (d. Stewart/Warwick 7–5 7–5 6–4), ***won 1987***.

ALEXANDER ANTONITSCH (Austria)
Born Villach, 8 February, 1966; lives Perchtoldsdorf; RH; 6ft 2in; 185lb; final 1987 ATP ranking 115; 1987 prize money $48,450.
Coached by Stan Franker. Left-handed for everything except tennis, in which he switched to the right hand after breaking his left arm playing ice-hockey. ***1982:*** Nat Jun Champ. ***1986:*** (217) Qf St Vincent. ***1987:*** Sf Livingston and Young Masters. ***1987 HIGHLIGHTS – SINGLES: French Open*** 2r (d. Laurendeau 6–3 2–6 6–3 7–6, lost Davin 5–7 6–3 6–2 6–3), ***Wimbledon*** 1r (lost Doohan 4–6 7–5 6–2 4–6 9–7), ***US Open*** 1r (lost Reneberg 6–3 6–2 6–2); ***sf*** Livingston (d. Goldie 6–4 7–5, Annacone 7–6 2–6 6–4, Freeman 0–6 7–6 6–4, lost Kriek 6–3 2–6 6–4), ***sf*** Young Masters (d. Stenlund 6–2 7–5, Wheaton 4–6 7–6 6–0, Bergstrom 3–6 7–6 6–4 in rr, lost Svensson 6–1 6–1).

JIMMY ARIAS (USA)
Born Buffalo, NY, 16 August 1964; lives Jericho, NY; RH; 5ft 9in; 145lb; final 1987 ATP ranking 34; 1987 prize money $129,711; career prize money $1,256,417.
Coached by Brian Gottfried. ***1981:*** (81) Under guidance of Nick Bollettieri, climbed into top 100, beat Teltscher on USTA Penn circuit and won French Open mixed doubles with A. Jaeger. ***1982:*** (20) Beaten in 1r of 6 of first 8 tournaments, he then made tremendous surge to reach f Washington and US CC and won his first GP event (Japan Asian Open) in autumn. ***1983:*** (6) Won 4 tournaments, including Italian Open and US CC; sf US Open. ***1984:*** (14) Reached qf French Open and 6 sf. ***1985:*** (21) Had disappointing results until end of year when he reached sf Canadian Open, f Japan Open and sf South African Open. ***1986:*** (48) Helped US past Ecuador in D Cup. ***1987:*** After D Cup loss in Paraguay he consulted sports psychologist Jim Loehe, who helped him to improve his attitude, enjoy his tennis more and reach f Monte Carlo. Yet, still lacking motivation, he took 3 months off from Aug. ***1987 HIGHLIGHTS – SINGLES: French Open*** last 16, unseeded (d. Scanlon 6–2 7–6 6–2, J. B. Svensson 6–4 6–0 6–2, Arrese 4–6 7–6 6–2 4–6 6–2, lost Becker [seed 2] 5–7 6–3 6–2 6–0), ***Wimbledon*** 1r (lost Cane 6–7 6–2 7–6 6–3), ***US Open*** 1r (lost Fleming 7–6 6–7 6–2 7–6); ***r/u*** Monte Carlo (d. Westphal, Becker 6–3 6–3, Krickstein 7–5 6–1, K. Carlsson 6–0 2–2 ret'd, Skoff 7–5 6–1, lost Wilander 4–6 7–5 6–1 6–3). ***CAREER HIGHLIGHTS – SINGLES: Italian Open – won 1983*** (d. Higueras 6–2 6–7 6–1 6–4); ***US CC – won 1983*** (d. Gomez 6–4 2–6 6–4), ***r/u 1982*** (lost Higueras 7–5 5–7 6–3); ***US Open – sf 1983*** (d. Nystrom 6–0 fs, Noah 7–5 fs, lost Lendl 6–2 7–6 6–1). ***CAREER HIGHLIGHTS – MIXED DOUBLES:*** (with A. Jaeger) ***French Open – won 1981*** (d. Gonzalez/Teeguarden 4–6 6–3 11–9, McNair/Stove [seed 2] 7–6 6–4).

DIANNE FROMHOLTZ BALESTRAT (Australia)
Born Albury, NSW, 10 August, 1956; lives Sydney; LH; 5ft 4in; 120lb; final 1987 WITA ranking 21; 1987 prize money $69,245.
1973: Displayed her considerable promise by winning ten minor tournaments, mostly in Great Britain. ***1974:*** R/u South African Open (d. M. Court in sf, lost K. Reid). ***1975:*** (20) Won Wimbledon Plate; r/u US CC; sf Canadian Open. ***1976:*** (5) Sf US Open and US Indoor; upset world No. 1 Chris Evert in 1r VS Boston. ***1977:*** (8) R/u Australian Open singles, won doubles with Gourlay Cawley. ***1978:*** (10) R/u VS Detroit. ***1979:*** (6) Sf Avon Champs; sf French Open. ***1980:*** (12) R/u US Indoor. ***1981:*** (38) Sf Berlin (d. Mandlikova). ***1982:*** (32). ***1983:*** (75) Married French businessman Claude Balestrat and decided to quit tennis at US Open, only to return 15 months later. ***1984:*** (99). ***1985:*** (30) R/u Sydney and was named the Comeback Player of Year. ***1986:*** (21) Had wins over M. Maleeva, Sabatini and Lindqvist, winning 19 of 32 matches across the year. ***1987:*** Reached qf Wimbledon and f Arizona. ***1987 HIGHLIGHTS – SINGLES: Australian Open*** 3r, seed 15 (bye, d. Rush 6–3 6–4 6–2, lost Hobbs 6–4 6–2), ***French Open*** 2r (d. Holladay 6–2 6–3, lost M. Maleeva [seed 7] 6–2 6–0), ***Wimbledon*** qf, unseeded (d. Byrne 6–4 6–1, M. Maleeva 6–7 6–1 8–6, Fulco 7–6 6–0, M. J. Fernandez 7–5 6–2, lost Navratilova [seed 1] 6–2 6–1), ***US Open*** 1r (lost Bassett 6–4 6–2); ***r/u*** VS Arizona (d. Wasserman 6–4 6–4, Cueto 6–3 6–2, Suire 6–2 6–0, Walsh Pete 7–5 7–5, lost A. White 6–1 6–2). ***CAREER HIGHLIGHTS – SINGLES: Australian Open – r/u Jan. 1977*** (d. Krantzcke, lost Reid 7–5 6–2); ***South African Open – r/u 1974*** (d. DuPlooy 8–6 fs, Court 6–4 6–4, lost Reid 6–3 7–5); ***US CC – r/u 1975*** (d. Riedel, Ebbinghaus, lost Evert 6–3 6–4); ***US Indoor – r/u 1979*** (d. Navratilova 6–1 fs, lost Goolagong Cawley 6–3 6–4); ***French Open – sf 1979*** (d. Ruzici 6–0 6–4, lost Evert Lloyd

6–1 6–3), ***sf 1980*** seed 5 (d. King 6–1 6–4, lost Ruzici 7–6 6–1); ***US Open – sf 1976*** (d. Russell, Newberry, Liess, lost Goolagong Cawley 7–6 6–0); ***Italian Open – sf 1975*** (lost Navratilova 7–6 6–3); ***Avon Champs – sf 1979*** (d. Stevens, Evert Lloyd 6–2 6–3, lost Austin 7–5 6–2); ***US Indoor – r/u 1980*** (d. King 7–6 6–3, lost Austin 6–1 2–6 6–2). ***CAREER HIGHLIGHTS – DOUBLES: Australian Open*** – [Gourlay Cawley] ***won Jan. 1977*** (d. Reid/Nagelsen 5–7 6–1 7–5); ***South African Open*** – [Court] ***r/u 1974***.

JEREMY BATES (Great Britain)
Born Solihull, 19 June, 1962 and lives there; RH; 5ft 11in; 163lb; 1987 ATP ranking 89; 1987 prize money $51,612.
Coached by Warren Jacques. ***1982:*** (329) Joined British D Cup squad. ***1983:*** (256). ***1984:*** (185). ***1985:*** (99) Sf Tel Aviv, qf Bristol. ***1986:*** (187) Qf Bristol. ***1987:*** Sf Hong Kong and won Wimbledon mixed doubles with Durie. ***1987 HIGHLIGHTS – SINGLES: Australian Open*** 2r (bye, lost Mecir [seed 6] 4–6 6–2 6–1 6–3), ***Wimbledon*** 3r (d. Fleming 7–6 7–6 7–6, Giammalva 6–3 6–3 6–2, lost Zivojinovic 7–6 7–5 7–6); ***sf*** Hong Kong (d. Kratzmann 2–6 7–5 6–3, Rive 5–7 6–4 6–4, Nijssen 6–4 6–4, lost Fitzgerald 6–3 6–4). ***1987 HIGHLIGHTS – MIXED DOUBLES:*** (with Durie) ***won Wimbledon*** (d. Cahill/Provis 7–6 6–3).

BORIS BECKER (West Germany)
Born Leimen, 22 November, 1967; lives Monte Carlo; RH; 6ft 2in; 175lb; final 1987 ATP ranking 5 singles, 16 (13) doubles; 1987 prize money $558,979; career prize money $2,658,929.
Coached by Bob Brett. Girlfriend Benedicte Courtin. ***1982:*** Won first of three consecutive German Nat Jun Champs. ***1983:*** (564) R/u Orange Bowl 16s. ***1984:*** (65) R/u US Open Jun and qf Australian Open in first big men's showing. ***1985:*** (6) Won Queens Club, Wimbledon, Cincinnati, becoming youngest men's titlist at Wimbledon, the first German, and the first unseeded player to capture the world's most prestigious event. Closed year with D Cup wins over Edberg and Wilander in f as Germany lost 3–2 to Sweden. Won inaugural Young Masters. ***1986:*** (2) Won tournaments in Chicago, Toronto, Sydney, Tokyo and Paris Indoor, but most notably won Wimbledon again in even more convincing fashion, dismissing Lendl in f without loss of a set and still younger than any other champ. Closed year with streak of 3 straight tournaments and 21 matches in a row before losing Masters f to Lendl. Won Young Masters in Jan. and Dec. ***1987:*** Split with coach Gunther Bosch Jan; trained by Frank Dick. At end of year Bob Brett became coach. Missed LIPC suffering from a form of typhus which seemed to weaken him and restrict his performance for several weeks, and he was further restricted by tendonitis of left knee for last 5 months of year. Won only 3 titles all year and going for his third consecutive Wimbledon singles title, fell 2r to Doohan. After US Open took time off in Germany with his family, returning refreshed in Oct. and qualified for Masters where he extended Lendl to 3s, but lost his Young Masters title. ***1987 HIGHLIGHTS – SINGLES: Australian Open*** last 16, seed 2 (bye, d. Dyke 6–7 6–1 6–4 6–7 6–2, Zivojinovic 6–3 6–3 3–6 6–3, lost Masur 4–6 7–6 6–4 6–7 6–2), ***French Open*** sf, seed 2 (d. Perez 6–0 6–1 7–5, Buckley 6–1 4–6 6–3 6–2, Sundstrom 6–1 3–6 6–3 6–1, Arias 5–7 6–3 6–2 6–0, Connors [seed 8] 6–3 6–3 7–5, lost Wilander [seed 4] 6–4 6–1 6–2), ***Wimbledon*** 2r, seed 1 (d. Novacek 6–4 6–2 6–4, lost Doohan 7–6 4–6 6–2 6–4), ***US Open*** last 16, seed 4 (d. Wilkison 4–6 4–6 7–5 6–4 6–2, Canter 6–4 6–2 7–6, Castle 6–4 5–7 6–2 7–5, lost Gilbert [seed 13] 2–6 6–7 7–6 7–5 6–1); ***won*** Indian Wells (d. Wilkison, S. Davis, E. Sanchez 6–3 7–5, Noah 6–4 6–2, Edberg 6–4 6–4 7–5), ***won*** Milan (d. Birner 6–1 6–3, Casal 6–2 6–4, Zivojinovic 6–2 3–6 6–2, Mecir 6–4 6–3), ***won*** Queens (d. Doohan 6–2 6–4, Fleming 6–4 6–2, Sadri 6–4 6–4, Pate 6–4 7–6, Mayotte 4–6 7–6 6–4, Connors 6–7 6–3 6–4); ***r/u*** Cincinnati (d. Freeman 3–6 6–3 6–1, Testerman 3–6 6–4 6–3, Rostagno 6–4 7–6, Pernfors 6–3 2–1 ret'd, Jarryd 6–3 6–3, lost Edberg 6–4 6–1); ***sf*** Tourn of Champs (d. Maciel 7–6 5–7 6–2, Avendano, de la Pena 6–4 7–6, Vilas 7–6 6–2, lost Gomez 4–6 6–4 6–3), ***sf*** Washington (d. Matuszewski 6–4 7–5, Ross 6–4 6–2, Berger 6–3 6–2, lost Gilbert 3–6 6–3 6–0), ***sf*** Montreal (d. K. Jones 7–5 6–4, Reneberg 6–2 6–2, Lundgren 1–6 6–2 6–1, lost Edberg 6–2 6–4), ***sf*** Sydney (d. Pawsat 6–4 6–0, Giammalva 6–2 6–4, Annacone 6–3 6–2, lost Cash 6–3 2–6 7–6). ***1987 HIGHLIGHTS – DOUBLES:*** (with Zivojinovic unless stated) ***won*** Brussels (d. Hooper/Leach 7–6 7–6), ***won*** Milan (d. Casal/Sanchez 3–6 6–3 6–4), [Kuhnen] ***won*** Frankfurt (d. Davis/Pate 6–4 6–3); [Jelen] ***r/u*** Indian Wells (lost Forget/Noah 6–4 7–6), [Seguso] ***r/u*** Sydney (lost

Cahill/Kratzmann 6–3 6–2). ***CAREER HIGHLIGHTS – SINGLES: Wimbledon – won 1985*** unseeded, d. Nystrom 3–6 7–6 6–1 4–6 9–7, Mayotte 6–3 4–6 6–7 7–6 6–2, Leconte 7–6 3–6 6–3 6–4, Jarryd 2–6 7–6 6–3 6–3, Curren 6–3 6–7 7–6 6–4), ***won 1986*** (d. Bengoechea, Tom Gullikson, McNamee, Pernfors 6–3 7–6 6–2, Mecir 6–4 6–2 7–6, Leconte 6–2 6–4 6–7 6–3, Lendl 6–4 6–3 7–5); ***Nabisco Masters – r/u 1985*** (lost Lendl 6–2 7–6 6–1), ***r/u 1986*** (d. Nystrom, Leconte, Wilander 6–3 fs, Edberg 6–4 6–4, lost Lendl 6–4 6–4 6–4); ***US Open – sf 1986*** (d. Michibata, Motta, Casal, Donnelly 6–4 6–3 6–7 6–4, Srejber 6–3 6–2 6–1, lost Mecir 4–6 6–3 6–4 3–6 6–3); ***French Open – qf 1986*** (d. Potier, Oresar, Teltscher, E. Sanchez 6–0 4–6 4–6 6–4 6–2, lost Pernfors 2–6 6–4 6–2 6–0).

EDUARDO BENGOECHEA (Argentina)
Born Cordoba, 2 July, 1959; lives Buenos Aires; RH; 6ft 1in; 172lb; final 1987 ATP ranking 24; 1987 prize money $110,748.
Coached by Daniel Garcia. ***1983:*** (271) won Argentine Nat Champ. ***1984:*** (111). ***1985:*** (103) Sf Marbella and Florence. ***1986:*** (79) Sf Geneva. ***1987:*** Reached 5 sf and had some big wins during the year, including Noah 1r Italian Open, Nystrom in Hamburg and Mecir in Barcelona. ***1987 HIGHLIGHTS – SINGLES: French Open*** 2r (d. Hlasek 6–4 6–7 7–5 4–6 6–4, lost Novacek 6–0 6–0 6–0); ***sf*** Hamburg (d. Purcell, Chesnokov 6–4 4–6 6–2, Nystrom 7–6 6–3, Pernfors 7–5 6–4, lost Mecir 7–6 6–1), ***sf*** Florence (d. Baldoni, Tous, Cane 6–3 6–2, lost De Minicis 6–3 4–6 6–4), ***sf*** Gstaad (d. Bahrami 6–4 6–2, Novacek 6–3 6–4, Tous 7–5 3–6 6–4, lost E. Sanchez 6–1 7–5), ***sf*** Hilversum (d. Aprili 6–4 7–6, Arrese 6–7 6–4 6–2, Steeb 3–6 7–6 6–2, lost Mecir 6–1 7–5), ***sf*** Barcelona (d. J. Sanchez 2–6 7–6 10–8, Vajda 7–5 6–3, Mecir 6–4 6–1, lost Jaite 6–2 6–4).

TARIK BENHABILES (France)
Born Algiers, Algeria, 5 February, 1965; lives Paris and London; RH; 5ft 9in; 132lb; final 1987 ATP ranking 65; 1987 prize money $77,350.
1980: Won European Jun Champs. ***1981:*** Won European Jun Champs again. ***1982:*** (616) Won French Open Jun. ***1983:*** (275). ***1984:*** (71) R/u Treviso and sf Florence. ***1985:*** (133). ***1986:*** (46) Best showing was qf Nice, and he took Noah to 5s 1r French Open. ***1987:*** Beat Perfors and Jarryd *en route* to last 16 French Open, where he took a set off Wilander. ***1987 HIGHLIGHTS – SINGLES: French Open*** last 16, unseeded (d. Pernfors [seed 13] 4–6 6–3 6–4 6–0, Jarryd 7–6 0–6 2–6 6–3 9–7, Chesnokov 5–7 6–4 7–5 6–3, lost Wilander [seed 4] 5–7 6–1 6–3 6–3), ***US Open*** 2r (d. Parker 6–3 3–6 6–4 6–4, lost Forget 7–6 4–6 6–3 6–4); ***won*** Marrakech Challenger (d. Yunis 6–2 7–5).

CAMILLE BENJAMIN (USA)
Born Cleveland, 22 June, 1966; lives Bakersfield, Cal.; LH; 2HB; 5ft 10in; 130lb; final 1987 WITA ranking 66; 1987 prize money $65,040.
1981: Ranked No. 1 in US 16s. ***1982:*** (63) Qf US Indoor and San Diego. ***1983:*** (49) Qf Richmond; sf Mahwah. ***1984:*** (33) Sf French Open and Tampa. ***1985:*** (62) R/u VS Utah. ***1986:*** (84). ***1987:*** R/u Puerto Rico. ***1987 HIGHLIGHTS – SINGLES: Australian Open*** 3r (d. E. Minter 0–6 6–4 6–4, Kelesi 4–6 6–4 6–4, lost Navratilova 6–2 6–1), ***French Open*** 3r (d. Mochizuki 7–5 6–3, Laval 6–0 6–2, lost Sabatini [seed 7] 6–0 2–6 6–2), ***Wimbledon*** 2r (d. Bykova 7–5 6–4, lost Lindqvist [seed 11] 7–5 7–6), ***US Open*** 2r (d. Torres 6–3 7–5, lost McNeil [seed 11] 6–4 6–2); ***r/u*** Puerto Rico (d. Reynolds 6–4 4–6 6–2, Sloane 6–2 7–6, G. Fernandez 5–7 6–3 6–0, Reis 4–6 6–2 6–3, Vasquez 6–2 4–6 7–5, lost Rehe 7–5 7–6). ***CAREER HIGHLIGHTS – SINGLES: French Open – sf 1984*** (d. Bonder 6–3 fs, lost Evert Lloyd 6–0 6–0).

JAY BERGER (USA)
Born Fort Dix, NJ, 26 November 1966; lives Plantation, Fla.; 5ft 9in; 150lb; RH; final 1987 ATP ranking 47; 1987 prize money $104,096.
Coached by Brian Gottfried. ***1984:*** R/u Orange Bowl 18s. ***1985:*** (249) Won US Boys' 18, US Boys' 18 CC, Florida State Open and Florida State Jun titles as well as reaching last 16 US Open all before his jun year at Clemson, where he was an All-American. ***1986:*** (82) Made the most of his 8 tournament appearances, winning Buenos Aires at end of year. ***1987:*** Qf LIPC (d. Gomez), r/u Buenos Aires where he retired v Perez Roldan with ankle injury, sf Sao Paulo. ***1987 HIGHLIGHTS – SINGLES: French Open*** 3r (d. Pistolesi 6–1

6–3 6–3, Mattar 7–6 6–3 6–3, lost Gomez [seed 10] 5–7 6–1 4–6 6–3 6–4), ***US Open*** 2r (d. Gurfein 4–6 6–3 6–2 6–2, lost Gilbert [seed 13] 4–6 6–2 6–4 6–3); ***r/u*** Buenos Aires (d. Filippini 6–4 6–2, Davin 6–2 4–6 6–4, de la Pena 6–7 6–3 6–4, Arraya 2–6 7–6 6–4, lost Perez Roldan 3–2 ret'd); ***sf*** Sao Paulo (d. Arguello 6–4 6–3, Frana 7–6 6–0, Meinecke 6–3 6–2, lost Yzaga 6–2 6–1).

CHRISTIAN BERGSTROM (Sweden)
Born Gothenburg, 19 July, 1967 and lives there; RH; 5ft 10½in; 145lb; final 1987 ATP ranking 69; 1987 prize money $50,754.
Coached by Tim Klein. ***1984:*** Nat Jun Champ. ***1985:*** (410) European Jun Champ. ***1986:*** (120) Won Tampere Challenger. ***1987:*** Qf Nancy, won Porto Challenger. ***1987 HIGHLIGHTS – SINGLES: French Open*** 2r (d. J. Carlsson 6–2 6–1 6–3, lost Noah [seed 6] 7–5 6–7 7–5 6–1), ***Wimbledon*** 2r (d. Lundgren 6–4 6–2 1–6 3–6 13–11, lost Van Rensburg 6–3 6–2 6–2), ***US Open*** 2r (d. Pernfors 6–3 3–0 ret'd, lost Muster 6–7 6–2 6–7 6–3 6–4); ***won*** Porto Challenger (d. Antonitsch 6–1 6–3).

LISA BONDER (USA)
Born Columbus, 16 October, 1965; lives Saline, Mich. and Largo, Fla.; RH; 2HB; 5ft 10in; 135lb; final 1987 WITA ranking 49; prize money $42,292.
1980: Co-ranked No. 1 in US 14s. ***1981:*** (22) Captured US Nat 18 title at age 15. ***1982:*** (41) Reached sf Italian Open. ***1983:*** (36) Became toast of Tokyo when she took two singles titles there in the space of one month, stunning Evert Lloyd in 2r and A. Jaeger in f of first. ***1984:*** (16) Had her most successful season, reaching sf Italian Open, qf French Open and last 16 US Open. ***1985:*** (36) Bad draws contributed to lowering of confidence but she reached sf New Orleans. ***1986:*** (53) She did not pass last 16 of any singles event. ***1987:*** Reached qf LIPC. ***1987 HIGHLIGHTS – SINGLES: French Open*** 2r (d. McNeil 6–3 6–3, lost Schimper 4–6 6–3 6–4), ***Wimbledon*** 1r (lost M. J. Fernandez 6–0 6–2), ***US Open*** 3r (d. Santrock 6–4 7–5, Casale 6–4 6–1, lost Navratilova [seed 2] 6–2 6–1). ***CAREER HIGHLIGHTS – SINGLES: French Open – qf 1984*** (lost Benjamin 7–6 5–7 6–3); ***Italian Open – sf 1982*** (d. Rinaldi, lost Evert Lloyd 6–2 6–4); ***sf 1984*** (lost Evert Lloyd 6–1 6–1).

FEDERICA BONSIGNORI (Italy)
Born Rome, 20 November, 1967, and lives there; RH; 5ft 3in; 110lb; final 1987 WITA ranking 91; 1987 prize money $22,661.
1987: Sf Paris Open and qf Belgian Open. ***1987 HIGHLIGHTS – SINGLES: French Open*** 1r (lost Porwik 7–6 6–4), ***US Open*** 2r (d. Krapl 6–2 6–4, lost Halard 6–2 7–6); ***sf*** Paris (d. Paradis 6–4 2–6 7–5, Ter Riet 6–1 6–7 6–2, Cecchini 4–6 7–6 6–4, lost Wasserman 6–1 6–2).

BEVERLY BOWES (USA)
Born Highland Park, Ill., 9 September, 1965; lives Lubbock, Texas; RH; 5ft 7in; 145lb; final 1987 WITA ranking 75; 1987 prize money $35,068.
Coached by her father, Mickey. ***1976–77:*** Won Nat 12s doubles title with A. Jaeger. ***1978:*** Won Nat 14s doubles title with A. Jaeger. ***1982:*** Ranked 6 in US Girls' 18s and played Jun W Cup. ***1983:*** Wimbledon Jun qf. ***1984:*** R/u USTA Flemington. ***1985:*** (111). ***1986:*** (100). ***1987:*** Turned pro before French Open. Sf Tampa. ***1987 HIGHLIGHTS – SINGLES: Australian Open*** 3r (bye, d. Bryant 6–2 6–7 6–3, lost Thompson 6–3 7–5), ***French Open*** 1r (lost Marsikova 4–6 6–3 6–2), ***Wimbledon*** 1r (lost Reggi 6–4 6–2), ***US Open*** 1r (lost Sabatini 6–3 6–3); ***sf*** Tampa (d. Mascotti, Burgin 7–5 7–5, Phelps 6–3 5–7 6–1, lost Evert 6–0 6–0).

JIMMY BROWN (USA)
Born Hialeah, Fla., 28 April, 1965; lives Largo, Fla.; RH; 5ft 11in; 150lb; 1987 ATP ranking 85; 1987 prize money $37,586.
Brother of Ricky. ***1981:*** Won Nat 18s. ***1983:*** (44) R/u Venice. ***1984:*** (100) R/u Florence. ***1985:*** (65) R/u Bordeaux. ***1986:*** (235). ***1987:*** Married Lisa Hache 24 Oct. Qf Bologna. ***1987 HIGHLIGHTS – SINGLES: US Open*** 2r (d. Tulasne 6–2 6–4 6–1, lost Castle 7–6 6–1 6–3); ***won*** Raleigh Challenger (d. Parker 1–6 6–0 6–1).

BETTINA BUNGE (West Germany)
Born Adliswil, Switzerland, 13 June, 1963; lives Monte Carlo, Monaco; RH; 5ft 8in; 125lb; final 1987 WITA ranking 15 singles, 21 doubles; 1987 prize money $171,855; career prize money $1,095,881.
Coached by Heinz Gildemeister and Roy Emerson. This German citizen (her father is German) spent part of her childhood in Peru and won Peruvian Nat at 13. ***1978:*** Reached sf Orange Bowl 18s not far from her home in Coral Gables, Florida. ***1979:*** (32) R/u Toronto; qf Eastbourne. ***1980:*** (19) R/u Stockholm. ***1981:*** (9) Sf Avon Champs and sf Mahwah. ***1982:*** (9) Sf Wimbledon; won German Open, Houston and Tokyo. ***1983:*** (7) Won VS Oakland then underwent ear surgery. ***1984:*** (21) Sf Birmingham. ***1985:*** (23) Sf German Open (d. Kohde-Kilsch). ***1986:*** (13) Reached qf Wimbledon, unseeded, then made late-season surge including two wins over Sukova to qualify for VS Champ, where she beat Rinaldi *en route* to qf. ***1987:*** At the Belgian Open reached first f since winning Oakland in 1983 and was voted WITA Comeback Player of the Year. Qualified for VS Champs, where she fell 1r to Sabatini. ***1987 HIGHLIGHTS – SINGLES: Wimbledon*** 3r, seed 9 (d. C. Wood 6–3 6–1, W. White 6–4 6–4, lost Fairbank 7–6 6–4), ***US Open*** last 16, seed 12 (d. Piatek 6–3 7–5, Fendick 6–2 6–4, Henricksson 6–3 6–4, lost Sabatini [seed 8] 1–6 6–1 6–1); ***r/u*** Belgian Open (d. Dechaume 6–4 6–2, Etchemendy 6–4 6–2, Cueto 6–2 6–1, Herreman 7–5 6–2, lost Horvath 6–1 7–6); ***sf*** Canadian Open (d. Perez Roldan 6–1 6–2, Horvath 6–3 6–2, Potter 6–2 6–0, lost Garrison 6–2 6–0). ***1987 HIGHLIGHTS – DOUBLES:*** [M. Maleeva] ***won*** Belgian Open (d. Horvath/Mesker 4–6 6–4 6–4); [McNeil] ***r/u*** Plymouth (lost Turnbull/Evert Lloyd 6–1 7–5), [Pfaff] ***r/u*** New England (lost Burgin/Fairbank 6–4 6–4). ***CAREER HIGHLIGHTS – SINGLES: Wimbledon – sf 1982*** seed 11 (d. Leslie Allen 6–3 7–5, A. Smith 6–2 3–6 6–0, lost Navratilova [seed 1] 6–2 6–2, ***qf 1986*** unseeded (d. G. Fernandez 4–6 6–4 6–1, Savchenko 6–7 6–0 7–5, Fendick 6–2 6–3, M. Maleeva [seed 8] 3–6 6–2 6–3, lost Navratilova [seed 1] 6–1 6–3). ***CAREER HIGHLIGHTS – DOUBLES:*** (with Kohde) ***French Open – sf 1981*** (lost Fairbank/Harford 6–2 fs); ***Wimbledon – sf 1982*** (lost Navratilova/Shriver 6–3 6–4); ***US Open – sf 1982*** (d. K. Jordan/A. Smith 6–7 7–5 6–3, lost Casals/Turnbull 6–4 6–1).

ELISE BURGIN (USA)
Born Baltimore, 5 March, 1962 and lives there; LH; 2HB; 5ft 5in; 120lb; final 1987 WITA ranking 65 singles, 16 (11) doubles; 1987 prize money £130,133.
Coached by Lenny Scheuermann. ***1980:*** Always among the top American jun in her age group, she capped a successful jun career by beating Horvath *en route* to f US Open jun. ***1981:*** (85) Moved into world top 100. ***1982:*** (48) Reached qf Wimbledon doubles with Stanford Univ. friend, Moulton, and beat Bunge on way to last 16 of US Open singles. ***1983:*** (42) Sf Canadian Open with upset of K. Jordan. ***1984:*** (51) Returned to circuit after 6 months out with back injury; graduated from Stanford and won NCAA doubles. ***1985:*** (27) Had best year in singles, including r/u showings at VS Houston and Indianapolis. Played Fed Cup. ***1986:*** (43) Won Wild Dunes in singles, made debut as US W Cup captain and proved to be a born leader as the Americans routed British 7–0 at Albert Hall. Sf Wimbledon and US Open doubles with Fairbank. ***1987:*** Best singles showing was qf Strasbourg, but reached 5 f in doubles, winning 2. ***1987 HIGHLIGHTS – SINGLES: Australian Open*** 2r (bye, lost McNeil [seed 8] 6–3 6–4), ***French Open*** 1r (lost Sanchez 7–5 6–3), ***Wimbledon*** 3r (d. E. Reinach 6–1 6–3, A. Smith 6–4 7–5, lost Lindqvist [seed 11] 6–4 6–1), ***US Open*** 2r (d. Javer 7–5 6–4, lost Sukova [seed 6] 6–3 6–4). ***1987 HIGHLIGHTS – DOUBLES:*** (with Shriver unless stated) ***won*** VS Washington (d. Garrison/McNeil 6–1 3–6 6–4), [Fairbank] ***won*** VS New England (d. Bunge/Pfaff 6–4 6–4); ***r/u*** Bridgestone (lost Kohde-Kilsch/Sukova 6–1 7–6), [R. White] ***r/u*** VS Dallas (lost Piatek/A. White 7–5 6–3), [Fairbank] ***r/u*** Tampa (lost Evert/Turnbull 6–4 6–3). ***CAREER HIGHLIGHTS – DOUBLES:*** (with Fairbank) ***Wimbledon – sf 1986*** (lost Navratilova/Shriver [seed 1] 6–4 6–3).

NATALIA BYKOVA (USSR)
Born Moscow, 13 September, 1966 and lives there; RH; 5ft 7in; 138lb; final 1987 WITA ranking 93; 1987 prize money $24,285.
Amateur. Coached by Volkov Anatoliy. ***1986:*** (220). ***1987:*** Qf VS Kansas and Oklahoma. ***1987 HIGHLIGHTS – SINGLES: Wimbledon*** 1r (lost Benjamin 7–5 6–4), ***US Open*** 1r

(lost Kelesi 7–6 7–5). ***1987 HIGHLIGHTS – DOUBLES:*** (with Meskhi) ***r/u*** Hamburg (d. Bunge/Graf, lost Kohde-Kilsch/Novotna 7–6 7–6).

DARREN CAHILL (Australia)
Born Adelaide, 2 October, 1965 and lives there; RH; 6ft 1in; 154lb; 1987 ATP ranking 82; 1987 prize money $101,507.
1985: (132). ***1986:*** (132) Formed an effective doubles partnership with Kratzmann, reaching f Queens. ***1987:*** Sf Kitzbuhel and Hong Kong. Broke into top 100 in Aug. and underwent a knee operation at end of year. ***1987 HIGHLIGHTS – SINGLES: Australian Open*** 1r (lost Barr 6–3 6–4 6–4), ***French Open*** 3r (d. Kratzmann 6–0 6–3 4–6 6–4, Robertson 6–4 7–6 6–3, lost Nystrom 6–4 7–6 6–4), ***US Open*** 2r (d. Kures 6–2 7–5 6–4, lost Flach 1–6 6–4 3–6 6–1 7–6); ***won*** New Haven Challenger (d. Cassidy 6–0 6–3); ***sf*** Kitzbuhel (d. Novacek 6–3 6–3, Colombo 6–3 6–3, Smid 6–7 7–6 7–6, Osterthun 6–3 1–6 7–5, lost Mecir 6–1 6–2), ***sf*** Hong Kong (d. Mmoh 7–6 6–2, Muller 6–4 7–6, Ross 6–4 4–6 6–4, lost Teltscher 7–5 6–0). ***1987 HIGHLIGHTS – DOUBLES:*** [Kratzmann] ***won*** Sydney (d. Becker/Seguso 6–3 6–2); [Woodforde] ***r/u*** Bordeaux (lost Casal/E. Sanchez 6–3 6–3). ***MIXED DOUBLES:*** (with Provis) ***r/u Wimbledon*** (lost Bates/Durie 7–6 6–3).

OMAR CAMPORESE (Italy)
Born Bologna, 8 May, 1968 and lives there; RH; 6ft 1in; 168lb; final 1987 ATP ranking 283; 1987 prize money $11,592.
1986: (766) Won Italian Jun and r/u European Jun Champs. ***1987:*** R/u Mediterranean Games.

FRANCESCO CANCELLOTTI (Italy)
Born Perugia, 27 February, 1963 and lives there; RH; 5ft 11in; 167lb; 1987 ATP ranking 74; 1987 prize money $57,882.
1982: (267). ***1983:*** (72) Won Nat singles, r/u Florence and joined Italian D Cup squad. ***1984:*** (26) Won Florence and Palermo, r/u Bordeaux. ***1985:*** (58) Last 16 French Open; qf Monte Carlo and Palermo. ***1986:*** (242) Qf Florence. ***1987:*** R/u Bari and St Vincent as he reached 1st f since 1984. ***1987 HIGHLIGHTS – SINGLES: r/u*** Bari (d. Lopez-Maeso 6–2 6–3, Yunis 6–3 4–6 6–2, Tulasne 6–3 4–6 6–2, de la Pena 6–3 6–3, lost Pistolesi 6–7 7–5 6–3), ***r/u*** St Vincent (d. Bassanelli 6–3 6–3, Cierro 7–6 6–0, K. Carlsson w.o., Cane 6–3 6–2, lost Rebolledo 7–6 4–6 6–3).

PAOLO CANE (Italy)
Born Bologna, 9 April, 1965 and lives there; RH; 5ft 11in; 150lb; final 1987 ATP ranking 51; 1987 prize money $79,068.
1983: (353) R/u Italian Nat Champs. ***1984:*** (552) Won bronze medal at Olympics in LA. ***1985:*** (197) Played nine tourns in singles, but performed better in doubles, earning a ranking of 44. ***1986:*** (44) Burst out of the pack on GP tour, winning Bordeaux, reaching f Bologna, and beating Nystrom to reach qf Bastad. Played D Cup. ***1987:*** Sf Bologna and St Vincent. Began 1 year's military service in June, but was granted special leave to play Wimbledon, where he extended Lendl to 5s, and US Open. ***1987 HIGHLIGHTS – SINGLES: French Open*** 1r (lost McNamee 6–0 6–3 6–2), ***Wimbledon*** 2r (d. Arias 6–7 6–2 7–6 6–3, lost Lendl [seed 2] 3–6 7–6 6–7 7–5 6–1), ***US Open*** 1r (lost Svensson 5–7 6–4 6–2 7–6); ***sf*** Bologna (d. A. Sundstrom 6–4 1–6 6–2, Panatta 0–6 6–0 6–2, Tulasne 7–5 4–6 6–0, lost K. Carlsson 6–1 6–0), ***sf*** St Vincent (d. Cox 6–3 7–6, DeMinicis 6–3 7–5, Colombo 7–5 6–3, Cancellotti 6–2 6–2, lost Rebolledo 7–6 4–6 6–3).

TOMAS CARBONELL (Spain)
Born Barcelona, 23 August 1968; lives Cabrera; RH; 5ft 11½in; 158lb; final 1987 ATP ranking 242; 1987 prize money $21,021.
Coached by Pato (Bill) Alvarez. ***1985:*** Nat Jun champ. ***1986:*** No. 1 in ITF Jun Doubles World Rankings. Won US Open Jun (with J. Sanchez), Wimbledon Jun (with Korda) and r/u French Open Jun (with J. Sanchez). ***1987:*** Qf Barcelona and won Buenos Aires doubles with Casal. ***1987 HIGHLIGHTS – SINGLES: French Open*** 2r (d. Bathman 5–7 7–5 7–6 6–3, lost Chesnokov 6–2 6–2 6–0). ***1987 HIGHLIGHTS – DOUBLES:*** (with Casal) ***won*** Buenos Aires (d. Gildemeister/Motta, Berger/de la Pena w.o.).

KENT CARLSSON (Sweden)
Born Eskilstuna, 3 January, 1968, and lives there; RH; 5ft 11in; 158lb; final 1987 ATP ranking 12; 1987 prize money $167,541.
1981–83: Won European Jun titles. ***1983:*** (794) Won Orange Bowl 18-and-under title at age 15 with steady, precocious baseline game reminding many of Borg and Wilander. ***1984:*** (139) Became one of four-member SIAB under captain Peter Ronsjo along with Johan Carlsson (no relation), Jonas Svensson and Helena Dahlstrom. Won French Open Jun. ***1985:*** (48) R/u Hilversum. ***1986:*** (13) Won his first GP tournament in Bari and first Super Series in Barcelona, aged 18. Made début on Swedish D Cup squad and routed Mecir in crucial opening-day match as SWE d. TCH in Prague. ***1987:*** Knee injury suffered at LIPC kept him out of action for 7 weeks in spring and in Sept. he underwent arthroscopic knee surgery for 3rd time and was out of action for rest of year. Between injuries he won Nice and Bologna and was r/u Boston and USCC. ***1987 HIGHLIGHTS – SINGLES: French Open*** last 16, seed 11 (d. Boetsch 6–1 6–0 6–3, Casal 6–3 6–1 6–3, Yunis 7–5 6–2 6–1, lost Noah [seed 6] 7–6 6–3 6–7 7–5); ***won*** Bologna (d. Meinecke, Rebolledo 6–0 6–1, Davin 6–0 6–0, Cane 6–1 6–0, E. Sanchez 6–2 6–1), ***won*** Nice (d. Pugh 2–6 6–1 9–7, Arraya 6–1 6–1, Agenor 6–2 6–1, Chesnokov 6–0 7–5, E. Sanchez 7–6 6–3); ***r/u*** Boston (d. J. Brown 6–4 6–3, Vilas 6–3 6–2, Nystrom 6–1 7–5, Gomez 7–5 4–6 7–5, lost Wilander 7–6 6–1), ***r/u*** US CC (d. Cassidy 6–3 6–1, Frana 6–4 6–4, Kuhnen 7–6 6–1, Perez Roldan 6–2 6–2, lost Wilander 7–5 6–3); ***sf*** Hamburg (d. Steeb, Teltscher, E. Sanchez 6–2 6–1, lost Lendl 3–6 7–5 6–0).

SERGIO CASAL (Spain)
Born Barcelona, 8 September, 1962, and lives there; RH; 6ft 2in; 155lb; final 1987 ATP ranking 92 singles, 7 (27) doubles; 1987 prize money $269,851.
Coached by Pato (Bill) Alvarez. ***1980:*** Stopped S. Giammalva and Wilander to reach qf Orange Bowl. ***1982:*** (159) Joined Spanish D Cup squad. ***1985:*** (38) Won first GP at Florence and reached sf Kitzbuhel. Started successful partnership with E. Sanchez, winning Kitzbuhel, Geneva and Barcelona and reaching 4 other f. ***1986:*** (62) Had great run to final of new Paris tourn, won 5 doubles titles with E. Sanchez, and won US Open mixed doubles with Reggi. ***1987:*** Qf Munich and Itaparica; with E. Sanchez won 6 doubles titles, r/u Wimbledon and sf Masters. ***1987 HIGHLIGHHTS – SINGLES: French Open*** 2r (d. Tauson 6–4 6–1 6–3, lost K. Carlsson [seed 11] 6–3 6–1 6–3), ***Wimbledon*** 1r (lost Pate [seed 15] 6–4 7–6 7–5), ***US Open*** 1r (lost Perez 1–6 6–1 5–7 6–4 6–4). ***1987 HIGHLIGHTS – DOUBLES:*** (with E. Sanchez unless stated) ***r/u Wimbledon*** (d. Edberg/Jarryd 6–3 7–5 6–2, lost Flach/Seguso 7–6 6–1 6–4); ***won*** US Pro Indoor (d. Flach/Smid 6–2 6–7 6–3, Steyn/Visser 3–6 6–1 7–6), ***won*** Nice (d. Mezzadri/Ocleppo 6–4 6–3), ***won*** Bologna (d. Panatta/Willenborg 6–3 6–2), ***won*** Bordeaux (d. Cahill/Woodforde 6–3 6–3), ***won*** Kitzbuhel (d. Mecir/Smid 7–6 7–6), [Carbonell] ***won*** Buenos Aires (d. Gildemeister/Motta, Berger/de la Pena w.o.), ***won*** Itaparica (d. Lozano/Perez 6–2 6–2); ***r/u*** Milan (lost Becker/Zivojinovic 3–6 6–3 6–4), ***r/u*** Memphis (d. Anger/Holmes, lost Jarryd/Svensson 6–4 6–2), ***r/u*** Munich (lost Pugh/Willenborg 7–6 4–6 6–4), ***r/u*** Madrid (lost DiLaura/J. Sanchez 6–3 3–6 7–6). ***CAREER HIGHLIGHTS – DOUBLES:*** (with E. Sanchez) ***Wimbledon – r/u 1987. MIXED DOUBLES –*** (with Reggi) ***US Open – won 1986*** (d. Navratilova/Fleming 6–4 6–4).

PAM CASALE (USA)
Born Camden, NJ, 20 December, 1963; lives Fairfield, NJ; RH; 2HB; 5ft 7in; 127lb; final 1987 WITA ranking 113; 1987 prize money $18,268.
1980: Emerging from the training camp of Nick Bollettieri, she won Orange Bowl and Easter Bowl 16 titles. ***1981:*** (22) Turned pro after winning Avon Futures Bakersfield, reaching f Mahwah and rising to No. 16. ***1982:*** (39) Reached qf WTA Champs. ***1983:*** (38) Reached qf German Open. ***1984:*** (15) Restoring herself, she reached 4 sfs. ***1985:*** (34) R/u Marco Island and US CC. ***1986:*** (46) Began year slowly but recovered, using her Françoise Durr-style backhand and never-say-die attitude to reach last 16 French Open. ***1987 HIGHLIGHTS – SINGLES: Wimbledon*** 1r (lost Sloane 6–4 2–6 6–2), ***US Open*** 2r (d. Budarova 7–5 6–2, lost Bonder 6–4 6–1).

PAT CASH (Australia)
Born Melbourne, 27 May, 1965; lives Ringwood and London; RH; 5ft 11in; 170lb; final 1987 ATP ranking 7; 1987 prize money $565,934.
Coached by Ian Barclay, trainer Anne Quinn. Girlfriend Anna Britt Kristiansen; son Daniel born May 1986. ***1982:*** (44) In Melbourne he became the youngest to win a GP title (Krickstein broke the record the following year); earlier in year he won Wimbledon and US Open Jun. ***1983:*** (38) Won Brisbane and led Australia to victory in D Cup. ***1984:*** (8) Sf Wimbledon and US Open, where he had mp in sf with Lendl, upset Connors in dead rubber D Cup match and reached f Melbourne. ***1985:*** (67) Sidetracked by injuries, he achieved his best effort to reach sf Brussels. R/u Wimbledon doubles 2nd straight year. ***1986:*** (24) Only 3 weeks after having emergency appendectomy he reached qf Wimbledon with win over Wilander and later in year he led Australia to victory over Sweden in D Cup f. ***1987:*** After reaching f Australian Open (d. Lendl sf), where he took Edberg to 5s, won Nancy for 1st title since 1983. He followed in tremendous style by winning 1st GS title at Wimbledon (d. Lendl in ss in f), becoming 1st Australian to win the singles there since Newcombe in 1971 and the only player to d. Lendl twice in 1987. Won Johannesburg and qualified for Masters 1st time. ***1987 HIGHLIGHTS – SINGLES: r/u Australian Open*** seed 11 (bye, d. Pistolesi 7–5 2–6 7–6 6–2, Testerman 6–3 6–7 6–1 6–2, Annacone 6–4 6–1 6–7 1–6 6–2, Noah [seed 3] 6–4 6–2 2–6 6–0, Lendl [seed 1] 7–6 5–7 7–6 6–4, lost Edberg [seed 4] 6–3 6–4 3–6 5–7 6–3), ***French Open*** 1r, seed 12 (lost Pugh 3–6 6–3 6–2 7–6), ***won Wimbledon*** seed 11 (d. Freeman 6–0 6–3 6–2, McNamee 7–5 6–4 6–2, Schapers 7–6 6–2 2–6 6–4, Forget 6–2 6–3 6–4, Wilander [seed 3] 6–3 7–5 6–4, Connors [seed 7] 6–4 6–4 6–1, Lendl [seed 2] 7–6 6–2 7–5), ***US Open*** 1r, seed 7 (lost Lundgren 6–4 4–6 6–4 6–4); ***won*** Nancy (d. Schultz 6–3 6–4, Nelson 6–3 6–1, Grabb 7–6 6–2, Krishnan 7–5 6–3, Masur 6–2 6–3), ***won*** Johannesburg (d. Robertson 6–2 6–2, Anger 6–3 6–2, Curren 2–6 6–3 6–4, Mansdorf 6–3 7–6, Gilbert 7–6 4–6 2–6 6–0 6–1); ***r/u*** Sydney (d. Evernden 6–3 7–6, J. Frawley 6–3 7–6, S. Davis 6–3 7–5, Becker 6–3 2–6 7–6, lost Lendl 6–4 6–2 6–4); ***sf*** Queens (d. Matuszewski 6–4 6–4, Fitzgerald 6–4 3–6 6–3, Curren 7–5 6–3, Edberg 7–6 7–6, lost Connors 7–6 6–4). ***1987 HIGHLIGHTS – DOUBLES:*** (with Edberg) ***won*** Montreal (d. Doohan/Warder 6–7 6–3 6–4). ***CAREER HIGHLIGHTS – SINGLES: Wimbledon – won 1987, sf 1984*** unseeded (d. Wilander, Motta, Curren, Gomez, lost McEnroe 6–3 7–6 6–4), ***qf 1986*** unseeded (d. Vilas, Simpson, Lapidus, Wilander 4–6 6–4 7–5 6–3, lost Leconte 4–6 7–6 7–6 6–3); ***Australian Open – r/u 1987, qf 1984*** (lost Kriek 7–5 6–1 7–6); ***US Open – sf 1984*** (d. Wilander, lost Lendl [seed 2] 3–6 6–3 6–4 6–7 7–6 after having 1 mp). ***CAREER HIGHLIGHTS – DOUBLES:*** (with Fitzgerald unless stated) [McNamee] ***Wimbledon – r/u 1984*** (lost McEnroe/Fleming 6–2 5–7 6–2 3–6 6–3), ***r/u 1985*** (d. McEnroe/Fleming, lost Gunthardt/Taroczy 6–4 6–3 4–6 6–3); ***Australian Open – sf 1984*** (lost Nystrom/Wilander 6–4 6–4 2–6 6–3).

ANNA MARIA (SANDRA) CECCHINI (Italy)
Born Bologna, 27 February, 1965; lives Ceriva; RH; 5ft 5in; 135lb; final 1987 WITA ranking 18; 1987 prize money $88,775.
Prefers to be known by her nickname, Sandra. ***1983:*** R/u to Spence at Orange Bowl 18s, ranked second among world juniors and third among Italy's women. ***1984:*** (49) Won Rio de Janeiro. ***1985:*** (49) Reached qf French Open and won Barcelona, restoring herself after 8 consecutive 1r losses early in year. ***1986:*** (76) Produced the upset of the year when she stunned Evert Lloyd in Fed Cup, the first time the American had lost in the international team competition. ***1987:*** Extended Graf to 3s sf Berlin, won VS Arkansas and reached f Strasbourg. ***1987 HIGHLIGHTS – SINGLES: French Open*** 1r (lost M. Maleeva [seed 6] 3–6 6–3 6–3), ***US Open*** 3r (d. A. White 6–4 6–2, Hy 6–4 5–7 7–5, lost Kohde-Kilsch [seed 9] 6–4 6–3; ***won*** Bastad (d. Van Der Torre 6–1 6–2, Schultz 6–2 6–4, Joensson 6–4 7–6, K. Maleeva 4–6 6–3 6–4, Lindqvist 6–4 6–4), ***won*** VS Arkansas (d. Golarsa 6–2 4–6 6–3, Cammie MacGregor 6–2 6–0, Sodupe 6–4 6–2, A. Smith 6–4 6–3, Zvereva 0–6 6–1 6–3); ***r/u*** Strasbourg (d. Demongeot 6–4 6–2, Kelesi 7–5 5–7 6–3, Cueto 6–2 6–3, Horvath 6–0 7–6, lost Bassett 6–3 6–4); ***sf*** Berlin (d. Nozzoli 6–2 6–1, Kelesi 6–3 6–3, Huber 6–2 7–5, Field 6–2 6–2, lost Graf 6–3 6–7 6–4), ***sf*** Hamburg (d. Porwik 6–2 6–2, Sanchez 6–2 6–1, Reggi 6–3 1–6 6–4, lost Graf 6–0 6–2). ***1987 HIGHLIGHTS – DOUBLES:*** (with Goles) ***r/u*** Paris (lost Demongeot/Tauziat 1–6 6–3 6–3). ***CAREER HIGHLIGHTS – SINGLES: French Open – qf 1985*** (lost Navratilova 6–2 6–2).

MICHAEL CHANG (USA)
Born Hoboken, NJ, 22 February, 1972; lives Placentia, Cal.; RH; 5ft 8in; 135lb; final 1987 ATP ranking 163; 1987 prize money $25,681.
Amateur until Feb. 1988. Parents from Taipei. ***1987:*** At 15 yrs 6 mths was youngest player to compete in men's singles at US Open since 1918, and was the youngest ever to win a match in GS tourn, having been granted a wild card after winning US 18s at Kalamazoo. At 15 yrs 7 mths was youngest to win a pro tourn at Las Vegas Challenger and was youngest ever GP semi-finalist at Scottsdale. ***1987 HIGHLIGHTS – SINGLES: US Open*** 2r (d. McNamee 6–3 6–7 6–4 6–4, lost Odizor 6–1 6–2 6–7 3–6 6–4); ***won*** Las Vegas Challenger (d. J. Levine 6–3 4–6 6–2); ***sf*** Scottsdale (d. Berger 6–3 6–2, Testerman 4–6 6–1 6–3, Lozano 6–4 6–1, lost Gilbert 6–3 6–4).

ANDREI CHESNOKOV (USSR)
Born Moscow, 2 February, 1966 and lives there; RH; 2HB; 6ft 2in; 163lb; final 1987 ATP ranking 52; 1987 prize money $112,980.
Coached by Tatiana Naoumko. ***1980:*** Won Russian Nat Jun Champ. ***1982:*** Won Russian Nat Jun Champ again. ***1984:*** Beat Glickstein and Perkis in D Cup. ***1985:*** (136) Upset Teltscher at French Open. ***1986:*** (36) Reached qf French Open, upsetting No. 2 seed Wilander in 3r, and last 16 US Open. ***1987:*** Reached last 16 US Open and won his 1st GP title in his 1st f at Florence, becoming 1st from his country to win a title since Metreveli won S Orange in 1974. ***1987 HIGHLIGHTS – SINGLES: French Open*** 3r (d. Donnelly 6–1 6–3 6–3, Carbonell 6–2 6–2 6–0, lost Benhabiles 5–7 6–4 7–5 6–3), ***US Open*** last 16, unseeded (d. Hooper 6–4 6–1 6–4, Lundgren 6–2 7–5 2–6 6–0, Perez 6–1 6–2 6–2, lost Krishnan 6–4 6–1 6–2); ***won*** Florence (d. Olkhovski, Pistolesi, Yzaga 7–6 6–1, Perez Roldan 3–6 7–5 7–6, De Minicis 6–1 6–3); ***sf*** Nice (d. Meinecke 7–6 6–3, Benhabiles 6–4 1–6 6–2, Jaite 7–6 6–2, lost K. Carlsson 6–0 7–5). ***CAREER HIGHLIGHTS – SINGLES: French Open – qf 1986*** unseeded (d. J. B. Svensson 6–3 2–6 6–4 6–2, Osterthun, Wilander [seed 2] 6–2 6–3 6–2, Maciel, lost Leconte [seed 8] 6–3 6–4 6–3).

JOSEF CIHAK (Czechoslovakia)
Born Plzen, 19 March, 1963; lives Prague; RH; 5ft 11in; 158lb; final 1987 ATP ranking 77; 1987 prize money $20,675.
1986: Out of action all year with hepatitis. ***1987:*** Cracked top 100 in Oct after reaching sf Palermo. ***1987 HIGHLIGHTS – SINGLES: sf*** Palermo (d. Stenlund 6–3 6–1, Filippini 6–1 6–1, Miniussi 7–5 7–6, lost Jaite 6–2 6–3).

HALLE CIOFFI (USA)
Born Cleveland, 5 August, 1969; lives Knoxville; RH; 2HB; 5ft 7in; 130lb; final 1987 WITA ranking 55; amateur.
1987: Won VS Indianapolis. Out of action 4 months in summer with back problems. ***1987 HIGHLIGHTS – SINGLES: French Open*** 2r (d. Fairbank 6–2 6–3, lost Kanellopoulou 6–1 0–6 6–3), ***Wimbledon*** 1r (lost Louie Harper 6–2 6–1), ***US Open*** 1r (lost Hakami 6–1 6–1); ***won*** VS Indianapolis (d. Purdy 6–3 6–3, Louie Harper 6–0 6–3, Mesker 2–6 7–6 6–3, Potter 5–7 5–2 ret'd, Meskhi 5–7 6–0 6–4, A. Smith 4–6 6–4 7–6).

GRANT CONNELL (Canada)
Born Vancouver, 17 November, 1965; lives North Vancouver; LH; 6ft 1in; 175lb; final 1987 ATP ranking 123; 1987 prize money $33,520.
1985: (570) All-American at Texas A & M. ***1986:*** (191) Won Nat doubles with Greenan. ***1987:*** Won Vancouver Challenger and r/u Nancy doubles with Scott. ***1987 HIGHLIGHTS – SINGLES: Australian Open*** 1r (lost Nelson 6–4 6–4 6–4); ***won*** Vancouver Challenger (d. Mronz 7–6 6–1).

JIMMY CONNORS (USA)
Born East St Louis, Ill., 2 September, 1952; lives Sanibel Island, Fla. and Santa Barbara, Cal., with wife Patti, son Brett (born 1979) and daughter Aubree (born Dec. 1984); LH; 2HB; 5ft 10in; 153lb; final 1987 ATP ranking 4; 1987 prize money $422,026; career prize money $7,489,978.
One of the game's greatest players, he was taught by his mother and grandmother,

growing up outside St Louis in Bellville, Ill. Moving to California, he received expert tutelage from the two great Panchos – Gonzales and Segura – during his crucial late teenage years. His exceptional record from the mid-70s into the mid-80s is an enormous tribute to his skill and willpower. ***1971:*** Won NCAA title as UCLA freshman. ***1972:*** Won first pro title in Jacksonville and made Wimbledon début, upsetting 7th seed Hewitt *en route* to qf, where he lost to Nastase. ***1973:*** Won first important title – US Pro – signalling that he was ready to take over American tennis when he stopped Smith in 1r and Ashe in f. Won Wimbledon doubles with Nastase. ***1974:*** (1) Rose to No. 1 in world, winning Wimbledon, US and Australian Opens and 99 of 103 matches. ***1975:*** (1) He slipped to No. 2 in minds of most experts, losing in f Wimbledon, US and Australian Opens, falling to Ashe in most critical match of the year in Wimbledon f. Won US Open doubles with Nastase. ***1976:*** (1) Won second US Open crown (on clay this time). ***1977:*** (1) Beaten again in Wimbledon and US Open f by Borg and Vilas, but salvaged year with triumph at Masters. ***1978:*** (1) Avenged Wimbledon f loss to Borg at US Open. ***1979:*** (2) Beaten in sf Wimbledon by Borg and sf US Open by McEnroe, he slipped to third in world on most experts' lists. ***1980:*** (3) Ousted by McEnroe in both Wimbledon and US semis he nevertheless played with renewed inspiration and conviction. ***1981:*** (3) Lost Wimbledon and US semis to Borg and returned briefly to represent US in D Cup for first time since Dec. 75. ***1982:*** (2) Despite No. 2 computer ranking behind McEnroe, he was everyone else's choice for No. 1 as he won second Wimbledon and fourth US Open crowns and 7 of 18 tournaments entered; was deservedly awarded ITF World Champion's award. ***1983:*** (3) Took fifth US Open title after disappointment of 4r loss to Curren at Wimbledon, the first time in 12 years he had failed to reach qf. ***1984:*** (2) Reached fifth Wimbledon f and joined forces with McEnroe to lead US into D Cup f where they lost to Sweden. Won his 105th tournament – a record – at Seiko, Toyko. ***1985:*** (4) For first time since 1972, did not win a singles title but he appeared in his 12th consecutive US Open sf. ***1986:*** (8) Again did not win a title but reached 4 f. Missed the Masters and suffered first Wimbledon 1r loss in 15 years, then beaten in 3r at US Open after an early-year suspension had kept him out of French Open. ***1987:*** After taking a 3-month break Nov–Jan, he played a lighter winter schedule and, with the pressure off him to win, he enjoyed his best season for 4 years, reaching f 3 times, with a win–loss record of 52–16 going into Masters for which he qualified a record 11th time. Played superbly and with tremendous spirit to reach sf Wimbledon, coming back from 1–6 1–6 1–4 to d. Pernfors in last 16; sf US Open, qf French Open, r/u Memphis, Orlando and Queens and reached sf 5 more times. ***1987 HIGHLIGHTS – SINGLES: French Open*** qf, seed 8 (d. Nelson 7–5 6–2 6–3, Westphal 6–4 3–6 7–6 6–2, Davin 6–3 6–1 6–2, Osterthun 4–6 7–5 6–0 6–3, lost Becker [seed 2] 6–3 6–3 7–5), ***Wimbledon*** sf, seed 7 (d. M. Davis 6–1 7–6 7–6, Shaw 6–2 2–6 6–3 6–4, Evernden 6–1 6–2 6–7 6–3, Pernfors 1–6 1–6 7–5 6–4 6–2, Zivojinovic 7–6 7–5 6–3, lost Cash [seed 11] 6–4 6–4 6–1), ***US Open*** sf, seed 6 (d. Rive 6–1 6–4 6–4, Hearn 6–3 6–2 6–1, Grabb 6–3 6–2 6–4, Leconte [seed 11] 6–7 6–4 6–4 6–3, Gilbert [seed 13] 4–6 6–3 6–4 6–0, lost Lendl [seed 1] 6–4 6–2 6–2); ***r/u*** Memphis (d. Chesnokov, Teltscher 6–1 4–6 6–1, Curren 7–5 6–7 6–3, Pernfors 6–7 7–6 6–3, lost Edberg 6–3 2–1 ret'd), ***r/u*** Orlando (d. Evernden 7–6 6–2, Holmes 6–2 7–6, Wilkison 6–2 5–2 ret'd, Gilbert 3–6 6–4 6–2, lost Van Rensburg 6–3 3–6 6–1), ***r/u*** Queens (d. Visser 6–3 6–4, Shaw 6–4 6–7 7–5, Odizor 7–5 7–5, Jelen 6–4 6–4, Cash 7–6 6–4, lost Becker 6–7 6–3 6–4); ***sf*** LIPC (d. Testerman 6–1 6–1 6–3, Lundgren 2–6 6–4 6–2 6–3, Cahill 6–3 6–3 6–1, J. Carlsson 6–0 6–1 6–0, Rostagno 6–4 4–6 6–1 6–2, lost Lendl 3–6 7–6 7–6 6–3), ***sf*** Washington (d. K. Jones 6–3 6–4, Pugh 6–3 6–1, Witsken 6–3 2–6 6–2, lost Lendl 6–4 7–6), ***sf*** Montreal (d. Rostagno 7–6 6–1, Berger 4–6 7–5 4–0 ret'd, McEnroe 6–3 3–6 6–3, lost Lendl 7–5 6–4), ***sf*** Cincinatti (d. Berger 4–6 6–2 6–1, Chamberlin 6–1 6–3, Evernden 6–3 6–2, Odizor 6–1 6–7 6–3, lost Edberg 6–2 6–3), ***sf*** Tel Aviv (d. Paris 6–1 6–2, Westphal 6–4 6–2, Van Boeckel 6–1 6–1, lost Mansdorf 7–6 6–3). ***CAREER HIGHLIGHTS – SINGLES: Wimbledon – won 1974*** (d. Rosewall 6–1 6–1 6–4), ***won 1982*** (d. Alexander 7–6 4s, Gitlin 7–5 4s, G. Mayer 6–1 6–2 7–6, Edmondson 6–4 6–3 6–1, McEnroe 3–6 6–3 6–7 7–6 6–4), ***r/u 1975*** (lost Ashe 6–1 6–1 5–7 6–4), ***r/u 1977*** (lost Borg 3–6 6–2 6–1 5–7 6–4), ***r/u 1978*** (lost Borg 6–2 6–2 6–3), ***r/u 1984*** (d. Lendl 6–7 6–3 7–5 6–1, lost McEnroe 6–1 6–1 6–2), ***sf 1979*** (lost Borg 6–2 6–3 6–2), ***sf 1980*** seed 3 (lost McEnroe 6–3 3–6 6–3 6–4), ***sf 1981*** (d. V. Amritraj 2–6 5–7 6–4 6–3 6–2, lost Borg 0–6 4–6 6–3 6–0 6–4), ***sf 1985*** (lost Curren 6–2 6–2 6–1), ***sf 1987***; ***US Open – won 1974*** (d. Rosewall 6–1 6–0 6–1), ***won 1976*** (d. Borg 6–4 3–6 7–6 6–4), ***won 1978*** (d. McEnroe 6–2

Right: *In another profitable year Dianne Balestrat reached the quarter-finals at Wimbledon and the final at Arizona.* ***Below left:*** *Patty Fendick won the NCAA Championships for the second successive season.* ***Below right:*** *Elly Hakami won her first title at the California Women's Open and broke into the top 50.*
(T. Hindley, Carol L. Newsom)

6–2 7–5, Borg 6–4 6–2 6–2), ***won 1982*** (d. Arias 6–4 4–6 6–4 6–1, Nastase 6–3 6–3 6–4, Vilas 6–1 3–6 6–4, Vilas 6–1 3–6 6–2 6–3, Lendl 6–3 6–2 4–6 6–4), ***won 1983*** (d. Lendl 6–3 6–7 7–5 6–0), ***r/u 1975*** (lost Orantes 6–4 6–3 6–3), ***r/u 1977*** (lost Vilas 2–6 6–3 7–6 6–0), ***sf 1979*** (lost McEnroe 6–3 6–3 7–5), ***sf 1980*** seed 3 (lost McEnroe 6–4 5–7 0–6 6–3 7–6), ***sf 1981*** (lost Borg 6–2 7–5 6–4), ***sf 1984*** (lost McEnroe 6–4 4–6 7–5 4–6 6–3), ***sf 1985*** (lost Lendl 6–2 6–3 7–5), ***sf 1987; Australian Open – won 1974*** (d. Dent 7–6 6–4 4–6 6–3), ***r/u 1975*** (lost Newcombe 7–5 3–6 6–4 7–6); ***Masters – won 1978*** (d. Borg 6–4 1–6 6–4), ***sf 1979*** seed 3 (lost Gerulaitis 7–5 6–2), ***sf 1980*** seed 4 (lost Borg 6–4 6–7 6–3), ***sf 1982*** (lost Lendl 6–3 6–1), ***sf 1983*** (lost Lendl 6–3 6–4), ***sf 1984*** (lost Lendl 7–6 5–7 7–5); ***WCT Finals – won 1977*** (d. Stockton 6–7 6–1 6–4 6–3), ***won 1980*** seed 2 (d. Scanlon, Lendl, McEnroe 2–6 7–6 6–1 6–2); ***US CC – won 1974*** (d. Borg 5–7 6–3 6–4), ***won 1976*** (d. Fibak 6–2 6–4), ***won 1978*** (d. Higueras 7–5 6–1), ***won 1978*** (d. Vilas 6–1 2–6 6–4), ***r/u 1972*** (lost Hewitt 6–1 7–6), ***r/u 1977*** (lost Orantes 6–1 6–3); ***US Pro Indoor – won 1976*** (d. Borg 7–6 6–4 6–0), ***won 1978*** (d. Tanner 6–4 6–2 6–3), ***won 1979*** (d. Ashe 6–3 6–4 6–1), ***won 1980*** (d. McEnroe 6–3 2–6 6–3 3–6 6–4); ***US Indoor – won 1973*** (d. Meiler), ***won 1974*** (d. McMillan), ***won 1975*** (d. Gerulaitis 6–1 fs), ***won 1978*** (d. Tim Gullikson 7–6 6–3), ***won 1979*** (d. Ashe 6–4 5–7 6–3), ***won 1983*** (d. G. Mayer 7–5 6–0), ***won 1984*** (d. Leconte 6–3 4–6 7–5); ***South African Open – won 1973*** (d. Ashe), ***won 1974*** (d. Ashe); ***French Open – sf 1979*** seed 2 (lost Pecci 7–6 6–4 5–7 6–3), ***sf 1980*** (lost Gerulaitis 6–1 3–6 6–7 6–2 6–4), ***qf 1981*** (lost Clerc 4–6 6–2 4–6 7–5 6–0), ***sf 1985*** (d. Edberg, lost Lendl 6–2 6–3 6–1). ***CAREER HIGHLIGHTS – DOUBLES:*** (with Nastase) ***Wimbledon – won 1973*** (d. Cooper/Fraser 3–6 6–3 6–4 8–9 6–1); ***US Open – won 1975*** (d. Okker/Riessen); ***French Open – r/u 1973*** (lost Newcombe/Okker 6–4 fs). ***MIXED DOUBLES:*** (with Evert) ***US Open – r/u 1974*** (lost Masters/Teeguarden 6–1 7–6).

ANNABEL CROFT (Great Britain)
Born London, 12 July, 1966; lives Farnborough, Kent; RH; 5ft 7in; 130lb; final 1987 WITA ranking 140; 1987 prize money $24,185.
Coached by Owen Davidson. ***1981:*** Reached sf Orange Bowl 16s. ***1982:*** R/u at Trophe Pernod Lee-on-Solent and Solihull British satellite events. ***1983:*** (140) Reached qf Fort Myers on USTA satellite circuit. ***1984:*** (82) As if by design, she saved her best for Wimbledon, winning jun event after reaching 3r in main draw. Made impressive W Cup début with victory over more experienced Moulton. ***1985:*** (24) Rose to No. 1 in her country, won San Diego, and defeated the likes of Turnbull, Sukova and Gurney. ***1986:*** (70) Victorious in only 10 of 29 singles matches, she lost 11 1r matches but on her good days beat Phelps, Temesvari, Torres and Durie. ***1987 HIGHLIGHTS – SINGLES: French Open*** 1r (lost Dinu 2–6 6–3 6–1), ***Wimbledon*** 2r (d. Lake 6–3 6–1, lost Smylie 6–3 6–1), ***US Open*** 2r (d. Kanellopoulou 7–5 7–5, lost Hobbs 6–2 7–6).

ISABEL CUETO (West Germany)
Born Kehl, Rhein, 3 December, 1968; lives Aspach; LH; 2HB; 5ft 7in; 124lb; final 1987 WITA ranking 29; 1987 prize money $48,268.
1984: Won Valencia. ***1985:*** Won Nat 18s for 2nd time; qf Taranto and Bregenz. ***1986:*** (96) Qf Athens, Bregenz and Perugia. ***1987:*** At Hamburg reached first f since 1984. ***1987 HIGHLIGHTS – SINGLES: French Open*** 2r (d. Medrado 6–3 6–2, lost Tauziat 6–2 0–6 6–3), ***US Open*** 3r (d. Rush Magers 1–6 7–5 7–5, Louie Harper 6–3 6–2, lost Sukova [seed 6] 7–6 6–1); ***r/u*** Hamburg (d. Weigl 6–4 6–1, Huber 7–5 6–7 6–1, Meskhi 6–3 6–3, Goles 6–1 3–6 6–1, Horvath 6–4 1–6 6–2, lost Graf 6–2 6–2); ***sf*** Athens (d. Bonsignori 6–3 6–0, Villagran 6–1 6–2, Dechaume 2–6 7–5 7–5, lost Halard 7–6 7–6).

KEVIN CURREN (USA)
Born Durban, South Africa, 2 March, 1958; lives Austin, Tex.; RH; 2HB; 6ft 1in; 170lb; final 1987 ATP ranking 37 singles, 19 doubles; 1987 prize money $171,458; career prize money $1,785,282.
Coached by Warren Jacques. Became US citizen in 1985. ***1979:*** (195) A huge server with a two-handed forehand (a shot he has since abandoned), he won NCAA champs while attending University of Texas. ***1980:*** (47) Last 16 Wimbledon. ***1981:*** (57) Won Johannesburg in spring; last 16 US Open. ***1982:*** (17) Won Cologne singles, US Open doubles with Steve Denton and 2nd straight US Open mixed and Wimbledon mixed with A. Smith.

1983: (9) R/u Milan and reached sf Wimbledon, upsetting Connors in last 16. ***1984:*** (15) R/u to Wilander at Australian Open (d. Lendl). ***1985:*** (10) R/u to Becker at Wimbledon (d. McEnroe and Connors) and won Toronto Indoor. ***1986:*** (18) Won his 1st SS title in Atlanta and was one of only four players to beat Lendl, upsetting world No. 1 at Canadian Open. ***1987:*** Reached qf only 3 times in singles but won 3 doubles titles. ***1987 HIGHLIGHTS – SINGLES: Australian Open*** 3r, seed 8 (bye, d. Fitzgerald 7–5 6–2 6–7 4–6 6–3, lost Doohan 4–6 6–7 6–4 7–6), Wimbledon 2r, seed 16 (d. Testerman 7–6 7–6 6–3, lost Kriek 6–4 3–6 6–3 6–2). ***1987 HIGHLIGHTS – DOUBLES:*** (with Pate unless stated) [Annacone] ***won*** Tokyo (d. Gomez/Jarryd 6–4 7–6), ***won*** Los Angeles (d. Gilbert/Wilkison 6–3 6–4), ***won*** Johannesburg (d. Korita/Pearce 6–4 6–4). ***CAREER HIGHLIGHTS – SINGLES: Wimbledon – r/u 1985*** (d. Edberg 7–6 6–3 7–6, McEnroe 6–2 6–2 6–4, Connors 6–2 6–2 6–1, lost Becker 6–3 6–7 7–6 6–4), ***sf 1983*** (d. Connors 6–3 6–7 6–3 7–6, Mayotte, lost C. Lewis 6–7 6–4 7–6); ***Australian Open – r/u 1984*** (d. Lendl, S. Davis, Testerman, lost Wilander 6–7 6–4 7–6 6–2). ***CAREER HIGHLIGHTS – DOUBLES:*** (with Denton) ***US Open – won 1982*** (d. Amaya/Pfister 6–2 6–7 5–7 6–2 6–4); ***US CC – won 1980*** (d. Fibak/Lendl 3–6 7–6 6–4), ***won 1981*** (d. Ramirez/Winitsky 7–5 fs); ***US Pro Indoor – won 1983*** (d. McEnroe/Fleming 6–4 7–6); ***Wimbledon – sf 1982*** (lost McEnroe/Fleming 6–2 6–4 2–6 6–3), ***sf 1983*** (lost Tim/Tom Gullikson 7–6 6–7 7–6 6–3); ***Australian Open – sf 1981*** (lost Edmondson/Warwick). ***MIXED DOUBLES:*** (with A. Smith) ***Wimbledon – won 1982*** (d. Lloyd/Turnbull 2–6 6–3 7–5); ***US Open – won 1981*** (d. Denton/Russell 6–4 7–6), ***won 1982*** (d. Taygan/Potter 6–3 7–6).

MARY LOU PIATEK DANIELS (USA)
Born Whiting, Ind., 6 August, 1961; lives Munster, Ind.; RH; 2HB; 5ft 6in; 125lb; final 1987 WITA ranking 92; 1987 prize money $39,831.
Coached by Emille Foster and her father, Joseph. ***1979:*** Ranked 1 in US 18s, she won Wimbledon and Italian Jun titles and was r/u at US and French Open Jun. ***1980:*** (23) Turned pro after an impressive season for Trinity Univ in Texas. R/u Richmond. ***1981:*** (17) Won Richmond. ***1982:*** (37) Sf French Open doubles with Walsh. ***1983:*** (64) Sf Washington. ***1984:*** (60). ***1985:*** (61) Qf VS Denver. ***1986:*** (98). ***1987:*** Married Paul Daniels 19 Oct. ***1987 HIGHLIGHTS – SINGLES: Wimbledon*** 1r (lost Meier 6–2 6–2), ***US Open*** 1r (lost Bunge [seed 12] 6–3 7–5). ***1987 HIGHLIGHTS – DOUBLES:*** [A. White] ***won*** VS Dallas (d. Burgin/R. White 7–5 6–3), [R. White] ***won*** VS Arkansas (d. Antonoplis/Gerken 6–2 6–4). ***CAREER HIGHLIGHTS – DOUBLES: French Open*** – [Walsh] ***sf 1982*** (d. Madruga Osses/Tanvier 7–6 6–4, lost Casals/Turnbull 6–0 2–6 6–3); ***Wimbledon*** – [Leand] ***qf 1983*** (lost Casals/Turnbull 6–3 5–7 6–2).

FRANCO DAVIN (Argentina)
Born Buenos Aires, 11 January, 1970; LH; 5ft 8in; 140lb; final 1987 ATP ranking 166; 1987 prize money $39,163.
Coached by Raul Perez Roldan. ***1985:*** (508). ***1986:*** (111) R/u Buenos Aires. ***1987:*** Qf Bari and Bologna. ***1987 HIGHLIGHTS – SINGLES: French Open*** 3r (d. Vekemans 7–5 3–6 2–6 6–2 9–7, Antonitsch 5–7 6–3 6–2 6–3, lost Connors [seed 8] 6–3 6–1 6–2); ***sf*** Madrid (d. Kist 6–3 5–7 7–5, Tous 5–7 6–2 7–6, Bardou 3–6 7–5 6–1, lost E. Sanchez 7–5 6–1).

MARTY DAVIS (USA)
Born San José, Cal., 15 November, 1958; lives Harbor Bay Isle, Cal.; RH; 6ft; 180lb; final 1987 ATP ranking 96; 1987 prize money $64,976.
Wife Jill. ***1981:*** (117) Sf Hong Kong. ***1982:*** (141) All-American at Cal-Berkeley. Reached sf Bristol, qf LA, Hong Kong, Bangkok and won Mexico City doubles with Dunk. ***1983:*** (85) Improved his ranking. ***1984:*** (63) Won first GP tourn in Honolulu. ***1985:*** (63) Captured GP events in Bristol and Melbourne. ***1986:*** (89) Toppled S. Davis and Arias but results were less spectacular. ***1987:*** Qf Washington was his best showing. ***1987 HIGHLIGHTS – SINGLES: Australian Open*** 2r (d. Eagle 7–6 6–4 7–6, lost Kratzmann 6–4 6–2 6–4), ***Wimbledon*** 1r (lost Connors [seed 7] 6–1 7–6 7–6).

SCOTT DAVIS (USA)
Born Santa Monica, Cal., 27 August, 1962, and lives Bardmoor CC, Fla.,RH; 6ft 2in; 170lb; final 1987 ATP ranking 59 singles, 23 doubles; 1987 prize money $145,438.

1977–80: No. 1 US Jun. in his age group. ***1980:*** (457) Broke Dick Stockton's previous record of 20 US Nat Jun titles, concluding jun career with 24. ***1983:*** (24) Graduated from Stanford, turned pro, won Maui (first GP title), r/u Seiko Tokyo (d. Leconte, Gomez, Connors, lost Lendl 6–4 fs), Newport and Taipei. Won Columbus doubles with Teacher. ***1984:*** (48) Married Suzy Jaeger (sister of Andrea). Reached last 16 Wimbledon, extending Lendl to 7–5 in 5s, and qf Australian Open. ***1985:*** (17) Finalist LIPC and sf at US Pro Indoor and Chicago; won Japan Open and qualified for Masters first time. Won doubles at Stratton Mountain, Japan Open (with Pate) and LA (with Van't Hof). ***1986:*** (39) An off year in which injuries and bad draws contributed to his woes. Began working with Australian Bob Brett in autumn in effort to build up stamina and confidence and finished on a high note as r/u WCT Houston. ***1987:*** Beat Mecir and Connors to reach sf Tokyo. Continued to work with Bob Brett until end of year. ***1987 HIGHLIGHTS – SINGLES: Australian Open*** 2r (d. McNamara 7–6 6–4 2–6 3–6 6–4), ***French Open*** 1r (lost Schapers 7–6 5–7 6–4 6–4), ***Wimbledon*** 3r (d. de Miguel 6–1 6–1 6–3, V. Amritraj 6–3 6–0 6–4, lost Kriek 5–7 6–4 6–7 6–1 8–6), ***US Open*** 1r (lost Hlasek 3–6 6–3 2–6 6–4 6–4); ***sf*** Tokyo (d. Lapidus 6–4 6–3, Hogstedt 5–2 ret'd, Mecir 7–5 6–1, Connors 6–3 6–4, lost Pate 7–5 6–1). ***1987 HIGHLIGHTS – DOUBLES:*** (with Pate) ***r/u*** Frankfurt (lost Becker/Kuhnen 6–4 6–3).

HORACIO de la PENA (Argentina)
Born Buenos Aires, 1 August, 1966, and lives there; LH; 5ft 11in; 138lb; final 1987 ATP ranking 88; 1987 prize money $57,177.
Has twin sister, Nuria. ***1984:*** (90) Won two satellite events, beginning to fulfil promise he had exhibited in sweeping Nat 12, 14, 16, and 18 jun crowns. ***1985:*** (70) Joined Argentine D Cup team. Won GP Marbella and reached sf Buenos Aires. ***1986:*** (38) Producing superior CC results, he reached last 16 at French Open, was r/u at Bari, and reached sf Boston (d. Tulasne). ***1987:*** Sf Bari, qf Buenos Aires and stunned McEnroe 1r French Open. ***1987 HIGHLIGHTS – SINGLES: French Open*** 3r (d. McEnroe [seed 7] 4–6 6–2 6–4 6–2, Purcell 6–3 6–4 6–3, lost E. Sanchez 6–3 6–3 4–6 6–3); ***sf*** Bari (d. Baldoni 7–6 6–4, Allgaardh 6–3 7–5, Avendano 6–3 1–6 7–6, lost Cancellotti 6–3 6–3).

ISABELLE DEMONGEOT (France)
Born Gassin, 18 September, 1966; lives St Tropez; RH; 5ft 7in; 123lb; final 1987 WITA ranking 53; 1987 prize money $59,810.
Coached by Regis DeCamaret. ***1983:*** (245) No. 1 player on Israeli satellite circuit. ***1984:*** (165) No. 15 in ITF World Jun rankings. R/u French Nat. ***1985:*** (135) Won Chicago on USTA satellite circuit and reached sf Hilversum. ***1986:*** (64) Reached last 16 Wimbledon and qf Mahwah. ***1987:*** Played Fed Cup; qf San Francisco and San Diego. ***1987 HIGHLIGHTS – SINGLES: French Open*** 2r (d. Tarabini 6–2 7–5, lost Evert [seed 3] 6–3 7–5), ***Wimbledon*** 3r (d. Miro 6–3 6–1, Garrone 3–6 6–2 8–6, lost Sabatini [seed 6] 6–3 6–4), ***US Open*** 3r (d. Perez Roldan 6–2 6–2, Nagelsen 6–4 6–1, lost Hanika [seed 13] 6–4 6–2). ***1987 HIGHLIGHTS – DOUBLES:*** (with Tauziat) ***won*** Paris (d. Cecchini/Goles 1–6 6–3 6–3).

ANN DEVRIES (Belgium)
Born Bree, 27 February, 1970; lives Maaseik; RH; 2HB; 5ft 6in; 125lb; final 1987 WITA ranking 100; 1987 prize money $23,910.
Coached by Nick Carr. ***1986:*** (170). ***1987:*** Won Australian Open Jun doubles with Provis and in senior tournaments reached qf Belgian Open, Taipei, Singapore and Auckland. ***1987 HIGHLIGHTS – SINGLES: Australian Open*** 2r (d. Okamoto 6–2 2–6 6–4, lost Lindqvist [seed 10] 6–2 6–3), ***French Open*** 1r (lost Krapl 6–4 6–4), ***Wimbledon*** 1r (lost Kohde-Kilsch [seed 8] 6–0 6–1), ***US Open*** 2r (d. Van Nostrand 6–3 6–2, lost Kijimuta 6–3 1–6 6–2).

NIEGE DIAS (Brazil)
Born Rio Grande, 5 December, 1966; lives Porto Alegre; 5ft 5in; 130lb; RH; final 1987 WITA ranking 117; 1987 prize money $30,164.
Coached by Luis Enck. ***1985:*** (116) Ranked 1 in her country. ***1986:*** (72) Played Fed Cup. ***1987 HIGHLIGHTS – SINGLES: French Open*** 1r (lost Hanika [seed 5] 6–2 6–1), ***Wimbledon*** 1r (lost Smylie 6–2 6–3), ***US Open*** 2r (d. Sanchez 6–4 6–2, lost Evert [seed 3] 6–0 6–1). ***1987 HIGHLIGHTS – DOUBLES:*** (with Medrado) ***won*** Brazilian Open (d. Gildemeister/Huber 4–6 6–4 7–6).

GARY DONNELLY (USA)
Born Phoenix, 3 June, 1962; lives Scottsdale; RH; 6ft 3in; 180lb; final 1987 ATP ranking 439 singles, 20 (23) doubles; 1987 prize money $101,647.
Coached by Kim Warwick. ***1983:*** Turned pro. ***1985:*** (257) Ranked 40 in doubles. ***1986:*** (50) Reached last 16 US Open singles and Wimbledon doubles f with Fleming. ***1987:*** Lost 1r singles 1st 18 tourns but was one of the most successful doubles players. Took 3 months off Nov. to Jan. 1988 to refresh his mind and work out with Carl Coombs. ***1987 HIGHLIGHTS – SINGLES: Australian Open*** 1r (lost Simpson 7–6 6–7 6–3 7–6), ***French Open*** 1r (lost Chesnokov 6–1 6–3 6–3), ***Wimbledon*** 1r (lost Bailey 4–6 7–6 7–5 7–6), ***US Open*** 2r (d. Limberger 4–6 6–7 7–5 6–4 6–4, lost Svensson 6–4 4–6 3–6 6–2 7–6). ***1987 HIGHLIGHTS – DOUBLES:*** (with Fleming unless stated) [Holmes] ***won*** Livingston (d. Flach/Seguso 7–6 6–3), [Muller] ***won*** Schenectady (d. Pearce/Pugh 7–6 6–2), ***won*** Washington (d. Warder/Willenborg 6–2 7–6); [DePalmer] ***r/u*** Chicago (lost Annacone/Van Rensburg 6–3 7–6), ***r/u*** Tourn of Champs (lost Forget/Noah). ***CAREER HIGHLIGHTS – DOUBLES:*** (with Fleming) ***Wimbledon – r/u 1986*** (lost Nystrom/Wilander 7–6 6–3 6–3).

PETER DOOHAN (Australia)
Born Newcastle, 2 May, 1961 and lives there; RH; 6ft 3in; 165lb; final 1987 ATP ranking 72 singles, 27 doubles; 1987 prize money $101,020.
1982: All-American at Univ. of Arkansas; won NCAA doubles with Serrett. ***1983:*** (281). ***1984:*** (84) Won Adelaide. ***1985:*** (101) R/u Adelaide and Melbourne. ***1986:*** (301) Out of action 5 months with tendonitis of the shoulder suffered late in year. ***1987:*** Confirmed his grass-court ability by reaching last 16 Australian Open and f Sydney before bringing off the upset of the year at Wimbledon where he stunned Becker 2r *en route* to last 16. Formed a successful doubles partnership with Warder, reaching f Australian Open. ***1987 HIGHLIGHTS – SINGLES: Australian Open*** last 16, unseeded (d. Tyson 7–6 7–6 6–1, Scanlon 6–3 1–6 7–5 7–6, Curren [seed 8] 4–6 6–3 6–4 6–4, lost Jarryd [seed 9] 6–1 6–7 6–4 7–6), ***Wimbledon*** last 16, unseeded (d. Antonitsch 4–6 7–5 6–2 4–6 9–7, Becker [seed 1] 7–6 4–6 6–2 6–4, Shiras 6–7 4–6 6–3 6–4 12–10, lost Zivojinovic 6–2 6–4 7–6), ***US Open*** 1r (lost Gilbert [seed 13] 6–1 6–2 6–2); ***won*** Martinique Challenger (d. Nelson 6–3 6–2); ***r/u*** Sydney (d. Mmoh, Jarryd 6–3 3–6 6–1, Odizor 6–4 6–3, Drewett 6–7 6–4 6–4, lost Mecir 6–2 6–4). ***1987 HIGHLIGHTS – DOUBLES:*** (with Warder) ***r/u Australian Open*** seed 16 (d. Flach/Seguso 6–1 3–6 6–1 4–6 10–8 [seed 3], lost Edberg/Jarryd [seed 1] 6–4 6–4 7–6); ***r/u*** Adelaide (lost Lendl/Scanlon 6–7 6–3 6–4), ***r/u*** Sydney (lost Drewett/Edmondson 6–4 4–6 6–2), ***r/u*** Montreal (lost Cash/Edberg 6–7 6–3 6–4). ***CAREER HIGHLIGHTS – DOUBLES:*** (with Warder) ***Australian Open – r/u 1987.***

VICKI NELSON DUNBAR (USA)
Born Wooster, Ohio, 25 September, 1962; lives North Ridgeville; RH; 5ft 6in; 120lb; final 1987 WITA ranking 99; 1987 prize money $27,611.
1980: Ranked 11 in US 18s. ***1981:*** (87) Reached last 16 US CC. ***1982:*** (65) Sf Hong Kong and last 16 US Open. ***1983:*** (110) Qf Fort Myers and Tokyo. ***1984:*** (92) Won longest officially recorded match in modern women's pro tennis 6–4 7–6 in 6 hours and 31 minutes over Jean Hepner at Richmond Ginny. ***1985:*** (79) Married tennis pro Keith Dunbar. R/u Italian Open. ***1986:*** (116). ***1987:*** Won first major singles title at Brazilian Open. ***1987 HIGHLIGHTS – SINGLES: Australian Open*** 2r (bye, lost Durie [seed 14] 7–5 6–1), ***French Open*** 1r (lost Rinaldi [seed 10] 6–2 6–0), ***Wimbledon*** 1r (lost Tanvier 6–1 7–5), ***US Open*** 1r (lost K. Maleeva 6–2 6–3); ***won*** Brazilian Open (d. Pennington, Golder, Nozzoli 7–5 6–2, Schwartz 6–4 6–3, Klitch 6–2 7–6).

LAWSON DUNCAN (USA)
Born Asheville, NC, 26 October, 1964 and lives there; RH; 6ft 1in; 165lb; final 1987 ATP ranking 93; 1987 prize money $46,293.
Coached by Woody Blocher. ***1984:*** (165) In his only year at Clemson Univ., was r/u NCAA to Pernfors. ***1985:*** (59) R/u Bari, Marbella and Madrid. ***1986:*** (174) Qf Bari and St Vincent. ***1987:*** Won 2 titles in Challenger Series. ***1987 HIGHLIGHTS – SINGLES: US Open*** 1r (lost Flach 6–2 7–6 6–0); ***won*** Agadir Challenger (d. Pugh 6–4 6–2), ***won*** Casablanca Challenger (d. Narducci 7–5 6–1).

JO DURIE (Great Britian)
Born Bristol, 27 July, 1960; lives there and London; RH; 6ft; 150lb; final 1987 WITA ranking (73); 1987 prize money $78,765.
Coached by Alan Jones. ***1978:*** Top-ranked British jun. ***1979:*** (73) Sf Wimbledon Plate. ***1980:*** (53) Out of action 8 months following back surgery. Sf German Indoor Open. ***1981:*** (31) Last 16 US Open; won British HC. ***1982:*** (28) No. 1 in Great Britain, taking over from Wade. ***1983:*** (6) Best year of career when she reached sf US and French Opens, qf Australian Open, and won Sydney and Mahwah. ***1984:*** (24). ***1985:*** (26) Sf Brighton (d. Graf). ***1986:*** (23) Played 17 tournaments and W and Fed Cups, winning 24 of 44 matches, beating McNeil, Lindqvist and K. Jordan, but best showing was sf Mahwah in summer. ***1987:*** In W Cup ended 23-match winning streak by US when she d. Garrison, but otherwise suffered a poor year. ***1987 HIGHLIGHTS – SINGLES: Australian Open*** last 16, seed 14 (bye, d. Nelson Dunbar 7–5 6–1, Polzl 6–1 6–4, lost Shriver [seed 3] 6–1 6–2), ***French Open*** 1r (lost Novotna 6–3 6–1), ***Wimbledon*** 3r (d. Van Nostrand 6–2 6–0, Mesker 6–3 6–3, lost Sukova [seed 4] 6–1 6–3), ***US Open*** 2r (d. A. Minter 6–3 2–6 6–2, lost Mandlikova [seed 4] 6–3 6–7 6–2). ***CAREER HIGHLIGHTS – SINGLES: US Open – sf 1983*** (d. Madruga Osses 6–2, lost Evert Lloyd 6–4 6–4); ***French Open – sf 1983*** (d. Moulton, Shriver, Rinaldi, Austin 6–0 fs, lost Jausovec 6–2 fs); ***Australian Open – qf 1983*** (lost Navratilova 4–6 6–3 6–4). ***CAREER HIGHLIGHTS – DOUBLES:*** (with Hobbs unless stated) ***Wimbledon – sf 1983*** (lost Navratilova/Shriver 6–3 7–5), [Evert Lloyd] ***qf 1985*** (d. Bunge/Pfaff, lost Navratilova/Shriver [seed 1] 6–4 6–2); ***French Open – sf 1983*** (lost Fairbank/Reynolds 6–3 6–2); ***Australian Open – sf 1985*** (lost Navratilova/Shriver 7–6 6–2).

STEFAN EDBERG (Sweden)
Born Vastervik, 19 January, 1966; lives London; RH; 6ft 2in; 158lb; final 1987 ATP ranking 2 singles, 3 (3) doubles; 1987 prize money $1,587,467; career prize money $3,573,502.
Coached by Tony Pickard. ***1983:*** (53) Won jun Grand Slam, proving prowess on 3 different surfaces, and played 11 events on men's tour. ***1984:*** (20) Won Milan and contributed crucial triumph in D Cup f as Sweden d. USA with doubles win alongside Jarryd over McEnroe/Fleming, repeating their success over that duo at US Open, where they were r/u. ***1985:*** (5) Reached top 5 with first GS men's success, upending Lendl and Wilander for Australian Open title. Also won San Francisco, Basle and Memphis. ***1986:*** (5) Won Gstaad, Basle and Stockholm, lost four other finals (two to Becker, one to McEnroe, one to Gilbert) and reached sf US Open. In doubles with Jarryd won Masters and r/u French Open. ***1987:*** Won 2nd Australian singles title, sf Wimbledon and US Open, won titles in Memphis, Rotterdam, Tokyo (2), Cincinnati and Stockholm, reached 4 more f and achieved win-loss singles record of 70–11 going into Masters, where he reached sf. In doubles with Jarryd won Australian and US Opens, and reached sf Masters. ***1987 HIGHLIGHTS – SINGLES: won Australian Open*** seed 4 (bye, d. Letts 3–6 6–1 6–0 6–2, Frawley 6–4 6–3 6–1, Seguso [seed 13] 6–1 6–0 6–1, Mecir [seed 6] 6–1 6–4 6–4, Masur 6–2 6–4 7–6, Cash [seed 11] 6–3 6–4 3–6 5–7 6–3), ***French Open*** 2r, seed 3 (d. Leach 6–2 6–3 6–3, lost Winogradsky 7–6 7–6 7–5), ***Wimbledon*** sf, seed 4 (d. Eriksson 6–0 6–0 6–0, Purcell 6–4 6–3 6–4, Anger 7–6 6–2 6–2, Hlasek 6–3 6–7 6–1 6–4, Jarryd 4–6 6–4 6–1 6–3, lost Lendl 3–6 6–4 7–6 6–4), ***US Open*** sf, seed 2 (d. Rostagno 6–3 7–6 6–2, Goldie 6–7 6–4 6–2 6–4, Evernden 6–2 6–1 6–4, Svensson 6–2 7–6 6–3, Krishnan 6–2 6–2 6–2, lost Wilander [seed 3] 6–4 3–6 6–3 6–4); ***won*** Memphis (d. Reneberg, Krishnan, Mayotte 6–3 6–4, Gilbert 6–4 7–6, Connors 6–3 2–1 ret'd), ***won*** Rotterdam (d. Birner 6–1 6–2, Maurer 6–0 6–0, Jarryd 6–3 6–7 6–4, Grabb 6–3 6–4, McEnroe 3–6 6–3 6–1), ***won*** Tokyo (d. Grabb 7–5 6–4, Goldie 6–3 7–5, Jarryd 6–3 6–2, Gomez 4–6 7–6 6–2, Pate 7–6 6–4), ***won*** Cincinnati (d. Arias 6–4 6–4, Hlasek 7–6 7–5, Benhabiles 6–3 6–1, Gilbert 6–1 6–3, Connors 6–2 6–3, Becker 6–4 6–1), ***won*** Tokyo Seiko (d. Fukui, J. Carlsson 6–0 6–2, Annacone 3–6 6–1 6–2, Zivojinovic 7–6 4–6 6–2, Lendl 6–7 6–4 6–4), ***won*** Stockholm (d. Reneberg 6–7 6–0 6–2, Stenlund 7–6 6–3, Lundgren 6–1 7–6, Jarryd 6–4 6–2, J. B. Svensson 7–5 6–2 4–6 6–4); ***r/u*** Indian Wells (d. Arraya, Witsken, Mecir 4–6 6–4 6–2, Wilander 6–1 7–6, lost Becker 6–4 6–4 7–5), ***r/u*** Bastad (d. Eriksson 6–3 6–2, Haldin 6–2 6–0, Vojtisek 6–3 6–4, E. Sanchez 6–4 6–0, lost Nystrom 4–6 6–0 6–3), ***r/u*** Montreal (d. Pridham 7–5 7–6, Arias 7–5 6–2, Curren 7–6 7–5, Becker 6–2 6–4, lost Lendl 6–4 7–6), ***r/u*** Los Angeles (d. Flur 6–2 6–2, Berger 6–3 7–6, Annacone 6–1 7–5, Wilkison 6–2 6–3, lost Pate 6–4 6–4); ***sf*** WCT Finals (d. Mayotte, lost McEnroe), ***sf*** Masters (d. Cash 6–4 4–6 6–1, Mecir 6–3 6–3, Wilander 6–2 7–6 in rr,

lost Wilander 6–2 4–6 6–3). ***1987 HIGHLIGHTS – DOUBLES:*** (with Jarryd unless stated) ***won Australian Open*** seed 1 (d. Annacone/Van Rensburg [seed 4] 6–3 7–6 6–3, Doohan/Warder [seed 16] 6–4 6–4 7–6), ***won US Open*** (d. Casal/E. Sanchez, Flach/Seguso 7–6 6–2 4–6 5–7 7–6); ***won*** Rotterdam (d. Mecir/Smid, Hooper/M. Leach 3–6 6–3 6–4), ***won*** Bastad (d. E./J. Sanchez 7–6 6–3), [Cash] ***won*** Montreal (d. Doohan/Warder 6–7 6–3 6–4), ***won*** Stockholm (d. Grabb/Pugh 6–3 6–4). ***CAREER HIGHLIGHTS – SINGLES: Australian Open – won 1985*** (D. Masur 6–7 2–6 7–6 6–4 6–2 [saving 2 mps], Schapers, Lendl [seed 1] 6–7 7–5 6–1 4–6 9–7, Wilander [seed 3] 6–4 6–3 6–3), ***won 1987; Wimbledon – sf 1987; US Open – sf 1986*** (d. Bonneau, Curren, Krishnan, Goldie, Wilkison 6–3 6–3 6–3, lost Lendl [seed 1] 7–6 6–2 6–3), ***sf 1987. CAREER HIGHLIGHTS – DOUBLES:*** (with Jarryd) ***US Open – won 1987, r/u 1984*** (d. McEnroe/Fleming 3–6 7–6 7–5 7–6, lost Fitzgerald/Smid 7–6 6–3 6–3); ***Australian Open – won 1987; Masters – won 1985*** (d. Wilander/Nystrom 4–6 6–2 6–3), ***won 1986*** (d. Forget/Noah 6–3 7–6 6–3); ***French Open – r/u 1986*** (lost Fitzgerald/Smid 6–3 4–6 6–3 6–7 14–12).

KELLY EVERNDEN (New Zealand)
Born Gisborne, 21 September, 1961; lives Sydney, Australia; RH; 5ft 9½in; 155lb; final 1987 ATP ranking 36; 1987 prize money $167, 667.
Coached by Jeff Simpson. Has only one lung following a serious motor accident when he was 16. ***1983:*** (527). ***1984:*** (255). ***1985:*** (86) R/u Brisbane and Sydney. Joined New Zealand D Cup squad. ***1986:*** (289). ***1987:*** Began the year well by reaching qf Australian Open, unseeded, won his 1st GP title at Bristol, following with Brisbane singles and doubles in Oct. ***1987 HIGHLIGHTS – SINGLES: Australian Open*** qf, unseeded (d. Canter 7–6 6–3 6–4, Kriek [seed 10] 6–2 2–6 6–4 6–4, Pearce 6–2 6–2 6–4, Rostagno 6–7 6–2 6–4 5–7 7–5, lost Masur 6–3 7–5 6–4), ***Wimbledon*** 3r (d. Goldie 6–3 4–6 6–4 7–5, Visser 6–2 7–6 6–1, lost Connors [seed 7] 6–1 6–2 6–7 6–3), ***US Open*** 3r (d. Sundstrom 6–2 6–2 7–6, Flur 4–6 7–6 3–6 6–4 6–3, lost Edberg [seed 2] 6–2 6–1 6–4); ***won*** Bristol (d. Layendecker 6–4 6–2, Goldie 6–2 6–2, J. B. Svensson 3–6 6–3 6–3, Edwards 3–6 6–3 6–4, Jelen 6–7 6–3 6–2, Wilkison 6–4 7–6), ***won*** Brisbane (d. Eagle 5–7 7–5 6–1, Shaw 6–0 6–3. Krishnan 7–6 6–1, J. Frawley 5–7 6–3 6–4, Jelen 3–6 6–1 6–1). ***1987 HIGHLIGHTS – DOUBLES:*** (with Anger) ***won*** Brisbane (d. Dyke/Masur 7–6 6–2). ***CAREER HIGHLIGHTS – SINGLES: Australian Open – qf 1987.***

CHRIS EVERT (USA)
Born Fort Lauderdale, Fla., 21 December, 1954; lives Amelia Island, Fla.; RH; 2HB; 5ft 6in; 125lb; final 1987 WITA ranking 3; 1987 prize money $769,943; career prize money $7,965,861.
1970: At age 15, only weeks after Margaret Court had won GS, she stunned the world No. 1 7–6 7–6 in sf Charlotte. ***1971:*** Watched by her coach and proud father Jimmy Evert, she became the youngest sf in history of US Champ (now US Open), upsetting Eisel (saving 6 mps after trailing 6–4 6–5 40–0), Durr, and Hunt, finally losing to King. In W Cup début at Cleveland demolished Wade 6–1 6–1 and closed jun career with triumph at US Nat 18 Champ. ***1972:*** Reached sf on début at Wimbledon before losing first career showdown with Goolagong after leading by a set and 3–0. Won 4 tourns including US CC over Goolagong and VS Champ over Melville to be ranked No. 3 by most experts behind King and Goolagong. ***1973:*** R/u Wimbledon, French and Italian Opens and won SA Open and 11 other tourns to remain No. 3 behind Court and King. ***1974:*** Universally regarded as No. 1 in the world, winning 16 of 23 tourns, 100 of 107 matches and 10 straight tourns from March until September. ***1975:*** (1) Won first US Open, second French Open, 16 of 22 tourns and 94 of 100 matches. ***1976:*** (1) Swept 2nd Wimbledon and 3rd US Open titles, winning 12 of 17 tourns and 75 of 80 matches. ***1977:*** (1) Won third straight US Open, 11 of 14 tourns and 70 of 74 matches. ***1978:*** (2) Ranked first by most experts after winning fourth consecutive US Open and first on cement at Flushing Meadow, being r/u at Wimbledon and winning 7 of 11 tourns and 56 of 59 matches, losing only to Goolagong in Boston and Navratilova at Eastbourne and Wimbledon. ***1979:*** (3) R/u Wimbledon, losing to Navratilova, and at US Open, losing to Austin in f. Married John Lloyd 17 April. ***1980:*** (1) Regained top ranking with third French Open triumph and fifth US Open title, defeating Austin in sf. Won 8 of 15 tourns and 71 of 78 matches. ***1981:*** (1) Just beat Austin and Navratilova to No. 1 position after capturing third Wimbledon singles title without loss of a set (the first

since King in 1967 to achieve that feat), and winning 9 of 15 tourns and 73 of 79 matches. ***1982:*** (2) Closed year with strong surge, including 6th US Open over Mandlikova and first Australian title over Navratilova. Won 10 of 16 tourns, 75 of 81 matches. ***1983:*** (2) Won fifth French Open and was r/u to Navratilova at US Open, although 3r Wimbledon loss to K. Jordan, when she was unwell, was first pre-sf defeat in 35 GS career events. Won 6 of 15 tourns, 57 of 65 matches. ***1984:*** (2) Captured Australian Open at end of season to win GS singles title for the 11th consecutive year, and was r/u to Navratilova at French, Wimbledon and US Opens, being the only player of either sex to appear in every GS f. Won 6 of 14 tourns and 69 of 77 matches. ***1985:*** (2) Ended 13-match losing streak against Navratilova with 6–2 6–4 win in f VS Florida and won sixth French Open with 6–3 6–7 7–5 triumph over Navratilova after Martina rallied from 2–4, 15–40 down in 2s and from 2–0 3–1 and 5–3 down in fs. Won 10 of 18 tourns, 81 of 89 matches. ***1986:*** (2) Won record 7th French Open to extend GS streak to at least one for each of the last 13 years. Won 6 of 12 tourns, 59 of 66 matches, did not play after US Open as knee injury forced first sustained absence of her career. ***1987:*** After 5½ months out of action with injuries to left knee and right heel, she slipped out of the top 2 on March 3 for the first time since 1981, and on 12 April dropped briefly from the top 3 – behind Navratilova, Graf and Mandlikova – for the first time since the early 1970s. At Dallas in March she won her first tourn since French Open 1986 and at New Orleans won a record 153rd title – more than any man or woman in the Open era. However, she lost to Navratilova at French Open and Wimbledon and McNeil at US Open, thus failing for the first time in 14 years to win a GS title. It was only the second time in 16 years she had failed to reach sf of GS tourn. After ss defeat by Hanika in 1r VS Champs, she took a break to reconsider her future. Divorced from John April 1987. ***1987 HIGHLIGHTS – SINGLES: French Open*** sf, seed 3 (d. Pfaff 6–1 6–3, Demongeot 6–3 7–5, Krapl 6–2 6–0, K. Maleeva [seed 12] 6–3 6–1, Reggi [seed 14] 6–2 6–2, lost Navratilova [seed 1] 6–2 6–2), ***Wimbledon*** sf (d. Gomer 6–1 6–0, Golarsa 7–5 6–0, Okamoto 7–5 6–0, Fairbank 6–2 2–6 7–5, Kohde-Kilsch [seed 8] 6–1 6–3, lost Navratilova 6–2 5–7 6–4), ***US Open*** qf, seed 3 (d. Sloane 6–1 6–0, Dias 6–0 6–1, Zvereva 6–0 6–2, M. Maleeva [seed 10] 7–5 6–4, lost McNeil [seed 11] 3–6 6–2 6–4); ***won*** VS Dallas (d. K. Maleeva 2–6 6–3 6–1, Bassett 6–0 6–1, Rehe 6–1 6–0, Garrison 3–6 6–1 6–0, Shriver 7–5 6–3), ***won*** Houston (d. Herreman 6–1 6–1, Perez Roldan 6–2 6–1, Gompert 6–3 6–3, Mandlikova 6–3 7–5, Navratilova 3–6 6–1 7–6), ***won*** Tampa (d. Dinu, Benjamin, Gildemeister 6–2 6–1, Bowes 6–0 6–0, Gompert 6–3 6–2), ***won*** Geneva (d. Derly 6–1 6–4, Gompert 6–3 6–1, McNeil 6–0 6–2, M. Maleeva 6–3 4–6 6–2), ***won*** New Orleans (d. A. Minter 6–0 6–1, Gerken 6–4 6–1, A. Smith 6–2 6–0, Turnbull 4–2 ret'd, McNeil 6–3 7–5); ***r/u*** VS LA (d. R. White 6–0 7–5, Novotna 7–6 6–3, McNeil 6–1 7–5, Navratilova 6–2 6–1, lost Graf 6–3 6–4), ***r/u*** Filderstadt (d. Marsikova 6–2 7–5, Reggi 6–4 6–1, M. J. Fernandez 6–2 5–7 6–4, Shriver 7–5 6–3, lost Navratilova 7–5 6–1), ***r/u*** VS New England (d. Torres, Holikova, Potter 1–6 6–1 6–3, Sabatini 6–4 7–6, lost Shriver 6–4 4–6 6–0); ***sf*** LIPC (d. Mundel 6–0 6–1, Kijimuta 6–1 6–1, Nelson Dunbar 6–0 6–0, Rehe 6–3 6–2, Kohde-Kilsch 6–2 7–5, Mandlikova 7–5 6–0, lost Graf 6–1 6–2), ***sf*** FC Cup (d. Huber 7–5 6–2, Spence 6–3 6–0, Bunge 6–3 6–2, lost M. Maleeva 6–1 2–6 7–6), ***sf*** Eastbourne (d. Walsh Pete 6–2 6–1, Bonder 6–1 6–1, W. White 6–3 6–4, Savchenko 6–1 6–3, lost Sukova 4–6 6–4 8–6), ***sf*** Canadian Open (d. Gomer 6–3 6–2, Tauziat 6–3 6–2, Kelesi 6–2 6–0, lost Shriver 6–4 6–1). ***1987 HIGHLIGHTS – DOUBLES:*** (with Turnbull unless stated) ***won*** Plymouth (d. McNeil/Bunge 3–6 6–3 6–2, ***won*** Tampa (d. Burgin/Fairbank 6–4 6–3); [Shriver] ***r/u*** VS Florida (lost Parkhomenko/Savchenko 6–0 3–6 6–2). ***CAREER HIGHLIGHTS – SINGLES: French Open – won 1974*** (d. Morozova 6–1 6–2), ***won 1975*** (d. Navratilova 2–6 6–2 6–0), ***won 1979*** (d. Turnbull 6–2 6–0), ***won 1980*** seed 1 (d. Mandlikova 6–3 3–6 6–3, Ruzici 6–0 6–3), ***won 1983*** (d. Sukova, Mandlikova 4–6 6–3 6–2, Jaeger 6–3 6–1, Jausovec 6–1 6–2), ***won 1985*** (d. Navratilova 6–3 6–7 7–5), ***won 1986*** (d. Calmette 6–0 6–1, Herreman 6–2 6–1, A. Smith 6–3 6–1, Sabatini 1–6 6–3 6–3, Bassett 5–7 6–2 6–1, Mandlikova 6–1 6–1, Navratilova 2–6 6–3 6–3), ***r/u 1973*** (lost Court 6–7 7–6 6–4), ***r/u 1984*** (lost Navratilova 6–3 6–1), ***sf 1981*** (lost Mandlikova [seed 5] 7–5 6–4), ***sf 1982*** (lost Jaeger 6–3 6–1), ***sf 1987***; ***Wimbledon – won 1974*** (d. Hunt 8–6 5–7 11–9, Masthoff 6–4 6–2, Reid 6–2 6–3, Morozova 6–0 6–4), ***won 1976*** (d. Navratilova 6–3 4–6 6–4, Goolagong Cawley 6–3 4–6 8–6), ***won 1981*** (d. Jausovec 6–2 6–2, Shriver 6–3 6–1, Mandlikova 6–2 6–2), ***r/u 1973*** (d. Court 6–1 1–6 6–1, lost King 6–0 7–5), ***r/u 1978*** (d. Wade 8–6 6–2, lost Navratilova 2–6 6–4 7–5), ***r/u 1979*** (d. Goolagong Cawley 6–3 6–2, lost Navratilova 6–4 6–4), ***r/u 1980*** seed 3 (d.

Jaeger 6–1 6–1, Navratilova [seed 1] 4–6 6–4 6–2, lost Goolagong Cawley [seed 4] 6–1 7–6), ***r/u 1982*** seed 2 (d. King 7–6 2–6 6–3, lost Navratilova 6–2 3–6 6–2), ***r/u 1984*** (d. Mandlikova 6–1 6–2, lost Navratilova 7–6 6–2), ***r/u 1985*** (lost Navratilova 4–6 6–3 6–2), ***sf 1972*** (lost Goolagong 4–6 6–3 6–4), ***sf 1975*** (lost King 2–6 6–2 6–3), ***sf 1977*** (lost Wade 6–2 4–6 6–1), ***sf 1986*** (d. M. J. Fernandez 6–4 6–1, Casale 6–0 5–7 6–1, Horvath 6–4 6–1, K. Jordan 7–5 6–2, Sukova 7–6 4–6 6–4, lost Mandlikova [seed 3] 3–6 7–5), ***sf 1987***; ***US Open – won 1975*** (d. Navratilova 6–4 6–4, Goolagong Cawley 5–7 6–4 6–2), ***won 1976*** (d. Goolagong Cawley 6–3 6–0), ***won 1977*** (d. King 6–2 6–0, Stove 6–3 7–5, Turnbull 7–6 6–2), ***won 1978*** (d. Turnbull 6–3 6–0, Shriver 7–5 6–4), ***won 1980*** seed 3 (d. Austin [seed 1] 4–6 6–1 6–1, Mandlikova 5–7 6–1 6–1), ***won 1982*** seed 2 (d. Gadusek 4–6 6–1 6–0, Jaeger 6–1 6–2, Mandlikova 6–3 6–1), ***r/u 1979*** (d. King 6–1 6–1, lost Austin 6–4 6–3), ***r/u 1983*** (d. Mandlikova 6–4 6–3, Durie 6–4 6–4, lost Navratilova 6–4 6–3), ***r/u 1984*** (lost Navratilova 4–6 6–4 6–4), ***sf 1971*** (d. Eisel 4–6 7–6 6–1 [saved 6 m-ps at 5–6 2s], Durr 2–6 6–2 6–3, Hunt 4–6 6–2 6–3, lost King 6–3 6–2), ***sf 1972*** (d. Morozova 3–6 6–3 7–6, lost Reid 6–4 6–2), ***sf 1973*** (lost Court 7–5 2–6 6–2), ***sf 1974*** (lost Goolagong 6–1 6–7 6–3), ***sf 1981*** (d. Mandlikova, lost Navratilova 7–6 4–6 6–4), ***sf 1985*** (lost Mandlikova 4–6 6–2 6–3), ***sf 1986*** (d. Gerken 6–2 6–1, Marsikova 6–0 6–0, M. J. Fernandez 6–4 6–2, Lindqvist 6–2 2–6 6–2, M. Maleeva 6–2 6–2, lost Sukova [seed 7] 6–2 6–4); ***Australian Open – won 1982*** seed 2 (d. King 6–2 6–2, Jaeger 6–1 6–0, Navratilova 6–3 2–6 6–2), ***won 1984*** (d. Sukova 6–7 6–1 6–3), ***r/u 1974*** (lost Goolagong 7–6 4–6 6–0), ***r/u 1981*** (lost Navratilova 6–7 6–4 7–5), ***r/u 1985*** (lost Navratilova 6–2 4–6 6–2); ***Italian Open – won 1974*** (d. Navratilova 6–3 6–3), ***won 1975*** (d. Navratilova 6–1 6–0), ***won 1980*** (d. Ruzici 5–7 6–2 6–3), ***won 1981*** (d. Ruzici 6–1 6–2), ***won 1982*** (d. Mandlikova 6–0 6–3), ***r/u 1973*** (lost Goolagong 7–6 6–0); ***CS Champ – won 1977*** (d. King 6–2 6–2), ***won 1978*** (d. Navratilova 6–3 6–3), ***VS Champ – won 1972*** (d. Reid 7–5 6–4), ***won 1973*** (d. Richey 6–3 6–3), ***won 1975*** (d. Navratilova 6–4 6–2), ***won 1977*** (d. Barker 2–6 6–1 6–1), ***r/u 1974*** (lost Goolagong 6–3 6–4), ***r/u 1976*** (lost Goolagong Cawley 6–4 5–7 6–3), ***r/u 1984*** (lost Navratilova 6–3 7–5 6–1), ***sf 1985–86*** (lost Mandlikova 6–3 7–5); ***US CC – won 1972*** (d. Goolagong 7–6 6–1), ***won 1973*** (d. V. Burton 6–4 6–3), ***won 1974*** (d. Chanfreau 6–0 6–0), ***won 1975*** (d. Fromholtz 6–3 6–4), ***won 1979*** (d. Goolagong Cawley 6–4 6–3); ***US Indoor – won 1978*** (d. Wade 6–7 6–2 6–4); ***South African Open – won 1973*** (d. Goolagong 6–3 6–3). ***CAREER HIGHLIGHTS – DOUBLES:*** (with Navratilova unless stated) ***Wimbledon – won 1976*** (d. King/Stove 6–1 3–6 7–5); ***French Open –*** [Morozova] ***won 1974*** (d. Chanfreau/Ebbinghaus 6–4 2–6 6–1), ***won 1975*** (d. Anthony/Morozova); ***Italian Open –*** [Morozova] ***won 1974*** (w.o. Masthoff/Orth), ***won 1975*** (d. Barker/Coles), [Ruzici] ***r/u 1981*** (lost Reynolds/P. Smith 7–5 6–1); ***Australian Open –*** [Turnbull] ***sf 1984*** (lost Navratilova/Shriver 6–4 6–3). ***MIXED DOUBLES:*** (with Connors) ***US Open – r/u 1974*** (lost Teeguarden/Masters).

ROSALYN FAIRBANK (South Africa)

Born Durban, 2 November, 1960; lives San Diego, Cal.; RH; 5ft 8in; 140lb; final 1987 WITA ranking 37 singles, 19 (12) doubles; 1987 prize money $113,258.

Coached by Rod Nideffer. ***1978:*** Seemingly shy and somewhat portly, she displayed extraordinary court sense and a fine flat forehand in her drive to f Orange Bowl, losing to A. Jaeger. ***1979:*** Established herself firmly on women's tour, winning 22 of 23 matches on Australian satellite tour and reaching f NSW Open. ***1980:*** (33) Won Wimbledon Plate. ***1981:*** (43) Won French Open doubles with Harford. ***1982:*** (17) Won Indianapolis, sf Detroit and Fort Myers. ***1983:*** (26) Won Richmond. ***1984:*** (32) Sf VS LA. ***1985:*** (38) Beat Rehe in San Diego. ***1986:*** (30) Sf Canadian Open (d. Sabatini) and Brighton, r/u French Open mixed doubles with Edmondson, and sf Wimbledon and US Open doubles with Burgin. ***1987:*** Reached last 16 Wimbledon, extending Evert to 7–5 fs. ***1987 HIGHLIGHTS – SINGLES: Australian Open*** 2r, seed 16 (bye, lost Thompson 3–6 6–4 8–6), ***French Open*** 1r (lost Cioffi 6–2 6–3), ***Wimbledon*** last 16, unseeded (d. Werdel 6–2 6–3, Fendick 6–2 5–7 6–2, Bunge [seed 9] 7–6 6–4, lost Evert 6–2 2–6 7–5), ***US Open*** 2r (d. Gerken 1–6 6–4 6–2, lost Tarabini 6–2 4–6 6–3); ***sf*** Newport (d. Reis 7–5 6–3, E. Minter 6–0 6–4, McNeil 5–7 6–4 6–4, lost W. White 6–3 6–4). ***1987 HIGHLIGHTS – DOUBLES:*** (with Burgin unless stated) [R. White] ***won*** Beckenham (d. Hy/Inoue 6–2 6–2), ***won*** VS New England (d. Bunge/Pfaff 6–4 6–4); ***r/u*** Tampa (lost Evert/Turnbull 6–4 6–3), [Smylie] ***r/u*** Eastbourne (lost Parkhomenko/Savchenko 7–6 4–6 7–5). ***CAREER HIGHLIGHTS – DOUBLES:*** (with Harford unless stated) ***French Open – won 1981*** (d. K. Jordan/A. Smith, Reynolds/P. Smith 6–1

6–3), [Reynolds] ***won 1983*** (d. Durie/Hobbs, K. Jordan/A. Smith 5–7 7–5 6–2); ***US Open*** – [Reynolds] ***r/u 1983*** (d. Burgin/Russell 7–5 fs, King/Walsh 7–5 fs, lost Navratilova/Shriver 6–7 6–1 6–3), ***qf 1981*** (lost K. Jordan/A. Smith 6–4 6–4); ***Wimbledon – sf 1981*** (lost K. Jordan/A. Smith 6–1 6–2); [Burgin] ***sf 1986*** (lost Navratilova/Shriver 6–4 6–3). ***MIXED DOUBLES:*** (with Edmondson) ***French Open – r/u 1986*** (lost Flach/K. Jordan 3–6 7–6 6–3).

PATTY FENDICK (USA)
Born Sacramento, Cal., 31 March, 1965, and lives there; RH; 5ft 5in; 117lb; final 1987 WITA ranking 78; 1987 prize money $30,092.
Scar tissue in her eye from an old injury expands and restricts her vision in brightness, obliging her to wear a baseball cap to play tennis. ***1983:*** Won Wimbledon Jun doubles with Hy, and Orange Bowl 18s singles and doubles. ***1984:*** Member US Jun Fed Cup team. All-American for Stanford, playing No. 1 on that team. ***1985:*** (83). ***1986:*** (94) Sf Wimbledon doubles with Hetherington and won NCAA Champs. ***1987:*** NCAA Champ for second time. ***1987 HIGHLIGHTS – SINGLES: Wimbledon*** 2r (d. Bohmova 6–1 6–4, lost Fairbank 6–2 5–7 6–2), ***US Open*** 2r (d. Field 6–3 2–6 6–0), lost Bunge [seed 12] 6–2 6–4). ***CAREER HIGHLIGHTS – DOUBLES:*** (with Hetherington) ***Wimbledon – sf 1986*** (lost Mandlikova/Turnbull 6–3 6–7 6–3).

GIGI FERNANDEZ (Puerto Rico)
Born Puerto Rico, 22 February, 1964; lives there and Fort Worth, Texas; 5ft 7in; 145lb; final 1987 WITA ranking 39 singles, 20 (20) doubles; 1987 prize money $101,841.
Coached by Don Usher. ***1983:*** (84) Narrowly beaten 7–6 fs by Herr in f AIAW. ***1984:*** (27) Buoyed by praise she received from Navratilova after coming within two points of upsetting Shriver at Wimbledon, she reached f Newport as 'Lucky Loser' and pushed Navratilova to 2s tb. ***1985:*** (64) Won LIPC doubles with Navratilova. ***1986:*** (62) Qualified with R. White for VS Champ doubles in Nov. ***1987:*** Reached last 16 Wimbledon unseeded, qf VS Florida and San Diego and won 3 doubles titles with McNeil. ***1987 HIGHLIGHTS – SINGLES: Australian Open*** 2r (d. McCann 6–4 6–3, lost Werdel 6–2 6–3), ***French Open*** 2r (d. Herr 6–2 6–4, lost Wasserman 6–3 6–2), ***Wimbledon*** last 16, unseeded (d. K. Maleeva 7–6 1–6 6–4, Parkhomenko 6–2 3–6 6–4, Cordwell 7–6 6–1, lost Navratilova 6–3 6–1), ***US Open*** 1r (lost Paz 6–4 6–2); ***sf*** New Jersey (d. Forman 6–1 6–0, Gurney 6–3 6–0, Kim 6–1 7–6, lost Sukova 6–3 7–5). ***1987 HIGHLIGHTS – DOUBLES:*** (with McNeil) ***won*** New Jersey (d. Nagelsen/Smylie 6–1 6–4), ***won*** VS Newport (d. Hobbs/K. Jordan 7–6 7–5), ***won*** Mahwah (d. Hobbs/Smylie 6–3 6–2. ***CAREER HIGHLIGHTS – DOUBLES:*** [Navratilova] ***LIPC – won 1985*** (d. K. Jordan/Mandlikova 7–6 6–2).

MARY JOE FERNANDEZ (USA)
Born Dominican Republic, 19 August, 1971; lives Miami, Fla.; RH; 2HB; final 1987 WITA ranking 20; 1987 prize money $57,567.
Coached by Fred Stolle. ***1982:*** Won Orange Bowl 12s, beating Sabatini in f. ***1983:*** Won Orange Bowl 14s, beating Sabatini in sf. ***1984:***Won Orange Bowl 16s, US 16 Nat, US 16 CC and was ranked 1 in US 16s. ***1985:*** (99) Won Orange Bowl 18s, ranked second behind Rehe in US 18s. ***1986:*** (27) Demonstrating her uncanny court sense, her excellent anticipation, her extraordinary determination and formidable flat forehand and two-handed backhand, she stopped 4th-seeded Kohde-Kilsch to reach qf French Open; had other good CC wins over Rehe and Sabatini during year. ***1987:*** Reached last 16 Wimbledon, qf Geneva and Filderstadt. ***1987 HIGHLIGHTS – SINGLES: French Open*** 2r, seed 13 (d. Horvath 4–6 6–0 6–2, lost Rehe 7–6 1–6 6–4), ***Wimbledon*** last 16, unseeded (d. Bonder 6–0 6–2, Potter 6–0 6–1, Moulton 7–6 6–2, lost Balestrat 7–5 6–2), ***US Open*** 3r (d. Marsikova 6–3 6–0, Savchenko 6–1 6–4, lost M. Maleeva [seed 10] 6–0 0–6 6–3). ***CAREER HIGHLIGHTS – SINGLES: French Open – qf 1986*** (d. Temesvari, Hobbs, Kohde-Kilsch 7–6 7–5, lost Sukova 6–2 6–4).

LOUISE FIELD (Australia)
Born Melbourne, 25 February, 1967; lives Pearcedale; RH; 5ft 5in; 130lb; final 1987 WITA ranking 114; 1987 prize money $35,688.
1981: Won Australian Nat 14s. ***1984:*** Won Australian Open Jun doubles with Savchenko.

1985: (123) Won Wimbledon Jun doubles with Thompson, r/u Australian Jun singles. ***1986:*** (127). ***1987 HIGHLIGHTS – SINGLES: Australian Open*** 2r (d. Gerken 7–6 1–6 6–4, lost E. Reinach 6–1 6–2), ***French Open*** 1r (lost Herreman 6–4 6–2), ***Wimbledon*** 2r (d. Torres 7–6 6–1, lost Kohde-Kilsch 7–6 6–0), ***US Open*** 1r (lost Fendick 6–3 2–6 6–0).

JOHN FITZGERALD (Australia)
Born Cummins, 28 December, 1960, and lives there; RH; 6ft 1in; 170lb; final 1987 ATP ranking 73; 1987 prize money $90,384.
1979: (301). ***1980:*** (136) Won $25,000 tourn in Tokyo. ***1981:*** (60) Last 16 Wimbledon and won Kitzbuhel over Vilas. ***1982:*** (78) Won Australian Open doubles with Alexander, and in singles won Hawaii and r/u Sydney. ***1983:*** (35) Last 16 Australian Open, where he won mixed doubles with Sayers, and won Newport and Stowe. Member of winning Australian D Cup team. ***1984:*** (29) Won Sydney NSW and r/u Melbourne; sf Australian Open doubles with Cash. ***1985:*** (91) In doubles won Auckland with C. Lewis, Las Vegas with Cash and Sydney Indoor with Jarryd, also reaching f Wimbledon (d. McEnroe/Fleming) and Queens Club, both with Cash. ***1986:*** (102) Won French Open doubles with Smid. In victorious Australian D Cup squad, winning doubles in f over Edberg/Jarryd with Cash. Married Jenny Harper 18 Nov. ***1987:*** Underwent shoulder surgery in Feb. Reached 1st f in 3 years at Hong Kong and d. Connors 2r Tokyo Seiko. ***1987 HIGHLIGHTS – SINGLES: Australian Open*** 2r (bye, lost Curren [seed 8] 7–5 6–2 6–7 4–6 6–3), ***French Open*** 1r (lost Anger 7–6 7–5 6–3), ***Wimbledon*** 1r (lost Hlasek 6–1 6–4 7–6), ***US Open*** 2r (d. Williamson 6–3 7–5 6–4, lost Mecir [seed 5] 6–3 6–1 6–0); ***r/u*** Hong Kong (d. Drewett 6–2 1–6 6–4, Pugh 6–1 7–6, Saceanu 6–1 4–6 6–2, Bates 6–3 6–4, lost Teltscher 6–7 3–6 6–1 6–2 7–5). ***1987 HIGHLIGHTS – DOUBLES:*** (with Denton) ***r/u Cincinnati*** (lost Flach/Seguso 7–5 6–3). ***CAREER HIGHLIGHTS – DOUBLES:*** (with Cash unless stated) ***French Open*** – [Smid] ***won 1986*** (d. Edberg/Jarryd 6–3 4–6 6–3 6–7 14–12); ***Australian Open*** – [Alexander] ***won 1982*** (d. Taygan/Rennert, Andrews/Sadri 6–4 7–6), ***sf 1984*** (lost Nystrom/Wilander 6–4 6–4 2–6 6–3); ***Wimbledon – r/u 1985*** (d. McEnroe/Fleming, lost Gunthardt/Taroczy).

KEN FLACH (USA)
Born St Louis, 19 May, 1963; lives Sebring, Fla.; RH; 6ft 1in; 160lb; final 1987 ATP ranking 100 singles, 5 (19) doubles; 1987 prize money $226,371.
1983: All-American at Southern Ill. Univ. with Seguso. ***1984:*** (154) In doubles with Seguso won Italian Open, US Pro, US CC, Los Angeles, Hong Kong, Taipei and WCT London. ***1985:*** (60) With Seguso won US Open, Fort Myers, WCT Forest Hills, Queens Club, US CC, Canadian Open, Tokyo Seiko. ***1986:*** (223) Won mixed doubles with K. Jordan at French Open and Wimbledon. Married Sandra Freeman 9 Sept. ***1987:*** Last 16 US Open and qf Livingston in singles; won Wimbledon and r/u US Open and Masters in doubles with Seguso. ***1987 HIGHLIGHTS – SINGLES: Australian Open*** 3r (bye, d. Srejber [seed 12] 3–6 2–6 7–5 6–3 6–3, lost Kratzmann 6–4 6–2 6–3), ***Wimbledon*** 3r (d. Saad 6–1 6–4 6–4, Sadri 3–6 6–3 7–6 6–3, lost Gomez [seed 8] 6–4 6–3 3–6 7–5), ***US Open*** last 16, unseeded (d. Duncan 6–2 7–6 6–0, Cahill 1–6 6–4 3–6 6–1 7–6, E. Sanchez [seed 14] 5–7 7–6 7–6 7–5, lost Wilander [seed 3] 6–3 6–3 7–6). ***1987 HIGHLIGHTS – DOUBLES:*** (with Seguso unless stated) ***won Wimbledon*** (d. Casal/Sanchez 3–6 6–7 7–6 6–1 6–4), ***r/u US Open*** (lost Edberg/Jarryd 7–6 6–2 4–6 5–7 7–6); ***won*** Cincinnati (d. Denton/Fitzgerald 7–5 6–3), Stratton Mountain divided with Annacone/Van Rensburg; ***r/u*** LIPC (lost Annacone/Van Rensburg 6–2 6–4 6–4), [Grabb] ***r/u*** Seoul (lost Korita/Leach 6–7 6–1 7–5), ***r/u*** Livingston (lost Donnelly/Holmes 7–6 6–3), ***r/u*** Wembley (lost Mecir/Smid 7–5 6–4), ***r/u*** Masters (lost Mecir/Smid 6–4 7–5 6–7 6–3). ***CAREER HIGHLIGHTS – DOUBLES:*** (with Seguso) ***Wimbledon – won 1987; US Open – won 1985*** (d. Noah/Leconte 7–6 6–7 7–6 6–0), ***r/u 1987; Italian Open – won 1984*** (d. Alexander/M. Leach 3–6 6–3 6–4); ***Masters – r/u 1987. MIXED DOUBLES:*** (with K. Jordan) ***French Open – won 1986*** (d. Edmondson/Fairbank 3–6 6–7 6–3); ***Wimbledon – won 1986*** (d. Gunthardt/Navratilova 6–3 7–6).

PETER FLEMING (USA)
Born Chatham, NJ, 21 January, 1955; lives London and Glen Cove, NY; RH; 6ft 5in; 185lb; final 1987 ATP ranking 174 singles, 21 (4) doubles; 1987 prize money $75,192; career prize money $1,986,717.
Wife Jennifer, children Joe (born 1984) and Alexandra (born 31 Jan. 1987). ***1976:*** R/u to

Scanlon at NCAA Champ. ***1977:*** (47). ***1978:*** (26) Won Bologna, r/u WCT Challenge Cup and Maui and r/u Wimbledon doubles with McEnroe. ***1979:*** (13) Moved as high as No. 7 during the year. Won ATP Champs over Roscoe Tanner and LA over McEnroe; r/u to McEnroe San Francisco. Won Wimbledon and US Open doubles with McEnroe and played D Cup. ***1980:*** (38) Qf Wimbledon singles. ***1981:*** (106) Won Wimbledon and US Open doubles with McEnroe and played doubles on winning US D Cup team. ***1982:*** (389) Played doubles on winning US D Cup team again. ***1983:*** (32) Won Wimbledon and US Open doubles with McEnroe. ***1984:*** (49) Won Masters doubles with McEnroe for 7th year in a row. ***1985:*** (94) Sf Houston. ***1986:*** (103) Reached 7th Wimbledon doubles f but with a different partner – Donnelly, and won 5 doubles titles with Forget (4) and McEnroe (1). ***1987:*** Qf Chicago singles and won only 1 doubles title – Washington with Donnelly. ***1987 HIGHLIGHTS – SINGLES: Wimbledon*** 1r (lost Bates 7–6 7–6 7–6), ***US Open*** 2r (d. Arias 7–6 6–7 6–2 7–6, lost Jarryd [seed 16] 6–3 6–4 6–2). ***1987 HIGHLIGHTS – DOUBLES:*** (with Donnelly) ***won*** Washington (d. Warder/ Willenborg 6–2 7–6); ***r/u*** Tourn of Champs (lost Forget/Noah). ***CAREER HIGHLIGHTS – SINGLES: ATP Champs – won 1979*** (d. Tanner 6–4 6–2); ***Wimbledon – qf 1980*** (d. Dowdeswell, Birner, Nastase 6–4 3–6 7–6 7–6, Parun 6–3 6–2 6–7 7–6, lost McEnroe 6–3 6–2 6–2). ***CAREER HIGHLIGHTS – DOUBLES:*** (with McEnroe unless stated) ***Wimbledon – won 1979*** (d. Gottfried/Ramirez 4–6 6–4 6–2), ***won 1981*** (d. Lutz/Smith 6–4 6–4 6–4), ***won 1983*** (d. Tim/Tom Gullikson 6–4 6–3 6–4), ***won 1984*** (d. Cash/McNamee 6–2 5–7 6–2 3–6 6–3), ***r/u 1978*** (lost Hewitt/McMillan 6–1 6–4 6–2), ***r/u 1982*** (lost McNamara/McNamee 6–3 6–2), [Donnelly] ***r/u 1986*** (lost Nystrom/Wilander 7–6 6–3 6–3), ***sf 1985*** (lost Cash/Fitzgerald); ***US Open – won 1979*** (d. Smith/Lutz 6–2 6–4), ***won 1981*** (d. Newcombe/Stolle 6–2 6–2 6–7 5–7 7–6, McNamara/Gunthardt def.), ***won 1983*** (d. Buehning/Winitsky 6–3 6–4 6–2); ***Masters – won 1978*** (d. Lutz/Smith 6–4 6–2 6–4), ***won 1979*** (d. Fibak/Okker 6–4 6–2 6–4), ***won 1980*** (d. McNamara/McNamee 6–4 6–3), ***won 1981*** (d. Curren/Denton 6–3 6–3), ***won 1982*** (d. Stewart/Taygan 7–5 6–3), ***won 1983*** (d. Slozil/Smid 6–2 6–2), ***won 1984*** (d. Edmondson/Stewart 6–3 6–1); ***Italian Open –*** [Smid] ***won 1979*** (d. Clerc/Nastase 4–6 6–1 7–5). ***MIXED DOUBLES:*** [Navratilova] ***US Open – r/u 1986*** (lost Reggi/Casal 6–4 6–4).

GUY FORGET (France)

Born Casablanca, Morocco, 4 January, 1965; lives Marseilles and London; LH; 6ft 2in; 160lb; final 1987 ATP ranking 54 singles 6 (8) doubles; 1987 prize money $224,273.

1982: (70) Was world's second best jun, winning Orange Bowl in Dec. and making presence felt on GP tour. ***1983:*** (188) String of 1r losses as he joined men's tour. ***1984:*** (36) Confidence restored by reaching 3r Wimbledon and last 16 Australian Open where he beat V. Amritraj (seed 15). Qf Queens, Bordeaux, Stockholm and Wembley where he beat Jarryd and Becker. ***1985:*** (61) Despite sf appearances in Gstaad and Toulouse, he suffered a hard year. ***1986:*** (25) Reached last 16 French Open where he held m-p before bowing to Vilas. Won Toulouse, as his grandfather (1946) and father (1966) had done, and lifted his ranking again. R/u Masters doubles with Noah. ***1987:*** Last 16 Wimbledon, d. Noah with whom he was r/u French Open, and won 5 titles. ***1987 HIGHLIGHTS – SINGLES: French Open*** 1r (lost Wahlgren 6–3 6–4 6–4), ***Wimbledon*** last 16, unseeded (d. Muster 6–4 6–4 6–4, Noah [seed 6] 3–6 7–6 4–6 6–4 9–7, Annacone 4–6 6–4 4–6 6–2 6–4, lost Cash [seed 11] 6–2 6–3 6–4), ***US Open*** 3r (d. Seguso 3–6 7–5 6–3 6–2, Benhabiles 7–6 4–6 4–6 6–3 6–4, lost Gilbert [seed 13] 6–4 6–7 7–5 6–4); ***sf*** Basel (d. Limberger 6–3 6–2, Mezzadri 7–5 4–6 6–4, Zivojinovic 5–7 6–4 6–4, lost Noah 6–1 6–2). ***1987 HIGHLIGHTS – DOUBLES:*** (with Noah unless stated) ***r/u French Open*** (lost Jarryd/Seguso 6–7 6–7 6–3 6–4 6–2); ***won*** Lyon (d. Jones/Pate 4–6 6–3 6–4), ***won*** Indian Wells (d. Casal/E. Sanchez 6–2 6–4, Becker/Jelen 6–4 7–6), ***won*** Tourn of Champs (d. Donnelly/Fleming 4–6 6–4 6–1), ***won*** Italian Open (d. Mecir/Smid 6–2 6–7 6–3), ***won*** Queens (d. Leach/Pawsat 6–4 6–4); [Courteau] ***r/u*** Gstaad (lost Gunnarsson/Smid 7–6 6–2). ***CAREER HIGHLIGHTS – DOUBLES:*** (with Noah) ***French Open – r/u 1987.***

JOHN FRAWLEY (Australia)

Born Redcliffe, 4 July, 1965 and lives there; RH; 5ft 8in; 165lb; final 1987 ATP ranking 42; 1987 prize money $25,099.

Brother of Rod. ***1983:*** (152). ***1984:*** (67) Sf Munich, qf Los Angeles and Brisbane. ***1985:***

Peter Doohan of Australia, who leapt from 301 to 72 in the rankings, confirmed his grass-court ability by reaching the last 16 of the Australian Open and the final at Sydney before ending Boris Becker's quest for a third Wimbledon title by beating him there in the second round. *(T. Hindley)*

(174). ***1986:*** (249) Kept off GP circuit by back injuries; r/u Lisbon Challenger. ***1987:*** Plagued all year by injuries again but upset Cash *en route* to sf Brisbane. ***1987 HIGHLIGHTS – SINGLES: Australian Open*** 3r (bye, d. P. Carlsson 6–2 6–3 3–2 ret'd, lost Edberg [seed 4] 6–4 6–3 6–1); ***won*** Brisbane Challenger (d. Kratzmann 6–2 6–2); ***sf*** Brisbane (d. Muller 6–4 6–4, Anger 6–2 6–2, Cash 6–4 6–3, lost Evernden 5–7 6–3 6–4).

BETTINA FULCO (Argentina)
Born Mar Del Plata, 23 October, 1968 and lives there; RH; 5ft 3in; 120lb; final 1987 WITA ranking 44; 1987 prize money $39,620.
Coached by Patricio Apey. ***1986:*** (118) Won 3 singles titles on Italian Circuit. ***1987:*** Sf Wild Dunes, qf Argentine Open. ***1987 HIGHLIGHTS – SINGLES: French Open*** 2r (d. Calleja 6–0 6–0, lost K. Maleeva [seed 12] 6–3 2–6 6–4), ***Wimbledon*** 3r (d. Budarova 6–0 6–3, Hobbs 6–4 6–3, Balestrat 7–6 6–0), ***US Open*** 1r (lost Graf 6–0 6–3); ***sf*** Wild Dunes (d. Nelson Dunbar 6–1 6–1, Paz 5–7 6–4 6–1, Jaeger 6–1 6–1, Cecchini 6–0 2–6 6–2, lost M. Maleeva 6–4 6–1).

ZINA GARRISON (USA)
Born Houston, 16 November, 1963, and lives there; RH; 5ft 4½in; 128lb; final 1987 WITA ranking 9 singles, 7 (18) doubles; 1987 prize money $328,694; career prize money $1,198,961.
1981: Won Wimbledon and US Open Jun. ***1982:*** (16) Qf French Open and last 16 Wimbledon. ***1983:*** (10) Sf Australian Open, Eastbourne and Detroit. ***1984:*** (9) Won Zurich; r/u VS Washington and New Orleans. ***1985:*** (8) Won WTA Champs (d. Mandlikova and Evert Lloyd), sf Wimbledon and r/u US CC. ***1986:*** (11) Won 48 of 69 matches as she won VS Indianapolis, reached f Tampa and sf Canadian Open. ***1987:*** Suffering stress fracture to foot, was obliged to pull out of French Open and missed Wimbledon. Won NSW Open and VS California, reached f Canadian Open, 5 sf, and qf Australian Open. In doubles was r/u Australian Open with McNeil and won Australian Open mixed with Stewart. Qualified for VS Champs in singles and doubles. ***1987 HIGHLIGHTS – SINGLES: Australian Open*** qf, seed 7 (bye, d. Ludloff 6–1 6–1, Pfaff 6–2 3–6 7–5, Turnbull [seed 11] 6–1 6–3, lost Navratilova [seed 1] 6–0 6–3), ***US Open*** last 16, seed 7 (d. Scheuer-Larsen 6–1 6–3, Phelps 7–6 6–1, K. Maleeva 7–6 7–6, lost McNeil [seed 11] 7–6 3–6 7–6); ***won*** NSW Open (d. Turnbull 6–3 6–4, Shriver 6–2 6–4), ***won*** VS California (d. Demongeot 6–3 6–3, Louie Harper 6–1 6–1, W. White 6–1 6–2, Mandlikova 7–5 4–6 6–2, Hanika 1–6 6–3 6–2); ***r/u*** Canadian Open (d. Torres 6–1 6–4, Pfaff 5–7 6–3 6–4, A. Minter 6–1 2–6 6–4, Bunge 6–2 6–0, lost Shriver 6–4 6–1); ***sf*** VS Washington (d. A. Minter 6–2 6–4, Bassett 6–3 6–1, Henricksson 6–2 6–2, lost Potter 3–6 6–3 7–6), ***sf*** VS Dallas (d. Moulton 7–6 6–0, Mochizuki 6–1 6–2, Bunge 6–3 6–4, lost Evert Lloyd 3–6 6–1 6–0), ***sf*** Amelia Island (d. G. Fernandez 6–1 6–1, Bassett 6–1 7–5, Rinaldi 6–4 6–4, lost Mandlikova 6–3 6–3), ***sf*** VS Houston (d. Cioffi, Burgin 6–0 6–0, Reggi 6–1 6–0, lost Navratilova 6–1 7–6), ***sf*** New Orleans (d. Henricksson 6–2 6–1, Lindstrom 7–6 6–4, Werdel 3–6 6–1 6–4, lost McNeil 6–2 6–4). ***1987 HIGHLIGHTS – DOUBLES:*** (with McNeil unless stated) ***r/u Australian Open*** (d. Mandlikova/Turnbull 3–6 6–3 8–6, Kohde-Kilsch/Sukova 7–6 7–6, lost Navratilova/Shriver 6–1 6–0); ***won*** Canadian Open (d. Kohde/Kilsch/Sukova 6–1 6–2), ***won*** New Orleans (d. Louie Harper/Ludloff 6–3 6–3); [Sabatini] ***r/u*** VS California (lost Mandlikova/Turnbull 6–4 7–6), ***r/u*** VS Washington (lost Burgin/Shriver 6–1 3–6 6–4), ***r/u*** FC Cup (lost Paz/Pfaff 7–6 7–5), ***r/u*** VS Houston (lost K. Jordan/Navratilova 6–2 6–4), ***r/u*** VS LA (lost Navratilova/Shriver 6–3 6–4), ***r/u*** Filderstadt (lost Navratilova/Shriver 6–1 6–2), ***r/u*** VS Chicago (lost Kohde-Kilsch/Sukova 6–4 6–3). ***MIXED DOUBLES:*** (with Stewart) ***won Australian Open*** (d. Castle/Hobbs 3–6 7–6 6–3). ***CAREER HIGHLIGHTS – SINGLES: USCC – r/u 1983*** (lost Temesvari 6–2 6–2), ***r/u 1985*** (lost Temesvari 7–6 6–3); ***Wimbledon – sf 1985*** (d. Tanvier, Van Nostrand, lost Navratilova [seed 1] 6–4 7–6); ***Australian Open – sf 1983*** (d. Pfaff, Turnbull 6–2 7–6, lost K. Jordan), ***qf 1985*** (d. Henricksson, lost Mandlikova [seed 3] 2–6 6–3 6–3); ***French Open – qf 1982*** unseeded (d. Bunge, Herr, Jausovec 7–5 6–1, lost Navratilova 6–3 6–2); ***US Open – qf 1985*** (d. Gompert, lost Navratilova [seed 1] 6–2 6–3). ***CAREER HIGHLIGHTS – DOUBLES:*** [Rinaldi] ***US Open – sf 1985*** unseeded (d. Bassett/Evert Lloyd, lost Kohde-Kilsch/Sukova 5–7 6–4 6–3); ***Australian Open*** – [McNeil] ***r/u 1987. MIXED DOUBLES:*** (with Stewart) ***Australian Open – won 1987.***

LAURA GARRONE (Italy)
Born Milan, 15 November, 1967, and lives there; RH; 5ft 5in; 125lb; final 1987 WITA ranking 85; 1987 prize money $28,280.
1985: (108) Won French Open Jun and US Open Jun, was ranked 1 in ITF Jun World Rankings, and 3 in her country behind Reggi and Cecchini. ***1986:*** (38) Reached last 16 French Open, unseeded. ***1987:*** Sf Belgian Open. ***1987 HIGHLIGHTS – SINGLES: French Open*** 3r (d. A. M. Fernandez 6–1 6–2, Bollegraf 6–4 2–6 6–3, lost Hanika [seed 15] 6–4 6–3), ***Wimbledon*** 2r (d. Holladay 3–6 6–3 6–4, lost Demongeot 3–6 6–2 8–6), ***US Open*** 1r (lost Gildemeister 6–3 2–6 6–4); ***sf*** Belgian Open (d. La Fratta 6–3 6–1, Ter Riet 6–2 6–7 6–0, Bonsignori 2–6 7–5 6–3, lost Horvath 6–4 6–2).

BARBARA GERKEN (USA)
Born Santa Monica, Cal., 3 July, 1964; lives Thousand Oaks, Cal.; RH; 2HB; 5ft 5in; 125lb; final 1987 WITA ranking 63; 1987 prize money $49,657.
1981: At 17, she reached qf US Open with wins over Turnbull and Durie. ***1982:*** (60) Ranked 5 in US 18s. ***1983:*** Qf NCAA Champs and was All-American at UCLA. ***1984:*** Qf Wimbledon Plate. ***1985:*** (78) Qf Filderstadt. ***1986:*** (97) Sf Taipei. ***1987:*** R/u Japan/Asian Open and Singapore. ***1987 HIGHLIGHTS – SINGLES: Australian Open*** 1r (lost Field 7–6 1–6 6–4), ***Wimbledon*** 1r (lost Sabatini [seed 6] 6–3 6–3), ***US Open*** 1r (lost Fairbank 1–6 6–4 6–2); ***r/u*** Japan/Asian Open (d. Hy, A. Minter 3–6 6–1 6–3, K. Jordan 6–3 3–6 7–5, Inoue 6–2 7–6, lost K. Maleeva 6–2 6–3), ***r/u*** Singapore (d. O'Neill, Okamoto, Cammie MacGregor 6–4 6–4, Okagawa 6–4 6–3, lost A. Minter 6–4 6–1). ***1987 HIGHLIGHTS – DOUBLES:*** (with Ludloff) ***r/u*** Singapore (lost A. M. Fernandez/Richardson 6–1 6–4).

BRAD GILBERT (USA)
Born Oakland. 9 August, 1961; lives Piedmont, Cal; RH; 6ft 1in; 160lb; final 1987 ATP ranking 13; 1987 prize money $507,187.
Coached by Shivington. ***1982:*** (54) The brother of 1978 US CC titlist Dana Gilbert he played for Allan Fox's Pepperdine team in California and reached f NCAA, losing to M. Leach. Won Taipei. ***1983:*** (62). ***1984:*** (23) Won Columbus and Taipei and reached last 16 Australian Open. ***1985:*** (18) Moved into top 20 winning Livingston, Cleveland and Tel Aviv and capping best year with 1r victory over McEnroe at Masters. ***1986:*** (11) Made further strides, downing Connors and Edberg for US Indoor crown, adding GP titles in Livingston, Israel and Vienna, reaching last 16 Wimbledon and US Open, and playing D Cup. ***1987:*** Qf US Open, won Scottsdale and reached 4 more f to qualify for Masters, where he d. Connors and Becker. ***1987 HIGHLIGHTS – SINGLES: Australian Open*** 3r, seed 7 (bye, d. Drewett 7–5 6–3 6–2, lost Rostagno 4–6 6–2 6–3 6–1), ***French Open*** 2r, seed 15 (d. Oresar 1–6 7–5 2–6 6–4 6–4, lost Arrese 7–5 6–2 6–1), ***Wimbledon*** 3r, seed 12 (d. Bale 7–6 6–4 6–3, Bailey 4–6 7–6 7–5 7–6, lost Volkov 7–6 0–6 6–3 6–4), ***US Open*** qf, seed 13 (d. Doohan 6–1 6–2 6–2, Berger 4–6 6–2 6–4 6–3, Forget 6–4 6–7 7–5 6–4, Becker [seed 4] 2–6 6–7 7–6 7–5 6–1, lost Connors [seed 6] 4–6 6–3 6–4 6–0); ***won*** Scottsdale (d. DePalmer 6–3 6–2, Rostagno 6–4 6–0, Kriek 6–2 6–4, Chang 6–3 6–4, Teltscher 6–2 6–2); ***r/u*** Washington (d. Hooper 6–3 2–6 6–1, Odizor 6–3 6–4, M. Davis 6–4 6–4, Becker 3–6 6–3 6–0, lost Lendl 6–1 6–0), ***r/u*** Tel Aviv (d. Weidenfeld 6–3 4–6 6–0, Perkis 6–1 6–3, Bloom 6–3 6–3, Lundgren 6–3 6–3, lost Mansdorf 3–6 6–3 6–4), ***r/u*** Paris Open (d. Mezzadri 6–0 6–3, Smid 6–2 6–2, Curren 7–5 6–4, Schapers 7–5 5–7 6–4, lost Mayotte 2–6 6–3 7–5 6–7 6–3), ***r/u*** Buenos Aires (d. Westphal 6–2 6–0, Aldrich 6–2 6–1, Hlasek w.o., Gomez 6–4 6–1, lost Cash 7–6 4–6 2–6 6–0 6–1); ***sf*** Memphis (d. Sadri, Jelen 6–3 6–3, Kriek 6–2 7–6, lost Edberg 6–4 7–6), ***sf*** Orlando (d. Dickson 6–1 6–4, Anger 6–1 7–6, Freeman 4–6 6–3 6–1, lost Connors 3–6 6–4 6–2), ***sf*** Los Angeles (d. Witsken 6–2 6–3, Evernden 6–3 7–6, Teltscher 6–1 6–4, lost Page 6–3 6–7 6–3). ***1987 HIGHLIGHTS – DOUBLES:*** (with Wilkison) ***r/u*** Los Angeles (lost Curren/Pate 6–3 6–4). ***CAREER HIGHLIGHTS – SINGLES: US Indoor – won 1986*** (d. Connors 6–4 fs, Jarryd 6–3 6–0, Edberg 7–5 7–6); ***Masters – qf 1985*** (d. McEnroe 5–7 6–4 6–1, lost Jarryd 6–1 6–2).

HANS GILDEMEISTER (Chile)
Born Lima, Peru, 6 Feburary, 1956; lives Santiago and Bardmoor Club, Fla.; RH; 2HF and 2HB; 6ft; 160lb; final 1987 ATP ranking (–) singles, 22 (7) doubles; 1987 prize money $33,063.

1980: (33) Qualified for Masters with Gomez but was unable to play owing to illness. ***1981:*** (29) Won 5 tourns including Italian Open with Gomez. ***1982:*** (35) Reached French Open f with Prajoux, but back injury forced retirement. ***1983:*** (134) Advised to retire owing to back injury, but continued to play limited schedule. ***1984:*** (59) Played only 11 tourns. ***1985:*** (145) Won Hamburg with Gomez and Washington with Pecci. ***1986:*** (161). ***1987:*** Played almost exclusively doubles, winning Monte Carlo and Boston with Gomez. ***1987 HIGHLIGHTS – DOUBLES:*** (with Gomez) ***won*** Monte Carlo (d. Smid/Van Rensburg, Bahrami/Mortensen 6–2 6–4), ***won*** Boston (d. Nystrom/Wilander 7–6 3–6 6–1). ***CAREER HIGHLIGHTS – DOUBLES:*** (with Gomez) ***Italian Open – won 1981*** (d. Manson/Smid 7–5 6–2).

LAURA ARRAYA GILDEMEISTER (Peru)
Born Cordoba, Argentina, 12 January, 1964; lives Miami, Fla.; married Heinz Gildemeister Dec. 1984; RH; 5ft 8in; 125lb; final 1987 WITA ranking 46; 1987 prize money $50,221.
Having lived in Argentina until age 7, she moved with family to Peru and became citizen of that country, but now lives in Miami. ***1982:*** (69) She burst into her own, beating Bonder, Nagelsen, Temesvari and Horvath with her big-hitting game featuring an explosive forehand. ***1983:*** (86) R/u Freiburg, qf Hilton Head. ***1984:*** (34) R/u Tourn of Champs. ***1985:*** (63) Sf VS Utah and Japan Open; played Fed Cup. ***1986:*** (31) Upset Lindqvist, M. Maleeva and Kohde-Kilsch during year. ***1987 HIGHLIGHTS – SINGLES: French Open*** 1r (lost Gomer 6–2 6–4), ***Wimbledon*** 3r (d. Paz 7–5 4–6 6–3, Kijimuta 6–2 6–4, lost Graf [seed 2] 6–2 6–1), ***US Open*** 2r (d. Garrone 6–3 2–6 6–4, lost Golarsa 7–6 6–4). ***1987 HIGHLIGHTS – DOUBLES:*** [Scheuer-Larsen] ***won*** Wild Dunes (d. Paz/Reynolds 6–4 6–4); [Tanvier] ***r/u*** Geneva (lost Nagelsen/Smylie 4–6 6–4 6–3).

DAN GOLDIE (USA)
Born Sioux City, Iowa, 3 October, 1963; lives McLean, Va.; RH; 6ft 2in; 170lb; final 1987 ATP ranking 50; 1987 prize money $107,042.
Coached by Jack Shore and Dick Gould. ***1983:*** (794). ***1984:*** (102) Broke into top 100 during year. ***1985:*** (265). ***1986:*** (113) Last 16 US Open and won NCAA singles playing for Stanford. ***1987:*** Last 16 Australian Open, won 1st pro title in singles and doubles at Newport and broke into top 50. ***1987 HIGHLIGHTS – SINGLES: Australian Open*** last 16, unseeded (d. DePalmer 1–6 6–4 1–6 6–1 6–2, Simpson 6–3 7–6 7–6, Krishnan [seed 16] 4–6 5–7 6–1 6–3 6–3, lost Lendl [seed 1] 2–6 6–4 7–6 6–3), ***Wimbledon*** 1r (lost Evernden 6–3 4–6 6–4 7–5), ***US Open*** 2r (d. Steyn 3–6 6–3 7–5 6–7 6–2, lost Edberg [seed 2] 6–7 6–4 6–2 6–4); ***won*** Newport (d. Scott 7–6 7–6, Pate 6–0 4–6 6–4, Flur 6–4 7–5, Masur 6–2 4–6 6–2, Giammalva 6–7 6–4 6–4). ***1987 HIGHLIGHTS – DOUBLES:*** (with L. Scott) ***won*** Newport (d. Hooper/M. Leach 6–3 4–6 6–4).

SABRINA GOLES (Yugoslavia)
Born Stari Mikanovci, 3 June, 1965; lives Zagreb; 5ft 7in; 130lb; RH; final 1987 WITA ranking 64; 1987 prize money $49,762.
1983: (109) Won Italian Open Jun Champ and made Fed Cup début. ***1984:*** (55) Won Olympic silver medal in LA where she upset Horvath. ***1985:*** (54) Had good wins over Bonder, K. Maleeva and Louie but lacked consistency. ***1986:*** (29) Had best win of her career over Kohde-Kilsch in Hilton Head. ***1987:*** Took Navratilova to 2s tb in 2r Italian Open and won Paris in autumn. ***1987 HIGHLIGHTS – SINGLES: French Open*** 1r (lost Scheuer-Larsen 7–5 6–2), ***Wimbledon*** 2r (d. Bassett 6–4 0–6 6–4, lost Okamoto 4–6 6–3 6–0), ***US Open*** 2r (d. Schultz 7–6 6–3, lost Lindqvist [seed 14] 6–2 6–0); ***won*** Paris (d. Fulco 6–4 4–6 6–3, Halard 4–6 7–6 6–2, Reggi 7–5 7–5, Torres 6–2 6–4, Wasserman 7–5 6–1). ***1987 HIGHLIGHTS – DOUBLES:*** (with Cecchini) ***r/u*** Paris (lost Demongeot/Tauziat 1–6 6–3 6–3).

SARA GOMER (Great Britain)
Born Torquay, 13 May, 1964, and lives there; LH; 6ft 2in; 165lb; final 1987 WITA ranking 72; 1987 prize money $42,495.
1985: (77) One of the tallest players on the tour, this former member of the British Annie Soisbault and Maureen Connolly Brinker Cup teams won USTA San Antonio and was named first time to W Cup squad. ***1986:*** (56) With a record of 15 wins, 15 losses for the

year, she demonstrated her prowess and improvement with wins over Reggi, R. White and Burgin. ***1987 HIGHLIGHTS – SINGLES: Australian Open*** 2r (d. Betzner 4–6 6–2 8–6, lost Hobbs 6–2 6–3), ***French Open*** 2r (d. Gildemeister 6–2 6–4, lost Reggi [seed 14] 6–3 6–3), ***Wimbledon*** 1r (lost Evert [seed 3] 6–1 6–0), ***US Open*** 2r (d. Probst 6–3 6–0, lost Sabatini [seed 8] 6–3 6–1).

ANDRES GOMEZ (Ecuador)
Born Guayaquil, 27 February, 1960 and lives there and Bardmoor Club, Fla.; LH; 6ft 4in; 190lb; final 1987 ATP ranking 11 singles, 11 (2) doubles; 1987 prize money $433,813; career prize money $2,499,454.
1980: (43). ***1981:*** (37) Won first GP title in Bordeaux. ***1982:*** (15) Won Italian Open and Quito, showing the talent that had been blossoming under the guidance of Harry Hopman. ***1983:*** (14) Won Dallas GP event. ***1984:*** (5) Qf French and US Opens and Wimbledon. Won second Italian, US CC, Washington, Nice and Hong Kong. ***1985:*** (15) Won Hong Kong again and r/u US CC. ***1986:*** (10) Won US CC, Florence, US Pro and Itaparica in singles and US Open doubles with Zivojinovic. Married Anna Maria Estrada 13 June. ***1987:*** Qf French Open, won Tourn of Champs, r/u Frankfurt and reached sf on 5 other occasions, but failed to qualify for Masters. Son born Dec. ***1987 HIGHLIGHTS – SINGLES: French Open*** qf, seed 10 (d. Stadler 6–4 6–2 6–1, Champion 7–5 6–2 6–2, Berger 5–7 6–1 4–6 6–3 6–4, E. Sanchez 5–7 1–6 7–6 7–5 6–4, lost Lendl [seed 1] 5–7 6–4 6–1 6–1), ***Wimbledon*** last 16, seed 8 (d. Skoff 6–4 6–4 7–6, Stenlund 6–3 6–2 7–6, Flach 6–4 6–3 3–6 7–5, lost Leconte [seed 9] 7–5 7–5 7–5), ***US Open*** last 16, seed 9 (d. Schapers 7–6 6–4 7–5, Agenor 6–4 6–2 4–6 7–6, Muster 1–6 6–7 6–3 6–3 6–3, lost McEnroe [seed 8] 6–4 7–6 6–3); ***won*** Tourn of Champs (d. Aerts, Bengoechea, Moir, Jaite 6–4 3–6 6–4, Becker 4–6 6–4 6–3, Noah 6–4 7–6 7–6); ***r/u*** Frankfurt (d. Navratil, Reneberg 7–6 3–6 6–1, Pimek 6–2 6–4, Pugh 6–3 6–3, lost Mayotte 7–6 6–4); ***sf*** WCT Finals (d. Curren 6–7 7–6 6–7 6–4 6–2, lost Mecir 6–7 7–6 6–4 6–2), ***sf*** Tokyo (d. Westphal 6–1 7–5, Scanlon 6–3 6–4, Agassi 6–2 6–0, lost Edberg 4–6 7–6 6–2), ***sf*** Boston (d. Dickson 7–5 3–6 7–6, Perez 6–4 6–4, Arias 2–6 7–5 7–6, lost K. Carlsson 7–5 4–6 7–5), ***sf*** Geneva (d. Agenor 3–6 6–3 6–2, Vilas 7–6 6–4, Tulasne 7–6 6–4, lost Smid 7–6 4–6 6–0), ***sf*** Johannesburg (d. Visser 6–1 7–5, Forget 6–2 6–4, Muller 6–1 6–3, lost Gilbert 6–4 6–1). ***1987 HIGHLIGHTS – DOUBLES:*** (with Gildemeister unless stated) ***won*** Monte Carlo (d. Smid/Van Rensburg, Bahrami/Mortensen 6–2 6–4), ***won*** Boston (d. Nystrom/Wilander 7–6 3–6 6–1); [Jarryd] ***r/u*** Tokyo (lost Annacone/Curren 6–4 7–6). ***CAREER HIGHLIGHTS – SINGLES: Italian Open – won 1982*** (d. Noah 6–0 fs, Higueras 6–3 fs, Wilander 5–7 6–4 6–3, Teltscher 6–2 6–3 6–2), ***won 1984*** (d. Krickstein 2–6 6–1 6–2 6–2); ***French Open – qf 1984*** (lost Lendl [seed 2] 6–3 6–7 6–4 6–3), ***qf 1986*** (lost Lendl [seed 1] 6–7 7–6 6–0 6–0), ***qf 1987; Wimbledon – qf 1984*** (lost Cash 6–4 6–4 6–7 7–6); ***US Open – qf 1984*** (lost Lendl [seed 2] 6–4 6–4 6–1). ***CAREER HIGHLIGHTS – DOUBLES: US Open –*** [Zivojinovic] ***won 1986*** (d. Nystrom/Wilander 4–6 6–3 6–3 4–6 6–3); ***Italian Open –*** [Gildemeister] ***won 1981*** (d. Manson/Smid 7–5 6–2).

KATE GOMPERT (USA)
Born Ames, Iowa, 11 January, 1963; lives Rancho Mirage, Cal.; LH; 5ft 10in; 136lb; final 1987 WITA ranking 22; 1987 prize money $54,603.
1980: Won Nat 18 title. ***1981:*** R/u Nat 18 and US Open Jun; member US Jun W Cup team. ***1982–83:*** All-American at Stanford Univ. ***1984:*** (98) Won two titles on USTA satellite circuit. ***1985:*** (25) Upset Phelps and both Maleevas to reach sf US CC. ***1986:*** (33) Won 20 of 39 matches and upset Shriver on way to last 16 LIPC. ***1987:*** Had a win over Evert Lloyd in 3r VS Florida, was r/u to her at Tampa, and reached 4 qf. ***1987 HIGHLIGHTS – SINGLES: French Open*** 3r (d. E. Reinach 6–7 6–3 8–6, Niox-Chateau 6–4 6–3, lost K. Maleeva [seed 12] 7–6 6–1), ***Wimbledon*** 1r (lost Inoue 7–5 6–4), ***US Open*** 1r (lost Navratilova [seed 2] 6–1 6–1); ***r/u*** Tampa (d. Sodupe, Nelson Dunbar, Reis 6–1 3–6 6–1, Rinaldi 6–0 6–1, lost Evert 6–3 6–2).

JIM GRABB (USA)
Born Tucson, Arizona, 14 April, 1964, and lives there; RH; 6ft 3in; 175lb; final 1987 ATP ranking 66; 1987 prize money $126,208.
1984: (313) Sf NCAA Champs. ***1985:*** (250) Senior year at Stanford; reached sf Livingston. ***1986:*** (94) Qf San Francisco and Scottsdale. ***1987:*** Won 1st GP title at Seoul. ***1987***

HIGHLIGHTS – SINGLES: Wimbledon 1r (lost Panatta 6–4 6–7 6–7 6–4 6–3), ***US Open*** 3r (d. Cannon 6–3 6–2 6–2, Smith 6–0 6–1 6–3, lost Connors 6–3 6–2 6–4); ***won*** Seoul (d. Levine, Michibata, Schapers 6–3 6–3, Fleurian 6–2 7–6, Agassi 1–6 6–4 6–2); ***sf*** Rotterdam (d. Canter 7–6 6–3, Pimek 6–4 4–1 ret'd, Hooper 6–1 7–6, lost Edberg 6–3 6–4). ***1987 HIGHLIGHTS – DOUBLES:*** [P. McEnroe] ***won*** San Francisco (d. Flach/Seguso, Layendecker/Witsken 6–2 0–6 6–4); [Flach] ***r/u*** Seoul (lost Korita/Leach 6–7 6–1), [Pugh] ***r/u*** Stockholm (lost Edberg/Jarryd 6–3 6–4).

STEFFI GRAF (West Germany) **Official World Champion**
Born Bruehl, 14 June, 1969 and lives there; 5ft 8in; 116lb; RH; final 1987 WITA ranking 1 singles, 13 (4) doubles; 1987 prize money $1,063,785; career prize money $1,909,312.
Coached by her father, Peter. Trained by Pavel Slozil. ***1981:*** Won Orange Bowl 12s. ***1982:*** (214) At the time the youngest to receive a WTA ranking at 13 years, 4 months; won European 14-and-under and European circuit Masters. ***1983:*** (98) Sf Freiburg. ***1984:*** (22) Won Olympic Demonstration event in LA and reached last 16 Wimbledon. ***1985:*** (6) Sf US Open and LIPC; last 16 French Open and Wimbledon. ***1986:*** (3) Won 8 of her last 11 tourns and 52 of her last 55 matches. Won her first pro tourn by beating Evert Lloyd in Hilton Head f, then beat Navratilova in German Open f and had 3 mps in memorable US Open sf loss to Navratilova. Won 4 straight tourns and 23 consecutive matches in the spring. A virus infection affected her performance in Paris and kept her out of Wimbledon, and a freak accident in Prague (a heavy umbrella stand blew over and broke a toe) prevented her from playing in Fed Cup. ***1987:*** After a 2-month break Dec–Jan, missing Australian Open, she took over No. 2 ranking from Evert Lloyd end Feb, and No. 1 from Navratilova 16 Aug. Won her first GS title at French Open, becoming, at 17 years 11 months and 23 days, the youngest-ever winner of the women's singles there. Unbeaten from 23 Nov 1986 (VS Champs) until Wimbledon f, where she fell to Navratilova, losing to her again in f US Open when suffering from flu. She won 75 of 77 matches to take 11 titles, confirming her No.1 ranking by taking the VS Champs and being named Official World Champion by virtue of her position at head of VS points table. She became only the 2nd player after Navratilova to earn more than $1m in prize-money in a year. ***1987 HIGHLIGHTS – SINGLES: won French Open*** seed 2 (d. Bartos Cserepy 6–1 6–1, Budarova 6–1 6–1, Novotna 6–0 6–1, Kelesi 7–6, 6–2, M. Maleeva [seed 6] 6–4 6–1, Sabatini 6–4 4–6 7–5, Navratilova 6–4 4–6 8–6), ***r/u Wimbledon*** seed 2 (d. Villagran 6–0 6–2, Scheuer-Larsen 6–0 6–0, Gildemeister 6–2 6–1, Novotna 6–4 6–3, Sabatini [seed 6] 4–6 6–1 6–1, Shriver [seed 5] 6–0 6–2, lost Navratilova 7–5 6–3), ***r/u US Open*** seed 1 (d. Fulco 6–0 6–3, Huber 6–2 6–3, Tarabini 6–2 6–0, Hanika [seed 13] 7–5 6–2, Shriver [seed 5] 6–4 6–3, McNeil 4–6 6–2 6–4, lost Navratilova 7–6 6–1); ***won*** VS Florida (d. Kanellopoulou 6–2 6–0, Gomer 6–0 6–0, Kohde-Kilsch 7–6 6–2, Shriver 6–4 6–3, Sukova 6–2 6–3), ***won*** LIPC (d. Bollegraf 6–1 6–2, Burgin 6–3 6–4, Gomer 6–1 6–0, Keil 6–0 6–1, Bonder 6–0 6–1, Navratilova 6–3 6–2, Evert Lloyd 6–1 6–2), ***won*** FC Cup (d. Perez Roldan 6–2 6–0, Calleja 6–1 6–2, Kelesi 6–2 6–2, Sabatini 6–3 2–6 7–6, M. Maleeva 6–1 2–6 7–6), ***won*** Amelia Island (d. Nelson Dunbar 6–2 6–2, Fulco 6–0 6–1, M. Maleeva 6–1 6–0, Sabatini 6–2 6–2, Mandlikova 6–3 6–4), ***won*** Italian Open (d. Huber 6–2 6–2, Cecchini 6–1 7–5, Fulco 6–4 6–4, Sukova 6–3 6–3, Sabatini 7–5 4–6 6–0), ***won*** Berlin (d. Thompson 6–4 6–1, Porwik 6–0 6–1, Tauziat 6–2 6–1, Cecchini 6–3 6–7 6–4, Kohde-Kilsch 6–2 6–3), ***won*** VS LA (d. Phelps 6–3 6–2, Paradis 6–0 6–0, Bunge 6–1 6–1, Sabatini 7–5 7–5, Evert 6–3 6–4), ***won*** Hamburg (d. Field 6–1 6–2, Fulco 6–2 6–4, Probst 6–2 6–0, Cecchini 6–0 6–2, Cueto 6–2 6–2), ***won*** Zurich (d. Porwik 6–0 6–1, Halard 6–1 6–2, K. Maleeva 6–2 6–3, M. Maleeva 6–4 6–7 6–1, Mandlikova 6–2 6–2), ***won*** VS Champs (d. Garrison 6–0 6–3, Sukova 6–2 6–0, Hanika 6–1 6–4, Sabatini 4–6 6–4 6–0 6–4). ***1987 HIGHLIGHTS – DOUBLES:*** (with Sabatini) ***r/u French Open*** (lost Navratilova/Shriver 6–2 6–1), ***US Open*** sf (lost Navratilova/Shriver def.); ***won*** Amelia Island (d. Mandlikova/Turnbull 3–6 6–3 7–5). ***CAREER HIGHLIGHTS – SINGLES: French Open – won 1987; Wimbledon – r/u 1987; US Open – r/u 1987, sf 1985*** (d. M. Maleeva 6–4 6–2, Shriver 7–6 6–7 7–6, lost Navratilova [seed 2] 6–2 6–3), ***sf 1986*** (d. Mascarin, Temesvari, Bowes, Reggi 6–1 3–6 6–0, Gadusek 6–3 6–1, lost Navratilova [seed 1] 6–1 6–7 7–6); ***VS Champs – won 1987, r/u Nov. 1986*** (d. McNeil 6–3 fs, M. Maleeva 7–5 fs, Sukova 6–1 fs, lost Navratilova 7–6 6–3 6–2), ***sf March 1986***

(lost Navratilova 6–3 6–2). ***CAREER HIGHLIGHTS – DOUBLES:*** (with Sabatini) ***French Open r/u 1986*** (lost Navratilova/Temesvari 6–1 6–2), ***r/u 1987.***

JAN GUNNARSSON (Sweden)
Born Olofstroem, 30 May, 1962 and lives Monte Carlo: RH; 6ft; 165lb; final 1987 ATP ranking 39; 1987 prize money $128,239.
Girlfriend Catharin, daughter Anna. ***1979:*** (392) R/u US Open Jun. ***1980:*** (247) Sf Pepsi GS Jun; finished 3rd Swedish satellite circuit. ***1983:*** (100) Qf Bastad and Barcelona. R/u doubles Nancy with Jarryd and Rome with Leach. ***1984:*** (47) Won Vienna ($25,000), r/u Metz, qf 4 tourns and last 16 French Open. Won doubles at Nice, Bastad, Toulouse with Mortensen. ***1985:*** (25) Won Vienna and sf LIPC. ***1986:*** (57) Sf Gstaad and Vienna, last 16 Boca West. ***1987:*** R/u Stuttgart and d. Wilander, E. Sanchez and Gilbert during the year. ***1987 HIGHLIGHTS – SINGLES: French Open*** 2r (d. P. Carlsson 6–1 7–6 6–3, lost Tulasne 6–2 6–3 6–3), ***Wimbledon*** 2r (d. Leach 6–4 6–4 6–4, lost Wilander [seed 3] 6–2 6–1 6–2); ***r/u*** Stuttgart (d. Sundstrom 6–7 7–6 4–1 ret'd, Gilbert 6–4 3–6 7–5, Hlasek 6–4 6–4, Steeb 6–4 7–6, lost Mecir 6–0 6–2). ***1987 HIGHLIGHTS – DOUBLES:*** (with Smid) ***won*** Gstaad (d. Courteau/Forget 7–6 6–2).

MELISSA GURNEY (USA)
Born Palos Verdes, Cal., 24 June, 1969 and lives there; RH; 5ft 6½in; 128lb; final 1987 WITA ranking 90; 1987 prize money $28,150.
1983: Coached by Robert Lansdorp (former coach of Tracy Austin), she was ranked second in US Girls' 16s after finishing third in 14s previous year. ***1984:*** (84) Extended Evert Lloyd to 4–6 6–4 6–0 at VS LA. Co-ranked first with Rehe in US Girls' 18s and won US Nat 18s. ***1985:*** (81) Sf San Diego. ***1986:*** (25) Won back-to-back tournaments in Berkeley and VS San Diego, r/u VS Indianapolis and qualified first time for VS Champ in Nov. ***1987:*** Reached 1st f at California Women's Open. ***1987 HIGHLIGHTS – SINGLES: French Open*** 1r, seed 16 (lost Provis 6–4 6–2), ***US Open*** 1r (lost Sukova [seed 6] 6–7 6–3 6–4); ***r/u*** California Women's Open (d. Green 7–5 6–2, Allen 6–3 6–2, Barg 6–7 6–3 6–3, Perez Roldan 6–3 6–1, lost Hakami 6–3 6–4).

MAGNUS GUSTAFSSON (Sweden)
Born Lund, 3 January, 1967; lives Lindome; RH; 6ft 1½in; 172lb; final 1987 ATP ranking 53; 1987 prize money $36,960.
Coached by Tim Klein. ***1986:*** (273) Nat 16 Champ. ***1987:*** Reached 1st GP sf at Stockholm, won Tampere Challenger and broke into top 50. ***1987 HIGHLIGHTS – SINGLES: won*** Tampere Challenger (d. Falk 6–2 6–4); ***sf*** Stockholm (d. Cancellotti 4–6 6–3 6–2, Pernfors 6–2 6–2, Jelen 7–6 6–2, Anger 6–2 6–4, lost Svensson 6–3 6–4), ***sf*** Young Masters (d. Pistolesi 3–6 6–3 6–3, Kulti 6–2 6–1, Becker 2–6 6–4 6–2 in rr, lost Muster 6–2 6–4).

ELLY HAKAMI (USA)
Born San Francisco, 25 August, 1969; lives Tiburon; RH; 2HB; 2HF; 5ft 8in; 135lb; final 1987 WITA ranking 42; 1987 prize money $43,983.
Coached by her father, Ray. ***1986:*** (114) Won US Open Jun. ***1987:*** Won her first pro title at California Women's Open. ***1987 HIGHLIGHTS – SINGLES: US Open*** 3r (d. Cioffi 6–1 6–1, Paz 6–2 6–4, lost Sabatini [seed 8] 6–1 6–3); ***won*** California Women's Open (d. Benjamin 6–1 6–3, Graham 6–2 6–2, K. Jordan 2–6 6–2 6–1, Phelps 6–3 6–4, Gurney 6–3 6–4).

JULIE HALARD (France)
Born Versailles, 10 September, 1970; lives La Baule; RH; 2HB; 5ft 7in; 110 lb; final 1987 WITA ranking 62; 1987 prize money $29,960.
1986: Won French Open Jun. ***1987:*** Turned pro June. R/u Wimbledon Jun to Zvereva and reached f Athens. ***1987 HIGHLIGHTS – SINGLES: French Open*** 2r (d. Fukarkova 5–7 7–6 6–2, lost Rinaldi [seed 10] 3–6 6–1 7–5), ***US Open*** 3r (d. Inoue 4–6 6–2 7–5, Bonsignori 6–2 7–6, lost Novotna 6–4 6–0); ***r/u*** Athens (d. Kanellopoulou 6–3 7–5, Horvath 7–5 6–1, Meskhi 6–3 1–6 6–3, Cueto 7–6 7–6, lost K. Maleeva 6–1 6–0).

SYLVIA HANIKA (West Germany)
Born Munich, 30 November, 1959; lives Ottendichl; LH; 5ft 8in; 135lb; final 1987 WITA ranking 14; 1987 prize money $135,774; career prize money $1,049,946.
Coached by Franz Humar. ***1979:*** (16) Athletic and clever, capable of producing heavy topspin groundstrokes along with a pronounced slice backhand, she found her way to f Italian Open, extending Tracy Austin to 6–3 fs. ***1980:*** (14) Had wins over Goolagong and Mandlikova and was r/u Swiss Open. ***1981:*** (6) Won indoor Avon event in Seattle and ousted Navratilova and Jaeger to reach f French Open, losing to Mandlikova. ***1982:*** (10) Was one of only three players (Shriver and Evert Lloyd were the others) to beat Navratilova, producing a huge upset from 1s and 1–3 down over her fellow left-hander in f Avon Champ indoors in New York's Madison Square Garden. ***1983:*** (5) Reached f 5 tournaments. ***1984:*** (17) Reached qf US Open, won Brighton Indoor. ***1985:*** (21) Reached sf Swiss Open and VS Central NY. ***1986:*** (50) Played reduced schedule of 15 tournaments and won Greek Open. ***1987:*** Reached f VS California with wins over Sabatini, Turnbull and Rinaldi, r/u Mahwah and appeared in last 16 Wimbledon, Australian, US and French Opens. Rising nearly 100 places on the computer from an all-time low during 1986, she qualified for VS Champs where she stunned Evert in ss 1r, going on to reach sf. ***1987 HIGHLIGHTS – SINGLES: Australian Open*** last 16, unseeded (d. Van Der Torre 7–5 5–7 10–8, Inoue 6–4 6–4, Kijimuta 6–3 6–3, lost Kohde-Kilsch [seed 5] 6–3 6–1), ***French Open*** last 16 seed 15 (d. Dias 6–2 6–1, Perez Roldan 6–2 6–4, Garrone 6–4 6–3, lost Navratilova [seed 1] 6–0 6–2), ***Wimbledon*** last 16, seed 16 (d. Van Rensburg 7–5 6–2, Savchenko 6–3 6–3, Kuczynska 6–3 6–4, lost Shriver [seed 5] 6–7 7–5 10–8), ***US Open*** last 16, seed 13 (d. Okamoto 6–0 6–1, Meier 6–3 6–0, Demongeot 6–4 6–2, lost Graf [seed 1] 7–5 6–2); ***r/u*** VS California (d. Sabatini 4–6 6–1 6–2, Garrone 6–0 6–2, Turnbull 6–4 6–1, Rinaldi 1–6 6–3 6–2, lost Garrison 7–5 4–6 6–3), ***r/u*** Mahwah (d. Demongeot 6–3 6–2, Nagelsen 6–0 6–2, Balestrat 6–2 7–5, McNeil 6–4 2–6 6–2, lost M. Maleeva 1–6 6–4 6–1); ***sf*** VS Champs (d. Evert 6–4 6–4, Reggi 6–2 4–6 6–0, lost Graf 6–1 6–4). ***CAREER HIGHLIGHTS – SINGLES: French Open – r/u 1981*** seed 6 (bye, d. Jevans 6–2 4–6 6–3, Rossi 6–3 6–2, Marsikova 6–1 6–3, Navratilova [seed 2] 6–2 6–4, Jaeger [seed 3] 4–6 6–1 6–4, lost Mandlikova [seed 4] 6–2 6–4); ***Avon Champ – won 1982*** (d. Turnbull 7–6 fs. Navratilova 1–6 6–3 6–4); ***Italian Open – r/u 1979*** (d. Tomanova 6–2 6–2, Fromholtz 6–3 1–6 6–2, Goolagong Cawley 7–5 3–6 7–5, lost Austin 6–4 1–6 6–3); ***VS Champ – sf 1987.***

MAREEN 'PEANUT' LOUIE HARPER (USA)
Born San Francisco, 15 August, 1960 and lives there; RH; 2HB; 5ft 5in; 120lb; final 1987 WITA ranking 97; 1987 prize money $40,929.
1977: One of five children including Marcie Louie (ranked 5 in US in 1975), she was r/u Wimbledon Jun. ***1978:*** (36) Won San Carlos. ***1979:*** (80). ***1980:*** (35) Won Columbus. ***1981:*** (32) Qf Chicago, Boston. ***1982:*** (90). ***1983:*** (52) Qf Hershey. ***1984:*** (53) Won Durban. ***1985:*** (22) Her best year, in which she reached sf Fort Lauderdale, sf VS Florida and won VS Denver (d. Sabatini and Garrison). ***1986:*** (65) Married Tim Harper 31 May. Overcame four consecutive 1r losses at start of season to beat Kelesi and Spence. ***1987 HIGHLIGHTS – SINGLES: Wimbledon*** 3r (d. Cioffi 6–2 6–1, Gould 7–6 6–2, lost Navratilova [seed 1] 6–2 6–2), ***US Open*** 2r (d. Spence 6–4 6–1, lost Cueto 6–3 6–2). ***1987 HIGHLIGHTS – DOUBLES:*** (with Ludloff) ***r/u*** New Orleans (lost Garrison/McNeil 6–3 6–3).

ANN HENRICKSSON (USA)
Born St Paul, Minnesota, 31 October, 1959; lives Mahtomedi, Minnesota; RH; 5ft 5in; 145lb; final 1987 WITA ranking 60; 1987 prize money $61,031.
Coached by Gordon Smith. ***1979:*** Became All-American as freshman at UCLA. ***1980:*** Won US Nat 21 singles title. ***1981:*** Reached qf Swiss Open and led UCLA to AIAW team title. ***1982:*** (82). ***1983:*** (124). ***1984:*** (40) R/u Sydney where she beat Turnbull and lost to Navratilova. ***1985:*** (53). ***1986:*** (41) R/u VS Arizona, sf VS Kansas. ***1987:*** Qf VS Washington and Arizona. ***1987 HIGHLIGHTS – SINGLES: Australian Open*** 2r (d. Marsikova 6–4 6–4, lost Polzl 7–6 6–4), ***French Open*** 1r (lost Rehe 6–3 6–2), ***Wimbledon*** 3r (d. Keil 6–2 6–1, Tauziat 6–4 6–4, lost Zvereva 6–3 6–3), ***US Open*** 3r (d. Polzl Wiesner 7–6 6–2, Schimper 6–4 5–7 6–4, lost Bunge [seed 12] 6–3 6–4).

NATHALIE HERREMAN (France)
Born St Adresse, 28 March, 1966; lives Paris; RH; 5ft 4in; 132lb; final 1987 WITA ranking 89; 1987 prize money $40,561.
Coached by Patrick Faviere. ***1983:*** Won French Nat Champs and reached sf Wimbledon Jun singles and doubles and qf Tokyo. ***1985:*** (126) Qf Hewlett-Packard Trophy. ***1986:*** (42) Won first title at Perugia and surprised Rinaldi 1r Wimbledon. Wore a cast to correct wrist injury for 2 months at end of year. ***1987:*** Stunned Mandlikova in ss at French Open, reached sf Belgian Open and qf San Diego. ***1987 HIGHLIGHTS – SINGLES: French Open*** 3r (d. Field 6–4 6–2, Mandlikova [seed 4] 6–4 7–6, lost C. Karlsson 6–3 4–6 7–5), ***Wimbledon*** 1r (lost Walsh Pete 6–3 3–6 8–6), ***US Open*** 1r (lost Mandlikova [seed 4] 6–1 6–3); ***sf*** Belgian Open (d. Simmonds 7–6 6–3, Schilder 6–4 6–1, Paz 6–2 3–6 7–6, lost Bunge 7–5 6–2). ***1987 HIGHLIGHTS – DOUBLES:*** (with Paradis) ***won*** Zurich (d. Novotna/Suire 6–3 2–6 6–3).

JAKOB HLASEK (Switzerland)
Born Prague, Czechoslovakia, 12 November, 1964; lives Zurich; 6ft 3in; 165lb; final 1987 ATP ranking 23; 1987 prize money $207,416.
Coached by Georges Deniau. Family moved to Zurich in 1968. ***1984:*** (88) Joined both Olympic and D Cup squads for Switzerland and played prolific schedule including 22 tournaments. ***1985:*** (33) R/u Rotterdam, sf Milan, Hong Kong and qf 4 times. Won Toulouse doubles with Acuna. ***1986:*** (32) Played consistent tennis all season, reaching f Hilversum and 8 qf. ***1987:*** Reached last 16 Wimbledon with 2nd win over Nystrom, sf Toulouse and Wembley (d. Mecir). ***1987 HIGHLIGHTS – SINGLES: Australian Open*** 2r, seed 15 (bye, lost Van Rensburg 4–6 6–3 6–3 6–7 6–4), ***French Open*** 1r (lost Bengoechea 6–4 6–7 7–5 4–6 6–4), ***Wimbledon*** last 16, unseeded (d. Fitzgerald 6–1 6–4 7–6, Maurer 6–3 3–6 6–3 6–3, Nystrom [seed 13] 5–7 6–3 6–0 7–6, lost Edberg [seed 4] 6–3 6–7 6–1 6–4), ***US Open*** 3r (d. S. Davis 3–6 6–3 2–6 6–4 6–4, Navratil 7–5 7–5 6–4, lost Mecir [seed 5] 6–4 6–4 2–6 6–4); ***sf*** Toulouse (d. De Miguel 6–1 7–5, Schapers 6–3 6–4, Kuhnen 6–4 1–6 6–2, lost Mayotte 6–3 6–1), ***sf*** Wembley (d. Novacek 7–6 6–4, Gunnarsson 7–5 6–0, Mecir 6–3 6–3, lost Jarryd 7–6 6–1). ***1987 HIGHLIGHTS – DOUBLES:*** (with Mezzadri) ***won*** Paris Open (d. Mecir/Smid, S. Davis/Pate 7–6 6–2).

ANNE HOBBS (Great Britain)
Born Nottingham, 21 August, 1959; lives London; RH; 5ft 6in; 120lb; final 1987 WITA ranking 41 singles, 18 doubles; 1987 prize money $75,733.
1977: Ranked 1 among British jun. ***1978:*** (61) Qf Eastbourne. ***1979:*** (82). ***1980:*** (41) Sf Wimbledon Plate. ***1981:*** (34) Last 16 Wimbledon (d. Wade first time). ***1982:*** (104). ***1983:*** (47) Won Canadian Open doubles. ***1984:*** (59) Last 16 Wimbledon. ***1985:*** (40) Won Auckland and British Closed. ***1986:*** (61) Won only 6 of 22 matches but stopped Durie at French Open, Garrison at Wimbledon and Bunge at Eastbourne. ***1987:*** Reached last 16 Australian and US Opens. ***1987 HIGHLIGHTS – SINGLES: Australian Open*** last 16, unseeded (d. A. M. Fernandez 3–0 def., Gomer 6–2 6–3, Balestrat [seed 15] 6–4 6–2, lost McNeil 7–6 6–3), ***Wimbledon*** 2r (d. Probst 6–2 4–6 6–0, lost Fulco 6–4 6–3), ***US Open*** last 16, unseeded (d. E. Minter 6–4 7–5, Croft 6–2 7–6, Kijimuta 6–4 2–6 6–4, lost Sukova [seed 6] 6–4 6–2). ***1987 HIGHLIGHTS – DOUBLES:*** [K. Jordan] ***r/u*** VS Newport (lost G. Fernandez/McNeil 7–6 7–5), [Smylie] ***r/u*** Mahwah (lost G. Fernandez/McNeil 6–3 6–2). ***MIXED DOUBLES:*** (with Castle) ***r/u Australian Open*** (lost Stewart/Garrison 3–6 7–6 6–3). ***CAREER HIGHLIGHTS – DOUBLES:*** (with Durie unless stated) ***Australian Open –*** [Turnbull] ***r/u 1983*** (d. Durie/Kiyomura, lost Navratilova/Shriver 6–4 6–7 6–2), ***sf 1985*** (d. Evert Lloyd/Lindqvist, lost Navratilova/Shriver 7–6 6–2); ***French Open – sf 1983*** (d. Kohde-Kilsch/Pfaff, lost Fairbank/Reynolds 6–3 6–2); ***Wimbledon – sf 1983*** (lost Navratilova/Shriver 7–6 6–4); ***US Open –*** [Turnbull] ***r/u 1984*** (d. Potter/Walsh 5–7 7–5 6–4, lost Navratilova/Shriver 6–2 6–4), [Jaeger] ***qf 1983*** (lost Navratilova/Shriver 6–3 6–3). ***MIXED DOUBLES:*** (with Castle) ***Australian Open – r/u 1987.***

KATHLEEN HORVATH (USA)
Born Chicago, 25 August, 1965; lives Bardmoor CC, Largo, Fla., RH; 2HB; 5ft 7in; 115lb; final 1987 WITA ranking 31; 1987 prize money $52,704.
1979: A precocious, ambitious player, she became the youngest participant in the history

of the US Open when, aged 13, she entered qualifying rounds and played main draw shortly after her 14th birthday. Earlier in year she had won US Nat 16 and Nat 21 Champs and later in year she won Orange Bowl 18s. ***1980:*** Won French Open Jun, r/u Italian Jun, and won Pepsi Jun at Boca Raton. ***1981:*** (28) Won three tournaments and had two mps against Evert Lloyd at Italian Open. ***1982:*** (49) Won Italian Open doubles with Vermaak. ***1983:*** (15) Was only player to beat Navratilova all year, ousting the favourite in last 16 French Open; r/u to Evert Lloyd at German Open and beat Bassett to win Ginny Champ in Honolulu. ***1984:*** (29) R/u German Open and qf French Open second straight year. ***1985:*** (50) Won VS Indianapolis and Palm Beach Gardens. ***1986:*** (51) Reached two qf early in season but finished year with only 16 victories in 31 singles matches. ***1987:*** At Belgian Open won first tourn since 1985 after being out of action 3 months at beginning of year with leg injury. ***1987 HIGHLIGHTS – SINGLES: French Open*** 1r (lost M. J. Fernandez [seed 13] 4–6 6–0 6–2), ***Wimbledon*** 1r (lost Bartos Cserepy 6–4 7–5), ***US Open*** 1r (lost Savchenko 6–3 6–4); ***won*** Belgian Open (d. Jagerman 6–4 6–3, Krapl 6–3 7–5, Devries 6–4 6–3, Garrone 6–4 6–2, Bunge 6–1 7–6); ***sf*** Strasbourg (d. Balestrat 6–4 6–3, Paulus 7–5 3–6 6–4, Burgin 2–6 6–2 6–1, lost Cecchini 6–0 7–6), ***sf*** Hamburg (d. Nelson Dunbar 6–3 6–2, Torres 6–3 6–2, Kuczynska 6–1 6–7 6–3, lost Cueto 6–4 1–6 6–2). ***1987 HIGHLIGHTS – DOUBLES:*** [Mesker] ***r/u*** Strasbourg (lost Novotna/Suire 6–0 6–2), [Van Rensburg] ***r/u*** Athens (lost Betzner/Polzl Wiesner 6–4 7–6). ***CAREER HIGHLIGHTS – SINGLES: French Open – qf 1983*** (d. Navratilova 6–4 0–6 6–3, lost Jausovec 6–1 6–1), ***qf 1984*** (d. Rinaldi, A. White, lost Navratilova 6–4 6–2). ***CAREER HIGHLIGHTS – DOUBLES:*** (with Vermaak unless stated) ***Italian Open – won 1982*** (d. King/Kloss 2–6 6–4 7–6), ***r/u 1984*** (lost Budarova/Skronska); ***French Open – sf 1982*** (d. Reynolds/P. Smith 6–2 6–4, lost Navratilova/A. Smith 2–6 6–2 6–2), [Ruzici] ***sf 1984*** (lost Navratilova/Shriver 6–0 7–6).

PETRA HUBER (Austria)

Born Vienna, 15 February, 1966 and lives there; RH; 5ft 7in; 138lb; final 1987 WITA ranking 84; 1987 prize money $27,394.

1983: Ranked No. 1 in Austria. Reached sf French Open Jun and Orange Bowl. ***1984:*** (48) Reached last 16 US Open with upset of Temesvari. ***1985:*** (73) Qf Hilton Head, losing 7–5 fs to Graf and made Fed Cup début. ***1986:*** (58) Won Kitzbuhel and Spanish Open, upset Bassett in Fed Cup at Prague and reached qf German Open. ***1987 HIGHLIGHTS – SINGLES: French Open*** 3r (d. Kim 7–5 7–5, Vanhille 6–3 6–1, lost Navratilova [seed 1] 6–1 6–1), ***US Open*** 2r (d. Cammie MacGregor 6–1 6–4, lost Graf [seed 1] 6–2 6–3).

HU NA (USA)

Born People's Republic of China, 16 April, 1963; lives Los Angeles, Cal.; RH; 5ft 8in; 128lb; final 1987 WITA ranking 58; 1987 prize money $42,457.

Coached by Vic Braden and Walter Redondo. ***1981:*** Top-ranked player in her country, having been top jun 1979–81. ***1982:*** Defected to US after Fed Cup matches in California. Won Hong Kong singles and doubles. ***1983:*** (205) Won VS New Jersey. ***1984:*** (278) Won Michigan and Fayetteville. ***1985:*** (96) Qf VS San Diego and reached 3r Wimbledon after qualifying. ***1986:*** (99) Became US citizen. ***1987:*** Sf VS Indianapolis, qf Oklahoma. ***1987 HIGHLIGHTS – SINGLES: Australian Open*** 2r (d. Jaggard 7–6 2–6 6–0, lost Sukova [seed 4] 6–4 7–6), ***Wimbledon*** 2r (d. Pfaff 6–2 6–3, lost Novotna 6–2 6–3), ***US Open*** 1r (lost E. Reinach 6–1 6–0); ***sf*** VS Indianapolis (d. A. Minter 6–3 1–6 6–0, Mundel Reinbold 6–2 6–3, Zvereva 6–3 6–3, Rush Magers 6–1 6–2, lost A. Smith 0–6 6–2 6–4).

PATRICIA HY (Hong Kong)

Born Cambodia, 22 August, 1965; lives Kowloon; RH; 5ft 4in; 125lb; final 1987 WITA ranking 101; 1987 prize money $38,403.

1983: R/u Wimbledon Jun. ***1986:*** (101) Won Taipei. ***1987 HIGHLIGHTS – SINGLES: Australian Open*** 2r (d. A. Minter 6–4 6–4, lost Smylie 6–2 6–3), ***French Open*** 1r (lost Kohde-Kilsch [seed 8] 6–2 6–3), ***Wimbledon*** 1r (lost Kijimuta 6–4 7–5), ***US Open*** 2r (d. Reis 4–6 6–4 6–2, lost Cecchini 6–4 5–7 7–5). ***1987 HIGHLIGHTS – DOUBLES:*** (with Inoue) ***r/u*** Beckenham (lost Fairbank/R. White) 6–2 6–2).

ETSUKO INOUE (Japan)
Born Tokyo, 18 October, 1964 and lives there; RH; 5ft 4in; 114lb; final 1987 WITA ranking 30; 1987 prize money $49,289.
Coached by Jun Kuki. ***1983:*** (81) Ranked first in Japan and won Japan-Asian Open. ***1984:*** (68) Won Borden Classic in Tokyo over Herr. ***1985:*** (98) Had wins over Mesker, Schropp and Scheuer-Larsen. ***1986:*** (81) Played exceptional grass-court tennis to reach qf Birmingham and Eastbourne, producing wins over Durie, Pfaff, Gildemeister and Nagelsen. ***1987:*** Sf Japan/Asian Open, Singapore and Edgbaston. ***1987 HIGHLIGHTS – SINGLES: Australian Open*** 2r (d. Van Rensburg, lost Hanika 6–4 6–4), ***Wimbledon*** 2r (d. Gompert 7–5 6–4, lost Navratilova [seed 1] 6–1 6–2), ***US Open*** 1r (lost Halard 4–6 6–2 7–5); ***sf*** Japan/Asian Open (d. C. Karlsson, Kijimuta, Gurney 6–3 6–0, lost Gerken 6–2 7–6), ***sf*** Singapore (d. Cordwell, Dahlstrom, Porwik 6–3 6–2, lost A. Minter 2–6 6–4 6–2), ***sf*** Edgbaston (d. Jagerman 6–3 6–4, Herr 6–4 6–2, Parkhomenko 6–1 6–4, Bassett 6–7 7–6 6–1, lost Shriver 6–2 6–4). ***1987 HIGHLIGHTS – DOUBLES:*** (with Hy) ***r/u*** Beckenham (lost Fairbank/R. White 6–2 6–2).

MARTIN JAITE (Argentina)
Born Buenos Aires, 9 October, 1964 and lives there; RH; 5ft 11in; 150lb; final 1987 ATP ranking 14; 1987 prize money $287,923.
Coached by Daniel Garcia. Lived in Spain 1976–83. ***1984:*** (54) Burst into top 100 with upset of Gerulaitis at French Open and qf appearances at US CC and Barcelona. ***1985:*** (20) Won his first tournament of year in Buenos Aires, r/u Boston and Washington, and reached qf French Open over Mecir and Gunthardt. ***1986:*** (17) Won Bologna and Stuttgart, r/u Boston, sf Forest Hills (d. Becker) and US CC and last 16 French Open. Married Beatrice Kleinman 1 Nov. ***1987:*** Last 16 French Open, r/u Italian Open (d. Nystrom), won Barcelona (d. Wilander) and Palermo back-to-back in autumn. ***1987 HIGHLIGHTS – SINGLES: French Open*** last 16, seed 14 (d. Schwaier 6–2 6–3 6–4, Pham 6–4 6–2 6–2, Muster 6–2 3–6 7–6 6–0, lost Novacek 7–6 6–4 6–7 6–3), ***US Open*** 1r, seed 15 (lost Smid 7–6 6–4 6–2); ***won*** Barcelona (d. Motta 7–6 4–6 6–1, Osterthun 6–3 6–3, E. Sanchez 6–3 7–6, Bengoechea 6–2 6–4, Wilander 7–6 6–4 4–6 0–6 6–4), ***won*** Palermo (d. Pistolesi 7–5 6–2, Arraya 6–1 6–3, Duncan 7–6 6–3, Cihak 6–2 6–3, Novacek 7–6 6–7 6–4); ***r/u*** Italian Open (d. Sundstrom 6–3 5–7 6–0, Agassi 6–2 7–5, Leconte 6–2 2–0 ret'd, Cane 3–6 7–6 6–4, Nystrom 6–3 6–4, lost Wilander 6–3 6–4 6–4); ***sf*** Bologna (d. Maciel 6–0 6–2, Narducci 7–5 6–2, J. Brown 6–1 6–1, lost E. Sanchez 6–3 6–0), ***sf*** Boston (d. Moir 6–4 6–3, Cancellotti 6–2 6–2, Krickstein 1–6 6–4 6–1, lost Wilander 0–6 7–5 6–0), ***sf*** Hilversum (d. McNamee 6–4 6–0, Nijssen 7–6 6–0, Chesnokov 6–2 6–4, lost Perez Roldan 3–6 7–5 7–6), ***sf*** Itaparica (d. Arraya 6–3 3–6 6–1, Perez 7–6 6–3, Meinecke 6–2 6–2, lost Agassi 6–2 7–5). ***CAREER HIGHLIGHTS – SINGLES: French Open – qf 1985*** (d. Mecir [seed 11] 2–6 7–6 6–3 6–4, Gunthardt 6–1 6–2 6–3, lost Lendl [seed 2] 6–4 6–2 6–4).

ANDERS JARRYD (Sweden)
Born Lidkoping, 13 July 1961 and lives there and London: RH; 2HB; 5ft 11in; 155lb; final 1987 ATP ranking 15 singles, 2 (10) doubles; 1987 prize money $561,977; career prize money $2,209,259.
1981: (100). ***1982:*** (60) Playing second singles in D Cup v US, he stunned Gottfried in straight sets. Won Linz and Ancona. ***1983:*** (19) Won French Open doubles with H. Simonsson, d. McEnroe in sf Canadian Open, losing f to Lendl, and was r/u Bastad. ***1984:*** (6) Won 2 GP tourns, including Australian Indoor at Sydney where he d. Lendl in f and was r/u US Open doubles with Edberg. Played on winning Swedish D Cup team, contributing decisive win in doubles with Edberg over McEnroe/Fleming. ***1985:*** (8) Sf Wimbledon, won Brussels over Wilander; r/u Toronto, Milan and Stockholm and won Masters doubles with Edberg. ***1986:*** (19) Won WCT Finals in Dallas over Wilander and Becker, and r/u French Open doubles, but slowed down after knee surgery, returning to win Masters doubles with Edberg again in Dec. ***1987:*** In singles reached qf Australian Open and Wimbledon, r/u Wembley; in doubles won Australian and US Opens with Edberg and French Open with Seguso and sf Masters with Edberg. ***1987 HIGHLIGHTS – SINGLES: Australian Open*** qf, seed 9 (bye, d. J. Carlsson 6–0 7–5 6–0, Champion 6–0 7–6 2–6 6–2, Doohan 6–1 6–7 6–4 7–6, lost Lendl [seed 1] 7–6 6–1 6–3), ***French Open*** 2r (d. Fioroni 6–3 4–6 6–3 6–1, lost Benhabiles 7–6 0–6 2–6 6–3 9–7), ***Wimbledon*** qf, unseeded (d. Osterthun

6–3 7–6 6–4, Rostagno 6–0 6–3 3–6 6–3, Mecir [seed 5] 6–3 6–3 6–3, Volkov 7–6 7–5 6–7 6–4, lost Edberg [seed 4] 4–6 6–4 6–1 6–3), ***US Open*** last 16, seed 16 (d. Acuna 6–3 6–4 6–4, Fleming 6–3 6–4 6–2, Mansdorf 6–3 6–2 6–3, lost Lendl [seed 1] 6–2 7–6 6–4); ***r/u*** Wembley (d. Forget 6–4 6–3, Mezzadri 6–4 6–3, Cash 3–6 7–6 6–2, Hlasek 7–6 6–1, lost Lendl 6–3 6–2 7–5); ***sf*** Brussels (d. Pimek 6–3 6–3, Chesnokov 6–2 6–3, Becker 4–6 6–3 6–4, lost McEnroe 6–3 6–3), ***sf*** Cincinnati (d. Tulasne 6–2 6–4, V. Amritraj 7–5 1–6 7–5, Moir 6–1 7–6, Lundgren 6–4 6–4, lost Becker 6–3 6–3), ***sf*** Stockholm (d. Odizor 6–3 6–4, Bates 6–1 6–1, Laurendeau 6–2 6–4, lost Edberg 6–4 6–2). ***1987 HIGHLIGHTS – DOUBLES:*** (with Edberg unless stated) ***won Australian Open*** (d. Doohan/Warder [seed 16] 6–4 6–4 7–6), [Seguso] ***won French Open*** (d. Forget/Noah 6–7 6–7 6–3 6–4 6–2), ***won US Open*** (d. Casal/E. Sanchez, Flach/Seguso 7–6 6–2 4–6 5–7 7–6); [Svensson] ***won*** Memphis (d. Casal/Sanchez 6–4 6–2), ***won*** Rotterdam (d. Hooper/Leach 3–6 6–3 6–4), ***won*** Bastad (d. E./J. Sanchez 7–6 6–3), [Smid] ***won*** Basel (d. Birner/Navratil 6–4 6–3), ***won*** Stockholm (d. Grabb/Pugh 6–3 6–4); [Gomez] ***r/u*** Tokyo (lost Annacone/Curren 6–4 7–6). ***CAREER HIGHLIGHTS – SINGLES: Wimbledon – sf 1985*** (d. Visser, Gunthardt 6–4 6–3 6–2, lost Becker 2–6 7–6 6–3 6–3). ***CAREER HIGHLIGHTS – DOUBLES:*** (with Edberg unless stated) ***French Open*** – [H. Simonsson] ***won 1983*** seed 8 (d. Edmondson/Stewart 7–6 6–4 6–2), [Seguso] ***won 1987, r/u 1986*** (lost Fitzgerald/Smid 6–3 4–6 6–3 6–7 14–12), ***sf 1985*** (d. Annacone/Van Rensburg, lost Glickstein/H. Simonsson 6–3 6–4 6–1), ***US Open – won 1987, r/u 1984*** (d. McEnroe/Fleming 3–6 7–6 7–5 7–6, lost Fitzgerald/Smid 7–6 6–3 6–3); ***Australian Open – won 1987; Masters – won 1985*** (d. Nystrom/Wilander 4–6 6–2 6–3), ***won 1986*** (d. Forget/Noah 6–3 7–6 6–3); ***D Cup – f 1984.***

ERIC JELEN (West Germany)
Born Trier, 11 March, 1965 and lives there; RH; 6ft 0½in; 168lb; final 1987 ATP ranking 40; 1987 prize money $162,184.
Coached by Olle Palmer. ***1985:*** (192) Qf Tel Aviv. ***1986*** (31) Ousted 1985 r/u Curren 1r Wimbledon *en route* to last 16, sf Rotterdam, and had wins during year over Wilander, Zivojinovic and Krishnan. ***1987:*** Underwent surgery in Jan. to relieve severe sinus condition. R/u Brisbane in 1st GP f. ***1987 HIGHLIGHTS – SINGLES: French Open*** 2r (d. Hogstedt 6–4 6–0 3–6 6–1, lost Sundstrom 2–6 6–3 6–0 5–7 8–6), ***Wimbledon*** 2r (d. Yzaga 7–6 0–6 6–2 4–6 6–2, lost E. Sanchez 5–7 6–1 2–6 7–6 6–2), ***US Open*** 2r (d. Oresar 6–3 6–2 6–4, lost Perez 2–6 6–2 6–1 6–3); ***r/u*** Brisbane (d. Shiras 7–6 6–4, Cahill 6–4 6–3, Fitzgerald 7–5 6–3, Freeman 6–2 6–3, lost Evernden 3–6 6–1 6–1); ***sf*** Bristol (d. Laurendeau 6–2 7–5, Yzaga 7–6 6–2, Winogradsky 6–4 6–4, lost Evernden 6–7 6–3 6–2). ***1987 HIGHLIGHTS – DOUBLES:*** (with Becker) ***r/u*** Indian Wells (d. Annacone/Van Rensburg 6–4 6–4, lost Forget/Noah 6–4 7–6).

CHRISTIANE JOLISSAINT (Switzerland)
Born Vevey, 12 September, 1961; lives Port; RH; 5ft 7½in; 145lb; final 1987 WITA ranking 86; 1987 prize money $15,708.
Coached by Nick Kelaidis. ***1977:*** Played Fed Cup. ***1982:*** (103) Sf Hong Kong. ***1983:*** (29) Qf Italian Open and Indianapolis and upset Bunge 1r Wimbledon. ***1984:*** (58) Qf Hilton Head, last 16 Australian Open. ***1985:*** (33) Qf Sydney, Brighton and Zurich; d. Sukova French Open. ***1986:*** (122) Qf Hilversum. ***1987:*** Qf VS Arizona, then out of action 8 months from April owing to knee injury. ***1987 HIGHLIGHTS – SINGLES: Australian Open*** 3r (bye, d. Nagelsen 6–4 1–6 6–3, lost Sukova [seed 4] 6–2 6–1).

KATHY JORDAN (USA)
Born Bryn Mawr, Pa., 3 December. 1959; lives King of Prussia, Pa.; RH; 5ft 8in; 130lb; final 1987 WITA ranking 36 singles, 10 (10) doubles; 1987 prize money $78,130; career prize money $1,283,214.
1977: R/u US Nat 18 Champs. ***1979:*** (11) Won AIAW Champs while at Stanford and came within 2 points of beating eventual champ Tracy Austin in last 16 US Open. ***1980:*** (13) Won Wimbledon and French Open doubles with A. Smith. ***1981:*** (15) Won US and Australian doubles with A. Smith. ***1982:*** (21) Won Boston indoors over Turnbull. ***1983:*** (14) Reached qf Wimbledon, upsetting Evert Lloyd in 3r to hand her fellow-American her first pre-semi-final defeat in 35 GS events. R/u Australian Open to Navratilova. ***1984:*** (10) Ranked 5 for 9 months in her finest year, reaching sf Wimbledon with upset of Shriver

and f Eastbourne with win over Evert Lloyd. ***1985:*** (19) Won Wimbledon doubles again with Smylie, ending the 109-match winning streak of Navratilova/Shriver in memorable 3s f. ***1986:*** (15) Had first career win in 13 meetings with Navratilova in sf VS Oakland and won French Open and Wimbledon mixed doubles with Flach. ***1987:*** Out of action for first half of year with a string of injuries, returning to form in autumn to be r/u US Open doubles with Smylie and d. Garrison to reach sf Brighton. ***1987 HIGHLIGHTS – SINGLES: Wimbledon*** 1r (lost Lindqvist [seed 11] 6–2 6–2), ***US Open*** 1r (lost M. Maleeva [seed 10] 7–5 6–2); ***sf*** Brighton (d. Garrison 6–7 6–2 6–0, Burgin 6–3 6–3, Cecchini 6–1 6–3, lost Shriver 6–1 7–5). ***1987 HIGHLIGHTS – DOUBLES:*** [Smylie] ***r/u US Open*** (lost Navratilova/Shriver 5–7 6–4 6–2); [Nagelsen] ***won*** Tokyo (d. Collins/Walsh Pete 6–3 7–5), [Navratilova] ***won*** VS Houston (d. Garrison/McNeil 6–2 6–4), [R. White] ***won*** California Women's Open (d. Antonoplis/Gerken 6–1 6–0), [Sukova] ***won*** Brighton (d. Scheuer-Larsen/Tanvier 7–5 6–1); [Hobbs] ***r/u*** VS Newport 7–6 7–5). ***CAREER HIGHLIGHTS – SINGLES: Wimbledon – qf 1983*** (d. Evert Lloyd 6–1 7–6, lost King), ***sf 1984*** (d. Shriver 2–6 6–3 6–4, lost Navratilova 6–3 6–4). ***CAREER HIGHLIGHTS – DOUBLES:*** (with A. Smith unless stated) ***French Open – won 1980*** (d. Madruga/Villagran 6–1 6–0); ***Wimbledon – won 1980*** (d. Casals/Turnbull 3–6 7–6 6–1), [Smylie] ***won 1985*** (d. Kohde-Kilsch/Sukova, Navratilova/Shriver 5–7 6–3 6–4), ***r/u 1981*** (d. Fairbank/Harford, lost Navratilova/Shriver 6–3 7–6), ***r/u 1982*** (lost Navratilova/Shriver 6–4 6–1), ***r/u 1984*** (d. Potter/Walsh, lost Navratilova/Shriver 6–3 6–1), [Jausovec] ***qf 1983*** (lost Navratilova/Shriver 3–6 6–3 6–3); ***US Open – won 1981*** (d. Casals/Turnbull 6–3 6–3), [Smylie] ***r/u 1987,*** [Jausovec] ***sf 1983*** (lost Navratilova/Shriver 6–3 6–2); ***Australian Open – won 1981*** (d. Navratilova/Shriver 6–2 7–5). ***CAREER HIGHLIGHTS – MIXED DOUBLES:*** (with Flach) ***French Open – won 1986*** (d. Edmondson/Fairbank 4–6 7–5 6–3); ***Wimbledon – won 1986*** (d. Navratilova/Gunthardt 6–3 7–6).

KATHRIN KEIL (USA)
Born La Jolla, 28 November, 1962; lives Los Angeles; RH; 5ft 6in; 118lb; final 1987 WITA ranking 68; 1987 prize money $28,650.
1987: Engaged to Judson Rothschild. Sf Brazilian Open and Auckland. ***1987 HIGHLIGHTS – SINGLES: Australian Open*** 2r (bye, lost Smith 6–2 6–4), ***Wimbledon*** 1r (lost Henricksson 6–2 6–1), ***US Open*** 2r (d. Herr 6–3 6–1), lost Provis 6–4 6–2); ***sf*** Brazilian Open (d. Hack, Murgo 6–1 6–1. Cueto 6–2 7–6, Jagerman 6–2 6–0, lost Klitch 6–1 4–6 6–3), ***sf*** Auckland (d. Newman, Gerken 2–6 7–6 6–0, Field 6–3 6–2, DeVries 6–4 2–6 6–1, lost Rush Magers 7–6 6–1).

HELEN KELESI (Canada)
Born Victoria, 15 November, 1969; lives Toronto; RH; 2HB; 5ft 5in; 130lb; final 1987 WITA ranking 33; 1987 prize money $66,203.
Coached by her father, Milan. ***1985:*** (48) The daughter of Czech parents who left that country for Canada a year before her birth, this feisty, gritty backcourt player made her mark on the tour, reaching f VS Central NY. ***1986:*** (40) Won her first pro event – Japan Open – and d. Mandlikova VS New England. ***1987:*** Upset Kohde-Kilsch at Amelia Island and Lindqvist at French Open, where she held sp against Graf last 16. Reached qf Canadian Open, played Fed Cup and took over No. 1 ranking in Canada from Bassett Seguso. ***1987 HIGHLIGHTS – SINGLES: Australian Open*** 2r (d. Monteiro 6–4 6–4, lost Benjamin 4–6 6–4 6–4), ***French Open*** last 16, unseeded (d. Meier 2–6 6–0 6–2, Lindqvist [seed 11] 7–5 7–5, Torres 6–1 6–3, lost Graf [seed 2] 7–6 6–2), ***Wimbledon*** 1r (lost M. Maleeva [seed 7] 6–3 6–2), ***US Open*** 3r (d. Bykova 7–6 7–5, E. Reinach 4–6 6–1 6–4, lost Lindqvist [seed 14] 4–6 7–5 6–4).

AKIKO KIJIMUTA (Japan)
Born Tokyo, 1 May, 1968; lives Kanagawa; RH; 2HB; 5ft 4in; 121lb; final 1987 WITA ranking 79; 1987 prize money $28,327.
1986: (128) Qf Singapore. ***1987:*** Upset Potter 1r US Open and played Fed Cup. ***1987 HIGHLIGHTS – SINGLES: Australian Open*** 3r (bye, d. Phelps [seed 13] 6–3 4–6 6–0, lost Hanika 6–3 6–3), ***French Open*** 1r (lost Bassett 6–1 6–3), ***Wimbledon*** 2r (d. Hy 6–4 7–5, lost Gildemeister 6–2 6–4), ***US Open*** 3r (d. Potter [seed 15] 7–6 6–3, Devries 6–3 1–6 6–2, lost Hobbs 6–4 2–6 6–4).

Slobodan Zivojinovic (above left) reached four semi-finals and the last 16 at Wimbledon, where Paolo Cane (above right) took Lendl to five sets in the second round. Jan Gunnarsson (below left) was a finalist in Stuttgart, while Eduardo Bengoechea (below right) leapt up in the rankings to No. 24. *(T. Hindley, A. Evans, M. Cole)*

CLAUDIA KOHDE-KILSCH (West Germany)
Born Saarbrucken, 11 December, 1963; lives Marbella, Spain and Monte Carlo; RH; 6ft 0½in; 150lb; final 1987 WITA ranking 10 singles, 3 (5) doubles; 1987 prize money $321,773; career prize money $1,617,388.
Coached by Bob Rheinberger. ***1979:*** Ranked in top 10 jun, she won German Int Jun event. ***1980:*** (78). ***1981:*** (20) Upset Navratilova 1r VS Oakland and won Swiss Open. ***1982:*** (19) Won Avon Futures Champs, reached sf Mahwah and r/u Australian Open doubles. ***1983:*** (24) Adopted by her step-father, Jurgen Kilsch, and added his name to hers. ***1984:*** (8) Won German Open and r/u Australian and French Open doubles. ***1985:*** (5) Reached sf French and Australian Opens; upset Navratilova in qf on way to f Canadian Open, won US Open doubles, and r/u French Open and Australian Open doubles with Sukova. ***1986:*** (7) R/u WITA Champs. ***1987:*** Sf Australian Open, qf Wimbledon and French and US Opens; won Wimbledon doubles with Sukova and qualified for VS Champs in singles and doubles. ***1987 HIGHLIGHTS – SINGLES: Australian Open*** sf, seed 5 (bye, d. Provis 6–2 6–2, Mochizuki 6–2 6–2, Hanika 6–3 6–1, Smylie 7–6 4–6 6–2, lost Mandlikova [seed 2] 6–1 0–6 6–3), ***French Open*** qf, seed 8 (d. Hy 6–2 6–3, Kuczynska 6–2 6–2, Bassett 7–5 6–3, Tauziat 6–1 3–6 6–0, lost Navratilova [seed 1] 6–1 6–2), ***Wimbledon*** qf, seed 8 (d. De Vries 6–0 6–1, Field 7–5 6–0, Smylie 6–2 6–1, Lindqvist [seed 11] 6–4 6–2, lost Evert 6–1 6–3), ***US Open*** qf, seed 9 (d. Moulton 6–2 7–5, Bassett 7–6 6–0, Cecchini 6–4 6–3, Mandlikova [seed 4] 6–7 6–4 6–1, lost Sukova [seed 6] 6–1 6–3); ***r/u*** Berlin (d. Villagran 6–2 6–4, Gildemeister 6–4 7–6, Reggi 7–5 6–3, Tarabini 6–4 7–6, lost Graf 6–2 6–3). ***1987 HIGHLIGHTS – DOUBLES:*** (with Sukova unless stated) ***won Wimbledon*** (d. Nagelsen/Smylie 6–4 6–7 6–4); ***won*** Bridgestone (d. Burgin/Shriver 6–1 7–6), won Berlin (d. Lindqvist/Scheuer-Larsen 6–1 6–2), [Novotna] ***won*** Hamburg (d. Bykova/Meskhi 7–6 7–6), ***won*** VS Chicago (d. Garrison/McNeil 6–4 6–3); ***r/u*** LIPC (lost Navratilova/Shriver 6–3 7–6), ***r/u*** Italian Open (lost Navratilova/Sabatini 6–4 6–1), ***r/u*** Canadian Open (lost Garrison/McNeil 6–1 6–2), ***r/u*** VS Champs (lost Navratilova/Shriver 6–1 6–1). ***CAREER HIGHLIGHTS – SINGLES: French Open – sf 1985*** (d. Mandlikova [seed 3] 6–4 6–4, lost Navratilova [seed 1] 6–4 6–4); ***Australian Open – sf 1985*** (lost Evert Lloyd [seed 1] 6–1 7–6), ***sf 1987; US Open – sf 1985*** (lost Evert Lloyd [seed 1] 6–3 6–3). ***CAREER HIGHLIGHTS – DOUBLES:*** (with Sukova unless stated) ***Wimbledon – won 1987,*** [Bunge] ***sf 1982*** (d. Barker/Kiyomura 6–3 3–6 6–4, Piatek/W. White, Blackwood/Leo, lost Navratilova/Shriver 6–3 6–4), ***sf 1985*** (lost Jordan/Smylie 5–7 6–1 6–4); ***US Open – won 1985*** (d. Navratilova/Shriver 6–7 6–2 6–3), [Bunge] ***sf 1982*** (d. K. Jordan/A. Smith 6–3 fs, lost Casals/Turnbull 6–4 6–1); ***French Open –*** [Mandlikova] ***r/u 1984*** (lost Navratilova/Shriver 5–7 6–3 6–2), ***r/u 1985*** (lost Navratilova/Shriver 4–6 6–2 6–2); ***Australian Open –*** [Pfaff] ***r/u 1982*** (d. Casals/Turnbull 6–3 5–7 6–2, Potter/Walsh 7–6 fs, lost Navratilova/Shriver 6–4 6–2), ***r/u 1984*** (lost Navratilova/Shriver 6–3 6–4), ***r/u 1985*** (lost Navratilova/Shriver 6–3 6–4); ***VS Champs – r/u 1984–85*** (lost Navratilova/Shriver 6–7 6–4 7–6), ***r/u 1985–86*** (lost Mandlikova/Turnbull 6–4 6–7 6–3), ***r/u Nov. 1986*** (lost Navratilova/Shriver 7–6 6–3), ***r/u 1987.***

PETR KORDA (Czechoslovakia)
Born Prague, 23 January, 1968 and lives there; LH; 6ft 3in; 145lb; final 1987 ATP ranking 87; 1987 prize money $28,344.
1986: (511) Won Wimbledon Jun doubles with Carbonell. ***1987:*** Won Budapest Challenger, qf Prague (d. Srejber) and broke into top 100. ***1987 HIGHLIGHTS – SINGLES: won*** Budapest Challenger (d. Zverev 5–7 6–3 6–2).

AARON KRICKSTEIN (USA)
Born Ann Arbor, Mich., 2 August, 1967; lives Grosse Pointe, Mich.; RH; 2HB; 5ft 10in; 150lb; final 1987 ATP ranking 61; 1987 prize money $53,140.
1982: Won US Nat 16 at Kalamazoo. ***1983:*** (94) Won Nat 18 at Kalamazoo and turned pro in autumn, after arriving in last 16 at US Open where he upended Edberg and Gerulaitis in 5s before Noah stopped him. He won his first pro event in Tel Aviv to become youngest ever to capture GP tournament at 16 years, 2 months, 13 days. ***1984:*** (12) Won US Pro and two other GP titles and reached f Italian Open, including Wilander among his major victims. ***1985:*** (30) Despite r/u showing in Hong Kong and last 16 French Open, he did not live up to promise of previous two years. ***1986:*** (26) Made history at US Open with two straight triumphs from two-sets-to-love down against Novacek and Annacone, and

added a straight-sets dismissal of Purcell to reach last 16. R/u Tel Aviv and contributed to US D Cup win over Ecuador with win over Viver. ***1987:*** Reached qf 3 times, but progressed no further. Stress fracture of left tibia kept him out Aug-Sept, and before he could return to action, a rib injury sustained in a motor accident sidelined him for rest of year. ***1987 HIGHLIGHTS – SINGLES: French Open*** 3r (d. Masur 6–3 6–3 6–4, Wahlgren 6–4 6–1 6–1, lost Wilander [seed 4] 5–7 6–1 6–3 6–3). ***CAREER HIGHLIGHTS – SINGLES: US Pro – won 1984*** (d. Clerc 7–6 3–6 6–4); ***Italian Open – r/u 1984*** (d. Teltscher, Nystrom, lost Gomez 2–6 6–1 6–2 6–2).

JOHAN KRIEK (USA)

Born Pongola, South Africa, 5 April, 1958; lives Naples, Fla., with wife Tish; RH; 5ft 8in; 155lb; final 1987 ATP ranking 48; 1987 prize money $141,398; career prize money $2,053,250.

1978: (27) Emerged from satellite American Express circuit to reach qf of US Open. ***1979:*** (35) Reached qf US Open again. ***1980:*** (18) Reached sf US Open where he established lead of two sets to love against Borg. ***1981:*** (13) R/u to McEnroe at WCT Finals, he won first GS title in Australia at end of season. ***1982:*** (12) He became US citizen, beat McEnroe for US Indoor title, repeated GS triumph at Australian Open and reached qf Wimbledon. ***1983:*** (15) Achieved first career win over Connors in LA but was erratic. ***1984:*** (13) Achieved his highest world ranking of 7 during the year, winning Bristol and Livingston and reaching f Boca West and sf Australian Open. ***1985:*** (14) Qf Australian Open, won Las Vegas over Mayotte, Smid and Arias, beat McEnroe in San Francisco and upset Edberg in 1r Masters. ***1986:*** (23) An otherwise disappointing year was highlighted by sf French Open in only his second appearance there. ***1987:*** Last 16 Wimbledon and won Livingston. ***1987 HIGHLIGHTS – SINGLES: Australian Open*** 2r (bye, lost Evernden 6–2 2–6 6–4 6–4), ***French Open*** 1r, seed 16 (lost Nystrom 6–7 6–2 6–2 6–1), ***Wimbledon*** last 16, unseeded (d. Avendano 6–2 6–1 4–6 6–4, Curren [seed 16] 6–4 3–6 6–3 6–2, S. Davis 5–7 6–4 6–7 6–1 8–6, lost Lendl [seed 2] 6–3 7–6 6–2), ***US Open*** 3r (d. Drewett 6–1 6–2 6–1, R. Leach 6–3 7–6 3–6 6–3, lost Krishnan 6–3 6–4 6–3); ***won*** Livingston (d. Cannon 6–1 6–4, Matuszewski 6–2 6–2, Bonneau 6–2 6–1 6–2, Antonitsch 6–3 2–6 6–4, Saceanu 7–6 3–6 6–2). ***CAREER HIGHLIGHTS – SINGLES: Australian Open – won 1981*** (d. T. Mayotte, Edmondson, Denton 6–2 7–6 6–7 6–4), ***won 1982*** (d. McNamee 7–6 7–6 4–6 3–6 7–5 [saving 1 m-p], Denton 6–3 6–3 6–2), ***sf 1984*** (lost Wilander 6–1 6–0 6–2), ***qf 1985*** (d. Mustard, Doohan, Lapidus, lost Wilander [seed 3] 6–3 7–5 6–2); ***US Indoor – won 1982*** (d. Gerulaitis 6–3 fs, Mottram 6–4 fs, McEnroe 6–3 3–6 6–4); ***S. African Open – won 1983*** (d. Dowdeswell 6–4 4–6 1–6 7–5 6–3); ***WCT Final – r/u 1981*** (d. Fibak, Tanner 6–4 fs, lost McEnroe 6–1 6–2 6–4); ***French Open – sf 1986*** (d. Kirmayr, Srejber, Mattar, Noah def., Vilas 3–6 7–6 7–6 7–6, lost Lendl [seed 1] 6–2 6–1 6–0); ***US Open – sf 1980*** (d. Birner, Fleming [seed 9], A. Giammalva, Mottram, Fibak [seed 14], lost Borg [seed 1] 4–6 4–6 6–1 6–1 6–1), ***qf 1978*** (d. Teacher, lost Gerulaitis 6–2 6–1 6–2), ***qf 1979*** (d. Pecci, Noah 6–4 5s, lost Gerulaitis 5–7 6–3 6–4 6–3); ***Wimbledon – qf 1982*** (d. Elter 6–4 5s, Rennert, Saviano, lost McEnroe 4–6 6–2 7–5 6–3); ***Masters – qf 1983*** (d. Arias, lost McEnroe), ***qf 1984*** (lost Wilander 6–4 6–3 7–6), ***qf 1985*** (d. Edberg 6–2 4–6 6–2, lost Gomez 6–3 6–2).

RAMESH KRISHNAN (India)

Born Madras, 5 June, 1961; lives there and Bardmoor Club, Fla.; RH; 5ft 7in; 160lb; final 1987 ATP ranking 58; 1987 prize money $145,185.

Wife Priya. ***1979:*** (179) Became top jun in world, sweeping French and Wimbledon Jun. ***1981:*** (66) Had long slump brought about by playing with injuries but rebounded to win Manila and reach qf US Open, taking 1s from eventual champion McEnroe. ***1982:*** (100) Won Stuttgart. ***1983:*** (84). ***1984:*** (24) Upset Wilander to reach sf Seiko Tokyo and won Metz. ***1985:*** (40) Got married a few weeks before Wimbledon. R/u Cologne. ***1986:*** (35) Reached qf Wimbledon, and won Tokyo and Hong Kong. ***1987:*** Reached qf US Open, sf Nancy and Rye Brook and helped India to f D Cup for 1st time since 1966, when his father played. Troubled by recurring knee injury. ***1987 HIGHLIGHTS – SINGLES: Australian Open*** 3r, seed 16 (bye, d. Edwards 4–6 5–7 6–1 6–3 6–3, lost Goldie 3–6 7–5 6–7 6–2 6–2), ***Wimbledon*** 2r (d. Westphal 6–3 6–1 6–3, lost Anger 6–2 6–4 6–2), ***US Open*** qf, unseeded (d. Annacone 6–0 7–5 6–1, Nystrom [seed 10] 6–4 7–5 6–2, Kriek 6–3 6–4 6–3, Chesnokov 6–4 6–1 6–2, lost Edberg [seed 2] 6–2 6–2 6–2); ***won*** Nagoya Challenger (d.

Lapidus 6–3 6–0); ***sf*** Nancy (d. Lacombrade 6–0 6–2, Stadler 7–5 6–4, Bahrami 6–4 4–6 6–4, lost Cash 7–6 6–3), ***sf*** Rye Brook (d. Maciel 6–2 6–3, Kures 6–3 3–6 6–3, J. Sanchez 6–0 6–1, lost Lundgren 6–2 7–5). ***1987 HIGHLIGHTS – DOUBLES:*** (with Mezzadri) ***won*** Nancy (d. Connell/Scott 6–4 6–4). ***CAREER HIGHLIGHTS – SINGLES: Wimbledon – qf 1986*** unseeded (d. Maciel, Bauer, Nystrom [seed 6] 6–7 6–2 7–6 6–4, Jelen, lost Zivojinovic 6–2 7–6 4–6 6–3); ***US Open – qf 1981*** (d. S. Smith 6–4 6–3 6–3, M. Davis 6–2 7–5 6–7 6–4, G. Mayer [seed 7] 4–6 1–6 7–6 7–5 ret'd, lost McEnroe [seed 1] 6–7 7–6 6–4 6–2), ***qf 1987.***

OLA KRISTIANSSON (Sweden)
Born Helsingborg, 23 September, 1971 and lives there; RH; 6ft 1in; 147lb.
1986: Was Donald Duck winner.

NICLAS KROON (Sweden)
Born Karistad, 5 February, 1966; lives Vakjo; RH; 6ft 0½in; 182lb; final 1987 ATP ranking 90; 1987 prize money $24,251.
1987: Upset Wilander *en route* to qf Frankfurt. ***1987 HIGHLIGHTS – SINGLES: won*** Montabaur Challenger (d. Popp 6–1 6–3).

PATRICK KUHNEN (West Germany)
Born Pugglingen, 2 November, 1966; RH; 6ft 2in; 177lb; final 1987 ATP ranking 83; 1987 prize money $60,912.
1987: Qf Indianapolis and won Bergen on Satellite circuit. ***1987 HIGHLIGHTS – SINGLES: Australian Open*** 1r (lost Saltz 6–4 6–3 6–3), ***French Open*** 1r (lost Pham 7–6 6–3 6–2), ***Wimbledon*** 1r (lost Bloom 6–3 6–3 6–2); ***won*** Bergen Challenger (d. Connell 6–4 3–6 7–6). ***1987 HIGHLIGHTS – DOUBLES:*** (with Becker) ***won*** Frankfurt (d. Davis/Pate 6–4 6–3).

IWONA KUCZYNSKA (Poland)
Born Wroctaw, 22 February, 1961; lives Paris and Palm Beach Gardens, Fla.; RH; 5ft 10in; 130lb; final 1987 WITA ranking 89; 1987 prize money $28,656.
1982: (170). ***1983:*** (188). ***1984:*** (231). ***1985:*** (253). ***1986:*** (338) Sidelined much of year with elbow injury. ***1987:*** Upset Kohde-Kilsch 3r Hamburg, won 1st pro title at Bayonne on Satellite circuit and reached qf Athens. ***1987 HIGHLIGHTS – SINGLES: French Open*** 2r (d. Van Nostrand 6–1 6–3, lost Kohde-Kilsch [seed 8] 6–2 6–2), ***Wimbledon*** 3r (d. A. M. Fernandez 6–4 7–5, Meier 6–3 6–3, lost Hanika [seed 16] 6–3 6–4), ***US Open*** 2r (d. Kim 6–4 6–1, lost Shriver [seed 5] 6–3 6–2); ***won*** Bayonne Satellite (d. Mothes 2–6 6–3 6–4).

LEONARDO LAVALLE (Mexico)
Born Mexico City, 14 July, 1967 and lives there; LH; 6ft 4½in; 170lb; final 1987 ATP ranking 224; 1987 prize money $33,778.
Coached by Carlos Alvarado. ***1984:*** (741) Won US Open Jun doubles with Nastase. ***1985:*** (87) Won Wimbledon Jun singles; reached qf Geneva and Hong Kong. ***1986:*** (105) Upset Edberg at Philadelphia and Cash in 5s at US Open and helped Mexico d. West Germany in D Cup. ***1987:*** Won Bancen Challenger. ***1987 HIGHLIGHTS – SINGLES: Australian Open*** 1r (lost Van Rensburg 6–3 6–4 0–6 6–4); ***won*** Bancen Challenger (d. Lozano 6–4 3–6 6–4). ***1987 HIGHLIGHTS – DOUBLES:*** (with Panatta) ***won*** Palermo (d. Korda/Smid 3–6 6–4 6–4).

HENRI LECONTE (France)
Born Lillers, 4 July, 1963; lives Geneva; LH; 6ft 1in; 160lb; final 1987 ATP ranking 21; 1987 prize money $196,190; career prize money $1,372,685.
Coached by Wojtek Fibak. Wife Brigitte, son Maxim born 6 March 1986. ***1982:*** (28) Won Stockholm Open over Wilander and played No. 2 singles on D Cup team behind Noah as France lost to US in f. Beat Borg in 2r Monte Carlo as the Swede attempted a come-back. ***1983:*** (30) Beat Lendl twice (on clay at WCT Forest Hills and indoors at Sydney) and was r/u at Kitzbuhel and Sydney. ***1984:*** (27) Won Stuttgart (d. Borg in 2r), r/u to Connors at Memphis and won French Open doubles with Noah. ***1985:*** (16) Won Nice and Sydney

NSW as well as reaching qf French Open and Wimbledon and last 16 US Open. R/u US Open doubles with Noah. ***1986:*** (6) Won Geneva and Hamburg, qualified for Masters first time, reached sf French Open and qf Wimbledon and US Open, finally arriving as expected in world's top 10. ***1987:*** Underwent laser surgery Feb. to repair herniated disc, and was not fully fit until Wimbledon, where he reached qf again and followed with last 16 US Open. But then he was sidelined again in Oct, suffering from an illness similar to mononucleosis, returning to reach 1st sf of year at Paris Open. ***1987 HIGHLIGHTS – SINGLES: Australian Open*** 3r, seed 5 (bye, d. Nelson 4–6 7–6 6–2 6–3, lost Annacone 1–6 4–6 6–3 6–4 10–8), ***French Open*** 1r, seed 9 (lost Osterthun 6–3 6–3 6–7 6–1), ***Wimbledon*** qf, seed 9 (d. Agassi 6–2 6–1 6–2, Mansdorf 6–2 7–6 2–6 1–6 6–2, Bloom 6–3 7–6 7–5, Gomez [seed 8] 7–5 7–5 7–5, lost Lendl [seed 2] 7–6 6–3 7–6), ***US Open*** last 16, seed 11 (d. Agassi 6–4 7–6 4–6 6–3, Pozzi 6–3 6–2 6–3, Odizor 6–7 6–2 6–1 6–2, lost Connors [seed 6] 6–7 6–4 6–4 6–3); ***sf*** Paris Open (d. Fleurian 7–5 6–1, Bengoechea 6–2 6–1, Cash 6–4 6–7 6–3, lost Mayotte 6–3 4–6 6–3). ***CAREER HIGHLIGHTS – SINGLES: French Open – sf 1986*** (d. de Miguel, Mansdorf, Motta, de la Pena, Chesnokov 6–3 6–4 6–3, lost Pernfors 2–6 7–5 7–6 6–3), ***qf 1985*** (d. Gomez [seed 5], Noah [seed 9] 6–3 6–4 6–7 4–6 6–1, lost Wilander [seed 4] 6–4 7–6 6–7 7–5); ***Wimbledon – qf 1985*** (d. Lendl [seed 2] 3–6 6–4 6–3 6–1, lost Becker 7–6 3–6 6–3 6–4), ***qf 1986*** (d. Fitzgerald, Cash 4–6 7–6 7–6 6–3, lost Becker [seed 4] 6–2 6–4 6–7 6–3), ***qf 1987; US Open – qf 1986*** (d. Mansdorf, Krickstein 6–3 7–5 6–4, lost Lendl [seed 1] 7–6 6–1 1–6 6–1). ***CAREER HIGHLIGHTS – DOUBLES:*** (with Noah) ***French Open – won 1984*** (d. Gunthardt/Taroczy, Slozil/Smid 6–4 2–6 3–6 6–3 6–2); ***US Open – r/u 1985*** (d. Nystrom/Wilander, lost Flach/Seguso 7–6 6–7 7–6 6–0).

IVAN LENDL (Czechoslovakia) **Official World Champion**

Born Ostrava, 7 March, 1960; lives Greenwich, Conn.; RH; 6ft 2in; 175lb; final 1987 ATP ranking 1; 1987 prize money $2,003,656; career prize money $12,278,031.

Girlfriend Samantha Frankel. ***1977:*** Won Orange Bowl 18. ***1978:*** (74) Won Wimbledon, French, Italian Jun and became first ITF world jun champ. ***1979:*** (20) R/u Brussels. ***1980:*** (6) Won Houston, Toronto, Barcelona, Basle, Tokyo, Hong Kong, Taipei, beating world No. 1 Borg in Toronto and Basle. ***1981:*** (2) Won Stuttgart, Las Vegas, Montreal, Madrid, Barcelona, Basle, Vienna, Cologne, Buenos Aires, Masters, closing season with seven straight tourn wins and 35 straight matches, a streak which ended at 44 in Feb. 1982. ***1982:*** (3) Won 15 of 23 tourns and 106 of 115 matches, taking Frankfurt, Washington, North Conway, Cincinnati, WCT Delray Beach, WCT Genoa, WCT Munich, Strasbourg, Houston, Dallas, Forest Hills, LA, Naples, Hartford, Masters and r/u US Open. ***1983:*** (2) Won Detroit, Milan, Houston, Hilton Head, Montreal, San Francisco, Tokyo, r/u US Open and Australian Open. ***1984:*** (3) Won French Open for first GS success in 5 finals, coming from two-sets-to-love down to oust McEnroe in f. Won Wembley and Luxembourg and reached sf Wimbledon and f US Open. ***1985:*** (1) Won 84 of 91 matches (31 consecutively from US Open to sf Australian Open) and 11 of 18 tournaments, capturing first US Open in fourth straight f and third Masters to cement his status as No. 1 in the world. ***1986:*** (1) Won 74 of 80 matches and 9 of 15 tournaments to take second consecutive US Open, second French Open, second consecutive Nabisco Masters and fourth in all, being beaten by only Becker, Noah, Edberg and Curren all year. ***1987:*** Underwent arthroscopic knee surgery March, returning to win Hamburg in May. Still vulnerable on grass, he fell in sf Australian Open and 2nd consecutive Wimbledon f, both to Cash. However, he won 3rd French Open, 2nd US Open crown, a record 5th Masters, 5 other titles and finished the year undisputed No. 1 for 3rd consecutive year. ***1987 HIGHLIGHTS – SINGLES: Australian Open*** sf, seed 1 (bye, d. Saltz 6–4 3–6 6–1 6–1, Anger 6–4 6–2 6–7 6–2, Goldie 2–6 6–4 7–6 6–3, Jarryd [seed 9] 7–6 6–1 6–3, lost Cash [seed 11] 7–6 5–7 7–6 6–4), ***won French Open*** seed 1 (d. Agenor 7–5 7–6 0–6 6–3, Canter 3–6 6–1 6–1 6–2, Tulasne 7–6 6–2 6–2, Nystrom 2–6 6–1 5–7 6–0 6–2, Gomez [seed 10] 5–7 6–4 6–1 6–1, Mecir [seed 5] 6–3 6–3 7–6, Wilander [seed 4] 7–6 6–3 3–6 7–6), ***r/u Wimbledon*** seed 2 (d. Saceanu 6–2 3–6 6–3 7–5, Cane 3–6 7–6 6–7 7–5 6–1, Reneberg 6–4 6–7 6–3 7–6, Kriek 6–3 7–6 6–2, Leconte [seed 9] 7–6 6–3 7–6, Edberg [seed 4] 3–6 6–4 7–6 6–4, lost Cash [seed 11] 7–6 6–2 7–5), ***won US Open*** seed 1 (d. Moir 6–0 6–0 6–0, Fleurian 6–4 6–2 6–2, Pugh 6–1 6–1 6–2, Jarryd [seed 16] 6–2 7–6 6–4, McEnroe [seed 8] 6–4 7–6 6–3, Connors [seed 6] 6–4 6–2 6–2, Wilander [seed 3] 6–7 6–0 7–6 6–4); ***won*** Hamburg (d. Cahill 6–2 6–1, Gunnarsson 6–2 6–1, Tulasne 4–6 6–4 6–3, K. Carlsson 3–6 7–5 6–0, Mecir 6–1 6–3 6–3),

won Washington (d. Pearce 7–6 6–3, Wheaton 6–7 6–3 6–2, Arias 6–3 4–6 6–4, Connors 6–4 7–6, Gilbert 6–1 6–0), ***won*** Montreal (d. Witsken 6–3 6–2, Sznajder 6–1 6–1, Zivojinovic 6–1 6–1, Connors 7–5 6–4, Edberg 6–4 7–6), ***won*** Sydney (d. Doohan 6–2 6–4, Jelen w.o., Krishnan 6–2 6–3, Zivojinovic 6–3 7–5, Cash 6–4 6–2 6–4), ***won*** Wembley (d. Agenor 6–2 6–1, Volkov 6–4 6–3, Annacone 3–6 6–3 6–4, Leconte 6–4 7–6, Jarryd 6–3 6–2 7–5); Stratton Mountain ***divided*** with McEnroe (d. Flur 6–4 6–3, Pugh 7–6 6–3, Seguso 6–3 6–7 6–2, K. Jones 6–3 6–1, Agassi 6–2 5–7 6–3), ***won*** Masters (d. Gilbert 6–2 6–2, Connors 4–3 ret'd, Becker 6–4 6–7 6–3 in rr, Gilbert 6–2 6–4, Wilander 6–2 6–2 6–3); ***r/u*** LIPC (d. Acuna 6–2 6–3 6–2, Annacone 5–7 7–6 4–6 6–2 6–2, Muster 3–6 6–4 6–0 6–2, Gilbert 6–2 6–2 6–4, Berger 6–3 6–1 6–1, Connors 3–6 7–6 7–6 6–3, lost Mecir 7–5 5–1 ret'd), ***r/u*** Tokyo Seiko (d. Canter 6–1 6–4, Seguso 6–2 6–0, Jelen 6–3 6–0, Pernfors 6–0 6–2, lost Edberg 6–7 6–4 6–4); ***sf*** San Francisco (d. Purcell 6–2 6–3, Grabb 7–5 6–2, Goldie 5–7 6–4 6–3, lost Lundgren 6–3 4–6 7–6). ***1987 HIGHLIGHTS – DOUBLES:*** [Scanlon] ***won*** Adelaide (d. Doohan/Warder 6–7 6–3 6–4). ***CAREER HIGHLIGHTS – SINGLES: French Open – won 1984*** (d. Wilander, McEnroe 3–6 2–6 6–4 7–5 7–5), ***won 1986*** (d. Westphal, Hlasek, Miniussi, Keretic, Gomez 6–7 7–6 6–0 6–0, Kriek 6–2 6–1 6–0, Pernfors 6–3 6–2 6–4), ***won 1987, r/u 1981*** (d. McNamee 6–2 4–6 7–6 7–6, McEnroe 6–4 6–4 7–5, Clerc 3–6 6–4 4–6 7–6 6–2, lost Borg 6–1 4–6 6–2 3–6 6–1), ***r/u 1985*** (lost Wilander 3–6 6–4 6–2 6–2); ***US Open – won 1985*** (d. Noah, Connors 6–2 6–3 7–5, McEnroe [seed 1] 7–6 6–3 6–4), ***won 1986*** (d. Svensson, Gilbert, Leconte, Edberg 7–6 6–2 6–3, Mecir 6–4 6–2 6–0), ***won 1987, r/u 1982*** (d. McEnroe 6–4 6–4 7–6, lost Connors 6–3 6–2 0–6 6–4), ***r/u 1983*** (d. Wilander, Arias 6–2 7–6 6–1, lost Connors 6–3 6–7 7–5 6–0), ***r/u 1984*** (d. Cash 3–6 6–3 6–4 6–7 7–6 [saving 1 mp], lost McEnroe 6–3 6–4 6–4); ***Masters – won 1981*** (d. Gerulaitis, Vilas in rr, McEnroe 6–4 6–2, Gerulaitis 6–7 2–6 7–6), ***won 1982*** (d. Noah 6–4 7–5, Connors 6–3 6–1, McEnroe 6–4 6–4 6–2), ***won 1985*** (d. Becker 6–2 7–6 6–3), ***won 1986*** (d. Gomez, Edberg, Noah 6–4 6–4, Wilander 6–4 6–2, Becker 6–4 6–4 6–4), ***won 1987, r/u 1980*** (d. Mayer 6–3 6–4, lost Borg 6–4 6–2 6–2), ***r/u 1983*** (d. Connors 6–3 6–4, lost McEnroe 6–3 6–4 6–4), ***r/u 1984*** (d. Connors, lost McEnroe 7–5 6–0 6–4); ***Wimbledon – r/u 1986*** (d. Lavalle, Freeman, Mansdorf, Anger, Mayotte 6–4 4–6 6–4 3–6 9–7, Zivojinovic 6–2 6–7 6–3 6–7 6–4, lost Becker 6–4 6–3 7–5), ***r/u 1987, sf 1983*** (d. Tanner, lost McEnroe 7–6 6–4 6–4), ***sf 1984*** (lost Connors 6–7 6–3 7–5 6–1); ***Australian Open – r/u 1983*** (d. Mayotte 6–1 7–6 6–3, lost Wilander 6–1 6–4 6–4), ***sf 1985*** (lost Edberg 6–7 7–5 6–1 4–6 9–7), ***sf 1987; D Cup – 1980 winning team*** TCH.

CATARINA LINDQVIST (Sweden)

Born Malmo, 13 June, 1963; lives Hollviksnas; RH; 5ft 5in; 125lb; final 1987 WITA ranking 16; 1987 prize money $145,883.

Coached by John Lloyd. ***1983:*** (114). ***1984:*** (18) Won Hershey and Filderstadt and reached sf Canadian Open. ***1985:*** (13) Won Ginny Champs, and using superior topspin ground-strokes off both sides she upset Shriver at Australian Open, to reach qf, and Mandlikova at Key Biscayne. ***1986:*** (16) R/u to Graf at Brighton, had 4mps v Navratilova qf Filderstadt, reached first Wimbledon qf and won Bastad. ***1987:*** Sf Australian Open, last 16 Wimbledon and US Open, r/u Bastad and qualified for VS Champs. ***1987 HIGHLIGHTS – SINGLES: Australian Open*** sf, seed 10 (bye, d. Devries 6–2 6–3, Calleja 4–6 6–1 6–3, M. Maleeva [seed 6] 6–3 6–3, Shriver [seed 3] 6–3 6–1, lost Navratilova [seed 1] 6–3 6–2), ***French Open*** 2r [seed 11] (d. Paz 6–0 7–6, lost Kelesi 7–5 7–5), ***Wimbledon*** last 16, seed 11 (d. K. Jordan 6–2 6–2, Benjamin 7–5 7–6, Burgin 6–4 6–1, lost Kohde-Kilsch [seed 8] 6–4 6–2), ***US Open*** last 16, seed 14 (d. Frazier 6–2 6–2, Goles 6–2 6–0, Kelesi 4–6 7–5 6–4, lost Navratilova [seed 2] 6–0 6–4); ***r/u*** Bastad (d. Ferrando 2–6 6–2 6–4, Golarsa 6–2 7–5, Villagran 7–6 6–3, Polzl Wiesner 6–4 6–3, lost Cecchini 6–4 6–4); ***sf*** VS Oklahoma (d. Probst 7–5 6–1, C. Karlsson 4–6 7–6 6–4, E. Minter 6–4 6–2, lost Smylie 6–4 6–4), ***sf*** Beckenham (lost Moulton 3–6 6–3 6–0), ***sf*** Tokyo (d. Okamoto 6–2 6–4, W. White 6–0 6–0, Potter 7–5 5–7 6–4, lost M. Maleeva 6–3 3–6 6–4). ***1987 HIGHLIGHTS – DOUBLES:*** [Scheuer-Larsen] ***r/u*** Berlin (lost Kohde-Kilsch/Sukova 6–1 6–2). ***CAREER HIGHLIGHTS – SINGLES: Australian Open – sf 1987, qf 1985*** (d. Shriver, lost Kohde-Kilsch [seed 5] 6–4 6–0); ***Wimbledon – qf 1986*** (d. Rush, Kelesi, E. Minter, Balestrat 7–6 7–5, lost Sabatini 6–2 6–3).

HEATHER LUDLOFF (USA)
Born Honolulu, 11 June, 1961; lives Foster City, Cal; RH; 5ft 5in; 115lb; final 1987 WITA ranking 74; 1987 prize money $41,548.
Coached by Todd Mitchell. ***1981:*** (162) All-American at Brigham Young Univ. ***1982:*** (97). ***1983:*** (76) All-American at UCLA. ***1984:*** (129). ***1985:*** (139) Suffered severe ankle injury. ***1986:*** (231). ***1987:*** Sf Taipei for best singles result since r/u Californian Open 1978. ***1987 HIGHLIGHTS – SINGLES: Australian Open*** 2r (d. Okagawa 7–5 6–3, lost Garrison 6–1 6–1), ***Wimbledon*** 1r (lost Zvereva 6–2 6–4), ***US Open*** 1r (lost Tauziat 6–4 6–2); ***sf*** Taipei (d. A. M. Fernandez, Walsh Pete 6–1 6–2, Nozzoli 6–3 6–4, lost Porwik 4–6 6–1 6–2). ***1987 HIGHLIGHTS – DOUBLES:*** [with Gerken] ***r/u*** Singapore (lost A. M. Fernandez/Richardson 6–1 6–4), [Louie Harper] ***r/u*** New Orleans (lost Garrison/McNeil 6–3 6–3).

PETER LUNDGREN (Sweden)
Born Sundsvall, 29 January, 1965; lives Stockholm; RH; 5ft 11in; 155lb; final 1987 ATP ranking 26; 1987 prize money $171,038.
Coached by Per Hjertqvist. ***1985:*** (27) The most improved player among the Swedes, he won first GP title in Cologne. ***1986:*** (98) Won only 7 matches in first 13 tournaments, with best showing sf Los Angeles, and dropped in the rankings. ***1987:*** After a poor start in which he failed to pass 2r in all tournaments until end July, he had his best season yet, upsetting Wilander 2r Cincinnati, winning Rye Brook to break into top 50, stunning Cash 3r Canadian Open and 1r US Open and beating Lendl *en route* to 1st SS title in San Francisco. ***1987 HIGHLIGHTS – SINGLES: French Open*** 1r (lost DePalmer 7–5 7–5 6–4), ***Wimbledon*** 1r (lost Bergstrom 6–4 6–2 1–6 3–6 13–11), ***US Open*** 2r (d. Cash [seed 7] 6–4 4–6 6–4 6–4, lost Chesnokov 6–2 7–5 2–6 6–0); ***won*** Rye Brook (d. Shiras 7–6 6–3, Chesnokov 6–3 7–6, M. Davis 6–2 6–3, Krishnan 6–2 7–5, Ross 6–7 7–5 6–3), ***won*** San Francisco (d. Muller 6–4 6–3, Pate 3–6 6–1 6–3, Wilkison 6–3 6–4, Lendl 6–3 4–6 7–6, Pugh 6–1 7–5): ***sf*** Tel Aviv (d. Levine 6–0 6–1, Masso 7–6 6–4, Campbell 6–3 3–6 6–2, lost Gilbert 6–3 6–3).

JOHN McENROE (USA)
Born Wiesbaden, West Germany, 16 February 1959; lives New York; LH; 5ft 11in; 165lb; final 1987 ATP ranking 10; 1987 prize money $391,766; career prize money $9,586,625.
Coached by Tony Palafox, and also old doubles partner Peter Fleming for 1988. ***1976:*** (264) R/u to Larry Gottfried at US Nat 18 Champs and won Orange Bowl 18s. ***1977:*** (21) Stunned tennis world by reaching sf Wimbledon as qualifier and taking set off Connors. ***1978:*** (4) Turned pro in June after winning NCAA title as Stanford freshman. Won Hartford, San Francisco, Stockholm and Wembley in autumn, led US D Cup triumph, and closed year by saving 2 mps to beat Ashe in Masters f. ***1979:*** (3) Won US Open, WCT Finals, New Orleans, Milan, San José, Queens Club, South Orange, San Francisco, Stockholm and Wembley and again led US D Cup triumph. ***1980:*** (2) Lost epic Wimbledon f to Borg after saving 7 mps in 4s, finally falling 8–6 5s. Won second straight US Open with 5s triumph over Borg as well as Richmond, Memphis, Milan, Queens Club, Brisbane, Sydney, Wembley and WCT Montreal. ***1981:*** (1) Became first male player since Connors in 1974 to win Wimbledon and US Open in same year, stopping Borg in both f to replace the Swede as the No. 1 player in the world. Led US to D Cup victory. ***1982:*** (1) Lost to Connors in 5s Wimbledon f, coming within three points of victory at 4–3 in 4s tb. After losing to Lendl in sf US Open and f Masters, he was regarded by many experts as No. 3 behind Connors and Lendl. Led US to D Cup victory for 4th time in 5 years and won US Pro Indoor, San Francisco, Sydney, Tokyo and Wembley. ***1983:*** (1) Won his second Wimbledon and Masters titles, beating Lendl in sf former and f latter. Also won US Pro Indoor, WCT Dallas, Forest Hills, Sydney and Wembley to become undisputed No. 1. ***1984:*** (1) Won 13 of 15 tournaments and 79 of 82 matches, losing only to Lendl in f French Open, V. Amritraj at Cincinnati and Sundstrom in D Cup f. For the second time he won Wimbledon and US Open, producing glorious form to rout Connors in Wimbledon f and dismissing Lendl with relative ease 6–3 6–4 6–1 in US Open f. Only his loss to Lendl from 2 sets to 0 ahead in f French Open spoiled a nearly perfect year. ***1985:*** (2) Won Philadelphia, Houston, Chicago, Milan, Atlanta, Stratton, Montreal and Stockholm, but was soundly beaten by Curren in qf Wimbledon and Lendl in f US Open. When he lost to Gilbert in 1r Masters, he elected to take a 6-month sabbatical from the game. ***1986:*** (14) Returning to competition in

Stratton Mountain in July, he lost to Becker in sf after holding 4 mps, then lost to Seguso in 3r Canadian Open and suffered his first 1r defeat at US Open to Annacone. He rebounded with three straight tourn wins (LA, San Francisco and Scottsdale), but was beaten thereafter by Casal in qf of Paris Indoor and Cash in 1r Wembley. Son, Kevin, born in May; married Tatum O'Neal 1 Aug. ***1987:*** In f World Team Cup v Mecir he walked off the court following two disputed umpiring decisions, later claiming that a back injury had prompted his withdrawal, and avoided threatened suspension when MIPTC accepted that he was indeed injured. However, following US Open, when he accumulated fines exceeding $7,500 for the second time in the year, he was suspended for 2 months from 28 Sept. Continuing to be plagued by injuries, and missing Wimbledon with a leg injury, he began working with physical trainer Dae-Shik Seo in summer. Reached f 5 times but won no title. Son Sean Timothy born 23 Sept. ***1987 HIGHLIGHTS – SINGLES: French Open*** 1r, seed 7 (lost de la Pena 4–6 6–2 6–4 6–2), ***US Open*** qf, seed 8 (d. Anger 6–3 6–2 6–2, Reneberg 7–6 2–6 6–4 6–2, Zivojinovic 6–4 5–7 6–7 6–4 6–3, Gomez [seed 9] 6–4 7–6 6–3, lost Lendl [seed 1] 6–3 6–3 6–4); Stratton Mountain ***divided*** with Lendl (d. Canter 6–3 6–2, Lundgren 6–3 6–4, Testerman 7–6 0–6 6–1, Gilbert 6–3 6–2, Van Rensburg 6–4 6–2); ***r/u*** US Pro Indoor (d. Purcell 6–2 6–1, Smid 6–2 6–1, Hlasek 6–2 6–3, Mansdorf 5–7 6–2 6–3, lost Mayotte 3–6 6–1 6–3 6–1), ***r/u*** Rotterdam (d. Chesnokov 6–4 6–4, Schapers 6–4 6–0, Mansdorf 6–4 7–5, Mecir 6–1 7–5, lost Edberg 3–6 6–3 6–1), ***r/u*** Brussels (d. Cane 6–3 6–1, Hogstedt 7–6 6–1, Hlasek 6–3 7–5, Jarryd 6–3 6–3, lost Wilander 6–3 6–4), ***r/u*** WCT Finals (d. Noah 7–6 6–2 4–6 6–3, Edberg 7–6 6–7 7–6 6–4, lost Mecir 6–0 3–6 6–2 6–2); ***sf*** Italian Open (d. Davin 3–6 6–2 6–3, de la Pena 6–2 6–4, Krickstein 4–6 6–3 7–5, Mezzadri 6–1 6–7 6–3, lost Wilander 6–1 6–3). ***CAREER HIGHLIGHTS – SINGLES: Wimbledon – won 1981*** seed 2 (d. Ramirez, Smith, Kriek, Frawley 7–6 6–4 7–5, Borg 4–6 7–6 7–6 6–4), ***won 1983*** (d. Lendl 7–6 6–4 6–4, C. Lewis 6–2 6–2 6–2), ***won 1984*** (d. Connors 6–1 6–1 6–2), ***r/u 1980*** seed 2 (d. Connors 6–3 3–6 6–3 6–4, lost Borg 1–6 7–5 6–3 6–7 8–6), ***r/u 1982*** (lost Connors 3–6 6–3 6–7 7–6 6–4), ***sf 1977*** unseeded after qualifying (lost Connors 6–3 6–3 4–6 6–4); ***US Open – won 1979*** (d. Connors 6–3 6–3 7–5, Gerulaitis 7–5 6–4 6–3), ***won 1980*** seed 2 (d. Lendl 4–6 6–3 6–2 7–5, Connors 6–4 5–7 0–6 6–3 7–6, Borg 7–6 6–1 6–7 5–7 6–4), ***won 1981*** (d. Gerulaitis 5–7 6–3 6–2 4–6 6–3, Borg 4–6 6–2 6–4 6–3), ***won 1984*** (d. Connors 6–4 4–6 7–5 4–6 6–3, Lendl 6–3 6–4 6–4), ***r/u 1985*** (d. Wilander 3–6 6–4 4–6 6–3 6–3, lost Lendl 7–6 6–3 6–4), ***sf 1982*** (lost Lendl 6–4 6–4 7–6); ***WCT Final – won 1979*** (d. Connors 6–1 6–4 6–4, Borg 7–5 4–6 6–2 7–6), ***won 1981*** (d. Kriek 6–1 6–2 6–4), ***won 1983*** (d. Lendl 6–2 4–6 6–7 7–6), ***won 1984*** (d. Connors 6–1 6–2 6–3); ***Masters – won 1979*** (d. Ashe 6–7 6–3 7–5), ***won 1983*** (d. Wilander 6–2 7–5, Lendl 6–3 6–4 6–4), ***won 1984*** (d. Wilander 6–1 6–1, Lendl 7–5 6–0 6–4), ***r/u 1982*** (d. Vilas, lost Lendl 6–4 6–4 6–2), ***sf 1981*** (lost Lendl 6–4 6–2); ***French Open – r/u 1984*** (lost Lendl 3–6 2–6 6–4 7–5 7–5); ***sf 1985*** (lost Wilander 6–1 7–5 7–5). ***CAREER HIGHLIGHTS – DOUBLES:*** (wi th Fleming) ***Wimbledon – won 1979*** (d. Gottfried/Ramirez 6–2 4s), ***won 1981*** (d. Smith/Lutz 6–4 6–4 6–4), ***won 1983*** (d. Tim/Tom Gullikson 6–4 6–3 6–4), ***won 1984*** (d. Cash/McNamee 6–2 5–7 6–2 3–6 6–3), ***r/u 1978*** (lost Hewitt/McMillan 6–1 6–4 6–2), ***r/u 1982*** (lost McNamara/McNamee 6–3 6–1), ***sf 1980*** (lost McNamara/McNamee 6–3 6–3 6–3), ***sf 1985*** (lost Cash/Fitzgerald 7–6 2–6 6–1 6–4), ***US Open – won 1979*** (d. Smith/Lutz), ***won 1981*** (d. Newcombe/Stolle 6–2 6–2 6–7 5–7 7–6, McNamara/Gunthardt def.), ***won 1983*** (d. Buehning/Winitsky 6–3 6–4 6–2), ***sf 1984*** (lost Edberg/Jarryd 3–6 7–6 7–5 7–6); ***Masters – won 1978*** (d. Lutz/Smith 6–4 6–2 6–4), ***won 1979*** (d. Fibak/Okker 6–4 6–2 6–4), ***won 1980*** (d. McNamara/McNamee 6–4 6–4), ***won 1981*** (d. Curren/ Denton 6–3 6–3), ***won 1982*** (d. Stewart/Taygan 7–5 6–3), ***won 1983*** (d. Slozil/Smid 6–2 6–2), ***won 1984*** (d. Edmondson/Stewart 6–3 6–1).

LORI McNEIL (USA)

Born San Diego, 18 December, 1963; lives Houston; 5ft 7in; 135lb; RH; final 1987 WITA ranking 11 singles, 4 doubles; 1987 prize money $401,524.

1983: Member US Jun Fed Cup team, ranked 8 US Intercollegiate list and 4 on USTA satellite circuit. ***1984:*** (97) Reached last 16 US Open and led Mandlikova by a set and 4–2 before losing. ***1985:*** (93). ***1986:*** (14) Burst out of the pack and established herself as one of top 15 players in world. Won Key Largo – over Garrison in first VS Series final between two black women – and VS Tulsa back-to-back in Sept. Ably coached by John Wilkerson, who is also Garrison's instructor, she reached qf Wimbledon unseeded and qualified first time for VS Champ in Nov., clearly the most improved fast-court player in the world. ***1987:*** Qf Australian Open and sf US Open, where she spoiled Evert's record of winning at least one GS event each year by beating her in qf. Won no singles title but reached f Oklahoma, New Orleans and New Jersey. In doubles r/u Australian Open with Garrison, won 6 titles and r/u 7 more with 5 different partners. Qualified for VS Champs in singles and doubles. ***1987 HIGHLIGHTS – SINGLES: Australian Open*** qf, seed 8 (bye, d. Burgin 6–3 6–4, Werdel 6–2 7–5, Hobbs 7–6 6–3, lost Mandlikova [seed 3] 6–0 6–0), ***French Open*** 1r, seed 9 (lost Bonder 6–3 6–3), ***Wimbledon*** 2r, seed 10, (d. Calleja 6–2 6–3, lost Zvereva 6–4 6–4), ***US Open*** sf, seed 11 (d. Zrubakova 6–3 6–1, Benjamin 6–4 6–2, Provis 5–7 6–1 7–6, Garrison [seed 7] 7–6 3–6 7–5, Evert [seed 3] 3–6 6–2 6–4, lost Graf [seed 1] 4–6 6–2 6–4); ***r/u*** VS Oklahoma (d. Dechaume 6–2 6–3, Meier 6–1 6–3, Hu Na 6–1 7–6, Savchenko 7–6 6–2, lost Smylie 4–6 6–3 7–5), ***r/u*** New Orleans (d. Louise Allen 6–4 6–2, Ludloff 7–6 2–6 6–2, Gompert 6–4 6–4, Garrison 6–2 6–4, lost Evert 6–3 7–5); ***sf*** Argentine Open (d. Rapponi Longo, Bonsignori 6–4 4–6 6–3, Golarsa 6–2 6–2, lost Sabatini 6–2 6–3), ***sf*** VS New Jersey (d. Rimes 6–0 6–4, Ludloff 6–3 6–1, Turnbull 4–6 6–1 6–2, Mandlikova def., lost Sukova 6–0 6–3), ***sf*** VS Dallas (d. Hanika 6–2 4–6 6–2, Potter 6–4 6–4, M. Maleeva 5–7 7–6 6–2, lost Shriver 7–5 6–3), ***sf*** Geneva (d. Benjamin 2–6 6–4 6–2, Cioffi 6–3 7–5, Perez Roldan 6–1 6–0, lost Evert 6–0 6–2), ***sf*** San Diego (d. Goles 6–4 6–3, Louie Harper 5–7 6–3 6–1, Hakami 6–3 7–6, lost A. Minter 2–6 6–4 7–5), ***sf*** Mahwah (d. Cecchini 6–3 6–3, Lindqvist 4–6 6–4 6–3, lost Hanika 6–4 2–6 6–2), ***1987 HIGHLIGHTS – DOUBLES:*** (with Garrison unless stated) ***r/u Australian Open*** (d. Mandlikova/Turnbull 3–6 6–3 8–6, Kohde-Kilsch/Sukova 7–6 7–6, lost Navratilova/Shriver 6–1 6–0); [G. Fernandez] ***won*** New Jersey (d. Nagelsen/Smylie 6–1 6–4); [Paz] ***won*** Argentine Open (d. Jagerman/Bollegraf 6–1 2–6 6–1), [G. Fernandez] ***won*** VS Newport (d. Hobbs/K. Jordan 7–6 7–5), ***won*** Canadian Open (d. Kohde-Kilsch/Sukova 6–1 6–2), [G. Fernandez] ***won*** Mahwah (d. Hobbs/Smylie 6–3 6–2), ***won*** New Orleans (d. Louie Harper/Ludloff 6–3 6–3); [Sands] ***r/u*** VS Oklahoma (lost Parkhomenko/Savchenko 6–4 6–4), ***r/u*** VS Washington (lost Burgin/Shriver 6–1 3–6 6–4), [Bunge] ***r/u*** Plymouth (lost Turnbull/Evert Lloyd 6–1 7–5), ***r/u*** FC Cup (lost Paz/Pfaff 7–6 7–5), ***r/u*** VS Houston (lost K. Jordan/Navratilova 6–2 6–4), ***r/u*** VS LA (lost Navratilova/Shriver 6–3 6–4), ***r/u*** Filderstadt (lost Navratilova/Shriver 6–1 6–2), ***r/u*** Chicago (lost Kohde-Kilsch/Sukova 6–4 6–3). ***CAREER HIGHLIGHTS – SINGLES: US Open – sf 1987; Wimbledon – qf 1986*** unseeded (d. Bryant, Mesker, Burgin 6–3 6–2, Nagelsen 7–5 6–1, lost Mandlikova [seed 3] 6–7 6–0 6–2); ***Australian Open – qf 1987. CAREER HIGHLIGHTS – DOUBLES:*** (with Garrison) ***Australian Open – r/u 1987.***

GRETCHEN RUSH MAGERS (USA)

Born Pittsburgh, Pa., 7 February, 1964; lives San Antonio, Texas; RH; 5ft 7in; 135lb; final 1987 WITA ranking 52; 1987 prize money $54,407.

1981: Won US CC 18s. ***1982:*** Qf US Open (d. Jausovec and Turnbull). Top of ITF Jun World Rankings, r/u US Open Jun, won Italian Open Jun and US 18 GC and played Jun W Cup. ***1983:*** (55) Qf French Open. At Trinity, won NCAA doubles with Louise Allen. Won 3 doubles titles on US circuit and played Jun Fed Cup. ***1984:*** (81) All-American for 2nd year and played W Cup. ***1985:*** (176) R/u NCAA Champs singles and doubles with Sassano. ***1986:*** (74) Married Stephen Magers Dec. ***1987:*** Won Auckland. ***1987 HIGHLIGHTS – SINGLES: Australian Open*** 2r (bye, lost Balestrat [seed 15] 6–3 4–6 6–2), ***French Open*** 2r (d. Spence 6–2 6–3, lost Sukova [seed 5] 6–3 6–1), ***Wimbledon*** 1r (lost Savchenko 3–6 6–4 6–4), ***US Open*** 1r (lost Cueto 1–6 7–5 7–5); ***won*** Auckland (d. Seeman, Vasquez 6–2 6–4, Provis 6–0 6–1, Keil 7–6 6–1, Phelps 6–2 6–3). ***CAREER HIGHLIGHTS – SINGLES: French Open – qf 1983*** (d. M. Maleeva, Madruga Osses, lost Jaeger [seed 3] 6–2 6–2); ***US Open – qf 1982*** (d. Jausovec [seed 11] 7–5 2–6 6–4, Mundel, Turnbull [seed 6] 6–3 4–6 6–2, lost Jaeger [seed 4] 3–6 6–1 6–0).

KATERINA MALEEVA (Bulgaria)

Born Sofia, 7 May, 1969 and lives there; RH; 2HB; 5ft 6in; 120lb; final 1987 WITA ranking 13; 1987 prize money $135,393.

Coached by her mother, 9 times Bulgarian champion Yulia Berberian. Sister of Manuela. ***1984:*** (93) Won US Open Jun and was r/u to Sabatini at both Orange Bowl and French Open Jun while making her mark in women's play as well. ***1985:*** (28) Won Seabrook Island and Hilversum and stopped some of the big names in the sport like Shriver, Sukova and Garrison. ***1986:*** (28) Did not pass qf in 20 tournaments but won 26 of 47 matches. Played Fed Cup again with sister and mother. ***1987:*** Beat Sukova 3r Mahwah, won Japan/Asian Open for first title since 1985, following with Athens and qualifying for VS Champs 1st time. ***1987 HIGHLIGHTS – SINGLES: French Open*** last 16, seed 12 (d. Barg 6–2 6–1, Fulco 6–3 2–6 6–4, Gompert 7–6 6–1, lost Evert [seed 3] 6–3 6–1), ***Wimbledon*** 1r, seed 14 (lost G. Fernandez 7–6 1–6 6–4), ***US Open*** 3r (d. Nelson Dunbar 6–1 6–1, Van Rensburg 6–2 6–3, lost Garrison [seed 7] 7–6 7–6); ***won*** Japan/Asian Open (d. Dias, Cammie MacGregor, Herr 6–1 6–1, Nagelsen 1–6 7–6 6–3, Gerken 6–2 6–3), ***won*** Athens (d. Bykova 6–2 6–0, Paz 6–2 6–1, Tsarbopoulou 6–1 7–5, Polzl Wiesner 7–5 6–0, Halard 6–1 6–0); ***sf*** Bastad (d. Rapponi Longo 6–4 6–1, Lindstrom 6–3 6–4, Scheuer-Larsen 6–3 6–2, lost Cecchini 4–6 6–3 6–4), ***sf*** Mahwah (d. Frazier 6–0 6–3, Durie 6–2 6–3, Sukova 6–2 6–3, lost M. Maleeva 6–3 6–4), ***sf*** Tokyo (d. Provis 6–4 6–2, Balestrat 6–2 6–0, lost Sabatini 7–6 6–4). ***1987 HIGHLIGHTS – DOUBLES:*** (with M. Maleeva) ***r/u*** Tokyo (lost A./R. White 6–1 6–2).

MANUELA MALEEVA (Bulgaria)
Born Sofia, 14 February, 1967 and lives there; RH; 2HB; 5ft 8in; 127lb; final 1987 WITA ranking 8, 1987 prize money $245,100; career prize money $1,102,030.
Coached by her mother, 9 times Bulgarian women's champion Yulia Berberian. Sister of Katerina. ***1981:*** Won Orange Bowl 14s. ***1982:*** (60) This stylish groundstroker made inroads in women's events but concluded jun career on sad note when her mother ordered her off the court as she trailed Bassett 3–6 3–4 in Orange Bowl f at Miami Beach. ***1983:*** (31) Upsets of Mandlikova and Bunge signalled her swift advance. ***1984:*** (6) In her most productive season, she won 5 tourns, including Italian Open, on the last day of which she completed qf win over Ruzici and then dismissed Bassett and Evert Lloyd. ***1985:*** (7) Won Tokyo Pacific to close year with her only singles title. ***1986:*** (8) Reached qf or better in 11 of 22 tournaments entered, including US Open qf, and joined sister Katerina and mother Yulia to represent Bulgaria in Fed Cup at Prague. ***1987:*** Upset Evert FC Cup and at Wild Dunes won 1st tourn since 1985, qualifying for VS Champs, where she reached sf. Married François Fragniere, a Swiss tennis coach, 12 Dec. ***1987 HIGHLIGHTS – SINGLES: Australian Open*** last 16, seed 6 (bye, d. Koizumi 6–4 6–1, Bartos Cserepy 6–3 6–7 7–5, lost Lindqvist [seed 10] 6–3 6–3), ***French Open*** qf, seed 6 (d. Cecchini 3–6 6–3 6–3, Balestrat 6–2 6–0, Wasserman 5–7 6–3 6–1, Rehe 7–6 6–1, lost Graf [seed 2] 6–4 6–1), ***Wimbledon*** 2r, seed 7 (d. Kelesi 6–3 6–2, lost Balestrat 6–7 6–1 8–6), ***US Open*** last 16, seed 10 (d. K. Jordan 7–5 6–2, Tauziat 6–1 6–3, M. J. Fernandez 6–2 0–6 6–3, lost Evert [seed 3] 7–5 6–4); ***won*** WIld Dunes (d. Mosca 6–1 6–1, Suire 6–3 6–1, Cioffi 6–0 6–4, Fulco 6–4 6–1, Reggi 6–3 2–6 7–5), ***won*** Mahwah (d. Tauziat 6–1 6–4, Reggi 6–4 6–3, K. Maleeva 6–3 6–4, Hanika 1–6 6–4 6–1); ***r/u*** FC Cup (d. Barg 6–1 6–1, Torres 6–2 6–0, Garrison 6–2 7–5, Evert 6–1 2–6 7–6, lost Graf 6–2 4–6 6–3), ***r/u*** Geneva (d. Devries 7–5 6–0, Sloane 6–3 6–2, K. Maleeva 6–1 6–2, Reggi 6–4 2–6 6–2, lost Evert 6–3 4–6 6–2), ***r/u*** Tokyo (d. Van Nostrand 6–0 6–3, Werdel 4–6 7–5 6–1, Lindqvist 6–3 3–6 6–4, lost Sabatini 6–4 7–6); ***sf*** NSW Open (d. A. Smith 7–5 6–1, lost Shriver 6–3 6–3), ***sf*** Zurich (d. Paradis 6–1 6–0, Pfaff 7–5 6–2, Reggi 6–2 6–4, lost Graf 6–4 6–7 6–1), ***sf*** VS Champs (d. Kohde-Kilsch 4–6 6–3 6–4, Shriver 6–2 3–6 7–5, lost Sabatini 6–3 4–6 6–3). ***1987 HIGHLIGHTS – DOUBLES:*** [Bunge] ***won*** Belgian Open (d. Horvath/Mesker 4–6 6–4 6–4); [K. Maleeva] ***r/u*** Tokyo (lost A./R. White 6–1 6–2). ***CAREER HIGHLIGHTS – SINGLES: Italian Open – won 1984*** (d. Bassett 6–2 6–2, Evert Lloyd 6–3 6–3); ***US CC – won 1984*** (d. Bonder 6–4 6–3); ***VS Champs – sf 1987; French Open – qf 1985*** (lost Sabatini 6–3 3–6 6–1); ***Wimbledon – qf 1984*** (lost Navratilova [seed 1] 6–3 6–2); ***US Open – qf 1986*** (d. Kohde-Kilsch 6–2 2–6 7–6, lost Evert Lloyd [seed 2] 6–2 6–2); ***Australian Open – qf 1985*** (lost Evert Lloyd 6–3 6–3).

HANA MANDLIKOVA (Australia)
Born Prague, Czechoslovakia, 19 February, 1962; lives Sydney; RH; 5ft 8in; 132lb; final 1987 WITA ranking 5 singles, 12 (7) doubles; 1987 prize money $340,410; career prize money $3,005,091.
Became a naturalised Australian 1 Jan, 1988. ***1977:*** Won Orange Bowl 16s in Miami Beach, already flashing a brilliant range of strokes at age 15. ***1978:*** (45) R/u to Austin at Wimbledon Jun, she was ITF World Jun Champ with countryman Lendl. ***1979:*** (17) Won

5 tourns. ***1980:*** (5) Won 6 of 24 tourns including Australian Open, Mahwah, Atlanta and Stockholm and was r/u US Open. ***1981:*** (4) Won French Open (d. Evert Lloyd in sf), and was r/u at Wimbledon but won only 3 of 18 tourns. ***1982:*** (7) Played only 13 tourns and won none, although r/u Italian Open. ***1983:*** (12) Reached f only twice in 15 events. ***1984:*** (3) Won 5 of 16 events. ***1985:*** (3) Won second GS title with back-to-back triumphs over Evert Lloyd and Navratilova at US Open, the first player since Tracy Austin at TS Champs 1981 to beat both in same tourn. Since Austin won 1981 US Open, Navratilova or Evert Lloyd had won the intervening 15 GS titles. Won 3 of 18 tourns and 59 of 73 matches, defeating Evert Lloyd and Navratilova twice each. ***1986:*** (4) Won no tournament in 15 appearances but was r/u Wimbledon to Navratilova, reached sf French Open and was r/u at VS Champs March. Married Sydney restaurant owner Jan Sedlak during Fed Cup in Prague in July. ***1987:*** Won Australian Open for 1st title since 1985, but missed Wimbledon owing to foot injury and retired 1r VS Champs with pulled hamstring. ***1987 HIGHLIGHTS – SINGLES: won Australian Open*** seed 2 (bye, d. Richardson 4–6 6–2 6–2, Smith 6–3 6–2, Bassett [seed 12] 6–2 4–6 6–2, McNeil [seed 8] 6–0 6–0, Kohde-Kilsch [seed 5] 6–1 0–6 6–3, Navratilova [seed 1] 7–5 7–6), ***French Open*** 2r (d. Jausovec 6–0 6–0, lost Herreman 6–4 7–6), ***US Open*** last 16, seed 4 (d. Herreman 6–1 6–3, Durie 6–3 6–7 6–2, Reggi 6–3 6–1, lost Kohde-Kilsch [seed 9] 6–7 6–4 6–1); ***won*** Brisbane (d. Calleja, Marsikova, Kelesi 6–3 6–3, Sukova 4–6 6–1 6–4, Shriver 6–2 2–6 6–4), ***won*** VS Washington (d. G. Fernandez 6–3 6–4, Hy 6–1 7–6, Rinaldi 7–6 6–1, Sukova 6–3 6–2, Potter 6–4 6–2); ***r/u*** Amelia Island (d. Cueto 6–4 6–1, Fairbank 6–2 6–4, Phelps 7–6 6–2, Garrison 6–3 6–3, lost Graf 6–3 6–4, ***r/u*** Zurich (d. Herreman 6–3 7–5, Demongeot 6–1 6–2, Polzl Wiesner 6–3 7–5, Tauziat 6–1 3–6 6–3, lost Graf 6–2 6–2); ***sf*** VS California (d. E. Reinach 6–3 6–2, Moulton 6–0 4–6 6–3, M. Maleeva 6–3 7–6, lost Garrison 7–5 4–6 6–2), ***sf*** LIPC (d. Kelesi 6–1 7–5, Bonsignori 6–0 6–1, Parkhomenko 7–5 6–4, Bunge 6–2 6–4, Sukova 6–4 6–3, lost Evert Lloyd 7–5 6–0), ***sf*** New Jersey (d. Smylie 3–6 6–2 6–3, Werdel 6–1 6–3, Hanika 6–4 6–1, lost McNeil def.), ***sf*** VS Houston (d. Louise Allen 6–2 6–1, Fulco 6–1 6–4, Sabatini 7–5 6–4, lost Evert 6–3 7–5). ***1987 HIGHLIGHTS – DOUBLES:*** (with Turnbull) ***won*** Brisbane (d. Smylie/Nagelsen 6–4 6–3), ***won*** VS California (d. Garrison/Sabatini 6–1 3–6 6–1); ***r/u*** Amelia Island (lost Graf/Sabatini 3–6 6–3 7–5). ***CAREER HIGHLIGHTS – SINGLES: French Open – won 1981*** (d. Romanov, Casals, Vasquez, Rinaldi, Evert Lloyd [seed 1], Hanika 6–2 6–4), ***sf 1980*** seed 7 (d. Redondo, Fairbank, Delhees, Madruga, lost Evert Lloyd [seed 1] 6–7 6–2 6–2), ***sf 1982*** (d. Austin 7–6 6–7 6–2, lost Navratilova 6–0 6–2), ***sf 1984*** (lost Navratilova 3–6 6–2 6–2), ***sf 1986*** (d. Goles, Paquet, Marsikova 6–1 6–2, Gildemeister 6–1 6–3, Graf [seed 3] 2–6 7–6 6–1, lost Evert Lloyd 6–1 6–1); ***US Open – won 1985*** (d. Evert Lloyd 4–6 6–2 6–3, Navratilova 7–6 1–6 7–6), ***r/u 1980*** seed 9 (d. Collins, Guissani, P. Smith, Navratilova [seed 2] 7–6 6–4, Hallquist, Jaeger [seed 8] 6–1 3–6 7–6, lost Evert Lloyd 5–7 6–1 6–1), ***r/u 1982*** (d. Austin 4–6 6–4 6–4, Shriver 6–4 2–6 6–2, lost Evert Lloyd 6–3 6–1, ***qf 1981*** seed 5 (lost Evert Lloyd 6–1 6–3), ***qf 1983*** (lost Evert Lloyd 6–4 6–3), ***qf 1984*** (lost Bassett 6–4 6–3); ***Australian Open – won 1980*** seed 3 (d. Little, Hallquist, Ruzici [seed 6] 6–1 3–6 6–4, Jausovec 6–4 6–1, Turnbull [seed 4] 6–0 7–5), ***won 1987, qf 1981*** (d. Sukova 6–4 7–6, lost Evert Lloyd 6–4 7–6); ***Wimbledon – r/u 1981*** seed 2 (d. Turnbull, Navratilova, lost Evert Lloyd [seed 1] 6–2 6–2), ***r/u 1986*** (d. Tacon, Tanvier, Budarova, Bassett 6–4 7–6, McNeil 6–7 6–0 6–2, Evert Lloyd [seed 2] 7–6 7–5, lost Navratilova [seed 1] 7–6 6–3), ***sf 1984*** (lost Evert Lloyd 6–1 6–2); ***VS Champs – r/u 1985–86*** (d. Evert Lloyd 6–3 7–5, lost Navratilova 6–2 6–0 3–6 6–1). ***CAREER HIGHLIGHTS – DOUBLES:*** (with Turnbull unless stated) ***VS Champs – won 1985–86*** (d. Kohde-Kilsch/Sukova 6–4 6–7 6–3); ***French Open*** – [Kohde-Kilsch] ***r/u 1984*** (lost Navratilova/Shriver 5–7 6–3 6–2); ***Wimbledon – r/u 1986*** (lost Navratilova/Shriver 6–1 6–3), ***sf 1985*** (lost Navratilova/Shriver 6–4 6–2), ***US Open – r/u 1986*** (lost Navratilova/Shriver 6–4 3–6 6–3), ***sf 1985*** (lost Navratilova/Shriver 6–3 6–4).

AMOS MANSDORF (Israel)

Born Tel Aviv, 20 October, 1965, and lives there; RH; 5ft 8in; 140lb; final 1987 ATP ranking 27; 1987 prize money $194,417.

Coached by Peter Fishbach. ***1984:*** (268) Joined Israeli Olympic team; qf US Open Jun. ***1985:*** (84) R/u Tel Aviv. ***1986:*** (37) Won first GP title in Johannesburg. ***1987:*** Beat Mecir and Novacek as he led his country to major upset of TCH in D Cup, d. Connors and Gilbert to win Tel Aviv, and appeared in top 20 in Nov.

1987 HIGHLIGHTS – SINGLES: Australian Open 2r (bye, lost Anger 7–6 6–3 3–6 6–3), ***French Open*** 1r (lost Srejber 5–7 7–6 7–6 6–3), ***Wimbledon*** 2r (d. Fulwood 6–2 7–5 6–1, lost Leconte [seed 9] 6–2 7–6 1–6 6–2), ***US Open*** 3r (d. Pistolesi 6–4 6–2 6–3, Freeman 2–6 6–3 6–2 6–2, lost Jarryd [seed 16] 6–3 6–2 6–3); ***won*** Tel Aviv (d. Panatta 6–1 7–5, Merenstein 6–0 6–2, Popp 6–7 6–4 6–2, Connors 7–6 6–3, Gilbert 3–6 6–3 6–4); ***r/u*** Vienna (d. Novacek 6–1 6–4, Dickson 4–6 6–0 6–2, Jarryd 4–6 7–5 6–2, Muster 2–6 6–4 6–2, lost J. B. Svensson 1–6 1–6 6–2 6–3 7–5); ***sf*** US Pro Indoor (d. Blackman, Gunnarsson, Novacek 6–7 6–3 6–4, lost McEnroe 5–7 6–2 6–3), ***sf*** Johannesburg (d. Steyn 7–6 6–2, Reneberg 6–4 6–4, Cancellotti 0–6 6–3 6–3, lost Cash 6–3 7–6).

REGINA MARSIKOVA (Czechoslovakia)
Born Prague, 11 December, 1958 and lives there; RH; 5ft 10in; 145lb; final 1987 WITA ranking 71; 1987 prize money $33,382.
1975: R/u Wimbledon Jun. ***1976:*** (23) Qf French Open. ***1977:*** (20) Won Canadian Open, reached sf French Open; in doubles won French Open with Teeguarden. ***1978:*** (14) Won Italian Open, Canadian Open, last 16 Wimbledon and US Open. ***1979:*** (14) Sf French Open, r/u German Open. ***1980:*** (18) R/u FC Cup. ***1981:*** (13) Won German Open. Forced out of game at end of year by Czech government after tragic car accident. ***1982–84:*** Out of game. ***1985:*** (80) Made a notable comeback, reaching sf Barcelona. ***1986:*** Won 23 of 43 matches, upsetting Horvath and Bonder. ***1987 HIGHLIGHTS – SINGLES: Australian Open*** 1r (lost Henricksson 6–4 6–4), ***French Open*** 2r (d. Bowes 4–6 6–3 6–2, lost Bassett 6–2 6–7 6–3), ***Wimbledon*** 2r (d. Phelps 6–4 6–3, lost Tanvier 6–0 6–2), ***US Open*** 1r (lost M. J. Fernandez 6–3 6–0). ***CAREER HIGHLIGHTS – SINGLES: Italian Open – won 1978*** (d. Nagelsen, Newberry, Ruzici 7–5 7–5); ***French Open – sf 1979*** (lost Turnbull 6–4 6–3), ***sf 1977*** (lost Jausovec 6–3 fs). ***CAREER HIGHLIGHTS – DOUBLES:*** (with Teeguarden) ***French Open – won 1977*** (d. Fox/H. Cawley 5–7 6–4 6–2).

WALLY MASUR (Australia)
Born Southampton, England, 13 May, 1963; lives Canberra; RH; 5ft 11in; 165lb; final 1987 ATP ranking 35; 1987 prize money $165,259.
1981: (287) Won Australian Open Jun. ***1982:*** (125). ***1983:*** (66) Qf Australian Open and won Hong Kong. ***1984:*** (106) R/u Taipei. ***1985:*** (101) R/u Auckland. ***1986:*** (87) Sf Livingston and Auckland. ***1987:*** In Adelaide won first tourn since 1983, then upset Becker *en route* to sf Australian Open. ***1987 HIGHLIGHTS – SINGLES: Australian Open*** sf, unseeded (d. Sadri 6–3 6–7 6–4 6–0, Jones 6–7 6–2 6–0 6–4, Van Rensburg 6–3 1–6 7–5 4–6 6–0, Becker [seed 2] 4–6 7–6 6–4 6–7 6–2, Evernden 6–3 7–5 6–4, lost Edberg [seed 4] 6–2 6–4 7–6), ***French Open*** 1r (lost Krickstein 6–3 6–3 6–4), ***Wimbledon*** 2r (d. Motta 6–2 6–4 6–4, lost Annacone 6–7 6–4 7–6 6–7 6–3), ***US Open*** 1r (lost E. Sanchez [seed 14] 1–6 6–4 7–6 6–3); ***won*** Adelaide (d. K. Jones, Woodforde, Mansdorf 6–2 6–4, Schapers 6–4 6–0, Scanlon 6–4 7–6); ***r/u*** Nancy (d. Cahill 3–6 6–2 6–2, P. Carlsson 7–5 6–3, Dickson 6–4 3–6 6–3, Drewett 6–4 7–6, lost Cash 6–2 6–3); ***sf*** Sydney (d. Lavalle, Warder, Evernden, lost Mecir 6–4 6–2), ***sf*** Newport (d. Freeman 6–2 6–4, Visser 7–6 6–4, Fitzgerald 6–4 6–3, lost Goldie 6–2 4–6 6–2). ***CAREER HIGHLIGHTS – SINGLES: Australian Open – sf 1987, qf 1983*** (d. Flach, Jarryd [seed 8] 6–3 6–3 4–6 6–1, lost McEnroe [seed 2] 6–2 6–1 6–2).

LUIZ MATTAR (Brazil)
Born Sao Paulo, 18 August, 1963 and lives there; RH; 5ft 11½in; 168lb; final 1987 ATP ranking 38; 1987 prize money $163,769.
1985: (230). ***1986:*** (95) Qf Madrid. Played D Cup. ***1987:*** Won Guaruja, r/u Sao Paulo and Itaparica. ***1987 HIGHLIGHTS – SINGLES: French Open*** 2r (d. Vojtisek 3–6 0–6 6–4 7–5 6–4, lost Berger 7–6 6–3 6–3), ***Wimbledon*** 1r (lost Visser 3–6 7–6 6–4 6–4); ***won*** Guaruja (d. Willenborg, Tarr, Werner, Oresar 4–6 7–6 6–4, Motta 7–5 6–2), ***won*** Campos do Jordao Challenger (d. Motta 6–3 6–1); ***r/u*** Sao Paulo (d. Ross 0–6 7–6 6–2, J. Sanchez 7–5 6–0, Filippini 6–3 6–4, Cassidy 6–2 6–4, lost Yzaga 6–2 4–6 6–2), ***r/u*** Itaparica (d. Kley 6–4 6–7 6–3, Motta 6–1 6–2, Casal 7–5 5–7 7–6, Smid 4–6 7–6 6–4, lost Agassi 7–6 6–2). ***1987 HIGHLIGHTS – DOUBLES:*** [Motta] ***won*** Guaruja (d. Hipp/Meinecke 7–6 6–1), [Acioly] ***won*** Geneva (d. Gildemeister/Gomez 6–3 6–2, lost Bahrami/Perez 3–6 6–4 6–2).

Emilio Sanchez and Sergio Casal (foreground) won six doubles titles and were runners-up at Wimbledon, where they were beaten by Ken Flach and Robert Seguso (below r–l), who also reached the US Open and Masters finals. *(M. Cole, A. Evans)*

TIM MAYOTTE (USA)
Born Springfield, Mass., 3 August, 1960; lives Bradenton, Fla.; RH; 6ft 3in; 180lb; final 1987 ATP ranking 9; 1987 prize money $458,821.
Coached by Bill Drake. ***1978:*** Top-ranked player in US Boys' 18. ***1981:*** (30) Won NCAA Champs while playing for Stanford, reached qf Wimbledon and Australian Open and f Maui to be named ATP Newcomer of the Year. ***1982:*** (29) Reached sf Wimbledon, f WCT Strasbourg and Bristol. ***1983:*** (16) Qf Wimbledon, sf Australian Open. ***1984:*** (44) R/u Newport. ***1985:*** (12) Won inaugural LIPC Champs and r/u to Lendl at WCT Dallas. ***1986:*** (15) Won Queens Club (d. Becker, Edberg, Connors), qf Wimbledon, r/u US Pro Indoor and D Cup début for US, winning crucial 5s match over Lavalle to lead US into sf v Australia. ***1987:*** Took a 2-month break at beginning of year to concentrate on improving his backcourt game, returning to win US Pro Indoor, Chicago, Toulouse, Paris Open and Frankfurt. ***1987 HIGHLIGHTS – SINGLES: Wimbledon*** 3r, seed 10 (d. Fleurian 6–2 6–3 6–3, Wilkison 6–3 4–6 6–7 6–2 6–4, lost Pernfors 2–6 4–6 6–4 6–3 7–5), ***US Open*** 2r, seed 12 (d. Giammalva 6–1 6–0 6–1, lost Woodforde 7–6 7–6 3–6 2–6 7–6); ***won*** US Pro Indoor (d. Muller, Testerman, Annacone 7–5 6–4, Srejber 6–2 6–2, McEnroe 3–6 6–1 6–3 6–1), ***won*** Chicago (d. Rostagno 6–1 6–1, Nelson 6–4 6–7 6–3, Fleming 6–2 6–3, Teltscher 3–6 7–5 6–2, Pate 6–3 6–2), ***won*** Toulouse (d. Jones 6–4 6–3, Odizor 7–6 6–3, Mezzadri 6–2 6–1, Hlasek 6–3 6–1, Osterthun 6–2 5–7 6–4), ***won*** Paris Open (d. Bloom, Zivojinovic 4–6 6–2 6–2, Mansdorf 6–4 6–2, Leconte 6–3 4–6 6–3, Gilbert 2–6 6–3 7–5 6–7 6–3), ***won*** Frankfurt (d. Odizor 6–2 6–2, Testerman 6–1 6–3, Goldie 7–6 6–4, Rostagno 6–4 6–1, Gomez 7–6 6–4); ***sf*** Orlando (d. Berger 6–4 7–6, Steyn 6–4 7–5, Annacone 6–1 7–5, lost Van Rensburg 2–6 7–6 6–4), ***sf*** Queens (d. Nelson 6–2 6–4, McNamee 6–2 7–5, Van Rensburg 6–4 7–6, Krishnan 6–2 6–3, lost Becker 4–6 7–6 6–4). ***CAREER HIGHLIGHTS – SINGLES: LIPC – won 1985*** (d. Becker 6–2 6–3, S. Davis 4–6 4–6 6–3 6–2 6–4); ***Wimbledon – sf 1982*** (d. Mayer 3–6 6–7 6–4 6–2 6–4, Mottram 6–2 7–5 6–3, Teacher 6–7 7–6 7–5 3–6 6–1, lost McEnroe [seed 1] 6–1 6–3 6–2), ***qf 1981*** (d. Mitton, Fancutt, Sadri, A. Mayer 6–3 6–4 7–6, lost Frawley 4–6 7–6 6–3 6–3), ***qf 1983*** (d. Dickson, Teacher, McCurdy, lost Curren 4–6 7–6 6–2 7–6); ***qf 1986*** (d. Canter, Smid, Edwards, lost Lendl [seed 1] 6–4 4–6 6–4 3–6 9–7); ***Australian Open – sf 1983*** (d. Nystrom, Teltscher, lost Lendl 6–1 7–6 6–3), ***qf 1981*** (d. Van't Hof, DuPre, lost Kriek 7–6 6–3 7–5).

MILOSLAV MECIR (Czechoslovakia)
Born Bojnice, 19 May, 1964; lives Prievidza; RH; 2HB; 6ft 3in; 180lb; final 1987 ATP ranking 6 singles, 12 doubles; 1987 prize money $1,205,326.
Wife Petra (married Aug 1987). ***1982:*** (215). ***1983:*** (101) Immensely talented, deceptive with his lethal forehand down the line and sharp two-handed backhand crosscourt, he won Czech Closed Champs and r/u Adelaide. ***1984:*** (60) R/u Palermo and Cologne. ***1985:*** (9) Won Rotterdam and Hamburg, r/u to McEnroe at US Pro Indoor following win over Connors and r/u Italian Open (d. Wilander, lost Noah). ***1986:*** (9) Played his best tennis in the two biggest tournaments, upsetting Edberg at Wimbledon *en route* to qf and downing Wilander, Nystrom and Becker to reach US Open f. Won Kitzbuhel over Gomez. Missed Masters owing to knee injury. ***1987:*** Was the first since McEnroe in 1984 to win GP titles on all four surfaces – Auckland and LIPC on HC, Sydney on GC, WCT Finals on carpet, Stuttgart and Hilversum on CC – and was one of the few players to beat Lendl all year. Sf French Open, qf Australian and US Opens, won LIPC mixed doubles with Novotna, and qualified for Masters in singles and doubles, winning doubles with Smid. ***1987 HIGHLIGHTS – SINGLES: Australian Open*** qf, seed 6 (bye d. Bates 4–6 6–2 6–1 6–3, Muller 7–5 5–7 4–6 7–6 6–4, Kratzmann 6–4 6–2 6–3, lost Edberg [seed 4] 6–1 6–4 6–4), ***French Open*** sf, seed 5 (d. Witsken 6–2 6–1 6–3, Skoff 7–6 6–4 6–1, Srejber 6–1 6–2 6–1, Kuchna 6–0 6–1 6–3, Novacek 7–6 6–1 6–2, lost Lendl [seed 1] 6–3 6–3 7–6), ***Wimbledon*** 3r, seed 5 (d. DePalmer 6–3 6–2 7–5, Woodforde 6–1 6–3 6–3, lost Jarryd 6–3 6–3 6–3), ***US Open*** qf, seed 5 (d. Novacek 6–3 6–4 7–6, Fitzgerald 6–3 6–1 6–0, Hlasek 6–4 6–4 2–6 6–4, Woodforde 6–4 3–6 6–2 6–2, lost Wilander [seed 3] 6–3 6–7 6–4 7–6); ***won*** Auckland (d. Doohan, Michibata, Derlin, Rostagno 6–2 6–1, Schapers 6–2 6–3 6–4), ***won*** Sydney (d. Frawley, Stoltenberg, Scanlon, Masur 6–4 6–2, Doohan 6–2 6–4), ***won*** LIPC (d. Motta 6–3 6–1 6–0, Yzaga 6–4 6–3 6–2, Arias 6–3 6–4 6–4, Zivojinovic 2–6 6–1 6–1 6–4, Edberg 3–6 6–2 6–2 6–4, Lendl 7–5 5–1 ret'd), ***won*** WCT Finals (d. Wilander 6–1 6–1 6–3, Gomez 6–7 7–6 6–4 6–2, McEnroe 6–0 3–6 6–2 6–2), ***won*** Stuttgart (d. Tideman 6–2 6–4, Muster 6–2

6–1, Vajda 6–3 6–2, Smid 6–3 6–3, Gunnarsson 6–0 6–2), ***won*** Hilversum (d. Davin 6–3 4–6 6–2, Osterthun 4–6 6–3 6–4, Skoff 7–5 6–2, Bengoechea 6–1 7–5, Perez Roldan 6–4 1–6 6–3 6–2); ***r/u*** Milan (d. Colombini 6–2 6–3, Jelen 6–1 6–4, Smid 6–4 6–4, Wilander 6–0 6–2, lost Becker 6–4 6–3), ***r/u*** Hamburg (d. Motta, Srejber 7–6 6–3, Jaite 6–1 6–3, Bengoechea 7–6 6–1, lost Lendl 6–1 6–3 6–3), ***r/u*** Kitzbuhel (d. Champion 7–5 4–6 6–4, Popp 6–3 6–4, Maurer 6–2 6–3, Agenor 6–4 6–4, Cahill 6–1 6–2, lost E. Sanchez 6–4 6–1 4–6 6–1); ***sf*** Rotterdam (d. Cahill 6–2 6–3, Forget 7–5 7–5, J. B. Svensson 6–2 7–5, lost McEnroe 6–1 7–5). ***1987 HIGHLIGHTS – DOUBLES:*** (with Smid unless stated) ***won*** Hamburg (d. Mezzadri/Pugh 4–6 7–6 6–2), [Fibak] ***won*** Hilversum (d. Nijssen/Vekemans 7–6 5–7 6–2), ***won*** Prague (d. Birner/Navratil 6–3 6–7 6–3), ***won*** Barcelona (d. Frana/Miniussi 6–1 6–2), ***won*** Wembley (d. Flach/Seguso 7–5 6–4), ***won*** Masters (d. Edberg/Jarryd 3–6 6–3 2–6 6–3 6–4, Flach/Seguso 6–4 7–5 6–7 6–3); ***r/u*** Italian Open (lost Forget/Noah 6–2 6–7 6–3), ***r/u*** Kitzbuhel (lost Casal/E. Sanchez 7–6 7–6). ***1987 HIGHLIGHTS – MIXED DOUBLES:*** (with Novotna) ***won*** LIPC (d. Van Rensburg/M. Reinach). ***CAREER HIGHLIGHTS – SINGLES: US Open – r/u 1986*** (d. Tim Gullikson, Forget, Edwards, Wilander [seed 2] 6–7 6–3 6–3 6–4, Nystrom [seed 7] 6–4 6–2 3–6 6–2, Becker [seed 3] 4–6 6–3 6–4 3–6 6–3, lost Lendl [seed 1] 6–4 6–2 6–0), ***qf 1987; French Open – sf 1987; Wimbledon – qf 1986*** unseeded (d. Edberg [seed 5] 6–4 6–4 6–4, Gilbert [seed 12] 3–6 7–6 6–1 6–2, lost Becker [seed 4] 6–4 6–2 7–6); ***Australian Open – qf 1987. CAREER HIGHLIGHTS – DOUBLES:*** (with Smid) ***Masters – won 1987. MIXED DOUBLES:*** (with Novotna) ***LIPC – won 1987.***

NATALIA MEDVEDEVA (USSR)
Born 15 November, 1971; final 1987 WITA ranking 196; 1987 prize money $10,761.
Known as Natasha in USSR. ***1987:*** ITF Jun Champ in doubles; won French Open and Wimbledon Jun doubles with Zvereva. In autumn won 3 consec. titles on LTA British circuit. ***1987 HIGHLIGHTS – SINGLES:*** Wimbledon 1r (lost Shriver [seed 5] 6–2 6–1).

SILKE MEIER (West Germany)
Born Wiesbaden, 13 July, 1968; lives Enkenback-Alsenborn; RH; 5ft 8in; 135lb; final 1987 WITA ranking 50; 1987 prize money $52,025.
1985: (167). ***1986:*** (86) Sf VS Arkansas. ***1987:*** Upset M. Maleeva at LIPC and Sukova in Berlin. ***1987 HIGHLIGHTS – SINGLES: French Open*** 1r (lost Kelesi 2–6 6–0 6–2), ***Wimbledon*** 2r (d. Piatek 6–2 6–2, lost Kuczynska 6–3 6–3), ***US Open*** 2r (d. Walsh Pete 7–5 6–3, lost Hanika [seed 13] 6–3 6–0).

TORE MEINECKE (West Germany)
Born Hamburg, 21 July, 1967; lives Berlin; RH; 5ft 11in; 159lb; final 1987 ATP ranking 64; 1987 prize money $101,341.
Coached by brother Bjorn. ***1983:*** (603) R/u Nat Indoor. ***1984:*** (292). ***1985:*** (178). ***1986:*** (123) Qf Madrid. ***1987:*** Reached first GP f in Athens, sf Kitzbuhel and d. Zivojinovic Monte Carlo. ***1987 HIGHLIGHTS – SINGLES: r/u*** Athens (d. Pimek 6–1 6–0, Pistolesi 6–2 6–2, Rebolledo 6–1 6–7 6–3, Yunis 6–4 6–4, lost Perez Roldan 6–2 6–3); ***sf*** Kitzbuhel (d. Vilas 6–1 2–6 6–4, Tulasne 6–2 6–2, Miniussi 6–2 6–0, Perez Roldan 1–6 6–3 6–4, lost E. Sanchez 6–2 6–2). ***1987 HIGHLIGHTS – DOUBLES:*** [Osterthun] ***won*** Athens (d. Navratil/Nijssen).

LEILA MESKHI (USSR)
Born Minsk, 5 January, 1968; lives Tbilisi; RH; 2HB; 5ft 4½in; 120lb; final 1987 WITA ranking 45; 1987 prize money $25,772.
Amateur. Coached by Kakulia and Olga Morozova. ***1986:*** (241) No. 1 in ITF Jun doubles world rankings. In singles r/u Wimbledon Jun; in doubles won French Open Jun (with Zvereva), r/u Wimbledon (with Zvereva) and US Open Jun (with Brioukhovets). ***1987:*** Reached 1st sf at VS Indianapolis, qf Athens and Chicago, and upset Bunge 2r Hamburg. ***1987 HIGHLIGHTS – SINGLES: won*** USTA Tarzana (d. C. Wood 1–6 6–4 6–2); ***sf*** VS Indianapolis (d. Gurney 7–5 6–0, Reece 6–4 6–3, Kelesi 6–3 6–1, Phelps 6–2 6–4, lost Cioffi 5–7 6–0 6–4). ***1987 HIGHLIGHTS – DOUBLES:*** [Bykova] ***r/u*** Hamburg (d. Bunge/Graf lost Kohde-Kilsch/Novotna 7–6 7–6).

CLAUDIO MEZZADRI (Switzerland)
Born Locarno, 10 June, 1965; lives Milan, Italy; RH; 5ft 11in; 155lb; final 1987 ATP ranking 28; 1987 prize money $175,282.
1984: (150). ***1985:*** (135). ***1986:*** (138) Sf Florence and Palermo. ***1987:*** Ranked No. 2 in Switzerland. Won his 1st pro title at Geneva, qf Italian Open, sf Gstaad and Vienna (d. Mayotte after qualifying) and broke into top 50 in Oct. ***1987 HIGHLIGHTS – SINGLES: US Open*** 1r (lost Zivojinovic 6–3 6–0 6–4); ***won*** Geneva (d. Allgaardh 6–2 4–6 6–0, Nystrom 3–6 6–2 6–3, Stadler 6–4 6–1, Stenlund 6–2 6–7 7–6, Smid 6–4 7–5); ***sf*** Gstaad (d. Beutel 6–4 7–6, Jarryd 7–6 6–3, Forget 7–6 6–3, lost Agenor 6–7 6–4), ***sf*** Vienna (d. Osterthun 6–1 7–5, Bergstrom 6–2 6–4, Mayotte 7–6 6–7 7–6, lost Svensson 6–2 6–3). ***1987 HIGHLIGHTS – DOUBLES:*** [Krishnan] ***won*** Nancy (d. Connell/Scott 6–4 6–4), [Hlasek] ***won*** Paris Open (d. Mecir/Smid, S. Davis/ Pate 7–6 6–2); [Pugh] ***r/u*** Hamburg (lost Mecir/Smid 4–6 7–6 6–3).

ANNE MINTER (Australia)
Born Melbourne, 4 March, 1963, and lives there; RH; 5ft 4½in; 120lb; final 1987 WITA ranking 38; 1987 prize money $73,972.
Coached by fiancé Graeme Harris (wedding planned for Nov. 1988). Sister of Elizabeth. Plays flute to state orchestra standard. ***1980:*** Won Australian Open Jun and was ranked 5 on ITF world jun list. ***1981:*** Australian Jun champ. ***1982:*** (77) Won Goldair on Australian satellite circuit. ***1983:*** (95). ***1984:*** (43) Sf Salt Lake City and Newport in singles, qf Australian Open doubles with her sister. Joined Fed Cup team. ***1985:*** (72) Qf Marco Island. ***1986:*** (82) Won 20 of 40 matches, upsetting Lindqvist 1r VS LA. ***1987:*** Won her first major title at Taipei, following with Singapore a week later, and d. Sukova 2r Canadian Open. ***1987 HIGHLIGHTS – SINGLES: Australian Open*** 1r (lost Hy 6–4 6–4), ***French Open*** 3r (d. Probst 6–3 6–0, Sloane 7–6 6–4, lost Reggi [seed 14] 7–5 6–2), ***Wimbledon*** 2r (d. Mochizuki 7–5 6–3, lost Shriver [seed 5] 6–2 6–2), ***US Open*** 1r (lost Durie 6–3 2–6 6–2); ***won*** Taipei (d. Cordwell, Koizumi, Devries 6–2 6–3, Villagran 0–6 6–3 6–1, Porwik 6–4 6–1), ***won*** Singapore (d. Xinyi, Nozzoli, Croft 6–1 6–0, Inoue 2–6 6–4 6–2, Gerken 6–4 6–1); ***r/u*** VS San Diego (d. Allred 6–2 6–1, Novotna 6–7 6–4 6–2, Phelps 7–5 6–3, Herreman 6–2 6–4, McNeil 2–6 6–4 7–5, lost Reggi 6–0 6–4).

ELIZABETH MINTER (Australia)
Born Melbourne, 23 August, 1965, and lives there; LH; 5ft 7in; 135lb; final 1987 WITA ranking 76; 1987 prize money $30,740.
Younger sister of Anne. ***1982:*** Won Victorian Open. ***1983:*** (135) Ranked 1 in Australian 18s, became first Australian to win US Open Jun, r/u Bari, sf Taranto. ***1984:*** (65) In doubles won Salt Lake City (with her sister), Richmond (with Russell), qf Australian Open (with her sister) and r/u NCAA Champs (with L. Lewis). Played Fed Cup as AUS r/u to TCH in f. ***1985:*** (127). ***1986:*** (93). ***1987:*** Sf Auckland and Puerto Rico, qf VS Oklahoma. ***1987 HIGHLIGHTS – SINGLES: Australian Open*** 1r (lost Benjamin 0–6 6–4 6–4), ***French Open*** 1r (lost C. Karlsson 7–5 6–3), ***Wimbledon*** 1r (lost Mesker 6–1 6–1), ***US Open*** 1r (lost Hobbs 6–4 7–5); ***sf*** Auckland (d. Carney 6–2 6–7 6–4, Golder 6–1 6–0, Jaggard 7–5 4–6 7–6, lost Phelps 6–1 7–5), ***sf*** Puerto Rico (d. Mascarin 6–3 6–4, Labuschagne 6–1 ret'd, Gurney 6–4 6–2, Sodupe 6–3 7–6, lost Rehe 6–3 6–1).

ALYCIA MOULTON (USA)
Born Sacramento Cal., 18 February, 1961; lives Palo Alto, Cal.; RH; 5ft 10½in; 145lb; final 1987 WITA ranking 51; 1987 prize money $49,224.
Coached by Jeff Arons. ***1979:*** (70) Won US Open Jun and r/u Wimbledon Jun. ***1980:*** (114) R/u AIAW Champs, playing for Stanford. ***1981:*** (88) R/u AIAW Champs second consecutive year. ***1982:*** (38) Won AIAW in her third straight f. ***1983:*** (32) Won Newport. ***1984:*** (19) R/u Canadian Open beating Mandlikova. ***1985:*** (35) Reached sf Sydney. ***1986:*** (37) Beat Potter, K. Jordan and Bassett among others, but lacked consistency. ***1987 HIGHLIGHTS – SINGLES: Australian Open*** 2r (d. Porwik 4–6 6–4 6–3, lost Shriver 6–2 4–6 11–9), ***Wimbledon*** 3r (d. Nagelsen 6–2 7–5, Polzl Wiesner 6–4 6–4, lost M. J. Fernandez 7–6 6–2), ***US Open*** 1r (lost Kohde-Kilsch [seed 9] 6–2 7–5); ***r/u*** Beckenham (d. Lindqvist 3–6 6–3 6–0, lost Potter 7–6 7–5); ***sf*** VS Newport (d. Van Rensburg 6–2 6–1, Turnbull 6–4 6–0, Phelps 6–4 6–3, lost Shriver 6–3 6–2).

GARY MULLER (South Africa)
Born Durban, 27 December, 1964; lives Johannesburg; LH; 6ft 4in; 180lb; final 1987 ATP ranking 68; 1987 prize money $73,845.
Coached by José Higueras. ***1985:*** (186). ***1986:*** (236) Qf Basle, sf US Open doubles with Nelson. ***1987:*** Qf Indianapolis (d. Gomez) Schenectady and Johannesburg. ***1987 HIGHLIGHTS – SINGLES: Australian Open*** 3r (d. Denton 6–7 6–3 6–4 6–4, Woodforde 7–5 5–7 4–6 7–6 6–4, lost Mecir [seed 6] 6–4 6–4 6–4), ***Wimbledon*** 1r (lost Wilander [seed 3] 6–2 6–1 6–4), ***US Open*** 2r (d. Osterthun 7–5 6–3 6–2, lost Pugh 7–5 6–3 6–4). ***1987 HIGHLIGHTS – DOUBLES:*** (with Donnelly) ***won*** Schenectady (d. Pearce/Pugh 7–6 6–2).

THOMAS MUSTER (Austria)
Born Leibnitz, 2 October, 1967; lives Monte Carlo; LH; 5ft 11in; 156lb; final 1987 ATP ranking 56; 1987 prize money $73,325.
1985: (98) Won Banana Bowl, r/u French Open Jun and Rolex. Became a member of Austrian D Cup squad and finished 6 on Austrian satellite circuit. ***1986:*** (47) Won first GP title in Hilversum. ***1987:*** Sf Vienna (d. E. Sanchez) and won Young Masters. ***1987 HIGHLIGHTS – SINGLES: French Open*** 3r (d. Perez Roldan 6–1 6–3 6–2, Stenlund 6–2 6–2 6–2, lost Jaite [seed 14] 6–2 3–6 7–6 6–0), ***Wimbledon*** 1r (lost Forget 6–4 6–4 6–4), ***US Open*** 3r (d. Lozano 7–6 6–2 6–4, Bergstrom 6–7 6–2 6–7 6–3 6–4, lost Gomez [seed 9] 1–6 6–7 6–3 6–3 6–3); ***won*** Young Masters (d. Steeb 7–6 6–3, Schaffner 6–0 6–0, Winogradsky 6–4 3–6 6–3 in rr, Gustafsson 6–2 6–4, Svensson 6–4 4–6 7–5 6–2); ***sf*** Vienna (d. Smid 7–6 6–3, Skoff 6–4 6–4, E. Sanchez 6–4 6–4, lost Mansdorf 2–6 6–4 6–2).

BETSY NAGELSEN (USA)
Born St Petersburg, Fla., 23 October, 1956; lives Kapalua Bay, Hawaii; RH; 5ft 10in; 135lb; final 1987 WITA ranking 61 singles, 14 (15) doubles; 1987 prize money $98,786.
1974: At 17, she stunned Morozova and Wade to reach f Newport, displaying superior serve-and-volley skills and delighting the galleries. ***1975:*** (51) Beset by back injuries which plagued her for several years. ***1977:*** (30) Won first Avon Futures Champ. ***1978:*** (87) R/u Australian Open. ***1981:*** (23) Won Surbiton, d. Navratilova in sf. ***1982:*** (54) Achieved highest career ranking of 17 in March. ***1984:*** (77) Reached sf US Open doubles with A White. ***1985:*** (45) Reached sf French Open doubles with A. White. ***1986:*** (47) Married Mark McCormack in March. R/u VS Kansas and last 16 Wimbledon (d. Shriver for first time in 1r). ***1987:*** Sf Brisbane and Japan/Asian Open in singles, r/u Wimbledon doubles with Smylie and r/u US Open mixed with Annacone. ***1987 HIGHLIGHTS – SINGLES: Australian Open*** 2r (d. Antonoplis 6–2 6–7 6–1, lost Jolissaint 6–4 1–6 6–3), ***Wimbledon*** 1r (lost Moulton 6–2 7–5), ***US Open*** 2r (d. Tanvier 7–6 6–1, lost Demongeot 6–4 6–1); ***sf*** Brisbane (d. Mochizuki, Hy 6–1 6–1, Ludloff 6–3 3–6 7–6, Smylie 3–6 6–2 6–3, lost Shriver 6–1 6–3), ***sf*** Japan/Asian Open (d. Okagawa, Paradis 6–1 6–0, Okamoto 7–6 6–4, lost K. Maleeva 1–6 7–6 6–3). ***1987 HIGHLIGHTS – DOUBLES:*** (with Smylie unless stated) ***r/u Wimbledon*** (lost Kohde-Kilsch/Sukova 7–5 7–5); ***won*** NSW Open (d. Byrne/Thompson 6–7 7–5 6–1), [K. Jordan] ***won*** Japan/Asian Open (d. Collins/Walsh Pete 6–3 7–5), ***won*** Geneva (d. Gildemeister/Tanvier 4–6 6–4 6–3); ***r/u*** Brisbane (lost Mandlikova/Turnbull 6–4 6–3), ***r/u*** New Jersey (lost G. Fernandez/McNeil). ***1987 HIGHLIGHTS – MIXED DOUBLES:*** (with Annacone) ***r/u US Open*** (lost Navratilova/Sanchez 6–4 6–7 7–6). ***CAREER HIGHLIGHTS – SINGLES: Australian Open – r/u 1978*** (d. Tomanova 6–4 6–4, Matison 7–5 6–4, lost C. O'Neill 6–3 7–6). ***CAREER HIGHLIGHTS – DOUBLES: Australian Open*** – [Tomanova] ***won 1978*** (d. Sato/Whytcross 7–5 6–2), [Reid] ***r/u 1977*** [Jan.] (lost Fromholtz/H. Cawley 5–7 6–1 7–5); ***Wimbledon*** [Smylie] ***r/u 1987; Italian Open*** – [Mihai] ***r/u 1978*** (lost Jausovec/Ruzici 6–2 2–6 7–5); ***French Open*** – [Navratilova] ***sf 1981*** (d. Evert Lloyd/Ruzici [seed 6], lost Reynolds/P. Smith [seed 2] 6–4 7–5), [A. White] ***sf 1985*** (lost Navratilova/Shriver 6–3 6–4); ***US Open*** [Shriver] ***sf 1978*** (d. Stove/Evert [seed 3] 6–3 6–2, lost Reid/Turnbull [seed 2] 6–4 1–6 7–5), [A. White] ***sf 1984*** (d. Evert Lloyd/King 7–6 4–6 6–3, lost Navratilova/Shriver 6–4 7–5).

DIEGO NARGISO (Italy)
Born Naples, 15 March, 1970; lives Monte Carlo; LH; 2HB; 6ft 2in; 176lb; final 1987 ATP ranking 191; 1987 prize money $15,995.

Coached by Roberto Lombardi. ***1987:*** Won Wimbledon Jun singles over Stoltenberg, and US Open Jun doubles with Ivanisevic.

JAROSLAV NAVRATIL (Czechoslovakia)
Born Prerov, 28 July, 1957 and lives there; RH; 6ft 5in; 180lb; final 1987 ATP ranking 78; 1987 prize money $61,451.
1984: (93) Qf Bastad and Toulouse. ***1985:*** (181). ***1986:*** (183). ***1987:*** Pulled off one of the upsets of the year when he d. countryman Mecir *en route* to 1st GP sf in Prague. ***1987 HIGHLIGHTS – SINGLES: US Open*** 2r (d. DePalmer 4–6 6–3 1–6 6–2 7–5, lost Hlasek 7–5 7–5 6–4); ***sf*** Prague (d. Mecir 6–3 5–7 7–6, Roubicek 6–3 6–4, Popp 6–4 6–4, lost Smid 6–1 7–5). ***1987 HIGHLIGHTS – DOUBLES:*** (with Birner) ***r/u*** Prague (lost Mecir/Smid 6–3 6–7 6–3), ***r/u*** Basel (d. Casal/E. Sanchez 7–6 4–6 7–6, lost Jarryd/Smid 6–4 6–3).

MARTINA NAVRATILOVA (USA)
Born Prague, 18 October, 1956; lives Fort Worth, Texas; single; LH; 5ft 7½in; 145lb; final 1987 WITA ranking 2 singles, 1 (1) doubles; 1987 prize money $932,102; career prize money $12,724,417.
1973: Displaying enormous promise, she reached qf French Open and extended Goolagong to 7–6 6–4 in memorable match after eliminating 1968 champion Nancy Richey. ***1974:*** Won first major tournament in Orlando and was r/u to Evert at Italian Open. ***1975:*** (3) Led Czechoslovakia to Fed Cup title (d. Goolagong in f), and was r/u to Evert at VS Champs, French and Italian Opens, reaching f in 13 of 25 tourns. The day after losing to Evert in US Open sf Forest Hills she announced her defection from Czechoslovakia. ***1976:*** (4) Reached first sf at Wimbledon and won first doubles there with Evert, but made tearful exit from US Open after losing 1r. ***1977:*** (3) Won 6 tourns and reached f of 5 other events in 20 appearances. ***1978:*** (1) Ranked 1 on computer in close race with Evert, whom she beat to win first Wimbledon singles title. Won 80 of 89 matches and 11 of 20 tourns, including 37-match winning streak as she won 7 straight VS tourns in winter. ***1979:*** (1) Defended Wimbledon title safely and won 11 of 23 tourns, reaching f of 19 events and closing year with resounding victory over Austin at TS Champs. ***1980:*** (3) Won 11 of 24 tourns but no majors. ***1981:*** (3) Linking with Renee Richards at US Open, she received sound technical and tactical advice, leading to sf win there over Evert Lloyd, another f Australian Open, and sucess in 8 of 19 tourns. ***1982:*** (1) Won 15 of 18 tourns 90 of 93 matches, including 41 straight from March until September, with third Wimbledon singles and first French Open. ***1983:*** (1) Won 16 of 17 tourns, including first US Open and third Wimbledon, and 86 of 87 matches, closing season with streak of 50 straight match victories, her only defeat being by Kathleen Horvath in last 16 of French Open. Her .988 winning percentage set an 'Open Tennis' record for men and women. ***1984:*** (1) Won 78 of 80 matches, 13 of 15 tourns, and set modern pro record of 74 straight matches won, beginning immediately after her 54-match streak was broken at start of season by Mandlikova at VS Oakland. Won bonus of $1m from ITF for achieving a modern GS, culminating with French Open where she played possibly the best match of her career to beat Evert Lloyd in f. She extended her GS streak to six with her fifth Wimbledon and second US Open victories, but her bid for traditional GS, as well as her 74-match winning streak, were stopped by Sukova in sf Australian Open. ***1985:*** (1) Won her 6th Wimbledon and 3rd Australian titles, 84 of 89 matches and 12 of 17 tourns. Was challenged for No. 1 ranking by Evert Lloyd, who took over top spot for virtually half the year, but Martina clinched No. 1 with 3s triumph over Chris in Australian f. ***1986:*** (1) Won 14 of 17 tourns and 89 of 92 matches, including 5th straight Wimbledon (the first since Lenglen 1919–23 to achieve that feat) and her 3rd US Open. Won two VS Champs and closed season with streak of 53 straight matches. ***1987:*** Coached by Randy Crawford Jan. to March, by Angel Gimenez (who helped her to develop a faster game) and Virginia Wade Jan.–May, by Renee Richards to end of year, and Tim Gullikson from Jan. 1988. Losing Australian Open to Mandlikova, French Open to Graf, who also beat her in sf LIPC, she won no singles tournament from Nov. 1986 until triumphing over Graf at Wimbledon. This was her longest spell without a win since mid 1970s and cost her the No. 1 computer ranking which she had held continuously since July 1985. However, she won her 1st triple crown at US Open, her 2 GS singles titles confirming her as No. 1 in some eyes until she fell to Sabatini in qf VS Champs. In doubles, won 3rd GS with Shriver in Paris and their 6th VS Champs together.

Following Italian Open switched to the same type of racket that Graf uses. ***1987 HIGHLIGHTS – SINGLES: r/u Australian Open*** seed 1 (bye, d. Golder 6–0 6–2, Benjamin 6–2 6–1, Thompson 6–4 6–1, Garrison 6–0 6–3, Lindqvist 6–3 6–2, lost Mandlikova 7–5 7–6), ***r/u French Open*** seed 1 (d. Tanvier 6–3 7–6, Villagran 6–0 2–6 6–2, Huber 6–1 6–1, Hanika 6–0 6–2, Kohde-Kilsch 6–1 6–2, Evert 6–2 6–2, lost Graf 6–4 4–6 8–6), ***won Wimbledon*** seed 1 (d. Porwik 6–1 6–0, Inoue 6–1 6–2, Louie Harper 6–2 6–2, G. Fernandez 6–3 6–1, Balestrat 6–2 6–1, Evert [seed 3] 6–2 5–7 6–4, Graf [seed 2] 7–5 6–3), ***won US Open*** seed 2 (d. Gompert 6–1 6–1, R. White 6–1 6–3, Bonder 6–2 6–1, Lindqvist [seed 14] 6–0 6–4, Sabatini [seed 8] 7–5 6–3, Sukova [seed 6] 6–2 6–2, Graf [seed 1] 7–6 6–1), ***won*** Filderstadt (d. Fairbank 6–1 6–4, Demongeot 6–2 6–0, McNeil 6–4 6–2, Sabatini 6–2 6–2, Evert 7–5 6–1), ***won*** VS Chicago (d. Suire 6–0 6–1, M. J. Fernandez 6–4 6–3, McNeil 6–1 6–4, Sukova 7–5 7–5, Zvereva 6–1 6–2); ***r/u*** VS Houston (d. Benjamin 6–2 6–1, Gildemeister 6–3 6–4, McNeil 6–1 6–2, Garrison 6–1 7–6, lost Evert 3–6 6–1 7–6), ***r/u*** Eastbourne (d. Werdel 6–1 6–0, Magers 6–1 6–0, R. White 6–4 6–3, Demongeot 7–5 6–3, Shriver 6–4 4–6 6–3, lost Sukova 7–6 6–3); ***sf*** LIPC (d. Sanchez 7–5 6–4, A. Minter 6–3 6–1, Cioffi 6–1 6–0, Sabatini 6–1 6–3, Tauziat 6–1 6–1, lost Graf 6–3 6–2), ***sf*** Italian Open (d. Goles 7–6 7–6, Zrubakova 6–2 6–3, Kohde-Kilsch 6–2 6–3, lost Sabatini 7–6 6–1), ***sf*** VS LA (d. Magers 6–3 6–2, Pfaff 7–6 6–1, Hakami 6–3 6–2, lost Evert 6–2 6–1). ***1987 HIGHLIGHTS – DOUBLES:*** (with Shriver unless stated) ***won Australian Open*** (d. Hy/Inoue 6–1 6–0, Garrison/McNeil 6–1 6–0), ***won French Open*** (d. Graf/Sabatini 6–2 6–1), ***won US Open*** (d. K. Jordan/Smylie 5–7 6–4 6–2); ***won*** LIPC (d. Graf/Sabatini, Kohde-Kilsch/Sukova 6–3 7–6), [K. Jordan] ***won*** VS Houston (d. Garrison/McNeil 6–2 6–4), [Sabatini] ***won*** Italian Open (d. Kohde-Kilsch/Sukova), ***won*** VS LA (d. Garrison/McNeil 6–3 6–4), ***won*** Filderstadt (d. Garrison/McNeil 6–1 6–2), ***won*** VS Champs (d. Kohde-Kilsch/Sukova 6–1 6–1). ***1987 HIGHLIGHTS – MIXED DOUBLES:*** (with E. Sanchez) ***won US Open*** (d. Nagelsen/Annacone 6–4 6–7 7–6). ***CAREER HIGHLIGHTS – SINGLES: French Open – won 1982*** (d. Mandlikova 6–0 6–2, Jaeger 7–6 6–1), ***won 1984*** (d. Mandlikova 3–6 6–2 6–2, Evert Lloyd 6–3 6–1), ***r/u 1975*** (lost Evert 2–6 6–2 6–0), ***r/u 1985*** (lost Evert Lloyd 6–3 6–7 7–5), ***r/u 1986*** (d. Cecchini, Savchenko, Porwik, Garrone 6–1 6–2, Rinaldi 7–5 6–4, Sukova 4–6 7–6 6–2, lost Evert Lloyd 2–6 6–3 6–3), ***r/u 1987; Wimbledon – won 1978*** (d. Goolagong Cawley 2–6 6–4 6–4, Evert 2–6 6–4 7–5), ***won 1979*** (d. Austin 7–5 6–1, Evert Lloyd 6–4 6–4), ***won 1982*** (d. Russell 6–3 6–4, Bunge 6–2 6–2, Evert Lloyd 6–1 3–6 6–2), ***won 1983*** (d. Vermaak 6–1 6–1, Jaeger 6–0 6–3), ***won 1984*** (d. Evert Lloyd 7–6 6–2), ***won 1985*** (d. Garrison 6–4 7–6, Evert Lloyd 4–6 6–3 6–2), ***won 1986*** (d. Dingwall, Forman, Kinney, Demongeot 6–3 6–3, Bunge 6–1 6–3, Sabatini 6–2 6–2, Mandlikova 7–6 6–3), ***r/u 1987; US Open – won 1983*** (d. Hanika 6–0 6–3, Shriver 6–2 6–1, Evert Lloyd 6–1 6–3), ***won 1984*** (d. Evert Lloyd 4–6 6–4 6–4), ***won 1986*** (d. Holikova, Nagelsen, Horvath, Sabatini 6–4 6–2, Shriver 6–2 6–4, Graf 6–1 6–7 7–6, Sukova 6–3 6–2), ***won 1987, r/u 1981*** (d. K. Jordan, A. Smith, Evert Lloyd [seed 1], lost Austin [seed 3] 1–6 7–6 7–6), ***r/u 1985*** (d. Garrison, Graf, lost Mandlikova 7–6 1–6 7–6); ***Australian Open – won 1981*** seed 3 (d. Tobin, K. Jordan, Goolagong Cawley, Shriver, Evert Lloyd [seed 1] 6–7 6–4 7–5), ***won 1983*** (d. Durie 4–6 6–3 6–4, Shriver 6–4 6–3, K. Jordan 6–2 7–6), ***won 1985*** (d. Mandlikova 6–7 6–1 6–4, Evert Lloyd 6–2 4–6 6–2), ***r/u 1982*** (d. Shriver 6–3 6–4, lost Evert Lloyd 6–3 2–6 6–3), ***r/u 1987; VS Champs – won 1978*** (d. Goolagong Cawley 7–6 6–4), ***won 1984*** (d. Evert Lloyd 6–3 7–5 6–1), ***won 1985*** (d. Mandlikova, Sukova 6–3 7–5 6–4), ***won 1985–86*** (d. Mandlikova 6–2 6–0 3–6 6–1), ***won 1986*** (d. Shriver 6–2 4–6 6–4, Graf 7–6 6–3 6–2), ***r/u 1975*** (lost Evert Lloyd 6–4 6–2); ***Avon Champs – won 1979*** (d. Austin 6–3 3–6 6–2), ***won 1981*** (d. Jaeger 6–3 7–6), ***r/u 1982*** (lost Hanika 1–6 6–3 6–4); ***TS Final – won 1982*** (d. Evert Lloyd 4–6 6–1 6–2), ***r/u 1981*** (lost Austin 2–6 6–4 6–2); ***Italian Open – r/u 1974*** (lost Evert 6–3 6–3), ***r/u 1975*** (lost Evert 6–1 6–0); ***CS Finals – r/u 1978*** (lost Evert 6–3 6–3). ***CAREER HIGHLIGHTS – DOUBLES:*** (with Shriver unless stated) ***French Open*** – [Evert] ***won 1975*** (d. Anthony/Morozova, [A. Smith] ***won 1982*** (d. Casals/Turnbull 6–3 6–4), ***won 1984*** (d. Kohde-Kilsch/Mandlikova 5–7 6–3 6–2), ***won 1985*** (d. Kohde-Kilsch/Sukova 4–6 6–2 6–2), [Temesvari] ***won 1986*** (d. Graf/Sabatini 6–1 6–2), ***won 1987; Wimbledon*** – [Evert] ***won 1976*** (d. King/Stove 6–1 3–6 7–5), [King] ***won 1979*** (d. Stove Turnbull 5–7 6–3 6–2), ***won 1981*** (d. K. Jordan/A. Smith 6–3 7–6), ***won 1982*** (d. K. Jordan/A. Smith 6–4 6–1), ***won 1983*** (d. Casals/Turnbull 6–2 6–2), ***won 1984*** (d. K. Jordan/A. Smith 6–3 6–4), ***won 1986*** (d. Mandlikova/Turnbull 6–1 6–3), ***r/u 1985*** (lost K. Jordan/Smylie 5–7 6–3 6–4); ***US Open*** – [Stove] ***won 1977*** (d. Richards/Stuart), [King] ***won 1978*** (d. Stove/Turnbull 7–6 6–4),

[King] ***won 1980*** (d. Shriver/Stove 6–7 7–5), ***won 1983*** (d. Reynolds/Fairbank 6–7 6–1 6–3), ***won 1984*** (d. Turnbull/Hobbs 6–2 6–4), ***won 1986*** (d. Mandlikova/Turnbull 6–4 3–6 6–3), ***won 1987,*** [King] ***r/u 1979*** (lost Stove/Turnbull), ***r/u 1985*** (lost Kohde-Kilsch/Sukova 6–7 6–2 6–3); ***Australian Open*** – [Nagelsen] ***won 1980*** (d. Kiyomura/Reynolds), ***won 1982*** (d. Kohde/Pfaff 6–4 6–2), ***won 1983*** (d. Hobbs/Turnbull 6–4 6–7 6–2), ***won 1984*** (d. Kohde-Kilsch/Sukova 6–3 6–4), ***won 1987,*** [Tomanova] ***r/u 1974, r/u 1981*** (lost K. Jordan/A. Smith 6–2 7–5); ***Italian Open*** – [Evert] ***won 1975*** (d. Barker/Coles), [Tomanova] ***r/u 1973*** (lost Wade/Morozova 7–5 fs); ***CS Finals*** – [King] ***won 1978*** (d. Reid/Turnbull), [King] ***won 1979*** (d. Casals/Evert Lloyd); ***TS Champs – won 1981*** (d. Casals/Turnbull 6–3 6–4), ***won 1982*** (d. Reynolds/P. Smith); ***VS Champs – won 1984*** (d. Durie/Kiyomura 6–3 6–1), ***won 1985–86*** (d. Kohde-Kilsch/Sukova 6–7 6–4 7–6), ***won 1986*** (d. Kohde-Kilsch/Sukova 7–6 6–3), ***won 1987; US Indoor*** – [King] ***won 1979*** (d. Stove/Turnbull), ***won 1984*** (d. Durie/Kiyomura Hayashi 6–4 6–3); ***Avon Champs – won 1980*** (d. Casals/Turnbull 6–3 fs), [King] ***won 1981*** (d. Potter/Walsh 6–0 7–6), ***won 1982*** (d. K. Jordan/A. Smith). ***MIXED DOUBLES:*** (with J. Sanchez) ***US Open – won 1987.***

YANNICK NOAH (France)
Born Sedan, 18 May, 1960; lives Paris and New York; RH; 6ft 4in; 180lb; final 1987 ATP ranking 8 singles, 4 (6) doubles; 1987 prize money $394,503; career prize money $2,497,400.
Wife Cecilia, son Joakim Simon (born Dec. 1984), daughter Yelenah Tara (born April 1986). ***1977:*** Won French Open Jun and r/u to Lendl Orange Bowl 18s. ***1978:*** (49) R/u Nice, won Manila and Calcutta. ***1979:*** (25) Won Nancy, Madrid and Bordeaux. ***1980:*** (23) R/u to Vilas Italian Open. ***1981:*** (12) Won Nice and Richmond WCT, r/u Gstaad, qf French Open. ***1982:*** (9) Won Palm Springs (d. Lendl to end 44-match winning streak), South Orange, Basle, Toulouse, r/u Nice, qf French Open and led France into D Cup f with crucial win over Lendl. ***1983:*** (5) Became first from his country to win French Open since Marcel Bernard in 1946. Also won Madrid and Hamburg, was r/u Lisbon and reached qf US Open. ***1984:*** (10) R/u La Quinta to Connors. ***1985:*** (7) Won Italian Open, Washington, Toulouse and was r/u Memphis and Basle. ***1986:*** (4) Played 15 tourns, winning WCT Forest Hills and Wembley, was r/u to Nystrom at La Quinta and Monte Carlo and was one of only four players to beat Lendl (at WCT Forest Hills). ***1987:*** Won Lyon but lost 1r Italian Open to K. Carlsson, fell 2r Wimbledon to his doubles partner, Forget, and further discouraged by 1r loss to Bates at Bordeaux, he pulled out of French D Cup tie v Sweden, talking of retiring from competitive tennis. However, he returned refreshed ten weeks later to win Basel, but a torn stomach muscle in the autumn sidelined him for rest of year. Qf Australian and French Opens and r/u French Open doubles with Forget. ***1987 HIGHLIGHTS – SINGLES: Australian Open*** qf, seed 3 (bye, d. MacPherson 4–6 6–1 6–4 6–3, Schultz 7–6 4–6 4–6 7–6 6–4, Wilkison [seed 14] 6–2 6–1 7–6, lost Cash [seed 11] 6–4 6–2 2–6 6–0), ***French Open*** qf, seed 6 (d. Kley 6–0 6–2 6–2, Bergstrom 7–5 6–7 7–5 6–1, Schapers 6–3 6–3 6–2, K. Carlsson [seed 11] 7–6 6–3 6–7 7–5, lost Wilander [seed 4] 6–4 6–3 6–2), ***Wimbledon*** 2r, seed 6 (d. Drewett 6–4 6–4 6–4, lost Forget 3–6 7–6 4–6 6–4 9–7); ***won*** Lyon (d. Panatta, Boetsch, Willenborg 6–2 6–3, K. Jones 5–7 6–4 7–6, Nystrom 6–4 7–5), ***won*** Basel (d. H. Gunthardt 7–5 4–6 6–4, Casal 4–6 6–2 7–5, Skoff 6–2 6–4, Forget 6–1 6–2, Agenor 7–6 6–4 6–4); ***r/u*** Tourn of Champs (d. Yzaga, Keretic, Forget 6–1 6–1, Krickstein 6–2 6–2, Zivojinovic 6–3 7–5, lost Gomez 6–4 7–6 7–6); ***sf*** Indian Wells (d. Pate 3–6 6–2 6–3, Benhabiles 6–3 6–4, Tulasne 6–0 3–6 6–4, lost Becker 6–4 6–2), ***sf*** LIPC (d. Panatta 6–3 6–7 6–2 6–3, J. Sanchez 6–7 4–6 6–3 6–4 7–5, Stenlund 1–6 6–0 6–4 2–6 6–3, Kriek 4–6 6–2 6–3 7–6, Wilander 6–4 6–2 4–6 2–6 7–6, lost Mecir 6–4 6–2 4–6 2–6 7–6). ***1987 HIGHLIGHTS – DOUBLES:*** (with Forget) ***r/u French Open*** (lost Jarryd/Seguso 6–7 6–7 6–3 6–4 6–2); ***won*** Lyon (d. Jones/Pate 4–6 6–3 6–4), ***won*** Indian Wells (d. Casal/E. Sanchez 6–2 6–4, Becker/Jelen 6–4 7–6), ***won*** Tourn of Champs (d. Donnelly/Fleming 4–6 6–4 6–1), ***won*** Italian Open (d. Mecir/Smid 6–2 6–7 6–3), ***won*** Queens (d. R. Leach/Pawsat 6–4 6–4). ***CAREER HIGHLIGHTS — SINGLES: French Open – won 1983*** (d. Jarryd 6–1 6–0 6–2, Pecci, DuPre, Alexander, Lendl 7–6 6–2 5–7 6–0, Roger-Vasselin, Wilander 6–2 7–5 7–6), ***qf 1981*** seed 11 (d. Vilas [seed 6], lost Pecci 3–6 6–4 6–4 6–4), ***qf 1982*** (d. Fibak 4–6 6–7 6–4 6–4 6–3, lost Vilas 7–6 6–3 6–4), ***qf 1984*** (lost Wilander 7–6 3–6 2–6 6–3 6–3), ***qf 1987***; ***Italian Open – won 1985*** (d. Becker, Mecir 6–3 3–6 6–2 7–6), ***r/u 1980*** (d. Dibbs, Barazzutti, Smid 6–1 6–1, lost Vilas 6–0 6–4 6–4); ***US Pro Indoor – sf 1981*** (d. Gerulaitis 6–3 fs, lost

Fibak 6–2 4s); ***US Open – qf 1983*** (lost Arias 7–5 fs), ***qf 1985*** (lost Lendl 6–2 6–2 6–4); ***Australian Open – qf 1987. CAREER HIGHLIGHTS – DOUBLES:*** (with Leconte unless stated) ***French Open – won 1984*** (d. Slozil/Smid 6–4 2–6 3–6 6–3 6–2); ***US Open – r/u 1985*** (lost Flach/Seguso 7–6 6–7 7–6 6–0, ***r/u 1987; Nabisco Masters*** – [Forget] ***r/u 1986*** (lost Edberg/Jarryd 6–3 7–6 6–3).

KAREL NOVACEK (Czechoslovakia)
Born Prostejov, 30 March, 1965: lives Prevov; RH; 6ft 3in; 180lb; final 1987 ATP ranking 76; 1987 prize money $115,777.
Coached by Petr Hutka. Won Nat 12s, 14s, 18s. ***1984:*** Joined Olympic team. ***1985:*** (158) Sf Madrid. ***1986:*** (33) R/u Vienna and captured his first GP title in Washington. ***1987:*** Reached qf French Open unseeded (d. Jaite), US Pro and Prague. ***1987 HIGHLIGHTS – SINGLES: French Open*** qf, unseeded (d. Nijssen 6–2 6–1 6–0, Bengoechea 6–0 6–0 6–0, Winogradsky 6–1 6–0 2–6 6–4, Jaite [seed 14] 7–6 6–4 6–7 6–3, lost Mecir [seed 5] 7–6 6–1 7–6), ***Wimbledon*** 1r (lost Becker [seed 1] 6–4 6–2 6–4), ***US Open*** 1r (lost Mecir [seed 5] 6–3 6–4 7–6); ***r/u*** Palermo (d. Lavalle 6–1 2–6 6–1, Davin 6–0 4–6 6–2, Arrese 6–3 1–6 6–3, Keretic 6–2 6–3, lost Jaite 7–6 6–7 6–4). ***CAREER HIGHLIGHTS – SINGLES: French Open – qf 1987.***

JANA NOVOTNA (Czechoslovakia)
Born Prague, 2 October, 1968, and lives there; RH; 5ft 6in; 135lb; final 1987 WITA ranking 47 singles, 24 (–) doubles; 1987 prize money $95,347.
1986: (182) Won US Open Jun doubles with Zrubakova. ***1987:*** Reached last 16 Wimbledon and US Open, qf VS Kansas. In doubles formed a formidable partnership with Suire, qualifying for VS Champs and taking a set off Navratilova/Shriver. ***1987 HIGHLIGHTS – SINGLES: French Open*** 3r (d. Durie 6–3 6–1, Zrubakova 6–3 4–6 6–4, lost Graf 6–0 6–1), ***Wimbledon*** last 16, unseeded (d. Reis 6–3 3–6 8–6, Hu Na 6–2 6–3, Walsh Pete 6–2 4–6 6–4, lost Graf [seed 2] 6–4 6–3), ***US Open*** last 16, unseeded (d. Parkhomenko 6–1 7–6, Turnbull [seed 16] 6–2 6–4, Halard 6–4 6–0, lost Shriver [seed 5] 6–3 7–6); ***sf*** Wild Dunes (d. Medrado 6–1 6–2, Benjamin 6–2 6–3, Sanchez 6–1 6–4, Gompert 6–1 7–6, lost Reggi 6–3 2–6 7–5). ***1987 HIGHLIGHTS – DOUBLES:*** (with Suire unless stated) ***won*** Strasbourg (d. Horvath/Mesker 6–0 6–2), ***won*** VS San Diego (d. Burgin/Walsh Pete 6–3 6–4), [Kohde-Kilsch] ***won*** Hamburg (d. Bykova/Meskhi 7–6 7–6); ***r/u*** Zurich (d. Mandlikova/Pfaff, lost Herreman/Paradis 6–3 2–6 6–3).

JOAKIM NYSTROM (Sweden)
Born Skelleftea, 20 February, 1963; lives there and Monte Carlo; RH; 2HB; 6ft 2in; 155lb; final 1987 ATP ranking 16 singles, 24 (5) doubles; 1987 prize money $268,215; career prize money $1,949,162.
Wife Suzanne, daughters Caroline and Jacqueline. ***1980:*** Won Orange Bowl 18 singles, playing with the same effortless, smooth style he exhibits today. ***1981:*** (73). ***1982:*** (167) Last 16 French Open. ***1983:*** (27) Won Sydney NSW Open, r/u Munich and played No.2 singles for Sweden in D Cup f. ***1984:*** (11) Won Gstaad, North Conway, Basle and Cologne. ***1985:*** (11) Won Munich and Gstaad and reached qf French and US Opens and sf US Open doubles with Wilander. ***1986:*** (7) Won 5 of first 8 tourns, but could not keep up the pace. Won Wimbledon doubles with Wilander, and reached qf US Open singles. ***1987:*** Defeated Lendl 1st time at Italian Open, but suffered a poor year by his standards, dropping to No. 29 in May, until he beat Wilander and Edberg to win his first title of the year at Bastad. Out of action Oct. with a recurring knee injury. ***1987 HIGHLIGHTS – SINGLES: French Open*** last 16, unseeded (d. Kriek [seed 16] 6–7 6–2 6–2 6–1, Vajda 6–3 6–3 6–1, Cahill 6–4 7–6 6–4, lost Lendl [seed 1] 2–6 6–1 5–7 6–0 6–2), ***Wimbledon*** 3r, seed 13 (d. Sundstrom 6–2 6–7 6–4 6–3, Smid 6–3 6–1 6–4, lost Hlasek 5–7 6–3 6–0 7–6), ***US Open*** 2r, seed 10 (d. J. Sanchez 7–6 7–6 3–6 6–3, lost Krishnan 6–4 7–5 6–2); ***won*** Bastad (d. Cancellotti 6–3 6–2, Navratil 6–0 6–1, K. Carlsson 6–2 5–7 7–5, Wilander 6–3 6–2, Edberg 4–6 6–0 6–3); ***r/u*** Lyon (d. Champion, Agenor, Potier, Nelson 7–6 4–6 7–6, lost Noah 6–4 7–5); ***sf*** Munich (d. Schwaier, Mattar 6–4 4–6 6–3, Limberger 7–6 6–3, lost Vajda 6–4 6–4), ***sf*** Italian Open (d. Schwaier 6–3 6–0, Skoff 6–3 6–4, Lendl 6–4 2–6 6–3, K. Carlsson 5–7 7–5 6–1, lost Jaite 6–3 6–4), ***sf*** US CC (d. Mmoh 6–0 6–2, Vilas 6–1 4–6 6–4, Jaite 7–6 6–0, lost Wilander 6–4 7–5). ***1987 HIGHLIGHTS – DOUBLES:*** (with Wilander) ***r/u*** Boston (lost

Gildemeister/Gomez 7–6 3–6 6–1), ***r/u*** US CC (lost Warder/Willenborg 6–0 6–3). ***CAREER HIGHLIGHTS – DOUBLES:*** (with Wilander) ***Wimbledon – won 1986*** (d. Donnelly/Fleming 7–6 6–3 6–3); ***Australian Open – r/u 1984*** (d. Cash/Fitzgerald 6–4 6–4 2–6 6–3, lost Edmondson/Stewart 6–2 7–5); ***French Open – sf 1985*** (d. Giammalva/Willenborg, lost Edmondson/Warwick 6–4 6–1 7–5); ***US Open – sf 1985*** (d. Denton/Fleming, lost Leconte/Noah 6–3 7–6 6–4).

NDUKA ODIZOR (Nigeria)
Born Lagos, 8 August, 1958; lives Houston, Texas; RH; 6ft; 165lb; final 1987 ATP ranking 98; 1987 prize money $73,896.
Wife Karen, son Nicholas. ***1982:*** (80). ***1983:*** (65) Won Taipei and reached last 16 Wimbledon, eliminating 4th seed Vilas from mp down in 1r. ***1984:*** (110). ***1985:*** (106) Qf Bristol. ***1986:*** (75). ***1987:*** Sf Adelaide, qf Sydney and Cincinnati. ***1987 HIGHLIGHTS – SINGLES: Australian Open*** 1r (lost Rostagno 7–5 6–2 6–3), ***Wimbledon 1r*** (lost Giammalva 6–3 6–7 6–3 6–3), ***US Open*** 3r (d. Nelson 2–6 2–6 7–6 7–5 6–3, Chang 6–1 6–2 6–7 3–6 6–4, lost Leconte [seed 11] 6–7 6–2 6–1 6–2); ***sf*** Adelaide (d. Carter, Lane, Krishnan 6–3 6–2, lost Scanlon 6–7 6–4 6–4).

BRUNO ORESAR (Yugoslavia)
Born Zagreb, 21 April, 1967 and lives there; RH; 5ft 10in; 147lb; final 1987 ATP ranking 111; 1987 prize money $40,711.
Won Nat 12s, 14s, 16s and 18s in singles, doubles and mixed. ***1983:*** Won Orange Bowl 16s having also won 12s and 14s. ***1984:*** (464) Won Madrid on Spanish Satellite circuit. ***1985:*** (82) Sf US Pro (d. Arias). ***1986:*** (159) Reached qf Athens but was restricted by back injury. ***1987:*** Sf Guaruja. ***1987 HIGHLIGHTS – SINGLES: French Open*** 1r (lost Gilbert [seed 15] 1–6 7–5 2–6 6–4 6–4), ***US Open*** 1r (lost Jelen 6–3 6–2 6–4); ***won*** Clermont Ferrand Challenger (d. Pimek 6–2 6–4); ***sf*** Guaruja (d. Arraya 6–3 2–6 6–3, Levine, Goes, lost Mattar 4–6 7–6 6–4).

RICKI OSTERTHUN (West Germany)
Born Hamburg, 2 May, 1964 and lives there; RH; 6ft 1½in; 170lb; final 1987 ATP ranking 75; 1987 prize money $107,555.
Coached by Claud Hofsass. ***1984:*** (192). ***1985:*** (119) Won Hilversum and briefly broke into top 100 in summer. ***1986:*** (110) R/u Munich, qf Vienna. ***1987:*** Removed Leconte 1r *en route* to last 16 French Open and was r/u Toulouse. ***1987 HIGHLIGHTS – SINGLES: French Open*** last 16, unseeded (d. Leconte 6–3 6–3 6–7 6–1, Anger 6–2 7–6 6–2, Keretic 6–4 5–7 6–2 6–4, lost Connors [seed 8] 6–4 7–5 6–0 6–3), ***Wimbledon*** 1r (lost Jarryd 6–3 7–6 6–4), ***US Open*** 1r (lost Muller 7–5 6–3 6–2); ***r/u*** Toulouse (d. Ostoja 1–6 7–5 7–6, Limberger 6–4 6–2, Mattar 3–6 6–4 6–3, Wilkison 5–7 6–4 6–2, lost Mayotte 6–2 5–7 6–4). ***1987 HIGHLIGHTS – DOUBLES:*** [Meinecke] ***won*** Athens (d. Navratil/Nijssen 6–2 3–6 6–2).

PASCALE PARADIS (France)
Born Troyes, 24 April, 1966; lives Paris; RH; 5ft 9in; 135lb; final 1987 WITA ranking 103; 1987 prize money $28,257.
1981: Won French Open Jun. ***1983:*** (87) Won French and Wimbledon Jun and reached last 16 US Open in main draw. ***1984:*** (28) R/u Indianapolis and Pittsburgh; sf Brisbane and Brighton. ***1985:*** (46) Beat Hanika and Turnbull to reach last 16 Wimbledon. Played Fed Cup. ***1986:*** (129). ***1987: HIGHLIGHTS – SINGLES: Wimbledon*** 1r (lost A. White 6–3 7–5), ***US Open*** 1r (lost Zvereva 6–3 6–3). ***1987 HIGHLIGHTS – DOUBLES:*** (with Herreman) ***won*** Zurich (d. Novotna/Suire 6–3 2–6 6–3).

SVETLANA CHERNEVA PARKHOMENKO (USSR)
Born Moscow, 8 October, 1962, and lives there; RH; 5ft 4in; 124lb; final 1987 WITA ranking 112 singles; 9 (28) doubles; 1987 prize money $54,642.
Coached by Olga Morozova. ***1981:*** Upset Mandlikova in Fed Cup début in Tokyo. ***1983:*** Reached her first of three straight qfs Wimbledon doubles with Savchenko. ***1984:*** (122). ***1985:*** (74) Qf Sydney (d. Garrison). ***1986:*** (90) Beat M. J. Fernandez, Benjamin and Paz twice; married Alexander Parkhomenko, a wrestling coach. ***1987:*** In doubles with Sav-

chenko d. Navratilova/Shriver to reach Wimbledon sf, and won 4 titles. ***1987 HIGHLIGHTS – SINGLES: Wimbledon*** 2r (d. Wood 7–5 6–3, lost G. Fernandez 6–2 3–6 6–4), ***US Open*** 1r (lost Novotna 6–1 7–6). ***1987 HIGHLIGHTS – DOUBLES:*** (with Savchenko) ***Wimbledon*** sf (d. Navratilova/Shriver 6–2 6–4, lost Kohde-Kilsch/Sukova 1–6 6–4 7–5); ***won*** VS Florida (d. Mandlikova/Turnbull, Evert Lloyd/Shriver 6–0 3–6 6–2), ***won*** VS Kansas (d. Potter/White 6–2 6–4), ***won*** VS Oklahoma (d. McNeil/Sands 6–3 4–6 6–1), ***won*** Eastbourne (d. Fairbank/Smylie 7–6 4–6 7–5).

DAVID PATE (USA)
Born Los Angeles, 16 April, 1962; lives Las Vegas; RH; 6ft; 170lb; final 1987 ATP ranking 18 singles, 15 doubles; 1987 prize money $251,121.
Coached by Pancho Gonzales. Wife Debra. ***1981:*** (662) A two-time All-American at Texas Christian University, he won NCAA doubles title with Richter. ***1983:*** (103) Helped considerably by Pancho Gonzales. ***1984:*** (31) Won first GP event – Japan Open in Tokyo. ***1985:*** (26) R/u La Quinta to Stefanki and sf Newport and Wembley where he d. Edberg and Nystrom. ***1986:*** (30) Sf Atlanta and Scottsdale and 7 qfs. ***1987:*** Had his biggest wins of the year at Tokyo, where he beat Lendl on his way to f, and at LA where he beat Edberg *en route* to his first title since Tokyo 1984. ***1987 HIGHLIGHTS – SINGLES:*** Wimbledon 2r, seed 15 (d. Casal 6–4 7–6 7–5, lost Zivojinovic 3–6 7–6 6–4 6–1), ***US Open*** 1r (lost Castle 7–5 1–6 2–6 7–6 6–4); ***won*** Los Angeles (d. Chang 6–3 7–6, Lundgren 6–4 6–4, Agassi 5–7 7–6 6–2, Gilbert 6–3 6–7 6–3, Edberg 6–4 6–4); ***r/u*** Chicago (d. Pearce 6–2 6–4, Annacone 7–6 6–2, Purcell 7–5 6–4, Scanlon 6–3 6–2, lost Mayotte 6–4 6–2), ***r/u*** Tokyo (d. Van't Hof 6–3 6–4, Levine 7–6 4–6 6–3, Lendl 7–6 4–6 7–6, Kriek 7–5 6–2, S. Davis 7–5 6–1, lost Edberg 7–6 6–4); ***sf*** Scottsdale (d. Purcell 6–3 6–1, Witsken 7–5 6–1, Curren 6–2 7–6, lost Teltscher 7–6 7–5). ***1987 HIGHLIGHTS – DOUBLES:*** (with Curren unless stated) ***won*** Los Angeles (d. Gilbert/Wilkison 6–3 6–4), ***won*** Johannesburg (d. Korita/Pearce 6–4 6–4); [Jones] ***r/u*** Lyon (lost Forget/Noah 4–6 6–3 6–4), [S. Davis] ***r/u*** Frankfurt (lost Becker/Kuhnen 6–4 6–3).

BARBARA PAULUS (Austria)
Born Vienna, 1 September, 1970; lives Hinterbruehl; RH; 5ft 8in; 117lb; final 1987 WITA ranking 80; 1987 prize money $17,933.
Coached by Nicki Spear. ***1982:*** Won Nat 12s 2nd time. ***1985:*** Won Nat 18s. ***1986:*** (187) Won Nat Indoor and Outdoor; qf Bregenz and played Fed Cup. ***1987 HIGHLIGHTS – SINGLES: French Open*** 3r (d. Mascarin 6–2 6–4, Provis 6–4 6–4, lost Sanchez 6–4 6–2), ***Wimbledon*** 1r (lost Tauziat 2–6 6–1 6–1).

MERCEDES PAZ (Argentina)
Born Tucuman, 27 June, 1966; lives Key Biscayne, Fla.; RH; 5ft 11½in; 145lb; final 1987 WITA ranking 88; 1987 prize money $54,355.
Coached by Patricio Apey. ***1984:*** Won Rolex Jun Port Washington and US Open Jun doubles and Orange Bowl 18 doubles with Sabatini. ***1985:*** (115) Won Sao Paulo and was ranked 2 in Argentina. ***1986:*** (59) Last 16 French Open, r/u Singapore, sf USCC. ***1987:*** Qf Belgian Open. ***1987 HIGHLIGHTS – SINGLES: French Open*** 1r (lost Lindqvist [seed 11] 6–0 7–6), ***Wimbledon*** 1r (lost Gildemeister 7–5 4–6 6–3), ***US Open*** 2r (d. G. Fernandez 6–4 6–2, lost Hakami 6–2 6–4). ***1987 HIGHLIGHTS – DOUBLES:*** [McNeil] ***won*** Argentine Open (d. Jagerman/Bollegraf 6–1 2–6 6–1), [Pfaff] ***won*** FC Cup (d. Garrison/McNeil 7–6 7–5).

GUILLERMO PEREZ ROLDAN (Argentina)
Born Tandil, Buenos Aires, 20 October, 1969 and lives there; RH; 5ft 9in; 165lb; final 1987 ATP ranking 19; 1987 prize money $193,226.
Coached by his father, Raul. Won Nat. and S. American 14s, 16s, 18s. Brother of Mariana. ***1985:*** (485). ***1986:*** (109) Sf St Vincent and Buenos Aires and won French Open Jun singles and doubles. ***1987:*** When he won Munich aged 17 years, 6 months, 10 days he became the second-youngest (after Krickstein) to win a GP title, following with Athens 7 weeks later and Buenos Aires in Nov to take him into top 20. Won French Open Jun singles again over Stoltenberg. ***1987 HIGHLIGHTS – SINGLES: French Open*** 1r (lost Muster 6–1 6–3 6–2); ***won*** Munich (d. Van Boeckel, Muster 6–2 6–3, Casal 6–7 7–5 6–1, Purcell 1–6 7–6

6–1, Vajda 6–3 7–6), ***won*** Athens (d. Kalovelonis 6–2 6–2, Hennemann 6–4 6–2, Vajda 6–4 6–4, Vojtisek 6–7 6–4 6–2, Meinecke 6–2 6–3), ***won*** Buenos Aires (d. DiLaura 6–3 6–0, Mancini 6–3 6–0, Motta 4–6 6–1 6–4, Aguilera 6–3 6–1, Berger 3–2 ret'd); ***r/u*** Hilversum (d. Limberger 6–1 6–1, Maurer 6–7 7–6 7–6, Muster 7–6 1–6 6–1, Jaite 3–6 7–5 7–6, lost Mecir 6–4 1–6 6–3 6–2); ***sf*** Florence (d. Winogradsky, Bloom, Panatta 6–3 6–1, lost Chesnokov 3–6 7–5 7–6), ***sf*** US CC (d. Moraing 6–4 6–4, Youl 4–6 6–1 6–3, Pimek 6–3 6–0, Muller 1–6 6–3 6–4, lost K. Carlsson 6–2 6–2), ***sf*** Barcelona (d. Srejber 6–4 1–6 8–6, Vilas 6–4 7–6, Gomez 6–3 1–0 ret'd, lost Wilander 6–3 6–0).

MARIANA PEREZ ROLDAN (Argentina)
Born Buenos Aires, 7 October, 1967; lives Tandil; RH; 5ft 4in; 117lb; final 1987 WITA ranking 70; 1987 prize money $26,113.
Coached by her father, Raul. Sister of Guillermo. ***1985:*** Was among the 10 best jun, winning French Open Jun doubles with Tarabini and was joint No. 1 in ITF Jun doubles rankings. ***1986:*** (87) Playing predominantly on satellite circuit, she won Lyon. ***1987:*** Qf Geneva. Underwent surgery for torn cartilege in autumn. ***1987 HIGHLIGHTS – SINGLES: French Open*** 2r (d. Drescher 0–6 6–0 6–1, lost Hanika [seed 15] 6–2 6–4), ***US Open*** 1r (lost Demongeot 6–2 6–2); ***sf*** Argentine Open (d. Bollegraf 6–1 6–1, Ter Riet 6–1 6–4, Jagerman 6–2 6–2, lost Sanchez 7–6 7–5), ***sf*** California Women's Open (d. Bartos Cserepy 6–6 ret'd, Kuczynska 6–4 7–6, Mascarin 6–4 6–3, lost Gurney 6–3 6–1).

MIKAEL PERNFORS (Sweden)
Born Malmo, 16 July, 1963; lives Hollviksnas and Athens, Ga; RH; 5ft 8in; 150lb; final 1987 ATP ranking 33; 1987 prize money $117,133.
Coached by Olga Malmqvist. ***1983:*** Won US Nat Jun College singles and doubles titles playing for Seminole Jun College in Florida. ***1984:*** (434) Won NCAA singles title as transfer student for Univ. of Georgia and led his school to sf in team champ. ***1985:*** (164) Won NCAA Champ, the first since Dennis Ralston (1963–64) to do so twice. ***1986:*** (12) In first full year on tour, he twice beat Edberg, once ousted Becker, and reached his first GS f at French Open, where he lost to Lendl. ***1987:*** Ankle injury kept him out of Monte Carlo. Reached last 16 at Wimbledon, where he was 6–1 6–1 4–1 up to Connors before losing the match; sf Memphis and Tokyo Seiko. ***1987 HIGHLIGHTS – SINGLES: French Open*** 1r, seed 12 (lost Benhabiles 4–6 6–3 6–4 6–0), ***Wimbledon*** last 16, unseeded (d. Seguso 3–6 6–3 6–2 6–7, Steyn 6–3 6–3 6–2, Mayotte [seed 10] 2–6 4–6 6–4 6–3 7–5, lost Connors [seed 7] 1–6 1–6 7–5 6–4 6–2), ***US Open*** 1r (lost Bergstrom 6–3 3–0 ret'd); ***sf*** Memphis (d. Hogstedt, Mansdorf 7–6 7–6, Holmes 6–4 3–6 6–3, lost Connors 6–7 7–6 6–3), ***sf*** Tokyo Seiko (d. Nijssen 6–3 4–6 6–2, Giammalva 6–3 6–2, Fitzgerald 6–2 6–1, lost Lendl 6–0 6–2). ***1987 HIGHLIGHTS – DOUBLES:*** (with Tideman) ***r/u*** Stuttgart (lost R. Leach/Pawsat 6–3 6–4). ***CAREER HIGHLIGHTS – SINGLES: French Open – r/u 1986*** (d. Delaitre, Edberg [seed 5] 6–7 7–5 6–3 2–6 6–4, Seguso, Jaite [seed 11], Becker [seed 3] 2–6 6–4 6–3 6–0, Leconte [seed 8] 2–6 7–5 7–6 6–3, lost Lendl [seed 1] 6–3 6–2 6–4).

SHARON WALSH PETE (USA)
Born San Francisco, 24 February, 1952; lives Albequerque; RH; 5ft 8in; 140lb; final 1987 WITA ranking 83; 1987 prize money $52,659.
Primarily a doubles specialist. ***1970:*** Won Wimbledon Jun; won US Nat 18s 2nd time. ***1974:*** Joined Fed Cup squad. ***1975:*** (65) Sf South African Open. ***1976:*** Sf Beckenham. ***1977:*** (41) R/u Avon Boise, sf South African Open, qf Seattle and Detroit; r/u Italian Open doubles with Bruning. ***1978:*** (44) Won Tuscon Futures, qf Detroit. ***1979:*** (61) R/u Australian Open, won Pasadena Futures. ***1980:*** (39). ***1981:*** (26) Won Manchester, last 16 US Open. ***1982:*** (64) Last 16 Australian Open; r/u US Open doubles with Potter and French Open with Piatek, sf Australian Open doubles with Potter. Played W Cup. ***1983:*** (45) Sf Detroit, qf Birmingham in singles; in doubles won 6 titles and reached sf Wimbledon and Australian Open (with Potter) and US Open (with King). ***1984:*** (38) Qf Australian Open (d. Garrison 1r); in doubles won 3 titles, reached 6 more f and sf Wimbledon and Australian Open. ***1985:*** (130) Qf Denver and Melbourne; sf Australian Open doubles. Married Michael Pete in spring. ***1986:*** (195). ***1987:*** At age 35 returned to top 100 and reached sf Arizona. ***1987 HIGHLIGHTS – SINGLES: Australian Open*** 1r (lost Polzl 6–2 6–4), ***French Open*** 1r (lost Kanellopoulou 6–2 6–3), ***Wimbledon*** 3r (d. Herreman 6–3 3–6 6–4, Turnbull [seed 12] 6–4

6–4, lost Novotna 6–2 4–6 6–4), ***US Open*** 1r (lost Meier 7–5 6–3); ***sf*** VS Arizona (d. Richardson 6–3 6–3, Nelson Dunbar 6–4 6–3, C. Karlsson 7–5 6–4, Henricksson 7–6 6–3, lost Balestrat 7–5 7–5). ***1987 HIGHLIGHTS – DOUBLES:*** (with Collins) ***r/u*** Taipei (lost Cammie/Cynthia MacGregor 7–6 5–7 6–4), ***r/u*** Tokyo (lost K. Jordan/Nagelsen 6–3 7–5). ***CAREER HIGHLIGHTS – SINGLES: Australian Open – r/u 1979*** (d. Mesker, Gurdal, Sawyer, lost B. Jordan 6–3 6–3). ***CAREER HIGHLIGHTS – DOUBLES:*** (with Potter) ***US Open – r/u 1982*** (d. Navratilova/Shriver 7–5 2–6 6–4, lost Casals/Turnbull 6–3 6–4).

EVA PFAFF (West Germany)
Born Konigstein, 10 February, 1961, and lives there; RH; 5ft 9in; 144lb; final 1987 WITA ranking 43 singles, 25 doubles; 1987 prize money $77,208.
Coached by Dieter Ecklebe, she is an immensely talented player troubled frequently by knee injuries. ***1982:*** (35) Joined Fed Cup team; won Nashville. ***1983:*** (22) Reached last 16 Wimbledon and had 2 mps v Navratilova at Canadian Open. ***1984:*** (31). ***1985:*** (31) Upset Sukova at VS LA. ***1986:*** (60) Sf Zurich and beat Bassett at Canadian Open. ***1987 HIGHLIGHTS – SINGLES: Australian Open*** 3r (bye, d. Rimes 7–5 6–3, lost Garrison [seed 7] 6–2 3–6 7–5), ***French Open*** 1r (lost Evert [seed 3] 6–1 6–3), ***Wimbledon*** 1r (lost Novotna 6–3 3–6 8–6), ***US Open*** 1r (lost Smylie 6–4 7–5); ***sf*** Edgbaston (d. Benjamin 7–6 6–4, Demongeot 6–4 6–2, A. White 5–7 6–4 8–6, Smylie 6–1 6–3, lost Savchenko 6–3 6–0). ***1987 HIGHLIGHTS – DOUBLES:*** [Paz] ***won*** FC Cup (d. Garrison/McNeil 7–6 7–5); [Bunge] ***r/u*** VS New England (lost Burgin/Fairbank 6–4 6–4). ***CAREER HIGHLIGHTS – SINGLES: Australian Open – qf 1982*** (d. Mandlikova, Durie, lost Jaeger 7–5 6–2).

TERRY PHELPS (USA)
Born Larchmont, NY, 18 December, 1966 and lives there; RH; 2HB; 5ft 10in; 135lb; final 1987 WITA ranking 48; 1987 prize money $67,121.
Coached by Nick Bollettieri. ***1982:*** (107) Ranked 4 in US 16s. ***1983:*** (54) Won US 16 Nat; ranked 4 in 18s; turned pro. ***1984:*** (26) Played 27 tournaments and reached sf Filderstadt. ***1985:*** (29) Reached qf French Open, beat Rehe and Potter at US Open and took a set off Navratilova in Fort Lauderdale. ***1986:*** (22) Qualified for VS Champ in both March and Nov., demonstrating her consistency and high standards. ***1987:*** R/u Auckland and qf San Diego. ***1987 HIGHLIGHTS – SINGLES: Australian Open*** 2r, seed 13 (bye, lost Kijimuta 6–3 6–4 6–0), ***French Open*** 3r (d. Rajchrtova 6–3 0–6 6–4, Polzl Wiesner 6–3 6–3, lost Schimper 6–7 6–2 6–2), ***Wimbledon*** 1r (lost Marsikova 6–4 6–3), ***US Open*** 2r (d. Stafford 6–3 6–3, lost Garrison [seed 7] 7–6 6–1); ***r/u*** Auckland (d. Salmon 6–0 6–2, Faulkner 6–0 6–3, A. M. Fernandez 6–4 6–3, E. Minter 6–1 7–5, lost Rush Magers 6–2 6–3); ***sf*** California Women's Open (d. Nelson Dunbar 6–2 6–1, Schimper 6–4 6–0, Cammie MacGregor 6–3 6–1, lost Hakami 6–3 6–4). ***CAREER HIGHLIGHTS – SINGLES: French Open – qf 1985*** (d. Bassett [seed 8] 4–6 6–0 6–3, lost Evert Lloyd 6–4 6–0).

LIBOR PIMEK (Czechoslovakia)
Born Most, 3 August, 1963; lives Ostrava; RH; 6ft 5in; 172lb; final 1987 ATP ranking 95; 1987 prize money $59,225.
1983: (57) Tall and wiry, he reached sf Lisbon, qf Barcelona and South Orange and won doubles at Nice with Boileau. ***1984:*** (25) Won first GP title in Munich and reached sf Indianapolis, Columbus and Geneva. ***1985:*** (34) R/u Vienna and reached sf La Quinta and Basle. ***1986:*** (71) Despite qf appearances in Cologne, Bordeaux and Italian Open, and sf St Vincent, he was less productive. ***1987:*** Qf Frankfurt. ***1987 HIGHLIGHTS – SINGLES: French Open*** 1r (lost Westphal 7–5 5–7 6–2 6–3), ***US Open*** 3r (d. Teltscher 7–5 6–3 1–6 7–6, Winogradsky 6–4 6–0 6–4, lost Wilander [seed 3] 6–2 6–0 6–1).

CLAUDIO PISTOLESI (Italy)
Born Rome, 25 August, 1967 and lives there; RH; 5ft 9in; 168lb; final 1987 ATP ranking 97; 1987 prize money $63,384.
1985: (211) ITF Jun Champ and won Orange Bowl 18s. ***1986:*** (179). ***1987:*** Won 1st GP title at Bari (d. Krickstein). ***1987 HIGHLIGHTS – SINGLES: Australian Open*** 2r (d. Robertson 5–7 2–6 6–3 7–6 9–7, lost Cash [seed 11] 7–5 2–6 7–6 6–2), ***French Open*** 1r (lost Berger 6–1 6–3 6–3), ***US Open*** 1r (lost Mansdorf 6–4 6–2 6–3); ***won*** Bari (d. Krickstein 7–5 5–7 6–0, Panatta 6–3 6–4, Davin 7–6 6–3, Stenlund 6–1 0–6 6–1, Cancellotti 6–7 7–5

Doubles experts; Svetlana Parkhomenko and Larisa Savchenko (above l–r) won four titles together and ousted Navratilova and Shriver at Wimbledon, while Gary Donnelly (below left) and Paul Annacone (below right) each won three titles with different partners, finishing the year ranked 20 and 9 respectively. *(Carol L. Newsom, T. Hindley, M. Cole)*

6–3); ***sf*** St Vincent (d. Bahrami 3–6 6–3 6–2, Luna 6–2 6–4, Miniussi 6–2 5–7 6–3, lost Rebolledo 6–1 6–4).

CLAUDIA PORWIK (West Germany)
Born Coburg, 14 November, 1968; lives Furth; RH; 5ft 10in; 135lb; final 1987 WITA ranking 44; 1987 prize money $31,855.
1985: (244) Won Mexico. ***1986:*** (95) Won 20 of 28 matches. Underwent operation to remove cysts from right wrist end of year. ***1987:*** Reached first f at Taipei. ***1987 HIGHLIGHTS – SINGLES: Australian Open*** 1r (lost Moulton 4–6 6–4 6–3), ***French Open*** 2r (d. Bonsignori 7–6 6–4, lost C. Karlsson 6–4 3–6 9–7), ***Wimbledon*** 1r (lost Navratilova [seed 1] 6–1 6–0), ***US Open*** 1r (lost Provis 4–6 7–5 6–1); ***r/u*** Taipei (d. Gerken, Derly 3–6 6–1 7–6, Golarsa 7–6 6–2, Ludloff 4–6 6–1 6–1, lost A. Minter 6–4 6–1).

BARBARA POTTER (USA)
Born Waterbury, Conn., 22 October, 1961; lives Woodbury Conn.; LH; 5ft 9in; 135lb; final 1987 WITA ranking 12 singles, 26 (25) doubles; 1987 prize money $114,533; career prize money $1,169,248.
Coached by Tim Gullikson and Roy Emerson. ***1978:*** (62). ***1979:*** (47) Played W Cup. ***1980:*** (25). ***1981:*** (10) Sf US Open, Chicago, Brighton and Detroit and last 16 Wimbledon. ***1982:*** (8) Qf Wimbledon, won US Indoors (d. Austin in sf) and Cincinnati. In doubles with Walsh won Kansas City, Oakland, Tampa, r/u US Open, WTA Champs and sf Australian Open. In mixed doubles with Taygan r/u US Open. ***1983:*** (25) Wimbledon qf singles and sf doubles (with Walsh), r/u US Open mixed doubles with Taygan. ***1984:*** (12) Qf Australian Open singles, sf doubles there and Wimbledon. ***1985:*** (17) Won VS New York singles and VS Dallas doubles, qf Wimbledon both singles and doubles, qf US Open doubles, sf Australian Open doubles. ***1986:*** (24) Forced out for 5 months with herniated disks. ***1987:*** After resting her back injury again, she returned to win VS Kansas in Feb – her first title since Aug. 1985. ***1987 HIGHLIGHTS – SINGLES: Wimbledon*** 2r, seed 13 (d. Suire 6–4 4–6 6–1, lost M. J. Fernandez 6–0 6–1), ***US Open*** 1r, seed 15 (lost Kijimuta 7–5 6–3); ***won*** VS Kansas (d. Sanchez 6–1 6–2, Reynolds 6–4 7–5, Novotna 7–6 6–3, Derly 5–7 6–2 6–3, Savchenko 7–6 7–6), ***won*** Beckenham (d. R. White 6–1 4–6 7–6, Moulton 7–6 7–5); ***r/u*** VS Washington (d. Van Rensburg 6–4 6–2, Lindqvist 6–4 7–5, Hanika 4–6 7–6 7–6, Garrison 3–6 6–3 7–6, lost Mandlikova 6–4 6–2); ***sf*** VS Chicago (d. Lindqvist 6–3 6–2, Adams 6–2 6–4, Garrison 6–3 6–4, lost Zvereva 6–4 2–6 6–4). ***1987 HIGHLIGHTS – DOUBLES:*** (with W. White) ***r/u*** VS Kansas (lost Parkhomenko/Savchenko 6–2 6–4). ***CAREER HIGHLIGHTS – SINGLES: US Open – sf 1981*** (d. Leand, Gerken, lost Austin 6–1 6–3); ***Wimbledon – qf 1982*** (d. Shriver 6–2 6–4, lost Evert Lloyd 6–2 6–1), ***qf 1983*** (d. Benjamin 6–1 fs, Bonder 7–5 6–4, lost Jaeger 6–4 6–1), ***qf 1985*** (unseeded, d. Lindqvist [seed 12], Gomer, Fendick, Durie, lost Evert Lloyd [seed 1] 6–2 6–1); ***Australian Open – qf 1984*** (d. Temesvari, lost Navratilova 6–3 6–2). ***CAREER HIGHLIGHTS – DOUBLES:*** (with Walsh) ***US Open – r/u 1982*** (d. Navratilova/Shriver 7–5 2–6 6–4, lost Casals/Turnbull 6–3 6–4), ***qf 1985*** (d. Mesker/Paradis, lost Kohde-Kilsch/Sukova 6–7 6–4 6–2); ***Wimbledon – sf 1983*** (lost Casals/Turnbull 6–1 6–7 6–4), ***sf 1984*** (lost K. Jordan/A. Smith 3–6 6–3 6–2), ***qf 1985*** (d. Mould/P. Smith, lost Kohde-Kilsch/Sukova 7–6 4–6 6–3); ***Australian Open – sf 1982*** (lost Kohde-Kilsch/Pfaff 5–7 7–5 7–6), ***sf 1984*** (lost Kohde-Kilsch/Sukova), ***sf 1985*** (lost Kohde-Kilsch/Sukova 3–6 6–4 6–1). ***MIXED DOUBLES:*** (with Taygan) ***US Open – r/u 1982*** (lost Curren/A. Smith), ***r/u 1983*** (lost Fitzgerald/Sayers 3–6 6–3 6–4).

WILTRUD PROBST (West Germany)
Born Nuremburg, 29 May, 1969, and lives there; RH; 5ft 7in; 135lb; final 1987 WITA ranking 98; 1987 prize money $26,411.
1987: Qf Wild Dunes and Hamburg. ***1987 HIGHLIGHTS – SINGLES: Australian Open*** 2r (d. Bowrey 6–1 6–4, lost Holikova 5–7 6–4 8–6), ***French Open*** 1r (lost A. Minter 6–3 6–0), ***Wimbledon*** 1r (lost Hobbs 6–2 4–6 6–0), ***US Open*** 1r (lost Gomer 6–3 6–0).

NICOLE PROVIS (Australia)
Born Melbourne, 22 September, 1969; lives Cheltenham, Vic.; RH; 5ft 9in; 141lb; final 1987 WITA ranking 77; 1987 prize money $51,695.
Coached by Ken Richardson. ***1986:*** (105) R/u French Open Jun. ***1987:*** R/u Australian Open

Jun to Jaggard; won doubles with Devries. On senior tour qf Auckland and r/u Wimbledon mixed doubles with Cahill. ***1987 HIGHLIGHTS – SINGLES: Australian Open*** 2r (bye, lost Kohde-Kilsch [seed 5] 6–2 6–2), ***French Open*** 2r (d. Gurney 6–4 6–2, lost Paulus 6–4 6–4), ***Wimbledon*** 1r (lost Polzl Wiesner 5–7 6–1 6–3), ***US Open*** 3r (d. Porwik 4–6 7–5 6–1, Keil 6–4 6–2, lost McNeil [seed 11] 5–7 6–1 7–6); ***won*** Australian HC (d. Peters, Peetz, Jaggard 4–6 6–4 6–1, Bowrey 6–3 6–3). ***1987 HIGHLIGHTS – MIXED DOUBLES:*** (with Cahill) ***r/u Wimbledon*** (lost Bates/Durie 7–6 6–3).

JIM PUGH (USA)
Born Burbank, Cal., 5 February, 1964; lives Palos Verdes, Cal.; RH; 2HF and 2HB; 6ft 4in; 170lb; final 1987 ATP ranking 45; 1987 prize money $167,568.
1982: Suffered severe shoulder injury, amazingly cured by taking thyroid tablets. ***1983:*** All-American at UCLA. ***1985:*** (344). ***1986:*** (99) Won Istanbul Challenger. ***1987:*** Stunned Cash 1r French Open and reached first GP f at Schenectady, following with San Francisco (d. Mayotte). ***1987 HIGHLIGHTS – SINGLES: French Open*** 3r (d. Cash [seed 12] 3–6 6–3 6–2 7–6, Limberger 6–1 6–2 6–2, lost Kuchna 6–4 6–2 3–6 6–2), ***Wimbledon*** 1r (lost Wilkison 7–5 6–7 6–4 6–4), ***US Open*** 3r (d. Yunis 6–3 6–2 6–2, Muller 7–5 6–3 6–4, lost Lendl [seed 1] 6–1 6–1 6–2); ***r/u*** Schenectady (d. Donnelly 7–6 7–6, Laurendeau 6–3 6–3, Testerman 6–2 6–3, Hogstedt 6–3 6–4, lost Yzaga 0–6 7–6 6–1), ***r/u*** San Francisco (d. Mayotte 7–5 6–7 7–5, Hunt 6–2 6–2, Giammalva 6–3 7–5, Nelson 6–3 6–7 6–4, lost Lundgren 6–1 7–5); ***sf*** Frankfurt (d. Jones 6–3 4–6 7–6, Stenlund 6–7 6–3 7–6, Gilbert 7–5 0–6 6–2, lost Gomez 6–3 6–3). ***1987 HIGHLIGHTS – DOUBLES:*** [Willenborg] ***won*** Munich (d. Casal/E. Sanchez 7–6 4–6 6–4), [Leach] ***won*** Scottsdale (d. Goldie/Purcell 6–3 6–2), [Kratzmann] ***won*** Hong Kong (d. M. Davis/Drewett 6–7 6–4 6–2); [Mezzadri] ***r/u*** Hamburg (lost Mecir/Smid 4–6 7–6 6–2), [Pearce] ***r/u*** Schenectady (lost Donnelly/Muller 7–6 6–2), [Grabb] ***r/u*** Stockholm (lost Edberg/Jarryd 6–3 6–4).

REGINA RAJCHRTOVA (Czechoslovakia)
Born Havlickuv Brod, 5 February, 1968; lives Prague; RH; 5ft 11in; 148lb; final 1987 WITA ranking 87; 1987 prize money $24,267.
1985: (282). ***1986:*** (226) Won Mali Losinj Satellite. ***1987:*** Reached 4 f on Satellite circuit, winning Mald. ***1987 HIGHLIGHTS – SINGLES: French Open*** 1r (lost Phelps 6–3 0–6 6–4).

PEDRO REBOLLEDO (Chile)
Born Santiago, 17 December, 1960 and lives there; RH; 5ft 7in; 150lb; final 1987 ATP ranking 94; 1987 prize money $58,502.
Wife Alejandra, son Pedro Pablo born Nov. 1987. Having undergone operations on both knees, has been advised by doctors to avoid HC. ***1981:*** (43) R/u Palermo. ***1982:*** (129) Won first GP title at Vina Del Mar. ***1983:*** (133). ***1984:*** (99) R/u Bari. ***1985:*** (143). ***1986:*** (172) Qf Athens. ***1987:*** Won second GP title at St Vincent. ***1987 HIGHLIGHTS – SINGLES: won*** Tarbes Challenger (d. Agenor 6–3 6–4), ***won*** St Vincent (d. C. Panatta 7–6 6–1, Mezzadri 2–6 6–3 6–3, McNamee 6–2 6–1, Pistolesi 6–1 6–4, Cancellotti 7–6 4–6 6–3).

RAFFAELLA REGGI (Italy)
Born Faenza, 27 November, 1965, and lives there; RH; 2HB; 5ft 6in; 125lb; final 1987 WITA ranking 17; 1987 prize money $138,527.
Coached by Ferruccio Bonetti. ***1981:*** One of the most spirited performers in the sport, an unwavering competitor, she won Orange Bowl 16s and was ranked No. 1 in Italian 16s. ***1982:*** (127) Moved up to No. 3 among Italian women and joined Fed Cup team. ***1983:*** (48) No. 1 in Italy. ***1984:*** (62) Sf Swiss Open and qf Italian Open. ***1985:*** (42) Won Taranto and r/u Barcelona. ***1986:*** (26) Won Puerto Rican Open and Lugano with victories over Bunge and M. Maleeva, reached last 16 Wimbledon and US Open both unseeded, and won US Open mixed doubles with Casal, becoming 1st Italian to win GS title. Qualified for VS Champ Nov. ***1987:*** Beat Sukova *en route* to qf French Open, reached last 16 Wimbledon and won VS San Diego. Qualified for VS Champs again. ***1987 HIGHLIGHTS – SINGLES: French Open*** qf, seed 14 (d. Singer 6–4 6–1, Gomer 6–3 6–3, A. Minter 7–5 6–2, Sukova [seed 5] 6–3 4–6 6–2, lost Evert [seed 3] 6–2 6–2), ***Wimbledon*** last 16, seed 15 (d. Bowes 6–4 6–2, Sloane 6–2 6–2, Tanvier 6–3 6–4, lost Sukova 6–0 6–0), ***US Open*** 3r (d. Grossman 6–4 6–0, Derly 6–2 4–6 6–2, lost Mandlikova [seed 4] 6–3 6–1); ***won*** VS

San Diego (d. Walsh Pete 6–2 6–3, Garrone 6–0 6–0, Demongeot 4–6 6–3 6–4, Tauziat 6–4 6–3, A. Minter 6–0 6–4); ***r/u*** Wild Dunes (d. Villagran 6–3 6–1, Louise Allen 7–6 6–2, Probst 6–4 6–3, Novotna 6–3 2–6 7–5, lost M. Maleeva 5–7 6–2 6–3); ***sf*** Geneva (d. C. Karlsson 4–6 6–2, Cohen 2–6 6–4 6–4, Budarova 6–4 6–4, lost M. Maleeva 6–4 2–6 6–2). ***CAREER HIGHLIGHTS – SINGLES: French Open – qf 1987. MIXED DOUBLES:*** (with Casal) ***US Open – won 1986*** (d. Navratilova/Fleming 6–4 6–4).

STEPHANIE REHE (USA)
Born Fontana, Cal., November 5, 1969; lives Highland, Cal; RH; 2HB; 5ft 11in; 130lb; final 1987 WITA ranking 28; 1987 prize money $49,150.
Coached by Olaf Merkel. ***1981:*** Won US Nat 12 singles. ***1982:*** Youngest to compete in VS tourn at 13 years 1 month. Won US Nat 14 indoor singles and Orange Bowl 14s. ***1983:*** At 13 years 2 months, youngest to receive computer ranking. Won US Nat 14 and Nat 16 Clay. ***1984:*** Won 18 Clay and 18 Nat Indoor. ***1985:*** (18) Won Nat 18, VS Utah and Tampa, and climbed into top 20 with wins over Sabatini and Bassett. ***1986:*** (17) Consolidated position in game, doing better early in season. ***1987:*** Won Puerto Rico and reached last 16 French Open. Out of action 6 weeks in late summer with pulled stomach muscle. ***1987 HIGHLIGHTS – SINGLES: French Open*** last 16, unseeded (d. Henricksson 6–3 6–2, M. J. Fernandez [seed 13] 7–6 1–6 6–4, Kanellopoulou 7–6 6–3, lost M. Maleeva [seed 6] 7–6 6–1); ***won*** Puerto Rico (d. Byrne 6–4 6–2, Keil 7–5 7–6, Hakami 6–3 6–4, E. Minter 6–3 6–1, Benjamin 7–5 7–6).

ELNA REINACH (South Africa)
Born Pretoria, 2 December, 1968; lives Johannesburg; RH; 5ft 10in; 130lb; final 1987 WITA ranking 94; 1987 prize money $44,788.
Coached by her mother, Elna. Sister of Monica. ***1984:*** R/u Wimbledon Jun, won South African Int jun event and South African satellite circuit Masters. ***1985:*** Won Wimbledon Plate and 2 tourns on satellite circuits. ***1986:*** (55) Upset Rinaldi at Mahwah. ***1987 HIGHLIGHTS – SINGLES: Australian Open*** 3r (bye, d. Field 6–1 6–2, lost Shriver [seed 3] 6–2 6–4), ***French Open*** 1r (lost Gompert 6–7 6–3 8–6), ***Wimbledon*** 1r (lost Burgin 6–1 6–3), ***US Open*** 2r (d. Hu Na 6–1 6–0, lost Kelesi 4–6 6–1 6–4).

RICHEY RENEBERG (USA)
Born Phoenix, Ariz., 5 October, 1965; lives Houston; RH; 5ft 11in; 170lb; final 1987 ATP ranking 79; 1987 prize money $49,875.
1987: Qf Indianapolis. ***1987 HIGHLIGHTS – SINGLES: Wimbledon*** 3r (d. Stadler 6–7 7–6 6–3 7–6, Castle 6–4 4–6 6–3 6–4, lost Lendl [seed 2] 6–4 6–7 6–3 7–6), ***US Open*** (d. Antonitsch 6–2 6–3 6–2, lost McEnroe [seed 8] 7–6 2–6 6–4 6–2).

KATHY RINALDI (USA)
Born Stuart, Fla., 24 March, 1967; lives Amelia Island Plantation, Fla.; RH; 2HB; 5ft 6in; 121lb; final 1987 WITA ranking 26 singles, 26 (23) doubles; 1987 prize money $68,479.
Coached by Andy Brandi. ***1979:*** Quietly precocious, she became first to win a US Girls' 12 GS, winning Indoor, HC, CC and Nat Champ. ***1980:*** Won Nat Girls' 14 CC and was ranked 3rd in division. ***1981:*** (33) Youngest to reach qf French Open and youngest to win a match at Wimbledon (14 years and 3 months). Turned pro in July. ***1982:*** (12) R/u German Open and San Diego. ***1983:*** (16) Sf US CC and WTA Champs, last 16 Wimbledon and French Open, and played W Cup. ***1984:*** (23) Sf Fort Lauderdale. ***1985:*** (11) Sf Wimbledon, won Mahwah over Graf and had wins over Sukova, Kohde-Kilsch and Mandlikova. ***1986:*** (9) Had a strong start with qf French Open, overcame mid-season injuries and returned to win VS Arkansas at end of year. ***1987:*** Out of action 2 months with fractured thumb and missed Wimbledon. Qf Washington. ***1987 HIGHLIGHTS – SINGLES: French Open*** 3r, seed 10 (d. Nelson Dunbar 6–2 6–0, Halard 3–6 6–1 7–5, lost Tauziat 6–1 6–3); ***sf*** VS California (d. Fendick 4–6 7–5, A. White 6–0 6–1 7–6, Rehe 1–6 6–4 6–4, lost Hanika 1–6 6–3 6–2), ***sf*** Tampa (d. Tarabini, Marsikova 4–6 6–3 6–3, Miro 7–5 6–4, lost Gompert 6–0 6–1). ***CAREER HIGHLIGHTS – SINGLES: German Open – r/u 1982*** (d. Jausovec 1–6 6–3 7–5, Hanika 6–3 7–5, lost Bunge 6–2 6–2), ***sf 1984*** (lost Kohde-Kilsch 6–4 6–0); ***Wimbledon – sf 1985*** (lost Sukova 6–1 1–6 6–1); ***French Open – qf 1981*** (d. Fromholtz [seed 8], A. Smith [seed 11], lost Mandlikova [seed 4] 6–1 6–3), ***qf 1986*** (d. Hu Na,

Burgin, Fairbank 6–1 6–2, Lindqvist 6–4 ret'd, lost Navratilova [seed 1] 7–5 6–4). ***CAREER HIGHLIGHTS – DOUBLES:*** (with Garrison) ***US Open – sf 1985*** (lost Kohde-Kilsch/Sukova 6–3 fs).

JOEY RIVE (USA)
Born Hato Bay, Puerto Rico, 8 July, 1963; lives Fort Lauderdale, Fla.; LH; 6ft 1in; 175lb; final 1987 ATP ranking 102; 1987 prize money $43,837.
Coached by Craig Wittus. ***1985:*** (497). ***1986:*** (363). ***1987:*** Qf Newport and Stratton Mountain (d. Mayotte). ***1987 HIGHLIGHTS – SINGLES: US Open*** 1r (lost Connors [seed 6] 6–1 6–4 6–4).

DERRICK ROSTAGNO (USA)
Born Los Angeles, 25 October, 1965; lives Brentwood, Cal.; RH; 6ft 1in; 165lb; final 1987 ATP ranking 60; 1987 prize money $101,908.
1983: Won New Zealand Masters satellite circuit. ***1984:*** Played in Olympic demonstration event in Los Angeles. ***1985:*** (427). ***1986:*** (70) Sf Houston, qf LA. ***1987:*** Reached last 16 Australian Open, sf Auckland and Frankfurt, with wins across the year over Gilbert, Becker and Gomez. ***1987 HIGHLIGHTS – SINGLES: Australian Open*** last 16, unseeded (d. Odizor 7–5 6–2 6–3, Matuszewski 7–5 6–1 6–1, Gilbert [seed 7] 4–6 6–2 6–3 6–1, lost Evernden 6–7 6–2 6–4 5–7 7–5), ***French Open*** 1r (lost Tulasne 3–6 6–3 1–6 6–4 6–2), ***Wimbledon*** 2r (d. Dyke 6–2 6–3 6–4, lost Jarryd 6–0 6–3 3–6 6–3), ***US Open*** 1r (lost Edberg [seed 2] 6–3 7–6 6–2); ***sf*** Auckland (d. Lapidus, M. Davis, Krishnan 6–3 6–7 10–8, lost Mecir 6–2 6–1), ***sf*** Frankfurt (d. Arias 6–7 6–4 6–4, Woodforde 6–3 6–4, Kroon 7–6 4–6 6–1, lost Mayotte 6–4 6–1).

GABRIELA SABATINI (Argentina)
Born Buenos Aires, 16 May, 1970; lives there and Key Biscayne, Fla.; 5ft 7½in; 130lb; final 1987 WITA ranking 6 singles, 5 (9) doubles; 1987 prize money $465,933.
Coached by Angel Gimenez. ***1984:*** (74) Top of ITF Jun rankings, she won French and Italian Jun and Orange Bowl 18s, where she conceded only 9 games in 6 matches. Meanwhile she tested the waters in women's tennis and reached 3r US CC and US Open, where she was youngest to win a match. ***1985:*** (12) Youngest sf at French Open, won Japan Open and was r/u to Evert Lloyd at Hilton Head, following big wins over Garrison, Shriver and M. Maleeva. ***1986:*** (10) Youngest sf Wimbledon and qf or better in 12 of 21 tournaments. Established a successful doubles partnership with Graf, r/u French Open. ***1987:*** With a win-loss record of 56–16, she was one of the few players to trouble Graf during the year, frequently taking her to 3s but never beating her. Sf French Open, r/u Italian Open and won her first major titles at Tokyo and Brighton in autumn. R/u VS Champs where she d. Navratilova in ss and took Graf to 4s. R/u French Open doubles with Graf. ***1987 HIGHLIGHTS – SINGLES: French Open*** sf, seed 7 (d. Van Der Torre 6–0 6–2, Ferrando 6–2 6–4, Benjamin 6–0 2–6 6–2, Schimper 6–4 6–1, Sanchez 6–4 6–0, lost Graf 6–4 4–6 7–5), ***Wimbledon*** qf, seed 6 (d. Gerken 6–3 6–3, Bartos Cserepy 6–1 6–3, Demongeot 6–3 6–4, Zvereva 6–0 6–2 6–4, lost Graf [seed 2] 4–6 6–1 6–1), ***US Open*** qf, seed 8 (d. Bowes 6–3 6–3, Gomer 6–3 6–1, Hakami 6–1 6–3, Bunge [seed 12] 1–6 6–1 6–1, lost Navratilova [seed 2] 7–5 6–3); ***won*** Argentine Open (d. Lindstrom 6–2 6–2, Nelson Dunbar 6–1 6–0, Tarabini 6–3 6–0, McNeil 6–2 6–3, Sanchez 6–1 6–1), ***won*** Tokyo (d. Gerken 6–1 6–0, Inoue 6–2 6–3, K. Maleeva 7–6 6–4, M. Maleeva 6–4 7–6), ***won*** Brighton (d. Nagelsen 4–6 6–3 6–4, Demongeot 6–2 6–0, Bunge 5–0 ret'd, Sukova 6–1 6–3, Shriver 7–5 6–4); ***r/u*** Italian Open (d. Calleja 6–2 6–1, M. J. Fernandez 6–1 6–3, Sanchez 6–0 6–0, Navratilova 6–2 6–3, lost Graf 7–5 4–6 6–0), ***r/u*** VS Champs (d. Bunge 6–2 7–6, Navratilova 6–4 7–5, M. Maleeva 6–3 4–6 6–3, lost Graf 4–6 6–4 6–0 6–4); ***sf*** VS Florida (d. Croft 6–2 6–4, Reggi 6–7 6–1 6–4, Gompert 6–2 6–1, lost Sukova 4–6 6–3 6–1), ***sf*** FC Cup (d. Scheuer-Larsen 6–0 6–2, Hu Na 6–2 6–2, Kohde-Kilsch 7–6 6–4, lost Graf 6–3 2–6 7–6), ***sf*** Amelia Island (d. Sanchez 6–0 6–2, M. J. Fernandez 6–1 6–4, Kelesi 6–4 4–6 6–2, lost Graf 6–2 6–2), ***sf*** VS LA (d. Tauziat 7–5 6–4, Demongeot 7–5 6–1, Mandlikova 7–6 2–6 7–5, lost Graf 7–5 7–5), ***sf*** Filderstadt (d. Hanika 6–2 6–1, Meier 6–2 6–2, Sukova 6–7 7–6 6–3, lost Navratilova 6–2 6–2), ***sf*** VS New England (d. Hy 6–3 6–3, K. Jordan 2–2 ret'd, McNeil 6–2 6–3, lost Evert 6–4 7–6). ***1987 HIGHLIGHTS – DOUBLES:*** (with Graf unless stated) ***r/u French Open*** (lost Navratilova/Shriver 6–2 6–1), ***sf*** US Open (lost Navra-

tilova/Shriver def.); ***won*** Amelia Island (d. Mandlikova/Turnbull 3–6 6–3 7–5), [Navratilova] ***won*** Italian Open (d. Kohde-Kilsch/Sukova 6–4 6–1); [Garrison] ***r/u*** VS California (lost Mandlikova/Turnbull 6–4 7–6). ***CAREER HIGHLIGHTS – SINGLES: VS Champs – r/u 1987; French Open – sf 1985*** (d. M. Maleeva 6–1 fs, lost Evert Lloyd 6–4 6–1), ***sf 1987; Wimbledon – sf 1986*** (d. Jolissaint, Suire, Gerken, Reggi 6–4 1–6 6–3, Lindqvist 6–2 6–3, lost Navratilova [seed 1] 6–2 6–2). ***CAREER HIGHLIGHTS – DOUBLES:*** (with Graf) ***French Open – r/u 1986*** (lost Navratilova/Temesvari 6–1 6–2), ***r/u 1987.***

CHRISTIAN SACEANU (West Germany)
Born Klausenburg, Rumania, 8 July, 1968; lives Neuss; RH; 6ft 3in; 177lb; final 1987 ATP ranking 84; 1987 prize money $77,324.
Coached by Gunther Bosch. ***1987:*** Won Graz Challenger (after qualifying), Valkenswaard Challenger and reached 1st GP f at Livingston. ***1987 HIGHLIGHTS – SINGLES: Australian Open*** 1r (lost J. Carlsson 4–6 7–6 6–3 7–6), ***Wimbledon*** 1r (lost Lendl 6–2 3–6 6–3 7–5), ***US Open*** 1r (lost Flur 0–6 6–1 7–5 6–7 6–4); ***r/u*** Livingston (d. Seguso 6–2 6–3, Hooper 7–6 6–4, Flach 6–1 3–6 6–3, Flur 6–3 6–4, lost Kriek 7–6 3–6 6–2).

ARANTXA SANCHEZ (Spain)
Born Barcelona, 18 December, 1971, and lives there; RH; 5ft 6in; 106lb; final 1987 WITA ranking 54; 1987 prize money $49,125.
Sister of Emilio and Javier. ***1986:*** (124) Emerging from satellite circuit, she reached sf Spanish Open and played Fed Cup. ***1987:*** Qf French Open in first GS appearance. ***1987 HIGHLIGHTS – SINGLES: French Open*** qf, unseeded (d. Burgin 7–5 6–3, Dinu 6–0 6–2, Paulus 6–4 6–2, C. Karlsson 6–1 6–4, lost Sabatini [seed 7] 6–4 6–0), ***Wimbledon*** 1r (lost Cordwell 6–1 2–6 6–4), ***US Open*** 1r (lost Dias 6–4 6–2); ***r/u*** Argentine Open (d. Keil, Drescher 6–1 6–4, Huber 6–2 6–1, Fulco 6–3 6–4, Perez Roldan 7–6 7–5, lost Sabatini 6–1 6–1).

EMILIO SANCHEZ (Spain)
Born Madrid, 29 May, 1965; lives Barcelona; RH; 5ft 11in; 164lb; final 1987 ATP ranking 17 singles, 8 (20) doubles; 1987 prize money $538,158.
Coached by Pato (Bill) Alvarez. Brother of Javier and Arantxa. ***1983:*** (208) R/u Orange Bowl and won Spanish Champs. ***1984:*** (112) Last 16 French Open. ***1985:*** (64) Upset Nystrom and Jarryd and reached 7 f doubles with Casal, winning 3 titles. ***1986:*** (16) Emerged as the most improved slow-court player, winning Nice, Munich, and Bastad, r/u Italian Open reaching 5 sfs and twice stopping Wilander and also claiming Becker and Edberg as his victims. ***1987:*** In singles won Gstaad, Bordeaux, Kitzbuhel, Madrid and reached last 16 French Open and Wimbledon. In doubles with Casal r/u Wimbledon, won 6 titles and qualified for Masters, reaching sf. In mixed doubles won French Open with Shriver and US Open with Navratilova. ***1987 HIGHLIGHTS – SINGLES: French Open*** last 16, unseeded (d. Zivojinovic 6–4 6–3 3–6 7–6, McNamee 6–3 6–1 6–1, de la Pena 6–3 6–3 4–6 6–3, lost Gomez [seed 10] 5–7 1–6 7–6 7–5 6–4), ***Wimbledon*** last 16, seed 14 (d. Bauer 6–4 3–6 6–2 7–5, Jelen 5–7 6–1 2–6 7–6 6–2, Van Rensburg 7–5 6–4 7–6, lost Wilander [seed 3] 2–6 7–6 6–3 7–5), ***US Open*** 3r, seed 14 (d. Masur 1–6 6–4 7–6 6–3, Witsken 6–1 6–4 6–3, lost Flach 5–7 7–6 7–6 7–5); ***won*** Gstaad (d. Kriek 6–1 6–4, Gunnarsson 6–7 6–4 6–4, Pernfors 5–7 6–4 6–1, Bengoechea 6–1 7–5, Agenor 6–2 6–3 7–6), ***won*** Bordeaux (d. Arguello 6–1 6–2, Bardou 6–2 6–3, Champion 6–4 6–2, Urpi 6–1 6–2, Agenor 5–7 6–4 6–4), ***won*** Kitzbuhel (d. Arguello 6–1 6–3, Schwaier 6–4 6–2, Arraya 6–3 6–2, Meinecke 6–2 6–2, Mecir 6–4 6–1 4–6 6–1), ***won*** Madrid (d. Gustafsson 6–2 7–5, Maciel 6–3 4–6 6–4, Aguilera 6–3 6–0, Davin 7–5 6–1, J. Sanchez 6–3 3–6 6–2); ***r/u*** Nice (d. Casal 6–1 6–0, Purcell 6–0 6–1, Vajda 6–2 6–2, Tulasne 7–5 6–2, lost K. Carlsson 7–6 6–3), ***r/u*** Bologna (d. Osterthun 6–3 6–3, Perez 6–0 4–6 6–3, Jaite 6–3 6–0, lost K. Carlsson 6–2 6–1); ***sf*** Bastad (d. Wahlgren 6–1 6–4, Bergstrom 4–6 6–3 6–1, Jarryd 6–3 6–2, lost Edberg 6–4 6–0). ***1987 HIGHLIGHTS – DOUBLES:*** (with Casal unless stated) ***r/u Wimbledon*** (lost Flach/Seguso 3–6 6–7 7–6 6–1 6–4); ***won*** US Pro Indoor (d. Flach/Smid 6–2 6–7 6–3, Steyn/Visser 3–6 6–1 7–6), ***won*** Nice (d. Mezzadri/Ocleppo 6–4 6–3), ***won*** Bologna (d. Panatta/Willenborg 6–3 6–2), ***won*** Bordeaux (d. Cahill/Woodforde 6–3 6–3), ***won*** Kitzbuhel (d. Mecir/Smid 7–6 7–6), ***won*** Itaparica (d. Lozano/Perez 6–2 6–2); ***r/u*** Memphis (d. Anger/Holmes, lost Jarryd/Svensson 6–4 6–2), ***r/u*** Milan (lost Becker/Zivojinovic 3–6 6–3 6–4),

r/u Munich (lost Pugh/Willenborg 7–6 4–6 6–4), [J. Sanchez] ***r/u*** Bastad (lost Edberg/Jarryd 7–6 6–3), ***r/u*** Madrid (lost DiLaura/J. Sanchez 6–3 3–6 7–6). ***1987 HIGHLIGHTS – MIXED DOUBLES:*** [Shriver] ***won French Open*** (d. McNeil/Stewart 6–3 7–6), [Navratilova] ***won US Open*** (d. Nagelsen/Annacone 6–4 6–7 7–6). ***CAREER HIGHLIGHTS – DOUBLES:*** (with Casal) ***Wimbledon – r/u 1987. MIXED DOUBLES: French Open*** – [Shriver] ***won 1987; US Open*** – [Navratilova] ***won 1987.***

JAVIER SANCHEZ (Spain)
Born Pamplona, 1 February, 1968; lives Barcelona; RH; 5ft 10in; 155lb; final 1987 ATP ranking 110; 1987 prize money $79,084.
Coached by Pato (Bill) Alvarez. Brother of Emilio and Arantxa. ***1986:*** No. 1 in ITF Jun world rankings. Won Orange Bowl 18s, US Open Jun singles and doubles (with Carbonell), r/u Wimbledon Jun singles and French Open Jun doubles (with Carbonell). ***1987:*** R/u Madrid to his brother, Emilio. ***1987 HIGHLIGHTS – SINGLES: French Open*** 2r (d. Fleurian 6–2 6–3 6–4, lost Schapers 6–4 6–2 7–5), ***Wimbledon*** 1r (lost Schapers 7–5 6–2 6–2), ***US Open*** 1r (lost Nystrom [seed 10] 7–6 7–6 3–6 6–3); ***r/u*** Madrid (d. DiLaura 6–0 6–1, Arrese 7–6 7–6, Rebolledo 6–4 6–4, Windahl 6–3 6–4, lost E. Sanchez 6–3 3–6 6–2). ***1987 HIGHLIGHTS – DOUBLES:*** [DiLaura] ***won*** Madrid (d. Casal/E. Sanchez 6–3 3–6 7–6), [Bloom] ***won*** Sao Paulo (d. Carbonell/Casal 6–3 6–7 6–4); [E. Sanchez] ***r/u*** Bastad (lost Edberg/Jarryd 7–6 6–3).

LARISA SAVCHENKO (USSR)
Born Lvov, Ukraine, 21 July, 1966, and lives there; RH; 5ft 2in; 139lb; final 1987 WITA ranking 24 singles, 11 (20) doubles; 1987 prize money $83,732.
Amateur. ***1983:*** Ranked 10 on ITF jun list after reaching qf Wimbledon Jun and first Wimbledon doubles qf with Parkhomenko. ***1984:*** (138) Wimbledon doubles qf again. ***1985:*** (55) Third Wimbledon doubles qf and sf VS Denver in singles. Joined Fed Cup team. ***1986:*** (35) Showed affinity for grass courts, reaching sf Birmingham, qf Eastbourne, and upsetting Rehe at Wimbledon. Qualified with Parkhomenko for VS Champ doubles March and Nov. ***1987:*** Won 4 doubles titles with Parkhomenko and ousted Navratilova/Shriver *en route* to sf Wimbledon. ***1987 HIGHLIGHTS – SINGLES: US Open*** 2r (d. Horvath 6–3 6–4, lost M. J. Fernandez 6–1 6–4); ***Wimbledon*** 2r (d. Magers 3–6 6–4 6–4, lost Hanika [seed 16] 6–3 6–3); ***r/u*** VS Kansas (d. Demongeot 6–4 7–5, Benjamin 7–6 6–2, Hanika 6–3 6–3, W. White 5–7 6–2 6–4, lost Potter 7–6 7–6), ***r/u*** Edgbaston (d. Cordwell 6–1 6–2, Hobbs 6–3 6–1, Fairbank 7–5 6–4, Pfaff 6–3 6–0, lost Shriver 4–6 6–2 6–2); ***sf*** VS Oklahoma (d. Zvereva 4–6 6–4 6–4, Gerken 6–2 7–5, Bykova 7–5 7–6, lost McNeil 7–6 6–2), ***sf*** VS Arkansas (d. Parkhomenko 7–5 6–2, Ter Riet 6–3 6–3, Bollegraf 6–1 6–1, lost Zvereva 6–3 6–1). ***1987 HIGHLIGHTS – DOUBLES:*** (with Parkhomenko) ***won*** VS Florida (d. Mandlikova/Turnbull, Evert Lloyd/Shriver 6–0 3–6 6–2), ***won*** VS Kansas (d. Potter/W. White 6–2 6–4), ***won*** VS Oklahoma (d. McNeil/Sands 6–3 4–6 6–1), ***won*** Eastbourne (d. Fairbank/Smylie 7–6 4–6 7–5).

BILL SCANLON (USA)
Born Dallas, 13 November, 1956, and lives there; RH; 6ft 1in; 170lb; final 1987 ATP ranking 99; 1987 prize money $71,545; career prize money $1,366,150.
1976: (52) All-American at Trinity Univ, he won NCAA singles (d. Fleming in f). ***1977:*** (37) Last 16 Australian Open Dec. ***1978:*** (95) Won Maui as 'lucky loser'. ***1979:*** (43) Won Maui 2nd straight year, r/u Birmingham and Jackson, and qf Wimbledon. ***1980:*** (26) Qf Australian Open. ***1981:*** (35) Won Auckland and Bangkok. ***1982:*** (71) Won WCT Zurich, r/u Vienna, Paris Indoor, WCT Chicago and WCT Hartford. ***1983:*** (12) Sf US Open (d. McEnroe), last 16 Wimbledon and r/u Columbus. ***1984:*** (55) Last 16 Wimbledon. ***1985:*** (180) Hampered by persistent knee injury, he reached only one qf – at Melbourne. ***1986:*** (85) Won Newport. ***1987:*** R/u Adelaide. ***1987 HIGHLIGHTS – SINGLES: Australian Open*** 2r (d. Lane 6–7 3–6 6–3 6–2 6–2, lost Doohan 6–3 1–6 7–5 7–6), ***French Open*** 1r (lost Arias 6–2 7–6 6–2), ***Wimbledon*** 2r (d. Mmoh 4–6 6–7 6–2 6–4 6–4, lost Volkov 7–6 7–6 6–2), ***US Open*** 1r (lost Woodforde 6–2 6–4 6–2); ***r/u*** Adelaide (d. Frana, Derlin, Michibata 7–6 7–5, Odizor 6–7 6–4 6–4, lost Masur 6–4 7–6); ***sf*** Chicago (d. Leach 6–3 6–4, Gilbert 7–5 6–4, S. Davis 6–3 6–3, lost Pate 6–3 6–2). ***1987 HIGHLIGHTS – DOUBLES:*** [Lendl] ***won*** Adelaide (d. Anger/Flach, Doohan/Warder 6–7 6–3 6–4). ***CAREER HIGHLIGHTS –***

SINGLES: US Open – sf 1983 (d. Sundstrom 6–2 4s, C. Lewis, Cash, McEnroe 7–6 7–6 4–6 6–3, lost Connors 6–2 6–3 6–2); ***US Pro Indoor – sf 1983*** (d. Wilander, McNamara, lost Lendl); ***Wimbledon – qf 1979*** (lost Connors [seed 2] 6–3 4–6 7–6 6–4).

MICHIEL SCHAPERS (Netherlands)
Born Rotterdam, 11 October, 1959 and lives there; RH; 6ft 5½in; 176lb; final 1987 ATP ranking 49; 1987 prize money $148,121.
Coached by Martin Simek. ***1982:*** Won Dutch Nat Indoor. ***1983:*** (107) Won Dutch Nat Outdoor. ***1984:*** (78). ***1985:*** (100) Upset Becker *en route* to qf Australian Open. ***1986:*** (84) Sf Metz. ***1987:*** R/u Auckland, sf Adelaide, Bristol, Paris Open. ***1987 HIGHLIGHTS – SINGLES: Australian Open*** 2r (d. Levine 6–1 6–4 6–4, lost Testerman 7–6 6–1 6–4), ***French Open*** 3r (d. S. Davis 7–6 5–7 6–4 6–4, J. Sanchez 6–4 6–2 7–5, lost Noah [seed 6] 6–3 6–3 6–2), ***Wimbledon*** 3r (d. J. Sanchez 7–5 6–2 6–2, Scott 7–6 6–3 6–2, lost Cash [seed 11] 7–6 6–2 2–6 6–4), ***US Open*** 1r (lost Gomez [seed 9] 7–6 6–4 7–5); ***r/u*** Auckland (d. Guy, Woodforde, Schultz, Limberger 6–2 3–6 6–4, lost Mecir 6–2 6–3 6–4); ***sf*** Adelaide (d. Youl, Anger 7–5 6–3, Fitzgerald 7–6 6–4, lost Masur 6–4 6–0), ***sf*** Bristol (d. Velez 6–4 6–4, Amritraj 6–1 6–4, Leconte 7–6 6–7 7–5, lost Wilkison 4–6 6–4 10–8), ***sf*** Paris Open (d. Tulasne 6–3 6–3, Volkov 6–3 4–6 6–3, Noah w.o., lost Gilbert 7–5 5–7 6–4). ***1987 HIGHLIGHTS – DOUBLES:*** [Fibak] ***won*** Toulouse (d. Forget/Smid, Jones/Kuhnen 6–2 6–4). ***CAREER HIGHLIGHTS – SINGLES: Australian Open – qf 1985*** (unseeded, d. Becker [seed 4] 3–6 6–4 7–6 4–6 6–3, Van Boeckel, Tim Gullikson, lost Edberg [seed 5] 6–0 7–5 6–4).

TINE SCHEUER-LARSEN (Denmark)
Born Olstykke, 13 March, 1966 and lives there; RH; 5ft 6in; 140lb; final 1987 WITA ranking 129 singles, 22 doubles; 1987 prize money $52,721.
Coached by Martin Bohm. ***1978:*** Won her first of 4 Danish Nat Jun Champs. ***1982:*** Won her last Danish Nat Jun Champ. ***1983:*** (162) Joined Danish Fed Cup team. ***1984:*** (73) Ranked No. 1 in Denmark for second year running. ***1985:*** (52) Reached last 16 French Open, 2 sf and was r/u Filderstadt doubles. ***1986:*** (45) R/u Charleston. ***1987:*** Qf Bastad in singles and won Wild Dunes and Bastad doubles. ***1987 HIGHLIGHTS – SINGLES: French Open*** 2r (d. Goles 7–5 6–2, lost Torres 4–6 6–4 6–3), ***Wimbledon*** 2r (d. Jagerman 6–2 6–0, lost Graf [seed 2] 6–0 6–0), ***US Open*** 1r (lost Garrison [seed 7] 6–1 6–3). ***1987 HIGHLIGHTS – DOUBLES:*** [Gildemeister] ***won*** Wild Dunes (d. Paz/Reynolds 6–4 6–4), [Barg] ***won*** Bastad (d. Cecchini/Tarabini 6–1 6–2); [Lindqvist] ***r/u*** Berlin (lost Kohde-Kilsch/Sukova 6–1 6–2), [Tanvier] ***r/u*** Brighton (lost K. Jordan/Sukova 7–5 6–1).

KAREN SCHIMPER (South Africa)
Born Marguard, 26 May, 1967, and lives there; RH; 5ft 9in; 135lb; final 1987 WITA ranking 102; 1987 prize money $31,328.
1986: (281) Won 2 tourns on USTA circuit. ***1987:*** Last 16 French Open. ***1987 HIGHLIGHTS – SINGLES: French Open*** last 16, unseeded (d. Lindstrom 7–6 6–2, Bonder 4–6 6–3 6–4, Phelps 6–7 6–2 6–2, lost Sabatini [seed 7] 6–4 6–1), ***Wimbledon*** 1r (lost A. Smith 6–2 2–6 6–1), ***US Open*** 2r (d. Russell 6–2 6–3, lost Henricksson 6–4 5–7 6–4).

CARLING BASSETT SEGUSO (Canada)
Born Toronto, 9 October, 1967; lives there and Gulf Island Resort, Fla.; RH; 2HB; 5ft 6in; 118lb; final 1987 WITA ranking 32; 1987 prize money $67,259.
1982: After winning Orange Bowl 18s she consulted with coach Nick Bollettieri and elected to turn pro. She had already demonstrated with her sound groundstrokes, first-rate forehand drop-shot and her extraordinary determination that she is her country's best prospect ever. ***1983:*** (20) Playing with uncommon assurance, she reached f WTA Champs and led Evert Lloyd 4–2 fs in f before losing memorable match; reached qf Australian Open. ***1984:*** (11) Made her mark in big championships, reaching qf French Open and sf US Open, where she downed Mandlikova. ***1985:*** (15) Played best tennis at LIPC where she accounted for Sabatini and Mandlikova. ***1986:*** (19) Began working with Dennis Ralston (Evert Lloyd's coach) and played her finest tennis at LIPC (qf), French Open (qf), and Wimbledon (last 16). Handled the death of her father, John Bassett, with great maturity. ***1987:*** At Strasbourg won first title since Ginny Hershey 1983. Married Robert Seguso 26

Sept; baby due March 1988. ***1987 HIGHLIGHTS – SINGLES: Australian Open*** last 16, seed 12 (bye, d. Salmon 6–1 6–1, Holikova 6–1 7–6, lost Mandlikova 6–2 4–6 6–2), ***French Open*** 3r (d. Kijimuta 6–1 6–3, Marsikova 6–2 6–7 6–3, lost Kohde-Kilsch [seed 8] 7–5 6–3), ***Wimbledon*** 1r (lost Goles 6–4 0–6 6–4), ***US Open*** 2r (d. Balestrat 6–4 6–2, lost Kohde-Kilsch [seed 9] 7–6 6–0); ***won*** Strasbourg (d. Lindstrom 6–0 7–5, Kijimuta 1–6 7–6 6–1, Ruzici 6–4 7–5, Tauziat 6–0 6–1, Cecchini 6–0 7–6). ***CAREER HIGHLIGHTS – SINGLES: US Open – sf 1984*** (lost Evert Lloyd 4–6 6–1 6–0); ***French Open – qf 1984*** (d. Mandlikova 6–4 6–3, lost Evert Lloyd 6–2 6–2), ***qf 1986*** (d. Tanvier 7–5 6–3, Etchemendy 3–6 6–4 7–5, Byrne 6–3 6–2, Paz 6–4 2–6 6–0, lost Evert Lloyd [seed 2] 5–7 6–2 6–1); ***Australian Open – qf 1983*** (lost Shriver 6–0 6–1).

ROBERT SEGUSO (USA)

Born Minneapolis, 1 May, 1963; lives Sebring, Fla.; 6ft 3in; 182lb; final 1987 ATP ranking 135 singles, 1 (16) doubles; 1987 prize money $367,022.

Coached by Bob Brett, until end 1987. ***1983:*** (146) All-American with Flach at Southern Ill. Univ. ***1984:*** (208). ***1985:*** (56) Sf Stratton Mountain, last 16 Wimbledon and won US Open doubles with Flach. ***1986:*** Beat Connors at Wimbledon and McEnroe at Canadian Open; sf Queens. Knee surgery postponed after US Open. ***1987:*** Underwent knee surgery in Jan. in an attempt to solve problems caused by scar tissue. Last 16 Australian Open; in doubles won French Open with Jarryd, Wimbledon with Flach and r/u Masters with Flach. Married Carling Bassett 26 Sept. ***1987 HIGHLIGHTS – SINGLES: Australian Open*** last 16, seed 13 (bye, d. Green 6–3 3–6 7–6 6–4, Frana 6–3 3–6 7–6 6–4, lost Edberg [seed 4] 6–1 6–0 6–1), ***French Open*** 1r (lost Vajda 6–4 3–6 6–2 7–6), ***Wimbledon*** 1r (lost Pernfors 3–6 6–3 6–2 6–7), ***US Open*** 1r (lost Forget 3–6 7–5 6–3 6–2). ***1987 HIGHLIGHTS – DOUBLES:*** (with Flach unless stated) [Jarryd] ***won French Open*** (d. Forget/Noah 6–7 6–7 6–3 6–4 6–2), ***won Wimbledon*** (d. Casal/E. Sanchez 3–6 6–7 7–6 6–1 6–4), ***r/u US Open*** (lost Edberg/Jarryd 7–6 6–2 4–6 5–7 7–6); ***won*** Cincinnati (d. Denton/Fitzgerald 7–5 6–3), Stratton Mountain divided with Annacone/Van Patten; ***r/u*** LIPC (lost Annacone/Van Rensburg 6–2 6–4 6–4), ***r/u*** Livingston (lost Donnelly/Holmes 7–6 6–3), [Becker] ***r/u*** Sydney (lost Cahill/Kratzmann 6–3 6–2), ***r/u*** Wembley (lost Mecir/Smid 7–5 6–4), ***r/u*** Masters (lost Mecir/Smid 6–4 7–5 6–7 6–3). ***CAREER HIGHLIGHTS – DOUBLES:*** (with Flach unless stated) [Jarryd] ***French Open – won 1987; Wimbledon – won 1987; US Open – won 1985*** (d. Noah/Leconte 7–6 6–7 7–6 6–0), ***r/u 1987; Italian Open – won 1984*** (d. Alexander/M. Leach 3–6 6–3 6–4); ***Masters r/u 1987.***

PAM SHRIVER (USA)

Born Baltimore, 4 July, 1962; lives Lutherville, Md; single; RH; 6ft; 150lb; final 1987 WITA ranking 4 singles, 2 (2) doubles; 1987 prize money $703,030; career prize money $3,375,777.

Coached by Don Candy and Hank Harris. ***1978:*** (13) At age 16 upset top-seeded Navratilova to become youngest finalist in US Open. ***1979:*** (33) Troubled by nagging shoulder injury, lost 1r US Open. ***1980:*** (9) Won La Costa and r/u Sydney (d. Navratilova). ***1981:*** (7) Won first Wimbledon doubles title with Navratilova, sf Wimbledon and Australian Open singles (d. Austin in both) and won Perth. ***1982:*** (6) Sf US Open (d. Navratilova). ***1983:*** (4) Sf US Open and won Brisbane. ***1984:*** (4) Won VS Chicago and r/u Mahwah. ***1985:*** (4) Won Sydney, Melbourne and Birmingham. Completed double GS with Navratilova by collecting 8th straight GS title in Paris, but record 109-match winning streak broken in f Wimbledon by Jordan/Smylie. ***1986:*** (6) Won 5th Wimbledon doubles title in 6 years with Navratilova. Won Birmingham and Newport and reached sf VS Champs in Nov. ***1987:*** Played no singles from March until June, returning to win Edgbaston, Canadian Open (d. Evert 1st time), VS Newport and New England, beating Evert again. With Navratilova won Australian and French Opens for 3rd GS in doubles, won US Open doubles, VS Champs for the 6th time and won French Open mixed doubles with E. Sanchez. ***1987 HIGHLIGHTS – SINGLES: Australian Open*** qf, seed 3 (bye, d. Moulton 6–2 4–6 11–9, Reinach 6–2 6–4, Durie [seed 14] 6–1 6–2, lost Lindqvist [seed 10] 6–3 6–1), ***Wimbledon*** sf, seed 5 (d. Medvedeva 6–2 6–1, A. Minter 6–2 6–2, Herr 6–2 6–2, Hanika [seed 16] 6–7 7–5 10–8, Sukova [seed 4] 4–6 7–6 10–8, lost Graf 6–0 6–2), ***US Open*** qf, seed 5 (d. W. White 6–3 6–3, Kuczynska 6–3 6–2, Golarsa 6–1 6–2, Novotna 6–3 7–6, lost Graf 6–4 6–3); ***won*** Edgbaston (d. E. Reinach 6–4 6–2, Van Rensburg 6–2 6–3, Tauziat 6–0 6–1, Inoue 6–2 6–4, Savchenko 4–6

6–2 6–2), ***won*** VS Newport (d. K. Jordan 6–3 6–0, Fendick 6–2 6–1, G. Fernandez 7–6 4–6 6–2, Moulton 6–3 6–2, W. White 6–2 6–4), ***won*** Canadian Open (d. Hakami 6–3 6–3, K. Jordan 6–3 6–3, Sabatini 6–2 6–1, Evert 6–4 6–1, Garrison 6–4 6–1), ***won*** VS New England (d. Gompert 6–3 6–3, Louie Harper 6–4 6–2, Bunge 6–4 6–4, Sukova 7–5 6–3, Evert 6–4 4–6 6–0); ***r/u*** Brisbane (d. Hobbs 7–5 7–6, Jolissaint, Pfaff 6–1 6–3, Nagelsen 6–1 6–3, lost Mandlikova 6–2 2–6 6–4), ***r/u*** NSW Open (d. Rush 6–3 6–1, M. Maleeva 6–3 6–3, lost Garrison 6–2 6–4), ***r/u*** VS Dallas (d. Schimper 6–2 6–2, Bonder 6–3 6–3, Turnbull 6–4 6–4, McNeil 7–5 6–3, lost Evert Lloyd 6–1 6–3), ***r/u*** Brighton (d. Provis 7–6 6–4, Gomer 6–3 6–3, K. Maleeva 6–2 6–1, K. Jordan 6–1 7–5, lost Sabatini 7–5 6–4); ***sf*** VS Florida (d. Van Rensburg 6–3 6–2, M. J. Fernandez 6–2 6–1, G. Fernandez 6–3 6–3, lost Graf 6–4 6–3), ***sf*** Eastbourne (d. Louis 6–0 6–2, E. Reinach 4–6 6–1 6–2, Smylie 6–4 6–1, Sabatini 6–3 6–3, lost Navratilova 6–4 4–6 6–3), ***sf*** Filderstadt (d. Porwik 6–3 6–2, Novotna 6–2 7–5, Garrison 6–4 6–2, lost Evert 7–5 6–3). ***1987 HIGHLIGHTS – DOUBLES:*** (with Navratilova unless stated) ***won Australian Open*** (d. Hy/Inoue 6–1 6–0, Garrison/McNeil 6–1 6–0), ***won French Open*** (d. Graf/Sabatini 6–2 6–1), ***won US Open*** (d. K. Jordan/Smylie 5–7 6–4 6–2); ***won*** LIPC (d. Graf/Sabatini, Kohde-Kilsch/Sukova 6–3 7–6), [Burgin] ***won*** VS Washington (d. Garrison/McNeil 6–1 3–6 6–4), ***won*** VS LA (d. Garrison/McNeil 6–3 6–4), ***won*** Filderstadt (d. Garrison/McNeil 6–7 7–6 6–4), ***won*** VS Champs (d. Kohde-Kilsch/Sukova 6–1 6–1); [Burgin] ***r/u*** Bridgestone (lost Kohde-Kilsch/Sukova 6–1 7–6), [Evert Lloyd] ***r/u*** VS Florida (lost Parkhomenko/Savchenko 6–0 3–6 6–2). ***MIXED DOUBLES:*** (with E. Sanchez) ***won French Open*** (d. McNeil/Stewart 6–3 7–6). ***CAREER HIGHLIGHTS – SINGLES: US Open – r/u 1978*** (d. Reid, Hunt, Navratilova 7–6 7–6, lost Evert 7–5 6–4), ***sf 1982*** (d. Navratilova 1–6 7–6 6–2, lost Mandlikova 6–4 2–6 6–2), ***sf 1983*** (d. Jaeger 7–6 6–3, lost Navratilova 6–2 6–1); ***Wimbledon – sf 1981*** seed 7 (d. Ekblom, Little, Coles, Durie, Austin [seed 3] 7–5 6–4, lost Evert Lloyd [seed 1] 6–3 6–1); ***Australian Open – sf 1981*** seed 6 (d. Desfor, Durie, Austin [seed 2] 7–5 7–6, lost Navratilova [seed 3] 6–3 7–5), ***sf 1982*** (lost Navratilova 6–3 6–4), ***sf 1983*** (d. Bassett 6–0 6–1, lost Navratilova 6–4 6–3); ***VS Champs – sf 1984*** (d. Mandlikova, lost Navratilova), ***sf 1986*** (lost Navratilova 6–2 4–6 6–4). ***CAREER HIGHLIGHTS – DOUBLES:*** (with Navratilova unless stated) ***French Open – won 1984*** (d. Kohde-Kilsch/Mandlikova 5–7 6–3 6–2), ***won 1985*** (d. Kohde-Kilsch/Sukova 4–6 6–2 6–2), ***won 1987; Wimbledon – won 1981*** (d. K. Jordan/A. Smith 6–3 7–6), ***won 1982*** (d. K. Jordan/A. Smith 6–4 6–1), ***won 1983*** (d. Casals/Turnbull 6–2 6–2), ***won 1984*** (d. K. Jordan/A. Smith 6–3 6–4), ***won 1986*** (d. Mandlikova/Turnbull 6–1 6–3), ***r/u 1985*** (d. Mandlikova/Turnbull, lost K. Jordan/Smylie 5–7 6–3 6–4); ***US Open – won 1983*** (d. Fairbank/Reynolds 6–7 6–1 6–3), ***won 1984*** (d. Turnbull/Hobbs 6–2 6–4), ***won 1986*** (d. Mandlikova/Turnbull 6–4 3–6 6–3), ***won 1987,*** [Stove] ***r/u 1980*** (lost King/Navratilova 7–6 7–5), ***r/u 1985*** (lost Kohde-Kilsch/Sukova 6–7 6–2 6–3), ***sf 1982*** (lost Potter/Walsh 7–5 2–6 6–4); ***Australian Open – won 1982*** (d. Kohde/Pfaff 6–4 6–2), ***won 1983*** (d. Hobbs/Turnbull 6–4 6–7 6–2), ***won 1984*** (d. Kohde-Kilsch/Sukova 6–3 6–4), ***won 1985*** (d. Kohde-Kilsch/Sukova 6–3 6–4), ***won 1987, r/u 1981*** (lost K. Jordan/A. Smith 6–2 7–5); ***TS Champs – won 1982*** (d. P. Smith/Reynolds 6–4 7–5); ***VS Champs – won 1984*** (d. Durie/Kiyomura 6–3 6–1), ***won 1985*** (d. Kohde-Kilsch/Sukova 6–7 6–4 7–6), ***won 1986*** (d. Kohde-Kilsch/Sukova 7–6 6–3), ***won 1987.***

CHRISTINA SINGER (West Germany)
Born Goppiugeu, 27 July, 1968, and lives there; RH; 5ft 10in; 148lb; final 1987 WITA ranking 82; 1987 prize money $18,668.
1985: (295) Won Stockholm on Swedish Satellite circuit. ***1986:*** (162) Won Wahlingen on German Satellite circuit. ***1987:*** Qf Zurich (d. Hanika). ***1987 HIGHLIGHTS – SINGLES: Australian Open*** 2r (d. Pazderova 6–1 6–4, lost Mochizuki 6–3 6–3), ***French Open*** 1r (lost Reggi [seed 14] 6–4 6–1).

HORST SKOFF (Austria)
Born Klagensuart, 22 August, 1968, and lives there; RH; 5ft 9in; 157lb; final 1987 ATP ranking 63; 1987 prize money $77,508.
Coached by Jan Kukal. ***1984:*** (555) Won Orange Bowl 16. ***1985:*** (299) Won Austrian Nat Indoor. ***1986:*** (42) Austrian Nat Indoor Champ again, sf Barcelona, qf Kitzbuhel and Stuttgart. ***1987:*** Upset Noah and Gomez *en route* to sf Monte Carlo. ***1987 HIGHLIGHTS – SINGLES: French Open*** 2r (d. Delaitre 6–4 7–6 6–1, lost Mecir [seed 5] 7–6 6–4 6–1),

Wimbledon 1r (lost Gomez [seed 8] 6–4 6–4 7–5); ***sf*** Monte Carlo (d. Arraya, Noah 3–6 7–5 6–2, Benhabiles 7–5 3–6 7–6, Gomez 7–5 2–6 6–4, lost Arias 7–5 6–1).

TOMAS SMID (Czechoslovakia)
Born Plzen, 20 May, 1956; lives Prague; RH; 6ft 3in; 175lb; final 1987 ATP ranking 31; singles, 13 (14) doubles; 1987 prize money $433,783; career prize money $3,342,005.
Son Tomas born 1979. ***1978:*** (36) Won first GP title in Sarasota. ***1979:*** (28) Won Stuttgart. ***1980:*** (24 Won Stuttgart, Bologna and r/u Vienna. ***1981:*** (31) R/u Frankfurt and Vienna. ***1982:*** (23) Won WCT Mexico City and Cap d'Agde. ***1983:*** (17) Won Munich and Hilversum, r/u Bournemouth, Gstaad and Stockholm and qf Australian Open. ***1984:*** (16) R/u Madrid, Luxembourg, Hilversum and Hong Kong; qf Wimbledon, won US Open doubles with Fitzgerald. ***1985:*** (19) Won Geneva over Wilander and r/u Toulouse. ***1986:*** (54) At 30, he had his least productive year since 1977, apart from winning French Open doubles with Fitzgerald. ***1987:*** Despite suffering from arthritis in one foot, he returned to his old territory in the rankings, reaching f Prague and Geneva, sf Stuttgart and Itaparica, and winning 7 doubles titles, including Masters with Mecir. ***1987 HIGHLIGHTS – SINGLES: French Open*** 1r (lost Courteau 7–5 6–2 6–3), Wimbledon 2r (d. Tyson 6–4 6–4 6–7 6–3, lost Nystrom [seed 13] 6–3 6–1 6–4), ***US Open*** 2r (d. Jaite [seed 15] 7–6 6–4 6–2, lost Yzaga 6–3 6–4 6–1); ***won*** Neu Ulm Challenger (d. Champion 6–3 6–4); ***r/u*** Prague (d. Kuchna 6–2 6–2, Cihak 6–4 6–4, Muster 7–5 5–7 7–5, Navratil 6–1 7–5, lost Vajda 6–1 6–3), ***r/u*** Geneva (d. de Miguel 1–6 6–4 6–2, Bengoechea 6–3 6–2, Perez Roldan 6–2 7–6, Gomez 7–6 4–6 6–0, lost Mezzadri 6–4 7–5); ***sf*** Stuttgart (d. Osterthun 6–3 7–6, Stenlund 7–6 6–3, Skoff 7–6 4–6 6–4, Bengoechea 6–3 6–2, lost Mecir 6–3 6–3), ***sf*** Itaparica (d. Rebolledo 6–3 6–0, J. Sanchez 3–6 7–6 6–4, Gomez 7–6 7–6, lost Mattar 4–6 7–6 6–4). ***1987 HIGHLIGHTS – DOUBLES:*** (with Mecir unless stated) ***won*** Hamburg (d. Gunnarsson/Nystrom, lost Mezzadri/Pugh), [Gunnarsson] ***won*** Gstaad (d. Courteau/Forget 7–6 6–2), ***won*** Prague (d. Birner/Navratil 6–3 6–7 6–3), ***won*** Barcelona (d. Frana/Miniussi 6–1 6–2), [Jarryd] ***won*** Basel (d. Birner/Navratil 6–4 6–3), ***won*** Wembley (d. Flach/Seguso 7–5 6–4), ***won*** Masters (d. Edberg/Jarryd 3–6 6–3 2–6 6–3 6–4, Flach/Seguso 6–4 7–5 6–7 6–3); ***r/u*** Italian Open (lost Forget/Noah 6–2 6–7 6–3), ***r/u*** Kitzbuhel (lost Casal/E. Sanchez 7–6 7–6). ***CAREER HIGHLIGHTS – SINGLES: Wimbledon – qf 1984*** (lost Lendl 6–1 7–6 6–3), ***Australian Open – qf 1983*** (d. Fitzgerald, lost Lendl [seed 1] 7–6 2–6 6–1 6–2). ***CAREER HIGHLIGHTS – DOUBLES: French Open*** – [Fitzgerald] ***won 1986*** (d. Edberg/Jarryd 6–3 4–6 6–3 6–7 14–12), [Slozil] ***r/u 1984*** (lost Leconte/Noah 6–4 2–6 3–6 6–3 6–2); ***US Open*** – [Fitzgerald] ***won 1984*** (d. Edberg/Jarryd 7–6 6–3 6–3); ***Italian Open*** [Fleming] ***won 1979*** (d. Clerc/Nastase 7–5 fs), [Manson] ***r/u 1981*** (lost Gildemeister/Gomez 7–5 6–2); ***German Open*** – [Slozil] ***won 1982*** (d. Jarryd/H. Simonsson 6–4 6–3); ***Masters*** – [Mecir] ***won 1987,*** [Slozil] ***r/u 1983*** (lost McEnroe/Fleming 6–2 6–2).

ANNE SMITH (USA)
Born Dallas, 1 July, 1959; lives San Antonio, Texas; RH; 5ft 5in; 120lb; final 1987 WITA ranking 40; 1987 prize money $38,820.
1976: R/u Orange Bowl. ***1977:*** Won Orange Bowl and became 1st American to win French Open Jun. ***1978:*** (20) Last 16 US Open. ***1979:*** (24) Last 16 US Open. ***1980:*** (24) With K. Jordan won French Open and Wimbledon doubles. ***1981:*** (16) With Jordan won US and Australian Opens and r/u Wimbledon. Won US Open mixed with Curren. ***1982:*** (13) R/u Washington, qf Wimbledon singles. With Jordan won French Open and r/u Wimbledon. In mixed won Wimbledon and US Open with Curren. ***1983:*** (28) After r/u French Open with Jordan, took a 6-month break to coach at Trinity Univ. ***1984:*** (Not ranked) Still coaching, but with Jordan won WTA Champs, r/u Wimbledon; with Curren won French Open mixed. Played Fed Cup. ***1985:*** (Not ranked) Playing sparingly, she reached last 16 Wimbledon. ***1986:*** (79) Won only 8 of 21 singles matches. ***1987:*** At VS Indianapolis reached 1st f since 1982. ***1987 HIGHLIGHTS – SINGLES: Australian Open*** 3r (d. Paquet 7–5 6–3, Kell 6–2 6–4, lost Mandlikova [seed 2] 6–3 6–2), ***Wimbledon*** 2r (d. Schimper 6–2 2–6 6–1, lost Burgin 6–4 7–5); ***r/u*** Indianapolis (d. Baranski 5–7 6–1 6–3, Moulton 6–1 6–2, Ter Riet 6–3 6–4, Hakami 6–4 6–0, Hu Na 0–6 6–2 6–4, lost Cioffi 4–6 6–4 7–6); ***sf*** VS Arkansas (d. R. White 1–6 6–4 6–2, Piatek Daniels 6–2 6–4, Sloane 6–2 6–2, lost Cecchini 6–4 6–3). ***CAREER HIGHLIGHTS – DOUBLES:*** (with K. Jordan unless stated) ***French Open – won 1980*** (d. Madruga/Villagran 6–1 6–0), [Navratilova] ***won 1982*** (d. Casals/Turnbull 6–3 6–4),

r/u 1983 (lost Reynolds/Fairbank 5–7 7–5 6–2); ***Wimbledon – won 1980*** (d. Casals/ Turnbull 3–6 7–6 6–1), ***r/u 1981*** (d. Fairbank/Harford 6–1 6–2, lost Navratilova/Shriver 6–3 7–6), ***r/u 1982*** (d. Casals/Turnbull 6–4 fs, lost Navratilova/Shriver 7–5 6–1), ***r/u 1984*** (d. Potter/Walsh, lost Navratilova/Shriver 6–3 6–4); ***US Open – won 1981*** (d. Casals/ Turnbull 6–3 6–3); ***Australian Open – won 1981*** (d. Navratilova/Shriver 6–2 7–5). ***MIXED DOUBLES:*** (with Curren unless stated) ***French Open*** – (Stockton) ***won 1984*** (d. Sayers/ Stewart, A. Minter/Warder 6–2 6–4); ***Wimbledon – won 1982*** (d. Turnbull/J. Lloyd 7–5 fs); ***US Open – won 1981*** (d. Denton/Russell 6–4 7–6), ***won 1982*** (d. Potter/Taygan 7–6 fs).

ELIZABETH SAYERS SMYLIE (Australia)
Born Perth, 11 April, 1963; lives Sydney and Hilton Head, SC; RH; 5ft 7in; 129lb; final 1987 WITA ranking 27 singles, 8 (8) doubles; 1987 prize money $145,642.
Coached by her husband, Peter. ***1981:*** Among world's top 10 jun. ***1982:*** (115) Won Sardinia on Italian satellite circuit and was ranked 7 in Australia. ***1983:*** (70) Won Kansas City. ***1984:*** (36) Ranked 2 in Australia behind Turnbull and played Fed Cup. Married Peter Smylie Nov. 10. ***1985:*** (43) Joined K. Jordan to beat Navratilova/Shriver in Wimbledon f, ending the record 109-match winning streak by world's top pair. ***1986:*** (80) Won only 6 of 20 singles matches including 7 straight 1r losses at start of year. Won LIPC mixed doubles with Fitzgerald. ***1987:*** Qf Australian Open and won VS Oklahoma in Feb. in first singles f since Nov. 1984. In doubles r/u Wimbledon with Nagelsen and US Open with K. Jordan. ***1987 HIGHLIGHTS – SINGLES: Australian Open*** qf, unseeded (bye, d. Hy 6–2 6–3, R. White [seed 9] 6–1 6–2, Sukova [seed 4] 7–5 3–6 7–5, lost Kohde-Kilsch [seed 5] 7–6 4–6 6–2), ***French Open*** 1r (lost Polzl Wiesner 6–2 6–2), ***Wimbledon*** 3r (d. Dias 6–2 6–3, Croft 6–3 6–1, lost Kohde-Kilsch [seed 8] 6–2 6–1), ***US Open*** 2r (d. Pfaff 6–4 7–5, lost Zvereva 6–3 6–2); ***won*** VS Oklahoma (d. Mochizuki 6–4 6–2, Piatek 2–6 6–4 6–3, Benjamin 6–2 6–4, Lindqvist 6–4 6–4, McNeil 4–6 6–3 7–5). ***1987 HIGHLIGHTS – DOUBLES:*** (with Nagelsen unless stated) ***r/u Wimbledon*** (lost Kohde-Kilsch/Sukova 7–5 7–5), [K. Jordan] ***r/u US Open*** (lost Navratilova/Shriver 5–7 6–4 6–2); ***won*** NSW Open (d. Byrne/Thompson 6–7 7–5 6–1), ***won*** Geneva (d. Gildemeister/Tanvier 4–6 6–4 6–3); ***r/u*** Brisbane (lost Mandlikova/Turnbull 6–4 6–3), ***r/u*** New Jersey (lost G. Fernandez/McNeil), ***r/u*** Eastbourne (lost Parkhomenko/Savchenko), [Hobbs] ***r/u*** Mahwah (lost G. Fernandez/McNeil 6–3 6–2). ***CAREER HIGHLIGHTS – SINGLES: Australian Open – qf 1987. CAREER HIGHLIGHTS – DOUBLES:*** [K. Jordan] ***Wimbledon – won 1985*** (d. Kohde-Kilsch/Sukova 5–7 6–1 6–4, Navratilova/Shriver 5–7 6–3 6–4), [Nagelsen] ***r/u 1987;*** [B. Jordan] ***French Open – sf 1984*** (lost Kohde-Kilsch/Mandlikova 6–7 6–3 6–4). ***MIXED DOUBLES:*** (with Fitzgerald unless stated) ***US Open – won 1983*** (d. Taygan/Potter 3–6 6–3 6–4), ***r/u 1984*** (lost M. Maleeva/Tom Gullikson 2–6 7–5 6–4), ***r/u 1985*** (lost Gunthardt/Navratilova 6–3 6–4), [K. Jordan] ***r/u 1987.***

MILAN SREJBER (Czechoslovakia)
Born Prague, 30 December, 1963, and lives there; RH; 6ft 8in; 210lb; final 1987 ATP ranking 62; 1987 prize money $214,263.
1985: (169) Won Finnish Challenger and was r/u Brazil Challenger. ***1986:*** (27) Began year brilliantly with win over Becker at LIPC after reaching f Toronto Indoor and followed with qf US Open. Helped lead Czech D Cup team to sf, defeating Oresar and Zivojinovic in qf and extending Edberg to 7–5 fs in sf. ***1987:*** Less spectacular but reached sf US Pro Indoor, and collected wins over Connors and Vilas during the year. ***1987 HIGHLIGHTS – SINGLES: Australian Open*** 2r (bye, lost Flach 3–6 2–6 7–5 6–3 6–3), ***French Open*** 3r (d. Mansdorf 5–7 7–6 7–6 6–3, Vilas 6–3 6–4 6–2, lost Mecir [seed 5] 6–0 6–1 6–3), ***Wimbledon*** 1r (lost Annacone 7–6 6–4 6–1), ***US Open*** 3r (d. Matuszewski 6–7 7–6 7–5 7–6, Bourne 7–6 3–6 6–7 7–5 6–3, lost Woodforde 6–2 6–1 6–1); ***sf*** US Pro Indoor (d. S. Giammalva 7–6 7–6, Wilkison 2–6 6–4 6–2, Connors 6–3 7–6, lost Mayotte 6–2 6–2). ***CAREER HIGHLIGHTS – SINGLES: US Open – qf 1986*** unseeded (d. Arias 7–5 6–0 6–3, Dyke, Yzaga, Witsken, lost Becker [seed 3] 6–3 6–2 6–1).

BRANISLAV STANKOVIC (Czechoslovakia)
RH; final 1987 ATP ranking 86; 1987 prize money $16,287.
1987 HIGHLIGHTS – SINGLES: won Istanbul Challenger (d. Segarceanu 6–2 6–1).

Richey Reneberg (right) was voted ATP Newcomer of the Year in 1987, an honour accorded in 1986 to Ulf Stenlund (below right), who in 1987 beat Stefan Edberg in Monte Carlo. The high spot for Karel Novacek (below left) came at the French Open, where he reached the quarter-finals, but he fell at the first hurdle at Wimbledon.
(A. Evans, T. Hindley)

CARL-UWE STEEB (West Germany)
Born Aalen, 1 September, 1967; lives Stuttgart; LH; 6ft; 157lb; final 1987 ATP ranking 41; 1987 prize money $44,880.
Coached by Karl Meiler and Gunther Metzger. ***1985:*** (363). ***1986:*** (150) Won Hauptfeld and r/u Harren on German Satellite circuit; qf Buenos Aires. ***1987:*** Upset Krickstein, Forget and Leconte to reach first GP sf in Stuttgart; qf Munich and Hilversum. ***1987 HIGHLIGHTS – SINGLES: French Open*** 1r (lost Champion 6–2 6–4 2–6 6–4), ***Wimbledon*** 1r (lost Maurer 6–4 6–7 6–4 5–7 11–9); ***sf*** Stuttgart (d. Bergstrom 7–6 6–4, Krickstein 6–0 6–4, Forget 6–2 1–6 6–3, Leconte 7–5 6–3, lost Gunnarsson 6–4 7–6).

ULF STENLUND (Sweden)
Born Falun, 21 January, 1967; lives Hedemora; RH; 5ft 11in; 155lb; final 1987 ATP ranking 43; 1987 prize money $103,754.
A past semi-finalist of Kalle Anka Cup. ***1984:*** Won Swedish Jun Champs over C. Bergstrom and left school. ***1985:*** (274) In last jun tourn won Rolex 18s at Port Washington over Ohta. ***1986:*** (34) Upset countryman Jarryd on his way to last 16 of French Open, won Palermo and reached sf Bordeaux and Stuttgart in first full season on tour. ***1987:*** Upset Edberg *en route* to sf Monte Carlo and reached the same stage at Bari and Geneva. ***1987 HIGHLIGHTS – SINGLES: French Open*** 2r (d. Willenborg 6–2 6–2 6–2, lost Muster 6–2 6–2 6–2), ***Wimbledon*** 2r (d. Canter 6–7 6–3 6–4 6–4, lost Gomez [seed 8] 6–3 6–2 7–6), ***US Open*** 1r (lost Hearn 4–6 7–6 6–2 6–4); ***sf*** Bari (d. Castle 6–0 6–0, Bengoechea 6–1 1–6 6–4, Osterthun 6–3 1–6 6–1, lost Pistolesi 6–1 0–6 6–1), ***sf*** Monte Carlo (d. Holmes, Edberg 2–6 6–1 6–4, Meinecke 7–5 6–3, Jaite 2–6 6–0 7–6, lost Wilander 6–2 6–2), ***sf*** Geneva (d. Marmillo 6–2 6–3, Mattar 6–3 6–0, de la Pena 4–6 6–1 7–5, lost Mezzadri 6–2 6–7 7–6). ***1987 HIGHLIGHTS – DOUBLES:*** (with Allgaardh) ***won*** Bari (d. Azar/Ingaramo 6–3 6–3).

SHERWOOD STEWART (USA)
Born Goose Creek, Texas, 6 June, 1946; lives Woodlands, Texas; RH; 6ft 2in; 185lb; final 1987 ATP ranking singles —, doubles 37 (22); 1987 prize money $21,863; career prize money $1,584,555.
Wife Linda, daughter Shastyn. ***1972:*** Won French Open doubles with Taygan. ***1974:*** (63) Won Dublin. ***1975:*** (78) R/u Cincinnati. ***1976:*** (94) Won French Open doubles with McNair. ***1975:*** (78) R/u Cincinnati. ***1976:*** (76) R/u Towson and won French Open doubles with McNair. ***1978:*** (60) R/u US Open doubles with Riessen. ***1983:*** (Not ranked in singles) R/u French Open with Edmondson and Australian Open with Denton. ***1984:*** (673) Won Australian Open doubles with Edmondson. ***1986:*** (Not ranked) Sf French Open with Leconte. Won Stockholm doubles and r/u 5 more with various partners. ***1987:*** Played no singles, but was still a force in doubles, winning Australian Open mixed with Garrison. ***1987 HIGHLIGHTS – DOUBLES:*** (with Warwick) ***won*** Orlando (d. Annacone/Van Rensburg 2–6 7–6 6–4). ***MIXED DOUBLES:*** (with Garrison) ***won*** Australian Open (d. Castle/Hobbs 3–6 7–6 6–3). ***CAREER HIGHLIGHTS – DOUBLES:*** (with McNair unless stated) ***French Open – won 1976*** (d. Gottfried/Ramirez [seed 7] 7–6 6–3 6–1), [Taygan] ***won 1982*** seed 1 (d. Gildemeister/Prajoux 7–5 6–3 1–1 ret'd), [Taygan] ***r/u 1983*** (lost Jarryd/H. Simonsson 7–6 6–4 6–2); ***Australian Open*** – [Edmondson] ***won 1984,*** [Denton] ***r/u 1983*** (lost Edmondson/McNamee 6–3 7–6); ***US CC –*** [Taygan] ***won 1982*** (d. Venter/Willenborg 6–4 7–5); ***US Pro Indoor –*** [Riessen] ***won 1981*** (d. Gottfried/Ramirez 6–2 6–2), [Taygan] ***r/u 1982*** (lost Fleming/McEnroe [seed 1] 7–6 6–4); ***Masters – won 1976*** (d. Gottfried/Ramirez 6–3 5–7 5–7 6–4 6–4), [Taygan] ***r/u 1982*** (lost Fleming/McEnroe 6–2 6–2), [Edmondson] ***r/u 1984*** (lost McEnroe/Fleming); ***South African Open*** – [Gottfried] ***won 1976*** (d. S. Smith/Gisbert 1–6 6–1 6–2 7–6), [Gomez] ***r/u 1983*** (lost Teacher/Meister 6–7 7–6 6–2); ***US Open –*** [Riessen] ***r/u 1978*** seed 8 (lost Smith/Lutz [seed 3] 1–6 7–5 6–3); ***Italian Open – r/u 1977*** (d. Kodes/Nastase 7–5 7–6, lost Gottfried/Ramirez 7–6 6–7 7–5), [Edmondson] ***r/u 1986*** (lost Gildemeister/Gomez 7–6 6–2); ***Wimbledon*** – [Taygan] ***sf 1982*** seed 2 (lost McNamara/McNamee 4–6 6–4 6–7 7–6 6–4). ***MIXED DOUBLES:*** (with Garrison) ***Australian Open – won 1987.***

JASON STOLTENBERG (Australia)
Born Narrabri, 4 April, 1970, and lives there; RH; 6ft; 168lb; final 1987 ATP ranking 413; 1987 prize money $8,928.

1987: 1st to become ITF Jun champ in both singles and doubles in the same year. Won Australian Open Jun singles and Australian and Wimbledon Jun doubles (with Woodbridge); r/u French Open and Wimbledon Jun singles. ***1987 HIGHLIGHTS – SINGLES: Australian Open*** 1r (lost P. Carlsson 6–3 1–6 6–3 6–2).

CATHERINE SUIRE (France)
Born Madagascar, 15 September, 1959; lives Paris; RH; 5ft 6in; 130lb; final 1987 WITA ranking 135 singles, 27 doubles; 1987 prize money $46,641.
Coached by Virginia Wade. ***1983:*** (80) Ranked 3 in France and was r/u French Nat, d. Paradis in sf. ***1984:*** (115) Qf Pittsburgh. ***1985:*** (104). ***1986:*** (85) R/u VS Pennsylvania. ***1987:*** Reached qf VS Arizona and formed a successful doubles partnership with Novotna, qualifying for VS Champs and taking a set off Navratilova/Shriver. ***1987 HIGHLIGHTS – SINGLES: French Open*** 2r (d. Etchemendy 3–6 7–5 6–1, lost Zvereva 6–7 6–3 6–0), ***Wimbledon*** 1r (lost Potter [seed 13] 6–4 4–6 6–1). ***1987 HIGHLIGHTS – DOUBLES:*** (with Novotna) ***won*** Strasbourg (d. Horvath/Mesker 6–0 6–2), ***won*** VS San Diego (d. Burgin/Walsh Pete 7–6 3–6 7–5); ***r/u*** Zurich (d. Mandlikova/Pfaff, lost Herreman/Paradis 6–3 2–6 6–3).

HELENA SUKOVA (Czechoslovakia)
Born Prague, 23 February, 1965 and lives there; RH; 6ft 2in; 150lb; final 1987 WITA ranking 7 singles, 6 (3) doubles; 1987 prize money $490,792; career prize money $2,069,885.
Coached by Jan Kurz. Daughter of 1962 Wimbledon finalist, the late Vera Sukova, and Cyril Suk, President of Czech Tennis Federation. Brother Cyril. ***1981:*** (74) Beat Anne Smith and Barbara Potter to reach last 16 Australian Open at age 16. ***1982:*** (24) Qf Swiss Open, r/u US CC and Avon Futures Champs. ***1983:*** (17) Sf Sydney. ***1984:*** (7) R/u Australian Open (d. Navratilova) and won Brisbane. ***1985:*** (9) R/u VS Champ and Eastbourne. Qf Australian Open. ***1986:*** (5) Won Canadian Open and Hilversum and r/u US Open (d. Evert Lloyd first time in 15 career meetings). ***1987:*** Sf US Open, qf Wimbledon, won Eastbourne (d. Evert and Navratilova back to back) and New Jersey in singles and Wimbledon doubles with Kohde-Kilsch. Qualified for VS Champs in singles and doubles. ***1987 HIGHLIGHTS – SINGLES: Australian Open*** last 16, seed 4 (bye, d. Hu Na 6–4 7–6, Jolissaint 6–2 6–1, lost Smylie 7–5 3–6 7–5), ***French Open*** last 16, seed 5 (d. Van Rensburg 6–1 6–1, Rush Magers 6–3 6–1, Zvereva 6–1 6–3, lost Reggi [seed 14] 6–3 4–6 6–2), ***Wimbledon*** qf, seed 4 (d. Louis 6–1 6–4, R. White 6–2 3–6 6–3, Durie 6–1 6–3, Reggi [seed 15] 6–0 6–0, lost Shriver [seed 5] 4–6 7–6 10–8), ***US Open*** sf, seed 6 (d. Gurney 6–7 6–3 6–4, Burgin 6–3 6–4, Cueto 7–6 6–1, Hobbs 6–4 6–2, Kohde-Kilsch [seed 9] 6–1 6–3, lost Navratilova [seed 2] 6–2 6–2); ***won*** New Jersey (d. Balestrat 6–4 6–0, Henricksson 6–3 6–3, Lindqvist 6–4 6–3, G. Fernandez 6–3 7–5, McNeil 6–0 6–3), ***won*** Eastbourne (d. Durie 6–0 6–4, Casale 6–2 6–1, E. Minter 7–5 6–2, Fairbank 6–7 6–3 8–6, Evert 4–6 6–4 8–6, Navratilova 7–6 6–3); ***r/u*** VS Florida (d. Durie 6–4 6–3, Fendick 3–6 6–0 7–5, Bunge 3–6 6–3 7–6, Sabatini 4–6 6–3 6–1, lost Graf 6–2 6–3); ***sf*** Brisbane (d. Hu Na 7–6 6–4, Gomer 3–6 6–2 6–2, Fairbank 7–5 6–3, lost Mandlikova 4–6 6–1 6–4), ***sf*** VS Washington (d. Durie 6–3 6–1, Tanvier 7–6 6–0, McNeil 6–4 2–6 6–1, lost Mandlikova 6–3 6–2), ***sf*** Italian Open (d. Marsikova 7–6 7–5, Bykova 7–6 6–0 Polzl 6–4 6–2, lost Graf 6–3 6–3), ***sf*** Brighton (d. Durie 6–3 6–3, Paradis 7–6 6–1, Hanika 6–3 5–7 6–1, lost Sabatini 6–1 6–3), ***sf*** VS Chicago (d. Kelesi 3–6 6–3 6–2, Novotna 3–6 6–3 6–2, Meskhi 7–6 0–6 6–0, lost Navratilova 7–5 7–5), ***sf*** VS New England (d. Keil 6–1 6–1, Inoue 5–7 6–2 6–4, Pfaff 6–2 6–1, lost Shriver 7–5 6–3). ***1987 HIGHLIGHTS – DOUBLES:*** (with Kohde-Kilsch unless stated) ***won Wimbledon*** (d. Nagelsen/Smylie 7–5 7–5); ***won*** Bridgestone (d. Burgin/Shriver 6–1 7–6), ***won*** Berlin (d. Lindqvist/Scheuer-Larsen 6–1 6–2), [K. Jordan] ***won*** Brighton (d. Scheuer-Larsen/Tanvier 7–5 6–1), ***won*** VS Chicago (d. Garrison/McNeil 6–4 6–3); ***r/u*** LIPC (lost Navratilova/Shriver 6–3 7–6), ***r/u*** Italian Open (lost Navratilova/Sabatini 6–4 6–1), ***r/u*** Canadian Open (lost Garrison/McNeil 6–1 6–2), ***r/u*** VS Champs (lost Navratilova/Shriver 6–1 6–1). ***CAREER HIGHLIGHTS – SINGLES: Australian Open – r/u 1984*** (d. Kohde-Kilsch, Shriver, Navratilova 1–6 6–3 7–5, lost Evert Lloyd 6–7 6–1 6–3); ***US Open – r/u 1986*** (d. Drescher, Gomer, Bonder, Garrison 6–4 2–6 6–4, Turnbull 6–4 6–0, Evert Lloyd 6–2 6–4, lost Navratilova 6–3 6–2), ***sf 1987, qf 1984*** (d. K. Jordan, lost Navratilova); ***VS Champ – r/u 1985–86*** (lost Navratilova 6–3 7–5 6–4), ***sf 1986*** lost Graf 7–6 3–6 6–1); ***Wimbledon – qf 1986*** (d.

Parnell, Betzner, A. Minter, R. White 6–3 6–0, lost Evert Lloyd 7–6 4–6 6–4). ***CAREER HIGHLIGHTS – DOUBLES:*** (with Kohde-Kilsch) ***Wimbledon – won 1987; US Open – won 1985*** (d. Navratilova/Shriver [seed 1] 6–7 6–2 6–3); ***French Open – r/u 1985*** (lost Navratilova/Shriver 4–6 6–2 6–2); ***Australian Open – r/u 1984*** (lost Navratilova/Shriver 6–3 6–4), ***r/u 1985*** (lost Navratilova/Shriver 6–3 6–4); ***VS Champs – r/u 1984–85*** (lost Navratilova/ Shriver 6–7 6–4 7–6), ***r/u 1985–86*** (lost Mandlikova/Turnbull 6–4 6–7 6–3), ***r/u 1986*** (lost Navratilova/Shriver 7–6 6–3), ***r/u 1987.***

JONAS SVENSSON (Sweden)
Born Goteborg, 21 October, 1966; lives Kungsbacka and Monte Carlo; RH; 6ft 2in; 168lb; final 1987 ATP ranking 30; 1987 prize money $185,326.
Coached by Tim Klein. ***1983:*** (445) Sf Wimbledon Jun. ***1982:*** (741). ***1985:*** (122) Won Swiss Satellite. ***1986:*** (21). Clearly the most improved player in the top 25, winning Cologne, narrowly losing to Noah in f Wembley, r/u Stuttgart and beating Jarryd, Zivojinovic and Mecir. ***1987:*** Shortly after starting to work with psychologist Lars Ryberg, he reached last 16 US Open, won 1st GP title in Vienna and reached f Stockholm and Young Masters. ***1987 HIGHLIGHTS – SINGLES: French Open*** 2r (d. Shiras 6–4 6–0 6–2, lost Arias 7–5 6–1 2–6 6–4), ***Wimbledon*** 3r (d. Youl 5–7 6–1 6–3 2–6 6–3, Edwards 4–6 6–3 3–6 6–3 8–6, lost Wilander [seed 3] 7–6 6–1 6–3), ***US Open*** last 16, unseeded (d. Cane 5–7 6–4 6–2 7–6, Donnelly 6–4 4–6 3–6 6–2 7–6, Yzaga 2–6 6–4 3–6 6–2 6–2, lost Edberg [seed 2] 6–2 7–6 6–3); ***won*** Vienna (d. Birner 6–3 6–0, Gunnarsson 7–5 6–2, Srejber 6–1 5–7 6–2, Mezzadri 6–2 6–3, Mansdorf 1–6 1–6 6–2 6–3 7–5); ***r/u*** Stockholm (d. Antonitsch 3–6 6–3 6–1, Pimek 6–3 6–2, Grabb 6–1 6–3, Gustafsson 6–3 6–4, lost Edberg 7–5 6–2 4–6 6–4), ***r/u*** Young Masters (d. Kristiansson 6–1 6–2, J. Carlsson 6–0 6–1, Kuhnen 6–7 6–3 7–5 in rr, Antonitsch 6–1 6–1, lost Muster 6–4 4–6 7–5 6–2); ***sf*** Brussels (d. Arraya 6–3 6–3, Limberger 6–2 5–7 6–3, Gunnarsson 6–3 6–3, lost Wilander 6–3 6–2). ***1987 HIGHLIGHTS – DOUBLES:*** (with Jarryd) ***won*** Memphis (d. Casel/E. Sanchez 6–4 6–2).

CATHERINE TANVIER (France)
Born Toulouse, 28 May, 1965; lives Nice; RH; 2HB; 5ft 8in; 116lb; final 1987 WITA ranking 95; 1987 prize money $52,591.
Coached by Patrice Hagelhauer and Steve Myers. ***1979:*** Won French Nat 14s. ***1980:*** (173) Won French Nat 16s. ***1981:*** (95) Sf Columbus. ***1982:*** (24) Won Wimbledon Jun over Sukova. In singles r/u Hershey and in doubles won Monte Carlo and Bakersfield. ***1983:*** In singles won Freiburg, r/u Stuttgart and in doubles r/u Italian Open, Hittfeld and sf French Open. ***1984:*** (30) Sf German Open. ***1985:*** (39) Last 16 Wimbledon, sf US Indoor (d. Shriver). ***1986:*** (36) R/u Hilversum and Wild Dunes. ***1987 HIGHLIGHTS – SINGLES: French Open*** 1r (lost Villagran 6–0 6–4), ***Wimbledon*** 3r (d. Nelson Dunbar 6–1 7–5, Marsikova 6–0 6–2, lost Reggi [seed 15] 6–3 6–4), ***US Open*** 1r (lost Nagelsen 7–6 6–1). ***1987 HIGHLIGHTS – DOUBLES:*** [Gildemeister] ***r/u*** Geneva (lost Nagelsen/Smylie 4–6 6–4 6–3), [Scheuer-Larsen] ***r/u*** Brighton (lost K. Jordan/Sukova 7–5 6–1).

PATRICIA TARABINI (Argentina)
Born La Plata, 6 August, 1968; lives Tandil; RH; 5ft 5in; 135lb; final 1987 WITA ranking 69; 1987 prize money $39,560.
1984: R/u Orange Bowl 16s. ***1985:*** (305) No. 1 in ITF Jun World Rankings doubles after winning Italian Open Jun and r/u Orange Bowl singles, and winning French Open, Orange Bowl and r/u US Open Jun doubles (with Perez Roldan). ***1986:*** (125) Won French Open Jun, Orange Bowl and two titles on Italian circuit. ***1987:*** Sf Berlin, qf Argentine Open and Athens. ***1987 HIGHLIGHTS – SINGLES: French Open*** 1r (lost Demongeot 6–2 7–5), ***Wimbledon*** 1r (lost Okamoto 6–1 6–4), ***US Open*** 3r (d. Medrado 5–7 6–1 6–3, Fairbank 6–2 4–6 6–3, lost Graf 6–2 6–0); ***sf*** Berlin (d. Dirnu 6–3 6–1, Van Rensburg 6–1 6–1, Meier 6–1 5–0 ret'd, Provis 6–2 6–1, lost Kohde-Kilsch 6–4 7–6).

NATHALIE TAUZIAT (France)
Born Bangui, Africa, 17 October, 1967; lives St Tropez; RH; 5ft 4in; 120lb; final 1987 WITA ranking 25; 1987 prize money $92,208.
Coached by Regis DeCamaret. ***1985:*** (112) Reached 3r French Open, upsetting 16th seed Casale, and played Fed Cup. ***1986:*** (67), Qf Hilversum. ***1987:*** Last 16 French Open, sf

Strasbourg, San Diego and Zurich and d. Rinaldi to reach qf LIPC. ***1987 HIGHLIGHTS – SINGLES: French Open*** last 16, unseeded (d. Byrne 7–5 3–6 6–3, Cueto 6–2 0–6 6–3, Rinaldi 6–1 6–3, lost Kohde-Kilsch [seed 8] 6–1 3–6 6–0), ***US Open*** 2r (d. Ludloff 6–4 6–2, lost M. Maleeva 6–1 6–3); ***sf*** Strasbourg (d. Kim 6–3 6–0, Wood 7–5 6–2, Phelps 4–6 6–2 6–4, lost Bassett 6–0 6–1), ***sf*** VS San Diego (d. Burgin 6–0 6–3, Horvath 6–3 6–1, Gompert 6–3 2–6 6–4, lost Reggi 6–4 6–3), ***sf*** Zurich (d. Javer 6–1 6–1, Kohde-Kilsch def., Singer 7–5 6–4, lost Mandlikova 6–1 3–6 6–3). ***1987 HIGHLIGHTS – DOUBLES:*** [Demongeot] ***won*** Paris (d. Cecchini/Goles 1–6 6–3 6–3).

ELIOT TELTSCHER (USA)
Born Palos Verdes Estates, Cal., 15 March, 1959, and lives there; RH; 5ft 10in; 150lb; final 1987 ATP ranking 20; prize money $141,888; career prize money $1,601,173.
1976: (239) Closed jun career by reaching Orange Bowl f where he lost to McEnroe. ***1977:*** (106). ***1978:*** (42) Took first GP title in Hong Kong. ***1979:*** (27) Won Atlanta. ***1980:*** (10) Won Atlanta and Maui and reached US Open qf. ***1981:*** (8) US Open qf again and f French Open doubles with T. Moor. ***1982:*** (14) R/u Italian Open. ***1983:*** (13) Won Tokyo, qf Australian Open and US Open, last 16 French Open, won French Open mixed doubles with B. Jordan. ***1984:*** (9) Victorious in Brisbane, Tokyo and S. African Open. Played D Cup. ***1985:*** (24) Played only 12 events plus D Cup as injuries halted his progress. ***1986:*** (53) At age 27, played greatly reduced schedule; sf Munich and Houston. ***1987:*** Beat Connors to reach sf Chicago and at Hong Kong won 1st title for 3 years. ***1987 HIGHLIGHTS – SINGLES: US Open*** 1r (lost Pimek 7–5 6–3 1–6 7–6); ***won*** Hong Kong (d. Chamberlin 7–6 4–6 6–3, Dyke 6–4 3–6 6–3, R. Leach 4–6 6–2 6–3, Cahill 7–5 6–0, Fitzgerald 6–7 3–6 6–1 6–2 7–5); ***r/u*** Scottsdale (d. Rive 6–2 6–2, Grabb 6–3 6–3, Lundgren 3–6 6–3 6–4, Pate 7–6 7–5, lost Gilbert 6–2 6–2); ***sf*** Chicago (d. Devries 6–2 6–4, Van Rensburg 6–3 6–2, Connors 6–3 6–1, lost Mayotte 3–6 7–5 6–2). ***CAREER HIGHLIGHTS – SINGLES: South African Open – won 1984*** (d. Gerulaitis 6–3 6–1 7–6); ***Italian Open – r/u 1982*** seed 4 (d. Nystrom, Maurer, Mottram 6–4 6–3, Dibbs 6–2 6–2, Arraya 6–3 fs, lost Gomez 6–2 6–3 6–2); ***US Open – qf 1980*** (d. Davis, Pecci, Ocleppo, Gottfried, lost Connors 6–1 3–6 6–3 6–0), ***qf 1981*** seed 8 (d. Amaya, Austin, V. Armitraj, Gottfried [seed 16], lost Connors [seed 4] 6–3 6–1 6–2), ***qf 1983*** (d. S. Giammalva, Jarryd, Holmes, lost Connors 7–6 6–2 6–2). ***CAREER HIGHLIGHTS – DOUBLES:*** (with Moor) ***French Open – r/u 1981*** (d. Feigl/Martin, lost Gunthardt/Taroczy 6–2 7–6 6–3). ***MIXED DOUBLES:*** (with B. Jordan) ***French Open – won 1983*** (d. Allen/Strode 6–2 6–3).

MICHELLE TORRES (USA)
Born Chicago, Ill., 27 June, 1967; lives Northfield, Ill.; RH; 2HB; 5ft 4in; 114lb; final 1987 WITA ranking 67; 1987 prize money $31,415.
Coached by Steve Casati. ***1981:*** (92) Ranked 5 in US Girls 14 division, Illinois State High School Champ, and member US Jun W Cup team. ***1982:*** (61) Beat K. Jordan and reached qf US CC. ***1983:*** (30) Qf Wimbledon Jun and French Open Jun and sf Palm Springs on women's tour. Ranked 10 in ITF Jun rankings. ***1984:*** (20) Turned pro at US Open, r/u to Navratilova at Fort Lauderdale and beat Bassett to win Tampa. ***1985:*** (56) Qf Tampa and Fort Lauderdale. ***1986:*** (54) Salvaged year with sf showing in Tampa. ***1987:*** Sf Paris Open. ***1987 HIGHLIGHTS – SINGLES: French Open*** 3r (d. Okamoto 7–6 6–0, Scheuer-Larsen 4–6 6–4 6–3, lost Kelesi 6–1 6–3), Wimbledon 1r (lost Field 7–6 6–1), ***US Open*** 1r (lost Benjamin 6–3 7–5); ***sf*** Paris Open (d. Bakkum 6–3 5–7 7–5, Provis 7–6 7–5, Fukarkova 6–4 6–1, lost Goles 6–2 6–4).

ALBERTO TOUS (Spain)
Born Palma, 3 August, 1962; lives Barcelona; RH; 5ft 10in; 150lb; final 1987 ATP ranking 80; 1987 prize money $75,065.
1979: Won Nat 18s. ***1980:*** R/u French Open Jun. ***1981:*** (396). ***1982:*** (91) Had wins over Smid and Leconte and was r/u Brussels Satellite. ***1983:*** (195). ***1984:*** (103). ***1985:*** (227). ***1986:*** (259) Played only doubles. ***1987:*** Won Cairo Challenger and Waiblingen Challenger, qf Gstaad. ***1987 HIGHLIGHTS – SINGLES: won*** Cairo Challenger (d. DeMiguel 6–2 6–3), ***won*** Waiblingen Challenger (d. Fleurian 7–5 0–6 6–4, Stadler w.o.).

THIERRY TULASNE (France)
Born Aix-les-Bains, 12 July, 1963; lives Tours; RH; 2HB; 5ft 10in; 160lb; final 1987 ATP ranking 57; 1987 prize money $105,040.
Wife Nathalie (married June 1986). ***1980:*** (113) Exploding with potential even before he turned 17, he won Italian and Wimbledon Jun and upset former champion Gerulaitis at Italian Open men's. ***1981:*** (52) Won Bastad, reached sf US Pro Indoor and joined French D Cup squad. ***1982:*** (98) Reached qf Bournemouth, Geneva and Barcelona. ***1983:*** (83) Reached qf Madrid, Nice and Florence. ***1984:*** (52) Reached sf Washington and qf US CC. ***1985:*** (23) Following 7 1r and 3 2r losses in first 10 tournaments, he won Bologna, Palermo and Barcelona, playing best tennis of his career. ***1986:*** (20) Won Metz, was r/u at Washington, Geneva and Indianapolis and played with impressive consistency all year. ***1987:*** Sf Nice and reached 4 qf. ***1987 HIGHLIGHTS – SINGLES: French Open*** 3r (d. Rostagno 3–6 6–3 1–6 6–4 6–2, Gunnarsson 6–2 6–3 6–3, lost Lendl [seed 1] 7–6 6–2 6–2), ***US Open*** 1r (lost Brown 6–2 6–4 6–1); ***sf*** Nice (d. Holmes 3–6 6–0 6–1, Berger 5–7 6–2 6–3, Krickstein 7–5 7–6, lost E. Sanchez 7–5 6–2).

WENDY TURNBULL (Australia)
Born Brisbane, 26 November, 1952; lives Sandgate and Deer Creek, Fla.; RH; 5ft 4½in; 120lb; final 1987 WITA ranking 12 singles, 15 (6) doubles; 1987 prize money $207,467; career prize money $2,614,704.
1977: (9) R/u US Open. Joined Fed Cup team. ***1978:*** (7) Won Wimbledon doubles with Reid. ***1979:*** (9) A late bloomer, she burst into her own at 25 and reached US Open f with brilliant string of victories over Casals, Wade and Navratilova, losing to Evert. This lifted her into the top 10, where she remained every year until 1985. ***1978:*** (7) Won Wimbledon doubles with Kerry Reid and reached sf US Open. ***1979:*** (7) R/u French Open where she won mixed with Hewitt and women's doubles with Stove, won Detroit and Philadelphia, and took US Open doubles with Stove. ***1980:*** (8) R/u Australian Open (d. Navratilova in sf) and won US Open mixed doubles with Riessen. ***1981:*** (8) Sf Australian Open. ***1982:*** (5) Won Richmond, Brisbane singles and won US Open doubles with Casals and French Open mixed doubles with John Lloyd. ***1983:*** (8) Won Wimbledon mixed doubles with J. Lloyd and won Boston singles. ***1984:*** (5) Sf US and Australian Opens and won Wimbledon mixed with Lloyd again. Awarded OBE. ***1985:*** (14) R/u VS San Diego. ***1986:*** (18) Upset defending champion Mandlikova in last 16 US Open and in doubles won VS Champs March and was r/u Wimbledon and US Open with Mandlikova. ***1987:*** Upset Mandlikova at NSW Open and won 4 doubles titles. ***1987 HIGHLIGHTS – SINGLES: Australian Open*** last 16, seed 11 (bye, d. Byrne 2–6 6–4 6–3, Mundel 4–6 6–1 6–2, lost Garrison [seed 7] 6–1 6–3), ***Wimbledon*** 2r, seed 12 (d. Spence 6–4 6–2, lost Walsh Pete 6–4 6–4), ***US Open*** 2r, seed 16 (d. Gadusek 6–2 6–1, lost Novotna 6–2 6–4); ***sf*** NSW Open (d. Mandlikova 6–3 7–5, McNeil 6–4 7–5, lost Garrison 6–3 6–4), ***sf*** New Orleans (d. A. White 7–5 6–2, Keil 7–5 6–2, R. White 6–2 3–6 6–4, lost Evert 4–2 ret'd). ***1987 HIGHLIGHTS – DOUBLES:*** (with Mandlikova unless stated) ***won*** Brisbane (d. Nagelsen/Smylie 6–4 6–3), ***won*** VS California (d. Garrison/Sabatini 6–1 3–6 6–1), [Evert Lloyd] ***won*** Plymouth (d. McNeil/Bunge 3–6 6–3 6–2), [Evert] ***won*** Tampa (d. Burgin/Fairbank 6–4 6–3); ***r/u*** Amelia Island (lost Graf/Sabatini 3–6 6–3 7–5). ***CAREER HIGHLIGHTS – SINGLES: French Open – r/u 1979*** (d. Mandlikova 6–3 6–3, Marsikova 6–4 6–3, lost Evert Lloyd 6–2 6–0), ***qf 1980*** seed 3 (lost Ruzici [seed 8] 6–2 6–0); ***US Open – r/u 1977*** (d. Casals 4–6 6–0 6–0, Wade 6–2 6–1, Navratilova 2–6 7–5 6–4, lost Evert 7–6 6–2), ***sf 1978*** (lost Evert 6–3 6–0), ***sf 1984*** (d. Shriver 2–6 6–3 6–3, lost Navratilova 6–4 6–1); ***Australian Open – sf 1981*** seed 7 (d. Jaeger 6–3 7–6, lost Evert Lloyd 6–4 7–6), ***sf 1984*** (d. Graf, lost Evert Lloyd 6–3 6–3); ***Wimbledon – qf 1980*** seed 6 (lost Goolagong Cawley 6–3 6–3), ***qf 1981*** seed 6 (lost Mandlikova [seed 2] 6–0 6–0). ***CAREER HIGHLIGHTS – DOUBLES:*** (with Stove unless stated) ***French Open – won 1979*** (d. Wade/Durr 3–6 7–5 6–4), [Casals] ***r/u 1982*** (lost Navratilova/A. Smith 6–3 6–4); ***Wimbledon –*** [Reid] ***won 1978*** (d. Jausovec/Ruzici 4–6 9–8 6–3), ***r/u 1979*** (lost King/Navratilova 5–7 6–3 6–2), [Casals] ***r/u 1980*** (lost K. Jordan/A. Smith 3–6 7–6 6–1), [Casals] ***r/u 1983*** (d. Potter/Walsh 6–1 6–7 6–4, lost Navratilova/Shriver 6–2 6–2), [Mandlikova] ***r/u 1986*** (lost Navratilova/Shriver 6–1 6–3), [Mandlikova] ***sf 1985*** (lost Navratilova/Shriver 6–4 6–2); ***US Open – won 1979*** (d. King/Navratilova 7–5 6–2), [Casals] ***won 1982*** (d. Potter/Walsh 6–3 6–4), [Casals] ***r/u 1981*** (d. Navratilova/Shriver 6–4 fs, lost A. Smith/K. Jordan 6–3 6–3), [Hobbs] ***r/u 1984*** (lost Navratilova/Shriver 6–2 6–4), [Mandlikova] ***r/u***

1986 (lost Navratilova/Shriver 6–4 3–6 6–3, [Mandlikova] ***sf 1985*** (lost Navratilova/Shriver 6–3 6–4); ***Italian Open – won 1979*** (d. Goolagong Cawley/Reid 6–3 6–4); ***CS Final*** – [Casals] ***won 1980*** (d. Stove/Shriver 6–4 6–4, Reynolds/P. Smith 6–3 4–6 7–6); ***VS Champs*** – [Mandlikova] ***won 1985–86*** (d. Navratilova/Shriver, lost Kohde-Kilsch/Sukova 6–4 6–7 6–3); ***TS Champ*** – [Casals] ***r/u 1981*** (lost Navratilova/Shriver 6–3 6–4); ***Australian Open*** – [Hobbs] ***r/u 1983*** (d. Durie/Kiyomura, King/Walsh 6–4 6–1, lost Navratilova/Shriver 6–4 6–7 6–2). ***MIXED DOUBLES:*** (with J. Lloyd unless stated) ***French Open*** – [Hewitt] ***won 1979*** (d. Tiriac/Ruzici 6–3 2–6 6–1), ***won 1982*** (d. Motta/Monteiro 6–2 7–6); ***Wimbledon – won 1983*** (d. Denton/King 6–7 7–6 7–5), ***won 1984*** (d. Denton/Jordan 6–3 6–3), ***r/u 1982*** (lost Curren/A. Smith 2–6 6–3 7–5); ***US Open*** – [Riessen] ***won 1980*** (d. McMillan/Stove 7–6 6–2).

MARIAN VAJDA (Czechoslovakia)
Born Povazska, 24 March, 1965; lives Bratislava; RH; 5ft 8in; 150lb; final 1987 ATP ranking 46; 1987 prize money $119,124.
1985: (52) A former Czech Nat Jun Champ, he came from nowhere to reach sf Kitzbuhel and qf Geneva. ***1986:*** (88) Qf Nice, Hilversum, Itaparica. ***1987:*** After qualifying at Munich he upset Kriek and Nystrom in ss *en route* to f, following in Aug. with 1st GP title at Prague. ***1987 HIGHLIGHTS – SINGLES: French Open*** 2r (d. Seguso 6–4 3–6 6–2 7–6, lost Nystrom 6–3 6–3 6–1), ***US Open*** 1r (lost Smith 4–6 6–2 6–2 6–4); ***won*** Prague (d. Zdrazila 6–2 6–3, Stankovic 7–6 7–5, Novacek 6–4 4–6 6–3, Vilas 3–6 6–3 6–3, Smid 6–1 6–3); ***r/u*** Munich (d. Jelen 3–6 6–1 6–1, Eriksson 6–0 3–6 6–0, Kriek 6–2 7–5, Nystrom 6–4 6–4, lost Perez Roldan 6–3 7–6).

CHRISTO VAN RENSBURG (South Africa)
Born Uitenhage, 23 October, 1962, and lives there; RH; 6ft 1in; 165lb; final 1987 ATP ranking 29 singles, 10 (21) doubles; 1987 prize money $210,088.
Coached by Peter Fishbach. No relation to Dinky. ***1983:*** (291) Won South African Jun. ***1984:*** (120) Formed partnership with Annacone in Dec. ***1985:*** (252) Moves into top 10 in doubles after winning 4 GP titles with Annacone, including first GS success at Australian Open. ***1986:*** (69) Reached sf Wimbledon doubles with Annacone but his appearance in last 16 singles there was more surprising. ***1987:*** Won Orlando over Mayotte and Connors in 1st GP f. ***1987 HIGHLIGHTS – SINGLES: Australian Open*** 3r (d. Lavalle 6–3 6–4 0–6 6–4, Hlasek [seed 15] 4–6 6–3 6–3 6–7 6–4, lost Masur 6–3 1–6 7–5 4–6 6–0), ***Wimbledon*** 3r (d. Hogstedt 6–4 6–7 7–6 6–3, Bergstrom 6–3 6–2 6–2, lost E. Sanchez [seed 14] 7–5 6–4 7–6); ***won*** Orlando (d. Giammalva 6–3 6–4, S. Davis 6–0 6–1, Rostagno 2–6 6–1 7–5, Mayotte 2–6 7–6 6–4, Connors 6–3 3–6 6–1); ***sf*** Newport (d. Steyn 6–3 7–6, Wilder 6–1 6–4, Rive 2–6 6–3 6–4, lost Giammalva 6–3 6–1), ***sf*** Stratton Mountain (d. Odizor 6–4 6–3, Giammalva 7–6 6–4, Holmes 6–1 6–4, Visser 6–2 6–3, lost McEnroe 6–4 6–2). ***1987 HIGHLIGHTS – DOUBLES:*** (with Annacone) ***won*** LIPC (d. Gomez/Zivojinovic, Flach/Seguso 6–2 6–4 6–4), ***won*** Chicago (d. DePalmer/Donnelly 6–3 7–6), Stratton Mountain ***divided*** with Flach/Seguso; ***r/u*** Orlando (lost Stewart/Warwick 2–6 7–6 6–4). ***CAREER HIGHLIGHTS – DOUBLES:*** (with Annacone) ***Australian Open – won 1985*** (d. Edmondson/Warwick 3–6 7–6 6–4 6–4); ***LIPC – won 1987.***

DINKY VAN RENSBURG (South Africa)
Born Salisbury, 4 March, 1968; lives Johannesburg; RH; 5ft 7in; 123lb; final 1987 WITA ranking 96; 1987 prize money $33,816.
No relation to Christo. ***1985:*** R/u to Garrone at French Open Jun. ***1986:*** (69) Sf VS Tulsa and had wins over McNeil, Cecchini and Savchenko. ***1987 HIGHLIGHTS – SINGLES: Australian Open*** 1r (lost Inoue 6–3 7–6), ***French Open*** 1r (lost Sukova [seed 5] 6–1 6–1), ***Wimbledon*** 1r (lost Hanika [seed 16] 7–5 6–2), ***US Open*** 2r (d. Villagran 6–2 6–0, lost K. Maleeva 6–2 6–3). ***1987 HIGHLIGHTS – DOUBLES:*** [Horvath] ***r/u*** Athens (lost Betzner/Polzl Wiesner 6–4 7–6).

GUILLERMO VILAS (Argentina)
Born Buenos Aires, 17 August, 1952; lives Mar Del Plata; LH; 5ft 11in; 165lb; final 1987 ATP ranking 71; 1987 prize money $92,504; career prize money $4,839,190.
1974: (5) After a glorious second half of the season featuring six GP tournament triumphs,

he defied those who said he could not play on grass with an astonishing victory in CU Masters in Melbourne, stopping Newcombe, Borg and Nastase. ***1975:*** (2) Won 5 tourns, r/u to Borg at French Open and US Pro, r/u to Ashe in San Francisco and reached qf Wimbledon. ***1976:*** (6) Qf Wimbledon, sf US Open and won six tourns. ***1977:*** (2) Won 15 tourns and set Open tennis record with 50 straight match victories. Routed Gottfried for French Open and halted Connors for US Open crown, and at end of year many experts placed him at No. 1 over Borg and Connors. ***1978:*** (5) Won 7 tourns, including Australian Open and r/u French Open. ***1979:*** (6) Captured 4 tourns, including second straight Australian Open. ***1980:*** (5) Won Italian Open, Kitzbuhel and Palermo. ***1981:*** (6) Won 3 tourns, including Houston and Cairo. ***1982:*** (4) Won 7 tourns, including US Pro, was r/u to Wilander at French Open and reached sf US Open. ***1983:*** (11) After 9 straight years, he dropped out of top 10, but won 3 tourns including WCT Richmond and Delray Beach. Suffered agonising second half of season when notified by Pro Council that he faced a possible one-year suspension for allegedly accepting a $60,000 guarantee to play in Rotterdam. At hearing in New York in Dec. a three-man committee of Forrest Hainline, Bill Talbert and Vic Seixas decided his fine of $20,000 should stand, although his suspension was not enforced. ***1984:*** (28) For the first time since 1972, he did not reach a f. ***1985:*** (39) Sf Boston was his best showing. ***1986:*** (22) Recovering some of his old zest and form, he reached f WCT Forest Hills (d. Nystrom) and qf French Open. ***1987:*** Sf Prague, qf Forest Hills were his best showings. ***1987 HIGHLIGHTS – SINGLES: French Open*** 2r (d. Potier 6–3 7–6 6–4, lost Srejber 6–3 6–4 6–2); ***sf*** Prague (d. Arraya 6–3 6–1, Strelba 6–2 6–0, Korda 6–3 6–2, lost Vajda 3–6 6–3 6–3). ***CAREER HIGHLIGHTS – SINGLES: French Open – won 1977*** (d. S. Smith, Fibak 6–4 6–0 6–4, Ramirez 6–2 6–0 6–3, Gottfried 6–0 6–3 6–0), ***r/u 1975*** (lost Borg 6–2 6–3 6–4), ***r/u 1978*** (lost Borg 6–1 6–1 6–3), ***r/u 1982*** (d. Noah 7–6 6–3 6–4, Higueras 6–1 6–3 7–6, lost Wilander 1–6 7–6 6–0 6–4); ***US Open – won 1977*** (d. Moore 6–1 6–1 6–0, Solomon 6–2 7–6 6–2, Connors 2–6 6–3 7–6 6–0), ***sf 1982*** (d. Denton 3–6 4–6 7–6 6–3 6–3, Tom Gullikson, lost Connors 6–1 3–6 6–2 6–3); ***Australian Open – won 1978*** (d. Roche, Pfister, Marks 6–4 6–4 3–6 6–3), ***won 1979*** (d. Amaya, Sadri 7–6 6–3 6–2), ***r/u 1977*** (lost Tanner 6–3 6–3 6–3); ***Masters – won 1974*** (d. Newcombe, Borg, Parun, Ramirez, Nastase 7–6 6–2 3–6 3–6 6–4), ***sf 1977*** (d. Connors 6–4 3–6 7–5 in rr, lost Borg 6–3 6–3), ***sf 1982*** (d. Gomez, lost McEnroe 6–3 6–3); ***South African Open – won 1977*** (d. Smith, Mottram 7–6 6–3 6–4), ***r/u 1982*** (lost Gerulaitis 7–6 6–2 4–6 7–6); ***Italian Open – won 1980*** seed 1 (d. Ramirez, Teltscher, Noah 6–0 6–4 6–4), ***r/u 1976*** (lost Panatta 2–6 7–6 6–2 7–6), ***r/u 1979*** (lost Gerulaitis 6–7 7–6 6–7 6–4 6–2); ***Nations Cup – won 1980*** (d. Barazzutti, Gehring, Lendl in rr, Borg 6–3 1–6 6–1 in sf, Barazzutti 6–3 6–2 in f as Argentina won); ***US Pro – won 1982*** (d. Noah 6–3 6–2, Purcell 6–4 6–0).

PAUL VOJTISCHEK (West Germany)
Born Olomouc, 13 June, 1963; lives Munich; RH; 6ft 1½in; 176lb; final 1987 ATP ranking 81; 1987 prize money $43,182.
Wife Eva, son Petr. ***1985:*** (355). ***1986:*** (218) Won Riemerling on German Satellite circuit. ***1987:*** Sf Athens and d. Mayotte 1r Tourn of Champs. ***1987 HIGHLIGHTS – SINGLES: French Open*** 1r (lost Mattar 3–6 0–6 6–4 7–5 6–4), ***Wimbledon*** 1r (lost Laurendeau 7–5 6–3 6–0); ***sf*** Athens (d. Agenor 7–5 4–6 7–6, Champion 6–3 3–1 ret'd, Skoff 7–6 6–4, lost Perez Roldan 6–7 6–4 6–2).

ALEKSANDR VOLKOV (USSR)
Born Kaliningrad, 3 March, 1967; lives Moscow; LH; 6ft 2in; 175lb; final 1987 ATP ranking 104; 1987 prize money $39,124.
1986: (529) R/u Nat champs. ***1987:*** Upset Gilbert *en route* to last 16 Wimbledon after qualifying, surprised Jaite at Paris Open and broke into top 100 Nov. ***1987 HIGHLIGHTS – SINGLES: Wimbledon*** last 16, unseeded (d. Stefanki 6–4 4–6 6–3 6–4, Scanlon 7–6 7–6 6–2, Gilbert [seed 12] 7–6 0–6 6–3 6–4, lost Jarryd 7–6 7–5 6–7 6–4), ***US Open*** 1r (lost Bourne 7–5 6–2 3–6 2–6 7–5).

LAURIE WARDER)(Australia)
Born Sydney, 23 October, 1962 and lives there; RH; 6ft; 145lb; final 1987 ATP ranking 311 singles, 18 doubles; 1987 prize money $90,684.
1985: (339). ***1986:*** (281). ***1987:*** A formidable doubles player, he was r/u Australian Open

with Doohan. ***1987 HIGHLIGHTS – SINGLES: Australian Open*** 1r (lost Zivojinovic 6–7 3–6 6–3 6–4 6–1), ***French Open*** 1r (lost Canter 6–4 6–1 5–7 6–2). ***1987 HIGHLIGHTS – DOUBLES:*** (with Doohan unless stated) ***r/u Australian Open*** (d. Flach/Seguso 6–1 3–6 6–1 4–6 10–8, lost Edberg/Jarryd 6–4 6–4 7–6); ***won*** US CC (d. Nystrom/Wilander); ***r/u*** Montreal (lost Cash/Edberg 6–7 6–3 6–4), ***r/u*** Adelaide (lost Lendl/Scanlon 6–7 6–3 6–4), ***r/u*** Sydney (lost Drewett/Edmondson 6–4 4–6 6–2), [Willenborg] ***r/u*** Washington (lost Donnelly/Fleming 6–2 7–6).

MARIANNE WERDEL (USA)
Born Los Angeles, 17 October, 1967; lives Bakersfield; RH; 5ft 10in; 144lb; final 1987 WITA ranking 59; 1987 prize money $37,296.
1983: (221) R/u US Open Jun. ***1985:*** (122) Won USTA Key Biscayne and Fayetteville. ***1986:*** (32) Sf Puerto Rico, played Jun Fed Cup and was All-American at Stanford. ***1987:*** Qf VS New Orleans and Tokyo and upset Shriver 1r VS Washington. ***1987 HIGHLIGHTS – SINGLES: Australian Open*** 3r (d. Vasquez 6–4 6–2, G. Fernandez 6–2 6–3, lost McNeil 6–2 7–5), ***French Open*** 1r (lost Laval 6–2 6–4), ***Wimbledon*** 1r (lost Fairbank 6–2 6–3), ***US Open*** 1r (lost Golarsa 7–5 0–6 6–2).

DAVID WHEATON (USA)
Born Excelsior, Minn., 2 June, 1969; lives Deephaven, Minn.; RH; 6ft 3in; 171lb; final 1987 ATP ranking 345; 1987 prize money $10,549.
1986: A freshman at Stanford, was r/u Nat Jun Champs. ***1987:*** Extended Lendl to 3s at Washington and won US Open Jun singles over Cherkasov. ***1987 HIGHLIGHTS – SINGLES: US Open*** 1r (lost Witsken 7–5 5–7 6–3 6–4).

ANNE WHITE (USA)
Born Charleston, West Va., 28 September, 1961; lives Los Angeles, Cal., RH; 5ft 10½in; 135lb; final 1987 WITA ranking 57 singles, 23 (20) doubles; 1987 prize money $60,415.
Coached by John Lloyd. ***1979:*** Concluded jun career ranked 7 in US 18s. ***1981:*** (41) Turned pro with one year remaining at USC. ***1982:*** (51). ***1983:*** (35) Reached sf Atlanta and Birmingham. ***1984:*** (45) Reached last 16 French Open singles, sf US Open doubles, and qf Wimbledon doubles with Nagelsen. ***1985:*** (20) Sf appearances at New Orleans and Tampa contributed largely to highest-ever year-end status. Reached second GS doubles sf with Nagelsen in Paris, but created biggest stir by appearing in body suit for 1r singles v Shriver at Wimbledon. ***1986:*** (48) Her singles play was below par apart from sf showing in Newport. ***1987:*** Won first singles pro tourn at VS Arizona. ***1987 HIGHLIGHTS – SINGLES: Wimbledon*** 2r (d. Paradis 6–3 7–5, lost Herr 6–1 6–4), ***US Open*** 1r (lost Cecchini 6–4 6–2); ***won*** VS Arizona (d. Gerken 6–3 3–6 7–5, Croft 7–5 6–1, Jolissaint 6–3 6–2, Lindstrom 6–2 6–4, Balestrat 6–1 6–2). ***1987 HIGHLIGHTS – DOUBLES:*** [Piatek] ***won*** VS Dallas (d. Burgin/R. White 7–5 6–3), [R. White] ***won*** Tokyo (d. K./M. Maleeva 6–1 6–2). ***CAREER HIGHLIGHTS – DOUBLES:*** (with Nagelsen) ***French Open – sf 1985*** (lost Navratilova/Shriver 6–3 6–4); ***US Open – sf 1984*** (d. Evert Lloyd/King 7–6 4–6 6–3, lost Navratilova/Shriver 6–4 7–5).

ROBIN WHITE (USA)
Born San Diego, Cal., December 10, 1963; lives San José, Cal.; RH; 5ft 4½in; 125lb; final 1987 WITA ranking 56 singles, 17 (22) doubles; 1987 prize money $99,752.
Coached by John Hubble. ***1984:*** (105) R/u Wimbledon Plate. ***1985:*** (32) Last 16 US Open with win over Gadusek and won VS Hershey. ***1986:*** (20) Won 24 of 42 matches, upsetting Mandlikova and Sabatini to reach sf Eastbourne, and reaching last 16 Wimbledon. Qualified for VS Champ Nov. doubles with G. Fernandez. ***1987:*** Qf New Orleans and won 4 doubles titles. ***1987 HIGHLIGHTS – SINGLES: Australian Open*** 3r, seed 9 (bye, d. Cordwell 6–1 6–4, lost Smylie 6–1 6–2), ***Wimbledon*** 2r (d. Grunfeld 6–1 6–3, lost Sukova [seed 4] 6–2 3–6 6–3), ***US Open*** 2r (d. Mochizuki 7–5 7–5, lost Navratilova [seed 2] 6–1 6–3); ***sf*** Beckenham (lost Potter 6–1 4–6 7–6). ***1987 HIGHLIGHTS – DOUBLES:*** [Fairbank] ***won*** Beckenham (d. Hy/Inoue 6–2 6–2), [K. Jordan] ***won*** California Women's Open (d. Antonoplis/Gerken 6–1 6–0), [A. White] ***won*** Tokyo (d. K./M. Maleeva 6–1 6–2), [Piatek Daniels] ***won*** VS Arkansas (d. Antonoplis/Gerken 6–4 6–3); [Burgin] ***r/u*** VS Dallas (lost Piatek/A. White 7–5 6–3).

WENDY WHITE (USA)
Born Atlanta, 29 September, 1960 and lives there; RH; 5ft 7in; 125lb; final 1987 WITA ranking 35; 1987 prize money $54,428.
1978: Reached qf doubles US Open with K. Jordan. ***1979:*** (39). ***1980:*** (26) Playing for Rollins College in Florida, she won AIAW Champ and then turned pro. ***1982:*** (36) Sf Mahwah. ***1983:*** (34) Reached sf Richmond and qf US Open doubles with Gadusek. ***1984:*** (67) Never passed qf all year. ***1985:*** (95) Still excelled in doubles, but suffered a poor singles year, and took time off at end of year to try new training methods. ***1986:*** (39) Won first career singles title at VS Kansas. ***1987:*** Reached 1st major singles f at Newport. ***1987 HIGHLIGHTS – SINGLES: Wimbledon*** 2r (d. Jaggard 6–2 7–6, lost Bunge [seed 9] 6–4 6–4), ***US Open*** 1r (lost Shriver [seed 5] 6–3 6–3); ***r/u*** VS Newport (d. Cammie MacGregor 6–3 7–6, Henricksson 6–2 7–6, Ludloff 6–3 5–7 6–4, Fairbank 6–3 6–4, lost Shriver 6–2 6–4); ***sf*** VS Kansas (d. Porwik 6–2 6–3, Hu Na 6–3 7–6, Zvereva def., lost Savchenko 5–7 6–2 6–4). ***1987 HIGHLIGHTS – DOUBLES:*** (with Potter) ***r/u*** VS Kansas (lost Parkhomenko/Savchenko 6–2 6–4).

JUDITH POLZL WIESNER (Austria)
Born Hallein, 2 March, 1966; lives Salzburg; RH; 5ft 7in; 142lb; final 1987 WITA ranking 34; 1987 prize money $37,569.
Husband Heinz (married April 1987). Coached by Karel Safarik. ***1985:*** (305). ***1986:*** (142) R/u Kitzbuhel and played Fed Cup. ***1987:*** Sf Bastad and Athens and d. Bunge *en route* to qf VS Arizona and 2r Italian Open. ***1987 HIGHLIGHTS – SINGLES: Australian Open*** 3r (d. Walsh Pete 6–2 6–4, Henricksson 7–6 7–6, lost Durie 6–1 6–4), ***French Open*** 2r (d. Smylie 6–2 6–2, lost Phelps 6–3 6–3), ***Wimbledon*** 2r (d. Provis 5–7 6–1 6–3, lost Moulton 6–4 6–4), ***US Open*** 1r (lost Henricksson 7–6 6–2); ***sf*** Bastad (d. Dinu 6–0 6–3, O'Neill 6–3 6–3, K. Karlsson 6–3 6–1, lost Lindqvist 6–4 6–3), ***sf*** Athens (d. Byrne 6–3 6–1, Ter Riet 6–1 6–2, Tarabini 7–5 6–0, lost K. Maleeva 6–3 6–2). ***1987 HIGHLIGHTS – DOUBLES:*** [Betzner] ***won*** Athens (d. Horvath/Van Rensburg 6–4 7–6).

MATS WILANDER (Sweden)
Born Vaxjo, 22 August, 1964; lives there, Greenwich, Conn., and Monte Carlo; RH; 2HB; 5ft 11½in; 170lb; final 1987 ATP ranking 3 singles, 25 (9) doubles; 1987 prize money $1,164,674; career prize money $5,101,332.
Coached by Jan-Anders Sjogren. Married Sonya Mulholland 3 Jan. 1987. ***1981:*** (68) Won European Jun Champ and French Open Jun. ***1982:*** (7) Became youngest ever to win a GS event when he captured his first GP title at French Open aged 17 years, 9 months, 6 days with wins over Lendl, Gerulaitis, Clerc and Vilas. He was also the first unseeded player to win a GS event in the Open era. ***1983:*** (4) The only player in men's tennis to win tournaments on clay (6), grass (1), indoor (1) and cement (1), he won more tournaments than anyone else (9) including his second GS triumph at Australian Open over McEnroe and Lendl. ***1984:*** (4) Retained his Australian crown and also won Cincinnati and Barcelona. ***1985:*** (3) Won 2nd French Open as well as Boston and Bastad, and was r/u to Edberg at Australian Open. ***1983:*** (3) After winning at least one GS title for four straight years, he lost 3r French Open and 4r Wimbledon and US Open, but won Brussels and Cincinnati in singles, and in doubles with Nystrom won Wimbledon and reached f US Open. ***1987:*** R/u to Lendl French Open, US Open, and Masters; qf Wimbledon, won his first Italian Open crown and titles in Brussels, Monte Carlo, Boston and USCC. ***1987 HIGHLIGHTS – SINGLES: r/u French Open*** seed 4 (d. Colombo 3–6 6–2 6–1 ret'd, Annacone 6–3 6–4 4–6 6–4, Krickstein 6–1 6–7 6–0 6–2, Benhabiles 5–7 6–1 6–3 6–3, Noah [seed 6] 6–4 6–3 6–2, Becker [seed 2] 6–4 6–1 6–2, lost Lendl [seed 1] 7–5 6–2 3–6 7–6), ***Wimbledon*** qf, seed 3 (d. Muller 6–2 6–1 6–4, Gunnarsson 6–2 6–1 6–2, Svensson 7–6 6–1 6–3, E. Sanchez [seed 14] 2–6 7–6 6–3 7–5, lost Cash [seed 11] 6–3 7–5 6–4), ***r/u US Open*** seed 3 (d. Ross 6–1 6–1 6–1, J. Carlsson 6–2 6–3 6–1, Pimek 6–2 6–0 6–1, Flach 6–3 6–3 7–6, Mecir [seed 5] 6–3 6–7 6–4 7–6, Edberg [seed 2] 6–4 3–6 6–3 6–4, lost Lendl [seed 1] 6–7 6–0 7–6 6–4); ***won*** Brussels (d. Masso 7–5 6–2, Kratzmann 6–0 6–2, Bloom 5–7 6–3 6–2, J. B. Svensson 6–3 6–2, McEnroe 6–3 6–4), ***won*** Monte Carlo (d. Gunnarsson 6–3 6–2, Tulasne 7–5 6–3, Chesnokov 6–1 6–3, Stenlund 6–2 6–2, Arias 4–6 7–5 6–1 6–3), ***won*** Italian Open (d. Chesnokov 6–2 6–3, Mattar 6–2 6–1, Motta 6–3 6–2, Gomer 6–1 7–6, McEnroe 6–1 6–3, Jaite 6–3 6–4 6–4), ***won*** Boston (d. Hogstedt 6–2 7–5, Davin 6–2 6–2,

Nijssen 6–2 7–5, Jaite 0–6 7–5 6–0, K. Carlsson 7–6 6–1), ***won*** US CC (d. Shiras 6–1 7–5, Perez 7–5 7–5, Reneberg 6–4 6–4, Nystrom 6–4 7–5, K. Carlsson 7–5 6–3); ***r/u*** Barcelona (d. Windahl 6–3 7–6, Aguilera 6–4 7–5, Carbonell 6–0 6–3, Perez Roldan 6–3 6–0, lost Jaite 7–6 6–4 4–6 0–6 6–4), ***r/u*** Masters (d. Mecir 6–4 6–1, Cash 7–6 6–3, lost Edberg in rr, d. Edberg 6–2 4–6 6–3, lost Lendl 6–2 6–2 6–3); ***sf*** Indian Wells (d. Casal, Srejber 3–6 6–0 6–4, Hlasek 6–3 6–0, lost Edberg 6–1 7–5), ***sf*** Milan (d. Skoff 6–3 6–7 6–3, Gunnarsson 6–3 6–4, E. Sanchez 6–3 6–1, lost Mecir 6–0 6–2), ***sf*** Bastad (d. Perez 7–5 4–6 6–3, Luna 6–2 6–3, Gunnarsson 6–4 7–6, lost Nystrom 6–3 6–2). ***1987 HIGHLIGHTS – DOUBLES:*** (with Nystrom) ***won*** Boston (d. Gildemeister/Gomez 7–6 3–6 6–1); ***r/u*** US CC (lost Warder/Willenborg 6–0 6–3). ***CAREER HIGHLIGHTS – SINGLES: French Open – won 1982*** unseeded (d. Lendl 4–6 7–5 3–6 6–4 6–2, Gerulaitis 6–3 6–3 4–6 6–4, Clerc 7–5 6–2 1–6 7–5, Vilas 1–6 7–6 [saving one s-p] 6–0 6–4), ***won 1985*** (d. Leconte, McEnroe [seed 1] 6–1 5–7 7–5, Lendl [seed 2] 3–6 6–4 6–2 6–2), ***r/u 1983*** (d. Sundstrom, McEnroe 1–6 6–2 6–4 6–0, Higueras, lost Noah 6–2 7–5 7–6), ***r/u 1987, sf 1984*** (lost Lendl 6–3 6–3 7–5); ***Australian Open – won 1983*** (d. McEnroe 4–6 6–3 6–4 6–3, Lendl 6–1 6–4), ***won 1984*** (d. Curren 6–7 6–4 7–6 6–2), ***r/u 1985*** (d. Kriek, Zivojinovic, lost Edberg 6–4 6–3 6–3); ***US Open – r/u 1987, sf 1985*** (d. Annacone, Holmes, Jarryd 2–6 6–2 5–0 ret'd, lost McEnroe [seed 1] 3–6 6–4 4–6 6–3 6–3), ***qf 1984*** (lost Cash 7–6 6–4 2–6 6–3); ***Masters – r/u 1987, sf 1983*** (lost McEnroe 6–2 6–4), ***sf 1984*** (lost McEnroe 6–1 6–1). ***CAREER HIGHLIGHTS – DOUBLES:*** (with Nystrom) ***Wimbledon – won 1986*** (d. Donnelly/Fleming 7–6 6–3 6–3); ***US Open – r/u 1986*** (lost Gomez/Zivojinovic 4–6 6–3 6–3 4–6 6–3), ***sf 1985*** (lost Leconte/Noah 6–3 7–6 6–4); ***Australian Open – r/u 1984*** (lost Cash/Fitzgerald 6–4 6–4 2–6 6–3); ***French Open – sf 1985*** (lost Edmondson/Warwick 6–4 6–1 7–5).

TIM WILKISON (USA)
Born Shelby, NC, 21 November, 1959; lives Asheville, NC; LH; 5ft 11in; 160lb; final 1987 ATP ranking 55; 1987 prize money $127,953.
Coached by Woody Blocher. Wife Vicki. ***1976:*** (360) Won US Nat 16. ***1977:*** (114) Won US Nat 21. ***1978:*** (54) Won NSW Open. ***1979:*** (73) Won Auckland. ***1980:*** (85) R/u Auckland. ***1981:*** (67) R/u Auckland and won NSW. ***1982:*** (55) Won Auckland. ***1983:*** (103) Reached qf Rotterdam and Tampa. ***1984:*** (39) Won Vienna, r/u North Conway and Basle. ***1985:*** (44) Won Nancy. ***1986:*** (29) Enjoyed finest GS showing at US Open when he reached qf unseeded, upsetting Noah before falling to Edberg; r/u Atlanta and Newport. ***1987:*** Twice underwent arthroscopic surgery on right knee. Last 16 Australian Open, r/u Bristol. ***1987 HIGHLIGHTS – SINGLES: Australian Open*** last 16, seed 14 (bye, d. Barr 6–2 6–2 3–6 7–6, Edmondson 6–2 6–1 7–6, lost Noah [seed 3] 4–6 4–6 6–3 6–4 6–2), ***Wimbledon*** 2r (d. Pugh 7–5 6–7 6–4 6–4, lost Mayotte [seed 10] 6–3 4–6 6–7 6–2 6–4), ***US Open*** 1r (lost Becker [seed 4] 4–6 4–6 7–5 6–4 6–2); ***r/u*** Bristol (d. Acioly 7–5 2–6 6–2, Frawley 6–1 ret'd, Testerman 6–7 6–2 6–2, Schapers 4–6 6–4 10–8, lost Evernden 6–4 7–6); ***sf*** Los Angeles (d. Giammalva 6–7 6–4 6–2, Muller 6–4 6–4, M. Davis 4–6 7–6 6–4, lost Edberg 6–2 6–3), ***sf*** Toulouse (d. de la Pena 6–0 6–1, Woodforde 5–7 6–4 7–6, Potier 6–4 6–7 6–3, lost Osterthun 5–7 6–4 6–2). ***1987 HIGHLIGHTS – DOUBLES:*** [Purcell] ***won*** Vienna (d. E./J. Sanchez 6–3 7–5); [Gilbert] ***r/u*** Los Angeles (lost Curren/Pate 6–3 6–4). ***CAREER HIGHLIGHTS – SINGLES: US Open – qf 1986*** unseeded (d. Skoff 7–6 6–2 6–0, McNamee 6–1 6–2 6–1, Noah [seed 5] 7–6 3–6 4–6 6–1 6–4, Chesnokov 6–0 6–2 6–3, lost Edberg [seed 4] 6–3 6–3 6–3).

BLAINE WILLENBORG (USA)
Born Miami, Fla., 4 January, 1960; lives Miami Shore; RH; 5ft 7in; 150lb; final 1987 ATP ranking 145 singles, 17 doubles; 1987 prize money $64,988.
1984: (79) Qf North Conway. ***1985:*** (188). ***1986:*** (160) Enjoyed success in doubles with a variety of partners. ***1987 HIGHLIGHTS – SINGLES: French Open*** 1r (lost Stenlund 6–2 6–2 6–2). ***1987 HIGHLIGHTS – DOUBLES:*** (with Warder unless stated) [Pugh] ***won*** Munich (d. Casal/E. Sanchez 7–6 4–6 6–4), ***won*** US CC (d. Nystrom/Wilander 6–0 6–3); [Panatta] ***r/u*** Bologna (lost Casal/E. Sanchez 6–3 6–2), ***r/u*** Washington (lost Donnelly/Fleming 6–2 7–6).

Above left: *Four titles enabled Robin White to improve her doubles ranking to 17.* **Above right:** *Wendy White reached her first major singles final at Newport.* **Below:** *Kathy Jordan suffered a string of injuries in 1987.* *(Carol L. Newsom, T. Hindley)*

ERIC WINOGRADSKY (France)
Born Paris, 22 April, 1966; lives Agen; RH; 6ft 3in; 177lb; final 1987 ATP ranking 131; 1987 prize money $43,621.
Coached by Georges Goven. ***1985:*** (255). ***1986:*** (156) Won 2 titles on French satellite circuit. ***1987:*** Upset Edberg in ss 2r French Open, reached qf Bristol and won Vienna Challenger. Married Angelique Mateu 12 Dec. ***1987 HIGHLIGHTS – SINGLES: French Open*** 3r (d. Freeman 7–6 7–5 6–3, Edberg [seed 3] 7–6 7–6 7–5, lost Novacek 6–1 6–0 2–6 6–4), ***US Open*** 2r (d. Kennedy 6–4 7–5 2–6 7–6, lost Pimek 6–4 6–0 6–4); ***won*** Vienna Challenger (d. Woodforde 6–3 6–2).

TODD WOODBRIDGE (Australia)
Born Sydney, 2 April, 1971; lives Woolooware; RH; 5ft 10in; 150lb; final 1987 ATP ranking 420; 1987 prize money $860.
1987: R/u Australian Open Jun to Stoltenberg with whom he won the doubles there and at Wimbledon.

MARK WOODFORDE (Australia)
Born Adelaide, 23 September, 1965 and lives there; LH; 6ft 2in; 164lb; final 1987 ATP ranking 67; 1987 prize money $79,454.
Coached by Barry Phillips-Moore. ***1984:*** (385). ***1985:*** (127). ***1986:*** (181) Won 1st pro title at Auckland, sf Bristol. ***1987:*** Last 16 US Open (d. Mayotte) after qualifying. ***1987 HIGHLIGHTS – SINGLES: Australian Open*** 2r (d. Baroch 6–3 6–4 6–4, lost Muller 7–5 5–7 4–6 7–6 6–4), ***Wimbledon*** 2r (d. K. Jones 4–6 3–6 6–3 6–3 6–1, lost Mecir [seed 5] 6–1 6–3 6–3), ***US Open*** last 16, unseeded (d. Scanlon 6–2 6–4 6–2, Mayotte [seed 12] 7–6 7–6 3–6 2–6 7–6, Srejber 6–2 6–1 6–1, lost Mecir [seed 5] 6–3 3–6 6–2 6–2). ***1987 HIGHLIGHTS – DOUBLES:*** [Limberger] ***r/u*** Auckland (lost Jones/Pearce 6–7 6–7), [Cahill] ***r/u*** Bordeaux (lost Casal/E. Sanchez).

JAIME YZAGA (Peru)
Born Lima, 23 October, 1967, and lives there; RH; 5ft 7in; 134lb; final 1987 ATP ranking 70; 1987 prize money $114,979.
Coached by Colar Nunez. Has suffered from recurring shoulder injury since 1982. ***1984:*** Joined Peruvian D Cup squad. ***1985:*** (45) Won French Jun and Wimbledon Jun doubles before bursting into last 16 US Open, after qualifying, where he was the only player to take a set off Lendl. ***1986:*** (64) Played D Cup for Peru, scored wins over Hlasek, Pecci and Pate and reached sf Tokyo. ***1987:*** Won first GP singles title at Schenectady, following with Sao Paulo. ***1987 HIGHLIGHTS – SINGLES: French Open*** 1r (lost Buckley 2–6 6–1 6–4 7–6), ***Wimbledon*** 1r (lost Jelen 7–6 0–6 6–2 4–6 6–2), ***US Open*** 3r (d. Hogstedt 6–3 6–2 7–6, Smid 6–3 6–4 6–1, lost Svensson 2–6 6–4 3–6 6–2 6–2); ***won*** Schenectady (d. Moraing 6–7 6–3 6–1, M. Davis 5–7 6–2 6–2, Lapidus 6–2 6–0, Mmoh 6–3 6–2, Pugh 0–6 7–6 6–1), ***won*** Sao Paulo (d. Casal 6–3 6–4, Daher 7–6 6–3, Saad 6–4 7–6, Berger 6–2 6–1, Mattar 6–2 4–6 6–2).

SLOBODAN ZIVOJINOVIC (Yugoslavia)
Born Belgrade, 23 July, 1963; lives Monte Carlo; RH; 6ft 4in; 223lb; final 1987 ATP ranking 22 singles, 14 (2) doubles; 1987 prize money $256,824.
Wife Zorcia, son Filip. Coached by brother Ceda (born 1948). ***1985:*** (35) Having proved his potential by capturing Yugoslav Nat Champ in 12, 13, 14, 16, 18 and 21 categories, he burst into prominence by upsetting 4th-seeded Wilander in 1r Wimbledon and then stunning No. 2 seed McEnroe in qf Australian Open before falling to Wilander in sf. ***1986:*** (40) Displaying again his superior grass-court skills, he surged into Wimbledon sf where he extended Lendl to 5 hard sets, and then won first GS trophy in US Open doubles with Gomez, and first GP singles at Houston. ***1987:*** Last 16 Wimbledon; sf Milan, Tourn of Champs, Sydney, Tokyo Seiko. ***1987 HIGHLIGHTS – SINGLES: Australian Open*** 3r (d. Warder 6–7 3–6 6–3 6–4 6–1, Limberger 6–1 6–4 6–2, lost Becker [seed 2] 6–7 6–1 6–4 6–7 6–2), ***French Open*** 1r (lost E. Sanchez 6–4 6–3 3–6 7–6), ***Wimbledon*** last 16, unseeded (d. Flur 3–6 6–3 6–4 6–0, Pate [seed 15] 3–6 7–6 6–4 6–1, Bates 7–6 7–5 7–6, Doohan 6–2 6–4 7–6, lost Connors [seed 7] 7–6 7–5 6–3), ***US Open*** 3r (d. Mezzadri 6–3 6–0 6–4, Dyke 2–6 4–6 6–1 6–2 6–0, lost McEnroe [seed 8] 6–4 5–7 6–7 6–4 6–3); ***sf*** Milan (d. J. B. Svensson 6–7

Former South African Johan Kriek, Australian Open Champion of 1981 and 1982, won Livingston for his first title since 1985, and reached the last 16 at Wimbledon to take his career prize money past $2 million. *(A. Evans)*

6–3 6–2, Drewett 7–6 6–3, Cane 6–1 6–1, lost Becker 6–2 3–6 6–2), ***sf*** Tourn of Champs (d. Dickson 7–6 4–6 7–5, Banck, Wostenholme, Annacone 5–7 7–5 6–4, lost Noah 6–3 7–5), ***sf*** Sydney (d. Mmoh 4–6 6–3 6–1, Saceanu 6–3 6–4, M. Davis 7–5 6–4, lost Lendl 6–3 7–5), ***sf*** Tokyo Seiko (d. Rive 6–4 7–5, Mmoh 6–2 6–3, Becker 6–3 1–6 3–0 ret'd, lost Edberg 7–6 4–6 6–2). ***1987 HIGHLIGHTS – DOUBLES:*** (with Becker) ***won*** Brussels (d. Hooper/Leach 6–7 6–7), ***won*** Milan (d. Casal/E. Sanchez 3–6 6–3 6–4). ***CAREER HIGHLIGHTS – SINGLES: Wimbledon – sf 1986*** unseeded (d. Youl, Wostenholme, Flach, Van Rensburg, Krishnan 6–2 7–6 4–6 6–3, lost Lendl [seed 1] 6–2 6–7 6–3 6–7 6–4); ***Australian Open – sf 1985*** (d. McEnroe 6–0 5s, lost Wilander 7–5 6–1 6–3). ***CAREER HIGHLIGHTS – DOUBLES:*** (with Gomez) ***US Open – won 1986*** (d. Nystrom/Wilander 4–6 6–3 6–3 4–6 6–3).

NATALIA ZVEREVA (USSR)

Born Minsk, 16 April, 1971, and lives there; RH; 2HB; 5ft 5in; 125lb; final 1987 WITA ranking 19; final 1987 prize money $64,333.

Nicknamed Natasha. Coached by Anatoli Volkov and Olga Morozova. Amateur. ***1985:*** Won Bethesda on USTA circuit and World Jun Champs. ***1986:*** (92) In singles won Soviet Nat Champs (d. Savchenko), won Wimbledon Jun singles, USTA Bethesda, and was r/u to Rinaldi at VS Arkansas after qualifying, becoming youngest player to reach f of VS Series event, at 15 years 7 months. In doubles won French Open Jun and r/u Wimbledon Jun with Meskhi. ***1987:*** ITF Jun Champ; won Nat Champ, Jun singles at French Open, Wimbledon and US Open and Jun doubles at French Open and Wimbledon with Medvedeva. Did not compete in Australian Open Jun. Last 16 Wimbledon, beating McNeil and extending Sabatini to 3s, won Taranto on Italian Satellite and reached f in Arkansas and Chicago in consecutive weeks. ***1987 HIGHLIGHTS – SINGLES: French Open*** 3r (d. Mesker 6–3 6–3, Suire 6–7 6–3 6–0, lost Sukova [seed 5] 6–1 6–3), ***Wimbledon*** last 16, unseeded (d. Ludloff 6–2 6–4, McNeil [seed 10] 6–4 6–4, Henricksson 6–3 6–3, lost Sabatini [seed 6] 6–0 2–6 6–4), ***US Open*** 3r (d. Pfaff 6–3 6–3, Smylie 6–3 6–2, lost Evert [seed 3] 6–0 6–2); ***won*** Taranto (d. Lundqvist, Segura, Lapi 6–2 6–0, Zrubakova 6–2 6–2, Rajchrtova 7–6 4–6 6–3); ***r/u*** Arkansas (d. Cammie MacGregor 6–2 6–3, E. Minter 6–3 6–1, Gerken 6–0 6–3, Savchenko 6–3 6–1, lost Cecchini 0–6 6–1 6–3), ***r/u*** VS Chicago (d. Nagelsen 6–3 6–2, Kohde-Kilsch 6–4 6–2, Gompert 5–7 6–4 6–0, Potter 6–4 2–6 6–4, lost Navratilova 6–1 6–2).

ALL-TIME GREATS

David Gray and John Barrett

WILMER LAWSON ALLISON (USA)
Born 8/1/04. Died 30/4/77. One of the greatest and most spectacular of American doubles specialists, he also gained some notable singles successes. Possessing a fierce smash, a serve 'with the kick of a Texas mustang', considerable power on the volley, and a fine backhand drive, he found an ideal doubles partner in John Van Ryn. They won at Wimbledon in ***1929–30*** and were runners-up in ***1935.*** They took the US title in ***1931*** and ***1935*** and reached the final in ***1930/32/34/36.*** His singles form was less consistent, but on his day he could play brilliantly. He defeated Perry to win the US title in ***1935,*** and in ***1930,*** after beating Cochet, he was runner-up to Tilden at Wimbledon. Between ***1929–35*** he played in 45 D Cup rubbers, winning 18 out of 29 singles and 14 of his 16 doubles.

JOSEPH ASBOTH (Hungary)
Born 18/9/17. A stylish righthander whose victory in the ***1947*** French singles, when he beat Petra, Tom Brown and Sturgess, was Hungary's most important tennis success before their victory in the Saab King's Cup in 1976; 7 times nat champ; 6 times winner of the Hungarian int title; he played 1st at Wimbledon in ***1939*** and impressed those who saw him against Austin in 1 r. Lost to Bromwich in the ***1948*** sfs. From ***1938–57*** he played 41 D Cup rubbers in 16 ties.

ARTHUR ROBERT ASHE (USA)
Born 10/7/43. A cool, thoughtful, dogged competitor, he was the first black American to win the Wimbledon men's singles title and, in ***1968,*** playing as an amateur, he became the first US Open champion. Always happier on fast courts, he tried hard to succeed on clay but endured regular disappointments in Paris and never progressed further than the semi-finals ***(1971)*** in Rome. He was a semi-finalist at Wimbledon ***1968–69*** before surprising Connors in the ***1975*** final. He defeated Okker to win the US title in ***1968*** but in ***1972*** lost to Nastase after leading by two sets to one and 4–2 in the final. He won Australian singles ***1970*** and the WCT title ***1975.*** Refused a visa to South Africa in 1970, he broke through apartheid laws to play in Johannesburg ***1973,*** losing to Connors in the final and winning the doubles with Okker. After missing most of the 1977 season, he regained his place among the leaders of the circuit in ***1978*** and reached match-point against McEnroe in the Masters final. Between ***1963*** and ***1978,*** he appeared in 18 Davis Cup ties, winning 27 out of 32 singles and one of two doubles. US Davis Cup captain ***1980–85,*** following his retirement from active play owing to a heart condition that had necessitated triple bypass surgery.

CILLY AUSSEM (Germany)
Born 4/1/09. Died 22/3/63. Later the Contessa della Corta Brae. The only German to win the women's singles at Wimbledon. Her strokes were not strong but she was a model of steadiness and persistence. 'Quite small and more of a girl in appearance with round brown eyes and a cherub face', wrote Helen Wills. 'Her agility on court and the distance that she covers in spite of her shortness are really astonishing.' ***1931*** – when the Californian did not compete – was her best year. She beat Betty Nuthall in the French f and then defeated Hilde Krahwinkel in Wimbledon's only all-German final. That was a disappointing match, because both women were handicapped by blistered feet. Her victory compen-

sated for an unlucky failure in ***1930.*** Then she slipped and sprained an ankle at 4–4 in the fs of her sf against Elizabeth Ryan and had to be carried from the court.

HENRY WILFRED AUSTIN (Great Britain)
Born 20/8/06. Bunny Austin's Wimbledon record was remarkable (and unlucky), but his most important contribution to British tennis was in the D Cup. The possessor of elegant groundstrokes, which compensated for a lack of power in his serving and smashing, he played many of the crucial singles, alongside Perry, in Britain's successful campaigns in the 1930s. A former Cambridge Univ captain, he played in 24 ties between ***1929–37,*** winning 36 of his 48 rubbers, all singles. He won 8 rubbers out of 12 and 5 out of 8 'live' rubbers in his 6 Challenge Rounds. At Wimbledon he failed only once to reach the qf or go further between ***1929–39.*** R/u to Vines ***1932*** and Budge ***1938,*** in sf ***1929*** and ***1936/37,*** and r/u to Henkel in ***1937*** French singles.

WILFRED BADDELEY (Great Britain)
Born 11/1/1872. Died 30/1/1929. Youngest winner – at 19 years, 5 months and 23 days – of Wimbledon singles in ***1891*** until Becker in 1985. Also won singles in ***1892/95,*** and doubles (with twin brother Herbert) ***1891/94/95/96.***

MARCEL BERNARD (France)
Born 18/6/14. Shrewd and stylish, a canny lefthander with considerable touch, he is one of only two French players to have won in Paris since the days of the 'Musketeers' (the other is Noah, 1983); demonstrated his promise early, reaching the French singles sf and, with Boussus, the doubles in ***1932,*** still in sufficient form to be chosen for the French D Cup team in ***1956.*** In ***1946*** he won 5 set matches against Petra in the sf and Drobny in the final to take the French title; in sf on 3 other occasions; won the doubles with Borotra ***(1936)*** and with Petra ***(1946)*** and the mixed with Lollette Payot ***(1935)*** and Billie Yorke ***(1936).*** Between ***1935–56*** he played 42 D Cup rubbers in 25 ties and he has also served as president of the French Tennis Federation.

PAULINE MAY BETZ (USA)
Born 6/8/19. Now Mrs Addie. An agile, athletic competitor, who might have gained many more titles if the war had not interrupted international competition. She was ranked eighth in the US in ***1939*** and was the most successful player in wartime competitions there, winning the national title from ***1942–44.*** She won Wimbledon at a cost of only 20 games in ***1946,*** defeating Louise Brough 6–2 6–4 in the final. She and Miss Hart were runners-up to Miss Brough and Miss Osborne in the doubles and, if she was disappointed in Paris, where Miss Osborne beat her 1–6 8–6 7–5 in the final, after saving two match-points with drop-shots at 5–6 in the second set, she asserted her supremacy again at Forest Hills by defeating Doris Hart 11–9 6–3 in the final. Soon afterwards she turned professional.

BLANCHE BINGLEY (Great Britain)
Born 3/11/1863. Died 6/8/1946. Became Mrs Hillyard. One of the determined pioneers of women's tennis. She competed in the first women's tournament at Wimbledon in ***1884*** and lost to Maud Watson, the eventual champion, in sfs. The following year Miss Watson defeated her in f, but she avenged those failures by beating the champion in the challenge round in ***1886.*** That was the first of her six victories. Further successes followed in ***1889, 1894, 1897, 1899*** and ***1900.*** Only Lottie Dod, who retired in 1893, troubled her until Mrs Sterry ended her supremacy in 1901. Like many early players, her game was founded on a powerful forehand and strict command of length. A reluctant volleyer who invariably ran round her backhand, she was so quick and so fit that she was difficult to outmanoeuvre. She wore white gloves to give her a better grip and her follow-through on the forehand was said to have been so complete 'that her left shoulder was often a mass of bruises from the impact of the racket'. She

married Commander G. W. Hillyard, secretary of the All England Club from 1907–24; altogether she competed in the championships 24 times.

PENELOPE DORA HARVEY BOOTHBY (Great Britain)
Born 2/8/1881. Died 22/2/1970. Became Mrs Green. One of the group of players from the county of Middlesex who dominated the early years of women's tennis at Wimbledon. She won one of the most exciting of the pre-1914 f, defeating Miss A. M. Morton 6–4 4–6 8–6 ('Few closer or more interesting struggles have ever been witnessed on the famous old court', wrote G. W. Hillyard) in ***1909,*** and lost the most dismal in the history of the championships to Mrs Lambert Chambers, who beat her 6–0 6–0, in the ***1911*** challenge round. Mrs Lambert Chambers had beaten her by the same score at the Beckenham tournament two weeks earlier and had allowed her only four games in the challenge round in ***1910.*** Somewhat fortunately she and Mrs McNair became Wimbledon's first women's doubles champions in 1913. They were down 2–6 2–4 to Mrs Lambert Chambers and Mrs Sterry in the final when Mrs Sterry fell and retired with a torn tendon. She and Mrs McNair were also semi-finalists in ***1922.***

BJORN BORG (Sweden)
Born 6/6/56. One of the coolest match players the game has ever known, he matured early, winning his first important title, the ***1974*** Italian Open, shortly before his 18th birthday and the first of his six French Championships just after it. With fierce topspin on both his forehand and his double-handed backhand, a powerful serve and speedy court coverage plus an indomitable will to win, he was virtually invincible on European clay between ***1974*** and ***1981*** adding the French Open in ***1975, 1978, 1979, 1980*** and ***1981*** and a second Italian title in ***1978*** as well as the US Pro Championship on US clay in ***1974, 1975*** and ***1976***. Never an instinctive volleyer, he confounded those observers who thought his game was unsuited to grass by setting a modern record at Wimbledon where he won five successive titles between ***1976*** and ***1980***. Only William Renshaw, in the days of the Challenge Round, won more (1881–86). He learned to win indoors, taking the WCT title in ***1976*** and the Masters twice ***(1979*** and ***1980)*** and leading Sweden to their first D Cup success, a 3–2 victory over Czechoslovakia in Stockholm in ***1975***. But he never solved the problems of the high, fast bounce and positive foothold of US hard courts. Four times he was beaten in the US Open final, twice by Connors ***(1976, 1978)*** and twice by McEnroe ***(1980, 1981)***, the last three being on asphalt at Flushing Meadow. By the autumn of ***1981*** this great champion felt burnt out and virtually retired from the mainstream, restricting his play to exhibitions and special events. Although he attempted two comebacks, in ***1982*** and ***1984***, he could no longer make the total commitment that had once made him supreme and turned to other interests. His legacy to Swedish tennis is immeasurable for he sparked the flame that has burned so brightly ever since through Wilander, Sundstrom, Jarryd, Nystrom and Edberg. His style of errorless, counter-attacking topspin inspired a whole generation of players around the world.–J.B.

JEAN BOROTRA (France)
Born 13/8/1898. A brilliantly agile volleyer and a shrewd player. One of the 'Four Musketeers' who won the D Cup for France from ***1927–32.*** Enthusiastic and popular, he continued to play competitive lawn tennis long past his 80th year, regularly appearing for France in International Club matches against Britain. Won Wimbledon singles ***1924*** and ***1926*** and doubles (with R. Lacoste) ***1925*** and (with J. Brugnon) ***1932/33.*** French singles ***1924/31,*** and doubles ***1925/28/29/34/36.*** Won Australian singles and doubles ***1928.*** Had long and spectacular covered court record, winning French singles title 12 times, British 11, and US 4. Played 54 D Cup rubbers ***1922–47,*** winning 36 in 32 ties.

MAUREEN CONNOLLY BRINKER (USA)
Born 17/9/34. Died 21/6/69. The most determined and concentrated of post-war women's champions she hit her groundstrokes with remorseless accuracy. Won US singles in ***1951*** at the age of 16 and thereafter lost only 4 matches – 2 to Doris Hart, one to Shirley Fry,

and another to Beverley Fleitz – before she broke her leg in a riding accident in 1954 and retired. She was never beaten in singles at Wimbledon, winning ***1952/53/54.*** US singles ***1951/52/53.*** French singles ***1953/54*** and (with Mrs H. C. Hopman) doubles ***1954.*** Australian singles and doubles (with Julie Sampson) ***1953.*** Italian singles ***1954.*** She won all 9 of her W Cup rubbers and in ***1953*** she was the first woman to bring off the Grand Slam of the 4 major singles titles in the same year.

JOHN EDWARD BROMWICH (Australia)
Born 14/11/18. A gracefully unorthodox player whose career might have been even more successful if it had not been interrupted by World War II. Ambidextrous but using both hands on the forehand, he used a very light, softly strung racket to control the ball with great subtlety. He won the Australian singles in ***1939*** and regained the title from Quist in ***1946.*** Those were his only major singles victories, although he was agonisingly close to success in f of ***1948*** Wimbledon when he lost to Falkenburg after leading 5–2 in the fs and holding three match-points. But it was in doubles, mostly with Quist or Sedgman, that he earned most honours. He won at Wimbledon in ***1948*** (with Sedgman) ***/50*** (with Quist), took the US title three times, and he and Quist ruled in Australia from ***1938–40*** and ***1946–50.*** Won the Wimbledon mixed with Louise Brough, ***1947/48,*** and played in 53 D Cup rubbers between ***1937–50.***

SIR NORMAN EVERARD BROOKES (Australia)
Born 14/11/1877. Died 10/1/1968. The first overseas winner of men's singles at Wimbledon. Left-handed and a notable volleyer, he lost to H. L. Doherty in Challenge Round on first visit to Wimbledon 1905. Won singles and doubles (with A. F. Wilding) ***1907*** and ***1914*** and Australian singles in ***1911*** and doubles in ***1924*** with J. O. Anderson. With Wilding won the D Cup for Australasia in ***1907.*** Between ***1905–20*** he played 39 rubbers and was 6 times a member of a side which won the Challenge Round. Returned to Wimbledon in ***1924*** at 46 and reached the 4r.

ALTHEA LOUISE BROUGH (USA)
Born 11/3/23. Now Mrs Clapp. An aggressive server and volleyer, she played a major part in establishing American domination of women's tennis immediately after World War II. Won Wimbledon singles ***1948/49/50*** and again in ***1955*** after the retirement of Maureen Connolly, who beat her in ***1952*** and ***1954*** f, US in ***1947,*** and Australian, ***1950.*** She and Margaret Osborne du Pont formed a redoubtable doubles partnership, winning 5 times at Wimbledon and 3 times in Paris, and holding the US title from ***1942–50*** and ***1955/56/57.*** She was mixed doubles champ at Wimbledon ***1946/47/48/50*** and took all 3 titles in ***1948*** and ***1950.*** She played 22 W Cup rubbers between ***1946–57*** and was never beaten.

JACQUES BRUGNON (France)
Born 11/6/1895. Died 20/3/1978. The doubles specialist of the 'Four Musketeers', he gained most of his early success with Cochet and then formed a partnership with Borotra, which was still capable of reaching the ***1939*** French f, when he was 44 and Borotra 40, and coming three times within a point of the title. He and Borotra returned to Wimbledon and reached the 3r in ***1948.*** Won Wimbledon doubles ***1926/28*** (Cochet) ***/32/33*** (Borotra). Between ***1927–34*** won French doubles 3 times with Cochet and twice with Borotra. Also Australian doubles (with Borotra) in ***1928.*** Reached singles sf at Wimbledon, ***1926.*** Played 31 D Cup doubles and 6 singles ***1921–34.***

JOHN DONALD BUDGE (USA)
Born 13/6/15. The first player to bring off the Grand Slam of the 4 historic singles titles in one year – ***1938.*** A relentless competitor with a majestic backhand he won all 3 titles at Wimbledon in ***1937*** and ***1938.*** Won doubles (with G. Mako) and mixed (with Alice Marble). US singles ***1937/38*** and doubles (with Mako) ***1936/38.*** French and Australian singles ***1938*** and between ***1935–38*** won 25 out of 29 D Cup rubbers in 11 ties. Turned professional in ***1938.***

MARIA ESTHER ANDION BUENO (Brazil)
Born 11/10/39. The most gracefully artistic of post-war women's champions. For nearly a decade her rivalry with Margaret Court provided the principal excitement of the women's game, but at the end she was plagued by injury. Won Wimbledon singles ***1959/60/64,*** and doubles (with Althea Gibson) ***1958,*** (with Darlene Hard) ***1960/63,*** (with Billie Jean King) ***/65,*** and (with Nancy Gunter) ***/66.*** US singles ***1959/63/64/66*** and doubles (with Darlene Hard) ***1960/62,*** (with Nancy Gunter) ***/66,*** and (with Margaret Court) ***/68.*** French doubles (with Darlene Hard) ***1960.*** Australian doubles (with Christine Truman) ***1960.*** Italian singles, ***1958/61/65.***

MAY SUTTON BUNDY (USA)
Born in Plymouth, England, 25/9/1886. Died 4/10/1975. In ***1905*** the first overseas player to win a Wimbledon title. The seventh and youngest child of a British naval officer, Captain A. de G. Sutton, she learnt tennis on asphalt courts after her family moved to California in 1893. She was forceful and vigorous with a disconcerting top-spin forehand. F. R. Burrow commented: 'She took a deep breath before every stroke and then hit the ball with all her force to the accompaniment of a very audible expiration.' After winning the US singles and doubles in ***1904*** she went, aged 18, to Wimbledon ***1905*** and defeated the holder, Miss Douglass, in the Challenge Round. Miss Douglass regained the title the following year, but then lost a third battle with the Californian in ***1907.*** After winning the US Clay Court singles ***1912,*** Miss Sutton married Thomas Bundy, 3 times a US doubles champ. She played doubles in the ***1925*** W Cup and in ***1929*** returned to Wimbledon at 42 to defeat Eileen Bennett, seeded 4, and reach the qf. She was still playing 44 years later. Her daughter Dorothy represented the US 3 times in the W Cup and won the Australian singles 1938 and a nephew, John Doeg, was US champ in 1930.

DOROTHEA LAMBERT CHAMBERS (Great Britain)
Born 3/9/1878. Died 7/1/1960. Née Douglass. The most successful British woman player before 1914, she won Wimbledon singles 7 times and lost dramatically to Suzanne Lenglen in ***1919*** Challenge Round after holding 2 match-points. Played in ***1926*** W Cup – 23 years after first success at Wimbledon. The daughter of an Ealing vicar, she became a coach in ***1928.*** Won Wimbledon singles ***1903/04/06/10/11/13/14.***

HENRI COCHET (France)
Born 14/12/01. The great instinctive genius of lawn tennis, swift and imaginative, a master of the volley and half-volley, whose play could rise to dizzy heights and sometimes slip to unexpected disaster. Won Wimbledon singles ***1927/29*** and doubles (with J. Brugnon) ***1926/28.*** US singles ***1928.*** French singles ***1922/26/28/30/32*** and doubles (with Brugnon) ***1927/30/32.*** With the other 'Musketeers', he played successfully in 6 Challenge Rounds. Between ***1922*** and ***1933,*** when he turned professional, he won 44 D Cup rubbers out of 58 in 26 ties. After the war reinstated as an amateur.

ASHLEY JOHN COOPER (Australia)
Born 15/9/36. A strong and determined competitor who maintained Australia's command of the international game after Hoad and Rosewall turned professional. After being overwhelmed by Hoad in the ***1957*** f at Wimbledon, he returned to beat Fraser in a stern test of endurance in ***1958.*** He was US champion ***1958*** and won Australia ***1957–58.*** His doubles victories included Australia ***1958,*** France ***1957–58*** and US ***1958.*** He played singles when Australia successfully defended the D Cup in ***1957*** and ***1958,*** winning one rubber in each match. He beat Seixas and lost to Mackay ***1957*** and beat Mackay and lost to Olmedo ***1958.***

CHARLOTTE COOPER (Great Britain)
Born 22/9/1870. Died 10/10/1970. Became Mrs Sterry. One of the first successful women volleyers, she won at Wimbledon ***1895/96/98/1901/08***. Overshadowed at first by Mrs Hillyard – her first three victories were gained in years when the older player did not

compete – she defeated her at last in ***1901,*** the year of her marriage, after losing to Mrs Hillyard in four previous matches at the championships. In ***1902*** she lost in the famous re-played challenge round to Muriel Robb (they stopped at 4–6 13–11 on the first evening, then began again and Miss Robb won 7–5 6–1) and then regained the title in ***1908*** after beating Mrs Lambert Chambers in the quarter-finals. She reached the all-comers' final in ***1912*** and took Mrs McNair to 9–7 in the third set of a qf in ***1913.*** Her attacking spirit delighted her contemporaries. 'Her smiling good temper and sportsmanship made her as popular a player as ever went on to the Centre Court', wrote Burrow. 'She had a constitution like the proverbial ostrich. She never knew what it was to be tired and was never sick or sorry', said Hillyard.

BARON GOTTFRIED VON CRAMM (Germany)
Born 7/7/09. Died in car accident in Egypt 9/11/76. An elegant stylist and Germany's most successful player. Won French singles ***1934/36*** and doubles (with H. Henkel) ***1937,*** and German singles ***1932/33/34/35/48/49*** and doubles ***1948/49/53/55.*** Like F. S. Stolle, he was losing singles finalist at Wimbledon for 3 successive years – 1935–37. Won Wimbledon mixed (with Hilda Krahwinkel) ***1933*** and US doubles (with Henkel) ***1937.*** Won 82 D Cup rubbers out of 102 in 37 ties between ***1932–53.***

JOHN HERBERT CRAWFORD (Australia)
Born 22/3/08. Classic stylist, he beat H. E. Vines in ***1933*** in one of the greatest of all Wimbledon f. Won Wimbledon doubles (with A. K. Quist) ***1935.*** French singles ***1933*** and doubles (with Quist) ***1935,*** Australian singles ***1931/33*** and doubles (with H. C. Hopman) ***1929/30,*** (with E. F. Moon) ***1932,*** and (with V. B. McGrath) ***1935.*** Won 36 out of 58 D Cup rubbers between ***1928–37.***

DWIGHT FILLEY DAVIS (USA)
Born 5/7/1879. Died 28/11/1945. The donor of the D Cup, the trophy at stake in the international team championship. A Harvard undergraduate, he played against the British Isles in the first two matches of that competition, winning a single and partnering Holcombe Ward successfully in the doubles in ***1900*** and, with Ward again, losing to the Dohertys in the doubles in ***1902.*** A lefthander, he won the US doubles with Ward from ***1899–1901,*** retiring undefeated, and also the all-comers' final at Wimbledon in ***1901,*** only to fall to the Dohertys. He was President of the US LTA in ***1923,*** US Secretary of War 1925–29 and later Governor-General of the Philippines.

MAX DECUGIS (France)
Born 24/9/1882. Died 6/9/1978. The first great French player. He spent his schooldays in England and won his first tournaments there. Short, quick, and wiry, he was an aggressive competitor, whom Lawrie Doherty described as 'the most promising young player in the world'. He dominated French tennis from ***1903,*** when he won in Paris for the first time, to the outbreak of World War I, winning the singles title 8 times in 12 years and the doubles from ***1902–14*** and again in ***1920*** when the Champs were resumed. He was still playing well enough to reach the singles final in ***1923*** when he was 41. By that time the age of the 'Musketeers' was dawning. Although he competed regularly at Wimbledon, he never progressed beyond the singles sf ***(1911/12)*** but, with Gobert, he gained France's first title by winning the doubles in ***1911.***

CHARLOTTE DOD (Great Britain)
Born 24/9/1871. Died 27/6/1960. The first lawn tennis prodigy. Won the first of 5 Wimbledon titles in ***1887*** at the age of 15 years and 10 months. When she retired, she became an international golfer and hockey player. Nicknamed 'the Little Wonder', she won Wimbledon singles ***1887/88/91/92/93.***

Evonne Goolagong Cawley charmed spectators with her grace and natural talent, but was equally frustrating with her 'walkabouts' and extravagant errors. She won Wimbledon twice, the Australian Open four times and the French Open once. *(A. Evans)*

HUGH LAWRENCE DOHERTY (Great Britain)
Born London 8/10/1875. Died 21/8/1919. Learnt game with elder brother, Reginald Frank ('Reggie'), at Westminster School. Played for Cambridge Univ against Oxford in 1896–98 and developed into one of the most spectacular, aggressive, stylish, and successful of British players. 'Lawrie' Doherty was celebrated for smashing and volleying, and for speed about the court. With his brother, formed one of the greatest doubles partnerships in the history of the game. Won all-comers' singles at Wimbledon, ***1898,*** and singles champ ***1902–06.*** Doubles champ (with R. F. Doherty) ***1897–1901, 1903–05.*** First overseas player to win US singles, ***1903,*** and doubles, ***1902/03.*** In 5 D Cup challenge rounds, ***1902–06,*** he was never beaten, winning 7 singles rubbers and 5 doubles.

REGINALD FRANK DOHERTY (Great Britain)
Born London 14/10/1872. Died 29/12/1910. The senior partner of the great Doherty combination and the most notable stylist of early lawn tennis. Contemporary observers called his backhand, produced with back swing, full follow-through and remarkable touch, 'a model of perfection'. Was Wimbledon singles champ ***1897–1900*** and doubles champ ***1897–1901*** and ***1903–05.*** Reached the doubles challenge round at Wimbledon for first time with H. A. Nisbet in 1896. Thereafter he and his brother, H. L. Doherty, were beaten only by S. H. Smith and F. L. Riseley at Wimbledon. They lost to this pair in 1902, then beat them in the next three challenge rounds before falling to them again in 1906. The Dohertys won the US doubles in ***1902/03.*** Won South African singles and doubles, ***1909.***

JAROSLAV DROBNY (Great Britain)
Born 12/10/21. Exiled himself from Czechoslovakia in 1949, became an Egyptian subject in 1950 and a naturalised Briton in 1960. One of the great post-war clay court competitors with tremendous left-hand serve and smash, and delicate touch, he played in some of Wimbledon's most dramatic and emotional matches and eventually won the singles in ***1954*** at the age of 33. In ***1946*** he beat Kramer, the favourite; he lost to Schroeder in the ***1949*** f; in ***1950*** he let a two-set lead slip against Sedgman; Mottram surprised him in ***1951;*** he fell to Sedgman again in the ***1952*** f; and in ***1953*** he never recovered from beating Patty 8–6 16–18 3–6 8–6 12–10 in Wimbledon's second longest singles. The following year, when his chance seemed to be slipping away, he beat Rosewall, then 19, in f. He won in Paris in ***1951/52*** (after another series of dramatic failures), Italy ***1950/51/53*** and Germany ***1950.*** In ***1946/47/48/49*** he played in 43 D Cup rubbers, and won 37.

FRANCOISE DURR (France)
Born 25/12/42. Now Mrs Browning. The outstanding French woman player of the 1960s and 1970s. Shrewd and unorthodox, particularly in her serve and on the backhand, she excelled in doubles. She gained her major singles successes in ***1967*** when she won the French and German titles and reached the US semi-finals, but in doubles won a host of titles with a variety of partners, including five successive French victories – with Gail Sheriff (later Mrs Chanfreau and now Mrs Lovera) ***1967*** and ***1970/71,*** and with Ann Jones, ***1968/69.*** Won US doubles ***1972*** with Betty Stove, and Italian and South African titles ***1969*** with Jones. She failed, however, in six Wimbledon doubles finals between ***1965*** and ***1975.*** Won Wimbledon mixed doubles with Tony Roche ***1976*** and the French with Jean-Claude Barclay in ***1968, 1971*** and ***1973.***

ROY STANLEY EMERSON (Australia)
Born 3/11/36. A remarkable athlete, 'lean, keen, and trained to the last ounce', who led Australia's international challenge for five years after Laver turned professional in 1962. A Queenslander, he won Wimbledon singles ***1964/65*** but injury in 1966 spoilt his chance of equalling Perry's record of three successive titles. Won the doubles with Fraser ***1959/61,*** US singles ***1961/64*** and doubles ***1959/60*** (with Fraser) and ***1965/66*** (with Stolle), Australian singles ***1961*** and ***1963/64/65/66/67*** and doubles ***1960/66.*** On clay courts won the French singles ***1963/67,*** Italian ***1959/61/66*** and German ***1967*** and his most interesting doubles achievement was to take the French title from

1960/61/63/64/65 with five different partners, Fraser ***1960/62,*** Laver ***1961,*** Santana ***1963,*** Fletcher ***1964,*** and Stolle ***1965.*** He won 36 of his 40 D Cup rubbers and played in 9 successive challenge rounds between ***1959*** and ***1967.***

ROBERT FALKENBURG (USA)
Born 29/1/26. Won the US Junior Championship in ***1943–44*** and came to Europe in ***1947*** with the reputation of possessing the fastest service in the US. He won at Queen's Club, but lost to Pails in qf at Wimbledon and then won the doubles with Kramer, defeating Mottram and Sidwell in f. The following year he won one of Wimbledon's most dramatic f, defeating Bromwich 7–5 0–6 6–2 3–6 7–5 after saving three match-points as 3–5 in 5s. He was born in New York, learnt most of his tennis in Los Angeles and moved to Brazil, for whom he played in D Cup on a residential qualification.

NEALE ANDREW FRASER (Australia)
Born 3/10/33. A consistently aggressive lefthander, with a plain, direct serve and volley game, he was trained by Hopman, winning 18 of 21 D Cup rubbers between ***1958*** and ***1963,*** and later captained the Australian team which recaptured the trophy at Cleveland in ***1973*** and at Melbourne in ***1978 and 1983.*** Fraser started his Wimbledon career in the qualifying competition and ended by winning the singles in ***1960*** after a remarkable escape in the qf. Buchholz, who had held 5 match-points against him, retired with cramp. He won the doubles with Emerson ***1959/61*** and mixed with du Pont in ***1962*** – the year in which he and his brother, John, a Melbourne doctor, both reached the singles sf. Neither got through to the f. He won the US singles ***1959/60*** and doubles ***1957/59/60,*** the French doubles ***1958/60/62,*** and Australian doubles ***1957/58/62.***

SHIRLEY JUNE FRY (USA)
Born 30/6/27. Now Mrs Irvin. A persistent competitor, whose most notable performances were in doubles. She was first ranked in the top ten in the US in 1944, but she did not gain her two major singles successes until ***1956*** when she won both Wimbledon and Forest Hills. Until then she had always been thwarted by fellow-Americans. She won the Wimbledon doubles from ***1951–53*** with Doris Hart, losing only four games in capturing the title in ***1953*** and beat Helen Fletcher and Jean Quertier 6–0 6–0 in sf and Julie Sampson and Maureen Connolly by the same score in f. They won the US title ***1951–54.*** Her other successes included the Wimbledon mixed, with Seixas, ***1956,*** the Australian singles and doubles, with Althea Gibson, ***1957,*** and the French singles, ***1951,*** and doubles, with Hart, ***1950–53.*** She played in six W Cup contests, winning 10 matches and losing twice.

ALTHEA GIBSON (USA)
Born 25/8/27. Now Mrs Darbin. The first black player to dominate international lawn tennis, relying on fierce serving and considerable strength and reach. Won Wimbledon singles ***1957/58*** and doubles (with Angela Buxton) ***1957*** and (with Maria Bueno) ***/58.*** US singles ***1957/58.*** French singles and doubles (with Angela Buxton) ***1956.*** Australian doubles (with Shirley Fry) ***1957.*** Italian singles ***1956.*** W Cup ***1957/58,*** turned professional ***1958.***

ANDRE HENRI GOBERT (France)
Born 30/9/1890. Died 6/12/1951. Wallis Myers described him as 'perhaps the greatest indoor player of all time'. With Decugis, he gained France's first Wimbledon title by defeating the holders, Ritchie and Wilding, in ***1911.*** Although they were beaten by Dixon and Roper Barrett the following year, the brilliant Gobert's compensation was a place in the all-comers' singles f in which he lost to the experienced A. W. Gore. He won the French covered court title from ***1911–13*** and again in ***1920*** and the British covered court event in ***1911–12*** and again from ***1920–22.*** He first played in D Cup in ***1911*** and his career ended when the 'Musketeers' arrived in ***1922.*** He also won two Olympic gold medals in ***1912.***

RICHARD (PANCHO) GONZALES (USA)
Born 9/5/28. A dramatic and spectacular competitor, who was undoubtedly the best player in the world for most of the 1950s. He turned pro in 1949 after winning the US singles in ***1948/49,*** taking the US Clay Court title ***1948/49,*** the US indoor title ***1949,*** and winning the doubles in Paris and at Wimbledon – in his only amateur appearances there – in ***1949*** with Parker. Thereafter he played his brilliant, angry tennis away from the main arenas of the game until, at last, open competition was allowed. By then he was 40, but he played one last great match for the Wimbledon crowd. In ***1969*** he beat Pasarell 22–24 1–6 16–14 6–3 11–9 in 5hr 12min – the longest singles seen at Wimbledon.

EVONNE FAY GOOLAGONG (Australia)
Born 31/7/51. Now Mrs Roger Cawley (married in 1975). One of the most naturally gifted of champions, she was the first of her Aborigine race to excel at the game. Suddenly in ***1971*** at the age of 19, 3 years before her coach Vic Edwards had forecast she would, she swept through both the French Championships and Wimbledon on a cloud of inspiration to win her first major titles. Although she reached the Wimbledon final again the following year and twice more, in ***1975*** and ***1976***, it was not until ***1980*** that she won again – four years after the birth of her daughter, Kelly. This was the first win by a mother since Dorothea Lambert-Chambers's success in 1914. The nine-year gap between her championships was also the greatest since Bill Tilden's wins in 1921 and 1930. She was always more at home on faster surfaces where her beautifully instinctive volleying paid handsome dividends and she won her native Australian Open on that surface four times – ***1974, 1975, 1976, 1978***. She was always a competent player on clay but tended to be rather erratic as her famous 'walkabouts' led to extravagant errors. Nevertheless, besides the French Open in ***1971*** she also won the Italian title in ***1973***. The other highlights of her singles career were the victories in the South African Championships ***(1972)*** and the Virginia Slims Champs ***(1974, 1976)***. She was a good doubles player and won once at Wimbledon ***(1974)***, four times in Melbourne ***(1971, 1974, 1975, 1976)*** and twice in Johannesburg ***(1971, 1972)***. In seven years of Fed Cup duty for Australia from ***1971*** to ***1982*** she won 33 of the 38 rubbers she contested in 24 ties. – J.B.

ARTHUR WENTWORTH GORE (Great Britain)
Born 2/1/1868. Died 1/12/1928. Wimbledon's oldest champ and probably the most persistent and industrious competitor in the history of the Champs. He played there for the first time in 1888 and although the Dohertys, Brookes, and Wilding were among his contemporaries, won the singles 3 times ***1901*** and ***1908/09*** and, at the age of 44 years and 6 months, won the right to challenge Wilding for the title in ***1912.*** That was his seventh appearance in the challenge round in 13 years. He was almost entirely a forehand player, hitting the ball flat with the racket in a dead line with his outstretched arm. His lightness of foot enabled him to protect his backhand which was no more than a safe push. He competed at every Wimbledon between ***1888–1927*** and captained the first British D Cup team at Boston in 1900, reaching sf US Champs on that trip.

KAREN HANTZE (USA)
Born 11/12/42. Now Mrs Susman. One of the new generation of aggressive Californians who arrived on the international scene at the start of the 1960s, she won the doubles at Wimbledon with the 17-year-old Billie Jean Moffitt in ***1961*** and then defeated Vera Sukova in the ***1962*** singles final. Marriage and motherhood restricted her tennis, but she won US doubles (again with Moffitt) ***1964.*** She played W Cup ***1960–62*** and ***1965,*** winning six of her nine matches, and Fed Cup ***1965.***

DARLENE R. HARD (USA)
Born 6/1/36. An energetic volleyer, a shrewd tactician, and one of the best doubles players of her generation, she won the US singles in ***1960*** and ***1961*** and the French singles ***1960,*** but she failed in both her Wimbledon finals, losing to Althea Gibson in ***1957*** and Maria Bueno ***1960.*** She won the Wimbledon doubles, with Gibson ***1957***, Jeanne Arth ***1959***, and

twice with Bueno ***(1960, 1963)*** and the mixed in ***1957*** (with Rose), ***1959–60*** (with Laver). She won the US doubles six times and the French doubles three times. Perhaps her most surprising American success came in ***1969,*** some years after she had retired from regular competition, when she and Francoise Durr defeated Margaret Court and Virginia Wade 0–6 6–3 6–4 in f.

DORIS HART (USA)
Born 20/6/25. In spite of childhood illness which impeded her movement, she became one of the subtlest and most graceful of post-war competitors. Won Wimbledon singles ***1951,*** doubles (with Pat Todd) ***1947*** and (with Shirley Fry) ***1951/52/53.*** US singles ***1954/55*** and doubles (with Shirley Fry) ***1951/52/53/54.*** French singles ***1950/52*** and doubles (with Pat Todd) ***1948*** and (with Shirley Fry) ***1950/51/53.*** Australian singles ***1949*** and doubles (with Louise Brough) ***1950.*** Italian singles ***1951/53*** and South African singles ***1952.*** Also won many mixed titles, notably with E. V. Seixas at Wimbledon ***1953/54/55.*** Turned professional ***1955.***

ADRIANNE SHIRLEY HAYDON (Great Britain)
Born 17/10/38. Now Mrs Jones. A shrewd, persistent lefthander, who reached sf at Wimbledon 7 times in 10 years, she captured the title at last in ***1969*** after beating Margaret Court in sf and Billie Jean King, to whom she had been r/u in ***1967,*** in f. She achieved international fame as a table tennis player, but decided to concentrate on lawn tennis after being r/u in three events in the 1957 World Table Tennis Champs. She won the French title in ***1961/66,*** Rome in ***1966*** and was twice r/u at Forest Hills ***1961/67.*** She took the French doubles (with Francoise Durr) in ***1968/69*** and won the Wimbledon mixed with Stolle in ***1969.*** Her W Cup record – 15 successful rubbers out of 32 in 12 matches – is another remarkable illustration of her tenacity and consistency.

ROBERT ANTHONY JOHN HEWITT (South Africa)
Born 12/1/40 in Sydney, Australia. He moved to South Africa in the early 1960s and started to represent that country when his residential qualification matured in 1967. A big brooding volcano of a man, he had deceptively fine touch and became one of the greatest right-court returners of the serve of modern times. He enjoyed two careers – first with fellow-Australian Fred Stolle and then with South Africa's Frew McMillan. With Stolle he won Wimbledon twice ***(1962/64)*** the Australian Championship twice ***(1963/64)*** and the Italian twice ***(1963/64)*** and with McMillan he added three more Wimbledon crowns ***(1967/74/78)***, two German ***(1967/70)***, one French ***(1972)***, one US ***(1977)***, one Masters ***(1977)*** and one WCT ***(1974)*** title as well as the Italian in ***1967*** and four at home in South Africa ***(1967/70/72/74)***. He registered four major mixed doubles successes with three different partners, winning in Australia with Jan Lehane in ***1961***, in Paris with Billie Jean King in ***1970*** and twice at Wimbledon with his pupil, Greer Stevens, in ***1977*** and ***1979***. He represented South Africa in D Cup ***1967–74*** and was a member of the successful team of ***1974*** that won by default from India. – J.B.

LEWIS ALAN HOAD (Australia)
Born 23/11/34. Capable of generating fierce power with great ease, he was one of the 'boy wonders' Harry Hopman produced to beat the US in the ***1953*** D Cup match. The other was Rosewall, 21 days his senior, who was to thwart his attempt on the Grand Slam in ***1956*** by beating him at Forest Hills, in the last of the 4 great f. That year Hoad had won the Australian and French titles, and had beaten Rosewall at Wimbledon. In ***1957*** he defeated Ashley Cooper in one of the most devastating Wimbledon f ever and then turned professional, but constant back trouble spoilt his pro career and also ended his attempt to return to the circuit when the game was opened to the pros. He won the Wimbledon doubles in ***1953/55/56,*** the US doubles in ***1956,*** the French doubles in ***1953,*** and the Australian doubles in ***1953/56/57.*** He won 17 rubbers out of 21 in D Cup play between ***1953–56.***

HAZEL HOTCHKISS (USA)
Born 20/12/1886. Died 5/12/1974. Became Mrs G. Wightman. One of the most remarkable and enthusiastic competitors that the game has known. She was the donor of the W Cup and a considerable influence in American tennis for more than 60 years. She gained the first of her four US singles titles ***(1909/10/11/19)*** in 1909 and won the US indoor doubles for the 10th ***(1919/21/24/27/28/29/30/31/33/43)*** and last time in 1943. A remarkable volleyer with great speed about the court, she and Helen Wills were never beaten in doubles. They won the Wimbledon doubles in ***1924*** and the US doubles – a title which she had won on 4 other occasions – in ***1924–28.*** She captained the first US W Cup team in 1923 and between ***1923–31*** won 3 doubles rubbers in 5 matches.

HELEN HULL JACOBS (USA)
Born 6/8/08. A tenacious competitor, notable for duels with fellow-Californian, Helen Wills Moody, 5 times a Wimbledon finalist between ***1929–39*** but won only in ***1936.*** US singles ***1932/33/34/35*** and doubles (with Sarah Palfrey Fabyan) ***1930/34/35.*** Italian singles ***1934.***

WILLIAM JOHNSTON (USA)
Born 2/11/1894. Died 1/6/1946. 'Little Bill', a Californian, small in physique but a brilliant volleyer and the possessor of a formidable top-spin forehand, was 'Big Bill' Tilden's principal rival at home in the first half of the 1920s. He defeated McLoughlin to win the US singles in ***1915,*** the first year at Forest Hills, lost to Williams in the ***1916*** final and then regained the title by beating Tilden in straight sets in ***1919.*** Tilden gained his revenge the following year and, although Johnston reached the final five times between ***1920*** and ***1925,*** Tilden always frustrated him. He beat Hunter in the ***1923*** Wimbledon final, losing only one set in the tournament. He won the US doubles with Griffin ***1915/16*** and ***1920*** and played in eight D Cup challenge rounds, winning 18 of his 21 D Cup rubbers.

BILLIE JEAN MOFFITT KING (USA)
Born 22/11/43. Perhaps the most important single figure in the history of tennis, as player, stateswoman, innovator and entrepreneur (usually with lawyer husband Larry King, whom she married in 1965), she has worked tirelessly to gain recognition and respect for the women's game. One of the founders of the women's pro tour in ***1970***, twice President of the Women's Tennis Association, and the prime mover behind Team Tennis, she has been involved in most aspects of the game. As a player her natural exuberance and bubbling personality suited her attacking serve-and-volley game and made her a fearsome opponent. She will best be remembered for her 'Battle of the Sexes' against Bobby Riggs at the Houston Astrodome on 20 September, ***1973*** where the world's largest-ever crowd of 30,492 and some 50 million more around the world on TV, saw her win 6–4 6–3 6–3. In ***1979*** she achieved her 20th Wimbledon title to pass the record she had jointly shared with fellow-Californian Elizabeth Ryan who, ironically, had died on the eve of that unique achievement. Her unparalleled record comprises 6 singles – ***1966, 1967, 1968, 1972, 1973*** and ***1975***; 10 women's doubles – ***1961, 1962, 1965, 1967, 1968, 1970, 1971, 1972, 1973*** and ***1979***; 4 mixed doubles – ***1967, 1971, 1973*** and ***1974***. She first played at Wimbledon in ***1961*** and won the doubles with Karen Hantze. At her last appearance in ***1983*** she was competing for the 22nd year (she had not entered in ***1981***) and reached the mixed doubles final with Steve Denton when she played her 265th and last match at Wimbledon. It was also her 29th final and, as they lost to John Lloyd and Wendy Turnbull 7–5 in the final set, she was losing at that stage for only the 9th time. She was almost as successful in her own US Championships where she won 13 titles, 4 in singles – ***1967, 1971, 1972, 1974***, five in doubles – ***1964, 1967, 1974, 1978, 1980*** and four in mixed – ***1967, 1971, 1973, 1976*** and, in addition she became the only woman to win US National titles on all four surfaces – grass, clay, hard and indoor – a feat she repeated in doubles with Rosie Casals with whom she had most of her major doubles successes. She won the French Open singles and doubles in ***1972*** and the mixed in ***1967*** and ***1970*** and was successful in singles and mixed at the Australian Open in ***1968***, the first year of open tennis. Her 39 Grand Slam titles put her second only to Margaret Court who won 62. She was also the singles and

doubles champion of Italy ***(1970)*** and of Germany ***(1971)*** and won the South African title 3 times ***(1966, 1967, 1969)***. With 21 winning rubbers from 26 played in 9 W Cup matches between ***1961*** and ***1978***, plus 52 wins from 58 rubbers in 6 years of Fed Cup play from ***1963*** to ***1979*** she contributed hugely to American dominance in those team competitions. – J.B.

JAN KODES (Czechoslovakia)
Born 1/3/46. A dogged, industrious player with great strength and determination. He won his first major victories on clay, winning the French singles ***1970/71*** and reaching the Italian final ***1970/71/72,*** but he won the Wimbledon singles in the boycott year of ***1973*** and was runner-up in the US Champs ***1971/73.*** Having served his apprenticeship in European junior team competitions (he was on a winning Galea Cup team), he first represented Czechoslovakia in D Cup in ***1966,*** took them to the final in ***1975*** and was a member of their winning team in ***1980.***

HILDE KRAHWINKEL (West Germany)
Born 26/3/08. Now Mrs Sperling. A tall German, later Danish by marriage, whose dogged ability to retrieve from the back of the court turned her matches into long tests of endurance. She won the German indoor title in ***1929*** and then, emerging rapidly as an international player, lost to Cilly Aussem in the only all-German women's f at Wimbledon ***1931.*** She reached the final again in ***1936,*** losing 6–2 4–6 7–5 to Helen Jacobs, and altogether she was in qf (or better) 8 times. She won the French singles ***1935–37,*** defeating Mrs Mathieu in each of the three f, the Italian title ***1935*** and she was German singles champ ***1933/35/37/39.*** There was no competition in 1936. Her last important victory was in the Scandinavian indoor final in ***1950.***

JACK ALBERT KRAMER (USA)
Born 1/8/21. A methodical and powerful exponent of the serve and volley game. Played for the US in the last pre-war D Cup challenge round against Australia. Won Wimbledon singles title in ***1947*** after losing dramatically to the then unknown Jaroslav Drobny in 1946. Won doubles ***1946/47.*** Won US singles ***1946/47*** and doubles ***1940/41/43/47.*** Turned pro ***1947*** and then controlled pro tennis for 15 years. Still appears occasionally as a television commentator and was executive director of ATP Sept. 1972–April 1975.

RENE LACOSTE (France)
Born 2/7/04. In spite of ill health, he became the best groundstroke player and most astute tactician of pre-war lawn tennis. Won Wimbledon singles ***1925/28*** and doubles (with J. Borotra) ***1925.*** Won US singles ***1926/27,*** French singles ***1925/27/29*** and French doubles (with Borotra) ***1924/25/29.*** Played in 51 D Cup rubbers between ***1923–28*** and won the crucial rubbers of the ***1927*** challenge round which brought France the trophy for the first time, when he beat Tilden and Johnston in the singles.

ARTHUR D. LARSEN (USA)
Born 6/4/25. A graceful, elegant lefthander with exquisite touch and some notable eccentricities, he was famous for his dressing-room superstitions, his physical twitches and his rituals on court. He was known as Tappy because he would have a lucky number for the day and would always tap the baseline, the umpire's chair – even his own toe – with his racket the required number of times before continuing. He won US singles ***1950,*** US Clay Courts ***1952*** and US Indoor ***1953.*** A motor-cycle accident in which he suffered severe head injuries ended his career in 1957.

RODNEY GEORGE LAVER (Australia)
Born 9/8/38. The first player to achieve the Grand Slam twice and the master of the old professional circuit, with Rosewall as his great rival, in its last days. A lefthander, red-haired like Budge, with a spectacularly aggressive style, he brought off the slam of the four major singles titles, as an amateur, in ***1962*** and then, as a professional, in ***1969.***

Disciplined, unassuming, quick and light in movement, he could produce sudden bombardments of shots, heavy with spin, which totally disconcerted his opponents. Born at Rockhampton, Queensland, 'Rocket' was a perfect nickname for the first tennis millionaire. If he had not turned professional in 1963, he would have won many more of the traditional titles. As it was, he won the singles at Wimbledon ***1961/62*** and ***1968/69,*** the doubles with Emerson ***1971*** and the mixed, with Darlene Hard, ***1959/60.*** He took the US singles and French singles ***1962*** and ***1969,*** also winning the French doubles with Emerson and the mixed with Hard in ***1961.*** His Australian singles victories came in ***1960, 1962*** and ***1969,*** with doubles ***1959/61*** (Mark) and ***1969*** (Emerson). He was Italian singles champion ***1962*** and ***1971,*** German champion ***1961/62*** and a member of the undefeated Australian D Cup team from ***1959–62.*** He returned to D Cup in ***1973,*** collecting three more rubbers in Australia's 5–0 victory over the US in the final at Cleveland.

SUZANNE LENGLEN (France)
Born 24/5/1899. Died 4/7/1938. The most exciting, and successful of women players. She survived 2 match-points to win at Wimbledon in ***1919*** against Mrs Lambert Chambers and thereafter lost only in a controversial match to Molla Mallory (US) in 1921 US Champs until her retirement in 1926. Quarrelled with the Wimbledon referee in 1926 and turned pro. Won Wimbledon singles and doubles (with Elizabeth Ryan) ***1919/20/21/22/23/25.*** French singles and doubles (with various partners) ***1920/21/22/23/25/26.***

KATHLEEN McKANE (Great Britain)
Born 7/5/1897. Now Mrs Godfree. A fine match-player with a quick, aggressive game, she achieved the notable distinction of winning the Wimbledon singles twice – even though she was a contemporary of Suzanne Lenglen and Helen Wills. In Lenglen's absence, she beat the Californian (a feat which no other player achieved in the next 14 years at Wimbledon) in the ***1924*** final after trailing by a set and 1–4, and in ***1926*** she regained the title after being within a point of 1–4 in the third set against Lili d'Alvarez. She won the Wimbledon mixed (with Gilbert) in ***1924*** and in ***1926*** (with her husband, Leslie Godfree). She was r/u to Miss Wills at Forest Hills in 1925 after beating Elizabeth Ryan and Molla Mallory, and she won the US doubles in ***1923*** (with Mrs Covell) ***/27*** (with Miss Harvey). She won 7 rubbers out of 17 in 7 W Cup matches between ***1923–34.***

CHARLES ROBERT McKINLEY (USA)
Born 5/1/41. An energetic and athletic match-player, who won the Wimbledon singles title in ***1963*** without meeting another seeded player in the course of the tournament. He was runner-up to Laver in ***1961,*** a disappointing competitor in ***1962*** but in ***1963*** bounced back to take the title. In the US Championships he never progressed further than the semi-finals, failing three times at that stage, but, with Ralston, he won the doubles in ***1961*** and ***1963–64.*** He played in 16 D Cup matches between ***1960*** and ***1965*** and won 29 of his 38 rubbers.

MAURICE EVANS McLOUGHLIN (USA)
Born 7/1/1890. Died 10/12/1957. 'The Californian Comet' was the first notable exponent of the cannonball service. Fiercely effective with volley and smash, he was US champ in ***1912–13*** and his appearance at Wimbledon was, as a contemporary remarked, a sign of the way the modern game was developing. His spectacular style had considerable appeal. When he met Wilding for the title in ***1913,*** 'there was such an indecent crush round the barriers of the Centre Court that, to avoid serious injury, several ladies had to be lifted over by policemen into the security of the arena'. Wilding beat him 8–6 6–3 10–8, but McLoughlin had the consolation of winning 2 rubbers in the American capture of the D Cup from Britain at Wimbledon. In the ***1914*** challenge round at Forest Hills he beat both Brookes and Wilding, but Australasia took the trophy. He did not play after the war. His aggressive style was said to have burnt him out.

FREW DONALD McMILLAN (South Africa)
Born 20/5/42 in Springs, a small Transvaal town. A gifted and unusual doubles player who invariably wore a peaked white cloth cap and held the racket with two hands on both sides to produce just the right blend of disguise, finesse and power. His partnership with ex-patriate Australian Bob Hewitt was particularly fruitful and they became one of the three greatest pairs of the post-Second World War years. Together they won their native South African title four times ***(1967/70/72/74)*** and succeeded at Wimbledon three times ***(1967/72/78)***. They won once each the French ***(1972)***, the US ***(1977)***, the Masters ***(1977*** played in Jan '78), the WCT ***(1974)*** and the Italian ***(1967)*** titles and won the German twice ***(1967/70)***. But it was in mixed doubles that he won his first and last major championships. In ***1966*** he partnered Annette Van Zyl to the French title and in ***1981*** he captured the Wimbledon mixed for the second time with Betty Stove, with whom he had been successful in 1978 – the same year they won a second US Open together ***(1977/78)***. He played D Cup from ***1965*** to ***1976*** and was a member of the only team ever to win the famous trophy by default – from India in 1974. – J.B.

ALICE MARBLE (USA)
Born 28/9/13. A brilliant server and volleyer whose career was interrupted by ill health and the war. Won Wimbledon singles ***1939*** and doubles (with Sarah Palfrey Fabyan) ***1938/39.*** US singles ***1936/38/39/40*** and doubles (with Sarah Palfrey Fabyan) ***1937/38/39/40.*** Turned pro ***1941.***

SIMONE MATHIEU (France)
Born 31/1/08. Died 7/1/80. A formidable clay court player, she succeeded Lenglen as the leader of the women's game in France. She was junior champ – as a married woman – at 18, and 3 years later reached the French f, losing 6–3 6–4 to Wills. She was r/u again in ***1933/36/37*** before she won at last in ***1938,*** defeating Landry, and then retained her title ***1939*** against Jedrzejowska. She won the French doubles 6 times and the Wimbledon doubles twice with Ryan ***1933/34*** and once with Yorke ***1937.*** Her soundness from the baseline carried her 4 times to the singles sf.

HELEN WILLS MOODY (USA)
Born 6/10/05. Later Mrs A. Roark. Lenglen's successor as ruler of Wimbledon. A relentless baseliner, she won the singles 8 times in 9 attempts, losing only to Kitty McKane in 1924. Between ***1927–32*** she won all the major singles champs, except Australia, without losing a set. Won Wimbledon singles ***1927/28/29/30/32/33/35/38*** and doubles (with Hazel Wightman) ***1924*** and (with Elizabeth Ryan) ***/27/30.*** US singles ***1923/24/25/27/28/29/31,*** and doubles (with Mrs J. B. Jessup) ***1922,*** (with Hazel Wightman) ***/24/28,*** and (with Mary K. Browne) ***/25.*** French singles ***1928/29/30/32*** and doubles (with Elizabeth Ryan) ***1930/31/32.***

ANGELA MORTIMER (Great Britain)
Born 21/4/32. Now Mrs Barrett. Britain's first post-war Wimbledon singles champ. Coached by Arthur Roberts at Torquay, she used an armoury of firmly controlled groundstrokes most effectively and considerable determination enabled her to overcome a certain frailty of physique. Her first notable success was the capture of the French title in ***1955*** – the first British victory in Paris since Peggy Scriven won in 1934 – and in the same year she won the Wimbledon doubles (with Anne Shilcock). She won the Australian title in ***1958,*** after travelling there to recover from illness, and 6 months later was r/u to Althea Gibson at Wimbledon. She won the title in ***1961*** by beating Christine Truman in the first all-British f of the modern Wimbledon. She won 5 rubbers out of 16 in 6 W Cup matches and became W Cup captain ***1964–70.***

ILIE NASTASE (Rumania)
Born 19/8/46. One of the most gifted shot-makers and fluid movers in the game's history, he never quite fulfilled his enormous potential. His two Grand Slam titles were won on

Anne Haydon Jones, winner of the British Hard Courts title in Bournemouth from 1963–66, further delighted the home crowds by winning Wimbledon in 1969, after seven appearances in the semi-finals. *(A. Evans)*

different surfaces – on grass in New York in ***1972*** and on clay in Paris the following year. He could also play beautifully indoors as his four Masters titles in ***1971, 1972, 1973, 1975*** testify. Sadly for his many admirers, a childlike and sometimes mischievous streak was his undoing on many occasions, particularly towards the end of his playing days when he fell foul of authority for his behaviour. Throughout his career the showman in him struggled constantly with the athlete so that there was often a lack of steel about his match play. This failing, and an inability to put the ball away with his somewhat lightweight volleys, cost him two chances to win the Wimbledon title – in ***1972*** when Smith beat him and in ***1976*** when Borg won the first of his five titles. His lightning reflexes made him an excellent doubles player and he won major titles in Paris ***(1970)*** and Rome ***(1970*** and ***1972)***, at Wimbledon ***(1973)*** and in New York ***(1975)***. He also won two mixed titles at Wimbledon with Rosie Casals ***(1970, 1972)***. His biggest disappointment was his failure to lead Rumania to victory in the ***1972*** D Cup final against the Americans on clay in Bucharest where his loss to Smith in the opening rubber proved decisive. – J.B.

JOHN DAVID NEWCOMBE (Australia)
Born 23/5/44. The supreme exponent of the simple, rugged style in modern tennis. Splendidly confident and with great strength of personality, Newcombe relied upon a heavy service, forceful volleying and solid, powerful groundstrokes. His best singles successes were on grass – Wimbledon ***1967, 1970/71,*** US Championships ***1967, 1973,*** and Australia ***1973, 1975*** – but he also won, by doggedness and determination, the German ***(1968)*** and Italian ***(1969)*** titles. He and Roche formed the most successful of modern doubles partnerships, winning Wimbledon in ***1965, 1968–70,*** and ***1974.*** When Roche was injured in ***1966,*** Fletcher replaced him at short notice and he and Newcombe won the title. He won the US doubles with Roche ***1967,*** with Taylor ***1971,*** and with Davidson ***1973,*** France twice with Roche ***(1967, 1969)*** and once with Okker ***(1973)*** and Australia four times with Roche ***(1965, 1967, 1971*** and ***1976)*** and once with Anderson ***(1973).*** In ***1981***, aged 37, he and Stolle (42) took McEnroe/Fleming to 5s tie-break in US Open sf. He first played in the Davis Cup in ***1963*** and finally against Italy in Rome, ***1976,*** but perhaps his best performance was in ***1973*** when he and Laver inflicted a 5–0 defeat upon the United States at Cleveland.

BETTY NUTHALL (Great Britain)
Born 23/6/11. Now Mrs Shoemaker. An aggressive and attractive competitor, with a remarkable record as a junior, she never progressed beyond qf at Wimbledon but gained her most impressive victories abroad. At 16, after beating Molla Mallory, No. 6 seed, at Wimbledon in ***1927,*** she astonished the tennis world by reaching f at F Hills, where Helen Wills beat her 6–1 6–4. In ***1930*** she became the first British player to win that title with a 6–4 6–1 victory over Mrs Harper. She won the US doubles ***1930/31/33*** and mixed ***1929/31*** and the French doubles ***1931*** and mixed ***1931/32.*** Her only British success in a nat singles event was the capture of the HC title in ***1927.*** She won the HC doubles ***1926/28/31/32*** and the mixed in ***1927.*** She played in 8 W Cup matches between ***1927*** and ***1939,*** winning 6 rubbers and losing 7.

ALEJANDRO OLMEDO (USA)
Born 24/3/36. The son of a groundsman in Peru, this superb natural athlete rose like a comet in ***1958*** to win D Cup for America in Brisbane almost single-handed. Selected by the captain, Perry T. Jones, Olmedo had rewarded him with two singles wins and a share with Ham Richardson in the doubles win that had sealed the victory. Success in the Australian Championships confirmed the quality of his play as he beat Neale Fraser in four sets. Six months later 'The Chief', as he was popularly known, won the ***1959*** Wimbledon from Rod Laver for the loss of only two sets, with one of the most competent displays of power tennis seen since the war. After taking part in the unsuccessful defence of D Cup where he lost to Fraser but beat Laver again, he reached the final of the US Championships but failed once more against Fraser. Immediately he turned professional. – J.B.

MANUEL ORANTES (Spain)
Born 6/2/49. A consumate artist on European clay whose exquisite touch and gentle, generous manners made him an international favourite. A left-hander who, after leading Spain to two Galea Cup victories in ***1968*** and ***1969***, won his first two important titles in ***1972*** – the German and Italian Opens. His best year was ***1975*** for, besides winning a second German title, the Canadian Open and the first of his two US Clay Court crowns (he won the second in ***1977***, he was triumphant on the clay at Forest Hills. After recovering miraculously to defeat Vilas in a night-time semi-final, having trailed one set to two and 0–5 in the fourth, he was back on court 15 hours later to thrash Jimmy Connors 6–4 6–3 6–3 in a near-perfect display of the clay-court art. In ***1976*** he won the Spanish Open and at the year's end won Masters in Houston against Fibak with another brave recovery, coming back from one set to two and 1–4. He played in the losing Spanish team in the D Cup challenge round of ***1967*** in Brisbane but led his country to victory in the World Team Cup in Düsseldorf 11 years later. – J.B.

MARGARET OSBORNE (USA)
Born 4/4/18. Now Mrs du Pont. One of the finest of American doubles players and a formidably successful competitor in singles. With her splendidly consistent serving and her strength and skill at the net, she did much to set the pattern for the period of American supremacy in women's tennis, which began in 1946. Won Wimbledon singles in ***1947*** Forest Hills ***1948/49/50*** and Paris in ***1946/49.*** She and Louise Brough won the Wimbledon doubles in ***1946/48/49/50/54.*** They ruled the US doubles from ***1942–50*** and ***1955–57,*** and held the French title ***1946/47/49.*** She won the Wimbledon mixed with Neale Fraser in ***1962*** – 15 years after her first singles victory.

SARAH PALFREY (USA)
Born 18/9/12. Now Mrs Danzig, formerly Mrs Fabyan, and Mrs Cooke. A fine volleyor with a sweeping backhand and a notable doubles player, she partnered Alice Marble to victory at Wimbledon in ***1938/39*** and won the US doubles title with a variety of partners – Betty Nuthall, Helen Jacobs (3 times), Alice Marble (4 times) and Margaret Osborne – 9 times between ***1930–41.*** She won the US singles in ***1941/45*** and was r/u to Helen Jacobs in ***1934/35.*** She was the US mixed champion on 4 occasions. She played in 10 W Cup matches and won 14 rubbers out of 21.

ADRIANO PANATTA (Italy)
Born 9/7/50. Without doubt, 1976 was the *annus mirabilis* of Panatta's career. Until then he had always been dashing and stylish, but had never made full use of his talent. In ***1976***, however, he lived dangerously and survived brilliantly. In Rome he became the first home player to win in Italy for 15 years after frustrating Warwick no fewer than 11 times at m-p in the first round. In Paris, against Hutka, he again faced a first-round m-p and again went on to take the championship. Four months later, when Italy won D Cup for the first time, Panatta played a major role in their victory. Paris, Rome and D Cup – this was Panatta's year! He was also the leading player in the Italian teams which reached the ***1977***, ***1979*** and ***1980*** D Cup finals. He reached the French sf in ***1973*** and ***1975*** and was runner-up in Rome ***1978*** and Hamburg ***1972***.

GERALD L. PATTERSON (Australia)
Born 17/12/1895. Died 13/6/1967. Formidably aggressive with a cannonball service modelled on McLoughlin's, he was the dominating player when international competition was resumed in 1919. After being r/u to O'Hara Wood in the ***1914*** Australian singles, he became Wimbledon's first post-war champ by defeating Brookes in ***1919.*** He lost his Wimbledon title to Tilden in ***1920*** but regained it against Lycett in ***1922.*** R/u doubles in ***1922*** (O'Hara Wood) and ***1928*** (Hawkes) and won the mixed with Suzanne Lenglen in ***1920.*** He won the Australian singles in his fourth final in ***1927.*** Between ***1919–28*** he played 46 D Cup rubbers for Australia and Australasia and won 4 out of 12 challenge round

rubbers. He was a nephew of Dame Nellie Melba and was the first man to win the Wimbledon singles by playing through when the challenge round was abolished there in 1922.

J. EDWARD PATTY (USA)
Born 11/2/24. An American who lived in Paris and developed his game there, 'Budge' Patty, with his elegant, effective forehand volley, was one of the great post-war stylists. ***1950*** – when he won both the Wimbledon and French singles – was the peak of his career, but his rivalry with Drobny captured the public's imagination. The most notable of their long and dramatic matches was in the third round at Wimbledon in 1953. After 4½ hours Patty lost 8–6 16–18 3–6 8–6 12–10 after holding 6 match-points. He had beaten the Czech at Wimbledon in ***1947*** and 3 years later by 6–1 6–2 3–6 5–7 7–5 in his French f. The last of their meetings was in ***1954.*** Drobny, on his way to the title, won a 4-set sf. Patty won his last title there in ***1957*** when he and Mulloy, then aged 43, beat Hoad and Fraser to take the men's doubles. He won the Italian singles ***1954,*** and the German singles ***1953/54*** and doubles ***1953/54/55.***

FRANK A. PARKER (USA)
Born 31/1/16. Shrewd, persistent, and accurate in spite of a certain lightness of shot, he shared with Trabert the distinction, rare for an American, of winning the French title twice. At his best on slow courts, he was ranked in the first 10 in the US for 17 consecutive years between ***1933,*** the year of the first of his 5 US Clay Court victories, and ***1949*** when he turned pro. His victories in Paris were in ***1948/49***, and in ***1949*** he won the doubles in Paris and Wimbledon with Gonzales. He won the US singles in ***1944*** and ***1945*** as an Army sergeant and the doubles with Kramer in ***1943.*** He played in the D Cup challenge round against Britain in ***1937*** when the US regained the trophy after 10 years and in the ***1939*** and ***1948*** challenge rounds. He was beaten only twice in 14 D Cup rubbers.

FREDERICK JOHN PERRY (Great Britain)
Born 18/5/09. A US citizen. The most successful modern British player, an aggressive competitor with boundless self-confidence and a remarkable running forehand. Won Wimbledon singles ***1934/35/36*** – the first player since A. F. Wilding (1910–13) to take the title 3 years in succession – and mixed (with Dorothy Round) ***1935/36.*** US singles ***1933/34/36.*** French singles ***1935*** and doubles (with G. P. Hughes) ***1933.*** Australian singles ***1934*** and doubles (with Hughes) ***1934.*** Won 45 out of 52 D Cup rubbers, 34 out of 38 singles, between ***1931–36.*** Turned pro in ***1936.***

YVON FRANCOIS MARIE PETRA (France)
Born 8/3/16 in Indo-China. Died 11/9/84. Wimbledon's first post-war men's singles champion. Reached mixed f at Wimbledon ***1937*** with Simone Mathieu and won French doubles ***1938*** with Destremau, defeating Budge and Mako in f. Between 1942, when he was released from a prisoner-of-war camp, and 1945, he consolidated his reputation as France's most aggressive competitor in wartime domestic competitions. At Wimbledon, ***1946,*** his strength, flair and, notably, the consistency of his heavy serving gained this formidably built player an unexpected title. Drobny beat Kramer, the favourite, in 4r. Petra disposed of Pails, the other expected finalist, in qf and then won 5s matches against Tom Brown and Geoff Brown. That was the peak of his career. Marcel Bernard beat him in the French sf – played in July that year – and his consolation was a doubles victory, partnered by Bernard, over Morea and Segura in f. Patty beat him easily on the second day at Forest Hills and in ***1947*** he lost to Tom Brown in qf at Wimbledon.

NICOLA PIETRANGELI (Italy)
Born 11/9/33. A master of the European clay court style, he was born in Tunis (of a French father and Russian mother) and between ***1954*** and ***1972*** played in 163 D Cup rubbers for Italy, more than anyone in history. Won most rubbers (120), played most singles (109) and won most (78), played most doubles (54), and won most (42), and played in most ties

(66). Appeared in the ***1960/61*** challenge rounds against Australia, but won only one 'dead' singles. Won French singles ***1959/60*** and doubles (with Sirola), Italian singles ***1957/61,*** and German singles ***1960.*** Reached sf at Wimbledon, ***1960,*** and doubles final (with Sirola) ***1956.***

DR JOSHUA PIM (Ireland)
Born 20/6/1869. Died 13/4/1942. A robust, adventurous competitor, regarded by contemporary critics as one of the great geniuses of early tennis. 'When Pim was at his best he was virtually unplayable', wrote Wallis Myers. 'It is scarcely exaggerating to say that he could hit a coin placed anywhere on the court.' He reached sf at Wimbledon ***1890,*** losing to Hamilton, who became Wimbledon's first Irish champ, then lost in ***1891*** to Wilfred Baddeley in the all-comers' f and again in ***1892*** challenge round. He gained his revenge, however, by beating Baddeley in the 2 following Wimbledon f. Pim won the Irish title for the 3rd and last time in ***1895*** but then played little first-class tennis until he was controversially picked for the D Cup match against USA at New York in 1902. He was preferred to Lawrie Doherty, lost both his singles badly and the British Isles were beaten 3–2. 'Although still very good, Pim had no more than a shadow of his former skill, but alas! a great deal more than the shadow of his former weight', wrote Commander Hillyard.

ADRIAN KARL QUIST (Australia)
Born 4/8/13. A shrewd, graceful doubles player, whose victories at Wimbledon were separated by a gap of 15 years. Won with J. H. Crawford in ***1935*** and, when almost a veteran, with J. E. Bromwich ***1950.*** Held Australian title from ***1936–50,*** winning twice with D. P. Turnbull and 8 times with Bromwich. Won US doubles (with Bromwich) ***1939,*** French doubles (with J. H. Crawford) ***1935,*** and Australian singles ***1936/40/48.*** Won 42 out of 55 D Cup rubbers in 28 ties between ***1933–48.***

WILLIAM CHARLES RENSHAW (Great Britain)
Born 3/1/1861. Died 12/8/1904. The first great champ. Learnt on asphalt at school at Cheltenham with twin brother, Ernest, a more graceful but less determined competitor. They were the first spectacular players and their skill – particularly in volleying and smashing – brought crowds to Wimbledon and contributed considerably to the development of lawn tennis as a spectator sport. 'Willie' Renshaw was singles champ at Wimbledon from ***1881–86*** and in ***1889.*** He held the doubles, with Ernest, in ***1884/85/86/88/89.*** Ernest won the singles title in ***1888*** and was beaten by William in the challenge rounds of 1882 and 1883.

NANCY ANN RICHEY (USA)
Born 23/8/42. Later Mrs Gunter. A Texan, famous for her shorts and peaked cap, she was, like her brother, George Clifford Richey, a tenacious baseliner, impressive on clay. Her determination occasionally brought unexpected success on grass. She reached the ***1969*** US final, losing 6–2 6–2 to Margaret Court. She won Australia ***1967,*** beating Lesley Turner, another clay-court specialist, in the final. At Wimbledon she reached qf seven times in nine years ***1964–72*** but was semi-finalist only in ***1968.*** She won Wimbledon doubles with Maria Bueno ***1966.*** On clay she won French singles ***1968,*** beating Ann Jones to avenge a defeat in the ***1966*** final, but the best evidence of her quality was her record in US Clay Courts. She won Indianapolis from ***1963–68*** and even as late as ***1975*** led Chris Evert 7–5 5–0 in the semi-finals there, twice reaching match-point before retiring with cramp at 2–4 in the final set. She played Wightman Cup from ***1962–68*** and Federation Cup ***1964–69.***

ROBERT LARIMORE RIGGS (USA)
Born 25/2/18. A shrewd, confident match-player, with remarkable versatility of shot, he won all 3 titles on his first appearance at Wimbledon in ***1939.*** He also won Forest Hills in ***1939,*** but lost to McNeill in the French f. He turned pro in 1941 and later became a notable

competitor in veterans' events, but his greatest fame came at the age of 55. Profiting from the Women's Lib controversy, he challenged and beat Margaret Court 6–2 6–1 in a singles match in Ramona, Cal, and then lost to Billie Jean King 6–4 6–3 6–3, before a record television audience of almost 50 million and 30,492 paying spectators at the Houston Astrodome in September 1973.

ANTHONY DALTON ROCHE (Australia)
Born 17/6/45. Strong, rugged and a fine volleyer, he was the lefthander in one of Wimbledon's most successful doubles partnerships. He won the doubles with John Newcombe in ***1965,*** from ***1968–70*** (the first hat-trick of titles since the Dohertys 1903–5) and in ***1974.*** Other doubles victories included US ***1967,*** French ***1967–69.*** Australia ***1965/67/71/76/77*** and Italy ***1965/71.*** He did not achieve as much as expected in singles, partly because of injury. The extraordinary operation on his left elbow, performed without knife or anaesthetic in the Philippines by a faith healer, received worldwide publicity. He never reached an Australian final in spite of numerous attempts, but was runner-up to Laver at Wimbledon in ***1968*** and lost two US Open finals: ***1969*** when Laver beat him to complete the Grand Slam and ***1970*** to Rosewall. His most successful year was ***1966*** when he won French and Italian titles. Played Davis Cup ***1964–78*** but did not play singles in a final until he beat Panatta in the opening match ***1977.***

KENNETH ROBERT ROSEWALL (Australia)
Born 2/11/34. For a quarter of a century Rosewall's grace and easy, economical style delighted the connoisseurs and the only regret about his long and distinguished career is that, in spite of four finals over a period of 20 years, he never won the Wimbledon singles title. He began as a Hopman prodigy and it was not until the end of ***1979*** that he retired from Grand Prix tennis. In ***1953,*** aged 18, he won the Australian and French singles and, with Hoad, the French and Wimbledon doubles. In ***1954*** he lost to Drobny in the Wimbledon final. Hoad beat him in the ***1956*** Wimbledon final, but Rosewall avenged that defeat in the US final, frustrating Hoad in the last leg of his attempt on the Grand Slam. Turning professional in ***1957,*** he took over the leadership of the professional circuit from Gonzales until Laver's arrival in ***1963.*** Rosewall's skills endured. In ***1968*** he won the first open tournament at Bournemouth and then recaptured some of his former titles. He regained the French singles and doubles (with Stolle) in ***1968.*** In ***1970*** – after 14 years and aged 35 – he won the US title again and reached his fourth final at Forest Hills in ***1974.*** The gap between his Australian successes was even wider. After his victories in ***1953*** and ***1955,*** he won again in ***1971*** and ***1972.*** But Wimbledon always eluded him. Newcombe beat him in ***1970,*** his third final, and Connors overwhelmed him in the ***1974*** final.

DOROTHY EDITH ROUND (Great Britain)
Born 13/7/09. Died 12/11/82. Became Mrs Little. Determined and efficient, possessing a fine forehand drive and shrewd drop-shot, she was one of the two British women's singles champs at Wimbledon between the wars. She gained her first notable victory there against Lili d'Alvarez in ***1931,*** was r/u to Helen Wills Moody in ***1933,*** then beat Helen Jacobs to win the title in ***1934*** and regained it against Jadwiga Jedrzejowska in ***1937.*** She won the Australian singles in ***1935*** and the Wimbledon mixed in ***1934*** (with Miki) and ***1935/36*** (with Perry). She won 4 of her 13 W Cup rubbers between ***1931–36.***

ELIZABETH RYAN (USA)
Born 5/2/1892. Died 6/7/1979. Suzanne Lenglen's doubles partner and the winner of 19 Wimbledon titles – 12 doubles and 7 mixed. A determined competitor with a cunningly chopped forehand and a great appetite for match-play, she was regarded by contemporaries as 'the best player never to win a great singles championship'. With a variety of partners, she won the Wimbledon doubles ***1914/19/20/21/22/23/25/26/27/30/33/34*** and the mixed ***1919/21/23/27/28/30/32.*** US doubles in ***1926,*** the French doubles ***1930/32/33/34.***

JOHN WILLIAM VAN RYN (USA)
Born 30/6/06. Formed one of the most famous of all doubles partnerships with Wilmer Allison. Pat Hughes described their combination as 'a perfect blending of styles . . . Van Ryn dipped the ball over from the right court and his partner stepped in at the psychological moment for the final volley'. George Lott thought that their deep personal friendship and knowledge of each other's movements and reactions played an important part in their success. With Allison, Van Ryn succeeded at Wimbledon in ***1929–30*** and took the US title in ***1931*** and ***1935.*** He won Paris and Wimbledon with Lott in ***1931.*** In the ***1929*** D Cup challenge round he and Allison beat Cochet and Borotra and in the ***1932*** match they defeated Cochet and Brugnon. He was a member of the US team from ***1929–36*** and won 29 of his 32 rubbers in 24 matches. He lost only two of his 24 D Cup doubles.

MANUEL SANTANA (Spain)
Born 10/5/38. Learnt the game as a ballboy and, after a period in which he was the most admired clay court player in Europe, won US singles ***1965,*** and Wimbledon singles ***1966.*** Possessed a remarkable forehand and great delicacy of touch. Won French singles ***1961*** and ***1964,*** defeating Pietrangeli in both finals, and doubles (with Emerson) ***1963,*** and South African singles ***1967.*** The most successful Spanish player in history, he won 91 D Cup rubbers out of 119 between ***1958*** and ***1973.***

RICHARD SAVITT (USA)
Born 4/3/27. His talent was discovered in the classic fashion by a complete stranger who saw him playing in a public park, and after a modest junior career he became a powerful exponent of the serve and volley game. Concentrating on tennis after a basketball injury in 1949, he rose rapidly on the US ranking-list, moving up from 16th to 6th after reaching sf at Forest Hills, ***1950,*** with victories over Seixas and Bromwich. His remarkable year was ***1951.*** He won both the Australian and Wimbledon titles, defeating McGregor in both finals. This was his first trip to Europe and he never achieved the same kind of success again, although he played some memorable matches, notably sf against Rosewall at Forest Hills, ***1956,*** and a vain defence of his US indoor title in a three-hour f in ***1959.*** He was a member of the US D Cup team in 1951, but was not chosen to play in the challenge round against Australia.

FREDERICK RUDOLPH SCHROEDER (USA)
Born 20/7/21. A powerful Californian whose aggressive serve-and-volley game brought him much success on fast surfaces. The US National Junior Champion in ***1939***, he won the NCAA Championships from Stanford in ***1942*** and the same year won the US Championships, defeating Frank Parker in the final. In ***1949*** he reached the final again but lost in five sets to Pancho Gonzales. Earlier that same year, on his only visit to Wimbledon he had won the singles in heroic fashion after surviving four five-set matches. In the first round he had beaten his doubles partner, Gardnar Mulloy, 7–5 in the fifth (later they reached the doubles final and lost to Gonzales and Parker). In the quarter-finals he had been match-point down to Frank Sedgman and, despite being foot-faulted on his first serve, had followed in his second serve to hit a winning volley and finally won 9–7 in the final set. In all he played 291 games. Only two champions played more – Boris Becker (292) in 1985 and Ashley Cooper (322) in 1958. In doubles he won the US Championships with Jack Kramer in ***1940, 1941*** and ***1947*** and the mixed with Louise Brough in ***1942***. A distinguished member of the US D Cup team between ***1946*** and ***1951***, he played in six challenge rounds, winning eight of his 11 singles and one of his four doubles. – J.B.

FRANCIS ARTHUR SEDGMAN (Australia)
Born 29/10/27. A superb volleyer who seemed to glide about the court, he was Australia's first post-war Wimbledon singles champ and, with Ken McGregor, he achieved the grand slam of the 4 major doubles titles in ***1953.*** Won Wimbledon singles ***1952*** and doubles (with J. E. Bromwich) ***1948*** and (with McGregor) ***/51/52.*** US singles ***1951/52*** and doubles (with Bromwich) ***1950*** and (with McGregor) ***/51.*** French doubles (with McGregor)

1951/52. Australian singles ***1949/50*** and (with McGregor) doubles ***1951/52.*** Italian singles and doubles (with McGregor) ***1952.*** Won 25 D Cup rubbers out of 28 between ***1949–52.*** Turned pro in ***1953.***

FRANCISCO 'PANCHO' SEGURA (Ecuador)
Born 20/6/21. An unorthodox showman who made his reputation in his pro years – he achieved little as an amateur. Won the US Clay Court title in ***1944*** and the US Indoor in ***1946,*** but made little mark at Wimbledon, losing to Tom Brown and to Drobny in his two singles appearances. He turned pro in 1947 and immediately became one of the great entertainers of the pro game. With his double-fisted forehand, his deadly lobs, his scuttling speed about the court, and his beaming smile, he was a most popular competitor for 20 years. If he did not win as many titles as he deserved, he was always capable of testing players of the quality of Kramer, Rosewall, and Gonzales.

ELIAS VICTOR SEIXAS (USA)
Born 30/8/23. A doggedly successful American competitor. Won Wimbledon singles ***1953*** and mixed ***1953/54/55/56,*** 3 times with Doris Hart and once with Shirley Fry. US singles ***1954*** and doubles (with M. G. Rose) ***1952*** and (with M. A. Trabert) ***/54.*** French doubles (with Trabert) ***1954/55.*** Played in 7 successive D Cup challenge rounds and won 38 out of 55 rubbers in 19 ties between ***1951–57.***

MARGARET SMITH (Australia)
Born 16/7/42. Now Mrs Court. In 1970 she became the second woman to achieve the Grand Slam of the major singles championships, having brought off a unique mixed doubles slam with Fletcher in ***1963.*** A powerful athlete, superbly fit, with a heavy service, great stamina and a formidable reach on the volley, she won a record number of 62 GS titles – and would have won more if she had not been afflicted by occasional and often inexplicable losses of confidence. Her major singles successes were Wimbledon ***1963, 1965, 1970,*** US Championships ***1962, 1965, 1969, 1970, 1973,*** French Championships ***1962, 1964, 1969, 1970, 1973,*** and Australia ***1960–66, 1969–71*** and ***1973.*** She was also three times the holder of the Italian, German and South African titles. In addition, she won the doubles at Wimbledon twice and the mixed five times, the US doubles five times and the mixed on eight occasions, the French four times in doubles and mixed, and she held eight Australian doubles and two mixed titles. She toured successfully, with the help of her husband, Barry, with two children, but retired in 1977 when she found that she was expecting a third baby.

STANLEY ROGER SMITH (USA)
Born 14/12/46. The very epitome of the All-American boy with his tall straight-backed figure, his fair hair and his clean-cut good looks, he became a national hero in ***1972***, as well as the world's No. 1 player, when he won a magnificent Wimbledon final against Nastase and then beat the Rumanian again in the opening rubber of the D Cup final on unfriendly clay in Bucharest to launch the United States towards an improbable victory against the odds. Earlier, in ***1969***, he had won the US Nationals and the following year had beaten Laver and Rosewall to capture the first-ever Masters which, that year, was a round-robin competition. When he won the US Open in ***1971*** on the grass of Forest Hills he was perfecting the serve-and-volley technique that made him such an awkward opponent. Although his groundstrokes were never his strength, he used them intelligently to secure the few breaks of serve that were necessary as he blanketed the net to secure his own service games. His doubles partnership with Lutz was one of the best American pairings there has ever been. They are the only pair to have won US National titles on all four surfaces – grass, clay, hard and indoor. Four times they won the US Open – ***1968, 1974, 1978, 1980*** and in ***1977*** they were successful both in South Africa and the US Pro at Boston. In D Cup they are the only American pair to have won three Challenge Round rubbers and two in the Final Round. Overall his D Cup record is 34 wins and 7 losses in 23 ties. – J.B.

FREDERICK SYDNEY STOLLE (Australia)
Born 8/10/38. Former Sydney bank clerk, regarded primarily as doubles specialist, who by diligence and determination became one of the most successful singles players of the 1960s. Powerful serving and volleying, added to dogged consistency in return of service on the backhand, compensated for his lack of mobility and flexibility. Shared with Von Cramm the unlucky distinction of losing in 3 successive Wimbledon singles f, falling to McKinley ***(1963)*** and Emerson ***(1964/65).*** Was also r/u to Lundquist in ***1964*** Italian f, but won French singles ***1965*** and US and German titles ***1966.*** Established himself first as a doubles player with Hewitt. They won Australia ***1963/64,*** Wimbledon ***1962/64*** and Italy ***1963/64.*** With Emerson, who had dominated him in singles, won French and US doubles ***1965*** and Australia, Italy and US ***1966.*** In ***1981,*** aged 42, he and Newcombe (37) took McEnroe/Fleming to 5s tie-break in US Open sf. Became contract professional ***1967*** and reached Wimbledon doubles f with Rosewall ***1968.*** Between ***1964–66*** he won 13 out of his 16 D Cup rubbers. Coached NY Sets to victory in World Team Tennis competition ***1976.***

ERIC WILLIAM STURGESS (South Africa)
Born 10/6/20. South Africa's most successful singles competitor and their nat champ on no fewer than 11 occasions, beginning a sequence of victories in ***1939/40*** and continuing in ***1946, 1948–54,*** and ***1957.*** Outside Johannesburg his major achievement was the capture of the German singles ***1952;*** r/u in Paris ***1947*** and ***1951*** and lost to Gonzales in ***1948*** US f. Twice he was in Wimbledon sf, but in spite of speed, steadiness, and elegance, he lacked the weight of shot to win in the highest class and his second service was vulnerable. He won the French doubles with Fannin ***1947*** and a number of mixed titles, notably Wimbledon ***1949*** (with Sheila Summers) and ***1950*** (with Louise Brough), and F Hills ***1949*** (with Brough).

WILLIAM F. TALBERT (USA)
Born 4/11/18. An expert in the practice, technique and strategy of doubles. The best right-court player of his generation, his most important victories were gained with Mulloy, with whom he won the US doubles ***1942/45/46/48***, and a total of 84 out of 90 tournaments in ten years. With a variety of partners, he won US Clay Court doubles ***1942/44/45/46*** and the US Indoor Doubles ***1949/50/51/52/54***. Abroad, with the young Trabert, also from Cincinnati, he won French and Italian doubles ***1950***. He was runner-up to Parker in US singles ***1944/45*** and US Indoor champion ***1948/51***. He won nine of his ten D Cup rubbers ***1946–53***, from ***1953–57*** he captained the US D Cup team and later became Tournament Director of the US Open. All this was achieved despite the disability of diabetes.

WILLIAM TATUM TILDEN (USA)
Born 10/2/1893. Died 5/6/1953. For many critics the greatest player and student of match-strategy in the history of the game. Tall, with a long reach and a long stride, great strength and versatility of shot, and a powerful sense of drama, Tilden did not win a major title until he was 27. Then won Wimbledon singles ***1920/21/30,*** and doubles (with F. T. Hunter) ***1927,*** and US singles ***1920/21/22/23/24/25/29,*** and doubles ***1918/21/22/23/27.*** Was first Italian champ in ***1930*** and played D Cup from ***1920–30*** winning 34 rubbers out of 41 and 21 out of 28 in challenge rounds. Between ***1920–26*** won 13 successive challenge round singles. Turned pro in ***1931.***

MARION ANTHONY TRABERT (USA)
Born 16/8/30. Won Wimbledon singles ***1955*** and US singles ***1953/55*** without losing a set. Won French singles ***1954,*** and doubles victories included US in ***1954*** (with E. V. Seixas), French ***1950*** (with W. F. Talbert) and ***1954/55*** (with Seixas) and Italian ***1950*** (with Talbert). Won 27 out of 35 D Cup rubbers between ***1951–55.*** Turned pro in ***1955.***

Rod Laver was the first tennis millionaire and the first player to achieve the Grand Slam twice – as an amateur in 1962 and as a professional in 1969. *(A. Evans)*

CHRISTINE CLARA TRUMAN (Great Britain)
Born 16/1/41. Now Mrs Janes. Britain's most popular post-war player. She possessed a powerful forehand, a disconcerting ability to hit her way out of crises, a remarkable capacity for unorthodox volleying, and temperament and court manners that made her a model for every schoolgirl in the country. She was always regarded as a potential Wimbledon champ and reached sf at the age of 16 at her first Wimbledon, where she lost to Althea Gibson, the eventual winner. Afterwards came a series of spectacular failures until she reached the ***1961*** f, only to fall to Angela Mortimer. Her best performances were a victory over Miss Gibson in the ***1958*** W Cup match, which helped to give Britain the trophy for the first time since the war, and the capture of the French and Italian singles titles in ***1959.*** Won ***1960*** Australian doubles with Maria Bueno. She and her sister, Nell, formed an aggressively effective – and sometimes erratic – doubles partnership. She won 10 rubbers out of 25 in 11 W Cup matches.

LESLEY ROSEMARY TURNER (Australia)
Born 16/8/1942. Now Mrs Bowrey. Clever, strong and persistent, she gained her principal successes on European clay courts. In ***1961*** on her first European tour she lost to Maria Bueno in the Italian final and was runner-up again ***1962*** and ***1964*** before winning the title

1967/68. She won the French singles ***1963,*** defeating Ann Jones, and ***1965,*** beating Margaret Court, and was runner-up ***1962*** and ***1967.*** She reached the Australian final ***1964*** and ***1967.*** In doubles, with Margaret Court, she won Wimbledon ***1964,*** Paris ***1964/65*** and Australia ***1965.*** Also took the Australian doubles title, with Judy Tegart, ***1964*** and ***1967*** and the US doubles, with Darlene Hard, ***1961.*** Won Wimbledon mixed doubles with Fred Stolle ***1961*** and ***1964.***

H. ELLSWORTH VINES (USA)
Born 28/9/11. The possessor of a fine forehand and one of the fastest services of all time. Defeated Bunny Austin in ***1932*** 6–4 6–2 6–0 in one of the shortest Wimbledon f and lost title next year in a classic f against Jack Crawford. Won US singles ***1931/32*** and Australian doubles ***1933.*** Played D Cup ***1932/33,*** winning 13 rubbers out of 16. Turned pro ***1934.***

SARAH VIRGINIA WADE (Great Britain)
Born 10/7/45. A spectacular and dramatic competitor, at her 16th attempt she finally achieved her ambition of winning the women's singles at Wimbledon in the Centenary year of ***1977***. Until then her career had been an extravagant mixture of bitter disappointments, many of the worst endured at Wimbledon, and dazzling successes. Her first major success was gained at US Open ***1968*** when she defeated Billie Jean King 6–4 6–2 in the final. She won the Australian title, beating Evonne Goolagong, in ***1972*** and gained her only major clay-court success in ***1971***, when she defeated Helga Masthoff in the Italian final. Her best doubles victories – France ***1973***, US ***1973/75***, Australia ***1975*** and Italy ***1968*** – were won with Margaret Court, but she also succeeded in Rome ***1971*** with Mrs Masthoff and ***1973*** with Olga Morozova. She also holds the record for the most appearances of any player of any nation in both Fed Cup (100 rubbers in 57 ties) and the W Cup (56 rubbers in 20 ties).

ANTHONY FREDERICK WILDING (New Zealand)
Born 31/10/1883. Killed in action in Belgium 9/5/1915. Coached by his father, a notable cricketer, he won the champ of Canterbury, New Zealand, at the age of 17 and went to Cambridge Univ for which he played ***1904–05.*** He became one of the great heroes of Edwardian tennis, winning the singles champ at Wimbledon ***1910/11/12/13.*** Won doubles (with N. E. Brookes) in ***1907*** and (with M. J. G. Ritchie) ***/08/10.*** He won 21 of the 30 D Cup rubbers which he played for Australasia between ***1905–14.***

SIDNEY BURR BEARDSLEE WOOD (USA)
Born 1/11/11. A nephew of the late Julian Myrick, a former President of the US LTA and the prime mover in 1913 in the development of Forest Hills as the national centre of tennis in the US, he made his first appearance at Wimbledon, aged 15, in ***1927,*** playing Lacoste on the Centre Court. In ***1931,*** aged 19 years and 243 days, he became Wimbledon's second youngest champion at the time. He won by default. Frank Shields fell in 4s of his sf against Borotra and damaged an ankle. Shields won, but was not fit enough to play in f. A shrewd strategist and a graceful stroke-maker, Wood was r/u to Allison at Forest Hills in ***1935*** but lost 6–2 6–2 6–3 in one of the tournament's most disappointing finals.

CHAMPIONSHIP ROLLS

AUSTRALIAN CHAMPIONSHIPS

MEN'S SINGLES

	CHAMPION	RUNNER-UP	SCORE
1905	R. W. Heath	A. H. Curtis	4–6 6–3 6–4 6–4
1906	A. F. Wilding	F. N. Fisher	6–0 6–0 6–4
1907	H. M. Rice	H. A. Parker	6–3 6–4 6–4
1908	F. B. Alexander	A. W. Dunlop	3–6 3–6 6–0 6–2 6–3
1909	A. F. Wilding	E. F. Parker	6–1 7–5 6–2
1910	R. W. Heath	H. M. Rice	6–4 6–3 6–2
1911	N. E. Brookes	H. M. Rice	6–1 6–2 6–3
1912	J. C. Parke	A. E. Beamish	3–6 6–2 1–6 6–1 7–5
1913	E. F. Parker	H. A. Parker	2–6 6–1 6–3 6–2
1914	A. O'Hara Wood	G. L. Patterson	6–4 6–3 5–7 6–1
1915	F. G. Lowe	H. M. Rice	4–6 6–1 6–1 6–4
1916–18	*Not held*		
1919	A. R. F. Kingscote	E. O. Pockley	6–4 6–0 6–3
1920	P. O'Hara Wood	R. V. Thomas	6–3 4–6 6–8 6–1 6–3
1921	R. H. Gemmell	A. Hedeman	7–5 6–1 6–4
1922	J. O. Anderson	G. L. Patterson	6–0 3–6 3–6 6–3 6–2
1923	P. O'Hara Wood	C. B. St John	6–1 6–1 6–3
1924	J. O. Anderson	R. E. Schlesinger	6–3 6–4 3–6 5–7 6–3
1925	J. O. Anderson	G. L. Patterson	11–9 2–6 6–2 6–3
1926	J. B. Hawkes	J. Willard	6–1 6–3 6–1
1927	G. L. Patterson	J. B. Hawkes	3–6 6–4 3–6 18–16 6–3
1928	J. Borotra	R. O. Cummings	6–4 6–1 4–6 5–7 6–3
1929	J. C. Gregory	R. E. Schlesinger	6–2 6–2 5–7 7–5
1930	E. F. Moon	H. C. Hopman	6–3 6–1 6–3
1931	J. H. Crawford	H. C. Hopman	6–4 6–2 2–6 6–1
1932	J. H. Crawford	H. C. Hopman	4–6 6–3 3–6 6–3 6–1
1933	J. H. Crawford	K. Gledhill	2–6 7–5 6–3 6–2
1934	F. J. Perry	J. H. Crawford	6–3 7–5 6–1
1935	J. H. Crawford	F. J. Perry	2–6 6–4 6–4 6–4
1936	A. K. Quist	J. H. Crawford	6–2 6–3 4–6 3–6 9–7
1937	V. B. McGrath	J. E. Bromwich	6–3 1–6 6–0 2–6 6–1
1938	J. D. Budge	J. E. Bromwich	6–4 6–2 6–1
1939	J. E. Bromwich	A. K. Quist	6–4 6–1 6–3
1940	A. K. Quist	J. H. Crawford	6–3 6–1 6–2
1941–45	*Not held*		
1946	J. E. Bromwich	D. Pails	5–7 6–3 7–5 3–6 6–2
1947	D. Pails	J. E. Bromwich	4–6 6–4 3–6 7–5 8–6
1948	A. K. Quist	J. E. Bromwich	6–4 3–6 6–3 2–6 6–3
1949	F. A. Sedgman	J. E. Bromwich	6–3 6–2 6–2
1950	F. A. Sedgman	K. McGregor	6–3 6–4 4–6 6–1
1951	R. Savitt	K. McGregor	6–3 2–6 6–3 6–1
1952	K. McGregor	F. A. Sedgman	7–5 12–10 2–6 6–2
1953	K. R. Rosewall	M. G. Rose	6–0 6–3 6–4
1954	M. G. Rose	R. N. Hartwig	6–2 0–6 6–4 6–2
1955	K. R. Rosewall	L. A. Hoad	9–7 6–4 6–4
1956	L. A. Hoad	K. R. Rosewall	6–4 3–6 6–4 7–5
1957	A. J. Cooper	N. A. Fraser	6–3 9–11 6–4 6–2
1958	A. J. Cooper	M. J. Anderson	7–5 6–3 6–4
1959	A. Olmedo	N. A. Fraser	6–1 6–2 3–6 6–3
1960	R. G. Laver	N. A. Fraser	5–7 3–6 6–3 8–6 8–6
1961	R. S. Emerson	R. G. Laver	1–6 6–3 7–6 6–4
1962	R. G. Laver	R. S. Emerson	8–6 0–6 6–4 6–4

				FIRST PRIZE (US $)
1963	R. S. Emerson	K. N. Fletcher	6–3 6–3 6–1	
1964	R. S. Emerson	F. S. Stolle	6–3 6–4 6–2	
1965	R. S. Emerson	F. S. Stolle	7–9 2–6 6–4 7–5 6–1	
1966	R. S. Emerson	A. R. Ashe	6–4 6–8 6–2 6–3	
1967	R. S. Emerson	A. R. Ashe	6–4 6–1 6–4	
1968	W. W. Bowrey	J. M. Gisbert	7–5 2–6 9–7 6–4	
1969	R. G. Laver	A. Gimeno	6–3 6–4 7–5	5,000
1970	A. R. Ashe	R. D. Crealy	6–4 9–7 6–2	3,800
1971	K. R. Rosewall	A. R. Ashe	6–1 7–5 6–3	10,000
1972	K. R. Rosewall	M. J. Anderson	7–6 6–3 7–5	2,240
1973	J. D. Newcombe	O. Parun	6–3 6–7 7–5 6–1	8,750
1974	J. S. Connors	P. Dent	7–6 6–4 4–6 6–3	9,750
1975	J. D. Newcombe	J. S. Connors	7–5 3–6 6–4 7–5	12,489
1976	M. Edmondson	J. D. Newcombe	6–7 6–3 7–6 6–1	32,000
1977	(Jan) R. Tanner	G. Vilas	6–3 6–3 6–3	32,000
1977	(Dec) V. Gerulaitis	J. M. Lloyd	6–3 7–6 5–7 3–6 6–2	28,000
1978	G. Vilas	J. Marks	6–4 6–4 3–6 6–3	41,000
1979	G. Vilas	J. Sadri	7–6 6–3 6–2	50,000
1980	B. Teacher	K. Warwick	7–5 7–6 6–3	65,000
1981	J. Kriek	S. Denton	6–2 7–6 6–7 6–4	65,000
1982	J. Kriek	S. Denton	6–3 6–3 6–2	70,000
1983	M. Wilander	I. Lendl	6–1 6–4 6–4	77,500
1984	M. Wilander	K. Curren	6–7 6–4 7–6 6–2	100,000
1985	S. Edberg	M. Wilander	6–4 6–3 6–3	100,000
1986	*Not held*			
1987	S. Edberg	P. Cash	6–3 6–4 3–6 5–7 6–3	103,875

WOMEN'S SINGLES

	CHAMPION	RUNNER-UP	SCORE
1922	Mrs M. Molesworth	Miss E. F. Boyd	6–3 10–8
1923	Mrs M. Molesworth	Miss E. F. Boyd	6–1 7–5
1924	Miss S. Lance	Miss E. F. Boyd	6–3 3–6 6–4
1925	Miss D. Akhurst	Miss E. F. Boyd	1–6 8–6 6–4
1926	Miss D. Akhurst	Miss E. F. Boyd	6–1 6–3
1927	Miss E. F. Boyd	Mrs S. Harper	5–7 6–1 6–2
1928	Miss D. Akhurst	Miss E. F. Boyd	7–5 6–2
1929	Miss D. Akhurst	Miss L. M. Bickerton	6–1 5–7 6–2
1930	Miss D. Akhurst	Mrs S. Harper	10–8 2–6 7–5
1931	Mrs C. Buttsworth	Mrs J. H. Crawford	1–6 6–3 6–4
1932	Mrs C. Buttsworth	Miss K. Le Messurier	9–7 6–4
1933	Miss J. Hartigan	Mrs C. Buttsworth	6–4 6–3
1934	Miss J. Hartigan	Mrs M. Molesworth	6–1 6–4
1935	Miss D. E. Round	Miss N. M. Lyle	1–6 6–1 6–3
1936	Miss J. Hartigan	Miss N. Wynne	6–4 6–4
1937	Miss N. Wynne	Mrs V. Westacott	6–3 5–7 6–4
1938	Miss D. M. Bundy	Miss D. Stevenson	6–3 6–2
1939	Mrs V. Westacott	Mrs H. C. Hopman	6–1 6–2
1940	Mrs N. Bolton	Miss T. Coyne	5–7 6–4 6–0
1941–45	*Not held*		
1946	Mrs N. Bolton	Miss J. Fitch	6–4 6–4
1947	Mrs N. Bolton	Mrs H. C. Hopman	6–3 6–2
1948	Mrs N. Bolton	Miss M. Toomey	6–3 6–1
1949	Miss D. J. Hart	Mrs N. Bolton	6–3 6–4
1950	Miss A. L. Brough	Miss D. J. Hart	6–4 3–6 6–4
1951	Mrs N. Bolton	Mrs T. D. Long	6–1 7–5
1952	Mrs T. D. Long	Miss H. Angwin	6–2 6–3
1953	Miss M. Connolly	Miss J. Sampson	6–3 6–2
1954	Mrs T. D. Long	Miss J. Staley	6–3 6–4
1955	Miss B. Penrose	Mrs T. D. Long	6–4 6–3
1956	Miss M. Carter	Mrs T. D. Long	3–6 6–2 9–7
1957	Miss S. J. Fry	Miss A. Gibson	6–3 6–4
1958	Miss A. Mortimer	Miss L. Coghlan	6–3 6–4
1959	Mrs S. J. Reitano	Miss R. Schuurman	6–2 6–3
1960	Miss M. Smith	Miss J. Lehane	7–5 6–2
1961	Miss M. Smith	Miss J. Lehane	6–1 6–4
1962	Miss M. Smith	Miss J. Lehane	6–0 6–2
1963	Miss M. Smith	Miss J. Lehane	6–2 6–2
1964	Miss M. Smith	Miss L. R. Turner	6–3 6–2
1965	Miss M. Smith	Miss M. E. Bueno	5–7 6–4 5–2 ret'd

				FIRST PRIZE (US $)
1966	Miss M. Smith	Miss N. Richey	w.o.	
1967	Miss N. Richey	Miss L. R. Turner	6–1 6–4	
1968	Mrs L. W. King	Mrs B. M. Court	6–1 6–2	
1969	Mrs B. M. Court	Mrs L. W. King	6–4 6–1	2,000
1970	Mrs B. M. Court	Miss K. Melville	6–1 6–3	700
1971	Mrs B. M. Court	Miss E. Goolagong	2–6 7–5 7–6	1,800
1972	Miss S. V. Wade	Miss E. Goolagong	6–4 6–4	1,200
1973	Mrs B. M. Court	Miss E. Goolagong	6–4 7–5	5,700
1974	Miss E. Goolagong	Miss C. M. Evert	7–6 4–6 6–0	9,000
1975	Miss E. Goolagong	Miss M. Navratilova	6–3 6–2	8,115
1976	Mrs E. Cawley	Miss R. Tomanova	6–2 6–2	12,000
1977	(Jan) Mrs G. Reid	Miss D. Fromholtz	7–5 6–2	12,000
1977	(Dec) Mrs E. Cawley	Mrs H. Cawley	6–3 6–0	9,000
1978	Miss C. O'Neil	Miss B. Nagelsen	6–3 7–6	6,000
1979	Miss B. Jordan	Miss S. Walsh	6–3 6–3	10,000
1980	Miss H. Mandlikova	Miss W. M. Turnbull	6–0 7–5	32,000
1981	Miss M. Navratilova	Mrs C. Evert Lloyd	6–7 6–4 7–5	34,000
1982	Mrs C. Evert Lloyd	Miss M. Navratilova	6–3 2–6 6–3	40,000
1983	Miss M. Navratilova	Miss K. Jordan	6–2 7–6	75,000
1984	Mrs J. M. Lloyd	Miss H. Sukova	6–7 6–1 6–3	100,000
1985	Miss M.Navratilova	Mrs J. M. Lloyd	6–2 4–6 6–2	100,000
1986	*Not held*			
1987	Miss H. Mandlikova	Miss M. Navratilova	7–5 7–6	115,000

MEN'S DOUBLES

	CHAMPIONS	RUNNERS-UP	SCORE
1905	R. Lycett/T. Tachell	E. T. Barnard/B. Spence	11–9 8–6 1–6 4–6 6–1
1906	R. W. Heath/A. F. Wilding	C. C. Cox/H. A. Parker	6–2 6–4 6–2
1907	W. A. Gregg/H. A. Parker	H. M. Rice/G. W. Wright	6–2 3–6 6–3 6–2
1908	F. B. Alexander/A. W. Dunlop	G. G. Sharpe/A. F. Wilding	6–3 6–2 6–1
1909	J. P. Keane/E. F. Parker	C. Crooks/A. F. Wilding	1–6 6–1 6–1 9–7
1910	A. Campbell/H. M. Rice	R. W. Heath/J. L. O'Dea	6–3 6–3 6–2
1911	H. W. Heath/R. Lycett	J. J. Addison/N. E. Brookes	6–2 7–5 6–0
1912	C. P. Dixon/J. C. Parke	A. E. Beamish/F. G. Lowe	6–0 6–4 6–2
1913	A. H. Hedemann/E. F. Parker	H. Parker/R. Taylor	8–6 4–6 6–4 6–4
1914	A. Campbell/G. L. Patterson	R. W. Heath/A. O'Hara Wood	7–5 3–6 6–3 6–3
1915	H. M. Rice/C. V. Todd	F. G. Lowe/C. St John	8–6 6–4 7–9 6–3
1916–1918	*Not held*		
1919	P. O'Hara Wood/R. V. Thomas	J. O. Anderson/A. H. Lowe	7–5 6–1 7–9 3–6 6–3
1920	P. O'Hara Wood/R. V. Thomas	H. Rice/R. Taylor	6–1 6–0 7–5
1921	S. H. Eaton/R. H. Gemmell	E. Stokes/N. Breasly	7–5 6–3 6–3
1922	J. B. Hawkes/G. L. Patterson	J. O. Anderson/N. Peach	8–10 6–0 6–0 7–5
1923	P. O'Hara Wood/C. B. St John	H. Rice/J. Bullough	6–4 6–3 3–6 6–0
1924	J. O. Anderson/N. E. Brookes	P. O'Hara Wood/G. L. Patterson	6–2 6–4 6–3
1925	P. O'Hara Wood/G. L. Patterson	J. O. Anderson/F. Kalms	6–4 8–6 7–5
1926	J. B. Hawkes/G. L. Patterson	J. O. Anderson/P. O'Hara Wood	6–1 6–4 6–2
1927	J. B. Hawkes/G. L. Patterson	I. McInnes/P. O'Hara Wood	8–6 6–2 6–1
1928	J. Borotra/J. Brugnon	E. F. Moon/J. Willard	6–2 4–6 6–4 6–4
1929	J. H. Crawford/H. C. Hopman	R. O. Cummings/E. F. Moon	6–1 6–8 4–6 6–1 6–3
1930	J. H. Crawford/H. C. Hopman	J. Fitchett/J. B. Hawkes	8–6 6–1 2–6 6–3
1931	C. Donohoe/R. Dunlop	J. H. Crawford/H. O. Hopman	8–6 6–2 5–7 7–9 6–4
1932	J. H. Crawford/E. F. Moon	H. C. Hopman/G. L. Patterson	12–10 6–3 4–6 6–4
1933	K. Gledhill/H. E. Vines	J. H. Crawford/E. F. Moon	6–4 10–8 6–2
1934	G. P. Hughes/F. J. Perry	A. K. Quist/D. P. Turnbull	6–8 6–3 6–4 3–6 6–3
1935	J. H. Crawford/V. B. McGrath	G. P. Hughes/F. J. Perry	6–4 8–6 6–2
1935	J. H. Crawford/V. B. McGrath	G. P. Hughes/F. J. Perry	6–4 8–6 6–2
1936	A. K. Quist/D. P. Turnbull	J. H. Crawford/V. B. McGrath	6–8 6–2 6–1 3–6 6–2
1937	A. K. Quist/D. P. Turnbull	J. E. Bromwich/J. E. Harper	6–2 9–7 1–6 6–8 6–4
1938	J. E. Bromwich/A. K. Quist	H. Henkel/G. Von Cramm	7–5 6–4 6–0
1939	J. E. Bromwich/A. K. Quist	C. F. Long/D. P. Turnbull	6–4 7–5 6–2
1940	J. E. Bromwich/A. K. Quist	J. H. Crawford/V. B. McGrath	6–3 7–5 6–1
1941–1945	*Not held*		
1946	J. E. Bromwich/A. K. Quist	M. Newcombe/L. A. Schwartz	6–4 6–2 6–3
1947	J. E. Bromwich/A. K. Quist	F. A. Sedgman/G. Worthington	6–1 6–3 6–1
1948	J. E. Bromwich/A. K. Quist	C. Long/F. A. Sedgman	1–6 6–8 9–7 6–3 8–6
1949	J. E. Bromwich/A. K. Quist	G. Brown/O. W. Sidwell	6–8 7–5 6–2 6–3
1950	J. E. Bromwich/A. K. Quist	J. Drobny/E. W. Sturgess	6–3 5–7 4–6 6–3 8–6
1951	K. McGregor/F. A. Sedgman	J. E. Bromwich/A. K. Quist	11–9 2–6 6–3 4–6 6–3
1952	K. McGregor/F. A. Sedgman	D. Candy/M. G. Rose	6–4 7–5 6–3

1953	L. A. Hoad/K. R. Rosewall	D. Candy/M. G. Rose	9–11 6–4 10–8 6–4
1954	R. N. Hartwig/M. G. Rose	N. A. Fraser/C. Wilderspin	6–3 6–4 6–2
1955	E. V. Seixas/M. A. Trabert	L. A. Hoad/K. R. Rosewall	6–3 6–2 2–6 3–6 6–1
1956	L. A. Hoad/K. R. Rosewall	D. Candy/M. G. Rose	10–8 13–11 6–4
1957	N. A. Fraser/L. A. Hoad	M. J. Anderson/A. Cooper	6–3 8–6 6–4
1958	A. Cooper/N. A. Fraser	R. S. Emerson/R. Mark	6–5 6–8 3–6 6–3 7–5
1959	R. G. Laver/R. Mark	D. Candy/R. N. Howe	9–7 6–4 6–2
1960	R. G. Laver/R. Mark	R. S. Emerson/N. A. Fraser	1–6 6–2 6–4 6–4
1961	R. G. Laver/R. Mark	R. S. Emerson/M. F. Mulligan	6–3 7–5 3–6 7–9 6–2
1962	R. S. Emerson/N. A. Fraser	R. A. J. Hewitt/F. S. Stolle	4–6 4–6 6–1 6–4 11–9
1963	R. A. J. Hewitt/F. S. Stolle	K. N. Fletcher/J. D. Newcombe	6–2 3–6 6–3 3–6 6–3
1964	R. A. J. Hewitt/F. S. Stolle	R. S. Emerson/K. N. Fletcher	6–4 7–5 3–6 4–6 14–12
1965	J. D. Newcombe/A. D. Roche	R. S. Emerson/F. S. Stolle	3–6 4–6 13–11 6–3 6–4
1966	R. S. Emerson/F. S. Stolle	J. D. Newcombe/A. D. Roche	7–9 6–3 6–8 14–12 12–10
1967	J. D. Newcombe/A. D. Roche	W. W. Bowrey/O. K. Davidson	3–6 6–3 7–5 6–8 8–6
1968	R. D. Crealy/A. J. Stone	T. Addison/R. Keldie	10–8 6–4 6–3
1969	R. S. Emerson/R. G. Laver	K. R. Rosewall/F. S. Stolle	6–4 6–4 6–4
1970	R. C. Lutz/S. R. Smith	J. G. Alexander/P. Dent	6–3 8–6 6–3
1971	J. D. Newcombe/A. D. Roche	T. S. Okker/M. C. Riessen	6–2 7–6
1972	O. K. Davidson/K. R. Rosewall	R. Case/G. Masters	3–6 7–6 6–3
1973	M. J. Anderson/J. D. Newcombe	J. G. Alexander/P. Dent	6–3 6–4 7–6
1974	R. Case/G. Masters	S. Ball/R. Giltinan	6–7 6–3 6–4
1975	J. G. Alexander/P. Dent	R. Carmichael/A. J. Stone	6–3 7–6
1976	J. D. Newcombe/A. D. Roche	R. Case/G. Masters	7–6 6–4
1977	A. R. Ashe/A. D. Roche	C. Pasarell/E. Van Dillen	6–4 6–4
1977	(Dec) R. O. Ruffels/A. J. Stone	J. G. Alexander/P. Dent	7–6 7–6
1978	W. Fibak/K. Warwick	P. Kronk/C. Letcher	7–6 7–5
1979	P. McNamara/P. McNamee	P. Kronk/C. Letcher	7–6 6–2
1980	M. R. Edmondson/K. Warwick	P. McNamara/P. McNamee	7–5 6–4
1981	M. R. Edmondson/K. Warwick	H. Pfister/J. Sadri	6–3 6–7 6–3
1982	J. G. Alexander/J. Fitzgerald	A. Andrews/J. Sadri	6–4 7–6
1983	M. R. Edmondson/P. McNamee	S. Denton/S. E. Stewart	6–3 7–6
1984	M. R. Edmondson/S. E. Stewart	J. Nystrom/M. Wilander	6–2 6–2 7–5
1985	P. Annacone/C. Van Rensburg	M. R. Edmondson/K. Warwick	3–6 7–6 6–4 6–4
1986	*Not held*		
1987	S. Edberg/A. Jarryd	P. Doohan/L. Warder	6–4 6–4 7–6

WOMEN'S DOUBLES

	CHAMPIONS	RUNNERS-UP	SCORE
1922	E. F. Boyd/M. Mountain	St George/H. S. Utz	1–6 6–4 7–5
1923	E. F. Boyd/S. Lance	M. Molesworth/H. Turner	6–1 6–4
1924	D. Akhurst/S. Lance	K. Le Mesurier/P. O'Hara Wood	7–5 6–2
1925	D. Akhurst/R. Harper	E. F. Boyd/K. Le Mesurier	6–4 6–3
1926	E. F. Boyd/P. O'Hara Wood	D. Akhurst/M. Cox	6–3 6–8 8–6
1927	L. M. Bickerton/P. O'Hara Wood	E. F. Boyd/R. Harper	6–3 6–3
1928	D. Akhurst/E. F. Boyd	K. Le Mesurier/D. Weston	6–3 6–1
1929	D. Akhurst/L. M. Bickerton	R. Harper/P. O'Hara Wood	6–2 3–6 6–2
1930	E. Hood/M. Molesworth	M. Cox/R. Harper	6–3 0–6 7–5
1931	L. M. Bickerton/R. Cozens	A. Lloyd/H. S. Utz	6–0 6–4
1932	C. Buttsworth/J. H. Crawford	K. Le Mesurier/D. Weston	6–2 6–2
1933	M. Molesworth/V. Westacott	J. Hartigan/J. Van Ryn	6–3 6–3
1934	M. Molesworth/V. Westacott	J. Hartigan/U. Valkenborg	6–8 6–4 6–4
1935	E. M. Dearman/N. M. Lyle	L. M. Bickerton/N. Hopman	6–3 6–4
1936	T. Coyne/N. Wynne	M. Blick/K. Woodward	6–2 6–4
1937	T. Coyne/N. Wynne	N. Hopman/V. Westacott	6–2 6–2
1938	T. Coyne/N. Wynne	D. M. Bundy/D. E. Workman	9–7 6–4
1939	T. Coyne/N. Wynne	M. Hardcastle/V. Westacott	7–5 6–4
1940	T. Coyne/N. Bolton	J. Hartigan/E. Niemeyer	7–5 6–2
1941–1945	*Not held*		
1946	M. Bevis/J. Fitch	Not available	
1947	N. Bolton/T. D. Long	M. Bevis/J. Fitch	6–3 6–3
1948	N. Bolton/T. D. Long	M. Bevis/N. Jones	6–3 6–3
1949	N. Bolton/T. D. Long	D./M. Toomey	6–0 6–1
1950	L. Brough/D. J. Hart	N. Bolton/T. D. Long	6–3 2–6 6–3
1951	N. Bolton/T. D. Long	J. Fitch/M. Hawton	6–2 6–1
1952	N. Bolton/T. D. Long	R. Baker/M. Hawton	6–1 6–1
1953	M. Connolly/J. Sampson	M. Hawton/B. Penrose	6–3 6–2
1954	M. Hawton/B. Penrose	H. Redick-Smith/J. Wipplinger	6–3 8–6
1955	M. Hawton/B. Penrose	N. Hopman/A. Thiele	7–5 6–1

1956	M. Hawton/T. D. Long	M. Carter/B. Penrose	6–3 5–7 9–7
1957	S. J. Fry/A. Gibson	M. Hawton/F. Muller	6–2 6–1
1958	M. Hawton/T. D. Long	L. Coghlan/A. Mortimer	7–5 6–8 6–2
1959	S. Reynolds/R. Schuurman	L. Coghlan/M. Reitano	7–5 6–4
1960	M. E. Bueno/C. Truman	L. Robinson/M. Smith	6–2 5–7 6–2
1961	M. Reitano/M. Smith	M. Hawton/J. Lehane	6–3 3–6 7–5
1962	E. Ebbern/M. Smith	D. R. Hard/M. Reintano	6–4 6–4
1963	R. Ebbern/M. Smith	J. Lehane/L. R. Turner	6–1 6–3
1964	J. A. M. Tegart/L. R. Turner	R. Ebbern/M. Smith	6–4 6–4
1965	M. Smith/L. R. Turner	R. Ebbern/B. J. Moffitt	1–6 6–2 6–3
1966	C. Graebner/N. Richey	M. Smith/L. R. Turner	6–4 7–5
1967	J. A. M. Tegart/L. R. Turner	L. Robinson/E. Terras	6–0 6–2
1968	K. Krantzcke/K. Melville	J. A. M. Tegart/L. R. Turner	6–4 3–6 6–2
1969	B. M. Court/J. A. M. Tegart	R. Casals/L. W. King	6–4 6–4
1970	B. M. Court/D. Dalton	K. Krantzcke/K. Melville	6–3 6–4
1971	B. M. Court/E. F. Goolagong	J. Emmerson/L. Hunt	6–0 6–0
1972	H. Gourlay/K. Harris	P. Coleman/K. Krantzcke	6–2 6–3
1973	B. M. Court/S. V. Wade	K. Harris/K. Melville	6–4 6–4
1974	E. F. Goolagong/M. Michel	K. Harris/K. Melville	7–5 6–3
1975	E. F. Goolagong/M. Michel	B. M. Court/O. Morozova	7–6 7–6
1976	E. F. Cawley/H. Gourlay	W. W. Bowrey/R. Tomanova	8–1 (one set)
1977	D. Fromholtz/H. Gourlay	B. Nagelsen/G. E. Reid	5–7 6–1 7–5
1977	(Dec) E. F. Cawley/H. Cawley div'd with M. Guerrant/G. E. Reid		
1978	B. Nagelsen/R. Tomanova	N. Sato/P. Whytcross	7–5 6–2
1979	D. D. Chaloner/D. R. Evers	L. Harrison/M. Mesker	6–2 1–6 6–0
1980	B. Nagelsen/M. Navratilova	A. Kiyomura/C. Reynolds	6–4 6–4
1981	K. Jordan/A. E. Smith	M. Navratilova/P. H. Shriver	6–2 7–5
1982	M. Navratilova/P. H. Shriver	C. Kohde/E. Pfaff	6–4 6–2
1983	M. Navratilova/P. H. Shriver	A. E. Hobbs/W. M. Turnbull	6–4 6–7 6–2
1984	M. Navratilova/P. H. Shriver	C. Kohde-Kilsch/H. Sukova	6–3 6–4
1985	M. Navratilova/P. H. Shriver	C. Kohde-Kilsch/H. Sukova	6–3 6–4
1986	*Not held*		
1987	M. Navratilova/P. H. Shriver	Z. Garrison/L. McNeil	6–1 6–0

MIXED DOUBLES

	CHAMPIONS	RUNNERS-UP	SCORE
1922	J. B. Hawkes/Miss E. F. Boyd	H. S. Utz/Mrs Utz	6–1 6–1
1923	H. M. Rice/Miss S. Lance	C. St John/Miss M. Molesworth	2–6 6–4 6–4
1924	J. Willard/Miss D. Akhurst	G. M. Hone/Miss E. F. Boyd	6–3 6–4
1925	J. Willard/Miss D. Akhurst	R. E. Schlesinger/Mrs R. Harper	6–4 6–4
1926	J. B. Hawkes/Miss E. F. Boyd	J. Willard/Miss D. Akhurst	6–2 6–4
1927	J. B. Hawkes/Miss E. F. Boyd	J. Willard/Miss Y. Anthony	6–1 6–3
1928	J. Borotra/Miss D. Akhurst	J. B. Hawkes/Miss E. F. Boyd	w.o
1929	E. F. Moon/Miss D. Akhurst	J. H. Crawford/Miss M. Cox	6–0 7–5
1930	H. C. Hopman/Miss N. Hall	J. H. Crawford/Miss M. Cox	11–9 3–6 6–3
1931	J. H. Crawford/Mrs Crawford	A. Willard/Mrs V. Westacott	Not available
1932	J. H. Crawford/Mrs Crawford	J. Satoh/Mrs P. O'Hara Wood	6–8 8–6 6–3
1933	J. H. Crawford/Mrs Crawford	H. E. Vines/Mrs J. Van Ryn	3–6 7–5 13–11
1934	E. F. Moon/Miss J. Hartigan	R. Dunlop/Mrs V. Westacott	6–3 6–4
1935	C. Boussus/Miss L. Bickerton	V. G. Kirby/Mrs Bond	1–6 6–3 6–3
1936	H. C. Hopman/Mrs Hopman	A. A. Kay/Miss M. Blick	6–2 6–0
1937	H. C. Hopman/Mrs Hopman	D. P. Turnbull/Miss D. Stevenson	3–6 6–3 6–2
1938	J. E. Bromwich/Miss J. Wilson	C. Long/Miss N. Wynne	6–3 6–2
1939	H. C. Hopman/Mrs Hopman	J. E. Bromwich/Miss J. Wilson	6–8 6–2 6–3
1940	C. Long/Mrs N. Bolton	H. C. Hopman/Mrs Hopman	7–5 2–6 6–4
1941–1945	*Not held*		
1946	C. Long/Mrs N. Bolton	J. Bromwich/Miss J. Fitch	6–0 6–4
1947	C. Long/Mrs N. Bolton	J. E. Bromwich/Miss J. Fitch	6–3 6–3
1948	C. Long/Mrs N. Bolton	O. W. Sidwell/Mrs T. D. Long	7–5 4–6 8–6
1949	F. A. Sedgman/Miss D. J. Hart	J. E. Bromwich/Miss J. Fitch	6–1 5–7 12–10
1950	F. A. Sedgman/Miss D. J. Hart	E. W. Sturgess/Miss J. Fitch	6–3 2–6 6–3
1951	G. A. Worthington/Mrs T. D. Long	J. May/Miss C. Proctor	4–6 6–3 6–2
1952	G. A. Worthington/Mrs T. D. Long	T. Warhurst/Mrs A. R. Thiele	9–7 7–5
1953	R. N. Hartwig/Miss J. Sampson	H. Richardson/Miss M. Connolly	6–4 6–3
1954	R. N. Hartwig/Mrs T. D. Long	J. E. Bromwich/Miss B. Penrose	8–6 9–7
1955	G. A. Worthington/Mrs T. D. Long	L. A. Hoad/Miss J. Staley	6–2 6–1
1956	N. A. Fraser/Miss B. Penrose	R. S. Emerson/Mrs M. Hawton	6–2 6–4
1957	M. J. Anderson/Miss F. Muller	W. A. Knight/Miss J. Langley	7–5 3–6 6–1
1958	R. N. Howe/Mrs M. Hawton	A. Newman/Miss A. Mortimer	9–11 6–1 6–2

1959	R. Mark/Miss S. Reynolds	R. G. Laver/Miss R. Schuurman	4–6 13–11 6–1
1960	T. Fancutt/Miss J. Lehane	R. Mark/Mrs M. Reitano	6–2 7–5
1961	R. A. J. Hewitt/Miss J. Lehane	J. Pearce/Mrs M. Reitano	9–7 6–2
1962	F. S. Stolle/Miss L. R. Turner	R. Taylor/Miss D. R. Hard	6–3 9–7
1963	K. N. Fletcher/Miss M. Smith	F. S. Stolle/Miss L. R. Turner	7–5 5–7 6–4
1964	K. N. Fletcher/Miss M. Smith	M. J. Sangster/Miss J. Lehane	6–1 6–2
1965	J. D. Newcombe/Miss M. Smith div'd with O. K. Davidson/Miss R. Ebbern		
1966	A. D. Roche/Miss J. A. Tegart	W. W. Bowrey/Miss R. Ebbern	6–1 6–3
1967	O. K. Davidson/Miss L. R. Turner	A. D. Roche/Miss J. A. M. Tegart	9–7 6–4
1968	R. D. Crealy/Mrs L. W. King	A. J. Stone/Mrs B. M. Court	6–2 9–7
1969	M. C. Riessen/Mrs B. M. Court div'd with F. S. Stolle/Mrs P. F. Jones		
1970–1986 Not held			
1987	S. E. Stewart/Miss Z. Garrison	A. Castle/Miss A. E. Hobbs	3–6 7–6 6–3

FRENCH CHAMPIONSHIPS

Up to 1924 entry was restricted to members of French clubs. In 1925 entry was open to all amateurs. The Championships became 'open' in 1968.

MEN'S SINGLES

1891	H. Briggs
1892	J. Schopfer
1893	L. Riboulet
1894–96	A. Vacherot
1897–1900	P. Ayme
1901	A. Vacherot
1902	M. Vacherot
1903–04	M. Decugis
1905–06	M. Germot
1907–09	M. Decugis
1910	M. Germot
1911	A. H. Gobert
1912–14	M. Decugis
1915–19	*Not held*
1920	A. H. Gobert
1921	J. Samazeuilh
1922	H. Cochet
1923	P. Blanchy
1924	J. Borotra

	CHAMPION	RUNNER-UP	SCORE	FIRST PRIZE *(in French francs)*
1925	R. Lacoste	J. Borotra	7–5 6–1 6–4	
1926	H. Cochet	R. Lacoste	6–2 6–4 6–3	
1927	R. Lacoste	W. T. Tilden	6–4 4–6 5–7 6–3 11–9	
1928	H. Cochet	R. Lacoste	5–7 6–3 6–1 6–3	
1929	R. Lacoste	J. Borotra	6–3 2–6 6–0 2–6 8–6	
1930	H. Cochet	W. T. Tilden	3–6 8–6 6–3 6–1	
1931	J. Borotra	C. Boussus	2–6 6–4 7–5 6–4	
1932	H. Cochet	G. de Stefani	6–0 6–4 4–6 6–3	
1933	J. H. Crawford	H. Cochet	8–6 6–1 6–3	
1934	G. von Cramm	J. H. Crawford	6–4 7–9 3–6 7–5 6–3	
1935	F. J. Perry	G. von Cramm	6–3 3–6 6–1 6–3	
1936	G. von Cramm	F. J. Perry	6–0 2–6 6–2 2–6 6–0	
1937	H. Henkel	H. W. Austin	6–1 6–4 6–3	
1938	J. D. Budge	R. Menzel	6–3 6–2 6–4	
1939	W. D. McNeill	R. L. Riggs	7–5 6–0 6–3	
1940–45	*Not held*			
1946	M. Bernard	J. Drobny	3–6 2–6 6–1 6–4 6–3	
1947	J. Asboth	E. W. Sturgess	8–6 7–5 6–4	
1948	F. A. Parker	J. Drobny	6–4 7–5 5–7 8–6	
1949	F. A. Parker	J. E. Patty	6–3 1–6 6–1 6–4	
1950	J. E. Patty	J. Drobny	6–1 6–2 3–6 5–7 7–5	
1951	J. Drobny	E. W. Sturgess	6–3 6–3 6–3	
1952	J. Drobny	F. A. Sedgman	6–2 6–0 3–6 6–3	
1953	K. R. Rosewall	E. V. Seixas	6–3 6–4 1–6 6–2	
1954	M. A. Trabert	A. Larsen	6–4 7–5 6–1	
1955	M. A. Trabert	S. Davidson	2–6 6–1 6–4 6–2	
1956	L. A. Hoad	S. Davidson	6–4 8–6 6–3	
1957	S. Davidson	H. Flam	6–3 6–4 6–4	
1958	M. G. Rose	L. Ayala	6–3 6–4 6–4	
1959	N. Pietrangeli	I. C. Vermaak	3–6 6–3 6–4 6–1	
1960	N. Pietrangeli	L. Ayala	3–6 6–3 6–4 4–6 6–3	
1961	M. Santana	N. Pietrangeli	4–6 6–1 3–6 6–0 6–2	
1962	R. G. Laver	R. S. Emerson	3–6 2–6 6–3 9–7 6–2	
1963	R. S. Emerson	P. Darmon	3–6 6–1 6–4 6–4	
1964	M. Santana	N. Pietrangeli	6–3 6–1 4–6 7–5	
1965	F. S. Stolle	A. D. Roche	3–6 6–0 6–2 6–3	
1966	A. D. Roche	I. Gulyas	6–1 6–4 7–5	
1967	R. S. Emerson	A. D. Roche	6–1 6–4 2–6 6–2	
1968	K. R. Rosewall	R. G. Laver	6–3 6–1 2–6 6–2	15,000
1969	R. G. Laver	K. R. Rosewall	6–4 6–3 6–4	35,000

1970	J. Kodes	Z. Franulovic	6–2 6–4 6–0	56,000
1971	J. Kodes	I. Nastase	8–6 6–2 2–6 7–5	48,000
1972	A. Gimeno	P. Proisy	4–6 6–3 6–1 6–1	48,000
1973	I. Nastase	N. Pilic	6–3 6–3 6–0	70,000
1974	B. Borg	M. Orantes	2–6 6–7 6–0 6–1 6–1	120,000
1975	B. Borg	G. Vilas	6–2 6–3 6–4	120,000
1976	A. Panatta	H. Solomon	6–1 6–4 4–6 7–6	130,000
1977	G. Vilas	B. E. Gottfried	6–0 6–3 6–0	190,000
1978	B. Borg	G. Vilas	6–3 6–1 6–3	210,000
1979	B. Borg	V. Pecci	6–3 6–1 6–7 6–4	208,200
1980	B. Borg	V. Gerulaitis	6–4 6–1 6–2	221,000
1981	B. Borg	I. Lendl	6–1 4–6 6–2 3–6 6–1	250,000
1982	M. Wilander	G. Vilas	1–6 7–6 6–0 6–4	400,000
1983	Y. Noah	M. Wilander	6–2 7–5 7–6	500,000
1984	I. Lendl	J. P. McEnroe	3–6 2–6 6–4 7–5 7–5	1,058,600
1985	M. Wilander	I. Lendl	3–6 6–4 6–2 6–2	1,338,200
1986	I. Lendl	M. Pernfors	6–3 6–2 6–4	1,397,250
1987	I. Lendl	M. Wilander	7–5 6–2 3–6 7–6	1,303,800

WOMEN'S SINGLES

1897–99	Mlle F. Masson
1900	Mlle Y. Prevost
1901	Mme P. Girod
1902–03	Mlle F. Masson
1904–05	Mlle K. Gillou
1906	Mme F. Fenwick
1907	Mme de Kermel
1908	Mme F. Fenwick
1909–12	Mlle J. Matthey
1913–14	Mlle M. Broquedis
1915–19	*Not held*
1920–23	Mlle S. Lenglen
1924	Mlle D. Vlasto

(Up to 1924 entry was restricted to members of French clubs. In 1925 entry was open to all amateurs.)

	CHAMPION	RUNNER-UP	SCORE	FIRST PRIZE (in French francs)
1925	Mlle S. Lenglen	Miss K. McKane	6–1 6–2	
1926	Mlle S. Lenglen	Miss M. K. Browne	6–1 6–0	
1927	Mlle K. Bouman	Mrs G. Peacock	6–2 6–4	
1928	Miss H. N. Wills	Miss E. Bennett	6–1 6–2	
1929	Miss H. N. Wills	Mme R. Mathieu	6–3 6–4	
1930	Mrs F. S. Moody	Miss H. H. Jacobs	6–2 6–1	
1931	Frl C. Aussem	Miss B. Nuthall	8–6 6–1	
1932	Mrs F. S. Moody	Mme R. Mathieu	7–5 6–1	
1933	Miss M. C. Scriven	Mme R. Mathieu	6–2 4–6 6–4	
1934	Miss M. C. Scriven	Miss H. H. Jacobs	7–5 4–6 6–1	
1935	Mrs H. Sperling	Mme R. Mathieu	6–2 6–1	
1936	Mrs H. Sperling	Mme R. Mathieu	6–3 6–4	
1937	Mrs H. Sperling	Mme R. Mathieu	6–2 6–4	
1938	Mme R. Mathieu	Mme N. Landry	6–0 6–3	
1939	Mme R. Mathieu	Miss J. Jedrzejowska	6–3 8–6	
1940–45	*Not held*			
1946	Miss M. E. Osborne	Miss P. M. Betz	1–6 8–6 7–5	
1947	Mrs P. C. Todd	Miss D. J. Hart	6–3 3–6 6–4	
1948	Mme N. Landry	Miss S. J. Fry	6–2 0–6 6–0	
1949	Mrs W. du Pont	Mme N. Adamson	7–5 6–2	
1950	Miss D. J. Hart	Mrs P. C. Todd	6–4 4–6 6–2	
1951	Miss S. J. Fry	Miss D. J. Hart	6–3 3–6 6–3	
1952	Miss D. J. Hart	Miss S. J. Fry	6–4 6–4	
1953	Miss M. Connolly	Miss D. J. Hart	6–2 6–4	
1954	Miss M. Connolly	Mme G. Bucaille	6–4 6–1	
1955	Miss A. Mortimer	Mrs D. P. Knode	2–6 7–5 10–8	
1956	Miss A. Gibson	Miss A. Mortimer	6–0 12–10	
1957	Miss S. J. Bloomer	Mrs D. P. Knode	6–1 6–3	
1958	Mrs Z. Kormoczy	Miss S. J. Bloomer	6–4 1–6 6–2	
1959	Miss C. C. Truman	Mrs Z. Kormoczy	6–4 7–5	
1960	Miss D. R. Hard	Miss Y. Ramirez	6–3 6–4	
1961	Miss A. S. Haydon	Miss Y. Ramirez	6–2 6–1	
1962	Miss M. Smith	Miss L. R. Turner	6–3 3–6 7–5	
1963	Miss L. R. Turner	Mrs P. F. Jones	2–6 6–3 7–5	
1964	Miss M. Smith	Miss M. E. Bueno	5–7 6–1 6–2	
1965	Miss L. R. Turner	Miss M. Smith	6–3 6–4	
1966	Mrs P. F. Jones	Miss N. Richey	6–3 6–1	
1967	Mlle F. Durr	Miss L. R. Turner	4–6 6–3 6–4	
1968	Miss N. Richey	Mrs P. F. Jones	5–7 6–4 6–1	5,000
1969	Mrs B. M. Court	Mrs P. F. Jones	6–1 4–6 6–3	10,000
1970	Mrs B. M. Court	Miss H. Niessen	6–2 6–4	17,800

1971	Miss E. Goolagong	Miss H. Gourlay	6–3 7–5	13,500
1972	Mrs L. W. King	Miss E. Goolagong	6–3 6–3	13,500
1973	Mrs B. M. Court	Miss C. M. Evert	6–7 7–6 6–4	25,000
1974	Miss C. M. Evert	Mrs O. Morozova	6–1 6–2	40,000
1975	Miss C. M. Evert	Miss M. Navratilova	2–6 6–2 6–1	40,000
1976	Miss S. Barker	Miss R. Tomanova	6–2 0–6 6–2	30,000
1977	Miss M. Jausovec	Miss F. Mihai	6–2 6–7 6–1	35,000
1978	Miss V. Ruzici	Miss M. Jausovec	6–2 6–2	100,000
1979	Mrs C. Evert Lloyd	Miss W. M. Turnbull	6–2 6–0	126,900
1980	Mrs C. Evert Lloyd	Miss V. Ruzici	6–0 6–3	178,500
1981	Miss H. Mandlikova	Miss S. Hanika	6–2 6–4	200,000
1982	Miss M. Navratilova	Miss A. Jaeger	7–6 6–1	300,000
1983	Mrs C. Evert Lloyd	Miss M. Jausovec	6–1 6–2	375,000
1984	Miss M. Navratilova	Mrs C. Evert Lloyd	6–3 6–1	791,600
1985	Mrs C. Evert Lloyd	Miss M. Navratilova	6–3 6–7 7–5	1,262,700
1986	Mrs C. Evert Lloyd	Miss M. Navratilova	2–6 6–3 6–3	1,278,400
1987	Miss S. Graf	Miss M. Navratilova	6–4 4–6 8–6	1,178,840

MEN'S DOUBLES

	CHAMPIONS	RUNNERS-UP	SCORE
1925	J. Borotra/R. Lacoste	J. Brugnon/H. Cochet	7–5 4–6 6–3 2–6 6–3
1926	H. O. Kinsey/V. Richards	J. Brugnon/H. Cochet	6–4 6–1 4–6 6–4
1927	J. Brugnon/H. Cochet	J. Borotra/R. Lacoste	2–6 6–2 6–0 1–6 6–4
1928	J. Borotra/J. Brugnon	R. de Buzelet/H. Cochet	6–4 3–6 6–2 3–6 6–4
1929	J. Borotra/R. Lacoste	J. Brugnon/H. Cochet	6–3 3–6 6–3 3–6 8–6
1930	J. Brugnon/H. Cochet	H. C. Hopman/J. Willard	6–3 9–7 6–3
1931	G. M. Lott/J. Van Ryn	N. G. Farquharson/V. G. Kirby	6–4 6–3 6–4
1932	J. Brugnon/H. Cochet	M. Bernard/C. Boussus	6–4 3–6 7–5 6–3
1933	G. P. Hughes/F. J. Perry	V. B. McGrath/A. K. Quist	6–2 6–4 2–6 7–5
1934	J. Borotra/J. Brugnon	J. H. Crawford/V. B. McGrath	11–9 6–3 2–6 4–6 9–7
1935	J. H. Crawford/A. K. Quist	V. B. McGrath/D. P. Turnbull	6–1 6–4 6–2
1936	M. Bernard/J. Borotra	G. P. Hughes/C. R. D. Tuckey	6–2 3–6 9–7 6–1
1937	G. Von Cramm/H. Henkel	N. G. Farquharson/V. G. Kirby	6–4 7–5 3–6 6–1
1938	B. Destremau/Y. Petra	J. D. Budge/G. Mako	3–6 6–3 9–7 6–1
1939	C. Harris/W. D. McNeil	J. Borotra/J. Brugnon	4–6 6–4 6–0 2–6 10–8
1940–1945	*Not held*		
1946	M. Bernard/Y. Petra	E. Morea/F. Segura	7–5 6–3 0–6 1–6 10–8
1947	E. Fannin/E. W. Sturgess	T. P. Brown/O. W. Sidwell	6–4 4–6 6–4 6–3
1948	L. Bergelin/J. Drobny	H. C. Hopman/F. A. Sedgman	8–6 6–1 12–10
1949	R. A. Gonzales/F. Parker	E. Fannin/E. W. Sturgess	6–3 8–6 5–7 6–3
1950	W. F. Talbert/M. A. Trabert	J. Drobny/E. W. Sturgess	6–2 1–6 10–8 6–2
1951	K. McGregor/F. A. Sedgman	G. Mulloy/R. Savitt	6–2 2–6 9–7 7–5
1952	K. McGregor/F. A. Sedgman	G. Mulloy/R. Savitt	6–3 6–4 6–4
1953	L. A. Hoad/K. R. Rosewall	M. G. Rose/C. Wilderspin	6–2 6–1 6–1
1954	E. V. Seixas/M. A. Trabert	L. A. Hoad/K. R. Rosewall	6–4 6–2 6–1
1955	E. V. Seixas/M. A. Trabert	N. Pietrangeli/O. Sirola	6–1 4–6 6–2 6–4
1956	D. W. Candy/R. M. Perry	A. J. Cooper/L. A. Hoad	7–5 6–3 6–3
1957	M. J. Anderson/A. J. Cooper	D. W. Candy/M. G. Rose	6–3 6–0 6–3
1958	A. J. Cooper/N. A. Fraser	R. N. Howe/A. Segal	3–6 8–6 6–3 7–5
1959	N. Pietrangeli/O. Sirola	R. S. Emerson/N. A. Fraser	6–3 6–2 14–12
1960	R. S. Emerson/N. A. Fraser	J. L. Arilla/A. Gimeno	6–2 8–10 7–5 6–4
1961	R. S. Emerson/R. G. Laver	R. N. Howe/R. Mark	3–6 6–1 6–1 6–4
1962	R. S. Emerson/N. A. Fraser	W. P. Bungert/C. Kuhnke	6–3 6–4 7–5
1963	R. S. Emerson/M. Santana	G. L. Forbes/A. Segal	6–2 6–4 6–4
1964	R. S. Emerson/K. N. Fletcher	J. D. Newcombe/A. D. Roche	7–5 6–3 3–6 7–5
1965	R. S. Emerson/F. S. Stolle	K. N. Fletcher/R. A. J. Hewitt	6–8 6–3 8–6 6–2
1966	C. E. Graebner/R. D. Ralston	I. Nastase/I. Tiriac	6–3 6–3 6–0
1967	J. D. Newcombe/A. D. Roche	R. S. Emerson/K. N. Fletcher	6–3 9–7 12–10
1968	K. R. Rosewall/F. S. Stolle	R. S. Emerson/R. G. Laver	6–3 6–4 6–3
1969	J. D. Newcombe/A. D. Roche	R. S. Emerson/R. G. Laver	4–6 6–1 3–6 6–4 6–4
1970	I. Nastase/I. Tiriac	A. R. Ashe/C. Pasarell	6–2 6–4 6–3
1971	A. R. Ashe/M. C. Riessen	T. W. Gorman/S. R. Smith	6–8 4–6 6–3 6–4 11–9
1972	R. A. J. Hewitt/F. D. McMillan	P. Cornejo/J. Fillol	6–3 8–6 3–6 6–1
1973	J. D. Newcombe/T. S. Okker	J. S. Connors/I. Nastase	6–1 3–6 6–3 5–7 6–4
1974	R. D. Crealy/O. Parun	R. C. Lutz/S. R. Smith	6–3 6–2 3–6 5–7 6–1
1975	B. E. Gottfried/R. Ramirez	J. G. Alexander/P. Dent	6–2 2–6 6–2 6–4
1976	F. McNair/S. E. Stewart	B. E. Gottfried/R. Ramirez	7–6 6–3 6–1
1977	B. E. Gottfried/R. Ramirez	W. Fibak/J. Kodes	7–6 4–6 6–3 6–4
1978	G. Mayer/H. Pfister	J. Higueras/M. Orantes	6–3 6–2 6–2

1979	A. A./G. Mayer	R. Case/P. Dent	6–4 6–4 6–4
1980	V. Amaya/H. Pfister	B. E. Gottfried/R. Ramirez	1–6 6–4 6–4 6–3
1981	H. Gunthardt/B. Taroczy	T. Moor/E. Teltscher	6–2 7–6 6–3
1982	S. E. Stewart/F. Taygan	H. Gildemeister/B. Prajoux	7–5 6–3 1–1 ret'd
1983	A. Jarryd/H. Simonsson	M. R. Edmondson/S. E. Stewart	7–6 6–4 6–2
1984	H. Leconte/Y. Noah	P. Slozil/T. Smid	6–4 2–6 3–6 6–3 6–2
1985	M. R. Edmondson/K. Warwick	S. Glickstein/H. Simonsson	6–3 6–4 6–7 6–3
1986	J. Fitzgerald/T. Smid	S. Edberg/A. Jarryd	6–3 4–6 6–3 6–7 14–12
1987	A. Jarryd/R. Seguso	G. Forget/Y. Noah	6–7 6–7 6–3 6–4 6–2

WOMEN'S DOUBLES

	CHAMPIONS	RUNNERS-UP	SCORE
1925	S. Lenglen/D. Vlasto	E. Colyer/K. McKane	6–1 9–11 6–2
1926	S. Lenglen/D. Vlasto	E. Colyer/L. A. Godfree	6–1 6–1
1927	E. L. Heine/G. Peacock	P. Saunders/P. H. Watson	6–2 6–1
1928	E. Bennett/P. H. Watson	S. Deve/A. Lafaurie	6–0 6–2
1929	L. de Alvarez/K. Bouman	E. L. Heine/A. Neave	7–5 6–3
1930	F. S. Moody/E. Ryan	S. Barbier/S. Mathieu	6–3 6–1
1931	B. Nuthall/E. F. Whittingstall	C. Aussem/E. Ryan	9–7 6–2
1932	F. S. Moody/E. Ryan	B. Nuthall/E. F. Whittingstall	6–1 6–3
1933	S. Mathieu/E. Ryan	S. Henrotin/C. Rosambert	6–1 6–3
1934	S. Mathieu/E. Ryan	H. H. Jacobs/S. Palfrey	3–6 6–4 6–2
1935	M. C. Scriven/K. Stammers	N. Adamoff/H. Sperling	6–4 6–0
1936	S. Mathieu/A. M. Yorke	S. Noel/J. Jedrzejowska	2–6 6–4 6–4
1937	S. Mathieu/A. M. Yorke	D. Andrus/S. Henrotin	3–6 6–2 6–2
1938	S. Mathieu/A. M. Yorke	A. Halff/N. Landry	6–3 6–3
1939	J. Jedrzejowska/S. Mathieu	A. Florian/H. Kovac	7–5 7–5
1940–1945	*Not held*		
1946	L. Brough/M. Osborne	P. Betz/D. Hart	6–4 0–6 6–1
1947	L. Brough/M. Osborne	D. Hart/P. C. Todd	7–5 6–2
1948	D. Hart/P. C. Todd	S. Fry/M. A. Prentiss	6–4 6–2
1949	L. Brough/W. du Pont	J. Gannon/B. Hilton	7–5 6–1
1950	S. Fry/D. Hart	L. Brough/W. du Pont	1–6 7–5 6–2
1951	S. Fry/D. Hart	B. Bartlett/B. Scofield	10–8 6–3
1952	S. Fry/D. Hart	H. Redick-Smith/J. Wipplinger	7–5 6–1
1953	S. Fry/D. Hart	M. Connolly/J. Sampson	6–4 6–3
1954	M. Connolly/N. Hopman	M. Galtier/S. Schmitt	7–5 4–6 6–0
1955	B. Fleitz/D. R. Hard	S. J. Bloomer/P. Ward	7–5 6–8 13–11
1956	A. Buxton/A. Gibson	D. R. Hard/D. Knode	6–8 8–6 6–1
1957	S. J. Bloomer/D. R. Hard	Y. Ramirez/R. M. Reyes	7–5 4–6 7–5
1958	Y. Ramirez/R. M. Reyes	M. K. Hawton/T. D. Long	6–4 7–5
1959	S. Reynolds/R. Schuurman	Y. Ramirez/R. M. Reyes	2–6 6–0 6–1
1960	M. E. Bueno/D. R. Hard	R. Hales/A. Haydon	6–2 7–5
1961	S. Reynolds/R. Schuurman	M. E. Bueno/D. R. Hard	w.o.
1962	S. Price/R. Schuurman	J. Bricka/M. Smith	6–4 6–4
1963	P. F. Jones/R. Schuurman	R. A. Ebbern/M. Smith	7–5 6–4
1964	M. Smith/L. R. Turner	N. Baylon/H. Schultze	6–3 6–1
1965	M. Smith/L. R. Turner	F. Durr/J. Lieffrig	6–3 6–1
1966	M. Smith/J. A. M. Tegart	J. Blackman/F. Toyne	4–6 6–1 6–1
1967	F. Durr/G. Sheriff	A. M. Van Zyl/P. Walkden	6–2 6–2
1968	F. Durr/P. F. Jones	R. Casals/L. W. King	7–5 4–6 6–4
1969	F. Durr/P. F. Jones	M. Court/N. Richey	6–0 4–6 7–5
1970	F. Durr/G. Chanfreau	R. Casals/L. W. King	6–1 3–6 6–3
1971	F. Durr/G. Chanfreau	H. Gourlay/K. Harris	6–4 6–1
1972	L. W. King/B. Stove	W. Shaw/F. E. Truman	6–1 6–2
1973	M. Court/S. V. Wade	F. Durr/B. Stove	6–2 6–3
1974	C. Evert/O. Morozova	G. Chanfreau/K. Ebbinghaus	6–4 2–6 6–1
1975	C. Evert/M. Navratilova	J. Anthony/O. Morozova	6–3 6–2
1976	F. Bonicelli/G. Lovera	K. Harter/H. Masthoff	6–4 1–6 6–3
1977	R. Marsikova/P. Teeguarden	R. Fox/H. Gourlay	5–7 6–4 6–2
1978	M. Jausovec/V. Ruzici	N. Bowey/G. Lovera	5–7 6–4 8–6
1979	B. Stove/W. M. Turnbull	F. Durr/S. V. Wade	6–4 7–6
1980	K. Jordan/A. E. Smith	I. Madruga/I. Villagran	6–1 6–0
1981	R. Fairbank/T. Harford	C. Reynolds/P. Smith	6–1 6–3
1982	M. Navratilova/A. E. Smith	R. Casals/W. M. Turnbull	6–3 6–4
1983	R. Fairbank/C. Reynolds	K. Jordan/A. E. Smith	5–7 7–5 6–2
1984	M. Navratilova/P. H. Shriver	C. Kohde-Kilsch/H. Mandlikova	5–7 6–3 6–2
1985	M. Navratilova/P. H. Shriver	C. Kohde-Kilsch/H. Sukova	4–6 6–2 6–2

1986	M. Navratilova/A. Temesvari	S. Graf/G. Sabatini	6–1 6–2
1987	M. Navratilova/P. H. Shriver	S. Graf/G. Sabatini	6–2 6–1

MIXED DOUBLES

	CHAMPIONS	RUNNERS-UP	SCORE
1925	J. Brugnon/Miss S. Lenglen	H. Cochet/Miss D. Vlasto	6–2 6–2
1926	J. Brugnon/Miss S. Lenglen	J. Borotra/Mrs Le Besnerais	6–4 6–3
1927	J. Borotra/Miss M. Broquedis	W. T. Tilden/Miss L. de Alvarez	6–4 2–6 6–2
1928	H. Cochet/Miss E. Bennett	F. T. Hunter/Miss H. Wills	3–6 6–3 6–3
1929	H. Cochet/Miss E. Bennett	F. T. Hunter/Miss H. Wills	6–3 6–2
1930	W. T. Tilden/Miss C. Aussem	H. Cochet/Mrs F. Whittingstall	6–4 6–4
1931	P. D. B. Spence/Miss B. Nuthall	H. W. Austin/Mrs D. C. Shepherd-Barron	6–3 5–7 6–3
1932	F. J. Perry/Miss B. Nuthall	S. B. Wood/Mrs F. S. Moody	6–4 6–2
1933	J. H. Crawford/Miss M. C. Scriven	F. J. Perry/Miss B. Nuthall	6–2 6–3
1934	J. Borotra/Miss C. Rosambert	A. K. Quist/Miss E. Ryan	6–2 6–4
1935	M. Bernard/Miss L. Payot	A. M. Legeay/Mrs S. Henrotin	4–6 6–2 6–4
1936	M. Bernard/Miss A. M. Yorke	A. M. Legeay/Mrs S. Henrotin	7–5 6–8 6–3
1937	Y. Petra/Mrs S. Mathieu	R. Journu/Miss M. Horne	7–5 7–5
1938	D. Mitic/Mrs S. Mathieu	C. Boussus/Miss N. Wynne	2–6 6–3 6–4
1939	E. T. Cooke/Mrs S. Fabyan	F. Kukuljevic/Mrs S. Mathieu	4–6 6–1 7–5
1940–1945	*Not held*		
1946	J. E. Patty/Miss P. M. Betz	T. P. Brown/Miss D. Bundy	7–5 9–7
1947	E. W. Sturgess/Mrs S. P. Summers	C. Caralulis/Miss J. Jedrzejowska	6–0 6–0
1948	J. Drobny/Mrs P. C. Todd	F. A. Sedgman/Miss D. Hart	6–3 3–6 6–3
1949	E. W. Sturgess/Mrs S. P. Summers	G. D. Oakley/Miss J. Quertier	6–1 6–1
1950	E. Morea/Miss B. Scofield	W. F. Talbert/Mrs P. C. Todd	w.o.
1951	F. A. Sedgman/Miss D. Hart	M. G. Rose/Mrs T. D. Long	7–5 6–2
1952	F. A. Sedgman/Miss D. Hart	E. W. Sturgess/Miss S. Fry	6–8 6–3 6–3
1953	E. V. Seixas/Miss D. Hart	M. G. Rose/Miss M. Connolly	4–6 6–4 6–0
1954	L. A. Hoad/Miss M. Connolly	R. N. Hartwig/Mrs J. Patorni	6–4 6–3
1955	G. L. Forbes/Miss D. R. Hard	L. Ayala/Miss J. Staley	5–7 6–1 6–2
1956	L. Ayala/Mrs T. D. Long	R. N. Howe/Miss D. R. Hard	4–6 6–4 6–1
1957	J. Javorsky/Miss V. Puzejova	L. Ayala/Miss E. Buding	6–3 6–4
1958	N. Pietrangeli/Miss S. J. Bloomer	R. N. Howe/Miss L. Coghlan	9–7 6–8 6–2
1959	W. A. Knight/Miss R. Ramirez	R. G. Laver/Miss R. Schuurman	6–4 6–4
1960	R. N. Howe/Miss M. Bueno	R. S. Emerson/Miss A. Haydon	1–6 6–1 6–2
1961	R. G. Laver/Miss D. R. Hard	J. Javorsky/Miss V. Puzejova	6–0 2–6 6–3
1962	R. N. Howe/Miss R. Schuurman	F. S. Stolle/Miss L. R. Turner	3–6 6–4 6–4
1963	K. N. Fletcher/Miss M. Smith	F. S. Stolle/Miss L. R. Turner	6–1 6–2
1964	K. N. Fletcher/Miss M. Smith	F. S. Stolle/Miss L. R. Turner	6–3 6–4
1965	K. N. Fletcher/Miss M. Smith	J. D. Newcombe/Miss M. Bueno	6–4 6–4
1966	F. D. McMillan/Miss A. M. Van Zyl	C. Graebner/Mrs P. F. Jones	1–6 6–3 6–2
1967	O. K. Davidson/Mrs L. W. King	I. Tiriac/Mrs P. F. Jones	6–3 6–1
1968	J. C. Barclay/Miss F. Durr	O. K. Davidson/Mrs L. W. King	6–1 6–4
1969	M. C. Riessen/Mrs. B. M. Court	J. C. Barclay/Miss F. Durr	7–5 6–4
1970	R. A. J. Hewitt/Mrs L. W. King	J. C. Barclay/Miss F. Durr	3–6 6–3 6–2
1971	J. C. Barclay/Miss F. Durr	T. Lejus/Miss W. Shaw	6–2 6–4
1972	K. Warwick/Miss E. Goolagong	J. C. Barclay/Miss F. Durr	6–2 6–4
1973	J. C. Barclay/Miss F. Durr	P. Dominguez/Miss B. Stove	6–1 6–4
1974	I. Molina/Miss M. Navratilova	M. Lara/Mrs R. M. Darmon	6–3 6–3
1975	T. Koch/Miss F. Bonicelli	J. Fillol/Miss P. Teeguarden	6–4 7–6
1976	K. Warwick/Miss I. Kloss	C. Dowdeswell/Miss L. Boshoff	5–7 7–6 6–2
1977	J. P. McEnroe/Miss M. Carillo	I. Molina/Miss F. Mihai	7–6 6–3
1978	P. Slozil/Miss R. Tomanova	P. Dominguez/Miss V. Ruzici	7–6 ret'd
1979	R. A. J. Hewitt/Miss W. M. Turnbull	I. Tiriac/Miss V. Ruzici	6–3 2–6 6–3
1980	W. Martin/Miss A. E. Smith	S. Birner/Miss R. Tomanova	2–6 6–4 8–6
1981	J. Arias/Miss A. Jaeger	F. D. McNair/Miss B. Stove	7–6 6–4
1982	J. M. Lloyd/Miss W. M. Turnbull	C. Motta/Miss C. Monteiro	6–2 7–6
1983	E. Teltscher/Miss B. Jordan	C. Strode/Miss L. Allen	6–2 6–3
1984	R. L. Stockton/Miss A. E. Smith	L. Warder/Miss A. Minter	6–2 6–4
1985	H. P. Gunthardt/Miss M. Navratilova	F. Gonzalez/Miss P. Smith	2–6 6–3 6–2
1986	K. Flach/Miss. K. Jordan	M. R. Edmondson/Miss. R. Fairbank	3–6 7–6 6–3
1987	E. Sanchez/Miss P. H. Shriver	S. E. Stewart/Miss L. McNeil	6–3 7–6

WIMBLEDON CHAMPIONSHIPS

For the years 1913, 1914, and 1919–23 inclusive, these records include the 'World's Championship on Grass' granted to the LTA by the ILTF. This title was then abolished. Prior to 1922 the holder did not

compete in the Championship but met the winner of the singles in the Challenge Round. The Challenge Round was abolished in 1922 and the holder subsequently played through. Modified 'seeding' was introduced in 1924. Full 'seeding', as we know it today, was first practised in 1927. The Championships became 'open' in 1968. From 1877–1921 the Championships were played at the Worple Road ground. Since 1922 they have been played at the present ground in Church Road.
There was a tie-break at 8–all in the years 1971–1978. Thereafter the tie-break was played at 6–all.
* *Holders did not defend the title.*

MEN'S SINGLES

	CHAMPION	RUNNER-UP	SCORE
1877	S. W. Gore	W. C. Marshall	6–1 6–2 6–4
1878	P. F. Hadow	S. W. Gore	7–5 6–1 9–7
1879*	J. T. Hartley	V. St L. Goold	6–2 6–4 6–2
1880	J. T. Hartley	H. F. Lawford	6–3 6–2 2–6 6–3
1881	W. Renshaw	J. T. Hartley	6–0 6–1 6–1
1882	W. Renshaw	E. Renshaw	6–1 2–6 4–6 6–2 6–2
1883	W. Renshaw	E. Renshaw	2–6 6–3 6–3 4–6 6–3
1884	W. Renshaw	H. F. Lawford	6–0 6–4 9–7
1885	W. Renshaw	H. F. Lawford	7–5 6–2 4–6 7–5
1886	W. Renshaw	H. F. Lawford	6–0 5–7 6–3 6–4
1887*	H. F. Lawford	E. Renshaw	1–6 6–3 3–6 6–4 6–4
1888	E. Renshaw	H. F. Lawford	6–3 7–5 6–0
1889	W. Renshaw	E. Renshaw	6–4 6–1 3–6 6–0
1890	W. J. Hamilton	W. Renshaw	6–8 6–2 3–6 6–1 6–1
1891*	W. Baddeley	J. Pim	6–4 1–6 7–5 6–0
1892	W. Baddeley	J. Pim	4–6 6–3 6–3 6–2
1893	J. Pim	W. Baddeley	3–6 6–1 6–3 6–2
1894	J. Pim	W. Baddeley	10–8 6–2 8–6
1895*	W. Baddeley	W. V. Eaves	4–6 2–6 8–6 6–2 6–3
1896	H. S. Mahony	W. Baddeley	6–2 6–8 5–7 8–6 6–3
1897	R. F. Doherty	H. S. Mahony	6–4 6–4 6–3
1898	R. F. Doherty	H. L. Doherty	6–3 6–3 2–6 5–7 6–1
1899	R. F. Doherty	A. W. Gore	1–6 4–6 6–2 6–3 6–3
1900	R. F. Doherty	S. H. Smith	6–8 6–3 6–1 6–2
1901	A. W. Gore	R. F. Doherty	4–6 7–5 6–4 6–4
1902	H. L. Doherty	A. W. Gore	6–4 6–3 3–6 6–0
1903	H. L. Doherty	F. L. Riseley	7–5 6–3 6–0
1904	H. L. Doherty	F. L. Riseley	6–1 7–5 8–6
1905	H. L. Doherty	N. E. Brookes	8–6 6–2 6–4
1906	H. L. Doherty	F. L. Riseley	6–4 4–6 6–2 6–3
1907*	N. E. Brookes	A. W. Gore	6–4 6–2 6–2
1908*	A. W. Gore	H. Roper Barrett	6–3 6–2 4–6 3–6 6–4
1909	A. W. Gore	M. J. G. Ritchie	6–8 1–6 6–2 6–2 6–2
1910	A. F. Wilding	A. W. Gore	6–4 7–5 4–6 6–2
1911	A. F. Wilding	H. Roper Barrett	6–4 4–6 2–6 6–2 ret'd
1912	A. F. Wilding	A. W. Gore	6–4 6–4 4–6 6–4
1913	A. F. Wilding	M. E. McLoughlin	8–6 6–3 10–8
1914	N. E. Brookes	A. F. Wilding	6–4 6–4 7–5
1915–18	*Not held*		
1919	G. L. Patterson	N. E. Brookes	6–3 7–5 6–2
1920	W. T. Tilden	G. L. Patterson	2–6 6–2 6–3 6–4
1921	W. T. Tilden	B. I. C. Norton	4–6 2–6 6–1 6–0 7–5
(Challenge Round abolished)			
1922*	G. L. Patterson	R. Lycett	6–3 6–4 6–2
1923*	W. M. Johnston	F. T. Hunter	6–0 6–3 6–1
1924	J. Borotra	R. Lacoste	6–1 3–6 6–1 3–6 6–4
1925	R. Lacoste	J. Borotra	6–3 6–3 4–6 8–6
1926	J. Borotra	Howard Kinsey	8–6 6–1 6–3
1927	H. Cochet	J. Borotra	4–6 4–6 6–3 6–4 7–5
1928	R. Lacoste	H. Cochet	6–1 4–6 6–4 6–2
1929	H. Cochet	J. Borotra	6–4 6–3 6–4
1930	W. T. Tilden	W. L. Allison	6–3 9–7 6–4
1931*	S. B. Wood	F. X. Shields	w.o.
1932	H. E. Vines	H. W. Austin	6–4 6–2 6–0
1933	J. H. Crawford	H. E. Vines	4–6 11–9 6–2 2–6 6–4
1934	F. J. Perry	J. H. Crawford	6–3 6–0 7–5
1935	F. J. Perry	G. von Cramm	6–2 6–4 6–4
1936	F. J. Perry	G. von Cramm	6–1 6–1 6–0

				FIRST PRIZE (£)
1937*	J. D. Budge	G. von Cramm	6–3 6–4 6–2	
1938	J. D. Budge	H. W. Austin	6–1 6–0 6–3	
1939*	R. L. Riggs	E. T. Cooke	2–6 8–6 3–6 6–3 6–2	
1940–45	*Not held*			
1946*	Y. Petra	G. E. Brown	6–2 6–4 7–9 5–7 6–4	
1947	J. A. Kramer	T. Brown	6–1 6–3 6–2	
1948*	R. Falkenburg	J. E. Bromwich	7–5 0–6 6–2 3–6 7–5	
1949	F. R. Schroeder	J. Drobny	3–6 6–0 6–3 4–6 6–4	
1950*	J. E. Patty	F. A. Sedgman	6–1 8–10 6–2 6–3	
1951	R. Savitt	K. McGregor	6–4 6–4 6–4	
1952	F. A. Sedgman	J. Drobny	4–6 6–2 6–3 6–2	
1953*	E. V. Seixas	K. Nielsen	9–7 6–3 6–4	
1954	J. Drobny	K. R. Rosewall	13–11 4–6 6–2 9–7	
1955	M. A. Trabert	K. Nielsen	6–3 7–5 6–1	
1956*	L. A. Hoad	K. R. Rosewall	6–2 4–6 7–5 6–4	
1957	L. A. Hoad	A. J. Cooper	6–2 6–1 6–2	
1958*	A. J. Cooper	N. A. Fraser	3–6 6–3 6–4 13–11	
1959*	A. Olmedo	R. G. Laver	6–4 6–3 6–4	
1960*	N. A. Fraser	R. G. Laver	6–4 3–6 9–7 7–5	
1961	R. G. Laver	C. R. McKinley	6–3 6–1 6–4	
1962	R. G. Laver	M. F. Mulligan	6–2 6–2 6–1	
1963*	C. R. McKinley	F. S. Stolle	9–7 6–1 6–4	
1964	R. S. Emerson	F. S. Stolle	6–1 12–10 4–6 6–3	
1965	R. S. Emerson	F. S. Stolle	6–2 6–4 6–4	
1966	M. Santana	R. D. Ralston	6–4 11–9 6–4	
1967	J. D. Newcombe	W. P. Bungert	6–3 6–1 6–1	
1968	R. G. Laver	A. D. Roche	6–3 6–4 6–2	2,000
1969	R. G. Laver	J. D. Newcombe	6–4 5–7 6–4 6–4	3,000
1970	J. D. Newcombe	K. R. Rosewall	5–7 6–3 6–2 3–6 6–1	3,000
1971	J. D. Newcombe	S. R. Smith	6–3 5–7 2–6 6–4 6–4	3,750
1972*	S. R. Smith	I. Nastase	4–6 6–3 6–3 4–6 7–5	5,000
1973*	J. Kodes	A. Metreveli	6–1 9–8 6–3	5,000
1974	J. S. Connors	K. R. Rosewall	6–1 6–1 6–4	10,000
1975	A. R. Ashe	J. S. Connors	6–1 6–1 5–7 6–4	10,000
1976	B. Borg	I. Nastase	6–4 6–2 9–7	12,500
1977	B. Borg	J. S. Connors	3–6 6–2 6–1 5–7 6–4	15,000
1978	B. Borg	J. S. Connors	6–2 6–2 6–3	19,000
1979	B. Borg	R. Tanner	6–7 6–1 3–6 6–3 6–4	20,000
1980	B. Borg	J. P. McEnroe	1–6 7–5 6–3 6–7 8–6	20,000
1981	J. P. McEnroe	B. Borg	4–6 7–6 7–6 6–4	21,600
1982	J. S. Connors	J. P. McEnroe	3–6 6–3 6–7 7–6 6–4	41,667
1983	J. P. McEnroe	C. J. Lewis	6–2 6–2 6–2	66,600
1984	J. P. McEnroe	J. S. Connors	6–1 6–1 6–2	100,000
1985	B. Becker	K. Curren	6–3 6–7 7–6 6–4	130,000
1986	B. Becker	I. Lendl	6–4 6–3 7–5	140,000
1987	P. Cash	I. Lendl	7–6 6–2 7–5	155,000

WOMEN'S SINGLES

	CHAMPION	RUNNER-UP	SCORE
1884	Miss M. Watson	Miss L. Watson	6–8 6–3 6–3
1885	Miss M. Watson	Miss B. Bingley	6–1 7–5
1886	Miss B. Bingley	Miss M. Watson	6–3 6–3
1887	Miss C. Dod	Miss B. Bingley	6–2 6–0
1888	Miss C. Dod	Mrs G. W. Hillyard	6–3 6–3
1889*	Mrs G. W. Hillyard	Miss H. Rice	4–6 8–6 6–4
1890*	Miss H. Rice	Miss M. Jacks	6–4 6–1
1891*	Miss C. Dod	Mrs G. W. Hillyard	6–2 6–1
1892	Miss C. Dod	Mrs G. W. Hillyard	6–1 6–1
1893	Miss C. Dod	Mrs G. W. Hillyard	6–8 6–1 6–4
1894*	Mrs G. W. Hillyard	Miss L. Austin	6–1 6–1
1895*	Miss C. Cooper	Miss H. Jackson	7–5 8–6
1896	Miss C. Cooper	Mrs W. H. Pickering	6–2 6–3
1897	Mrs G. W. Hillyard	Miss C. Cooper	5–7 7–5 6–2
1898*	Miss C. Cooper	Miss L. Martin	6–4 6–4
1899	Mrs G. W. Hillyard	Miss C. Cooper	6–2 6–3
1900	Mrs G. W. Hillyard	Miss C. Cooper	4–6 6–4 6–4
1901	Mrs A. Sterry	Mrs G. W. Hillyard	6–2 6–2
1902	Miss M. E. Robb	Mrs A. Sterry	7–5 6–1
1903*	Miss D. K. Douglass	Miss E. W. Thomson	4–6 6–4 6–2

				FIRST PRIZE (£)
1904	Miss D. K. Douglass	Mrs A. Sterry	6–0 6–3	
1905	Miss M. Sutton	Miss D. K. Douglass	6–3 6–4	
1906	Miss D. K. Douglass	Miss M. Sutton	6–3 9–7	
1907	Miss M. Sutton	Mrs Lambert Chambers	6–1 6–4	
1908*	Mrs A. Sterry	Miss A. M. Morton	6–4 6–4	
1909*	Miss D. P. Boothby	Miss A. M. Morton	6–4 4–6 8–6	
1910	Mrs Lambert Chambers	Miss D. P. Boothby	6–2 6–2	
1911	Mrs Lambert Chambers	Miss D. P. Boothby	6–0 6–0	
1912*	Mrs D. R. Larcombe	Mrs A. Sterry	6–3 6–1	
1913*	Mrs Lambert Chambers	Mrs R. J. McNair	6–0 6–4	
1914	Mrs Lambert Chambers	Mrs D. R. Larcombe	7–5 6–4	
1915–18 *Not held*				
1919	Mlle S. Lenglen	Mrs Lambert Chambers	10–8 4–6 9–7	
1920	Mlle S. Lenglen	Mrs Lambert Chambers	6–3 6–0	
1921	Mlle S. Lenglen	Miss E. Ryan	6–2 6–0	
(Challenge Round abolished)				
1922	Mlle S. Lenglen	Mrs F. Mallory	6–2 6–0	
1923	Mlle S. Lenglen	Miss K. McKane	6–2 6–2	
1924	Miss K. McKane	Miss H. N. Wills	4–6 6–4 6–4	
1925	Mlle S. Lenglen	Miss J. Fry	6–2 6–0	
1926	Mrs L. A. Godfree	Sta E. de Alvarez	6–2 4–6 6–3	
1927	Miss H. N. Wills	Sta E. de Alvarez	6–2 6–4	
1928	Miss H. N. Wills	Sta E. de Alvarez	6–2 6–3	
1929	Miss H. N. Wills	Miss H. H. Jacobs	6–1 6–2	
1930	Mrs F. S. Moody	Miss E. Ryan	6–2 6–2	
1931*	Frl C. Aussem	Frl H. Krahwinkel	6–2 7–5	
1932*	Mrs F. S. Moody	Miss H. H. Jacobs	6–3 6–1	
1933	Mrs F. S. Moody	Miss D. E. Round	6–4 6–8 6–3	
1934*	Miss D. E. Round	Miss H. H. Jacobs	6–2 5–7 6–3	
1935	Mrs F. S. Moody	Miss H. H. Jacobs	6–3 3–6 7–5	
1936*	Miss H. H. Jacobs	Mrs S. Sperling	6–2 4–6 7–5	
1937	Miss D. E. Round	Miss J. Jedrzejowska	6–2 2–6 7–5	
1938*	Mrs F. S. Moody	Miss H. H. Jacobs	6–4 6–0	
1939*	Miss A. Marble	Miss K. E. Stammers	6–2 6–0	
1940–45 *Not held*				
1946*	Miss P. M. Betz	Miss A. L. Brough	6–2 6–4	
1947*	Miss M. E. Osborne	Miss D. J. Hart	6–2 6–4	
1948	Miss A. L. Brough	Miss D. J. Hart	6–3 8–6	
1949	Miss A. L. Brough	Mrs W. du Pont	10–8 1–6 10–8	
1950	Miss A. L. Brough	Mrs W. du Pont	6–1 3–6 6–1	
1951	Miss D. J. Hart	Miss S. J. Fry	6–1 6–0	
1952	Miss M. Connolly	Miss A. L. Brough	6–4 6–3	
1953	Miss M. Connolly	Miss D. J. Hart	8–6 7–5	
1954	Miss M. Connolly	Miss A. L. Brough	6–2 7–5	
1955*	Miss A. L. Brough	Mrs J. G. Fleitz	7–5 8–6	
1956	Miss S. J. Fry	Miss A. Buxton	6–3 6–1	
1957*	Miss A. Gibson	Miss D. R. Hard	6–3 6–2	
1958	Miss A. Gibson	Miss A. Mortimer	8–6 6–2	
1959*	Miss M. E. Bueno	Miss D. R. Hard	6–4 6–3	
1960	Miss M. E. Bueno	Miss S. Reynolds	8–6 6–0	
1961*	Miss A. Mortimer	Miss C. C. Truman	4–6 6–4 7–5	
1962	Mrs J. R. Susman	Mrs V. Sukova	6–4 6–4	
1963*	Miss M. Smith	Miss B. J. Moffitt	6–3 6–4	
1964	Miss M. E. Bueno	Miss M. Smith	6–4 7–9 6–3	
1965	Miss M. Smith	Miss M. E. Bueno	6–4 7–5	
1966	Mrs L. W. King	Miss M. E. Bueno	6–3 3–6 6–1	
1967	Mrs L. W. King	Mrs P. F. Jones	6–3 6–4	
1968	Mrs L. W. King	Miss J. A. M. Tegart	9–7 7–5	750
1969	Mrs P. F. Jones	Mrs L. W. King	3–6 6–3 6–2	1,500
1970*	Mrs B. M. Court	Mrs L. W. King	14–12 11–9	1,500
1971	Miss E. Goolagong	Mrs B. M. Court	6–4 6–1	1,800
1972	Mrs L. W. King	Miss E. Goolagong	6–3 6–3	2,400
1973	Mrs L. W. King	Miss C. M. Evert	6–0 7–5	3,000
1974	Miss C. M. Evert	Mrs O. Morozova	6–0 6–4	7,000
1975	Mrs L. W. King	Mrs R. A. Cawley	6–0 6–1	7,000
1976*	Miss C. M. Evert	Mrs R. A. Cawley	6–3 4–6 8–6	10,000
1977	Miss S. V. Wade	Miss B. F. Stove	4–6 6–3 6–1	13,500
1978	Miss M. Navratilova	Miss C. M. Evert	2–6 6–4 7–5	17,100
1979	Miss M. Navratilova	Mrs C. Evert Lloyd	6–4 6–4	18,000
1980	Mrs R. A. Cawley	Mrs C. Evert Lloyd	6–1 7–6	18,000
1981	Mrs C. Evert Lloyd	Miss H. Mandlikova	6–2 6–2	19,440
1982	Miss M. Navratilova	Mrs C. Evert Lloyd	6–1 3–6 6–2	37,500

1983	Miss M. Navratilova	Miss A. Jaeger	6–0 6–3	60,000
1984	Miss M. Navratilova	Mrs C. Evert Lloyd	7–6 6–2	90,000
1985	Miss M. Navratilova	Mrs C. Evert Lloyd	4–6 6–3 6–2	117,000
1986	Miss M. Navratilova	Miss H. Mandlikova	7–6 6–3	126,000
1987	Miss M. Navratilova	Miss S. Graf	7–5 6–3	139,500

MEN'S DOUBLES

	CHAMPIONS	RUNNERS-UP	SCORE
1884	E./W. Renshaw	E. W. Lewis/E. L. Williams	6–3 6–1 1–6 6–4
1885	E./W. Renshaw	C. E. Farrer/A. J. Stanley	6–3 6–3 10–8
(Challenge Round instituted)			
1886	E./W. Renshaw	C. E. Farrer/A. J. Stanley	6–3 6–3 4–6 7–5
1887*	P. Bowes-Lyon H. W. W. Wilberforce	E. Barret-Smith/J. H. Crispe	7–5 6–3 6–2
1888	E./W. Renshaw	P. Bowes-Lyon H. W. W. Wilberforce	2–6 1–6 6–3 6–4 6–3
1889	E./W. Renshaw	G. W. Hillyard/E. W. Lewis	6–4 6–4 3–6 0–6 6–1
1890*	J. Pim/F. O. Stoker	G. W. Hillyard/E. W. Lewis	6–0 7–5 6–4
1891	H./W. Baddeley	J. Pim/F. O. Stoker	6–1 6–3 1–6 6–2
1892	H. S. Barlow/E. W. Lewis	H./W. Baddeley	4–6 6–2 8–6 6–4
1893	J. Pim/F. O. Stoker	H. W. Barlow/E. W. Lewis	4–6 6–3 6–1 2–6 6–0
1894*	H./W. Baddeley	H. S. Barlow/C. H. Martin	5–7 7–5 4–6 6–3 8–6
1895	H./W. Baddeley	W. V. Eaves/E. W. Lewis	8–6 5–7 6–4 6–3
1896	H./W. Baddeley	R. F. Doherty/H. A. Nisbet	1–6 3–6 6–4 6–2 6–1
1897	H. L./R. F. Doherty	H./W. Baddeley	6–4 4–6 8–6 6–4
1898	H. L./R. F. Doherty	C. Hobart/H. A. Nisbet	6–4 6–4 6–2
1899	H. L./R. F. Doherty	C. Hobart/H. A. Nisbet	7–5 6–0 6–2
1900	H. L./R. F. Doherty	H. A. Nisbet/H. Roper Barrett	9–7 7–5 4–6 3–6 6–3
1901	H. L./R. F. Doherty	D. F. Davis/H. Ward	4–6 6–2 6–3 9–7
1902	F. L. Riseley/S. H. Smith	H. L./R. F. Doherty	4–6 8–6 6–3 4–6 11–9
1903	H. L./R. F. Doherty	F. L. Riseley/S. H. Smith	6–4 6–4 6–4
1904	H. L./R. F. Doherty	F. L. Riseley/S. H. Smith	6–3 6–4 6–3
1905	H. L./R. F. Doherty	F. L. Riseley/S. H. Smith	6–2 6–4 6–8 6–3
1906	F. L. Riseley/S. H. Smith	H. L./R. F. Doherty	6–8 6–4 5–7 6–3 6–3
1907*	N. E. Brookes/A. F. Wilding	K. Behr/B. C. Wright	6–4 6–4 6–2
1908*	M. J. G. Ritchie/A. F. Wilding	A. W. Gore/H. Roper Barrett	6–1 6–2 1–6 1–6 9–7
1909*	A. W. Gore/H. Roper Barrett	S. N. Doust/H. A. Parker	6–2 6–1 6–4
1910	M. J. G. Ritchie/A. F. Wilding	A. W. Gore/H. Roper Barrett	6–1 6–1 6–2
1911	M. Decugis/A. H. Gobert	M. J. G. Ritchie/A. F. Wilding	9–7 5–7 6–3 2–6 6–2
1912	C. P. Dixon/H. Roper Barrett	M. Decugis/A. H. Gobert	3–6 6–3 6–4 7–5
1913	C. P. Dixon/H. Roper Barrett	H. Kleinschroth/F. W. Rahe	6–2 6–4 4–6 6–2
1914	N. E. Brookes/A. F. Wilding	C. P. Dixon/H. Roper Barrett	6–1 6–1 5–7 8–6
1915–1918	*Not held*		
1919*	P. O'Hara Wood/R. V. Thomas	R. W. Heath/R. Lycett	6–4 6–2 4–6 6–2
1920*	C. S. Garland/R. N. Williams	A. R. F. Kingscote/J. C. Parke	4–6 6–4 7–5 6–2
1921*	R. Lycett/M. Woosnam	A. H./F. G. Lowe	6–3 6–0 7–5
(Challenge Round abolished)			
1922	J. O. Anderson/R. Lycett	P. O'Hara Wood/G. L. Patterson	3–6 7–9 6–4 6–3 11–9
1923	L. A. Godfree/R. Lycett	E. Flaquer/Count de Gomar	6–3 6–4 3–6 6–3
1924	F. T. Hunter/V. Richards	W. M. Washburn/R. N. Williams	6–3 3–6 8–10 8–6 6–3
1925	J. Borotra/R. Lacoste	R. Casey/J. Hennessey	6–4 11–9 4–6 1–6 6–3
1926	J. Brugnon/H. Cochet	H. Kinsey/V. Richards	7–5 4–6 6–3 6–2
1927	F. T. Hunter/W. T. Tilden	J. Brugnon/H. Cochet	1–6 4–6 8–6 6–3 6–4
1928	J. Brugnon/H. Cochet	J. B. Hawkes/G. L. Patterson	13–11 6–4 6–4
1929	W. L. Allison/J. Van Ryn	I. G. Collins/J. C. Gregory	6–4 5–7 6–3 10–12 6–4
1930	W. L. Allison/J. Van Ryn	J. H. Doeg/G. M. Lott	6–3 6–3 6–2
1931	G. M. Lott/J. Van Ryn	J. Brugnon/H. Cochet	6–2 10–8 9–11 3–6 6–3
1932	J. Borotra/J. Brugnon	G. P. Hughes/F. J. Perry	6–0 4–6 3–6 7–5 7–5
1933	J. Borotra/J. Brugnon	R. Nunoi/J. Satoh	4–6 6–3 6–3 7–5
1934	G. M. Lott/L. R. Stoefen	J. Borotra/J. Brugnon	6–2 6–3 6–4
1935	J. H. Crawford/A. K Quist	W. L. Allison/J. Van Ryn	6–3 5–7 6–2 5–7 7–5
1936	G. P. Hughes/C. R. D. Tuckey	C. E. Hare/F. H. D. Wilde	6–4 3–6 7–9 6–1 5–4
1937	J. D. Budge/G. Mako	G. P. Hughes/C. R. D. Tuckey	6–0 6–4 6–8 6–1
1938	J. D. Budge/G. Mako	H. Henkel/G. von Metaxa	6–4 3–6 6–3 8–6
1939	E. T. Cooke/R. L. Riggs	C. E. Hare/F. H. D. Wilde	6–3 3–6 6–3 9–7
1940–1945	*Not held*		
1946	T. Brown/J. A. Kramer	G. E. Brown/D. Pails	6–4 6–4 6–2
1947	R. Falkenburg/J. A. Kramer	A. J. Mottram/O. W. Sidwell	8–6 6–3 6–3

				FIRST PRIZE *(£ per team)*
1948	J. E. Bromwich/F. A. Sedgman	T. Brown/G. Mulloy	5–7 7–5 7–5 9–7	
1949	R. A. Gonzales/F. A. Parker	G. Mulloy/F. R. Schroeder	6–4 6–4 6–2	
1950	J. E. Bromwich/A. K. Quist	G. E. Brown/O. W. Sidwell	7–5 3–6 6–3 3–6 6–2	
1951	K. McGregor/F. A. Sedgman	J. Drobny/E. W. Sturgess	3–6 6–2 6–3 3–6 6–3	
1952	K. McGregor/F. A. Sedgman	E. V. Seixas/E. W. Sturgess	6–3 7–5 6–4	
1953	L. A. Hoad/K. R. Rosewall	R. N. Hartwig/M. G. Rose	6–4 7–5 4–6 7–5	
1954	R. N. Hartwig/M. G. Rose	E. V. Seixas/M. A. Trabert	6–4 6–4 3–6 6–4	
1955	R. N. Hartwig/L. A. Hoad	N. A. Fraser/K. R. Rosewall	7–5 6–4 6–3	
1956	L. A. Hoad/K. R. Rosewall	N. Pietrangeli/O. Sirola	7–5 6–2 6–1	
1957	G. Mulloy/B. Patty	N. A. Fraser/L. A. Hoad	8–10 6–4 6–4 6–4	
1958	S. Davidson/U. Schmidt	A. J. Cooper/N. A. Fraser	6–4 6–4 8–6	
1959	R. Emerson/N. A. Fraser	R. Laver/R. Mark	8–6 6–3 1–6 9–7	
1960	R. H. Osuna/R. D. Ralston	M. G. Davies/R. K. Wilson	7–5 6–3 10–8	
1961	R. Emerson/N. A. Fraser	R. A. J. Hewitt/F. S. Stolle	6–4 6–8 6–4 6–8 8–6	
1962	R. A. J. Hewitt/F. S. Stolle	B. Jovanovic/N. Pilic	6–2 5–7 6–2 6–4	
1963	R. H. Osuna/A. Palafox	J. C. Barclay/P. Darmon	4–6 6–2 6–2 6–2	
1964	R. A. J. Hewitt/F. S. Stolle	R. Emerson/K. N. Fletcher	7–5 11–9 6–4	
1965	J. D. Newcombe/A. D. Roche	K. N. Fletcher/R. A. J. Hewitt	7–5 6–3 6–4	
1966	K. N. Fletcher/J. D. Newcombe	W. W. Bowrey/O. K. Davidson	6–3 6–4 3–6 6–3	
1967	R. A. J. Hewitt/F. D. McMillan	R. Emerson/K. N. Fletcher	6–2 6–3 6–4	
1968	J. D. Newcombe/A. D. Roche	K. R. Rosewall/F. S. Stolle	3–6 8–6 5–7 14–12 6–3	800
1969	J. D. Newcombe/A. D. Roche	T. S. Okker/M. C. Riessen	7–5 11–9 6–3	1,000
1970	J. D. Newcombe/A. D. Roche	K. R. Rosewall/F. S. Stolle	10–8 6–3 6–1	1,000
1971	R. Emerson/R. Laver	A. R. Ashe/R. D. Ralston	4–6 9–7 6–8 6–4 6–4	750
1972	R. A. J. Hewitt/F. D. McMillan	S. R. Smith/E. Van Dillen	6–2 6–2 9–7	1,000
1973	J. S. Connors/I. Nastase	J. R. Cooper/N. A. Fraser	3–6 6–3 6–4 8–9 6–1	1,000
1974	J. D. Newcombe/A. D. Roche	R. C. Lutz/S. R. Smith	8–6 6–4 6–4	2,000
1975	V. Gerulaitis/A. Mayer	C. Dowdeswell/A. J. Stone	7–5 8–6 6–4	2,000
1976	B. E. Gottfried/R. Ramirez	R. L. Case/G. Masters	3–6 6–3 8–6 2–6 7–6	3,000
1977	R. L. Case/G. Masters	J. G. Alexander/P. C. Dent	6–3 6–4 3–6 8–9 6–4	6,000
1978	R. A. J. Hewitt/F. D. McMillan	P. Fleming/J. P. McEnroe	6–1 6–4 6–2	7,500
1979	P. Fleming/J. P. McEnroe	B. E. Gottfried/R. Ramirez	4–6 6–4 6–2 6–2	8,000
1980	P. McNamara/P. McNamee	R. C. Lutz/S. R. Smith	7–6 6–3 6–7 6–4	8,400
1981	P. Fleming/J. P. McEnroe	R. C. Lutz/S. R. Smith	6–4 6–4 6–4	9,070
1982	P. McNamara/P. McNamee	P. Fleming/J. P. McEnroe	6–3 6–2	16,666
1983	P. Fleming/J. P. McEnroe	T. E./T. R. Gullikson	6–4 6–3 6–4	26,628
1984	P. Fleming/J. P. McEnroe	P. Cash/P. McNamee	6–2 5–7 6–2 3–6 6–3	40,000
1985	H. P. Gunthardt/B. Taroczy	P. Cash/J. Fitzgerald	6–4 6–3 4–6 6–3	47,500
1986	J. Nystrom/M. Wilander	G. Donnelly/P. Fleming	7–6 6–3 6–3	48,500
1987	K. Flach/R. Seguso	S. Casal/E. Sanchez	3–6 6–7 7–6 6–1 6–4	53,730

WOMEN'S DOUBLES

	CHAMPIONS	RUNNERS-UP	SCORE
1913	R. J. McNair/D. P. Boothby	A. Sterry/D. Lambert Chambers	4–6 2–4 ret'd
1914	A. M. Morton/E. Ryan	G. Hannam/D. R. Larcombe	6–1 6–3
1915–1918	*Not held*		
1919	S. Lenglen/E. Ryan	D. Lambert Chambers/D. R. Larcombe	4–6 7–5 6–3
1920	S. Lenglen/E. Ryan	D. Lambert Chambers/D. R. Larcombe	6–4 6–0
1921	S. Lenglen/E. Ryan	A. E. Beamish/G. Peacock	6–1 6–2
1922	S. Lenglen/E. Ryan	K. McKane/A. D. Stocks	6–0 6–4
1923	S. Lenglen/E. Ryan	J. Austin/E. L. Colyer	6–3 6–1
1924	H. Wightman/H. N. Wills	B. C. Covell/K. McKane	6–4 6–4
1925	S. Lenglen/E. Ryan	A. V. Bridge/C. G. McIlquham	6–2 6–2
1926	M. K. Browne/E. Ryan	L. A. Godfree/E. L. Colyer	6–1 6–1
1927	H. N. Wills/E. Ryan	E. L. Heine/G. Peacock	6–3 6–2
1928	P. Saunders/M. Watson	E. Bennett/E. H. Harvey	6–2 6–3
1929	L. R. C. Michell/M. Watson	B. C. Covell/D. C. Shepherd-Barron	6–4 8–6
1930	F. S. Moody/E. Ryan	E. Cross/S. Palfrey	6–2 9–7
1931	D. C. Shepherd-Barron/P. E. Mudford	D. Metaxa/J. Sigart	3–6 6–3 6–4
1932	D. Metaxa/J. Sigart	H. H. Jacobs/E. Ryan	6–4 6–3
1933	S. Mathieu/E. Ryan	F. James/A. M. Yorke	6–2 9–11 6–4
1934	S. Mathieu/E. Ryan	D. B. Andrus/S. Henrotin	6–3 6–3
1935	F. James/K. E. Stammers	S. Mathieu/H. Sperling	6–1 6–4
1936	F. James/K. E. Stammers	S. Fabyan/H. H. Jacobs	6–2 6–1
1937	S. Mathieu/A. M. Yorke	P. King/E. Pittman	6–3 6–3
1938	S. Fabyan/A. Marble	S. Mathieu/A. M. Yorke	6–2 6–3
1939	S. Fabyan/A. Marble	H. H. Jacobs/A. M. Yorke	6–1 6–0
1940–1945	*Not held*		
1946	A. L. Brough/M. E. Osborne	P. M. Betz/D. J. Hart	6–3 2–6 6–3

				FIRST PRIZE (*£ per team)*
1947	D. J. Hart/P. C. Todd	A. L. Brough/M. E. Osborne	3–6 6–4 7–5	
1948	A. L. Brough/W. du Pont	D. J. Hart/P. C. Todd	6–3 3–6 6–3	
1949	A. L. Brough/W. du Pont	G. Moran/P. C. Todd	8–6 7–5	
1950	A. L. Brough/W. du Pont	S. J. Fry/D. J. Hart	6–4 5–7 6–1	
1951	S. J. Fry/D. J. Hart	A. L. Brough/W. du Pont	6–3 13–11	
1952	S. J. Fry/D. J. Hart	A. L. Brough/M. Connolly	8–6 6–3	
1953	S. J. Fry/D. J. Hart	M. Connolly/J. Sampson	6–0 6–0	
1954	A. L. Brough/W. du Pont	S. J. Fry/D. J. Hart	4–6 9–7 6–3	
1955	A. Mortimer/J. A. Shilcock	S. J. Bloomer/P. E. Ward	7–5 6–1	
1956	A. Buxton/A. Gibson	F. Muller/D. G. Seeney	6–1 8–6	
1957	A. Gibson/D. R. Hard	K. Hawton/T. D. Long	6–1 6–2	
1958	M. E. Bueno/A. Gibson	W. du Pont/M. Varner	6–3 7–5	
1959	J. Arth/D. R. Hard	J. G. Fleitz/C. C. Truman	2–6 6–2 6–3	
1960	M. E. Bueno/D. R. Hard	S. Reynolds/R. Schuurman	6–4 6–0	
1961	K. Hantz/B. J. Moffitt	J. Lehane/M. Smith	6–3 6–4	
1962	B. J. Moffitt/J. R. Susman	L. E. G. Price/R. Schuurman	5–7 6–3 7–5	
1963	M. E. Bueno/D. R. Hard	R. A. Ebbern/M. Smith	8–6 9–7	
1964	M. Smith/L. R. Turner	B. J. Moffitt/J. R. Susman	7–5 6–2	
1965	M. E. Bueno/B. J. Moffitt	F. Durr/J. Lieffrig	6–2 7–5	
1966	M. E. Bueno/N. Richey	M. Smith/J. A. M. Tegart	6–3 4–6 6–4	
1967	R. Casals/L. W. King	M. E. Bueno/N. Richey	9–11 6–4 6–2	
1968	R. Casals/L. W. King	F. Durr/P. F. Jones	3–6 6–4 7–5	500
1969	B. M. Court/J. A. M. Tegart	P. S. A. Hogan/M. Michel	9–7 6–2	600
1970	R. Casals/L. W. King	F. Durr/S. V. Wade	6–2 6–3	600
1971	R. Casals/L. W. King	B. M. Court/E. Goolagong	6–3 6–2	450
1972	L. W. King/B. Stove	D. E. Dalton/F. Durr	6–2 4–6 6–3	600
1973	R. Casals/L. W. King	F. Durr/B. Stove	6–1 4–6 7–5	600
1974	E. Goolagong/M. Michel	H. F. Gourlay/K. M. Krantzcke	2–6 6–4 6–3	1,200
1975	A. Kiyomura/K. Sawamatsu	F. Durr/B. Stove	7–5 1–6 7–5	1,200
1976	C. Evert/M. Navratilova	L. W. King/B. Stove	6–1 3–6 7–5	2,400
1977	H. Gourlay-Cawley/J. C. Russell	M. Navratilova/B. Stove	6–3 6–3	5,200
1978	G. E. Reid/W. Turnbull	M. Jausovec/V. Ruzici	4–6 9–8 6–3	6,500
1979	L. W. King/M. Navratilova	B. Stove/W. M. Turnbull	5–7 6–3 6–2	6,930
1980	K. Jordan/A. E. Smith	R. Casals/W. M. Turnbull	4–6 7–5 6–1	7,276
1981	M. Navratilova/P. H. Shriver	K. Jordan/A. E. Smith	6–3 7–6	7,854
1982	M. Navratilova/P. H. Shriver	K. Jordan/A. E. Smith	6–4 6–1	14,450
1983	M. Navratilova/P. H. Shriver	R. Casals/W. M. Turnbull	6–2 6–2	23,100
1984	M. Navratilova/P. H. Shriver	K. Jordan/A. E. Smith	6–3 6–4	34,700
1985	K. Jordan/E. Smylie	M. Navratilova/P. H. Shriver	5–7 6–3 6–4	41,100
1986	M. Navratilova/P. H. Shriver	H. Mandlikova/W. M. Turnbull	6–1 6–3	42,060
1987	C. Kohde-Kilsch/H. Sukova	B. Nagelsen/E. Smylie	7–5 7–5	46,500

MIXED DOUBLES

	CHAMPIONS	RUNNERS-UP	SCORE
1913	Hope Crisp/Mrs C. O. Tuckey	J. C. Parke/Mrs D. R. Larcombe	3–6 5–3 ret'd
1914	J. C. Parke/Mrs D. R. Larcombe	A. F. Wilding/Mlle M. Broquedis	4–6 6–4 6–2
1915–1918	*Not held*		
1919	R. Lycett/Miss E. Ryan	A. D. Prebble/Mrs D. Lambert Chambers	6–0 6–0
1920	G. L. Patterson/Mlle S. Lenglen	R. Lycett/Miss E. Ryan	7–5 6–3
1921	R. Lycett/Miss E. Ryan	M. Woosnam/Miss P. L. Howkins	6–3 6–1
1922	P. O'Hara Wood/Mlle S. Lenglen	R. Lycett/Miss E. Ryan	6–4 6–3
1923	R. Lycett/Miss E. Ryan	L. S. Deane/Mrs D. C. Shepherd-Barron	6–4 7–5
1924	J. B. Gilbert/Miss K. McKane	L. A. Godfree/Mrs D. C. Shepherd-Barron	6–3 3–6 6–3
1925	J. Borotra/Mlle S. Lenglen	H. L. de Morpurgo/Miss E. Ryan	6–3 6–3
1926	L. A./Mrs Godfree	H. Kinsey/Miss M. K. Browne	6–3 6–4
1927	F. T. Hunter/Miss E. Ryan	L. A./Mrs Godfree	8–6 6–0
1928	P. D. B. Spence/Miss E. Ryan	J. H. Crawford/Miss D. Akhurst	7–5 6–4
1929	F. T. Hunter/Miss H. N. Wills	I. G. Collins/Miss J. Fry	6–1 6–4
1930	J. H. Crawford/Miss E. Ryan	D. Prenn/Frl H. Krahwinkel	6–1 6–3
1931	G. M. Lott/Mrs L. A. Harper	I. G. Collins/Miss J. C. Ridley	6–3 1–6 6–1
1932	E. Maier/Miss E. Ryan	H. C. Hopman/Mlle J. Sigart	7–5 6–2
1933	G. von Cramm/Frl H. Krahwinkel	N. G. Farquharson/Miss M. Heeley	7–5 8–6
1934	R. Miki/Miss D. E. Round	H. W. Austin/Mrs D. C. Shepherd-Barron	3–6 6–4 6–0
1935	F. J. Perry/Miss D. E. Round	H. C./Mrs Hopman	7–5 4–6 6–2
1936	F. J. Perry/Miss D. E. Round	J. D. Budge/Mrs S. Fabyan	7–9 7–5 6–4
1937	J. D. Budge/Miss A. Marble	Y. Petra/Mme S. Mathieu	6–4 6–1
1938	J. D. Budge/Miss A. Marble	H. Henkel/Mrs S. Fabyan	6–1 6–4
1939	R. L. Riggs/Miss A. Marble	F. H. D. Wilde/Miss N. B. Brown	9–7 6–1
1940–1945	*Not held*		

1946	T. Brown/Miss A. L. Brough	G. E. Brown/Miss D. Bundy	6–4 6–4	
1947	J. E. Bromwich/Miss A. L. Brough	C. F. Long/Mrs N. M. Bolton	1–6 6–4 6–2	
1948	J. E. Bromwich/Miss A. L. Brough	F. A. Sedgman/Miss D. J. Hart	6–2 3–6 6–3	
1949	E. E. Sturgess/Mrs S. P. Summer	J. E. Bromwich/Miss A. L. Brough	9–7 9–11 7–5	
1950	E. W. Sturgess/Miss A. L. Brough	G. E. Brown/Mrs P. C. Todd	11–9 1–6 6–4	
1951	F. A. Sedgman/Miss D. J. Hart	M. G. Rose/Mrs N. M. Bolton	7–5 6–2	
1952	F. A. Sedgman/Miss D. J. Hart	E. Morea/Mrs T. D. Long	4–6 6–3 6–4	
1953	E. V. Seixas/Miss D. J. Hart	E. Morea/Miss S. J. Fry	9–7 7–5	
1954	E. V. Seixas/Miss D. J. Hart	K. R. Rosewall/Mrs W. du Pont	5–7 6–4 6–3	
1955	E. V. Seixas/Miss D. J. Hart	E. Morea/Miss A. L. Brough	8–6 2–6 6–3	
1956	E. V. Seixas/Miss S. J. Fry	G. Mulloy/Miss A. Gibson	2–6 6–2 7–5	
1957	M. G. Rose/Miss D. R. Hard	N. A. Fraser/Miss A. Gibson	6–4 7–5	
1958	R. N. Howe/Miss L. Coghlan	K. Nielsen/Miss A. Gibson	6–3 13–11	
1959	R. Laver/Miss D. R. Hard	N. A. Fraser/Miss M. E. Bueno	6–4 6–3	
1960	R. Laver/Miss D. R. Hard	R. N. Howes/Miss M. E. Bueno	13–11 3–6 8–6	
1961	F. S. Stolle/Miss L. R. Turner	R. N. Howe/Miss E. Buding	11–9 6–2	
1962	N. A. Fraser/Mrs W. du Pont	R. D. Ralston/Miss A. S. Haydon	2–6 6–3 13–11	
1963	K. N. Fletcher/Miss M. Smith	R. A. J. Hewitt/Miss D. R. Hard	11–9 6–4	
1964	F. S. Stolle/Miss L. R. Turner	K. N. Fletcher/Miss M. Smith	6–4 6–4	FIRST
1965	K. N. Fletcher/Miss M. Smith	A. D. Roche/Miss J. A. M. Tegart	12–10 6–3	PRIZE
1966	K. N. Fletcher/Miss M. Smith	R. D. Ralston/Mrs L. W. King	4–6 6–3 6–3	*(£ per*
1967	O. K. Davidson/Mrs L. W. King	K. N. Fletcher/Miss M. E. Bueno	7–5 6–0	*team)*
1968	K. N. Fletcher/Mrs B. M. Court	A. Metreveli/Miss O. Morozova	6–1 14–12	450
1969	F. S. Stolle/Mrs P. F. Jones	A. D. Roche/Miss J. A. M. Tegart	6–3 6–2	500
1970	I. Nastase/Miss R. Casals	A. Metreveli/Miss O. Morozova	6–3 4–6 9–7	500
1971	O. K. Davidson/Mrs L. W. King	M. C. Rieseen/Mrs B. M. Court	3–6 6–2 15–13	375
1972	I. Nastase/Miss R. Casals	K. Warwick/Miss E. Goolagong	6–4 6–4	500
1973	O. K. Davidson/Mrs L. W. King	R. Ramirez/Miss J. Newberry	6–3 6–2	500
1974	O. K. Davidson/Mrs L. W. King	M. J. Farrell/Miss L. J. Charles	6–3 9–7	1,000
1975	M. C. Riessen/Mrs B. M. Court	A. J. Stone/Miss B. Stove	6–4 7–5	1,000
1976	A. D. Roche/Miss F. Durr	R. L. Stockton/Miss R. Casals	6–3 2–6 7–5	2,000
1977	R. A. J. Hewitt/Miss G. R. Stevens	F. D. McMillan/Miss B. Stove	3–6 7–5 6–4	3,000
1978	F. D. McMillan/Miss B. Stove	R. O. Ruffels/Mrs L. W. King	6–2 6–2	4,000
1979	R. A. J. Hewitt/Miss G. R. Stevens	F. D. McMillan/Miss B. Stove	7–5 7–6	4,200
1980	J. R. Austin/Miss T. Austin	M. R. Edmondson/Miss D. L. Fromholtz	4–6 7–6 6–3	4,420
1981	F. D. McMillan/Miss B. Stove	J. R. Austin/Miss T. Austin	4–6 7–6 6–3	4,770
1982	K. Curren/Miss A. E. Smith	J. M. Lloyd/Miss W. M. Turnbull	2–6 6–3 7–5	6,750
1983	J. M. Lloyd/Miss W. M. Turnbull	S. Denton/Mrs L. W. King	6–7 7–6 7–5	12,000
1984	J. M. Lloyd/Miss W. M. Turnbull	S. Denton/Miss K. Jordan	6–3 6–3	18,000
1985	P. McNamee/Miss M. Navratilova	J. Fitzgerald/Mrs E. Smylie	7–5 4–6 6–2	23,400
1986	K. Flach/Miss K. Jordan	H. P. Gunthardt/Miss M. Navratilova	6–3 7–6	25,200
1987	M. J. Bates/Miss J. M. Durie	D. Cahill/Miss N. Provis	7–6 6–3	27,900

US NATIONAL CHAMPIONSHIPS 1881–1969

**Holders did not defend the title*

MEN'S SINGLES

	CHAMPION	RUNNER-UP	SCORE
1881	R. D. Sears	W. E. Glyn	6–0 6–3 6–2
1882	R. D. Sears	C. M. Clark	6–1 6–4 6–0
1883	R. D. Sears	J. Dwight	6–2 6–0 9–7
1884	R. D. Sears	H. A. Taylor	6–0 1–6 6–0 6–2
1885	R. D. Sears	G. M. Brinley	6–3 4–6 6–0 6–3
1886	R. D. Sears	R. L. Beeckman	4–6 6–1 6–3 6–4
1887	R. D. Sears	H. W. Slocum	6–1 6–3 6–2
1888*	H. W. Slocum	H. A. Taylor	6–4 6–1 6–0
1889	H. W. Slocum	Q. A. Shaw	6–3 6–1 4–6 6–2
1890	O. S. Campbell	H. W. Slocum	6–2 4–6 6–3 6–1
1891	O. S. Campbell	C. Hobart	2–6 7–5 7–9 6–1 6–2
1892	O. S. Campbell	F. H. Hovey	7–5 3–6 6–3 7–5
1893*	R. D. Wrenn	F. H. Hovey	6–4 3–6 6–4 6–4
1894	R. D. Wrenn	M. F. Goodbody	6–8 6–1 6–4 6–4
1895	F. H. Hovey	R. D. Wrenn	6–3 6–2 6–4
1896	R. D. Wrenn	F. H. Hovey	7–5 3–6 6–0 1–6 6–1
1897	R. D. Wrenn	W. V. Eaves	4–6 8–6 6–3 2–6 6–2

Year	Winner	Runner-up	Score
1898*	M. D. Whitman	D. F. Davis	3–6 6–2 6–2 6–1
1899	M. D. Whitman	J. P. Paret	6–1 6–2 3–6 7–5
1900	M. D. Whitman	W. A. Larned	6–4 1–6 6–2 6–2
1901*	W. A. Larned	B. C. Wright	6–2 6–8 6–4 6–4
1902	W. A. Larned	R. F. Doherty	4–6 6–2 6–4 8–6
1903	H. L. Doherty	W. A. Larned	6–0 6–3 10–8
1904*	H. Ward	W. J. Clothier	10–8 6–4 9–7
1905	B. C. Wright	H. Ward	6–2 6–1 11–9
1906	W. J. Clothier	B. C. Wright	6–3 6–0 6–4
1907*	W. A. Larned	R. LeRoy	6–2 6–2 6–4
1908	W. A. Larned	B. C. Wright	6–1 6–2 8–6
1909	W. A. Larned	W. J. Clothier	6–1 6–2 5–7 1–6 6–1
1910	W. A. Larned	T. C. Bundy	6–1 5–7 6–0 6–8 6–1
1911	W. A. Larned	M. E. McLoughlin	6–4 6–4 6–2
(Challenge Round abolished)			
1912	M. E. McLoughlin	W. F. Johnson	3–6 2–6 6–2 6–4 6–2
1913	M. E. McLoughlin	R. N. Williams	6–4 5–7 6–3 6–1
1914	R. N. Williams	M. E. McLoughlin	6–3 8–6 10–8
1915	W. M. Johnston	M. E. McLoughlin	1–6 6–0 7–5 10–8
1916	R. N. Williams	W. M. Johnston	4–6 6–4 0–6 6–2 6–4
1917	*Not held*		
1918	R. L. Murray	W. T. Tilden	6–3 6–1 7–5
1919	W. M. Johnston	W. T. Tilden	6–4 6–4 6–3
1920	W. T. Tilden	W. M. Johnston	6–1 1–6 7–5 5–7 6–3
1921	W. T. Tilden	W. F. Johnson	6–1 6–3 6–1
1922	W. T. Tilden	W. M. Johnston	4–6 3–6 6–2 6–3 6–4
1923	W. T. Tilden	W. M. Johnston	6–4 6–1 6–4
1924	W. T. Tilden	W. M. Johnston	6–1 9–7 6–2
1925	W. T. Tilden	W. M. Johnston	4–6 11–9 6–3 4–6 6–3
1926	P. Lacoste	J. Borotra	6–4 6–0 6–4
1927	R. Lacoste	W. T. Tilden	11–9 6–3 11–9
1928	H. Cochet	F. T. Hunter	4–6 6–4 3–6 7–5 6–3
1929	W. T. Tilden	F. T. Hunter	3–6 6–3 4–6 6–2 6–4
1930	J. H. Doeg	F. X. Shields	10–8 1–6 6–4 16–14
1931	H. E. Vines	G. M. Lott	7–9 6–3 9–7 7–5
1932	H. E. Vines	H. Cochet	6–4 6–4 6–4
1933	F. J. Perry	J. H. Crawford	6–3 11–13 4–6 6–0 6–1
1934	F. J. Perry	W. L. Allison	6–4 6–3 1–6 8–6
1935	W. L. Allison	S. B. Wood	6–2 6–2 6–3
1936	F. J. Perry	J. D. Budge	2–6 6–2 8–6 1–6 10–8
1937	J. D. Budge	C. Von Cramm	6–1 7–9 6–1 3–6 6–1
1938	J. D. Budge	G. Mako	6–3 6–8 6–2 6–1
1939	R. L. Riggs	S. W. van Horn	6–4 6–2 6–4
1940	W. D. McNeill	R. L. Riggs	4–6 6–8 6–3 6–3 7–5
1941	R. L. Riggs	F. Kovacs	5–7 6–1 6–3 6–3
1942	F. R. Schroeder	F. A. Parker	8–6 7–5 3–6 4–6 6–2
1943	J. R. Hunt	J. A. Kramer	6–3 3–6 10–8 6–0
1944	F. A. Parker	W. F. Talbert	6–4 3–6 6–3 6–3
1945	F. A. Parker	W. F. Talbert	14–12 6–1 6–2
1946	J. A. Kramer	T. P. Brown	9–7 6–3 6–0
1947	J. A. Kramer	F. A. Parker	4–6 2–6 6–1 6–0 6–3
1948	R. A. Gonzales	E. W. Sturgess	6–2 6–3 14–12
1949	R. A. Gonzales	F. R. Schroeder	16–18 2–6 6–1 6–2 6–4
1950	A. Larsen	H. Flam	6–3 4–6 5–7 6–4 6–3
1951	F. A. Sedgman	E. V. Seixas	6–4 6–1 6–1
1952	F. A. Sedgman	G. Mulloy	6–1 6–2 6–3
1953	M. A. Trabert	E. V. Seixas	6–3 6–2 6–3
1954	E. V. Seixas	R. N. Hartwig	3–6 6–2 6–4 6–4
1955	M. A. Trabert	K. R. Rosewall	9–7 6–3 6–3
1956	K. R. Rosewall	L. A. Hoad	4–6 6–2 6–3 6–3
1957	M. J. Anderson	A. J. Cooper	10–8 7–5 6–4
1958	A. J. Cooper	M. J. Anderson	6–2 3–6 4–6 10–8 8–6
1959	N. A. Fraser	A. Olmedo	6–3 5–7 6–2 6–4
1960	N. A. Fraser	R. G. Laver	6–4 6–4 9–7
1961	R. S. Emerson	R. G. Laver	7–5 6–3 6–2
1962	R. G. Laver	R. S. Emerson	6–2 6–4 5–7 6–4
1963	R. H. Osuna	F. Froehling	7–5 6–4 6–2
1964	R. S. Emerson	F. S. Stolle	6–4 6–2 6–4
1965	M. Santana	E. C. Drysdale	6–2 7–9 7–5 6–1
1966	F. S. Stolle	J. D. Newcombe	4–6 12–10 6–3 6–4
1967	J. D. Newcombe	C. Graebner	6–4 6–4 8–6

1968	A. R. Ashe	R. C. Lutz	4–6 6–3 8–10 6–0 6–4
1969	S. R. Smith	R. C. Lutz	9–7 6–3 6–1

WOMEN'S SINGLES

	CHAMPION	RUNNER-UP	SCORE
1887	Miss E. Hansell	Miss L. Knight	6–1 6–0
1888	Miss B. L. Townsend	Miss E. Hansell	6–3 6–5
1889	Miss B. L. Townsend	Miss L. D. Voorhes	7–5 6–2
1890	Miss E. C. Roosevelt	Miss B. L. Townsend	6–2 6–2
1891	Miss M. E. Cahill	Miss E. C. Roosevelt	6–4 6–1 4–6 6–3
1892	Miss M. E. Cahill	Miss E. H. Moore	5–7 6–3 6–4 4–6 6–2
1893*	Miss A. Terry	Miss A. Schultze	6–1 6–3
1894	Miss H. Hellwig	Miss A. Terry	7–5 3–6 6–0 3–6 6–3
1895	Miss J. Atkinson	Miss H. Hellwig	6–4 6–2 6–1
1896	Miss E. H. Moore	Miss J. Atkinson	6–4 4–6 6–2 6–2
1897	Miss J. Atkinson	Miss E. H. Moore	6–3 6–3 4–6 3–6 6–3
1898	Miss J. Atkinson	Miss M. Jones	6–3 5–7 6–4 2–6 7–5
1899*	Miss M. Jones	Miss M. Banks	6–1 6–1 7–5
1900*	Miss M. McAteer	Miss E. Parker	6–2 6–2 6–0
1901	Miss E. H. Moore	Miss M. McAteer	6–4 3–6 7–5 2–6 6–2
1902	Miss M. Jones	Miss E. H. Moore	6–1 1–0 ret'd
1903	Miss E. H. Moore	Miss M. Jones	7–5 8–6
1904	Miss M. G. Sutton	Miss E. H. Moore	6–1 6–2
1905*	Miss E. H. Moore	Miss H. Homans	6–4 5–7 6–1
1906*	Miss H. Homans	Mrs M. Barger-Wallach	6–4 6–3
1907*	Miss E. Sears	Miss C. Neely	6–3 6–2
1908	Mrs M. Barger-Wallach	Miss E. Sears	6–3 1–6 6–3
1909	Miss H. Hotchkiss	Mrs M. Barger-Wallach	6–0 6–1
1910	Miss H. Hotchkiss	Miss L. Hammond	6–4 6–2
1911	Miss H. Hotchkiss	Miss F. Sutton	8–10 6–1 9–7
1912*	Miss M. K. Browne	Miss Eleanora Sears	6–4 6–2
1913	Miss M. K. Browne	Miss D. Green	6–2 7–5
1914	Miss M. K. Browne	Miss M. Wagner	6–2 1–6 6–1
1915*	Miss M. Bjurstedt	Mrs G. W. Wightman	4–6 6–2 6–0
1916	Miss M. Bjurstedt	Mrs L. H. Raymond	6–0 6–1
1917	*Not held*		
1918	Miss M. Bjurstedt	Miss E. E. Goss	6–4 6–3
(*Challenge Round abolished*)			
1919	Mrs G. W. Wightman	Miss M. Zinderstein	6–1 6–2
1920	Mrs F. Mallory	Miss M. Zinderstein	6–3 6–1
1921	Mrs F. Mallory	Miss M. K. Browne	4–6 6–4 6–2
1922	Mrs F. Mallory	Miss H. N. Wills	6–3 6–1
1923	Miss H. N. Wills	Mrs F. Mallory	6–2 6–1
1924	Miss H. N. Wills	Mrs F. Mallory	6–1 6–3
1925	Miss H. N. Wills	Miss K. McKane	3–6 6–0 6–2
1926	Mrs F. Mallory	Miss E. Ryan	4–6 6–4 9–7
1927	Miss H. N. Wills	Miss B. Nuthall	6–1 6–4
1928	Miss H. N. Wills	Miss H. H. Jacobs	6–2 6–1
1929	Miss H. N. Wills	Mrs P. H. Watson	6–4 6–2
1930	Miss B. Nuthall	Mrs L. A. Harper	6–1 6–4
1931	Mrs F. S. Moody	Mrs F. Whittingstall	6–4 6–1
1932	Miss H. H. Jacobs	Miss C. A. Babcock	6–2 6–2
1933	Miss H. H. Jacobs	Mrs F. S. Moody	8–6 3–6 3–0 ret'd
1934	Miss H. H. Jacobs	Miss S. Palfrey	6–1 6–4
1935	Miss H. H. Jacobs	Mrs S. P. Fabyan	6–2 6–4
1936	Miss A. Marble	Miss H. H. Jacobs	4–6 6–3 6–2
1937	Miss A. Lizane	Miss J. Jedrzejowksa	6–4 6–2
1938	Miss A. Marble	Miss N. Wynne	6–0 6–3
1939	Miss A. Marble	Miss H. H. Jacobs	6–0 8–10 6–4
1940	Miss A. Marble	Miss H. H. Jacobs	6–2 6–3
1941	Mrs S. P. Cooke	Miss P. M. Betz	7–5 6–2
1942	Miss P. M. Betz	Miss A. L. Brough	4–6 6–1 6–4
1943	Miss P. M. Betz	Miss A. L. Brough	6–3 5–7 6–3
1944	Miss P. M. Betz	Miss M. E. Osborne	6–3 8–6
1945	Mrs S. P. Cooke	Miss P. M. Betz	3–6 8–6 6–4
1946	Miss P. M. Betz	Miss P. C. Todd	11–9 6–3
1947	Miss A. L. Brough	Miss M. E. Osborne	8–6 4–6 6–1
1948	Mrs W. D. du Pont	Miss A. L. Brough	4–6 6–4 15–13
1949	Mrs W. D. du Pont	Miss D. J. Hart	6–4 6–1

1950	Mrs W. D. du Pont	Miss D. J. Hart	6–4 6–3
1951	Miss M. Connolly	Miss S. J. Fry	6–3 1–6 6–4
1952	Miss M. Connolly	Miss D. J. Hart	6–3 7–5
1953	Miss M. Connolly	Miss D. J. Hart	6–2 6–4
1954	Miss D. J. Hart	Miss A. L. Brough	6–8 6–1 8–6
1955	Miss D. J. Hart	Miss P. E. Ward	6–4 6–2
1956	Miss S. J. Fry	Miss A. Gibson	6–3 6–4
1957	Miss A. Gibson	Miss A. L. Brough	6–3 6–2
1958	Miss A. Gibson	Miss D. R. Hard	3–6 6–1 6–2
1959	Miss M. E. Bueno	Miss C. C. Truman	6–1 6–4
1960	Miss D. R. Hard	Miss M. E. Bueno	6–4 10–12 6–4
1961	Miss D. R. Hard	Miss A. S. Haydon	6–3 6–4
1962	Miss M. Smith	Miss D. R. Hard	9–7 6–4
1963	Miss M. E. Bueno	Miss M. Smith	7–5 6–4
1964	Miss M. E. Bueno	Mrs C. Graebner	6–1 6–0
1965	Miss M. Smith	Miss B. J. Moffitt	8–6 7–5
1966	Miss M. E. Bueno	Miss N. Richey	6–3 6–1
1967	Mrs L. W. King	Mrs P. F. Jones	11–9 6–4
1968	Mrs B. M. Court	Miss M. E. Bueno	6–2 6–2
1969	Mrs B. M. Court	Miss S. V. Wade	4–6 6–3 6–0

MEN'S DOUBLES

** Holders did not defend the title.*

	CHAMPIONS	RUNNERS-UP	SCORE
1881	C. M. Clark/F. W. Taylor	A. Van Rennselaer/A. E. Newbold	6–5 6–4 6–5
1882	J. Dwight/R. D. Sears	W. Nightingale/G. M. Shields	6–2 6–4 6–4
1883	J. Dwight/R. D. Sears	A. Van Rennselaer/A. E. Newbold	6–0 6–2 6–2
1884	J. Dwight/R. D. Sears	A. Van Rennselaer/W. V. R. Berry	6–4 6–1 8–10 6–4
1885	J. S. Clark/R. D. Sears	W. P. Knapp/H. W. Slocum	6–3 6–0 6–2
1886	J. Dwight/R. D. Sears	G. M. Brinley/H. A. Taylor	7–5 5–7 7–5 6–4
1887	J. Dwight/R. D. Sears	H. W. Slocum/H. A. Taylor	6–4 3–6 2–6 6–3 6–3
1888	O. S. Campbell/V. G. Hall	C. Hobart/E. P. MacMullen	6–4 6–2 6–4
1889	H. W. Slocum/H. A. Taylor	O. S. Campbell/V. G. Hall	6–1 6–3 6–2
1890	V. G. Hall/C. Hobart	C. W. Carver/J. A. Ryerson	6–3 4–6 6–2 2–6 6–3
(Challenge Round instituted)			
1891	O. S. Campbell/R. P. Huntington	V. G. Hall/C. Hobart	6–3 6–4 8–6
1892	O. S. Campbell/R. P. Huntingdon	V. G. Hall/E. L. Hall	6–4 6–2 4–6 6–3
1893	C. Hobart/F. H. Hovey	O. S. Campbell/R. P. Huntington	6–3 6–4 4–6 6–2
1894	C. Hobart/F. H. Hovey	C. B. Neel/S. R. Neel	6–3 8–6 6–1
1895	M. G. Chase/R. D. Wrenn	C. Hobart/F. H. Hovey	7–5 6–1 8–6
1896*	C. B./S. R. Neel	M. G. Chase/R. D. Wrenn	6–3 1–6 6–1 3–6 6–1
1897	L. E. Ware/P. Sheldon	H. S. Mahony/H. A. Nisbet	11–13 6–2 9–7 1–6 6–1
1898	L. E. Ware/P. Sheldon	D. F. Davis/H. Ward	1–6 7–5 6–4 4–6 7–5
1899	D. F. Davis/H. Ward	L. E. Ware/P. Sheldon	6–4 6–4 6–3
1900	D. F. Davis/H. Ward	F. B. Alexander/R. D. Little	6–4 9–7 12–10
1901	D. F. Davis/H. Ward	L. E. Ware/B. C. Wright	6–3 9–7 6–1
1902	H. L./R. F. Doherty	D. F. Davis/H. Ward	11–9 12–10 6–4
1903	H. L./R. F. Doherty	L. Collins/L. H. Waldner	7–5 6–3 6–3
1904*	H. Ward/B. C. Wright	K. Collins/R. D. Little	1–6 6–2 3–6 6–4 6–1
1905	H. Ward/B. C. Wright	F. B. Alexander/H. H. Hackett	6–3 6–1 6–2
1906	H. Ward/B. C. Wright	F. B. Alexander/H. H. Hackett	6–3 3–6 6–3 6–3
1907*	F. B. Alexander/B. C. Wright	W. J. Clothier/W. A. Larned	6–3 6–1 6–4
1908	F. B. Alexander/H. H. Hackett	R. D. Little/B. C. Wright	6–1 7–5 6–2
1909	F. B. Alexander/H. H. Hackett	G. J. James/M. E. McLoughlin	6–4 6–1 6–0
1910	F. B. Alexander/H. H. Hackett	T. C. Bundy/T. W. Hendrick	6–1 8–6 6–3
1911	R. D. Little/G. F. Touchard	F. B. Alexander/H. H. Hackett	7–5 13–15 6–2 6–4
1912	T. C. Bundy/M. E. McLoughlin	R. D. Little/G. F. Touchard	3–6 6–2 6–1 7–5
1913	T. C. Bundy/M. E. McLoughlin	C. J. Griffin/J. R. Strachan	6–4 7–5 6–1
1914	T. C. Bundy/M. E. McLoughlin	G. M. Church/D. Mathey	6–4 6–2 6–4
1915	C. J. Griffin/W. M. Johnston	T. C. Bundy/M. E. McLoughlin	6–2 3–6 4–6 6–3 6–3
1916	C. J. Griffin/W. M. Johnston	W. Dawson/M. E. McLoughlin	6–4 6–3 5–7 6–3
1917	*Not held*		
(Challenge Round abolished)			
1918	V. Richards/W. T. Tilden	F. B. Alexander/B. C. Wright	6–3 6–4 3–6 2–6 6–2
(Challenge Round restored)			
1919	N. E. Brookes/G. L. Patterson	V. Richards/W. T. Tilden	8–6 6–3 4–6 6–2
(Challenge Round abolished)			
1920	C. J. Griffin/W. M. Johnston	W. E. Davis/R. Roberts	6–2 6–2 6–3
1921	V. Richards/W. T. Tilden	W. M. Washburn/R. N. Williams	13–11 12–10 6–1

1922	V. Richards/W. T. Tilden	P. O'Hara Wood/G. L. Patterson	4–6 6–1 6–3 6–4
1923	B. I. C. Norton/W. T. Tilden	W. M. Washburn/R. N. Williams	3–6 6–2 6–3 5–7 6–2
1924	H./R. Kinsey	P. O'Hara Wood/G. L. Patterson	7–5 5–7 7–9 6–3 6–4
1925	V. Richards/R. N. Williams	J. B. Hawkes/G. L. Patterson	6–2 8–10 6–4 11–9
1926	V. Richards/R. N. Williams	A. H. Chapin/W. T. Tilden	6–4 6–8 11–9 6–3
1927	F. T. Hunter/W. T. Tilden	W. M. Johnston/R. N. Williams	10–8 6–3 6–3
1928	J. F. Hennessey/G. M. Lott	J. B. Hawkes/G. L. Patterson	6–2 6–1 6–2
1929	J. H. Doeg/G. M. Lott	B. Bell/L. N. White	10–8 16–14 6–1
1930	J. H. Doeg/G. M. Lott	W. L. Allison/J. Van Ryn	8–6 6–3 4–6 13–15 6–4
1931	W. L. Allison/J. Van Ryn	B. Bell/G. S. Mangin	6–4 8–6 6–3
1932	K. Gledhill/H. E. Vines	W. L. Allison/J. Van Ryn	6–4 6–3 6–2
1933	G. M. Lott/L. R. Stoefen	F. A. Parker/F. X. Shields	11–13 9–7 9–7 6–3
1934	G. M. Lott/L. R. Stoefen	W. L. Allison/J. Van Ryn	6–4 9–7 3–6 6–4
1935	W. L. Allison/J. Van Ryn	J. D. Budge/G. Mako	6–4 6–2 3–6 2–6 6–1
1936	J. D. Budge/G. Mako	W. L. Allison/J. Van Ryn	6–4 6–2 6–4
1937	G. Von Cramm/H. Henkel	J. D. Budge/G. Mako	6–4 7–5 6–4
1938	J. D. Budge/G. Mako	J. E. Bromwich/A. K. Quist	6–3 6–2 6–1
1939	J. E. Bromwich/A. K. Quist	J. H. Crawford/H. C. Hopman	8–6 6–1 6–4
1940	J. A. Kramer/F. R. Schroeder	G. Mulloy/H. J. Prussoff	6–4 8–6 9–7
1941	J. A. Kramer/F. R. Schroeder	G. Mulloy/W. Sabin	9–7 6–4 6–2
1942	G. Mulloy/W. F. Talbert	F. R. Schroeder/S. B. Wood	9–7 7–5 6–1
1943	J. A. Kramer/F. A. Parker	D. Freeman/W. F. Talbert	6–2 6–4 6–4
1944	R. Falkenburg/W. D. McNeill	F. Segura/W. F. Talbert	7–5 6–4 3–6 6–1
1945	G. Mulloy/W. F. Talbert	R. Falkenburg/J. Tuero	12–10 8–10 12–10 6–2
1946	G. Mulloy/W. F. Talbert	G. Guernsey/W. D. McNeill	3–6 6–4 2–6 6–3 20–18
1947	J. A. Kramer/F. R. Schroeder	W. F. Talbert/O. W. Sidwell	6–4 7–5 6–3
1948	G. Mulloy/W. F. Talbert	F. A. Parker/F. R. Schroeder	1–6 9–7 6–3 3–6 9–7
1949	J. Bromwich/O. W. Sidwell	F. A. Sedgman/G. Worthington	6–4 6–0 6–1
1950	J. Bromwich/F. A. Sedgman	G. Mulloy/W. F. Talbert	7–5 8–6 3–6 6–1
1951	K. McGregor/F. A. Sedgman	D. Candy/M. G. Rose	10–8 6–4 4–6 7–5
1952	M. G. Rose/E. V. Seixas	K. McGregor/F. A. Sedgman	3–6 10–8 10–8 6–8 8–6
1953	R. N. Hartwig/M. G. Rose	G. Mulloy/W. F. Talbert	6–4 4–6 6–2 6–4
1954	E. V. Seixas/M. A. Trabert	L. A. Hoad/K. R. Rosewall	3–6 6–4 8–6 6–3
1955	K. Kamo/A. Miyagi	G. Moss/W. Quillian	6–3 6–3 3–6 1–6 6–4
1956	L. A. Hoad/K. R. Rosewall	H. Richardson/E. V. Seixas	6–2 6–2 3–6 6–4
1957	A. J. Cooper/N. A. Fraser	G. Mulloy/J. E. Patty	4–6 6–3 9–7 6–3
1958	A. Olmedo/H. Richardson	S. Giammalva/B. McKay	3–6 6–3 6–4 6–4
1959	R. S. Emerson/N. A. Fraser	E. Buchholz/A. Olmedo	3–6 6–3 5–7 6–4 7–5
1960	R. S. Emerson/N. A. Fraser	R. G. Laver/R. Mark	9–7 6–2 6–4
1961	C. McKinley/R. D. Ralston	A. Palafox/R. H. Osuna	6–3 6–4 2–6 13–11
1962	A. Palafox/R. H. Osuna	C. McKinley/R. D. Ralston	6–4 10–12 1–6 9–7 6–3
1963	C. McKinley/R. D. Ralston	A. Palafox/R. H. Osuna	9–7 4–6 5–7 6–3 11–9
1964	C. McKinley/R. D. Ralston	G. Stilwell/M. Sangster	6–3 6–2 6–4
1965	R. S. Emerson/F. S. Stolle	F. Froehling/C. Pasarell	6–4 10–12 7–5 6–3
1966	R. S. Emerson/F. S. Stolle	C. Graebner/R. D. Ralston	6–4 6–4 6–4
1967	J. D. Newcombe/A. D. Roche	O. K. Davidson/W. W. Bowrey	6–8 9–7 6–3 6–3
1968	R. C. Lutz/S. R. Smith	R. A. J. Hewitt/R. J. Moore	6–4 6–4 9–7
1969	R. D. Crealy/A. Stone	W. W. Bowrey/C. Pasarell	9–11 6–3 7–5

WOMEN'S DOUBLES

	CHAMPIONS	RUNNERS-UP	SCORE
1889	M. Ballard/B. L. Townsend	M. Wright/L. Knight	6–0 6–2
1890	E. C. Roosevelt/G. W. Roosevelt	B. L. Townsend/M. Ballard	6–1 6–2
1891	M. E. Cahill/W. F. Morgan	E. C. Roosevelt/G. W. Roosevelt	2–6 8–6 6–4
1892	M. E. Cahill/A. M. McKinley	A. H. Harris/A. R. Williams	6–1 6–3
1893	H. Butler/A. M. Terry	A. L. Schultz/Stone	6–4 6–3
1894	J. P. Atkinson/H. R. Helwig	A. R. Williams/A. C. Wistar	6–4 7–5
1895	J. P. Atkinson/H. R. Helwig	E. H. Moore/A. R. Williams	6–2 6–2 12–10
1896	J. P. Atkinson/E. H. Moore	A. R. Williams/A. C. Wistar	6–4 7–5
1897	J. P. Atkinson/K. Atkinson	F. Edwards/E. J. Rastall	6–2 6–1 6–1
1898	J. P. Atkinson/K. Atkinson	C. B. Neely/M. Weimar	6–1 2–6 4–6 6–1 6–2
1899	J. W. Craven/M. McAteer	M. Banks/E. J. Rastall	6–1 6–1 7–5
1900	H. Champlin/E. Parker	M. McAteer/M. Weimar	9–7 6–2 6–2
1901	J. P. Atkinson/M. McAteer	M. Jones/E. H. Moore	w.o.
1902†	J. P. Atkinson/M. Jones	M. Banks/N. Closterman	6–2 7–5
1903	E. H. Moore/C. B. Neely	M. Jones/M. Hall	6–4 6–1 6–1
1904	M. Hall/M. G. Sutton	E. H. Moore/C. B. Neely	3–6 6–3 6–3*
1905	H. Homans/C. B. Neely	V. Maule/M. F. Oberteuffer	6–0 6–1
1906	Mrs L. S. Coe/Mrs D. S. Platt	C. Boldt/H. Homans	6–4 6–4

1907	C. B. Neely/M. Weimer	E. Wildey/N. Wildey	6–1 2–6 6–4
1908	M. Curtis/E. Sears	C. B. Neely/M. Steever	6–3 5–7 9–7
1909	H. V. Hotchkiss/E. E. Rotch	D. Green/L. Moyes	6–1 6–1
1910	H. V. Hotchkiss/E. E. Rotch	A. Browning/E. Wildey	6–4 6–4
1911	H. V. Hotchkiss/E. Sears	D. Green/F. Sutton	6–4 4–6 6–2
1912	M. K. Browne/D. Green	Mrs M. Barger-Wallach/Mrs F. Schmitz	6–2 5–7 6–0
1913	M. K. Browne/Mrs R. H. Williams	D. Green/E. Wildey	12–10 2–6 6–3
1914	M. K. Browne/Mrs R. H. Williams	Mrs E. Raymond/E. Wildey	8–6 6–2
1915	E. Sears/Mrs G. W. Wightman	Mrs G. L. Chapman/Mrs M. McLean	10–8 6–2
1916	M. Bjurstedt/E. Sears	Mrs E. Raymond/E. Wildey	4–6 6–2 10–8
1917	*Not held*		
(Challenge Round abolished)			
1918	E. E. Goss/M. Zinderstein	M. Bjurstedt/Mrs J. Rogge	7–5 8–6
(Challenge Round restored)			
1919	E. E. Goss/M. Zinderstein	E. Sears/Mrs G. W. Wightman	9–7 9–7
(Challenge Round abolished)			
1920	E. E. Goss/M. Zinderstein	H. Baker/E. Tennant	13–11 4–6 6–3
1921	M. K. Browne/Mrs L. Williams	H. Gilleaudeau/Mrs L. G. Morris	6–3 6–2
1922	J. B. Jessup/H. N. Wills	Mrs F. I. Mallory/E. Sigourney	6–4 7–9 6–3
1923	Mrs B. C. Covell/K. McKane	E. E. Goss/Mrs G. W. Wightman	2–6 6–2 6–1
1924	Mrs G. W. Wightman/H. N. Wills	E. E. Goss/Mrs J. B. Jessup	6–4 6–3
1925	M. K. Browne/H. N. Wills	Mrs T. C. Bundy/E. Ryan	6–4 6–3
1926	E. E. Goss/E. Ryan	M. K. Browne/Mrs A. H. Chapin	3–6 6–4 12–10
1927	Mrs L. A. Godfree/E. H. Harvey	J. Fry/B. Nuthall	6–1 4–6 6–4
1928	Mrs G. W. Wightman/H. N. Wills	E. Cross/Mrs L. A. Harper	6–2 6–2
1929	Mrs L. R. C. Michell/Mrs P. H. Watson	Mrs B. C. Covell/Mrs D. C. Shepherd-Barron	2–6 6–3 6–4
1930	B. Nuthall/S. Palfrey	E. Cross/Mrs L. A. Harper	3–6 6–3 7–5
1931	B. Nuthall/Mrs E. F. Whittingstall	H. H. Jacobs/D. E. Round	6–2 6–4
1932	H. H. Jacobs/S. Palfrey	A. Marble/Mrs M. Painter	8–6 6–1
1933	F. James/B. Nuthall	Mrs F. S. Moody/E. Ryan	w.o.
1934	H. H. Jacobs/S. Palfrey	Mrs D. B. Andrus/C. A. Babcock	4–6 6–3 6–4
1935	H. H. Jacobs/Mrs M. Fabyan	Mrs D. B. Andrus/C. A. Babcock	6–4 6–2
1936	C. A. Babcock/Mrs J. Van Ryn	H. H. Jacobs/Mrs M. Fabyan	9–7 2–6 6–4
1937	Mrs M. Fabyan/A. Marble	C. A. Babcock/Mrs J. Van Ryn	7–5 6–4
1938	Mrs M. Fabyan/A. Marble	J. Jedrzejowska/Mrs R. Mathieu	6–8 6–4 6–3
1939	Mrs M. Fabyan/A. Marble	Mrs S. H. Hammersley/K. E. Stammers	7–5 8–6
1940	Mrs M. Fabyan/A. Marble	D. M. Bundy/Mrs J. Van Ryn	6–4 6–3
1941	Mrs E. T. Cooke/M. E. Osborne	D. M. Bundy/D. J. Hart	3–6 6–1 6–4
1942	A. L. Brough/M. E. Osborne	P. M. Betz/D. J. Hart	9–7 6–2 6–1
1943	A. L. Brough/M. E. Osborne	P. M. Betz/D. J. Hart	6–4 6–3
1944	A. L. Brough/M. E. Osborne	P. M. Betz/D. J. Hart	4–6 6–4 6–3
1945	A. L. Brough/M. E. Osborne	P. M. Betz/D. J. Hart	6–4 6–4
1946	A. L. Brough/M. E. Osborne	Mrs P. C. Todd/Mrs M. A. Prentiss	6–1 6–3
1947	A. L. Brough/M. E. Osborne	Mrs P. C. Todd/D. J. Hart	5–7 6–3 7–5
1948	A. L. Brough/Mrs W. D. du Pont	Mrs P. C. Todd/D. J. Hart	6–4 8–10 6–1
1949	A. L. Brough/Mrs W. D. du Pont	S. J. Fry/D. J. Hart	6–4 10–8
1950	A. L. Brough/Mrs W. D. du Pont	S. J. Fry/D. J. Hart	6–2 6–3
1951	S. J. Fry/D. J. Hart	N. Chaffee/Mrs P. C. Todd	6–4 6–2
1952	S. J. Fry/D. J. Hart	A. L. Brough/M. Connolly	10–8 6–4
1953	S. J. Fry/D. J. Hart	A. L. Brough/Mrs W. D. du Pont	6–2 7–9 9–7
1954	S. J. Fry/D. J. Hart	A. L. Brough/Mrs W. D. du Pont	6–4 6–4
1955	A. L. Brough/Mrs W. D. du Pont	S. J. Fry/D. J. Hart	6–3 1–6 6–3
1956	A. L. Brough/Mrs W. D. du Pont	Mrs B. R. Pratt/S. J. Fry	6–3 6–0
1957	A. L. Brough/Mrs W. D. du Pont	A. Gibson/D. R. Hard	6–2 7–5
1958	J. M. Arth/D. R. Hard	A. Gibson/M. E. Bueno	2–6 6–3 6–4
1959	J. M. Arth/D. R. Hard	S. Moore/M. E. Bueno	6–2 6–3
1960	M. E. Bueno/D. R. Hard	D. M. Catt/A. A. Haydon	6–1 6–1
1961	D. R. Hard/L. Turner	E. Buding/Y. Ramirez	6–4 5–7 6–0
1962	M. E. Bueno/D. R. Hard	Mrs J. B. Susman/B. J. Moffitt	4–6 6–3 6–2
1963	R. Ebbern/M. Smith	M. E. Bueno/D. R. Hard	4–6 10–8 6–3
1964	Mrs J. B. Susman/B. J. Moffitt	M. Smith/L. Turner	3–6 6–2 6–4
1965	N. Richey/Mrs C. Graebner	Mrs J. B. Susman/B. J. Moffitt	6–4 6–4
1966	M. E. Bueno/N. Richey	R. Casals/Mrs L. W. King	6–3 6–4
1967	R. Casals/Mrs L. W. King	M. A. Eisel/Mrs D. Fales	4–6 6–3 6–4
1968	M. E. Bueno/M. Smith	S. V. Wade/Mrs G. M. Williams	6–3 7–5
1969	Mrs B. M. Court/S. V. Wade	Mrs P. W. Curtis/V. Ziegenfuss	6–1 6–3

** There is some doubt about the accuracy of this result.*
† 5-set finals abolished.

MIXED DOUBLES

** Not recognised as an official championship*

	CHAMPIONS	RUNNERS-UP	SCORE
1887*	J. S. Clark/Miss V. Stokes	Not known	
1888*	J. S. Clark/Miss M. Wright	P. Johnson/Miss A. Robinson	1–6 6–5 6–4 6–3
1889*	J. S. Clark/Miss M. Wright	Not known	
1890*	R. Beach/Miss M. E. Cahill	Not known	
1891*	M. R. Wright/Miss M. E. Cahill	C. T. Lee/Miss G. W. Roosevelt	6–4 6–0 7–5
1892	C. Hobart/Miss M. E. Cahill	R. Beach/Miss E. H. Moore	6–1 6–3
1893	C. Hobart/Miss E. C. Roosevelt	R. N. Wilson/Miss Bankson	6–1 4–6 10–8 6–1
1894	E. P. Fischer/Miss J. P. Atkinson	A. Remak/Mrs McFaddon	6–2 6–2 6–1
1895	E. P. Fischer/Miss J. P. Atkinson	M. Fielding/Miss A. R. Williams	4–6 6–1 6–2
1896	E. P. Fischer/Miss J. P. Atkinson	M. Fielding/Miss A. R. Williams	6–2 6–3 6–3
1897	D. L. Magruder/Miss L. Henson	R. A. Griffin/Miss M. Banks	6–4 6–3 7–5
1898	E. P. Fischer/Miss C. B. Neely	J. A. Hill/Miss H. Chapman	Not known
1899	A. L. Hoskins/Miss E. J. Rastall	J. P. Gardner/Miss J. W. Craven	6–4 6–0 ret'd
1900	A. Codman/Miss M. J. Hunnewell	G. Atkinson/Miss T. Shaw	11–9 6–3 6–1
1901	R. D. Little/Miss M. Jones	C. Stevens/Miss M. McAteer	6–4 6–4 7–5
1902	W. C. Grant/Miss E. H. Moore	A. L. Hoskins/Miss E. J. Rastall	6–2 6–1
1903	H. F. Allen/Miss H. Chapman	W. H. Rowland/Miss C. B. Neely	6–4 7–5
1904	W. C. Grant/Miss E. H. Moore	F. B. Dallas/Miss M. Sutton	6–2 6–1
1905	C. Hobart/Mrs Hobart	E. B. Dewhurst/Miss E. H. Moore	6–2 6–4
1906	E. B. Dewhurst/Miss S. Coffin	J. B. Johnson/Miss M. Johnson	6–3 7–5
1907	W. F. Johnson/Miss M. Sayres	H. M. Tilden/Miss N. Wildey	6–1 7–5
1908	N. W. Niles/Miss E. E. Rotch	R. D. Little/Miss L. Hammond	6–4 4–6 6–4
1909	W. F. Johnson/Miss H. V. Hotchkiss	R. D. Little/Miss L. Hammond	6–2 6–0
1910	J. R. Carpenter/Miss H. V. Hotchkiss	H. M. Tilden/Miss E. Wildey	6–2 6–2
1911	W. F. Johnson/Miss H. V. Hotchkiss	H. M. Tilden/Miss E. Wildey	6–4 6–4
1912	R. N. Williams/Miss M. K. Browne	W. J. Clothier/Miss E. Sears	6–4 2–6 11–9
1913	W. T. Tilden/Miss M. K. Browne	C. S. Rogers/Miss D. Green	7–5 7–5
1914	W. T. Tilden/Miss M. K. Browne	J. R. Rowland/Miss M. Myers	6–1 6–4
1915	H. C. Johnson/Mrs G. W. Wightman	I. C. Wright/Miss M. Bjurstedt	6–0 6–1
1916	W. E. Davis/Miss E. Sears	W. T. Tilden/Miss F. A. Ballin	6–4 7–5
1917	*Not held*		
(Challenge Round abolished)			
1918	I. C. Wright/Mrs G. W. Wightman	F. B. Alexander/Miss M. Bjurstedt	6–2 6–4
(Challenge Round restored)			
1919	V. Richards/Miss M. Zinderstein	W. T. Tilden/Miss F. A. Ballin	2–6 11–9 6–1
(Challenge Round abolished)			
1920	W. F. Johnson/Mrs G. W. Wightman	C. Biddle/Mrs F. I. Mallory	6–4 6–3
1921	W. M. Johnston/Miss M. K. Browne	W. T. Tilden/Miss F. I. Mallory	3–6 6–4 6–3
1922	W. T. Tilden/Mrs F. I. Mallory	H. Kinsey/Miss H. N. Wills	6–4 6–3
1923	W. T. Tilden/Mrs F. I. Mallory	J. B. Hawkes/Miss K. McKane	6–3 2–6 10–8
1924	V. Richards/Miss H. N. Wills	W. T. Tilden/Mrs F. I. Mallory	6–8 7–5 6–0
1925	J. B. Hawkes/Miss K. McKane	V. Richards/Miss E. H. Harvey	6–2 6–4
1926	J. Borotra/Miss E. Ryan	R. Lacoste/Mrs G. W. Wightman	6–4 7–5
1927	H. Cochet/Miss E. Bennett	R. Lacoste/Mrs G. W. Wightman	2–6 6–0 6–2
1928	G. M. Lott/Miss B. Nuthall	H. W. Austin/Mrs B. C. Covell	6–3 6–3
1930	W. L. Allison/Miss E. Cross	F. X. Shields/Miss M. Morrill	6–4 6–4
1931	G. M. Lott/Miss B. Nuthall	W.L. Allison/Mrs L. A. Harper	6–3 6–3
1932	F. J. Perry/Miss S. Palfrey	H. E. Vines/Miss H. H. Jacobs	6–3 7–5
1933	H. E. Vines/Miss E. Ryan	G. M. Lott/Miss S. Palfrey	11–9 6–1
1934	G. M. Lott/Miss H. H. Jacobs	L. R. Stoefen/Miss E. Ryan	4–6 13–11 6–2
1935	E. Maier/Mrs M. Fabyan	R. Menzel/Miss K. E. Stammers	6–3 3–6 6–4
1936	G. Mako/Miss A. Marble	J. D. Budge/Mrs M. Fabyan	6–3 6–2
1937	J. D. Budge/Mrs M. Fabyan	Y. Petra/Mme S. Henrotin	6–2 8–10 6–0
1938	J. D. Budge/Miss A. Marble	J. E. Bromwich/Miss T. Coyne	6–1 6–2
1939	H. C. Hopman/Miss A. Marble	E. T. Cooke/Mrs M. Fabyan	9–7 6–1
1940	R. L. Riggs/Miss A. Marble	J. A. Kramer/Miss D. M. Bundy	9–7 6–1
1941	J. A. Kramer/Mrs E. T. Cooke	R. L. Riggs/Miss P. M. Betz	4–6 6–4 6–4
1942	F. R. Schroeder/Miss A. L. Brough	A. D. Russell/Mrs P. C. Todd	3–6 6–1 6–4
1943	W. F. Talbert/Miss M. E. Osborne	F. Segura/Miss P. M. Betz	10–8 6–4
1944	W. F. Talbert/Miss M. E. Osborne	W. D. McNeill/Miss D. M. Bundy	6–2 6–3
1945	W. F. Talbert/Miss M. E. Osborne	R. Falkenburg/Miss D. J. Hart	6–4 6–4
1946	W. F. Talbert/Miss M. E. Osborne	R. Kimbrell/Miss A. L. Brough	6–3 6–4
1947	J. Bromwich/Miss A. L. Brough	F. Segura/Miss G. Moran	6–3 6–1
1948	T. P. Brown/Miss A. L. Brough	W. F. Talbert/Mrs W. D. du Pont	6–4 6–4
1949	E. W. Sturgess/Miss A. L. Brough	W. F. Talbert/Mrs W. D. du Pont	4–6 6–3 7–5
1950	K. McGregor/Mrs W. D. du Pont	F. A. Sedgman/Miss D. J. Hart	6–4 3–6 6–3

1951	F. A. Sedgman/Miss D. J. Hart	M. G. Rose/Miss S. J. Fry	6–3 6–2
1952	F. A. Sedgman/Miss D. J. Hart	L. A. Hoad/Mrs T. C. Long	6–3 7–5
1953	E. V. Seixas/Miss D. J. Hart	R. N. Hartwig/Miss J. A. Sampson	6–2 4–6 6–4
1954	E. V. Seixas/Miss D. J. Hart	K. R. Rosewall/Mrs W. D. du Pont	4–6 6–1 6–1
1955	E. V. Seixas/Miss D. J. Hart	L. A. Hoad/Miss S. J. Fry	9–7 6–1
1956	K. R. Rosewall/Mrs W. D. du Pont	L. A. Hoad/Miss D. R. Hard	9–7 6–1
1957	K. Nielsen/Miss A. Gibson	R. N. Howe/Miss D. R. Hard	6–3 9–7
1958	N. A. Fraser/Mrs W. D. du Pont	A. Olmedo/Miss M. E. Bueno	6–3 3–6 9–7
1959	N. A. Fraser/Mrs W. D. du Pont	R. Mark/Miss J. Hopps	7–5 13–15 6–2
1960	N. A. Fraser/Mrs W. D. du Pont	A. Palafox/Miss M. E. Bueno	6–3 6–2
1961	R. Mark/Miss M. Smith	R. D. Ralston/Miss D. R. Hard	w.o.
1962	F. S. Stolle/Miss M. Smith	F. Froehling/Miss L. Turner	7–5 6–2
1963	K. Fletcher/Miss M. Smith	E. Rubinoff/Miss J. Tegart	3–6 8–6 6–2
1964	J. D. Newcombe/Miss M. Smith	E. Rubinoff/Miss J. Tegart	10–8 4–6 6–3
1965	F. S. Stolle/Miss M. Smith	F. Froehling/Miss J. Tegart	5–2 6–2
1966	O. K. Davidson/Mrs D. Fales	E. Rubinoff/Miss C. A. Aucamp	6–1 6–3
1967	O. K. Davidson/Mrs L. W. King	S. R. Smith/Miss R. Casals	6–3 6–2
1968	P. W. Curtis/Miss M. A. Eisel	R. N. Perry/Miss T. A. Fretz	6–4 7–5
1969	P. Sullivan/Miss P. S. A. Hogan	T. Addison/Miss K. Pigeon	6–4 2–6 12–10

US OPEN CHAMPIONSHIPS

Played at West Side Club, Forest Hills, New York, on grass courts 1968–74, on Har-Tru courts 1975–77. Played at National Tennis Centre, Flushing Meadow, New York, on cement courts, 1978 on.

MEN'S SINGLES

	CHAMPION	RUNNER-UP	SCORE	WINNER'S PRIZE ($)
1968	A. R. Ashe	T. S. Okker	14–12 5–7 6–3 3–6 6–3	14,000
1969	R. G. Laver	A. D. Roche	7–9 6–3 6–1 6–2	16,000
1970	K. R. Rosewall	A. D. Roche	2–6 6–4 7–6 6–3	20,000
1971	S. R. Smith	J. Kodes	3–6 6–3 6–2 7–6	15,000
1972	I. Nastase	A. R. Ashe	3–6 6–3 6–7 6–4 6–3	25,000
1973	J. D. Newcombe	J. Kodes	6–4 1–6 4–6 6–2 6–3	25,000
1974	J. S. Connors	K. R. Rosewall	6–1 6–0 6–1	22,500
1975	M. Orantes	J. S. Connors	6–4 6–3 6–3	25,000
1976	J. S. Connors	B. Borg	6–4 3–6 7–6 6–4	30,000
1977	G. Vilas	J. S. Connors	2–6 6–3 7–6 6–0	33,000
1978	J. S. Connors	B. Borg	6–4 6–2 6–2	38,000
1979	J. P. McEnroe	V. Gerulaitis	7–5 6–3 6–3	39,000
1980	J. P. McEnroe	B. Borg	7–6 6–1 6–7 5–7 6–4	46,000
1981	J. P. McEnroe	B. Borg	4–6 6–2 6–4 6–3	60,000
1982	J. S. Connors	I. Lendl	6–3 6–2 4–6 6–4	90,000
1983	J. S. Connors	I. Lendl	6–3 6–7 7–5 6–0	120,000
1984	J. P. McEnroe	I. Lendl	6–3 6–4 6–1	160,000
1985	I. Lendl	J. P. McEnroe	7–6 6–3 6–4	187,500
1986	I. Lendl	M. Mecir	6–4 6–2 6–0	210,000
1987	I. Lendl	M. Wilander	6–7 6–0 7–6 6–4	250,000

WOMEN'S SINGLES

	CHAMPION	RUNNER-UP	SCORE	WINNER'S PRIZE ($)
1968	Miss S. V. Wade	Mrs L. W. King	6–4 6–2	6,000
1969	Mrs B. M. Court	Miss N. Richey	6–2 6–2	6,000
1970	Mrs B. M. Court	Miss R. Casals	6–2 2–6 6–1	7,500
1971	Mrs L. W. King	Miss R. Casals	6–4 7–6	5,000
1972	Mrs L. W. King	Miss K. Melville	6–3 7–5	10,000
1973	Mrs B. M. Court	Miss E. Goolagong	7–6 5–7 6–2	25,000
1974	Mrs L. W. King	Miss E. Goolagong	3–6 6–3 7–5	22,500
1975	Miss C. M. Evert	Mrs R. A. Cawley	5–7 6–4 6–2	25,000
1976	Miss C. M. Evert	Mrs R. A. Cawley	6–3 6–0	30,000
1977	Miss C. M. Evert	Miss W. Turnbull	7–6 6–2	33,000
1978	Miss C. M. Evert	Miss P. Shriver	7–5 6–4	38,000
1979	Miss T. A. Austin	Miss C. M. Evert	6–4 6–3	39,000
1980	Mrs J. M. Lloyd	Miss H. Mandlikova	5–7 6–1 6–1	46,000
1981	Miss T. A. Austin	Miss M. Navratilova	1–6 7–6 7–6	60,000
1982	Mrs J. M. Lloyd	Miss H. Mandlikova	6–3 6–1	90,000

The remarkable Jimmy Connors, the five-times US Open champion who turned 35 in September, enjoyed his best season for four years in 1987, returning to the top four and qualifying for a record 11th Masters. *(M. Cole)*

1983	Miss M. Navratilova	Mrs J. M. Lloyd	6–1 6–3	120,000
1984	Miss M. Navratilova	Mrs J. M. Lloyd	4–6 6–4 6–4	160,000
1985	Miss H. Mandlikova	Miss M. Navratilova	7–6 1–6 7–6	187,500
1986	Miss M. Navratilova	Miss H. Sukova	6–3 6–2	210,000
1987	Miss M. Navratilova	Miss S. Graf	7–6 6–1	250,000

MEN'S DOUBLES

	CHAMPIONS	RUNNERS-UP	SCORE
1968	R. C. Lutz/S. R. Smith	A. R. Ashe/A. Gimeno	11–9 6–1 7–5
1969	K. R. Rosewall/F. S. Stolle	C. Pasarell/R. D. Ralston	2–6 7–5 13–11 6–3
1970	P. Barthes/N. Pilic	R. S. Emerson/R. G. Laver	6–3 7–6 4–6 7–6
1971	J. D. Newcombe/R. Taylor	S. R. Smith/E. van Dillen	6–7 6–3 7–6 4–6 7–6
1972	E. C. Drysdale/R. Taylor	O. K. Davidson/J. D. Newcombe	6–4 7–6 6–3
1973	O. K. Davidson/J. D. Newcombe	R. G. Laver/K. R. Rosewall	7–5 2–6 7–5 7–5
1974	R. C. Lutz/S. R. Smith	P. Cornejo/J. Fillol	6–3 6–3
1975	J. S. Connors/I. Nastase	T. S. Okker/M. C. Riessen	6–4 7–6
1976	T. S. Okker/M. C. Riessen	P. Kronk/C. Letcher	6–4 6–4
1977	R. A. J. Hewitt/F. D. McMillan	B. E. Gottfried/R. Ramirez	6–4 6–0
1978	R. C. Lutz/S. R. Smith	M. C. Riessen/S. E. Stewart	1–6 7–5 6–3
1979	P. Fleming/J. P. McEnroe	R. C. Lutz/S. R. Smith	6–2 6–4
1980	R. C. Lutz/S. R. Smith	P. Fleming/J. P. McEnroe	7–6 3–6 6–1 3–6 6–3
1981	P. Fleming/J. P. McEnroe	H. Gunthardt/P. McNamara	w.o.
1982	K. Curren/S. Denton	V. Amaya/H. Pfister	6–2 6–7 5–7 6–2 6–4
1983	P. Fleming/J. P. McEnroe	F. Buehning/V. Winitsky	6–3 6–4 6–2
1984	J. Fitzgerald/T. Smid	S. Edberg/A. Jarryd	7–6 6–3 6–3
1985	K. Flach/R. Seguso	H. Leconte/Y. Noah	7–6 6–7 7–6 6–0
1986	A. Gomez/S. Zivojinovic	J. Nystrom/M. Wilander	4–6 6–3 6–3 4–6 6–3
1987	S. Edberg/A. Jarryd	K. Flach/R. Seguso	7–6 6–2 4–6 5–7 7–6

WOMEN'S DOUBLES

	CHAMPIONS	RUNNERS-UP	SCORE
1968	M. E. Bueno/Mrs B. M. Court	R. Casals/Mrs L. W. King	4–6 9–7 8–6
1969	F. Durr/D. R. Hard	Mrs B. M. Court/S. V. Wade	0–6 6–4 6–4
1970	Mrs B. M. Court/Mrs D. Dalton	R. Casals/S. V. Wade	6–3 6–4
1971	R. Casals/Mrs D. Dalton	Mrs J. B. Chanfreau/F. Durr	6–3 6–3
1972	F. Durr/B. Stove	Mrs B. M. Court/S. V. Wade	6–3 1–6 6–3
1973	Mrs B. M. Court/S. V. Wade	R. Casals/Mrs L. W. King	3–6 6–3 7–5
1974	R. Casals/Mrs L. W. King	F. Durr/B. Stove	7–6 6–7 6–4
1975	Mrs B. M. Court/S. V. Wade	R. Casals/Mrs L. W. King	7–5 2–6 7–5
1976	L. Boshoff/I. Kloss	O. Morozova/S. V. Wade	6–1 6–4
1977	M. Navratilova/B. Stove	R. Richards/B. Stuart	6–1 7–6
1978	Mrs L. W. King/M. Navratilova	Mrs G. E. Reid/W. M. Turnbull	7–6 6–4
1979	B. Stove/W. M. Turnbull	Mrs L. W. King/M. Navratilova	7–5 6–3
1980	Mrs L. W. King/M. Navratilova	P. H. Shriver/B. Stove	7–6 7–5
1981	K. Jordan/A. E. Smith	R. Casals/W. M. Turnbull	6–3 6–3
1982	R. Casals/W. M. Turnbull	B. Potter/S. A. Walsh	6–4 6–4
1983	M. Navratilova/P. H. Shriver	R. Fairbank/C. Reynolds	6–7 6–1 6–3
1984	M. Navratilova/P. H. Shriver	A. E. Hobbs/W. M. Turnbull	6–2 6–4
1985	C. Kohde-Kilsch/H. Sukova	M. Navratilova/P. H. Shriver	6–7 6–2 6–3
1986	M. Navratilova/P. H. Shriver	H. Mandlikova/W. M. Turnbull	6–4 3–6 6–3
1987	M. Navratilova/P. H. Shriver	K. Jordan/E. Smylie	5–7 6–4 6–2

MIXED DOUBLES

	CHAMPIONS	RUNNERS-UP	SCORE
1968	*Not held*		
1969	M. C. Riessen/Mrs B. M. Court	R. D. Ralston/Miss F. Durr	7–5 6–3
1970	M. C. Riessen/Mrs B. M. Court	F. D. McMillan/Mrs D. Dalton	6–4 6–4
1971	O. K. Davidson/Mrs L. W. King	R. R. Maud/Miss B. Stove	6–3 7–5
1972	M. C. Riessen/Mrs B. M. Court	I. Nastase/Miss R. Casals	6–3 7–5
1973	O. K. Davidson/Mrs L. W. King	M. C. Riessen/Miss B. M. Court	6–3 3–6 7–6
1974	G. Masters/Miss P. Teeguarden	J. S. Connors/Miss C. M. Evert	6–1 7–6

1975	R. L. Stockton/Miss R. Casals	F. S. Stolle/Mrs L. W. King	6–3 7–6
1976	P. Dent/Mrs L. W. King	F. D. McMillan/Miss B. Stove	3–6 6–2 7–5
1977	F. D. McMillan/Miss B. Stove	V. Gerulaitis/Mrs L. W. King	6–2 3–6 6–3
1978	F. D. McMillan/Miss B. Stove	R. O. Ruffels/Mrs L. W. King	6–3 7–6
1979	R. A. J. Hewitt/Miss G. Stevens	F. D. McMillan/Miss B. Stove	6–3 7–5
1980	M. C. Riessen/Miss W. M. Turnbull	F. D. McMillan/Miss B. Stove	7–5 6–2
1981	K. Curren/Miss A. E. Smith	S. Denton/Miss J. Russell	6–4 7–6
1982	K. Curren/Miss A. E. Smith	F. Taygan/Miss B. Potter	6–7 7–6 7–6
1983	J. Fitzgerald/Miss E. Sayers	F. Taygan/Miss B. Potter	3–6 6–3 6–4
1984	Tom Gullikson/Miss M. Maleeva	J. Fitzgerald/Miss E. Sayers	2–6 7–5 6–4
1985	H. Gunthardt/Miss M. Navratilova	J. Fitzgerald/Mrs E. Smylie	6–3 6–4
1986	S. Casal/Miss R. Reggi	P. Fleming/Miss M. Navratilova	6–4 6–4
1987	E. Sanchez/Miss M. Navratilova	P. Annacone/Miss B. Nagelsen	6–4 6–7 7–6

US CLAY COURT CHAMPIONSHIPS

** Played as 'Patriotic Tournament' without championship status.*

MEN'S SINGLES

	CHAMPION	RUNNER-UP	SCORE
1910	M. H. Long	W. M. Hall	6–0 6–1 6–1
1911	W. T. Hayes	P. Siverd	7–5 6–2 6–1
1912	R. N. Williams	W. T. Hayes	6–3 6–1 8–6
1913	J. R. Strachan	W. M. Hall	6–0 6–4 4–6 6–4
1914	C. J. Griffin	E. Fottrell	3–6 6–8 8–6 6–0 6–2
1915	R. N. Williams	G. M. Church	7–5 6–3 2–6 8–6
1916	W. E. Davis	C. B. Doyle	6–2 7–5 6–3
1917*	S. Hardy	C. S. Garland	3–6 6–1 1–6 6–3 6–3
1918	W. T. Tilden	C. S. Garland	6–4 6–4 3–6 6–2
1919	W. M. Johnston	W. T. Tilden	6–0 6–1 4–6 6–2
1920	R. Roberts	V. Richards	6–3 6–1 6–3
1921	W. T. Hayes	A. Squair	6–0 6–2 6–4
1922	W. T. Tilden	Z. Shimizu	6–5 6–3 6–1
1923	W. T. Tilden	M. Alonso	6–2 6–8 6–1 7–5
1924	W. T. Tilden	H. B. Snodgrass	6–2 6–1 6–1
1925	W. T. Tilden	G. M. Lott	3–6 6–3 2–6 6–2 8–6
1926	W. T. Tilden	B. I. C. Norton	w.o.
1927	W. T. Tilden	J. Hennessey	5–4 6–1 6–2
1928	*Not held*		
1929	E. Pare	J. B. Hall	6–4 6–3 4–6 3–6 6–1
1930	B. M. Grant	W. F. Coen	6–2 4–6 6–2 6–4
1931	H. E. Vines	K. Gledhill	6–3 6–3 6–3
1932	G. M. Lott	B. M. Grant	3–6 6–2 3–6 6–3 6–3
1933	F. A. Parker	G. Mako	6–3 6–3 6–3
1934	B. M. Grant	J. D. Budge	6–2 8–6 6–3
1935	B. M. Grant	F. A. Parker	4–6 6–1 3–6 6–3 6–0
1936	R. L. Riggs	F. A. Parker	6–1 6–8 6–4
1937	R. L. Riggs	J. R. Hunt	6–3 4–6 6–3 6–4
1938	R. L. Riggs	G. Mulloy	6–4 5–7 4–6 6–1 7–5
1939	F. A. Parker	G. Mulloy	6–3 6–0 5–7 6–3
1940	D. McNeill	R. L. Riggs	6–1 6–4 6–9 6–3
1941	F. A. Parker	R. L. Riggs	6–3 7–5 6–8 4–6 6–3
1942	S. Greenberg	H. W. Everett	5–7 7–5 7–9 7–5 8–6
1943	S. Greenberg	W. F. Talbert	6–1 4–6 6–3 6–3
1944	F. Segura	W. F. Talbert	6–1 2–6 7–5 6–3
1945	W. F. Talbert	F. Segura	6–4 4–6 6–2 2–6 6–2
1946	F. A. Parker	W. F. Talbert	6–4 6–4 6–2
1947	F. A. Parker	F. R. Schroeder	8–6 6–2 6–4
1948	R. A. Gonzales	C. Carter	7–5 6–2 6–3
1949	R. A. Gonzales	F. A. Parker	6–1 3–6 8–6 6–3
1950	H. Flam	F. R. Schroeder	6–1 6–2 6–2
1951	M. A. Trabert	A. Larsen	6–8 2–6 6–4 6–3 8–6
1952	A. Larsen	R. Savitt	4–6 6–4 6–2 6–4
1953	E. V. Seixas	H. Richardson	6–2 6–4 6–3
1954	B. Bartzen	M. A. Trabert	6–2 4–6 6–0 6–2
1955	M. A. Trabert	B. Bartzen	10–8 6–1 6–4
1956	H. Flam	E. Moylan	3–6 6–3 1–6 6–3 6–3
1957	E. V. Seixas	H. Flam	1–6 8–6 6–1 6–3
1958	B. Bartzen	S. Giammalva	3–6 7–5 6–2 6–2

1959	B. Bartzen	W. Reed	6–0 8–6 7–5
1960	B. MacKay	B. Bartzen	4–6 7–5 6–4 6–0
1961	B. Bartzen	D. Dell	6–1 2–6 6–2 6–0
1962	C. R. McKinley	F. S. Stolle	6–3 8–6 6–4
1963	C. R. McKinley	R. D. Ralston	6–2 6–2 6–4
1964	R. D. Ralston	C. R. McKinley	6–2 6–2 6–1
1965	R. D. Ralston	C. Richey	6–4 4–6 6–4 6–3
1966	C. Richey	F. A. Froehling	13–11 6–1 6–3
1967	A. R. Ashe	M. C. Riessen	4–6 6–3 6–1 7–5
1968	C. Graebner	S. R. Smith	6–3 7–5 6–0
1969	Z. Franulovic	A. R. Ashe	8–6 6–3 6–4
1970	C. Richey	S. R. Smith	6–2 10–8 3–6 6–1
1971	Z. Franulovic	C. Richey	6–3 6–4 0–6 6–3
1972	R. A. J. Hewitt	J. S. Connors	7–6 6–1 6–2
1973	M. Orantes	R. Ramirez	6–4 6–1 6–4
1974	J. S. Connors	B. Borg	5–7 6–3 6–4
1975	M. Orantes	A. R. Ashe	6–2 6–2
1976	J. S. Connors	W. Fibak	6–2 6–4
1977	M. Orantes	J. S. Connors	6–1 6–3
1978	J. S. Connors	J. Higueras	7–5 6–1
1979	J. S. Connors	G. Vilas	6–1 2–6 6–4
1980	J. L. Clerc	M. Purcell	7–5 6–3
1981	J. L. Clerc	I. Lendl	4–6 6–4 6–2
1982	J. Higueras	J. Arias	7–6 5–7 6–3
1983	J. Arias	A. Gomez	6–4 2–6 6–4
1984	A. Gomez	B. Taroczy	6–0 7–6
1985	I. Lendl	A. Gomez	6–1 6–3
1986	A. Gomez	T. Tulasne	6–4 7–6
1987	M. Wilander	K. Carlsson	7–5 6–3

WOMEN'S SINGLES

	CHAMPION	RUNNER-UP	SCORE
1912	Miss M. Sutton	Miss M. K. Browne	6–4 6–2
1913	*Not held*		
1914	Miss M. K. Browne	Miss R. H. Williams	6–1 3–6 6–2
1915	Miss M. Bjurdstedt	Mrs G. W. Wightman	3–6 6–1 6–3
1916	Miss M. Bjurdstedt	Miss M. Guthrie	6–3 6–3
1917*	Miss R. Sanders	Mrs W. Ellis	6–1 6–3
1918	Miss C. B. Neely	Mrs A. Yager	6–4 6–2
1919	Miss C. Gould	Miss C. B. Neely	6–4 6–2
1920	Miss M. Zinderstein	Miss C. Gould	6–0 6–1
1921	Mrs B. E. Cole	Mrs F. Godfrey	6–0 6–3
1922	Mrs H. Bickle	Miss L. Bancroft	3–6 6–1 7–5
1923	Miss M. MacDonald	Miss L. Scharman	7–5 1–6 6–4
1924–39	*Not held*		
1940	Miss A. Marble	Miss G. W. Wheeler	7–5 6–0
1941	Miss P. M. Betz	Miss M. Arnold	6–3 6–1
1942	*Not held*		
1943	Miss P. M. Betz	Miss N. Corbett	6–1 6–0
1944	Miss D. M. Bundy	Miss M. Arnold	7–5 6–4
1945	Mrs S. P. Cooke	Miss P. M. Betz	6–3 7–5
1946	Miss B. Krase	Mrs V. W. Kovacs	10–8 6–4
1947	Mrs M. A. Prentiss	Miss D. Head	6–1 6–1
1948	Mrs M. Rurac	Miss D. Head	1–6 7–5 6–3
1949	Mrs M. Rurac	Miss B. Baker	2–6 9–7 6–3
1950	Miss D. J. Hart	Miss S. J. Fry	6–1 6–3
1951	Miss D. Head	Mrs P. C. Todd	4–6 6–2 6–2
1952	Miss A. Kanter	Mrs L. Davidson	6–4 6–3
1953	Miss M. Connolly	Miss A. Gibson	6–4 6–4
1954	Miss M. Connolly	Miss D. J. Hart	6–3 6–1
1955	Mrs D. H. Knode	Miss B. Breit	6–4 6–3
1956	Miss S. J. Fry	Miss A. Gibson	7–5 6–1
1957	Miss A. Gibson	Miss D. R. Hard	6–2 6–3
1958	Mrs D. H. Knode	Miss K. Fageros	6–3 6–8 6–2
1959	Miss S. Moore	Miss S. Reynolds	6–2 2–6 6–3
1960	Mrs D. H. Knode	Miss G. Thomas	6–3 6–3
1961	Miss E. Buding	Miss K. Hantze	6–4 2–6 6–4
1962	Miss D. Floyd	Miss C. Caldwell	6–3 6–1
1963	Miss N. Richey	Miss V. Palmer	6–1 6–1

1964	Miss N. Richey	Miss C. Caldwell	6–2 6–1
1965	Miss N. Richey	Miss J. M. Heldman	5–7 6–3 9–7
1966	Miss N. Richey	Miss S. De Fina	6–2 6–2
1967	Miss N. Richey	Miss R. Casals	6–2 6–3
1968	Miss N. Richey	Miss L. Tuero	6–3 6–3
1969	Mrs G. Chanfreau	Miss L. Tuero	6–2 6–2
1970	Miss L. Tuero	Mrs G. Chanfreau	7–5 6–1
1971	Mrs L. W. King	Miss L. Tuero	6–4 7–5
1972	Miss C. M. Evert	Miss E. F. Goolagong	7–6 6–1
1973	Miss C. M. Evert	Miss V. Burton	6–4 6–3
1974	Miss C. M. Evert	Mrs G. Lovera	6–0 6–0
1975	Miss C. M. Evert	Miss D. Fromholtz	6–3 6–4
1976	Miss K. May	Miss B. Cuypers	6–4 4–6 6–2
1977	Miss L. DuPont	iss N. Richey	6–4 6–3
1978	Miss D. Gilbert	Miss V. Gonzalez	6–2 6–3
1979	Mrs J. M. Lloyd	Mrs E. Cawley	6–4 6–3
1980	Mrs J. M. Lloyd	Miss A. Jaeger	6–4 6–3
1981	Miss A. Jaeger	Miss V. Ruzici	6–1 6–0
1982	Miss V. Ruzici	Miss H. Sukova	6–2 6–0
1983	Miss A. Temesvari	Miss Z. Garrison	6–2 6–2
1984	Miss M. Maleeva	Miss L. Bonder	6–4 6–3
1985	Miss A. Temesvari	Miss Z. Garrison	7–6 6–3
1986	Miss S. Graf	Miss G. Sabatini	2–6 7–6 6–2
1987	*Not held*		

MEN'S DOUBLES

	CHAMPION	RUNNER-UP	SCORE
1910	F. G. Anderson/W. T. Hayes	M. H. Long/A. Scribner	2–6 3–6 6–1 6–3 6–3
1911	H. G. Whitehead/J. H. Winston	F. G. Anderson/W. T. Hayes	6–3 2–6 7–5 6–1
1912	H. H. Hackett/W. M. Hall	H. G. Whitehead/J. H. Winson	4–6 6–1 6–0 6–1
1913	C. J. Griffin/J. R. Strachan	W. M. Hall/F. Harris	w.o.
1914	N. Browne/C. Wayne	E. Fottrell/C. J. Griffin	6–3 6–4 6–3
1915	G. M. Church/D. Mathey	W. M. Washburn/R. N. Williams	6–3 2–6 6–3
1916	G. M. Church/D. Mathey	W. Davis/H. V. D. Johns	7–5 6–0 6–2
1917*	C. S. Garland/S. Hardy	H. T. Emerson/W. H. Hopple	6–4 6–2 6–3
1918	C. S. Garland/S. Hardy	R. H. Burdick/W. T. Hayes	6–4 1–6 6–2 7–9 6–2
1919	S. Hardy/W. M. Johnston	A. Gravem/R. Kinsley	6–3 6–1 2–6 6–3
1920	V. Richards/R. Roberts	R. Burdick/W. T. Hayes	6–2 6–2 7–5
1921	W. T. Hayes/C. B. Herd	R. Burdick/J. Hennessey	6–1 6–3 6–2
1922	F. Bastian/R. Burdick	J. Hennessey/W. Wesbrook	6–3 3–6 7–5 5–7 6–4
1923	H./R. Kinsey	J. Hennessey/W. Wesbrook	6–4 13–11 6–3
1924	H./R. Kinsey	W. T. Tilden/S. Wiener	6–4 7–5 6–2
1925	H. Snodgrass/W. Wesbrook	W. T. Tilden/S. Wiener	6–1 6–2 6–1
1926	L. Thalheimer/L. N. White	H. Chapin/B. I. C. Norton	w.o.
1927	J. Hennessey/R. N. Williams	W. T. Tilden/S. Wiener	6–4 6–3 3–6 9–7
1928	*Not held*		
1929	J. G. Hall/F. Mercur	B. Gerschakoff/A. Kussman	10–12 3–6 6–2 9–7 6–4
1930	J. G. Hall/F. Mercur	W. Brown/H. Coggeshell	3–6 6–3 7–5 6–2
1931	K. Gledhill/H. E. Vines	B. Barnes/B. Bell	6–3 7–9 10–8 9–7
1932	B. M. Grant/G. M. Lott	C./E. Sutter	6–4 6–4 1–6 4–6 6–3
1933	G. Mako/J. Tidball	R. Bryan/J. McDiarmid	6–2 2–6 7–5 4–6 6–0
1934	J. D. Budge/G. Mako	R. Bryan/J. McDiarmid	4–6 6–3 6–4 6–4
1935	B. Bell/J. G. Hall	R. Bruan/J. McDiarmid	6–4 6–4 5–7 9–11 6–2
1936	R. L. Riggs/W. Sabin	E. McCauliff/J. McDiarmid	4–6 6–2 7–5 6–4
1937	E. McCauliff/J. McDiarmid	N. Bickett/N. Burgess	3–6 6–3 11–13 7–5 6–1
1938	J. R. Hunt/L. Wetherel	E. Cooke/C. Hare	6–4 8–6 6–2
1939	G. Mako/F. A. Parker	J. H. Doeg/W. Sabin	6–3 3–6 6–3 6–4
1940	R. Harmon/R. C. Peacock	W. D. McNeill/F. A. Parker	w.o.
1941	J. A. Kramer/F. R. Schroeder	J. R. Hunt/C. Oliwine	6–4 7–5 6–1
1942	W. Reedy/W. F. Talbert	C. Mattman/G. Richards	6–3 6–3 6–3
1943	E. Cochell/R. Kimbrell	S. Greenberg/W. F. Talbert	1–6 6–3 6–4 6–2
1944	F. Segura/W. F. Talbert	H. Manire/H. Wrobbel	6–3 6–1 5–7 6–1
1945	F. Segura/W. F. Talbert	E. Cooke/H. Surface	6–4 7–5 6–2
1946	G. Mulloy/W. F. Talbert	J. Cushingham/R. Falkenburg	12–10 6–2 6–4
1947	F. R. Schroeder/J. Tuero	S. Greenberg/E. V. Seixas	6–3 3–6 2–6 8–6 6–4
1948	T. Chambers/S. Match	T. P. Brown/R. A. Gonzales	1–6 7–5 6–3
1949	S. Match/E. V. Seixas	R. A. Gonzales/H. Stewart	6–1 1–6 5–7 8–6 9–7
1950	H. Flam/A. Larsen	F. R. Schroeder/M. A. Trabert	3–6 1–6 6–2 6–2 6–4

1951	H. Richardson/M. A. Trabert	H. Burrows/S. Clark	3–6 8–6 6–2 6–2
1952	G. Golden/A. Larsen	N. Brown/H. Stewart	6–2 6–4 8–6
1953	B. Bartzen/G. Holden	A. Larsen/G. Worthington	8–6 2–6 8–6 6–4
1954	E. V. Seixas/M. A. Trabert	B. Bartzen/A. Larsen	6–3 11–9 6–2
1955	H. Richardson/M. A. Trabert	B. Bartzen/E. Moylan	6–1 6–2
1956	F. Contreras/A. Olmedo	H. Flam/A. Larsen	6–3 5–7 6–4
1957	A. J. Cooper/N. A. Fraser	H. Flam/E. V. Seixas	4–6 7–5 6–4 6–3
1958	S. Giammalva/B. MacKay	B. Bartzen/G. Golden	6–2 6–4 5–7 3–6 6–0
1959	B. Bartzen/G. Golden	W. Bond/R. D. Ralston	12–10 6–2 6–4
1960	R. A. J. Hewitt/M. F. Mulligan	R. Earnhart/M. C. Riessen	6–3 6–2 11–13 6–4
1961	C. R. McKinley/R. D. Ralston	R. Earnhart/M. C. Riessen	6–3 6–4 6–2
1962	R. Earnhart/M. C. Riessen	C. Crawford/F. S. Stolle	6–4 6–2 6–3
1963	C. Graebner/M. C. Riessen	C. R. McKinley/R. D. Ralston	6–4 0–6 6–4 5–7 6–3
1964	C. R. McKinley/R. D. Ralston	C. Graebner/M. C. Riessen	6–1 6–4 6–2
1965	C. Graebner/M. C. Riessen	R. D. Ralston/H. Richardson	3–6 6–3 6–1 ret'd
1966	C. Graebner/R. D. Ralston	F. A. Froehling/C. Pasarell	6–1 8–10 6–4 6–8 6–4
1967	C. Graebner/M. C. Riessen	J. Brown/B. Tobin	6–2 6–4 6–4
1968	R. C. Lutz/S. R. Smith	M. Mosur/M. C. Riessen	3–6 6–2 6–4 6–2
1969	W. W. Bowrey/C. Graebner	R. D. Crealy/A. J. Stone	6–4 4–6 6–4
1970	A. R. Ashe/C. Graebner	I. Nastase/I. Tiriac	2–6 6–4 6–4
1971	Z. Franulovic/J. Kodes	C. Graebner/E. Van Dillen	7–6 5–7 6–3
1972	R. A. J. Hewitt/F. D. McMillan	O. Cornejo/J. Fillol	6–2 6–3
1973	R. Carmichael/F. D. McMillan	M. Orantes/I. Tiriac	6–3 7–4
1974	J. S. Connors/I. Nastase	J. Fassbender/H. J. Pohmann	6–7 6–3 6–4
1975	J. Gisbert/M. Orantes	W. Fibak/H. J. Pohmann	7–5 6–0
1976	B. E. Gottfried/R. Ramirez	F. McNair/S. E. Stewart	6–2 6–2
1977	P. Cornejo/J. Fillol	R. D. Crealy/C. Letcher	6–7 6–4 6–3
1978	G. Mayer/H. Pfister	J. Borowiak/C. J. Lewis	6–3 6–0
1979	J. P. McEnroe/G. Mayer	J. Kodes/T. Smid	6–4 7–6
1980	K. Curren/S. Denton	W. Fibak/I. Lendl	3–6 7–6 6–4
1981	K. Curren/S. Denton	R. Ramirez/V. Winitsky	6–3 5–7 7–5
1982	S. E. Stewart/F. Taygan	R. Venter/B. Willenborg	6–4 7–5
1983	M. R. Edmondson/S. E. Stewart	C. Kirmayr/C. Motta	6–3 6–2
1984	K. Flach/R. Seguso	H. Gunthardt/B. Taroczy	7–6 7–5
1985	K. Flach/R. Seguso	P. Slozil/K. Warwick	6–4 6–4
1986	H. Gildemeister/A. Gomez	J. Fitzgerald/S. E. Stewart	6–4 6–3
1987	L. Warder/B. Willenborg	J. Nystrom/M. Wilander	6–0 6–3

WOMEN'S DOUBLES

	CHAMPIONS	RUNNERS-UP	SCORE
1914	M. K. Brown/Mrs R. Williams	M. Dodd/M. Lyons	6–1 6–2
1915–16	*Not held*		
1917*	Mrs C. Gregg/R. Sanders	Mrs W. Ellis/A. Levy	6–4 6–2
1918	B. Esch/Mrs R. Field	C. B. Neely/Mrs A. Yager	6–4 4–6 6–4
1919	C. B. Neely/K. Vorhees	C. Gould/Mrs H. Peters	6–4 6–2
1920	F. Ballin/E. Tennant	B. Esch/C. Gould	6–3 6–2
1921	Mrs B. E. Cole/Mrs F. Godfrey	L. Bancroft/Mrs E. V. Lynch	6–3 8–6
1922	L. Bancroft/Mrs F. Godfrey	Mrs H. Bickle/H. Hooker	3–6 7–5 6–1
1923	Mrs R. Leqchman/E. Sigourney	M. MacDonald/L. Scharman	6–1 6–0
1924–39	*Not held*		
1940	M. Arnold/A. Marble	H. I. Bernard/G. W. Wheeler	7–5 6–1
1941	B. Bradley/Mrs J. S. Gallagher	D. J. Hart/N. Sheer	4–6 8–6 6–4
1942	*Not held*		
1943	P. M. Betz/N. Corbett	M. Hernando/M. Siriwaitis	6–3 6–3
1944	P. M. Betz/D. J. Hart	M. Warnold/C. Wolf	8–6 6–3
1945	P. M. Betz/D. J. Hart	M. Arnold/Mrs S. P. Cooke	3–6 6–4 9–7
1946	S. J. Fry/Mrs M. A. Prentiss	Mrs V. W. Kovacs/B. Scofield	6–4 6–1
1947	G. Moran/Mrs M. A. Prentiss	S. J. Fry/B. Krase	6–4 6–4
1948–49	*Not held*		
1950	S. J. Fry/D. J. Hart	B. Baker/Mrs M. Rurac	2–6 6–4 6–4
1951	Mrs M. Rurac/Mrs P. C. Todd	D. Head/A. Kanter	3–6 6–2 6–2
1952	Mrs L. Davidson/D. Popple	A. Kanter/J. Merciadis	7–5 6–4
1953	A. Kanter/Mrs T. D. Long	M. Connolly/J. Sampson	6–3 6–0
1954	M. Connolly/D. J. Hart	A. Gibson/E. Norton	6–3 6–2
1955	J. Hopps/Mrs D. H. Knode	B. Breit/P. Shaffer	6–2 3–6 6–3
1956	S. J. Fry/Mrs D. H. Knode	M. Hernandez/Y. Ramirez	6–2 6–1
1957	A. Gibson/D. R. Hard	J. Arth/K. Fageros	6–3 6–0
1958	K. Fageros/Mrs D. H. Knode	M. Hernandez/M. Montgomery	2–6 6–5 ret'd
1959	S. Reynolds/R. Schuurman	J. Arth/J. Hopps	4–6 6–0 6–3

1960	D. R. Hard/B. J. Moffitt	J. Bricka/C. Hanks	6–3 6–4
1961	J. Bricka/C. Hanks	D. Floyd/B. Gunderson	6–3 6–2
1962	S. Behlmar/D. R. Hard	C. Hanks/M. Montgomery	6–2 6–3
1963	M. E. Bueno/D. R. Hard	C. Caldwell/B. J. Moffitt	6–2 6–2
1964	Mrs C. Graebner/N. Richey	J. Danilovich/S. Shrader	6–1 6–4
1965	Mrs C. Graebner/N. Richey	R. Casals/J. M. Heldman	7–5 6–4
1966	K. Krantzcke/K. Melville	E. Emanuel/M. Godwin	1–6 6–4 6–4
1967	K. Krantzcke/K. Melville	R. Casals/Mrs L. W. King	6–4 6–1
1968	N. Richey/V. Ziegenfuss	J. Bartkowicz/S. De Fina	6–2 6–0
1969	Mrs W. W. Bowrey/Mrs G. Chanfreau	E. Burrer/L. Tuero	6–0 10–8
1970	P. Austin/M. Cooper	M. Gengler/A. Lebedeff	2–6 6–3 7–5
1971	Mrs D. E. Dalton/Mrs L. W. King	J. M. Heldman/L. Tuero	6–1 6–2
1972	E. F. Goolagong/L. Hunt	Mrs B. M. Court/P. Teeguarden	6–2 6–1
1973	P. S. A. Hogan/S. A. Walsh	F. Bonicelli/I. Fernandez	6–4 6–4
1974	Mrs G. Chanfreau/J. M. Heldman	C. M./J. C. Evert	6–3 6–1
1975	F. Bonicelli/I. Fernandez	Mrs G. Chanfreau/J. M. Heldman	3–6 7–5 6–3
1976	L. Boshoff/I. Kloss	L. DuPont/W. M. Turnbull	6–2 6–3
1977	L. Boshoff/I. Kloss	M. Carillo/W. Overton	5–7 7–5 6–3
1978	H. Anliot/Mrs H. Sparre-Viragh	B. Hallquist/S. McInerney	6–3 6–1
1979	K. Jordan/A. E. Smith	P. Johnson/P. Smith	6–1 6–0
1980	A. E. Smith/P. Smith	V. Ruzici/R. Tomanova	6–4 3–6 6–4
1981	J. Russell/V. Ruzici	S. Barker/P. Smith	6–2 6–2
1982	I. Madruga Osses/C. Tanvier	J. Russell/V. Ruzici	7–5 7–6
1983	K. Horvath/V. Ruzici	G. Fernandez/B. Herr	4–6 7–6 6–2
1984	B. Mould/P. Smith	E. Burgin/J. Russell	6–2 7–5
1985	K./M. Maleeva	P. Barg/P. Smith	2–6 6–3 6–4
1986	S. Graf/G. Sabatini	G. Fernandez/R. White	6–2 6–0
1987	*Not held*		

MIXED DOUBLES

This event was staged intermittently

	CHAMPIONS	RUNNERS-UP	SCORE
1912	F. Harris/Miss M. Sutton	R. N. Williams/Miss M. K. Browne	6–3 2–6 6–2
1915	H. Johnson/Mrs G. W. Wightman	P. D. Siverd/Miss C. Cassel	6–2 6–0
1916	G. Church/Miss M. Bjurdstedt	C. Doyle/Mrs H. Bickle	6–1 6–2
1917*	H. Cordes/Miss R. Sanders	C. S. Garland/Miss L. Hofer	6–1 6–2
1923	A. J. Castle/Miss M. MacDonald	A. Misner/Miss E. Sigourney	6–1 7–5
1945	E. Cooke/Mrs J. P. Cooke	W. F. Talbert/Miss P. M. Betz	7–5 4–6 6–3

ITALIAN CHAMPIONSHIPS

Staged in Milan 1930 to 1934. Moved to the Foro Italico in Rome in 1935. Not held 1936 to 1949 because of the Abyssinia War and World War II. In 1961 the tournament was staged in Turin. Men's and women's events were held at different dates in 1979. In 1980–1985 the women's events moved to Perugia.

MEN'S SINGLES

	CHAMPION	RUNNER-UP	SCORE
1930	W. T. Tilden	H. L. de Morpurgo	6–1 6–1 6–2
1931	G. P. Hughes	H. Cochet	6–4 6–3 6–2
1932	A. Merlin	G. P. Hughes	6–1 5–7 6–0 8–6
1933	E. Sertorio	A. Martin Legeay	6–3 6–1 6–3
1934	G. Palmieri	G. de Stefani	6–3 6–0 7–5
1935	W. Hines	G. Palmieri	6–3 10–8 9–7
1936–49	*Not held*		
1950	J. Drobny	W. F. Talbert	6–4 6–3 7–9 6–2
1951	J. Drobny	G. Cucelli	6–3 10–8 6–1
1952	F. A. Sedgman	J. Drobny	7–5 6–3 1–6 6–4
1953	J. Drobny	L. A. Hoad	6–2 6–1 6–2
1954	J. E. Patty	E. Morea	11–9 6–4 6–4
1955	F. Gardini	G. Merlo	6–1 1–6 3–6 5–6ret'd
1956	L. A. Hoad	S. Davidson	7–5 6–2 6–0
1957	N. Pietrangeli	G. Merlo	8–6 6–2 6–4
1958	M. G. Rose	N. Pietrangeli	5–7 8–6 6–4 1–6 6–2

1959	L. Ayala	N. A. Fraser	6–3 1–6 6–3 6–3
1960	B. MacKay	L. Ayala	7–5 7–5 0–6 0–6 6–1
1961	N. Pietrangeli	R. G. Laver	6–8 6–1 6–1 6–2
1962	R. G. Laver	R. S. Emerson	6–1 1–6 3–6 6–3 6–1
1963	M. F. Mulligan	B. Jovanovic	6–2 4–6 6–3 8–6
1964	J. E. Lundquist	F. S. Stolle	1–6 7–5 6–3 6–1
1965	M. F. Mulligan	M. Santana	1–6 6–4 6–3 6–1
1966	A. D. Roche	N. Pietrangeli	11–9 6–1 6–2
1967	M. F. Mulligan	A. D. Roche	6–3 0–6 6–4 6–1
1968	T. S. Okker	R. A. J. Hewitt	10–8 6–8 6–1 1–6 6–0
1969	J. D. Newcombe	A. D. Roche	6–3 4–6 6–2 5–7 6–3
1970	I. Nastase	J. Kodes	6–3 1–6 6–3 8–6
1971	R. G. Laver	J. Kodes	7–5 6–3 6–3
1972	M. Orantes	J. Kodes	4–6 6–1 7–5 6–2
1973	I. Nastase	M. Orantes	6–1 6–1 6–1
1974	B. Borg	I. Nastase	6–3 6–4 6–2
1975	R. Ramirez	M. Orantes	7–6 7–5 7–5
1976	A. Panatta	G. Vilas	2–6 7–6 6–2 7–6
1977	V. Gerulaitis	A. Zugarelli	6–2 7–6 3–6 7–6
1978	B. Borg	A. Panatta	1–6 6–3 6–1 4–6 6–3
1979	V. Gerulaitis	E. Dibbs	6–7 7–6 6–7 6–4 6–2
1980	G. Vilas	Y. Noah	6–0 6–4 6–4
1981	J. L. Clerc	V. Pecci	6–3 6–4 6–0
1982	A. Gomez	E. Teltscher	6–2 6–3 6–2
1983	J. Arias	J. Higueras	6–2 6–7 6–1 6–4
1984	A. Gomez	A. Krickstein	2–6 6–1 6–2 6–2
1985	Y. Noah	M. Mecir	6–3 3–6 6–2 7–6
1986	I. Lendl	E. Sanchez	7–5 4–6 6–1 6–1
1987	M. Wilander	M. Jaite	6–3 6–4 6–4

WOMEN'S SINGLES

	CHAMPION	RUNNER-UP	SCORE
1930	Miss E. de Alvarez	Miss L. Valerio	3–6 8–6 6–0
1931	Mrs L. Valerio	Mrs D. Andrus	2–6 6–2 6–2
1932	Miss I. Adamoff	Miss L. Valerio	6–4 7–5
1933	Miss E. Ryan	Miss I. Adamoff	6–1 6–1
1934	Miss H. Jacobs	Miss L. Valerio	6–3 6–0
1935	Miss H. Sperling	Miss L. Valerio	6–4 6–1
1936–49	*Not held*		
1950	Mrs A. Bossi	Miss P. J. Curry	6–4 6–4
1951	Miss D. J. Hart	Miss S. J. Fry	6–3 8–6
1952	Miss S. Partridge	Miss M. P. Harrison	6–3 7–5
1953	Miss D. J. Hart	Miss M. Connolly	4–6 9–7 6–3
1954	Miss M. Connolly	Miss P. E. Ward	6–3 6–0
1955	Miss P. E. Ward	Miss E. Vollmer	6–4 6–3
1956	Miss A. Gibson	Mrs S. Kormoczy	6–3 7–5
1957	Miss S. J. Bloomer	Mrs D. P. Knode	1–6 9–7 6–2
1958	Miss M. E. Bueno	Miss L. Coghlan	3–6 6–3 6–3
1959	Miss C. C. Truman	Miss S. Reynolds	6–0 6–1
1960	Mrs S. Kormoczy	Miss A. S. Haydon	6–4 4–6 6–1
1961	Miss M. E. Bueno	Miss L. R. Turner	6–4 6–4
1962	Miss M. Smith	Miss M. E. Bueno	8–6 5–7 6–4
1963	Miss M. Smith	Miss L. R. Turner	6–3 6–4
1964	Miss M. Smith	Miss L. R. Turner	6–1 6–1
1965	Miss M. E. Bueno	Miss N. Richey	6–1 1–6 6–3
1966	Mrs P. F. Jones	Miss A. Van Zyl	8–6 6–1
1967	Miss L. R. Turner	Miss M. E. Bueno	6–3 6–3
1968	Mrs W. W. Bowrey	Mrs B. M. Court	2–6 6–2 6–3
1969	Miss J. M. Heldman	Miss K. Melville	7–5 6–4
1970	Mrs L. W. King	Miss J. M. Heldman	6–1 6–3
1971	Miss S. V. Wade	Mrs H. Masthoff	6–4 6–4
1972	Miss L. Tuero	Mrs O. Morozova	6–4 6–3
1973	Miss E. F. Goolagong	Miss C. M. Evert	7–6 6–0
1974	Miss C. M. Evert	Miss M. Navratilova	6–3 6–3
1975	Miss C. M. Evert	Miss M. Navratilova	6–1 6–0
1976	Miss M. Jausovec	Miss L. Hunt	6–1 6–3
1977	Miss J. Newberry	Miss R. Tomanova	6–3 7–6
1978	Miss R. Marsikova	Miss V. Ruzici	7–5 7–5
1979	Miss T. A. Austin	Miss S. Hanika	6–4 1–6 6–3

1980	Mrs J. M. Lloyd	Miss V. Ruzici	5–7 6–2 6–2
1981	Mrs J. M. Lloyd	Miss V. Ruzici	6–1 6–2
1982	Mrs J. M. Lloyd	Miss H. Mandlikova	6–0 6–3
1983	Miss A. Temesvari	Miss B. Gadusek	6–1 6–0
1984	Miss M. Maleeva	Mrs J. M. Lloyd	6–3 6–3
1985	Miss R. Reggi	Miss V. Nelson	6–4 6–4
1986	*Not held*		
1987	Miss S. Graf	Miss G. Sabatini	7–5 4–6 6–0

MEN'S DOUBLES

	CHAMPIONS	RUNNERS-UP	SCORE
1930	W. F. Coen/W. T. Tilden	H. L. de Morpurgo/P. Gaslini	6–0 6–3 6–3
1931	A. del Bono/G. P. Hughes	H. Cochet/A. Merlin	3–6 8–6 4–6 6–4 6–3
1932	G. P. Hughes/G. de Stafani	J. Bonte/A. Merlin	6–2 6–2 6–4
1933	J. Lesuer/A. M. Legeay	G. Palmieri/E. Sertorio	6–2 6–4 6–2
1934	G. Palmieri/G. L. Rogers	G. P. Hughes/G. de Stefani	3–6 6–4 9–7 0–6 6–2
1935	J. H. Crawford/V. B. McGrath	J. Borotra/J. Brugnon	4–6 4–6 6–4 6–2 6–2
1936–49	*Not held*		
1950	W. F. Talbert/M. A. Trabert	J. E. Patty/O. W. Sidwell	6–3 6–1 4–6 ret'd
1951	J. Drobny/R. Savitt	G. Cucelli/M. Del Bello	6–2 7–9 6–1 6–3
1952	J. Drobny/F. A. Sedgman	G. Cucelli/M. Del Bello	3–6 7–5 3–6 6–3 6–2
1953	L. A. Hoad/K. R. Rosewall	J. Drobny/J. E. Patty	6–2 6–4 6–2
1954	J. Drobny/E. Morea	M. A. Trabert/E. V. Seixas	6–4 0–6 3–6 6–3 6–4
1955	A. Larsen/E. Morea	N. Pietrangeli/O. Sirola	6–1 6–4 4–6 7–5
1956	J. Drobny/L. A. Hoad	N. Pietrangeli/O. Sirola	11–9 6–2 6–3
1957	N. A. Fraser/L. A. Hoad	N. Pietrangeli/O. Sirola	6–1 6–8 6–0 6–2
1958	A. Jancso/K. Nielsen	L. Ayala/D. Candy	8–10 6–3 6–2 1–6 9–7
1959	R. S. Emerson/N. A. Fraser	N. Pietrangeli/O. Sirola	8–6 6–4 6–4
1960	N. Pietrangeli/O. Sirola	R. S. Emerson/N. A. Fraser	3–6 7–5 2–6 11–11 ret'd
1961	R. S. Emerson/N. A. Fraser	N. Pietrangeli/O. Sirola	6–2 6–4 11–9
1962	N. A. Fraser/R. G. Laver	K. N. Fletcher/J. D. Newcombe	11–9 6–2 6–4
1963	R. A. J. Hewitt/F. S. Stolle	N. Pietrangeli/O. Sirola	6–3 6–3 6–1
1964	R. A. J. Hewitt/F. S. Stolle	A. D. Roche/J. D. Newcombe	7–5 6–3 3–6 7–5
1965	A. D. Roche/J. D. Newcombe	C. Barnes/T. Koch	1–6 6–4 2–6 12–10 ret'd
1966	R. S. Emerson/F. S. Stolle	N. Pietrangeli/E. C. Drysdale	6–4 12–10 6–3
1967	R. A. J. Hewitt/F. D. McMillan	W. W. Bowrey/O. K. Davidson	6–3 2–6 6–3 9–7
1968	T. S. Okker/M. C. Riessen	A. Stone/N. Kalogeropoulos	6–3 6–4 6–2
1969	A. D. Roche/J. D. Newcombe	T. S. Okker/M. C. Riessen	6–4 1–6 ret'd
1970	I. Nastase/I. Tiriac	W. W. Bowrey/O. K. Davidson	0–6 10–8 6–3 6–8 6–1
1971	A. D. Roche/J. D. Newcombe	A. Gimeno/R. Taylor	6–4 6–4
1972	I. Nastase/I. Tiriac	L. A. Hoad/F. D. McMillan	3–6 3–6 6–4 6–3 5–3 ret'd
1973	J. D. Newcombe/T. S. Okker	R. Case/G. Masters	6–3 6–2 6–4
1974	B. E. Gottfried/R. Ramirez	J. Gisbert/I. Nastase	6–3 6–2 6–3
1975	B. E. Gottfried/R. Ramirez	J. S. Connors/I. Nastase	6–4 7–6 2–6 6–1
1976	B. E. Gottfried/R. Ramirez	G. Masters/J. D. Newcombe	7–6 5–7 6–3 3–6 6–3
1977	B. E. Gottfried/R. Ramirez	F. McNair/S. E. Stewart	7–6 6–7 7–5
1978	V. Pecci/B. Prajoux	J. Kodes/T. Smid	6–7 7–6 6–1
1979	P. Fleming/T. Smid	J. L. Clerc/I. Nastase	4–6 6–1 7–5
1980	M. R. Edmondson/K. Warwick	B. Taroczy/E. Teltscher	7–6 7–6
1981	H. Gildemeister/A. Gomez	B. Manson/T. Smid	7–5 6–2
1982	H. Gunthardt/B. Taroczy	W. Fibak/J. Fitzgerald	6–4 4–6 6–3
1983	F. Gonzalez/V. Pecci	J. Gunnarsson/M. Leach	6–2 6–7 6–4
1984	K. Flach/R. Seguso	J. G. Alexander/M. Leach	3–6 6–3 6–4
1985	A. Jarryd/M. Wilander	K. Flach/R. Seguso	4–6 6–3 6–2
1986	G. Forget/Y. Noah	M. R. Edmondson/S. E. Stewart	7–6 6–2
1987	G. Forget/Y. Noah	M. Mecir/T. Smid	6–2 6–7 6–3

WOMEN'S DOUBLES

	CHAMPIONS	RUNNERS-UP	SCORE
1930	E. de Alvarez/L. Valerio	C. Anet/M. Neufeld	7–5 5–7 7–5
1931	A. Luzzatti/J. Prouse	Mrs D. Andrus Burke/L. Valerio	6–3 1–6 6–3
1932	C. Rosambert/L. Payot	Mrs D. Andrus Burke/L. Valerio	7–5 6–3
1933	I. Adamoff/Mrs D. Andrus Burke	E. Ryan/L. Valerio	6–3 1–6 6–4
1934	H. H. Jacobs/E. Ryan	I. Adamoff/Mrs D. Andrus Burke	7–5 9–7

1935	E. M. Dearman/N. Lyle	C. Aussem/E. Ryan	6–2 6–4
1936–49	*Not held*		
1950	J. Quertier/J. Walker-Smith	B. E. Hilton/K. L. A. Tuckey	1–6 6–3 6–2
1951	S. J. Fry/D. J. Hart	L. Brough/T. D. Long	6–1 7–5
1952	N. Hopman/Mrs T. D. Long	N. Migliori/V. Tonoli	6–2 6–8 6–1
1953	M. Connolly/J. Sampson	S. J. Fry/D. J. Hart	6–8 6–4 6–4
1954	P. E. Ward/E. M. Watson	N. Adamson/G. Bucaille	3–6 6–3 6–4
1955	C. Mercellis/P. E. Ward	M. Muller/B. Penrose	6–4 10–8
1956	M. Hawton/Mrs T. D. Long	A. Buxton/D. R. Hard	6–4 6–8 9–7
1957	M. Hawton/Mrs T. D. Long	Y. Ramirez/R. M. Reyes	6–1 6–1
1958	S. J. Bloomer/C. Truman	M. Hawton/Mrs T. D. Long	6–3 6–2
1959	Y. Ramirez/R. M. Reyes	M. E. Bueno/J. Hopps	4–6 6–4 6–4
1960	M. Hellyer/Y. Ramirez	S. J. Brasher/A. Haydon	6–4 6–4
1961	J. Lehane/L. R. Turner	M. Reitano/M. Smith	2–6 6–1 6–1
1962	M. E. Bueno/D. R. Hard	S. Lazzarino/L. Pericoli	6–4 6–4
1963	R. Ebbern/M. Smith	S. Lazzarino/L. Pericoli	6–2 6–3
1964	L. R. Turner/M. Smith	S. Lazzarino/L. Pericoli	6–1 6–2
1965	M. Schacht/A. Van Zyl	S. Lazzarino/L. Pericoli	2–6 6–2 12–10
1966	N. Baylon/A. Van Zyl	Mrs P. F. Jones/E. Starkie	6–3 1–6 6–2
1967	R. Casals/L. R. Turner	S. Lazzarino/L. Pericoli	7–5 7–5
1968	Mrs B. M. Court/S. V. Wade	A. Van Zyl/P. Walkden	6–2 7–5
1969	F. Durr/Mrs P. F. Jones	R. Casals/Mrs L. W. King	6–3 3–6 6–2
1970	R. Casals/L. W. King	F. Durr/S. V. Wade	6–2 3–6 9–7
1971	Mrs H. Masthoff/S. V. Wade	Mrs L. Bowrey/H. Gourlay	5–7 6–2 6–2
1972	L. Hunt/Mrs O. Morozova	Mrs G. Chanfreau/R. Vido	6–3 6–4
1973	Mrs O. Morozova/S. V. Wade	M. Navratilova/R. Tomanova	3–6 6–2 7–5
1974	C. M. Evert/Mrs O. Morozova	H. Masthoff/H. Orth	w.o.
1975	C. M. Evert/M. Navratilova	S. Barker/G. Coles	6–1 6–2
1976	L. Boshoff/I. Kloss	M. Simionescu/V. Ruzici	6–1 6–2
1977	B. Cuypers/M. Kruger	B. Bruning/S. A. Walsh	3–6 7–5 6–2
1978	M. Jausovec/V. Ruzici	F. Mihai/B. Nagelsen	6–2 2–6 7–5
1979	B. Stove/W. M. Turnbull	Mrs E. Crawley/G. E. Reid	6–3 6–4
1980	H. Mandlikova/R. Tomanova	I. Madruga/I. Villagran	6–4 6–4
1981	C. Reynolds/P. Smith	Mrs J. M. Lloyd/V. Ruzici	7–5 6–1
1982	K. Horvath/Y. Vermaak	Mrs L. W. King/I. Kloss	2–6 6–4 7–6
1983	V. Ruzici/S. V. Wade	I. Madruga Osses/C. Tanvier	6–3 2–6 6–1
1984	I. Budarova/M. Skuherska	K. Horvath/V. Ruzici	7–6 1–6 6–4
1985	A. M. Cecchini/R. Reggi	P. Murgo/B. Romano	1–6 6–4 6–3
1986	*Not held*		
1987	M. Navratilova/G. Sabatini	C. Kohde-Kilsch/H. Sukova	6–4 6–1

MIXED DOUBLES

	CHAMPIONS	RUNNERS-UP	SCORE
1930	H. L. de Morpurgo/Miss E. de Alvarez	G. P. Hughes/Miss L. Valerio	4–6 6–4 6–2
1931	G. P. Hughes/Miss L. Valerio	A. del Bono/Mrs D. Andrus Burke	6–0 6–1
1932	J. Bonte/Miss L. Payot	A. del Bono/Mrs D. Andrus Burke	6–1 6–2
1933	A. M. Legeay/Mrs D. Andrus Burke	E. Gabrowitz/Miss Y. Orlandini	6–4 6–3
1934	H. M. Culley/Miss E. Ryan	F. Puncec/Miss R. Couquerque	6–1 6–3
1935	H. C. Hopman/Miss J. Jedrzejowska	G. P. Hughes/Miss E. M. Dearman	6–3 1–6 6–3
1936–49	*Not held*		
1950	A. K. Quist/Miss G. Moran	div'd with G. Cucelli/Miss A. Bossi	6–3 1–1 unf.
1951	F. Ampon/Miss S. J. Fry	L. Bergelin/Miss D. J. Hart	8–6 3–6 6–4
1952	K. Nielsen/Miss A. McGuire	E. Migone/Mrs M. J. de Riba	4–6 6–3 6–3
1953	E. V. Seixas/Miss D. J. Hart	M. G. Rose/Miss M. Connolly	6–4 6–4
1954	E. V. Seixas/Miss M. Connolly	div'd with M. A. Trabert/Miss B. M. Kimbrell	3–6 11–9 3–3 unf.
1955	E. Morea/Miss P. E. Ward	div'd with M. G. Rose/Miss B. Penrose	
1956	L. Ayala/Mrs T. D. Long	G. Fachini/Miss S. J. Bloomer	6–4 6–3
1957	L. Ayala/Mrs T. D. Long	R. N. Howe/Miss S. J. Bloomer	6–1 6–1
1958	G. Fachini/Miss S. J. Bloomer	L. Ayala/Mrs T. D. Long	4–6 6–2 9–7
1959	F. Contreras/Miss R. M. Reyes	W. A. Knight/Miss Y. Ramirez	9–7 6–1
1960	*Not held*		
1961	R. S. Emerson/Miss M. Smith	R. A. J. Hewitt/Miss J. Lehane	6–1 6–1
1962	F. S. Stolle/Miss L. R. Turner	S. Davidson/Miss M. Schacht	6–4 6–1
1963	*Not held*		
1964	J. D. Newcombe/Miss M. Smith	T. Koch/Miss M. E. Bueno	3–6 7–5 6–2
1965	J. E. Mandarino/Miss M. Coronado	V. Zarazua/Miss E. Subirats	6–1 6–1
1966	*Not held*		
1967	W. W. Bowrey/Miss L. R. Turner	F. D. McMillan/Miss F. Durr	6–2 7–5

1968	M. C. Riessen/Mrs B. M. Court	T. S. Okker/Miss S. V. Wade	8–6 6–3
	Event ceased		

SOUTH AFRICAN CHAMPIONSHIPS

MEN'S SINGLES

	CHAMPION	RUNNER-UP	SCORE
1891	L. A. Richardson	L. Winslow	Not available
1892	L. A. Richardson	R. Davis	Not available
1893	W. L. Edwards	L. A. Richardson	Not available
1894	L. Giddy	W. T. Edmonds	Not available
1895	L. Giddy	S. Bayly	Not available
1896	L. Giddy	H. R. Eaton	Not available
1897	L. Giddy	Not available	
1898	L. Giddy	Not available	
1899	L. G. Heard	Not available	
1900–02	*Not held*		
1903	R. W. G. Clarke	Not available	
1904	P. W. Sherwell	Not available	
1905	H. A. Kitson	Not available	
1906	J. Richardson	Not available	
1907	A. Rowan	Not available	
1908	H. A. Kitson	V. R. Gauntlett	6–2 5–7 6–2 7–9 6–2
1909	R. F. Doherty	Not available	
1910	A. F. Wilding	Not available	
1911	H. A. Kitson	Father Kelly	6–4 6–3 6–2
1912	G. H. Dodd	Not available	
1913	H. A. Kitson	Not available	
1914	C. L. Winslow	Not available	
1915–19	*Not held*		
1920	B. I. C. Norton	Not available	
1921	L. B. Raymond	M. Davies	6–3 6–0 6–1
1922	L. B. Raymond	Not available	
1923	L. B. Raymond	J. Condon	6–3 7–5 4–6 6–2
1924	L. B. Raymond	Not available	
1925	I. J. Richardson	Not available	
1926	J. Condon	C. R. Blackbeard	6–0 6–3 6–2
1927	G. Eaglestone	Not available	
1928	G. Eaglestone	Not available	
1929	C. J. J. Robbins	Not available	
1930	L. B. Raymond	C. J. J. Robbins	6–2 5–7 6–3 6–4
1931	L. B. Raymond	M. Bertrams	6–3 4–6 6–4 6–2
1932	M. Bertram	C. J. J. Robbins	2–6 9–7 9–7 6–1
1933	C. J. J. Robbins	V. G. Kirby	6–1 1–6 4–6 9–7 6–4
1934	N. G. Farquharson	R. Malcolm	4–6 6–2 6–3 14–12
1935	N. G. Farquharson	V. G. Kirby	6–0 6–4 6–1
1936	N. G. Farquharson	M. Bertram	6–4 6–4 1–6 6–3
1937	J. Pallada	V. G. Kirby	6–2 0–6 4–6 6–1 6–0
1938	N. G. Farquharson	V. G. Kirby	4–6 4–6 6–3 7–5 6–0
1939	E. W. Sturgess	E. E. Fannin	6–2 9–7 3–6 6–8 7–5
1940	E. W. Sturgess	R. H. M. Bertram	6–2 2–6 6–0 6–2
1941–45	*Not held*		
1946	E. W. Sturgess	N. G. Farquharson	6–0 6–2 6–3
1947	E. Fannin	E. W. Sturgess	6–1 6–2 1–6 0–6 6–4
1948	E. W. Sturgess	A. J. Mottram	6–3 6–4 6–8 6–1
1949	E. W. Sturgess	G. E. Brown	4–6 6–4 6–2 7–5
1950	E. W. Sturgess	A. Larsen	6–1 6–1 3–6 6–1
1951	E. W. Sturgess	S. Levy	6–3 6–2 7–5
1952	E. W. Sturgess	S. Levy	6–2 6–2 6–3
1953	E. W. Sturgess	W. R. Seymour	6–1 6–3 6–3
1954	E. W. Sturgess	J. Drobny	5–7 6–4 6–3 8–6
1955	W. R. Seymour	G. L. Forbes	1–6 9–7 6–1 8–6
1956	I. C. Vermaak	T. Johansson	6–2 4–6 3–6 6–3 8–6
1957	E. W. Sturgess	G. Koening	9–7 6–3 6–1
1958	U. Schmidt	T. Ulrich	1–6 12–10 6–2 6–8 6–2
1959	G. L. Forbes	I. C. Vermaak	6–3 6–4 6–2
1960	E. Buchholz	J. Frost	6–1 7–5 6–3

1961	G. L. Forbes	J. C. Mayers	8–6 3–6 4–6 6–4 6–4
1962	R. Mark	G. L. Forbes	6–1 6–1 2–6 8–6
1963	W. P. Bungert	G. L. Forbes	6–4 6–4 8–6
1964	A. A. Segal	G. L. Forbes	4–6 7–5 6–3 6–3
1965	E. C. Drysdale	J. C. Couder	1–6 6–3 6–4 1–6 6–3
1966	R. S. Emerson	R. A. J. Hewitt	6–3 2–6 3–6 6–4 7–5
1967	M. Santana	J. Leschly	2–6 6–2 4–6 6–3 6–4
1968	T. S. Okker	M. C. Riessen	12–10 6–1 6–4
1969	R. G. Laver	T. S. Okker	6–3 10–8 6–3
1970	R. G. Laver	F. D. McMillan	4–6 6–2 6–1 6–2
1971	K. R. Rosewall	F. S. Stolle	6–4 6–0 6–4
1972	C. Richey	M. Orantes	6–4 7–5 3–6 6–4
1973	J. S. Connors	A. R. Ashe	6–4 7–6 6–3
1974	J. S. Connors	A. R. Ashe	7–6 6–3 6–1
1975	H. Solomon	B. E. Gottfried	6–2 6–4 5–7 6–1
1976	H. Solomon	B. E. Gottfried	6–2 6–7 6–3 6–4
1977	G. Vilas	C. J. Mottram	7–6 6–3 6–4
1978	Tim Gullikson	H. Solomon	2–6 7–6 7–6 6–7 6–4
1979	A. Pattison	V. Pecci	2–6 6–3 6–2 6–3
1980	K. Warwick	F. Buehning	6–2 6–1 6–2
1981	V. Gerulaitis	J. Borowiak	6–4 7–6 6–1
1982	V. Gerulaitis	G. Vilas	7–6 6–2 4–6 6–3
1983	J. Kriek	C. Dowdeswell	6–4 4–6 1–6 7–5 6–3
1984	E. Teltscher	V. Gerulaitis	6–3 6–2 7–6
1985	M. Anger	B. Gilbert	6–4 3–6 6–3 6–2
1986	A. Mansdorf	M. Anger	6–3 3–6 6–2 7–5
1987	P. Cash	B. Gilbert	7–6 4–6 2–6 6–0 6–1

WOMEN'S SINGLES

	CHAMPION	RUNNER-UP	SCORE
1891	Miss H. Grant	Miss Blackburn	Not available
1892	Miss H. Grant	Mrs McLagon	Not available
1893	Miss H. Grant	Mrs McLagon	Not available
1894	Miss H. Grant	Miss B. Grant	Not available
1895	Miss R. Biddulph	Miss Fry	Not available
1896	Mrs H. Green	Miss L. Biddulph	Not available
1897	Miss N. Hickman	Not available	
1898	Miss N. Hickman	Not available	
1899	Miss N. Hickman	Not available	
1900–02	*Not held*		
1903	Miss F. Kuys	Not available	
1904	Mrs H. A. Kirby	Not available	
1905	Mrs H. A. Kirby	Not available	
1906	Mrs H. A. Kirby	Not available	
1907	Mrs H. A. Kirby	Not available	
1908	Miss M. Kelly	Mrs Gillmore	6–2 6–1
1909	Mrs G. Washington	Not available	
1910	Mrs H. A. Kirby	Not available	
1911	Mrs G. Washington	Miss M. Kelly	6–0 6–1
1912	Mrs H. A. Kirby	Not available	
1913	Miss M. Coles	Not available	
1914	Miss O. Mathias	Not available	
1915–19	*Not held*		
1920	Mrs C. L. Winslow	Not available	
1921	Miss N. Edwards	Mrs W. F. du Plessis	6–1 6–2
1922	Mrs T. J. McJannett	Not available	
1923	Mrs C. K. Pitt	Mrs Moor	6–4 6–3
1924	Mrs I. E. Peacock	Not available	
1925	Mrs I. E. Peacock	Not available	
1926	Mrs I. E. Peacock	Miss A. de Smit	6–2 6–1
1927	Mrs T. J. McJannett	Not available	
1928	Miss E. L. Heine	Not available	
1929	Mrs T. J. McJannett	Not available	
1930	Miss R. D. Tapscott	Mrs V. Everett	7–5 6–2
1931	Miss E. L. Heine	Miss W. Miller	6–3 6–3
1932	Mrs E. Heine Miller	Mrs F. H. Lowe	6–0 6–3
1933	Mrs C. J. J. Robbins	Mrs F. H. Lowe	6–4 3–6 6–1
1934	Mrs C. J. J. Robbins	Mrs F. H. Lowe	6–0 6–3
1935	Mrs A. Allister	Mrs C. J. J. Robbins	6–4 6–3

1936	Mrs E. Heine Miller	Mrs V. Everett	6–2 4–6 6–4
1937	Mrs E. Heine Miller	Mrs A. Neave	6–4 4–6 6–0
1938	Mrs C. J. J. Robbins	Miss O. Craze	6–4 6–4
1939	Miss O. Craze	Miss S. Piercey	4–6 6–3 6–4
1940	Miss O. Craze	Miss S. Piercey	4–6 6–4 6–4
1941–45	*Not held*		
1946	Mrs M. Muller	Mrs O. Plessis	6–4 6–4
1947	Mrs M. Muller	Mrs S. P. Summers	6–2 6–8 6–2
1948	Mrs S. P. Summers	Mrs M. Menzies	6–1 6–4
1949	Mrs S. P. Summers	Mrs T. D. Long	6–1 6–1
1950	Miss S. J. Fry	Miss D. J. Hart	4–6 7–5 6–3
1951	Mrs S. P. Summers	Mrs H. Redick-Smith	8–6 2–6 7–5
1952	Miss D. J. Hart	Mrs J. Whipplinger	6–1 7–5
1953	Mrs H. Redick-Smith	Mrs J. Whipplinger	6–2 6–2
1954	Mrs H. Redick-Smith	Miss G. Love	4–6 6–3 6–2
1955	Mrs H. Redick-Smith	Miss L. van der Westhuizen	6–4 6–3
1956	Miss D. Kilian	Miss G. Love	4–6 7–5 6–4
1957	Mrs W. Brewer	Miss G. Love	8–10 6–2 6–3
1958	Miss B. Carr	Mrs A. A. Segal	3–6 7–5 6–4
1959	Miss S. Reynolds	Mrs B. Vukovich	6–0 8–6
1960	Mrs B. Vukovich	Miss S. Reynolds	6–1 2–6 12–10
1961	Miss S. Reynolds	Miss L. Hutchings	6–4 7–5
1962	Mrs A. A. Segal	Miss J. Forbes	6–1 7–5
1963	Miss A. Van Zyl	Miss M. Hunt	6–4 2–6 6–3
1964	Miss D. R. Hard	Mrs P. F. Jones	6–3 7–5
1965	Miss C. C. Truman	Miss A. Van Zyl	6–2 6–3
1966	Mrs L. W. King	Miss M. Smith	6–3 6–2
1967	Mrs L. W. King	Miss M. E. Bueno	7–5 5–7 6–2
1968	Mrs B. M. Court	Miss S. V. Wade	6–4 6–4
1969	Mrs L. W. King	Miss N. Richey	6–3 6–4
1970	Mrs B. M. Court	Mrs L. W. King	6–4 1–6 6–3
1971	Mrs B. M. Court	Miss E. F. Goolagong	6–3 6–1
1972	Miss E. F. Goolagong	Miss S. V. Wade	4–6 6–3 6–0
1973	Miss C. M. Evert	Miss E. F. Goolagong	6–3 6–3
1974	Miss K. Melville	Miss D. Fromholtz	6–3 7–5
1975	Mrs A. du Plooy	Miss B. Cuypers	6–3 3–6 6–4
1976	Miss B. Cuypers	Miss L. DuPont	6–7 6–4 6–1
1977	Miss L. Boshoff	Miss B. Cuypers	6–1 6–4
1978	Miss B. Cuypers	Miss L. Siegel	6–1 6–0
1979	Miss B. Cuypers	Miss T. Harford	7–6 6–2
1980	Miss L. J. Charles	Miss R. R. Uys	7–5 6–4
1981	Miss K. Horvath	Miss K. Rinaldi	7–6 6–4
1982–83	*Not available*		
1984	Mrs J. M. Lloyd	Miss A. Jaeger	6–3 6–0
1985	*Not available*		
1986	Miss D. Van Rensburg	Miss R. Mentz	6–3 6–1
1987	Mrs G. Magers	Miss L. Allen	6–7 7–6 6–4

MEN'S DOUBLES

	CHAMPIONS	RUNNERS-UP	SCORE
1903	J. Orr/P. W. Sherwell	Not available	
1904	P. H. Hobbs/P. W. Sherwell	Not available	
1905	M. Hathorn/H. A. Kitson	Not available	
1906	D./S. Cockerell	Not available	
1907	A. Rowan/F. L. Scholtz	Not available	
1908	V. R. Gauntlett/H. A. Kitson	A. Rowan/F. L. Scholtz	6–2 6–2 7–5
1909	R. F. Doherty/G. W. Hillyard	Not available	
1910	V. R. Gauntlett/H. A. Kitson	Not available	
1911	F. E. Cochran/H. A. Kitson	E. Tapscott/J. Walscott	w.o.
1912	F. E. Cochran/C. N. Davis	Not available	
1913	F. E. Cochran/H. A. Kitson	Not available	
1914	F. E. Cochran/H. A. Kitson	Not available	
1915–19	*Not held*		
1920	B. I. C. Norton/L. B. Raymond	Not available	
1921	M. S. Davies/P. D. B. Spence	G. Eaglestone/A. Whiteley	Not available
1922	H. Hatton/W. F. Upton	Not available	
1923	C. R./D. Blackbeard	G. Eaglestone/C. H. Golborne	11–9 4–6 6–3 ret'd
1924	J. Condon/L. B. Raymond	Not available	
1925	M. S. Davies/I. J. Richardson	Not available	

1926	C. R. Blackbeard/C. L. Winslow	J. Condon/R. Le Suer	6–3 6–4 9–7
1927	F. H. Lowe/F. R. Shaw	Not available	
1928	G. Eaglestone/C. V. Kirby	Not available	
1929	R. W. Cornell/R. Klemp	Not available	
1930	J. Condon/V. G. Kirby	R. Malcolm/L. B. Raymond	7–5 6–1 10–8
1931	N. G. Farquharson/V. G. Kirby	F. H. Lowe/F. R. Shaw	4–6 8–6 2–6 6–0 6–1
1932	N. G. Farquharson/R. Malcolm	J. Condon/L. B. Raymond	6–4 1–6 6–1 6–4
1933	N. G. Farquharson/V. G. Kirby	J. Condon/R. Malcolm	5–7 6–2 6–4 12–10
1934	J. Condon/R. Malcolm	N. G. Farquharson/H. Silson	4–6 9–7 8–6
1935	N. Farquharson/R. Musgrove	M. Bertram/C. H. Robbs	6–4 7–5 4–6 6–3
1936	N. G. Farquharson/V. G. Kirby	M. Bertram/C. H. Robbs	6–3 8–6 6–2
1937	N. G. Farquharson/V. G. Kirby	J. Pallada/F. Puncec	1–6 2–6 6–4 7–5 6–4
1938	M. Bertram/E. Fannin	K. Hedley/F. H. Lowe	6–1 6–1 12–10
1939	N. G. Farquharson/V. G. Kirby	Not available	
1940	M. Bertram/E. Fannin	Not available	
1941–45	*Not held*		
1946	G. Ballance/E. W. Sturgess	N. G. Farquharson/V. G. Kirby	2–6 6–1 6–4 6–3
1947	E. Fannin/E. W. Sturgess	N. G. Farquharson/V. G. Kirby	6–3 10–8 10–8
1948	R. Fannin/E. W. Sturgess	N. Cockburn/S. Levy	6–3 6–2 7–5
1949	G. E. Brown/T. Warhurst	N. G. Cockburn/E. W. Sturgess	2–6 6–4 4–6 6–3 6–4
1950	A. Larsen/E. V. Seixas	P. Buckley/L. Norgarb	6–4 6–2 7–5
1951	L. Norgarb/E. W. Sturgess	N. Cockburn/S. Levy	9–7 6–3 3–6 6–4
1952	N. Cockburn/E. W. Sturgess	I. G. Ayre/D. Candy	6–4 8–6 3–6 6–3
1953	N. Cockburn/E. W. Sturgess	O. Williams/B. M. Woodroffe	9–7 8–6 6–4
1954	J. Drobny/J. E. Patty	A. Segal/E. W. Sturgess	6–2 6–3 4–6 3–6 6–3
1955	A. Segal/E. W. Sturgess	T. T. Fancutt/I. C. Vermaak	1–6 6–4 6–1 6–4
1956	S. Davidson/T. Johansson	E. W. Sturgess/B. M. Woodroffe	3–6 9–7 7–5 6–2
1957	N. A. Fraser/E. W. Sturgess	I. C. Vermaak/B. M. Woodroffe	6–4 6–2 2–6 5–7 6–3
1958	E. W. Sturgess/O. Williams	G. L. Forbes/A. Segal	6–4 5–7 8–6 7–5
1959	G. L. Forbes/A. Segal	A. Gaetner/B. M. Woodroffe	6–3 13–11 3–6 6–3
1960	G. L. Forbes/A. Segal	E. Buchholz/J. Frost	6–3 4–6 6–4 6–4
1961	G. L. Forbes/A. Segal	A. Gaetner/J. Mayers	14–12 6–3 12–10
1962	R. Mark/J. Mayers	G. Koenig/E. W. Sturgess	4–6 6–2 6–3 6–2
1963	G. L. Forbes/A. Segal	W. P. Bungert/W. Stuck	6–3 15–17 6–3 9–7
1964	K. Diepram/E. C. Drysdale	G. L. Forbes/A. Segal	6–3 6–4 6–4
1965	K. Diepram/F. D. McMillan	E. C. Drysdale/W. Stuck	10–8 6–4 1–6 6–2
1966	R. S. Emerson/F. S. Stolle	G. L. Forbes/A. Segal	6–3 3–6 6–3 7–5
1967	R. A. J. Hewitt/F. D. McMillan	W. W. Bowrey/O. K. Davidson	6–1 6–4 6–4
1968	T. S. Okker/M. C. Riessen	R. A. J. Hewitt/F. D. McMillan	6–2 6–3 3–6 4–6 6–3
1969	R. A. Gonzales/R. J. Moore	R. A. J. Hewitt/F. D. McMillan	6–3 4–6 6–1 6–3
1970	R. A. J. Hewitt/F. D. McMillan	E. C. Drysdale/R. Taylor	6–3 6–3 6–2
1971	K. R. Rosewall/F. S. Stolle	R. A. J. Hewitt/F. D. McMillan	5–7 6–2 6–1 6–2
1972	R. A. J. Hewitt/F. D. McMillan	G. Goven/R. J. Moore	6–2 6–2 6–4
1973	A. R. Ashe/T. S. Okker	L. A. Hoad/R. R. Maud	6–2 4–6 6–2 6–4
1974	R. A. J. Hewitt/F. D. McMillan	T. S. Okker/M. C. Riessen	7–6 6–4 6–3
1975	R. A. J. Hewitt/F. D. McMillan	K. Meiler/C. Pasarell	7–5 6–4
1976	B. E. Gottfried/S. E. Stewart	J. Gisbert/S. R. Smith	1–6 6–1 6–2 7–6
1977	R. C. Lutz/S. R. Smith	R. J. Moore/P. Fleming	6–3 7–5 6–7 7–6
1978	R. J. Moore/P. Fleming	R. A. J. Hewitt/F. D. McMillan	6–3 7–6
1979	R. A. J. Hewitt/F. D. McMillan	M. Cahill/C. J. Mottram	1–6 6–1 6–4
1980	R. C. Lutz/S. R. Smith	H. Gunthardt/P. McNamee	6–7 6–3 6–4
1981	T. Moor/J. Yuill	F. Buehning/R. Simpson	6–3 5–7 6–4 6–7 12–10
1982	B. E. Gottfried/F. D. McMillan	S. Glickstein/A. Pattison	6–2 6–2
1983	S. Meister/B. Teacher	A. Gomez/S. E. Stewart	6–7 7–6 6–2
1984	T. Delatte/F. Gonzalez	E. Teltscher/S. Meister	7–6 6–1
1985	C. Dowdeswell/C. Van Rensburg	A. Mansdorf/S. Perkis	3–6 7–6 6–4
1986	M. DePalmer/C. Van Rensburg	A. Gomez/S. E. Stewart	6–2 3–6 7–6
1987	K. Curren/D. Pate	E. Korita/B. Pearce	6–4 6–4

WOMEN'S DOUBLES

	CHAMPIONS	RUNNERS-UP	SCORE
1905	Mrs Auret/Mrs H. A. Kirby	Not available	
1906	Mrs Stevenson/Mrs G. Washington	Not available	
1907	Mrs H. A. Kirby/A. Tudhope	Not available	
1908	Mrs J. Reid/A. Tudhope	Mrs Middleton/Mrs G. Washington	2–6 6–2 7–5
1909	M. Kelly/Mrs G. Washington	Not available	
1910	Mrs J. Reid/A. Tudhope	Not available	
1911	O. Mathias/Mrs G. Washington	M. Kelly/A. Pringle	4–6 6–2 6–1

1912	M. Coles/A. Tudhope	Not available	
1913	M. Coles/A. Tudhope	Not available	
1914	Mrs Botting/O. Mathias	Not available	
1915–19	*Not held*		
1920	N. Edwards/Mrs C. K. Pitt	Not available	
1921	E. Kellar/W. Vesfeld	Mrs Ellis/A. Gradwell	7–5 6–3
1922	Mrs H. A. Kirby/Mrs C. L. Winslow	Not available	
1923	Mrs T. J. McJannett/Mrs McArthur	Mrs Beck/Mrs W. F. du Plessis	4–6 6–2 6–2
1924	Mrs Moor/Mrs I. E. Peacock	Not available	
1925	A. Foote/Mrs I. E. Peacock	Not available	
1926	Mrs E. C. Hall/A. de Smit	Mrs F. H. Lowe/Mrs I. E. Peacock	6–2 6–0
1927	W. Miller/A. Williams	Not available	
1928	Mrs T. J. McJannett/A. de Smit	Not available	
1929	Mrs T. J. McJannett/Mrs Tanner	Not available	
1930	D. Cole/R. D. Tapscott	Mrs V. Everett/A. Hopkins	6–4 6–4
1931	D. Cole/Mrs E. L. Heine	Not available	
1932	F. H. Lowe/Mrs E. Heine Miller	Mrs V. Everett/A. de Smit	6–1 6–3
1933	Mrs E. C. Hall/D. Kitson	Not available	
1934	D. Kitson/A. de Smit	Mrs F. H. Lowe/K. Rodd	9–7 5–7 6–4
1935	Mrs A. Allister/D. Kitson	Mrs C. J. J. Robbins/Mrs F. H. Lowe	6–3 6–3
1936	E. M. Dearman/N. M. Lyle	R. M. Hardwick/F. James	6–3 6–4
1937	Mrs E. Heine Miller/M. Morphew	Mrs F. H. Lowe/S. Piercey	9–7 6–3
1938	Mrs E. Heine Miller/M. Morphew	O. Craze/S. Piercey	6–4 6–4
1939	Mrs E. Heine Miller/M. Morphew	Not available	
1940	O. Craze/S. Piercey	Not available	
1941–45	*Not held*		
1946	Mrs M. Muller/Mrs O. Plessis	J. Austin/B. Nichols	6–2 4–6 8–6
1947	Mrs E. Heine Miller/J. Scott	M. Morphew/Mrs O. Plessis	4–6 6–3 6–2
1948	Mrs B. E. Hilton/Mrs M. Menzies	Mrs M. Muller/Mrs S. P. Summers	6–1 6–3
1949	J. Fitch/Mrs T. D. Long	Mrs B. Bartlett/M. Morphew	6–0 6–4
1950	S. J. Fry/D. J. Hart	Mrs S. P. Summers/Mrs E. Watermeyer	6–3 0–6 6–2
1951	Mrs M. Muller/Mrs H. Redick-Smith	Mrs B. Bartlett/Mrs E. Watermeyer	6–4 6–2
1952	S. J. Fry/D. J. Hart	Mrs H. Redick-Smith/Mrs S. P. Summers	7–5 7–5
1953	Mrs H. Redick-Smith/Mrs S. P. Summers	Mrs T. Hale/Mrs R. Stevens	11–13 6–3 6–3
1954	Mrs T. Hale/Mrs R. Stevens	Mrs H. Redick-Smith/Mrs J. Wipplinger	6–2 3–6 9–7
1955	Mrs B. Bartlett/G. Love	D. Kilian/L. van der Westhuizen	6–4 6–2
1956	Mrs B. Bartlett/G. Love	D. Kilian/L. van der Westhuizen	6–3 6–8 8–6
1957	Mrs B. Bartlett/G. Love	Mrs T. Hale/Mrs T. T. Fancutt	6–2 6–4
1958	S. Reynolds/R. Schuurman	S. J. Bloomer/L. Brough	4–6 8–6 6–3
1959	Mrs T. Hale/Mrs D. Shaw	S. Reynolds/R. Schurman	6–3 6–4
1960	S. Reynolds/R. Schuurman	Mrs A. Segal/Mrs B. Vukovich	13–11 7–9 6–1
1961	S. Reynolds/R. Schuurman	J. Lehane/Mrs M. Reitano	6–1 6–1
1962	M. Hunt/A. Van Zyl	J. Forbes/Mrs G. L. Forbes	7–5 6–8 6–4
1963	M. Hunt/A. Van Zyl	A. Betlehem/Mrs B. Vukovich	6–2 9–7
1964	M. E. Bueno/D. R. Hard	M. Hunt/A. Van Zyl	6–4 6–8 6–0
1965	Mrs L. E. G. Price/C. C. Truman	Mrs A. Segal/A. Van Zyl	6–3 6–2
1966	M. Smith/A. Van Zyl	Mrs C. Graebner/Mrs L. W. King	6–4 6–4
1967	R. Casals/Mrs L. W. King	M. E. Bueno/J. A. M. Tegart	4–6 6–1 6–3
1968	Mrs A. Du Ploy/P. M. Walkden	Mrs B. M. Court/S. V. Wade	0–6 6–4 7–5
1969	F. Durr/Mrs P. F. Jones	N. Richey/S. V. Wade	6–2 3–6 6–4
1970	R. Casals/Mrs L. W. King	K. Krantzcke/K. Melville	6–2 6–2
1971	Mrs B. M. Court/E. F. Goolagong	B. Kirk/L. Rossouw	6–3 6–2
1972	E. F. Goolagong/H. Gourlay	W. M. Shaw/Mrs G. Williams	6–1 6–4
1973	L. Boshoff/I. Kloss	C. M. Evert/S. V. Wade	7–6 2–6 6–1
1974	I. Kloss/K. Melville	Mrs B. M. Court/D. Fromholtz	6–2 6–3
1975	D. Boshoff/I. Kloss	L. Du Pont/S. A. Walsh	4–6 6–3 6–3
1976	L. Du Pont/V. Ziegenfuss	Y. Vermaak/Mrs E. Vlotman	6–1 6–4
1977	L. Boshoff/I. Kloss	B. Cuypers/M. Kruger	6–1 6–4
1978	L. Charles/T. Harford	A, McDade/E. Vlatman	6–2 6–3
1979	L. J. Charles/T. Harford	F. Durr/M. Kruger	6–1 6–3
1980	S. Rollinson/J. Mundel	L. Gordon/N. Gregory	6–3 6–2
1981	B. Mould/R. Uys	I. Kloss/Y. Vermaak	6–4 1–6 6–3
1982	*Not available*		
1983	*Not available*		
1984	R. Fairbank/B. Mould	S. Collins/A. Leand	6–1 6–2
1985	*Not available*		
1986	*Not available*		
1987	*Not available*		

MIXED DOUBLES

	CHAMPIONS	RUNNERS-UP	SCORE
1903	V. M. Lumsden/Miss M. E. Lumsden	Not available	
1904	H. A. Kirby/Mrs H. A. Kirby	Not available	
1905	M. Hathorn/Mrs H. A. Kirby	Not available	
1906	H. A. Kitson/Mrs H. A. Kirby	Not available	
1907	H. A. Kitson/Mrs H. A. Kirby	Not available	
1908	V. R. Gauntlett/Mrs J. Reid	H. A. Kitson/Miss M. Kelly	7–5 6–2
1909	A. Rowan/Miss M. Kelly	Not available	
1910	H. A. Kitson/Mrs H. A. Kirby	Not available	
1911	H. A. Kitson/Miss O. Mathias	S. L. Taylor-Taswell/Miss Wells	6–2 6–4
1912	F. E. Cochran/Miss O. Mathias	Not available	
1913	F. E. Cochran/Mrs G. Washington	Not available	
1914	C. L. Winslow/Miss O. Mathias	Not available	
1915–19	*Not held*		
1920	C. L. Winslow/Mrs C. L. Winslow	Not available	
1921	L. B. Raymond/Miss N. Edwards	R. Le Suer/Miss W. Versfeld	6–1 6–1
1922	G. Eaglestone/Miss Parker	Not available	
1923	I. J. Richardson/Mrs Moor	R. Le Suer/Mrs Beck	6–8 6–1 6–3
1924	L. B. Raymond/Miss A. Foote	Not available	
1925	V. G. Kirby/Mrs I. E. Peacock	Not available	
1926	I. J. Richardson/Mrs V. Everett	J. Haywood/Mrs I. E. Peacock	6–4 6–2
1927	I. J. Richardson/Mrs V. Everett	Not available	
1928	G. Eaglestone/Miss A. de Smit	Not availble	
1929	M. J. Connor/Miss Stone	Not available	
1930	N. G. Farquharson/Miss E. L. Heine	L. B. Raymond/Mrs V. Everett	0–6 6–2 6–2
1931	F. H. Lowe/Miss W. Miller	N. G. Farquharson/Miss E. L. Heine	6–4 6–2
1932	V. G. Kirby/Miss A. de Smit	G. Eaglestone/Mrs E. Heine Miller	8–6 7–9 6–3
1933	R. J. Malcolm/Miss D. Cole	F. H. Lowe/Mrs F. H. Lowe	3–6 7–5 6–3
1934	N. G. Farquharson/Miss A. de Smit	J. Condon/Mrs F. H. Lowe	6–1 2–6 6–1
1935	F. H. Lowe/Mrs F. H. Lowe	J. Hendrie/Miss K. Rodd	6–3 6–3
1936	N. G. Farquharson/Miss W. Miller	V. G. Kirby/Mrs A. Allister	6–3 6–3
1937	N. G. Farquharson/Miss W. Miller	V. G. Kirby/Mrs V. Everett	6–3 8–6
1938	N. G. Farquharson/Miss W. Miller	V. G. Kirby/Miss M. Morphew	7–9 8–6 6–3
1939	N. G. Farquharson/Miss W. Miller	Not available	
1940	E. W. Sturgess/Miss S. Piercey	Not available	
1941–45	*Not held*		
1946	E. W. Sturgess/Mrs S. P. Summers	N. G. Farquharson/Mrs E. Heine Miller	2–6 6–4 10–8
1947	E. W. Sturgess/Mrs S. P. Summers	E. Fanin/Mrs M. Muller	6–4 6–3
1948	E. W. Sturgess/Mrs S. P. Summers	N. G. Farquharson/Mrs E. Heine Miller	6–4 6–1
1949	G. E. Brown/Miss J. Fitch	E. W. Sturgess/Mrs S. P. Summers	6–0 7–5
1950	E. V. Seixas/Miss D. J. Hart	E. W. Sturgess/Mrs S. P. Summers	6–3 4–6 6–3
1951	E. W. Sturgess/Mrs S. P. Summers	N. Cockburn/Mrs B. Bartlett	6–4 6–3
1952	D. Candy/Mrs N. Bolton	B. M. Woodroffe/Mrs T. Hale	6–2 6–3
1953	E. W. Sturgess/Mrs S. P. Summers	B. M. Woodroffe/Mrs T. Hale	2–6 6–3 6–4
1954	W. R. Seymour/Mrs H. Redick-Smith	A. Segal/Mrs J. Wipplinger	w.o.
1955	W. R. Seymour/Mrs H. Redick-Smith	B. M. Woodroffe/D. Kilian	6–4 6–4
1956	J. Hurry/Miss G. Love	S. Davidson/Miss P. E. Ward	1–6 7–5 6–3
1957	G. L. Forbes/Miss J. Forbes	O. Williams/Miss S. Reynolds	10–8 6–3
1958	G. L. Forbes/Miss J. Forbes	B. M. Woodroffe/Mrs T. Hale	6–2 3–6 6–3
1959	G. L. Forbes/Miss J. Forbes	B. Farrer/Mrs B. Bartlett	6–4 7–5
1960	R. N. Howe/Mrs B. Vukovich	A. Gaetner/Miss S. Reynolds	6–3 6–3
1961	R. Weedon/Miss M. Hunt	A. Gaetner/Miss R. Schuurman	4–6 6–0 6–1
1962	N. Pietrangeli/Mrs L. E. G. Price	B. M. Woodroffe/Mrs T. Hale	6–3 6–3
1963	G. L. Forbes/Miss J. Forbes	D. Phillips/Miss I. Frohling	6–2 7–5
1964	R. Mark/Miss D. R. Hard	F. D. McMillan/Miss M. Hunt	3–6 6–4 6–4
1965	F. D. McMillan/Mrs L. E. G. Price	D. Dell/Miss F. Durr	8–6 9–7
1966	F. S. Stolle/Miss M. Smith	F. D. McMillan/Mrs L. W. King	6–4 5–7 6–4
1967	O. K. Davidson/Mrs L. W. King	K. N. Fletcher/Miss M. E. Bueno	6–1 6–3
1968	M. C. Riessen/Miss P. M. Walkden	R. A. J. Hewitt/Mrs B. M. Court	6–8 6–4 6–4
1969	T. S. Okker/Mrs A. Du Ploy	R. R. Maud/Miss S. V. Wade	8–6 5–7 6–4
1970	M. C. Riessen/Mrs B. M. Court	F. D. McMillan/Miss P. M. Walkden	7–5 3–6 7–5
1971	F. S. Stolle/Mrs B. M. Court	R. O. Ruffels/Mrs P. M. Walkden	6–3 7–6
1972	M. F. Mulligan/Miss S. V. Wade	F. D. McMillan/Mrs Q. Pretorius	6–0 4–6 6–4
1973	J. Fassbender/Miss E. F. Goolagong	B. Mitton/Miss I. Kloss	6–3 6–2
1974	M. Riessen/Mrs B. M. Court	J. Fassbender/Miss I. Kloss	6–0 6–2
1975	B. Bertram/Miss I. Kloss	S. Cornchon/Miss J. Russell	div'd
1976	R. A. J. Hewitt/Miss B. Nagelsen	D. Joubert/Mrs A. Du Ploy	6–2 7–6
1977	C. Dowdeswell/Miss L. Boshoff	S. E. Stewart/Miss I. Kloss	6–4 4–6 7–5

1978	B. Mitton/Miss B. Cuypers	D. Joubert/Mrs A. Du Plooy	6–3 6–2
1979	S. Carnahan/Miss M. Depalmer	S. Van Der Merwe/Miss Y. Vermaak	div'd
	Event ceased		

THE *DAVIS CUP*

The International Men's Team Championship of the World was initiated in 1900 when the British Isles, then comprising Great Britain and Ireland, challenged the United States for the trophy presented by Dwight F. Davis. The competition was enlarged in 1904 when Belgium and France took part. Each tie has comprised two players engaged in reverse singles plus a doubles match with the best of five sets throughout.

From 1900 to 1971 the Champion Nation stood out until challenged by the winner of a knock-out competition between the challenging nations and had the choice of venue. The format was changed in 1972 with all nations taking part in a knock-out event. The format was amended in 1981, when the competition became sponsored by NEC. The Champion Nation was the winner of the World Group of 16 nations. Other nations competed in four zonal groups, two European, an American and an Eastern Zone, with the four winners earning promotion to the World Group. The four bottom nations of the top group, as decided by a relegation round, fell back to the zonal competition.

Between 1900 and 1984 the total number of participating nations was 72, including Hawaii and Estonia which have ceased to exist as distinct tennis nations.

CHALLENGE ROUNDS (In playing order)

1900 USA d. British Isles 3–0, Boston: M. D. Whitman d. A. W. Gore 6–1 6–3 6–2; D. F. Davis d. E. D. Black 4–6 6–2 6–4 6–4; Davis/H. Ward d. Black/H. Roper Barrett 6–4 6–4 6–4; Davis div'd with Gore 9–7 9–9.

1901 *Not held*

1902 USA d. British Isles 3–2, Brooklyn, New York: W. A. Larned lost to R. F. Doherty 6–2 6–3 3–6 4–6 4–6; M. D. Whitman d. J. Pim 6–1 6–1 1–6 6–0; Larned d. Pim 6–3 6–2 6–3; Whitman d. R. F. Doherty 6–1 7–5 6–4; D. F. Davis/H. Ward lost to R. F./H. L. Doherty 6–3 8–10 3–6 4–6.

1903 British Isles d. USA 4–1, Boston: H. L. Doherty d. R. D. Wrenn 6–0 6–3 6–4; R. F. Doherty lost to W. A. Larned ret'd; R. F./H. L. Doherty d. R. D./G. L. Wrenn 7–5 9–7 2–6 6–3; H. L. Doherty d. Larned 6–3 6–8 6–0 2–6 7–5; R. F. Doherty d. R. D. Wrenn 6–4 3–6 6–3 6–8 6–4.

1904 British Isles d. Belgium 5–0, Wimbledon: H. L. Doherty d. P. de Borman 6–4 6–1 6–1; F. L. Riseley d. W. Lemaire 6–1 6–4 6–2; R. F./H. L. Doherty d. de Borman/Lemaire 6–0 6–1 6–3; H. L. Doherty w.o. Lemaire; Riseley d. de Borman 4–6 6–2 8–6 7–5.

1905 British Isles d. USA 5–0, Wimbledon: H. L. Doherty d. H. Ward 7–9 4–6 6–1 6–2 6–0; S. H. Smith d. W. A. Larned 6–4 6–4 5–7 6–4; R. F./H. L. Doherty d. Ward/B. Wright 8–10 6–2 6–2 4–6 8–6; Smith d. W. J. Clothier 4–6 6–1 6–4 6–3; H. L. Doherty d. Larned 6–4 2–6 6–8 6–4 6–2.

1906 British Isles d. USA 5–0, Wimbledon: S. H. Smith d. R. D. Little 6–4 6–4 6–1; H. L. Doherty d. H. Ward 6–2 8–6 6–3; R. F./H. L. Doherty d. Little/Ward 3–6 11–9 9–7 6–1; Smith d. Ward 6–1 6–0 6–4; H. L. Doherty d. Little 3–6 6–3 6–8 6–1 6–3.

1907 Australasia d. British Isles 3–2, Wimbledon: N. E. Brookes d. A. W. Gore 7–5 6–1 7–5; A. F. Wilding d. H. Roper Barrett 1–6 6–4 6–3 7–5; Brookes/Wilding lost to Gore/Roper Barrett 6–3 6–4 5–7 2–6 11–13; Wilding lost to Gore 6–3 3–6 5–7 2–6; Brookes d. Roper Barrett 6–2 6–0 6–3.

1908 Australasia d. USA 3–2, Melbourne: N. E. Brookes d. F. B. Alexander 5–7 9–7 6–2 4–6 6–3; A. F. Wilding lost to B. Wright 6–3 5–7 3–6 1–6; Brookes/Wilding d. Alexander/Wright 6–4 6–2 5–7 1–6 6–4; Brookes lost to Wright 6–0 6–3 5–7 2–6 10–12; Wilding d. Alexander 6–3 6–4 6–1.

1909 Australasia d. USA 5–0, Sydney: N. E. Brookes d. M. E. McLoughlin 6–2 6–2 6–4; A. F. Wilding d. M. H. Long 6–2 7–5 6–1; Brookes/Wilding d. Long/McLoughlin 12–10 9–7 6–3; Brookes d. Long 6–4 7–5 8–6; Wilding d. McLoughlin 3–6 8–6 6–2 6–3.

1910 *Not held*

1911 Australasia d. USA 5–0, Christchurch, NZ: N. E. Brookes d. B. Wright 6–4 2–6 6–3 6–3; R. W. Heath d. W. A. Larned 2–6 6–1 7–5 6–2; Brookes/A. W. Dunlop d. Wright/M. E. McLoughlin 6–4 5–7 7–5 6–4; Brookes d. McLoughlin 6–4 3–6 4–6 6–3 6–4; Heath w.o. Wright.

1912 British Isles d. Australasia 3–2, Melbourne: J. C. Parke d. N. E. Brookes 8–6 6–3 5–7 6–2; C. P. Dixon d. R. W. Heath 5–7 6–4 6–4 6–4; A. E. Beamish/Parke lost to Brookes/A. W. Dunlop 4–6 1–6 5–7; Dixon lost to Brookes 2–6 4–6 4–6; Parke d. Heath 6–2 6–4 6–4.

1913 USA d. British Isles 3–2, Wimbledon: M. E. McLoughlin lost to J. C. Parke 10–8 5–7 4–6 6–1 5–7; R. N. Williams d. C. P. Dixon 8–6 3–6 6–2 1–6 7–5; H. Hackett/McLoughlin d. Dixon/H. Roper Barrett 5–7 6–1 2–6 7–5 6–4; McLoughlin d. Dixon 8–6 6–3 6–2; Williams lost to Parke 2–6 7–5 7–5 4–6 2–6.

1914 Australasia d. USA 3–2, Forest Hills, NY: A. F. Wilding d. R. N. Williams 7–5 6–2 6–3; N. E. Brookes lost to M. E. McLoughlin 15–17 3–6 3–6; Brookes/Wilding d. T. C. Bundy/McLoughlin 6–3 8–6 9–7; Brookes d. Williams 6–1 6–2 8–10 6–3; Wilding lost to McLoughlin 2–6 3–6 6–2 2–6.

1915–18 *Not held*

1919 Australasia d. British Isles 4–1, Sydney: G. L. Patterson d. A. H. Lowe 6–4 6–3 2–6 6–3; J. O. Anderson lost to A. R. F. Kingscote 5–7 2–6 4–6; N. E. Brookes/Patterson d. A. E. Beamish/Kingscote 6–0 6–0 6–2; Patterson d. Kingscote 6–4 6–4 8–6; Anderson d. Lowe 6–4 5–7 6–3 4–6 12–10.

1920 USA d. Australasia 5–0, Auckland: W. T. Tilden d. N. E. Brookes 10–8 6–4 1–6 6–4; W. M. Johnston d. G. L.

Patterson 6–3 6–1 6–1; Johnston/Tilden d. Brookes/Patterson 4–6 6–4 6–0 6–4; Johnston d. Brookes 5–7 7–5 6–3 6–3; Tilden d. Patterson 5–7 6–2 6–3 6–3.

1921 ***USA d. Japan 5–0, Forest Hills, NY:*** W. M. Johnston d. I. Kumagae 6–2 6–4 6–2; W. T. Tilden d. Z. Schimidzu 5–7 4–6 7–5 6–2 6–1; W. Washburn/R. N. Williams d. Kumagae/Shimidzu 6–2 7–5 4–6 7–5; Tilden d. Kumagae 9–7 6–4 6–1; Johnston d. Shimidzu 6–3 5–7 6–2 6–4.

1922 ***USA d. Australasia 4–1, Forest Hills, NY:*** W. T. Tilden d. G. L. Patterson 7–5 10–8 6–0; W. M. Johnston d. J. O. Anderson 6–1 6–2 6–3; V. Richards/Tilden lost to P. O'Hara Wood/Patterson 4–6 0–6 3–6; Johnston d. Patterson 6–2 6–2 6–1; Tilden d. Anderson 6–4 5–7 3–6 6–4 6–2.

1923 ***USA d. Australia 4–1, Forest Hills, NY:*** W. M. Johnston lost to J. O. Anderson 6–4 2–6 6–2 5–7 2–6; W. T. Tilden d. J. B. Hawkes 6–4 6–2 6–1; Tilden/R. N. Williams d. Anderson/Hawkes 17–15 11–13 2–6 6–3 6–2; Johnston d. Hawkes 6–0 6–2 6–1; Tilden d. Anderson 6–2 6–3 1–6 7–5.

1924 ***USA d. Australia 5–0, Philadelphia:*** W. T. Tilden d. G. L. Patterson 6–4 6–2 6–3; V. Richards d. P. O'Hara Wood 6–3 6–2 6–4; W. M. Johnston/Tilden d. O'Hara Wood/Patterson 5–7 6–3 6–4 6–1; Tilden d. O'Hara Wood 6–2 6–1 6–1; Richards d. Patterson 6–3 7–5 6–4.

1925 ***USA d. France 5–0, Philadelphia:*** W. T. Tilden d. J. Borotra 4–6 6–0 2–6 9–7 6–4; W. M. Johnston d. R. Lacoste 6–1 6–1 6–8 6–3; V. Richards/R. N. Williams d. Borotra/Lacoste 6–4 6–4 6–3; Tilden d. Lacoste 3–6 10–12 8–6 7–5 6–2; Johnston d. Borotra 6–1 6–4 6–0.

1926 ***USA d. France 4–1, Philadelphia:*** W. M. Johnston d. R. Lacoste 6–0 6–4 0–6 6–0; W. T. Tilden d. J. Borotra 6–2 6–3 6–3; V. Richards/R. N. Williams d. J. Brugnon/H. Cochet 6–4 6–4 6–2; Johnston d. Borotra 8–6 6–4 9–7; Tilden lost to Lacoste 6–4 4–6 6–8 6–8.

1927 ***France d. USA 3–2, Philadelphia:*** R. Lacoste d. W. M. Johnston 6–3 6–2 6–2; H. Cochet lost to W. T. Tilden 4–6 6–2 2–6 6–8; J. Borotra/J. Brugnon lost to F. Hunter/Tilden 6–3 3–6 3–6 6–4 0–6; Lacoste d. Tilden 6–4 4–6 6–3 6–3; Cochet d. Johnston 6–4 4–6 6–2 6–4.

1928 ***France d. USA 4–1, Paris:*** R. Lacoste lost to W. T. Tilden 6–1 4–6 4–6 6–2 3–6; H. Cochet d. J. Hennessey 5–7 9–7 6–3 6–0; J. Borotra/Cochet d. F. Hunter/Tilden 6–4 6–8 7–5 4–6 6–2; Lacoste d. Hennessey 4–6 6–1 7–5 6–3; Cochet d. Tilden 9–7 8–6 6–4.

1929 ***France d. USA 3–2, Paris:*** H. Cochet d. W. T. Tilden 6–3 6–1 6–2; J. Borotra d. G. M. Lott 6–1 3–6 6–4 7–5; Borotra/Cochet lost to W. Allison/J. Van Ryn 1–6 6–8 4–6; Cochet d. Lott 6–1 3–6 6–0 6–3; Borotra lost to Tilden 6–4 1–6 4–6 5–7.

1930 ***France d. USA 4–1, Paris:*** J. Borotra lost to W. T. Tilden 6–2 5–7 4–6 5–7; H. Cochet d. G. M. Lott 6–4 6–2 6–2; J. Brugnon/Cochet d. W. Allison/J. Van Ryn 6–3 7–5 1–6 6–2; Borotra d. Lott 5–7 6–3 2–6 6–2 8–6; Cochet d. Tilden 4–6 6–3 6–1 7–5.

1931 ***France d. Great Britain 3–2, Paris:*** H. Cochet d. H. W. Austin 3–6 11–9 6–2 6–4; J. Borotra lost to F. J. Perry 6–4 8–10 0–6 6–4 4–6; J. Brugnon/Cochet d. G. P Hughes/C. H. Kingsley 6–1 5–7 6–3 8–6; Cochet d. Perry 6–4 1–6 9–7 6–3; Borotra lost to Austin 5–7 3–6 6–3 5–7.

1932 ***France d. USA 3–2, Paris:*** H. Cochet d. W. Allison 5–7 7–5 3–6 7–5 6–2; J. Borotra d. H. E. Vines 6–4 6–2 2–6 6–4; J. Brugnon/Cochet lost to Allison/J. Van Ryn 3–6 13–11 5–7 6–4 4–6; Borotra d. Allison 1–6 3–6 6–4 6–2 7–5; Cochet lost to Vines 6–4 6–0 5–7 6–8 2–6.

1933 ***Great Britain d. France 3–2, Paris:*** H. W. Austin d. A. Merlin 6–3 6–4 6–0; F. J. Perry d. H. Cochet 8–10 6–4 8–6 3–6 6–1; G. P. Hughes/H. G. N. Lee lost to J. Borotra/J. Brugnon 3–6 6–8 2–6; Austin lost to Cochet 7–5 4–6 6–4 4–6 4–6; Perry d. Merlin 4–6 8–6 6–2 7–5.

1934 ***Great Britain d. USA 4–1, Wimbledon:*** F. J. Perry d. S. B. Wood 6–1 4–6 5–7 6–0 6–3; H. W. Austin d. F. X. Shields 6–4 6–4 6–1; G. P. Hughes/H. G. N. Lee lost to G. M. Lott/L. Stoefen 5–7 0–6 6–4 7–9; Perry d. Shields 6–4 4–6 6–2 15–13; Austin d. Wood 6–4 6–0 6–8 6–3.

1935 ***Great Britain d. USA 5–0, Wimbledon:*** F. J. Perry d. J. D. Budge 6–0 6–8 6–3 6–4; H. W. Austin d. W. Allison 6–2 2–6 4–6 6–3 7–5; G. P. Hughes/C. R. D. Tuckey d. Allison/J. Van Ryn 6–2 1–6 6–8 6–3 6–3; Perry d. Allison 4–6 6–4 7–5 6–3; Austin d. Budge 6–2 6–4 6–8 7–5.

1936 ***Great Britain d. Australia 3–2, Wimbledon:*** H. W. Austin d. J. H. Crawford 4–6 6–3 6–1 6–1; F. J. Perry d. A. K. Quist 6–1 4–6 7–5 6–2; G. P. Hughes/C. R. D. Tuckey lost to Crawford/Quist 4–6 6–2 5–7 8–10; Austin lost to Quist 4–6 6–3 5–7 2–6; Perry d. Crawford 6–2 6–3 6–3.

1937 ***USA d. Great Britain 4–1, Wimbledon:*** F. A. Parker lost to H. W. Austin 3–6 2–6 5–7; J. D. Budge d. C. E. Hare 15–13 6–1 6–2; Budge/G. Mako d. C. R. D. Tuckey/F. H. D. Wilde 6–3 7–5 7–9 12–10; Parker d. Hare 6–2 6–4 6–2; Budge d. Austin 8–6 3–6 6–4 6–3.

1938 ***USA d. Australia 3–2, Philadelphia:*** R. L. Riggs d. A. K. Quist 4–6 6–0 8–6 6–1; J. D. Budge d. J. E. Bromwich 6–2 6–3 4–6 7–5; Budge/G. Mako lost to Bromwich/Quist 6–0 3–6 4–6 2–6; Budge d. Quist 8–6 6–1 6–2; Riggs lost to Bromwich 4–6 6–4 0–6 2–6.

1939 ***Australia d. USA 3–2, Philadelphia:*** J. E. Bromwich lost to R. L. Riggs 4–6 0–6 5–7; A. K. Quist lost to F. A. Parker 3–6 6–2 4–6 6–1 5–7; Bromwich/Quist d. J. R. Hunt/J. Kramer 5–7 6–2 7–5 6–2; Quist d. Riggs 6–1 6–4 3–6 3–6 6–4; Bromwich d. Parker 6–0 6–3 6–1.

1940–45 *Not held*

1946 ***USA d. Australia 5–0, Melbourne:*** F. R. Schroeder d. J. E. Bromwich 3–6 6–1 6–2 0–6 6–3; J. Kramer d. D. Pails 8–6 6–2 9–7; Kramer/Schroeder d. Bromwich/A. K. Quist 6–2 7–5 6–4; Kramer d. Bromwich 8–6 6–4 6–4; G. Mulloy d. Pails 6–3 6–3 6–4.

1947 ***USA d. Australia 4–1, Forest Hills, NY:*** J. Kramer d. D. Pails 6–2 6–1 6–2; F. R. Schroeder d. J. E. Bromwich 6–4 5–7 6–3 6–3; Kramer/Schroeder lost to Bromwich/C. F. Long 4–6 6–2 2–6 4–6; Schroeder d. Pails 6–3 8–6 4–6 9–11 10–8; Kramer d. Bromwich 6–3 6–2 6–2.

1948 ***USA d. Australia 5–0, Forest Hills, NY:*** F. A. Parker d. O. W. Sidwell 6–4 6–4 6–4; F. R. Schroeder d. A. K. Quist 6–3 4–6 6–0 6–0; G. Mulloy/W. F. Talbert d. C. F. Long/Sidwell 8–6 9–7 2–6 7–5; Parker d. Quist 6–2 6–2 6–3; Schroeder d. Sidwell 6–2 6–1 6–1.

1949 ***USA d. Australia 4–1, Forest Hills, NY:*** F. R. Schroeder d. O. W. Sidwell 6–1 5–7 4–6 6–2 6–3; R. A. Gonzales d. F. A. Sedgman 8–6 6–4 9–7; G. Mulloy/W. F. Talbert lost to J. E. Bromwich/Sidwell 6–3 6–4 8–10 7–9 7–9; Schroeder d. Sedgman 6–4 6–3 6–3; Gonzales d. Sidwell 6–1 6–3 6–3.

1950 ***Australia d. USA 4–1, Forest Hills, NY:*** F. A. Sedgman d. T. Brown 6–0 8–6 9–7; K. McGregor d. F. R. Schroeder 13–11 6–3 6–4; J. E. Bromwich/Sedgman d. G. Mulloy/Schroeder 4–6 6–4 6–2 4–6 6–4; Sedgman d. Schroeder 6–2 6–2 6–2; McGregor lost to Brown 11–9 10–8 9–11 1–6 4–6.

1951 ***Australia d. USA 3–2, Sydney:*** M. G. Rose lost to E. V. Seixas 3–6 4–6 7–9; F. A. Sedgman d. F. R. Schroeder 6–4 6–3 4–6 6–4; K. McGregor/Sedgman d. Schroeder/M. A. Trabert 6–2 9–7 6–3; Rose lost to Schroeder 4–6 11–13 5–7; Sedgman d. Seixas 6–4 6–2 6–2.

1952 ***Australia d. USA 4–1, Adelaide:*** F. A. Sedgman d. E. V. Seixas 6–3 6–4 6–3; K. McGregor d. M. A. Trabert 11–9 6–4 6–1; McGregor/Sedgman d. Seixas/Trabert 6–3 6–4 1–6 6–3; Sedgman d. Trabert 7–5 6–4 10–8; McGregor lost to Seixas 3–6 6–8 8–6 3–6.

1953 ***Australia d. USA 3–2, Melbourne:*** L. A. Hoad d. E. V. Seixas 6–4 6–2 6–3; K. R. Rosewall lost to M. A. Trabert 3–6 4–6 4–6; R. Hartwig/Hoad lost to Seixas/Trabert 2–6 4–6 4–6; Hoad d. Trabert 13–11 6–3 2–6 3–6 7–5; Rosewall d. Seixas 6–2 2–6 6–3 6–4.

1954 ***USA d. Australia 3–2, Sydney:*** M. A. Trabert d. L. A. Hoad 6–4 2–6 12–10 6–3; E. V. Seixas d. K. R. Rosewall 8–6 6–8 6–4 6–3; Seixas/Trabert d. Hoad/Rosewall 6–2 4–6 6–2 10–8; Trabert lost to Rosewall 7–9 5–7 3–6; Seixas lost to R. Hartwig 6–4 3–6 2–6 3–6.

1955 ***Australia d. USA 5–0, Forest Hills, NY:*** K. R. Rosewall d. E. V. Seixas 6–3 10–8 4–6 6–2; L. A. Hoad d. M. A. Trabert 4–6 6–3 6–3 8–6; R. Hartwig/Hoad d. Seixas/Trabert 12–14 6–4 6–3 3–6 7–5; Rosewall d. H. Richardson 6–4 3–6 6–1 6–4; Hoad d. Seixas 7–9 6–1 6–4 6–4.

1956 ***Australia d. USA 5–0, Adelaide:*** L. A. Hoad d. H. Flam 6–2 6–3 6–3; K. R. Rosewall d. E. V. Seixas 6–2 7–5 6–3; Hoad/Rosewall d. S. Giammalva/Seixas 1–6 6–1 7–5 6–4; Hoad d. Seixas 6–2 7–5 6–3; Rosewall d. Giammalva 4–6 6–1 8–6 7–5.

1957 ***Australia d. USA 3–2, Melbourne:*** A. J. Cooper d. E. V. Seixas 3–6 7–5 6–1 1–6 6–3; M. J. Anderson d. B. MacKay 6–3 7–5 3–6 7–9 6–3; Anderson/M. G. Rose d. MacKay/Seixas 6–4 6–4 8–6; Cooper lost to MacKay 4–6 6–1 6–4 4–6 3–6; Anderson lost to Seixas 3–6 6–4 3–6 6–0 11–13.

1958 ***USA d. Australia 3–2, Brisbane:*** A. Olmedo d. M. J. Anderson 8–6 2–6 9–7 8–6; B. MacKay lost to A. J. Cooper 6–4 3–6 2–6 4–6; Olmedo/H. Richardson d. Anderson/N. A. Fraser 10–12 3–6 16–14 6–3 7–5; Olmedo d. Cooper 6–3 4–6 6–4 8–6; MacKay lost to Anderson 5–7 11–13 9–11.

1959 ***Australia d. USA 3–2, Forest Hills, NY:*** N. A. Fraser d. A. Olmedo 8–6 6–8 6–4 8–6; R. G. Laver lost to B. MacKay 5–7 4–6 1–6; R. S. Emerson/Fraser d. E. Buchholz/Olmedo 7–5 7–5 6–4; Laver lost to Olmedo 7–9 6–4 8–10 10–12; Fraser d. MacKay 8–6 3–6 6–2 6–4.

1960 ***Australia d. Italy 4–1, Sydney:*** N. A. Fraser d. O. Sirola 4–6 6–3 6–3 6–3; R. G. Laver d. N. Pietrangeli 8–6 6–4 6–3; R. S. Emerson/Fraser d. Pietrangeli/Sirola 10–8 5–7 6–3 6–4; Laver d. Sirola 9–7 6–2 6–3; Fraser lost to Pietrangeli 9–11 3–6 6–1 2–6.

1961 ***Australia d. Italy 5–0, Melbourne:*** R. S. Emerson d. N. Pietrangeli 8–6 6–4 6–0; R. G. Laver d. O. Sirola 6–1 6–4 6–3; Emerson/N. A. Fraser d. Pietrangeli/Sirola 6–2 6–3 6–4; Emerson d. Sirola 6–2 6–3 4–6 6–2; Laver d. Pietrangeli 6–3 3–6 4–6 6–3 8–6.

1962 ***Australia d. Mexico 5–0, Brisbane:*** N. A. Fraser d. A. Palafox 7–9 6–3 6–4 11–9; R. G. Laver d. R. H. Osuna 6–2 6–1 7–5; R. S. Emerson/Laver d. Osuna/Palafox 7–5 6–2 6–4; Fraser d. Osuna 3–6 11–9 6–1 3–6 6–4; Laver d. Palafox 6–1 4–6 6–4 8–6.

1963 ***USA d. Australia 3–2, Adelaide:*** R. D. Ralston d. J. D. Newcombe 6–4 6–1 3–6 4–6 7–5; C. R. McKinley lost to R. S. Emerson 3–6 6–3 5–7 5–7; McKinley/Ralston d. Emerson/N. A. Fraser 6–3 4–6 11–9 11–9; Ralston lost to Emerson 2–6 3–6 6–3 2–6; McKinley d. Newcombe 10–12 6–2 9–7 6–2.

1964 ***Australia d. USA 3–2, Cleveland, Ohio:*** F. S. Stolle lost to C. R. McKinley 1–6 7–9 6–4 2–6; R. S. Emerson d. R. D. Ralston 6–3 6–1 6–3; Emerson/Stolle lost to McKinley/Ralston 4–6 6–4 6–4 3–6 4–6; Stolle d. Ralston 7–5 6–3 3–6 9–11 6–4; Emerson d. McKinley 3–6 6–2 6–4 6–4.

1965 ***Australia d. Spain 4–1, Sydney:*** F. S. Stolle d. M. Santana 10–12 3–6 6–1 6–4 7–5; R. S. Emerson d. J. Gisbert 6–3 6–2 6–2; J. D. Newcombe/A. D. Roche d. J. L. Arilla/Santana 6–3 4–6 7–5 6–2; Emerson lost to Santana 6–2 3–6 4–6 13–15; Stolle d. Gisbert 6–2 6–4 8–6.

1966 ***Australia d. India 4–1, Melbourne:*** F. S. Stolle d. R. Krishnan 6–3 6–2 6–4; R. S. Emerson d. J. Mukerjea 7–5 6–4 6–2; J. D. Newcombe/A. D. Roche lost to Krishnan/Mukerjea 6–4 5–7 4–6 4–6; Emerson d. Krishnan 6–0 6–2 10–8; Stolle d. Mukerjea 7–5 6–8 6–3 5–7 6–3.

1967 ***Australia d. Spain 4–1, Brisbane:*** R. S. Emerson d. M. Santana 6–4 6–1 6–1; J. D. Newcombe d. M. Orantes 6–3 6–3 6–2; Newcombe/A. D. Roche d. Orantes/Santana 6–4 6–4 6–4; Newcombe lost to Santana 5–7 4–6 2–6; Emerson d. Orantes 6–1 6–1 2–6 6–4.

1968 ***USA d. Australia 4–1, Adelaide:*** C. Graebner d. W. W. Bowrey 8–10 6–4 8–6 3–6 6–1; A. R. Ashe d. R. O. Ruffels 6–8 7–5 6–3 6–3; R. C. Lutz/S. R. Smith d. J. G. Alexander/Ruffels 6–4 6–4 6–2; Graebner d. Ruffels 3–6 8–6 2–6 6–3 6–1; Ashe lost to Bowrey 6–2 3–6 9–11 6–8.

1969 ***USA d. Rumania 5–0, Cleveland, Ohio:*** A. R. Ashe d. I. Nastase 6–2 15–13 7–5; S. R. Smith d. I. Tiriac 6–8 6–3 5–7 6–4 6–4; R. C. Lutz/Smith d. Nastase/Tiriac 8–6 6–1 11–9; Smith d. Nastase 4–6 4–6 6–4 6–1 11–9; Ashe d. Tiriac 6–3 8–6 3–6 4–0 ret'd.

1970 ***USA d. West Germany 5–0, Cleveland, Ohio:*** A. R. Ashe d. W. Bungert 6–2 10–8 6–2; C. Richey d. C. Kuhnke 6–3 6–4 6–2; R. C. Lutz/S. R. Smith d. Bungert/Kuhnke 6–3 7–5 6–4; Richey d. Bungert 6–4 6–4 7–5; Ashe d. Kuhnke 6–8 10–12 9–7 13–11 6–4.

1971 ***USA d. Rumania 3–2, Charlotte, NC:*** S. R. Smith d. I. Nastase 7–5 6–3 6–1; F. A. Froehling d. I. Tiriac 3–6 1–6 6–1 6–3 8–6; Smith/E. Van Dillen lost to Nastase/Tiriac 5–7 4–6 8–6; Smith d. Tiriac 8–6 6–3 6–0; Froehling lost to Nastase 3–6 1–6 6–1 4–6.

Challenge Round abolished

FINAL ROUND SCORES

1972 ***USA d. Rumania 3–2, Bucharest:*** S. R. Smith d. I. Nastase 11–9 6–2 6–3; T. Gorman lost to I. Tiriac 6–4 6–2 4–6 3–6 2–6; Smith/E. Van Dillen d. Nastase/Tiriac 6–2 6–0 6–3; Smith d. Tiriac 4–6 6–2 6–4 2–6 6–0; Gorman lost to Nastase 1–6 2–6 7–5 8–10.

1973 Australia d. USA 5–0, Cleveland, Ohio (indoors): J. D. Newcombe d. S. R. Smith 6–1 3–6 6–3 3–6 6–4; R. G. Laver d. T. Gorman 8–10 8–6 6–8 6–3 6–1; Laver/Newcombe d. Smith/E. Van Dillen 6–1 6–2 6–4; Newcombe d. Gorman 6–2 6–1 6–3; Laver d. Smith 6–3 6–4 3–6 6–2.

1974 South Africa w.o. India

1975 Sweden d. Czechoslovakia 3–2, Stockholm (indoors): O. Bengtson lost to J. Kodes 4–6 6–2 5–7 4–6; B. Borg d. J. Hrebec 6–1 6–3 6–0; Bengtson/Borg d. Kodes/V. Zednik 6–4 6–4 6–4; Borg d. Kodes 6–4 6–2 6–2; Bengtson lost to Hrebec 6–1 3–6 1–6 4–6.

1976 Italy d. Chile 4–1, Santiago: C. Barazzutti d. J. Fillol 7–5 4–6 7–5 6–1; A. Panatta d. P. Cornejo 6–3 6–1 6–3; P. Bertolucci/Panatta d. Cornejo/Fillol 3–6 6–2 9–7 6–3; Panatta d. Fillol 8–6 6–4 3–6 10–8; A. Zugarelli lost to B. Prajoux 4–6 4–6 2–6.

1977 Australia d. Italy 3–1, Sydney: A. D. Roche d. A. Panatta 6–3 6–4 6–4; J. G. Alexander d. C. Barazzutti 6–2 8–6 4–6 6–2; Alexander/P. Dent lost to P. Bertolucci/Panatta 4–6 4–6 5–7; Alexander d. Panatta 6–4 4–6 2–6 8–6 11–9; Roche div'd with Barazzutti 12–12.

1978 USA d. Great Britain 4–1, Palm Springs, California: J. P. McEnroe d. J. M. Lloyd 6–1 6–2 6–2; B. E. Gottfried lost to C. J. Mottram 6–4 6–2 8–10 4–6 3–6; R. C. Lutz/S. R. Smith d. M. Cox/D. A. Lloyd 6–2 6–2 6–3; McEnroe d. Mottram 6–2 6–2 6–1; Gottfried d. J. M. Lloyd 6–1 6–2 6–4.

1979 USA d. Italy 5–0, San Francisco (indoors): V. Gerulaitis d. C. Barazzutti 6–3 3–2 ret'd; J. P. McEnroe d. A. Panatta 6–2 6–3 6–4; R. C. Lutz/S. R. Smith d. P. Bertolucci/Panatta 6–4 12–10 6–2; McEnroe d. A. Zugarelli 6–4 6–3 6–1; Gerulaitis d. Panatta 6–1 6–3 6–3.

1980 Czechoslovakia d. Italy 4–1, Prague (indoors): T. Smid d. A. Panatta 3–6 3–6 6–3 6–4 6–4; I. Lendl d. C. Barazzutti 4–6 6–1 6–1 6–2; Lendl/Smid d. P. Bertolucci/Panatta 3–6 6–3 3–6 6–3 6–4; Smid lost to Barazzutti 6–3 3–6 2–6; Lendl d. G. Ocleppo 6–3 6–3.

1981 USA d. Argentina 3–1, Cincinnati (indoors): J. P. McEnroe d. G. Vilas 6–3 6–2 6–2; R. Tanner lost to J. L. Clerc 5–7 3–6 6–8; P. Fleming/McEnroe d. Clerc/Vilas 6–3 4–6 6–4 4–6 11–9; McEnroe d. Clerc 7–5 5–7 6–3 3–6 6–3; Tanner div'd with Vilas 11–10.

1982 USA d. France 4–1, Grenoble (indoors): J. P. McEnroe d. Y. Noah 12–10 1–6 3–6 6–2 6–3; G. Mayer d. H. Leconte 6–2 6–2 7–9 6–4; P. Fleming/McEnroe d. Leconte/Noah 6–3 6–4 9–7; Mayer lost to Noah 1–6 0–6; McEnroe d. Leconte 6–2 6–3.

1983 Australia d. Sweden 3–2, Melbourne: P. Cash lost to M. Wilander 3–6 6–4 7–9 3–6; J. Fitzgerald d. J. Nystrom 6–4 6–2 4–6 6–4; M. R. Edmondson/P. McNamee d. A. Jarryd/H. Simonsson 6–4 6–4 6–2; Cash d. Nystrom 6–4 6–1 6–1; Fitzgerald lost to Wilander 8–6 0–6 1–6.

1984 Sweden d. USA 4–1, Gothenburg: M. Wilander d. J. S. Connors 6–1 6–3 6–3; H. Sundstrom d. J. P. McEnroe 13–11 6–4 6–3; S. Edberg/A. Jarryd d. P. Fleming/McEnroe 7–5 5–7 6–2 7–5; Wilander lost to McEnroe 3–6 7–6 3–6; Sundstrom d. J. Arias 3–6 8–6 6–3.

1985 Sweden d. West Germany 3–2, Munich: M. Wilander d. M. Westphal 6–3 6–4 10–8; S. Edberg lost to B. Becker 3–6 6–3 5–7 6–8; Wilander/J. Nystrom d. Becker/A. Maurer 6–4 6–2 6–1; Wilander lost to Becker 3–6 6–2 3–6 3–6; Edberg d. Westphal 3–6 7–5 6–4 6–3.

1986 Australia d. Sweden 3–2, Melbourne: P. Cash d. S. Edberg 13–11 13–11 6–4; P. McNamee lost to M. Pernfors 3–6 1–6 3–6; Cash/J. Fitzgerald d. Edberg/A. Jarryd 6–3 6–4 4–6 6–1; Cash d. Pernfors 2–6 4–6 6–3 6–4 6–3; McNamee lost to Edberg 8–10 4–6.

1987 Sweden d. India 5–0, Gothenburg (M. Wilander d. R. Krishnan 6–4 6–1 6–3; A. Jarryd d. V. Amritraj 6–3 6–3 6–1; Wilander/J. Nystrom d. An./V. Amritraj 6–3 3–6 6–1 6–2; Jarryd d. Krishnan 6–4 6–3; Wilander d. V. Amritraj 6–2 6–0).

ZONE WINNERS QUALIFYING FOR WORLD GROUP

	EUROPEAN ZONE A	EUROPEAN ZONE B	AMERICAN ZONE	EASTERN ZONE
1981	Spain	USSR	Chile	India
1982	Ireland	Denmark	Paraguay	Indonesia
1983	West Germany	Yugoslavia	Ecuador	India
1984	USSR	Spain	Chile	Japan
1985	Denmark	Great Britain	Mexico	New Zealand
1986	France	Israel	Argentina	Rep. of Korea
1987	Switzerland	Denmark	Brazil	New Zealand

DAVIS CUP *STALWARTS*

(Players participating in 100 or more rubbers)

	TOTAL MATCHES		SINGLES		DOUBLES			
	PL'D	WON	PL'D	WON	PL'D	WON	TIES	YEARS
N. Pietrangeli (ITA)	163	120	109	78	54	42	66	1954–72
I. Nastase (RUM)	146	110	96	74	50	36	51	1966–85
J. Brichant (BEL)	120	71	79	52	41	19	42	1949–65
M. Santana (ESP)	119	91	85	69	34	22	46	1958–73
T. Koch (BRA)	118	75	77	46	41	29	44	1962–81
J. E. Mandarino (BRA)	*109	67	*73	41	36	26	42	1961–76
I. Tiriac (RUM)	109	70	68	40	41	30	43	1959–77
A. Panatta (ITA)	103	65	65	38	38	27	39	1970–83
G. von Cramm (FRG)	102	82	69	58	33	24	37	1932–53

W. Bungert (FRG)	†102	66	†79	52	23	14	43	1958–71
U. Schmidt (SWE)	102	66	69	44	33	22	38	1955–64
P. Washer (BEL)	102	66	64	46	38	20	39	1946–61
T. Ulrich (DEN)	101	45	65	31	36	14	40	1948–77
A. Metreveli (URS)	†100	73	†67	51	33	22	36	1963–79

** Including one unfinished rubber. † Including two unfinished rubbers.*

FEDERATION CUP

International Women's Team Championship, staged on a knock-out basis at one venue with each tie comprising two singles and one doubles match.

FINAL ROUNDS

1963 USA d. Australia 2–1, Queen's Club, London, 18–21 June: D. R. Hard lost to M. Smith 3–6 0–6; B. J. Moffitt d. L. R. Turner 5–7 6–0 6–3; Hard/Moffitt d. Smith/Turner 3–6 13–11 6–3.

1964 Australia d. USA 2–1, Germanstown Cricket Club, Philadelphia, 2–5 September: M. Smith d. B. J. Moffitt 6–2 6–3; L. R. Turner d. N. Richey 7–5 6–1; Smith/Turner lost to Moffitt/Mrs J. R. Susman 6–4 5–7 1–6.

1965 Australia d. USA 2–1, Kooyong Stadium, Melbourne, 12–18 January: L. R. Turner d. Mrs C. Graebner 6–3 2–6 6–3; M. Smith d. B. J. Moffitt 6–4 8–6; Smith/J. M. Tegart lost to Graebner/Moffitt 5–7 6–4 4–6.

1966 USA d. West Germany 3–0, Turin, 11–15 May: J. M. Heldman d. H. Niessen 4–6 7–5 6–1; Mrs L. W. King d. E. Buding 6–3 3–6 6–1; Mrs C. Graebner/Mrs King d. Buding/H. Schultse 6–4 6–2.

1967 USA d. Great Britain 2–0, Rot-Weiss Club, Berlin, 7–11 June: R. Casals d. S. V. Wade 9–7 8–6; Mrs L. W. King d. Mrs P. F. Jones 6–3 6–4; Casals/Mrs King div'd with Mrs Jones/Wade 6–8 9–7.

1968 Australia d. Netherlands 3–0, Stade Roland Garros, Paris, 23–26 May: K. A. Melville d. M. Jansen 4–6 7–5 6–3; Mrs B. M. Court d. A. Suurbeck 6–1 6–3; Court/Melville d. Suurbeck/L. Venneboer 6–3 6–8 7–5.

1969 USA d. Australia 2–1, Athens, 19–25 May: N. Richey d. K. A. Melville 6–4 6–3; J. M. Heldman lost to Mrs B. M. Court 1–6 6–8; J. Bartkowicz/Richey d. Court/J. M. Tegart 6–4 6–4.

1970 Australia d. West Germany 3–0, Freiburg, Germany, 19–24 May: K. M. Krantzcke d. Mrs H. Hoesl 6–2 6–3; Mrs D. E. Dalton d. H. Niessen 4–6 6–3 6–3; Dalton/Krantzcke d. HoeslNiessen 6–2 7–5.

1971 Australia d. Great Britain 3–0, Perth, Australia, 26–29 December 1970: Mrs B. M. Court d. Mrs P. F. Jones 6–8 6–3 6–2; E. F. Goolagong d. S. V. Wade 6–4 6–1; Court/L. Hunt d. W. M. Shaw/Wade 6–4 6–4.

1972 South Africa d. Great Britain 2–1, Ellis Park, Johannesburg, 19–26 March: Mrs Q. C. Pretorius lost to S. V. Wade 3–6 2–6; B. Kirk d. W. M. Shaw 4–6 7–5 6–0; Kirk/Pretorius d. Wade/Mrs G. M. Williams 6–1 7–5.

1973 Australia d. South Africa 3–0, Bad Homburg, Germany, 30 April–6 May: E. F. Goolagong d. Mrs Q. C. Pretorius 6–0 6–2; P. Coleman d. B. Kirk 10–8 6–0; Goolagong/J. Young d. Kirk/Pretorius 6–1 6–2.

1974 Australia d. USA 2–1, Naples, 13–19 May: E. F. Goolagong d. J. M. Heldman 6–1 7–5; D. L. Fromholtz lost to C. M. Evert 6–2 5–7 3–6; Goolagong/J. Young d. Heldman/S. A. Walsh 7–5 8–6.

1975 Czechoslovakia d. Australia 3–0, Aix-en-Provence, 6–11 May: M. Navratilova* d. E. F. Goolagong 6–3 6–4; R. Tomanova d. H. Gourlay 6–4 6–2; Navratilova/Tomanova d. D. L. Fromholtz/Gourlay 6–3 6–1.

1976 USA d. Australia 2–1, Spectrum Stadium, Philadelphia, 22–29 August: R. Casals lost to Mrs G. Reid 6–1 3–6 5–7; Mrs L. W. King d. Mrs E. Cawley 7–6 6–4; Casals/King d. Cawley/Reid 7–5 6–3.

1977 USA d. Australia 2–1, Devonshire Park, Eastbourne, 13–18 June: Mrs L. W. King d. D. L. Fromholtz 6–1 2–6 6–2; C. M. Evert d. Mrs G. Reid 7–5 6–3; Casals/Evert lost to Reid/W. M. Turnbull 3–6 3–6.

1978 USA d. Australia 2–1, Kooyong Stadium, Melbourne, 27 November–3 December: T. A. Austin lost to Mrs G. Reid 3–6 3–6; C. M. Evert d. W. M. Turnbull 3–6 6–1 6–1; Evert/Mrs L. W. King d. Reid/Turnbull 4–6 6–1 6–4.

1979 USA d. Australia 3–0, Madrid, 30 April–6 May: T. A. Austin d. Mrs G. Reid 6–3 6–0; Mrs J. M. Lloyd d. D. L. Fromholtz 2–6 6–3 8–6; R. Casals/Mrs L. W. King d. Reid/W. M. Turnbull 3–6 6–3 8–6.

1980 USA d. Australia 3–0, Rot-Weiss Club, Berlin, 19–25 May: Mrs J. M. Lloyd d. D. L. Fromholtz 4–6 6–1 6–1; T. A. Austin d. W. M. Turnbull 6–2 6–3; R. Casals/K. Jordan d. Fromholtz/S. Leo 2–6 6–4 6–4.

1981 USA d. Great Britain 3–0, Tokyo, 9–15 November: A. Jaeger d. S. V. Wade 6–3 6–1; Mrs J. M. Lloyd d. S. Barker 6–2 6–1; R. Casals/K. Jordan d. J. M. Durie/Wade 6–4 7–5.

1982 USA d. West Germany 3–0, Santa Clara, California, 19–25 July: Mrs J. M. Lloyd d. C. Kohde 2–6 6–yy1 6–3; M. Navratilova* d. B. Bunge 6–4 6–4; Lloyd/Navratilova d. Bunge/Kohde 3–6 6–1 6–2.

1983 Czechoslovakia d. West Germany 2–1, Zurich, 18–24 July: H. Sukova d. C. Kohde 6–4 2–6 6–2; H. Mandlikova d. B. Bunge 6–2 3–0 ret'd; I. Budarova/M. Skuherska lost to E. Pfaff/Kohde 6–3 2–6 1–6.

1984 Czechoslovakia d. Australia 2–1, Sao Paulo, 15–22 July: H. Sukova lost to A. Minter 5–7 5–7; H. Mandlikova d. E. Sayers 6–1 6–0; Mandlikova/Sukova d. W. Turnbull/Sayers 6–2 6–2.

1985 Czechoslovakia d. USA 2–1, Nagoya, 7–13 October: H. Sukova d. E. Burgin 6–3 6–7 6–4; H. Mandlikova d. K. Jordan 7–5 6–1; A. Holikova/R. Marsikova lost to Burgin/Jordan 2–6 3–6.

1986 USA d. Czechoslovakia 3–0, Prague, 21–27 July: Mrs J. M. Lloyd d. H. Sukova 7–5 7–6; M. Navratilova d. H. Mandlikova 7–5 6–1; Navratilova/P. H. Shriver d. Mandlikova/Sukova 6–4 6–2.

1987 West Germany d. USA 2–1, Vancouver, 27 July–2 August: C. Kohde-Kilsch lost to P. H. Shriver 0–6 6–7; S. Graf d. C. M. Evert 6–2 6–1; Kohde-Kilsch/Graf d. Evert/Shriver 1–6 7–5 6–4.

** M. Navratilova became a US citizen in 1981.*

FEDERATION CUP *STALWARTS*

(Players participating in 30 or more rubbers)

	TOTAL RUBBERS PL'D	TOTAL RUBBERS WON	SINGLES PL'D	SINGLES WON	DOUBLES PL'D	DOUBLES WON	TIES	YEARS
S. V. Wade (GBR)	*100	66	56	36	*44	30	57	1967–83
Mrs L. W. King (USA)	*58	52	29	25	*29	27	36	1963–67,76–79
W. M. Turnbull (AUS)	59	43	25	17	34	26	42	1977–87
B. Stove (HOL)	55	41	26	21	29	20	29	1964,66,69–72,76–79,82,83
Mrs H. Masthoff (FRG)	53	35	31	21	22	14	31	1965–67,69,70,72–77
H. Mandlikova (TCH)	55	42	38	32	17	12	41	1978–87
Mrs J. M. Lloyd (USA)	55	51	37	35	18	16	37	1977–82, 86–87
Mrs G. E. Reid (AUS)	45	35	23	19	22	16	28	1967–69,76–79
D. M. Fromholtz (AUS)	45	34	33	24	12	10	36	1974–83
S. Barker (GBR)	45	32	24	16	21	16	27	1974–82
Mrs B. M. Court (AUS)	40	35	20	20	20	15	20	1963–65,68,69,71
R. Casals (USA)	*38	34	9	8	*29	26	29	1967,76–81
Mrs E. Cawley (AUS)	38	33	24	21	14	12	24	1971–76,82
F. Durr (FRA)	*35	22	18	12	*17	20	18	1963–67,71,72
Mrs P. F. Jones (GBR)	*34	21	17	10	*17	11	18	1963–67,71
B. Bunge (FRG)	35	26	19	16	16	10	21	1980–83, 86–87
H. Sukova (TCH)	38	26	28	21	10	5	28	1982–87
J. M. Heldman (USA)	30	21	19	13	11	8	19	1966,69,70,74,75

* *Including one unfinished rubber.*

WIGHTMAN CUP

Women's team contest between USA and Great Britain, each match comprising five singles and two doubles, with reverse singles played between the two top players.

1923 USA d. Great Britain 7–0, Forest Hills: H. Wills d. K. McKane 6–2 7–5, d. Mrs R. Clayton 6–2 6–3; Mrs F. Mallory d. Clayton 6–1 8–6, d. McKane 6–2 6–3; E. Goss d. Mrs W. G. Beamish 6–2 0–6 7–5; Mrs G. W. Wightman/Goss d. McKane/Mrs B. C. Covell 10–8 5–7 6–4; Mallory/Wills d. Beamish/Clayton 6–3 6–2.

1924 Great Britain d. USA 6–1, Wimbledon: Mrs B. C. Covell d. H. Wills 6–2 6–4, d. Mrs F. Mallory 6–2 5–7 6–3; K. McKane d. Mallory 6–3 6–3, d. Wills 6–2 6–2; Mrs W. G. Beamish d. E. Goss 6–1 8–10 6–3; Covell/Mrs D. C. Shepherd-Barron d. Mrs M. Z. Jessup/Goss 6–2 6–2; McKane/E. Colyer lost to Mrs G. W. Wightman/Wills 6–2 2–6 4–6.

1925 Great Britain d. USA 4–3, Forest Hills: K. McKane d. Mrs F. Mallory 6–4 5–7 6–0, lost to H. Wills 1–6 6–1 7–9; J. Fry lost to Wills 0–6 5–7, lost to Mallory 3–6 0–6; Mrs R. Lambert Chambers d. Goss 7–5 3–6 6–1; Lambert Chambers/E. H. Harvey d. Mallory/Mrs T. C. Bundy 10–8 6–1; McKane/E. Colyer d. Wills/M. K. Browne 6–0 6–3.

1926 USA d. Great Britain 4–3, Wimbledon: E. Ryan d. J. J. Fry 6–1 6–3, lost to Mrs L. A. Godfree 1–6 7–5 4–6; M. K. Browne lost to Godfree 1–6 5–7, lost to Fry 6–3 0–6 4–6; Mrs M. Z. Jessup d. Mrs D. C. Shepherd-Barron 6–1 5–7 6–4; Jessup/E. Goss d. Mrs R. Lambert Chambers/Shepherd-Barron 6–4 6–2; Browne/Ryan d. Godfree/E. L. Colyer 3–6 6–2 6–4.

1927 USA d. Great Britain 5–2, Forest Hills: H. Wills d. J. Fry 6–2 6–0, d. Mrs L. A. Godfree 6–1 6–1; Mrs F. Mallory d. Godfree 6–4 6–2, d. J. Fry 6–2 11–9; H. H. Jacobs lost to B. Nuthall 3–6 6–2 1–6; E. Goss/Mrs A. H. Chapin lost to G. Sterry/Mrs J. Hill 7–5 5–7 5–7; Wills/Mrs G. W. Wightman d. Godfree/E. H. Harvey 6–4 4–6 6–3.

1928 Great Britain d. USA 4–3, Wimbledon: Mrs P. H. Watson lost to H. Wills 1–6 2–6, d. Mrs F. Mallory 2–6 6–1 6–2; E. Bennett d. Mallory 6–1 6–3, lost to Wills 3–6 2–6; B. Nuthall lost to H. H. Jacobs 3–6 1–6; E. H. Harvey/P. Saunders d. E. Goss/Jacobs 6–4 6–1; Bennett/Watson d. Wills/P. Anderson 6–2 6–1.

1929 USA d. Great Britain 4–3, Forest Hills: H. Wills d. Mrs P. H. Watson 6–1 6–4, d. B. Nuthall 8–6 8–6; H. H. Jacobs d. Nuthall 7–5 8–6, lost to Watson 3–6 2–6; E. Goss d. Mrs L. R. C. Michell 6–3 3–6 6–3; Wills/Goss lost to Watson/Michell 4–6 1–6; Mrs G. W. Wightman/Jacobs lost to Mrs B. C. Covell/Mrs D. C. Shepherd-Barron 2–6 1–6.

1930 Great Britain d. USA 4–3, Wimbledon: J. Fry lost to H. Wills 1–6 1–6, lost to H. H. Jacobs 0–6 3–6; Mrs P. H. Watson d. Jacobs 2–6 6–2 6–4, lost to Wills 5–7 1–6; P. Mudford d. S. Palfrey 6–0 6–2; Fry/E. H. Harvey d. Palfrey/E. Cross 2–6 6–2 6–4; Watson/Mrs L. A. Godfree d. Jacobs/Wills 7–5 1–6 6–4.

1931 USA d. Great Britain 5–2, Forest Hills: Mrs F. S. Moody d. P. Mudford 6–1 6–4, d. B. Nuthall 6–4 6–2; H. H. Jacobs d. Nuthall 8–6 6–4, d. Mudford 6–4 6–2; Mrs L. A. Harper d. D. E. Round 6–3 4–6 9–7; S. Palfrey/Mrs G. W. Wightman lost to Mudford/Mrs D. C. Shepherd-Barron 4–6 8–10; Moody/Harper lost to Nuthall/Mrs Fearnley Whittingstall 6–8 7–5 3–6.

1932 USA d. Great Britain 4–3, Wimbledon: H. H. Jacobs d. D. E. Round 6–4 6–3, lost to Mrs Fearnley Whittingstall 4–6 6–2 1–6; Mrs F. S. Moody d. Fearnley Whittingstall 6–2 6–4, d. Round 6–2 6–3; Mrs L. A. Harper lost to Mrs M. R. King 6–3 1–6 1–6; Harper/Jacobs d. Mrs L. R. C. Michell/Round 6–4 6–1; Moody/Palfrey lost to Fearnley Whittingstall/B. Nuthall 3–6 6–1 8–10.

1933 USA d. Great Britain 4–3, Forest Hills: H. H. Jacobs d. D. E. Round 6–4 6–2, d. M. Scriven 5–7 6–2 7–5; S. Palfrey d. Scriven 6–3 6–1, lost to Round 4–6 8–10; C. Babcock lost to B. Nuthall 6–1 1–6 3–6; Jacobs/Palfrey d. Round/M. Heeley 6–4 6–2; A. Marble/Mrs J. Van Ryn lost to Nuthall/F. James 5–7 2–6.

1934 USA d. Great Britain 5–2, Wimbledon: S. Palfrey d. D. E. Round 6–3 3–6 8–6, d. M. Scriven 4–6 6–2 8–6; H. H. Jacobs d. Scriven 6–1 6–1, d. Round 6–4 6–4; C. Babcock lost to B. Nuthall 7–5 3–6 4–6; Babcock/J. Cruickshank lost to N. Lyle/E. M. Dearman 5–7 5–7; Jacobs/Palfrey d. Mrs L. A. Godfree/Nuthall 5–7 6–3 6–2.

1935 USA d. Great Britain 4–3, Forest Hills: H. H. Jacobs lost to K. Stammers 7–5 1–6 7–9, d. D. E. Round 6–3 6–2; Mrs E. B. Arnold lost to Round 0–6 3–6, d. Stammers 6–2 1–6 6–3; S. Palfrey d. Mrs M. R. King 6–0 6–3; Jacobs/Palfrey d. Stammers/F. James 6–3 6–2; Mrs D. B. Andrus/C. Babcock lost to N. Lyle/E. M. Dearman 6–3 4–6 1–6.

1936 USA d. Great Britain 4–3, Wimbledon: H. H. Jacobs lost to K. Stammers 10–12 1–6, lost to D. E. Round 3–6 3–6; S. Palfrey lost to Round 3–6 4–6, d. Stammers 6–3 6–4; C. Babcock d. M. Hardwick 6–4 4–6 6–2; Babcock/Mrs J. Van Ryn d. N. Lyle/E. M. Dearman 6–2 1–6 6–3; Jacobs/Palfrey d. Stammers/F. James 1–6 6–3 7–5.

1937 USA d. Great Britain 6–1, Forest Hills: A. Marble d. M. Hardwick 4–6 6–2 6–4, d. K. Stammers 6–3 6–1; H. H. Jacobs d. Stammers 6–1 4–6 6–4, d. Hardwick 2–6 6–4 6–2; S. Palfrey d. M. Lumb 6–3 6–1; Marble/Palfrey d. E. M. Dearman/J. Ingram 6–3 6–2; Mrs J. Van Ryn/D. M. Bundy lost to Stammers/F. James 3–6 8–10.

1938 USA d. Great Britain 5–2, Wimbledon: A. Marble lost to K. Stammers 6–3 5–7 3–6, d. M. Scriven 6–3 3–6 6–0; Mrs F. S. Moody d. Scriven 6–0 7–5, d. Stammers 6–2 3–6 6–3; S. Fabyan d. M. Lumb 5–7 6–2 6–3; Marble/Fabyan d. Lumb/F. James 6–4 6–2; Moody/D. Bundy lost to E. M. Dearman/J. Ingram 2–6 5–7.

1939 USA d. Great Britain 5–2, Forest Hills: A. Marble d. M. Hardwick 6–3 6–4, d. K. Stammers 3–6 6–3 6–4; H. H. Jacobs lost to Stammers 2–6 6–1 3–6, d. Hardwick 6–2 6–2; S. Fabyan lost to V. Scott 3–6 4–6; M. Arnold/D. M. Bundy d. B. Nuthall/N. Brown 6–3 6–1; Marble/Fabyan d. Stammers/Mrs S. H. Hammersley 7–5 6–2.

1940–45 *Not held.*

1946 USA d. Great Britain 7–0, Wimbledon: P. M. Betz d. Mrs J. Bostock 6–2 6–4, d. Mrs M. Menzies 6–4 6–4; M. Osborne d. Bostock 6–1 6–4, d. Menzies 6–3 6–2; L. Brough d. J. Curry 8–6 6–3; Brough/Osborne d. Bostock/Mrs M. Halford 6–2 6–1; Betz/D. Hart d. Mrs B. Passingham/M. Lincoln 6–1 6–3.

1947 USA d. Great Britain 7–0, Forest Hills: M. Osborne d. Mrs J. Bostock 6–4 2–6 6–2, d. Mrs M. Menzies 7–5 6–2; L. Brough d. Menzies 6–4 6–2, d. Bostock 6–4 6–4; D. Hart d. Mrs B. Hilton 4–6 6–3 7–5; Hart/Mrs P. C. Todd d. J. Gannon/J. Quertier 6–1 6–2; Brough/Osborne d. Bostock/Hilton 6–1 6–4.

1948 USA d. Great Britain 6–1, Wimbledon: Mrs W. du Pont d. Mrs J. Bostock 6–4 8–6, d. Mrs B. Hilton 6–3 6–4; L. Brough d. Hilton 6–1 6–1, d. Bostock 6–2 4–6 7–5; D. Hart d. J. Gannon 6–1 6–4; Brough/du Pont d. Mrs M. Menzies/Hilton 6–2 6–2; Hart/Mrs P. C. Todd lost to Bostock/Mrs N. W. Blair 3–6 4–6.

1949 USA d. Great Britain 7–0, Merion Cricket Club, Philadelphia: D. Hart d. Mrs J. Walker-Smith 6–3 6–1, d. Mrs B. Hilton 6–1 6–3; Mrs W. du Pont d. Hilton 6–1 6–3, d. Walker-Smith 6–4 6–2; B. Baker d. J. Quertier 6–4 7–5; Hart/S. Fry d. Quertier/Mrs N. W. Blair 6–1 6–2; G. Moran/Mrs P. C. Todd d. Hilton/K. Tuckey 6–4 8–6.

1950 USA d. Great Britain 7–0, Wimbledon: Mrs W. du Pont d. Mrs B. Hilton 6–3 6–4, d. Mrs J. Walker-Smith 6–3 6–2; L. Brough d. Hilton 2–6 6–2 7–5, d. Walker-Smith 6–0 6–0; D. Hart d. J. Curry 6–2 6–4; Hart/Mrs P. C. Todd d. Walker-Smith/J. Quertier 6–2 6–3; Brough/du Pont d. Hilton/K. Tuckey 6–2 6–0.

1951 USA d. Great Britain 6–1, Longwood Cricket Club, Boston: D. Hart d. J. Quertier 6–4 6–4, d. Mrs J. Walker-Smith 6–4 2–6 7–5; S. Fry d. Walker-Smith 6–1 6–4; lost to Quertier 3–6 6–8; M. Connolly d. K. Tuckey 6–1 6–3; Mrs P. C. Todd/N. Chaffee d. Mrs J. Mottram/P. Ward 7–5 6–3; Fry/D. Hart d. Quertier/Tuckey 6–3 6–3.

1952 USA d. Great Britain 7–0, Wimbledon: D. Hart d. Mrs J. Rinkel-Quertier 6–3 6–3, d. Mrs J. Walker-Smith 7–5 6–2; M. Connolly d. Walker-Smith 3–6 6–1 7–5, d. Rinkel-Quertier 9–7 6–2; S. Fry d. S. Partridge 6–0 8–6; Fry/Hart d. H. Fletcher/Rinkel-Quertier 8–6 6–4; L. Brough/Connolly d. Mrs J. Mottram/P. Ward 6–0 6–3.

1953 USA d. Great Britain 7–0, Westchester Club, Rye, NY: M. Connolly d. A. Mortimer 6–1 6–1, d. H. Fletcher 6–1 6–1; Hart d. Fletcher 6–4 7–5, d. Mortimer 6–1 6–1; S. Fry d. Rinkel-Quertier 6–2 6–4; L. Brough/Connolly d. Mortimer/A. Shilcock 6–2 6–3; Fry/Hart d. Fletcher/Rinkel-Quertier 6–2 6–1.

1954 USA d. Great Britain 6–0, Wimbledon: M. Connolly d. H. Fletcher 6–1 6–3, d. A. Shilcock 6–2 6–2; Hart d. Shilcock 6–4 6–1, d. Fletcher 6–1 6–8 6–2; L. Brough d. A. Buxton 8–6 6–2; L. Brough/Mrs W. du Pont d. Buxton/P. Hird 2–6 6–4 7–5; S. Fry/Hart v. Fletcher/Shilcock not played.

1955 USA d. Great Britain 6–1, Westchester Club, Rye, NY: D. Hart lost to A. Mortimer 4–6 6–1 5–7, d. S. J. Bloomer 7–5 6–3; L. Brough d. Bloomer 6–2 6–4, d. Mortimer 6–0 6–2; Mrs D. Knode d. A. Buxton 6–3 6–3; Brough/Mrs W. du Pont d. Bloomer/P. Ward 6–3 6–3; S. Fry/Hart d. Buxton/Mortimer 3–6 6–2 7–5.

1956 USA d. Great Britain 5–2, Wimbledon: L. Brough d. A. Mortimer 3–6 6–4 7–5, d. A. Buxton 3–6 6–3 6–4; S. Fry d. Buxton 6–2 6–8 7–5, lost to Mortimer 4–6 3–6; Mrs D. Knode lost to S. J. Bloomer 4–6 4–6; B. Baker/Knode d. Bloomer/P. Ward 6–1 6–4; Brough/Fry d. Buxton/Mortimer 6–2 6–2.

1957 USA d. Great Britain 6–1, Sewickley, Pennsylvania: A. Gibson d. S. J. Bloomer 6–4 4–6 6–2, d. C. Truman 6–4 6–2; Mrs D. Knode d. Truman 6–2 11–9, d. Bloomer 5–7 6–1 6–2; D. R. Hard lost to A. Haydon 3–6 6–3 4–6; Gibson/Hard d. Bloomer/S. M. Armonstrong 6–3 6–4; L. Brough/W. du Pont d. Haydon/A. Shilcock 6–4 6–1.

1958 Great Britain d. USA 4–3, Wimbledon: S. J. Bloomer lost to A. Gibson 3–6 4–6, lost to Mrs D. Knode 4–6 2–6; C. Truman d. Knode 6–4 6–4, d. Gibson 2–6 6–3 6–4; A. Haydon d. M. Arnold 6–3 5–7 6–3; Bloomer/Truman d. K. Fageros/Knode 6–2 6–3; A. Shilcock/P. Ward lost to Gibson/J. Jopps 4–6 6–3 3–6.

1959 USA d. Great Britain 4–3, Sewickley, Pennsylvania: Mrs B. Fleits d. A. Mortimer 6–2 6–1, d. C. Truman 6–4 6–4; D. R. Hard lost to Truman 4–6 6–2 3–6, d. Mortimer 6–3 6–8 6–4; S. Moore lost to A. Haydon 1–6 1–6; J. Arth/Hard d. S. J. Bloomer/Truman 9–7 9–7; J. Hopps/Moore lost to Haydon/Mortimer 2–6 4–6.

1960 Great Britain d. USA 4–3, Wimbledon: A. Haydon d. K. Hantze 2–6 11–9 6–1, lost to D. R. Hard 7–5 2–6 1–6; C. Truman lost to Hard 6–4 3–6 4–6, d. Hantze 7–5 6–3; A. Mortimer d. J. Hopps 6–8 6–4 6–1; Haydon/Mortimer lost to Hard/Hantze 0–6 0–6; S. J. Bloomer/Truman d. Hopps/Mrs D. Knode 6–4 9–7.

1961 USA d. Great Britain 6–1, Saddle & Cycle Club, Chicago: K. Hantze d. C. Truman 7–9 6–1 6–1, d. A. Haydon 6–1 6–4; B. J. Moffitt d. Haydon 6–4 6–4, lost to Truman 3–6 2–6; J. Bricka d. A. Mortimer 10–8 4–6 6–3; Hantze/Moffitt d. Truman/D. M. Catt 7–5 6–2; Mrs W. du Pont/M. Varner w.o. Mortimer/Haydon.

1962 USA d. Great Britain 4–3, Wimbledon: D. R. Hard d. C. Truman 6–2 6–2, d. A. Haydon 6–3 6–8 6–4; Mrs J. R. Susman lost to Haydon 8–10 5–7, d. Truman 6–4 7–5; N. Richey lost to D. M. Catt 1–6 5–7; Mrs W. du Pont/M. Varner d. Catt/E. Starkie 6–2 3–6 6–2; Hard/B. J. Moffitt lost to Haydon/Truman 4–6 3–6.

1963 USA d. Great Britain 6–1, Cleveland Skating Club, Cleveland: D. R. Hard lost to Mrs P. F. Jones 1–6 6–0 6–8,

d. C. Truman 6–3 6–0; B. J. Moffitt d. Truman 6–4 19–17, d. Jones 6–4 4–6 6–3; N. Richey d. D. M. Catt 14–12 6–3; Hard/Moffitt d. Truman/Jones 4–6 7–5 6–2; Richey/Mrs D. Fales d. Catt/E. Starkie 6–4 6–8 6–2.

1964 USA d. Great Britain 5–2, Wimbledon: N. Richey d. D. M. Catt 4–6 6–4 7–5, d. Mrs P. F. Jones 7–5 11–9; B. J. Moffitt d. Jones 4–6 6–2 6–3, d. Catt 6–3 4–6 6–3; C. Caldwell d. E. Starkie 6–4 1–6 6–3; Caldwell/Moffitt lost to Catt/Jones 2–6 6–4 0–6; Richey/Mrs D. Fales lost to A. Mortimer/Starkie 6–2 3–6 4–6.

1965 USA d. Great Britain 5–2, Clarke Stadium, Cleveland: B. J. Moffitt lost to Mrs P. F. Jones 2–6 4–6, d. E. Starkie 6–3 6–2; N. Richey d. Starkie 6–1 6–0, lost to Jones 4–6 6–8; Mrs C. Graebner d. S. V. Wade 3–6 10–8 6–4; Graebner/Richey d. F. E. Truman/Starkie 6–1 6–0; Moffitt/Mrs J. R. Susman d. Jones/Wade 6–3 8–6.

1966 USA d. Great Britain 4–3, Wimbledon: N. Richey lost to Mrs P. F. Jones 6–2 4–6 3–6, d. S. V. Wade 2–6 6–2 7–5; Mrs L. W. King d. Wade 6–3 6–3, d. Jones 5–7 6–2 6–3; M. A. Eisel lost to W. Shaw 2–6 3–6; King/J. Albert lost to Jones/Wade 5–7 2–6; Richey/Eisel d. R. Bentley/E. Starkie 6–1 6–2.

1967 USA d. Great Britain 6–1, Clarke Stadium, Cleveland: Mrs L. W. King d. S. V. Wade 6–3 6–2, d. Mrs P. F. Jones 6–1 6–2; N. Richey d. Jones 6–2 6–2, d. Wade 3–6 8–6 6–2; R. Casals lost to C. Truman 6–3 5–7 1–6; Casals/King d. Jones/Wade 10–8 6–4; M. A. Eisel/Mrs C. Graebner d. W. Shaw/Mrs J. Williams 8–6 12–10.

1968 Great Britain d. USA 4–3, Wimbledon: Mrs C. Janes lost to N. Richey 1–6 6–8, lost to M. A. Eisel 4–6 3–6; S. V. Wade d. Eisel 6–0 6–1, d. Richey 6–4 2–6 6–3; W. Shaw lost to J. Bartkowicz 5–7 6–3 4–6; Shaw/Wade d. Eisel/Richey 5–7 6–4 6–3; Janes/F. E. Truman d. S. De Fina/K. Harter 6–3 2–6 6–3.

1969 USA d. Great Britain 5–2, Clarke Stadium, Cleveland: J. M. Heldman d. S. V. Wade 3–6 6–1 8–6, d. W. Shaw 6–3 6–4; N. Richey d. Shaw 8–6 6–2, lost to Wade 3–6 6–2 4–6; J. Bartkowicz d. Mrs C. Janes 8–6 6–0; Mrs P. Curtis/V. Ziengenfuss lost to Janes/F. E. Truman 1–6 6–3 4–6; Heldman/Bartkowicz d. Shaw/Wade 6–4 6–2.

1970 USA d. Great Britain 4–3, Wimbledon: Mrs L. W. King d. S. V. Wade 8–6 6–4, d. Mrs P. F. Jones 6–4 6–2; N. Richey lost to Jones 3–6 3–6, lost to Wade 3–6 2–6; J. M. Heldman d. Mrs G. Williams 6–3 6–2; Mrs P. Curtis/Heldman lost to Jones/Williams 3–6 2–6; King/J. Bartkowicz d. W. Shaw/Wade 7–5 6–8 6–2.

1971 USA d. Great Britain 4–3, Clarke Stadium, Cleveland: C. Evert d. W. Shaw 6–0 6–4, d. S. V. Wade 6–1 6–1; J. M. Heldman lost to Wade 5–7 5–7; V. Ziegenfuss d. Shaw 6–4 4–6 6–3; K. Pigeon lost to Mrs G. Williams 5–7 6–3 4–6; Mrs P. Curtis/Ziegenfuss d. Mrs C. Janes/F. E. Truman 6–1 6–4; Mrs C. Graebner/Evert lost to Wade/Williams 8–10 6–4 1–6.

1972 USA d. Great Britain 5–2, Wimbledon: W. Overton lost to Mrs G. Williams 3–6 6–3 3–6, lost to S. V. Wade 6–8 5–7; C. Evert d. Wade 6–4 6–4, d. Williams 6–2 6–3; P. S. A. Hogan d. C. Molesworth 6–8 6–4 6–2; Evert/Hogan d. W. Shaw/F. E. Truman 7–5 6–4; Overton/V. Ziegenfuss d. Wade/Williams 6–3 6–3.

1973 USA d. Great Britain 5–2, Longwood Cricket Club, Boston: C. Evert d. S. V. Wade 6–4 6–2, d. V. Burton 6–3 6–0; P. S. A. Hogan d. Burton 6–4 6–3, lost to Wade 2–6 2–6; L. Tuero d. G. Coles 7–5 6–2; Evert/M. Redondo lost to Coles/Wade 3–6 4–6; J. Evert/Hogan d. L. Beaven/L. Charles 6–3 4–6 8–6.

1974 Great Britain d. USA 6–1, Deeside Leisure Centre, Queensferry, North Wales (indoors): S. V. Wade d. J. M. Heldman 5–7 9–7 6–4, d. J. Newberry 6–1 6–3; G. Coles d. Newberry 4–6 6–1 6–3, d. Heldman 6–0 6–4; S. Barker d. J. Evert 4–6 6–4 6–1; Barker/Charles d. Newberry/B. Nagelsen 4–6 6–2 6–1; Coles/Wade lost to Heldman/M. Schallau 5–7 4–6.

1975 Great Britain d. USA 5–2, Public Auditorium, Cleveland (indoors): S. V. Wade d. M. Schallau 6–2 6–2; lost to C. Evert 3–6 5–7; G. Coles lost to Evert 4–6 1–6, d. Schallau 6–3 7–6; S. Barker d. J. Newberry 6–4 7–5; Mrs P. F. Jones/Wade d. Newberry/J. Anthony 6–2 6–3; Coles/Barker d. Evert/Schallau 7–5 6–4.

1976 USA d. Great Britain 5–2, Crystal Palace, London (indoors): C. Evert d. S. V. Wade 6–2 3–6 6–2, d. S. Barker 2–6 6–2 6–2; R. Casals lost to Barker 6–1 3–6 2–6, lost to Wade 6–3 7–9 ret'd; T. Holladay d. G. Coles 3–6 6–1 6–4; Casals/Evert d. Barker/Wade 6–0 5–7 6–1; Mrs M. Guerrant/A. Kiyomura d. S. Mappin/L. Charles 6–2 6–2.

1977 USA d. Great Britain 7–0, Oakland, California (indoors): C. Evert d. S. V. Wade 7–5 7–6, d. S. Barker 6–1 6–2; Mrs L. W. King d. Barker 6–1 6–4, d. Wade 6–4 3–6 8–6; R. Casals d. M. Tyler 6–2 3–6 6–4; King/J. Russell d. S. Mappin/L. Charles 6–0 6–1; Casals/Evert d. Barker/Wade 6–2 6–4.

1978 Great Britain d. USA 4–3, Albert Hall, London (indoors): S. Barker lost to C. Evert 2–6 1–6, d. T. Austin 6–3 3–6 6–0; S. V. Wade d. Austin 3–6 7–5 6–3, lost to Evert 0–6 1–6; M. Tyler d. P. H. Shriver 5–7 6–2 6–3; S. Mappin/A. E. Hobbs lost to Mrs L. W. King/Austin 2–6 6–4 2–6; Barker/Wade d. Evert/Shriver 6–0 5–7 6–4.

1979 USA d. Great Britain 7–0, Palm Beach West, Florida: Mrs J. M. Lloyd d. S. Barker 7–5 6–2, d. S. V. Wade 6–1 6–1; T. Austin d. Wade 6–1 6–4, d. Barker 6–4 6–2; K. Jordan d. A. E. Hobbs 6–4 6–7 6–2; Austin/A. Kiyomura d. J. M. Durie/D. A. Jevans 6–3 6–1; Lloyd/R. Casals d. Barker/Wade 6–0 6–1.

1980 USA d. Great Britain 5–2, Albert Hall, London (indoors): Mrs J. M. Lloyd d. S. Barker 6–1 6–2, d. S. V. Wade 7–5 3–6 7–5; A. Jaeger d. Wade 3–6 6–3 6–2, lost to Barker 7–5 3–6 3–6; K. Jordan lost to A. E. Hobbs 6–4 4–6 1–6; Lloyd/R. Casals d. Hobbs/G. Coles 6–3 6–3; A. E. Smith/Jordan d. Barker/Wade 6–4 7–5.

1981 USA d. Great Britain 7–0, International Amphitheatre, Chicago (indoors): T. Austin d. S. Barker 7–5 6–3, d. S. V. Wade 6–3 6–1; Mrs J. M. Lloyd d. Wade 6–1 6–3, d. Barker 6–3 6–0; A. Jaeger d. A. E. Hobbs 6–0 6–0; Jaeger/P. H. Shriver d. J. M. Durie/Hobbs 6–1 6–3; Lloyd/R. Casals d. G. Coles/Wade 6–3 6–3.

1982 USA d. Great Britain 6–1, Albert Hall, London (indoors): B. Potter d. S. Barker 6–2 6–2, d. J. M. Durie 5–7 7–6 6–2; Mrs J. M. Lloyd d. Durie 6–2 6–2, d. Barker 6–4 6–3; A. E. Smith d. S. V. Wade 3–6 7–5 6–3; R. Casals/Smith lost to Durie/A. E. Hobbs 3–6 6–2 3–6; Potter/S. A. Walsh d. Barker/Wade 2–6 6–4 6–4.

1983 USA d. Great Britain 6–1, Williamsburg, Virginia (indoors): M. Navratilova d. S. Barker 6–2 6–0, d. J. M. Durie 6–3 6–3; P. H. Shriver d. Durie 6–3 6–2, d. Barker 6–0 6–1; K. Rinaldi d. S. V. Wade 6–3 6–2; C. Reynolds/P. Smith lost to Barker/Wade 5–7 6–3 1–6; Navratilova/Shriver d. Durie/A. Croft 6–2 6–1.

1984 USA d. Great Britain 5–2, Albert Hall, London (indoors): Mrs J. M. Lloyd d. A. E. Hobbs 6–2 6–2; A. Moulton lost to A. Croft 1–6 7–5 4–6; B. Potter lost to J. M. Durie 3–6 6–7; Lloyd/Moulton d. A. Brown/S. V. Wade 6–2 6–2; Potter d. Hobbs 6–1 6–3; Lloyd d. Durie 7–6 6–1; Potter/S. A. Walsh d. Durie/Hobbs 7–6 4–6 9–7.

1985 USA d. Great Britain 7–0, Williamsburg, Virginia (indoors): Mrs J. M. Lloyd d. J. M. Durie 6–2 6–3; K. Rinaldi d. A. E. Hobbs 7–5 7–5; P. H. Shriver d. A. Croft 6–0 6–0; B. Nagelsen/A. White d. Croft/S. V. Wade 6–4 6–1; Shriver d. Durie 6–4 6–4; Lloyd d. Croft 6–3 6–0; Lloyd/Shriver d. Durie/Hobbs 6–3 6–7 6–2.

1986 USA d. Great Britain 7–0, Albert Hall, London (indoors): K. Rinaldi d. S. Gomer 6–3 7–6; S. Rehe d. A. Croft

6–3 6–1; B. Gadusek d. J. M. Durie 6–2 6–4; Gadusek/Rinaldi d. Croft/Gomer 6–3 5–7 6–3; Gadusek d. Hobbs 2–6 6–4 6–4; Rinaldi d. Durie 6–4 6–2; E. Burgin/A. White d. Durie/Hobbs 7–6 6–3.

1987 USA d. Great Britain 5–2, Williamsburg, Virginia (indoors): Z. Garrison d. A. E. Hobbs 7–5 6–2; L. McNeil d. S. Gomer 6–2 6–1; P. H. Shriver d. J. M. Durie 6–1 7–5; G. Fernandez/R. White d. Gomer/C. Wood 6–4 6–1; Shriver d. Hobbs 6–4 6–3; Garrison lost to Durie 6–7 3–6; Garrison/McNeil lost to Durie/Hobbs 6–0 4–6 5–7.

WIGHTMAN CUP STALWARTS

(Players participating in 10 or more ties or playing 20 or more rubbers)

	TOTAL RUBBERS		SINGLES		DOUBLES			
	PL'D	WON	PL'D	WON	PL'D	WON	TIES	YEARS
S. V. Wade (GBR)	56	19	35	12	21	7	21	1965–85
Mrs J. M. Lloyd (USA)	38	34	26	26	12	8	13	1971–73,75–82,84–85
Mrs P. F. Jones (GBR)	32	16	21	10	11	6	13	1957–67,70,75
Mrs F. S. Moody (USA)	30	21	20	18	10	3	10	1923–25,27,29–32,38
H. H. Jacobs (USA)	30	19	22	14	8	5	12	1927–37,39
Mrs G. T. Janes (GBR)	27	12	21	10	11	6	13	1957–67,70,75
Mrs L. W. King (USA)	26	21	16	14	10	7	10	1961–67,70,77,78
S. Barker (GBR)	26	8	18	5	8	3	10	1974–83
D. Hart (USA)	24	22	15	14	9	8	10	1946–55
A. L. Brough (USA)	22	22	12	12	10	10	10	1946–48,50,52–57
Mrs S. P. Fabyan (USA)	21	14	11	7	10	7	10	1930–39
N. Richey (USA)	21	12	16	9	5	3	9	1962–70

EUROPEAN CUP

Formerly King's Cup

International Men's Team Championship on Indoor Courts. It was staged on a knock-out basis 1936–38, 1952–74, on a league basis 1976–83 with ties home and away. From 1984 the ties in each division were held concurrently at one venue. The Challenge Round system was used in the two opening years, with 1937 the only Challenge Round.

FINALS

1936 France d. Sweden 4–1, Stockholm: J. Borotra d. K. Schroder 2–6 6–2 6–1 6–3, d. C. Ostberg 6–1 6–3 7–5; B. Destremau d. Schroder 3–6 7–5 6–2 6–4, d. Ostberg 6–2 6–2 6–4; C. Boussus/J. Brugnon lost to Ostberg/Schroder 2–6 6–3 4–6 6–3 4–6.

1937 France d. Sweden 5–0, Paris: B. Destremau d. K. Schroder 8–6 1–6 2–6 11–9 8–6, d. N. Rohlsson 1–6 1–6 6–3 6–1 6–0; Y. Petra d. Rohlsson 6–1 6–4 6–2, d. Schroder 6–3 3–6 6–3 6–4; H. Bolelli/J. Lesueur d. Schroder/H. Wallen 10–8 6–4 6–4.

1938 Germany d. Denmark 5–0, Hamburg: R. Menzel d. H. Plougmann 6–3 6–2 8–6; H. Henkel d. I. Gerdes 6–4 6–0 6–3, d. Plougmann 6–2 6–1 6–3; R. Redl d. Gerdes 6–3 6–3 6–2; Henkel/Menzel d. Gerdes/Plougmann 6–0 6–4 6–2.

1939–51 *Not held*

1952 Denmark d. Sweden 3–2, Stockholm: K. Nielsen lost to S. Davidson 3–6 7–9 4–6; T. Ulrich d. T. Johansson 7–5 0–6 6–4 6–2; Nielsen/Ulrich d. Davidson/Johansson 6–2 2–6 4–6 8–6 7–5; Nielsen d. Johansson 6–3 6–4 6–1; Ulrich lost to Davidson 6–4 4–6 1–6 6–1 2–6.

1953 Denmark d. Sweden 3–2, Copenhagen: T. Ulrich d. S. Davidson 14–12 11–9 1–6 11–9; J. Ulrich lost to T. Johansson 0–6 2–6 7–9; J. Ulrich/T. Ulrich d. Davidson/N. Rohlsson 6–4 6–4 4–6 3–6 6–3; J. Ulrich lost to Davidson 3–6 4–6 0–6; T. Ulrich d. Johansson 6–3 2–6 6–4 5–7 6–3.

1954 Denmark d. Italy 3–2, Milan: T. Ulrich d. G. Merlo 7–5 2–6 9–7 9–7; K. Nielsen lost to O. Sirola 5–7 6–8 8–6 6–2 3–6; Nielsen/Ulrich d. N. Pietrangeli/Sirola 2–6 2–6 11–9 6–1 12–10; Nielsen lost to Pietrangeli 5–7 6–3 9–7 3–6 5–7; Ulrich d. Sirola 7–5 10–8 6–4.

1955 Sweden d. Denmark 4–1, Copenhagen: S. Davidson d. J. Ulrich 7–5 12–10 6–1; U. Schmidt lost to K. Nielsen 3–6 2–6 6–4 4–6; Davidson/T. Johansson d. Nielsen/J. Ulrich 11–9 6–3 14–12; Davidson d. Nielsen 8–10 6–2 7–9 12–10 7–5; Schmidt d. J. Ulrich 7–9 3–6 6–0 8–6 6–3.

1956 Sweden d. France 4–1, Paris: S. Davidson lost to P. Darmon 7–9 6–2 5–7 6–8; U. Schmidt d. R. Haillet 6–1 6–2 6–4; Davidson/Schmidt d. Darmon/P. Remy 8–6 3–6 6–1 6–4; Davidson d. Haillet 6–2 2–6 6–4 6–1; Schmidt d. Darmon 6–1 10–8 6–3.

1957 Sweden d. Denmark 3–2, Copenhagen: J. E. Lundqvist d. K. Nielsen 4–6 6–3 10–8 6–4; U. Schmidt lost to T. Ulrich 4–6 7–9 2–6; Lundqvist/Schmidt d. J. Ulrich/T. Ulrich 6–3 5–7 6–0 6–3; Lundqvist d. T. Ulrich 7–5 6–1 6–2; Schmidt lost to Nielsen 6–4 4–6 2–6 5–7.

1958 Sweden d. Denmark 3–2, Stockholm: B. Folke lost to J. Ulrich 11–13 3–6 4–6; S. Davidson d. K. Nielsen 6–0 6–1 6–4; Davidson/T. Johansson d. Nielsen/J. Ulrich 10–8 1–6 6–3 6–8 6–3; Folke lost to Nielsen 4–6 3–6 3–6; Davidson d. J. Ulrich 6–4 6–3 1–6 6–1.

1959 Denmark won, Stockholm: Denmark d. Italy 2–1, lost to Sweden 2–1, d. France 2–1 (12–11 sets); Sweden lost to France 2–1, d. Denmark 2–1, d. Italy 2–1 (10–10 sets); Italy lost to Denmark 2–1, d. France 2–1, lost to Sweden

2–1 (11–11 sets); France d. Sweden 2–1, lost to Italy 2–1, lost to France 2–1 (10–11 sets). Danish team: K. Nielsen and J. Ulrich.
***1960* Denmark d. West Germany 3–0, Paris:** J. Leschly d. B. Nitsche 6–4 8–6; J. Ulrich d. P. Scholl 6–2 6–3; Leschly/J. Ulrich d. Nitsche/Scholl 6–8 6–2 6–0.
***1961* Sweden d. Denmark 2–1, Cologne:** U. Schmidt d. J. Leschly 6–4 6–2; J. E. Lundqvist d. J. Ulrich 6–3 6–1; Lundqvist/Schmidt lost to Leschly/J. Ulrich 5–7 6–4 5–7.
***1962* Denmark d. Italy 3–0, Copenhagen:** J. Leschly d. G. Merlo 6–3 8–6; J. Ulrich d. N. Pietrangeli 6–4 6–2; Leschly/J. Ulrich d. Pietrangeli/O. Sirola 9–7 7–5.
***1963* Yugoslavia d. Denmark 3–0, Belgrade:** Yugoslav team: B. Jovanovic and N. Pilic.
***1964* Great Britain d. Sweden 3–0, Stockholm:** M. J. Sangster d. J. E. Lundquist 13–15 10–8 12–10; R. Taylor d. B. Holmstrom 6–3 9–7; Sangster/R. K. Wilson d. Holmstrom/L. Olander 4–6 12–10 6–4.
***1965* Great Britain d. Denmark 2–1, Torquay:** R. K. Wilson lost to J. Leschly 1–6 4–6; M. Cox d. C. Hedelund 6–4 6–3; A. R. Mills/Wilson d. Leschly/Hedelund 3–6 6–2 6–4 12–10.
***1966* Great Britain d. Italy 3–0, Milan:** R. Taylor d. N. Pietrangeli 6–4 6–4; M. J. Sangster d. G. Maioli 7–9 6–4 11–9; Sangster/R. K. Wilson d. D. di Maso/Maioli 6–4 6–1.
***1967* Great Britain d. Sweden 2–1, Stockholm:** R. Taylor d. O. Bengtson 2–6 6–3 9–7; R. K. Wilson d. M. Carlstein 8–6 6–2; M. Cox/Taylor lost to Bengtson/B. Homstrom 4–6 7–9.
***1968* Sweden d. Netherlands 2–1, Bratislava:** O. Bengtson lost to T. S. Okker 12–14 4–6; M. Carlstein d. J. Hordijk 6–4 6–3; Bengtson/Carlstein d. N. Fleury/Okker 1–6 4–6 7–5 6–3 6–4.
***1969* Czechoslovakia d. Sweden 2–1, Cologne:** V. Zednik d. H. Zahr 6–4 7–5; J. Kukal d. O. Bengtson 6–1 5–7 11–9; Kukal/Zednik lost to Bengtson/H. Nerell 4–6 4–6.
***1970* France d. Denmark 2–1, Copenhagen:** J. B. Chanfreau d. J. Ulrich 6–3 8–6; G. Goven lost to J. Leschly 1–6 3–6; Chanfreau/Goven d. Ulrich/Leschly 2–6 6–4 7–5.
***1971* Italy d. Spain 2–1, Ancona:** A. Panatta lost to M. Orantes 2–6 3–6; N. Pietrangeli d. J. Gisbert 7–9 8–6 6–4; Panatta/Pietrangeli d. Gisbert/Orantes 4–6 8–6 6–3 6–4.
***1972* Spain d. Hungary 3–0, Madrid:** A. Gimeno d. S. Baranyi 10–8 6–2; J. Gisbert d. B. Taroczy 6–1 7–9 6–3; J. Herrera/A. Munoz d. R. Machan/Taroczy 6–4 3–6 7–5.
***1973* Sweden d. Italy 2–1, Hanover:** L. Johansson d. A. Zugarelli 6–4 6–3; B. Borg d. A. Panatta 4–6 6–2 8–6; Borg/Johansson lost to P. Bertolucci/Zugarelli 6–3 5–7 4–6.
***1974* Italy d. Sweden 3–0, Ancona:** A. Panatta d. R. Norberg 6–3 6–4; A. Zugarelli d. T. Svensson 6–3 6–4; P. Bertolucci/A. Panatta d. B. Andersson/Norberg 6–2 6–4.
1975 *Not held*
***1976* Hungary 11 wins, Great Britain 10 wins** (played entirely as round robin, each tie home and away). Hungarian team: P. Szoke, B. Taroczy. British team: M. Cox, J. M. Lloyd, C. J. Mottram, R. Taylor.
1977* Sweden d. West Germany 5–1, Berlin:** R. Norberg d. U. Marten 6–2 4–6 6–4; K. Johansson d. K. Meiler 6–4 6–4; O. Bengtson/Norberg d. P. Elter/Meiler 6–2 6–2. ***Linköping: Norberg d. U. Pinner 7–6 6–2; Johansson d. Meiler 6–7 6–2 6–3; Bengtson/Norberg lost to Elter/Marten 6–3 4–6 4–6.
1978* Sweden d. Hungary 3–3 (9–7 sets), Uppsala:** T. Svensson d. P. Szoke 6–2 6–4; O. Bengtson lost to B. Taroczy 6–7 6–7; Bengtson/Svensson lost to Szoke/Taroczy 6–7 4–6; ***Debrecen: Svensson d. Szoke 6–2 6–2; Bengtson d. Taroczy 6–4 7–6; Bengtson/Svensson lost to Szoke/Taroczy 3–6 6–3 3–6.
1979* Czechoslovakia d. Hungary 4–2, Pécs:** I. Lendl lost to J. Benyik 6–7 7–5 6–7; T. Smid d. B. Taroczy 5–7 6–3 6–4; P. Slozil/T. Smid d. P. Szoke/Taroczy 6–4 6–4; ***Chrudin: Lendl lost to Benyik 6–4 2–6 0–6; Smid d. Szoke 6–3 3–6 6–2; Slozil/Smid d. Benyik/Szoke 6–4 6–2.
1980* Czechoslovakia d. Hungary 5–1, Chrudin:** T. Smid d. R. Machan 6–4 6–2; I. Lendl d. B. Taroczy 6–2 6–1; Smid/P. Slozil d. P. Szoke/Machan 6–4 7–5; ***Debreden: Smid d. J. Benyik 6–2 3–6 6–2; Lendl d. Machan 6–0 6–2; Smid/Slozil lost to Machan/Szoke 6–3 3–6 2–6.
***1981* West Germany d. USSR 3–3 (9–7 sets), Moscow, 2–1, and Hamburg, 1–2.**
***1982* West Germany d. Czechoslovakia 2–1, Dortmund:** K. Eberhard lost to J. Navratil 4–6 1–6; U. Pinnder d. P. Slozil 6–4 6–4; C. Zipf/H. D. Beutel d. Navratil/Slozil 6–3 6–4.
***1983* West Germany d. Czechoslovakia 2–1, Uppsala:** H. J. Schwaier lost to L. Pimek 6–4 2–6 3–6; M. Westphal d. J. Navratil 3–6 6–2 6–3; E. Jelen/W. Popp d. Navratil/Pimek 6–1 1–6 7–6.
***1984* Czechoslovakia d. Sweden 2–1, Essen:** M. Mecir d. J. Gunnarsson 7–6 6–4; L. Pimek lost to J. Nystrom 3–6 5–7; Pimek/J. Navratil d. Gunnarsson/Nystrom 3–6 6–2 6–4.
***1985* Sweden d. Switzerland 3–0, Essen:** T. Hogstedt d. R. Stadler 6–3 6–2; J. Gunnarsson d. J. Hlasek 7–5 4–6 6–2; H./S. Simonsson d. Hlasek/Stadler 6–3 3–6 6–3.
***1986* Switzerland d. Czechoslovakia 2–1, Queen's Club, London:** R. Stadler d. M. Vajda 6–4 7–5; J. Hlasek lost to L. Pimek 7–5 3–6 5–7; Hlasek/Stadler d. Pimek/P. Korda 6–2 6–3.
***1987* Switzerland d. Great Britain 2–1, Hanover:** R. Stadler lost to M. J. Bates 6–7 2–6; J. Hlasek d. A. Castle 6–3 6–7 6–2; Hlasek/Stadler d. Bates/Castle 3–6 7–5 6–0.

WORLD TEAM CUP

Eight-nation men's team event, qualification by individual ATP rating. Formerly Nations Cup.

FINALS

Played at Kingston, Jamaica
***1975* USA d. Great Britain 2–1:** R. Tanner d. R. Taylor 6–3 2–6 6–4; A. R. Ashe lost to C. J. Mottram 5–7 7–5 1–6; Ashe/Tanner d. Mottram/Taylor 6–1 1–6 6–4.
1976–77 *Not held*
Played at Düsseldorf
***1978* Spain d. Australia 2–1:** J. Higueras d. J. D. Newcombe 6–2 6–3; M. Orantes d. P. Dent 6–3 6–4; Higueras/Orantes lost to Dent/Newcombe 6–7 4–6.

***1979* Australia d. Italy 2–1:** J. G. Alexander d. C. Barazzutti 6–2 6–0; P. Dent lost to A. Panatta 3–6 3–6; Alexander/Dent d. P. Bertolucci/Panatta 6–3 7–6.
***1980* Argentina d. Italy 3–0:** G. Vilas d. C. Barazzutti 6–3 6–2; J. L. Clerc d. A. Panatta 7–6 6–3; Clerc/Vilas d. P. Bertolucci/Panatta 6–2 6–3.
***1981* Czechoslovakia d. Australia 2–1:** I. Lendl lost to P. McNamara 3–6 4–6; T. Smid d. P. McNamee 6–4 7–6; Lendl/Smid d. McNamara/McNamee 6–4 6–3.
***1982* USA d. Australia 2–1:** G. Mayer d. K. Warwick 7–6 6–2; E. Teltscher d. P. McNamara 6–4 7–6; Mayer/S. E. Stewart lost to M. R. Edmondson/McNamara 1–6 1–6.
***1983* Spain d. Australia 2–1:** J. Higueras d. M. R. Edmondson 6–2 6–4; M. Orantes d. P. Cash 6–3 6–2; A. Gimenez/Higueras lost to Cash/Edmondson 5–7 6–4 1–6.
***1984* USA d. Czechoslovakia 2–1:** J. P. McEnroe d. I. Lendl 6–3 6–2; J. Arias lost to T. Smid 6–4 6–7 4–6; P. Fleming/McEnroe d. Lendl/Smid 6–1 6–2.
***1985* USA d. Czechoslovakia 2–1:** J. P. McEnroe lost to I. Lendl 7–6 6–7 3–6; J. S. Connors d. M. Mecir 6–3 3–6 7–5; K. Flach/R. Seguso d. Lendl/T. Smid 6–3 7–6
***1986* France d. Sweden 2–1:** H. Leconte d. A. Jarryd 6–3 3–6 6–1; T. Tulasne lost to M. Wilander 1–6 4–6; G. Forget/Leconte d. Jarryd/Wilander 6–3 2–6 6–2.
***1987* Czechoslovakia d. USA 2–1:** M. Mecir d. J. P. McEnroe 7–5 2–6 2–1 disqual.; M. Srejber lost to B. Gilbert 4–6 7–5 4–6; Mecir/T. Smid d. Gilbert/R. Seguso 6–3 6–1.

MEN'S GRAND PRIX WINNERS

	SINGLES	BONUS	DOUBLES	BONUS	SPONSOR
1970	C. Richey	$25,000			Pepsi-Cola
1971	S. R. Smith	$25,000			Pepsi-Cola
1972	I. Nastase	$50,000			Commercial Union
1973	I. Nastase	$55,000			Commercial Union
1974	G. Vilas	$100,000			Commercial Union
1975	G. Vilas	$100,000	J. Gisbert	$25,000	Commercial Union
1976	R. Ramirez	$150,000	R. Ramirez	$40,000	Commercial Union
1977	G. Vilas	$300,000	R. A. J. Hewitt	$85,000	Colgate
1978	J. S. Connors	*$300,000	W. Fibak	$90,000	Colgate
1979	J. P. McEnroe	$300,000	S. E. Stewart	$90,000	Colgate
1980	J. P. McEnroe	$300,000	S. R. Smith	$90,000	Volvo
1981	I. Lendl	$300,000	H. Gunthardt	$90,000	Volvo
1982	J. S. Connors	$600,000	S. E. Stewart	$150,000	Volvo
1983	M. Wilander	$600,000	P. Fleming	$150,000	Volvo
1984	J. P. McEnroe	$600,000	T. Smid	$150,000	Volvo
1985	I. Lendl	$800,000	R. Seguso	$165,000	Nabisco
1986	I. Lendl	$800,000	G. Forget	$165,000	Nabisco
1987	I. Lendl	$800,000	A. Jarryd	$165,000	Nabisco

** Neither Connors nor second-placed B. Borg had played enough tournaments to qualify for the bonus payment, which was awarded to third-placed E. Dibbs.*

MEN'S GRAND PRIX MASTERS WINNERS

SINGLES

	VENUE	WINNER	RUNNER-UP	SCORE	FIRST PRIZE
1970	Tokyo	S. R. Smith	R. G. Laver	Round-Robin	$10,000
1971	Paris	I. Nastase	S. R. Smith	Round-Robin	$15,000
1972	Barcelona	I. Nastase	S. R. Smith	6–3 6–2 3–6 2–6 6–3	$15,000
1973	Boston	I. Nastase	T. S. Okker	6–3 7–5 4–6 6–3	$15,000
1974	Melbourne	G. Vilas	I. Nastase	7–6 6–2 3–6 3–6 6–4	$40,000
1975	Stockholm	I. Nastase	B. Borg	6–2 6–2 6–1	$40,000
1976	Houston	M. Orantes	W. Fibak	5–7 6–2 0–6 7–6 6–1	$40,000
1977*	New York	J. S. Connors	B. Borg	6–4 1–6 6–4	$100,000
1978*	New York	J. P. McEnroe	A. R. Ashe	6–7 6–3 7–5	$100,000
1979*	New York	B. Borg	V. Gerulaitis	6–2 6–2	$100,000
1980*	New York	B. Borg	I. Lendl	6–4 6–2 6–2	$100,000
1981*	New York	I. Lendl	V. Gerulaitis	6–7 2–6 7–6 6–2 6–4	$100,000
1982*	New York	I. Lendl	J. P. McEnroe	6–4 6–4 6–2	$100,000
1983*	New York	J. P. McEnroe	I. Lendl	6–3 6–4 6–4	$100,000
1984*	New York	J. P. McEnroe	I. Lendl	7–5 6–0 6–4	$100,000

1985*	New York	I. Lendl	B. Becker	6–2 7–6 6–3	$100,000
1986	New York	I. Lendl	B. Becker	6–4 6–4 6–4	$200,000
1987	New York	I. Lendl	M. Wilander	6–2 6–2 6–3	$200,000

* *Played in January of the following year.*

DOUBLES

	WINNERS	RUNNERS-UP	SCORE
1970	S. R. Smith/A. R. Ashe	R. G. Laver/J. Kodes	Round-Robin
1971–74	*Not held*		
1975	J. Gisbert/M. Orantes	J. Fassbender/H. J. Pohmann	Round-Robin
1976	F. McNair/S. E. Stewart	B. E. Gottfried/R. Ramirez	6–3 5–7 5–7 6–4 6–4
1977*	R. A. J. Hewitt/F. D. McMillan	R. C. Lutz/S. R. Smith	7–5 7–6 6–3
1978*	P. Fleming/J. P. McEnroe	W. Fibak/T. S. Okker	6–4 6–2 6–4
1979*	P. Fleming/J. P. McEnroe	W. Fibak/T. S. Okker	6–3 7–6 6–1
1980*	P. Fleming/J. P. McEnroe	P. McNamara/P. McNamee	6–4 6–3
1981*	P. Fleming/J. P. McEnroe	K. Curren/S. Denton	6–3 6–3
1982*	P. Fleming/J. P. McEnroe	S. E. Stewart/F. Taygan	6–2 6–2
1983*	P. Fleming/J. P. McEnroe	P. Slozil/T. Smid	6–2 6–2
1984*	P. Fleming/J. P. McEnroe	M. R. Edmondson/S. E. Stewart	6–3 6–1
1985*	A. Jarryd/S. Edberg	J. Nystrom/M. Wilander	6–1 7–6
1986†	A. Jarryd/S. Edberg	G. Forget/Y. Noah	6–3 7–6 6–3
1987†	M. Mecir/T. Smid	K. Flach/R. Seguso	6–4 7–5 7–6 6–3

* *Played in January of the following year.* † *Played separately from the singles at the Royal Albert Hall, London.*

WOMEN'S WORLD SERIES

	WINNER	BONUS	DOUBLES WINNERS	SPONSOR
1971	Mrs L. W. King	$10,000		Pepsi-Cola
1972	Mrs L. W. King	$20,000		Commerical Union
1973	Miss C. M. Evert	$23,000		Commercial Union
1974–76	*Not held*			
1977	Miss C. M. Evert	$100,000	Miss M. Navratilova/Miss B. Stove	Colgate
1978	Miss C. M. Evert	$100,000	Mrs G. E. Reid/Miss W. M. Turnbull	Colgate
1979	Mrs J. M. Lloyd	$115,000	Miss B. Stove/Miss W. M. Turnbull	Colgate
1980	Miss H. Mandlikova	$115,000	Miss K. Jordan/Miss A. E. Smith	Colgate
1981	Miss M. Navratilova	$125,000	Miss R. Casals/Miss W. M. Turnbull	Toyota
1982	Miss M. Navratilova	$130,000	Miss R. Casals/Miss W. M. Turnbull	Toyota
1983	Miss M. Navratilova	$150,000	Miss M. Navratilova/Miss P. H. Shriver	Virginia Slims
1984	Miss M. Navratilova	$150,000	Miss M. Navratilova/Miss P. H. Shriver	Virginia Slims
1985	Miss M. Navratilova	$150,000	Miss M. Navratilova/Miss P. H. Shriver	Virginia Slims
1986	Miss M. Navratilova	$200,000	Miss M. Navratilova/Miss P. H. Shriver	Virginia Slims
1987	Miss S. Graf	$225,000	Miss M. Navratilova/Miss P. H. Shriver	Virginia Slims

WOMEN'S INTERNATIONAL SERIES CHAMPIONSHIPS

SINGLES

	VENUE	WINNER	RUNNER-UP	SCORE	FIRST PRIZE
1977	Palm Springs	Miss C. M. Evert	Mrs L. W. King	6–2 6–2	$75,000
1978	Palm Springs	Miss C. M. Evert	Miss M. Navratilova	6–3 6–3	$75,000
1979*	Landover, Maryland	Miss M. Navratilova	Miss T. A. Austin	6–2 6–1	$75,000
1980*	Palm Springs	Miss T. A. Austin	Miss A. Jaeger	6–2 6–2	$75,000
1981	East Rutherford, NJ	Miss T. A. Austin	Miss M. Navratilova	2–6 6–4 6–2	$75,000
1982	East Rutherford, NJ	Miss M. Navratilova	Mrs J. M. Lloyd	4–6 6–1 6–2	$75,000
1983*	Madison Square Garden, NY	Miss M. Navratilova	Mrs J. M. Lloyd	6–3 7–5 6–1**	$125,000
1984*	Madison Square Garden, NY	Miss M. Navratilova	Miss H. Sukova	6–3 7–5 6–4**	$125,000
1985*	Madison Square Garden, NY	Miss M. Navratilova	Miss H. Mandlikova	6–2 6–0 3–6 6–1**	$125,000
1986	Madison Square Garden, NY	Miss M. Navratilova	Miss S. Graf	7–6 6–3 6–2**	$125,000
1987	Madison Square Garden, NY	Miss S. Graf	Miss G. Sabatini	4–6 6–4 6–0 6–4**	$125,000

* *Played in the following year.* ** *Best of five sets.*

DOUBLES

	WINNERS	RUNNERS-UP	SCORE
1977	Miss F. Durr/Miss S. V. Wade	Mrs H. Gourlay Cawley/Miss J. Russell	6–1 4–6 6–4
1978	Mrs L. W. King/Miss M. Navratilova	Mrs G. E. Reid/Miss W. M. Turnbull	6–3 6–4
1979*	Mrs L. W. King/Miss M. Navratilova	Miss R. Casals/Mrs J. M. Lloyd	6–4 6–3
1980*	Miss R. Casals/Miss W. M. Turnbull	Miss C. Reynolds/Miss P. Smith	6–3 4–6 7–6
1981	Miss M. Navratilova/Miss P. H. Shriver	Miss R. Casals/Miss W. M. Turnbull	6–3 6–4
1982	Miss M. Navratilova/Miss P. H. Shriver	Miss C. Reynolds/Miss P. Smith	6–4 7–5
1983*	Miss M. Navratilova/Miss P. H. Shriver	Miss J. M. Durie/Miss A. Kiyomura	6–3 6–1
1984*	Miss M. Navratilova/Miss P. H. Shriver	Miss C. Kohde-Kilsch/Miss H. Sukova	6–7 6–4 7–6
1985*	Miss H. Mandlikova/Miss W. M. Turnbull	Miss C. Kohde-Kilsch/Miss H. Sukova	6–4 6–7 6–3
1986	Miss M. Navratilova/Miss P. H. Shriver	Miss C. Kohde-Kilsch/Miss H. Sukova	7–6 6–3
1987	Miss M. Navratilova/Miss P. H. Shriver	Miss C. Kohde-Kilsch/Miss H. Sukova	6–1 6–1

** Played in the following year.*

WORLD CHAMPIONSHIP TENNIS

WCT FINALS, DALLAS

	WINNER	RUNNER-UP	SCORE	PRIZE
1971	K. R. Rosewall	R. G. Laver	6–4 1–6 7–6 7–6	$50,000
1972	K. R. Rosewall	R. G. Laver	4–6 6–0 6–3 6–7 7–6	50,000
1973	S. R. Smith	A. R. Ashe	6–3 6–3 4–6 6–4	50,000
1974	J. D. Newcombe	B. Borg	4–6 6–3 6–3 6–2	50,000
1975	A. R. Ashe	B. Borg	3–6 6–4 6–4 6–0	50,000
1976	B. Borg	G. Vilas	1–6 6–1 7–5 6–1	50,000
1977	J. S. Connors	R. D. Stockton	6–7 6–1 6–4 6–3	100,000
1978	V. Gerulaitis	E. Dibbs	6–3 6–2 6–1	100,000
1979	J. P. McEnroe	B. Borg	7–5 4–6 6–2 7–6	100,000
1980	J. S. Connors	J. P. McEnroe	2–6 7–6 6–1 6–2	100,000
1981	J. P. McEnroe	J. Kriek	7–6 6–3 4–6 0–6 6–4	100,000
1982	I. Lendl	J. P. McEnroe	6–2 3–6 6–3 6–3	150,000
1983	J. P. McEnroe	I. Lendl	6–2 4–6 6–3 6–7 7–6	150,000
1984	J. P. McEnroe	J. S. Connors	6–1 6–2 6–3	200,000
1985	I. Lendl	T. Mayotte	7–6 6–4 6–1	200,000
1986	A. Jarryd	B. Becker	6–7 6–1 6–1 6–4	200,000
1987	M. Mecir	J. P. McEnroe	6–0 3–6 6–2 6–2	200,000

WORLD DOUBLES CHAMPIONSHIPS

	VENUE	WINNERS	RUNNERS-UP	SCORE	PRIZE
1973	Montreal	R. C. Lutz/S. R. Smith	T. S. Okker/M. C. Riessen	6–2 7–6 6–0	$40,000
1974	Montreal	R. A. J. Hewitt/F. D. McMillan	J. D. Newcombe/O. K. Davidson	6–2 6–7 6–1 6–2	40,000
1975	Mexico City	B. R. Gottfried/R. Ramirez	M. Cox/C. Drysdale	7–6 6–7 7–6 7–6	40,000
1976	Kansas City	W. Fibak/K. Meiler	R. C. Lutz/S. R. Smith	6–3 2–6 3–6 6–3 6–4	40,000
1977	Kansas City	V. Amritraj/R. D. Stockton	V. Gerulaitis/A. Panatta	7–6 7–6 4–6 6–3	80,000
1978	Kansas City	W. Fibak/T. S. Okker	R. C. Lutz/S. R. Smith	6–7 6–4 6–0 6–3	80,000
1979	Olympia, London	J. P. McEnroe/P. Fleming	I. Nastase/S. E. Stewart	3–6 6–2 6–3 6–1	80,000
1980	Olympia, London	B. E. Gottfried/R. Ramirez	W. Fibak/T. S. Okker	3–6 6–4 6–4 3–6 6–3	80,000
1981	Olympia, London	P. McNamara/P. McNamee	V. Amaya/H. Pfister	6–3 2–6 3–6 6–3 6–2	80,000
1982	Birmingham	H. Gunthardt/B. Taroczy	K. Curren/S. Denton	6–7 6–3 7–5 6–4	80,000
1983	Royal Albert Hall, London	H. Gunthardt/B. Taroczy	B. E. Gottfried/R. Ramirez	6–3 7–5 7–6	80,000
1984	Royal Albert Hall, London	P. Slozil/T. Smid	A. Jarryd/H. Simonsson	1–6 6–3 3–6 6–4 6–3	80,000
1985	Royal Albert Hall, London	K. Flach/R. Seguso	H. Gunthardt/B. Taroczy	6–3 3–6 6–3 4–6 6–0	80,000

From 1986 this event was incorporated into the Masters Doubles.

GRAND SLAMS

The Grand Slam denotes holding the four championship titles of Australia, France, Wimbledon and the United States at the same time (originally in the same season)

MEN'S SINGLES

J. D. Budge: Wimbledon, US 1937, Australia, France, Wimbledon, US 1938
R. G. Laver: Australia, France, Wimbledon, US 1962
R. G. Laver: Australia, France, Wimbledon, US 1969

WOMEN'S SINGLES

Miss M. Connolly: Wimbledon, US 1952, Australia, France, Wimbledon, US 1953
Mrs B. M. Court: US 1969, Australia, France, Wimbledon, US 1970, Australia 1971
Miss M. Navratilova: Wimbledon, US, Australia 1983, France, Wimbledon, US 1984

MEN'S DOUBLES

F. A. Sedgman: (With J. E. Bromwich) US 1950, (with K. McGregor) Australia, France, Wimbledon, US 1951, Australia, France, Wimbledon 1952
K. McGregor: (With F. A. Sedgman) Australia, France, Wimbledon, US 1951, Australia, France, Wimbledon 1952

WOMEN'S DOUBLES

Miss A. L. Brough: (with Mrs W. du Pont) France, Wimbledon, US 1949, (with Miss D. J. Hart) Australia 1950
Miss M. E. Bueno: (With Miss C. C. Truman) Australia 1960, (with Miss D. R. Hard) France, Wimbledon, US 1960
Miss M. Navratilova/Miss P. H. Shriver: Wimbledon, US, Australia 1983, France, Wimbledon, US, Australia 1984, France 1985; *Wimbledon, US 1986, Australia, France 1987
* *Miss Navratilova also won France 1986 with Miss A. Temesvari.*

MIXED DOUBLES

Miss M. Smith: (With F. S. Stolle) US 1962, (with K. N. Fletcher) Australia, France, Wimbledon, US 1963, Australia, France 1964
K. N. Fletcher: (With Miss M. Smith) Australia, France, Wimbledon, US 1963, Australia, France 1964
O. K. Davidson: (With Mrs D. Fales) US 1966, (with Miss L. R. Turner) Australia 1967, (with Mrs L. W. King) France, Wimbledon, US 1967
Mrs L. W. King: (With O. K. Davidson) France, Wimbledon, US 1967, (with R. D. Crealy) Australia 1968

JUNIOR SINGLES

E. H. Buchholz: Australia, France, Wimbledon, US 1958 (*Note:* the US event was not then conducted as an international event)
S. Edberg: France, Wimbledon, US, Australia 1983

ITF VETERAN CHAMPIONSHIPS

MEN

	VENUE	45+ SINGLES	45+ DOUBLES	55+ SINGLES	55+ DOUBLES
1981	Sao Paulo	S. Davidson	S. Davidson/H. Stewart	S. Clark	S. Clark/T. Johansson
1982	Poertschach	I. Gulyas	J. Morton/J. Nelson	R. McCarthy	A. Hussmuller/L. Legenstein
1983	Bahia	I. Gulyas	K. Fuhrmann/F. Seeman	R. McCarthy	A. Hussmuller/L. Legenstein
1984	Cervia	I. Gulyas	K. Fuhrmann/F. Seeman	G. Merlo	J. Morton/H. Stewart
1985	Melbourne	I. Barclay	A. Duestler/J. Nelson	H. Stewart	J. Morton/H. Stewart
1986	Poertschach	J. Lemann	J. Lemann/I.Ribeiro	L. Maine	B. Howe/R. Seymour
1987	Garmisch-Partenkirchen	G. Rohrich	H. Gradischnig/P. Pokorny	I. Gulyas	I. Gulyas/H. Stewart

	VENUE	60+ SINGLES	60+ DOUBLES	65+ SINGLES	65+ DOUBLES
1982	Poertschach	T. Johansson	T. Johansson/A. Ritzenberg	F. Klein	J. Becker/F. Klein
1983	Bahia	—	—	R. San Martin	F. Barboza/H. H. Pizani

1984	Cervia			G. Mulloy	G. Mulloy/F. Klein
1985	Melbourne	R. Sorlein	T. Johansson/V. Zabrodsky	J. Gilchrist	F. Klein/R. Ritzenberg
1986	Poertschach	M. McCarthy	O. Jirkovsky/J. Karlhofer	T. Johansson	G. Mulloy/V. Hughes
1987	Garmisch-Partenkirchen	B. Howe	L. Legenstein/A. Stolpa	A. Swetka	B. Kempa/W. Kessler

WOMEN

	VENUE	40+ SINGLES	40+ DOUBLES	45+ DOUBLES
1981	Sao Paulo	E. de Molina	N. Reed/M. S. Plante	—
1982	Poertschach	R. Drisaldi	—	C. Hillebrand/N. Reed
1983	Bahia	H. Masthoff	H. Masthoff/H. Orth	—
1984	Cervia	H. Masthoff	H. Masthoff/H. Orth	—
1985	Melbourne	H. Orth	J. Dalton/H. Orth	—
1986	Poertschach	H. Masthoff	H. Masthoff/H. Orth	—
1987	Garmisch-Partenkirchen	M. Pinterova	G. Lovera/M. Pinterova	—

	VENUE	50+ SINGLES	50+ DOUBLES
1981	Sao Paulo	A. Cury	—
1982	Poertschach	E. Slytermann	E. Slytermann/I. Burmester
1983	Bahia	I. de Pla	G. Barboza/J. Borzone
1984	Cervia	C. Mazzoleni	H. Brabenec/P. Wearne
1985	Melbourne	I. Michael	A.Fotheringham/A. Pilkinghorne
1986	Poertschach	S. Brasher	S. Brasher/L. Cawthorn
1987	Garmisch-Partenkirchen	S. Brasher	S. Brasher/L. Cawthorn

DUBLER CUP

International Men's Team Championship for Over 45s

FINALS

	VENUE*	WINNERS	RUNNERS-UP	SCORE
1958	Monte Carlo	Italy	West Germany	3–1
1959	Zurich	Switzerland	Italy	4–1
1960	Merano, Italy	Italy	Switzerland	5–0
1961	Bologna	Italy	Austria	4–1
1962	Merano, Italy	Italy	France	3–2
1963	Merano, Italy	Italy	Belgium	4–1
1964	Merano, Italy	Italy	West Germany	5–0
1965	Merano, Italy	Italy	Sweden	3–0
1966	Florence	Sweden	Italy	4–1
1967	Avesta, Sweden	France	Sweden	3–2
1968	Paris	USA	France	5–0
1969	St Louis	USA	Sweden	4–1
1970	Cleveland	USA	Sweden	4–1
1971	La Costa, California	USA	Sweden	3–2
1972	Le Touquet	USA	France	4–1
1973	New York	Australia	USA	3–1
1974	New York	USA	Australia	3–2
1975	New York	Australia	USA	5–0
1976	Alassio, Italy	Italy	Canada	3–2
1977	New York	USA	France	4–1
1978	New York	USA	Australia	4–1
1979	Vienna	Austria	USA	3–2
1980	Cervia, Italy	Sweden	Austria	2–1
1981	Buenos Aires	USA	Great Britain	2–1
1982	Athens	USA	Great Britain	2–1
1983	New York	USA	West Germany	2–1
1984	Bastad	West Germany	USA	3–0

1985	Perth	West Germany	Australia	2–1
1986	Berlin	West Germany	Switzerland	3–0
1987	Poertschach	Italy	Austria	2–1

* *From 1958 to 1979 the early rounds were played zonally*

AUSTRIA CUP

International Men's Team Competition for Over 55s

	VENUE	WINNERS	RUNNERS-UP	FINAL SCORE
1977	Baden b. Wien	Great Britain	Austria	2–1
1978	Brand (Austria)	USA	Sweden	2–1
1979	Brand (Austria)	USA	Sweden	3–0
1980	Brand (Austria)	USA	Sweden	2–1
1981	Poertschach	USA	Sweden	3–0
1982	Cervia, Italy	Australia	USA	2–1
1983	New York	Australia	USA	2–1
1984	Poertschach	USA	Australia	2–1
1985	Perth	Australia	USA	3–0
1986	Poertschach	Australia	Canada	2–1
1987	Umag	Canada	Australia	3–0

YOUNG CUP

International Women's Team Competition for Over 40s

	VENUE	WINNERS	RUNNERS-UP	FINAL SCORE
1977	Malmo	Argentina	Not available	
1978	Ancona	Italy	Not available	
1979	Cannes	West Germany	USA	3–0
1980	Bad Wiessee, Germany	West Germany	Italy	3–0
1981	Bad Wiessee, Germany	France	Italy	2–1
1982	Brand, Austria	France	Italy	3–0
1983	Cervia, Italy	West Germany	France	2–1
1984	Cervia, Italy	USA	France	3–0
1985	Poertschach, Austria	West Germany	France	3–0
1986	Brand	West Germany	USA	2–1
1987	Venice	France	USA	2–1

MARIA ESTHER BUENO CUP

International Women's Team Competition for Over 50s

	VENUE	WINNERS	RUNNERS-UP	FINAL SCORE
1983	Poertschach	Great Britain	USA	2–1
1984	Le Touquet, France	USA	France	3–0
1985	Bremen	USA	Great Britain	3–0
1986	Brand	USA	Great Britain	2–1
1987	Helsinki	USA	Great Britain	2–1

ITALIA CUP

International Men's Team Competition for Over 35s

	VENUE	WINNERS	RUNNERS-UP	FINAL SCORE
1982	Cervia, Italy	Italy	USA	2–1
1983	Cervia, Italy	West Germany	USA	2–1
1984	Brand, Austria	West Germany	France	2–1
1985	Reggio Calabria, Italy	USA	Italy	2–0
1986	Normandy, France	West Germany	USA	3–0
1987	Grado	USA	Austria	2–1

BRITANNIA CUP

International Men's Team Competition for Over 65s

	VENUE	WINNERS	RUNNERS-UP	FINAL SCORE
1979	Queen's Club, London	USA	Great Britain	3–0
1980	Frinton-on-Sea	USA	Sweden	3–0
1981	Hurlingham Club, London	USA	Sweden	3–0
1982	New York	USA	Canada	3–0
1983	Poertschach	USA	Australia	3–0
1984	Poertschach	USA	Australia	3–0
1985	Poertschach	USA	Australia	3–0
1986	Bournemouth	USA	Norway	3–0
1987	Bastad	USA	Sweden	2–1

THE CRAWFORD CUP

International Men's Team Competition for Over 75s

	VENUE	WINNERS	RUNNERS-UP	FINAL SCORE
1983	Brand, Austria	USA	Sweden	3–0
1984	Helsinki, Finland	USA	Great Britain	3–0
1985	Brand, Austria	USA	Australia	3–0
1986	Seefeld, Austria	USA	France	3–0
1987	Poertschach	USA	Great Britain	3–0

AUSTRALIAN INTERNATIONAL JUNIOR CHAMPIONSHIPS

BOYS' SINGLES

1946	F. Sedgman	1956	R. Mark	1965	G. Goven
1947	D. Candy	1957	R. Laver	1966	K. Coombes
1948	K. McGregor	1958	M. Mulligan	1967	B. Fairlie (NZL)
1949	C. Wilderspin	1959	E. Buchholz (USA)	1968	P. Dent
1950	K. Rosewall	1960	W. Coghlan	1969	A. McDonald
1951	L. Hoad	1961	J. Newcombe	1970	J. Alexander
1952	K. Rosewall	1962	J. Newcombe	1971	C. Letcher
1953	W. Gilmour	1963	J. Newcombe	1972	P. Kronk
1954	W. Knight	1964	A. Roche	1973	P. McNamee
1955	G. Moss				

	WINNER	RUNNER-UP	SCORE
1974	H. Brittain		
1975	B. Drewett (AUS)		
1976	R. Kelly		
1977	(Jan.) B. Drewett (AUS)		
1977	(Dec.) R. Kelly		
1978	P. Serrett		
1979	G. Whitecross		
1980	C. Miller		
1981	J. Windahl (SWE)		
1982	M. Kratzmann (AUS)		
1983	S. Edberg (SWE)	S. Youl (AUS)	6–4 6–4
1984	M. Kratzmann (AUS)	P. Flyn	6–4 6–1
1985	S. Barr (AUS)	S. Furlong	7–6 6–7 6–3
1986	*Not held*		
1987	J. Stoltenberg (AUS)	T. Woodbridge (AUS)	6–2 7–6

GIRLS' SINGLES

1946	S. Grant	1956	L. Coghlan	1965	K. Melville
1947	J. Tuckfield	1957	M. Rayson	1966	K. Krantzcke
1948	B. Penrose	1958	J. Lehane	1967	A. Kenny
1949	J. Warnock	1959	J. Lehane	1968	L. Hunt
1950	B. McIntyre	1960	L. Turner	1969	L. Hunt
1951	M. Carter	1961	R. Ebbern	1970	E. Goolagong
1952	M. Carter	1962	R. Ebbern	1971	P. Coleman
1953	J. Staley	1963	R. Ebbern	1972	P. Coleman
1954	E. Orton	1964	K. Dening	1973	C. O'Neill
1955	E. Orton				

Vijay Amritraj (above left) led India to the 1987 Davis Cup *final; Anne Smith (above right), has collected nine Grand Slam doubles titles; Tomas Carbonell (below left), was the 1986 ITF Junior doubles champion, and Katerina Maleeva (below right) won the US Open Junior title in 1984.* *(T. Hindley, Carol L. Newsom)*

	WINNER	RUNNER-UP	SCORE
1974	J. Walker		
1975	S. Barker (GBR)		
1976	S. Saliba (AUS)		
1977	(Jan.) P. Bailey		
1977	(Dec.) A. Tobin (AUS)		
1978	E. Little (AUS)		
1979	A. Minter (AUS)		
1980	A. Minter (AUS)		
1981	A. Minter (AUS)		
1982	A. Brown (AUS)		
1983	A. Brown (AUS)	B. Randall	7–6 6–3
1984	A. Croft (GBR)	H. Dahlstrom (SWE)	6–0 6–1
1985	J. Byrne (AUS)	L. Field (AUS)	6–1 6–3
1986	*Not held*		
1987	M. Jaggard (AUS)	N. Provis (AUS)	6–2 6–4

BOYS' DOUBLES

	WINNERS	RUNNERS-UP	SCORE
1983	J. Harty/D. Tyson		
1984	B. Custer/D. Macpherson		
1985	B. Custer/D. Macpherson	C. Suk (TCH)/P. Korda (TCH)	7–5 6–2
1986	*Not held*		
1987	J. Stoltenberg (AUS)/T. Woodbridge (AUS)	S. Barr (AUS)/D. Roe (AUS)	6–2 6–4

GIRLS' DOUBLES

	WINNERS	RUNNERS-UP	SCORE
1983	B. Randall/K. Staunton		
1984	L. Field (AUS)/L. Savchenko (URS)		
1985	J. Byrne (AUS)/J. Thompson (AUS)	A. Scott/S. McCann	6–0 6–3
1986	*Not held*		
1987	N. Provis (AUS)/A. Devries (BEL)	D. Jones (AUS)/G. Dwyer (AUS)	6–3 6–1

FRENCH INTERNATIONAL JUNIOR CHAMPIONSHIPS

BOYS' SINGLES

	WINNER	RUNNER-UP	SCORE
1974	C. Casa (FRA)	U. Marten (FRG)	2–6 6–1 6–4
1975	C. Roger-Vasselin (FRA)	P. Elter (FRG)	6–1 6–2
1976	H. Gunthardt (SUI)	J. L. Clerc (ARG)	4–6 7–6 6–4
1977	J. P. McEnroe (USA)	R. Kelly (AUS)	6–1 6–1
1978	I. Lendl (TCH)	P. Hjertquist (SWE)	7–6 6–4
1979	R. Krishnan (IND)	B. Testerman (USA)	2–6 6–1 6–0
1980	H. Leconte (FRA)	A. Tous (ESP)	7–6 6–3
1981	M. Wilander (SWE)	J. Brown (USA)	7–5 6–1
1982	T. Benhabiles (FRA)	L. Courteau (FRA)	7–6 6–2
1983	S. Edberg (SWE)	F. Fevrier (FRA)	6–4 7–6
1984	K. Carlsson (SWE)	M. Kratzman (AUS)	6–3 6–3
1985	J. Yzaga (PER)	T. Muster (AUT)	2–6 6–3 6–0
1986	G. Perez Roldan (ARG)	S. Grenier (FRA)	4–6 6–3 6–2
1987	G. Perez Roldan (ARG)	J. Stoltenberg (AUS)	6–3 3–6 6–1

GIRLS' SINGLES

	WINNER	RUNNER-UP	SCORE
1974	M. Simionescu (RUM)	S. Barker (GBR)	6–3 6–3
1975	R. Marsikova (TCH)	L. Mottram (GBR)	6–3 5–7 6–2
1976	M. Tyler (GBR)	M. Zoni (ITA)	6–1 6–3
1977	A. E. Smith (USA)	H. Strachonova (TCH)	6–3 7–6
1978	H. Mandlikova (TCH)	M. Rothschild (FRG)	6–1 6–1

1979	L. Sandin (SWE)	M. L. Piatek (USA)	6–3 6–1
1980	K. Horvath (USA)	K. Henry (USA)	6–2 6–2
1981	B. Gadusek (USA)	H. Sukova (TCH)	6–7 6–1 6–4
1982	M. Maleeva (BUL)	P. Barg (USA)	7–5 6–2
1983	P. Paradis (FRA)	D. Spence (USA)	7–6 6–3
1984	G. Sabatini (ARG)	K. Maleeva (BUL)	6–3 5–7 6–3
1985	L. Garrone (ITA)	D. Van Rensburg (SAF)	6–1 6–3
1986	P. Tarabini (ARG)	N. Provis (AUS)	6–3 6–3
1987	N. Zvereva (URS)	J. Pospisilova (TCH)	6–1 6–0

BOYS' DOUBLES

	WINNERS	RUNNERS-UP	SCORE
1983	M. Kratzman (AUS)/S. Youl (AUS)	A. Chesnokov (URS)/A. Olkhovski (URS)	6–2 6–3
1985	P. Korda (TCH)/C. Suk (TCH)	V. Godrichidze (URS)/V. Volkov (URS)	4–6 6–0 7–5
1986	F. Davin (ARG)/G. Perez Roldan (ARG)	T. Carbonell (ESP)/J. Sanchez (ESP)	7–5 5–7 6–3
1987	J. Courier (USA)/J. Stark (USA)	F. Davin (ARG)/G. Perez Roldan (ARG)	6–7 6–4 6–3

GIRLS' DOUBLES

	WINNERS	RUNNERS-UP	SCORE
1983	C. Anderholm (SWE)/H. Olsson (SWE)	K./M. Maleeva (BUL)	6–4 6–1
1985	M. Perez Roldan (ARG)/P. Tarabini (ARG)	A. Holikova (TCH)/R. Szrubakova (TCH)	6–3 5–7 6–4
1986	L. Meskhi (URS)/N. Zvereva (URS)	J. Novotna (TCH)/R. Rajchrtova (TCH)	1–6 6–3 6–0
1987	N. Medvedeva (URS)/N. Zvereva (URS)	M. Jaggard (AUS)/N. Provis (AUS)	6–3 6–3

INTERNATIONAL WIMBLEDON JUNIOR CHAMPIONSHIPS

The event originated as an invitation tournament, boys' singles in 1947 and girls' singles in 1948. It became a championship event in 1975.

BOYS' SINGLES

1948	S. Stockenberg (SWE)	1957	J. I. Tattersall (GBR)	1966	V. Korotkov (URS)
1949	S. Stockenberg (SWE)	1958	E. Buchholz (USA)	1967	M. Orantes (ESP)
1950	J. A. T. Horn (GBR)	1959	T. Lejus (URS)	1968	J. G. Alexander (AUS)
1951	J. Kupferburger (RSA)	1960	A. R. Mandelstam (RSA)	1969	B. Bertram (RSA)
1952	R. K. Wilson (GBR)	1961	C. E. Graebner (USA)	1970	B. Bertram (RSA)
1953	W. A. Knight (GBR)	1962	S. Matthews (GBR)	1971	R. Kreiss (USA)
1954	R. Krishnan (IND)	1963	N. Kalogeropoulos (GRE)	1972	B. Borg (SWE)
1955	M. P. Hann (GBR)	1964	I. El Shafei (EGY)	1973	W. Martin (USA)
1956	R. Holmberg (USA)	1965	V. Korotkov (URS)	1974	W. Martin (USA)

	WINNER	RUNNER-UP	SCORE
1975	C. J. Lewis (NZL)	R. Ycaza (ECU)	6–1 6–4
1976	H. Gunthardt (SUI)	P. Elter (FRG)	6–4 7–5
1977	V. Winitsky (USA)	E. Teltscher (USA)	6–1 1–6 8–6
1978	I. Lendl (TCH)	J. Turpin (USA)	6–3 6–4
1979	R. Krishnan (IND)	D. Siegler (USA)	6–3 6–4
1980	T. Tulasne (FRA)	H. D. Beutel (FRG)	6–4 3–6 6–4
1981	M. Anger (USA)	P. Cash (AUS)	7–6 7–5
1982	P. Cash (AUS)	H. Sundstrom (SWE)	6–4 6–7 6–3
1983	S. Edberg (SWE)	J. Frawley (AUS)	6–3 7–6
1984	M. Kratzman (AUS)	S. Kruger (SAF)	6–4 4–6 6–3
1985	L. Lavalle (MEX)	E. Velez (MEX)	6–4 6–4
1986	E. Velez (MEX)	J. Sanchez (ESP)	6–3 7–5
1987	D. Nargiso (ITA)	J. Stoltenberg (AUS)	7–6 6–4

GIRLS' SINGLES

1948	O. Miskova (TCH)	1952	ten Bosch (HOL)	1956	A. S. Haydon (GBR)
1949	C. Mercelis (BEL)	1953	D. Kilian (RSA)	1957	M. Arnold (USA)
1950	L. Cornell (GBR)	1954	V. A. Pitt (GBR)	1958	S. M. Moore (USA)
1951	L. Cornell (GBR)	1955	S. M. Armstrong (GBR)	1959	J. Cross (RSA)

1960	K. Hantze (USA)	1965	O. Morozova (URS)	1970	S. Walsh (USA)
1961	G. Baksheeva (URS)	1966	B. Lindstrom (FIN)	1971	M. Kroschina (URS)
1962	G. Baksheeva (URS)	1967	J. Salome (HOL)	1972	I. Kloss (RSA)
1963	D. M. Salfati (FRA)	1968	K. Pigeon (USA)	1973	A. Kiyomura (USA)
1964	P. Bartkowicz (USA)	1969	K. Sawamatsu (JAP)	1974	M. Jausovec (YUG)

	WINNER	RUNNER-UP	SCORE
1975	N. Y. Chmyreva (URS)	R. Marsikova (TCH)	6–4 6–3
1976	N. Y. Chmyreva (URS)	M. Kruger (SAF)	6–3 2–6 6–1
1977	L. Antonoplis (USA)	Mareen Louie (USA)	6–5 6–1
1978	T. A. Austin (USA)	H. Mandlikova (TCH)	6–0 3–6 6–4
1979	M. L. Piatek (USA)	A. Moulton (USA)	6–1 6–3
1980	D. Freeman (AUS)	S. Leo (AUS)	7–6 7–5
1981	Z. Garrison (USA)	R. Uys (SAF)	6–4 3–6 6–0
1982	C. Tanvier (FRA)	H. Sukova (TCH)	6–2 7–5
1983	P. Paradis (FRA)	P. Hy (HKG)	6–2 6–1
1984	A. N. Croft (GBR)	E. Reinach (SAF)	3–6 6–3 6–2
1985	A. Holikova (TCH)	J. Byrne (AUS)	7–5 6–1
1986	N. Zvereva (URS)	L. Meskhi (URS)	2–6 6–2 9–7
1987	N. Zvereva (URS)	J. Halard (FRA)	6–4 6–4

BOYS' DOUBLES

	WINNERS	RUNNERS-UP	SCORE
1982	P. Cash (AUS)/F. Frawley (AUS)	R. Leach (USA)/J. Ross (USA)	6–3 6–2
1983	M. Kratzman (AUS)/S. Youl (AUS)	M. Nastase (RUM)/O. Rahnasto (FIN)	6–4 6–4
1984	R. Brown (USA)/R. Weiss (USA)	M. Kratzman (AUS)/J. Svensson (SWE)	1–6 6–4 11–9
1985	A. Moreno (MEX)/J. Yzaga (PER)	P. Korda (TCH)/C. Suk (TCH)	7–6 6–4
1986	T. Carbonell (ESP)/P. Korda (TCH)	S. Barr (AUS)/H. Karrasch (CAN)	6–1 6–1
1987	J. Stoltenberg (AUS)/T. Woodbridge (AUS)	D. Nargiso (ITA)/E. Rossi (ITA)	6–3 7–6

GIRLS' DOUBLES

	WINNERS	RUNNERS-UP	SCORE
1982	B. Herr (USA)/P. Barg (USA)	B. S. Gerken (USA)/G. Rush (USA)	6–1 6–4
1983	P. Fendick (USA)/P. Hy (HKG)	C. Anderholm (SWE)/H. Olsson (SWE)	6–1 7–5
1984	C. Kuhlman (USA)/S. Rehe (USA)	V. Milvidskaya (URS)/L. Savchenko (URS)	6–3 5–7 6–4
1985	L. Field (AUS)/J. Thompson (AUS)	E. Reinach (SAF)/J. Richardson (NZL)	6–1 6–2
1986	M. Jaggard (AUS)/L. O'Neill (AUS)	L. Meskhi (URS)/N. Zvereva (URS)	7–6 6–4
1987	N. Medvedeva (URS)/N. Zvereva (URS)	I. S. Kim (KOR)/P. M. Modeña (HKG)	2–6 7–5 6–0

US INTERNATIONAL JUNIOR CHAMPIONSHIPS

BOYS' SINGLES

	WINNER	RUNNER-UP	SCORE
1974	W. Martin (USA)	F. Taygan (USA)	6–4 6–2
1975	H. Schonfield (USA)	C. J. Lewis (NZL)	6–4 6–3
1976	Y. Ycaza (ECU)	J. L. Clerc (ARG)	6–4 5–7 6–0
1977	V. Winitsky (USA)	E. Teltscher (USA)	6–4 6–4
1978	P. Hjertquist (SWE)	S. Simonsson (SWE)	7–6 1–6 7–6
1979	S. Davis (USA)	J. Gunnarsson (SWE)	6–3 6–1
1980	M. Falberg (USA)	E. Korita (USA)	6–0 6–2
1981	T. Hogstedt (SWE)	H. Schwaier (FRG)	7–5 6–3
1982	P. Cash (AUS)	G. Forget (FRA)	6–3 6–3
1983	S. Edberg (SWE)	S. Youl (AUS)	6–2 6–4
1984	M. Kratzman (AUS)	B. Becker (FRG)	6–3 7–6
1985	T. Trigueiro (USA)	J. Blake (USA)	6–2 6–3
1986	J. Sanchez (ESP)	F. Davin (ARG)	6–2 6–2
1987	D. Wheaton (USA)	A. Cherkasov (URS)	7–5 6–0

GIRLS' SINGLES

	WINNER	RUNNER-UP	SCORE
1974	I. Kloss (SAF)	M. Jausovec (YUG)	6–4 6–3
1975	N. T. Chmyreva (URS)	G. Stevens (SAF)	6–7 6–2 6–2
1976	M. Kruger (SAF)	L. Romanov (RUM)	6–3 7–5
1977	C. Casabianca (ARG)	L. Antonoplis (USA)	6–3 2–6 6–2
1978	L. Siegel (USA)	I. Madruga (ARG)	6–4 6–4
1979	A. Moulton (USA)	M. L. Piatek (USA)	7–6 7–6
1980	S. Mascarin (USA)	K. Keil (USA)	6–3 6–4
1981	Z. Garrison (USA)	K. Gompert (USA)	6–0 6–3
1982	B. Herr (USA)	G. Rush (USA)	6–3 6–1
1983	E. Minter (AUS)	M. Werdel (USA)	6–3 7–5
1984	K. Maleeva (BUL)	N. Sodupe (USA)	6–1 6–2
1985	L. Garrone (ITA)	A. Holikova (TCH)	6–2 7–6
1986	E. Hakami (USA)	S. Stafford (USA)	6–2 6–1
1987	N. Zvereva (URS)	S. Birch (USA)	6–0 6–3

BOYS' DOUBLES

	WINNERS	RUNNERS-UP	SCORE
1982	J. Canter (USA)/M. Kures (USA)	P. Cash (AUS)/J. Frawley (AUS)	7–6 6–3
1983	M. Kratzman (AUS)/S. Youl (AUS)	P. McEnroe (USA)/B. Pearce (USA)	6–1 7–6
1984	L. Lavelle (MEX)/M. Nastase (RUM)	J. Icaza (PER)/A. Moreno (MEX)	7–6 1–6 6–1
1985	J. Blake (USA)/D. Yates (USA)	P. Flynn (USA)/D. McPherson (USA)	3–6 6–3 6–4
1986	T. Carbonell (ESP)/J. Sanchez (ESP)	J. Tarnago (USA)/D. Wheaton (USA)	6–4 1–6 6–1
1987	G. Ivanisevic (YUG)/D. Nargiso (ITA)	Z. Ali (IND)/B. Steven (NZL)	3–6 6–4 6–3

GIRLS' DOUBLES

	WINNERS	RUNNERS-UP	SCORE
1982	P. Barg (USA)/B. Herr (USA)	A. Hulbert (AUS)/B. Randall (AUS)	1–6 7–5 7–6
1983	A. Hulbert (AUS)/B. Randall (AUS)	N. Riva (URS)/L. Savchenko (URS)	6–4 6–2
1984	G. Sabatini (ARG)/M. Paz (MEX)	S. MacGregor (USA)/S. London (USA)	6–4 3–6 6–2
1985	R. Zrubakova (TCH)/A. Holikova (TCH)	P. Tarabini (ARG)/M. Perez Roldan (ARG)	6–4 2–6 7–5
1986	R. Zrubakova (TCH)/J. Novotna (TCH)	E. Brukhovets (URS)/L. Meskhi (URS)	6–4 6–2
1987	M. McGrath (USA)/K. Po (USA)	Il-Soon Kim (KOR)/Shi-Ting Wang (TPE)	6–4 7–5

ITF JUNIOR WORLD RANKING LEADERS

BOYS' SINGLES

1978 Ivan Lendl (TCH)
1979 Raul Viver (ECU)
1980 Thierry Tulasne (FRA)
1981 Pat Cash (AUS)
1982 Guy Forget (FRA)
1983 Stefan Edberg (SWE)
1984 Mark Kratzman (AUS)
1985 Claudio Pistolesi (ITA)
1986 Javier Sanchez (ESP)
1987 Jason Stoltenberg (AUS)

GIRLS' SINGLES

1978 Hana Mandlikova (TCH)
1979 Mary-Lou Piatek (USA)
1980 Susan Mascarin (USA)
1981 Zina Garrison (USA)
1982 Gretchen Rush (USA)
1983 Pascale Paradis (FRA)
1984 Gabriela Sabatini (ARG)
1985 Laura Garrone (USA)
1986 Patricia Tarabini (ARG)
1987 Natalia Zvereva (URS)

BOYS' DOUBLES

1982 Fernando Perez (MEX)
1983 Mark Kratzman (AUS)
1984 Augustin Moreno (MEX)
1985 Petr Korda (TCH) and Cyril Suk (TCH)
1986 Tomas Carbonell (ESP)
1987 Jason Stoltenberg (AUS)

GIRLS' DOUBLES

1982 Beth Herr (USA)
1983 Larisa Savchenko (URS)
1984 Mercedes Paz (ARG)
1985 Mariana Perez Roldan (ARG) and Patricia Tarabini (ARG)
1986 Leila Meskhi (URS)
1987 Natalia Medvedeva (URS)

WORLD YOUTH CUP

International Team Championship for boys and girls aged 16 and under. Early rounds played zonally.

BOYS' FINALS

1985 Australia d. USA 2–1, Kobe Japan: R. Fromberg lost to F. Montana 2–6 2–6, S. Barr d. J. A. Falbo 6–4 6–4; Barr/J. Stoltenberg d. Montana/Falbo 4–6 6–7 7–5.

1986 Australia d. USA 2–1, Kobe, Japan: J. Stoltenberg d. J. Courier 6–2 6–4; R. Fromberg lost to M. Chang 4–6 4–6; Stoltenberg/ Woolbridge d. Courier/Kass 7–6 6–2.

1987 Australia d. Netherlands 3–0, Freiburg, West Germany: T. Woodbridge d. P. Dogger 7–5 3–6 6–2; J. Anderson d. F. Wibier 6–0 6–1; J. Morgan/Woodbridge d. Dogger/Wibier 6–3 6–2.

GIRLS' FINALS

1985 Czechoslovakia d. Australia 3–0, Kobe, Japan: J. Pospisilova d. S. McCann 6–4 6–4; R. Zrubakova d. N. Provis 7–6 7–5; Pospisilova/Zrubakova d. Provis/W. Frazer 7–5 6–4.

1986 Belgium d. Czechoslovakia 2–1, Kobe, Japan: A. Devries d. R. Zrubakova 6–3 6–4; S. Wasserman d. P. Langrova 6–4 7–5; Devries/C. Neuprez lost to Langrova/Zrubakova.

1987 Australia d. USSR 2–1, Freiburg, West Germany: J. Faull lost to N. Medvedeva 6–4 2–6 2–6; R. McQuillan d. E. Brioukhovets 3–6 6–2 6–3; Faull/McQuillan d. Brioukhovets/Medvedeva 6–3 6–1.

ORANGE BOWL

International 18 and Under Championship

BOYS' SINGLES

	WINNER	RUNNER-UP	SCORE
1974	W. Martin (USA)	T. Smid (TCH)	6–7 4–6 6–2 6–1 7–6
1975	F. Luna (ESP)	B. E. Gottfried (USA)	6–4 6–4
1976	J. P. McEnroe (USA)	E. Teltscher (USA)	7–5 6–1
1977	I. Lendl (TCH)	Y. Noah (FRA)	4–6 7–6 6–3
1978	G. Urpi (ESP)	S. van der Merwe (SAF)	6–3 6–1
1979	R. Viver (ECU)	P. Arraya (PER)	7–6 6–4
1980	J. Nystrom (SWE)	C. Castellan (ARG)	7–5 7–6
1981	R. Arguello (ARG)	R. Joaquim (BRA)	6–2 6–1
1982	G. Forget (FRA)	J. Bardou (ESP)	7–5 2–6 6–1
1983	K. Carlsson (SWE)	E. Sanchez (ESP)	6–2 6–4
1984	R. Brown (USA)	J. Berger (USA)	6–3 6–3
1985	C. Pistolesi (ITA)	B. Oresar (YUG)	6–2 6–0
1986	J. Sanchez (ESP)	A. Parker (USA)	6–3 6–4
1987	J. Courier (USA)	A. Cherkasov (URS)	6–3 6–2

GIRLS' SINGLES

	WINNER	RUNNER-UP	SCORE
1974	L. Epstein (USA)	C. Penn (USA)	6–1 6–2
1975	L. Epstein (USA)	S. McInerny (USA)	6–2 6–1
1976	M. Kruger (SAF)	A. E. Smith (USA)	2–6 6–3 6–4
1977	A. E. Smith (USA)	H. Strachonova (TCH)	7–6 7–5
1978	A. Jaeger (USA)	R. Fairbank (SAF)	6–1 6–3
1979	K. Horvath (USA)	P. Murgo (ITA)	7–5 6–0
1980	S. Mascarin (USA)	R. Sasak (YUG)	6–3 3–6 6–4
1981	P. Barg (USA)	H. Fukarkova (TCH)	6–2 6–3
1982	C. Bassett (CAN)	M. Maleeva (BUL)	6–4 4–3 ret'd
1983	D. Spence (USA)	A. Cecchini (ITA)	2–6 7–5 6–4
1984	G. Sabatini (ARG)	K. Maleeva (BUL)	6–1 6–3
1985	M. J. Fernandez (USA)	P. Tarabini (ARG)	7–5 6–1
1986	P. Tarabini (ARG)	B. Fulco (ARG)	6–2 6–2
1987	N. Zvereva (URS)	L. Lapi (ITA)	6–2 6–0

GALEA CUP

International Men's Team Competition for Under 21s.

FINAL ROUNDS

Played at Deauville

1950 Italy d. France 4–1: U. Bergamo d. R. L. Haillet 6–2 6–3, d. A. Lemyze 8–10 7–5 7–5; F. Gardini d. Lemyze 6–1 6–2; A. Parri lost to F. Nys 3–6 2–6; Gardini/H. Clerici d. Lemyze/Nys 6–1 6–3.

1951 France d. West Germany 5–0: A. Lemyze d. B. Pottinger 8–6 10–8; R. L. Haillet d. F. Feldbausch 6–4 6–4; G.

Pilet d. C. Biederlack 1–6 6–2 6–2; P. Darmon d. J. Gulcz 6–4 1–6 6–1; Haillet/Lemyze d. Feldbausch/Pottinger 6–1 6–3 6–1.

Played at Vichy

1952 ***Italy d. France 4–1:*** N. Pietrangeli d. X. Perreau-Saussine 6–8 6–2 6–2, d. G. Pilet 7–5 6–1; A. Maggi lost to Pilet 3–6 6–2 3–6, d. Perreau-Saussine 6–4 7–5; Maggi/Pietrangeli d. J. N. Grinda/Pilet 10–8 6–3 6–3.

1953 ***France d. Italy 4–1:*** G. Pilet d. N. Pietrangeli 5–7 6–1 6–0, d. S. Jacobini 6–2 6–4; J. N. Grinda d. Jacobini 6–0 6–2, d. Pietrangeli 6–4 6–1; P. Darmon/Pilet lost to M. Pirro/Pietrangeli 3–6 5–7 7–9.

1954 ***Italy d. Yugoslavia 3–2:*** S. Jacobini d. L. Jagec 6–2 7–5, d. L. Backor 6–3 4–6 7–5; M. Pirro lost to Backor 6–3 4–6 4–6, lost to Jagec 0–6 5–7; Jacobsini/Pirro d. Backor/Jagec 10–8 4–6 6–4 6–3.

1955 ***Italy d. Spain 5–0:*** S. Jacobini d. A. Gimeno 3–6 6–3 6–4; F. Bonetti d. J. Moure 6–1 6–4; G. Morelli d. Moure 6–2 6–4; M. Drisaldi d. M. Santana 6–4 6–4; Drisaldi/Jacobini d. A. Arilla/Gimeno 6–3 6–4 2–6 6–1.

1956 ***Spain d. Italy 4–1:*** M. Santana d. F. Bonetti 6–3 5–7 7–5, d. G. Bonairi 4–6 6–5 7–5; A. Gimeno d. Bonetti 6–3 6–2, d. Bonairi 5–7 6–2 6–3: A. Arilla/A. Gimeno lost to M. Drisaldi/A. Maggi 6–1 4–6 3–6 3–6.

1957 ***Spain d. Italy 4–1:*** M. Santana d. G. Morelli 9–7 6–4, d. E. Casini 6–4 6–4; A. Gimeno d. F. Bonetti 6–3 6–4; J. L. Arilla lost to Morelli 3–6 6–8; A. Arilla/Gimeno d. Bonetti/A. Maggi 6–4 6–3 6–3.

1958 ***Spain d. West Germany 3–2:*** M. Santana d. W. Bungert 6–3 7–5 4–6 6–0, lost to D. Eklebe 1–6 5–7 6–1 3–6; A. Arilla d. Eklebe 6–1 9–7 4–6 7–5; J. Gisbert lost to W. Stuck 0–6 2–6 0–6; A. Arilla/Santana d. Eklebe/Stuck 7–6 6–3 6–3.

1959 ***West Germany d. USSR 4–1:*** W. Stuck d. A. Pontanin 6–3 6–0 6–1, d. T. Lejus 6–4 6–1 6–0; W. Bungert d. Lejus 6–2 6–3 6–2; L. Sanders lost to Pontanin 4–6 3–6 6–1 7–5 2–6; Bungert/Stuck d. Lejus/S. Likachev 6–4 5–7 3–6 7–5 6–4.

1960 ***France d. USSR 3–2:*** A. Bresson d. S. Likachev 6–3 6–2 6–4, d. T. Lejus 2–6 3–6 6–3 6–0 6–3; C. Duxin lost to Lejus 5–7 4–6 8–10, lost to Likachev 2–6 3–6 1–6; D. Contet/F. Jauffret d. Lejus/Likachev 8–6 6–2 4–6 6–2.

1961 ***France d. Spain 3–2:*** C. Duxin lost to J. Gisbert 1–6 3–6 2–6, d. T. Casado 6–2 6–1 6–1; F. Jauffret d. Casado 6–3 6–2 6–3, lost to Gisbert 6–1 4–6 3–6 6–4 3–6; D. Contet/Jauffret d. J. L. Arilla/Gisbert 6–2 6–0 6–2.

1962 ***France d. USSR 3–2:*** J. C. Barclay d. S. Mdzinarichvili 6–4 6–2 6–4, d. A. Metreveli 6–4 6–2 8–6; F. Jauffret lost to Metreveli 6–3 2–6 3–6 4–6, d. Mdzinarichvili 8–6 6–1 0–6 6–2; C. Duxin/Jauffret lost to Mdzinarichvili/Metreveli 8–6 3–6 4–6 5–7.

1963 ***Czechoslovakia d. Italy 3–2:*** S. Koudelka lost to G. Maioli 3–6 6–4 3–6 5–7; d. G. Di Maso 6–4 6–2 6–2; M. Holececk d. Di Maso 6–4 11–9 6–4, d. Maioli 6–0 6–3 8–6; Holecek/Koudelka lost to Di Maso/Maioli 6–8 4–6 9–7 7–9.

1964 ***USSR d. Czechoslovakia 3–2:*** A. Metreveli d. J. Kodes 6–3 6–3 4–6 17–15, d. S. Koudelka 6–1 6–4 6–1; A. Ivanov lost to Koudelka 6–4 8–10 6–8 2–6, lost to Kodes 7–5 6–4 8–10 6–8 3–6; Ivanov/Metreveli d. Koudelka/F. Pala 6–4 5–7 9–7 8–6.

1965 ***Czechoslovakia d. USSR 3–2:*** J. Kodes lost to A. Ivanov 5–7 6–3 6–3 2–6 1–6, d. V. Korotkov 6–2 5–7 7–5 6–1; M. Laudin d. Korotkov 6–2 9–7 6–0, lost to Ivanov 8–10 2–6 2–6; Kodes/J. Stoces d. Ivanov/Korotkov 6–2 6–3 6–1.

1966 ***Czechoslovakia d. USSR 4–1:*** J. Kodes d. S. Kakoulia 6–3 6–1 6–1; M. Laudin d. V. Korotkov 6–2 3–6 6–1 6–4, lost to Kakoulia 1–6 0–6 7–5 3–6; Kodes/J. Medonos d. A. Egorov/Korotkov 6–4 6–3 6–1.

1967 ***France d. Great Britain 3–1:*** J. B. Chanfreau d. G. Battrick 6–4 6–3 4–6 7–5, d. D. A. Lloyd 6–2 6–3 6–8 7–5; G. Goven d. D. A. Lloyd 3–6 6–3 6–2 6–2; Goven/Chanfreau d. Battrick/Lloyd 8–10 6–3 6–4 6–2.

1968 ***Spain d. France 3–2:*** M. Orantes d. G. Goven 6–4 6–2 6–3, d. P. Proisy 6–1 10–8 6–3; A. Munoz lost to Proisy 6–4 9–11 6–8 6–3 1–6, d. Goven 6–2 3–6 6–3 4–6 7–5; Munoz/Orantes lost to Goven/P. Dominguez 1–6 6–0 1–6 1–6.

1969 ***Spain d. Czechoslovakia 3–2:*** A. Munoz d. P. Hutka 1–6 6–3 6–1 6–3; M. Orantes d. J. Hrebec 6–2 6–4 7–5; J. Gisbert lost to Hutka 2–6 6–2 3–6 4–6; A. Muntanola lost to J. Pisecki 3–6 1–6 5–7; Munoz/Orantes d. Hrebec/Hutka 5–7 6–3 6–1 6–4.

1970 ***Czechoslovakia d. Spain 3–2:*** I. Pisecki lost to A. Munoz 7–5 4–6 4–6 2–6, d. A. Riba 6–1 6–2 6–2; J. Hrebec d. Riba 6–3 6–2 6–0, lost to Munoz 3–6 3–6 8–6 1–6; Hrebec/Pisecki d. Munoz/Riba 6–3 6–2 6–0.

1971 ***Sweden d. France 5–0:*** K. Johansson d. J. Lovera 6–1 0–6 6–1 6–3, d. E. Deblicker 10–12 6–4 6–3 1–6 7–5; T. Svensson d. Deblicker 6–2 6–2 6–2, d. Lovera 5–7 7–5 8–6; K./L. Johansson d. D. Naegelen/J. F. Caujoulle 6–4 6–4 6–2.

1972 ***Great Britain d. Spain 4–1:*** C. J. Mottram d. J. Herrera 6–1 4–6 6–0 2–6 7–5; S. Warboys d. J. Higueras 6–2 6–2 1–6 6–3, d. Herrera 6–3 6–2 0–6 2–6 7–5; J. M. Lloyd d. Higueras 6–2 10–8; Mottram/Warboys lost to Higueras/J. Moreno 6–3 3–6 4–6 6–1 5–7.

1973 ***Spain d. Great Britain 4–1:*** J. Higueras d. J. M. Lloyd 4–6 6–2 6–2 0–6 6–4; J. Moreno d. C. J. Mottram 3–6 3–6 6–3 6–1 6–3, d. Lloyd 6–1 6–1 6–3; Higueras/Moreno lost to S. Warboys/M. J. Farrell 7–9 3–6 2–6.

1974 ***Czechoslovakia d. Spain 4–1:*** P. Slozil d. S. Cabeza 6–4 6–2 6–1; T. Smid d. J. Soler 0–6 6–4 6–0 11–9, d. J. Garcia 6–3 1–6 6–3; J. Granat lost to A. Gimenez 4–6 2–6; Slozil/Smid d. Gimenez/Soler 6–4 6–2 6–4.

1975 ***Czechoslovakia d. Spain 3–2:*** T. Smid d. A. Gimenez 6–1 4–6 3–6 6–2 6–2, d. M. Mir 3–6 8–6 6–2 7–5; P. Slozil d. Mir 8–6 3–6 6–3 6–2, lost to A. Gimenez 4–6 8–6 1–6 5–7; Slozil/Smid lost to Gimenez/Mir 8–6 6–4 3–6 2–6 1–6.

1976 ***West Germany d. Italy 3–2:*** W. Zirngibl lost to F. Merlone 2–6 2–6 7–5 4–6, d. G. Ocleppo 6–1 6–1 6–4; P. Elter lost to Ocleppo 2–6 2–6 6–2 4–6, d. Merlone 6–3 3–6 6–4 6–4; U. Marten/K. Eberhard d. V. Vattuone/G. Marchetti 3–6 6–3 6–4 6–4.

1977 ***Argentina d. France 3–2:*** F. Dalla Fontana lost to C. Roger-Vasselin 4–6 6–1 4–6 4–6, d. C. Casa 6–3 7–6 6–3; J. L. Clerc lost to Casa 4–6 5–7 6–2 4–6, d. Roger-Vasselin 3–6 6–3 6–0 6–4; Clerc/A. Gattiker d. D. Bedel/Noah 2–6 4–6 7–5 6–1 6–4.

1978 ***France d. Czechoslovakia 4–1:*** Y. Noah d. D. Kulhaj 6–1 6–4 6–4; P. Portes d. I. Lendl 8–6 4–6 6–2 6–2; G. Morreton lost to Lendl 3–6 13–15; Portes d. M. Lacek 6–2 6–1; Morreton/Noah d. Kulhaj/Lendl 9–7 6–1 5–7 3–6 6–4.

1979 ***France d. Czechoslovakia 3–2:*** Y. Noah d. M. Lacek 6–3 6–1 6–1, d. D. Pohl 6–3 6–2 6–2; P. Portes lost to I. Lendl 1–6 3–6 5–7; T. Pham lost to Lacek 3–6 1–6; Noah/Portes d. Lacek/Lendl 14–12 5–7 8–6 7–5.
1980 ***France d. Spain 3–2:*** T. Tulasne d. A. Tous 6–4 6–3 6–2, d. J. B. Avendano 6–2 6–2 6–1; J. Potier lost to Avendano 6–8 2–6 2–6, lost to Tous 2–6 3–6; H. Leconte/Potier d. Avendano/Tous 6–0 7–5 3–6 6–1.
1981 ***West Germany d. Australia 5–0:*** C. Zipf d. G. Whitecross 5–7 7–5 9–11 6–2 6–2, d. C. Miller 8–6 3–6 11–9; H. D. Beutel d. Miller 3–6 8–6 6–2 6–1, d. Whitecross 6–4 6–2; Beutel/Zipf d. P. Doohan/Miller 6–4 7–5 6–2.
1982 ***Australia d. Spain 3–2:*** P. Cash d. A. Tous 4–6 6–2 8–10 6–4 6–1, lost to S. Casal 0–6 1–6; C. Miller d. Casal 6–4 1–6 9–7 6–3, lost to Tous 5–7 1–6; Cash/Miller d. Casal/M. Jaite 6–4 6–1 6–4.
1983 ***France d. Spain 5–0:*** G. Forget d. J. Bardou 6–2 6–2 5–7 4–6 10–8, d. M. Jaite 7–6 6–3; L. Courteau d. Jaite 6–4 10–8 3–6 6–2, d. Bardou 6–3 4–6 6–4; Courteau/Forget d. Bardou/Jaite 6–2 6–3 6–4.
1984 ***Czechoslovakia d. Argentina 4–1:*** M. Mecir d. G. Garetto 6–3 2–6 6–8 6–0 6–2, d. E. Masso 7–5 6–3; M. Vajda d. Masso 6–2 8–6 6–2, lost to Garetto 9–7 6–1; Mecir/K. Novacek d. Masso/Mena 6–4 6–4 6–1.
1985 ***Italy d. USA 3–2:*** P. Cane d. L. Jensen 6–2 6–1 8–6, d. R. Reneberg 6–3 6–0 6–4; C. Pistolesi lost to Reneberg 3–6 3–6 3–6, d. B. Pearce 10–8 4–6 4–6 6–1 6–1; Cane/M. Fioroni lost to Jensen/B. Pearce 1–6 6–3 1–6 2–6.
1986 ***Spain d. Czechoslovakia 3–2:*** J. Sanchez d. M. Strelba, d. P. Korda 6–2 6–3 6–2; F. Garcia lost to Strelba 4–6 12–14 8–10, d. Korda 1–6 6–4 6–4 10–8; Garcia/Sanchez lost to Korda/ C. Suk 11–13 4–6 3–6.
1987 ***France d. Czechoslovakia 3–1:*** O. Delaitre d. P. Korda 6–3 6–0, d. C. Suk 6–1 6–1; S. Grenier lost to P. Korda 7–6 2–6 11–13, d. C. Suk 6–3 6–2.

VASCO VALERIO CUP

International Team Championship for boys aged 18 and under. Played zonally with the final stages in Lesa, Italy.

FINALS

1970 ***Sweden d. France 4–1:*** L. Johansson d. F. Caujolle 10–8 6–3; T. Svensson d. E. Naegelen 6–4 6–0; R. Norbeg lost to E. Deblicker 4–6 0–6; M. Stig d. A. Collinot 6–3 6–1; Johansson/Stig d. Deblicker/Naegelen 6–3 6–3.
1971 ***Italy d. West Germany 4–0:*** M. Consolini d. U. Pinner 6–2 1–0 ret'd; N. Gasparini d. R. Gehring 6–1 3–6 6–0; C. Borea d. A. Hongsag 3–6 6–4 6–3; C. Barazzutti v L. Jelitto 5–1 abandoned; Barazzutti/Gasparini d. Gehring/Jelitto 6–4 6–4.
1972 ***Czechoslovakia d. USSR 3–2:*** I. Hora lost to V. Borisov 6–4 7–9 5–7; P. Slozil d. A. Machavez 6–2 2–6 6–4; Slozil/J. Granat d. A. Bogomolov/Borisov 6–3 7–5; T. Smid lost to K. Pugaev 3–6 8–6 4–6; Granat d. Bogomolov 6–3 6–4.
1973 ***Czechoslovakia d. USSR 4–1:*** A. Jankowski lost to V. Borisov 6–4 2–3 ret'd; P. Slozil d. A. Machavez 6–3 5–7 6–4: J. Granat d. K. Pugaev 3–6 6–4 6–3; T. Smid d. V. Katsnelson 6–4 6–4; Jankowski/Slozil d. Borisov/Pugaev 6–8 10–8 6–3.
1974 ***Spain d. Italy 3–2;*** L. Fargas d. A. Meneschincheri 6–1 6–1; A. Capitan /M. Mir lost to A. Marchetti/A. Vattuone 6–3 4–6 3–6; M. Mir lost to G. Ocleppo 4–6 2–6; A. Torralbo d. Vattuone 9–11 6–4 6–3; Capitan d. G. Marchetti 8–6 3–6 6–3.
1975 ***Italy d. USSR 3–2:*** G. Ocleppo d. S. Baranov 7–5 6–5 ret'd; A. Spiga d. S. Molodoikov 6–4 6–8 6–0; A. Merlone d. V. Gruzman 6–2 0–6 6–3; A. Meneschincheri lost to S. Elerdashvili 9–11 4–6; Ocleppo/Merlone lost to Baranov/-Gruzman 5–7 4–6.
1976 ***West Germany d. France 4–1:*** P. Elter d. P. Portes 6–3 6–2; W. Popp lost to Y. Noah 3–6 0–6; J. Henn d. J. Kuentz 6–2 6–2; A. Maurer d. G. Geniau 6–4 6–3; Elter/Popp d. G. Moretton/Noah 6–3 3–6 6–3.
1977 ***Italy d. Rumania 5–0:*** G. Rinaldini d. E. Pana 6–1 6–1; M. Rivaroli d. L. Mancas 6–2 6–4; N. Canessa d. A. Dirzu 6–3 2–6 6–4; P. Parrini d. F. Segarceanu 6–1 6–0; Canessa/Parrini d. Dirzu/Segarceanu 7–5 6–2.
1978 ***Sweden d. Italy 3–2:*** M. Wennberg d. F. Moscino 6–2 6–2; P. Hjertquist/S. Simonsson d. M. Alciati/C. Panatta 6–1 6–3; Hjertquist d. M. Ferrari 6–1 6–3; Simonsson lost to Alciati 4–6 1–6; A. Jarryd lost to Panatta 0–6 1–6.
1979 ***Sweden d. West Germany 4–1:*** S. Simonsson d. H. D. Beutel 6–4 6–0; T. Svensson d. C. Zipf 2–6 6–4 6–4; A. Jarryd d. K. Vogel 6–2 7–5; J. Gunnarsson d. A. Schulz 7–5 6–4; Simonsson/Svensson lost to Beutel/Zipf 3–6 6–2 6–8.
1980 ***Spain d. France 4–1:*** J. Aguilera d. T. Pham 6–4 1–6 6–3; A. Tous/S. Casal d. J. Potier/J. M. Piacentile 6–2 3–6 6–4; Tous lost to Potier 1–6 6–7; R. Mensua d. P. Kuchna 6–4 6–1; Casal d. Miacentile 6–1 6–1.
1981 ***Sweden d. Italy 3–2:*** H. Sundstrom d. S. Ercoli 6–4 6–2; J. Nystrom/M. Tideman lost to L. Botazzi/F. Cancellotti 6–1 3–6 4–6; Nystrom d. Botazzi 6–3 6–2; T. Hogstedt lost to Cancellotti 4–6 1–6; Tideman d. S. Colombo 6–2 7–6.
1982 ***Italy d. Spain 3–2:*** S. Ercoli lost to M. Jaite 2–6 6–7; M. Fiorini d. D. de Miguel 6–2 7–5; P. Cane d. E. Sanchez 6–1 3–6 6–4; M. Zampieri lost to J. Bardou 4–6 4–6; Cane/Fioroni d. Bardou/Jaite 4–6 6–3 8–6.
1983 ***Sweden d. Spain 4–1:*** J. Svensson d. G. R. Fernando 4–6 6–4 7–5; J./K. Carlsson d. D. de Miguel/J. Bardou 6–2 1–6 6–2; J. Carlsson lost to Bardou 4–6 2–6; K. Carlsson d. E. Sanchez 3–6 6–0 6–1; P. Lundgren d. L. F. Garcia 6–3 6–4.
1984 ***Italy d. France 3–1:*** F. Ricci d. G. Tournant 6–4 3–6 7–5; N. Devide d. P. Gardarein 6–3 6–4; I. Cappelloni d. O. Cayla 7–5 7–6; Gardarein/Winogradski d. Devide/Pistolesi 5–7 6–4 6–4.
1985 ***Italy d. Sweden 3–2:*** A. Baldoni lost to D. Engel 2–6 1–6; C. Pistolesi/S. Mezzadri d. C. Allgaardh/T. Nydahll 6–4 6–4; Pistolesi d. Allgaardh 6–3 6–4; U. Colombini d. C. Bergstrom 7–6 6–2; O. Camporese lost to U. Stenlund 0–6 3–6.
1986 ***Italy d. Spain 3–2:*** E. Rossi lost to J. Sanchez 6–7 4–6; O. Camporese lost to T. Carbonell 3–6 4–6; U. Pigato d. F. Anda 6–1 6–3; A. Baldoni d. F. Roig 7–5 6–4; Camporese/Rossi d. Carbonell/Sanchez 3–6 6–3 6–4.
1987 ***Czechoslovakia d. West Germany 2–0:*** D. Rikl d. C. Arriens 6–1 6–1; T. Zdrazila d. S. Nensel 6–1 4–6 6–2.

JEAN BOROTRA CUP

International Team Championship for boys aged 16 and under; originally the Jean Becker Cup. Finals played in Le Touquet.

1972 ***Spain d. France 4–1:*** M. Mir d. Ph. Gruthchet 6–3 6–2; F. Riba d. C. Freyss 6–2 1–6 6–4; A. Capitan d. R. Brunet 6–3 7–5; Masana/Mir lost to Frantz/Grutchet 6–4 6–7 3–6; Capitan/Riba d. Brunet/Freyss 7–5 3–6 9–7.

1973 ***Italy d. West Germany 3–2:*** M. Attolini lost to K. Eberhardt 1–6 1–6; G. Sileo d. P. Elter 7–5 6–4; M. Spiga d. U. Wellerdieck 6–2 7–5; Attolini/Sileo lost to Eberhardt/Elter 0–6 5–7; Mazzocchi/Spiga d. Liebthal/Wellerdieck 6–3 6–2.

1974 ***West Germany d. Italy 4–1:*** Buchbinder d. G. Rinaldi 6–2 6–2; P. Elter d. Risi 6–0 6–1; A. Maurer d. Gardi 6–7 7–5 6–1; Buchbinder/W. Popp lost to Gardi/Rinaldi 6–2 6–7 8–10; Elter/Maurer d. Risi/M. Rivarolli 6–0 6–3.

1975 ***Czechoslovakia d. Italy 3–2:*** M. Lacek d. G. Rinaldini 7–5 6–1; I. Lendl d. A. Ciardi 6–1 6–3; J. Kucera d. P. Parreni 6–4 6–4; Lacek/Kucera lost to Parreni/A. Rivaroli 4–6 4–6; Lendl/A. Vantuch lost to Ciardi/Rinaldini 6–1 4–6 3–6.

1976 ***Sweden d. Czechoslovakia 3–2:*** P. Hjertquist lost to I. Lendl 6–0 3–6 4–6; S. Simonsson d. A. Vikopa 6–3 6–0; H. Johansson d. T. Pitra 6–3 6–2; Simonsson/A. Fritzner lost to Lendl/J. Kerezek 6–4 3–6 1–6; Hjertquist/Johansson d. Pitra/J. Vikopal 6–3 6–2.

1977 ***Italy d. Sweden 3–2:*** A. Costa d. A. Jarryd 7–5 6–2; A. Giacomini lost to S. Simonsson 1–6 1–6; A. Moscino d. S. Svensson 6–4 6–4; Giacomini/A. Odling lost to Simonsson/Jarryd 3–6 4–6; Costa/Moscino d. Svensson/M. Wennberg 6–2 6–4.

1978 ***Sweden d. France 3–2:*** S. Svensson d. T. Tulasne 6–4 6–2; H. Simonsson lost to J. Potier 6–3 2–6 7–9 disqualified; J. Gunnarsson d. T. Pham 6–2 5–7 6–2; M. Wilander lost to J. L. Cotard 2–6 7–5 4–6; Svensson/Simonsson d. Cotard/J. M. Piacentile 6–3 6–1.

1979 ***Sweden d. France 4–1:*** J. Windahll lost to T. Tulasne 2–6 1–6; M. Wilander d. H. Leconte 6–2 1–6 6–3; T. Hogstedt d. P. Kuchna 6–2 6–1; J. Sjogren d. J. M. Piacentile 6–1 6–1; Hogstedt/Wilander d. Leconte/Piacentile 3–6 6–3 6–4.

1980 ***Sweden d. Czechoslovakia 3–0:*** M. Wilander d. M. Mecir 3–6 6–1 6–1; A. Mansson d. K. Novacek 6–3 6–3; H. Sundstrom/Wilander d. Mecir/B. Stankovic 6–3 3–0 ret'd.

1981 ***France d. Sweden 3–2:*** T. Benhabiles d. S. Edberg 6–4 6–4; F. Hamonet d. J. B. Svensson 6–0 6–2; T. Chamsion lost to P. Svensson 3–6 6–2 0–6; O. Cayla lost to A. Henricsson 6–1 4–6 3–6; Hamonet/G. Forget d. Edberg/P. Svensson 6–4 1–6 6–2.

1982 ***Sweden d. Spain 4–1:*** J. Svensson d. J. Maso 6–2 6–2; S. Edberg d. F. Garcia 6–4 6–4; P. Svensson d. J. M. Oltra 6–2 6–1; J. Carlsson lost to S. Castello 5–7 1–6; Edberg/P. Svensson d. Garcia/Oltra 6–2 6–1.

1983 ***Sweden d. USSR 3–2:*** D. Engel d. V. Gabritchidze 7–5 6–1; K. Carlsson d. A. Volkov 6–2 6–4; C. Allgaardh d. A. Tchernetsky 7–5 6–3; C. Bergstrom lost to I. Metreveli 6–0 6–7 3–6; Carlsson/Allgaardh d. Volkov/Metreveli 6–3 6–7 6–3.

1984 ***Italy d. Sweden 4–1:*** P. Chinellato lost to T. Nydhal 4–6 6–4 3–6; O. Camporese d. H. Holm 6–4 6–0; A. Baldoni d. A. Rosen 6–4 6–0; S. Sorensen d. N. Utgren 6–2 6–4; Baldoni/E. Rossi d. T. Nydal/P. Henricsson 7–6 1–6 6–3.

1985 ***Sweden d. France 3–2:*** P. Henricsson lost to A. Boetsch 3–6 2–6; P. Wennberg d. P. Ventura 6–2 6–2; N. Utgren d. S. Blanquie 6–1 6–2; M. Zeile d. C. Sebastiani 6–1 6–3; Henricsson/Utgren lost to Boetsch/R. Pedros 2–6 6–3 4–6.

1986 ***Italy d. Netherlands 3–2:*** F. Mordegan lost to P. Dogger 5–7 6–3 1–6; D. Nargiso lost to J. Eltingh 5–7 2–6; C. Caratti d. J. Siemerink 7–5 6–0; R. Furlan d. R. Heethius 7–5 5–7 7–5; Caratti/Nargiso d. Eltingh/Siemerink 4–6 7–5 6–3.

1987 ***Austria d. Italy 3–2:*** T. Buchmayer d. F. Pisilli 6–3 6–1; O. Fuchs lost to S. Pescosolido 4–6 1–6; H. Priller d. M. Ardinghi 6–3 6–4; G. Bohm lost to M. Boscatto 6–2 1–6 6–8; Buchmayer/Priller d. Boscatto/Pescosolido 1–6 6–4 6–4.

DEL SOL CUP

International Team Championship for boys aged 14 and under. Played in zones with finals in Barcelona.

1979 ***Italy d. France 3–2:*** M. Fioroni d. M. Cartier 6–0 6–2; G. Possani d. G. Forget 6–7 7–5 6–3; A. Paris lost to T. Benhabiles 0–6 5–7; L. Baglioni lost to F. Hamonet 0–6 0–6; Possani/Paris d. Benhabiles/Hamonet 6–1 6–4.

1980 ***Sweden d. Italy 4–1:*** P. Svensson d. R. Salemme 6–4 7–6; S. Edberg d. F. Ricci 7–5 6–3; R. Lofquist d. F. Filippi 6–3 6–4; J. Svensson lost to P. Poggioli 4–6 2–6; Edberg/P. Svensson d. Filippi/A. Vacca 6–4 6–1.

1981 ***Sweden d. Israel 3–2:*** T. Johansson lost to A. Naor 2–6 6–7; C. Allgaardh lost to G. Blom 4–6 6–2 4–6; K. Carlsson d. R. Weinberg 6–0 6–0; C. Bergstrom d. M. Osherov 2–6 7–5 7–5; Allgaardh/Carlsson d. Blom/Osherov 6–2 6–1.

1982 ***Sweden d. West Germany 4–1:*** H. Kolm d. U. Kraft 6–1 6–0; K. Carlsson d. O. Sachau 6–0 6–0; P. Ekstrand lost to I. Kroll 0–6 2–6; T. Nydahl d. C. Guhl 6–0 1–6 6–1; Carlsson/Nydahl d. Guhl/Kraft 6–1 6–4.

1983 ***Sweden d. West Germany 3–2:*** U. Persson d. H. Stang 6–2 6–2; P. Henricsson d. P. Pfleger 6–4 6–1; U. Eriksson lost to U. Kraft 7–6 3–6 2–6; P. Wennberg lost to L. Orzessek 2–6 3–6; Henricsson/M. Urgren d. Kraft/Orzessek 6–2 6–3.

1984 ***West Germany d. Spain 4–1:*** S. Scheider d. F. Alfonso 6–3 4–6 7–5; F. Loddenkemper/A. Thoms d. J. Olivert/S. Bruguera 6–3 6–2; Loddenkemper d. Olivert 7–6 7–6; D. Richter d. A. Martinez 6–1 7–5; A. Thoms lost to Bruguera 3–6 6–2 4–6.

1985 ***Austria d. Italy 5–0:*** G. Bohm d. F. Casa 6–4 6–2; T. Buchmayer/O. Fuchs d. S. Pescosolido/F. Pisilli 6–2 6–3; Buchmayer d. Pescosolido 6–3 4–6 6–4; Fuchs d. Pisilli 6–3 7–6; H. Prilled d. M. Ardinghi 6–2 6–1.
1986 ***Sweden d. Yugoslavia 4–1:*** J. Alven d. S. Hirszon 6–3 6–4; R. Pettersson lost to B. Trupy 2–6 3–6; M. Ekstrand d. A. Tonejc 3–6 6–4 6–3; J. Henriksson d. S. Ban 6–4 7–6; Alven/Pettersson d. Hirszon/Trupej 6–2 6–4.
1987 ***West Germany d. Austria 4–1:*** J. Weinzierl lost to R. Wawra 3–6 2–6; G. Paul d. N. Patzak 6–0 6–1; S. Petraschek d. J. Knowle 3–6 6–2 6–2; A. Kriebel d. H. Kugler 6–2 6–3; Paul/Petraschek d. Knowle/Wawra 4–6 6–2 6–2.

ANNIE SOISBAULT CUP

International Team Championship for women aged 20 and under. Played zonally with final stages in Le Touquet.

1965 ***Netherlands d. France 2–1:*** M. Jansen lost to J. Venturino 1–6 1–6; B. Stove d. C. Spinoza 6–1 1–6 6–3; Jansen/Stove d. Spinoza/Venturino 10–8 6–4.
1966 ***France d. Netherlands 2–1:*** A. A. Seghers lost to A. Bakker 4–6 7–5 2–6; J. Venturino d. M. Jansen 6–4 6–4; Seghers/Venturino d. Bakker/Jansen 7–5 6–8 6–4.
1967 ***Netherlands d. France 2–1:*** A. Bakker lost to O. de Roubin 3–6 0–1 ret'd; A. Suurbeck d. N. Cazeaux 8–6 6–2; Bakker/Suurbeck d. Cazeaux/de Roubin 6–0 6–0.
1968 ***USSR d. Czechoslovakia 3–0:*** O. Morozova d. M. Holubova 6–2 10–8; R. Islanova d. K. Vaneckova 7–5 6–2; Morozova/A. Eremeeva d. Holubova/Vaneckova 6–3 6–2.
1969 ***USSR d. Hungary 3–0:*** O. Morozova d. J. Szorenyi 6–0 6–1; S. Yansone d. A. Graczol 4–6 6–4 6–2; Yansone/E. Izopajitis d. Szorenyi/A. Barogh 8–6 6–1.
1970 ***USSR d. France 3–0:*** E. Izopajitis d. N. Fuchs 6–3 6–1; M. Kroshina d. A. M. Cassaigne 4–6 6–1 9–7; Izopajitis/K. Zincevic d. Fuchs/M. C. Brochard 6–4 2–6 6–3.
1971 ***France d. Czechoslovakia 2–1:*** N. Fuchs d. M. Kozeluhova 6–2 6–3; F. Guedy lost to R. Tomanova 4–6 1–6; M. C. Brochard/Fuchs d. Kozeluhova/Tomanova 1–6 7–5 6–3.
1972 ***USSR d. Great Britain 2–1:*** M. Kroshina d. G. L. Coles 6–3 6–4; E. Biriukova d. V. Burton 6–2 4–6 6–3; Biriukova/E. Granatuzova lost to L. J. Charles/Coles 3–6 2–6.
1973 ***Great Britain d. USSR 2–1:*** G. L. Coles d. M. Kroshina 7–5 4–6 6–3; S. Barker d. E. Granaturova 6–4 7–5; Barker/Coles lost to Granaturova/Kroshina 4–6 6–3 3–6.
1974 ***Czechoslovakia d. Great Britain 2–1:*** M. Navratilova d. G. L. Coles 6–1 6–2; R. Tomanova lost to S. Barker 3–6 2–6; Navratilova/Tomanova d. Baker/Coles 6–2 6–8 7–5.
1975 ***Great Britain d. Rumania 2–1:*** S. Barker d. V. Ruzici 4–6 6–4 6–2; L. J. Mottram lost to M. Simionescu 4–6 9–7 1–6; Barker/Mottram d. Ruzici/Simionescu 6–4 6–0.
1976 ***Czechoslovakia d. Great Britain 2–1:*** H. Strachonova lost to M. Tyler 7–5 4–6 4–6; R. Marsikova d. L. J. Mottram 6–2 6–4; Marsikova/K. Skronska d. Mottram/B. L. Thompson 6–3 8–10 6–1.
1977 ***Czechoslovakia d. Switzerland 3–0:*** H. Strachonova d. A. M. Ruegg 6–0 6–3; R. Marsikova d. M. Simmen 6–0 4–6 6–0; Marsikova/H. Mandlikova d. Ruegg/Simmen 8–6 6–4.
1978 ***USSR d. Switzerland 3–0:*** N. Chmyreva d. A. M. Ruegg 6–4 6–4; Eliseenko d. P. Delhees 7–5 6–4; Chmyreva/Eliseenko d. Ruegg/M. Simmen 6–1 6–0.
1979 ***Czechoslovakia d. Great Britain 2–1:*** H. Mandlikova d. A. E. Hobbs 4–6 6–3 6–3; I. Budarova lost to J. M. Durie 6–8 6–4 6–8; Budarova/Mandlikova d. Durie/D. Jevans 1–6 6–2 6–3.
1980 ***Czechoslovakia d. Australia 2–1:*** I. Budarova d. S. Leo 6–4 6–4; M. Skuherska lost to D. Evers 0–6 3–6; Budarova/Skuherska d. Evers/M. Sawyer 6–3 6–3.
1981 ***Netherlands d. USSR 2–0:*** M. Van Der Torre d. J. Salnikova 6–1 6–4; N. Shutte d. O. Zaitzeva 6–1 6–4.
1982 ***USSR d. Great Britain 2–1:*** O. Zaitseva d. S. Walpole 6–2 6–4; N. Reva d. A. Brown 6–1 6–3; J. Kashevarova/Zaitseva lost to Brown/J. Salmon 5–7 6–0 2–6.
1983 ***France d. Czechoslovakia 2–1:*** P. Paradis d. H. Fukarkova 7–5 1–6 6–2; N. Herreman d. O. Votavova 6–4 6–0; Paradis/P. Thanh lost to Fukarkova/Votavova 6–4 3–6 4–6.
1984 ***USA d. Czechoslovakia 3–0:*** G. Rush d. O. Votavova 6–3 6–1; D. Spence d. A. Holikova 6–2 7–5; Rush/N. Kuhlman d. Votavova/Holikova 6–3 6–2.
1985 ***Czechoslovakia d. Argentina 3–0:*** A. Holikova d. P. Tarabini 3–6 7–5 6–4; O. Votavova d. M. Perez Roldan 0–6 6–3 6–2; Holikova/J. Novotna d. Tarabini/Perez Roldan 7–5 7–5.
1986 ***Czechoslovakia d. West Germany 2–1:*** R. Zrubakova d. M. Schropp 6–2 6–2; R. Rajchrtova d. A. Betzner 6–1 6–2; Rajchrtova/Zrubakova lost to Betzner/Schropp 6–7 2–6.
1987 ***Australia d. Czechoslovakia 2–1:*** N. Provis d. R. Rajchrtova 2–6 6–2 6–1; J. Byrne lost to J. Novotna 5–7 6–3 3–6; Byrne/Provis d. Novotna/Rajchrtova 6–4 0–6 6–3.

HM QUEEN SOFIA CUP

International Team Championship for girls aged 18 and under. Played zonally with the final stages in Spain.

FINALS

1972 ***Rumania d. West Germany 3–2:*** F. Mihai d. A. Spiedel 6–4 7–5; V. Ruzici/M. Simionescu d. B. Portcheller/B. Kasler 8–6 6–1; Ruzici d. Portcheller 2–6 6–0 6–1; Simionescu lost to Kasler 4–6 3–6; M. Neuweiller lost to K. Pohmann 4–6 3–6.

1973 ***Great Britain d. Spain 4–1:*** B. L. Thompson d. G. Nogues 6–4 6–4; L. J. Mottram d. J. Mateo 6–3 12–10; S. Barker d. J. Alvarez 7–5 6–0; Barker/Mottram d. Mateo/C. Chillida 6–2 6–2; J. Potterton lost to Chillida 3–6 0–6.
1974 ***Czechoslovakia d. France 4–1:*** L. Plchova d. M. Cozaux 6–4 6–1; Y. Brzakova lost to B. Simon 6–8 6–2 4–6; H. Strachonova d. C. Gimmig 6–3 6–0; R. Marsikova d. F. Thibault 8–4 6–4; Brzakova/A. Kulankova d. Thibault/A. Duguy 9–7 4–6 6–4.
1975 ***Great Britain d. Czechoslovakia 4–1:*** M. Tyler d. A. Kulhankova 6–1 3–6 6–3; C. Harrison d. J. Kopekova 6–3 6–3; L. J. Mottram d. H. Strachonova 2–6 11–9 6–3; J. Cottrell lost to K. Skronska 1–6 1–6; A. Cooper/Cottrell d. Skronska/Kulhankova 1–6 6–4 6–4.
1976 ***Great Britain d. Switzerland 3–1:*** J. M. Durie d. C. Jolissaint 4–6 6–3 6–4; A. Cooper lost to M. Simmen 6–4 0–6 4–6; C. Harrison d. A. Ruegg 6–4 6–7 6–2; M. Tyler d. P. Delhees 6–2 6–2.
1977 ***Czechoslovakia d. Sweden 5–0:*** H. Mandlikova d. M. Wiedel 6–2 6–2; I. Budarova d. H. Brywe 6–1 6–1; Mandlikova/Budarova d. A. C. Mansson/A. Nilsson 6–1 6–3; M. Skuherska d. Nilsson 6–0 6–4; H. Strachonova d. Mansson 6–3 7–5.
1978 ***Czechoslovakia d. Sweden 5–0:*** M. Skuherska d. L. Jacobson 6–3 6–2; H. Mandlikova d. H. Brywe 6–1 6–1; I. Budarova/Mandlikova d. Jacobson/L. Sandin 6–3 6–1; I. Petru d. A. Nilsson 6–1 6–2; Budarova d. Sandin 6–3 5–7 7–5.
1979 ***Czechoslovakia d. Switzerland 3–1:*** I. Bendlova d. P. Frey 6–1 6–1; M. Skuherska/I. Petru lost to C. Jolissaint/I. Villiger 3–6 4–6; Skuherska d. Villiger 3–6 6–1 6–1; I. Novakova d. Jolissaint 6–7 6–3 6–3; Petru v C. Pasquale 5–7 abandoned.
1980 ***Switzerland d. USSR 3–2:*** K. Stampfli d. J. Kashevarova 6–3 6–3; I. Villiger/L. Drescher lost to O. Zaitseva/S. Cherneva 4–6 5–7; Villiger d. Zaitseva 6–2 7–5; C. Pasquale lost to Cherneva 4–6 7–5 7–9; Drescher d. J. Salnikova 7–6 6–4.
1981 ***Sweden d. Czechoslovakia 3–2:*** B. Bjort d. P. Dutkova 6–2 6–3; M. Lindstrom/C. Lindqvist d. H. Sukova/M. Pazderova 6–3 6–3; C. Jexell lost to Pazderova 6–3 2–6 0–6; Lindqvist d. N. Piskackova 6–2 6–2; Lindstrom lost to Sukova 6–7 3–6.
1982 ***Italy d. Czechoslovakia 4–1:*** R. Reggi d. I. Petru 6–3 6–4; N. Virgintino lost to H. Fukarkova 7–5 2–6 3–6; A. Cecchini d. P. Dutkova 7–6 7–6; F. Bonsignori d. A. Souckova 6–3 6–0; Reggi/Virgintino d. Petru/Fukarkova 7–5 4–6 6–2.
1983 ***Italy d. Czechoslovakia 4–1:*** L. Ferrando d. A. Souckova 6–0 6–3; B. Romano/N. Virgintino d. A. Holikova/-Souckova 6–3 6–7 6–3; A. M. Cecchini d. O. Votavova 6–7 6–3 6–1; Virgintino d. P. Tesarova 6–3 6–1; S. Dalla Valle lost to Holikova 5–7 3–6.
1984 ***Sweden d. Czechoslovakia 3–2:*** H. Dahlstrom d. O. Votavova 6–3 6–3; A. Karlsson d. A. Holikova 6–3 6–0; A. Souckova d. M. Lundquist 7–5 7–5; K. Karlsson d. P. Tesarova 6–1 6–2; Votavova/Holikova d. Lundquist/Olsson 6–4 6–2.
1985 ***Italy d. Sweden 4–1:*** L. Lapi lost to C. Dahlman 0–6 1–6; L. Garrone/L. Golarsa d. A. K. Ollson/M. Lundquist 6–1 6–3; Garrone d. H. Dahlstrom 6–2 6–7 6–2; C. Nozzoli d. Ollson 6–4 6–4; Golarsa d. Lundquist 6–2 6–0.
1986 ***Czechoslovakia d. Sweden 5–0:*** R. Rajchrtova d. C. Dahlstrom 6–4 6–0; R. Zbrubakova d. J. Jonerup 6–3 6–3; J. Novotna d. M. Stradlund 6–4 6–2; D. Krajcovicova d. M. Ekstrand 6–3 7–5; Novotna/Rajchrtova d. M. Nilsson/Stradlund 6–0 6–1.
1987 ***France d. Czechoslovakia 3–0:*** A. Dechaume d. R. Zrubakova 6–4 6–3; E. Derly d. P. Langrova 7–5 6–1; Dechaume/S. Niox-Chateau d. Langrova/Zrubakova 6–7 6–4 6–3.

HELVETIE CUP

International Team Championship for girls aged 16 and under. Played zonally with final stages at Leysin, Switzerland.

FINALS

1977 ***Italy d. Switzerland 3–2:*** P. Cigognani lost to C. Jolissaint 0–6 3–6; B. Rossi d. I. Villiger 6–3 6–7 8–6; M. Calabria d. K. Stampfli 6–1 6–2; P. Murgo d. C. Pasquale 6–3 6–3; Rossi/Murgo lost to Jolissaint/Villiger 4–6 3–6.
1978 ***Bulgaria d. West Germany 5–0:*** M. Condova d. C. Kohde 1–6 6–3 6–1; A. Veltcheva d. Haas 6–3 5–7 6–4; I. Chichkova d. Hammig 6–3 6–0; I. Christova d. Wilmsmeyer 3–6 7–6 6–3; Condova/Veltcheva d. Kohde/Haas 3–6 6–2 6–2.
1979 ***Sweden d. France 5–0:*** C. Lindqvist d. I. Vernhes 6–7 6–3 6–0; B. Bjork d. C. Vanier 4–6 6–3 6–3; A. Flodin d. S. Gardette 6–0 6–1; H. Olsson/K. Marivall d. M. Callejo/Vanier 6–3 6–3; Olsson d. Calleja 6–2 6–1.
1980 ***Sweden d. West Germany 3–2:*** C. Anderholm d. M. Schropp 6–1 6–2; H. Olsson lost to K. Reuter 5–7 4–6; M. Schultz d. P. Keppeler 6–4 6–4; N. Nielson d. M. Reinhard 6–7 6–3 6–2; Olsson/Schultz lost to Reuter/Reinhard 6–1 4–6 5–7.
1981 ***Sweden d. Italy 3–2:*** A. Bjork lost to F. Sollenti 2–6 6–7; H. Olsson/C. Anderholm d. R. Reggi/F. Virgintino 0–6 6–2 6–1; Olsson d. A. M. Cecchini 6–4 7–5; Anderholm d. Reggi 6–3 3–6 6–4; I. Sjogreen lost to Virgintino 0–6 0–6.
1982 ***USSR d. France 3–2:*** I. Fishkina d. I. Demongeot 6–1 6–2; L. Savchenko/V. Milvidskaya lost to P. Paradis/N. Phan-Thanh 4–6 7–5 4–6; N. Bykova lost to Paradis 1–6 2–6; Savchenko d. Phan-Thanh 6–2 6–3; Mildvidskaya d. N. Herreman 6–1 6–4.
1983 ***USSR d. Sweden 3–2:*** A. Kuzmina d. A. K. Olsson 6–3 1–6 6–3; V. Milvidskaya d. H. Dahlmstrom 3–6 6–2 6–4; I. Fischkina lost to M. Lundquist 4–6 4–6; I. Fateeva lost to E. Helmersson 2–6 3–6; Fishkina/Mildvidskaya d. Dahlstrom/Lundquist 6–4 7–5.
1984 ***Czechoslovakia d. West Germany 4–1:*** R. Wlona lost to M. Gartner 7–6 3–6 4–6; J. Novotna/R. Rajchrotova d. S. Meier/R. Weiser 6–0 7–6; Novotna d. Meier 7–5 6–2; Rajchrotova d. Weiser 6–3 4–6 6–1; P. Sedkackova d. S. Hack 6–4 4–6 6–2.

1985 ***West Germany d. Sweden 4–1:*** M. Schurhoff d. M. Ekstrand 6–2 4–6 6–4; M. Gartner/S. Hack lost to M. Strandlund/M. Nilsson 3–6 3–6; Gartner/J. Jonerup 7–6 6–2; Hack d. Strandlund 6–1 6–1; W. Probst d. M. Nilsson 6–1 6–1.
1986 ***Switzerland d. Czechoslovakia 3–1*** (one rubber not played): E. Zardo d. M. Frimmelova 6–4 6–2; M. Strebel d. L. Laskova 7–5 6–1; S. Jaquet v. P. Langróva not played; M. Plocher d. E. Sviglerova 6–4 6–2; Jacquet/Plocher lost to Frimmelova/Langrova 6–0 1–6 5–7.
1987 ***Netherlands d. Switzerland 3–2:*** N. Van Dierendonck lost to S. Jacquet 6–7 3–6; B. Sonneveld lost to M. Plocher 6–2 3–6 4–6; Y. Grubben d. G. Villiger 7–5 7–6; E. Haslinghuis d. S. Bregnard 6–1 6–0; Sonneveld/Van Dierendonck d. Jacquet/Plocher 7–5 6–3.

EUROPA CUP

International Team Championship for girls under 14.

FINALS

1981 ***West Germany d. France 3–2, Winterslag, Belgium:*** I. Cueto d. J. Clerin 6–3 2–6 6–1; R. Wieser lost to E. Folcher 1–6 6–3 1–6; S. Graf d. M. Phan-Thanh 7–5 6–3; S. Luidinant d. E. Grousseau 6–2 6–2; Graf/Wieser lost to Folcher/Grousseau 6–4 2–6 1–6.
1982 ***Sweden d. West Germany 3–2, Mons, Belgium:*** C. Dahlman d. S. Meier 7–5 7–5: H. Dahlstrom d. B. Herget 6–0 6–4; E. Helmersson lost to I. Cueto 3–6 7–6 0–6; I. Mattiasson lost to E. Walliser 5–7 2–6; Dahlstrom/Helmersson d. Cueto/Walliser 6–2 6–2.
1983 ***West Germany d. France 3–2, Lee-on-Solent, Hampshire:*** N. Vassen d. S. N. Chateau 4–6 6–3 6–2; W. Probst d. M. C. Rolet 7–5 5–7 ret'd; S. Hack lost to C. Bourdais 6–3 2–6 0–6; M. Gartner d. A. Dechaume 6–4 4–6 7–5; Gartner/Vassen lost to Bourdais/Dechaume 3–6 1–6.
1984 ***France d. Sweden 4–1:*** S. Dussault lost to A. Narbe 0–6 6–4 3–6; A. Dechaume/E. Derly d. M. Ekstrand/H. Johnsson 6–3 6–3; Dechaume d. Ekstrand 7–5 6–2; Derly d. Salsgard 6–4 3–6 6–1; M. Laval d. Johnsson 6–4 6–4.
1985 ***USSR d. Italy 3–2:*** N. Zvereva d. A. Dell'Orso 6–2 4–6 6–4; T. Tchernysova lost to F. Romano 3–6 2–6; E. Brihovec lost to S. Favini w.o.; A. Blumberga d. G. Boscheiro 6–3 4–6 6–4; Zvereva/Tchernysova d. Boscheiro/Dell'Orso 6–4 6–3.
1986 ***Netherlands d. Italy 3–2:*** Y. Grubben lost to Boscheiro 5–7 4–6; N. Van Lottum d. Favini 6–2 6–1; E. Markestein d. Migliori 6–4 6–4; E. Haslinghuis lost to Bertelloni 2–6 2–6; Grubben/Van Lottum d. Boscheiro/Migliori 6–2 6–2.
1987 ***Czechoslovakia d. Austria 3–2:*** P. Kucova lost to U. Priller 3–6 0–6; R. Bobkova d. D. Bidmon 6–2 6–4; P. Markova lost to N. Dobrovits 4–6 1–6; K. Matouskova d. S. Suchan 1–6 6–0 10–8; Bobkova/Kucova d. Dobrovits/Priller 6–4 4–6 7–5.

US INTERCOLLEGIATE CHAMPIONSHIPS

MEN'S SINGLES

	WINNER		WINNER
1883	*Spring:* J. S. Clark (Harvard)	1910	R. A. Holden (Yale)
1883	*Autumn:* H. A. Taylor (Harvard)	1911	E. H. Whitney (Harvard)
1884	W. P. Knapp (Yale)	1912	G. M. Church (Princeton)
1885	W. P. Knapp (Yale)	1913	R. N. Williams (Harvard)
1886	G. M. Brinley (Trinity, Con.)	1914	G. M. Church (Princeton)
1887	P. S. Sears (Harvard)	1915	R. N. Williams (Harvard)
1888	P. S. Sears (Harvard)	1916	G. C. Caner (Harvard)
1889	R. P. Huntington (Yale)	1917–18	*Not held*
1890	F. H. Hovey (Harvard)	1919	C. S. Garland (Yale)
1891	F. H. Hovey (Harvard)	1920	L. M. Banks (Yale)
1892	W. A. Larned (Cornell)	1921	P. Neer (Stanford)
1893	M. G. Chace (Brown)	1922	R. N. Williams (Yale)
1894	M. G. Chace (Yale)	1923	C. H. Fischer (Phil. Osteo.)
1895	M. G. Chace (Yale)	1924	W. Scott (Washington)
1896	M. D. Whitman (Harvard)	1925	E. G. Chandler (California)
1897	S. G. Thompson (Princeton)	1926	E. G. Chandler (California)
1898	L. E. Ware (Harvard)	1927	W. Allison (Texas)
1899	D. F. Davis (Harvard)	1928	H. Siligson (Lehigh)
1900	R. D. Little (Princeton)	1929	B. Bell (Texas)
1901	F. B. Alexander (Princeton)	1930	C. Sutter (Tulane)
1902	W. J. Clothier (Harvard)	1931	K. Gledhill (Stanford)
1903	E. B. Dewhurst (U of Penn)	1932	C. Sutter (Tulane)
1904	R. LeRoy (Columbia)	1933	J. Tidball (UCLA)
1905	E. B. Dewhurst (U of Penn)	1934	G. Mako (USC)
1906	R. LeRoy (Columbia)	1935	W. Hess (Rice)
1907	G. P. Gardner (Harvard)	1936	E. Sutter (Tulane)
1908	N. W. Niles (Harvard)	1937	E. Sutter (Tulane)
1909	W. F. Johnson (U of Penn)	1938	F. D. Guernsey (Rice)

Year	Winner
1939	F. D. Guernsey (Rice)
1940	D. McNeill (Kenyon Coll)
1941	J. R. Hunt (US Naval Acad)
1942	F. R. Schroeder (Stanford)
1943	F. Segura (Miami)
1944	F. Segura (Miami)
1945	F. Segura (Miami)
1946	R. Falkenburg (USC)
1947	G. Larned (Wm & Mary)
1948	H. E. Likas (U of San Francisco)
1949	J. Tuero (Tulane)
1950	H. Flam (USC)
1951	M. A. Trabert (U of Cincinnati)
1952	H. Stewart (USC)
1953	H. Richardson (Tulane)
1954	H. Richardson (Tulane)
1955	J. Aguero (Tulane)
1956	A. Olmedo (USC)
1957	B. McKay (U of Michigan)
1958	A. Olmedo (USC)
1959	W. Reed (San Jos;xae State)
1960	L. Nagler (UCLA)
1961	A. Fox (UCLA)
1962	R. H. Osuna (USC)
1963	R. D. Ralston (USC)
1964	R. D. Ralston (USC)
1965	A. R. Ashe (UCLA)
1966	C. Pasarell (UCLA)
1967	R. C. Lutz (USC)
1968	S. R. Smith (USC)
1969	J. Loyo-Mayo (USC)
1970	J. Borowiak (UCLA)
1971	J. S. Connors (UCLA)
1972	R. L. Stockton (Trinity, Texas)
1973	A. A. Mayer (Stanford)
1974	J. Whitlinger (Stanford)
1975	W. Martin (UCLA)
1976	W. Scanlon (Trinity, Texas)
1977	M. Mitchell (Stanford)
1978	J. P. McEnroe (Stanford)
1979	K. Curren (Texas)
1980	R. Van't Hof (USC)
1981	T. Mayotte (Stanford)
1982	M. Leach (Michigan)
1983	G. Holmes (Utah)
1984	M. Pernfors (Georgia)
1985	M. Pernfors (Georgia)
1986	D. Goldie (Stanford)
1987	A. Burrow (U of Miami)

WOMEN'S SINGLES

	WINNER
1958	D. R. Hard (Pomona)
1959	D. Floyd (Wm & Mary)
1960	L. Vail (Oakland City)
1961	T. A. Fretz (Occidental)
1962	R. Allison (Alabama)
1963	R. Allison (Alabama)
1964	J. Albert (Stanford)
1965	M. Henreid (UCLA)
1966	C. Martinez (San Francisco State)
1967	O. Rippy (Odessa Jr)
1968	E. Burrer (Trinity, Texas)
1969	E. Burrer (Trinity, Texas)
1970	L. DuPont (N Carolina)
1971	P. Richmond (Arizona State)
1972	J. Metcalf (Redlands)
1973	J. Metcalf (Redlands)
1974	C. Meyer (Marymount)
1975	S. Tolleson (Trinity, Texas)
1976	B. Hallquist (USC)
1977	B. Hallquist (USC)
1978	S. Margolin (USC)
1979	K. Jordan (Stanford)
1980	W. White (Rollins)
1981	A. M. Fernandez (Rollins)
1982	A. Moulton (Stanford)
1983	B. Herr (USC)
1984	L. Spain (Georgia)
1985	L. Gates (Stanford)
1986	P. Fendick (Stanford)
1987	P. Fendick (Stanford)

THE INTERNATIONAL TENNIS FEDERATION

ITF JUNIOR RESULTS
ITF VETERAN TENNIS
NATIONAL RANKINGS

Jason Stoltenberg of Australia, the ITF Junior World Champion in both singles and doubles in 1987, won the Australian Open Junior singles, also taking the doubles title there and at Wimbledon in partnership with Todd Woodbridge. *(P. Shephard-Lewis)*

Javier Sanchez, top of the junior rankings in 1986, made his mark in the men's game in 1987, reaching the final in Madrid, where he lost to his brother, Emilio, and finishing the year poised to crack the top 100. *(T. Hindley)*

THE INTERNATIONAL TENNIS FEDERATION

The International Tennis Federation
Palliser Road, Barons Court, London W14 9EN
Telephone: 01-381 8060. Cables: Intennis London W14. Telex: 919253 ITF G and 943119 ITF G. Telecopier: 01-381 3989

President 1987–89: Mr Philippe Chatrier.
Honorary Life Vice-Presidents: Mr Jean Borotra, Mr Derek N. Hardwick – posthumously elected, Mr Allan Heyman, Dr Giorgio de Stefani.
Honorary Life Counsellors: Dr Paolo Angeli, Mr Leslie E. Ashenheim, Mr Joseph Carrico, Mr Hunter L. Delatour Jnr, Mr Lazslo Gorodi, Mr John Harrison, Padma Bhushan R. K. Khanna, Mr Alvaro Pena, Mr Stan Malless, Mr W. Harcourt Woods.
Committee of Management 1987–89: Mr Philippe Chatrier, Mr Jim R. Cochrane, Mr Randolf Gregson, Dr Heinz Grimm, Mr Gordon D. Jorgensen, Mr Eiichi Kawatei, Mr Pablo Llorens, Mr Eduardo Moline O'Connor, Mr Radmilo Nikolic, Mr Francesco Ricci Bitti, Mr Brian R. Tobin.
Vice Presidents 1987–89: Mr Gordon D. Jorgensen, Mr Pablo Llorens, Mr Brian R. Tobin.
Honorary Treasurer 1987–89: Mr David Jude.
Auditors 1987–89: Messrs Ernst & Whinney, Becket House, 1 Lambeth Palace Road, London SE1 7EU.
Legal Counsel: Mr James W. Lillie.
Sub-Committees 1987–89: *Davis Cup*; *Federation Cup*; Finance; Junior Competitions; Olympic; Olympic Selection; Rules; Technical; Veterans.
Commissions: Media; Medical.
Secretariat: Mr Mike Davies – Director of Marketing; Mr Thomas Hallberg – Director of Men's Tennis; Miss Sally Holdsworth – Director of Administration and Personnel; Mr Doug MacCurdy – Director of Development; Miss Barbara Wancke – Director of Women's Tennis; Mr Leif Dahlgren – Development Administrator; Mr David Fechtman – Marketing Assistant; Mr Tony Gathercole – Administrator – Veteran Tennis; Mr George Pharr – Public Relations Officer; Mr Christopher S. Stokes – *Davis Cup* Sponsorship Administrator; Mr John Treleven – Junior Programmes Administrator; Mrs Frances Deed – Financial Co-ordinator; Miss Claire Hamilton – Membership Co-ordinator; Mrs Joyce Hume – Public Relations Co-ordinator; Mrs Debbie Jarrett – Project Co-ordinator, Olympic Tennis; Miss Kay Peters – Technical Co-ordinator.

MEN'S INTERNATIONAL PROFESSIONAL TENNIS COUNCIL
ITF Representatives: Mr Philippe Chatrier, Mr David Markin, Mr Brian R. Tobin. ***Player Representatives:*** Mr Weller B. Evans, Mr Hamilton Jordan, Mr Ray Moore. ***Tournament Representatives: North American:*** Mr Charles M. Pasarell. ***European:*** Mr Franco Bartoni. ***Rest of World:*** Mr Graham Lovett. ***Administrator:*** Mr M. Marshall Happer III. ***Assistant Administrators:*** Mr Bill Babcock, Mr David Cooper (New York), and Mr Paul Svehlik (Paris).

WOMEN'S INTERNATIONAL PROFESSIONAL TENNIS COUNCIL
ITF Representatives: Mr Robert Cookson, Mr Brian R. Tobin, Miss Barbara Wancke (Alternates Mr Philippe Chatrier, Mrs Ann Jones). ***WITA Representatives:*** Miss Peachy Kellmeyer, Miss Candy Reynolds, Mr Merrett Stierheim (Alternates Mrs Trish Faulkner and Miss Christianne Jolissaint). ***Tournament Representatives: North America:*** Mrs Edythe McGoldrick (Alternate Mr Bill Goldstein). ***Europe:*** Mr George Hendon (Alternate – Gunter Sanders). ***Rest of World:*** Mr Geoff Pollard (Alternate Mr Jack Butefish). ***Managing Director:*** Miss Jane Brown.

The following tennis manufacturers
and other groups whose interest
lie in the sport are members of the
ITF FOUNDATION

Any commercial tennis organisation is welcome to
apply for membership – details of the
I.T.F. Foundation and the benefits it brings
to both sport and member can be obtained from:-

The ITF Foundation
International Tennis Federation
Palliser Road
Barons Court
London W14 9EN.

THE AFRICAN YEAR

The year began with the tenth anniversary of the ITF West African Junior Championships Air Afrique Trophy held in Abidjan, Cote d'Ivoire. A film was made documenting the event and tennis development in Africa, which was later to be shown on television throughout the African continent. The African Zone of the *Davis Cup* was most exciting, with stunning upsets in the semi-finals, when Senegal defeated Egypt and Zimbabwe edged Nigeria. Both Senegal and Zimbabwe went forward to the European Zone, where Zimbabwe fell in the first round to Poland, but Senegal beat Norway before losing comprehensively to Bulgaria.

New circuits inaugurated in 1987 included men's satellite tournaments in Tunisia, Algeria, Morocco, Cote d'Ivoire, Senegal and Togo. The ITF East/Central Africa Junior Circuit was staged in Botswana, Zimbabwe, Zambia and Kenya, these competitions being supported by the ITF Grand Slam Trust Fund. The fourth All Africa Games were held in Nairobi in August. The champions were: Men's Singles – Byron Black; Women's Singles – Berthe Marie; Men's Doubles – Byron Black and Mark Gurr; Women's Doubles – Rolake Olagbegi and Veronika Oyibokia. Eighteen nations participated in the African Tennis Championships in Tripoli, Libya in September.

Encouraging results were being registered by African junior players in international competitions, which bodes well for the future. Byron Black of Zimbabwe won several tournaments as well as reaching the quarter-finals of the Wimbledon Junior Championships, while Clement N'Goran of Cote d'Ivoire ended the year on a high note by reaching the semi-finals of the Orange Bowl in Miami.

UNIVERSIADE

ZAGREB, YUGOSLAVIA, 15–17 JULY

MEN'S SINGLES – Quarter-finals: B. Oresar d. A. Deleval (FRA) 6–2 6–3; G. Dzelde (URS) d. R. Vogel (TCH) 6–3 6–3; M. Tabares (CUB) d. A. Olkhovski (URS) 6–7 6–4 6–4; I. Saric d. B. Stankovic (TCH) 6–1 6–2. ***Semi-finals:*** Oresar d. Dzelde 6–0 6–1; Saric d. Tabares 6–4 5–7 6–3. ***Final:*** Oresar d. Saric 6–3 6–0 6–0.

MEN'S DOUBLES – Final: Vogel/Stankovic d. Olkhovski/Dzelde 6–3 7–5 6–3.

WOMEN'S SINGLES – Quarter-finals: S. Goles (YUG) d. J. Santrock (USA) 6–1 7–5; L. Meskhi (URS) d. B. Rodriguez (CUB) 6–1 6–0; J. Lee (KOR) d. Y. Li (CHN) 6–3 6–0; I. Budarova (TCH) d. V. Milvidskaia (URS) 6–4 6–3. ***Semi-finals:*** Meskhi d. Goles 6–2 6–3; Budarova d. Lee 7–5 6–4. ***Final:*** Meskhi d. Budarova 7–5 7–6.

WOMEN'S DOUBLES – Final: Milvidskaia/Meskhi d. Budarova/N. Bajcikova (TCH) 7–5 6–2.

MIXED DOUBLES – Final: Goles/Oresar d. Meskhi/Olkhovski 6–4 6–3.

THE ITF FOUNDATION

The ITF Foundation was created in 1980 to establish a liaison and co-operation between the International Tennis Federation and manufacturers. The Foundation has grown from the first meeting attended by representatives of twelve companies to the present membership of some 30 companies. Three new companies joined the Federation in 1987: FTM from the United States, FILA from Italy and Junior Tennis World from Great Britain. The ITF development programme continues to benefit from the money and equipment donated, and with the formation of the Marketing Department in Dallas, the ITF is now able to offer a greatly improved service to its Foundation members.

ADIDAS, France; **AMF Head,** USA; **ASICS,** Japan; **ASICS,** West Germany; **Bolltex,** Sweden; **Diadora,** Italy; **Dunlop,** Great Britain; **FILA,** Italy; **FILA,** USA; **Fischer,** Austria; **FTM,** USA; **Gosen,** Japan; **Kim Top Line,** Italy; **Lacoste,** France; **Marlboro Leisure Wear,** Switzerland; **Mizuno,** Japan; **Nassau,** Korea; **Nassau,** France; **Nassau,** Great Britain; **Penn,** USA; **Penn,** France; **Penn,** Eire; **Pirelli,** Italy; **Prince,** USA; **Prince,** France; **Rossignol,** France; **Slazenger,** Great Britain; **Supreme,** USA; **Supreme,** West Germany; **Tacchini,** Italy; **Junior World Tennis,** Great Britain; **Tennis Australia,** Australia; **Tennis de France,** France; **Tennis World,** Great Britain; **Tretorn,** Sweden; **Wilson,** Great Britain; **Wilson,** USA; **Yamaha,** Japan; **Yamaha,** Great Britain.

THE JUNIOR GAME

The Russians are coming – hotly pursued by the Australians. No doubt inspired by the reintroduction of tennis to the Olympics, the Soviet players had an outstanding junior year.

Natalia Zvereva dominated the girls' singles, winning all six events she played, including five Group A events. By finishing 19th in the WITA rankings, she is no doubt the highest-ever senior-ranked Junior Champion. She amassed more than twice as many points as her nearest challenger, Gabriela Mosca, who maintained Argentina's excellent recent record in the girls' singles by finishing runner-up with a string of consistent results in the bigger events. Mosca's best performance was as runner-up in Venezuela, an event won by Tanja Weigl of West Germany, who finished third at the year's end – a position she also held in doubles.

The girls' doubles rankings were headed by Zvereva's compatriot, Natalia Medvedeva, who was almost as commanding a winner as Zvereva was of the singles. They played together for the first part of the year, winning the Italian, French and Wimbledon titles, and after Zvereva's senior commitments took her away from junior doubles, Elena Brioukhovets became Medvedeva's partner for the latter half of the year. The doughty Brioukhovets's singles play blossomed at the same time, taking her to fourth place; and with Medvedeva she won the Orange Bowl and Canadian Open doubles titles to take second spot in the doubles list. Brioukhovets and Medvedeva also took the USSR to the final of the World Youth Cup, and rounded the year off by winning the Continental Players Cup on behalf of their country.

The Russian boys made a valiant attempt to emulate their girls' successes, and with a late surge almost achieved it. Andrei Cherkasov, winner of the European Closed in July, followed with a win at Port Washington, as well as reaching the finals of the Canadian and US Opens plus the Orange Bowl, to finish in third place, as he did in the doubles, with his partner Vladimir Petrushenko immediately behind him. Together they won the Sunshine Cup as the USSR completed the double, the girls having won the equivalent competition, the Continental Players Cup, in the same week.

However, they narrowly failed to stop Jason Stoltenberg of Australia becoming the first to top both the junior singles and doubles in the same year. His singles success was based on a series of excellent results in the major tournaments. He started with two wins on his home circuit, before reaching at least the semi-finals of the JAL Cup, French Open, Wimbledon and US Open, to demonstrate his versatility on all surfaces. He gradually overhauled the runaway leader of the first half of the season – Alejandro Aramburo of Peru – who set the pace by winning six of the early South American circuit tournaments. He then followed with two more clay-court successes in Italy and Belgium, but eventually, needing to win the Orange Bowl to regain his lead, he fell in the quarter-finals.

Jim Courier, winner of the Italian Open and Orange Bowl, and David Wheaton, winner of the US Open, showed that the next generation of US players may be on the way. They finished fourth and seventh respectively, divided by Diego Nargiso, an Italian who proved his preference for grass by winning Wimbledon, and Todd Woodbridge, who won the JAL Cup as well as finishing runner-up to his doubles partner, Stoltenberg, in the New South Wales and Australian Opens.

The doubles race was a very close one, with Stoltenberg (first) and Woodbridge (fifth) winning the two grass-court Grand Slam events at Melbourne and Wimbledon, as well as being runners-up in the JAL Cup. They led from the start, but Nargiso got to within five points of the lead when he won the US Open with Goran Ivanisevic of Yugoslavia. How-

Top juniors in 1987 (clockwise from top left): Todd Woodbridge and Jason Stoltenberg pictured with the Wimbledon Junior doubles trophy, Marcus Barbosa, Jim Courier and David Wheaton. (A. Evans, P. Shephard-Lewis, T. Hindley)

ever, Nargiso failed to close this narrow advantage, and although Cherkasov and Petrushenko moved in to threaten, they failed to reach the semi-finals at Port Washington in the final event of the year, which would have given them top spots. They will no doubt rue a number of narrow defeats during the year.

While the Russians can look back on success in the team events of the 18s age group, it was the Australians who dominated the World Youth Cup for 16s. Held in 1987 in Freiburg, West Germany, the event was blessed with excellent weather and capacity crowds. Australia's boys, led by Woodbridge, who was ably assisted by John Anderson, won a final-set deciding doubles match against Sweden in the semi-finals before overcoming the Dutch in the final more easily, although Paul Dogger, winner of the Orange Bowl 16s, fully stretched Woodbridge in the top singles match. This completed a hat-trick for the Australian boys, who had won both previous events, but the triumph of their girls was a novel one. Jo-Anne Faull and Rachel McQuillan defeated the host nation on the deciding doubles in the semi-finals, and repeated the feat in the final against the USSR. It is therefore appropriate that the venue for 1988 is Perth, although this was decided before the 1987 event took place.

The Australian girls also won the Annie Soisbault Cup, defeating the Czechoslovakians, who none the less reached another four team finals and five other semi-finals. In a generally outstanding year they won the Valerio and Europa Cups, while France defeated them in the Galea and Queen Sofia finals.

Austria had high hopes going into the World Youth Cup, having won the Jean Borotra Cup, and although these were dashed perhaps their chance will come in two years' time, for their 14s teams reached the finals of the Del Sol and Europa Cups respectively. They were, however, defeated in both by the Czechoslovakian girls and the West German boys, who thus gained compensation for losing the Valerio Cup final. Italy had no such solace, losing both the Borotra and Continental Players Cup finals, as well as losing two other semi-finals. Sweden were also empty-handed, for after missing out so narrowly in the World Youth Cup, they also lost the Sunshine Cup final.

The closest of all the team competitions was the Helvetie Cup. Six of the seven ties from the quarter-finals onwards were decided by the odd rubber, and the final saw the Dutch come back from losing the top two singles to defeat the Swiss in the deciding doubles.

JUNIOR WORLD RANKING 1987

BOYS' SINGLES

1 Jason Stoltenberg (AUS); **2** Alejandro Aramburu (PER); **3** Andrei Cherkasov (URS); **4** Jim Courier (USA); **5** Diego Nargiso (ITA); **6** Todd Woodbridge (AUS); **7** David Wheaton (USA); **8** Nicklas Utgren (SWE); **9** Marcus Barbosa (BRA); **10** Goran Ivanisevic (YUG).

GIRLS' SINGLES

1 Natalia Zvereva (URS); **2** Gabriela Mosca (ARG); **3** Tanja Weigl (FRG); **4** Elena Brioukhovets (URS); **5** Il-Soon Kim (KOR); **6** Nany 'Yayuk' Basuki (INA); **7** Steffi Menning (FRG); **8** Natalia Medvedeva (URS); **9** Andrea Vieira (BRA); **10** Cristina Tessi (ARG).

BOYS' DOUBLES

1 Jason Stoltenberg (AUS); **2** Diego Nargiso (ITA); **3** Andrei Cherkasov (URS); **4** Vladimir Petrushenko (URS); **5** Todd Woodbridge (AUS); **6 eq** Jim Courier (USA), Jonathan Stark (USA); **8** Peter Nyborg (SWE); **9** Marcus Barbosa (BRA); **10** Fabio Silberberg (BRA).

GIRLS' DOUBLES

1 Natalia Medvedeva (URS); **2** Elena Brioukhovets (URS); **3** Tanja Weigl (FRG); **4** Patricia Miller (URU); **5** Eva-Maria Schuerhoff (FRG); **6** Cristina Tessi (ARG); **7** Andrea Vieira (BRA); **8** Steffi Menning (FRG); **9** Gabriela Mosca (ARG); **10** Luciana Tella (BRA).

JUNIOR WORLD RANKING 1987 – POINTS EXPLANATION

The Junior World Ranking is a world-wide points-linked circuit of 97 tournaments, five continental championships and four team competitions in 65 countries, under the management of the International Tennis Federation. There are ten separate points categories covering the three types of events. There is no limit to the number of tournaments in which a player may compete each year. The best six results from tournaments (Groups A and 1–5) and continental championships (Groups B1–B3) count towards a player's final ranking, plus the best result from a team competition (Group C). To qualify for a final ranking a player must have competed in at least six events, including at least three Group A tournaments and at least three outside his or her own country.

POINTS TABLE (Tournaments and Continental Championships)

SINGLES

	A	**1**	**2**	**3**	**4**	**5**	**B1**	**B2**	**B3**
Winner	200	100	70	55	40	30	150	100	55
Runner Up	150	80	55	40	30	20	100	80	40
Semi-Finalists	100	60	40	30	20	10	80	60	40
Quarter-Finalists	80	40	30	15	10	5	60	40	15
Losers in last 16	60	20	15	10	5	—	40	20	10
Losers in last 32 (only if 64 draw)	30	10	—	—	—	—	—	—	—

DOUBLES (each player)

	A	**1**	**2**	**3**	**4**	**5**	**B1**	**B2**	**B3**
Winners	150	80	55	40	30	20	100	80	40
Runners Up	100	60	40	30	20	10	80	60	30
Semi-Finalists	80	40	30	15	10	5	60	40	15
Quarter-Finalists	60	20	15	10	5	—	40	20	10
Losers in last 16 (only if 32 draw)	30	10	—	—	—	—	—	—	—

POINTS TABLE (Team Competitions)

	No. 1 Singles Player Win	**No. 2 Singles Player Win**	**Doubles Win Each Player**
Final	55	40	40
Semi-Final	40	30	30

POINTS TABLE (Group A Bonus Points)

	Singles	**Doubles**
Winner of 4 or more Group A events	150	150
Winner of 3 Group A events	100	100

ITF JUNIOR WORLD RANKING CIRCUIT 1987

DATE	TOURNAMENT	GROUP	BOYS' SINGLES FINAL	GIRLS' SINGLES FINAL
26–29 Dec	Western Australian Boys'	4	C. Turich d. N. Prickett 6–1 6–2	—
27 Dec–1 Jan	Queensland Girls'	3	—	K. Radford d. P. Parentich 6–1 5–7 6–4
28 Dec–3 Jan	African, Ivory Coast	B3	C. N'Goran d. M. Benyebka 6–4 6–2	O. Bouchabou d. N. Wagstaff 6–1 6–0
29 Dec–2 Jan	South Australian Boys'	3	S. Barr d. D. Nargiso 6–2 5–7 6–4	—
1–6 Jan	Salk, Sweden	5	N. Utgren d. M. Larsson 4–6 6–1 6–2	M. Nilsson d. A. Narbe 6–3 6–1
3–7 Jan	New South Wales, Australia	1	J. Stoltenberg d. T. Woodbridge 7–6 6–3	S. McCann d. K. Radford 6–2 6–2
5–10 Jan	Puerto Rico	2	J. Naves d. O. Braves 6–3 7–6	K. Nowak d. L. Albano 6–3 6–4
5–11 Jan	Caracas, Venezuela	A	A. Aramburu d. N. Marques 4–6 6–4 7–5	T. Weigl d. G. Mosca 7–6 6–1
12–16 Jan	Victorian, Australia	2	D. Nargiso d. A. Anderson 6–3 6–1	S. McCann d. K. Radford 7–6 6–2
12–18 Jan	Pony Malta Cup, Colombia	1	J. Eltingh d. C. Caratti 6–4 6–7 6–4	E. Schuerhoff d. S. Menning 6–2 6–2
12–18 Jan	Coffee Bowl, Costa Rica	3	J. Holtari d. A. Lindholm 4–6 6–3 6–1	K. Nowak d. M. Mroz 6–4 7–6
17–25 Jan	Australian Junior	A	J. Stoltenberg d. T. Woodbridge 6–2 7–6	M. Jaggard d. N. Provis 6–2 6–4
20–25 Jan	Ecuador Cup, Quito	3	R. Haas d. F. Silberberg 6–4 6–4	S. Menning d. T. Weigl 6–7 6–1 8–6
27 Jan–1 Feb	Inka Bowl, Peru	2	A. Aramburu d. A. Garizzio 7–5 3–6 6–3	S. Menning d. K. Strohmeier 6–2 4–6 6–2
27 Jan–1 Feb	Start, Bulgaria	4	R. Itu d. P. Vizner 6–2 6–0	E. Sviglerova d. M. Kraicheva 1–6 6–3 6–2
2–8 Feb	Indira Ghandi, India	4	Z. Ali d. P. Raman 6–3 6–1	D. Merchant d. S. Kanamwar 6–1 6–3
3–8 Feb	Condor de Plata, Bolivia	3	B. Laustroer d. S. Nensel 6–2 7–5	L. Tella d. P. Wallenfels 6–2 6–0
9–15 Feb	Sri Lanka Int.	4	N. Rajapakse d. J. Wijesekera 6–0 6–1	T. Viragh d. V. Premaratne 7–5 6–3
10–15 Feb	Milo Cup, Chile	2	A. Burga d. A. Garizzio 6–2 4–6 6–4	C. Chabalgoity d. M. Kemper 7–5 6–3
16–22 Feb	Indonesia Int.	4	D. Suhendar d. I. Yosep 6–3 7–6	N. Basuki d. W. Walalangi 6–2 6–2
17–22 Feb	Carrasco Bowl, Uruguay	2	A. Aramburu d. S. Sarli 6–4 6–1	A. Vieira d. S. Menning 6–2 2–6 6–3
23 Feb–1 March	Singapore Int.	5	U. Rahim d. R. Mirza 6–3 6–2	F. Khursheed d. T. Viragh 6–0 6–1
24 Feb–1 March	Argentina Cup	2	A. Aramburu d. J. Noriega 6–2 6–3	P. Wallenfels d. F. Labat 6–4 6–4
2–8 March	Brunei Int.	5	U. Rahim d. R. Mirza 6–1 6–3	—
3–7 March	Ascuncion Bowl, Paraguay	2	A. Aramburu d. M. Pacheco 6–2 6–4	M. Kemper d. G. Paiva 6–0 6–4
7–13 March	Qatar Champs.	5	J. Johnsen d. A. Asad 7–5 6–4	—
8–14 March	Banana Bowl, Brazil	1	A. Aramburu d. S. Sarli 6–3 6–3	M. Kemper d. G. Mosca 6–0 6–4
9–15 March	Sun Cup, Belgium	4	P. Nyborg d. G. Van Der Veeren 7–6 3–6 7–5	M. Mroz d. S. Appelmans 7–5 4–6 7–5
9–15 March	Manolo Elizalde, Philippines	3	J. Siemerink d. A. Navarossa 6–3 7–5	S. Rafael d. Jennifer Saberon 6–3 6–1
15–21 March	South American, Brazil	B2	J. Noriega d. G. Carbonari 6–3 6–4	F. Labat d. C. Tessi 6–1 4–6 6–4
16–21 March	Ershad Int., Bangladesh	4	D. Suhendar d. K. Masuda 6–1 6–3	Y. Yamagishi d. R. Noguchi 6–0 2–6 6–0
23–29 March	Thailand Int.	2	J. Morgan d. D. Heryanto 4–6 6–1 6–3	Y. Yamagishi d. W. Walalangi 6–0 4–6 6–3
23–29 March	South African Int.	3	P. Norval d. L. Bale 7–6 6–3	M. De Swardt d. A. Coetzer 7–5 4–6 6–0
30 March–5 April	Hong Kong Int.	2	R. Tsujino d. J. Shin 3–6 7–6 6–4	N. Basuki d. Jennifer Saberon 5–7 6–1 6–3
6–11 April	Katoro Cup, Yugoslavia	4	G. Ivanisevic d. M. Klesinger 7–5 6–2	E. Koljanin d. S. Reichel 6–2 6–0
6–12 April	Taipei Int.	2	M. Chang d. D. Suhendar 6–2 6–3	S. Wang d. S. Rafael 6–1 6–2
6–12 April	Grasse Int., France	4	F. Fontang d. C. N'Goran 4–6 6–3 6–1	M. Laval d. C. Menain 6–3 4–6 6–4
13–18 April	Tel Aviv Int.	4	R. Weidenfeld d. H. Zion 1–6 7–6 6–1	D. Coriat d. A. Varon 6–3 6–3
13–19 April	Suntory, Tokyo	2	Z. Ali d. D. Kirk 7–6 7–6	R. Yamaguchi d. I. Kim 6–4 6–2
13–19 April	Nice, France	2	R. Fromberg d. B. Wuyts 6–1 7–5	M. Strandlund d. S. Appelmans 6–1 3–6 6–1
13–19 April	Pascuas Bowl, Paraguay	5	R. Teofilo d. G. Ramos 6–2 6–2	M. Rodriguez d. X. Diaz De Vivar 6–2 6–3

DATE	TOURNAMENT	GROUP	BOYS' SINGLES FINAL	GIRLS' SINGLES FINAL
15–20 April	Florence Int., Italy	2	F. Mordegan d. R. Furlan 6–3 6–3	C. Martinez d. A. Grossman 3–6 7–5 6–3
20–26 April	Jal Cup, Tokyo	A	T. Woodbridge d. P. Henricsson 7–6 6–2	I. Kim d. R. Yamaguchi 4–6 6–3 6–3
20–26 April	Tbilisi Int.	4	A. Cherkasov d. D. Kacharava 6–1 6–0	E. Kislukha d. A. Mirza 6–1 6–1
21–26 April	Penn Spring Bowl, Austria	2	L. Jonsson d. J. Apell 6–4 6–3	M. Strandlund d. A. Vieira 6–3 6–1
27 April–3 May	Acropolis Cup, Greece	3	L. Jonsson d. P. Nyborg 6–3 6–3	R. Milorieva d. E. Nikolova 6–1 7–5
27 April–3 May	Tashkent Int., USSR	4	T. Zdrazila d. D. Kacharava 6–2 7–5	E. Kislukha d. M. Pecheanu 7–6 3–6 7–6
4–10 May	Alessandria Trophy, Italy	1	A. Aramburu d. O. Della 6–2 6–1	N. Medvedeva d. P. Miller 3–6 6–4 6–4
11–16 May	Verona Trophy, Italy	2	F. Davin d. A. Cherkasov 6–2 6–3	N. Zvereva d. N. Medvedeva 6–1 6–1
14–17 May	Berlin Int.	3	F. Loddenkemper d. M. Zillner 6–3 6–2	M. Kemper d. S. Menning 6–4 6–1
17–23 May	Italian Junior	A	J. Courier d. A. Aramburu 7–6 1–6 6–3	N. Zvereva d. C. Martinez 6–2 6–3
25–30 May	Astrid Bowl, Belgium	1	A. Aramburu d. O. Della 6–2 6–3	C. Tessi d. S. Appelmans 3–6 6–1 6–1
25–30 May	Cremona Trophy, Italy	4	R. Itu d. S. Pescosolido 6–2 6–3	A. Coetzer d. D. Samungi 6–4 6–1
1–7 June	French Junior	A	G. Perez Roldan d. J. Stoltenberg 6–3 3–6 6–2	N. Zvereva d. J. Pospisilova 6–0 6–1
8–13 June	White Devils, Belgium	2	B. Black d. C. Carbonari 6–4 6–2	N. Basuki d. R. Caldas 7–6 6–3
8–14 June	Apple Bowl, Spain	2	L. Ruette d. R. Furlan 7–5 6–3	N. Marcucci d. C. Martinez 7–6 6–1
15–21 June	LTA Int., Thames Ditton	2	D. Nargiso d. B. Black 6–1 6–4	I. Kim d. N. Medvedeva 6–3 7–5
16–20 June	OTP Danubius Cup, Hungary	5	S. Noszaly d. T. Klimek 5–7 6–4 6–3	A. Noszaly d. S. Witzova 7–6 6–2
22–28 June	LTA Int., Surbiton	1	B. Black d. B. Steven 6–2 6–1	R. Zrubakova d. N. Medvedeva 6–2 6–0
22–28 June	Danish Junior	5	F. Fetterlein d. T. Sorensen 6–4 6–4	K. Ptaszek d. S. Albinus 6–2 6–3
29 June–5 July	Wimbledon Junior	A	D. Nargiso d. J. Stoltenberg 7–6 6–4	N. Zvereva d. J. Halard 6–4 6–4
2–5 July	Panasonic Cup, Hamburg	5	J. Anderson d. F. Nilsson 6–4 6–1	J. Faull d. S. Remhke 4–6 6–3 7–5
6–11 July	Coca-Cola, Netherlands	4	O. Weinberg d. J. Asplund 6–0 3–6 6–3	N. Van Dierendonck d. Y. Segal 7–5 6–4
6–12 July	German Junior	2	J. Noriega d. G. Raoux 6–1 6–1	T. Weigl d. M. Zivec 7–5 6–2
6–12 July	Jamaican Junior	5	P. Lavergne d. C. Mark 6–3 6–3	D. Millington d. C. Walter 6–0 6–1
13–19 July	Ebel, Swiss	3	P. Sjoden d. M. Barbosa 7–6 6–2	E. Zardo d. A. Vieira 7–6 6–4
20–26 July	Luxembourg Int.	5	O. Casey d. S. Horowitz 2–6 6–2 6–4	A. Michailoff d. C. Toleafoa 6–2 6–1
21–25 July	Friendship Cup, Poland	4	B. Dabrawski d. M. Onila 7–6 6–0	A. Listowska d. S. Czopek 6–3 6–7 6–3
27 July–1 Aug	Slazenger, Winchester	5	C. Wilkinson d. J. Hunter 6–4 3–6 6–2	A. Hill d. L. Nimmo 5–7 6–4 6–3
27 July–2 Aug	European Championships, France	B1	A. Cherkasov d. N. Utgren 6–1 6–4	H. Adamkova d. A. Dechaume 6–2 6–0
1–9 Aug	USTA Nationals	2	M. Chang d. J. Courier 6–4 6–2	A. Grossman d. I. McCalla 6–2 6–0
3–9 Aug	Slovakia Cup, Czechoslovakia	5	R. Itu d. C. Dosedel 4–6 7–5 6–3	R. Smekalova d. J. Dubcova 1–6 6–1 6–4
9–16 Aug	USTA Int. Grass	2	T. Martin d. J. Falbo 7–6 6–7 7–6	A. Grossman d. Jennifer Saberon 6–3 6–2
10–16 Aug	Crystal Cup, Czechoslovakia	3	R. Itu d. P. Vizner 7–5 6–4	P. Langrova d. L. Laskova 6–1 6–1
10–16 Aug	McDonald's S-Sparkassen Cup, Austria	5	P. Peham d. H. Mair 6–2 7–5	N. Dobrovits d. U. Priller 6–3 7–6
18–22 Aug	Artex-Nyirfa Cup, Hungary	4	K. Keresztes d. V. Nagy 4–6 6–4 6–3	M. Pecheanu d. M. Koves 6–0 6–4
18–23 Aug	Tunisia Int.	5	S. Bruek d. H. Debbeche 6–2 6–4	M. Bey d. A. Bennacer 7–5 2–6 6–1
19–23 Aug	BMC, Botswana	5	K. El Salawy d. M. Birch w.o.	P. Iversen d. E. Cochery 7–5 6–4
24–27 Aug	USTA Int. Hard Courts	3	L. Ruette d. A. Aramburu 7–6 3–6 6–4	C. Toleafoa d. S. Reece 7–5 6–2
24–28 Aug	Zeralda Cup, Algeria	5	M. Benyebka d. T. Hegazi 6–1 6–3	A. Bennécer d. R. Pichardo 6–4 6–2
26–30 Aug	Bata, Zimbabwe	5	F. Ofori d. K. El Salawy 6–3 4–6 6–2	L. Barbour d. P. Iversen 7–6 6–4

DATE	TOURNAMENT	GROUP	BOYS' SINGLES FINAL	GIRLS' SINGLES FINAL
29 Aug–6 Sept	Caribbean & Central American	B3	M. Cuculiza d. C. Zuniga 6–4 7–5	I. Gonzalez d. R. Wachtler 6–4 6–3
31 Aug–6 Sept	Chipwich Canadian	1	A. Aramburu d. A. Cherkasov 6–4 6–4	E. Brioukhovets d. A. Farley 6–2 6–3
1–6 Sept	Romania Int	5	R. Itu d. D. Dobre 6–4 3–6 6–0	S. Czopek d. E. Kislukha 6–2 6–2
1–6 Sept	Albert Elgrichi, Morocco	5	F. Francqueville d. M. Ridaoui 7–6 0–6 6–2	A. Bennacer d. A. Fahmy 6–2 7–5
2–6 Sept	Colgate Palmolive, Zambia	3	F. Ofori d. M. Birch 6–2 6–4	L. Barbour d. S. Murnane 6–1 6–2
7–13 Sept	US Open Junior	A	D. Wheaton d. A. Cherkasov 7–5 6–0	N. Zvereva d. S. Birch 6–0 6–3
7–13 Sept	Kenya Junior	5	M. Birch d. J. Kouassi 6–1 6–1	S. Munane d. G. Seleka 6–4 5–7 10–8
14–20 Sept	26th Catalan Int., Spain	5	J. Sedeno d. J. Olivert 7–5 7–6	S. Tous d. P. Fas 6–7 6–4 6–4
14–20 Sept	Aphrodite Cup, Cyprus	5	C. Dosedel d. J. Kabakoglou 6–2 6–2	—
21–27 Sept	Guangzhou Int., China	4	Z. Jiuhua d. R. Rajpal 6–1 6–3	L. Fang d. C. Li 6–2 6–3
28 Sept–4 Oct	East Asian, Hong Kong	4	H. Shin d. D. Suhendar 6–2 6–2	T. Kim d. M. Tang 5–7 6–3 6–3
5–11 Oct	Asian Closed, Korea	B2	H. Shin d. E. Jang 7–6 6–4	S. Wang d. N. Smith-Miyagi 6–3 6–4
12–18 Oct	Mercu Buana, Indonesia	4	D. Suhendar d. D. Heryanto 7–6 6–1	W. Walalangi d. I. Moerid 2–6 6–0 6–2
2–8 Nov	Pakistan Int.	5	R. Rajpal d. G. Natekar 6–2 6–2	—
13–17 Nov	Swedish Int.	4	M. Larsson d. N. Kulti 6–3 6–2	J. Jonerup d. N. Dahlman 2–6 6–3 6–2
19–22 Nov	HBL Cup, Finland	4	J. Alven d. J. Holtari 6–2 7–5	N. Dahlman d. P. Thoren 7–6 4–6 6–3
7–12 Dec	Coffee Bowl, Costa Rica	2	J. Bianchi d. G. Koves 6–4 6–7 6–2	M. Zivec d. S. Czopek 6–3 6–2
20–23 Dec	Zibans Cup, Algeria	5	B. Bierkens d. M. Mahmoudi 6–1 6–1	O. Bouchabou d. A. Bennacer 6–2 6–1
21–28 Dec	Orange Bowl, USA	A	J. Courier d. A. Cherkasov 6–3 6–2	N. Zvereva d. L. Lapi 6–2 6–0
28 Dec–3 Jan	Port Washington, USA	1	A. Cherkasov d. V. Petrushenko 4–6 6–1 6–0	N. Smith-Miyagi d. E. Brioukhovets 6–1 6–1
28 Dec–3 Jan	Casablanca Cup, Mexico	3	G. Ivanisevic d. L. Herrera 7–6 6–3	M. Mroz d. S. Czopek 6–0 4–6 6–1

WORLD YOUTH CUP

Boys' and Girls' 16 & Under International Team Championships
51 nations competed, 50 taking part in the boys' event and 45 in the girls' event. Final stages took place in Freiburg, West Germany, 16–20 September.
FINAL POSITIONS – BOYS: Champion nation – Australia; runners-up – Netherlands; 3rd – Sweden; 4th – France; 5th – Argentina; 6th – West Germany; 7th – Brazil; 8th – Austria; 9th – USA; 10th – Hungary; 11th – Mexico; 12th – Japan; 13th – Israel; 14th – Egypt; 15th – Republic of Korea; 16th – Chile.
GIRLS: Champion nation – Australia; runners-up – USSR; 3rd – West Germany; 4th – USA; 5th – Argentina; 6th – Bulgaria; 7th – Italy; 8th – Switzerland; 9th – Spain; 10th – Japan; 11th – Chinese Taipei; 12th – Brazil; 13th – Canada; 14th – Peru; 15th – Zimbabwe; 16th – Republic of Korea.
BOYS' CHAMPIONSHIP – Semi-finals: Australia d. Sweden 2–1 (T. Woodbridge lost to N. Kulti 6–3 3–6 2–6; J. Anderson d. O. Kristiansson 6–2 6–3; Anderson/Woodbridge d. Kristiansson/Kulti 3–6 6–4 6–2); ***Netherlands d. France 2–1*** (P. Dogger d. S. Hette 6–4 7–5; F. Wibier lost to F. Santoro 2–6 7–5 3–6; Dogger/Woodbridge d. D. Durand/Santoro 6–4 6–4). ***Final: Australia d. Netherlands 3–0*** (Woodbridge d. Dogger 7–5 3–6 6–2; Anderson d. Wibier 6–0 6–1; J. Morgan/Woodbridge d. Dogger/Wibier 6–3 6–2).
GIRLS' CHAMPIONSHIP – Semi-finals: Australia d. West Germany 2–1 (J. Faull d. M. Kriebel 6–4 6–4; R. McQuillan lost to S. Menning 5–7 1–6; Faull/McQuillan d. Menning/P. Wallenfels 7–6 6–3); ***USSR d. USA 2–1*** (N. Medvedeva d. L. Poruri 6–1 5–7 6–3; E. Brioukhovets d. D. Moringiello 2–6 6–2 11–9; N. Biletskaia/Medvedeva lost to D. Herman/Poruri 6–7 7–6 2–6). ***Final: Australia d. USSR 2–1*** (Faull lost to Medvedeva 6–4 2–6 2–6; McQuillan d. Brioukhovets 3–6 6–2 6–3; Faull/McQuillan d. Brioukhovets/Medvedeva 6–3 6–1).

GALEA CUP

Men's 20 & Under International Team Championship
27 nations competed. Quarter-finals, semi-finals and final played in Vichy, France, 14–19 July.
Quarter-finals: France d. USSR 3–1 (one rubber not played); Spain d. USA 3–1 (one rubber not played); Australia d. West Germany 3–2; Czechoslovakia d. Sweden 3–2. ***Semi-finals:*** France d. Spain 3–2; Czechoslovakia d. Australia 3–1 (one rubber not played). ***Final:*** France d. Czechoslovakia 3–1 (one rubber not played) (O. Delaitre d. P. Korda 6–3 6–0, d. C. Suk 6–1 6–1; S. Grenier lost to P. Korda 7–6 2–6 11–13, d. C. Suk 6–3 6–2; Delaitre/Grenier v Korda/Suk not played.

ANNIE SOISBAULT CUP

Women's 20 & Under International Team Championship
15 nations competed. Played in Le Touquet, France, 6–11 July.
Quarter-finals: Australia d. Italy 2–1; USA d. West Germany 3–0; France d. Spain 2–1; Czechoslovakia d. USSR 3–0. ***Semi-finals:*** Australia d. USA 2–1; Czechoslovakia d. France 3–0. ***3rd place play-off:*** USA d. France 3–0. ***Final:*** Australia d. Czechoslovakia 2–1 (N. Provis d. R. Rajchrtova 2–6 6–2 6–1; J. Byrne lost to J. Novotna 5–7 6–3 3–6; Byrne/Provis d. Novotna/Rajchrtova 6–4 0–6 6–3).

SUNSHINE CUP

Boys' 18 & Under International Team Championship
40 nations competed. Played in Delray Beach, Florida, USA, 13–20 December.
Quarter-finals: USSR d. Italy 3–0; France d. West Germany 2–1; Great Britain d. Peru 2–1; Sweden d. USA 2–1. ***Semi-finals:*** USSR d. France 3–0; Sweden d. Great Britain 3–0. ***Final:*** USSR d. Sweden 2–1 (A. Cherkasov d. L. Jonsson 6–4 7–6; V. Petrushenko lost to N. Kulti 7–5 2–6 3–6; Cherkasov/Petrushenko d. Kulti/P. Nyborg 6–1 1–6 6–3).

MAUREEN CONNOLLY BRINKER CONTINENTAL PLAYERS CUP

Girls' 18 & Under International Team Championship
30 nations competed. Played in Coral Springs, Florida, USA, 13–19 December
Quarter-finals: USSR d. Netherlands 3–0; Brazil d. USA 2–1; Belgium d. Poland 2–1; Italy d. Sweden 3–0. ***Semi-finals:*** USSR d. Brazil 2–0 (one rubber not played); Italy d. Belgium 2–1. ***Final:*** USSR d. Italy 2–1 (N. Medvedeva lost to L. Lapi 2–6 4–6; E. Brioukhovets d. G. Boschiero 4–6 7–5 6–4; Brioukhovets/Medvedeva d. Boschiero/Lapi 6–1 6–3).

Left: *Joanne Faull played her part in Australia's triumph in the World Youth Cup, and began 1988 in style by winning both singles and doubles titles in the Australian Open Junior Championship.*
Below: *The victorious Australian boys' and girls' teams.* *(R. Guzzo)*

VASCO VALERIO CUP

Boys' 18 & Under International Team Championship
15 nations competed. Played in Novara, Italy, 21–25 July.
Quarter-finals: Czechoslovakia d. Italy 2–1; Spain d. Yugoslavia 3–0; France d. USSR 2–1; West Germany d. Sweden 2–1. ***Semi-finals:*** Czechoslovakia d. Spain 2–1; West Germany d. France 3–0. ***3rd place play-off:*** Spain v France 1–1 (one rubber not played). ***Final:*** Czechoslovakia d. West Germany 2–0 (one rubber not played) (D. Rikl d. C. Arriens 6–1 6–1; T. Zdrazila d. S. Nensel 6–1 4–6 6–2; Rikl/P. Vizner v. F. Loddenkemper/Nensel not played).

HM QUEEN SOFIA CUP

Girls' 18 & Under International Team Championship
13 nations competed. Semi-finals and final played in Lerida, Barcelona, Spain, 23–25 July.
Quarter-finals: France d. Sweden 2–1; Italy d. West Germany 2–1; Hungary d. USSR 2–1; Czechoslovakia d. Finland 3–0. ***Semi-finals:*** France d. Italy 3–0; Czechoslovakia d. Hungary 2–1. ***3rd place play-off:*** Hungary d. Italy 2–1. ***Final:*** France d. Czechoslovakia 3–0 (A. Dechaume d. R. Zrubakova 6–4 6–3; E. Derly d. P. Langrova 7–5 6–1; Dechaume/S. Niox-Chateau d. Langrova/Zrubakova 6–7 6–4 6–3).

JEAN BOROTRA CUP

Boys' 16 & Under International Team Championship
19 nations competed. Semi-finals and final played in Le Touquet, France, 17–19 July.
Quarter-finals: Austria d. Sweden 5–0; France d. Netherlands 4–1; West Germany d. Yugoslavia 3–2; Italy d. USSR 4–1. ***Semi-finals:*** Austria d. France 4–1; Italy d. West Germany 4–1. ***3rd place play-off:*** West Germany d. France 3–0 (two rubbers not played). ***Final:*** Austria d. Italy 3–2 (T. Buchmayer d. F. Pisilli 6–3 6–1; O. Fuchs lost to S. Pescosolido 4–6 1–6; H. Priller d. M. Ardinghi 6–3 6–4; G. Bohm lost to M. Boscatto 6–2 1–6 6–8; Buchmayer/Priller d. Boscatto/Pescosolido 1–6 6–4 6–4).

HELVETIE CUP

Girls' 16 & Under International Team Championship
19 nations competed. Semi-finals and final played in Leysin, Switzerland, 23–25 July.
Quarter-finals: Netherlands d. France 3–2; Czechoslovakia d. Sweden 3–2; Italy d. USSR 3–2; Switzerland d. Austria 3–2. ***Semi-finals:*** Netherlands d. Czechoslovakia 4–1; Switzerland d. Italy 3–2. ***3rd place play-off:*** Czechoslovakia d. Italy 3–1 (one rubber not played). ***Final:*** Netherlands d. Switzerland 3–2 (N. Van Dierendonck lost to S. Jaquet 6–7 3–6; B. Sonneveld lost to M. Plocher 6–2 3–6 4–6; Y. Grubben d. G. Villiger 7–5 7–6; E. Haslinghuis d. S. Bregnard 6–1 6–0; Sonneveld/Van Dierendonck d. Jaquet/Plocher 7–5 6–3).

DEL SOL CUP

Boys' 14 & Under International Team Championship
14 nations competed. Semi-finals and final played in Gerona, Spain, 10–12 July.
Quarter-finals: West Germany d. Sweden 4–1; Czechoslovakia d. France 4–1; Belgium d. Spain 4–1; Austria d. Italy 3–2. ***Semi-finals:*** West Germany d. Czechoslovakia 3–2; Austria d. Belgium 3–2. ***3rd place play-off:*** Czechoslovakia d. Belgium 5–0. ***Final:*** West Germany d. Austria 4–1 (J. Weinzierl lost to R. Wawra 3–6 2–6; G. Paul d. N. Patzak 6–0 6–1; S. Petraschek d. J. Knowle 3–6 6–2 6–2; A. Kriebel d. H. Kugler 6–2 6–3; Paul/Petraschek d. Knowle/Wawra 4–6 6–2 6–2).

EUROPA CUP

Girls' 14 & Under International Team Championship
16 nations competed. Semi-finals and final played in Maaseik, Brussels, Belgium, 10–12 July.
Quarter-finals: Czechoslovakia d. Spain 3–2; Netherlands d. USSR 4–1; Hungary d. Yugoslavia 3–2; Austria d. Italy 3–2. ***Semi-finals:*** Czechoslovakia d. Netherlands 3–2; Austria d. Hungary 3–2. ***3rd place play-off:*** Netherlands d. Hungary 3–2. ***Final:*** Czechoslovakia d. Austria 3–2 (P. Kucova lost to U. Priller 3–6 0–6; R. Bobkova d. D. Bidmon 6–2 6–4; P. Markova lost to N. Dobrovits 4–6 1–6; K. Matouskova d. S. Suchan 1–6 6–0 10–8; Bobkova/Kucova d. Dobrovits/Priller 6–4 4–6 7–5).

ITF VETERAN TENNIS

It seems that the older a tennis player becomes the more insatiable is his or her appetite for competitive tennis. In the ten years since 1977, the number of teams competing for seven age-group trophies has risen from 25 to 103. In 1987 the USA continued their dominance by retaining both the Britannia and Crawford Cups, which they have won since their inception. The wind of change may be on the horizon, though, with Canada winning the Austria Cup – their first success in any Cup event – while Italy and France also appeared in the winner's circle, being victorious in the Dubler and Young Cups respectively.

The ITF Veteran Championships again increased their list of entries to 547 competitors, and each year the calendar of events around the world becomes more universal. It is for this very reason of buoyancy and growth that the ITF now have a permanent office to control and guide the ever increasing popularity of Veteran tennis.

ITALIA CUP

Men's 35 and over
GRADO, ITALY 2–6 JUNE
Quarter-finals: France d. West Germany 2–0; Austria d. Sweden 2–0; Great Britain d. Italy 2–1; USA d. Spain 2–0. ***Semi-finals:*** Austria d. France 2–1; USA d. Great Britain 3–0. ***Final:*** USA d. Austria 2–1 (C. Owens d. M. Kary 6–2 6–2; J. Diaz lost to P. Feigl 5–7 6–3 6–4; A. Neely/C. Owens d. P. Feigl/M. Kary 6–1 6–7 6–3).

DUBLER CUP

Men's 45 and over
POERTSCHACH, AUSTRIA 8–13 JUNE
Quarter-finals: West Germany d. Australia 2–1; Austria d. Yugoslavia 3–0; Italy d. USA 2–1; Switzerland d. Sweden 3–0. ***Semi-finals:*** Austria d. West Germany 3–0; Italy d. Switzerland 3–0. ***Final:*** Italy d. Austria 2–1 (G. Rohrich d. P. Pokorny 6–2 6–2; G. Pozzi d. H. Gradischnig 7–5 6–0; P. Gilli/G. Morelli lost to H. Gradischnig/P. Pokorny 6–2 6–2).

AUSTRIA CUP

Men's 55 and over
UMAG, YUGOSLAVIA, 26–31 MAY
Quarter-finals: Australia d. Great Britain 3–0; Austria d. Sweden 3–0; USA d. New Zealand 3–0; Canada d. Switzerland 3–0; ***Semi-finals:*** Australia d. Austria 2–1; Canada d. USA 3–0. ***Final:*** Canada d. Australia 3–0 (K. Sinclair d. B. McCarthy 6–2 6–3; L. Main d. A. Kendall 6–2 6–3; L. Main/K. Sinclair d. T. Halliday/B. McCarthy 6–2 6–2).

BRITANNIA CUP

Men's 65 and over
BASTAD, SWEDEN 2–6 JUNE
Quarter-finals: USA d. Italy 3–0; West Germany d. Denmark 3–0; Australia d. France 2–1; Sweden d. Austria 3–0. ***Semi-finals:*** USA d. West Germany 3–0; Sweden d. Australia 3–0. ***Final:*** USA d. Sweden 2–1 (M. Miller d. L. Larsson 7–6 6–2; R. Sherman lost to T. Johansson 6–3 3–6 6–4; M. Miller/R. Sherman d. T. Johansson/L. Larsson 6–1 6–2).

CRAWFORD CUP

Men's 70 and over
POERTSCHACH, AUSTRIA 1–6 JUNE
Quarter-finals: USA d. Australia 3–0; Brazil d. Hungary 3–0; Great Britain d. Sweden 3–0; France d. Norway 3–0. ***Semi-finals:*** USA d. Brazil 3–0; Great Britain d. France 2–1. ***Final:*** USA d. Great Britain 3–0 (G. Mulloy d. R. Smith 6–0 6–2; F. Klein d. H. Walton 6–2 6–2; J. Behr/V. Hughes d. T. Anderson/R. Smith 6–1 6–3).

YOUNG CUP

Women's 40 and over
VENICE, ITALY, 19–23 MAY
Quarter-finals: West Germany d. Switzerland 3–0; France d. Norway 3–0; Great Britain d. Australia 2–1; USA d. Netherlands 2–1. ***Semi-finals:*** France d. West Germany 3–0; USA d. Great Britain 3–0. ***Final:*** France d. USA 2–1 (A. Casado lost to C. Hillebrand 3–6 6–3 6–2; G. Lovera d. B. Mueller 6–3 6–3; R. Darmon/G. Lovera d. C. Hillebrand/B. Mueller 6–4 6–7 4–6 7–5).

MARIA ESTHER BUENO CUP

Women's 50 and over
HELSINKI, FINLAND, 8–12 JUNE
Quarter-finals: USA d. Norway 3–0; Australia d. Argentina 2–1; West Germany d. Canada 2–1; Great Britain d. Italy 2–1. ***Semi-finals:*** USA d. Australia 3–0; Great Britain d. West Germany 3–0. ***Final:*** USA d. Great Britain 2–1 (J. Crofford d. R. Lauder 6–4 6–1; N. Reed lost to S. Brasher 6–3 6–3; J. Crofford/N. Reed d. R. Illingworth/R. Lauder 6–4 3–6 6–0).

ITF VETERAN CHAMPIONSHIPS

GARMISCH-PARTENKIRCHEN, 11–21 JUNE
MEN'S OVER 35 SINGLES – Final: R. Machan (HUN) d. M. Wunschig (FRG) 6–1 6–4
MEN'S OVER 35 DOUBLES – Final: J. Fassbender (FRG)/R. Machan (HUN) d. J. Hrebec/M. Wunschig (FRG) 3–6 6–3 6–4.
MEN'S OVER 45 SINGLES – Final: G. Rohrich (ITA) d. J. Pinto Bravo (CHI) 6–3 6–4.
MEN'S OVER 45 DOUBLES – Final: H. Gradischnig/P. Pokorny (AUT) d. F. Ali/G. Rohrich (ITA) 7–6 7–5.
MEN'S OVER 55 SINGLES – Final: I. Gulyas (HUN) d. K. Sinclair (CAN) 6–2 6–4.
MEN'S OVER 55 DOUBLES – Final: I. Gulyas (HUN)/H. Stewart (USA) d. L. Main/K. Sinclair (CAN) 7–6 3–6 6–3.
MEN'S OVER 60 SINGLES – Final: B. Howe (AUT) d. L. Legenstein (AUT) 6–1 6–0.
MEN'S OVER 60 DOUBLES – Final: L. Legenstein (AUT)/A. Stolpa (FRG) d. E. Halliday/B. McCarthy (AUS) 6–4 6–3.
MEN'S OVER 65 SINGLES – Final: A. Swetka (USA) d. T. Johansson (SWE) 6–4 3–6 6–4.
MEN'S OVER 65 DOUBLES – Final: B. Kempa/W. Kessler (FRG) d. E. Biller/H. Gieren (FRG) 7–5 7–5.
MEN'S OVER 70 SINGLES – Final: F. Klein (USA) d. G. Mulloy (USA) 6–3 6–4.
MEN'S OVER 70 DOUBLES – Final: G. Mulloy/V. Hughes (USA) d. G. Hunger/F. Schiemann (FRG) 3–6 6–0 6–1.
WOMEN'S OVER 40 SINGLES – Final: M. Pinterova (HUN) d. H. Masthoff (FRG) 6–2 6–4.
WOMEN'S OVER 40 DOUBLES – Final: G. Lovera (FRA)/M. Pinterova (HUN) d. H. Masthoff/H. Orth (FRG) 6–3 6–0.
WOMEN'S OVER 50 SINGLES – Final: S. Brasher (GBR) d. E. Molina (ARG) 6–4 6–3.
WOMEN'S OVER 50 DOUBLES – Final: S. Brasher/L. Cawthorn (GBR) d. N. Blom (HOL)/L. Burling (USA) 6–3 6–2.
WOMEN'S OVER 60 SINGLES – Final: D. Cheney (USA) d. M. Marczewski (FRG) 7–5 6–4.
WOMEN'S OVER 60 DOUBLES – Final: D. Cheney/C. Murdock (USA) d. R. Jung/R. Kohler (FRG) 6–3 6–3.

1987 ITF VETERAN WORLD RANKINGS

MEN

OVER 35
1 R. Machan (HUN); **2** Ch. Owens (USA); **3** P. Feigl (AUT); **4** M. Wunschig (FRG); **5** J. Camina (ESP); **6** R. Staguhn (FRG).

OVER 45
1 G. Roehrich (ITA); **2** J. Pinto-Bravo (CHI); **3** P. Saila (FIN); **4** C. Holm (SWE); **5** P. Pokorny (AUT); **6** G. Pozzi (ITA); **7** N. Klatil (AUT); **8** K. Fuhrmann (FRG); **9** T. Stalder (SUI); **10** K. Haas (FRG).

OVER 55
1 I. Gulyas (HUN); **2** K. Sinclair (CAN); **3** L. Main (CAN); **4** C. Devoe (USA); **5** S. Davidson (SWE); **6 eq** R. Seymour (USA), H. Stewart (USA); **8** W. Davis (USA); **9** H. Cruchet (FRA); **10** J. Morton (USA).

OVER 60
1 R. Howe (AUS); **2** R. McCarthy (AUS); **3** L. Legenstein (AUT); **4** A. Stolpa (HUN); **5** A. Hussmuller (FRG); **6** L. Lenart (HUN); **7** H. Lege (FRG); **8** L. Bollen (FRG); **9** W. Peikart (FRG); **10** G. Viziru (ROM).

OVER 65
1 M. Miller (USA); **2** A. Swetka (USA); **3** T. Johansson (SWE); **4** R. Sherman (USA); **5** R. Hay (AUS); **6** O. Nordvik (NOR); **7** M. Emery (FRA); **8 eq** R. Ruzic (MON), E. Smith (AUS); **10** R. Gay (FRA).

OVER 70
1 F. Klein (USA); **2** G. Mulloy (USA); **3 eq** J. Becker (FRA), A. Juchen (BRA); **5** E. Giffoni (BRA); **6** D. Laroye (FRA); **7 eq** V. Gierke (FRG), F. Schiemann (FRG), H. Walton (GBR); **10** G. Hunger (FRG).

WOMEN

OVER 40
1 M. Pinterova (HUN); **2** H. Masthoff (FRG); **3** G. Lovera (FRA); **4** J. Louie (USA); **5 eq** E. Grindvold (NOR), C. Hillebrand (USA); **7** A. Casado (FRA); **8** R. Schroeder (FRG); **9** T. Groenman (HOL); **10** B. Muller (USA).

OVER 50
1 S. Brasher (GBR); **2** E. Molina (ARG); **3** J. Crofford (USA); **4** N. Reed (USA); **5** L. Rank (FRG); **6** L. Burling (USA); **7** N. Marsh (AUS); **8** C. Mazzoleni (ITA); **9 eq** L. Forbes (AUS), F. Gaspar (ARG), L. Parsons (USA).

OVER 60
1 D. Cheney (USA); **2** K. Sorge (FRG); **3** R. Jung (FRG); **4** M. Marczewski (FRG); **5** G. Waliczek (FRG); **6** M. Frigerio (ITA).

NATIONAL ASSOCIATIONS, RANKINGS AND CHAMPIONSHIPS

MEMBERS WITH VOTING RIGHTS (85)

Abbreviations: C.=Cable address, T.=Telephone number, TX.=Telex number.
Number following country's name denotes year of foundation.

ALGERIA (1962)

Federation Algerienne de Tennis, Centre des Federations Sportives, Cite Olympique, BP 88 El Biar, Algers.
T. (213) 793939/786363; TX. 61379 CFSDZ; *Pres.* Mr L. Benazzi; *Sec.* Mr R. Bouakkaz.
MEN: **1** Galou Redha; **2** Boudjemline Djamel Eddine; **3** Zehar Moncef; **4** Amier Yacine; **5** Benyebka Mehdi; **6** Laslah Noreddine.
WOMEN: **1** Mahmoudi Samira; **2** Bouchabou Ouarda; **3** Bennacer Amina; **4** Chefri Nouara; **5** Hameurlaine Lamia; **6** Bouchabou Nabila.

National Closed Championships
MEN'S SINGLES – Semi-finals: B. Djamel d. A. Yacine 6–3 4–6 6–2 7–6; G. Reda d. L. Khaled 6–3 6–2 6–3. ***Final:*** Reda d. Djamel 6–2 6–7 7–5 6–1.
WOMEN'S SINGLES – Semi-finals: A. Aicha d. B. Aicha 6–2 6–3; C. Nouara d. I. Nadira 7–5 6–1. ***Final:*** Nouara d. Aicha 6–3 6–2.

ARGENTINA (1921)

Asociacion Argentina de Tenis, Av. San Juan 1315/17, (1148) Capital Federal, Buenos Aires.
C. Argtennis, Buenos Aires; T. (1) 26 1569/27 0101/26 4696; TX. 17336 ARGTEN AR; *Pres.* Mr J. J. Vasquez; *Secs.* Mr F. A. Turno, Mr J. C. Vasquez.

National Closed Championships
MEN'S SINGLES – Semi-finals: M. Jaite d. H. de la Pena 6–1 6–1; E. Bengoechea d. G. Perez Roldan 7–5 6–2. ***Final:*** Jaite d. Bengoechea 7–6 6–4.

AUSTRALIA (1904)

Tennis Australia, Private Bag 6060, Richmond South 3121, Victoria.
C. Tencourt, Melbourne; T. (3) 655 1277; TX. 36893 TENCRT; Fax. (3) 650 2743; *Pres.* Mr B. R. Tobin; *Tennis Manager* Mr B. F. McMillan; *Admin. Manager* Mr M. Daws.

AUSTRIA (1902)

Osterreichischer Tennisverband, Hainburgerstrasse 36, A 1030 Vienna.
C. Austriatennis, Vienna; T. (1) 753345/733352; TX. 131652 OETEN A; *Pres.* Dr T. Zeh; *Sec.* Mr P. Nader.

National Closed Championships
MEN'S SINGLES – Semi-finals: H. Skoff d. M. Bauer 6–2 6–4; T. Muster d. G. Schaller 6–0 6–2. ***Final:*** Muster d. Skoff 7–5 6–2 6–4.
WOMEN'S SINGLES – Semi-finals: B. Paulus d. H. Sprung 2–6 7–6 6–0; P. Huber d. P. Ritter 6–2 6–3. ***Final:*** Paulus d. Huber 7–6 7–6.

A qualifier at Munich, the Czech No. 5, Marian Vajda, upset Kriek and Nystrom on his way to the final, following with his first Grand Prix title at Prague. *(T. Hindley)*

BAHRAIN (1981)

Bahrain Lawn Tennis Federation, PO Box 26985, Bahrain.
C. Tennis, Bahrain; T. (973) 687236; TX. 8292 GPIC BN; *Pres.* Dr Tawfiq Almoaid; *Sec.* Mr Yousif Abdul Ghaffar.
MEN: **1** Esam Abdul Aal; **2** Geraud Laveissiere; **3** Jehad Rashid; **4** Abdul Jawad Mohamed; **5** Abdul Rahman Shehab; **6** Hamad Saleh; **7** Shehab Shehab; **8** Toby Marion.
WOMEN: **1** Hilary Sparks; **2** Anna Chalmers; **3** Kazuko Uchida; **4** Chrissie Stauffacher; **5** Scheherazade Rehman; **6** Ann Koheji; **7** Zina Crabtree; **8** Kuniko Nakano.

BANGLADESH (1972)

Bangladesh Tennis Federation, Tennis Complex, Ramna Green, Dhaka 1000.
C. Tennisfed Dhaka; T. (2) 506650; TX. 642401 SHER BJ (mark: for tennis); *Pres.* Mr H. M. Ershad; *Sec.* Mr M. H. Jamaly.
MEN: **1** Shovon Jamaly; **2** Sardar Iftekhar; **3** Mahtabur Rahman; **4** Haroon R. Bhuiya.
WOMEN: **1** Sharmin Siddiq; **2** Rehana Begum Bhuiya.

National Closed Championships
MEN'S SINGLES – Semi-finals: S. Jamaly d. M. Rhaman 6–4 6–2 2–6 6–1; S. Iftekhar d. H. R. Bhuiya 6–2 6–3 7–6. ***Final:*** Jamaly d. Iftekhar 7–6 7–6 6–4.
WOMEN'S SINGLES – Final: S. Siddiq d. R. B. Bhuiya 1–6 7–6 7–6.

BELGIUM (1902)

Royal Belgian Tennis Federation, Passage International Rogier 6, BTE 522, 1210 Brussels.
C. Tennisfeder, Brussels: T. (2) 217 2365; TX. 24023 TENFED B: *Pres.* Mr P. P. de Keghel; *Secs.* Mr W. Goethals, Mr F. Lemaire.
MEN: **1** Karel Demuynck; **2** Eric Brawerman; **3** Denis Langaskens; **4** Johan Depreter; **5** Bernard Boileau; **6** Jan Vanlangendonck; **7** Jean Fisette; **8** Jos Warmoes; **9** Xavier Daufresne; **10** Pierre Godfroid.
WOMEN: **1** Ann Devries; **2** Sandra Wasserman; **3** Sabine Appelmans; **4** Kathleen Schuurmans; **5** Ilse de Ruysscher; **6** Caroline Van Renterghem; **7** Marianne Vermijlen; **8** Isabelle Dumont; **9** Annick Claes; **10** Caroline Neuprez.

National Closed Championships
MEN'S SINGLES – Semi-finals: E. Brawerman d. E. Mampaey 6–3 6–3 6–3; K. Demuynck d. D. Langaskens 6–3 4–6 0–6 6–1 6–4. ***Final:*** Demuynck d. Brawerman 6–0 1–6 7–5 3–6 7–6.
WOMEN'S SINGLES – Semi-finals: S. Wasserman d. S. Hermans 3–6 6–2 6–4; S. Appelmans d. I. Dumont 6–2 6–4. ***Final:*** Appelmans d. Wasserman 7–6 6–2.

BOLIVIA (1937)

Federacion Boliviana de Tennis, Casilla de Correo 180, Cochabamba.
T. 26168-47876; TX. 6292 LAMBDA BV; *Pres.* Sr T. Sagarnaga P.; *Sec.* Sr J. T. Alejandre F.

BRAZIL (1956)

Confederacao Brasileira de Tenis, Av. Paulista Nr. 352 – Sala 64, 6 Andar, Conjunto, 64 CEP-01310, Sao Paulo.
C. Cebetenis, Rio de Janeiro T. (11) 251 3920/289 9404; TX. 1132733 CTEN-BR; *Pres.* Mr W. E. Checchia; *Sec.* Ms Marilia Silberberg.
MEN: **1** Luiz Mattar; **2** Cassio Motta; **3** Julio Goes; **4** Ivan Kley; **5** Cezar Kist; **6** Givaldo Barboza; **7** Dacio Campos; **8** Joao Soares; **9** Danilo Marcelino; **10** Jose Amin Daher.
WOMEN: **1** Niege Dias; **2** Gisele Miro; **3** Patricia Medrado; **4** Claudia Monteiro; **5** Luciana Corsatto; **6** Luciana Tella; **7** Andrea Vieira; **8** Claudia Faillace; **9** Roberta Caldas; **10** Gisele Faria.

BULGARIA (1930)

Bulgarian Tennis Federation, 18 Tolbuchin Blvd., 1040 Sofia.
C. Besefese Tennis, Sofia; T. 80-3710/8651; TX. 22723/22724 BSFS BG; *Pres.* Mr S. Ganev; *Sec.* Mr T. Tzevtkov.

MEN: **1** Ruslan Rainov; **2** Julian Stamatov; **3** Krasimir Lazarov; **4** Anton Radev; **5** Ivan Keskinov; **6** Teodor Batchev; **7** Milko Petkov; **8** Milen Velev; **9** Milen Ianakiev; **10** Toma Petkov.
WOMEN: **1** Manuela Maleeva; **2** Katerina Maleeva; **3** Dora Rangelova; **4** Ralitza Milorieva; **5** Galia Angelova; **6** Bogdana Marinova; **7** Elizabet Nikolova; **8** Plamena Gogovska; **9** Marina Kondova; **10** Tzvetelina Nikolova.

National Closed Championships
MEN'S SINGLES – Semi-finals: M. Petkov d. A. Radev 6–3 6–7 6–1 7–5; R. Rainov d. I. Kisinov 3–6 6–0 6–1 6–0. ***Final:*** Rainov d. Petkov 6–1 6–3 6–3.
WOMEN'S SINGLES – Semi-finals: D. Rangelova d. G. Angelova 3–6 7–5 6–2; E. Nikolova d. M. Kondova 7–6 6–1. ***Final:*** Rangelova d. Nikolova 6–1 7–5.

CAMEROON (1966)

Federation Camerounaise de Lawn Tennis, BP 1121, Yaounde.
C. Fecatennis-MJS Yaounde; T. (237) 233860/1310/224329; TX. 8568 KN/8261 MNFA; *Pres.* Brig. Gen. J. Tataw; *Sec.* Dr N. Mboulet.

CANADA (1890)

Canadian Tennis Association, 3111 Steeles Avenue West, Downsview, Ontario M3J 3H2, Canada.
T. (416) 665 9777; TX. 062 18419 CAN TENNIS TOR; Fax. (416) 665 9017; *Pres.* Mr B. Wright.
MEN: **1** Grant Connell; **2** Martin Laurendeau; **3** Chris Pridham; **4** Andrew Sznajder; **5** Martin Wostenholme; **6** Stephane Bonneau; **7** Glenn Michibata; **8** Doug Burke; **9** Hatem McDadi; **10** Geoff Roper.
WOMEN: **1** Helen Kelesi; **2** Carling Bassett Seguso; **3** Jill Hetherington; **4** Maureen Drake; **5** Jane Yates; **6** Jillian Alexander; **7** Karen Dewis; **8** Marianne Groat; **9** Jane Young; **10** Teresa Dobson.

National Closed Championships
MEN'S SINGLES – Semi-finals: A. Sznajder d. D. Burke 6–1 3–6 6–2; H. McDadi d. S. Bonneau 6–4 4–1 (ret). ***Final:*** Sznajder d. McDadi 6–7 6–2 6–3.
WOMEN'S SINGLES – Semi-finals: H. Kelesi d. M. Groat 6–1 7–5; J. Yates d. T. Dobson 3–6 6–1 7–5. ***Final:*** Kelesi d. Yates 6–1 6–0.

CHILE (1920)

Federacion de Tenis de Chile, Almirante Simpson No. 36 Providencia, Casilla 1149, Santiago.
T. (2) 2227279/342416; TX. 341416 FTCH CK; *Pres.* Mr J. Hinzpeter G.; *Sec.* Mr G. Pavez.
MEN: **1** Gonzalo Fernandez; **2** Rodrigo Urzua; **3** Sergio Cortes; **4** Alfredo Rivera; **5** Enrique Anglada; **6** Herman Urresti; **7** Horacio Matta; **8** Marcelo Giaverini; **9** Hans Jannaz; **10** Sergio Fuentes.
WOMEN: **1** Carolina Espinoza; **2** Marlene Zuleta; **3** Paula Castro; **4** Pamela Gonzalez; **5** Patricia Rivera; **6** Paulina Sepulveda; **7** Ana Orellana; **8** Manola Murillo; **9** Myriam Bardi; **10** Mariela Espinola.

National Closed Championships
MEN'S SINGLES – Semi-finals: F. Rivera d. H. Urresti 6–4 0–6 6–4; W. Macaya d. H. Matta 1–6 6–2 6–2. ***Final:*** Macaya d. Rivera 6–1 6–3.
WOMEN'S SINGLES – Semi-finals: P. Hermida d. P. Sepulveda w.o.; M. Zuleta d. P. Rivera 7–5 6–0. ***Final:*** Hermida d. Zuleta 6–4 3–6 7–5.

CHINA, PEOPLE'S REPUBLIC OF (1956)

Tennis Association of the People's Republic of China, 9 Tiyukuan Road, Beijing.
C. Sportschine, Beijing; T. 757231 Ext. 210; TX. 22323 CHOC CN/22034 ACSF CN; *Pres.* Mr L. Zhengcao; *Sec.* Ms Y. Xiaolan.

CHINESE TAIPEI (1973)

Chinese Taipei Tennis Association, 6th Floor, 120 Chung Yang Road, Nan Kang, Taipei, Taiwan, ROC.
C. Sinovision, Taipei; T. (02) 7829333; TX. 25080 CHINA TV; Fax. (02) 7828776; *Pres.* Mr H. P. Chung; *Sec.* Mr E. S. C. Wang.
MEN: **1** Chang-Rung Wu; **2** Huang-Jung Hsu; **3** Chung-Hsing Liu; **4** Tze-Shin Chen; **5** Yu-Hui Lien; **6** Hong-Rung Wu; **7** Kuo-Long Ho; **8** Fei-Piao Gong; **9** Tze-Ming Chung; **10** Fei-Shyong Gong.

WOMEN: **1** Shi-Ting Wang; **2** Su-Ling Lai; **3** Chiu-Mei Ho; **4** Shi-Min Lin; **5** Dai-Hwa Wang; **6** Ya-Hui Ling; **7** Su-Jen Lai; **8** Mei-Chu Hsu; **9** Yu-Chun Liao; **10** Fang-Lin Ling.

National Closed Championships
MEN'S SINGLES – Semi-finals: Chang-Rung Wu d. Chung-Hsing Liu 6–3 6–1; Huang-Jung Hsu d. Yu-Hui Lien 6–1 6–4. ***Final:*** Chang Rung Wu d. Huang-Jung Hsu 3–6 6–4 6–4 6–3.
WOMEN'S SINGLES – Semi-finals: Shi-Ting Wang d. Shi-Min Lin 6–2 6–0; Su-Lin Lai d. Chiu-Mei Ho 6–2 1–6 6–4. ***Final:*** Shi-Ting Wang d. Su-Lin Lai 6–0 3–6 6–3.

COLOMBIA (1932)

Federacion Colombiana de Tenis, Apartado No. 10.917, Calle 16 No. 9–64 Oficina 401, Bogota 1 D.E. C. Fedetenis, Bogota; T. (2) 822252; TX. 41275 ICJD CO; *Pres.* Mr G. Obando; *Exec. Sec.* Mr A. R. de Pedroza.

COTE D'IVOIRE (1969)

Federation Ivoirienne de Tennis, 01 BP V 273, Abidjan 01, Cote D'Ivoire.
T. (225) 44 13 54; TX. 23555 IHCHOT CI; *Pres.* Mr J. C. Delafosse; *Gen. Sec.* Mr K. Kouadje.
MEN: **1** Niamien Kouadio; **2** Kossokre Adjamoin; **3** Konate Karim; **4** Meh Kouadio; **5** Ouedraogo Lassine; **6** Assouan Ekue; **7** Kouassi Koffi; **8** Anoye Kablan; **9** Bahi Kanon; **10** Kouame N'Dri.

National Closed Championships
MEN'S SINGLES – Semi-finals: N'Goran d. Bado 6–0 6–4; Z. Kouame d. B. Norbert 7–5 7–5. ***Final:*** N'Goran d. Kouame 6–4 6–4.
WOMEN'S SINGLES – Semi-finals: Malan d. Kassi 6–2 6–4; Kouakou d. Assale 6–0 6–1. ***Final:*** Kouakou d. Malan 6–2 6–3.

CUBA

Federacion Cubana de Tenis de Campo, Calle 13 NR 601 ESQ AC, Vedado Habana 4.
C. Olimpicuba, Habana; T. (7) 418883/402921/415394; TX. 0511332 INDER CU; *Pres.* Mr R. M. Perez; *Sec.* Mr M. O. Rodriguez.
MEN: **1** Mario Tabares; **2** Juan Pino; **3** Tomas Rodriguez; **4** Wilfredo Henry; **5** Roberto Rodriguez; **6** Pedro Del Valle; **7** Ivan Perez; **8** Duviel Medina; **9** Jesus Borrego; **10** Ernesto Lopez.
WOMEN: **1** Belkis Rodriguez; **2** Maria Garcia; **3** Yoanis Montesino; **4** Paula Hernandez; **5** Yamile Cordova; **6** Rita Pichardo; **7** Lesvia Arteaga; **8** Katia Barrios; **9** Yilian Romero; **10** Mirna Marrero.

National Closed Championships
MEN'S SINGLES – Semi-finals: T. Rodriguez d. P. Valle 7–6 6–2; W. Henry d. R. Rodriguez 6–4 3–6 6–3. ***Final:*** T. Rodriguez d. Henry 7–5 5–7 7–5.
WOMEN'S SINGLES – Semi-finals: B. Rodriguez d. P. Hernandez 6–3 6–3; M. Garcia d. Y. Cordova 6–2 6–2. ***Final:*** Rodriguez d. Garcia 6–3 6–4.

CYPRUS (1951)

Cyprus Tennis Federation, Ionos Str. 20, PO Box 3931, Nicosia.
C. Tennis, Nicosia; T. (2) 450 875; TX. 5300 OLYMPIC CY; *Pres.* Mr P. Christodoulou; *Sec.* Mr D. Solomonides.
MEN: **1** Alkis Papamichael; **2** Yiannos Hadjigeorgiou; **3** Nicolas Georgallides; **4** Phivos Zachariades; **5** Neoclis Neocleous; **6** Antonis Indianos; **7** Simon Aynedjian; **8** Angus Cameron.
WOMEN: **1** Eleni Pilava; **2** Stalo Tritti; **3** Joanna Rossi; **4** Natia Iacovou; **5** Roulla Mina; **6** Mari Missirli; **7** Nitsa Stylianou; **8** Marina Potoudes.

National Closed Championships
MEN'S SINGLES – Semi-finals: A. Papamichael d. P. Zachariades 6–3 6–2; Y. Hadjigeorgiou d. S. Constantinou 6–2 7–5. ***Final:*** Papamichael d. Hadjigeorgiou 6–2 6–0.
WOMEN'S SINGLES – Semi-finals: E. Pilava d. N. Constantinidou 6–2 6–1; J. Rossi d. S. Tritti 6–3 6–0. ***Final:*** Pilava d. Rossi 7–6 6–4.

CZECHOSLOVAKIA (1906)

Czechoslovenska Tenisova Asociace, Ostrov Stvanice 38, 170 00 Prague 7.
C. Sportsvaz, Prague; T. (2) 2311484; TX. 122650 CSTVC; *Pres.* Mr C. Suk; *Sec.* Mr M. Polak.
MEN: **1** Ivan Lendl; **2** Miloslav Mecir; **3** Tomas Smid; **4** Milan Srejber; **5** Marian Vajda; **6** Karel Novacek; **7** Jaroslav Navratil; **8** Josef Cihak; **9** Petr Korda; **10** Libor Pimek.
WOMEN: **1 eq** Hana Mandlikova, Helena Sukova; **3** Jana Novotna; **4** Iva Budarova; **5** Regina Rajchrtova; **6** Regina Marsikova; **7** Radka Zrubakova; **8** Hana Fukarkova; **9** Denisa Krajcovicova; **10** Jana Pospisilova.

National Closed Championships
MEN'S SINGLES – Semi-finals: P. Korda d. B. Stankovic 7–5 6–3; M. Srejber d. R. Vogel 6–4 6–2. ***Final:*** Korda d. Srejber 6–4 6–4.
WOMEN'S SINGLES – Semi-finals: H. Sukova d. O. Vetavoa 6–2 3–6 6–3; H. Fukarkova d. P. Langrova 6–3 6–7 6–2. ***Final:*** Sukova d. Fukarkova 2–6 6–4 6–3.

DENMARK (1920)

Dansk Tennis Forbund, Idraettens Hus, Broendby Stadion 20, 2605 Broendby.
C. Tennisforbund, Copenhagen; T. (2) 455555 Ext. 235/236; TX. 33111 I DRAET DK (Mark: Attn Tennis); Fax (45 2) 456245; *Pres.* Mr J. Bertelsen; *Hon. Sec.* Mr J. Ahlstrand; *Gen. Sec.* Mr A. Nrodam.

National Closed Championships
MEN'S SINGLES – Semi-finals: M. Tauson d. P. Bastiansen 6–3 6–2; M. Christensen d. S. Nielsen 6–3 6–3. ***Final:*** Christensen d. Tauson 6–3 6–3.
WOMEN'S SINGLES – Semi-finals: T. Larsen d. A. Michailoff 6–1 6–1; L. Vandborg d. H. Nielsen 7–5 6–3. ***Final:*** Larsen d. Vandborg 6–0 6–2.

DJIBOUTI (1978)

Federation Djiboutienne de Tennis, Rue Pierre-Pascal, BP 728 Djibouti.
C. PO Box 728, Djibouti; T. 352286; *Pres.* Mr H. Houmed; *Sec.* Mme M. A. Farah.

ECUADOR (1960)

Federacion Ecuatoriana de Tennis, PO Box 4587, Guayaquil.
C. Fetenis, Guayaquil; T. 320233/322020; TX. 43482 NATURS; *Pres.* Mr N. Macchiavello; *Sec.* Mr C. Carbo.
MEN: **1** Andres Gomez; **2** Raul Viver; **3** Hugo Nunez; **4** Martin Aguirre; **5** Ernesto Lingen; **6** Hugo Molina; **7** Giorgio Carneade; **8** Andres Alarcon; **9** Eduardo Ayala; **10** Victor Moncayo.
WOMEN: **1** Maria Gallegos; **2** Nuria Niemes; **3** Cecilia Piedrahita; **4** Paola Sandoval; **5** Maria Robert; **6** Valeria Gallegos; **7** Ivette Donoso; **8** Priscilla Escobar; **9** Monica Escaleras; **10** Silvia Ramos.

EGYPT (1920)

Egyptian Lawn Tennis Federation, 13 Kasr el Nil Street, Cairo.
C. Gyplawnten, Cairo; T. (2) 753235; TX. 93697 SAFLM UN/21554 STC MN, (Mark: Att. Tennis); *Pres.* Mr G. El Nazer; *Sec.* Dr A. Tewfik.
MEN: **1** Hany Nasser; **2** Mostafa Naeem; **3** Aly Elsayed; **4** Ayman Azmy Galal; **5** Ahmed El Gamal; **6** Tamer El Sawy; **7** Mohamed Nael Zaki; **8** Tamer Rahmy; **9** Alaa Eldin Olwy; **10** Hisham Nasser.
WOMEN: **1** Shahira Tawfik; **2** Ayda Ismael; **3** Nahla Mohamed; **4** Racha El Sakka; **5** Linda Nagy; **6** Randha Helmy; **7** Hallah Abd Elwahab; **8** Ola Baligh.

FINLAND (1911)

Suomen Tennisliitto, Radiokatu 12, SF-00240 Helsinki.
C. Tennisliitto, Helsinki; T. (0) 158 2301; TX. 121797 SVUL SF; Fax: (0) 145237; *Pres.* Mr M. Huhtamaki; *Sec.* Mr E. Kiuttu.
MEN: **1** Veli Paloheimo; **2** Olli Rahnasto; **3** Mika Hedman; **4** Pasi Virtanen; **5** Aki Rahunen; **6** Alexander Lindholm; **7** Pasi Montonen; **8** Kimmo Alkio; **9** Janne Holtari; **10** Antti Eranne.
WOMEN: **1** Petra Thoren; **2** Nanne Dahlman; **3** Anne Aallonen; **4** Katja Kokko; **5 eq** Sarianna Ansio, Laura Mannisto; **7 eq** Marianna Ansio, Hanna Thoren, Anu Varpula; **10** Pirjo Ojala.

After a poor year in 1986, Stephen Shaw, ranked five in Great Britain, played Davis Cup *in 1987 and took Connors to four sets at Wimbledon.* *(A. Evans)*

National Closed Championships
MEN'S SINGLES – Semi-finals: V. Paloheimo d. J. Lemponen 6–4 6–2; M. Hedman d. A. Lindholm 6–4 6–2. ***Final:*** Paloheimo d. Hedman 5–7 6–2 7–5.
WOMEN'S SINGLES – Semi-finals: P. Thoren d. N. Dahlman 6–4 4–6 7–6; A. Aallonen d. L. Mannisto 6–2 6–0. ***Final:*** Thoren d. Aallonen 6–4 2–6 7–6.

FRANCE (1920)

Federation Francaise de Tennis, Stade Roland Garros, 2 Avenue Gordon Bennett, 75016 Paris.
C. Tenisfedet, Paris; T. (1) 47 43 48 00; TX. TENFED 611871F; Fax. (1) 47 43 04 94; *Pres.* Mr P. Chatrier; *Sec.* Mr J. C. Collinot.
MEN: **1** Henri Leconte; **2** Yannick Noah; **3** Thierry Tulasne; **4** Guy Forget; **5** Tarik Benhabiles; **6** Thierry Champion; **7** Thierry Pham; **8** Jean Philippe Fleurian; **9** Eric Winogradsky; **10** Thierry Van Den Daele.
WOMEN: **1** Nathalie Herreman; **2** Catherine Tanvier; **3** Isabelle Demongeot; **4** Nathalie Tauziat; **5** Catherine Suire; **6** Marie Christine Calleja; **7** Pascale Paradis; **8** Sybille Niox-Chateau; **9** Pascale Etchemendy; **10** Alexia Dechaume.

National Closed Championships
MEN'S SINGLES – Semi-finals: J. P. Fleurian d. J. Potier 6–4 2–6 8–6; T. Champion d. P. Kuchna 7–5 6–2. ***Final:*** Champion d. Fleurian 6–3 6–4.
WOMEN'S SINGLES – Semi-finals: C. Suire d. P. Paradis 0–6 6–3 6–2; A. Dechaume d. M. Damas 6–3 6–2. ***Final:*** Suire d. Dechaume 0–6 6–2 6–3.

GERMANY, DEMOCRATIC REPUBLIC OF

Deutscher Tennis-Verband der DDR, Storkower Strasse 118, 1055 Berlin.
T. (2) 54 98 533; TX. 114919 DTSB DD; *Pres.* Mr K. H. Sturm; *Sec.* Mr W. Joch.

GERMANY, FEDERAL REPUBLIC OF (1902)

Deutscher Tennis Bund e.V, Leisewitzstr. 26, D 3000 Hanover 1.
C. Tennisbund, Hanover; T. (511) 816063; TX. 921378 DTB D; Fax. (511) 813 711; *Pres.* Dr C. Stauder; *Exec. Dir.* Mr G. Sanders.
MEN: **1** Boris Becker; **2** Eric Jelen; **3** Paul Vojtisek; **4** Carl-Uwe Steeb; **5** Tore Meinecke; **6** Ricki Osterthun; **7** Damir Keretic; **8** Andreas Maurer; **9** Patrick Kuhnen; **10** Michael Westphal.
WOMEN: **1** Steffi Graf; **2** Claudia Kohde-Kilsch; **3** Sylvia Hanika; **4** Bettina Bunge; **5** Eva Pfaff; **6** Isabel Cueto; **7** Silke Meier; **8** Wiltrud Probst; **9** Claudia Porwik; **10** Heike Thoms.

National Closed Championships
MEN'S SINGLES – Semi-finals: P. Vojtisek d. Al Lesch 7–5 6–1; H. Beutel d. H. Schwaier 6–7 6–3 6–4. ***Final:*** Vojtisek d. Schwaier 6–4 6–2 7–5.
WOMEN'S SINGLES – Semi-finals: S. Meier d. C. Porwik 6–2 6–0; I. Cueto d. J. Thoms 6–0 4–6. ***Final:*** Cueto d. Meier 6–0 6–2.

GHANA (1909)

Ghana Tennis Association, c/o National Sports Council, PO Box 1272, Accra.
C. Ghansport; T. (021) 63924/63927; *Pres.* Mr E. Annan; *Sec.* Mr O. Schandorf-Adjei.

GREAT BRITAIN (1888)

Lawn Tennis Association, The Queens Club, Barons Court, West Kensington, London, W14 9EG.
C. Lawntenna, London W14; T. (1) 385 2366; TX. 8956036 THELTA G; Fax. (1) 381 5965; *Pres.* Mr R. J. Presley; *Exec. Dir.* Mr I. D. Peacock; *Sec.* Mr J. C. U. James.
MEN: **1** Andrew Castle; **2** Jeremy Bates; **3** John Lloyd; **4** Nick Fulwood; **5** Stephen Shaw; **6** Stuart Bale; **7** Stephen Botfield; **8** Jason Goodall; **9** James Turner; **10** Colin Dowdeswell.
WOMEN: **1** Jo Durie; **2** Sara Gomer; **3** Annabel Croft; **4** Anne Hobbs; **5** Julie Salmon; **6** Sally Reeves; **7** Lisa Pennington; **8** Clare Wood; **9** Belinda Borneo; **10** Joy Tacon.

National Closed Championships
MEN'S SINGLES – Semi-finals: S. Bale d. R. Whichello 6–1 6–0; A. Castle d. C. Bailey 6–4 6–1. ***Final:*** Castle d. Bale 7–6 6–2.

WOMEN'S SINGLES – Semi-finals: J. Durie d. S. Gomer 6–7 (6–8) 6–1 6–4; A. Hobbs d. C. Wood 6–7 (3–7) 7–6 (7–2) 6–3. ***Final:*** Durie d. Hobbs 7–5 6–1.

GREECE (1938)

Hellenic Tennis Federation, 89 Patission Str., 104 34 Athens.
C. Efotennis, Athens; T. (1) 2210478/8815804; TX. 222415 EFOA GR; *Pres.* Mr D. Stefanides; *Sec.* Mr D. Gangas.

National Closed Championships
MEN'S SINGLES – Semi-finals: G. Kalovelonis d. J. Rigas 6–1 6–0 6–3; A. Bavelas d. J. Kabakoglou 6–4 6–4 6–3. ***Final:*** Bavelas d. Kalovelonis 3–6 6–2 7–5 7–5.
WOMEN'S SINGLES – Semi-finals: O. Tsarbopoulou d. C. Papadaki 6–1 6–1; X. Anastasiadou d. B. Michalopoulou 6–0 6–2. ***Final:*** Tsarbopoulou d. Anastasiadou 6–1 6–1.

HAITI

Federation Haitienne de Tennis, PO Box 1442, Port-au-Prince.
C. Joetienne, Port-au-Prince; T. (1) 51461/1 51462; *Pres.* Mr I. Rampy; *Sec.* Mr F. Liautaud.
MEN: **1** Ronald Agenor; **2** Bertrand Lacombe; **3** Bertrand Madsen; **4** Laurent Lamothe; **5** Edouard Delphin; **6** Sylvio Germain; **7** Marc Myrthil; **8** Renald Etienne; **9** Patrice Baker; **10** Gille Antoine.
WOMEN: **1** Edna Jean; **2** Catherine Lenoire; **3** Eila Levy; **4** Marie Lisa Daelphin; **5** Vera Emina; **6** Vanessa Goscinny; **7** Carla Bertrand; **8** Rachel Dupuy; **9** Josette Deas; **10** Christine Duverge.

HONG KONG (1909)

Hong Kong Tennis Association Ltd., Tennis Office, The Jubilee Sports Centre, Shatin, New Territories.
C. Tennis, Hong Kong; T. 0 6944138/139/140/141/142; TX. 41224 JSCEN HX (Attn: Tennis Assoc.); Fax. (0) 695455 (Att. HKTA); *Pres.* Dr P. Kwok JP.

HUNGARY (1907)

Magyar Tenisz Szovetseg, Dosza Gyorgy ut 1-3, H-1143 Budapest.
C. Comsport Tennis, Budapest; T. (1) 630 852; TX. 225105 OTSH HV; *Sec.* Mr F. Zentai.

INDIA (1920)

All India Tennis Association 'Deepika', 6 Mohan Kumaramangalam Street, Nungambakkam High Road, Madras 600034.
C. 'Indtennis', Madras 34; T. (44) 478947; TX. 041 568 NEC IN/041 6541 NEC R; *Pres.* Mr R. Masturial; *Sec.* Gen. Mr L. Reddy.
MEN: **1** E. Piperino; **2** K. G. Ramesh; **3** Nandan Bal; **4** Narendranath; **5** Zubin Irani; **6** Surendra Kumar; **7** Mark Ferira; **8** Vivek Sathyash; **9** R. Dinesh; **10** Pradeep Raman.
WOMEN: **1** Nandhini Rangaraj; **2** Nasreen Shujathali; **3** Amritha Balchander; **4** Cristable Fernandez; **5** Reena Achrekar; **6** Anisha Mehta; **7** Malini Mukorkea; **8** Sohini Kumari; **9** Radha Pandit; **10** S. Kannamwar.

INDONESIA (1935)

Indonesian Tennis Association, c/o Tennis Stadium, Gelora Senayan, Jakarta Pusat 10270.
C. Tennis Indonesia, Jakarta; T. 021 581718; TX. 45214 KONI IA/44157 EDIKA IA; Fax. (21) 377169; *Pres.* Mr Moerdiono; *Sec.* Mr R. Witoelar.
MEN: **1** Suharyadi; **2** Donald Wailan Walalangi; **3** Abdul Kahar Mim; **4** Tintus Arianto Wibowo; **5** Justedjo Tarik; **6** Aga Soemarno; **7** Dede Suhendar; **8** Sulistiono; **9** Bunge Nahor; **10** Daniel Heryanto.
WOMEN: **1** Yayuk Basuki; **2** Suzanna Anggarkusuma; **3** Tania Soemarno; **4** Agustina Wibisono; **5** Waya Walalangi; **6** Irawati Moerid; **7** Tanti Trayono; **8** Utaminingsih; **9** Lukky Tedjamukti; **10** Dewi Fortuna Wibisono.

IRAN (1937)

Tennis Federation of Islamic Republic of Iran, Physical Education Organisation, Department of International Affairs, Park Shahr, Ave Shahid, Tehran.
C. Olympic, Tehran; T. (21) 674186; TX. 2677 VARZ IR; *Pres.* Mr G. H. Noorian; *Sec.* Mr M. Sefatti.
MEN: **1** Moharam-Ali Khoda-EE; **2** Kambiz Derafshi-Javan; **3** Jahan-Bakhsh Souri; **4** Seifollah Behzadpour; **5** Ali Reza Ra-Eiss Mohammadi; **6** Taghi Akbari; **7** Abbas Kheil-Tash; **8** Ahmad-Reza Jamalian; **9** Hossein Akbari; **10** Matin Bahadori.

IRAQ (1959)

Iraqi Tennis Federation, c/o Iraqi National Olympic Committee, PO Box No. 441, Baghdad.
C. Iroq, Baghdad; T. (1) 7748261; TX. 213409; *Pres.* Dr S. S. Tawfiq; *Sec.* M. A. A. Kennan.
MEN: **1** Faris Abdul Al-Hassan; **2** Ali Hussain Kadhim; **3** Yousif Araibi; **4** Kadhim Hussain Kadhim; **5** Sadoon Hassan; **6** Fasil Muhmood; **7** Murtidha Abdul-Karim; **8** Ali Muhmood; **9** Ahmed Araibi; **10** Dhia Ali.
WOMEN: **1** Zina Al Hijia; **2** Doris Serwan; **3** Zinab Al Janabi; **4** Ishraq Al Janabi; **5** Yasameen Al Janabi; **6** Tunis Meki; **7** Mehad Fakri; **8** Samar Louis; **9** Hala Muhmood; **10** Nagam Al-Dorra.

National Closed Championships
MEN'S SINGLES – Semi-finals: A. Hussain d. S. Hassan 6–1 6–3 6–0; Y. Araibi d. F. Abdul-Hassan 6–1 6–2 7–5. ***Final:*** Araibi d. Hussain 2–6 6–4 3–6 6–3 6–2.
WOMEN'S SINGLES – Semi-finals: Z. Al Hujia d. Y. Al Janabi 6–0 6–1; Z. Al Janabi d. D. Serwan 6–3 6–2. ***Final:*** Al Hujia d. Z. Al Janabi 6–0 6–2.

IRELAND (1895)

Irish Lawn Tennis Association, 22 Upper Fitzwilliam Street, Dublin 2.
C. Irishtennis, Dublin; T. (01) 606332; TX. 31295 ILTA EL; *Pres.* Mrs H. Clinton; *Chief Exec.* Mr J. Taylor; *Sec.* Mrs M. Hogg.
MEN: **1** Matt Doyle; **2** Michael Nugent; **3** Eoin Collins; **4** Robbie Dolan; **5** Michael Cowhie; **6** Sean Molloy; **7** Eric Crotty; **8** Liam Croke; **9** Peter Lowther; **10** John Fahy.
WOMEN: **1** Siobhan Nicholson; **2** Jennifer Thornton; **3** Lesley O'Halloran; **4** Rosemary Langford; **5** Jennifer O'Brien; **6** Philippa Palmer; **7** Sandra Fearon; **8** Carmel O'Sullivan; **9** Michelle Buckley; **10** Gina Niland; **11** Diane Craig; **12** Michelle Egan.

National Closed Championships
MEN'S SINGLES – Semi-finals: M. Nugent d. M. Cowhie 6–1 3–6 7–5; E. Collins d. R. Reid 4–6 6–0 6–3. ***Final:*** Nugent d. Collins 6–4 6–4.
WOMEN'S SINGLES – Semi-finals: L. O'Halloran d. R. Langford 6–3 6–1; M. Buckley d. M. Egan 6–4 6–2. ***Final:*** O'Halloran d. Buckley 6–2 6–2.

ISRAEL

Israel Tennis Association, PO Box 20073, Tel Aviv 61200.
C. ILTA, Tel Aviv; T. (3) 613911/625864; TX. 341118 BXTVIL Ext. 5348; *Chmn.* Mr D. Harnik; *Sec.* Mr Z. Meyer.
MEN: **1** Amos Mansdorf; **2** Shachar Perkis; **3** Gilad Bloom; **4** Amit Naor; **5** Shlomo Glickstein; **6** Boaz Merenstein; **7** Raviv Weidenfeld; **8** Yoram Baron; **9** Haim Zion; **10** Ohad Weinberg.
WOMEN: **1** Ilana Berger; **2** Dalia Koriat; **3** Yael Shavit; **4** Anat Varon; **5** Sofi Rafael; **6** Yael Segal; **7** Sariat Shalev; **8** Daniela Blanka; **9** Limor Zaltz; **10** Meddi Dadosch.

ITALY (1910)

Federazione Italiana Tennis, Viale Tiziano 70, 00100 Rome.
C. Italtennis, Rome; T. (6) 36858 213/210/3960092; TX. 613330 FIT I; *Pres.* Avv. P. Galgani; *Sec.* Dott G. Annibali.

JAMAICA

Jamaica Lawn Tennis Association, 2A Piccadilly Road, PO Box 175, Kingston 5.
C. Lawntenna, Kingston; T. New Kingston 2441/2442; TX. 2442; *Pres.* Mr W. A. Scholefield; *Sec.* Mrs Y. K. Walsh.

JAPAN (1921)

Japan Tennis Association, c/o Kishi Memorial Hall, 1-1-1 Jinnan, Shibuya-Ku, Tokyo 150.
C. Niplotenis, Tokyo; T. (3) 481 2321; TX. 2428222 JTENIS J. Fax. 03 467 5192; *Pres.* Mr T. Kosaka; *Sec.* Mr S. Shimizu.

National Closed Championships
MEN'S SINGLES – Semi-finals: E. Takeuchi d. T. Fukui 6–2 6–1 6–2; S. Nishio d. S. Shiraishi 6–1 6–4 7–6 (7–3). ***Final:*** Nishio d. Takeuchi 7–6 (7–5) 6–4 4–6 7–6 (7–4).
WOMEN'S SINGLES – Semi-finals: E. Inoue d. E. Okagawa 4–6 6–2 7–5; K. Okamoto d. K. Date 7–5 6–3. ***Final:*** Inoue d. Okamoto 6–4 6–0.

KENYA (1922)

Kenya Lawn Tennis Association, PO Box 43184, Nairobi.
C. Tennis, Nairobi; T. 745164; TX. 22575 KATE NBO; *Chmn.* Dr N. Wekesa; *Sec.* Mr B. Aggarwal.
MEN: **1** Paul Wekesa; **2** Duncan Odipo; **3** Salim Rana; **4** Sam Kipkoech; **5** Peter Orwa; **6** David Kiago; **7** Asif Karim; **8** Kush Bhardwaj; **9** Peter Mithamo; **10** Eno Polo.
WOMEN: **1** Jane Ndunda; **2** Camilla Wekesa; **3** Carol Hughes; **4** Wanjiku Murigu; **5** Louise De Mello; **6** Susan Githuku; **7** Judy Wakhungu; **8** Rosemary Strachan; **9** Louis Wekesa; **10** Selina Patel.

National Closed Championships
MEN'S SINGLES – Semi-finals: A. Karim d. P. Orwa 6–2 6–1; D. Odipo d. S. Rana 6–2 6–1. ***Final:*** Karim d. Odipo 6–2 6–3.
WOMEN'S SINGLES – Semi-finals: J. Wakhungu d. J. Ndunda 6–3 7–5; S. Githuku d. L. Mello 6–2 6–0. ***Final:*** Wakhungu d. Githuku 6–3 3–6 6–4.

KOREA, REPUBLIC OF (1945)

Korea Tennis Association, Room 505, Sports Building, 19 Mukyo-Dong, Chung-Ku, Seoul.
C. Kortennis, Seoul; T. (2) 777 4028/777 6081-9 Ext. 609, 610 or 757 5045; TX. 24989 KOCSEL K; *Pres.* Mr Choong-Kun Cho; *Sec.* Mr Young Moo-Huh.

KUWAIT (1985)

Kuwait Tennis Federation, PO Box 1462, Hawalli, Cod 32015.
C. Tennis, Kuwait; T. (965) 2685148 TX. 23192 COMITE KT (Attn. Tennis Assoc.); *Pres.* Mr K. A. Al-Bannai, *Sec.* Mr A. R. Alghareeb.

LEBANON (1945)

Federation Libanaise de Tennis, PO Box 113-5591, Hamra, Beyrouth.
C. Tennispong. Beyrouth; T. (961) 1 342282; TX. GESPA 20653 LE (mark for E. A. Yazbeck); *Pres.* Mr A. K. Matar; *Hon. Gen. Sec.* Mr E. A. Yazbeck.

LIBYA (1947)

Jamahiriya Tennis Federation, PO Box 879, Tripoli.
C. Almadrab, Tripoli; T. (21) 39156; TX. 20710 RIADAHLY/20420 LY LIBOLYMPIC; *Pres.* Mr A. Laweti; *Sec.* Mr M. Krewi.
MEN: **1** Jeteiii Ibrahim; **2** Bournal Abdoulmunim; **3** Jeteili Abdoulhakim; **4** Sediah Ali; **5** Zankouli Khaled; **6** Marajaiei Assayed; **7** Alaabdiah Ahmad; **8** Arragig Saad; **9** Hassan Muhammad; **10** Eddebri Assenousi.

National Closed Championships
MEN'S SINGLES – Semi-finals: Abdiah Ahmad d. Zankouli Khaled 7–5 4–6 6–4; Jeteili Abdoulhakim d. Marajaiei Assayed 6–3 6–4. ***Final:*** Abdoulim d. Ahmad 6–4 5–7 6–3 6–2.

Ranked No. 1 in Haiti, the likeable Ronald Agenor improved his world ranking to 44 during an impressive year, in which he extended Lendl to four sets at the French Open, appeared in his first Grand Prix final at Gstaad and reached the same stage at Bordeaux and Basel. *(T. Hindley)*

LUXEMBOURG (1946)

Federation Luxembourgeoise de Tennis, 7 Avenue Victor Hugo, Luxembourg L 1750.
C. Federation Luxembourgeoise de Tennis, Luxembourg; T. (352) 47 31 57; TX. 3556 COSL LU; *Pres.* Mr M. Wolter; *Gen. Sec.* Mrs J. Schockmel.
MEN: **1** Johnny Goudenbour; **2** Serge Bruck; **3** Jacques Radoux; **4** Paul Hoffmann; **5** Mike Van Kauvenbergh; **6** Jean-Marc Goy.
WOMEN: **1** Ginette Huberty; **2** Pascale Welter; 3 Marie-Christine; **4** Sandra Denis; **5** Nadia Faber.

National Closed Championships
MEN'S SINGLES – Semi-finals: S. Bruck d. J. Radoux 3–6 6–1 6–1; J. Goudenbour d. P. Hoffmann 6–1 6–3. ***Final:*** Goudenbour d. Bruck 6–2 6–4.
WOMEN'S SINGLES – Semi-finals: K. Kschwendt d. M. Goy 6–2 6–0; G. Huberty d. P. Welter 6–4 6–0. ***Final:*** Kschwendt d. Huberty 6–3 6–2.

MALAYSIA (1921)

Lawn Tennis Association of Malaysia, c/o 100 Jalan 2, 68000 Ampang Jaya, Selangor.
C. Tennis Kuala Lumpur; T. (3) 4571341; TX. NOCMAL MA 30644; *Pres.* Hon. Mr A. G. Baba; *Sec.* Lt. Col. Z. B. Razali.

MALTA (1966)

Malta Lawn Tennis Association, PO Box 50, Sliema Post Office, Sliema.
T. (356) 512368; TX. 1558 MERLIN MW; *Pres.* Mr J. P. Galea; *Hon. Sec.* Mr M. Xuereb.
MEN: **1** Gordon Asciak; **2** Christopher Gatt; **3** Daryl Delicata; **4** Steven Schranz; **5** Denis Galea.
WOMEN: **1** Carol Curmi; **2** Helen Asciak; **3** Alexia Gera; **4** Katherine Camilleri.

MEXICO (1952)

Mexican Tennis Federation, Miguel Angel de Quevedo No. 953 COL. El. Rosedal, Deleg. Coyoacan, Mexico 04330 D.F.
C. Mextenis, Mexico City; T. (5) 549 16 18/544 90 23 TX. 1761056 FMDTME; *Pres.* Mr L. G. Reyes; *Sec.* Mr E. Andonegui.
MEN: **1** Jorge Lozano; **2** Enrique Haro; **3** Francisco Maciel; **4** Leonardo Lavalle; **5** Alejandro Flores; **6** Javier Contreras; **7** Yves Lemaitre; **8** Eduardo Velez; **9** Roberto Lopez; **10** Agustin Moreno.
WOMEN: **1** Heliane Steden; **2** Claudia Hernandez; **3** Ma Elena Llamas; **4** Lucila Becerra; **5** Xochitl Escobedo; **6** Maricarmen Casta; **7** Leticia Herrera; **8** Blanca Borbolla; **9** Alejandra Vallejo; **10** Karin Dalwitz.

National Closed Championships
MEN'S SINGLES – Final: F. Maciel d. J. Ordaz 6–4 6–0 6–3.

MONACO (1927)

Federation Monagesque de Lawn Tennis, 46 Rue Grimaldi, 98000 Monaco.
C. Federation-Tennis-Monaco; T. (93) 30-01-02; TX. 469760 CONG MC (Att. LTA); *Pres.* Mr L. Caravel; *Sec.* Mr J. C. Riley.

MOROCCO (1956)

Federation Royale Marocaine de Tennis, Parc de la Ligue Arabe, Casablanca, BP 15794.
C. Tenisfede, Maroc; T. (212) 27-87-31; TX. 23745 FRTENNIS; *Pres.* Mr M. M'Jid; *Sec.* Mr A. Mansouri.
MEN: **1** Arafa Chekrouni; **2 eq** Houssine Saber, Khalid Outaleb; **4 eq** Mohamod Dlimi, Abdelkhalek Nadini; **6** Bouehaib Assouadi; **7** Mustapha Amechrat; **8** Mustapha Dislam; **9** Abdellah Bennio; **10** Mohamid Ridaoui.
WOMEN: **1** Salma Benzekri; **2** Mouua Kharchafi.

National Closed Championships
MEN'S SINGLES – Semi-finals: H. Saber d. K. Outaleb 6–4 6–2; A. Chekrouni d. A. Nadini 6–1 6–3. ***Final:*** Chekrouni d. Saber 6–1 6–2.

WOMEN'S SINGLES – Semi-finals: S. Benzekri d. Belgezar 6–2 6–2; M. Kharchafi d. Najemil 6–4 6–1. ***Final:*** Benzekri d. Kharchafi 6–4 6–3.

NETHERLANDS (1899)

Koninklijke Nederlandse Lawn Tennis Bond, PO Box 107, 1200 AC Hilversum.
C. Tennisbond, Hilversum; T. (35) 46941; TX. 43061 KNLTB NL; *Pres.* Mr K. T. M. Hehenkamp; *Vice Pres.* Mrs H. V. Mook-Gurnberg; *Sec.* Mr Y. Buruma.
MEN: **1** Michiel Schapers; **2** Tom Nijssen; **3** Menno Oosting; **4** Paul Haarhuis; **5** Huub Van Boeckel; **6** Mark Koevermans; **7** Christian Feenstra; **8** Chris Vermeeren; **9** Wim Groenveld; **10** Hendrik Jan Davids.
WOMEN: **1** Hester Witvoet; **2** Brenda Schultz; **3** Marianne Van Der Torre; **4** Marcella Mesker; **5** Nicole Jagerman; **6** Eveline Hamers; **7** Hellas Ter Riet; **8** Simone Schilder; **9** Yvonne Der Kinderen; **10** Manon Bollegraf.

National Closed Championships
MEN'S SINGLES – Semi-finals: M. Oosting d. J. Vekemans 7–6 2–6 6–4 7–6; T. Nijssen d. R. Kok 7–5 3–6 7–6 6–4. ***Final:*** Oosting d. Nijssen 7–6 1–6 6–2 2–6 6–2.
WOMEN'S SINGLES – Semi-finals: C. Bakkum d. B. Schultz 6–2 7–6; E. Hamers d. M. Rooimans 6–3 6–3. ***Final:*** Hamers d. Bakkum 2–6 6–4 6–3.

NEW ZEALAND (1886)

New Zealand Lawn Tennis Association, PO Box 11541, Manners Street, Wellington.
C. Tennis, Wellington; T. (4) 731115; *Pres.* Mr I. D. Wells.
MEN: **1** Russell Simpson; **2** Bruce Derlin; **3** Kelly Evernden; **4** Steve Guy; **5** David Mustard; **6** Brett Steven; **7** James Dunphy; **8** David Lewis; **9** Troy Turnbull; **10** Greg Long.
WOMEN: **1** Julie Richardson; **2** Belinda Cordwell; **3** Michelle Parun; **4** Ruth Seeman; **5** Brenda Perry; **6** Elizabeth Daly; **7** Claudine Toeafoa; **8** Robyn Hunt; **9** Sally Moorfield; **10** Tracey King.

National Closed Championships
MEN'S SINGLES – Semi-finals: K. Evernden d. S. Guy 3–6 6–2 6–3; B. Derlin d. D. Mustard 6–7 6–4 7–6. ***Final:*** Evernden d. Derlin 6–3 6–4.
WOMEN'S SINGLES – Semi-finals: B. Cordwell d. M. Parun 7–6 6–1; J. Richardson d. E. Daly 7–5 7–6. ***Final:*** Cordwell d. Richardson 6–1 6–2.

NIGERIA (1927)

Nigeria Lawn Tennis Association, National Stadium, Syrulere, PO Box 145, Lagos.
C. Tennis Natsports, Lagos; T. (1) 83 0649; TX. 26559 ADEFNL NG; *Pres.* Alhaji Raheem A. Adejumo; *Sec.* Mr L. A. Ayorinde.

NORWAY (1909)

Norges Tennisforbund, Hauger Skolevei 1, 1351 Rud.
C. Norsktennis, Oslo; T. (2) 139075; (after 15.45 (2) 519287); TX. 78586 NIF N (Att. Tennis); Fax. (2) 132989 (Att. Tennis); *Pres.* Mr A. Melander; *Sec.* Mr T. Kverneland.
MEN: **1** Anders Haseth; **2** Auoun Jensen; **3** Bentove Pedersen; **4** Johnerik Rustad; **5** Jan Svensen; **6** Geir Sjoberg; **7** Bent Rolland; **8** Kjetil Rannes; **9** Terje Persson; **10** Erland Efskind.
WOMEN: **1** Amy Jonsson; **2** Stine Vogt-Andersen; **3** Monica Wiese; **4** Bente Bomark; **5** Astrid Sunde; **6** Ida Ross; **7** Ulrikke Evensen; **8** Lena Falck; **9** Kjersti Jensen; **10** Cathrine Vigander.

National Closed Championships
MEN'S SINGLES – Semi-finals: A. Haseth d. J. Rustad 6–1 6–2; B. Pedersen d. J. Svensen 6–1 6–4. ***Final:*** Pedersen d. Haseth 6–2 3–6 7–5.
WOMEN'S SINGLES – Semi-finals: S. Andersen d. I. Ross 7–6 6–0; A. Jonsson d. A. Sunde 7–5 6–1. ***Final:*** Jonsson d. Andersen 6–1 6–0.

PAKISTAN (1947)

Pakistan Tennis Federation, Wah Cantt, Pakistan.
C. Paktennis, Wah Cantt; T. (51) 66031/9 Ext. 2060; TX. 5840 POFAC PK/54178 POFAC PK; *Pres.* Maj. Gen. Talat Masood; *Sec.* Mr Ahson Baig.

PARAGUAY (1936)

Asociacion Paraguaya de Tennis, Colon Avenue 1054, 1st Floor, Asuncion.
T. (21) 97756; TX. 124 PY DIESA; *Pres.* Mr L. Cubas; *Sec.* Mr M. Carrisoza; *Exec. Dir.* Mr D. L. Llamosas.
MEN: **1** Victor Caballero; **2** Ruben Alvarenga.
WOMEN: **1** Patricia Perez; **2** Ximena Diaz de Vivar.

National Closed Championships
MEN'S SINGLES – Final: V. Caballero d. Dominguez 6–0 6–1 6–0.
WOMEN'S SINGLES – Final: X. D. de Vivar d. Ugarriza 6–3 2–6 6–4.

PERU (1930)

Federacion Peruana de Tenis, Cercado Campo de Marte s/n. Jesus Maria, Lima.
T. (14) 249979; TX. 25056 PE FPTENIS; *Pres.* Ing. Y. Senno; *Sec.* Mr A. Pereda.

PHILIPPINES (1946)

Philippine Tennis Association, Rizal Memorial Sports Complex, Vito Cruz Street, Manila.
C. Philta, Manila; T. (2) 583535/588248; TX. 23297 ALTIS PH/40255 ALTA PM; *Pres.* Col. S. H. Andrada; *Sec.* Mr A. P. Alcaraz.
MEN: **1** Felix Barrientos; **2** Manuel Tolentino; **3** Roland So; **4** Rod Rafael; **5** Andres Battad; **6** Raymund Suarez; **7** Ringo Navarrosa; **8** Roselle Nilo Natividad; **9** Danilo Pila; **10** Robert Angelo.
WOMEN: **1** Dyan Castillejo; **2** Yvette Niña Castillejo; **3** Jennifer Saberon; **4** Sarah Rafael; **5** Mia Fernandez; **6** Sarah Castillejo; **7** Dorothy Jane Suarez; **8** Eva Olivarez; **9** Michelle Pangilinan; **10** Anita Toledo.

National Closed Championships
MEN'S SINGLES – Semi-finals: M. Tolentino d. D. Pila 7–6 6–1 6–2; A. Battad d. F. Demonstverde 4–6 6–2 6–4 6–4. ***Final:*** Tolentino d. Battad 6–1 6–4 6–2.
WOMEN'S SINGLES – Semi-finals: D. Castillejo d. D. Suarez 6–2 6–0; M. Fernandez d. S. Castillejo 1–6 6–1 6–3. ***Final:*** D. Castillejo d. Fernandez 6–3 7–5.

POLAND (1921)

Polski Zwiazek Tenisowy, Ul. Marszalkowska 2, 3rd Floor, 00-581 Warsaw.
C. Poltenis, Warsaw; T. (22) 21 80 01/29 26 21; TX. 816494 PAISP PL/812466 COS PL; *Pres.* Mr R. Garbaczewski; *Gen. Sec.* Mr P. Dudzinski.
MEN: **1** Wojciech Kowalski; **2** Lech Bienkowski; **3** Ryszard Major; **4** Waldemar Rogowski Walexx; **5** Marek Kaczynski; **6** Tomasz Maliszewski; **7** Michel Klak; **8** Tomasz Iwanski; **9** Olgierd Hoffman; **10** Michal Przybylski.
WOMEN: **1** Ewa Zerdecak; **2** Renata Wojtkiewicz; **3** Sylwia Czopek; **4** Elzbieta Zaboklicka; **5** Malgorzata Zydek; **6** Izabella Listowska; **7** Dorota Dziekonska; **8** Magdalena Mroz; **9** Anna Gabzdyl; **10** Zyta Rogowska.

National Closed Championships
MEN'S SINGLES – Semi-finals: W. Kowalski d. M. Koska 6–1 6–3 6–4; M. Przybylski d. L. Bienkowski 4–6 6–4 2–6 7–5 7–5. ***Final:*** Kowalski d. Przybylski 6–4 6–1 4–6 6–2.
WOMEN'S SINGLES – Semi-finals: R. Wojtkiewicz d. I. Listowska 6–1 7–5; K. Nowak d. M. Mroz 6–7 6–2 7–5. ***Final:*** Nowak d. Wojtkiewicz 6–1 6–1.

PORTUGAL (1925)

Federacao Portuguesa de Tenis, Estadio Nacional, Apartado 210, 2 796 Linda-a-Velha Codex, Portugal.
C. Portugaltenis, Lisbon; T. (1) 419 84 72/419 52 44; TX. 65257 TENFED P; *Pres.* Mr A. Vaz Pinto; *Sec.* Mr D. D. Silva.

National Closed Championships
MEN'S SINGLES – Semi-finals: J. Silva d. A. Figueiredo 6–2 6–1 6–1; P. Cordeiro d. M. Seruca 5–7 6–1 6–4 7–6. ***Final:*** Silva d. Cordeiro 6–4 7–5 6–1.
WOMEN'S SINGLES – Semi-finals: T. Couto d. I. Drummond 6–4 6–1; P. Valadas d. A. Ascenso 6–2 4–6 8–6. ***Final:*** Valadas d. Couto 7–5 6–3.

ROMANIA (1929)

Federatia Romana de Tennis, Str. Vasile Conta 16, 70139 Bucharest.
C. Sportrom, Bucharest; T. (90) 119787; TX. 11180 SPORT R; Fax. (00) 119787; *Pres.* Mr I. Gheorghe; *Gen. Sec.* Ms F. Mihai.

National Closed Championships
MEN'S SINGLES – Semi-finals: D. Andrie d. M. Adrian 6–3 2–6 4–6 7–5 6–2; V. Mihai d. S. Florin 6–2 7–6 4–0 ab. ***Final:*** Andrie d. Mihai 6–2 6–4 2–6 4–6 8–6.
WOMEN'S SINGLES – Semi-finals: S. Diane d. C. Florentina 6–3 7–6; V. Madalina d. P. Otilia 6–3 6–4. ***Final:*** Madalina d. Diane 6–4 6–3.

SAUDI ARABIA (1956)

Saudi Arabia Tennis Federation, PO Box 4674; Riyadh 11412.
C. Koratawla, Riyadh; T. (1) 4820188/4822829; TX. 404130 TENNIS SJ; *Pres.* Mr S. Al-Jabhan; *Sec.* Mr S. A. Abdulaziz.
MEN: **1** Fahmi Tan Mohamed; **2** Khalid Hussin Fitiani; **3** Gamal Hussan Ashban; **4** Abed Al-Aziz Kridis; **5** Adnan Hussan Hawary; **6 eq** Khalid Hussan El-Siah, Fouad Ali Ibrahim; **8** Mazen Mohamed Genede; **9** Abed-Allah El-Messned; **10** Asaad Ali El-Gizeri.

National Closed Championships
MEN'S SINGLES – Semi-finals: F. Mohamed d. A. Hawary 2–0; K. Fitiani d. F. Ibrahim 2–0. ***Final:*** Mohamed d. Fitiani 2–1.

SENEGAL (1960)

Federation Senegalaise de Tennis, Sporting Club, 28 Avenue Rossevelt, BP 510, Dakar.
T. 21 02 39; TX. 3159 SG CTDSENE; *Pres.* Mr Y. Nidaye; *Sec.* Mr C. S. Ndiaye.

SINGAPORE (1928)

Singapore Lawn Tennis Association, c/o Singapore Sports Council, National Stadium, Singapore 1439.
T. 3457111 Ext. 640; TX. 35467 NASTAD RS; Fax. 3409537; *Pres.* Dr D. Oon; *Sec.* Mr A. Koh.

SOUTH AFRICA (1903)

The South African Tennis Union, PO Box 2211, Johannesburg 2000.
C. Tennis, Johannesburg; T. (11) 402 3580; TX. 425976 SA; Fax. (11) 402 6940; *Pres.* Mr J. Barnard; *Sec./Treasurer* Mr G. L. Talbot.
MEN: **1** Christo Steyn; **2** Eddie Edwards; **3** Christo Van Rensburg; **4** Danie Visser; **5** Barry Moir; **6** Schalk Van Der Merwe; **7** P. Aldrich; **8** M. Robertson; **9** Denys Maasdorp; **10** Gary Muller.
WOMEN: **1** Rosalyn Fairbank; **2** Elna Reinach; **3** Dinky Van Rensburg; **4** Yvonne Vermaak; **5** Jennifer Mundel Rheinbold; **6** Karen Schimper; **7** René Mentz; **8** M. de Swardt; **9** René Uys; **10** A. Coetzer.

National Closed Championships
MEN'S SINGLES – Semi-finals: B. Moir d. B. Pirow 6–3 3–6 6–3; S. Van Der Merwe d. M. Robertson 6–3 6–1. ***Final:*** Van Der Merwe d. Moir 6–4 6–3.
WOMEN'S SINGLES – Semi-finals: K. Schimper d. R. Mentz 1–6 6–3 6–4; G. Boon d. M. Reinach 6–1 6–1. ***Final:*** Schimper d. Boon 6–4 6–2.

SPAIN (1909)

Real Federacion Espanola de Tenis, Avda Diagonal 618 3 D, 08021 Barcelona.
C. FEDETENNIS, Barcelona; T. (3) 2005355/2010844/2005878/2015586; TX. 99447 RFET E; *Pres.* Mr A. Pujol, *Sec.* Mr T. G. Balmaseda.

National Closed Championships
MEN'S SINGLES – Semi-finals: S. Casal d. T. Carbonell 6–4 6–1; F. Luna d. J. Arrese 6–3 6–3. ***Final:*** Luna d. Casal 3–6 7–5 6–4.
WOMEN'S SINGLES – Semi-finals: M. J. Llorca d. M. Vaquero 6–1 7–5; A. Sanchez d. R. Bielsa 6–3 6–1. ***Final:*** Sanchez d. Llorca 6–3 6–1.

The multilingual Czech-born Swiss, Eva Krapl, took over as her country's No. 1 in 1987 and began 1988 in style by beating Garrison at the Australian Open. *(T. Hindley)*

SRI LANKA (1915)

Sri Lanka Tennis Association, 45 Sir Marcus Fernando Mawatha, Colombo 7.
C. Tennis, Colombo; T. (1) 91425; TX. 25137 METALIX CE; Fax. 94 1 580721; *Pres.* Mr D. L. Seneviratne; *Sec.* Mr E. Pararajasingham.

National Closed Championships
MEN'S SINGLES – Semi-finals: A. Fernando d. R. Braeg 6–2 6–0; U. Wallooppillai d. F. Sebaratnam 7–6 6–3. ***Final:*** Fernando d. Wallooppillai 6–1 6–0 6–1.
WOMEN'S SINGLES – Semi-finals: L. Weerasooriya d. V. Premaratne 6–1 6–0; S. Silva d. P. Sebaratnam 6–2 4–6 6–1. ***Final:*** Weerasooriya d. Silva 6–2 7–5.

SUDAN (1956)

Sudan Lawn Tennis Association, PO Box 1553, Khartoum.
T. (11) 70081; *Pres.* Mr T. Aboukadouk, *Sec.* Mr T. Shoush.

SWEDEN (1906)

The Swedish Tennis Association, Lidingovagen 75, S 115 36 Stockholm.
C. Svensktennis, Stockholm; T. (8) 6679770; TX. 12235 TENNIS S; Fax. (8) 6646606; *Pres.* Mr L. Olander; *Sec. Gen.* Mr R. Levin.
MEN: **1** Stefan Edberg; **2** Mats Wilander; **3** Joakim Nystrom; **4** Mikael Pernfors; **5** Kent Carlsson; **6** Anders Jarryd; **7** Jonas Svensson; **8** Jan Gunnarsson; **9** Ulf Stenlund; **10** Peter Lundgren.
WOMEN: **1** Catarina Lindqvist; **2** Elisabeth Ekblom; **3** Maria Lindstrom; **4** Carina Karlsson; **5** Karolina Karlsson; **6** Monica Lundqvist; **7** Helena Dahlstrom; **8** Catrin Jexell; **9** Cecilia Dahlman; **10** Annika Karlsson.

National Closed Championships
MEN'S SINGLES – Semi-finals: S. Eriksson d. C. Bergstrom 7–6 2–6 6–3; J. Gunnarsson d. M. Gustasson 6–4 6–3. ***Final:*** Gunnarsson d. Eriksson 6–3 6–2.
WOMEN'S SINGLES – Semi-finals: C. Jexell d. L. Sandin 6–1 6–1; A. Bjork d. K. Schultz 6–4 6–2. ***Final:*** Jexell d. Bjork 6–3 6–2.

SWITZERLAND (1896)

Schweizerischer Tennisverband, Talgut Zentrum 5, PO Box 3063 Ittigen/Berne.
C. Suissetennis, Bern; T. (31) 587444; TX. 911391 STV CH; Fax. (61) 507196; *Pres.* Mr B. Frischknecht; *Sec.* Mr R. Julita.
MEN: **1** Jakob Hlasek; **2** Claudio Mezzadri; **3** Zoltan Kuharszky; **4** Roland Stadler; **5** Heinz Guenthardt; **6** Rolf Hertzog; **7** Stephen Medem; **8** Stefano Mezzadri; **9** Emmanuel Marmillod; **10** Stephane Oberer.
WOMEN: **1** Eva Krapl; **2** Christiane Jolissaint; **3** Liliane Drescher; **4** Csilla Bartos Cserepy; **5** Celine Cohen; **6** Emauela Zardo; **7** Sandrine Jaquet; **8** Cathy Caverzasio; **9** Petra Delhees Jauch; **10** Michele Strebel.

National Closed Championships
MEN'S SINGLES – Semi-finals: Z. Kuharszky d. R. Stadler 1–6 4–6 6–4 6–3 6–2; C. Mezzadri d. C. Fresneda 6–3 6–3 4–6 6–3. ***Final:*** Kuharszky d. Mezzadri 6–2 6–2.
WOMEN'S SINGLES – Semi-finals: E. Krapl d. A. Martinelli 6–1 6–2; C. Caverzasio d. S. Jaquet 6–2 6–2. ***Final:*** Krapl d. Caverzasio 6–2 6–1.

SYRIA ARAB REPUBLIC (1953)

Syrian Arab Tennis Federation, PO Box 421, Damascus.
T. 225026/34/52; TX. 411578 SPOFED SY; *Pres.* Prof. Dr Eng S. Jabi; *Sec.* Mr F. Masalkhi.

THAILAND

The Lawn Tennis Association of Thailand, c/o Sports Promotion Organisation of Thailand, Hua mark, Bangkok 10240.
C. Thai Tennis, Bangkok; T. (2) 3140808/3146142; TX. 20843 MIDASIA TH; Fax. (2) 2366950; *Pres.* Co. Surapit Amornwichet; *Sec.* Capt. B. Phantawong.

TRINIDAD & TOBAGO (1948)

The Lawn Tennis Association of Trinidad & Tobago, c/o Cosmic Book Services, Upper Level, Westmall, West Mooring.
C. Lawntenna, Port-of-Spain; T. (809) 6334318; *Pres.* Mr L. St Aubyn HBM; *Hon. Sec.* Mr G. A. Matthew.

TUNISIA (1954)

Federation Tunisienne de Tennis, Cite Sportive Bourguiba, El Menzah, 1004 Tunis.
T. (1) 238 144; TX. 13541 SOTPAH TN; *Pres.* Mr F. Farah; *Sec.* Mr M. A. Lazral.

TURKEY (1923)

Turkiye Tenis Federasyonu, Ulus is Hani, Ankara.
C. Tennis Sport, Ankara; T. (41) 3103960/261; TX. 42251 TFF TR; *Pres.* Mr E. Cireli; *Sec.* Mr Y. Dogru.
MEN: **1** Necvet Demir; **2** Atlihan Binoz; **3** Kaya Saydas; **4** Reha Demirdag; **5** Yaman Esin; **6** Aladdin Karagoz; **7** Ali Colak; **8** Yavuz Erkangil; **9** Hasan Guzel; **10** Erol Uyar.
WOMEN: **1** Elif Oguz; **2** Duygu Aksit; **3** Yasemin Kaya; **4** Cigdem Kayacan; **5** Zeynep Yazcan; **6** Mine Terliksitz; **7** Neslihan Gucum; **8** Gul Guzelbey; **9** Tuana Elgin; **10** Arzu Katikaya.

USSR (1932)

Lawn Tennis Federation of the USSR, Luzhnetskaya Naberezhnaya 8, 119270 Moscow.
C. Sportkomitet, Moscow; T. (095) 201 08 64; TX. 411287 PRIZ SU; *Pres.* Mr B. Volkynov; *Sec. Gen.* Mr V. Yanchuck.

USA (1881)

United States Tennis Association Inc., 12th Floor, 1212 Avenue of the Americas, New York, NY 10036.
C. Ustennis, New York; T. (212) 302 3322; TX. 424499 ULTA UI; Fax. (212) 764 1838; *Pres.* Mr G. Jorgensen; *Exec. Dir.* Mr J. T. Fogarty; *Exec. Sec.* Mr M. J. Burns.

URUGUAY (1915)

Asociacion Uruguaya de Lawn Tennis, Calle Pablo De Maria 1065, Montevideo.
C. Urutennis, Montevideo; T. (2) 4 63 63; TX. 22333 CADE UY; *Pres.* Mr C. Rymer; *Sec.* Dr G. Inda.

VENEZUELA (1927)

Federacion Venezolana de Tenis, Apartado 70539, Los Ruices, Caracus 1070-A.
C. Fevetenis, Caracus; T. (2) 9792421/1487; TX. 28465 FVT VC; Fax. (2) 5416024; *Pres.* Mr F. Perez; *Sec.* Mr R. Vento.
MEN: **1** Nicolas Pereira; **2** Carlos Claverie; **3** Juan Carlos Bianchi; **4** Harry Sycorvo; **5** Harold Castillo; **6** Valerio Boccitto; **7** Alan Benarroch; **8** Maurice Ruah; **9** Boro Colvee; **10** Erick Sydow.
WOMEN: **1** Elizabeth Nieto; **2** Emily Leonardi; **3** Nelly Pardo; **4** Meliza Mazzota; **5** Nathalie Acacio; **6** Henrriet Gemer; **7** Maria E. Vento; **8** Eleonora Vegliante; **9** Alizia Tabares; **10** Maria Vento.

YUGOSLAVIA (1922)

Tenis Savez Yuoslavije, Terazije 35, 11000 Belgrade.
C. Tesaj, Belgrade; T. (11) 33 33 36; TX. 12595 SFKJ YU; *Pres.* Mr B. Andrejevski; *Sec.* Mr Z. Peric.

ZIMBABWE (1904)

Tennis Association of Zimbabwe, PO Box A575, Avondale, Harare.
T. (01) 32901; TX. 2501 ZW LIQUOR; *Pres.* Mr I. D. F. Godden; *Sec.* Mrs C. Greener.
MEN: **1** Bryon Black; **2 eq** Mark Gurr, Haroon Ismail; **4** Greig Rodger; **5** Clive Wilson; **6** Martin Lock; **7** Graham Martin; **8** Larry Katz; **9** Garth Thomson; **10** Simon Dawson.

WOMEN: **1** Julia Muir; **2** Paula Iversen; **3** Lesley Barbour; **4** Lindsay Standen; **5** Nicky Wagstaff; **6 eq** Sally Ann Birch, Sally Stephens; **8** Sue Roux; **9** Lyn Anticevitch; **10** Alison Vaughan.

National Closed Championships
MEN'S SINGLES – Semi-finals: G. Rodger d. G. Martin 6–7 6–4 6–2; C. Wilson d. L. Katz 6–0 6–3. ***Final:*** Rodger d. Wilson 6–2 6–7 6–4.
WOMEN'S SINGLES – Semi-finals: J. Muir d. S. Hutchinson 6–3 6–3; S. Stephens d. V. McKenzie 6–3 6–2. ***Final:*** Muir d. Stephens 6–2 6–0.

Associate Members Without Voting Rights (54)

AFGHANISTAN Afghan Lawn Tennis Association, c/o National Olympic Committee of Afghanistan, National Stadium, Kabul.
C. Olympic Kabul; TX. 20579; *Pres.* Mr O. Saraj; *Sec.* Mr H. Osman.

AMERICAN SAMOA (1985) American Samoa Tennis Association, PO Box 298, Pago Pago, American Samoa 96799.
T. (684) 633 2085; *Pres.* Mr P. M. Galea'i; *Sec.* Ms. J. Yamasaki.

BAHAMAS (1947) The Bahamas Lawn Tennis Association, PO Box N-10169 Nassau.
T. (809) 326 3000/326 1263; *Pres.* Mr J. B. Farrington; *Sec.* Mrs S. Ryan.

BARBADOS (1948) Barbados Lawn Tennis Association, PO Box 615c, Bridgetown.
T. (809) 427 5298; *Pres.* Mr J. F. L. Tasker; *Sec.* Mr G. A. Whitehead.

BENIN Federation Beninoise de Lawn Tennis, BP 2028, Cotonou.
C. Lawn Tenkning Box 516; T. (229) 313494/301663/300348; *Pres.* Mr A. Mallam-Idi; *Sec.* Mr C. Martins.

BERMUDA Bermuda Lawn Tennis Association, PO Box HM 341, Hamilton HM BX.
C. Ernsaudit, Bermuda; T. (809) 295 0319/295 7272; TX. 3680 ERNST BA; Fax. (809) 295 5193; *Pres.* Mr G. K. Harris; *Sec.* Mrs G. Butterfield.

BHUTAN (1976) Bhutan Tennis Federation, PO Box 103, Thimphu.
C. Olympic; *Pres.* Mr. T. Dorji; *Sec.* Mr L. Tsering.

BOTSWANA (1964) Botswana Lawn Tennis Association, PO Box 1174, Gaborone.
T. (31) 52818/53574/5; TX. 2334 MANFS BD; Fax. 2326; *Pres.* Dr G. Mosam; *Sec.* Mr L. Ranasinghe.

BRITISH VIRGIN ISLANDS (1982) British Virgin Islands Tennis Association, PO Box 201, Road Town, Tortola.
C. Veritatem, Tortola; T. (809) 49 42616; TX. 7918; *Pres.* Dr K. Adamson; *Sec.* Mr N. Barton.

BRUNEI DARUSSALEM (1967) Brunei Darussalem Lawn Tennis Association, PO Box 1300, Bandar Seri Begawan.
T. (02) 22452; TX. BERSATU BU 2357; Fax. (02) 23897; *Pres.* Mr T. Butcher; *Sec.* Mrs M. Elton-Lein.

BURKINA FASO (1970) Federation Burkinabe de Tennis, BP 1935, Ouagadougou.
Pres. Mr I. Zongo; *Sec.* Mme L. Traore.

BURMA (1949) Burma Tennis Federation, Aung San Memorial Stadium, Kandawgalay Post Office, Rangoon.
C. Ubsped, Rangoon; T. (1) 0171731; *Pres.* Mr J. B. Maung; *Sec.* Mr A. Thein.

CAYMAN ISLANDS (1973) Tennis Federation of the Cayman Islands, PO Box 1352, George Town, Grand Cayman.
T. (1 809 94) 92077; TX. 4310 CORPSER CP; *Pres.* Mr D. Price; *Sec.* Mr G. Barlow.

CONGO Federation Congolaise de Lawn-Tennis, Stade de la Revolution BP 2061 Brazzaville.
Pres. Mr I. Dinghat; *Sec.* Mr A. Ouabonzi.

COOK ISLANDS (1947) Cook Islands Tennis Association, PO Box 610, Rarotonga.
T. (682) 22327; TX. 62026 SSIRARO; *Pres.* Mr B. R. Baudinet; *Sec.* Mr T. A. Faireka.

COSTA RICA (1960) Federacion Costarricense de Tenis; PO Box 326-1005, B Mexico, San José.
C. Hopec, San José; T. (506) 213131/236133; TX. 2101 HOPEC; *Pres.* Mr A. Rodriguez; *Sec.* Mr R. Mendieta.

DOMINICA (1960) Dominica Lawn Tennis Association, c/o PO Box 13, Roseau, Commonwealth of Dominica, British West Indies.
T. (1) 809 448 2681 Ext. 17; TX. 8655 DOMLEC DO; *Pres.* Mr C. Severin; *Sec.* Mr T. Dorsett.

DOMINICAN REPUBLIC Federacion Dominicana de Tenis, Club Deportivo Naco, Calle Central, Ens. Naco, Santo Domingo.
T. (809) 565 4836/685 8059; TX. 3460418 BONELLY; *Pres.* Mr G. Mejia; *Sec.* Mr J. Ravello.

EL SALVADOR Federacion Salvadorena de Tenis, Apartado Postal (01) 110, San Salvador.
C. Molino, San Salvador; T. (503) 23 3892; TX. 20542 MOLINO; *Pres.* Ing. R. S. Alegria; *Sec.* Ing. E. Gutierrez.

ETHIOPIA (1972) Ethiopian Lawn Tennis Federation, c/o Sports Commission, PO Box 3241, Addis Ababa.
C. Addis Ababa (c/o Sports Commission); T. (01) 156795; TX. 21377 NESCO ET; *Pres.* Mr H. Balcha; *Sec.* Mr H. Afework.

FIJI (1934) Fiji Lawn Tennis Association, PO Box 2399, Government Buildings, Suva-Fiji.
T. 315988; TX. FJ 2355; *Pres.* Mr C. Benson; *Sec.* Miss K. Pande.

GAMBIA (1938) Gambia Tennis Association, PO Box 570, Banjul, The Gambia.
TX. 2293 MEPID GV; *Pres.* Mr D. A. Ndon; *Sec.* Mr G. M. Renner.

GUAM Tennis Association of Guam, PO Box 4379, Agana, Guam 96910.
C. Chelsea, Guam; T. (671) 734 2624; *Pres.* Ms H. Hosie; *Sec.* Ms J. Nelsen.

GUATEMALA Federacion Nacionale de Tenis, Palacio de Los Deportes, Zona 4, Guatemala City.
T. (2) 310261; TX. 5744 CDAG GU; *Pres.* Mr J. M. Cordova; *Sec.* Mr E. Vaides.

GUINEE CONAKRY (1984) Federation Guineenne de Tennis, Au Secretariat d'Etat a la Jeunesse et aux Sports, BP 262.
C. FGT BP 262, Conakry Guinee; T. 441962; TX. 22302 MJ GE; *Pres.* Mr A. Sylla; *Sec.* Mme M. M. Diallo.

GUYANA (1933) Guyana Lawn Tennis Association, PO Box 10205, Georgetown.
C. Lawntenna, Georgetown; T. 02 71195 (President), 02 67826 (Secretary); TX. 2281 CALAGY; *Pres.* Mr K. Juman-Yassin; *Sec.* Dr G. Muller.

JORDAN (1980) Jordan Tennis Federation, PO Box 35121, Amman.
C. Tenfed, Amman; T. 962 6 662707; TX. 22500 HILALJO; *Chmn.* Dr M. Al-Fawwaz; *Sec.* Mr I. Jarallah.

KOREA, DEMOCRATIC PEOPLE'S REPUBLIC OF Tennis Association of the Democratic People's Republic of Korea, Munsin-Dong, Dongdaewon Dist. Pyongyang.
C. Tennis DPR Korea; T. 6-2386/6-3998; TX. 5472; *Pres.* K. Yong Sam; *Sec.* Mr Li Won-Gun.

LESOTHO (1920) Lesotho Lawn Tennis Association, PO Box 156, Maseru 100.
C. LIPAPALI; TX. 4330 FOREIN LO; *Pres.* Mr H. Phoofolo; *Sec.* Mr C. Notsi.

MALAWI (1954) Lawn Tennis Association of Malawi, PO Box 1417, Blantyre.
Sec. Ms J. Williams.

MALI (1961) Federation Malienne de Tennis, Ministere des Affairs Etrangeres, Koulouba.
T. 225489/225633/225092; *Pres.* Mr A. Nafo; *Sec.* Mr A. Traore.

MAURITIUS (1910) Mauritius Lawn Tennis Association, PO Box 46, Rose Hill.
C. Tennis, Mauritius; T. (230) 41666; TX. 4729 SPORTS IW (Att. MLTA); *Pres.* Mr A. Gufflet; *Sec.* Mlle C. de Maroussem.

MONTSERRAT (1984) Montserrat Tennis Association, PO Box 386, Plymouth, Montserrat, British West Indies.
T. (809) 491 5363/5368; *Pres.* Mr L. Arnold; *Sec.* Miss C. Williams.

MOZAMBIQUE (1979) Federacao Mocambicana de Tenis, Caixa Postal 4351, Maputo.
C. JOFIRES, MAPUTO; T. (258) 27027; TX. 6-614 BMS MO; *Pres.* Mr P. Figueiredo; *Sec.* Mr V. Nhabangue.

NEPAL (1968) All Nepal Tennis Association, PO Box 2090, Dasarath Stadium, Kathmandu.
T. (977) 211732/215712; TX. 2390 NSCNP; *Pres.* Mr S. Singh; *Sec.* Mr P. K. Shrestha.

NETHERLANDS ANTILLES Netherlands Antilles Tennis Association, PO Box 3360, Emmastad Curacao.
T. (9) 44192; *Pres.* Mr Ing M. R. Paula; *Sec.* Mr H. Thomas.

NORTHERN MARIANA ISLANDS Northern Mariana Islands Tennis Association, PO Box 456, Saipan CM 96950.
T. (234) 7222/(234) 6865; TX. 643 AIUP SPN; *Pres.* Mr D. Barcinas; *Sec.* Mr V. Taitano.

PANAMA, REPUBLIC OF (1964) Federacion Panemena de Tenis, Apartado 6-6717, El Dorado.
T. (507) 60 0019/26 2785/60; TX. 2534 INDE PG or 3429 OLIMPAN PG; *Pres.* Mr H. Spalding; *Sec.* Mr J. Wilkins.

PUERTO RICO (1952) Puerto Rico Tennis Association, Box 40456 – Minillas Station, Santurce, Puerto Rico 00940.
T. (809) 721 9112; TX. 4212 PRTA PD; *Pres.* Mr J. Baldrich Jr., *Sec.* Mr J. Ariza.

QATAR (1984) Qatar Tennis and Squash Federation, PO Box 4959, Doha.
T. (974) 831786/831788; TX. 4059 QTSF DH; *Pres.* HE Sheik Issa G. Al Kawari; *Sec.* Mr K. O. Al Dafa.
ST LUCIA St Lucia Lawn Tennis Association, c/o PO 308, Castries, Saint Lucia, West Indies.
T. (809) 45 22484; *Pres.* Mr O. Monplaisir.

SAN MARINO (1950) Federazione Sammarinese Tennes, Republic of San Marino 47031.
C. Piazza M. Tini n. 15-47031, DOGANA: T. (39451) 905303; TX. 550885 SP RSMI; *Pres.* Mr A. S. Belluzzi; *Sec.* Mr S. Castelli.

SEYCHELLES (1955) Seychelles Tennis Association, PO Box 602, Victoria, Mahé.
T. (248) 47414; TX. 2305 MINED SZ; *Pres.* Mr J. Adam; *Sec.* Mr B. Shirley.

SIERRA LEONE (1965) Seychelles Tennis Association, c/o National Sports Council, PO Box 1181, Freetown.
T. (22) 40562/40167/41340; *Pres.* Mr H. Moore; *Sec.* Mr E. T. Ngandi.

SOMALI Somali Amateur Tennis Association, PO Box 523, Mogadishu.
T. (1) 28042; *Pres.* Mr Y. H. Yousaf.

SURINAM Surinaamse Tennisbond, PO Box 2087, Zinniastraat 3, Paramaribo.
T. (597) 97272/76727; TX. 240 LBBANK; *Pres.* Dr C. Pigot; *Vice Pres.* Mr E. Samson Sr.; *Sec.* Mrs E. Robles.

SWAZILAND Swaziland National Tennis Union, c/o Box 495, Mbabane.
T. (268) 22482/3 or 42398; *Pres.* Dr M. J. Ziyane; *Sec.* Mr M. Maseko.

TANZANIA Tanzania Lawn Tennis Association; PO Box 965, Dar Es Salaam.
T. (51) 23351; TX. 41009 CMCDAR LZ; *Pres.* Mr A. Fernandes; *Sec.* Mr R. Rugimbana.

TOGO (1955) Federation Togolaise de Tennis, BP 3601, Lome.
T. (228) 210320/210920/210607; TX. 5234 CIMTOGO; Fax. 217132; *Pres.* Mr K. Aquereburu; *Sec.* Mr A-K. B. Figan.

TONGA (1959) Tonga Amateur National Tennis Association, c/o Tonga Sports Association, PO Box 1278, Nuku-Alofa.
T. (676) 21 283/21 288; TX. 66217 NEWEXPO TS; *Pres.* Mr Hon. L. Hu'akavameiliku; *Sec.* Mr S. T. Finau.

UNITED ARAB EMIRATES (1982) United Arab Emirates Tennis Association, PO Box 87, Dubai.
T. (4) 690393; TX. 46347 FAGEN EM; *Pres.* Mr H. Khansaheb; *Sec.* Mr N. Madani.

US VIRGIN ISLANDS (1973) Virgin Islands Tennis Association, PO Box 11181, St Thomas, USVI 00801.
T. (1) 809 774 8547; Fax. (1) 809 776 2760; *Pres.* Mr W. F. McComb; *Vice Pres.* Mr K. Clarke; *Sec.* Ms J. Wisby.

WESTERN SAMOA (1950) Western Samoa Lawn Tennis Association, PO Box 1297, Apia.
T. (685) 20050/21145; *Pres.* Dr W. Soonalole; *Sec.* Mrs H. Mihaljevich.

YEMEN (1902) Yemen Tennis Federation, PO Box 4601, Aden.
C. Madhrab, Aden; T. 53244/53639; *Pres.* Mr A. H. Salem; *Sec.* A. A. M. Rahman.

ZAIRE (1984) Federation Zairoise de Lawn Tennis; BP 20750 Kin 15; Kinshasa.
T. (12) 25614 or 23260; TX. 211670 SGA KIN ZR; *Pres.* Mr N'Joli Balanga; *Sec.* Mr E. Botuna.

ZAMBIA (1975) Zambia Lawn Tennis Association, PO Box 36013, Lusaka.
T. (01) 218212; TX. 45820 ZA; Fax. (01) 217767; *Chmn* Mr M. S. Mulenga; *Hon. Sec.* Mrs H. Bright.

INDEX